RON SHANDLER's
Baseball
Forecaster

2009

Gravity Defying Edition

TRIUMPH
BOOKS

This book is available in quantity at special discounts for your group or organization. For further information, contact:

Triumph Books
542 South Dearborn Street
Suite 750
Chicago, Illinois 60605
(312) 939-3330
Fax (312) 663-3557

Printed in U.S.A.
ISBN: 978-1-60078-222-0

Rotisserie League Baseball is a registered trademark of the
Rotisserie League Baseball Association, Inc.

Statistics provided by Baseball Info Solutions

Cover design by Jon Resh@Go-Undaunted.com
Front cover photograph by Matthew O'Haren/Icon Sports Media, Inc.
Author photograph by Kevin Hurley

Acknowledgments

Ron Shandler's BASEBALL FORECASTER

Editors
Ray Murphy
Rod Truesdell

Minor Leagues
Deric McKamey

Injuries
Rick Wilton

Data
Paul Petera

Player commentaries
Dave Adler
Brent Hershey
Brandon Kruse
Scott Monroe
Ray Murphy
Stephen Nickrand
Joshua Randall
Michael Roy
Jock Thompson
Rod Truesdell

Research and Articles
Patrick Davitt
Dylan Hedges
Brandon Kruse
Scott Monroe
Tom Mulhall
Ray Murphy
Frank Noto
Joshua Randall
Michael Roy

As "change" has become the new keyword for our country, so it has been here as well. Shandler Enterprises, LLC handed over the keys to the kingdom last spring and we are all embarking on new adventures with new leaders. It is an exciting time.

But by virtue of you holding this book in your hand, it is also comforting to know that some things are not changing. I am still here, and my band of merry men (and women) continue to pioneer onward in the Land of Fanalytics. Behold the list on the left; these are the great minds that bring you this year's *Baseball Forecaster*. Without them, well, I could probably still do this myself, but the book wouldn't get done until June and only with alternating hourly doses of espresso and Xanax. I am grateful to every name on that list for keeping me straight.

Those contributors are part of the larger Baseball HQ family. The other fanalytic superstars are Andy Andres, Matt Baic, Matt Beagle, Neil Bonner, Hal Cohen, Jeremy Deloney, Doug Dennis, Matt Dodge, Rob Gordon, Phil Hertz, Joe Hoffer, Gerald Holmes, Tom Kephart, Troy Martell, Craig Neuman, Harold Nichols, Frank Noto, Josh Paley, Brian Rudd, Mike Shears, Peter Sheridan, Skip Snow, Tom Todaro and Jeffrey Tomich. In total, this group writes more than 1,000 articles each year, not including stats, charts and forum posts. My sincere appreciation for making "prolific" an understatement.

Thanks to Mike Krebs, Rob Rosenfeld and Uri Foox, our tech team and the driving force behind the great advancements on our site. And never enough is said about Lynda Knezovich, who quietly keeps the machine purring on the other end of the 800 line.

Greg Ambrosius, Jeff Barton, Matthew Berry, Jim Callis, Don Drooker, Jeff Erickson, Brian Feldman, Jason Grey, Eric Karabell, Peter Kreutzer, Gene McCaffrey, Lenny Melnick, John Menna, Lawr Michaels, Steve Moyer, Rob Neyer, Alex Patton, Peter Schoenke, Joe Sheehan, John Sickels, Perry Van Hook, Sam Walker, Brian Walton, Jeff Winick, Trace Wood, Todd Zola and others beyond alphabetization... an elite club of baseball's top analysts, writers and fantasy players. But more than that, they are colleagues and friends who contribute to this book in ways they'll never know.

Thank you to all the folks at Fantasy Sports Ventures, USA Today and Triumph Books for helping to keep the dream alive and allowing me to recharge my batteries.

It is a time of change in the Shandler household too. Coming off a lead role in a Shakespeare play in Cambridge, UK, Darielle is narrowing down her list of potential college destinations. The future theater major is vowing to head north — NYU, Hofstra, Emerson — even though eight Virginia schools are recruiting *her* after she wowed them at a performing arts competition. I told her to pack a parka.

Justina also spent July in the UK and headlined her speech & debate team in the Cambridge Union, where Winston Churchill once spoke. She has been wowing her own audiences at coffee house "open mic nights" and is setting her 2011 sights on Berklee College of Music. Surrounded by all this talent, I decided to rekindle my 25-year dormant songwriting career on page 0. Even after having sold the business, it's clear that I am going to need more to finance these educations.

As the stress level has started to lift, the one thing I am noticing more and more is... my wife. After nearly 24 years, Sue has been an amazing support; I hate to admit that I often took her for granted. She is the sun around which this family orbits, and I mean that in the most literal sense. Without her energy, there is no life on this planet. I love her, and you should too (but not in the literal sense) for without her, I would have quit long ago.

Finally, thank *you*. Many of you have been on this joyous ride for nearly all 23 editions. READ SOMETHING ELSE!! No, no, really, I do appreciate your support. I can't guarantee I'll be around for another 23 — heck, I'd be *ancient* by then — but the organization is in place to keep this running for many more years to come. That is *very* good news.

CONTENTS

The PED Blues

Words and music by Ron Shandler

What am I gonna do without Roger?
What am I gonna do without Bonds?
How'm I gonna muster
some pop for my roster?
How'm I gonna score enough runs?

What'll I do if they nail Tejada?
His ribbys are important to me.
And Roberts and Zaun
Don't know what they've been on
But I need 'em for position scarcity.

CHORUS
I'm sitting here in last place in homers.
My ERA could sure use a boost.
All that matters to me
Is winning Rotisserie.
I don't care if all my players are juiced.

FAITH

The very first national experts league draft took place in March 1994. It was a Rotisserie auction conducted via telephone conference call. It took nearly seven hours.

Two years later, the League of Alternative Baseball Reality (LABR) graduated to a live event in a St. Petersburg, Florida, hotel conference room. It was the first time many of these experts had ever met, but there was one thing we all had in common... paper. We all came to the draft armed with a razed forest's worth of books, magazines, dot-matrix computer printouts and loose-leaf binders.

Laptops? Few were willing to lug around those unwieldy monstrosities back then. The background noise at these drafts was more a ruckus of ruffling pages than a cacophony of clicking of keystrokes.

By 1998's debut Tout Wars draft — a major event held at the now-defunct All Star Cafe in Manhattan that included celebrity auctioneers and a viewer gallery — we were beginning to see some electronic assistance. There were a few laptops present, but most of them were just running Excel for tracking purposes. More participants were still plugging away with their hard-copy draft lists and reference books.

Today, nearly everyone has gone electronic, and many have embraced one of the numerous draft software programs now available. It's tough not to find value in these programs. The one we work with, RotoLab, provides such diverse tools as recommended players and in-draft inflation rates, all in real time. It's a level of intelligence we would not have conceived of 10 years ago.

However, as much as I applaud these programs, they all have one major flaw... *their intelligence is completely driven by somebody's player projections.*

We're all pretty much in agreement these days that the best accuracy a projections system can reasonably expect is about 70%. That means, any data that a draft software program feeds you is potentially 30% off. So when you are searching for that last big speedster to bid on, and the program identifies either Jacoby Ellsbury (40 projected SBs) or Denard Span (30), the best option may not always be obvious. A 30% swing is huge, and in this case, could make Ellsbury and Span virtually interchangeable commodities.

The proof of these assertions might lay in one fact... the pro-forma standings that are calculated at the end of your draft typically look nothing like the real standings six months later. Yes, you would expect a good deal of churn during the season, especially in leagues that allow trades. But one would also think that an accurately projected team tabbed for 11th place would be hard-pressed to finish in the money by October. And that happens often.

To be honest, I have never used one of these programs, not even RotoLab. I am no technophobe. I have complete faith in the value of the program for what it's intended to do, but I reject the notion that projective "precision" is worth chasing. As such, I think that our geeky stat obsession has no business playing a part in drafting a fantasy team, and may, in fact, be counter-productive.

What's worse, I fear that we are becoming too overly reliant on these types of tools. It seems like software programs answer *too many* questions for us during the draft. We barely have to think for ourselves anymore. These programs direct us down the optimal path in real time, and all we have to do is point and click. We are not using our intelligence and instincts at the draft table, we are just reacting to a data feed.

A feed that is at least 30% wrong.

We need to stop deluding ourselves into thinking we can nail a player's statistical output and instead focus on general skills and tendencies. All we really need to know is that Ellsbury is fast, Troy Percival is a high risk source for saves, and Andy Sonnanstine has ERA upside. Attaching numbers to these situations — 40, 29, 3.75 — only provides false security that we actually know what we're doing.

All of this talk must seem strange coming from a book called the *Baseball Forecaster*. You have probably come here because you want to know what those numbers are going to look like in 2009. But I have no crystal ball. Neither does any other service that proclaims great projective accuracy. The truth is, perhaps the *least valuable part of this book are the statistical projections that appear at the bottom of each player box.*

The most valuable part? Just about everything else. In fact, the greatest value that you can take away from this book is gaining the ability to evaluate players within a fantasy context *without* using the numbers (or at least not the ones you think you'd use).

A .300 hitter is not someone who has a projection of .300. A .300 hitter is someone who sees the ball well (batting eye ratio), makes contact often (contact rate) and is fortunate enough to have those batted balls fall for hits (hit rate). Those components may equate to .300, or .329, or .317. If his luck is particularly good, it might equate to a .350 season. If his luck is particularly bad, he might come out of the year at .275. Or worse.

But my slapping a label of ".300" on a set of stats, representing some mean expectation, is at best misleading, and at worse, potentially dangerous at the draft table.

And all that laptops do is make ".300" seem more real.

In *Fantasyland*, Sam Walker separated the Tout Wars experts into two groups — those who use laptops and those who are "old school" pen-and-paper drafters. But you know something about us pen-and-paper guys? We are not eschewing technology. We are not really "old school" either. I believe we just have greater confidence in our abilities to play this game. After two decades of experience, participating in a Rotisserie auction has evolved into a higher level decision-making process that does not need to rely on the hard data.

Tout veterans Lawr Michaels, Steve Moyer and I are among the few non-draft-software types left. We are all former experts league winners and finish in the money as often as any of our wired colleagues. All three of us know the player pool inside and out, which used to be an advantage by itself. But these days, there needs to be more.

I asked Lawr and Steve to share with me what that "more" is. It was remarkable how similar their responses were. For these vets, simply, the players themselves are just names on a sheet of paper. There are no emotional attachments or "gotta-haves." Both drafters have a sense of where there is value and then just seek out bargains, constructing their teams by playing the table.

I've seen these guys draft; I think they are selling themselves short.

I would better liken the process to when Luke Skywalker blew up the Death Star in *Star Wars.* The Force was something "special" inside of him that he was able to tap into when he needed it. It was a level of faith in his abilities that a higher level decision-making process was at work.

In a similar vein, Sam Walker calls Lawr the "Zen Master." Zen is defined as "acceptance of the present moment, spontaneous action, and letting go of self-conscious, judgmental thinking." That's pretty accurate.

For me, it's more of a sixth sense (but without the dead people). I just feel it.

Perhaps the best description of this process was in Malcolm Gladwell's book, *Blink.* He talks about our abilities to understand and react to situations at a glance, and make better decisions than those who have access to mountains of data. We have the ability to make unconscious adjustments to situations long before we are consciously aware that adjustments need to be made. He shows many case studies that prove our abilities to do this.

Gladwell talks about the power of "adaptive unconscious." Psychologist Timothy D. Wilson wrote, "The mind operates most efficiently by relegating a good deal of high-level, sophisticated thinking to the unconscious, just as a modern jetliner is able to fly on automatic pilot with little or no input from the human, "conscious" pilot." But Gladwell notes, "I think we are innately suspicious of this kind of rapid cognition. We live in a world that assumes that the quality of a decision is directly related to the time and effort that went into making it." Excess information can be harmful; it can potentially confuse an issue. We often call this "analysis paralysis."

So how do we tap into our "adaptive unconscious"? Gladwell cites author John Gottman's concept of "thin-slicing," the ability of our unconscious to find patterns in situations and behavior based on very narrow slices of experience.

I believe that is what happens at the draft table. For me, anyway. I sit down, look around me, and take it all in. The players occupy one part of my brain. My $260 budget occupies another part of my brain. I don't worry too much about them until I need to. I click on "auto-pilot."

It probably took me about 10-15 years of live auction experience, in dozens of leagues, to get to that point. But perhaps the only difference between me and you, and our respective abilities to play the game at an "expert" level, is that amount of experience. You can be no less a "real" expert if you've spent years perfecting the craft. There is nothing magical about being able to do this.

If I had to distill the process down, it might start with a series of pre-requisites. You must have:

- Confidence in your knowledge of the player pool.
- A rough, general sense of player value.
- An exceedingly simple record-keeping system.
- A deadly accurate focus on everything else that is going on around you at the draft.

Some perspective on these pre-requisites:

The **player knowledge** is not "Vlad Guerrero is projected to hit 25 home runs, drive in 100 runs and bat .300." These are lifeless pieces of projected data. Vlad could hit 27 HRs, or 22. He could bat .317 or .292. There are dozens of variables that may impact the actual numbers. The only knowledge that you can count on even a little is "Vlad Guerrero is a fading slugger who will get regular at bats on a contending team." Anything more definitive is pointless.

The rough idea of **player value** is not "Vlad is worth $23." Again, this fixed piece of data is nearly irrelevant. Vlad's $23 projection could be $27 if there is too much money chasing too little talent, or $31 if you are drafting at someone's house in Anaheim. The only knowledge you need is "Vlad's real value is probably in the low $20s. In my league, his market value might be higher." In a snake draft league, it would be "Vlad's real value is probably in the 4th round, but in my league he could go as early as late 2nd."

These first two bullets are things that you need to know almost intuitively. They must live in your unconscious.

The **record-keeping system** can be a cheat sheet, but if you have to start scanning lists to trigger your memory when Scott Hairston's name comes up (Is it Jerry? Or Scott?), you're not ready yet. And if these sheets contain data in four point type, you're not ready yet either. This system is intended merely to organize, not inform.

What does Ron Shandler use? Three sheets of paper.

Actually, it's a three-page draft grid. Listed along the top of the report are all the positions. Down the side are draft value ranges in $5 increments (though, depending upon your style of play, these ranges can be points, runs above replacement values or any other evaluative system). In each cell are just names of players. There is not a projected home run or save to be found.

(Draft grids that are fully customizable to your own league's parameters are available at BaseballHQ.com.)

Grouping players into tiers and cells of like value is the first step towards divorcing yourself from the numbers and the false sense of security that a data-driven program gives you. Vlad Guerrero is listed under "OF" in the grid's $20-$25 cell. He is one of many names there, all of whom I will consider as interchangeable commodities on Draft Day.

I then do some color highlighting to denote high or low risk players, those who I might go to the bank for (typically those with the highest skill *and* lowest risk) and some high-upside sleepers who might drop to the end game. I cross off names as they are drafted and note their purchase price. This gives me a general sense of whether players are going for over or under value. I don't need to know that the inflation rate is exactly 23% since that's driven by the projections anyway.

I circle those players who end up on my team. In the margin, I keep a running total of my budget. When about 75% of the players are off the board, then I start following the budgets and rosters of the other owners, but only those who have more money than I or can outbid me on any individual player.

Finally, with all the necessary draft prep in place, it is time for the last bullet point. These are the **things you are going to be accurately observing at the draft:**

- The auctioneer's cadence.
- The bidding behavior of those owners who you believe will be your toughest opposition.
- Incidences of pre-emptive bidding, jump bids and sluggish pacing.
- The types of players who are tossed out as openers.
- A sampling of purchase prices for top level, questionable and position/categorically scarce players.
- Any unusual behaviors that might be tip-offs to more aggressive competitive tactics.

This sounds like a ton of information to keep track of. It's also more qualitative in scope, which is tougher to get a handle on. However, if you truly own the earlier pre-requisites, you won't need to *consciously* keep track. Just like the players and values, this information will also be processed in your unconscious, the underlying patterns shaping your decisions as you go.

Back in 1997, in the LABR league, I challenged the experts to "draft naked," that is, sit down at the table with no prep materials whatsoever. They balked. When I launched the Xperts Fantasy League (XFL) in 2003, the rules limited draft prep materials to Major League depth charts only. No ranking lists, no cheat sheets, no electronic devices of any kind. The 15 of us have found these drafts exhilarating because they are the ultimate test of our knowledge and challenge us to approach Rotisserie baseball in an entirely different way.

It's not easy. This mode of play requires you to completely change the way you draft. It requires a higher level of decision-making, perhaps even a higher level of consciousness. It requires faith. But if you want to be considered a real expert in this game, it is the challenge you need to accept.

If you think you are ready to make a commitment to play on this completely different ballfield, here is the first thing you need to do:

You need to give up your laptop.

Trust the Force.

Welcome to the *Baseball Forecaster*, Edition #23.

This is a book about using numbers as a tool to compete successfully in any of the many flavors of fantasy baseball. It is a reference volume containing ideas and concepts that have been compiled over the course of two-plus decades. But, again, it is just a tool. There is no magic.

This book was conceived as a well-timed collision of sabermetrics and fantasy. The unique, hybrid brand of analysis that we perpetrate here is what we call **fanalytics,** which is a measured, deliberate approach to evaluating and projecting player performance within the context of fantasy baseball. It takes from both schools and provides deeper insight than any other analytical process. Sabermetrics becomes more than just a bunch of incomprehensible formulas, and fantasy becomes more than just blindly picking a bunch of players and praying.

New Readers – Welcome!

The *Baseball Forecaster* was the first book to approach prognostication by breaking performance down into its component parts. Rather than predicting batting average, for instance, we look at the elements of skill that make up that stat and reverse-engineer those skills back into batting average. This process has proven itself as being a better predictor than any quantitative model using the actual gauges themselves.

In all, we call this "component skills analysis."

You should know that there is some rudimentary math involved and there is a bit of a learning curve. The nice thing about the math, though, is that most of it is logical and intuitive. For instance, when we talk about "contact rate," that's just the percentage of time a batter makes contact with the ball. It is calculated simply as $((AB - K) / AB)$. As you would expect, the more contact a batter makes, the higher his batting average tends to be. We have benchmarks at the upper and lower ends of the scale — 70% and 90% — and we can project a player's batting average off of that.

And the pieces all fit together very neatly in the end.

Naturally, I think this approach is the best way to evaluate and project performance — and 23 years of publication attest to at least some level of public acceptance — but I'll let you decide for yourself. I do ask, however, that you keep an open mind. These tools do work, but you may have to toss away some of your preconceptions in order to embrace the possibilities.

For instance, later on in the book, you will read that, Boone Logan, a pitcher who had a 5.95 ERA in 2008, is projected to improve his ERA by more than *two full runs* in 2009. Old school evaluators will scoff at that assertion. They might have also scoffed last year when we projected a similarly significant upside for J.P. Howell (1-6, 7.59 ERA in 2007, 6-1, 2.22 ERA in 2008). The stuff works.

There's a ton of information here. At first glance, it will seem overwhelming. But you don't have to take it in all at once. Start slow; take as much time as you need.

What's New in 2009?

1. *More players:* The number of disabled list days has spiked over the past two years, giving many more players time in the major leagues. As such, it has become tougher to figure out which ones will have a future impact worth analyzing. So we've added more than two dozen player boxes to the main section of the book.

2. *Batter consistency charts:* With the rapid rise of head-to-head gaming, there is a need for a more in-depth look at each batter's week-to-week consistency. We provide three year trends.

3. *Starting pitcher consistency charts:* The same need exists on the pitching side. We've modified our PQS pitching logs and now have six-year trends for every starter.

4. *Reliability grades:* Our previous reliability scores tried to do too much and ended up giving us less information, not more. We've re-engineered these into three separate A-F grades for each batter and pitcher, measuring health, experience and consistency.

5. *Formula tweaks:* Later in the book, you will read about our new formula for Base Performance Values. We have also added some normalization factors for Expected Batting Average and Expected ERA so that league totals better approximate actual BA and ERA league levels.

The final new things are a new owner and a new publisher. Last April, the Shandler Enterprises LLC line, which included this book along with BaseballHQ.com, the *Minor League Baseball Analyst* and First Pitch Forums, was sold to Fantasy Sports Ventures, Inc. Triumph Books has taken over as publisher of this book. This is all good news for you. It means that we will have more resources to do more things in the future, and I will have more time to spend on furthering fanalytics.

Change takes time, however, so you won't see too many new things right away. But the prospects for the future of the *Baseball Forecaster* and Baseball HQ are very exciting. As for my fledgling songwriting career, not so much.

Updates

Content Update page: If there are any corrections or clarifications on the information in this book, go to:
http://www.baseballhq.com/books/bfupdates.shtml

Free Projections Update: As a buyer of this book, you get one free 2009 projections update, available online at
http://www.baseballhq.com/books/freeupdate/index.shtml
These are spreadsheet data files, to be posted on or about March 1, 2009.

Electronic book: The complete PDF version of the *Forecaster* – plus MS Excel versions of most key charts – is available free to those who bought the book directly through the BaseballHQ.com website. These files will be available in January 2009; contact us if you do not receive information via e-mail about accessing them. If you purchased the *Forecaster* through an online vendor or bookstore, you can purchase these files from us for $9.95. Call 1-800-422-7820 for more information.

Beyond the *Forecaster*

The *Forecaster* is just the beginning. The following companion products and services are described in more detail in the back of the book.

BaseballHQ.com is our home website. It provides regular updates to everything in this book, including daily updated projections, plus a ton more. In 2009, we'll be adding some robust new tools for managing your teams.

First Pitch Forums are a series of conferences we run all over the country, where you can meet some of the top industry analysts and network with fellow fantasy leaguers. In 2009, we'll have local three-hour sessions in the San Francisco Bay area, Los Angeles, Chicago, Cleveland, the Baltimore/DC area, New York and Boston. Check in the back for the schedule. Our 15th annual three-day conference will once again be in Phoenix on November 6-8.

RotoHQ.com is a very, very large online library of fantasy strategy essays and tools.

Minor League Baseball Analyst, the fourth edition of Deric McKamey's book, is a minor league version of the *Forecaster*, with stat boxes for over 1000 prospects, and more. *Available in January.*

We still have copies available of *How to Value Players for Rotisserie Baseball*, Art McGee's ground-breaking book on valuation theory.

RotoLab is the best draft software on the market, and not just because it comes bundled with our player projections. I might not use it myself (because I'm a pen-and-paper guy and stubborn beyond reason), but it's a terrific tool for those who draft with laptops. It's no exaggeration when I say that not one person has ever said anything negative to me about this product. Not one. Ever. All I ever hear are endless accolades.

I am going to wrap up this year's introduction with the final photograph ever taken of me at my childhood home. This is where I spent dozens of amazing afternoons, after cutting out of 6th and 7th period (usually Spanish and P.E.) to catch the Q65 bus into Flushing. It is where I watched Tom Seaver and Willie Mays, Buzz Capra and "Stork" Theodore. It is where I cheered my home team into the World Series on the back of

an 82-79 record. Yes, compared to other venues, it was not a great place to watch a game, but for me, it was home.

II.
FANALYTICS

Foundation Principles

Forecasting is the systematic process of determining likely end results. Baseball, as in most disciplines, uses some type of quantitative analysis in this process.

Baseball performance forecasting is inherently a high-risk exercise with a very modest accuracy rate. This is because the process involves not only statistics, but also unscientific elements, from random chance to human volatility. And even from within the statistical aspect there are multiple elements that need to be evaluated, from skill to playing time to a host of external variables.

Every system is comprised of the same core elements:

- Players will tend to perform within the framework of past history and/or trends.
- Skills will develop and decline according to age.
- Statistics will be shaped by a player's health, expected role and home ballpark.

While all systems are built from these same elements, they also are constrained by the same limitations. We are all still trying to project a bunch of human beings, each one...

- with his own individual skill set
- with his own rate of growth and decline
- with his own ability to resist and recover from injury
- limited to opportunities determined by other people
- generating a group of statistics largely affected by tons of external noise. For instance, a pitcher's wins requires the analysis of not only skill, but the skills of his team's offense, defense, bullpen and the manager's tendencies. *All* these variables must be analyzed.

Based on the research of multiple sources, the best accuracy rate that can be attained by any system is about 70%. In fact, a simple system that uses three-year averages adjusted for age ("Marcel the Monkey") can attain a success rate of 65%. This means all the advanced systems are fighting for occupation of the remaining 5%.

Other Considerations

Perpetuity: Forecasting is not an exercise that produces a single set of numbers. It is dynamic, cyclical and ongoing. Conditions are constantly changing and we must react to those changes by adjusting our expectations. A pre-season projection is just a snapshot in time. Once the first batter steps to the plate on Opening Day, that projection has become obsolete. Its value is merely to provide a starting point, a baseline for what is about to occur.

During the season, if a projection appears to have been invalidated by current performance, the process continues. It is then that we need to ask... What went wrong? What conditions have changed? In fact, has *anything* changed? We need to analyze the situation and revise our expectation, if necessary. This process must be ongoing.

Process and outcomes: The outcomes of forecasted events should not be confused with the process itself. Outcomes may be the components that are the most closely scrutinized, but as long as the process is sound, the forecast has done the best job it can do. *In the end, forecasting is about analysis, not prophecy.*

Component Skills Analysis

Our brand of forecasting is more about finding logical journeys than blind destinations.

Familiar gauges like HR and ERA have long been used to measure skill. In fact, these gauges only measure the outcome of an individual event, or series of events. They represent statistical output. They are "surface stats."

Raw skill is the talent beneath the stats, the individual elements of a player's makeup. Players use these skills to create the individual events, or components, that we record using measures like HR and ERA. Our approach:

1. It's not about batting average, it's about seeing the ball and making contact. We target hitters based on elements such as their batting eye (walks to strikeouts ratio), how often they make contact and the type of contact they make. We then combine these components into an "expected batting average." By comparing each hitter's actual BA to how he *should* be performing, we can draw conclusions about the future.

2. It's not about home runs, it's about power. From the perspective of a round bat meeting a round ball, it may be only a fraction of an inch at the point of contact that makes the difference between a HR or a long foul ball. When a ball is hit safely, often it is only a few inches that separate a HR from a double. We tend to neglect these facts in our analyses, although the outcomes — the doubles, triples, long fly balls — may be no less a measure of that batter's raw power skill. We must incorporate all these components to paint a complete picture.

3. It's not about ERA, it's about getting the ball over the plate and keeping it in the park. Forget ERA. You want to draft pitchers who walk few batters (control), strike out many (dominance) and succeed at both in tandem (command). You also want pitchers who keep the ball on the ground (because home runs are bad). All of this translates into an "expected ERA" that you can use to compare to a pitcher's actual performance.

4. It's never about wins. For pitchers, winning ballgames is less about skill and more about offensive support. As such, projecting wins is futile and valuing hurlers based on their win history is dangerous. Target skill; wins will come.

5. It's not about saves, it's about opportunity first and skills second. While the highest skilled pitchers have the best potential to succeed as closers, they still have to be given the ball with the game on the line in the 9th inning, and that is a decision left to others. Over the past 10 years, about 40% of relievers drafted for saves failed to hold the role for the entire season. The lesson: Don't take chances on draft day. There will always be saves in the free agent pool.

Luck

Luck has been used as a catch-all term to describe random chance. When we use the term here, we're talking about unexplained variances that shape the statistics. Yes, these variances are random, but they are also often measurable and projectable. In order to get a better read on "luck," we use formulas that capture the external variability of the data.

Through our research and the work of others, we have learned that when raw skill is separated from statistical output, what's remaining is often unexplained variance. The aggregate totals of many of these variances, for all players, is often a constant. For instance, while a pitcher's ERA might fluctuate, the rate at which his opposition's batted balls fall for hits will always be about 30%. Large variances in this rate can be expected to regress to 30%.

Why is all this important? Analysts complain about the lack of predictability of many traditional statistical gauges. The reason they find it difficult is that they are trying to project performance using gauges that are loaded with external noise. Raw skills gauges are more pure and follow better defined trends during a player's career. Then, as we get a better handle on the variances — explained and unexplained — we can construct a complete picture of what a player's statistics really mean.

The Process

The next step is to assemble these evaluators in such a way that they can be used to validate our observations, analyze their relevance and project a likely future direction.

In a perfect world, if a player's raw skills improve, then so should his surface stats. If his skills decline, then his stats should follow as well. But, sometimes a player's skill may increase while his surface stats may decline. These variances may be due to a variety of factors.

Component skills analysis is based on the expectation that events tend to move towards universal order. Surface stats will eventually approach their raw skill levels. Unexplained variances will regress to a mean. And from this, we can identify players whose performance may potentially change.

This process provides an important starting point for any forecasting analysis. For most of us, that analysis begins with the previous season's numbers. Last season provides us with a point of reference, so it's a natural way to begin the process of looking at the future.

Component skills analysis allows us to validate last year's numbers. A batter with few HRs but a high linear weighted power level has a good probability of improving his future HR output. A pitcher whose ERA was solid while his command ratio was poor is a good bet for an ERA spike.

Of course, these leading indicators do not always follow the rules. There are more shades of greys than blacks and whites. When indicators are in conflict – for instance, a pitcher who is displaying both a rising strikeout rate and a rising walk rate – then we have to find ways to sort out what these indicators might be saying.

It is often helpful to look at leading indicators in a hierarchy, of sorts. In fact, a hierarchy of the most important pitching base performance indicators might look like this: command (k/bb), control (bb/9), dominance (k/9) and GB/FB rate. For batters, contact rate might top the list, followed by power, walk rate and speed.

Assimilating Additional Research

Once we've painted the statistical picture of a player's potential, we then use additional criteria and research results to help us add some more color. These other criteria include the player's health, age, changes in role, ballpark, and a variety of other factors. We also use our *Forecaster's Toolbox* research results, which are described in the next section. These analyses look at things like traditional periods of peak performance and breakout profiles.

The final element of the process is assimilating the news into the forecast. This is the element that many fantasy leaguers tend to rely on most since it is the most accessible. However, it is also the element that provides the most noise.

Players, management and the media have absolute control over what we are allowed to know. Factors such as hidden injuries, messy divorces and clubhouse unrest are routinely kept from us, while we are fed red herrings and media spam. *We will never know the entire truth.*

And so... as long as we do not know all the facts, we cannot dismiss the possibility that any one fact is true, no matter how often the media assures it, deplores it, or ignores it. Don't believe everything you read; use your own judgment. If your observations conflict with what is being reported, that's powerful insight that should not be ignored.

Quite often, all you are reading is just other people's opinions... a manager who believes that a player has what it takes to be a regular, a team physician whose diagnosis is that a player is healthy enough to play. These words from experts have some element of truth, but cannot be wholly relied upon to provide an accurate expectation of future events. As such, it is often helpful to develop an appropriate cynicism for what you read.

For instance, if a player is struggling for no apparent reason, and there are denials about health issues, don't dismiss the possibility that an injury does exist. There are often motives for such news to be withheld from the public.

Also remember that nothing lasts forever in major league baseball. *Reality is fluid.* One decision begets a series of events that lead to other decisions. Any reported action can easily be reversed based on subsequent events. My favorite examples are announcements of a team's new bullpen closer. Those are about the shortest realities known to man.

We need the media to provide us with context for our analyses, and the *real* news they provide is valuable intelligence. But separating the news from the noise is difficult. In most cases, the only thing you can trust is how that player actually performs.

Embracing Imprecision

Precision and accuracy in baseball prognosticating is a fool's quest. There are far too many unexpected variables and noise that can render our projections useless. The truth is, the best we can ever hope for is to accurately forecast general tendencies and percentage plays.

However, even when you follow an 80% percentage play, for instance, you will still lose 20% of the time. Those 20% worth of outlying players are what skeptics like to use as proof that all prognosticators are frauds. The paradox, of course, is that fantasy league titles are often won or lost by those exceptions. Still, long-term success dictates that you always chase the 80% and accept the fact that you will be wrong 20% of the time. Or, whatever that percentage play happens to be.

For fantasy league purposes, playing the percentages can take on an even less precise spin. The best projections are often the ones that are just far enough away from the field of expectation to alter decision-making. In other words, it doesn't matter if I project Player X to bat .320 and he only bats .295; it matters that I projected .320 and everyone else projected .280.

Or, perhaps we should evaluate projections based upon their intrinsic value. For instance, coming into 2008, would it have been more important for me to tell you that Adam Dunn was going to hit 40 HRs or that Juan Pierre would only get 290 at bats? By season's end, the Dunn projection would have been dead-on accurate, but the Pierre projection — even though it was off by 85 AB — would have been far more *valuable*.

And that should be enough. Actually, it *has* to be enough. Any tout who exactly projects any player's statistics dead-on will have just been lucky with his dart throws that day.

About Us Touts

As a group, there is a strong tendency for all pundits to provide numbers that are more palatable than realistic. That's because committing to either end of the range of expectation poses a high risk. Few touts possess the courage to put their credibility on the line like that, even though we all know that those outliers are inevitable. So they take the easy road and just split the difference. I am a member of that group and I can say that we are cowards, all of us.

In the world of prognosticating, this is called the *comfort zone*. This represents the outer tolerances for the public acceptability of a set of numbers. In most circumstances, even if the evidence is outstanding, prognosticators will not stray from within the comfort zone.

For instance, I know several published touts who thought that Tim Lincecum had the potential to put up Cy Young-caliber numbers in 2008. Yet none of them projected anything close to a sub-3.00 ERA or more than a dozen wins on a lackluster Giants club. Most gave the big numbers to the typical names — Brandon Webb, Jake Peavy and Johan Santana — because they were safe. More publicly palatable.

As for me, occasionally I do commit to outlying numbers when I feel the data supports it. But on the whole, most of my numbers can be nearly as cowardly as everyone else's. I get around this by providing "color" to the projections in the capsule commentaries. That is where you will find the players whose projection has the best potential to stray beyond the limits of the comfort zone.

As analyst John Burnson once wrote: "The issue is not the success rate for one player, but the success rate for all players. No system is 100% reliable, and in trying to capture the outliers, you weaken the middle and thereby lose more predictive pull than you gain. At some level, everyone is an exception!"

And Just So You Know

We began the conversation about component skills analysis right here in 1993, in the sixth edition of the *Baseball Forecaster*. The LIMA Plan in 1998 pioneered the application of these concepts for fantasy baseball. Since then, we continue to further the discussion, enhancing and refining the process of winning with such tools as Pure Quality Starts and strategies such as the Portfolio3 Plan.

Thanks to the internet, its community of sharing and the easy dissemination of information, other sources have picked up on the power of these tools. When you see things like contact rate and strand rate cited elsewhere, know that the research and application of these gauges originated *here*, whether these other services provide fair attribution or have adopted the concepts as their own. But the source of the original thought, and the place that continues to pioneer innovative new ideas, is the *Baseball Forecaster* and BaseballHQ.com. This is where you stay ahead of the curve.

For a deeper discussion about my take on baseball forecasting, read "The Great Myths of Projective Accuracy" online at **http://www.baseballhq.com/books/myths.shtml**

CONSUMER ADVISORY

AN IMPORTANT MESSAGE FOR FANTASY LEAGUERS:
THE TOP 10 WARNINGS ABOUT
INCORRECTLY USING THE *BASEBALL FORECASTER*

This document is provided in compliance with authorities to outline the prospective risks and hazards possible in the event that the *Baseball Forecaster* is used incorrectly. Please be aware of these potentially dangerous situations and avoid them. Ron Shandler assumes no risk related to any financial loss or stress-induced illnesses caused by ignoring the items as described below.

1. The statistical projections in this book are intended as general guidelines, not as gospel. It is highly dangerous to use the projected statistics alone, and then live and die by them. That's like going to a ballgame, being given a choice of any seat in the park, and deliberately choosing the last row in the right field corner with an obstructed view. The projections are there, you can look at them, but there are so many better places to sit.

We have to publish those numbers, but they are stagnant, inert pieces of data. This book focuses on a *live forecasting process* that provides the tools so that you can understand the leading indicators and draw your own conclusions. If you at least attempt your own analyses of the data, and enhance them with the player commentaries, you can paint more robust, colorful pictures of the future.

In other words...

If you bought this book purely for the projected statistics and do not intend to spend at least some time learning about the process, then you might as well just buy an $8 magazine.

2. The player commentaries in this book are written by humans, just like you. These commentaries provide an overall evaluation of performance and likely future direction, but 40-word capsules cannot capture everything. Your greatest value will be to use these as a springboard to your own analysis of the data. Odds are, if you take the time, you'll find hidden indicators that we might have missed. *Forecaster* veterans say that this self-guided excursion is the best part of owning the book.

3. This book does not attempt to tackle playing time. Rather than making arbitrary decisions about how roles will shake out, the focus is on performance. The playing time projections presented here are merely to help you better evaluate each player's talent. Our online pre-season projections update provides more current AB/IP expectations based on how roles are being assigned.

4. The dollar values in this book are intended solely for player-to-player comparisons. They are not driven by a finite pool of playing time – which is required for valuation systems to work properly – so they cannot be used for bid values to be used in your own draft.

There are two reasons for this:

a. The finite pool of players that will generate the finite pool of playing time will not be determined until much closer to Opening Day.

b. Your particular league's construction will drive the values; a $10 player in a 10-team mixed league will not be the same as a $10 player in a 13-team NL-only league.

Note that book dollar values also cannot be compared to those published on BaseballHQ.com as the online values *are* generated by a more finite player pool.

5. Do not pass judgment on the effectiveness of this book based on the performance of individual players. The test, rather, is on the collective predictive value of the book's methods. Are players with better underlying base skills more likely to produce good results that bad ones? Years of research suggest that the answer is "yes." Does that mean that every high skilled player will perform well? No. But many more of them will perform well than will the average low-skilled player. So you should always side with the better percentage plays, but recognize that there are factors we cannot predict. Good decisions that beget bad outcomes do not invalidate the methods used in this book.

6. If your copy of this book is not marked up and dog-eared by Draft Day, you probably did not get as much out of it as you might have.

7. This book is not intended to provide absorbency for spills of more than 6.5 ounces

8. This book is not intended to provide stabilizing weight for more than 15 sheets of 20 lb. paper in winds more than 45 mph.

9. The pages of this book are not recommended for avian waste collection. In independent laboratory studies, most migratory water fowl refuse to excrete on interior pages, even when coaxed.

10. This book, when rolled into a cylindrical shape, is not intended to be used as a weapon for any purpose, including but not limited to insect extermination, canine training or as a means to influence bidding behavior at a fantasy draft.

Forecaster's Toolbox

The following tools, rules and research findings represent the work of many authors, from industry icons like Bill James to the analysts at Baseball HQ.

There are two types of information here. There are analytical tools, which are methods to put events and performances into context. And there are actual research results. Generally, we only include the results of each particular piece of research, rather than take up space with all the methodologies and minutia. The back-up data have appeared in our other publications and on Baseball HQ in the past. Our purpose here is to give you the tools you need to make evaluations, and quickly. So pardon the lack of support data. Rest assured we're not making this stuff up.

Be aware that these research findings represent tendencies, not absolutes. If we tell you that 96% of batters with eye ratios grater than 1.50 will hit over .250, don't send us hate mail if the former batting champion you drafted in the second round falls into the other 4%. It happens. It's not our fault. Consider this a universal disclaimer.

Beyond that, there is great value here. Consider this your own fanalytic arsenal.

Validating Overall Performance

Performance Validation Criteria

When a player puts up numbers that vary from expectation, we can assemble a set of support variables that can help us determine whether his statistical output is an accurate reflection of his skills, or if other variables have come into play that have distorted the stats. Essentially, we're asking, is this performance a "fact or fluke?"

1. The player's age... Is he at the stage of development when we might expect a change in performance?

2. Health status... Is he coming off an injury, reconditioned and healthy for the first time in years, or a habitual resident of the disabled list?

3. Minor league performance... Has he ever shown the potential for greater things at some level of the minors? Or does his minor league history show a poor skill set that might indicate a lower skills ceiling?

4. Historical trends... Have his skill levels over time been on an upswing or downswing?

5. Hidden indicators behind traditional stats... Looking beyond batting averages and ERAs, what do his support ratios look like?

6. Change in ballpark, team, league... Pitchers going to Texas will see their ERA spike. Pitchers going to Petco Field will see their ERA improve. Stuff like that.

7. Change in team performance... Has a player's performance been affected by overall team chemistry or the environment fostered by a winning or losing club?

8. Change in batting stance, pitching style... Has a change in performance been due to an adjustment made during the off-season?

9. Change in usage, lineup position, etc.... Has a change in RBI opportunities been a result of moving further up or down in the batting order? Has pitching effectiveness been impacted by moving from the bullpen to the rotation?

10. Change in managerial strategy, or opportunity... Does his sudden change in performance have less to do with ability than with playing time, or perhaps not having a well-defined role?

11. Coaching effects... Has the coaching staff changed the way a player approaches his conditioning, or how he approaches the game itself?

12. Off-season activity... Has a player spent the winter frequenting workout rooms or banquet tables?

13. Personal factors... Has the player undergone a family crisis? Experienced spiritual rebirth? Given up red meat? Taken up testosterone?

Skills Ownership

Once a player displays a skill, he owns it. That display could occur at any time – earlier in his career, back in the minors, or even in winter ball play. And while that skill may lie dormant after its initial display, the potential is always there for him to tap back into that skill at some point, barring injury or age. That dormant skill can reappear at any time given the right set of circumstances.

Caveat... The initial display of skill must have occurred over an extended period of time. An isolated 1-hit shut-out in Single-A ball amidst a 5.00 ERA season is not enough. The shorter the display of skill in the past, the more likely it can be attributed to random chance. The longer the display, the more likely that any re-emergence is for real.

Corollaries:

1. Once a player displays a vulnerability or skills deficiency, he owns that as well. That vulnerability could be an old injury problem, an inability to hit breaking pitches, or just a tendency to go into prolonged slumps.

2. The probability of a player addressing and correcting a skills deficiency declines with each year he allows that deficiency to continue to exist.

Categories of Surprises

When a player has an uncharacteristically good or bad season, it is helpful to characterize that performance to determine its likelihood of being repeated. By answering a question such as, "Was Cliff Lee's 2008 performance a career year, maturation, or aberration?" we can start the process of projecting what he is likely to do in 2009.

Career year: These are players who have established a certain level of performance over several years, then suddenly put up exceptional numbers. Career years may be explained from the list of validation criteria, but are usually one-shot deals.

Maturation: These players have also established a certain level of performance over time, but the performance spike is truly indicative of a positive change in skills and will likely be maintained.

Off year: These are players who have established a certain level of performance over several years, then suddenly drop off. This could be a performance blip, an adjustment period or an injury-induced decline. These players have the potential to bounce back.

Comedown: These players have also established a certain level of performance over time, but their performance drop is indicative of a new level at which they will likely plateau.

Opportunity: Sometimes a surprise isn't a change in performance at all but the effect a change in playing time has on performance. Often, a role player moves into a full-time job and experiences a marked change in productivity. This can work both ways — he may rise to the occasion, or find that the regular day-to-day grind has an adverse effect on his numbers. Opportunity surprises are created by events like injuries or changes in managerial strategy and can last as long as the opportunity lasts.

No surprise: We sometimes form unrealistic expectations about players due to media hype or small samples of past performance. Rookies and injured players fall into this category, for instance, but the success or failure of unknown, untested or unproven commodities should not be unexpected.

Aberration: These are the performances that simply cannot be adequately explained by the validation criteria. Chance occurrences do happen, and sometimes in bunches. There are stretches in a player's career when a spray hitter might see a few week's worth of fat, juicy homer balls, or a pitcher might face a string of wiffle bats. It just happens, then it stops. Most times, it will never happen again.

Contract Year Performance

There is a contention that players step up their game when they are playing for a new contract. Research looked at contract year players, their performance during that year (as compared to career levels) and whether they reverted to form in the first year of their new contract. Of the batters and pitchers studied, 53% of the batters performed as if they were on a salary drive, while only 15% of the pitchers managed to exhibit some level of contract year behavior.

Risk Management and Reliability Grades

Forecasts are constructed with the best data available, but there are factors that can impact the variability around that projection. One way we manage this risk is to assign each player Reliability Grades. The more certainty we see in a data set, the higher the reliability grades assigned to that player. The following variables are evaluated:

Health: Players with a history of staying healthy and off the disabled list are valuable to own. Unfortunately, while the ability to stay healthy can be considered skill, it is not very projectable. We can track the number of days spent on the disabled list and draw only rough conclusions. The grades in the player boxes also include an adjustment for older players, who have a higher likelihood of getting hurt. That is the only forward-looking element of the grade.

"A" level players would have accumulated fewer than 30 days on the Major League DL over the past five years. "F" grades go to those who've spent more than 120 days on the DL. Recent DL stays are given a heavier weight in the calculation.

Playing Time and Experience (PT/Exp): The greater the pool of Major League history to draw from, the greater our ability to construct a viable forecast. Length of service is important, as is length of consistent service. So players who bounce up and down from the Majors to the minors are higher risk players. And rookies are all high risk.

For batters, we simply track plate appearances. Major league PAs have greater weight than minor league PAs. "A" level players would have averaged at least 550 major league PAs per year over the past three years. "F" graded players averaged fewer than 250 major league PAs per year.

For pitchers, workload can be a double-edged sword. On one hand, small IP samples are deceptive in providing a read on a pitcher's true potential. Even a consistent 65-inning reliever can be considered higher risk; just one bad outing can skew an entire year's work.

On the flipside, high workload levels also need to be monitored, especially in the formative years of a pitcher's career. Exceeding those levels elevates the risk of injury, burnout, or breakdown. So, tracking workload must be done within a range of innings. The grades capture this.

Consistency: Consistent performers are easier to project and garner higher reliability grades. Players that mix mediocrity with occasional flashes of brilliance or badness generate higher risk projections. Even those who exhibit a consistent upward or downward trend cannot be considered truly consistent as we do not know whether those trends will continue.

"A" level players are those whose runs created per game level (xERA for pitchers) has fluctuated by less than half a run during each of the past three years. "F" grades go to those whose RC/G has fluctuated by two runs or more.

Remember that these grades have nothing to do with *quality* of performance; they strictly refer to confidence in our expectations. So a grade of **AAA** for Jason Marquis, for instance, only means that there is a high probability he will perform as poorly as we've projected.

Reliability and Experience

Peak batting reliability occurs at ages 29 and 30, followed by a minor decline for four years. So, to draft the most reliable batters, and maximize the odds of returning at least par value on your investments, you should target the age range of 28-34.

The most reliable age range for pitchers is 29-34. While we are forever looking for "sleepers" and hot prospects, it is very risky to draft any pitcher under 27 or over 35.

IN-SEASON ANALYSIS

April Performance as a Leading Indicator

We isolated all players who earned at least $10 more or $10 less than we had projected in March. Then we looked at the April stats of these players to see if we could have picked out the $10 outliers after just one month.

	Identifiable in April
Earned $10+ more than projected	
BATTERS	39%
PITCHERS	44%
Earned -$10 less than projected	
BATTERS	56%
PITCHERS	74%

Nearly three out of every four pitchers who earned at least $10 less than projected also struggled in April. For all the other surprises — batters or pitchers — April was not a strong leading indicator. Another look:

	Pct.
Batters who finished +$25	45%
Pitchers who finished +$20	44%
Batters who finished under $0	60%
Pitchers who finished under -$5	78%

April surgers are less than a 50/50 proposition to maintain that level all season. Those who finished April at the bottom of the roto rankings were more likely to continue struggling, especially pitchers. In fact, of those pitchers who finished April with a value *under -$10*, 91% finished the season in the red. Holes are tough to dig out of.

Courtship Period

Any time a player is put into a new situation, he enters into what we might call a *courtship period*. This period might occur when a player switches leagues, or switches teams. It could be the first few games when a minor leaguer is called up. It could occur when a reliever moves into the rotation, or when a lead-off hitter is moved to another spot in the lineup. There is a team-wide courtship period when a manager is replaced. Any external situation that could affect a player's performance sets off a new decision point in evaluating that performance.

During this period, it is difficult to get a true read on how a player is going to ultimately perform. He is adjusting to the new situation. Things could be volatile during this time. For instance, a role change that doesn't work could spur other moves. A rookie hurler might buy himself a few extra starts with a solid debut, even if he has questionable skills.

It is best not to make a decision on a player who is going through a courtship period. Wait until his stats stabilize. Don't cut a struggling pitcher in his first few starts after a managerial change. Don't pick up a hitter who smacks a pair of HRs in his first game after having been traded. Unless, of course, talent and track record say otherwise.

Half-Season Fallacies

A popular exercise at the midpoint of each season is to analyze those players who are *consistent* first half to second half surgers or faders. There are several fallacies with this analytical approach.

1. Half-season consistency is rare. There are very few players who show consistent changes in performance from one half of the season to the other.

Research results from a three-year study conducted in the late-1990s: The total of all batters who compiled a minimum of 300 full season ABs, and a minimum of 150 first half ABs in this study was 98. Of that group, 40% demonstrated a consistent first half to second half trend in at least one statistical category for all three years. Only 18% demonstrated any half-season tendency in more than one category. Only 3% demonstrated consistent tendencies in more than two categories over the three-year period.

The total of all pitchers who compiled a minimum of 100 full season IPs, and a minimum of 50 first half IPs in this study was only 42. Of that group, 57% demonstrated a consistent first half to second half trend in at least one stat category for all three years. Only 21% demonstrated any half-season tendency in more than one category. And only 5% had consistent tendencies in more than two categories.

When the analysis was stretched to a fourth year, only 1% of all players showed consistency in even one category.

2. Analysts often use false indicators. Situational statistics provide us with tools that are often misused. Several sources offer up three and 5-year statistics intended to paint a picture of a long-term performance. Some analysts look at a player's half-season batting average swing over that multi-year period and conclude that he is demonstrating consistent performance.

The fallacy is that those multi-year scans may not show any consistency at all. They are not individual season performances but *aggregate* performances. A player whose 5-year batting average shows a 15-point rise in the 2nd half, for instance, may actually have experienced a BA *decline* in several of those years, a fact that might have been offset by a huge BA rise in one of the years.

3. It's arbitrary. The season's midpoint is really an arbitrary delineator of performance swings. Some players are slow starters and might be more appropriately evaluated as pre-May 1 and post-May 1. Others bring their game up a notch with a pennant chase and might see a performance swing with August 15 as the cut-off. Each player has his own individual tendency, if, in fact, one exists at all. There's nothing magical about mid-season as the break point, and certainly not over a multi-year period.

Batting Toolbox

Batting Eye as a Leading Indicator

There is a strong correlation between strike zone judgment and batting average. However, research shows that this is more descriptive than predictive:

	Batting Average				
Batting Eye	2004	2005	2006	2007	2008
0.00 - 0.25	.235	.244	.251	.250	.242
0.26 - 0.50	.262	.261	.267	.265	.261
0.51 - 0.75	.276	.274	.279	.276	.273
0.76 - 1.00	.279	.279	.286	.280	.280
1.01 and over	.300	.290	.287	.305	.285

We can create percentage plays for the different levels:

For Eye	Pct who bat	
Levels of	.300+	.250-
0.00 - 0.25	7%	39%
0.26 - 0.50	14%	26%
0.51 - 0.75	18%	17%
0.76 - 1.00	32%	14%
1.01 - 1.50	51%	9%
1.51 +	59%	4%

Any batter with an eye ratio over 1.50 has about a 4% chance of hitting under .250 over 500 at bats.

Of all .300 hitters, those with ratios of at least 1.00 have a 65% chance of repeating as .300 hitters. Those with ratios under 1.00 have less than a 50% chance of repeating.

Only 4% of sub-.250 hitters with ratios less than 0.50 will mature into .300 hitters the following year.

In a 1995-2000 study, only 37 batters hit .300-plus with a sub-0.50 eye ratio over at least 300 AB in a season. Of this group, 30% were able to accomplish this feat on a consistent basis. For the other 70%, this was a short-term aberration.

Contact Rate as a Leading Indicator

The more often a batter makes contact with the ball, the higher the likelihood that he will hit safely.

	Batting Average				
Contact Rate	2004	2005	2006	2007	2008
0% - 60%	.187	.207	.181	.204	.210
61% - 65%	.186	.221	.220	.228	.226
66% - 70%	.242	.244	.251	.237	.235
71% - 75%	.249	.252	.256	.250	.250
76% - 80%	.265	.266	.270	.269	.262
81% - 85%	.273	.270	.274	.277	.273
86% - 90%	.283	.279	.287	.284	.284
Over 90%	.298	.282	.295	.289	.285

Contact Rate & Walk Rate as Leading Indicators

A matrix of contact rates and walk rates can provide expectation benchmarks for a player's batting average:

		bb%			
		0-5	6-10	11-15	16+
ct%	65-	.179	.195	.229	.237
	66-75	.190	.248	.254	.272
	76-85	.265	.267	.276	.283
	86+	.269	.279	.301	.309

A contact rate of 65% or lower offers virtually no chance for a player to hit even .250, no matter how high a walk rate he has. The .300 hitters most often come from the group with a minimum 86% contact and 11% walk rate.

Hit Rate (BABIP) as a Leading Indicator
(Patrick Davitt)

Every hitter establishes his own individual hit rate (batting average on balls-in-play) that stabilizes over time. A batter whose seasonal hit rate (H%) varies significantly from the H% he has established over the preceding three seasons is likely to improve or regress to his individual H% mean (with over-performer declines more likely and sharper than under-performer recoveries). Three-year H% levels strongly predict a player's H% the following year.

Batting Eye and Power

We often ignore the batting eye ratio when evaluating power because so many batters achieve their lofty HR numbers by opening up their swing, thereby increasing their strikeout totals and depressing their eye ratio. However, this path to power success is a riskier one.

During a four-year study period, any batter who slammed 30 HRs in a season had less than a 3 in 10 chance of improving his power skills the following year.

	YEAR 2	
Batting eye	PX increased	PX declined
Less than 0.50	13%	87%
0.50 - 0.99	24%	76%
1.00 and over	31%	69%

Batters with lower eye ratios were more likely to see a power drop-off in the year following a 30-HR campaign.

Power Breakouts

It is not easy to predict which batters will experience a power spike. We can categorize power breakouts to determine the likelihood of a player taking a step up or of a surprise performer repeating his feat. Possibilities:

- Increase in playing time
- History of power skills at some time in the past
- Redistribution of already demonstrated extra base hit power
- Normal skills growth
- Situational breakouts, particularly in hitter-friendly venues
- Increased fly ball tendency
- Use of illegal performance-enhancing substances
- Miscellaneous unexplained variables

Fly Ball Tendency and Power *(Mat Olkin)*

There is a proven connection between a hitter's ground ball-fly ball tendencies and his power production.

1. Extreme ground ball hitters generally do not hit for much power. It's almost impossible for a hitter with a ground/fly ratio over 1.80 to hit enough fly balls to produce even 25 HRs in a season. However, this does not mean that a low G/F ratio necessarily guarantees power production. Some players have no problem getting the ball into the air, but lack the strength to reach the fences consistently.

2. Most batters' ground/fly ratios stay pretty steady over time. Most year-to-year changes are small and random, as they are in any other statistical category. A large, sudden change in G/F, on the other hand, can signal a conscious change in plate approach. And so...

3. If a player posts high G/F ratios in his first few years, he probably isn't ever going to hit for all that much power.

4. When a batter's power suddenly jumps, his G/F ratio often drops at the same time.

5. Every so often, a hitter's ratio will drop significantly even as his power production remains level. In these rare cases, impending power development is likely, since the two factors almost always follow each other.

HR/F Rate as a Leading Indicator *(Joshua Randall)*

Each batter establishes an individual home run to fly ball rate that stabilizes over rolling three-year periods; those levels strongly predict the HR/F in the subsequent year. A batter who varies significantly from his HR/F is likely to regress toward his individual HR/F mean, with over-performance decline more likely and more severe than under-performance recovery.

Handedness Notes

1. While pure southpaws account for about 27% of total ABs (RHers about 55% and switch-hitters about 18%), they hit 31% of the triples and take 30% of the walks.

2. The average lefty posts a batting average about 10 points higher than the average RHer. The on base averages of pure LHers are nearly 20 points higher than RHers, but only 10 points higher than switch-hitters.

3. LHers tend to have a better batting eye ratio than RHers, but about the same as switch-hitters.

4. Pure righties and lefties have virtually identical power skills. Switch-hitters tend to have less power, on average.

5. Switch-hitters tend to have the best speed, followed by LHers, and then RHers.

6. On an overall production basis, LHers have an 8% advantage over RHers and a 14% edge over switch-hitters.

Batting Average Perception

Early season batting average strugglers who surge later in the year get no respect because they have to live with the weight of their early numbers all season long. Conversely, quick starters who fade late get far more accolades than they deserve.

For instance, take Robinson Cano's 2008 month-by-month batting averages. Perception, which is typically based solely on a player's cumulative season stat line, was that he struggled in batting average pretty much all season. Reality is different. He had one truly off-month, and it happened to occur in April. How many people knew he batted .297 from May 1 on and .302 in the second half?

Month	BA	Cum BA
April	.151	.151
May	.295	.219
June	.287	.242
July	.327	.263
August	.290	.268
September	.287	.271

Wasted Talent on the Basepaths

We refer to some players as having "wasted talent," a high level skill that is negated by a deficiency in another skill. Among these types are players who have blazing speed that is negated by a sub-.300 on base average.

These players can have short-term value. However, their stolen base totals are tied so tightly to their "green light" that any change in managerial strategy could completely erase that value. A higher OB mitigates that downside; the good news is that plate patience *can* be taught.

Players in 2008 who had at least 20 SBs with an OB less than .300, and whose SB output could be at risk, are Michael Bourn (41 SB, .286), Carlos Gomez (33, .289), Rajai Davis (30, .278) and Cory Hart (23, .299). Even Wily Tavares (68, .303) seems ill-positioned to repeat his SB success.

Spring Training Leading Indicator *(John Dewan)*

A positive difference between a hitter's spring training slugging pct. and his lifetime slugging pct. of .200 or more is a leading indicator for a better than normal season.

Optimal Ages

Players develop at different paces, but in general terms, age can be helpful to determine where they should be along the developmental curve. Bill James' original research showed that batters tended to peak at about age 27. More recent research suggests that a variety of factors have pushed that average up closer to 30. More tendencies:

"26 With Experience" *(John Benson)*: While batters may peak at about age 27, the players most likely to exhibit the most dramatic spike in performance are those aged 26 who have several years of major league experience.

Power: Batting power skills tend to grow consistently between ages 24 and 29. Many batters experience a power peak at about age 30-31. Catchers often experience a power spike in the mid-30's.

Speed: Base-running and speed are skills of the young. When given the choice of two speedsters of fairly equivalent abilities and opportunity, always go after the younger one. A sharp drop-off in speed skills typically occurs at age 34.

Batting eye: For batters who continue to play into their 30's, this is a skill that can develop and grow throughout their career. A decline in this level, which can occur at any age, often indicates a decline in overall skills.

Thirtysomethings *(Ed Spaulding)*: Batters tend to lose points on their BA but draw more walks. While players on the outside of the defensive spectrum (1B, 3B, LF, RF, DH) often have their best seasons in their 30's, players in the middle (2B, SS, CF) tend to fade. Many former stars move to new positions (Ripken, Molitor, Banks, etc.).

Catchers *(Ed Spaulding)*: Many catchers — particularly second line catchers — have their best seasons late in their careers. Some possible reasons why:

1. Catchers, like shortstops, often get to the big leagues for defensive reasons and not their offensive skills. These skills take longer to develop.

2. The heavy emphasis on learning the catching/defense/pitching side of the game detracts from their time to learn about, and practice, hitting.

3. Injuries often curtail their ability to show offensive skills, though these injuries (typically jammed fingers, bruises on the arms, rib injuries from collisions) often don't lead to time on the disabled list.

4. The time spent behind the plate has to impact the ability to recognize, and eventually hit, all kinds of pitches.

Projecting Batting Breakout Performances
(Brandon Kruse)

A breakout performance is defined here as one where a player posts a Rotisserie value of $20 or higher after having never posted a value of $10 previously. These criteria are primarily used to validate an apparent breakout in the current season but may also be used carefully to project a potential breakout for an upcoming season.

- Age 27 or younger.
- An increase in at least two of the following categories: H%, PX or SX.
- Minimum league average PX or SX (100)
- Minimum contact rate of 75%
- Minimum xBA of .270

IN-SEASON ANALYSIS
Projecting Runs Batted In *(Patrick Davitt)*

Evaluating players in-season for RBI potential is a function of the interplay among four factors:

- Teammates' ability to reach base ahead of him and to run the bases efficiently;
- His own ability to drive them around by hitting, especially for extra bases
- Number of Games Played
- Place in the batting order

3-4-5 Hitters:
(0.69 x GP x TOB) + (0.30 x ITB) + (0.275 x HR) − (.191 x GP)

6-7-8 Hitters:
(0.63 x GP x TOB) + (0.27 x ITB) + (0.250 x HR) − (.191 x GP)

9-1-2 Hitters:
(0.57 x GP x TOB) + (0.24 x ITB) + (0.225 x HR) − (.191 x GP)

...where GP = games played, TOB = team on-base pct. and ITB = individual total bases (ITB).

Apply this pRBI formula after 70 games played or so (to reduce the variation from small sample size) to find players more than 9 RBI's over or under their projected RBI. There could be a correction coming.

You should also consider other factors, like injury or trade (involving the player or a top-of-the-order speedster) or team SB philosophy and success rate.

As well, remember that the player himself has an impact on his TOB. When we first did this study, we excluded the player from his TOB and got slightly better results. The formula overestimates projected RBI for players like Barry Bonds, whose high OBP skews his teams' OBP upwards but who can't benefit in RBI from that effect.

Starting Pitcher Toolbox
Fundamental Skills

Unreliable pitching performance is a fallacy driven by the practice of attempting to project pitching stats using gauges that are poor evaluators of skill.

How can we better evaluate pitching skill? We can start with the three statistical categories that are generally unaffected by external factors. These three stats capture the outcome of an individual pitcher versus batter match-up without regard to supporting offense, defense or bullpen:

Walks Allowed, Strikeouts and Ground Balls

Even with only these stats to observe, there is a wealth of insight that these measures can provide.

Command Ratio as a Leading Indicator

The ability to get the ball over the plate — command of the strike zone — is one of the best leading indicators for future performance. Command ratio (K/BB) can be used to project potential in ERA as well as other skills gauges.

1. Research indicates that there is a high correlation between a pitcher's Cmd ratio and his ERA.

	Earned Run Average				
Command	**2004**	**2005**	**2006**	**2007**	**2008**
0.0 - 1.0	6.24	6.22	6.42	6.48	7.00
1.1 - 1.5	5.16	4.93	5.06	5.12	5.07
1.6 - 2.0	4.63	4.41	4.65	4.58	4.60
2.1 - 2.5	4.30	4.28	4.48	4.28	3.96
2.6 - 3.0	3.80	3.60	4.15	3.89	3.89
3.1 and over	3.30	3.45	3.49	3.49	3.35

We can create percentage plays for the different levels:

For Cmd Levels of	Pct who post	
	3.50-	**4.50+**
0.0 - 1.0	0%	87%
1.1 - 1.5	7%	67%
1.6 - 2.0	7%	57%
2.1 - 2.5	19%	35%
2.6 - 3.0	26%	25%
3.1 +	53%	5%

In general, pitchers who maintain a command ratio of over 2.5 have a high probability of long-term success. Pitchers with a ratio over 3.0 have only a 5% chance of posting a 4.50-plus ERA. For fantasy drafting purposes, it is best to avoid pitchers with sub-2.0 ratios. Bullpen closers should be avoided if they have a ratio under 2.5.

2. A pitcher's command in tandem with dominance (strikeout rate) provides even greater predictive abilities.

	Earned Run Average	
Command	**-5.6 Dom**	**5.6+ Dom**
0.0-0.9	5.36	5.99
1.0-1.4	4.94	5.03
1.5-1.9	4.67	4.47
2.0-2.4	4.32	4.08
2.5-2.9	4.21	3.88
3.0-3.9	4.04	3.46
4.0+	4.12	2.96

This helps to highlight the limited upside potential of soft-tossers with pinpoint control. The extra dominance makes a huge difference.

3. Research also suggests that there is a strong correlation between a pitcher's command ratio and his propensity to win ballgames. Over three quarters of those with ratios over 3.0 post winning records, and the collective W/L record of those command artists is nearly .600.

The command/winning correlation holds up in both leagues, although the effect was much more pronounced in the NL. Over four times more NL hurlers than AL hurlers have command ratios over 3.0, and it appears that higher command ratios are required in the NL to maintain good winning percentages. While a ratio between 2.0 and 2.9 might be good enough for a winning record for over 70% of AL pitchers, that level in the NL will generate an above-.500 mark only slightly more than half the time.

In short, in order to have at least a 70% chance of drafting a pitcher with a winning record, you must target NL pitchers with at least a 3.0 command ratio. To achieve the same odds in the AL, a 2.0 command ratio will suffice.

Strand Rate as a Leading Indicator

Strand Rate finds great utility in explaining variances between a pitcher's ERA and his performance indicators.

Pitchers with rates more than 80% always have exemplary ERAs. Starters and middle relievers with 80%-plus rates in a given season have an 80% likelihood of seeing their ERA rise the following year. The percentage drops to 50% for short relievers.

Pitchers with strand rates less than 65% always have inflated ERAs, but have an 89% likelihood of seeing their ERA improve the following year. In addition, 83% will improve their ERA by more than one run.

Important! These 65% and 80% benchmarks are firm. Other analysts may project ERA regression off of rates closer to the mean of 71%. These analyses are wrong.

Hit Rate as a Leading Indicator *(Voros McCracken)*

In 2000, Voros McCracken published a study that concluded that "there is little if any difference among major league pitchers in their ability to prevent hits on balls hit in the field of play." His assertion was that, while a Johan Santana would have a better ability to prevent a batter from getting wood on a ball, or perhaps keeping the ball in the park, once that ball was hit in the field of play, the probability of it falling for a hit was virtually no different than for any other pitcher.

Among the findings in his study were:

- There is little correlation between what a pitcher does one year in the stat and what he will do the next. This is not true with other significant stats (BB, K, HR).
- You can better predict a pitcher's hits per balls in play from the rate of the rest of the pitcher's team than from the pitcher's own rate.

This last point brings a team's defense into the picture. It begs the question, when a batter gets a hit, is it because the pitcher made a bad pitch, the batter took a good swing, or the defense was not positioned correctly to field it? McCracken's findings take the onus away from the pitcher and puts it on the shoulders of the batter and defense.

Pitchers will often post hit rates per balls-in-play that are far off from the league average, but then revert to the mean the following year. As such, we can use that mean – approximately 30% – in much the same way we use strand rate to project the direction of a pitcher's ERA.

Subsequent research has shown that ground ball or fly ball propensity may have a small impact on hit rate.

HR/FB Rate as a Leading Indicator *(John Burnson)*

McCracken's work focused on "balls in play," omitting home runs from the study. However, pitchers also do not have much control over the percentage of fly balls that turn into HR. Research shows that there is an underlying rate of HR as a percentage of fly balls of 10%. A pitcher's HR/FB rate will vary each year but always tends to regress to that 10%. The element that pitchers *do* have control over is the number of fly balls they allow. That is the underlying skill or deficiency that controls their HR rate.

Pitchers who keep the ball out of the air more often correlate well with Roto value. The formula *(K + 0.3GB) / Batters Faced* provides a strong gauge for "air superiority."

Line Drive Pct. as a Leading Indicator *(Seth Samuels)*

Also beyond a pitcher's control is the percentage of balls-in-play that are line drives. Line drives do the most damage; from 1994-2003, here are the expected hit rates and number of total bases per type of BIP.

	|—— Type of BIP ——|	
	GB	FB	LD
H%	26%	23%	56%
Total bases	0.29	0.57	0.80

Despite the damage done by LDs, pitchers do not have any innate skill to avoid them. There is little relationship between a pitcher's LD% one year and his rate the next year. All rates tend to regress towards a mean of 22.6%.

However, ground ball pitchers do have a slight ability to prevent line drives (21.7%) and extreme ground ball hurlers even moreso (18.5%). Extreme fly ball pitchers have a slight ability to prevent LDs (21.1%) as well.

Ground Ball Tendency as a Leading Indicator
(John Burnson)

Ground ball pitchers tend to give up fewer HRs than do fly ball pitchers. There is also evidence that GB pitchers have higher hit rates. In other words, a ground ball has a higher chance of being a hit than does a fly ball that is not out of the park.

GB pitchers have lower strikeout rates. We should be more forgiving of a low strikeout rate (under 5.5 K/9) if it belongs to an extreme ground ball pitcher.

GB pitchers have a lower ERA than do fly ball pitchers but a higher WHIP. On balance, GB pitchers come out ahead, even when considering strikeouts, because a lower ERA also leads to more wins.

Groundball, Strikeout Tendencies as Indicators

(Mike Dranchak)

Pitchers were assembled into 9 groups based on the following profiles (minimum 23 starts in 2005):

Profile	Ground Ball Rate
Ground Ball	higher than 47%
Neutral	42% to 47%
Fly Ball	less than 42%

Profile	Strikeout Rate (k/9)
Strikeout	higher than 6.6 k/9
Average	5.4 to 6.6 k/9
Soft-Tosser	less than 5.4 k/9

Findings: Pitchers with higher strikeout rates had better ERA's and WHIPs than pitchers with lower strikeout rates, regardless of ground ball profile. However, for pitchers with similar strikeout rates, those with higher ground ball rates had better ERA's and WHIPs than those with lower ground ball rates.

Pitchers with higher strikeout rates tended to strand more baserunners than those with lower K rates. Fly ball pitchers tended to strand fewer runners than their GB or neutral counterparts within their strikeout profile.

Ground ball pitchers (especially those who lacked high-dominance) yielded more home runs per fly ball than did fly ball pitchers. However, the ERA risk was mitigated by the fact that ground ball pitchers (by definition) gave up fewer fly balls to begin with.

Projecting Wins

Using regression analyses, we can rank the importance of the variables that impact pitching win totals. In order:

1. Team offense (run support)
2. Pitching Effectiveness (base performance value)
3. Run Prevention (strand rate)
4. Bullpen support (inherited runners stranded %)
5. Managerial Tendencies (quick hooks/slow hooks)
6. Team Defense (fielding percentage)

When a fantasy leaguer needs to draft or beef up the Wins category, the most prudent approach is to target pitchers on teams with good offensive support.

Skill versus Consistency

Two pitchers have identical 4.50 ERAs and identical 3.0 PQS averages. Their PQS logs look like this:

PITCHER A:	3	3	3	3	3
PITCHER B:	5	0	5	0	5

Which pitcher would you rather have on your team? The risk-averse manager would choose Pitcher A as he represents the perfectly known commodity. Many fantasy leaguers might opt for Pitcher B because his occasional dominating starts show that there is an upside. His Achilles Heel is inconsistency. Is there any hope for Pitcher B?

- If a pitcher's inconsistency is characterized by more poor starts than good starts, his upside is limited.
- Pitchers with extreme inconsistency rarely get a full season of starts.
- However, inconsistency is neither chronic nor fatal.

The outlook for Pitcher A is actually worse. Disaster avoidance might buy these pitchers more starts, but history shows that the lack of dominating outings is more telling of future potential. In short, consistent mediocrity is bad.

Usage Warning Flags

Research suggests that there is a finite number of innings in a pitcher's arm. This number varies by pitcher, by development cycle, and by pitching style and repertoire. We can measure a pitcher's potential for future arm problems and/or reduced effectiveness:

- *Sharp increases in usage from one year to the next...* Any pitcher who increases his workload by 50 IP or more from year #1 to year #2 is a candidate for burnout symptoms in year #3.
- *Starters' overuse...* Consistent "batters faced per game" (BF/G) levels of 28.0 or higher, combined with consistent seasonal IP totals of 200 or more may indicate burnout potential. Within a season, a BF/G of over 30.0 with a projected IP total of 200 may indicate a late season fade.
- *Relievers' overuse...* Warning flags should be up for relievers who post in excess of 100 IP in a season, while averaging fewer than 2 IP per outing.

When focusing solely on minor league pitchers, research results are striking:

Stamina: Virtually every minor league pitcher who has had a BF/G of 28.5 or more in one season will experience a drop-off in BF/G the following year. Many will be unable to ever duplicate that previous level of durability.

Performance: Most pitchers experience an associated drop-off in their BPVs in the years following the 28.5 BF/G season. Some are able to salvage their effectiveness later on by moving to the bullpen.

Optimal Ages

As with batters, pitchers develop at different rates, but a look at their age can help determine where they should be along the developmental curve. Here are some tendencies...

While peaks vary, most all pitchers (who are still around) tend to experience a sharp drop-off in their skills at age 38.

Starting pitchers *(Rick Wilton)*: Their first productive season in the majors (10 wins, 150 IP, sub-4.00 ERA) is at age 25 or 26. Starters who experience a career year after age 31 are far less likely to repeat that performance than those who achieve their career year at a younger age.

Thirtysomethings *(Ed Spaulding)*: Older pitchers, as they lose velocity and movement on the ball, must rely on more variety and better location. Thus, if strikeouts are a priority, you don't want many pitchers over 30. The over-30 set that tends to be surprising includes finesse types, career minor leaguers who break through for 2-3 seasons often in relief, and knuckleballers (a young knuckleballer is 31).

Career Year Drop-off *(Rick Wilton)*

Research shows that a pitcher's post-career year drop-off, on average, looks like this...

- ERA increases by 1.00
- WHIP increases by 0.14.
- Nearly 6 fewer wins

Protecting Young Pitchers (*Craig Wright*)

There is a link between some degree of eventual arm trouble and a history of heavy workloads in a pitcher's formative years. Some recommendations from this research:

Teenagers (A-ball): No 200 IP seasons and no BF/G over 28.5 in any 150 IP span. No starts on three days rest.

Ages 20-22: Average no more than 105 pitches per start with a single game ceiling of 130 pitches.

Ages 23-24: Average no more than 110 pitches per start with a single game ceiling of 140 pitches.

When possible, a young starter should be introduced to the majors in long relief before he goes into the rotation.

Catchers' Effect on Pitching (*Thomas Hanrahan*)

A typical catcher handles a pitching staff better after having been with a club for a few years. Research has shown that there is an improvement in team ERA of approximately 0.37 runs from a catcher's rookie season to his prime years with a club. Expect a pitcher's ERA to be higher than expected if he is throwing to a rookie backstop.

Handedness Notes

1. LHers tend to peak about a year after RHers.
2. LH post only 15% of the total saves. Typically, LHers are reserved for specialist roles so few are frontline closers.
3. RHers have slightly better command and HR rate.
4. There is no significant variance in ERA.
5. On an overall basis, RHers have about a 6% advantage.

Projecting Pitching Breakout Performances
(*Brandon Kruse*)

A breakout performance is defined here as one where a player posts a Rotisserie value of $20 or higher after having never posted a value of $10 previously. These criteria are primarily used to validate an apparent breakout in the current season but may also be used carefully to project a potential breakout for an upcoming season.

- Age 27 or younger
- Minimum 5.6 Dom, 2.0 Cmd, 1.1 hr/9 and 50 BPV
- Maximum 30% hit rate
- Minimum 71% strand rate
- Starters should have a hit rate no greater than the previous year's hit rate. Relievers should show improved command
- Maximum xERA of 4.00

IN-SEASON ANALYSIS
Pitching Streaks

It is possible to find predictive value in strings of DOMinating or DISaster starts:

Once a pitcher enters into a DOM streak of any length, the probability for his subsequent start is going to be a better-than-average outing. The further a player is into a DOM streak, the *higher the likelihood* that the subsequent performance will be of high quality. In fact, once a pitcher has posted six DOM starts in a row, there is greater than a 70% probability that the streak will continue. When it does end, there is less than a 10% probability that the streak-

breaker is going to be a DISaster.

Once a pitcher enters into a DIS streak of any length, the probability is that his next start is going to be below average, even if it breaks the streak. However, DIS streaks erode quickly. Once a pitcher hits the skids, odds are low for him to start posting good numbers in the short term, though the duration of the plummet itself should be brief.

Pitch Counts as a Leading Indicator

Long-term analysis of workload is an ongoing science. However, there have also been questions whether we can draw any conclusions from short-term trends. For this analysis, all pitching starts from 2005-2006 were isolated — looking at pitch counts and PQS scores — and compared side-by-side with each pitcher's subsequent outing. So we were examining two-start trends, essentially the immediate impact that the length of one pitching performance would have on the very next start.

		NEXT	**START**		
Pitch Ct	**Pct.**	**PQS**	**DOM**	**DIS**	**qERA**
< 80	13%	2.5	33%	28%	4.90
80-89	14%	2.6	35%	29%	4.82
90-99	28%	2.7	37%	26%	4.82
100-109	30%	2.9	41%	23%	4.56
110-119	13%	3.1	46%	18%	4.40
120+	3%	3.0	43%	20%	4.56

There does appear to be merit to the concern over limiting hurlers to 120 pitches per start. The research shows a slight drop-off in performance in those starts following a 120+ pitch outing. However, the impact does not appear to be all that great and the fallout might just affect those pitchers who have no business going that deep into games anyway. Additional detail to this research (not displayed) showed that higher-skilled pitchers were more successful throwing over 120 pitches but less-skilled pitchers were not.

Days of Rest as a Leading Indicator

Workload is only part of the equation. The other part is how often a pitcher is sent out to the mound. For instance, it's possible that a hurler might see no erosion in skill after a 120+ pitch outing if he had enough rest between starts.

PITCH COUNTS		**NEXT**	**START**		
Three days rest	**Pct.**	**PQS**	**DOM**	**DIS**	**qERA**
< 100	72%	2.8	35%	17%	4.60
100-119	28%	2.3	44%	44%	5.21
Four Days rest					
< 100	52%	2.7	36%	27%	4.82
100-119	45%	2.9	42%	22%	4.56
120+	3%	3.0	42%	20%	4.44
Five Days rest					
< 100	54%	2.7	38%	25%	4.79
100-119	43%	3.0	44%	19%	4.44
120+	3%	3.2	48%	14%	4.28
Six Days rest					
< 100	58%	2.7	39%	30%	5.00
100-119	40%	2.8	40%	26%	4.82
120+	3%	1.8	20%	60%	7.98
20+ Days rest					
< 100	85%	1.8	20%	46%	6.12
100-119	15%	2.3	33%	33%	5.08

Managers are reluctant to put a starter on the mound with any fewer than four days rest, and the results for those who pitched deeper into games shows why. Four days rest is the most common usage pattern and even appears to mitigate the drop-off at 120+ pitches.

Perhaps most surprising is that an extra day of rest improves performance across the board and squeezes even more productivity out of the 120+ pitch outings.

Performance begins to erode at six days (and continues at 7-20 days, though those are not displayed). The 20+ Days chart represents pitchers who were primarily injury rehabs and failed call-ups, and the length of the "days rest" was occasionally well over 100 days. This chart shows the result of their performance in their first start back. The good news is that the workload was limited for 85% of these returnees. The bad news is that these are not pitchers you want active. So for those who obsess over getting your DL returnees activated in time to catch every start, the better percentage play is to avoid that first outing.

Relief Pitcher Toolbox

Origin of Closers

History has long maintained that ace closers are not easily recognizable early on in their careers, so that every season does see its share of the unexpected. Brian Wilson, Kerry Wood, Ryan Franklin, Brad Ziegler, Jensen Lewis... who would have thought it a year ago?

Accepted facts, all of which have some element of truth:

- You cannot find major league closers from pitchers who were closers in the minors.
- Closers begin their careers as starters.
- Closers are converted set-up men.
- Closers are pitchers who were unable to develop a third effective pitch.

More simply, closers are a product of circumstance.

Are the minor leagues a place to look at all?

From 1990-2004, there were 280 twenty-save seasons in Double-A and Triple-A, accomplished by 254 pitchers.

Of those 254, only 46 ever made it to the majors.

Of those 46, only 13 ever saved 20 games in a season.

Of those 13, only 5 ever posted more than one 20-save season in the majors: John Wetteland, Mark Wohlers, Ricky Bottalico, Braden Looper and Francisco Cordero.

Five out of 254 pitchers, over 15 years, a rate of 2%.

One of the reasons that minor league closers rarely become major league closers is because, in general, they do not get enough innings in the minors to sufficiently develop their arms into big-league caliber.

In fact, organizations do not look at minor league closing performance seriously, assigning that role to pitchers who they do not see as legitimate prospects.

Year	Avg age of all AA and AAA pitchers who posted 20-plus saves
2005	28
2006	27
2007	28
2008	27

Elements of Saves Success

The task of finding future closing potential comes down to looking at two elements:

Talent: The raw skills to mow down hitters for short periods of time. Optimal BPVs over 100, but not under 75.

Opportunity: The more important element, yet the one that pitchers have no control over.

There are pitchers that have *Talent, but not Opportunity*. These pitchers are not given a chance to close for a variety of reasons (e.g. being blocked by a solid front-liner in the pen, being left-handed, etc.), but are good to own because they will not likely hurt your pitching staff. You just can't count on them for saves, at least not in the near term.

There are pitchers that have *Opportunity, but not Talent*. MLB managers decide who to give the ball to in the 9th inning based on their own perceptions about what skills are required to succeed, even if those perceived "skills" don't translate into acceptable BPI levels. Those pitchers without the BPIs may have some initial short-term success, but their long-term prognosis is poor and they are high risks to your roster. Classic examples of the short life span of these types of pitchers include Matt Karchner, Heath Slocumb, Ryan Kohlmeier, Dan Miceli and Danny Kolb.

BPV as a Leading Indicator *(Doug Dennis)*

Research has shown that a reliever's base performance value (BPV) is an excellent indicator of long-term success in a closer's role. Here are the last nine 20-plus saves seasons recorded, by year:

		B P V	(Pct.)	
Year	No.	100+	75+	<75
1999	26	27%	54%	46%
2000	24	25	54	46
2001	25	56	80	20
2002	25	60	72	28
2003	25	36	64	36
2004	23	61	61	39
2005	25	36	64	36
2006	25	52	72	28
2007	23	52	74	26
MEAN	**25**	**45**	**66**	**34**

Though 20-saves success with a 75+ BPV is only a 66% percentage play in any given year, the below-75 group is composed of closers who are rarely able to repeat the feat in the following season:

Year	No. with BPV < 75	No. who followed up 20+ saves <75 BPV
1999	12	2
2000	11	2
2001	5	2
2002	7	3
2003	9	3
2004	9	2
2005	9	1
2006	7	3
2007	6	0

Projecting Holds (Doug Dennis)

Here are some general rules of thumb for identifying pitchers who might be in line to accumulate Holds. The percentages represent the portion of 2003's top Holds leaders who fell into the category noted.

1. Left-handed set-up men with excellent BPIs. (43%)

2. A "go-to" right-handed set-up man with excellent BPIs. This is the one set-up RHer that a manager turns to with a small lead in the 7th or 8th innings. These pitchers also tend to vulture wins. (43%, but 6 of the top 9)

3. Excellent BPIs, but not a firm role as the main LHed or RHed set-up man. Roles change during the season; cream rises to the top. Relievers projected to post great BPIs often overtake lesser set-up men during the season. (14%)

Optimal Ages (Rick Wilton)

The first 20-save season for a relief ace arrives at about age 26. About three of every four relievers who begin a run of 20-save seasons in their 20's will likely sustain that level for about four years, with their value beginning to decline at the beginning of the third year.

Many aces achieve a certain level of maturity in their 30's and can experience a run of 20-save seasons between ages 33 and 36. For some, this may be their first time in the role of bullpen closer. However, those who achieve their first 20-save season after age 34 are unlikely to repeat.

Minor League Toolbox

Minor League Prospecting in Perspective

In our perpetual quest to be the genius who uncovers the next Albert Pujols when he is in A-ball, there is often an obsessive fascination with minor league prospects. That's not to say that prospecting is not important. The issue is one of perspective. Some rules:

1. Some prospects are going to hit the ground running (Ryan Braun) and some are going to immediately struggle (Alex Gordon), no matter what level of hype follows them.

2. Some prospects are going to start fast (since the league is unfamiliar with them) and then fade (as the league figures them out). Others will start slow (since they are unfamiliar with the opposition) and then improve (as they adjust to the competition). So if you make your free agent and roster decisions based on small early samples sizes, you are just as likely to be a genius as an idiot.

3. How any individual player will perform relative to his talent is largely unknown because there is a psychological element that is vastly unexplored. Some make the transition to the majors seamlessly, some not, completely regardless of how talented they are.

4. Still, talent is the best predictor of future success, so major league equivalent base performance indicators still have a valuable role in the process. As do scouting reports, carefully filtered.

5. Follow the player's path to the majors. Did he have to repeat certain levels? Was he allowed to stay at a level long enough to learn how to adjust to the level of competition? A player with only two great months at Double-A is a good bet to struggle if promoted directly to the majors because he was never fully tested at Double-A, let alone Triple-A.

6. Younger players holding their own against older competition is a good thing. Older players reaching their physical peak, regardless of their current address, can be a good thing too. The Jorge Campillos and Ryan Ludwicks can have some very profitable years.

7. Remember team context. A prospect with superior potential is not going to unseat a steady but unspectacular incumbent, especially one with a large contract.

8. Don't try to anticipate how a team is going to manage their talent, both at the major and minor league level. You might think it's time to promote Jason Heyward and give him an everyday role. You are not running the Braves.

9. Those who play in shallow, one-year leagues should have little cause to be looking at the minor leaguers at all. The risk versus reward is so skewed against you, and there is so much talent available with a track record, that taking a chance on a call-up makes no sense.

10. Decide where your priorities really are. If your goal is to win, prospect analysis is just a *part* of the process, not the entire process.

Factors Affecting Minor League Stats (Terry Linhart)

1. Often, there is an exaggerated emphasis on short-term performance in an environment that is supposed to focus on the long-term. Two poor outings don't mean a 21-year-old pitcher is washed up.

2. Ballpark dimensions and altitude create hitters parks and pitchers parks, but a factor rarely mentioned is that many parks in the lower minors are inconsistent in their field quality. Minor league clubs have limited resources to maintain field conditions, and this can artificially depress defensive statistics while inflating stats like batting average.

3. Some players' skills are so superior to the competition at their level that you can't get a true picture of what they're going to do from their stats alone.

4. Many pitchers are told to work on secondary pitches in unorthodox situations just to gain confidence in the pitch. The result is an artificially increased number of walks.

5. The #3, #4, and #5 pitchers in the lower minors are truly longshots to make the majors. They often possess only two pitches and are unable to disguise the off-speed offerings. Hitters can see inflated statistics in these leagues.

Minor League Level versus Age

When evaluating minor leaguers, look at the age of the prospect in relation to the median age of the league he is in:

Low level A	Between 19-20
Upper level A	Around 20
Double-A	21
Triple-A	22

These are the ideal ages for prospects at the particular level. If a prospect is younger than most and holds his own against older and more experienced players, elevate his status. If he is older than the median, reduce his status.

Triple-A Experience as a Leading Indicator

The probability that a minor leaguer will immediately succeed in the Majors can vary depending upon the level of Triple-A experience he has amassed at the time of call-up.

	BATTERS		PITCHERS	
	< 1 Yr	Full	<1 Yr	Full
Performed well	57%	56%	16%	56%
Performed poorly	21%	38%	77%	33%
2nd half drop-off	21%	7%	6%	10%

The odds of a batter achieving immediate MLB success was slightly more than 50-50. More than 80% of all pitchers promoted with less than a full year at Triple-A struggled in their first year in the majors. Those pitchers with a year in Triple-A succeeded at a level equal to that of batters.

BPIs as a Leading Indicator for Pitching Success

The percentage of hurlers that were good investments in the year that they were called up varied by the level of their historical minor league BPIs *prior* to that year.

Pitchers who had:	Fared well	Fared poorly
Good indicators	79%	21%
Marginal or poor indicators	18%	82%

The data used here were MLE levels from the previous two years, not the season in which they were called up. The significance? Solid current performance is what merits a call-up, but this is not a good indicator of short-term MLB success, because a) the performance data set is too small, typically just a few month's worth of statistics, and b) for those putting up good numbers at a new minor league level, there has typically not been enough time for the scouting reports to make their rounds.

Minor League BPV as a Leading Indicator

(Al Melchior)

There is a link between minor league skill and how a pitching prospect will fare in his first 5 starts upon call-up.

	MLE BPV		
PQS Avg	< 50	50-99	100+
0.0-1.9	60%	28%	19%
2.0-2.9	32%	40%	29%
3.0-5.0	8%	33%	52%

Pitchers who demonstrate sub-par skills in the minors (sub-50 BPV) tend to fare poorly in their first big league starts. Three-fifths of these pitchers register a PQS average below 2.0, while only 8% average over 3.0.

Fewer than 1 out of 5 minor leaguers with a 100+ MLE BPV go on to post a sub-2.0 PQS average in their initial major league starts, but more than half average 3.0 or better.

Adjusting to the Competition

All players must "adjust to the competition" at every level of professional play. Players often get off to fast or slow starts. During their second tour at that level is when we get to see whether the slow starters have caught up or whether the league has figured out the fast starters. That second half "adjustment" period is a good baseline for projecting the subsequent season, in the majors or minors.

Premature major league call-ups often negate the ability for us to accurately evaluate a player due to the lack of this adjustment period. For instance, a hotshot Double-A player might open the season in Triple-A. After putting up solid numbers for a month, he gets a call to the bigs, and struggles. The fact is, we do not have enough evidence that the player has mastered the Triple-A level. We don't know whether the rest of the league would have caught up to him during his second tour of the league. But now he's labeled as an underperformer in the bigs when in fact he has never truly proven his skills at the lower levels.

Late Season Performance of Rookie SP *(Ray Murphy)*

Given that a rookie's second tour of the league provides insight as to future success, do rookie pitchers typically run out of gas? We studied 2002-2005, identified 56 rookies who threw at least 75 IP and analyzed their PQS logs. The group:

All rookies	#	#GS/P	DOM%	DIS%	qERA
before 7/31	56	13.3	42%	21%	4.56
after 7/31	56	9.3	37%	29%	4.82

There is some erosion, but a 0.26 run rise in qERA is hardly cause for panic. If we re-focus our study class, the qERA variance increased to 4.44-5.08 for those who made at least 16 starts before July 31. The variance also was larger (3.97-4.56) for those who had a PQS-3 average prior to July 31. The pitchers who intersected these two sub-groups:

PQS>3+GS>15	#	#GS/P	DOM%	DIS%	qERA
before 7/31	8	19.1	51%	12%	4.23
after 7/31	8	9.6	34%	30%	5.08

While the sample size is small, the degree of flameout by these guys (0.85 runs) is more significant.

Bull Durham Prospects

There is some potential talent in older players — age 26, 27 or higher — who, for many reasons (untimely injury, circumstance, bad luck, etc.), don't reach the majors until they have already been downgraded from prospect to suspect. Equating potential with age is an economic reality for Major League clubs, but not necessarily a skills reality.

Skills growth and decline is universal, whether it occurs at the major league level or in the minors. So a high skills journeyman in Triple-A is just as likely to peak at age 27 as a major leaguer of the same age. The question becomes one of opportunity — will the parent club see fit to reap the benefits of that peak performance?

Prospecting these players for your fantasy team is, admittedly, a high risk endeavor, though there are some criteria you can use. Look for a player who is/has:

- Optimally, age 27-28 for overall peak skills, age 30-31 for power skills, or age 28-31 for pitchers.
- At least two seasons of experience at Triple-A. Career Double-A players are generally not good picks.
- Solid base skills levels.
- Shallow organizational depth at their position.
- Notable winter league or spring training performance.

Players who meet these conditions are not typically draftable players, but worthwhile reserve or FAAB picks.

Japanese Baseball Toolbox (Tom Mulhall)
Comparing MLB and Japanese Besuboru

The Japanese major leagues are generally considered to be equivalent to very good Triple-A ball and the pitching may be even better. However, statistics are difficult to convert due to differences in the way the game is played in Japan.

1. While strong on fundamentals, Japanese baseball's guiding philosophy is risk avoidance. Mistakes are not tolerated. Runners rarely take extra bases, batters focus on making contact rather than driving the ball, and managers play for one run at a time. As a result, offenses score fewer runs than they should given the number of hits. Pitching stats tend to look better than the talent behind them.

2. Stadiums in Japan usually have shorter fences. Normally this would mean more HRs, but given #1 above, it is the American players who make up the majority of Japan's power elite. Power hitters do not make an equivalent transition to the MLB.

3. There are more artificial turf fields, which increases the number of ground ball singles. Only a few stadiums have infield grass and some still use dirt infields.

4. The quality of umpiring is questionable; there are no sanctioned umpiring schools in Japan. Fewer errors are called, reflecting the cultural philosophy of low tolerance for mistakes and the desire to avoid publicly embarrassing a player. Moreover, umpires are routinely intimidated.

5. Teams have smaller pitching staffs, sometimes no more than about seven deep. Three-man pitching rotations are not uncommon and the best starters often work out of the pen between starts. Despite superior conditioning, Japanese pitchers tend to burn out early due to overuse.

6. Japanese leagues use a slightly smaller baseball, making it easier for pitchers to grip and control.

7. Tie games are allowed. If the score remains even after 12 innings, the game goes into the books as a tie.

Japanese Players as Fantasy Farm Selections

Many fantasy leagues have large reserve or farm teams with rules allowing them to draft foreign players before they sign with a MLB team. With increased coverage by fantasy experts, the internet, and exposure from the World Baseball Classic, anyone willing to do a minimum of research can compile an adequate list of good players.

However, the key is not to identify the *best* Japanese players – the key is to identify impact players who have the desire and opportunity to sign with a MLB team. It is easy to overestimate the value of drafting these players. Since 1995, only about three dozen Japanese players have made a big league roster, and about half of them were middle relievers. But for owners who are allowed to carry a large reserve or farm team at reduced salaries, these players could be a real windfall, especially if your competitors do not do their homework.

A list of Japanese League players who could jump to the Majors appears in the Prospects section.

Team Toolbox

Johnson Effect *(Bryan Johnson)*: Teams whose actual won/loss record exceeds or falls short of their statistically projected record in one season will tend to revert to the level of their projection in the following season.

Law of Competitive Balance *(Bill James)*: The level at which a team (or player) will address its problems is inversely related to its current level of success. Low performers will tend to make changes to improve; high performers will not. This law explains the existence of the Plexiglass and Whirlpool Principles.

Plexiglass Principle *(Bill James)*: If a player or team improves markedly in one season, it will likely decline in the next. The opposite is true but not as often (because a poor performer gets fewer opportunities to rebound).

Whirlpool Principle *(Bill James)*: All team and player performances are forcefully drawn to the center. For teams, that center is a .500 record. For players, it represents their career average level of performance.

Other Diamonds
The Fanalytic Fundamentals

1. This is not a game of accuracy or precision. It is a game of human beings and tendencies.

2. This is not a game of projections. It is a game of market value versus real value.

3. Draft skills, not stats.

4. A player's ability to post acceptable stats despite lousy BPIs will eventually run out.

5. Once you display a skill, you own it.

6. Virtually every player is vulnerable to a month of aberrant performance. Or a year.

7. Exercise excruciating patience.

Aging Axioms

1. Age is the only variable for which we can project a rising trend with 100% accuracy. (Or, age never regresses.)

2. The aging process slows down for those who maintain a firm grasp on the strike zone. Plate patience and pitching command can preserve any waning skill they have left.

3. Negatives tend to snowball as you age.

Age 26 Paradox: 26 is when a player begins to reach his peak skill, no matter what his address is. If circumstances have him celebrating that birthday in the majors, he is a breakout candidate. If circumstances have him celebrating that birthday in the minors, he is washed up.

A-Rod 10-Step Path to Stardom: Not all well-hyped prospects hit the ground running. More often they follow an alternative path...

1. Prospect puts up phenomenal minor league numbers.
2. The media machine gets oiled up.
3. Prospect gets called up, but struggles, Year 1.
4. Prospect gets demoted.
5. Prospect tears it up in the minors, Year 2.
6. Prospect gets called up, but struggles, Year 2.
7. Prospect gets demoted.
8. The media turns their backs. Fantasy leaguers reduce their expectations.

9. Prospect tears it up in the minors, Year 3. The public shrugs its collective shoulders.

10. Prospect is promoted in Year 3 and explodes. Some lucky fantasy leaguer lands a franchise player for under $5.

Some players that are currently stuck at one of the interim steps, and may or may not ever reach Step 10, include Andy Marte, Dallas McPherson and Homer Bailey.

Steve Avery List: Players who hang onto MLB rosters for six years searching for a skill level they only had for three.

Bylaws of Badness

1. Some players are better than an open roster spot, but not by much.

2. Some players have bad years because they are unlucky. Others have *many* bad years because they are bad... and lucky.

Rickey Bones List: Pitchers with BPIs so incredibly horrible that you have to wonder how they can possibly draw a major league paycheck year after year.

George Brett Path to Retirement: Get out while you're still putting up good numbers and the public perception of you is favorable. *(See Steve Carlton Path to Retirement.)*

Steve Carlton Path to Retirement: Hang around the major leagues long enough for your numbers to become so wretched that people begin to forget your past successes. *(See George Brett Path to Retirement.)*

Among the many players who have taken this path include Jose Mesa, Doc Gooden, Matt Morris, Hideo Nomo and of course, Steve Carlton. Current players who look to be on the same course include Andruw Jones, Nomar Garciaparra, Jason Isringhausen and Barry Zito.

Chaconian: Having the ability to post many saves despite sub-Mendoza BPIs and an ERA in the stratosphere.

Christie Brinkley Law of Statistical Analysis: Never get married to the model.

Chicken and Egg Problem: Did irregular playing time take its toll on the player's performance or did poor performance force a reduction in his playing time?

Chronology of the Classic Free-Swinger with Pop

1. Gets off to a good start.

2. Thinks he's in a groove.

3. Gets lax, careless.

4. Pitchers begin to catch on.

5. Fades down the stretch.

Crickets: The sound heard when someone's opening draft bid on a player is also the only bid.

Developmental Dogmata

1. Defense is what gets a minor league prospect to the majors; offense is what keeps him there. *(Deric McKamey)*

2. The reason why rapidly promoted minor leaguers often fail is that they are never given the opportunity to master the skill of "adjusting to the competition."

3. Rookies who are promoted in-season often perform better than those that make the club out of spring training. Inferior March competition can inflate the latter group's perceived talent level.

4. Young players rarely lose their inherent skills. Pitchers may uncover weaknesses and the players may have difficulty adjusting. These are bumps along the growth curve, but they do not reflect a loss of skill.

5. Late bloomers have smaller windows of opportunity and much less chance for forgiveness.

6. The greatest risk in this game is to pay for performance that a player has never achieved.

7. Some outwardly talented prospects simply have a ceiling that's spelled AAA.

Bull Durham List: Older minor leaguers who sneak onto major league rosters and shine for brief periods, showing what a mistake it is to pigeon-hole talented players just because they are not 24 and beautiful.

Edwhitsonitis: A dreaded malady marked by the sudden and unexplained loss of pitching ability upon a trade to the New York Yankees.

Scott Elarton List: Players you drop out on when the bidding reaches $1.

Employment Standards

1. If you are right-brain dominant, own a catcher's mitt and are under 40, you will always be gainfully employed.

2. Some teams believe that it is better to employ a pitcher with *any* experience because it has to be better than the devil they don't know.

3. It's not so good to go pffft in a contract year.

FAAB Forewarnings

1. Spend early and often.

2. Emptying your budget for one prime league-crosser is a tactic that should be reserved for the desperate.

3. If you chase two rabbits, you will lose them both.

Fantasy Economics 101: The market value for a player is generally based on the aura of past performance, not the promise of future potential. Your greatest advantage is to leverage the variance between market value and real value.

Fantasy Economics 102: The variance between market value and real value is far more important than the absolute accuracy of any individual player projection.

Brad Fullmer List: Players whose leading indicators indicate upside potential, year after year, but consistently fail to reach that full potential. Current list members include Bronson Arroyo, Jeremy Bonderman, David Bush, Rafael Furcal and Austin Kearns.

The Gravity Principles

1. It is easier to be crappy than it is to be good.

2. All performance starts at zero, ends at zero and can drop to zero at any time.

3. The odds of a good performer slumping are far greater than the odds of a poor performer surging.

4. Once a player is in a slump, it takes several 3-for-5 days to get out of it. Once he is on a streak, it takes a single 0-for-4 day to begin the downward spiral.

Corollary: Once a player is in a slump, not only does it take several 3-for-5 days to get out of it, but he also has to get his name back on the lineup card.

5. Eventually all performance comes down to earth. It may take a week, or a month, or may not happen until he's 45, but eventually it's going to happen.

Health Homilies

1. Staying healthy is a skill.

2. A $40 player can get hurt just as easily as a $5 player but is eight times tougher to replace.

3. Chronically injured players never suddenly get healthy.

4. There are two kinds of pitchers: those that are hurt and those that are not hurt... yet.

5. Players with back problems are always worth $10 less.

6. "Opting out of surgery" usually means it's coming anyway, just later.

The Health Hush: Players get hurt. Hurt players can potentially lose a lot. Therefore, there is an incentive for players to hide injuries. HIPAA laws restrict the disclosure of health information. Team doctors and trainers have been instructed not to talk with the media. So, when it comes to information on players' health status, we're all pretty much in the dark.

Jason Jennings Rationalization: Occasional nightmares (2/3 inning, 11 ER) are just a part of the game.

The Knuckleballers Rule: Knuckleballers don't follow any of the rules.

Monocarp: A player whose career consists of only one productive season.

Lance Painter Lesson: Six months of solid performance can be screwed up by one bad outing. (In 2000, Painter finished with an ERA of 4.76. However, prior to his final appearance of the year — in which he pitched 1 inning and gave up 8 earned runs — his ERA was 3.70.)

The Pitching Postulates

1. Never sign a soft-tosser to a long-term contract.

2. Right-brain dominance has a very long shelf life.

3. A fly ball pitcher who gives up a lot of HRs is expected. A ground ball pitcher who gives up a lot of HRs is making mistakes.

4. Never draft a contact fly ball pitcher who plays in a hitter's park.

5. Only bad teams ever have a need for an inning-eater.

6. Never chase wins.

Quack!: An exclamation in response to the educated speculation that a player has used performance enhancing drugs. While it is rare to have absolute proof, there is often enough information to suggest that, "if it looks like a duck and quacks like a duck, then odds are it's a duck."

Reclamation Conundrum: The problem with stockpiling bench players in the hope that one pans out is that you end up evaluating performance using data sets that are far too small to be reliable.

Rule 5 Reminder: Don't ignore the Rule 5 draft lest you ignore the 1% possibility of a Johan Santana.

The Five Saves Certainties:

1. On every team, there *will* be save opportunities and *someone* will get them. At a bare minimum, there will be at least 30 saves to go around, and not unlikely over 45.

2. *Any* pitcher could end up being the chief beneficiary. Bullpen management is a fickle endeavor.

3. Relief pitchers are often the ones that require the most time at the start of the season to find a groove. The weather is cold, the schedule is sparse and their usage is erratic.

4. Despite the talk about "bullpens by committee," managers prefer a go-to guy. It makes their job easier.

5. As many as 50% of the available saves in any given year will come from pitchers who are in the free agent pool at the end of Draft Day.

Small Sample Certitude: If players' careers were judged based what they did in a single game performance, then Tuffy Rhodes and Mark Whiten would be in the Hall of Fame.

Esix Snead List: Players with excellent speed and sub-.300 on base averages who get a lot of practice running down the line to first base, and then back to the dugout. Also used as an adjective, as in "Esix-Sneadian."

Standings Vantage Points

First Place: It's lonely at the top, but it's comforting to look down upon everyone else.

Sixth Place: The toughest position to be in is mid-pack at dump time.

Last Place in April: The sooner you fall behind, the more time you will have to catch up.

Last Place, Yet Again: If you can't learn to do something well, learn to enjoy doing it badly.

Tenets of Optimal Timing

1. If a second half fader had put up his second half stats in the first half and his first half stats in the second half, then he probably wouldn't even have had a second half.

2. Fast starters can often buy six months of playing time out of one month of productivity.

3. Poor 2nd halves don't get recognized until it's too late.

4. "Baseball is like this. Have one good year and you can fool them for five more, because for five more years they expect you to have another good one." — Frankie Frisch

The Three True Outcomes

1. Strikeouts 2. Walks 3. Homeruns

The Three True Handicaps

1. Has power but can't make contact.

2. Has speed but can't hit safely.

3. Has potential but is too old.

Mike Timlin List: Players who you are unable to resist drafting even though they have burned you multiple times in the past.

Walbeckian: Possessing below replacement level stats, as in "Guzman's season was downright Walbeckian." *Alternate usage:* "Guzman's stats were so bad that I might as well have had Walbeck in there."

Mark Wohlers Lament: When a closer posts a 65% strand rate, he has nobody to blame but himself.

Seasonal Assessment Standard: If you still have reason to be reading the boxscores during the last weekend of the season, then your year has to be considered a success.

The Three Cardinal Rules for Winners: If you cherish this hobby, you will live by them or die by them...

1. Revel in your success; fame is fleeting.

2. Exercise excruciating humility.

3. 100% of winnings must be spent on significant others.

Research Abstracts

The power outage of 2007-2008

by Joshua Randall

Over the past two seasons, a vocal faction of Baseball HQ forum regulars have posted that MLB is experiencing a power outage. At least by one crude measure of power, 2008 was a down year: only 4,878 HR were hit MLB-wide, compared to 4,957 HR hit in 2007 and 5,386 HR hit in 2006. In fact, 2008's HR total was the lowest since 1997. However, examining raw HR output quickly becomes a fool's errand. The number of teams has fluctuated over time, rendering a simple count of HR meaningless.

Enter LWPwr

A better tool is Linear Weighted Power (LWPwr), the numerator of our Power Index (PX). The more familiar PX normalizes a player's power skills for a given year, and is effective for player-to-player comparisons (a player with his own history, or one player to another). LWPwr is a better gauge for league-wide comparisons.

The chart below shows aggregate LWPwr levels for the past 25 seasons. With the exception of a spike in 1987 (often blamed on livelier balls), LWPwr ranged between 8.5 and 9.6 for 10 years. It then jumped to 10.8 in 1994 (one year after the first wave of expansion teams), and has remained between 10.6 and 11.7 ever since.

LWPwr has its ups and downs, but not to an alarming degree. As for the supposed power outage in 2007-2008, note that 2006's 11.5 LWPwr was on the high side of the range, which made the minor decline to 2007's and 2008's levels (11.1 and 11.2) appear more severe.

Segmenting Batters by LWPwr

What about the concern that the power outage was concentrated in the upper echelon of sluggers? We examined various cuts of the data from 2002-2008, looking for evidence that the upper quartile or decile of HR-hitters experienced a notable drop-off, but found nothing to support that notion. On the contrary, LWPwr remained stable over time, regardless of the group of hitters under examination.

Another approach is to group batters into three tiers that correspond to those in our LWPwr definition: top sluggers (LWPwr greater than 17), weak hitters (LWPwr less than 10), and everyone else. (The sample is restricted to batters with at least 100 AB, to weed out pitchers, rookies getting a "cup of coffee", and other marginal players.)

	Number of Batters						
LWPwr	**2002**	**2003**	**2004**	**2005**	**2006**	**2007**	**2008**
< 10	191	186	172	182	154	183	199
10-17	201	200	204	199	212	206	199
> 17	33	40	43	36	39	38	38
	425	426	419	417	405	427	436

There has been some fluctuation in the number of batters within each tier, but the 38 who were top sluggers in 2007 and 2008 hardly constitute a power outage. On a percentage basis, they represented about 9% of the entire sample in both years, compared to a little under 10% in 2006. Even 2002's apparent shortfall in top sluggers weighed in at almost 8% of the sample. So for the past six seasons, about 8%-10% of batters had LWPwr more than 17 —a fairly narrow range of results.

Perception Isn't Reality

Putting aside our advanced metrics, what about the number of batters who hit certain amounts of HR each season?

	Number of Batters						
HR	**2002**	**2003**	**2004**	**2005**	**2006**	**2007**	**2008**
0-10	399	401	427	442	378	420	468
11-20	99	118	104	113	106	107	92
21-30	49	47	55	45	51	58	52
31-40	17	20	23	19	23	15	27
41+	8	9	9	7	10	4	1
	572	595	618	626	568	604	640

LWPwr by Year, 1984-2008

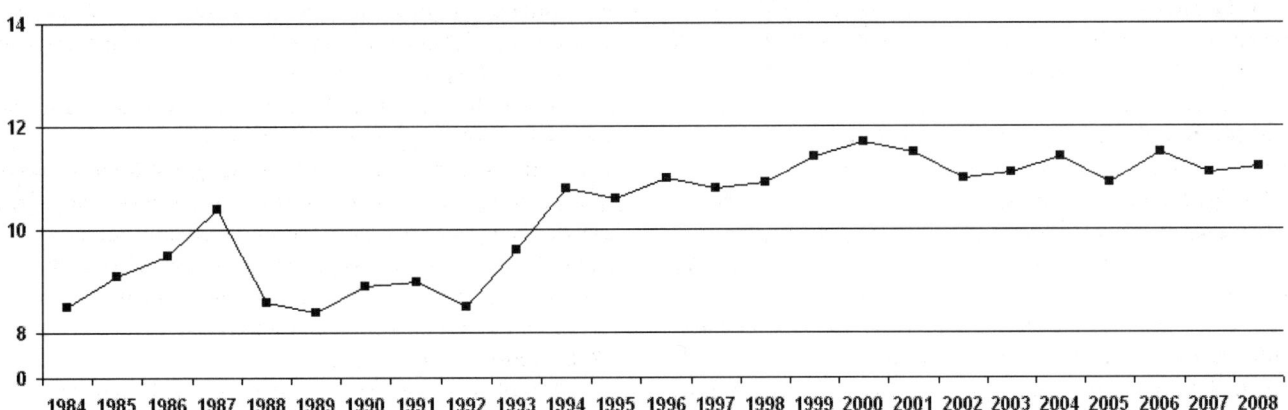

Here, at last, we find evidence to support the perception of a power outage in 2007 and 2008. While in the prior five seasons at least eight batters hit 41 or more HR, in 2007 only four managed that feat and in 2008 only one. These were noticeable drop-offs from 10 such players in 2006.

Consider also the number of players who hit 31 or more HR and the implications for fantasy baseball. In 2006, if the 31+ HR-hitters were equally distributed across a typical 15-team mixed league, each team would have had at least two such players. By contrast, in 2007, only four teams would have had two such players; the remaining 11 teams would have had to make do with just one each. In a game that revolves around individual player achievement, that sort of disparity immediately stands out. That 28 players hit 31+ HR in 2008 somewhat alleviated the problem, giving 14 of the 15 fantasy teams two top producers.

Conclusions

As measured by LWPwr, 2007-2008's power output was not substantially different from the power outputs of prior seasons. Instead, what was perceived as a power outage was a combination of two factors: first, the contrast between 2006's power output being on the high side and 2007's being on the low side; second, the temporary scarcity of 31+ HR hitters in 2007.

Looking forward, there is no data-driven reason to think that 2009's power output will fall outside the range of results observed since 1994. Some may believe that stricter testing for performance enhancing drugs (PEDs) will encourage players to go "off the juice", leading to a league-wide decline in power. That same argument has been trotted out for the past several years, but the data simply do not show any real power outages over the last 15 seasons.

The shift to speed

by Scott Monroe

In 2001, there were a total of 4,511 SB attempts in 4,858 total games played - almost one SB attempt per game. There were 31 players in the Major Leagues who stole 25 or more bases. The overall Stolen Base Opportunity Percent (SBO) for the AL and NL combined was more than 10%. In short, life was good for base stealers in MLB.

After 2001, SB numbers began to steadily drop. For four straight years (2002-2005), the total number of SB attempts decreased each year. But in 2006 the numbers started to trend upwards once again, and that shift continued in 2007 as well. 2008 saw the overall attempts drop, but SBO% was actually slightly higher than in 2006 and 2007. This influx of speed begs the question: Are we seeing the return of the stolen base, or is this a short-lived anomaly?

The chart below details the stolen base data over the past nine years:

Year	SBA	#25 SB	#50 SB	SBO%	SB%
2000	4246	23	3	8.86%	69%
2001	4511	31	2	10.14	69
2002	4032	24	0	8.99	68
2003	3705	14	3	8.24	69
2004	3689	17	2	8.11	70
2005	3635	16	4	8.18	71
2006	3877	26	5	8.53	71
2007	3920	28	6	8.53	74
2008	3826	23	3	8.55	73

What is interesting to note is that even though there were almost 600 more SBAs in 2001 vs. 2007, there were less than 200 more successful SBs in 2001 (3,103 SB in 2001 vs. 2,918 SB in 2007). This is reflected in the SB% column - base stealers were successful 74% of the time in 2007 and 73% in 2008, as compared to a 69% success rate in 2001. So teams

may not be stealing quite as often as six or seven years ago, but they are running "smarter" and with more success.

What else do these trends mean? Well, one possible explanation for the downward trend in SB from 2003-2005 can be summed up in one word - *Moneyball*. In 2003, many teams began to follow the example of the Oakland A's by placing more emphasis on OBA and OPS and less emphasis on potentially giving up outs via sacrifices or stolen base attempts.

One prime example of this is the Boston Red Sox. Each year from 2003-2005, the Red Sox led not only the AL but all of the Major Leagues in both Runs Scored and OPS. During that same period, however, their average MLB ranking in SBs was 20th. The Red Sox and A's were not alone in this philosophical shift, and the rise of the Moneyball philosophy certainly helped to curtail the overall SB numbers during those years.

In the past three years, it appears that teams are more willing to take chances on the basepaths if the right opportunity presents itself. This is evidenced by the climb in SBO% from 2006-2008 as compared to 2003-2005, and also by the volume of players with at least 25 SB. Also, the number of elite base stealers has grown; six players had 50+ SBs in 2007 - more than any other year since 2000.

So what does this mean from a fantasy perspective? Primarily, it means that you can achieve successful SB numbers without having to grab one SB "anchor" that will help you dominate the SB category but may not help as much in other areas (think Willy Taveras or Michael Bourn). Now that there are more players who will manage a moderate number of SBs, fantasy teams can look to draft several of these players and compete in the SB category without having to sacrifice production in other areas.

Quality and consistency

It's good to be good. It's also good to be consistent. In 2008, both John Danks and Dan Haren had ERAs around 3.40. But Haren posted nearly 30% more dominating starts than Danks, and 15% fewer disasters. In head-to-head leagues, there is no comparison between these two pitchers when it comes to value. Heck, consistency is something that all fantasy formats can find value in.

We use DOM/DIS splits to judge the consistency of pitchers (and this book has 5-year charts for the first time this year). But I've always wondered how to judge the relative value of a pitcher with a 60/20 split versus one with a 50/15 or 40/7. Which one is better?

We know that the DOM value can be considered a measure of quality of performance. The variance between DOM and DIS can be considered a measure of consistency. The larger that variance, the more consistently good or bad a pitcher is. We could also say that a pitcher with a DOM/DIS of 10/10 — and thus 80% neutral starts — could be considered consistently mediocre, probably. But that provides little actionable value for our analysis. Keying in on consistency at the extremes provides more opportunity to manage our rosters.

I like analyses that are both insightful and accessible, even if that means sacrificing a bit of precision. As such, a quick-and-dirty, back-of-the-envelope-when-it's-10-minutes-until-deadline method for evaluating both quality and consistency in tandem is just to combine DOM with the variance between DOM and DIS. We'd probably also want to add more of a penalty for those DISastrous starts because they can be real killers.

This is one way to approach it:

(DOM - DIS) x 2 = Quality/Consistency score (QC)

We'll multiply these values by 100 just so we have nice, whole numbers to deal with. It's a simple calculation that makes sense because the wider the variance, the higher the pitcher's DOM must be, right?

But there's more. HQ reader Arik Florimonte wrote:

"My gut tells me that a DIS hurts more than a DOM helps. I think that DOM - (2 * DIS) would be more realistic. I know I'd rather have a 40/0 pitcher than a 60/20. In my opinion, the avoidance of disasters is crucial, especially when you're looking at middle of the rotation guys.

"I went through a quick analysis using the 2008 PQS logs for the AL. I totaled up all the stats for each PQS value. I found the following averages for DIS starts, DOM starts, and 2s and 3s:

PQS	IP	H	ER	BB	K	HR	ERA	WHIP
0 or 1	3.9	6.9	4.8	2.5	2.2	1.0	11.08	2.41
2 or 3	5.9	6.1	2.8	2.0	4.0	0.7	4.27	1.37
4 or 5	6.9	5.3	1.7	1.4	5.7	0.4	2.22	0.97

"So that an entire 32-start season with no DOM and no DIS starts would look like this (all values rounded to whole numbers):

PQS	IP	H	ER	BB	K	HR	ERA	WHIP
0/32/0	189	195	90	64	128	22	4.29	1.37

"That would be a PQS season of "0/32/0", i.e. 0 DOM, 32 neutral, and 0 DIS starts.

"Below are the season values if you replace a typical PQS 2 or 3 start with a DIS, and then replace a 2-3 with a DOM, and then another DOM...

PQS	IP	H	ER	BB	K	HR	ERA	WHIP
0/31/1	187	196	92	65	126	22	4.43	1.40
1/30/1	188	195	91	64	128	22	4.36	1.38
2/29/1	189	194	90	63	130	22	4.29	1.36

"At a first pass, the 0/32/0 season is closest to the 2/29/1 season in the typical roto categories. The initial conclusion appears to me that **on average, it takes two DOMinating starts to erase the damage of one DISaster.**" And so...

QC = (DOM - (2 x DIS)) x 2

(Multiplying by 2 is solely intended to get it back on the 0-100 scale.)

QC is not a perfect gauge, but it is simple and easy to calculate, which alone makes it useful. QC scores are easy to read. Anything 100 or more represents your most skillful and consistent hurlers. You would probably have a decent percentage play with a QC of even 75. Here are the members of the elite 100 list in 2008:

Pitcher	DOM	DIS	QC
Halladay,Roy	76%	0%	152
Santana,Ervin	75%	0%	150
Santana,Johan	79%	3%	146
Lincecum,Tim	79%	6%	134
Haren,Dan	82%	9%	128
Harden,Rich	72%	4%	128
Lee,Cliff	68%	3%	124
Dempster,Ryan	64%	3%	116
Hamels,Cole	70%	6%	116
Sabathia,CC	74%	9%	112
Sheets,Ben	65%	6%	106
Wellemeyer,Todd	63%	6%	102
Meche,Gil	62%	6%	100
Lackey,John	58%	4%	100

As Arik noted, disaster avoidance has value in H2H leagues. Regarding pitchers with DOM levels less than 50% and DIS levels less than 20%, HQ analyst Dylan Hedges wrote: "If you are going to be successful at H2H, you'll need to draft a few of these guys to round out your staff. Because at the end of the week it is important to have pitchers who can avoid disaster starts rather than be volatile and blow a weekly lead on Sunday."

QC doesn't give overly high scores to these types, but you can cherry pick. Of those extreme disaster avoiders, these were the pitchers who registered a QC greater than zero:

Pitcher	DOM	DIS	QC
Matsuzaka,Daisuke	48%	14%	40
Floyd,Gavin	42%	12%	36
Sonnanstine,Andy	41%	13%	30
Zambrano,Carlos	47%	17%	26
Cook,Aaron	25%	6%	26
Verlander,Justin	48%	18%	24
Slowey,Kevin	48%	19%	20
Galarraga,Armando	32%	11%	20
Maddux,Greg	39%	15%	18
Litsch,Jesse	36%	14%	16
Moyer,Jamie	30%	12%	12
Bush,David	38%	17%	8
Olsen,Scott	39%	18%	6

QC and other percentage plays

Decision-making in fantasy baseball is all about percentage plays. It's not just about choosing the right players, or bidding the right amounts, or timing, or luck. You can't find success in those activities unless you understand percentage plays.

We choose Hanley Ramirez over Angel Berroa because, based on all the information we have, the percentage play is higher that Ramirez will provide better stats for our team. What is the exact percentage? Tough to say, but it would probably be pretty high. Perhaps a 95% certainty that Ramirez will outperform Berroa.

Most people would be pretty satisfied with a 95% chance of being correct, and in truth, decision-making within that percentage play will make you very successful. But you *are* going to be wrong 5% of the time, and as such, you have to maintain some humility. I always remind myself of that old list entitled, "If 99.9% Were Good Enough," and it keeps my expectations in perspective. *(See excerpt below.)*

For us, and playing fantasy baseball, most percentage plays we are faced with are nowhere near 99.9%, or 95%. Most are not even near 80%, the number I tend to toss around as the level we should try to set as our goal. We know that the best projective accuracy rate we can reasonably expect is about 70%. That means we'll be wrong 30% of the time. When it comes to individual game outcomes, we're often playing with a percentage play that might top out at 55%. Then we're wrong 45% of the time.

But for some applications, the good outcomes and bad outcomes don't necessarily have to add up to 100%. Sometimes the good outcomes are "good enough" and the bad outcomes are "rare enough" that actionable percentage plays are still possible. It's all in the spread.

The QC score in the previous article is based on the spread between acceptable outcomes. As such, we can also use this method to evaluate other percentage plays. There are a few charts from this book that provide good examples.

For instance, when considering batting eye as a leading indicator for batting average, we have the following chart:

For Eye Levels of	Pct who bat .300+	.250-
0.00 - 0.25	7%	39%
0.26 - 0.50	14%	26%
0.51 - 0.75	18%	17%
0.76 - 1.00	32%	14%
1.01 - 1.50	51%	9%
1.51 +	59%	4%

There are no strong percentage plays here for any individual expected outcome. For instance, if I want to draft a player with a .300-plus batting average, even a 1.51 eye ratio only provides a 59% chance of succeeding. However, if we evaluate the odds of a good

outcome and the odds of a poor outcome *in tandem*, then we might have a stronger percentage play from which to make a decision. To wit:

For Eye Levels of	Pct who bat .300+	.250-	QC
0.00 - 0.25	7%	39%	-142
0.26 - 0.50	14%	26%	-76
0.51 - 0.75	18%	17%	-32
0.76 - 1.00	32%	14%	8
1.01 - 1.50	51%	9%	66
1.51 +	59%	4%	102

Using the QC calculation, targeting players with an eye ratio of 1.51 or better becomes a stronger percentage play as the potential spread between good and bad outcomes registers a QC score greater than 100. Even eye ratios between 1.01 and 1.50 provide a marginal play.

We can look similarly at pitching command ratios (K/BB) as a leading indicator for ERA:

For Cmd Levels of	Pct who post 3.50-	4.50+	QC
0.0 - 1.0	0%	87%	-348
1.1 - 1.5	7%	67%	-254
1.6 - 2.0	7%	57%	-214
2.1 - 2.5	19%	35%	-102
2.6 - 3.0	26%	25%	-48
3.1 +	53%	5%	86

Here, even the high-end comparison does not clear the 100 hurdle, though it is probably strong enough for decision-making purposes. However, if we were to recalculate this chart using an ERA of 5.00+ as the benchmark for futility, we would probably create a stronger play. This shows the utility of the method; you can adjust the scope of the analysis based upon your needs. If you absolutely had to draft a pitcher with an ERA no worse than 4.00, for instance, you could re-run the percentages (and clearly end up with a weaker percentage play).

One more... the probability of a minor leaguer succeeding immediately in the majors depending upon the amount of Triple-A experience:

	Performed well	Performed poorly	QC
Batters, full year	56%	38%	-40
Batters, less than full year	57%	21%	30
Pitchers, full year	56%	33%	-20
Pitchers, less than full year	16%	77%	-276

There are no percentage plays strong enough for a positive outcome, but we can see that QC offers the opportunity to evaluate negative outcomes as well. This chart shows that pitchers with less than a full year of Triple-A are poor percentage plays to succeed immediately in the majors. We can use a benchmark of -100 here. A scan of the earlier charts provides similar insight for avoiding risk.

If 99.9% were good enough then....

- 268,500 defective tires would be shipped every year.
- 103,260 income tax returns would be processed incorrectly every year.
- Two plane landings at O'Hare International Airport would be unsafe every day.
- 20,000 incorrect drug prescriptions would be written every year.
- 107 incorrect medical procedures would be performed every day.
- 315 entries in *Webster's Third New International Dictionary of English Language* would be misspelled.

BPV: The next generation

Back in the *1993 Baseball Forecaster*, I introduced a gauge called Pure Pitching Potential, or *P Value* for short. Its intent was to give us a better view of minor league ERAs. It wasn't until I applied it to the major league population that I realized its true power. I wrote:

"While many pitchers' ERAs fluctuate wildly over the years, their P values remain fairly stable. Trends are easier to spot. P values surge, peak and decline as other stats swing wildly from one year to the next. One example...

"Since 1988, Frank Viola's ERA has fluctuated every year, from a low of 2.65 (1988) to a high of 3.97 (1991). In 1992, he appeared to have rebounded from a horrible 1991 to have a decent season with a lousy team. But his P values each year from 1988 have displayed a consistent trend, going 97, 90, 87, 60 and 42. Might his rapidly eroding base skill levels tumble off the charts in 1993?"

They declined further in 1993, and tumbled in 1994.

Re-dubbed Base Performance Value (BPV) in 1995, this gauge has gone through several iterations in the past 16 years. The current version looks like this:

(Strikeout Rate x 6)
+ (Command ratio x 21)
- (Expected Opposition HR Rate x 30)
- ((Opposition Batting Average - .275) x 200)

As rudimentary and outwardly unscientific as this seems, research has shown that BPV fares as well, or better, in evaluating pitching talent as any other measurement that has been developed since. And while other gauges, such as xERA, tend to measure much of the same skill, BPV remains widely used. Why? There is something about a 0-100 scale that is immediately understandable to even the most math-averse among us.

BPV has been working well for all these years; why tinker now? Our fanalytic arsenal has grown immensely over that time, so couldn't this gauge be improved?

I had one main goal for this overdue revision: Simplify the formula by focusing on the three true outcomes — strikeouts, walks and home runs. That meant Opposition BA would be in danger of getting axed. Command Ratio, as it was currently stated, was vulnerable as well.

I also had a secondary goal: Don't invalidate all the years of BPV history. This new iteration would have to remain on its familiar 0-100+ scale with those 100-BPV superstars remaining no more than 15% of the total player population.

Here is how the thought process went:

1. Strikeout Rate would stay.

2. Command Ratio was problematic. First, it often caused highly inflated and volatile values. A pitcher with pinpoint control, say, a walk rate of 1.0, could potentially earn a BPV over 80 with a strikeout rate as low as 4.0. If that pitcher walked just one more batter per game, his BPV would plummet by half. Second, it essentially double-counted strikeouts. All we really needed to capture here was a pitcher's walk rate. So we'd simply replace K/BB with bb/9.

3. Opposition home run rate was good, but we were already calculating that off of a pitcher's fly ball rate, so it seemed that we could bring this down to even more basic levels. Over the past few years, we've discovered how extreme ground ball pitchers can overcome mediocre strikeout rates. We needed to reward hurlers for this skill. We could replace xHR/9 with GB%.

4. Opposition batting average was pointless.

The new BPV would have just three elements: *Strikeout Rate, Walk Rate and Ground Ball Rate.*

The next step was to set benchmarks for what would be considered an acceptable level for each of these three elements. I decided that the offset to each element in the formula would be a value just below acceptable levels. In this way, the minimum acceptable level for each skill — 6.0 k/9 (I know 5.6 is our new norm but I wanted to keep round numbers, for now anyway), 3.0 bb/9 and 45% GB% -- would generate a BPV of 50, much like it does now. So, we'd start by calculating... (Strikeout rate - 5.0), (4.0 - Walk rate) and (Groundball rate - 40%), and assign multipliers so that our new formula would be:

(Strikeout rate - 5.0) x 17
+ (4.0 - Walk rate) x 28
+ (Groundball rate - 40%)

How does the distribution of values compare between the old version and the new version?

	Per	Cent
BPV	**OLD**	**NEW**
140+	3%	1%
120-139	5	3
100-119	6	9
80-99	14	13
60-79	22	19
40-59	27	20
20-39	19	18
< 20	6	18

As a group, the distribution of new BPV values is a bit off from the old formula. New BPV depresses values at the low end, though I'm not sure that's a bad thing. It provides a wider spread and more differentiation between skills. Using 2008 data and eliminating two high-end outliers (Mariano Rivera and Jon Papelbon), the range of old BPV values is -2 to 163, a spread of 165 points. New BPV has a range of -53 to 149, a spread of 202 points.

An important part of this exercise is to compare the two sets of values and see which players moved in the rankings. One of our objectives was to reward groundball pitchers and New BPV succeeds. Brandon Webb (65% GB rate), arguably one of the better pitchers in baseball, appropriately rises from 37th to 24th in the new rankings. Sinkerballers Rafael Perez (55%) and Chad Qualls (57%) rise as well.

On the flipside are those who give up more flyballs, and thus could be homer-prone. Brian Fuentes (33% GB rate) drops in the rankings from 13th to 16th; Jon Rauch (32%) drops from 17th to 22nd. Kerry Wood (37%) might have been expected to see a sharp drop as well, but his K and BB rates are so strong as to offset the low groundball rate; he only drops from 4th to 5th in the rankings.

Analyzing probable pitchers

During the first week of July, fantasy leaguers were faced with a "start or sit" decision for Kevin Millwood facing the Yankees in New York. Here was a struggling pitcher with a .348 opponent batting average in away games, facing the Yankees in the House the Ruth Built. A no-brainer to sit, correct?

Those who own Millwood know that he pitched five innings of one-run baseball. Where did that come from? Heck, if a bad pitcher can't lie down against a good offense under ideal conditions, is all our analysis worth the effort?

Some might say that sitting him was probably still the best percentage play for that start. Good decision, bad outcome. Some might say it's all a crapshoot.

The truth is somewhere in between.

Predicting individual game outcomes is an exercise fraught with uncertainty. We did some research several years ago and determined that the best percentage play we could expect is about 53%. Not much better than flipping a coin. But here is a little perspective...

Consider... the difference between the best team and the worst team in baseball is perhaps one win per week. If a team posts a record of 4-3 in each week's contests, they'd finish with a winning percentage of .571 yielding a record of 93-69. The team that goes 3-4 each week would have a winning percentage of .429 and a record of 69-93. While the real best and worst records usually exceed these limits a bit, the difference is still not much more than one win per week.

In essence, these are the levels to which each game's results will regress. The best and worst players will push their game outcomes toward the direction of their skills, but each is just one of many on a team. The aggregate team effort dilutes each individual performance, preventing clubs from escaping the pull of the .429-.571 range.

Except for the starting pitcher, or so it seems.

That is why we set our pitching rotations. We are under the perception that the guys on the hill have much more influence over game outcomes than anyone else on the field. And we are probably correct, to an extent. But even the very best arm is fighting a battle against regression to, at best, a .617 winning percentage (100 wins)... which is still just a 61.7% play. We think/hope that a confluence of factors pointing in a certain direction will elevate that percentage play on any day. But then Cliff Lee, with his 110 BPV, hurls a PQS-1 against the lowly Cincinnati Reds.

Good decision, bad outcome. Right?

So, how *should* we approach this decision-making process? Right now, we're doing it by inundating ourselves in data.

Most sources of probable pitchers will provide stats-to-date, stats over the last three starts, and perhaps home versus away stats. Sites that focus more on handicapping may add things like team record vs. LHP and RHP, in day and night games, head-to-head match-ups and the like. This is all helpful as a rough scan, but how predictive is it?

To begin with, most all of these scans use faulty stats — won-loss record and ERA. Really now. We can immediately do better just by looking at BPIs. Baseball HQ's Weekly Planner report shows each pitcher's last five PQS starts, which we determined several years ago to be marginally predictive of future outings. The report also shows each pitcher's PQS levels versus his opponent, this year and last. And finally, there is the opposing team's complete BPI scan, either at home or away, depending on where that game is being played. It is a wealth of insight and far more valuable than anything you can get elsewhere.

But even these tools are faulty. How a pitcher will do against aggregate team numbers assumes that, in this particular game, the opposing team contains the same players performing at more or less the same level as when the snapshot was taken.

Perhaps more helpful is to consider how to manage your pitching staff *tactically*. For instance, if you have to choose between two pitchers of equal skill, one who is making a single start or one making a pair of starts, how do you decide? Most fantasy leaguers will opt for the 2-start pitcher, even if he will be facing tough competition in one of those starts. The need for strikeouts and wins tends to trump the need to protect ERA and WHIP.

But look back at the recent lesson we learned... *"on average, it takes two DOMinating starts to erase the damage of one DISaster."* So, given a choice between a single start against a moderate or poor team, or a pair of starts, one of which is against a strong team, the better percentage play may be to opt for the single start hurler. The damage incurred by the single bad match-up cannot be offset by that week's second start, even if it is superb. Of course, the strikeout category needs to be considered, but this still provides some interesting food-for-thought.

We can also use a bit of decision theory to help us. Let's break down the process, looking at the two options — going with the 1-start pitcher or going with the 2-start pitcher — and each of the possible outcomes of those choices. For simplicity's sake, let's just consider outcomes of PQS-0 and PQS-5; even though there are more possible outcomes, analyzing the best and worst case scenarios is still helpful. We'll also once again assume that both pitchers are of roughly equivalent skill. Our grid will look like this:

	Possible PQS outcomes					
CHOOSE	A: 5 B: 00	A: 5 B: 05	A: 5 B: 55	A: 0 B: 00	A: 0 B 05	A: 0 B:55
A: 1-start pitcher						
B: 2-start pitcher						

Each cell of the grid considers one possible outcome. For instance, the top left cell represents your choice of the 1-start pitcher with the result being a PQS-5 while the 2-start pitcher gets bombed in both his outings (two PQS 0s).

The next step is to rank each of these cells according to desirability.

The very best scenario would be to select the 2-start pitcher and have him hurl two PQS-5 gems while the 1-start pitcher hurls a PQS-0 disaster. So, that cell we would rank as #1. The very worst possible outcome would be to select the 2-start pitcher, have him post two PQS-0 disasters while the 1-start pitcher posts a PQS-5. Given the 12 cells in the grid, we'll rank that cell #12. And so...

Possible PQS outcomes

CHOOSE	A: 5 B: 00	A: 5 B: 05	A: 5 B: 55	A: 0 B: 00	A: 0 B 05	A: 0 B:55
A: 1-start pitcher						
B: 2-start pitcher	12					1

We then proceed to rank the remaining cells in the grid. Some of this is no-brainer stuff, some of it is subjective based on your own goals. Here is how my grid looks:

Possible PQS outcomes

CHOOSE	A: 5 B: 00	A: 5 B: 05	A: 5 B: 55	A: 0 B: 00	A: 0 B 05	A: 0 B:55
A: 1-start pitcher	3	4	5	8	9	10
B: 2-start pitcher	12	7	2	11	6	1

The last step is to use what we call the Minimax Theorem to make your decision. Simply, you choose the option that has the least bad outcome. This is particularly relevant in our application where PQS-0 outings are so deadly. And our choice here would be to go with the 1-start pitcher since the worst case scenario (#10) is not as bad as two other downside possibilities for the 2-start pitcher.

Obviously, this is simplistic. However, you can add all the complexity you want by including the other PQS scores or by assigning weights to each cell. If you are comparing two pitchers of different skill, for instance, weighting each cell based on its probability of occurrence will provide a bit more precision.

The bottom line, though, is that we're still making decisions using very weak percentage plays. Even if you maximize your odds to the highest reasonable level, you are still likely going to be wrong at least 40% of the time.

Where do starting pitchers come from?

by Frank Noto

How can we identify in advance those who will succeed as major league starting pitchers? A look at 2007's top 30 aces (based on 2007 Rotisserie 5x5 earnings) yields some interesting answers.

	RookYr	HQPr	Base Perf Values			
			RY	**RY-1**	**RY-2**	**$07**
Carmona	2006	*	58	69	80	$22
Hamels	2006	9	113	70	na	24
Hill,R	2006	*	108	104	na	18
Maine	2006	65	58	39	62	17
Shields,J	2006	#	89	98	-18	20
Verlander	2006	22	51	117	na	20
Blanton	2005	27	44	89	128	16
Kazmir	2005	8	75	123	na	17
Young,C	2005	*	81	43	42	22
Wang	2005	*	36	78	48	15
Bedard	2004	88	57	--	94	24
Haren	2003	92	75	na	na	23
Webb	2003	*	96	70	na	29
Beckett	2003	1	86	116	na	25
Harang	2002	*	71	64	na	26
Lackey	2002	*	68	88	77	24
Perez,Ol	2002	*	79	na	na	17
Peavy	2002	13	84	120	na	39
Zambrano	2002	69	69	99	78	17
Lilly	2001	*	60	55	73	22
Oswalt	2001	15	152	134	na	19
Sabathia	2001	9	70	72	na	27
Burnett	2000	*	42	48	na	16
Penny	2000	6	42	90	na	20
Santana	2000	#	26	na	na	27
Halladay	1999	15	18	63	92	17
Hudson	1999	na	96	35	na	22
Escobar	1998	na	77	93	12	19
Vazquez	1998	na	35	186	na	22
Smoltz	1988	na	?	?	?	26

RookYr	Rookie year
HQPr	Rank in Baseball HQ Top 100 Prospects list
*	Organizational prospect list
#	"Bull Durham contributor" on org prospect list
RY	BPV for Rookie year (includes MLE).
RY-1	BPV for year prior to rookie year (includes MLE)
RY-2	BPV two years prior to rookie year (includes MLE)

There are several nuggets to be gleaned here, starting first with the relatively obvious findings:

The top major league SPs began as starting pitchers in the minors, apparently without exception. Though it is not uncommon for a minor league starter to later succeed as a closer or setup reliever in the majors, the reverse was not the case in this group. A look at all the names on our 2007 list shows that not one made it by going that route.

These aces also rarely started their major league careers primarily as relievers. All of the above started out in the majors *primarily* as starters, except for Johan Santana, who mostly relieved between occasional spot starts during his first two years, and Fausto Carmona, who pitched one more inning as a reliever than as a starter his first year. A number of pitchers did throw several games in relief their first year; many teams prefer to ease their rookies into the SP role.

Many SPs achieve success early in their careers. While no 2007 rookies made the top 30 rankings their first year, fully 20% of 2007 aces were sophomores, the most numerous class represented in these rankings (tied with 6th year pitchers from the class of 2002).

Many aces developed fairly early. The top SPs were not concentrated among pitchers with many years of experience. Almost two-thirds (63%) had six or fewer years in the majors. Long-term stars such as Smoltz whose careers span more than a decade were the exception among aces, rather than the rule. Of course, it's also possible that we are seeing a short-term trend here, as older stars from past years (e.g., Maddux, Martinez and Randy Johnson) decline or retire.

Good pitchers come up virtually every year. Each annual class has at least one representative stretching all the way back to 1998. Then there is a ten year gap until the phenomenal John Smoltz of the class of 1988 appears.

How good is Baseball HQ at predicting future aces among minor leaguers? While we aren't really in the business of projecting that "X will one day rank in the top 30 Roto starters," the evidence nonetheless shows that HQ's prospecting has done well.

Beginning in 2000, every one of these aces made HQ's lists of top minor league prospects, either as one of the top 100 prospects in baseball, or ranked on the lesser lists of top prospects in each organization. Two (Santana and Shields) showed up only on the Bull Durham list (2000 season) or as a likely major league "contributor" to his team, while others were only posted on organizational lists, meaning readers had to do a bit of digging. Still, this is a significant prognosticating feat, given that there are almost 2,000 minor league pitchers in any given year. Deric McKamey didn't miss any of the top 30 on the list stretching back to 1999, when HQ began running this feature.

Many of these top 30 SPs were prominently featured among HQ's top ten (including both hitters and pitchers) in past annual prospect lists, including Beckett (a #1 pick), Hamels, Kazmir, Sabathia and Penny. Still others ranked among the top 20 prospects, including Peavy, Oswalt and Halladay.

The other side of the coin is that some pitchers who were never ranked among HQ's Top 100 Prospects nonetheless went on to achieve fantasy stardom. SPs such as Wang (rated #10 prospect for NYY), Webb (#13, ARI) and Carmona (#12, CLE) were seen as potential assets within their respective organizations, but were not viewed as prospective aces while in the minors, or at least not good enough to crack the Top 100 list. It's interesting to note that all are extreme groundball pitchers.

BPV Is an Excellent Early Indicator

Base Performance Value (BPV) is a useful predictor of future success. Virtually every SP on our list generated a BPV of at least 60 during or prior to his rookie season, and frequently both. At the high end of the scale, Vazquez, Oswalt, Peavy, Beckett, Kazmir, Verlander, and Hill all showed very strong base skills in the minors, posting BPVs greater than 100. Similarly, Hamels, Hill and Sabathia posted excellent BPVs over 100 scores in their first MLB seasons.

There are a few exceptions, but even these prove the rule. Rule 5 pick Santana spent two mediocre years in major league relief instead of developing in the minors. After being sent back down to the minors in 2002, he posted a combined majors/MLE 113 BPV breakout which served as a precursor to his coming Roto breakout in 2003 ($22).

While minor league BPVs are not available for Oliver Perez and Dan Haren because they did not pitch above Single-A before promotion to the majors, both posted strong BPVs (79 and 75, respectively) in their first year in big league ball.

Virtually everyone on the Top 30 2007 list earned a solid BPV of at least 60 in his first year in the majors, even those few who did not excel BPV-wise in the minors. A.J. Burnett is the only clear outlier, posting marginal BPVs in both his inaugural 2000 season (42) and 1999 (48) while in the minors.

A determination of whether 2007 trends are valid over past years would require more study. But it appears BPV is a clear indicator of future success for our top listed pitchers.

Rate expectations for relievers

by Patrick Davitt

Do hit rates (H%) and strand rates (S%) for relief pitchers (RP) regress to some "normal" mean level as they do for starters? HQ studies suggest that we can't rely on regression when making roster decisions for relievers.

For this study, we used 2003-2007 pitching stats from both leagues, removing unrosterable pitchers (less than $1 Roto value in a particular season). The resulting large cohort— about 3,100 pitcher-seasons and 215,000 IP — had overall rates we've come to expect: 30% hit rate, 70% strand rate.

We then separated RPs (<2.9 IP/G) from SPs (>5.0 IP/G).

Results

The H% stats for SPs and RP were similar, with a common norm around 29% and about three-quarters of all pitchers in the 28-32% range. But there was a key difference: While 77% of SPs were in the normal range, just 53% of RPs were. Further, 38% of RPs were *below* the range — 185 RPs sustained sub-28% levels.

The S% outcomes showed RPs had a baseline five points higher than SPs (~78% to ~73%). So even if we accept that pitchers regress to a group mean (far from certain, given variance in skills), the higher RP mean suggests we again adjust our general expectation of "normality."

This is also shown in the distributions: While the "normal" 68-77% overall range captured 81% of SPs, it included just 48% of RPs. *Nearly half (46%) of all RPs had full seasons with a strand rate greater than 77%!* That includes 50 pitchers who maintained 85% for a full season (seven of those more than 90%). Like H%, it seems prudent not to assume automatic corrections to low reliever S%, because *a RP's low S% is sustainable over a full season.*

The HQ Forums and past HQ research suggest some explanations for RPs' advantages:

Pitching from the stretch is a skill. SPs might suffer in S% because they lose effectiveness pitching from the stretch. RPs are used to the stretch.

Hitters see particular RPs less often. Hitters see SPs two to four times per game, and multiple times per season. Hitters see RPs less often, making it harder to get a "book."

Shorter outings mean **RPs can get outs with one or two good pitches**, especially strikeouts, which depress S%. In the study, RPs had higher Dom (7.8 K/9 to 6.6), and lower HR/9 (0.8 to 1.0).

Relievers start some appearances with outs in the scorebook. S% measures how many of *your* baserunners score. If you come into an inning with one out, there's less chance that your allowed baserunners will score. With two outs, that advantage grows.

In a related issue, **relievers often enter the game with runners on**, potentially turning some groundballs into force outs, reducing H%, and double plays, reducing S% by ending innings.

Finally, **smaller samples add volatility.** Ten solid (or lucky) games have greater impact on a 70-inning season than on 210 IP.

In-season S% Correction

Our second study compared first- and second-half H%, S% and ERAs of 437 RPs who had 30 first-half IP in the 2003-06 individual seasons. We broke each cohort into five rough quintiles.

In this table of aggregated S% results. "Med" is the median change, "-" counts pitchers who had downward shifts more than five points, "+" counts pitchers with upshifts over five points, and "NC" counts changes between those two thresholds. The counts and the medians showed the expected movement, especially in the extreme quintiles, but with enough exceptions to challenge any rule:

STRAND RATE

1H S%	#	Med	-	+	NC
82-97	91	-11	64	3	24
77-81	78	- 3	33	15	30
73-76	90	- 3	33	18	39
68-72	96	+ 3	21	39	36
40-71	82	+ 8	6	49	27

Also, the range of changes was very wide. The top quintile maximum downward shift was 35 points, but the maximum upshift was 12! In the bottom quintile, the maximum upshift was 57 points, but there was a maximum downshift of 37. In the middle three quintiles, the movements were essentially random.

We see similar outcomes for ERA ("+" means an increase of 0.5 runs, "-" means any decline, "NC" means a result between those two):

EARNED RUN AVERAGE

1H S%	Med	-	+	NC
82-97	+1.33	69	16	6
77-81	+0.75	41	27	10
73-76	+0.08	39	42	9
68-72	-0.01	38	48	10
40-71	-1.00	12	64	6

Again, we see the expected shifts, especially at the extremes, with slightly fewer counterexamples. However, there is again a wide range of individual outcomes. Many top RPs' low first-half ERAs went up as we'd expect, but even at these higher ERAs were well worth retaining or adding to a fantasy roster.

In 2003, John Smoltz' first-half ERA was 0.83, thanks in part to a 89% S%. Anyone selling high was technically correct: His second-half S% fell — by one point — and his ERA "soared" — to 1.74. Similarly, anyone looking at Joaquin Benoit's 2006 first half might have bought in on the "inevitable" correction to his 63% S% and 5.02 ERA. They'd have been disappointed: His ERA fell just a few points to 4.71, and his second-half S% actually *dropped* two points.

The results for H% were similar.

Conclusion

So we know that H% and especially S% can't be reliably expected to regress to the mean of *all* pitchers, because of sample sizes and role differences. The best we can do is to focus on skills, understand that the short run is different from the long, and not automatically assume that RPs will regress to expected levels—because for RPs, there are no expected levels.

Pure Quality Relief

by Patrick Davitt

It has long been our belief that a sharp fantasy baseball owner can win a league with judicious management of relief pitching, from the LIMA Plan to avoiding risk in closers. It could even be argued that relievers are as important as starters.

Yet while we have a powerful tool to measure and monitor starters' performance with the Pure Quality Start (PQS) metric, we did not have such a tool for relievers (RP).

So in 2008, we developed **Pure Quality Relief** (PQR), an attempt to analyze relief pitcher effectiveness emulating the three critical elements of PQS: Its 5-point scoring system, its focus on the skills we monitor as Base Performance Indicators, and its game-by-game "snapshot" approach with rolling five-game averages for trend spotting.

Events and Values

We used detailed game log data from all MLB relievers in 2006-2007, defining a relief appearance as three innings or less, obviously excluding starters who got knocked out early. We had about 27,000 RP game records.

We first tried to correlate the value of the monitored events with overall R$ value for the season, but too much fantasy value was locked up in saves, making any potential PQR formula too dependent on situations and manager decisions. Correlating events with ERA and WHIP worked slightly better, and gave us a foundation to continue.

Regression analysis gave us an idea of the event values relative to one another, allowing us to draft a rough formula to test against the real-world outcomes, monitoring the resulting overall values to see if the cream rose to the top, to check the spread of values from top to bottom, to see game-by-game PQR results, and, overall, to assess the general utility of results in assessing RP performance.

Then came about 100 passes through the valuations, tweaking the values until we had a workable result. After the results were reported at Baseball HQ.com, we further refined and simplified the PQR formula.

PQS gives SPs a point for meeting a per-game innings target, but we thought this was unsuitable for PQR because an effective RP performance can be just one-third of an inning. So we decided to change the basic unit of measurement to the out, and to award one point per out recorded.

This approach was generally workable, but had a problem: It undervalued usefully "clean" (no-baserunner) one- and two-out stints. Giving two points per out overvalued longer stints, even when they weren't so clean. Half-points wasn't going to work because we wanted to have the crispness of whole numbers like PQS.

The solution turned out to be giving **two points for the first out made, and one point for each subsequent out**, to a maximum of four. At first glance, this might seem to penalize relievers who go 2-3 IP, but such outings get countervailing benefits in scoring negative events, as we shall see.

We also wanted to recognize the added value of a strikeout, in keeping with our desire to monitor core pitching skills and the theoretical belief that a strikeout is more valuable than other outs because baserunners don't advance. Strikeouts also had higher relative values in our regression analyses. Giving one point per "K" seemed the obvious solution, but created the problem of pushing positive points well beyond five—a reliever striking out the side would end up with seven points.

So we modified a PQS-style rule by giving a **bonus point for getting at least one K per every full four outs**. That is, at least 1 K for 1-4 outs, 2 K for 5-8 outs, and 3 K for 9-12 outs. This corresponds to a Dom rate of 6.8 K/9 or higher, well above the HQ minimum.

So we had outs and Ks contributing positive values. We also had to score the negative events. Here we departed from the binary PQS model, which awards a "1" for avoiding each particular outcome and a "0" for allowing it.

Instead, we **subtract a point for each Earned Run** (ER). To give allowance for longer appearances, we allowed one unpenalized ER for appearances of eight or nine outs, an ERA of 3.38 or lower.

We also **give one point for zero BR, and subtract one point for each baserunner**, allowing one unpenalized baserunner for every three full outs. So the RP gets no "free" BR for 1-2 outs, one BR for 3-5 outs, two BR for 6-8 outs, and three BR for 9 outs. This is the equivalent of a 1.00 WHIP or better.

Allowing these occasional BRs and ERs in longer outings offsets the disadvantage of the maximum of 4 out-points.

Finally, we had to deal with HRs. PQS allows one unpenalized HR, but we decided that a homer is such a catastrophic event for a reliever, **surrendering any HR would mean an automatic PQR of zero**. To avoid negative scores, we said that any total under zero would be set to zero, which is sufficiently bad.

If the K and zero-BR bonuses pushed the score to 6, it was reset to 5.

Validation: Cumulative Results

To test the new PQR scoring system, we looked at the 8,159 relief appearances from 2008 game logs through the All-Star break.

As with the PQS logs, we noted DOMinating (PQR 4 or 5) and DISaster (PQR 0 or 1) appearances, and generated five-game PQR rolling averages and DOM/DIS splits.

Using these rules resulted in this set of outcomes:

PQR	#	Pct
0	1,745	21%
1	466	6%
2	550	7%
3	949	12%
4	1,524	19%
5	2,925	36%

The average score was 3.1, and the median was 4. Scores weren't distributed in a bell-shaped curve, but that seemed okay given relief pitching's all-or-nothing nature. DOM/DIS was 55%/27%, with 19% in the middle.

We also checked all 235 relievers with at least 10 appearances, which again showed we were on a reasonable track. Median and Average were in the middle of the 0-5 range, and the gap from best to worst was what we might expect between a top reliever and a poor one:

MAX	4.37
MIN	2.13
AVE	2.79
MEDIAN	2.97

We also dug into individual reliever seasons in the top, middle and bottom cohorts by PQR ratings:

Rk	Pitcher	App	PQR	DOM/DIS
1	Rivera,Mariano	38	4.37	87%/ 8%
2	Soria,Joakim	40	4.28	83%/13%
3	Lidge,Brad	40	4.28	78%/ 0%
4	Nathan,Joe	40	4.20	85%/10%
5	Wood,Kerry	44	4.09	80%/11%
101	Franklin,Ryan	44	3.18	57%/25%
102	McClellan,Kyle	45	3.18	60%/27%
103	Meredith,Cla	47	3.17	49%/21%
104	Wade,Cory	30	3.17	60%/20%
105	Grabow,John	42	3.17	50%/24%
231	Chulk,Vinnie	27	2.22	37%/44%
232	Baek,Cha Seung	11	2.18	45%/45%
233	Sanches,Brian	12	2.17	50%/50%
234	Bass,Brian	35	2.14	37%/46%
235	Lewis,Jensen	23	2.13	35%/43%

This review passed the smell test, with relievers broadly scaling where we might expect. Interestingly, the Top 30 identified intriguing pickups like Joey Devine, Mike Gonzalez (in only 10 appearances at the time), Hong-Chih Kuo, Jonathon Broxton, Edwar Ramirez and Brad Ziegler. Also, the middle 30 identified guys like Todd Jones, Jason Isringhausen, and J.J. Putz as potential trouble spots. Because PQR is based on getting outs without giving up runners and runs, it did a good job identifying relievers not getting the job done consistently — the kind managers notice.

It was also worth noting the major differences in DOM/ DIS from the elite group's 80-10 or so to the bottom group's 35-45 or so.

Another use for PQR, as for PQS, was to find effective performers not getting full value for their consistent results. We filtered for pitchers outside the top 30 who met LIMA standards as well as these PQR criteria:

Rating >= 3.5
DOM >= 60%
DIS <= 20%

That test found such nuggets as Jose Arredondo, Matt Thornton and Scott Downs, among others.

Using the Logs

Finally, we wanted to see how the individual PQR game logs reflected trends or patterns for RPs. Brad Ziegler's log (at right) was typical:

Leaving aside Ziegler's remarkable zero-ER track record, we see that from June 21 forward, Ziegler

was simply not allowing baserunners. After a poor stretch June 14-20, culminating with a PQR-0 outing, Ziegler saw his 5-game PQR average rise steadily until he stumbled on July 10. His DOM/DIS is headed towards elite status (the DIS component is there). His low Dom of 4.1 K/9 might have given pause, but the log suggests he was being effective.

Conclusion

Like PQS, the PQR system can identify how well relievers are performing (the rating) and how consistently (DOM/ DIS). Both factors, in conjunction with our usual skills metrics, are important in assessing potential additions to a roster, especially in formats where weekly consistency is important, and for picking out potential future closers.

The logs themselves, like the PQS logs which inspired them, can also help pick out relievers who are "on a roll," and perhaps have the potential to improve their roles and their fantasy value.

Here's the scoring again:
- Two points for the first out, and one point for each subsequent out, to a maximum of four points
- A bonus point for having at least one strikeout for every four full outs (one K for 1-4 outs, two Ks for 5-8 outs, three Ks for 9 outs)
- One point for zero baserunners, minus one point for each baserunner, allowing the pitcher one BR for each three full outs (one BR for 3-5 outs, two for 6-8 outs, three for 9 outs)
- Minus one point for each ER, allowing one ER for 8- or 9-out appearances
- An automatic PQR-0 for allowing a home run.

When looking at the PQR results, we will have to remember that a PQR rating is only part of the analysis. Especially when trying to spot a future closer, we will have to check DOM/DIS splits to get a proper feel for effectiveness.

BRAD ZIEGLER

Date	Outs (Pts)	K (Pts)	ER (Pts)	BR (Pts)	HR	PQR	5-gm Ave	DOM/DIS
5/31	1 (2)	0 (0)	0 (0)	1 (-1)	0	1		0%/100%
6/3	5 (4)	0 (0)	0 (0)	0 (1)	0	5		50%/50%
6/4	3 (4)	0 (0)	0 (0)	1 (0)	0	4		67%/33%
6/7	5 (4)	2 (1)	0 (0)	1 (0)	0	5		75%/25%
6/8	5 (4)	0 (0)	0 (0)	1 (0)	0	4	3.8	80%/20%
6/12	3 (4)	0 (0)	0 (0)	0 (1)	0	5	4.6	83%/17%
6/14	2 (3)	0 (0)	0 (0)	1 (-1)	0	2	4.0	71%/14%
6/18	3 (4)	0 (0)	0 (0)	2 (-1)	0	3	3.8	63%/13%
6/19	4 (4)	0 (0)	0 (0)	2 (-1)	0	3	3.4	56%/11%
6/20	1 (2)	0 (0)	0 (0)	2 (-2)	0	0	2.6	50%/20%
6/21	2 (3)	0 (0)	0 (0)	0 (1)	0	4	2.4	55%/18%
6/27	2 (3)	1 (1)	0 (0)	0 (1)	0	5	3.0	58%/17%
6/29	3 (4)	1 (1)	0 (0)	0 (1)	0	5	3.4	62%/15%
7/1	6 (4)	3 (1)	0 (0)	0 (1)	0	5	3.8	64%/14%
7/4	3 (4)	1 (1)	0 (0)	0 (1)	0	5	4.8	67%/13%
7/7	6 (4)	0 (0)	0 (0)	1 (0)	0	4	4.8	69%/13%
7/10	3 (4)	0 (0)	0 (0)	3 (-2)	0	2	4.2	65%/12%
7/12	4 (4)	1 (1)	0 (0)	0 (1)	0	5	4.2	67%/11%
7/13	1 (2)	0 (0)	0 (0)	0 (1)	0	3	3.8	63%/11%

Speculating on Breakouts—1

by Brandon Kruse

Over the last two seasons, we have developed and refined a set of breakout profiles for batters and pitchers (these can now be found in the Forecaster's Toolbox section). We've defined a breakout season as one where a player who had never previously posted a Rotisserie value of $10 posts a value of $20 or higher. As a qualifier, he must have had at least one season of MLE (Double-A or higher) or MLB skill stats prior to their $20 season.

Until now, we've only used the profiles to assess the legitimacy of in-season breakouts. This time, we'd like to apply the profile before the season starts, to see if we can identify some breakout candidates for 2009. This was not the focus of the original research, so we're going out on a bit of a limb here. To try this out, we looked for players who had a Rotisserie value of $10 or less in 2008, and who met all of the filters for their respective breakout profile. This left us with nine players who, with a change in role or simply increased playing time, could be good speculative investments for 2009:

Brian Anderson (OF, CHW) flashed some strong power (143 PX) in 2008, a skill he hasn't owned since college and the low minors. But all of his 8 HR came against LHP; his slugging percentage against RHP was just .337. If he can't balance that out, he doesn't offer much hope for a breakout, because his 75% contact rate and .278 xBA barely meet our profile filters. Power would be his best shot at moving beyond a fourth outfielder role; at age 27, next season may be his last chance.

A good April (.318 BA, 15 R, 4 SB) had **Erick Aybar** (SS, LAA) earning at a $20 level early on in 2008, but he couldn't keep it up. He has a good ground ball/speed combo, but needs to have a contact rate above 90% to really make it work. A .280 xBA and 4% walk rate aren't enough to pump up his stolen base totals to elite levels, and steals are his most likely path to breaking out.

Saves are the missing ingredient for **Manny Delcarmen** (RHP, BOS) to reach the $20 level, and he has the misfortune of being stuck behind one of the league's best closers. Still, anything can happen, and Delcarmen has built up enough closer-worthy skills (8.7 Dom, 2.6 Cmd, 94 BPV) to become a solid Plan B option for the Red Sox. He's a great LIMA pick.

Joe Mather (OF, STL) impressed with terrific power (151 PX), and while his .241 BA was low, his .280 xBA shows promise. His contact rate dropped from an 85% MLE mark

in Double-A in 2007 to 76% in the majors in 2008, but at the same time, his PX shot up 43 points, and trading contact for power is a not uncommon trait for breakout hitters. Is 26 the age where he puts the power and the contact together? That possibility makes him worth keeping on your radar.

Martin Prado (3B/2B/1B, ATL) turned an 87% contact rate and a line drive swing into a .320 BA in 2008, though his .296 xBA says that might come down a bit in the future. His power and speed skills are merely average, but even average skills represent growth from his MLEs in the minors. He'll need to find a way to further at least a little of that growth to increase his value potential, because batting average alone won't cut it.

Ramon Ramirez (RHP, KC) quietly put together the best season of his career in 2008, with a 8.8 Dom, 2.3 Cmd, 86 BPV and 3.97 xERA, and his 2.64 ERA in 71.7 IP likely grabbed the attention of the Royals. Like Delcarmen, he's currently stuck behind a top-notch closer, but is emerging as a solid LIMA candidate.

Anytime a Rockies hitter shows a little power, it gets your attention, and **Seth Smith** (OF, COL) did that in 2008. His 119 PX was intriguing, but it was what he did in the second half that's really worth noting: 0.92 Eye, 137 PX and a .309 xBA. Granted, it was only in 66 AB, so it comes with a small sample size warning, but he does have a track record of high contact rates and above-average power in the minors. If he does get increased playing time, it would likely come as the left-handed half of a platoon role, but that could still mean 450 AB.

Fifteen SB in 275 AB may be the main thing owners noticed about **Eugenio Velez** (2B/OF, SF) in 2008, but when you look at his skills, there's more to like. He has a good ground ball/speed/contact combo (though as with Aybar, you'd like to see a little more contact), and it added up to a .288 xBA. He hit .328 in near full-time play over the final two months of last season. A regular role in 2009 may give him a chance to really shine.

Ben Zobrist (SS/OF, TAM) doesn't appear to be in Tampa Bay's long-term plans anymore, so he may require a change to scenery to break out in what will be his age 27 season. There was much to like in his skills in 2008, including a 148 PX and .292 xBA. That xBA also included an abnormally low 13% line drive rate that will probably revert to something closer to 20%. If the power's for real — and the 4 HRs he hit in the season's final week look even more intriguing now — he may have the skills of a .300+ hitter. Hope for a trade.

Speculating on Breakouts—2

by Ray Murphy

For those lucky enough to roster Carlos Pena's unlikely 2007 rebound season, the effect was massive. A 40+ HR bat scooped from the waiver wire is a major leg up in a fanalytic pennant chase. When we conducted a search for the 2008 version of Pena's breakout in a March column at BaseballHQ.com, among the candidates we identified were Jorge Cantu and Ryan Ludwick, both of whom did credible impersonations of Pena's career year.

So, who are the 2009 candidates? To frame the discussion, we will identify the following qualities describing Pena's pre-breakout profile:

- Owns a significant power skill from prior seasons, preferably displayed at the major league level.
- Lost his last job due to ineffectiveness. (we will also accept injury here)
- Lacking a clear path to playing time.
- Still at a prime age for a power spike.

With those ground rules set, here are some candidates for your consideration:

Ryan Shealy made this list in 2008, but still qualifies for 2009. In fact, he enhanced his candidacy by hitting 29 HR between Triple-A and KC, including seven in a 73-AB September callup. At 29, there is still time for him. What he really needs is an opportunity, the kind that Pena was handed in April 2007.

Another holdover from the 2008 search is **Dan Johnson**. He has a longer MLB track record than Shealy, although his PX history from 2005-07 with OAK (107-87-112) was not inspiring. But as a 28-year old sent back to Triple-A in 2008, he slugged .556, with 25 HR in fewer than 400 AB. Johnson is like Shealy in that the only thing he really lacks is a job.

Juan Rivera had a relatively successful 2008. Returning from a broken leg that cost him nearly all of 2007, he started slowly but improved as the season went on. He posted a 131 PX in the 2nd half, back in line with the 121 PX he posted pre-injury in 2006. Reflecting on other leg injuries where full recovery took multiple seasons, Rivera may have another step forward coming, even beyond what you might anticipate by doubling his 2nd half of 2008 (.268-12-42).

Dallas McPherson's big-league resume is somewhat lighter than the rest of this group, but the primary culprits are the back problems that eventually led LAA to give up on him. But his minor-league career (150 career HR) speaks to his prodigious power, and his 2008 season (42 HR in 448 Triple-A AB) speaks to the health of his back. Whether in FLA or elsewhere, McPherson certainly deserves regular playing time somewhere in 2009.

The American League equivalent of McPherson is **Nelson Cruz** in TEX. After a couple of failed cups of coffee in the bigs, Cruz finally flashed his power at the highest level, socking 7 HR and a 184 PX in 115 late-season AB. That surge came on top of 37 HR in Triple-A. In terms of his draft-day value, he would best serve fantasy leaguers by *not* being handed a starting job in March. The question is whether the breakout starts on Opening Day, or is briefly delayed. Either way, it's coming.

Mike Fontenot has now shown glimpses of real power in both 2007 (1H PX: 130) and 2008 (146 PX). Currently typecast as a utility IF in CHC, he is only one injury or hot streak away from shedding that label and racking up some impressive counting stats as an everyday player.

Another holdover from last year's list is **Jeff Baker**. An MLE PX of 120 in 2006 put him on our radar screen a year ago, and now a half-season in COL with a 149 PX in 2008 has reaffirmed our interest. Baker's biggest drawback is that he has not separated himself from Ian Stewart and Clint Barmes in the Rockies' 2B picture. It bears watching how COL reconstructs their infield this winter If they clear the logjam in front of Baker, the "buy" rating will only grow stronger.

Travis Buck was a former #1 draft pick and cornerstone of the OAK youth movement when he debuted in 2007. Injuries and a glut of young OF in OAK cost him his sophomore 2008 season. But that 130 PX he put up in his half-season as a rookie is still part of his skill set, and he flashed that potential at the end of 2008 with a post-injury September cameo in OAK (187 PX). There is still competition in the OAK OF, but Buck's skill set should win out if his health cooperates.

Similar to Buck, **Josh Fields** followed a credible rookie season with a sophomore wipeout. The return of Joe Crede exiled Fields to the minors, where he proceeded to lose half the season to the DL. If you give him a pass on 2008, he still owns the 166 (MLE) PX he posted in that rookie campaign, and it should not take him long to bounce back toward that level of production.

Former prospect **Wily Mo Pena** is all but completely forgotten. Having changed teams twice, coming off of season-ending shoulder surgery, and in a suddenly-crowded WAS OF, there are plenty of reasons to avoid him. But there is still one compelling reason to monitor his recovery: he owns elite power skills (see 2004-07 PX: 174-189-137-136). 2009 is his age 27 season, and he's still never received an unfettered opportunity in the majors (career-high AB: 336). There is still 40-HR power here if someone shows the patience to let it emerge.

III.
GAMING

Gaming Research

The changing face of fantasy

Each year at BaseballHQ.com, we keep tabs on ongoing fantasy baseball industry trends by means of our weekly HQ Poll, which we've been running since December 1998. In each edition of the *Forecaster*, we look back at some of these questions and share the results. There are dozens of trends that we track so we rotate the topics each year.

Since these questions are asked at Baseball HQ, they only represent the opinions of folks who a) visit Baseball HQ, and b) respond to online polls. So these are clearly not scientific representations of the industry as a whole. However, even from among our smaller group (note that all poll results had at least 500 responses) we can glean some interesting tidbits about where our hobby may be headed and how fantasy leaguers play the game.

When do you typically start getting into the upcoming baseball season?

	2006	2007	2008
Following the end of the World Series	36%	33%	36%
Following end of fantasy football season	44%	41%	43%
Following the end of the Super Bowl	14%	18%	14%
Opening of spring camps	6%	7%	6%

One way to read these results is that more than half of respondents tie their baseball fandom to football, and about two thirds spend 3 1/2 winter months without any baseball interest at all. Of course, another way to look at this is that about one third of respondents are 24/7/365 baseball lifers. The three-year trend is essentially flat.

What is your primary, underlying draft strategy?

	2006	2007	2008
Draft a balanced team all around	25%	29%	29%
Draft for value (trade for balance)	25%	23%	24%
Focus on position scarcity	11%	7%	9%
Target a specific group of players	17%	22%	21%
Take whatever bargains the table gives me	17%	15%	14%
Only strategy is making sure cooler is full	6%	4%	4%

There are many ways to skin a cat, I suppose. The strength of balanced drafting might be a reflection of leagues that do not allow trading, or owners that do not like to trade (otherwise, drafting for value and trading for balance is the more prudent approach). The recent bump in those who target specific players might be due to the adoption of strategies like LIMA and Portfolio3.

Perhaps the most heartening trend is the percentage of respondents who employ at least *some* type of active draft strategy: 77% in 2006, 81% in 2007 and 82% in 2008.

What is your approach to draft inflation?

	2003	2007	2008
I calculate one rate for the entire league	37%	38%	34%
I calc separate rates for batters & pitchers	27%	28%	29%
I don't bother calculating draft inflation.	35%	34%	34%

For those in keeper leagues, you really can't get a read on market value without calculating draft inflation. And if you are going to go through the process, you might as well do it correctly and calculate separate rates for batters and pitchers.

Which of these players would you most want to own?

	2006	2007	2008
20-HR hitter who broke out with 45 HRs last year. Reliability grade of CCC	15%	16%	11%
Consistent 45-HR hitter who slumped to 20 HRs last year. REL of BBB	36%	56%	43%
Consistent 25-HR hitter. REL of AAA	48%	27%	46%

Interesting swing in results, year-to-year. The only conclusion we can draw is that most folks would not trust the high-risk 45-HR breakout player. For the other two, it is almost an even split between forgiving the high-level off-year and banking on reliable low-level productivity.

I don't agree. If I had the choice between a hitter I am confident is going to hit 25 HRs versus one who has a moderate chance to return to the 45-HR level (and at worst, hit 20), I think I would opt for that shot at 45 HRs.

For those who participate in more than one league, how do you manage your time?

	2005	2007	2008
I try to devote an equal amount of time to all my teams.	38%	39%	42%
I have one or two primary leagues that I focus the most on; the rest I manage whenever I find extra time.	54%	56%	53%
I focus my time only on the teams that are doing well. Once a team drops, I abandon it.	5%	3%	2%
I generally don't spend much regular time on any of my teams. It's whenever I have a free moment.	3%	2%	2%

It was nice to see that more than 90% of respondents are committed to at least their primary teams, and the number that are committed to all their teams has been slowly growing. However, the primary mode of play is such that fantasy leaguers do over-commit and have several core leagues that they pay the most attention to.

Previous polls showed that the average number of leagues folks participate in is about 2.5. It's those "half-leagues" that tend to receive the least amount of attention.

How long do you wait to cut a struggling frontline pitcher (Round 1-6, $20+ draft pick)?

	2005	2007	2008
Three consecutive blowout starts. I can't afford to wait.	3%	3%	3%
4-6 weeks of poor performance.	8%	13%	11%
You have to give a frontliner at least 2-3 months	33%	35%	38%
I'll ride him all year if I have to. Odds of a turnaround are greater than any free agent option.	49%	43%	43%
I can't cut players in my league unless they are DLed or demoted.	7%	6%	6%

The issues here are the depth of the player pool, the ease in which owners can access that pool, the frequency at which transactions can be made, and patience. About 80% of respondents will wait a minimum of two months to make a move — which would have been a good thing for pitchers like C.C. Sabathia this year — but ultimately, it comes down to the age-old question... How long do you wait? Perhaps it depends on the player...

How long do you wait to cut an end-game pitcher (Round 18-23, $1-$5 draft pick) who started strong but is now struggling?

	2005	2007	2008
Three consecutive blowout starts.	52%	47%	42%
4-6 weeks of poor performance.	35%	34%	34%
If there's any hope of a turnaround, at least 2-3 months.	5%	8%	13%
Longer than 3 months. Pitching is a commodity not easy to find.	2%	3%	4%
I can't cut players in my league unless they are DLed or demoted.	6%	7%	7%

These results are fascinating as they show a marked trend towards exercising more patience at the low end of the talent scale. Driving this might be owners' increased confidence in their abilities to draft skilled pitchers (and thus more reluctant to give up on them), the increased volatility of pitching commodities, or perhaps just a dogged stubbornness.

You have $75 FAAB left, the most of any team in your league; the second ranked team has $70. How do you approach the MLB trading deadline?

	2006	2007	2008
I bid $71 on the best league-crosser, no matter who it is. There will be nothing else to spend it on after July 31.	59%	53%	52%
I bid a reasonable amount on the best league-crosser unless he's a stud, saving some dollars for late buys.	32%	40%	40%
I try to split my bids among several players so I can buy more than one.	8%	7%	8%

When it comes to FAAB, we always advise to "spend early and often." Those who heed that advice are rarely in the position of being able to control the board at the trading deadline. The dangers are always that there is not a suitable commodity to bid on, no guarantee that the stud league-crosser will justify his cost and the fact that even the best acquisition will only give you two months of production.

That said, if you do have the deepest FAAB wallet on July 31 — in this case, $75 — the only thing you can guarantee with 100% certainty is the acquisition of one player for $71. That's what you have to do. Then you have to hope that the best league-crosser is a Mark Teixeira-caliber player like it was this year, and not Jarrod Saltalamacchia who was the best AL deadline crossover last year.

From a purely Rotisserie strategy standpoint (stability, tradeability, etc.), which position is the most desirable to be in right now?

	2001	2004	2007	2008
1st place in batting average by 10 points (0.010)	3%	13%	14%	10%
1st place in HRs by 10 and RBIs by 30	13%	16%	18%	20%
1st place in stolen bases by 15	11%	21%	14%	11%
1st place in wins by 10	23%	21%	27%	24%
1st place in saves by 10	6%	6%	6%	6%
1st place in ERA by 0.25 and WHIP by 0.05	42%	23%	20%	29%

This poll merits a more in-depth look because I find these results to be so counter-intuitive. The core question is, which of these categorical leads are safest and/or most tradeable? For perspective, the poll was run in mid-August of each of these four years.

For starters, all of these leads are reasonably safe in mid-August. However, some are safer than others.

For instance, a closer on a 40-saves pace would be expected to amass about 9 more saves from mid-August through the end of the season. If you traded that closer in mid-August with a 10-save lead, you might still be able to hold onto that lead, but it would be close.

The tactical element to this, though, is how marketable a 40-save closer is in mid-August. Given that the saves category tends to be bunched tightly in most leagues, it would seem that you could get a good deal in trade for that pitcher while possibly not giving up your lead in saves.

So, I'd think that being in first place in saves by 10 would be *very* desirable, yet only 6% voted that way.

About a quarter of respondents polled said that being in first place in Wins by 10 is most desirable. I can buy into this a little more since wins are tough to chase. However, wins — by themselves — are also tough to trade.

The largest percentage of those polled chose being in first place in ERA by 0.25 and WHIP by 0.05 as the most desirable. Frankly, this boggles my mind. There are hundreds of horror stories about pitching staffs that go belly-up down the stretch. While these leads are reasonably safe, they are likely the *least* safe of all the options.

If you were to trade a Tim Lincecum-caliber starting pitcher, that means you would have to replace him with someone of a lower caliber. While that transaction alone might not be enough to chip away at a 0.25 lead in ERA, remember that you are also opening the door for other teams to close the gap as well. Average categories can be volatile, even in September.

Battling dwindling attention spans

If we were to try to pinpoint the reason why baseball has lost ground to football as America's most popular major sport, perhaps we can blame the internet.

Our online activity has become an extension of ourselves. Each time we log on, we are bombarded with information. Perhaps our brain can only process a finite amount of this information in a given period of time. More information in a fixed amount of time can only mean that there is less time for us to view and process any single piece of information.

Over the past decade, we have become conditioned to process data in smaller and smaller chunks so that we can amass more and more information in less and less time.

So.... it seems that a 6-month marathon of 162 four-hour ballgames would not fit into that model of information processing. For a child of the 1990s, sitting through an entire baseball game has got to be like watching paint dry.

I watch my two teenage daughters as they participate in the sport of Xtreme Homework... four IM windows open at one time, IPod in ear and texting on their phones, all while allegedly doing homework. They are both "A with the occasional B" students, so their brains *must* be functioning sufficiently well, right? Yet I can't get them to sit through a ballgame without 47 trips to the Dippin' Dots stand.

I'd think that this situation is not going to change any time soon, which could mean that our stodgy old game might have no hope of returning to its former prominence. Thank goodness for fantasy, though. If not for the interactivity of our hobby — drawing us back into the game on our own terms — then MLB might have fallen even further back behind the NFL.

This can be fixed. Sort of. All that is required is a minor restructuring of the Major League schedule. The minor leagues have had the right idea by splitting their seasons. But they don't go far enough.

Here is the tonic to cure our ever-dwindling attention spans: the Major League schedule needs to be divided into three 50-game split-seasons. The benefits:

Fifty games at a time might be just the length to maintain fan interest. Every game will have more meaning as pennant races will start at the opening gun, not four months into the season when the pretenders have already been eliminated. Teams that fall behind quickly can reassess and retool for the other two thirds. While statistical anomalies might not wash out at 50 games, the shorter segments will promote parity, which is hope for anyone who's been living in Pittsburgh or KC the past two decades.

The 150-game total season will allow us to closely approximate the records and benchmarks that we've become accustomed to. It might be a little more of a stretch for a pitcher to win 20 games, but at least we won't have to worry about 73 HR seasons any more. The fresh start might even be a good thing for the sport.

There are some exciting analytical implications. We revel in the chance to analyze the stats when they stop accumulating each October; with this new system, we'd have two additional opportunities *during* the season to stop, breathe, and analyze. Consider that the one off-week between each split could be used as a massive media blowout period — evaluating the previous 50 games, analyzing the next 50 games — so it would be like having the information crush of the last week of spring training (or better yet, Super Bowl weekend) three times each year.

The split-seasons would force a change in how we determine the winners. There could potentially be four "winners" from each division: the first place team from each split, plus the team with the best overall won-loss record for the entire year. In this case, it might mean elongating the play-off season a bit. However, there won't be a need for a wild card any more, which would offset the added rounds. Also, the post-season could begin a week earlier so we still might not have to play ball in November.

Yes, there may be play-off byes and scheduling hassles; it's not perfect. But these do not seem to be deal-breakers when there are so many other positives.

Obviously, the odds of this happening are pretty remote. We don't have control over what the Major Leagues do, but we can certainly look at this for fantasy baseball. After all, the fantasy game faces the same challenges from short attention spans. Look at all the benefits:

Fewer abandoned teams. Fifty game split seasons mean three shots at a title each year. There would always be something to look forward to and plan for.

More drafts. Given that drafting is the funnest activity in the game, the in-season breaks provide more opportunities to experience that fun. For those with very short attention spans, you can always do a complete re-draft and treat the year as three distinct mini-seasons. Or, you might allow teams to drop their five worst players and conduct a restocking draft at each break. Or, you could shorten your pre-season time commitment and conduct your minor league draft at each break. Lots of options.

Less isolation. The internet has turned fantasy into a solitary pursuit. The in-season breaks are a great excuse to get owners together for trade talk over wings and beer.

Bigger business. The primary obstacle when considering a change like this is the fact that support systems are not in place. Most commissioner services, game companies, even information providers are not set up to accommodate a 3-season year. But they'd *have to* provide support if there was demand in the marketplace. And what greater benefit could there be for them than offering triple the number of opportunities to play each year? ("Your team out of contention by May 1? Just draft a new team for the June 1 second season!") All we have to do is ask. A lot.

Even if the Major Leagues don't adopt such a radical system (though, when you think about it, interleague play and the wild card were not all that "ordinary"), there is nothing stopping fantasy from dividing up the season. I know that this is a huge departure from the norm, and many folks are naturally resistant to change, but if you take a step back and look at it objectively, it's tough to find much downside. The biggest obstacle? It requires change.

Batting Order and Fantasy Value

by Michael Roy

Rewind to the start of Nick Markakis' career in 2006: he spent the first half batting last in the Orioles' order. He took off in the summer, and by year-end he was hitting in the coveted three-hole. Have you ever wondered how much more valuable, in fantasy dollars, it is to move from last to cleanup in the batting order? Just how much of Markakis' jump from $2 to $12 was due to the lineup promotion?

Where do dollar values lie as you move up and down the average lineup? Then, how much value derives directly from batting order position and how much derives from the individual quality of the player, unrelated to where he hits?

Here is a profile of the average American League lineup from 2005 to 2007, ranking each position by dollar value:

Pos	PA	R	RBI	HR	SB	BA	R$
Bat #4	697	97	113	29	5	.283	$20.91
Bat #1	747	108	67	14	26	.281	$20.41
Bat #3	715	99	104	25	9	.280	$20.39
Bat #2	728	100	80	15	14	.280	$18.00
Bat #5	682	86	97	24	6	.276	$17.72
Bat #6	665	81	81	21	6	.266	$14.88
Bat #7	645	76	75	17	6	.261	$13.24
Bat #8	623	70	71	14	7	.251	$11.37
Bat #9	600	69	62	11	9	.251	$10.79

The AL lineup falls into four levels of value. No surprise that the cleanup hitter tops the chart, but the leadoff batter is only 50 cents behind, virtually tied with the key Bat #3. All three elite $20 spots are close. The next group, Bats #2 and #5, is still valuable at $18. These spots are also interchangeable in value, as #5 nosed out #2 in 2006 and 2007.

Value declines at Bat #6 and Bat #7. They get fewer AB and lurk outside the heart of the run-producing center. The final drop to Bat #8-9 signals the fantasy danger zone. There are 150 fewer PA from leadoff to last in the order.

What about the National League? Does the absence of the DH affect the relative values in the batting order?

Pos	PA	R	RBI	HR	SB	BA	R$
Bat #3	715	103	102	27	10	.287	$20.97
Bat #4	699	98	108	30	6	.278	$19.95
Bat #1	747	107	63	14	28	.276	$18.81
Bat #5	682	87	97	24	6	.272	$16.82
Bat #2	724	102	70	15	16	.276	$16.71
Bat #6	665	77	86	21	7	.273	$15.17
Bat #7	645	67	77	16	6	.263	$12.06
Bat #8	624	63	66	12	5	.251	$ 9.13

The NL landscape looks somewhat different. The meat of the order, batters three and four, comes out on top every year. While the leadoff hitter still commands almost $19, surprisingly the emphasis on speed and "small ball" in the NL does not produce higher fantasy value for Bat #1 and Bat #2 compared with the AL.

Like the AL profile, Bat #2 and Bat #5 are close at $17. But Bat #6 has more fantasy value in the NL, even outranking Bat #2 in 2007. Without the DH, the NL lineup puts more weight on the six-hole, after which the value drops a big $3

to Bat #7. And no fantasy owner wants to roster an NL #8 hitter, who gets few AB and few good pitches to hit ahead of the pitcher.

The tougher question: now that we grasp the relative dollar value of the batting order groups, just how much traces to batting order position ("BOP")? How much of that value simply derives from the individual quality ("IQ") of the hitters that occupy those spots, namely that David Ortiz has better hitting skills and fantasy value than Nick Punto, whether he bats cleanup or last.

We first construct a lineup featuring the same AL hitter with average hitting skills at each of the nine slots. Meet Joe Average, the average AL fantasy hitter from 2005-2007:

PA	R	RBI	HR	SB	BA	BB	Slg	R$
453	60	58	13	7	.276	39	.440	$11.90

To isolate the BOP factor from IQ, we make three adjustments: (1) we make Joe Average an everyday player at each batting slot, increasing his PA; (2) we alter his RBI at each BOP to conform to the RBI/TB ratio for each average slot from the above AL profile, neutralizing the hitter's IQ as it affects RBI; and (3) we alter his Runs at each BOP to conform to the Runs/(Hits plus Walks) ratio for each average slot, neutralizing the hitter's IQ as it affects Runs. Here is the resulting profile:

Pos	PA	R	RBI	HR	SB	BA	R$
Bat #1	747	107	72	22	12	.276	$18.75
Bat #2	728	102	84	22	12	.276	$19.00
Bat #3	715	95	100	21	11	.276	$19.45
Bat #4	698	93	104	21	11	.276	$19.36
Bat #5	682	86	94	20	11	.276	$18.18
Bat #6	665	85	82	20	11	.276	$17.19
Bat #7	645	81	80	19	10	.276	$16.60
Bat #8	623	78	80	18	10	.276	$16.19
Bat #9	600	78	73	18	10	.276	$15.50

This exercise is like having David DeJesus hit in each spot in your lineup: boring on the BA, HR, and SB fronts, but interesting on the contextual issues of playing time and run production. By promoting Joe Average from last to third in the lineup, we increase his dollar value by four bucks, or 26% — nothing to sneeze at. The big event to watch for here is a move into the top 4 slots in the order; this adds over 20% of value. After the first four slots, there is a sliding scale of value worth about 67 cents per spot, a lesser factor in a fantasy transaction.

The BOP differential is more pronounced if you substitute better players for Joe Average. What would Alex Rodriguez's dollar value be if we moved him from cleanup to last in the lineup?

Pos	PA	R	RBI	HR	SB	BA	R$
Bat #4	678	143	156	54	24	.314	$38.35
Bat #9	600	94	101	48	21	.314	$29.56

For an elite player like A-Rod, that degree of demotion would cost almost $9, a diminution in value of 23%. Of course, that's the extreme case. But it does illustrate the potential impact of lineup moves.

Fanalytic Gaming Strategies

The LIMA Plan

The LIMA Plan is a strategy for Rotisserie leagues (though the underlying concept can be used in other formats) that allows you to target high skills pitchers at very low cost, thereby freeing up dollars for offense. LIMA is an acronym for Low Investment Mound Aces, and also pays tribute to Jose Lima, a $1 pitcher in 1998 who exemplified the power of the strategy. In a $260 league:

1. *Budget a maximum of $60 for your pitching staff.*

2. *Allot no more than $30 of that budget for acquiring saves.* In 5x5 leagues, it is reasonable to forego saves at the draft (and acquire them during the season) and re-allocate this $30 to starters ($20) and offense ($10).

3. *Draft only pitchers with:*
  - Command ratio (K/BB) of 2.0 or better.
  - Strikeout rate of 5.6 or better.
  - Expected home run rate of 1.0 or less.

4. *Draft as few innings as your league rules will allow.* This is intended to manage risk. For some game formats, this should be a secondary consideration.

5. *Maximize your batting slots.* Target batters with:
  - Contact rate of at least 80%
  - Walk rate of at least 10%
  - PX or SX level of at least 100

Spend no more than $29 for any player and try to keep the $1 picks to a minimum.

The goal is to ace the batting categories and carefully pick your pitching staff so that it will finish in the upper third in ERA, WHIP and saves (and IP or K's in 5x5), and an upside of perhaps 9th in wins. In a competitive league, that should be enough to win, and definitely enough to finish in the money. Worst case, you should have an excess of offense available that you can deal for pitching.

The strategy works because it better allocates resources. Fantasy leaguers who spend a lot for pitching are not only paying for expected performance, they are also paying for better defined roles – #1 and #2 rotation starters, ace closers, etc. – which are expected to translate into more IP, wins and saves. But roles are highly variable. A pitcher's role will usually come down to his skill and performance; if he doesn't perform, he'll lose the role.

The LIMA Plan says, let's invest in skill and let the roles fall where they may. In the long run, better skills should translate into more innings, wins and saves. And as it turns out, pitching skill costs less than pitching roles do.

In *snake draft leagues*, don't start drafting starting pitchers until Round 10. In *shallow mixed leagues*, the LIMA Plan may not be necessary; just focus on the BPI benchmarks. In *simulation leagues*, also build your staff around BPI benchmarks.

Variations on the LIMA Plan

LIMA Extrema: Limit your total pitching budget to only $30, or less. This can be particularly effective in shallow leagues where LIMA-caliber starting pitcher free agents are plentiful during the season.

SANTANA Plan: Instead of spending $30 on saves, you spend it on a starting pitcher anchor. In 5x5 leagues where you can reasonably punt saves at the draft table, allocating those dollars to a high-end LIMA-caliber starting pitcher can work well as long as you pick the right anchor.

One way to approach that selection is...

The RIMA Plan

LIMA is based on optimal resource allocation. These days, however, no matter how good of a team you draft, player inconsistency, injuries and unexpected *risk factors* can wreak havoc with your season. The RIMA Plan adds the element of **RI**sk **MA**nagement.

Players are not risks by virtue of their price tags alone. A $30 Johan Santana, for example, might be a very good buy since he is a healthy, stable commodity. But most LIMA drafters would not consider him because of the price.

The RIMA Plan involves setting up two pools of players. The first pool consists of those who meet the LIMA criteria. The second pool includes players with high Reliability grades. The set of players who appear in both pools are our prime draft targets. We then evaluate the two pools further, integrating different levels of skill and risk, and creating six hierarchical tiers of players to draft from:

> **TIER A:** LIMA-caliber with high Reliability grades
> **TIER B:** LIMA-caliber with moderate Reliability grades
> **TIER C:** Non-LIMA with high Reliability grades
> **TIER D:** LIMA-caliber with low Reliability grades
> **TIER E:** Non-LIMA with moderate Reliability grades
> **TIER F:** Non-LIMA with low Reliability grades

Tier C is where RIMA opens up more opportunities. While we'd typically stay away from low-skilled players, carefully-chosen "C" bodies can provide valuable support if you are careful. In this group you might find inning-eater hurlers who could help boost your strikeout totals, though might have elevated ERAs. If the rest of your staff has a solid skills foundation, you can often weather the mediocre numbers that come along with these arms. The fact that they are low risk means that you know exactly what you will be getting and so you can better plan for it.

The goal for your roster is to assemble a balanced portfolio of solid performers and steady AB and IP-eaters that provide good return on your investment.

The RIMA concept is also applicable in non-Rotisserie formats. The process of integrating skill and risk management is universal for all types of league formats.

Total Control Drafting

Part of the reason we play this game is the aura of "control," our ability to create a team of players we want and manage them to a championship. We make every effort to control as many elements as possible. But in reality, the players that end up on our teams are largely controlled by the other owners. *Their* bidding affects your ability to roster the players you want. In a snake draft, the other owners control your roster to an even greater extent. We are really only able to get the players we want within the limitations set by others.

However, an optimal roster can be constructed from a fanalytic assessment of skill and risk. We can create our teams from that "perfect player pool" and not be forced to roster players that don't fit our criteria. It's now possible. It's just a matter of taking *Total Control*.

Why this makes sense

1. Our obsession with projected player values is holding us back. Fact: Only about 65% of players drafted provide a return within +/-$5 of projection. To get that percentage up to about 85%, you'd have to open the range to +/- $9. This is not indicative of poor forecasting; it's the nature of the beast. So, if a player on your draft list is valued at $20 and you agonize when the bidding hits $23, odds are about two chances in three that he could really earn anywhere from $15 to $25. What this means is, in some cases, and within reason, you should just pay what it takes to get the players you want.

2. There are no such things as bargains. Most of us *don't* just pay what it takes because we are always on the lookout for players who go under value. But we really don't know which players will cost less than they will earn because prices are still driven by the draft table. The concept of "bargain" assumes that we even know what a player's true value is. To wit:

If we target a player at $23 and land him for $20, we might *think* we got a bargain. In reality, this player might earn anywhere from $19 to $26, making that $3 in perceived savings virtually irrelevant.

The point is, a "bargain" is defined by your particular marketplace at the time of your particular draft, not by any list of canned values, or an "expectation" of what the market value of any player might be. So any contention that TCD forces you to overpay for your players is false.

3. "Control" is there for the taking. Most owners are so focused on their own team that they really don't pay much attention to what you're doing. There are some exceptions, and bidding wars do happen, but in general, other owners will not provide that much resistance.

How it's done

1. Create your optimal draft pool.
2. Get those players.

Start by identifying which players will be draftable based on the RIMA criteria. Then, at the draft:

Early Game: Your focus has to be on your roster only. When it's your bid opener, toss a player you need at about 50%-75% of your projected value. Bid aggressively. Forget about bargain-hunting; just pay what you need to pay. Of course, don't spend $40 for a $25 player, but it's okay to exceed your projected value within reason.

Mix up the caliber of openers. Instead of tossing out an Albert Pujols at $35 in the first round, toss out a Randy Winn at $11. *Wise Guy Baseball's* Gene McCaffrey suggests tossing all lower-end players early, which makes sense. It helps you bottom-fill your roster with players most others won't chase early, and you can always build the top end of your roster with players others toss out.

Another good early tactic is to gauge the market value of scarce commodities with a $19 opener for Joe Nathan or a $29 opener for Jose Reyes.

Other owners may pick up on the fact that you are only throwing out names of players you want, so mix in a few non-targets to throw them off. Also, bid aggressively on *every player*; it will obscure which ones you really want.

Mid-Game: If you've successfully rostered 10-12 players with high skills and Reliability grades, you will have likely built a solid foundation for your team. At that point, you can relax some of the reliability constraints and take a few chances on players with high upside, but higher risk, like upwardly mobile rookies.

End game: You will need to relax the reliability targets for your last picks, so it might be a good idea to make sure those last buys are all pitchers (who are inherently more risky). You'll note that most high-skilled end-game LIMA pitchers have low reliability grades by nature.

At the end of the draft, you may have rostered 23 players who could have been purchased at somewhat lower cost. It's tough to say. Those extra dollars likely won't mean much anyway; in fact, you might have just left them on the table. TCD almost ensures that you spend all your money.

In the end, it's okay to pay a slight premium to make sure you get the players with the highest potential to provide a good return on your investment. It's no different than the premium you'd pay to get the last valuable shortstop, or for the position flexibility a player like Mark DeRosa provides. With TCD, you're just spending those extra dollars up front on players with high skill and low risk.

The best part is that you take more control of your destiny. You build your roster with what you consider are the best assemblage of players. You keep the focus on your team. And you don't just roster whatever bargains the rest of the table leaves for you, because a bargain is just a fleeting perception of value we have in March.

The Portfolio3 Plan

2008 UPDATE

The previously discussed strategies have had important roles in furthering our potential for success. The problem is that they all take a broad-stroke approach to the draft. The $35 first round player is evaluated and integrated into the plan in the same way that the end-gamer is. But each player has a different role on your team by virtue of his skill set, dollar value, position and risk profile. When it comes to a strategy for how to approach a specific player, one size does not fit all...

We need some players to return fair value more than others. When you spend $40 on a player, you are buying the promise of putting over 15% of your budget in the hands of 4% of your roster. By contrast, the $1 players are easily replaceable. If you're in a snake draft league, you know that a first-rounder going belly-up is going to hurt you far more than a 23rd round bust.

We rely on some players for profit more than others. Those first-rounders are not where we are likely going to see the most profit potential. The $10-$20 players are likely to return more pure dollar profit; the end-gamers are most likely to return the highest profit percentage.

We can afford to weather more risk with some players than with others. Since those high-priced early-rounders need to return at least fair value, we cannot afford to take on excessive risk. Since we need more profit potential from the lower priced, later-round picks, that means opening up our tolerance for risk more with those players.

Players have different risk profiles based solely on what roster spot they are going to fill. Catchers are more injury prone. A closer's value is highly dependent on fickle managerial whim. These types of players are high risk even if they have the best skills on the planet. That needs to affect their draft price or draft round.

For some players, the promise of providing a scarce skill, or productivity at a scarce position, may trump risk. Not always, but sometimes. At minimum, we need to be open to the possibility. The determining factor is usually price. A $7, 15th round Frank Francisco is not something you pass up, even with a Reliability Grade of FDF.

In the end, we need a way to integrate all these different types of players, roles and needs. We need to put some form to the concept of a diversified draft approach. Thus:

The **Portfolio3 Plan** provides a three-tiered approach to the draft. Just like most folks prefer to diversify their stock portfolio, P3 advises to diversify your roster with three different types of players. Depending upon the stage of the draft (and budget constraints in auction leagues), P3 uses a different set of rules for each tier that you'll draft from. The three tiers are:

1. Core Players
2. Mid-Game Players
3. End-Game Players

One of the complaints about P3 when we debuted it in 2007 was that it was difficult to find enough players to meet the performance filters. Admittedly, the player pool can get pretty thin quickly during the course of the draft, particularly in AL-only or NL-only leagues. Early trials showed that rostering enough Tier 1 players was challenging, but doable; however, limiting T3 players to $25 was darned near impossible.

In 2008, we made a few tweaks to the filters to open up the player pool a bit. The new reliability grades also expand the player pool a bit. Here is the new structure:

TIER 1: CORE PLAYERS

Roster Slots	Budget	BATTERS Rel	Ct%	PX or SX		PITCHERS Rel	BPV
5-8	Up to $160	BBB	80%	100	100	BBB	75

These are the players who will provide the foundation to your roster. These are your prime stat contributors and where you will invest the largest percentage of your budget. In snake drafts, these are the names you pick in the early rounds. There is no room for risk here. Given their price tags, there is usually little potential for profit. The majority of your core players should be batters.

The above chart shows general roster goals. In a snake draft, you need to select core-caliber players in the first 5-8 rounds. In an auction, any player purchased for $20 or more should meet the Tier 1 filters.

The filters are not terribly strict, but they are important, so you should stick to them as best as possible. An 80% contact rate ensures that your batting average category is covered. PX and SX ensure that you draft players with a minimum league average power or speed. On the pitching side, a BPV of 75 ensures that, if you must draft a pitcher in your core, it will be one with high-level skill. For both batters and pitchers, minimum reliability grades of BBB should cover your risk.

Since these are going to be the most important players on your roster, the above guidelines help provide a report card, of sorts, for your draft. For instance, if you leave the table with only three Tier 1 players, then you know you have likely rostered too much risk or not enough skill. If you manage to draft nine Tier 1 players, that doesn't necessarily mean you've got a better roster, just a better core. There still may be more work to do in the other tiers.

Tier 1 remains the most important group of players as they are the blue chips that allow you to take chances elsewhere. However, there can be some play within this group on the batting side.

The 80% contact rate is important to help protect the batting average category. However, with some care, you can roster a few BA Suzuki-esque studs to allow you the flexibility to take on some low-contact hitters who excel in other areas (typically power). The tactic would work like this... If you are short on Tier 1 players and have exhausted the pool of those who meet all the filters, you can work your way down the following list...

TIER 1 BATTERS

	Rel	Ct%	PX	or	SX
Primary group	BBB	80%	100		100
Secondary	BBB	75%	110		110
Tertiary	BBB	70%	120		120

...knowing full well that, for every player you roster from these lower groups, you are putting your batting average at greater risk. You should only do this if you think the power/speed gains will sufficiently offset any BA shortfalls.

These two sub-groups are not fixed filters; they form a continuum. So if you have a player with a 78% contact rate, your PX/SX requirement would probably be somewhere around 105. However, for Tier 1, I would not go anywhere near a player with a contact rate less than 70%. This approach can be used with the other two tiers as well, though the risk elevates with the lower reliability grades.

TIER 2: MID-GAME PLAYERS

Roster		BATTERS				PITCHERS	
Slots	Budget	Rel	Ct%	PX	or SX	Rel	BPV
7-13	$50-$100	BBC	80%	100	100	BBC	50
	All players must be less than $20						

In Tier 2, we start relaxing the filters a bit. On the batting side, we hold tight to the skills requirements but are now starting to take on a bit more risk. Reliability grades can now include up to one "C" in any of the three elements.

On the pitching side, both skill and risk filters are relaxed so that we can open up more opportunities for starting pitchers (who tend to have somewhat lower BPVs). For those who opted to pass on pitchers in Tier 1, Tier 2 will provide many solid-skilled arms. Closers who drop to this level may be rostered carefully.

Tier 2 is often where the biggest auction bargains tend to be found as the blue-chippers are already gone and owners are reassessing their finances. It is in that mid-draft lull where you can scoop up tons of profit.

In a snake draft, these players should take you down to about round 16-18.

TIER 3: END-GAME PLAYERS

Roster		BATTERS				PITCHERS	
Slots	Budget	Rel	Ct%	PX	or SX	Rel	BPV
5-10	Up to $50	n/a	80%	100	100	n/a	75
	All players must be less than $10						

For some fantasy leaguers, the end game is when the beer is gone and you have to finish your roster with any warm body whose name pops out of a magazine. In the Portfolio3 Plan, these are your gambling chips, but every end-gamer must provide the promise of upside. For that reason, the focus must remain fixed on high skills and conditional opportunity. P3 drafters should fill the majority of their pitching slots from this group.

By definition, end-gamers are typically high risk players, but risk is something you'll want to embrace here. You probably don't want a Jason Kendall-type player at the end of the draft. His AAB reliability grade would provide stability, but there is no upside in his skill set, so there is little profit potential. This is where you need to look for profit opportunity so it is better here to ignore reliability; instead, take a few chances in your quest for those pockets

of possible profit. If the player does not pan out, he can be easily replaced.

As such, a Tier 3 end-gamer should possess the BPI skill levels noted above, and...

- playing time upside as a back-up to a risky front-liner
- an injury history that has depressed his value
- solid skills demonstrated at some point in the past
- minor league potential even if he has been more recently a major league bust

Notes on draft implementation...

Auction leagues: Optimal player acquisition — particularly Tier 1's — should be via the Total Control Drafting method. Simply, pay whatever it takes, within reason. Be willing to pay a small premium for the low risk and high skills combination.

Snake drafters will have choices in the first six rounds or so. There are no guarantees — a swing-pick seed might negate any chance you have for rostering some players — but at least there are some options. If you miss out on the cream, you can either drop down and select a lower round player early, or relax the filters a bit to grab someone who might have higher value but perhaps greater risk.

Position scarcity: While we still promote the use of position scarcity in snake drafts, it may be more important to have solid foundation players in the early rounds.

Drafting pitchers early is still something we advise against. However, if you are going to grab a pitcher in the first six rounds, at least make sure it's a Tier 1 name. It is still a viable strategy to hold off on starting pitchers until as late as Round 10 or 11; however, if it's Round 7 and Josh Beckett is still sitting out there, by all means jump.

LIMA Plan: Although LIMA says no starting pitchers over $20, Tier 1 typically provides a few options for which it would be okay to break the rules. You can adjust your $60 pitching budget up to accommodate, or downgrade your saves targets.

Punting saves: Still viable, unless a Tier 1 closer falls into your lap. These are extremely rare commodities anyway.

Keeper leagues: When you decide upon your freeze list, you should be looking for two types of keepers — the best values *and* the most valuable players. Freezing a $6 Tim Lincecum is a no-brainer; where some drafters struggle is with the $25 Aramis Ramirez. Given that TCD says that we should be willing to pay a premium for the Tier 1-type players above, any name on the Tier 1 list should be a freeze consideration.

Adding in the variable of potential draft inflation, you should be more flexible with the prices you'd be willing to freeze players at. For instance, if you currently own a $48 Alex Rodriguez, you might be tempted to throw him back. After all, his projected value is likely to be a bit lower than that. However, between draft inflation and the premium you should be willing to pay for a Tier 1 commodity, his real value is probably well over $50.

The 2009 lists of Tier 1,2 and 3 players appear in the Ratings & Rankings section.

The looong term plan

The entire concept of keeper leagues forces us to think about our teams in completely different ways. "Patience" takes on a whole new meaning. "Value" is tougher to pin down. A more holistic view of "league" and "team" is a requirement for success.

Depending upon the depth and rules of the league, many fantasy players have found success using a two-year cycle. Trade off the future in contending years, then stockpile young talent during rebuilding years. In shallow mixed leagues, adept strategists can turn this into league titles every other year. This is not so easy in deeper leagues.

But there are teams that can never seem to find the momentum to latch onto that cycle. They enter each year with the best of intentions but neither contend nor rebuild. One year it's 5th place. The next year it's 9th place.

There is a single, underlying obstacle that tends to keep these teams from making progress. *There is no long-term planning.* They go one season to the next, assessing their team's makeup, and deciding simply, *"this year* or *next year"*? But a two-year time-horizon is often not realistic to build and maintain a team. It is no less of a challenge for a Major League club, so why should we think otherwise for ourselves?

I know we play this game to have fun. Going into a new season with the knowledge that your team is not going to contend seems to fly in the face of why we play. But perhaps like life itself, the joy is more in the journey than the destination. The longer the journey, the greater the joy.

Or something like that.

Last summer, I detailed the decision-making process for my XFL team at BaseballHQ.com. This is a keeper league in which I finished 3rd or 4th for three consecutive seasons, selling off my future in that last season for a failed title bid. In the three years since, I have not finished higher than 7th.

I studied my roster and discovered that, if I stuck to my annual muddled title drive, my roster value would be lower than if I bit the bullet for a year and completely rebuilt.

TWO YEAR PLAN	2009	2010	
No. protectable players	15	11	
Value	$114	$117	
No. players to draft	9	12	
Average value	**$16.22**	**$11.92**	

THREE YEAR PLAN	2009	2010	2011
No. protectable players	15	14	13
Value	$59	$81	$110
No. players to draft	15	14	12
Average value	**$13.40**	**$12.79**	**$12.50**

In the two-year plan, I would have protected 15 players, most of whom were major leaguers with good value and could have a positive impact on my 2009 season. But using these players as a base for 2010, I'd only have 11 protectable players as some would have priced themselves out.

In the three-year plan, I raise the white flag on 2009 up front. I clean house of all players who won't have an impact in 2010. I would still protect 15 but most of them would be farm players (thus the lower $59 value). In the subsequent years, my cost per player is considerably lower and the available dollars to fill out my roster is higher than in the two-year plan.

From a strategic and tactical standpoint, there are several ways to approach this...

Draft Day

Strategically, if you know you are not going to contend, don't worry about buying players that will help your team specifically. The 2009 draft day purchases should continue the process of building towards 2010. Tactically...

1. Don't view your farm as a fixed resource. Even if your current farm keepers are among the top prospects in the game, there are no guarantees that they will become productive major league players. As such, you must always be stockpiling talent. Stockpiling gives you the flexibility to pick and choose the best players at cut-down time, and an abundance of resources from which to trade up. After ensuring you have 23 players to fill your active roster, everyone else on your reserve and farm should be futures commodities. In order to maximize this...

2. Buy players at the auction who can be easily flipped. What are the most tradeable stats? There is always a market for scarce commodities like saves and steals, particularly for stable, low-risk players, so one approach is to stock up on these types. Frontline starters are good too, but riskier. It's useless to pay $25 for Dan Haren and have him blow out his elbow. Home runs and productivity numbers are more plentiful, so the market won't be as active, but there will always be a taker for the A-Rods, Utleys and MCabs.

3. Price is not a consideration. Spend, overpay, it doesn't matter. When the contenders are looking for their summer boost, cost is irrelevant (though, you will have to be a bit more conservative in leagues with in-season salary caps). In a keeper league, inflation might make A-Rod a bargain at $60; pay it.

4. Stars and Scrubs to the max. Buying up tradeable high-priced talent means that you will end up with your fair share of $1 end-gamers. Play your cards right and there could be a few juicy keepers for 2010 among those 23rd rounders. So never mail it in during the end game. In fact, if you fear losing out on a prime minor leaguer during the farm draft, offer him up for $1 during the auction. Best case is you get him for a buck or three; worst case, you would have lost him later on anyway.

5. Take some long chances with those end-gamers. Fantasy leaguers who spent a few dollars on perpetually-hobbled players like Rich Harden and Kerry Wood this year were duly rewarded. Your $1 players next draft should have names like Mark Prior, Jason Schmidt, Kelvim Escobar or any half-forgotten, once-productive player who has a chance, however tiny, of coming back in 2010. Andruw

Jones. Kris Benson. Mark Mulder. It doesn't take much thought to come up with a million of them.

The names that made it onto my XFL end-game roster were Tim Hudson, Noah Lowry and Chris Carpenter. If even one of them becomes a protectable commodity for 2010, then I'm in the black.

In-Season

Your tactical approach during the season will depend upon how well, or poorly, your team performs. Although you are not *trying* to contend, neither were the Tampa Bay Rays this year. Surprise miracles can occur. If you find yourself suddenly in contention, there are only two hard-and-fast rules:

Make sure you are *really* in contention. Take an honest look at your talent and make sure they have the staying power for six months. Odds are they don't. But if all your farm players really have hit the ground running...

Go for it. As the ancient sages once said... "Never pass up the opportunity to sit down, go to the bathroom, or make a run for the title. You never know when that opportunity will come again."

The more likely scenario is that your team will be somewhere around middle of the pack, driven by your keepers and high-priced draftees. This is where you want to be. Here are a few in-season tactical moves:

1. Initiate bidding wars on your high-priced stars early. Owners tend to try to classify themselves as contenders as early as possible. Seek these owners out before their team starts to sputter. The earlier you do this, the less likely they'll be thinking about hanging onto their future stars.

2. Trade off players as soon as they hit the disabled list. As long as your league allows the trading of DLed players, move them while they still have any value at all. They are worthless to you on the DL, and might never rebound to pre-DL levels, but some other owner might be willing to speculate. Even if you have to take 50 cents on the dollar in trade, that's still a 50-cent profit for a player that is not (or should not be) in your future plans anyway.

3. Hold your FAAB. Don't spend a penny until after the All-Star break. This gives you a leg up on two types of important players:
- Prime cross-over players (who can either be kept or traded for more future talent)
- Late-season call-ups who may have future upside

And of course... **4. Follow all minor league players and situations carefully.** You don't want to stockpile just any future talent. Prospect smart.
- Keep tabs on players who were being watched in spring training but sent down.
- Keep tabs on in-season minor league performances, especially outliers.
- Look at underlying peripherals more than outward stats
- Track MLB positional battles that might create openings

There is one huge danger in all this. It's when the thrill of the chase overtakes the thrill of reaching that destination. Yes, the journey has to be enjoyable and challenging, but some owners can be so enamored by their prospecting abilities that they are never able to close the deal on a title.

At some point, you have to make the conscious decision that all the pieces are in place to make a run. And if the building blocks are positioned correctly, and you manage to stay healthy, and everyone performs up to expectation, and all the other teams experience just normal levels of luck... you just might win.

Fanalytic Gaming Formats

It's a game we love, but nobody says we need to be married to any specific set of rules.
The following alternative game formats provide different fanalytic challenges and experiences...

Rotisserie7

Rules

1. Mixed league. Any number of teams.

2. 25-man roster, stocked any way you like so long as all your positions are covered. Each week, 16 of those players will be designated as "active:" 9 position players (1B, 2B, 3B, SS, CA, OF, OF, OF, DH), 5 man starting rotation and 2 relief pitchers. Nine reserves at any position.

3. 4x4 game with the following categories:

> **BATTERS: HR, (Runs scored + RBIs - HR), SB, BatAvg**
> **PITCHERS: Wins, Saves, Strikeouts, ERA**

4. Snake draft or auction is fine. For auctions, budget for the 16 active players only, followed by a snake draft for the remaining 9 players.

5. Rotisserie's category ranking system is converted into a weekly won-loss record. Depending upon where your team finishes for that week's isolated statistics determines how many games you win for that week. Each week, your team will play seven games, hence Rotisserie7.

*Place	Record	*Place	Record
1st	7-0	7th	3-4
2nd	6-1	8th	2-5
3rd	6-1	9th	2-5
4th	5-2	10th	1-6
5th	5-2	11th	1-6
6th	4-3	12th	0-7

* Based on overall Rotisserie category ranking for the week.

At the end of each week, all the roto stats revert to zero and you start over. You never dig a hole in any category that you can't climb out of, because all categories themselves are incidental to the standings.

6. There is unlimited once-weekly movement allowed between the active and reserve rosters during the season. Access to the free agent pool is limited to one player per week per team. Free agents are acquired via a snake draft in reverse order of the standings.

7. The regular season lasts for 23 weeks, which is 161 games. Weeks 24, 25 and 26 are for play-offs. The top six teams make the play-offs. In larger leagues (minimum 15 teams), the top eight teams can make the play-offs. Here it becomes a head-to-head game, but Rotisserie standings again determine the victors.

> **Week 24**: Teams 1 and 2 get byes. Team 3 meets Team 6, Team 4 meets Team 5. In larger leagues, Teams 1 and 2 would meet teams 8 and 7, respectively.
> **Week 25**: Team 1 versus Team 4 or Team 5; Team 2 versus Team 3 or Team 6
> **Week 26**: Two winners meet for the championship

The pot is divided 70% for regular season standing and 30% for play-off results.

Stratified Rotisserie

Rules

1. Start with the same basic rules as a standard Rotisserie competition, but this is a pick-a-player contest.

2. A league may include any number of owners. You will be drafting from both American and National leagues.

3. Each team will have a 25-man roster and a 15-man reserve squad. Each active roster will have 15 batters and 10 pitchers. Standard roto positional structure applies, with two DH/utility slots on the offense side. Reserve rosters have no positional restrictions.

4. *The only players available are those who posted a dollar value of $5 or less in the previous season.*

5. Each team stocks its roster individually. There is no draft or auction. While players may end up on more than one team, the narrow spread of talent will likely ensure that no two teams look exactly alike.

6. There is unlimited once-weekly movement allowed between the active and reserve rosters during the season. There is no trading in this league.

7. On June 1 and August 1, you may select up to five new players to add to your team. For each player who is added, an active or reserve player must be dropped. New players cannot come from the original list of ineligibles (over $5).

Strategic considerations

The players with the best upside value are last year's injury rehabs and minor leaguers looking at significant playing time.

In drafting for your active roster, your key goal is to accumulate quality playing time.

Since you will be playing most of the season from the roster you draft, your reserve squad becomes very important. Naturally, you'll want to grab as many positional backups as possible to protect against injury and excessive bench-sitting of your active players. Your reserve also is a good place to stash upwardly mobile minor leaguers who could get promoted mid-season and have an impact.

Rule modification options for the truly masochistic

1. Draft from only one league, rather than both.

2. Reduce the strata threshold to $3 instead of $5.

3. Make all injury rehabs ineligible if they posted a roto value over $5 in their last healthy season.

4. Limit the number of players with less than 20 games of major league experience to 5 per roster.

5. No more than 3 players with less than 20 games of major league experience can be active at any time.

Quint-Inning

Object: To assemble a group of players that will amass the most points during a single baseball game.

Auction draft: A player auction is conducted among five "owners" before the ballgame and must be completed prior to the start of the game. Each owner must acquire 5 players from the current 25-man rosters of the two major league teams playing in that game, at a cost not to exceed $55. There are no positional requirements for the 5 players other than one must be a pitcher. All 5 roster spots must be filled.

An owner need not spend his entire auction dollar allotment. Any unspent dollars may be added to an owner's Free Agent Acquisition Budget (FAAB).

The "salaries" paid for the five players have no further relevance once the draft is over. They are essentially acquisition costs only.

Points and standings: Team standings are calculated based on a ranking of points accumulated by players at the time they are on an owner's roster.

BATTERS accumulate points for bases gained or lost:

Single = +1	Double = +2
BB = +1	Triple = +3
HBP = +1	Home run = +4
SB = +1	Error = -2
CS = -1	

Batting stats accumulated by pitchers in the National League do count, however, the pitcher must be drafted or acquired separately as a batter. A pitcher may appear as both a batter and a pitcher in a given game, accumulate points separately, and appear on two different rosters.

PITCHERS accumulate points for IP minus ER:

IP = +1	Earned Run allowed = -1

The IP point is awarded to the pitcher who is on the mound when the third out of the inning is registered.

Win = +5	Save = +3

These points are awarded to the owner who has the pitcher of record on his team at the end of the game, even if the owner did not draft that pitcher. If an unrostered pitcher gets a win or save, these points are not awarded.

"The Quint:" At the beginning of the 5th inning, any owner has the option of doubling the points (positive and negative) for one player on his roster for the remainder of the game. Should that player be traded, or dropped and then re-acquired, his "Quint" status remains for the game.

Ninth Inning: Beginning in the 9th inning, all batting points (positive and negative) are doubled.

FAAB points: Unused FAAB units can be converted to scoring points at the end of the game. The conversion rate is 10 FAAB = 1 point.

In-game roster management: The five drafted players must remain on each owner's roster for at least the first inning. Then, players may be dropped, added or traded, and all roster size restrictions are then lifted, except:

- Rosters must contain at least one player at all times.
- Rosters must contain at least one pitcher at all times.

All player moves take effect at the beginning of each half inning. All player moves must be announced prior to the first pitch of that half inning; otherwise, the move will not take effect until the following half inning.

Dropping players: Any player can be cut from an owner's roster at any time after the first inning. Players who are cut may not be re-acquired by the original owner.

Adding players: Each owner is allotted a free agent acquisition budget (FAAB) of $50 per game for the purpose of acquiring players. Available for FAABing are...

- undrafted players on one of the 25-man rosters
- players that had been cut by other owners
- players of those owners who drop out of the game

An owner can announce that he is placing a bid on a free agent at any time after the first inning. Other owners can then bid until a winner is determined. No other player needs to be dropped. All players accumulate points from the half inning after which they were acquired. Owners are limited to one player per half inning acquired via FAAB.

Trading: A trade can be consummated at any time after the first inning, between any two or more owners. The only commodities that may be traded are rostered players and FAAB dollars. Uneven trades are allowed and roster sizes do not have to be squared up at any time. However, should a team's only pitcher be traded to another owner, a pitcher must be received in return or a free agent pitcher acquired immediately. If a pitcher is not added to a roster before the first pitch of the next half-inning, the trade is nullified.

Stakes: Quint-Inning can be played as a no-stakes, low stakes, moderate or higher stakes competition.

- It costs ($1/$5/$55) to get in the game.
- It costs (25 cents/$1/$5) per inning to stay in the game for the first four innings.
- Beginning with the 5th inning, the stakes go up to (50 cents/$2/$10) per inning to stay in the game.
- Should the game go into extra innings, the stakes rise to ($1/$5/$25) to stay in the game until its conclusion.

Each owner has to decide whether he is still in the game at the end of each full inning. Owners can drop out at the end of any inning, thus forfeiting any monies they've already contributed to the pot. When an owner drops, his players go back into the pool and can be FAABed by the other owners.

Determining the winner: The winner is the owner who finishes the game with the most points. Tie-breakers:

The anti-Internet gambling bill that was signed into law in October 2006 has carve-out language that clearly defines the legality of fantasy sports. This language states that fantasy games are exempt as long as they follow several stipulations. The second stipulation states:

2. Winning outcomes are determined by skill for contests that use results from multiple real-life games.

Quint-Inning fails at this stipulation, which only means we won't be setting up QI games on the internet. But you can feel free to continue playing at home.

IV.

MAJOR

LEAGUES

The Teams

The following four pages contain stat boxes for all 30 major league teams plus summary boxes for both leagues. The stats themselves will be mostly familiar to you from the player boxes, however, we have included both batter and pitcher BPIs on each line.

Each team box is divided into three sections.

At Home represents all batting and pitching statistics accumulated by that team in its home ballpark.

Away represents all batting and pitching statistics accumulated by that team in its games on the road.

Opp@ represents all batting and pitching statistics accumulated by all visiting teams when they played at the home ballpark.

Within each section are BPIs from the past three years, 2006-2008. Teams that have changed ballparks during that time may cause some inconsistent data.

To get a sense of ballpark effects, look at both the At Home and Opp@ sections in tandem. If the levels are similar, then it may indicate a particular ballpark tendency. If the levels are not similar, then it may be team dependent. You can compare this data from one team's box to another for additional insight.

As an example, the Dodgers' batters have a contact rate at home in the low-to-mid 80%'s but the opposition at Dodger Stadium has levels consistently about 4%-7% lower. This could indicate the success of the Dodgers pitching staff as opposed to any park effects. In contrast, Milwaukee's At Home and Opp@ contact rates are both in the high 70%'s, which might be more telling of Miller Park park effects.

In the pitching section of each chart, we also show the number of wins (W) each team had, the Pythagorean projected wins (Py) they should have had based on their runs scored and runs allowed, and the percentage of save opportunities successfully converted. The Braves have consistently under-performed in road games the past three years (not an unusual occurrence), but in 2008, that shortfall was a massive 11 games. They only won 29 road games while they should have won 40!

The save opportunities data are interesting. We don't typically consider that a closer's success might hinge on the friendliness of his environment. However, if you wonder how the Tampa Bay Rays fared so well in 2008, one reason might be their offense's ability to get to opposition bullpens. Visiting teams in Tropicana Field were only able to close out 44% of their save opportunities, the lowest percentage of any team in either league over the past five years! Conversely, the Cardinals have been less and less effective at getting to opposition bullpens; during the past three years, the saves success rate of visiting teams has been 56%, 65% and 74%.

Other things to look at include a team's SX and SBO rates, which provide insight into which teams are easier or more difficult to run on. No surprise that opposing runners visiting San Diego have been running 14% of the time — the highest percentage in both leagues — with SX rates far above league average. Compare that to the opposition coming into Houston, which ran just 6% of the time with below average success.

Some other interesting tidbits...

There are wider home/road splits for pitchers than for batters. You find much larger variances between Home and Away BPVs than you do for RC/G.

Opposing pitchers have a horrible time in Fenway Park, posting a 5.56 ERA there over the past three years. There were only two teams whose home offense brutalized opposing pitchers more than the Red Sox' 5.53 ERA did in 2008... the White Sox (5.63) and Rangers (5.77).

Home runs per fly ball tend to regress to 10%, but there are a few ballparks where the base rate has been consistently higher over the past three years, including Chicago White Sox, Cincinnati, Colorado, Houston and Philadelphia. As you'd expect, consistent sub-10% rates can be found in places like Anaheim, Oakland, Pittsburgh, San Diego and San Francisco.

BATTING / PITCHING

ARI	Yr	Avg	OB	Slg	OPS	bb%	ct%	h%	Eye	G	L	F	PX	SX	SBO	xBA	RC/G	W	Py	Sv%	ERA	WHIP	H%	S%	xERA	Ctl	Dom	Cmd	hr/f	hr/9	BPV
At Home	06	283	342	461	803	8	84	31	0.57	46	20	35	108	102	7%	282	5.42	39	38	64%	4.81	1.45	31%	70%	4.47	3.5	6.9	2.0	13%	1.2	53
	07	260	331	445	776	10	81	29	0.56	41	18	41	112	121	10%	265	5.15	50	42	70%	4.11	1.39	30%	73%	4.18	3.4	6.5	1.9	10%	1.1	47
	08	268	341	446	786	10	78	32	0.49	40	21	39	116	114	6%	261	5.36	48	43	74%	4.10	1.27	31%	70%	4.04	2.6	7.8	2.9	11%	1.0	91
Away	06	251	312	388	701	8	82	28	0.48	43	19	38	87	99	8%	250	4.15	37	42	62%	4.16	1.34	31%	70%	4.27	3.1	6.9	2.2	9%	0.8	63
	07	241	305	382	687	8	78	28	0.41	41	17	42	92	108	9%	236	3.95	40	37	88%	4.17	1.38	30%	72%	4.17	3.4	7.1	2.1	10%	1.0	56
	08	234	308	385	693	10	75	28	0.43	39	21	40	103	92	5%	241	4.09	34	39	52%	3.88	1.32	31%	72%	3.94	3.0	7.7	2.5	9%	0.8	77
Opp @ ARI	06	273	340	453	793	9	80	31	0.51	47	20	33	111	107	8%	276	5.33	42	43	60%	4.55	1.46	31%	71%	4.49	3.2	5.6	1.8	10%	1.1	39
	07	265	332	427	759	9	81	30	0.52	43	19	38	100	91	8%	258	4.90	31	39	67%	4.75	1.38	29%	68%	4.91	3.6	6.4	1.8	10%	1.2	37
	08	254	307	404	712	7	78	30	0.34	46	19	35	100	100	9%	251	4.21	33	38	62%	4.78	1.46	32%	69%	4.77	3.8	7.8	2.0	10%	1.0	53

ATL	Yr	Avg	OB	Slg	OPS	bb%	ct%	h%	Eye	G	L	F	PX	SX	SBO	xBA	RC/G	W	Py	Sv%	ERA	WHIP	H%	S%	xERA	Ctl	Dom	Cmd	hr/f	hr/9	BPV
At Home	06	280	342	457	800	9	80	32	0.46	42	22	36	111	82	5%	270	5.37	40	43	59%	4.33	1.41	31%	73%	4.07	3.2	7.1	2.2	13%	1.2	61
	07	266	335	416	751	9	79	31	0.50	45	19	36	94	94	6%	253	4.80	44	42	75%	3.96	1.34	29%	74%	4.03	3.4	7.0	2.0	11%	1.1	54
	08	278	353	411	764	10	82	32	0.65	46	22	32	84	98	5%	265	5.09	43	39	58%	4.44	1.41	30%	70%	4.38	3.7	6.8	1.8	11%	1.0	46
Away	06	261	324	453	777	9	79	29	0.44	45	19	36	119	91	6%	267	5.06	39	42	54%	4.87	1.51	31%	70%	4.81	3.9	6.0	1.5	11%	1.1	25
	07	282	339	452	790	8	80	33	0.43	43	19	38	110	91	6%	262	5.24	40	46	67%	4.27	1.38	30%	72%	4.21	3.2	6.7	2.1	11%	1.1	58
	08	263	332	405	737	9	81	30	0.56	44	22	34	92	85	5%	266	4.70	29	40	60%	4.50	1.40	30%	70%	4.39	3.6	6.7	1.8	12%	1.0	48
Opp @ ATL	06	271	333	433	765	8	80	31	0.46	44	22	33	102	104	9%	270	4.93	41	38	71%	4.79	1.47	32%	71%	4.44	3.3	7.2	2.2	13%	1.3	58
	07	254	323	407	730	9	79	29	0.49	44	19	37	94	110	9%	252	4.54	37	39	61%	4.41	1.43	31%	72%	4.34	3.6	7.1	2.0	11%	1.1	53
	08	263	334	426	761	10	80	30	0.54	47	21	32	105	117	9%	274	4.99	38	42	57%	4.58	1.55	32%	71%	4.60	4.1	6.4	1.5	8%	0.8	25

BAL	Yr	Avg	OB	Slg	OPS	bb%	ct%	h%	Eye	G	L	F	PX	SX	SBO	xBA	RC/G	W	Py	Sv%	ERA	WHIP	H%	S%	xERA	Ctl	Dom	Cmd	hr/f	hr/9	BPV
At Home	06	290	344	454	798	8	86	31	0.57	43	20	36	94	109	10%	276	5.27	40	41	55%	4.73	1.47	30%	71%	4.50	3.6	6.2	1.7	13%	1.3	37
	07	280	338	430	768	8	84	31	0.57	44	17	38	88	106	12%	258	4.97	35	33	48%	5.38	1.54	31%	66%	5.40	4.2	6.5	1.5	9%	1.0	24
	08	275	338	444	782	9	83	30	0.56	42	19	38	102	96	7%	267	5.15	37	36	63%	5.14	1.54	30%	70%	4.96	4.1	5.9	1.4	12%	1.3	16
Away	06	265	323	393	717	8	83	30	0.51	46	19	35	81	97	10%	256	4.37	30	29	72%	6.02	1.63	32%	65%	5.63	4.2	6.7	1.6	13%	1.4	22
	07	264	324	395	719	8	82	30	0.50	44	18	38	86	108	12%	250	4.42	34	38	61%	4.99	1.50	30%	68%	5.03	4.5	7.2	1.6	10%	1.0	28
	08	260	325	414	739	9	81	30	0.52	43	19	38	97	96	8%	259	4.68	31	37	55%	5.17	1.60	31%	69%	5.29	4.6	5.8	1.3	9%	1.0	1
Opp @ BAL	06	277	345	442	787	9	82	31	0.57	44	20	36	98	81	9%	266	5.22	41	40	71%	4.91	1.49	31%	70%	4.72	2.9	5.2	1.8	12%	1.3	36
	07	276	354	423	777	11	82	31	0.65	45	17	38	92	98	7%	251	5.22	46	48	72%	4.64	1.44	31%	70%	4.78	3.1	5.5	1.8	9%	1.0	37
	08	277	352	448	801	10	83	30	0.70	45	18	37	101	104	10%	269	5.46	43	44	65%	4.91	1.46	31%	69%	4.84	3.4	6.0	1.8	11%	1.2	37

BOS	Yr	Avg	OB	Slg	OPS	bb%	ct%	h%	Eye	G	L	F	PX	SX	SBO	xBA	RC/G	W	Py	Sv%	ERA	WHIP	H%	S%	xERA	Ctl	Dom	Cmd	hr/f	hr/9	BPV
At Home	06	285	360	448	808	10	82	32	0.65	41	20	39	105	72	3%	264	5.61	48	42	65%	4.70	1.41	32%	68%	4.70	3.0	6.8	2.2	9%	0.9	61
	07	297	376	465	841	11	82	34	0.71	41	18	40	107	115	7%	264	6.08	51	51	79%	4.13	1.30	31%	70%	4.40	2.7	7.0	2.6	8%	0.9	73
	08	292	371	468	839	11	82	33	0.70	43	20	38	114	117	9%	276	6.06	56	52	70%	3.78	1.34	30%	74%	4.04	3.4	7.2	2.1	8%	0.8	58
Away	06	253	335	422	757	11	80	28	0.62	39	20	41	103	82	6%	256	4.93	38	39	69%	4.97	1.48	31%	70%	4.66	3.3	6.6	2.0	13%	1.4	49
	07	262	341	424	764	11	81	30	0.62	42	18	40	101	101	7%	254	5.07	45	50	81%	3.60	1.24	28%	75%	3.85	3.3	7.4	2.2	10%	1.0	62
	08	268	338	428	766	10	80	31	0.52	40	20	39	99	96	10%	255	5.00	39	43	66%	4.26	1.31	29%	70%	4.35	3.4	7.5	2.2	10%	1.0	63
Opp @ BOS	06	274	332	432	764	8	81	32	0.45	44	20	35	105	110	8%	269	4.94	33	39	45%	5.28	1.60	32%	68%	5.26	4.2	6.4	1.5	9%	1.1	19
	07	261	315	407	721	7	80	31	0.39	43	17	40	98	97	8%	247	4.38	30	30	63%	5.86	1.72	34%	67%	5.75	4.6	6.5	1.4	9%	1.0	9
	08	253	321	398	719	9	79	30	0.47	44	19	37	98	87	8%	250	4.45	25	29	57%	5.53	1.65	33%	68%	5.44	4.5	6.4	1.4	9%	1.0	13

CHW	Yr	Avg	OB	Slg	OPS	bb%	ct%	h%	Eye	G	L	F	PX	SX	SBO	xBA	RC/G	W	Py	Sv%	ERA	WHIP	H%	S%	xERA	Ctl	Dom	Cmd	hr/f	hr/9	BPV
At Home	06	281	342	480	822	8	82	30	0.51	42	20	38	116	90	9%	277	5.55	49	46	70%	4.43	1.36	30%	72%	4.31	2.8	6.3	2.2	12%	1.3	58
	07	247	316	419	735	9	80	27	0.51	43	18	40	103	80	10%	250	4.55	38	32	70%	4.94	1.43	32%	67%	4.83	2.9	6.4	2.2	10%	1.1	59
	08	272	340	481	821	9	82	29	0.57	38	20	42	122	79	7%	273	5.57	54	52	57%	3.75	1.23	29%	73%	3.81	2.8	7.5	2.7	11%	1.0	82
Away	06	280	336	448	785	8	81	32	0.44	42	20	38	103	93	10%	262	5.13	41	41	76%	4.82	1.36	31%	67%	4.79	2.5	6.3	2.5	10%	1.1	65
	07	246	311	390	701	9	78	29	0.42	45	17	37	93	86	7%	239	4.14	34	35	60%	4.60	1.42	30%	70%	4.73	3.3	6.2	1.9	9%	1.1	41
	08	253	316	414	730	8	81	28	0.49	42	19	39	99	85	7%	256	4.50	35	36	72%	4.50	1.43	32%	70%	4.42	2.9	6.6	2.3	9%	0.9	64
Opp @ CHW	06	268	322	440	763	7	82	29	0.45	43	18	39	102	107	10%	262	4.82	32	35	50%	5.47	1.47	30%	68%	4.90	3.3	6.4	2.0	16%	1.7	46
	07	282	337	437	774	8	82	32	0.45	44	19	37	96	102	8%	259	4.99	43	49	60%	4.26	1.32	27%	73%	4.21	3.5	6.8	2.0	13%	1.4	48
	08	242	300	388	688	8	78	28	0.38	46	19	35	95	111	12%	252	3.93	28	30	60%	5.63	1.46	29%	66%	5.26	3.6	6.3	1.8	15%	1.8	32

CHC	Yr	Avg	OB	Slg	OPS	bb%	ct%	h%	Eye	G	L	F	PX	SX	SBO	xBA	RC/G	W	Py	Sv%	ERA	WHIP	H%	S%	xERA	Ctl	Dom	Cmd	hr/f	hr/9	BPV
At Home	06	279	327	440	767	7	84	31	0.44	47	20	33	96	112	12%	275	4.88	36	35	60%	4.68	1.35	29%	70%	4.33	3.8	8.5	2.2	15%	1.5	66
	07	278	340	439	779	9	81	32	0.49	45	19	36	104	106	8%	264	5.15	44	44	75%	4.19	1.35	30%	72%	4.38	3.6	7.7	2.1	9%	1.0	57
	08	290	365	471	836	11	79	33	0.57	44	20	36	114	93	6%	268	5.92	55	51	76%	3.77	1.26	30%	73%	3.87	3.1	8.2	2.6	10%	1.0	81
Away	06	256	305	405	710	7	83	28	0.41	47	19	34	87	108	13%	261	4.17	30	34	67%	4.81	1.55	31%	71%	4.82	4.8	7.1	1.5	10%	1.1	15
	07	265	321	404	725	8	82	30	0.46	45	19	36	90	90	8%	257	4.45	41	43	72%	3.89	1.29	28%	73%	4.10	3.5	7.4	2.1	10%	1.0	56
	08	267	340	417	757	10	78	32	0.51	42	23	35	101	95	8%	262	4.96	40	45	53%	4.07	1.35	29%	73%	4.22	3.8	7.4	2.0	10%	1.0	49
Opp @ CHC	06	244	321	441	762	10	75	28	0.46	43	18	39	125	117	10%	256	4.96	45	46	63%	4.36	1.37	31%	71%	4.27	2.5	5.7	2.3	11%	1.0	61
	07	251	322	408	730	10	77	30	0.47	41	18	42	104	110	11%	244	4.57	37	37	61%	4.61	1.47	32%	71%	4.46	3.4	6.9	2.0	10%	1.1	55
	08	242	305	391	696	8	76	29	0.38	42	20	38	100	94	8%	245	4.08	26	30	57%	5.51	1.61	33%	68%	4.97	4.2	7.4	1.8	14%	1.4	39

CIN	Yr	Avg	OB	Slg	OPS	bb%	ct%	h%	Eye	G	L	F	PX	SX	SBO	xBA	RC/G	W	Py	Sv%	ERA	WHIP	H%	S%	xERA	Ctl	Dom	Cmd	hr/f	hr/9	BPV
At Home	06	271	350	459	809	11	78	30	0.56	43	19	38	116	92	10%	263	5.54	42	38	58%	4.78	1.38	31%	70%	4.50	2.8	6.9	2.5	13%	1.4	66
	07	265	333	456	789	9	80	29	0.51	40	19	41	118	102	7%	264	5.24	39	39	48%	4.94	1.37	30%	67%	4.83	2.8	6.7	2.4	12%	1.4	62
	08	253	327	428	755	10	80	28	0.54	45	19	36	108	90	8%	264	4.85	43	38	69%	4.51	1.41	31%	72%	4.15	3.3	7.7	2.3	13%	1.3	68
Away	06	244	314	407	721	9	78	28	0.47	44	19	37	106	97	11%	257	4.43	38	38	62%	4.28	1.44	31%	74%	4.10	3.0	6.2	2.1	11%	1.2	52
	07	269	328	418	746	8	80	31	0.45	44	19	37	93	93	10%	252	4.68	33	36	61%	4.98	1.51	33%	69%	4.85	3.2	6.6	2.1	10%	1.1	49
	08	241	308	388	696	9	79	28	0.46	45	20	36	93	85	10%	251	4.09	31	33	55%	4.59	1.50	33%	72%	4.27	3.7	7.6	2.1	12%	1.2	56
Opp @ CIN	06	273	327	460	788	7	80	31	0.41	41	20	39	116	71	5%	267	5.12	39	43	60%	4.84	1.51	30%	73%	4.34	4.2	7.5	1.8	16%	1.6	39
	07	272	326	455	781	7	81	30	0.42	40	18	42	114	95	8%	261	5.05	42	42	67%	4.90	1.42	30%	70%	4.69	3.6	7.0	2.0	13%	1.5	46
	08	272	335	456	791	9	78	32	0.43	42	21	37	118	97	8%	266	5.27	38	43	56%	4.40	1.38	28%	72%	4.23	3.7	6.9	1.9	14%	1.3	45

CLE	Yr	Avg	OB	Slg	OPS	bb%	ct%	h%	Eye	G	L	F	PX	SX	SBO	xBA	RC/G	W	Py	Sv%	ERA	WHIP	H%	S%	xERA	Ctl	Dom	Cmd	hr/f	hr/9	BPV
At Home	06	280	349	458	807	10	78	33	0.49	41	21	38	116	91	4%	266	5.55	44	47	58%	4.05	1.36	31%	72%	4.09	2.7	6.1	2.2	9%	0.9	60
	07	277	348	444	792	10	79	32	0.53	42	19	40	104	93	7%	252	5.33	49	44	74%	4.25	1.35	33%	70%	4.22	2.5	7.3	2.8	9%	0.9	85
	08	272	346	439	785	10	79	32	0.55	40	20	40	108	99	7%	257	5.31	45	47	58%	4.03	1.34	31%	71%	4.17	2.8	6.4	2.3	8%	0.8	63
Away	06	281	342	456	798	8	79	33	0.43	43	20	37	112	97	6%	264	5.36	34	42	46%	4.84	1.47	32%	70%	4.65	2.7	5.9	2.2	11%	1.2	55
	07	260	327	411	737	9	78	31	0.45	40	19	41	100	86	7%	242	4.66	44	45	79%	3.92	1.29	29%	72%	4.21	2.5	5.6	2.3	9%	0.9	57
	08	254	314	410	724	8	77	30	0.39	40	21	39	105	90	7%	252	4.42	36	38	64%	4.92	1.41	31%	69%	4.69	2.7	5.9	2.2	12%	1.4	55
Opp @ CLE	06	273	325	408	733	7	83	31	0.45	46	21	34	84	104	12%	261	4.49	37	34	71%	5.21	1.52	33%	68%	4.89	3.8	7.6	2.0	12%	1.2	52
	07	274	323	409	731	7	79	32	0.35	46	19	35	88	83	9%	246	4.44	28	33	60%	5.08	1.52	32%	69%	4.83	3.9	7.4	1.9	12%	1.3	46
	08	268	324	394	717	8	81	31	0.44	46	21	33	81	81	6%	254	4.33	36	34	65%	5.13	1.50	32%	68%	5.07	4.0	7.4	1.8	10%	1.1	40

BATTING / PITCHING

COL	Yr	Avg	OB	Slg	OPS	bb%	ct%	h%	Eye	G	L	F	PX	SX	SBO	xBA	RC/G	W	Py	Sv%	ERA	WHIP	H%	S%	xERA	Ctl	Dom	Cmd	hr/f	hr/9	BPV
At Home	06	294	362	459	821	10	82	34	0.60	45	23	32	101	114	9%	281	5.74	44	44	55%	4.72	1.47	31%	70%	4.50	3.4	5.9	1.8	12%	1.1	41
	07	298	369	480	849	10	82	34	0.61	43	22	35	111	106	7%	281	6.06	51	48	64%	4.34	1.36	30%	70%	4.43	2.8	5.6	2.0	10%	1.0	52
	08	278	346	454	801	10	80	32	0.52	42	23	35	112	120	11%	277	5.46	43	40	61%	4.83	1.43	32%	68%	4.64	3.1	6.3	2.1	11%	1.0	56
Away	06	247	312	408	720	9	78	29	0.43	42	19	38	105	94	9%	253	4.41	32	36	60%	4.60	1.43	31%	69%	4.92	3.5	5.9	1.7	7%	0.8	33
	07	261	332	395	727	10	78	31	0.48	44	20	37	89	107	8%	245	4.55	39	42	53%	4.29	1.36	29%	71%	4.44	3.4	6.2	1.8	10%	1.0	44
	08	249	317	377	694	9	77	30	0.43	45	20	35	87	94	12%	241	4.09	31	34	61%	4.70	1.49	31%	69%	4.75	4.0	6.7	1.7	9%	0.8	35
Opp @ COL	06	282	345	454	800	9	83	31	0.57	48	20	32	104	112	8%	281	5.40	37	37	71%	5.41	1.57	33%	66%	5.20	3.8	6.3	1.7	10%	1.0	32
	07	274	327	438	765	7	84	30	0.49	46	19	35	100	113	7%	276	4.92	31	34	52%	5.68	1.65	34%	68%	5.18	4.1	6.6	1.6	13%	1.3	29
	08	280	337	435	772	8	82	32	0.48	47	21	31	97	105	7%	275	5.03	38	41	51%	4.96	1.49	32%	69%	4.69	3.7	7.1	1.9	12%	1.2	46

DET	Yr	Avg	OB	Slg	OPS	bb%	ct%	h%	Eye	G	L	F	PX	SX	SBO	xBA	RC/G	W	Py	Sv%	ERA	WHIP	H%	S%	xERA	Ctl	Dom	Cmd	hr/f	hr/9	BPV
At Home	06	273	325	424	749	7	81	31	0.41	43	19	37	92	96	6%	255	4.68	46	45	72%	3.92	1.33	29%	73%	4.07	3.0	6.1	2.0	10%	1.0	51
	07	287	345	475	819	8	82	32	0.50	40	21	39	111	126	9%	275	5.59	45	43	64%	4.65	1.43	30%	70%	4.72	3.5	6.4	1.8	10%	1.1	42
	08	287	349	478	827	9	83	31	0.56	42	19	38	112	105	6%	274	5.68	40	41	63%	4.84	1.48	31%	70%	4.82	3.7	6.4	1.7	10%	1.1	36
Away	06	276	327	472	799	7	79	31	0.35	41	19	40	121	93	8%	263	5.25	49	51	76%	3.78	1.31	29%	74%	3.87	3.1	6.4	2.1	10%	1.0	56
	07	286	338	442	779	7	81	33	0.41	43	19	38	100	108	8%	260	5.08	43	46	72%	4.51	1.43	30%	71%	4.49	3.6	6.6	1.9	11%	1.1	45
	08	256	327	411	738	10	79	30	0.51	44	18	38	98	92	6%	250	4.67	34	37	47%	4.98	1.54	30%	69%	5.18	4.4	5.9	1.4	9%	1.0	6
Opp @ DET	06	259	318	404	722	8	82	29	0.50	46	19	35	87	84	6%	255	4.41	35	36	59%	4.53	1.37	31%	69%	4.53	2.7	6.6	2.4	10%	1.0	67
	07	268	334	431	765	9	82	30	0.54	44	18	38	99	102	7%	259	4.99	36	38	74%	5.36	1.50	32%	66%	5.15	3.1	6.3	2.0	11%	1.3	46
	08	276	344	437	781	9	82	31	0.58	44	19	38	99	96	6%	261	5.20	41	40	57%	5.23	1.52	31%	69%	4.90	3.4	6.2	1.8	13%	1.4	38

FLA	Yr	Avg	OB	Slg	OPS	bb%	ct%	h%	Eye	G	L	F	PX	SX	SBO	xBA	RC/G	W	Py	Sv%	ERA	WHIP	H%	S%	xERA	Ctl	Dom	Cmd	hr/f	hr/9	BPV
At Home	06	258	326	427	754	9	77	31	0.44	44	19	37	110	103	11%	254	4.87	42	39	63%	4.07	1.43	31%	74%	4.20	3.9	7.3	1.9	9%	1.0	43
	07	271	333	466	800	9	76	32	0.40	40	20	40	127	112	9%	260	5.41	36	36	58%	4.80	1.58	34%	71%	4.72	4.4	7.9	1.8	9%	0.9	38
	08	247	319	419	738	10	73	30	0.39	42	19	39	116	110	8%	244	4.69	45	39	63%	4.31	1.39	31%	71%	4.46	3.6	7.6	2.1	9%	0.9	55
Away	06	270	324	442	766	7	78	32	0.36	44	20	37	111	109	12%	260	4.91	36	41	58%	4.69	1.48	30%	71%	4.68	3.9	6.4	1.6	11%	1.1	30
	07	263	326	431	756	8	76	32	0.39	40	19	41	112	106	10%	248	4.86	35	36	67%	5.13	1.58	32%	70%	4.90	3.8	6.3	1.7	11%	1.3	30
	08	261	323	446	769	8	77	30	0.40	42	20	38	120	87	7%	260	4.97	39	42	58%	4.58	1.41	29%	70%	4.63	3.7	6.5	1.7	11%	1.1	36
Opp @ FLA	06	262	337	415	752	10	79	31	0.54	41	20	39	96	88	7%	250	4.90	39	42	74%	4.15	1.37	31%	73%	4.07	3.5	7.9	2.3	11%	1.1	68
	07	280	361	431	792	11	78	34	0.56	41	21	38	101	109	9%	253	5.48	45	45	71%	4.70	1.41	32%	71%	4.37	3.2	8.2	2.5	13%	1.4	76
	08	257	328	400	727	9	78	31	0.47	40	21	39	95	101	9%	248	4.53	36	42	62%	4.47	1.35	31%	70%	4.21	3.7	9.4	2.6	13%	1.2	86

HOU	Yr	Avg	OB	Slg	OPS	bb%	ct%	h%	Eye	G	L	F	PX	SX	SBO	xBA	RC/G	W	Py	Sv%	ERA	WHIP	H%	S%	xERA	Ctl	Dom	Cmd	hr/f	hr/9	BPV
At Home	06	254	328	430	758	10	81	28	0.57	42	19	40	108	87	5%	259	4.91	44	41	72%	4.03	1.27	29%	72%	3.94	2.7	7.2	2.6	12%	1.1	79
	07	266	333	422	755	9	82	30	0.56	43	18	39	94	98	6%	255	4.86	42	40	48%	4.05	1.33	31%	74%	3.88	2.9	7.7	2.6	12%	1.3	80
	08	277	332	451	783	8	82	31	0.44	46	19	36	107	107	13%	270	5.10	47	40	78%	4.28	1.36	30%	72%	4.11	3.2	7.3	2.3	12%	1.2	65
Away	06	256	325	390	714	9	80	29	0.52	45	19	36	84	92	10%	246	4.36	38	42	68%	4.16	1.33	29%	72%	4.16	3.2	7.0	2.2	11%	1.1	62
	07	254	319	403	722	9	81	29	0.49	44	17	39	95	75	7%	246	4.42	31	33	72%	5.42	1.51	31%	66%	5.25	3.4	5.9	1.8	11%	1.3	37
	08	254	311	389	700	8	80	29	0.42	45	20	34	86	89	11%	253	4.09	39	38	70%	4.48	1.38	30%	71%	4.34	3.1	6.6	2.1	12%	1.2	56
Opp @ HOU	06	255	310	419	729	7	79	29	0.38	46	20	35	104	93	7%	261	4.43	37	40	59%	4.43	1.36	28%	71%	4.54	3.7	6.5	1.8	12%	1.2	36
	07	262	319	439	758	8	78	30	0.38	44	16	40	114	95	8%	250	4.81	39	41	63%	4.26	1.40	30%	72%	4.48	3.4	6.1	1.8	9%	1.0	38
	08	261	323	438	761	8	79	30	0.44	44	19	37	113	89	6%	263	4.88	31	38	55%	4.60	1.40	31%	70%	4.36	2.9	6.5	2.3	12%	1.2	63

KC	Yr	Avg	OB	Slg	OPS	bb%	ct%	h%	Eye	G	L	F	PX	SX	SBO	xBA	RC/G	W	Py	Sv%	ERA	WHIP	H%	S%	xERA	Ctl	Dom	Cmd	hr/f	hr/9	BPV
At Home	06	289	348	437	785	8	81	34	0.49	47	20	32	96	103	6%	269	5.23	34	35	59%	5.68	1.62	31%	67%	5.46	4.1	5.4	1.3	12%	1.3	8
	07	267	321	403	724	7	82	31	0.44	46	20	34	88	105	7%	260	4.46	35	36	76%	4.61	1.47	32%	70%	4.72	3.3	6.1	1.9	9%	1.0	41
	08	275	323	396	719	7	83	32	0.42	46	21	33	79	89	7%	259	4.34	38	37	76%	4.13	1.33	30%	71%	4.43	3.1	6.2	2.0	8%	0.9	50
Away	06	254	308	385	693	7	81	29	0.42	48	19	33	85	91	7%	255	4.05	28	28	49%	5.66	1.59	32%	67%	5.36	3.9	6.0	1.5	12%	1.4	20
	07	256	309	373	682	7	79	31	0.37	48	18	33	77	102	10%	240	3.87	34	38	59%	4.39	1.41	30%	72%	4.46	3.3	6.3	1.9	10%	1.1	44
	08	263	310	398	708	6	81	30	0.36	47	19	34	85	94	9%	252	4.15	37	35	71%	4.89	1.42	32%	68%	4.85	3.4	7.3	2.2	10%	1.1	58
Opp @ KC	06	294	367	477	844	10	85	32	0.76	44	21	36	110	87	5%	286	6.02	47	46	72%	4.80	1.50	34%	69%	4.64	3.2	6.6	2.0	9%	0.8	56
	07	283	343	450	794	8	83	32	0.53	41	20	39	109	91	6%	271	5.34	46	45	93%	4.29	1.32	31%	68%	4.62	2.7	6.2	2.3	7%	0.6	63
	08	260	320	402	722	8	82	30	0.49	43	19	38	88	96	7%	253	4.43	43	44	70%	3.92	1.35	32%	72%	4.14	2.5	6.0	2.4	7%	0.6	64

LA	Yr	Avg	OB	Slg	OPS	bb%	ct%	h%	Eye	G	L	F	PX	SX	SBO	xBA	RC/G	W	Py	Sv%	ERA	WHIP	H%	S%	xERA	Ctl	Dom	Cmd	hr/f	hr/9	BPV
At Home	06	293	369	463	831	11	84	32	0.74	42	21	37	102	113	12%	276	5.90	49	47	71%	4.11	1.37	31%	72%	4.11	3.2	7.1	2.2	10%	0.9	67
	07	277	344	407	750	9	84	31	0.65	48	18	34	77	106	13%	256	4.83	43	41	72%	4.24	1.34	32%	70%	4.28	3.0	7.8	2.5	9%	0.9	78
	08	266	332	397	729	9	81	31	0.52	46	21	33	82	102	12%	257	4.53	48	51	72%	3.01	1.13	29%	75%	3.31	2.6	8.0	3.1	7%	0.6	101
Away	06	260	324	404	727	9	82	30	0.53	46	19	36	88	121	9%	259	4.55	39	40	61%	4.35	1.39	31%	70%	4.35	2.9	6.1	2.1	10%	0.9	56
	07	273	328	405	732	8	85	30	0.54	44	19	37	81	100	10%	259	4.57	39	41	71%	4.16	1.37	30%	72%	4.20	3.4	6.9	2.0	10%	0.9	56
	08	263	328	400	729	9	82	30	0.53	47	21	32	87	103	10%	265	4.56	36	37	57%	4.40	1.45	32%	72%	4.16	3.4	6.9	2.0	11%	0.9	59
Opp @ LA	06	265	326	408	734	8	80	31	0.45	48	17	35	94	103	12%	250	4.56	32	34	74%	5.36	1.63	32%	69%	5.26	4.3	5.8	1.4	10%	1.1	8
	07	263	323	394	717	8	77	32	0.39	45	19	36	88	90	10%	240	4.33	38	40	71%	4.50	1.48	31%	71%	4.61	3.5	5.5	1.5	9%	0.9	29
	08	228	284	333	617	7	76	28	0.32	50	18	32	74	96	8%	228	3.01	33	30	73%	4.09	1.40	30%	73%	4.13	3.4	6.5	1.9	10%	0.9	48

LAA	Yr	Avg	OB	Slg	OPS	bb%	ct%	h%	Eye	G	L	F	PX	SX	SBO	xBA	RC/G	W	Py	Sv%	ERA	WHIP	H%	S%	xERA	Ctl	Dom	Cmd	hr/f	hr/9	BPV
At Home	06	279	339	418	757	8	84	31	0.55	44	18	38	86	103	13%	253	4.86	45	43	81%	3.76	1.27	30%	73%	4.01	2.7	7.2	2.7	8%	0.9	77
	07	305	368	445	813	9	85	34	0.66	47	17	36	88	109	12%	261	5.61	54	51	68%	3.85	1.32	31%	73%	4.18	2.9	7.1	2.5	7%	0.8	68
	08	277	329	414	744	7	83	31	0.45	46	18	36	85	101	11%	254	4.62	50	43	76%	4.07	1.28	30%	71%	4.21	2.5	6.6	2.6	10%	1.0	73
Away	06	270	326	432	757	8	84	30	0.51	45	20	36	97	109	14%	272	4.82	44	42	77%	4.33	1.32	29%	70%	4.44	3.2	7.2	2.3	10%	1.1	63
	07	263	319	393	712	8	83	30	0.50	47	18	35	82	96	13%	253	4.29	39	37	88%	4.64	1.41	32%	69%	4.53	3.0	7.5	2.5	10%	1.0	72
	08	260	324	411	736	9	82	29	0.52	47	18	35	92	106	12%	258	4.59	50	44	73%	3.92	1.36	31%	74%	3.92	3.2	7.2	2.3	10%	1.0	64
Opp @ LAA	06	257	310	392	702	7	79	30	0.37	42	19	39	88	90	9%	241	4.10	36	38	71%	4.38	1.45	31%	71%	4.60	3.2	5.8	1.8	8%	0.9	40
	07	260	316	397	713	8	80	31	0.41	42	17	41	91	100	10%	240	4.28	27	30	64%	5.43	1.62	34%	66%	5.46	3.6	5.4	1.5	7%	0.8	26
	08	260	310	404	714	7	81	30	0.38	45	18	37	89	102	10%	249	4.21	31	38	54%	4.47	1.39	31%	69%	4.54	2.8	6.1	2.2	9%	0.9	59

MIL	Yr	Avg	OB	Slg	OPS	bb%	ct%	h%	Eye	G	L	F	PX	SX	SBO	xBA	RC/G	W	Py	Sv%	ERA	WHIP	H%	S%	xERA	Ctl	Dom	Cmd	hr/f	hr/9	BPV
At Home	06	260	329	438	767	9	77	30	0.46	41	19	40	116	99	7%	256	5.02	48	39	71%	4.46	1.31	30%	68%	4.53	3.2	7.7	2.5	10%	1.0	73
	07	268	333	476	809	9	80	30	0.48	41	17	41	129	110	10%	268	5.48	51	47	81%	4.06	1.32	30%	72%	4.16	3.2	7.6	2.3	10%	1.0	67
	08	251	324	433	756	10	77	29	0.47	42	18	40	117	101	10%	255	4.89	49	45	63%	3.51	1.32	29%	76%	3.56	3.4	7.1	2.1	11%	0.9	58
Away	06	256	312	403	715	8	77	30	0.36	44	20	36	97	76	8%	249	4.26	27	32	55%	5.22	1.46	31%	66%	5.05	3.3	6.7	2.0	11%	1.2	48
	07	256	314	437	750	8	79	29	0.41	41	19	40	110	104	8%	257	4.69	32	37	61%	4.85	1.48	34%	69%	4.80	3.1	7.0	2.3	9%	1.0	61
	08	254	317	429	746	8	79	29	0.44	42	19	39	112	110	11%	261	4.71	41	42	64%	4.26	1.35	29%	73%	4.10	3.1	6.6	2.1	13%	1.3	58
Opp @ MIL	06	251	314	412	725	8	77	30	0.41	43	19	38	107	110	9%	254	4.47	33	42	52%	4.54	1.39	30%	71%	4.42	3.6	7.8	2.2	12%	1.3	61
	07	252	316	401	717	9	78	30	0.43	42	18	40	98	92	8%	243	4.33	30	34	74%	5.23	1.43	30%	68%	4.91	3.4	7.2	2.1	14%	1.6	54
	08	252	321	386	706	9	79	29	0.48	46	21	33	84	82	9%	251	4.24	32	36	52%	4.33	1.36	29%	72%	4.25	3.7	7.7	2.1	12%	1.3	58

BATTING / PITCHING

MIN	Yr	Avg	OB	Slg	OPS	bb%	ct%	h%	Eye	G	L	F	PX	SX	SBO	xBA	RC/G	W	Py	Sv%	ERA	WHIP	H%	S%	xERA	Ctl	Dom	Cmd	hr/f	hr/9	BPV
At Home	06	298	351	439	790	8	84	33	0.52	45	23	32	83	106	8%	274	5.21	54	52	95%	3.40	1.16	30%	74%	3.48	1.8	7.5	4.1	10%	1.0	107
	07	263	326	376	702	9	85	29	0.64	50	18	33	69	110	10%	252	4.29	41	39	70%	3.84	1.27	30%	73%	4.02	2.6	7.1	2.8	9%	1.0	78
	08	289	348	429	777	8	84	33	0.55	46	21	33	87	118	9%	270	5.15	53	53	83%	3.27	1.22	29%	77%	3.45	2.2	6.3	2.9	9%	1.0	76
Away	06	276	338	412	750	9	84	31	0.60	49	20	31	82	94	9%	266	4.79	42	41	71%	4.54	1.41	32%	72%	4.14	2.6	7.1	2.7	13%	1.3	76
	07	266	328	405	733	8	84	29	0.58	50	17	33	84	108	9%	259	4.60	38	41	76%	4.54	1.42	32%	72%	4.24	2.7	6.5	2.4	12%	1.3	67
	08	269	333	388	722	9	82	31	0.53	47	19	34	76	105	9%	247	4.48	35	37	50%	5.12	1.50	32%	68%	4.89	2.9	6.0	2.1	11%	1.3	50
Opp @ MIN	06	251	289	392	681	5	78	30	0.24	44	19	37	91	84	8%	243	3.71	27	29	59%	4.91	1.51	33%	68%	4.78	2.9	5.5	1.9	9%	0.9	45
	07	255	307	403	711	7	79	30	0.36	42	18	40	95	84	7%	244	4.18	40	42	76%	3.82	1.36	29%	72%	4.26	3.2	5.0	1.6	6%	0.6	32
	08	255	299	396	694	6	82	29	0.35	43	20	37	87	83	9%	254	3.93	28	28	66%	5.19	1.49	33%	65%	5.24	3.2	5.8	1.8	8%	0.7	42

NYM	Yr	Avg	OB	Slg	OPS	bb%	ct%	h%	Eye	G	L	F	PX	SX	SBO	xBA	RC/G	W	Py	Sv%	ERA	WHIP	H%	S%	xERA	Ctl	Dom	Cmd	hr/f	hr/9	BPV
At Home	06	256	325	434	759	9	81	28	0.54	44	17	38	110	125	13%	266	4.92	50	45	70%	3.77	1.27	29%	73%	3.99	3.1	7.2	2.3	10%	1.0	64
	07	270	335	425	760	9	83	30	0.58	44	19	37	94	114	16%	264	4.92	41	40	65%	4.20	1.33	29%	70%	4.50	3.5	7.1	2.0	9%	1.0	51
	08	267	348	430	778	11	82	30	0.68	46	22	32	98	104	9%	275	5.23	48	45	57%	3.78	1.27	28%	73%	3.96	3.5	7.4	2.1	10%	0.9	60
Away	06	272	335	455	790	9	81	31	0.48	42	20	38	113	118	12%	271	5.26	47	45	79%	4.58	1.38	30%	70%	4.41	3.4	7.1	2.1	12%	1.3	58
	07	280	344	439	783	9	82	31	0.55	45	20	35	98	116	15%	268	5.18	47	46	73%	4.34	1.41	30%	72%	4.45	3.6	6.9	1.9	10%	1.1	45
	08	265	330	411	741	9	82	30	0.54	46	24	30	90	120	12%	276	4.70	41	45	62%	4.39	1.48	32%	73%	4.25	3.8	7.1	1.9	11%	1.1	43
Opp @ NYM	06	245	309	388	697	9	79	29	0.44	43	19	38	92	91	12%	245	4.08	31	36	54%	4.56	1.37	29%	70%	4.60	3.5	6.5	1.9	11%	1.2	44
	07	247	316	393	709	9	79	29	0.49	41	18	41	94	106	9%	244	4.29	40	41	63%	4.40	1.42	30%	71%	4.48	3.4	5.9	1.7	10%	1.1	37
	08	236	307	369	676	9	78	28	0.47	44	21	36	87	71	5%	244	3.85	33	36	62%	4.47	1.51	30%	74%	4.23	4.3	6.4	1.5	13%	1.2	21

NYY	Yr	Avg	OB	Slg	OPS	bb%	ct%	h%	Eye	G	L	F	PX	SX	SBO	xBA	RC/G	W	Py	Sv%	ERA	WHIP	H%	S%	xERA	Ctl	Dom	Cmd	hr/f	hr/9	BPV
At Home	06	284	358	470	829	10	82	31	0.66	44	18	37	112	107	10%	273	5.79	50	49	74%	3.97	1.29	29%	72%	4.19	2.9	6.2	2.1	10%	1.0	54
	07	300	374	474	848	11	84	33	0.72	45	19	36	103	113	10%	275	6.05	52	52	65%	4.32	1.37	30%	71%	4.51	3.3	6.7	2.1	9%	1.0	52
	08	281	342	440	783	9	82	31	0.53	45	19	36	97	105	10%	264	5.15	48	45	82%	4.11	1.30	30%	70%	4.26	3.1	7.4	2.4	9%	0.8	71
Away	06	285	358	453	811	10	80	33	0.58	46	20	34	106	104	10%	271	5.61	47	46	69%	4.90	1.42	31%	67%	4.94	3.3	6.5	2.0	10%	1.1	49
	07	280	348	453	801	9	82	31	0.58	46	19	35	106	105	9%	273	5.45	42	45	59%	4.69	1.50	31%	70%	4.95	3.9	5.8	1.5	8%	0.9	19
	08	262	328	414	743	9	81	30	0.52	47	20	33	94	94	11%	264	4.69	41	42	83%	4.47	1.43	33%	71%	4.36	3.0	6.9	2.3	10%	1.0	65
Opp @ NYY	06	253	311	400	711	8	82	28	0.47	44	18	38	91	89	10%	252	4.25	31	32	67%	5.47	1.58	31%	69%	5.10	4.1	6.3	1.5	13%	1.5	22
	07	263	326	412	738	9	81	30	0.49	42	18	39	96	97	10%	251	4.63	29	29	60%	6.32	1.70	33%	65%	5.79	4.3	6.0	1.4	13%	1.4	14
	08	253	315	387	702	8	78	30	0.42	46	19	35	88	91	11%	246	4.16	33	36	55%	4.83	1.48	32%	70%	4.64	3.3	6.3	1.9	11%	1.2	45

OAK	Yr	Avg	OB	Slg	OPS	bb%	ct%	h%	Eye	G	L	F	PX	SX	SBO	xBA	RC/G	W	Py	Sv%	ERA	WHIP	H%	S%	xERA	Ctl	Dom	Cmd	hr/f	hr/9	BPV
At Home	06	259	334	409	743	10	83	28	0.67	42	18	41	90	89	4%	250	4.77	49	43	75%	3.97	1.38	30%	73%	4.29	3.1	5.9	1.9	8%	0.9	43
	07	240	325	385	709	11	82	27	0.71	41	19	40	88	90	4%	250	4.42	40	38	55%	3.79	1.31	29%	72%	4.24	3.4	6.2	1.8	7%	0.7	44
	08	243	314	368	682	9	78	29	0.47	40	19	41	85	95	7%	234	3.97	42	40	67%	3.53	1.27	28%	75%	4.03	3.5	6.5	1.9	8%	0.8	43
Away	06	261	342	414	756	11	82	29	0.67	43	21	36	93	90	6%	263	4.96	44	42	71%	4.47	1.46	31%	72%	4.39	3.5	6.6	1.9	11%	1.2	43
	07	271	346	427	773	10	78	32	0.51	40	19	41	103	66	4%	246	5.13	36	41	63%	4.85	1.45	32%	68%	4.80	3.2	6.7	2.1	9%	1.0	54
	08	241	313	367	681	10	77	29	0.46	43	18	38	84	102	8%	233	3.95	32	34	63%	4.55	1.44	31%	70%	4.78	3.8	6.7	1.8	8%	0.9	35
Opp @ OAK	06	268	328	410	738	8	83	30	0.53	43	19	38	88	95	8%	254	4.64	32	38	64%	4.33	1.43	29%	72%	4.62	3.9	5.9	1.5	9%	1.1	19
	07	249	317	372	689	9	82	29	0.54	46	18	36	76	114	10%	245	4.08	41	43	69%	3.85	1.37	27%	75%	4.30	4.2	6.0	1.4	9%	1.0	11
	08	240	311	368	679	9	80	28	0.53	42	18	40	81	83	8%	238	3.94	37	39	64%	3.77	1.32	30%	73%	4.21	3.6	7.5	2.1	7%	0.8	55

PHI	Yr	Avg	OB	Slg	OPS	bb%	ct%	h%	Eye	G	L	F	PX	SX	SBO	xBA	RC/G	W	Py	Sv%	ERA	WHIP	H%	S%	xERA	Ctl	Dom	Cmd	hr/f	hr/9	BPV
At Home	06	274	346	462	808	10	80	31	0.54	46	20	34	116	106	6%	276	5.52	41	43	61%	4.70	1.42	31%	71%	4.11	3.1	7.5	2.4	16%	1.5	73
	07	280	350	475	825	10	79	32	0.52	43	19	38	119	128	10%	271	5.73	47	43	60%	4.79	1.43	30%	71%	4.31	3.4	6.8	2.0	16%	1.5	53
	08	262	336	447	784	10	80	29	0.57	41	23	36	113	124	13%	277	5.23	48	48	68%	3.67	1.33	30%	75%	3.67	3.0	6.7	2.2	11%	1.0	60
Away	06	260	334	433	767	10	78	30	0.51	42	20	38	107	115	8%	259	5.04	44	43	68%	4.52	1.42	31%	71%	4.48	3.2	6.5	2.0	10%	1.1	50
	07	268	345	442	787	10	78	31	0.54	40	19	41	113	120	10%	256	5.35	42	44	73%	4.74	1.47	31%	69%	4.89	3.5	6.1	1.7	8%	0.9	35
	08	249	318	429	747	9	79	28	0.49	44	19	37	111	116	9%	266	4.73	44	45	81%	4.13	1.40	30%	73%	4.12	3.6	6.7	1.9	11%	1.0	46
Opp @ PHI	06	275	334	471	805	8	79	31	0.42	45	21	34	123	106	9%	280	5.40	40	38	68%	5.10	1.50	31%	70%	4.58	3.9	7.2	1.9	15%	1.4	47
	07	273	338	474	811	9	80	30	0.49	44	21	35	124	82	7%	282	5.49	34	38	63%	5.34	1.54	32%	69%	4.84	3.9	7.4	1.9	14%	1.5	47
	08	258	318	400	718	8	81	30	0.45	44	23	33	91	92	10%	267	4.35	33	33	64%	4.91	1.44	29%	70%	4.65	3.9	6.9	1.8	14%	1.4	36

PIT	Yr	Avg	OB	Slg	OPS	bb%	ct%	h%	Eye	G	L	F	PX	SX	SBO	xBA	RC/G	W	Py	Sv%	ERA	WHIP	H%	S%	xERA	Ctl	Dom	Cmd	hr/f	hr/9	BPV
At Home	06	283	339	423	762	8	80	33	0.42	43	21	35	92	96	7%	258	4.90	43	42	68%	4.09	1.44	32%	73%	4.22	3.5	6.5	1.8	8%	0.8	45
	07	272	327	415	742	8	80	32	0.41	42	20	38	95	86	6%	254	4.65	37	39	54%	4.55	1.39	31%	69%	4.64	2.9	6.0	2.1	9%	0.9	54
	08	263	318	410	728	8	83	30	0.47	42	21	36	93	93	5%	265	4.47	39	36	75%	4.52	1.53	31%	72%	4.58	3.9	5.6	1.4	9%	0.9	16
Away	06	243	299	370	669	7	77	29	0.35	46	19	36	85	78	5%	235	3.66	24	29	62%	5.06	1.58	32%	71%	4.75	4.3	6.8	1.6	13%	1.2	27
	07	254	312	408	720	8	79	29	0.41	42	17	41	99	102	7%	244	4.35	31	31	74%	5.36	1.58	33%	68%	5.10	3.6	6.4	1.8	11%	1.3	39
	08	254	314	396	710	8	80	29	0.44	43	20	38	92	89	5%	252	4.24	28	31	46%	5.73	1.61	32%	66%	5.38	4.2	6.3	1.5	12%	1.3	21
Opp @ PIT	06	275	342	408	750	9	81	32	0.54	46	20	34	87	90	10%	257	4.85	38	39	68%	4.40	1.44	33%	71%	4.34	3.0	7.1	2.4	9%	0.9	67
	07	280	335	425	760	8	83	32	0.48	45	20	36	93	86	8%	262	4.86	44	42	79%	4.42	1.36	32%	68%	4.62	2.8	6.8	2.4	8%	0.8	67
	08	282	355	434	789	10	84	31	0.70	44	22	34	96	83	8%	277	5.38	42	45	64%	4.26	1.32	30%	70%	4.49	2.8	6.0	2.1	9%	0.9	52

SD	Yr	Avg	OB	Slg	OPS	bb%	ct%	h%	Eye	G	L	F	PX	SX	SBO	xBA	RC/G	W	Py	Sv%	ERA	WHIP	H%	S%	xERA	Ctl	Dom	Cmd	hr/f	hr/9	BPV
At Home	06	245	316	388	705	9	80	28	0.51	41	18	41	89	111	10%	242	4.25	43	38	73%	3.77	1.23	28%	73%	3.95	2.8	7.1	2.5	10%	1.1	69
	07	235	305	378	684	9	76	28	0.42	41	18	41	94	103	6%	233	3.96	47	46	86%	3.02	1.16	29%	75%	3.60	2.6	7.1	2.7	6%	0.5	80
	08	239	311	366	677	9	77	29	0.46	43	19	38	83	79	4%	233	3.88	35	35	53%	3.65	1.27	29%	73%	3.95	3.1	7.0	2.2	9%	0.8	62
Away	06	279	344	443	786	9	81	32	0.51	43	21	36	105	112	10%	269	5.25	45	48	68%	4.00	1.31	29%	73%	4.19	2.9	6.4	2.2	10%	1.1	56
	07	265	330	440	770	9	80	30	0.49	40	19	42	113	80	5%	258	5.04	42	44	53%	4.46	1.37	31%	69%	4.54	3.2	6.7	2.1	9%	0.9	58
	08	260	316	412	729	8	78	31	0.37	43	20	37	99	75	3%	250	4.44	28	33	54%	5.24	1.53	32%	68%	5.03	3.9	6.6	1.7	12%	1.2	33
Opp @ SD	06	244	302	396	698	8	79	28	0.40	41	20	40	95	113	12%	249	4.04	38	43	65%	3.74	1.32	29%	74%	4.09	3.5	6.9	1.9	9%	0.9	46
	07	235	290	336	626	7	79	28	0.37	45	18	37	67	115	14%	229	3.17	34	35	72%	3.87	1.25	29%	71%	4.20	3.4	8.0	2.4	9%	0.9	70
	08	246	310	368	677	8	79	29	0.45	43	20	37	77	105	14%	241	3.84	46	46	73%	3.38	1.28	29%	76%	3.69	3.5	7.7	2.2	8%	0.8	62

SEA	Yr	Avg	OB	Slg	OPS	bb%	ct%	h%	Eye	G	L	F	PX	SX	SBO	xBA	RC/G	W	Py	Sv%	ERA	WHIP	H%	S%	xERA	Ctl	Dom	Cmd	hr/f	hr/9	BPV
At Home	06	265	315	416	731	7	82	30	0.41	45	18	37	90	107	10%	256	4.43	44	39	71%	4.26	1.38	29%	72%	4.41	3.7	6.9	1.9	10%	1.0	43
	07	283	334	417	752	7	84	32	0.47	47	18	35	80	95	9%	251	4.70	49	39	74%	4.50	1.43	32%	70%	4.66	3.3	6.8	2.0	8%	0.9	53
	08	271	320	398	718	7	84	30	0.46	46	19	35	79	94	7%	256	4.33	35	36	69%	4.40	1.47	31%	72%	4.50	4.0	6.8	1.7	9%	0.9	36
Away	06	277	325	432	757	7	83	31	0.42	44	19	37	91	111	9%	264	4.73	34	39	69%	4.96	1.47	31%	69%	4.73	3.3	6.3	1.9	12%	1.2	47
	07	290	331	432	763	6	86	32	0.43	47	19	34	85	97	5%	269	4.80	39	40	75%	4.98	1.52	32%	68%	5.01	3.5	6.0	1.7	9%	0.9	35
	08	260	312	381	692	7	84	29	0.47	47	20	33	74	87	9%	255	4.02	26	31	40%	5.08	1.56	32%	69%	4.94	3.9	5.9	1.5	11%	1.1	24
Opp @ SEA	06	255	327	410	737	10	80	29	0.53	42	19	39	100	83	8%	253	4.67	37	42	73%	4.35	1.30	30%	69%	4.45	2.5	6.2	2.5	10%	1.0	67
	07	272	335	416	751	9	81	32	0.49	44	17	39	94	82	8%	246	4.81	32	42	55%	4.34	1.42	32%	72%	4.34	2.7	5.8	2.1	9%	1.0	56
	08	268	343	409	751	10	80	31	0.58	45	19	37	90	85	9%	250	4.89	46	45	72%	3.85	1.34	31%	73%	4.14	2.6	5.5	2.2	7%	0.7	55

BATTING

PITCHING

SF

SF	Yr	Avg	OB	Slg	OPS	bb%	ct%	h%	Eye	G	L	F	PX	SX	SBO	xBA	RC/G
At Home	06	264	329	415	744	9	85	29	0.63	44	19	37	93	114	6%	267	4.81
	07	259	325	382	706	9	84	29	0.62	47	17	35	75	106	10%	251	4.33
	08	264	322	391	712	8	82	31	0.47	50	18	31	84	107	11%	257	4.34
Away	06	254	312	428	740	8	83	28	0.49	43	18	39	102	94	6%	261	4.59
	07	249	314	391	706	9	83	28	0.56	44	17	39	86	109	11%	251	4.26
	08	260	314	374	688	7	81	31	0.40	47	19	34	76	94	10%	245	3.98
Opp @ SF	06	253	321	392	713	9	81	29	0.54	42	19	38	88	105	9%	252	4.38
	07	270	333	412	745	9	82	31	0.51	44	19	37	91	112	8%	257	4.76
	08	259	336	412	749	10	78	31	0.53	39	21	39	101	114	9%	253	4.89

SF	Yr	W	Py	Sv%	ERA	WHIP	H%	S%	xERA	Ctl	Dom	Cmd	hr/f	hr/9	BPV
At Home	06	43	40	67%	4.38	1.33	29%	68%	4.79	3.4	6.4	1.9	8%	0.8	42
	07	39	38	62%	4.02	1.41	31%	73%	4.28	3.3	6.4	2.0	7%	0.8	49
	08	37	32	62%	4.45	1.44	31%	71%	4.62	4.0	7.6	1.9	9%	0.9	42
Away	06	33	36	60%	4.92	1.48	30%	69%	5.05	3.9	6.1	1.6	10%	1.1	22
	07	32	39	61%	4.39	1.39	29%	70%	4.81	4.1	6.7	1.6	8%	0.9	27
	08	35	37	74%	4.30	1.43	31%	72%	4.44	4.1	7.9	1.9	9%	0.9	45
Opp @ SF	06	38	41	61%	4.49	1.38	29%	68%	4.94	3.3	5.3	1.6	7%	0.8	28
	07	42	43	68%	3.74	1.36	29%	73%	4.21	3.3	5.3	1.6	7%	0.7	32
	08	44	49	60%	3.54	1.33	31%	74%	3.82	2.9	6.3	2.1	7%	0.6	62

STL

STL	Yr	Avg	OB	Slg	OPS	bb%	ct%	h%	Eye	G	L	F	PX	SX	SBO	xBA	RC/G
At Home	06	273	339	429	768	9	84	30	0.62	44	20	36	94	89	5%	268	5.03
	07	283	343	405	749	8	85	31	0.62	43	19	38	76	79	6%	252	4.79
	08	285	350	430	780	9	83	32	0.58	43	22	35	87	85	6%	266	5.16
Away	06	265	327	434	761	8	83	29	0.53	45	19	36	102	89	7%	269	4.87
	07	265	326	405	731	8	82	30	0.51	44	18	37	88	71	6%	250	4.52
	08	277	346	436	783	10	82	31	0.59	45	21	34	98	92	7%	270	5.21
Opp @ STL	06	253	315	410	725	8	82	28	0.51	47	19	34	95	83	7%	263	4.44
	07	269	326	409	735	8	84	30	0.53	43	20	38	87	98	7%	260	4.60
	08	261	322	416	738	8	83	29	0.54	44	21	34	97	89	5%	274	4.63

STL	Yr	W	Py	Sv%	ERA	WHIP	H%	S%	xERA	Ctl	Dom	Cmd	hr/f	hr/9	BPV
At Home	06	49	45	70%	3.93	1.30	28%	73%	3.96	3.1	6.0	2.0	12%	1.1	51
	07	43	39	78%	4.17	1.37	30%	71%	4.52	3.0	5.6	1.9	7%	0.8	41
	08	46	42	61%	4.06	1.35	29%	72%	4.18	3.1	5.8	1.9	10%	1.0	43
Away	06	34	38	63%	5.20	1.48	31%	68%	4.85	3.3	6.2	1.9	13%	1.3	45
	07	35	33	72%	5.21	1.45	30%	67%	5.05	3.4	6.2	1.8	12%	1.3	42
	08	40	44	54%	4.35	1.42	31%	72%	4.26	3.0	6.1	2.0	11%	1.0	52
Opp @ STL	06	31	35	56%	4.78	1.46	30%	69%	4.79	3.5	5.7	1.6	10%	1.1	29
	07	38	42	65%	4.29	1.45	31%	72%	4.64	3.2	5.2	1.6	7%	0.8	28
	08	35	39	74%	4.47	1.50	32%	72%	4.40	3.5	6.1	1.7	10%	1.0	35

TAM

TAM	Yr	Avg	OB	Slg	OPS	bb%	ct%	h%	Eye	G	L	F	PX	SX	SBO	xBA	RC/G
At Home	06	259	321	437	758	8	80	29	0.45	44	18	38	107	114	14%	260	4.83
	07	256	320	421	741	9	77	30	0.42	42	18	40	103	107	11%	246	4.63
	08	273	353	440	793	11	78	32	0.57	42	20	38	105	121	13%	256	5.44
Away	06	250	300	403	703	7	80	29	0.35	44	20	36	95	98	13%	255	4.06
	07	276	341	442	782	9	75	34	0.40	43	20	38	112	111	12%	251	5.25
	08	248	319	405	724	9	78	29	0.47	46	19	35	102	98	11%	254	4.48
Opp @ TAM	06	275	345	446	791	10	82	31	0.59	43	19	37	104	98	10%	267	5.33
	07	284	347	452	799	9	78	34	0.44	42	18	40	109	104	7%	253	5.41
	08	231	299	367	665	9	79	27	0.45	41	19	39	87	88	7%	240	3.72

TAM	Yr	W	Py	Sv%	ERA	WHIP	H%	S%	xERA	Ctl	Dom	Cmd	hr/f	hr/9	BPV
At Home	06	41	37	66%	4.70	1.49	31%	71%	4.59	3.8	6.4	1.7	11%	1.2	33
	07	34	32	55%	5.06	1.49	34%	68%	4.86	3.4	7.7	2.3	10%	1.1	65
	08	54	48	79%	3.33	1.22	27%	75%	3.75	3.2	7.1	2.2	8%	0.9	59
Away	06	20	29	53%	5.26	1.62	33%	69%	5.16	3.9	6.0	1.5	9%	1.1	21
	07	29	33	58%	6.09	1.62	34%	64%	5.57	3.8	7.3	2.0	12%	1.4	48
	08	40	42	72%	4.34	1.37	30%	72%	4.41	3.3	7.1	2.2	10%	1.2	56
Opp @ TAM	06	40	44	67%	4.34	1.34	29%	72%	4.22	3.1	7.0	2.2	12%	1.3	62
	07	44	46	62%	4.25	1.33	30%	72%	4.18	3.2	7.7	2.4	12%	1.2	70
	08	24	30	44%	4.86	1.53	32%	71%	4.67	4.3	7.6	1.8	12%	1.2	38

TEX

TEX	Yr	Avg	OB	Slg	OPS	bb%	ct%	h%	Eye	G	L	F	PX	SX	SBO	xBA	RC/G
At Home	06	283	343	458	801	8	81	32	0.47	42	20	38	112	84	5%	270	5.38
	07	277	338	451	789	8	78	33	0.42	42	20	38	109	118	8%	258	5.25
	08	297	369	494	863	10	79	34	0.55	42	23	35	125	117	7%	283	6.29
Away	06	272	331	434	765	8	82	31	0.48	44	20	37	101	91	5%	264	4.92
	07	249	311	402	712	8	78	29	0.40	42	18	40	100	102	8%	245	4.27
	08	268	331	431	762	9	79	31	0.44	42	21	37	107	94	6%	262	4.94
Opp @ TEX	06	273	333	420	753	8	83	30	0.53	47	21	33	90	84	7%	268	4.78
	07	263	336	402	738	10	82	30	0.60	47	19	34	88	88	8%	256	4.72
	08	289	354	468	822	9	83	32	0.59	42	21	37	109	122	10%	278	5.70

TEX	Yr	W	Py	Sv%	ERA	WHIP	H%	S%	xERA	Ctl	Dom	Cmd	hr/f	hr/9	BPV
At Home	06	39	42	61%	4.68	1.42	31%	69%	4.58	3.2	5.9	1.9	11%	1.0	46
	07	47	42	76%	4.30	1.45	30%	72%	4.39	3.9	6.4	1.7	9%	0.9	36
	08	40	39	50%	5.47	1.55	32%	66%	5.28	3.6	6.2	1.7	11%	1.2	33
Away	06	41	44	68%	4.54	1.45	32%	71%	4.45	3.1	6.3	2.0	10%	1.0	54
	07	28	36	74%	5.25	1.63	31%	69%	5.18	4.6	5.9	1.3	10%	1.1	4
	08	39	37	62%	5.26	1.61	32%	68%	5.19	4.2	5.8	1.4	10%	1.0	13
Opp @ TEX	06	42	39	83%	5.12	1.49	33%	68%	4.86	3.2	6.9	2.1	11%	1.2	56
	07	34	39	67%	5.00	1.45	33%	68%	4.70	3.3	7.8	2.4	12%	1.2	70
	08	41	42	61%	5.77	1.66	35%	68%	5.09	4.1	7.6	1.8	14%	1.4	42

TOR

TOR	Yr	Avg	OB	Slg	OPS	bb%	ct%	h%	Eye	G	L	F	PX	SX	SBO	xBA	RC/G
At Home	06	295	352	505	858	8	84	31	0.57	41	20	39	124	94	6%	287	6.01
	07	260	328	433	761	9	80	30	0.50	40	20	40	111	94	5%	261	4.94
	08	264	329	413	742	9	83	30	0.55	44	21	36	92	112	6%	266	4.73
Away	06	274	337	421	758	9	83	31	0.57	44	19	37	92	81	7%	259	4.89
	07	258	321	406	727	8	82	29	0.52	40	20	40	94	89	6%	256	4.51
	08	264	326	386	712	8	83	30	0.56	44	20	36	78	92	8%	252	4.36
Opp @ TOR	06	252	313	409	722	8	80	29	0.44	47	20	33	96	109	11%	262	4.36
	07	235	292	385	677	7	79	27	0.38	49	19	32	95	110	12%	259	3.78
	08	234	298	361	659	8	77	29	0.39	48	19	33	87	92	9%	241	3.64

TOR	Yr	W	Py	Sv%	ERA	WHIP	H%	S%	xERA	Ctl	Dom	Cmd	hr/f	hr/9	BPV
At Home	06	50	49	65%	4.04	1.31	29%	73%	3.90	3.0	7.0	2.3	13%	1.1	68
	07	49	46	71%	3.67	1.18	27%	72%	3.70	2.7	7.1	2.6	12%	1.0	81
	08	47	48	83%	3.12	1.21	29%	76%	3.39	3.0	7.7	2.5	8%	0.7	82
Away	06	37	37	71%	4.74	1.43	31%	70%	4.54	3.3	6.6	2.0	12%	1.2	51
	07	34	40	58%	4.35	1.39	30%	71%	4.43	3.2	6.1	1.9	9%	0.9	49
	08	39	44	74%	3.89	1.28	30%	73%	3.92	2.8	7.0	2.5	11%	1.0	73
Opp @ TOR	06	31	32	81%	5.60	1.53	31%	67%	5.21	3.2	5.6	1.8	13%	1.6	34
	07	32	35	73%	4.61	1.39	30%	70%	4.64	3.5	7.0	2.0	11%	1.2	49
	08	34	33	53%	4.20	1.39	30%	71%	4.42	3.4	6.1	1.8	9%	0.9	40

WAS

WAS	Yr	Avg	OB	Slg	OPS	bb%	ct%	h%	Eye	G	L	F	PX	SX	SBO	xBA	RC/G
At Home	06	262	334	409	743	10	80	30	0.55	41	19	40	94	100	9%	250	4.76
	07	259	323	383	706	9	81	31	0.49	47	18	35	84	93	5%	247	4.29
	08	251	323	368	691	10	81	30	0.54	49	21	29	76	88	9%	252	4.12
Away	06	261	334	425	759	10	78	31	0.49	46	20	34	110	86	14%	263	4.95
	07	254	319	397	716	9	79	30	0.44	45	20	35	93	97	7%	251	4.36
	08	250	311	378	689	8	80	29	0.44	46	21	33	84	86	7%	251	4.00
Opp @ WAS	06	263	323	423	746	8	82	29	0.50	39	18	43	97	110	9%	254	4.70
	07	259	325	402	726	9	83	29	0.56	39	17	43	89	99	8%	245	4.52
	08	269	334	434	768	9	82	30	0.54	43	21	36	102	101	9%	271	5.00

WAS	Yr	W	Py	Sv%	ERA	WHIP	H%	S%	xERA	Ctl	Dom	Cmd	hr/f	hr/9	BPV
At Home	06	41	37	59%	4.66	1.36	29%	68%	4.96	3.1	6.1	2.0	9%	1.1	44
	07	40	37	65%	4.08	1.36	29%	72%	4.58	3.3	6.0	1.8	8%	0.9	34
	08	34	29	55%	4.57	1.42	30%	71%	4.49	3.4	6.3	1.9	12%	1.2	43
Away	06	30	33	58%	5.43	1.60	31%	69%	5.28	4.3	5.9	1.4	11%	1.3	8
	07	33	33	62%	5.11	1.53	30%	70%	5.02	3.9	5.6	1.4	12%	1.4	13
	08	25	33	47%	4.76	1.49	31%	71%	4.61	4.0	7.0	1.8	12%	1.2	36
Opp @ WAS	06	40	44	57%	4.37	1.40	30%	71%	4.63	3.7	6.7	1.8	9%	0.9	40
	07	41	44	74%	3.81	1.34	31%	72%	4.18	3.2	6.6	2.0	6%	0.6	56
	08	46	51	72%	3.71	1.33	29%	73%	3.93	3.5	6.5	1.8	8%	0.6	48

AL

AL	Yr	Avg	OB	Slg	OPS	bb%	ct%	h%	Eye	G	L	F	PX	SX	SBO	xBA	RC/G
At Home	06	280	342	447	789	9	82	31	0.53	43	20	37	100	100	8%	265	5.23
	07	274	340	432	772	9	82	31	0.55	44	19	38	100	100	9%	261	5.07
	08	276	341	436	777	9	82	31	0.54	43	20	37	100	100	8%	265	5.13
Away	06	270	331	427	758	8	82	30	0.49	44	20	36	100	100	8%	265	4.85
	07	266	328	414	742	8	81	31	0.47	44	18	37	100	100	8%	257	4.68
	08	259	323	404	727	9	80	30	0.48	44	19	36	100	100	9%	260	4.49

AL	Yr	W	Py	Sv%	ERA	WHIP	H%	S%	xERA	Ctl	Dom	Cmd	hr/f	hr/9	BPV
At Home	06	45	43	69%	4.30	1.37	30%	71%	4.33	3.1	6.4	2.1	10%	1.1	54
	07	44	42	68%	4.38	1.38	31%	70%	4.49	3.2	6.8	2.1	9%	0.9	57
	08	46	44	70%	4.07	1.34	30%	72%	4.23	3.2	6.7	2.1	9%	0.9	56
Away	06	38	39	67%	4.84	1.46	31%	69%	4.70	3.3	6.5	2.0	11%	1.2	48
	07	37	40	68%	4.67	1.44	31%	70%	4.68	3.5	6.5	1.9	10%	1.1	44
	08	37	38	64%	4.67	1.45	31%	70%	4.66	3.5	6.6	1.9	10%	1.1	45

NL

NL	Yr	Avg	OB	Slg	OPS	bb%	ct%	h%	Eye	G	L	F	PX	SX	SBO	xBA	RC/G
At Home	06	271	338	437	775	9	81	31	0.53	43	20	37	100	100	9%	262	5.11
	07	269	335	430	765	9	81	31	0.52	43	19	38	100	100	8%	259	4.97
	08	265	334	422	756	9	80	31	0.52	44	21	35	100	100	9%	263	4.89
Away	06	259	321	418	739	8	80	30	0.46	44	19	37	100	100	9%	258	4.62
	07	263	325	416	741	9	80	30	0.47	43	19	38	100	100	9%	255	4.66
	08	256	321	405	726	9	79	30	0.46	44	21	35	100	100	8%	261	4.47

NL	Yr	W	Py	Sv%	ERA	WHIP	H%	S%	xERA	Ctl	Dom	Cmd	hr/f	hr/9	BPV
At Home	06	43	41	65%	4.33	1.36	30%	71%	4.29	3.2	7.0	2.1	11%	1.1	59
	07	43	41	66%	4.22	1.36	30%	71%	4.34	3.2	6.8	2.1	10%	1.0	56
	08	44	41	65%	4.09	1.35	30%	72%	4.13	3.3	7.1	2.1	10%	1.0	59
Away	06	36	39	63%	4.67	1.45	31%	70%	4.63	3.6	6.5	1.8	11%	1.1	41
	07	37	39	66%	4.67	1.44	31%	70%	4.68	3.5	6.5	1.9	10%	1.1	44
	08	35	39	60%	4.52	1.44	31%	71%	4.43	3.6	6.9	1.9	11%	1.1	47

The Batters

QUALIFICATION: All batters who had at least 100 at bats in the majors in 2008, nearly all who accumulated 50-99 AB and a handful with fewer than 50 AB have been included. The decision often comes down to whether they will have an impact in 2009. Those who may have a role but have battled injuries for several years are often not included, though an injury status update appears on page 183. All of these players will appear on Baseball HQ as roles become clearer.

POSITIONS: Up to three positions are listed for each batter and represent those for which he appeared a minimum of 20 games in 2008. Positions are shown with their numeric designation (2=CA, 3=1B, 7=LF, 0=DH, etc.)

AGE: Each batter's current age is shown.

BATS: Shows which side of the plate he bats from — right (R), left (L) or switch-hitter (S).

RELIABILITY GRADES: An analysis of each player's forecast risk, on an A-F scale. High grades go to those batters who have accumulated few disabled list days (Health), have a history of substantial and regular major league playing time (PT/Exp) and have displayed consistent performance over the past three years, using RC/G (Consist).

LIMA PLAN GRADE: Rating that evaluates how well a batter would fit into a team using the LIMA Plan. Best grades go to batters who have excellent base skills, are expected to see a good amount of playing time, and are in the $10-$30 Rotisserie value range. Lowest grades will go to poor skills, few AB and values less than $5 or more than $30.

+/- SCORE: A score that measures the probability that a batter's 2009 performance will exceed or fall short of 2008's numbers. Two types of variables are tracked: 1) Multi-year trends in bb%, ct%, PX and SX, and 2) Outlying 2008 levels for h%, hr/f, xBA and LH/RH variance. Positive scores indicate both rebounds and potential breakouts. Negative scores indicate both corrections and breakdowns.

PLAYER STAT LINES: The past five years' statistics represent the total accumulated in the majors as well as in Triple-A, Double-A ball and various foreign leagues during each year. All non-major league stats used have been converted to a major league equivalent (MLE) performance level. Minor league levels below AA are not included.

Nearly all baseball publications separate a player's statistical experiences in the major leagues from the minor leagues and outside leagues. While this may be appropriate for the sake of official record-keeping, it is not an accurate snapshot of a player's complete performance for the year.

Bill James has proven that minor league statistics (converted to MLEs), at Double-A level or above, provide as accurate a record of a player's performance as Major League statistics. Other researchers have also devised conversion factors for foreign leagues. Since these are accurate barometers, we include them in the pool of historical data.

TEAM DESIGNATIONS: An asterisk (*) appearing with a team name means that major league equivalent Triple-A and/or Double-A numbers are included in that year's stat line. A designation of "a/a" means the stats were accumulated at both levels that year. Other designations: JPN (Japan), MEX (Mexico), KOR (Korea), CUB (Cuba), VNZ (Venezuela) and ind (independent league). All these stats are converted to major league equivalents.

The designation "2TM" appears whenever a player was on more than one major league team, crossing leagues, in a season. "2AL" and "2NL" represent more than one team in the same league. Complete season stats are presented for players who crossed leagues during the season.

SABERMETRIC CATEGORIES: Descriptions of all the categories appear in the glossary. The decimal point has been suppressed on some categories to conserve space.

- Platoon data (vL, vR) and Ball-in-play data (G/L/F) are for major league performance only.
- xBA only appears for years in which G/L/F data is available.

2009 FORECASTS: It is far too early to be making definitive projections for 2009, especially on playing time. Focus on the skill levels and trends, then consult Baseball HQ for playing time revisions as players change teams and roles become finalized. A free projections update will also be available online in March.

Forecasts are computed from a player's trends over the past five years. Adjustments were made for leading indicators and variances between skill and statistical output. After reviewing the leading indicators, you might opt to make further adjustments.

Although each year's numbers include all playing time at the Double-A level or above, the 2009 forecast only represents potential playing time at the major league level, and again is highly preliminary.

CAPSULE COMMENTARIES: For each player, a brief analysis of their BPIs and the potential impact on performance in 2009 is provided. For those who played only a portion of 2008 at the major league level, and whose isolated MLB stats are significantly different from their full-season total, their MLB stats are listed here. Note that these commentaries generally look at performance related issues only. Playing time expectations may impact these analyses, so you will have to adjust accordingly. Upside (UP) and downside (DN) statistical potential appears for some players. These are less grounded in hard data and more speculative of skills potential.

DO-IT-YOURSELF ANALYSIS: Here are some data points you can look at in doing your own player analysis:

- Variance between vLH and vRH batting averages
- Growth or decline in walk rate (bb%)
- Growth or decline in contact rate (ct%)
- Variance in 2008 hit rate (h%) to 2005-2007 three-year avg
- Variance between Avg and xBA each year
- Growth or decline in power index (PX) rate
- Variance in 2008 hr/f rate to 2005-2007 three-year average
- Growth or decline in speed index (SX) rate
- Concurrent growth/decline of gauges like ct%, PX, F
- Concurrent growth/decline of gauges like SX, SBO, OB

Abreu,Bobby			AB	R	H	HR	RBI	SB	Avg	vL	vR	OB	Slg	OPS	bb%	ct%	h%	Eye	xBA	G	L	F	PX	hr/f	SX	SBO	RC/G	RAR	R$
Pos	9	04 PHI	574	118	173	30	105	40	301	267	318	428	544	972	18	80	33	1.09	302	42	21	37	154	18%	115	20%	8.05	44.0	$37
Age	35	05 PHI	588	104	168	24	102	31	286	275	292	404	474	879	17	77	33	0.87	291	47	24	29	129	18%	101	18%	6.84	26.7	$32
Bats	Left	06 2TM	548	98	163	15	107	30	297	293	299	427	462	889	18	75	37	0.90	277	45	26	29	117	13%	105	16%	7.23	30.8	$27
Health	A	07 NYY	605	123	171	16	101	25	283	262	289	370	445	815	12	81	33	0.73	278	46	20	34	109	9%	129	17%	5.83	5.6	$26
PT/Exp	A	08 NYY	609	100	180	20	100	22	296	315	287	371	471	842	11	82	33	0.67	295	48	23	30	114	13%	106	17%	6.03	11.6	$27
Consist	B	1st Half	311	44	88	10	53	11	283			352	457	808	10	81	32	0.56	285	50	19	31	112	13%	105	18%	5.56	1.8	$13
LIMA Plan	B	2nd Half	298	56	92	10	47	11	309			391	487	877	12	83	34	0.80	306	45	26	29	116	14%	95	17%	6.52	9.6	$15
+/- Score	-14	09 Proj	578	105	168	18	98	20	291			383	464	847	13	80	33	0.77	289	46	23	31	116	13%	103	15%	6.25	14.4	$25

Three straight seasons of consistent value. Still, note the Eye and SB trends. Eye hasn't hurt his BA or power yet, but at his age, decline can set in fast. SB% fell to 66% in '08; '09 may be the year he fails to steal 20.

Alou,Moises			AB	R	H	HR	RBI	SB	Avg	vL	vR	OB	Slg	OPS	bb%	ct%	h%	Eye	xBA	G	L	F	PX	hr/f	SX	SBO	RC/G	RAR	R$
Pos	7	04 CHC	601	106	176	39	106	3	293	298	292	365	557	922	10	87	28	0.85	310	39	19	43	144	18%	79	2%	6.78	22.4	$28
Age	42	05 SF	427	67	137	19	63	5	321	372	303	400	518	917	12	90	32	1.30	302	42	20	38	109	13%	85	4%	6.90	17.8	$21
Bats	Right	06 SF	345	52	104	22	74	2	301	349	286	354	571	925	8	91	28	0.90	328	40	20	40	142	18%	52	4%	6.65	13.3	$17
Health	F	07 NYM	328	51	112	13	49	3	341	360	335	392	524	916	8	91	35	0.90	298	42	20	38	102	11%	65	3%	6.61	10.6	$16
PT/Exp	D	08 NYM	49	4	17	0	9	1	347	462	306	373	388	760	4	92	38	0.50	266	46	24	30	32	0%	43	12%	4.75	-0.9	$2
Consist	B	1st Half	49	4	17	0	9	1	347			373	388	760	4	92	38	0.50	266	46	24	30	32	0%	43	12%	4.75	-0.9	$2
LIMA Plan	D	2nd Half	0	0	0	0	0	0	0							0			0										
+/- Score	-94	09 Proj	204	32	60	7	29	0	294			344	468	813	7	90	30	0.76	297	42	21	37	99	11%	58	1%	5.47	0.5	$7

Torn hamstring caps a 4-year period when injuries have undermined his value. If he decides to return, still has the skills to hit .300, but you really can't trust him with anything more than an end-game bid.

Amezaga,Alfredo			AB	R	H	HR	RBI	SB	Avg	vL	vR	OB	Slg	OPS	bb%	ct%	h%	Eye	xBA	G	L	F	PX	hr/f	SX	SBO	RC/G	RAR	R$
Pos	8	04 aaa	135	11	29	1	10	5	216			263	280	543	6	90	23	0.65	0				38		101	15%	2.51	-9.0	$1
Age	31	05 aaa	185	20	54	1	9	10	293			337	375	712	6	89	33	0.59	0				58		99	35%	4.37	-0.3	$6
Bats	Both	06 FLA	334	42	87	3	19	20	260	91	294	327	332	659	9	86	29	0.72	243	51	17	33	41	3%	111	30%	3.85	-6.0	$9
Health	A	07 FLA	400	46	105	2	30	13	263	224	269	322	358	679	8	87	30	0.67	261	47	21	33	54	2%	122	17%	4.11	-5.0	$8
PT/Exp	C	08 FLA	311	41	82	3	32	8	264	254	266	306	367	673	6	85	30	0.40	258	47	20	34	64	3%	131	13%	3.81	-8.4	$8
Consist	A	1st Half	151	19	37	1	8	4	245			305	338	643	8	86	28	0.62	259	50	18	33	60	2%	112	13%	3.64	-5.0	$2
LIMA Plan	F	2nd Half	160	22	45	2	24	4	281			307	394	701	4	84	33	0.23	257	44	21	35	67	4%	132	13%	3.98	-3.5	$5
+/- Score	-1	09 Proj	196	24	52	2	17	5	265			314	356	671	7	86	30	0.51	255	47	20	33	54	3%	110	14%	3.86	-4.4	$4

If he's not going to run, then what's the point? Three-year SBO decline matches FLA team trend, so he could probably use a change of scenery. But who wants a sub-replacement level hitter with a .258 xBA?

Anderson,Brian			AB	R	H	HR	RBI	SB	Avg	vL	vR	OB	Slg	OPS	bb%	ct%	h%	Eye	xBA	G	L	F	PX	hr/f	SX	SBO	RC/G	RAR	R$
Pos	8	04 aa	185	25	49	4	26	3	265			330	400	730	9	84	30	0.62	0				81		98	10%	4.62	-0.3	$5
Age	27	05 CHW *	474	61	124	17	48	4	262	83	227	314	424	738	7	78	30	0.34	272	36	27	36	107	13%	71	5%	4.49	2.9	$12
Bats	Right	06 CHW	365	46	82	8	33	4	225	226	223	284	359	642	8	75	28	0.33	249	44	21	35	97	8%	68	14%	3.37	-14.6	$4
Health	A	07 aaa	200	26	49	9	28	3	243			305	421	725	8	78	27	0.41	0				108		74	10%	4.34	-1.2	$5
PT/Exp	F	08 CHW	181	24	42	8	26	5	232	225	238	272	436	709	5	75	27	0.22	273	45	17	38	145	15%	84	19%	4.05	-7.1	$5
Consist	B	1st Half	119	11	27	4	13	2	227			264	395	659	5	76	27	0.21	253	49	14	37	122	12%	54	14%	3.41	-7.1	$2
LIMA Plan	F	2nd Half	62	13	15	4	13	3	242			288	516	804	6	74	26	0.25	299	37	22	41	191	21%	119	30%	5.30	-0.1	$3
+/- Score	25	09 Proj	196	29	47	9	28	5	240			291	431	722	7	76	27	0.31	269	42	19	38	130	15%	80	16%	4.27	-4.1	$6

PRO: Intriguing power burst, xBA upside, nice second half.
CON: All 8 of his HR came vs LH; PX vs. RH was only 102. Career .221 hitter with 74% contact rate in 597 AB.
Verdict: Worth a flyer.

Anderson,Garret			AB	R	H	HR	RBI	SB	Avg	vL	vR	OB	Slg	OPS	bb%	ct%	h%	Eye	xBA	G	L	F	PX	hr/f	SX	SBO	RC/G	RAR	R$
Pos	70	04 ANA	442	57	133	14	75	2	301	262	321	344	446	790	6	83	34	0.39	272	42	23	35	87	11%	56	2%	5.07	1.5	$15
Age	36	05 ANA	575	68	163	17	96	1	283	330	259	311	435	746	4	85	31	0.27	276	42	21	38	97	9%	43	1%	4.45	-4.4	$17
Bats	Left	06 LAA	543	63	152	17	85	1	280	248	294	327	433	760	7	83	31	0.40	269	41	22	37	94	10%	51	1%	4.75	-6.5	$14
Health	C	07 LAA	417	67	124	16	80	1	297	288	300	340	492	832	6	87	31	0.50	295	40	19	41	121	11%	60	1%	5.59	6.3	$16
PT/Exp	B	08 LAA	557	66	163	15	84	7	293	290	293	328	433	760	5	86	32	0.38	276	42	21	36	86	9%	77	7%	4.70	-2.4	$18
Consist	B	1st Half	290	29	74	6	35	5	255			289	372	662	5	84	29	0.30	262	43	21	35	73	7%	86	10%	3.53	-11.3	$6
LIMA Plan	D+	2nd Half	267	37	89	9	49	2	333			369	498	867	5	88	35	0.48	290	41	21	37	98	10%	60	5%	5.91	7.5	$12
+/- Score	-21	09 Proj	458	60	131	11	72	3	286			325	427	752	6	86	31	0.41	274	42	21	38	89	8%	69	4%	4.66	-3.7	$14

Skills were a near match for 2005-06, and judging by RAR, that's not a good thing. Second year in a row it took big 2nd half to save his season. Be wary of age and what happens if those 1st half numbers ever stick.

Anderson,Josh			AB	R	H	HR	RBI	SB	Avg	vL	vR	OB	Slg	OPS	bb%	ct%	h%	Eye	xBA	G	L	F	PX	hr/f	SX	SBO	RC/G	RAR	R$
Pos	8	04	0	0	0	0	0	0	0							0			0						0				
Age	26	05 aa	524	61	140	1	23	46	267			300	335	635	5	86	31	0.34	0				42		157	47%	3.33	-17.2	$17
Bats	Left	06 aa	561	67	152	3	41	35	271			298	339	637	4	88	30	0.33	0				43		123	34%	3.34	-20.1	$16
Health	A	07 HOU *	580	58	138	2	43	31	238	389	347	274	292	566	5	87	27	0.37	275	64	19	17	34	2%	120	28%	2.55	-35.0	$10
PT/Exp	C	08 ATL *	630	82	172	6	43	43	272	200	341	307	356	664	5	86	31	0.37	277	52	22	26	56	4%	134	31%	3.65	-19.9	$22
Consist	B	1st Half	299	32	72	1	18	15	242			278	292	569	5	89	27	0.46	0				32		119	23%	2.67	-18.6	$6
LIMA Plan	D+	2nd Half	331	50	99	5	26	28	300			334	415	749	5	84	35	0.32	285	52	22	26	79	7%	139	38%	4.60	-1.3	$16
+/- Score	6	09 Proj	401	49	106	6	28	27	264			298	362	660	5	86	29	0.36	283	55	21	24	60	7%	130	34%	3.58	-12.4	$13

3-12-.294 in 136 AB at ATL. Terrific GB/speed combo, but with this PX, needs elite ct% to maximize BA. For now, lots of SB with a BA that won't hurt you. 118 PX in Sept gives sliver of hope for more.

Anderson,Marlon			AB	R	H	HR	RBI	SB	Avg	vL	vR	OB	Slg	OPS	bb%	ct%	h%	Eye	xBA	G	L	F	PX	hr/f	SX	SBO	RC/G	RAR	R$
Pos	7	04 STL	253	31	60	8	28	6	237	160	246	272	379	651	5	85	25	0.32	273	48	19	33	85	11%	82	15%	3.37	-15.8	$6
Age	35	05 NYM	235	31	62	7	19	6	264	267	264	316	391	708	7	81	30	0.40	258	42	22	36	82	10%	79	11%	4.12	-8.3	$7
Bats	Left	06 2NL	279	43	83	12	38	4	297	254	310	355	513	868	8	82	33	0.51	290	39	23	38	123	14%	90	13%	6.16	7.2	$11
Health	B	07 2NL	95	17	28	3	27	4	295	143	307	350	463	813	8	82	33	0.47	270	41	18	41	112	9%	87	19%	5.49	0.3	$5
PT/Exp	D	08 NYM	138	16	29	1	10	2	210		213	259	275	534	6	80	25	0.33	227	49	17	34	50	3%	70	10%	2.03	-14.6	$1
Consist	F	1st Half	92	10	18	1	7	2	196			229	283	512	4	82	23	0.24	243	43	20	37	65	4%	82	19%	1.71	-10.9	$0
LIMA Plan	F	2nd Half	46	6	11	0	3	0	239			314	261	575	10	78	31	0.50	184	61	11	28	20	0%	37	0%	2.65	-3.8	$0
+/- Score	-1	09 Proj	99	13	27	4	14	2	273			317	435	751	6	82	30	0.36	272	43	21	36	100	13%	61	13%	4.58	-2.3	$3

Dealt with a hamstring injury most of the season, so there's reason to believe he can return to his righty-mashing ways. That's his niche, and at his age, it's good to start accepting your limitations.

Ankiel,Rick			AB	R	H	HR	RBI	SB	Avg	vL	vR	OB	Slg	OPS	bb%	ct%	h%	Eye	xBA	G	L	F	PX	hr/f	SX	SBO	RC/G	RAR	R$
Pos	8	04 aa	5	0	0	0	0	0	0			167	0	167	17	80	0	1.00	0						0	0%	-2.27	-1.4	($0)
Age	29	05 aa	136	11	24	6	19	0	179			214	352	566	4	81	17	0.24	0				105		17	0%	2.22	-9.6	$1
Bats	Left	06	0	0	0	0	0	0	0							0			0						0				
Health	A	07 STL *	559	72	132	31	97	3	236	391	246	275	445	720	5	77	25	0.23	256	44	15	41	125	18%	68	6%	4.06	-7.9	$16
PT/Exp	D	08 STL	413	65	109	25	71	2	264	224	279	332	506	838	9	76	29	0.42	275	36	19	45	154	18%	69	3%	5.84	13.1	$16
Consist	D	1st Half	263	45	68	15	38	1	259			332	506	838	10	78	28	0.49	280	40	16	45	157	16%	80	3%	5.88	8.8	$10
LIMA Plan	C	2nd Half	150	20	41	10	33	1	273			331	507	838	8	73	31	0.32	271	30	25	45	149	21%	37	3%	5.78	4.5	$7
+/- Score	-38	09 Proj	522	69	134	31	92	3	257			307	483	790	7	76	28	0.31	268	36	20	44	138	18%	59	3%	5.06	6.5	$18

If we treat him like a 29-year-old, this looks like his peak. If we treat him like a second-year player, this looks like growth. For now, 30 HR and $20 value are within reach. Long-term, ct%, Eye merit some caution.

Antonelli,Matt			AB	R	H	HR	RBI	SB	Avg	vL	vR	OB	Slg	OPS	bb%	ct%	h%	Eye	xBA	G	L	F	PX	hr/f	SX	SBO	RC/G	RAR	R$
Pos	4	04	0	0	0	0	0	0	0							0			0						0				
Age	24	05	0	0	0	0	0	0	0							0			0						0				
Bats	Right	06	0	0	0	0	0	0	0							0			0						0				
Health	A	07 aa	187	31	50	6	22	9	267			360	422	782	13	82	30	0.79	0				97		103	20%	5.38	5.7	$7
PT/Exp	F	08 SD *	508	57	93	6	35	5	184	83	222	278	265	543	12	82	21	0.75	232	46	17	37	53	4%	75	7%	2.48	-37.7	$0
Consist	F	1st Half	279	27	45	2	19	3	162			265	228	493	12	84	19	0.85	0				44		80	7%	1.97	-25.9	($2)
LIMA Plan	D+	2nd Half	229	30	48	4	17	2	211			295	310	605	11	81	24	0.63	236	46	17	37	65	6%	69	8%	3.12	-11.9	$2
+/- Score	26	09 Proj	463	63	110	10	41	12	238			328	349	677	12	82	27	0.75	244	46	17	37	71	7%	87	12%	4.09	-8.8	$9

1-3-.193 in 57 AB at SD. Top prospect took a major step back in Triple-A, though h% indicates some bad luck. Steady Eye is a positive sign. Don't give up on him, but don't expect much '09 value either.

BRANDON KRUSE

Arias,Joaquin

		Year	AB	R	H	HR	RBI	SB	Avg	vL	vR	OB	Slg	OPS	bb%	ct%	h%	Eye	xBA	G	L	F	PX	hr/f	SX	SBO	RC/G	RAR	R$
Pos	4	04	0	0	0	0	0	0	0							0			0						0				
Age	24	05 aa	499	52	147	5	45	16	295			314	393	707	3	93	31	0.39	0				58		110	22%	4.14	-2.9	$15
Bats	Right	06 aaa	493	56	139	4	48	26	281			308	383	691	4	89	31	0.34	0				53		144	29%	3.97	-5.6	$15
Health	A	07 aa	432	44	110	6	36	17	256			280	358	637	3	90	27	0.34	0				56		125	23%	3.35	-12.8	$9
PT/Exp	D	08 TEX	* 542	59	142	6	45	21	263	417	256	291	368	659	4	90	28	0.39	277	48	20	32	60	4%	135	22%	3.65	-19.8	$13
Consist	A	1st Half	272	29	68	2	17	14	251			266	328	594	2	89	28	0.19	0				42		144	30%	2.78	-17.2	$6
LIMA Plan	D	2nd Half	270	30	74	4	28	7	275			315	408	723	5	91	29	0.64	294	48	20	32	78	5%	115	15%	4.50	-3.0	$7
+/- Score	14	09 Proj	**212**	**23**	**57**	**2**	**19**	**10**	**269**			**296**	**378**	**674**	**4**	**90**	**29**	**0.39**	**279**	**48**	**20**	**32**	**61**	**4%**	**133**	**27%**	**3.81**	**-4.1**	**$6**

0-9-.291 in 110 AB at TEX. Speed and contact skills aren't in doubt, but OBP and PT are. If given a shot, bb% and Eye in 2H give reason for optimism. At age 24, time is on his side.
UP: 25 SB

Atkins,Garrett

		Year	AB	R	H	HR	RBI	SB	Avg	vL	vR	OB	Slg	OPS	bb%	ct%	h%	Eye	xBA	G	L	F	PX	hr/f	SX	SBO	RC/G	RAR	R$
Pos	53	04 COL	* 473	63	157	13	72	0	332	333	385	386	510	896	8	93	34	1.31	308	58	15	27	105	11%	40	0%	6.55	18.4	$19
Age	29	05 COL	519	62	149	13	89	0	287	291	285	344	426	770	8	86	31	0.63	289	46	24	30	90	10%	34	1%	5.02	3.5	$17
Bats	Right	06 COL	602	117	198	29	120	4	329	341	327	407	556	963	12	87	34	1.04	308	37	22	41	131	13%	67	2%	7.44	30.9	$32
Health	A	07 COL	605	83	182	25	111	3	301	286	307	371	486	856	10	84	32	0.70	283	31	24	44	111	11%	48	2%	6.09	8.0	$24
PT/Exp	A	08 COL	611	86	175	21	99	1	286	357	265	330	452	782	6	84	31	0.40	273	37	22	41	101	10%	62	1%	4.99	-6.5	$21
Consist	C	1st Half	318	45	95	10	42	0	299			332	459	791	5	86	32	0.37	276	37	22	41	93	9%	66	1%	5.04	-2.9	$11
LIMA Plan	C	2nd Half	293	41	80	11	57	1	273			328	444	772	8	81	31	0.42	271	37	22	41	111	11%	46	1%	4.93	-3.6	$10
+/- Score	-14	09 Proj	**578**	**85**	**167**	**20**	**97**	**2**	**289**			**348**	**459**	**807**	**8**	**85**	**31**	**0.58**	**280**	**36**	**23**	**41**	**105**	**10%**	**62**	**2%**	**5.43**	**0.5**	**$21**

The slide continues. bb% and PX are in a freefall and ct% didn't bounce back, so HR and BA won't either. If he can't turn things around vs. RHers, .280/20/90 might be his new baseline. Don't overbid.

Aurilia,Rich

		Year	AB	R	H	HR	RBI	SB	Avg	vL	vR	OB	Slg	OPS	bb%	ct%	h%	Eye	xBA	G	L	F	PX	hr/f	SX	SBO	RC/G	RAR	R$
Pos	35	04 2TM	399	49	98	6	44	1	246	257	240	310	353	663	8	82	29	0.52	237	40	18	42	72	4%	67	1%	3.77	-20.0	$6
Age	37	05 CIN	426	61	120	14	68	2	282	272	286	339	444	783	8	84	31	0.55	277	41	21	38	101	10%	70	2%	5.13	-5.7	$15
Bats	Right	06 CIN	440	61	132	23	70	3	300	347	276	350	518	868	7	88	30	0.67	296	38	20	42	117	14%	59	3%	6.00	0.0	$18
Health	B	07 SF	329	40	83	5	33	0	252	240	260	299	368	667	6	86	28	0.49	266	39	22	38	74	5%	52	0%	3.79	-22.6	$5
PT/Exp	C	08 SF	407	33	115	10	52	1	283	321	263	332	413	745	7	86	31	0.54	255	41	18	41	81	7%	33	2%	4.65	-12.4	$10
Consist	D	1st Half	213	14	62	6	31	1	291			352	437	789	9	87	31	0.71	256	38	17	45	92	7%	18	3%	5.27	-2.7	$6
LIMA Plan	F	2nd Half	194	19	53	4	21	0	273			309	387	695	5	86	30	0.36	252	44	19	37	70	6%	42	0%	3.95	-9.8	$4
+/- Score	-42	09 Proj	**261**	**28**	**68**	**7**	**32**	**1**	**261**			**310**	**399**	**709**	**7**	**86**	**28**	**0.52**	**265**	**40**	**20**	**40**	**85**	**8%**	**49**	**1%**	**4.24**	**-12.4**	**$6**

Used to be good for pop and a decent BA. Now, xBA trend says the BA is gone for good and 2H PX says his power might follow suit. At age 37, the chances of an 2006-esque rebound are getting slimmer.

Ausmus,Brad

		Year	AB	R	H	HR	RBI	SB	Avg	vL	vR	OB	Slg	OPS	bb%	ct%	h%	Eye	xBA	G	L	F	PX	hr/f	SX	SBO	RC/G	RAR	R$
Pos	2	04 HOU	403	38	100	5	31	2	248	308	234	305	325	630	8	86	28	0.59	246	52	18	30	48	5%	49	4%	3.40	-4.9	$5
Age	40	05 HOU	387	35	100	3	47	5	258	293	251	345	331	675	12	88	29	1.06	268	54	21	25	52	3%	47	6%	4.25	5.2	$7
Bats	Right	06 HOU	439	37	101	2	39	3	230	266	220	302	285	586	9	84	27	0.63	238	53	19	28	38	2%	52	3%	2.95	-18.5	$2
Health	A	07 HOU	349	38	82	3	25	6	235	239	234	308	324	632	10	79	29	0.50	239	51	17	31	63	3%	95	7%	3.42	-10.6	$4
PT/Exp	C	08 HOU	216	15	47	3	24	0	218	277	192	299	296	595	10	81	26	0.61	219	45	18	36	55	5%	15	3%	2.98	-8.3	$1
Consist	A	1st Half	119	6	26	1	12	0	218			262	294	556	6	82	26	0.33	231	46	19	34	57	3%	19	4%	2.33	-6.9	$0
LIMA Plan	F	2nd Half	97	9	21	2	12	0	216			339	299	638	16	79	25	0.90	208	44	17	39	52	7%	21	3%	3.68	-1.6	$1
+/- Score	-43	09 Proj	**31**	**3**	**7**	**0**	**3**	**0**	**226**			**308**	**293**	**601**	**11**	**81**	**27**	**0.64**	**223**	**49**	**18**	**33**	**46**	**4%**	**33**	**4%**	**3.08**	**-1.1**	**$0**

If he doesn't hang 'em up, let's hope MLB clubs realize that intangibles alone aren't worth seven figures. His pop is gone, and xBA confirms BA tank is for real. Only value now is in 75-team mixed leagues.

Aviles,Mike

		Year	AB	R	H	HR	RBI	SB	Avg	vL	vR	OB	Slg	OPS	bb%	ct%	h%	Eye	xBA	G	L	F	PX	hr/f	SX	SBO	RC/G	RAR	R$
Pos	64	04	0	0	0	0	0	0	0							0			0						0				
Age	28	05 aa	521	56	119	9	57	8	228			259	348	607	4	91	24	0.44	0				73		95	15%	3.11	-18.5	$8
Bats	Right	06 aaa	469	46	115	6	42	12	245			283	340	623	5	91	26	0.60	0				56		94	15%	3.34	-14.7	$7
Health	A	07 aa	538	58	129	11	57	3	239			270	362	632	4	90	25	0.40	0				71		73	8%	3.31	-17.2	$8
PT/Exp	D	08 KC	* 633	100	198	17	83	11	313	348	313	341	495	836	4	88	34	0.34	305	46	20	33	113	9%	123	9%	5.57	21.4	$25
Consist	C	1st Half	308	49	92	10	47	5	299			327	528	855	4	88	31	0.36	327	44	21	35	140	11%	124	9%	5.82	12.6	$12
LIMA Plan	C	2nd Half	325	51	106	7	36	6	326			354	465	819	4	87	36	0.33	283	47	20	33	86	8%	105	9%	5.34	8.8	$13
+/- Score	5	09 Proj	**570**	**75**	**158**	**12**	**66**	**9**	**277**			**308**	**422**	**729**	**4**	**89**	**29**	**0.39**	**290**	**47**	**20**	**33**	**87**	**7%**	**102**	**10%**	**4.39**	**0.7**	**$15**

10-51-.325 in 419 AB at KC. MLB debut couldn't have gone much better, but don't expect a repeat. PX history and 2H PX dip suggest a HR decline looms. And H% spike fueled his BA, so that will regress too.

Aybar,Erick

		Year	AB	R	H	HR	RBI	SB	Avg	vL	vR	OB	Slg	OPS	bb%	ct%	h%	Eye	xBA	G	L	F	PX	hr/f	SX	SBO	RC/G	RAR	R$
Pos	6	04	0	0	0	0	0	0	0							0			0						0				
Age	25	05 aa	535	78	142	7	42	38	265			294	376	670	4	93	28	0.55	0				65		144	53%	3.84	-6.9	$19
Bats	Both	06 LAA	* 379	56	98	5	39	27	259	250	250	291	370	660	4	91	27	0.48	275	70	3	27	66	6%	137	58%	3.70	-8.5	$13
Health	C	07 LAA	194	18	46	1	19	4	237	304	216	275	289	563	5	84	28	0.31	213	52	12	36	35	2%	79	16%	2.40	-11.3	$2
PT/Exp	D	08 LAA	346	53	96	3	39	7	277	286	274	306	384	690	4	87	31	0.31	274	52	18	30	69	3%	129	11%	3.94	-3.8	$9
Consist	C	1st Half	191	26	53	2	18	5	277			292	372	664	2	86	31	0.15	274	52	20	28	64	4%	106	16%	3.48	-4.7	$5
LIMA Plan	D+	2nd Half	155	27	43	1	21	2	277			321	400	721	6	88	31	0.53	273	52	15	32	74	2%	129	5%	4.50	0.8	$4
+/- Score	13	09 Proj	**401**	**56**	**109**	**3**	**43**	**18**	**272**			**304**	**368**	**672**	**4**	**87**	**30**	**0.37**	**261**	**53**	**15**	**32**	**60**	**3%**	**132**	**26%**	**3.77**	**-6.8**	**$12**

Young speedster who showed some bb% and Eye gains down the stretch. Leg injury and lack of green light kept his SB low. While his skill trends appear stagnant, he's still got 30 SB wheels. Watch him.

Aybar,Willy

		Year	AB	R	H	HR	RBI	SB	Avg	vL	vR	OB	Slg	OPS	bb%	ct%	h%	Eye	xBA	G	L	F	PX	hr/f	SX	SBO	RC/G	RAR	R$
Pos	50	04 aa	482	51	120	14	70	7	249			313	384	697	9	85	27	0.63	0				81		46	14%	4.16	-12.1	$11
Age	26	05 LA	* 487	44	126	4	51	4	258	250	382	320	350	669	8	91	28	0.96	264	53	16	31	62	3%	50	11%	4.08	-10.2	$8
Bats	Both	06 2NL	* 450	57	125	11	62	2	278	328	263	346	420	766	9	87	30	0.82	254	44	14	42	86	7%	42	6%	5.10	-5.0	$12
Health	C	07	0	0	0	0	0	0	0							0			0						0				
PT/Exp	F	08 TAM	324	33	82	10	33	2	253	266	245	320	410	731	9	86	27	0.73	276	40	21	40	95	9%	55	5%	4.62	-2.5	$6
Consist	A	1st Half	126	16	33	3	11	1	260			342	409	751	11	90	27	1.21	286	39	20	41	97	7%	43	6%	5.11	0.8	$3
LIMA Plan	D	2nd Half	198	17	49	7	22	1	249			306	412	717	8	84	26	0.52	270	41	21	39	94	11%	57	4%	4.31	-3.3	$4
+/- Score	-15	09 Proj	**319**	**34**	**83**	**8**	**37**	**2**	**260**			**326**	**400**	**726**	**9**	**87**	**28**	**0.77**	**268**	**41**	**19**	**40**	**87**	**7%**	**46**	**7%**	**4.60**	**-2.6**	**$7**

He's becoming an effective utility guy, but is there still upside for more? Base skills confirm he handles the plate well. The problem? Neither his power nor speed are unique skills. Don't bet on an age 26 breakout.

Baker,Jeff

		Year	AB	R	H	HR	RBI	SB	Avg	vL	vR	OB	Slg	OPS	bb%	ct%	h%	Eye	xBA	G	L	F	PX	hr/f	SX	SBO	RC/G	RAR	R$
Pos	43	04	0	0	0	0	0	0	0							0			0						0				
Age	27	05 aaa	228	25	60	8	26	2	263			294	439	733	4	89	27	0.38	0				105		66	6%	4.37	0.2	$6
Bats	Right	06 COL	* 539	65	158	22	101	7	292	438	341	335	497	832	6	83	32	0.38	312	44	28	28	120	17%	89	6%	5.59	14.9	$21
Health	A	07 COL	144	17	32	4	12	0	222	246	205	287	347	634	8	72	28	0.33	218	40	20	39	75	10%	72	0%	3.20	-6.6	$1
PT/Exp	D	08 COL	299	55	80	12	48	4	268	290	256	326	468	794	8	72	34	0.31	275	43	24	33	148	17%	100	6%	5.44	5.7	$12
Consist	F	1st Half	140	26	39	5	24	1	279			322	493	815	6	70	37	0.21	281	41	24	36	175	14%	72	4%	5.77	4.0	$6
LIMA Plan	D	2nd Half	159	29	41	7	24	3	258			330	447	776	10	73	31	0.40	271	44	25	31	126	20%	105	7%	5.16	1.8	$6
+/- Score	9	09 Proj	**254**	**38**	**66**	**10**	**36**	**3**	**260**			**315**	**453**	**769**	**8**	**75**	**31**	**0.33**	**273**	**42**	**23**	**35**	**127**	**16%**	**94**	**4%**	**4.95**	**1.8**	**$8**

Remove '07 and you've got a hitter with surging power skills. But he still hits too many GB to expect a HR spike, and his ct% isn't showing signs of coming back. He's a guy to lease for short periods; don't ride him.

Baker,John

		Year	AB	R	H	HR	RBI	SB	Avg	vL	vR	OB	Slg	OPS	bb%	ct%	h%	Eye	xBA	G	L	F	PX	hr/f	SX	SBO	RC/G	RAR	R$
Pos	2	04 a/a	489	62	125	12	70	1	256			304	409	713	7	80	30	0.35	0				102		63	3%	4.24	2.5	$11
Age	28	05 aaa	346	33	70	4	32	1	202			252	312	564	6	80	24	0.33	0				82		68	2%	2.43	-15.9	$1
Bats	Left	06 aaa	293	39	70	3	30	5	240			312	338	650	9	79	29	0.51	0				72		92	6%	3.65	-6.4	$4
Health	A	07 aa	270	26	61	6	30	2	226			283	338	622	7	77	27	0.36	0				79		45	3%	3.07	-10.6	$3
PT/Exp	F	08 FLA	* 390	58	109	10	55	1	281	213	327	361	424	785	11	79	33	0.60	282	49	25	26	101	12%	49	2%	5.38	13.0	$12
Consist	C	1st Half	178	25	47	5	23	1	263			328	410	737	9	83	29	0.57	0				95		68	6%	4.67	2.4	$5
LIMA Plan	D	2nd Half	212	33	63	5	32	0	295			387	436	824	13	76	37	0.62	270	49	25	26	106	12%	29	0%	6.04	10.7	$7
+/- Score	-14	09 Proj	**312**	**41**	**80**	**7**	**40**	**2**	**256**			**328**	**387**	**715**	**10**	**79**	**31**	**0.50**	**275**	**49**	**25**	**26**	**92**	**10%**	**64**	**3%**	**4.42**	**1.6**	**$7**

5-32-.299 in 197 AB at FLA. .300 BA in Aug/Sept was nice, but don't bet on a repeat. 2H BA surge was h% driven. And as a GB hitter, we can't bank on sustained power. He's a good 2nd catcher, not a frontliner.

STEPHEN NICKRAND

Bako,Paul

		Year	AB	R	H	HR	RBI	SB	Avg	vL	vR	OB	Slg	OPS	bb%	ct%	h%	Eye	xBA	G	L	F	PX	hr/f	SX	SBO	RC/G	RAR	R$
Pos	2	04 CHC	138	13	28	1	10	1	203	95	222	281	283	564	10	79	25	0.52	234	49	19	33	63	3%	46	3%	2.57	-5.4	($0)
Age	36	05 LA	40	1	10	0	4	0	250	250	250	362	300	662	15	70	36	0.58	115	67	19	15	52	0%	0	0%	4.02	0.3	$0
Bats	Left	06 KC	153	7	32	0	10	0	209	200	210	262	229	491	7	70	30	0.24	175	56	19	24	20	0%	11	0%	1.21	-15.2	($1)
Health	C	07 BAL	156	13	32	1	8	0	205	192	208	275	256	531	9	68	30	0.30	211	56	23	21	40	5%	52	2%	1.83	-12.1	($1)
PT/Exp	F	08 CIN	299	30	65	6	35	0	217	197	224	297	328	625	10	70	29	0.38	226	56	18	26	81	11%	49	3%	3.21	-9.2	$3
Consist	C	1st Half	183	22	41	6	24	0	224			300	377	678	10	71	28	0.38	245	52	19	29	103	16%	72	4%	3.88	-1.9	$3
LIMA Plan	F	2nd Half	116	8	24	0	11	0	207			292	250	542	11	68	30	0.38	185	62	17	21	46	0%	17	0%	2.11	-7.6	($0)
+/- Score	22	09 Proj	199	16	42	2	17	0	211			285	283	568	9	70	29	0.35	216	57	19	23	57	5%	46	2%	2.41	-11.3	$0

Hot in April (.310, 125 PX, 77% ct%), but back to being crummy afterwards (.189, 65 PX, 68% ct%). Rising bb% and xBA may mean late career skills spike. But that only takes him from horrible to just really bad.

Baldelli,Rocco

		Year	AB	R	H	HR	RBI	SB	Avg	vL	vR	OB	Slg	OPS	bb%	ct%	h%	Eye	xBA	G	L	F	PX	hr/f	SX	SBO	RC/G	RAR	R$
Pos	0	04 TAM	518	79	145	16	74	17	280	331	264	319	436	756	5	83	31	0.34	267	52	13	35	94	11%	119	16%	4.65	-9.6	$19
Age	27	05 TAM	0	0	0	0	0	0	0							0			0						0				
Bats	Right	06 TAM	* 411	66	128	16	61	10	311	297	303	340	527	867	4	81	36	0.22	293	51	16	34	134	14%	134	13%	5.96	-5.2	$18
Health	F	07 TAM	137	16	28	5	12	4	204	156	219	253	358	611	6	74	24	0.26	236	38	18	44	106	11%	78	19%	2.78	-14.9	$2
PT/Exp	F	08 TAM	80	12	21	4	13	0	263	292	219	322	475	797	8	69	33	0.28	250	49	15	36	159	20%	31	0%	5.50	1.3	$3
Consist	F	1st Half	0	0	0	0	0	0	0							0			0										
LIMA Plan	F	2nd Half	80	12	21	4	13	0	263			322	475	797	8	69	33	0.28	250	49	15	36	159	20%	31	0%	5.50	1.3	$3
+/- Score	-49	09 Proj	230	34	62	8	32	0	270			313	448	761	6	76	32	0.26	259	48	15	37	122	13%	66	3%	4.77	-5.2	$7

With rare cellular disorder, he's now highly unlikely to play every day. Returned 8/10 and peaked at 1.105 OPS on 9/6, but .483 OPS after that highlights the fatigue. Power skills intact, but let someone else take the risk.

Balentien,Wladimir

		Year	AB	R	H	HR	RBI	SB	Avg	vL	vR	OB	Slg	OPS	bb%	ct%	h%	Eye	xBA	G	L	F	PX	hr/f	SX	SBO	RC/G	RAR	R$
Pos	98	04	0	0	0	0	0	0	0							0			0						0				
Age	24	05	0	0	0	0	0	0	0							0			0						0				
Bats	Right	06 aa	444	72	96	21	77	13	216			322	412	734	13	69	26	0.50	0				136		90	17%	4.78	-6.0	$13
Health	A	07 aaa	477	65	122	19	71	13	256			324	433	757	9	79	29	0.48	0				111		88	14%	4.82	-5.3	$15
PT/Exp	D	08 SEA	* 476	61	102	20	67	2	214	218	194	277	406	684	8	74	24	0.34	254	47	14	39	137	15%	42	8%	3.85	-22.6	$9
Consist	B	1st Half	215	26	41	10	27	1	191			268	377	645	9	75	21	0.43	248	46	14	40	125	15%	44	7%	3.36	-13.8	$3
LIMA Plan	C	2nd Half	261	35	61	11	40	1	232			286	430	716	7	73	28	0.28	259	48	14	38	146	15%	46	10%	4.26	-8.8	$6
+/- Score	25	09 Proj	418	57	96	18	62	7	230			300	420	720	9	75	26	0.40	257	47	14	39	130	15%	73	12%	4.37	-12.9	$11

7-24-.202 in 243 AB with SEA.
PROS:
- Solid power and bb%
CONS:
- Short high-minors time, ct% should develop into low-BA, high-HR hitter, just not this year.

Barajas,Rod

		Year	AB	R	H	HR	RBI	SB	Avg	vL	vR	OB	Slg	OPS	bb%	ct%	h%	Eye	xBA	G	L	F	PX	hr/f	SX	SBO	RC/G	RAR	R$
Pos	2	04 TEX	362	51	91	15	58	0	251	248	249	277	453	730	3	82	27	0.20	250	29	13	57	125	9%	55	2%	4.22	-1.2	$9
Age	33	05 TEX	410	53	104	21	60	0	254	272	251	298	466	764	6	83	26	0.37	279	29	20	51	131	12%	27	0%	4.70	8.2	$12
Bats	Right	06 TEX	344	49	88	11	41	0	256	156	279	291	410	701	5	85	27	0.33	250	32	17	51	94	7%	41	0%	3.97	-4.4	$7
Health	B	07 PHI	122	16	28	4	10	0	230	226	231	343	393	736	15	80	26	0.88	239	31	15	54	109	8%	29	3%	4.91	1.8	$2
PT/Exp	D	08 TOR	349	44	87	11	49	0	249	204	270	284	410	694	5	83	27	0.28	258	37	17	46	107	8%	34	0%	3.87	-3.3	$8
Consist	B	1st Half	159	20	45	6	25	0	283			325	478	803	6	82	31	0.36	274	39	17	44	131	10%	26	0%	5.26	4.8	$5
LIMA Plan	D	2nd Half	190	24	42	5	24	0	221			249	353	601	4	83	24	0.21	243	35	18	47	87	7%	43	0%	2.71	-8.6	$3
+/- Score	-10	09 Proj	381	50	93	12	47	0	244			288	398	687	6	82	27	0.35	249	34	17	49	102	8%	38	1%	3.86	-4.4	$7

For a player with below average hr/f, sure hits a lot of FB. This leads to lots of routine flyouts, limiting h% and BA and leaving those few balls that clear the fence as his only contribution. Value here is AB driven.

Bard,Josh

		Year	AB	R	H	HR	RBI	SB	Avg	vL	vR	OB	Slg	OPS	bb%	ct%	h%	Eye	xBA	G	L	F	PX	hr/f	SX	SBO	RC/G	RAR	R$
Pos	2	04 a/a	186	22	36	3	16	0	194			245	285	530	6	86	21	0.47	0				60		42	0%	2.17	-11.2	$0
Age	31	05 CLE	83	6	16	1	9	0	193	148	214	272	277	549	10	87	21	0.82	233	43	18	39	59	4%	16	0%	2.63	-3.6	($0)
Bats	Both	06 2TM	249	30	83	9	40	1	333	333	333	405	522	927	11	83	37	0.71	295	52	21	27	120	16%	30	1%	7.05	17.4	$10
Health	D	07 SD	389	42	111	5	51	0	285	376	250	367	404	770	11	85	33	0.86	267	52	18	30	81	5%	39	1%	5.31	9.6	$9
PT/Exp	D	08 SD	178	11	36	1	16	0	202	135	230	276	270	545	9	86	23	0.72	246	47	22	31	51	2%	14	0%	2.55	-9.2	($0)
Consist	F	1st Half	130	9	26	0	7	0	200			278	262	539	10	86	23	0.78	256	46	23	31	52	0%	18	0%	2.56	-6.7	($1)
LIMA Plan	D	2nd Half	48	2	10	1	9	0	208			269	292	561	8	85	22	0.57	187	51	17	32	48	8%	1	0%	2.52	-2.5	$0
+/- Score	19	09 Proj	342	35	90	6	38	0	263			336	383	719	10	85	30	0.72	271	50	21	29	82	7%	28	1%	4.57	3.2	$6

Wrist surgery after '07 season; still needed cortisone injection in May '08. Lost two months to ankle sprain. Injuries explain this power outage; poor h% a combo of that plus bad luck. Kept Eye intact; some BA rebound likely.

Barmes,Clint

		Year	AB	R	H	HR	RBI	SB	Avg	vL	vR	OB	Slg	OPS	bb%	ct%	h%	Eye	xBA	G	L	F	PX	hr/f	SX	SBO	RC/G	RAR	R$
Pos	46	04 aaa	533	70	155	13	35	14	292			316	442	758	3	93	30	0.48	0				88		95	20%	4.71	5.5	$16
Age	30	05 COL	350	55	101	10	46	6	289	289	283	320	434	754	4	90	30	0.44	282	36	23	41	87	8%	90	11%	4.63	0.7	$13
Bats	Right	06 COL	478	57	105	7	56	5	220	267	209	254	335	589	4	85	25	0.31	236	34	18	48	72	4%	92	10%	2.75	-27.4	$5
Health	C	07 COL	* 465	50	106	8	30	6	229	444	143	255	337	592	3	86	25	0.26	205	21	17	63	64	3%	87	12%	2.73	-28.2	$4
PT/Exp	C	08 COL	393	47	114	11	44	13	290	307	283	320	468	788	4	82	33	0.25	261	29	22	49	112	7%	128	19%	5.01	2.7	$14
Consist	C	1st Half	151	17	48	5	20	3	318			352	530	882	5	84	35	0.33	296	31	24	44	135	9%	93	14%	6.18	5.8	$6
LIMA Plan	D+	2nd Half	242	30	66	6	24	10	273			299	430	729	4	81	31	0.20	238	27	21	52	97	6%	138	23%	4.27	-3.5	$8
+/- Score	-11	09 Proj	423	50	112	10	42	10	265			294	415	709	4	82	30	0.23	249	30	21	48	95	6%	112	16%	4.06	-8.0	$11

	OPS	PX
Home:	.932	142
Away:	.644	78

He owes Coors a nice note. Also, while others see BA back to '05 level, you see ct% decline, inflated h%. Heed xBA warning.

Barrett,Michael

		Year	AB	R	H	HR	RBI	SB	Avg	vL	vR	OB	Slg	OPS	bb%	ct%	h%	Eye	xBA	G	L	F	PX	hr/f	SX	SBO	RC/G	RAR	R$
Pos	2	04 CHC	456	55	131	16	65	1	287	248	299	335	489	824	7	86	31	0.52	304	48	20	32	118	13%	70	5%	5.59	22.9	$14
Age	32	05 CHC	424	48	117	16	61	0	276	320	254	338	479	817	9	86	29	0.66	312	43	24	33	127	13%	44	3%	5.60	22.1	$13
Bats	Right	06 CHC	375	54	115	16	53	0	307	313	305	363	517	880	8	89	31	0.80	304	45	20	36	116	13%	50	1%	6.27	19.7	$14
Health	F	07 2NL	344	29	84	9	41	2	244	222	249	284	372	656	5	83	27	0.33	249	40	19	41	81	8%	35	5%	3.46	-10.0	$5
PT/Exp	D	08 SD	94	9	19	2	9	0	202	296	164	272	298	570	9	83	22	0.56	242	41	22	38	60	7%	24	0%	2.61	-4.7	$0
Consist	D	1st Half	91	9	18	2	9	0	198			270	297	567	9	82	22	0.56	244	39	22	38	63	7%	25	0%	2.57	-4.7	$0
LIMA Plan	F	2nd Half	3	0	1	0	0	0	333			333	333	666	0	100	33		0	67	0	33	0	0%		0%	3.66	-0.0	$0
+/- Score	15	09 Proj	254	28	65	8	32	0	256			313	414	727	8	85	27	0.56	277	42	21	37	96	10%	45	2%	4.48	1.7	$6

Lost much of '07 to concussion; lost '08 after fouling ball off face. Still owns '04-'06 BPIs, though, and h% plus hr/f rebounds should help his ailing BA and power. Possible sleeper if he can regain pre-injury form.

Bartlett,Jason

		Year	AB	R	H	HR	RBI	SB	Avg	vL	vR	OB	Slg	OPS	bb%	ct%	h%	Eye	xBA	G	L	F	PX	hr/f	SX	SBO	RC/G	RAR	R$
Pos	6	04 aaa	269	46	83	2	25	6	309			376	439	815	10	88	35	0.88	0				76		129	10%	5.81	11.2	$9
Age	29	05 MIN	* 453	68	123	7	44	6	272	290	226	339	375	714	9	85	31	0.68	256	47	18	35	67	5%	92	6%	4.47	-1.2	$11
Bats	Right	06 MIN	* 568	85	172	3	51	16	303	314	307	339	407	746	5	87	35	0.42	273	44	22	34	72	2%	112	15%	4.69	4.4	$16
Health	A	07 MIN	510	75	135	5	43	23	265	319	245	330	361	691	9	86	30	0.68	254	44	20	36	60	3%	140	17%	4.23	-0.9	$14
PT/Exp	B	08 TAM	454	48	130	1	37	20	286	379	248	319	361	681	5	85	34	0.32	261	49	21	30	56	1%	107	21%	3.84	-6.3	$12
Consist	A	1st Half	266	23	67	0	18	16	252			289	282	571	5	85	30	0.35	239	51	20	28	23	0%	105	26%	2.55	-14.1	$6
LIMA Plan	C+	2nd Half	188	25	63	1	19	4	335			362	473	836	4	85	39	0.28	290	46	21	33	104	2%	95	14%	5.68	6.8	$7
+/- Score	-34	09 Proj	511	68	149	3	45	23	292			335	390	725	6	85	34	0.45	267	46	21	33	69	2%	125	20%	4.48	1.9	$16

A few extra 2B and 3B inflated 2H PX, but don't read too much into that -- he's no power hitter. Few 2H steals due to knee sprain; when healthy, will run. But beware his problems vs. RHP, which could limit his AB.

Barton,Brian

		Year	AB	R	H	HR	RBI	SB	Avg	vL	vR	OB	Slg	OPS	bb%	ct%	h%	Eye	xBA	G	L	F	PX	hr/f	SX	SBO	RC/G	RAR	R$
Pos	7	04	0	0	0	0	0	0	0							0			0						0				
Age	27	05	0	0	0	0	0	0	0							0			0						0				
Bats	Right	06 aa	151	29	47	5	23	13	308			357	434	791	7	83	35	0.43	0				73		111	37%	5.10	-0.5	$9
Health	B	07 a/a	476	54	126	8	55	18	265			325	359	684	8	77	33	0.38	0				67		82	20%	3.92	-18.1	$13
PT/Exp	F	08 STL	* 226	33	57	4	22	4	252	258	281	332	381	713	11	71	34	0.42	237	51	17	32	94	8%	108	14%	4.52	-6.2	$5
Consist	B	1st Half	117	18	30	2	11	3	256			341	385	726	11	74	33	0.50	0				95		103	11%	4.70	-2.5	$3
LIMA Plan	F	2nd Half	109	15	27	2	11	1	248			322	376	698	10	68	35	0.34	224	51	17	32	93	9%	103	16%	4.35	-3.6	$2
+/- Score	7	09 Proj	159	22	42	3	18	5	264			331	378	710	9	74	34	0.39	238	51	17	32	80	8%	99	20%	4.33	-5.0	$5

2-13-.268 in 153 AB at STL. Ct% trend highlights struggles as he's moved up. That plus low LD% suggest he has some work to do to bring that '06 BA to the Majors. Could use more Triple-A time.

JOSHUA RANDALL

Barton,Daric

			AB	R	H	HR	RBI	SB	Avg	vL	vR	OB	Slg	OPS	bb%	ct%	h%	Eye	xBA	G	L	F	PX	hr/f	SX	SBO	RC/G	RAR	R$
Pos	3	04	0	0	0	0	0	0	0							0			0						0				
Age	23	05 aa	212	32	62	4	30	1	292			376	451	826	12	89	31	1.24	0				106		60	3%	6.04	4.1	$7
Bats	Left	06 aaa	147	22	36	2	19	1	247			366	367	732	16	88	27	1.51	0				68		88	2%	5.16	-2.4	$3
Health	A	07 OAK	* 588	87	164	11	67	4	279	296	378	360	423	784	11	89	30	1.12	285	32	24	44	96	5%	67	5%	5.50	4.1	$15
PT/Exp	C	08 OAK	451	59	101	9	47	2	224	273	208	322	344	665	13	78	27	0.66	226	35	19	46	78	6%	81	2%	3.93	-18.5	$6
Consist	B	1st Half	252	34	58	3	24	0	230			333	325	659	13	73	30	0.58	213	34	22	44	68	4%	73	1%	3.87	-10.7	$3
LIMA Plan	D+	2nd Half	199	25	43	6	23	2	216			307	367	673	12	84	23	0.81	244	35	16	49	90	7%	83	4%	4.04	-7.5	$3
+/- Score	7	09 Proj	**459**	**64**	**113**	**10**	**53**	**3**	**246**			**341**	**386**	**726**	**13**	**84**	**27**	**0.90**	**250**	**35**	**19**	**47**	**88**	**6%**	**80**	**3%**	**4.78**	**-6.6**	**$9**

Forgot how to make contact in 1H, but promising signs in 2H:
- ct% recovered
- Nearly doubled hr/f
- 6 HR, 50% FB% in Aug-Sept

Troubles vs RH should correct. Still young enough to blossom.

Bautista,Jose

			AB	R	H	HR	RBI	SB	Avg	vL	vR	OB	Slg	OPS	bb%	ct%	h%	Eye	xBA	G	L	F	PX	hr/f	SX	SBO	RC/G	RAR	R$
Pos	5	04 2TM	88	6	18	0	2	0	205			263	239	502	7	55	38	0.18	0				44		31	5%	1.54	-9.6	($1)
Age	28	05 PIT	* 515	53	122	16	69	7	238			294	390	684	7	82	26	0.45	0				98		66	10%	3.89	-13.9	$12
Bats	Right	06 PIT	* 501	70	122	18	60	4	243	283	216	323	420	743	11	74	29	0.46	233	40	13	47	117	10%	71	7%	4.79	-10.6	$11
Health	A	07 PIT	532	75	135	15	63	6	254	256	253	338	414	752	11	81	29	0.67	255	40	16	43	106	8%	73	6%	4.97	-10.0	$13
PT/Exp	B	08 2TM	370	45	88	15	54	1	238	250	233	312	405	718	10	75	28	0.44	241	46	15	39	113	14%	35	2%	4.34	-8.7	$9
Consist	A	1st Half	232	32	60	9	35	1	259			331	431	762	10	75	31	0.44	251	44	17	39	119	13%	42	3%	4.95	-1.2	$7
LIMA Plan	F	2nd Half	138	13	28	6	19	0	203			281	362	643	10	75	22	0.44	211	50	11	39	101	15%	14	0%	3.32	-7.8	$2
+/- Score	-22	09 Proj	**252**	**31**	**60**	**9**	**33**	**2**	**238**			**315**	**407**	**721**	**10**	**77**	**27**	**0.49**	**246**	**44**	**14**	**42**	**111**	**11%**	**58**	**4%**	**4.44**	**-5.3**	**$5**

Turned more doubles into HR, but worsening FB% puts a crimp in power upside. Returned to his strikeout ways, placing BA at risk. Throw in the lack of speed and you get a player consistently below replacement level.

Bay,Jason

			AB	R	H	HR	RBI	SB	Avg	vL	vR	OB	Slg	OPS	bb%	ct%	h%	Eye	xBA	G	L	F	PX	hr/f	SX	SBO	RC/G	RAR	R$
Pos	7	04 PIT	411	61	116	26	82	4	282	265	287	347	550	897	9	69	35	0.32	268	40	17	43	183	22%	81	10%	6.97	18.1	$19
Age	30	05 PIT	599	110	183	32	101	21	306	342	292	401	559	960	14	76	36	0.67	295	38	22	40	170	17%	133	11%	7.76	39.6	$34
Bats	Right	06 PIT	570	101	163	35	109	11	286	304	280	394	532	926	15	73	34	0.65	262	41	15	44	155	19%	87	7%	7.43	35.0	$27
Health	A	07 PIT	538	78	133	21	84	4	247	227	254	322	418	740	10	74	30	0.42	236	38	17	45	114	12%	73	3%	4.68	-10.8	$14
PT/Exp	A	08 2TM	577	111	165	31	101	10	286	252	296	374	522	896	12	76	33	0.59	272	38	17	46	154	15%	111	6%	6.80	26.9	$27
Consist	F	1st Half	292	56	83	16	43	6	284			389	531	920	15	78	32	0.77	281	36	17	47	160	15%	101	6%	7.21	17.0	$14
LIMA Plan	B	2nd Half	285	55	82	15	58	4	288			358	512	870	10	75	34	0.43	263	39	16	45	147	16%	102	5%	6.36	9.8	$14
+/- Score	13	09 Proj	**587**	**103**	**163**	**33**	**104**	**9**	**278**			**363**	**516**	**878**	**12**	**75**	**32**	**0.52**	**268**	**38**	**17**	**45**	**155**	**17%**	**101**	**6%**	**6.57**	**23.5**	**$26**

Across the board skills rebound means that 2007 likely an injury driven outlier. So hr/f could revert even higher. After trade he opened up swing, hit more fly balls. Ceiling now looks like: UP: 2005 with 8-10 more HRs

Belliard,Ronnie

			AB	R	H	HR	RBI	SB	Avg	vL	vR	OB	Slg	OPS	bb%	ct%	h%	Eye	xBA	G	L	F	PX	hr/f	SX	SBO	RC/G	RAR	R$
Pos	354	04 CLE	599	78	169	12	70	3	282	319	263	347	426	773	9	84	32	0.61	270	44	19	37	98	6%	54	3%	5.17	3.0	$14
Age	34	05 CLE	536	71	152	17	78	2	284	287	285	327	450	777	6	87	30	0.49	284	45	18	37	105	10%	50	3%	4.98	-1.7	$17
Bats	Right	06 2TM	544	63	148	13	67	2	272	220	295	317	403	720	6	85	30	0.44	261	46	19	35	81	8%	44	4%	4.31	-21.8	$12
Health	B	07 WAS	511	57	148	11	58	3	290	329	275	334	427	761	6	86	32	0.47	264	44	17	39	89	6%	59	2%	4.83	-18.6	$13
PT/Exp	B	08 WAS	296	37	85	11	46	3	287	307	279	366	473	839	11	80	33	0.64	289	42	23	35	125	13%	44	6%	6.01	2.3	$11
Consist	B	1st Half	122	18	26	6	20	1	213			333	426	760	15	79	22	0.85	276	38	19	43	139	14%	45	3%	5.14	-2.2	$3
LIMA Plan	F	2nd Half	174	19	59	5	26	2	339			392	506	897	8	82	39	0.47	299	45	26	29	116	12%	38	7%	6.55	3.8	$8
+/- Score	-18	09 Proj	**288**	**35**	**82**	**9**	**40**	**2**	**285**			**347**	**444**	**791**	**9**	**83**	**32**	**0.56**	**276**	**44**	**20**	**36**	**105**	**10%**	**44**	**4%**	**5.29**	**-4.8**	**$9**

Slow start, injuries reduced playing time. Can we attribute power spike to increased plate patience and a bunch more line drives? With more AB, we'd see if it was sustainable. This sample size is just too small.

Beltran,Carlos

			AB	R	H	HR	RBI	SB	Avg	vL	vR	OB	Slg	OPS	bb%	ct%	h%	Eye	xBA	G	L	F	PX	hr/f	SX	SBO	RC/G	RAR	R$
Pos	8	04 2TM	599	121	160	38	104	42	267	276	264	365	548	912	13	83	27	0.91	298	39	15	46	157	17%	167	27%	6.92	38.9	$35
Age	32	05 NYM	582	83	155	16	78	17	266	308	254	331	414	745	9	84	30	0.58	272	44	19	37	96	9%	102	14%	4.75	3.2	$20
Bats	Both	06 NYM	510	127	140	41	116	18	275	247	288	388	594	983	16	81	27	0.96	311	37	17	47	186	21%	108	14%	7.87	50.2	$31
Health	A	07 NYM	554	93	153	33	112	23	276	304	265	356	525	882	11	80	29	0.62	290	38	19	43	150	17%	113	16%	6.44	30.1	$28
PT/Exp	A	08 NYM	606	116	172	27	112	25	284	326	266	378	500	878	13	84	30	0.96	309	45	22	33	131	16%	127	15%	6.57	31.4	$32
Consist	B	1st Half	303	58	82	12	54	11	271			376	479	854	14	83	29	0.96	304	48	20	32	130	15%	124	12%	6.39	14.4	$14
LIMA Plan	B+	2nd Half	303	58	90	15	58	14	297			381	521	902	12	86	31	0.95	314	41	24	35	131	17%	122	17%	6.74	16.9	$18
+/- Score	-4	09 Proj	**550**	**101**	**154**	**26**	**106**	**18**	**280**			**371**	**501**	**872**	**13**	**83**	**30**	**0.84**	**295**	**41**	**20**	**39**	**134**	**15%**	**117**	**12%**	**6.46**	**28.7**	**$27**

Swapping out power for speed, an oddity for a 32-year-old coming off knee surgeries. His sudden GB tendency explains the power decline. Stable BPIs, we will continue to hold out for that long-projected .300 season.

Beltre,Adrian

			AB	R	H	HR	RBI	SB	Avg	vL	vR	OB	Slg	OPS	bb%	ct%	h%	Eye	xBA	G	L	F	PX	hr/f	SX	SBO	RC/G	RAR	R$
Pos	5	04 LA	598	104	200	48	121	7	334	291	347	389	629	1017	8	85	33	0.61	319	41	18	40	159	23%	61	5%	7.67	41.0	$38
Age	30	05 SEA	603	69	154	19	87	3	255	281	249	300	413	712	6	82	28	0.35	271	46	19	35	104	11%	56	3%	4.16	-6.0	$15
Bats	Right	06 SEA	620	88	166	25	89	11	268	280	264	319	465	784	7	81	30	0.40	276	37	21	42	121	12%	98	11%	5.07	1.1	$19
Health	A	07 SEA	595	87	164	26	99	14	276	280	274	319	482	801	6	83	30	0.37	289	44	17	39	132	13%	101	12%	5.21	5.7	$23
PT/Exp	A	08 SEA	556	74	148	25	77	8	266	338	240	327	457	784	8	84	28	0.56	287	40	22	39	116	14%	70	7%	5.09	3.4	$18
Consist	A	1st Half	299	40	74	15	41	7	247			322	441	764	10	83	25	0.66	282	38	22	40	115	15%	69	10%	4.91	0.3	$10
LIMA Plan	C	2nd Half	257	34	74	10	36	1	288			332	475	807	6	84	31	0.43	293	42	22	37	116	13%	55	3%	5.28	2.9	$9
+/- Score	-10	09 Proj	**594**	**82**	**163**	**26**	**89**	**9**	**274**			**326**	**473**	**799**	**7**	**83**	**29**	**0.45**	**287**	**41**	**20**	**39**	**122**	**14%**	**85**	**8%**	**5.22**	**5.8**	**$21**

Played through thumb and shoulder woes without a DL stint until he decided to go under the knife in Sept, but managed to maintain rock steady BPI levels. Assuming full recovery, you can ink in yet another similar year.

Berkman,Lance

			AB	R	H	HR	RBI	SB	Avg	vL	vR	OB	Slg	OPS	bb%	ct%	h%	Eye	xBA	G	L	F	PX	hr/f	SX	SBO	RC/G	RAR	R$
Pos	3	04 HOU	544	104	172	30	106	9	316	272	329	446	566	1012	19	81	34	1.26	303	40	21	39	151	17%	74	7%	8.57	38.9	$30
Age	33	05 HOU	468	76	137	24	82	4	293	296	295	408	524	931	16	85	30	1.26	320	46	23	32	142	19%	62	3%	7.37	23.0	$21
Bats	Both	06 HOU	536	95	169	45	136	3	315	266	335	421	621	1042	15	80	32	0.92	307	39	19	42	173	25%	35	3%	8.58	37.4	$32
Health	A	07 HOU	561	95	156	34	102	7	278	265	282	382	510	891	14	78	30	0.75	279	44	18	38	139	21%	70	5%	6.75	9.9	$24
PT/Exp	A	08 HOU	554	114	173	29	106	18	312	276	327	417	567	983	15	81	35	0.92	307	43	18	39	163	17%	113	11%	8.03	34.7	$33
Consist	D	1st Half	296	72	108	22	68	12	365			447	699	1146	13	83	39	0.86	344	44	16	39	202	23%	129	14%	9.75	30.0	$25
LIMA Plan	B+	2nd Half	258	42	65	7	38	6	252			383	415	798	18	78	30	0.96	267	40	21	38	116	9%	82	9%	5.90	1.3	$8
+/- Score	15	09 Proj	**532**	**98**	**157**	**30**	**102**	**8**	**295**			**405**	**537**	**941**	**16**	**80**	**32**	**0.91**	**294**	**42**	**19**	**39**	**150**	**18%**	**76**	**6%**	**7.48**	**23.8**	**$27**

Monster 1st half buoyed by fluky h%. Opened up swing in 2H only to be hurt by fluky hr/f. Remove the fluky and you're still left with elite skill set. However, at 33, armor cracks can't be ignored completely. Don't overbid.

Bernadina,Rogearvi

			AB	R	H	HR	RBI	SB	Avg	vL	vR	OB	Slg	OPS	bb%	ct%	h%	Eye	xBA	G	L	F	PX	hr/f	SX	SBO	RC/G	RAR	R$
Pos	8	04	0	0	0	0	0	0	0							0			0						0				
Age	24	05	0	0	0	0	0	0	0							0			0						0				
Bats	Left	06	0	0	0	0	0	0	0							0			0						0				
Health	A	07 a/a	413	56	96	5	33	35	232			300	317	617	9	80	28	0.49	0				58		125	45%	3.19	-17.5	$12
PT/Exp	F	08 WAS	* 533	74	148	7	45	37	277	300	197	334	385	719	8	79	34	0.42	275	67	15	17	71	9%	141	33%	4.41	-5.1	$20
Consist	C	1st Half	276	37	74	4	30	20	268			324	379	704	8	79	33	0.40	0	50	33	17	70	11%	148	40%	4.21	-4.4	$11
LIMA Plan	F	2nd Half	257	37	74	3	15	16	286			344	391	735	8	80	35	0.43	273	70	13	17	72	8%	136	26%	4.63	-0.8	$10
+/- Score	4	09 Proj	**55**	**8**	**14**	**1**	**4**	**4**	**255**			**316**	**364**	**680**	**8**	**80**	**31**	**0.45**	**274**	**68**	**15**	**17**	**68**	**9%**	**143**	**38%**	**3.97**	**-1.1**	**$2**

0-2-.211 in 76 AB at WAS. Light is always green for speedster who runs at every opportunity, but can he get on base? He's a grounder machine and draws walks, but not enough contact to be valuable.

Berroa,Angel

			AB	R	H	HR	RBI	SB	Avg	vL	vR	OB	Slg	OPS	bb%	ct%	h%	Eye	xBA	G	L	F	PX	hr/f	SX	SBO	RC/G	RAR	R$
Pos	6	04 KC	* 563	78	147	10	51	16	261	259	263	293	385	678	4	83	30	0.26	262	53	16	32	77	7%	126	20%	3.72	-12.4	$14
Age	31	05 KC	608	68	164	11	55	7	270	278	266	291	375	666	3	82	31	0.17	256	49	20	31	66	7%	88	8%	3.44	-19.8	$13
Bats	Right	06 KC	474	45	111	9	54	3	234	217	241	256	333	589	3	81	27	0.16	246	53	17	30	63	8%	65	4%	2.51	-27.2	$5
Health	A	07 aa	307	30	64	5	26	2	208			248	293	541	5	84	23	0.33	0				58		48	5%	2.15	-21.3	$1
PT/Exp	D	08 LA	* 415	51	96	8	36	3	232	219	235	277	351	628	6	84	26	0.39	270	44	22	34	80	7%	69	5%	3.24	-17.5	$6
Consist	B	1st Half	249	29	55	7	20	3	222			254	356	610	4	85	24	0.29	284	51	21	28	85	12%	64	9%	2.91	-13.2	$3
LIMA Plan	F	2nd Half	166	22	41	1	16	0	247			309	343	653	8	83	29	0.54	257	41	22	36	72	2%	58	0%	3.72	-4.5	$2
+/- Score	29	09 Proj	**189**	**22**	**44**	**3**	**17**	**1**	**233**			**274**	**343**	**617**	**5**	**83**	**27**	**0.34**	**260**	**47**	**20**	**33**	**73**	**6%**	**74**	**5%**	**3.08**	**-8.1**	**$2**

1-16-.230 in 226 AB at LA. Former Rookie of the Year made the descent to Double-A before rebounding slightly in LA. But until he can manage a full season with an OBA over.300, there is no value here at all.

MICHAEL ROY

Betancourt,Yunies			AB	R	H	HR	RBI	SB	Avg	vL	vR	OB	Slg	OPS	bb%	ct%	h%	Eye	xBA	G	L	F	PX	hr/f	SX	SBO	RC/G	RAR	R$
Pos	6	04	0	0	0	0	0	0	0							0			0						0				
Age	27	05 SEA	* 621	57	157	7	58	17	253	283	248	282	367	649	4	91	27	0.47	251	38	17	45	66	3%	113	25%	3.60	-18.0	$12
Bats	Right	06 SEA	558	68	161	8	47	11	289	240	303	310	403	713	3	90	31	0.31	270	46	18	36	67	4%	101	14%	4.16	-3.9	$13
Health	A	07 SEA	536	72	155	9	67	5	289	333	277	309	418	726	3	91	30	0.31	284	43	19	38	84	5%	78	7%	4.31	0.3	$14
PT/Exp	A	08 SEA	559	66	156	7	51	4	279	273	281	300	392	692	3	92	29	0.40	276	40	20	40	72	3%	75	6%	4.01	-5.1	$12
Consist	A	1st Half	283	32	76	3	25	1	269			279	385	664	1	93	28	0.21	287	43	20	36	75	3%	70	5%	3.65	-5.6	$5
LIMA Plan	C	2nd Half	276	34	80	4	26	3	290			322	399	720	4	92	31	0.57	264	37	20	44	69	4%	72	7%	4.37	0.3	$7
+/- Score	-1	09 Proj	562	68	158	8	56	5	281			304	398	701	3	92	30	0.39	273	41	19	39	73	4%	75	8%	4.09	-4.1	$12

Consistency would be great if he was consistently above replacement level. As is, utter lack of selectivity is limiting his growth. At least ct% keeps the BA decent. And at least you know what to expect.

Betemit,Wilson			AB	R	H	HR	RBI	SB	Avg	vL	vR	OB	Slg	OPS	bb%	ct%	h%	Eye	xBA	G	L	F	PX	hr/f	SX	SBO	RC/G	RAR	R$
Pos	35	04 aaa	356	42	91	11	52	3	256			310	421	731	7	76	31	0.33	0				111		70	7%	4.48	-10.4	$9
Age	27	05 ATL	246	36	75	4	20	1	305	260	323	362	435	797	8	78	38	0.40	271	48	25	27	88	8%	91	5%	5.44	-1.1	$7
Bats	Both	06 2NL	373	49	98	18	53	3	263	189	281	328	469	797	9	73	32	0.35	264	42	21	37	139	18%	48	4%	5.40	-6.5	$11
Health	B	07 2TM	240	33	55	14	50	0	229	239	227	335	454	789	14	66	28	0.46	245	42	18	40	167	22%	20	0%	5.64	-0.4	$7
PT/Exp	D	08 NYY	189	24	50	6	25	0	265	233	274	287	429	716	3	70	35	0.11	259	43	25	33	129	14%	41	3%	4.17	-6.1	$5
Consist	B	1st Half	79	12	21	4	12	0	266			275	494	769	1	71	33	0.04	285	35	28	37	170	19%	60	8%	4.74	-1.2	$3
LIMA Plan	F	2nd Half	110	12	29	2	13	0	264			296	382	677	4	70	36	0.15	237	48	22	30	100	9%	29	0%	3.74	-4.8	$2
+/- Score	-10	09 Proj	223	29	57	9	34	0	256			308	438	746	7	70	33	0.26	258	43	23	34	137	16%	38	3%	4.73	-3.5	$6

Done in by an abysmal July (.504 OPS) which sunk overall numbers. But that's what a bad stretch does when you don't play much. PX solid otherwise, and bb% should rebound. But getting AB will still be an issue.

Bixler,Brian			AB	R	H	HR	RBI	SB	Avg	vL	vR	OB	Slg	OPS	bb%	ct%	h%	Eye	xBA	G	L	F	PX	hr/f	SX	SBO	RC/G	RAR	R$
Pos	6	04	0	0	0	0	0	0	0							0			0						0				
Age	26	05	0	0	0	0	0	0	0							0			0						0				
Bats	Right	06 aa	226	32	64	3	16	6	283			324	386	710	6	77	36	0.26	0				75		96	13%	4.17	-1.4	$6
Health	A	07 aa	475	62	116	4	41	23	244			305	342	647	8	76	31	0.36	0				70		138	22%	3.53	-12.0	$10
PT/Exp	F	08 PIT	* 429	52	97	6	31	20	226	182	151	273	310	582	6	69	32	0.21	213	63	11	25	59	8%	139	26%	2.47	-28.8	$8
Consist	B	1st Half	210	28	45	4	15	7	214			252	318	570	5	72	28	0.18	228	61	13	27	68	9%	142	21%	2.24	-15.7	$3
LIMA Plan	F	2nd Half	219	24	52	2	16	13	237			292	302	594	7	66	35	0.23	201	73	7	20	50	7%	127	30%	2.72	-12.9	$5
+/- Score	1	09 Proj	98	12	22	1	8	4	224			277	308	585	7	72	30	0.26	222	64	11	25	59	6%	125	24%	2.57	-5.8	$2

0-2-.157 in 108 AB at PIT. Runs like a deer, whiffs like Rob Deer. Or Mark Reynolds, for you kids. Seriously, GB says if he could put it in play, get on, and use those wheels, he'd be worth a flier. But he doesn't, and isn't.

Blake,Casey			AB	R	H	HR	RBI	SB	Avg	vL	vR	OB	Slg	OPS	bb%	ct%	h%	Eye	xBA	G	L	F	PX	hr/f	SX	SBO	RC/G	RAR	R$
Pos	53	04 CLE	587	93	159	28	88	5	271	243	284	347	486	832	10	76	31	0.49	268	43	17	40	137	16%	70	8%	5.88	16.7	$20
Age	35	05 CLE	523	72	126	23	58	4	241	241	241	299	438	736	8	78	27	0.37	271	37	20	42	132	13%	63	8%	4.49	-0.1	$13
Bats	Right	06 CLE	401	63	113	19	68	6	282	272	286	354	479	833	10	77	33	0.48	273	40	23	37	124	17%	82	5%	5.84	9.4	$15
Health	B	07 CLE	588	81	159	18	78	4	270	256	276	332	437	769	8	79	32	0.44	257	39	18	43	113	9%	71	6%	5.01	2.4	$16
PT/Exp	A	08 2TM	536	71	147	21	81	3	274	287	270	335	463	798	8	78	32	0.41	273	38	22	40	129	13%	63	2%	5.35	3.4	$17
Consist	B	1st Half	261	37	73	7	46	2	280			338	433	771	8	79	33	0.42	271	41	23	36	110	9%	57	3%	5.03	-0.7	$9
LIMA Plan	C	2nd Half	275	34	74	14	35	1	269			332	491	823	9	76	31	0.40	276	34	22	44	147	15%	50	1%	5.66	4.2	$9
+/- Score	-16	09 Proj	525	73	142	21	76	2	270			334	461	795	9	78	31	0.43	269	38	21	41	126	13%	57	3%	5.32	2.8	$16

A decent skills rebound fueled by mid-year power spike. At 35, there's more chance he falls below this projection than exceeds it. But overall, this is a fairly stable skills set, and any drop-off should be small.

Blalock,Hank			AB	R	H	HR	RBI	SB	Avg	vL	vR	OB	Slg	OPS	bb%	ct%	h%	Eye	xBA	G	L	F	PX	hr/f	SX	SBO	RC/G	RAR	R$
Pos	35	04 TEX	627	108	173	33	114	2	276	282	273	354	504	858	11	76	31	0.51	265	34	18	48	144	15%	68	2%	6.23	22.1	$24
Age	28	05 TEX	647	80	170	25	92	1	263	196	290	317	431	748	7	80	30	0.39	277	39	24	36	111	13%	38	1%	4.61	-9.0	$18
Bats	Left	06 TEX	591	76	157	16	89	1	266	216	284	324	401	725	8	83	30	0.52	262	42	21	37	81	9%	62	1%	4.44	-16.7	$14
Health	F	07 TEX	208	32	61	10	33	4	293	298	292	358	543	901	9	82	32	0.55	298	33	21	46	157	13%	103	9%	6.65	8.1	$9
PT/Exp	C	08 TEX	258	37	74	12	38	1	287	277	291	336	508	843	7	84	30	0.48	299	36	21	43	137	13%	59	2%	5.75	3.5	$9
Consist	D	1st Half	87	9	26	3	7	0	299			358	460	818	8	90	31	0.89	281	38	21	41	96	9%	14	0%	5.59	0.8	$2
LIMA Plan	C+	2nd Half	171	28	48	9	31	1	281			324	532	856	6	82	30	0.35	306	35	22	44	160	15%	76	3%	5.87	2.9	$7
+/- Score	2	09 Proj	419	60	119	20	62	3	284			340	509	850	8	83	30	0.51	295	36	21	42	138	14%	77	3%	5.89	7.3	$15

Skills are back to early form, and it's easy to forget he's only 28. But lingering shoulder worries mean the risk remains. It all adds up to roughly equal odds for this projection, an '07-'08 repeat, or: UP: 600 AB, 30 HR, .300 BA

Blanco,Gregor			AB	R	H	HR	RBI	SB	Avg	vL	vR	OB	Slg	OPS	bb%	ct%	h%	Eye	xBA	G	L	F	PX	hr/f	SX	SBO	RC/G	RAR	R$
Pos	78	04	0	0	0	0	0	0	0							0			0						0				
Age	25	05 aa	401	56	92	5	32	24	229			335	332	667	14	73	30	0.59	0				67		141	28%	4.01	-12.9	$10
Bats	Left	06 a/a	520	84	146	0	27	30	281			390	344	734	15	79	35	0.87	0				51		107	22%	5.07	-2.2	$15
Health	A	07 aaa	464	73	124	3	31	21	267			346	341	687	11	83	32	0.72	0				49		105	26%	4.23	-13.7	$12
PT/Exp	C	08 ATL	430	52	108	1	38	13	251	248	252	361	309	670	15	77	32	0.75	239	50	24	26	43	1%	100	11%	4.15	-16.2	$8
Consist	A	1st Half	211	22	57	1	16	6	270			366	336	703	13	77	35	0.65	242	49	25	26	43	2%	103	9%	4.50	-5.6	$5
LIMA Plan	D	2nd Half	219	30	51	0	22	7	233			356	283	639	16	77	30	0.84	237	51	23	27	43	0%	89	13%	3.82	-10.8	$4
+/- Score	-2	09 Proj	332	46	85	1	26	14	256			359	322	680	14	79	32	0.75	246	50	24	26	47	2%	106	18%	4.26	-11.2	$8

High bb%, OB, and some steals make him intriguing as a sim end-game bat off the bench in a pinch, despite the RAR at his position. But no power and mediocre ct% are a huge downside with this many AB.

Blanco,Henry			AB	R	H	HR	RBI	SB	Avg	vL	vR	OB	Slg	OPS	bb%	ct%	h%	Eye	xBA	G	L	F	PX	hr/f	SX	SBO	RC/G	RAR	R$
Pos	2	04 MIN	315	36	65	10	37	0	206	204	207	256	368	624	6	82	22	0.38	242	36	14	50	101	8%	52	5%	3.13	-11.9	$3
Age	37	05 CHC	161	16	39	6	25	0	242	194	254	291	391	682	6	85	25	0.46	251	42	17	41	88	11%	19	0%	3.81	0.1	$4
Bats	Right	06 CHC	241	23	64	6	37	0	266	325	236	306	419	725	5	84	29	0.37	278	38	24	38	93	8%	42	0%	4.35	0.1	$5
Health	C	07 CHC	54	3	9	0	4	0	167	50	235	196	222	419	4	78	21	0.17	189	29	17	55	51	0%	24	0%	0.44	-7.0	($1)
PT/Exp	F	08 CHC	120	15	35	3	12	0	292	316	270	325	392	717	5	82	34	0.27	221	42	17	42	61	7%	30	0%	4.08	-0.4	$3
Consist	F	1st Half	60	8	18	1	5	0	300			344	350	694	6	78	37	0.31	197	38	20	42	27	5%	32	0%	3.85	-0.6	$2
LIMA Plan	F	2nd Half	60	7	17	2	7	0	283			306	433	740	3	85	31	0.22	246	45	14	41	92	10%	27	0%	4.30	0.2	$2
+/- Score	-85	09 Proj	166	19	40	5	21	0	241			280	368	648	5	83	26	0.32	244	40	18	41	79	8%	33	0%	3.34	-4.5	$3

Don't get too excited by this BA; as usual, xBA knows better. Tempting to see that FB% and "wishcast" a HR spike, but the AB just won't ever be there. Bottom line: if you pay a buck in end game, he might get you 3-4.

Bloomquist,Willie			AB	R	H	HR	RBI	SB	Avg	vL	vR	OB	Slg	OPS	bb%	ct%	h%	Eye	xBA	G	L	F	PX	hr/f	SX	SBO	RC/G	RAR	R$
Pos	8	04 SEA	188	27	46	2	18	13	245	281	212	283	330	613	5	74	32	0.21	222	42	20	38	67	4%	121	34%	2.87	-10.4	$6
Age	31	05 SEA	249	27	64	0	22	14	257	247	262	288	333	622	4	85	30	0.29	264	45	24	32	59	0%	131	26%	3.16	-8.1	$6
Bats	Right	06 SEA	251	36	62	1	15	16	247	253	243	313	299	612	9	84	29	0.60	223	46	17	37	32	1%	132	25%	3.22	-10.8	$6
Health	C	07 SEA	173	28	48	2	13	7	277	238	290	317	329	646	5	80	34	0.29	243	61	19	20	35	7%	89	23%	3.28	-6.4	$5
PT/Exp	F	08 SEA	165	32	46	0	9	14	279	351	220	374	285	659	13	82	34	0.86	227	56	20	24	5	0%	108	24%	3.97	-6.6	$7
Consist	A	1st Half	84	19	21	0	5	8	250			364	250	614	15	75	33	0.71	223	56	25	19	0	0%	114	28%	3.32	-5.2	$3
LIMA Plan	F	2nd Half	81	13	25	0	4	6	309			385	321	706	11	90	34	1.25	230	56	15	29	10	0%	89	21%	4.60	-1.7	$3
+/- Score	-40	09 Proj	158	27	43	1	10	11	272			341	303	644	9	83	33	0.60	233	54	19	27	23	2%	102	24%	3.58	-6.3	$5

The good news about his power outage: "You can't fall off the floor." But for him, new SX base is more troubling. With his multi-position benefit gone,steals are all he brings, making that $5 floor very shaky.

Blum,Geoff			AB	R	H	HR	RBI	SB	Avg	vL	vR	OB	Slg	OPS	bb%	ct%	h%	Eye	xBA	G	L	F	PX	hr/f	SX	SBO	RC/G	RAR	R$
Pos	5	04 TAM	339	38	73	8	35	2	215	288	193	267	348	615	7	83	24	0.41	244	46	14	40	87	7%	51	7%	3.08	-19.3	$3
Age	36	05 2TM	319	32	73	6	25	3	229	213	236	291	345	636	8	87	25	0.65	262	40	21	39	73	6%	69	8%	3.52	-11.0	$4
Bats	Both	06 SD	276	27	70	4	34	0	254	167	267	297	366	663	6	82	30	0.33	252	36	23	41	77	4%	41	2%	3.62	-15.2	$4
Health	A	07 SD	330	34	83	5	33	0	252	238	256	318	367	684	9	84	29	0.62	250	36	20	44	79	4%	32	0%	4.10	-14.6	$4
PT/Exp	D	08 HOU	325	36	78	14	53	1	240	229	242	286	418	705	6	83	25	0.39	268	36	20	44	105	12%	45	4%	4.02	-13.2	$8
Consist	A	1st Half	134	10	31	5	17	1	231			259	373	632	4	85	24	0.25	244	37	17	45	81	10%	31	4%	3.05	-9.4	$2
LIMA Plan	D	2nd Half	191	26	47	9	36	0	246			304	450	755	8	82	26	0.47	283	36	22	42	123	14%	55	5%	4.71	-3.8	$6
+/- Score	2	09 Proj	312	33	76	7	42	0	244			295	371	667	7	83	27	0.44	252	37	20	43	81	7%	45	2%	3.71	-15.8	$5

Another vintage season: Nine weeks over .300, 12 at .200 or below. And it always ends up at about the same level. Credit hr/f luck, not the Juice Box, for career-high HR. History suggests not to pay for a repeat.

ROD TRUESDELL

Bocock,Brian

Bocock,Brian			AB	R	H	HR	RBI	SB	Avg	vL	vR	OB	Slg	OPS	bb%	ct%	h%	Eye	xBA	G	L	F	PX	hr/f	SX	SBO	RC/G	RAR	R$
Pos	6	04	0	0	0	0	0	0	0							0			0						0				
Age	24	05	0	0	0	0	0	0	0							0			0						0				
Bats	Right	06	0	0	0	0	0	0	0							0			0						0				
Health	A	07	0	0	0	0	0	0	0							0			0						0				
PT/Exp	F	08 SF	* 200	16	30	0	5	10	148		167	239	168	406	11	69	22	0.38	182	51	18	31	21	0%	82	30%	0.08	-31.3	($1)
Consist	A	1st Half	200	16	30	0	5	10	148			239	168	406	11	69	22	0.38	182	51	18	31	21	0%	82	30%	0.08	-31.3	($1)
LIMA Plan	F	2nd Half	0	0	0	0	0	0	0							0			0										
+/- Score	17	09 Proj	31	3	6	0	1	2	194			288	226	513	12	66	30	0.38	181	51	18	31	35	0%	67	28%	1.65	-2.9	$0

0-2-.143 in 77 AB at SF. First year above A-ball didn't turn out well. Flashed some speed in the minors, but desperately needs to cut down on K's. A work in progress, a few years away from contributing.

Boggs,Brandon

Boggs,Brandon			AB	R	H	HR	RBI	SB	Avg	vL	vR	OB	Slg	OPS	bb%	ct%	h%	Eye	xBA	G	L	F	PX	hr/f	SX	SBO	RC/G	RAR	R$
Pos	7	04	0	0	0	0	0	0	0							0			0						0				
Age	26	05	0	0	0	0	0	0	0							0			0						0				
Bats	Both	06	0	0	0	0	0	0	0							0			0						0				
Health	A	07 aa	354	55	85	16	45	9	239			343	445	788	14	75	28	0.63	0				137		98	12%	5.49	3.1	$10
PT/Exp	F	08 TEX	* 351	38	82	8	46	4	233	227	226	327	394	721	12	69	32	0.45	245	39	24	37	123	9%	96	7%	4.75	-1.1	$6
Consist	B	1st Half	217	20	56	4	30	3	257			322	412	734	9	71	35	0.32	242	36	24	40	118	7%	93	11%	4.79	-0.4	$5
LIMA Plan	D	2nd Half	134	18	26	4	16	1	194			333	366	699	17	66	26	0.62	246	43	24	33	131	14%	92	2%	4.56	-1.2	$1
+/- Score	14	09 Proj	246	33	60	8	31	4	244			347	425	773	14	71	31	0.54	258	41	24	35	131	13%	93	8%	5.43	3.6	$6

8-41-.226 in 283 AB at TEX. Power, bb% are building blocks. 1H BA propped up by h% spike, won't hit above .250 until he cuts down on K's. Given ABs, could be a decent end-game power source.

Bonifacio,Emilio

Bonifacio,Emilio			AB	R	H	HR	RBI	SB	Avg	vL	vR	OB	Slg	OPS	bb%	ct%	h%	Eye	xBA	G	L	F	PX	hr/f	SX	SBO	RC/G	RAR	R$
Pos	4	04	0	0	0	0	0	0	0							0			0						0				
Age	24	05	0	0	0	0	0	0	0							0			0						0				
Bats	Both	06	0	0	0	0	0	0	0							0			0						0				
Health	A	07 aa	574	72	152	2	36	34	265			308	326	634	6	84	31	0.40	280	63	21	16	42	3%	120	31%	3.34	-17.3	$15
PT/Exp	D	08 2NL	* 567	76	150	1	40	24	264	163	270	311	343	653	6	82	32	0.37	265	55	21	23	53	1%	136	25%	3.59	-20.0	$14
Consist	A	1st Half	359	40	103	1	25	14	287			329	369	697	6	86	33	0.43	0				55		117	22%	4.14	-6.6	$10
LIMA Plan	D	2nd Half	208	36	47	0	16	10	225			281	298	578	7	75	30	0.31	243	55	21	23	51	0%	164	33%	2.60	-14.3	$4
+/- Score	5	09 Proj	393	54	96	1	27	20	244			292	314	606	6	81	30	0.36	261	56	21	23	48	1%	135	30%	3.00	-20.6	$9

0-14-.243 in 169 AB at ARI and WAS. No power, but that's not why you draft him. Speed to burn and runs frequently. More plate patience would boost OBA; that could come with time. For now, he's a one-trick pony.

Boone,Aaron

Boone,Aaron			AB	R	H	HR	RBI	SB	Avg	vL	vR	OB	Slg	OPS	bb%	ct%	h%	Eye	xBA	G	L	F	PX	hr/f	SX	SBO	RC/G	RAR	R$
Pos	3	04 2AL	0	0	0	0	0	0	0							0			0						0				
Age	36	05 CLE	511	61	124	16	60	9	243	229	246	291	378	669	6	82	27	0.38	263	43	21	35	84	11%	82	10%	3.62	-22.4	$12
Bats	Right	06 CLE	354	50	89	7	46	5	251	280	239	304	370	675	7	82	29	0.44	259	36	25	40	78	6%	79	10%	3.81	-17.0	$7
Health	F	07 FLA	189	27	54	5	28	2	286	213	310	357	423	780	10	78	34	0.51	250	26	26	48	95	7%	53	3%	5.24	-4.7	$6
PT/Exp	D	08 WAS	232	23	56	6	28	0	241	275	220	296	384	680	7	78	29	0.35	249	42	20	38	98	9%	41	2%	3.82	-13.3	$4
Consist	C	1st Half	155	17	40	5	17	0	258			311	426	737	7	79	30	0.36	263	43	19	38	111	11%	54	3%	4.53	-5.4	$3
LIMA Plan	F	2nd Half	77	6	16	1	11	0	208			265	299	564	7	75	26	0.32	222	40	21	40	72	4%	20	0%	2.33	-8.1	$0
+/- Score	-21	09 Proj	194	22	48	4	26	1	247			306	368	674	8	78	29	0.39	245	37	22	41	84	7%	46	4%	3.77	-12.1	$4

Power and speed have been MIA since 2003. 2008 shows that 2007 was a h%-fueled anomaly. While PX remained consistent, FB% drop is a bad sign for future power. Platoon work is in his future.

Bourn,Michael

Bourn,Michael			AB	R	H	HR	RBI	SB	Avg	vL	vR	OB	Slg	OPS	bb%	ct%	h%	Eye	xBA	G	L	F	PX	hr/f	SX	SBO	RC/G	RAR	R$
Pos	8	04	0	0	0	0	0	0	0							0			0						0				
Age	26	05 aa	539	68	134	6	37	32	249			315	334	649	9	81	30	0.50	0				55		132	29%	3.59	-13.6	$15
Bats	Left	06 a/a	470	91	129	5	39	42	274			345	379	724	10	81	33	0.56	0				56		181	31%	4.61	0.8	$20
Health	B	07 PHI	119	29	33	1	6	18	277	154	312	348	378	727	10	82	33	0.62	266	58	18	24	56	4%	198	49%	4.67	0.5	$7
PT/Exp	D	08 HOU	467	57	107	5	29	41	229	190	242	286	300	586	7	76	29	0.33	226	54	17	29	46	5%	146	41%	2.61	-30.9	$14
Consist	C	1st Half	297	36	68	4	15	31	229			287	306	593	7	76	29	0.34	227	54	17	30	48	6%	152	48%	2.71	-18.8	$10
LIMA Plan	C+	2nd Half	170	21	39	1	14	10	229			284	288	572	7	76	30	0.32	223	55	17	29	43	3%	120	29%	2.45	-12.0	$4
+/- Score	-20	09 Proj	417	68	104	4	28	40	249			313	330	643	8	79	31	0.43	241	55	17	27	49	4%	168	38%	3.47	-14.5	$16

PRO: Change of scenery gave him plenty of ABs, resulting in tons of SBs.
CON: falling plate patience, 2H decline, and can't hit lefties. Needs growth for the Bourn identity to be more than speed.

Bowker,John

Bowker,John			AB	R	H	HR	RBI	SB	Avg	vL	vR	OB	Slg	OPS	bb%	ct%	h%	Eye	xBA	G	L	F	PX	hr/f	SX	SBO	RC/G	RAR	R$
Pos	3	04	0	0	0	0	0	0	0							0			0						0				
Age	25	05	0	0	0	0	0	0	0							0			0						0				
Bats	Left	06	0	0	0	0	0	0	0							0			0						0				
Health	A	07 aa	522	63	139	16	71	2	266			308	437	745	6	83	29	0.36	0				107		63	8%	4.58	-17.1	$13
PT/Exp	F	08 SF	326	31	83	10	43	1	255	152	266	296	408	704	6	77	30	0.26	261	37	25	38	99	11%	62	3%	4.01	-16.5	$7
Consist	B	1st Half	198	23	55	8	35	1	278			313	465	777	5	79	32	0.24	274	33	26	41	115	12%	76	2%	4.85	-4.9	$7
LIMA Plan	F	2nd Half	128	8	28	2	8	0	219			270	320	590	7	74	28	0.27	237	45	23	32	72	7%	50	3%	2.63	-12.3	$0
+/- Score	5	09 Proj	202	20	51	6	24	1	252			296	406	702	6	79	29	0.29	267	39	25	36	98	10%	67	5%	4.03	-11.0	$4

Couldn't build on strong 1H; ct%, hr/f, FB declines caught up to him. Flashes of power and decent BA in the minors give hope for growth. For now, a platoon player, but he could turn into a contributor.

Bradley,Milton

Bradley,Milton			AB	R	H	HR	RBI	SB	Avg	vL	vR	OB	Slg	OPS	bb%	ct%	h%	Eye	xBA	G	L	F	PX	hr/f	SX	SBO	RC/G	RAR	R$
Pos	09	04 LA	516	72	138	19	67	15	267	295	257	356	424	780	12	76	32	0.58	253	47	19	34	102	14%	66	16%	5.30	0.0	$18
Age	31	05 LA	283	49	82	13	38	6	290	278	294	347	484	832	8	83	31	0.53	299	45	23	32	117	17%	99	9%	5.65	-2.9	$13
Bats	Both	06 OAK	351	53	97	14	52	10	276	293	270	368	447	815	13	81	31	0.78	269	52	15	33	99	15%	94	10%	5.75	-6.8	$13
Health	F	07 2TM	209	37	64	13	37	5	306	304	307	396	545	941	13	80	33	0.76	284	39	19	43	141	18%	81	10%	7.25	5.8	$11
PT/Exp	C	08 TEX	414	78	133	22	77	5	321	341	312	431	563	994	16	73	40	0.71	295	41	25	34	173	21%	62	5%	8.51	39.8	$22
Consist	C	1st Half	239	50	76	16	49	4	318			432	603	1035	17	74	37	0.77	310	38	24	38	198	24%	58	7%	8.96	26.1	$14
LIMA Plan	C+	2nd Half	175	28	57	6	28	1	326			430	509	939	15	71	43	0.64	275	45	26	29	137	17%	61	3%	7.87	13.7	$8
+/- Score	-44	09 Proj	348	60	101	17	59	6	290			390	501	892	14	77	34	0.70	282	43	21	35	139	18%	76	7%	6.85	12.6	$15

Feel lucky? Plenty of bumps and bruises, but no DL time after spending 239 days on the shelf from 05-07. H% will revert so BA shouldn't repeat. hr/f should also revert so a power encore is history too.

Branyan,Russell

Branyan,Russell			AB	R	H	HR	RBI	SB	Avg	vL	vR	OB	Slg	OPS	bb%	ct%	h%	Eye	xBA	G	L	F	PX	hr/f	SX	SBO	RC/G	RAR	R$
Pos	5	04 2TM	* 499	76	120	32	97	7	240	167	250	330	493	823	12	62	32	0.35	237	29	19	53	190	20%	86	7%	6.37	20.7	$18
Age	33	05 MIL	202	23	52	12	31	1	257	50	280	378	490	868	16	60	36	0.49	245	29	24	47	192	21%	24	1%	7.36	15.2	$7
Bats	Left	06 2TM	241	37	55	18	36	2	228	220	230	324	498	822	12	63	28	0.38	247	29	19	52	194	23%	49	3%	6.18	6.8	$7
Health	C	07 2NL	163	22	32	10	26	1	196	158	201	314	423	737	15	58	26	0.41	214	29	18	53	178	20%	66	2%	5.25	-1.8	$3
PT/Exp	F	08 MIL	* 285	40	75	21	44	4	262		280	345	548	892	11	69	31	0.40	273	22	21	57	206	18%	50	6%	6.92	12.9	$12
Consist	C	1st Half	240	31	66	20	42	3	274			354	588	942	11	67	32	0.38	278	18	19	63	227	19%	37	6%	7.69	16.0	$11
LIMA Plan	D	2nd Half	45	9	9	1	2	1	200			294	333	627	12	76	24	0.55	238	29	24	47	101	6%	90	9%	3.36	-2.8	$1
+/- Score	12	09 Proj	117	16	28	8	19	1	239			338	503	841	13	63	30	0.40	249	27	20	53	199	21%	36	4%	6.56	4.0	$4

12-20-.250 in 132 AB at MIL. The epitome of a "three true outcomes" hitter. Pitiful '08 ct% was a career high, by far. Not draftable, but streaks (9 HR in 67 July AB) mean you should keep an eye on him as a FA.

Braun,Ryan

Braun,Ryan			AB	R	H	HR	RBI	SB	Avg	vL	vR	OB	Slg	OPS	bb%	ct%	h%	Eye	xBA	G	L	F	PX	hr/f	SX	SBO	RC/G	RAR	R$
Pos	7	04	0	0	0	0	0	0	0							0			0						0				
Age	25	05	0	0	0	0	0	0	0							0			0						0				
Bats	Right	06 aa	231	40	68	15	38	11	294			353	580	933	8	81	31	0.47	0				173		119	20%	6.92	10.9	$13
Health	A	07 MIL	* 568	116	183	43	116	19	322	450	282	370	637	1007	7	79	35	0.35	309	39	16	45	190	21%	124	19%	7.78	37.3	$37
PT/Exp	C	08 MIL	611	92	174	37	106	14	285	287	284	331	553	884	6	79	31	0.33	294	39	17	44	166	17%	115	14%	6.24	14.3	$29
Consist	C	1st Half	333	45	94	20	58	8	282			315	544	859	5	79	30	0.23	289	36	18	46	162	16%	102	17%	5.81	3.7	$15
LIMA Plan	D+	2nd Half	278	47	80	17	48	6	288			349	565	913	9	79	31	0.44	301	42	16	41	171	19%	122	10%	6.75	10.4	$14
+/- Score	5	09 Proj	552	97	165	37	101	17	299			349	587	937	7	79	32	0.37	302	39	17	44	176	19%	124	16%	6.93	23.8	$31

Monster numbers... only a slow start and end (6 HR in Apr/Sep) denied a 40 HR repeat. Fewer K's would be nice, but that's a quibble. With this PX and hr/f, change some GBs to FBs, and: UP: 50 HR, 125 RBI.

DAVE ADLER

Brown,Emil

			AB	R	H	HR	RBI	SB	Avg	vL	vR	OB	Slg	OPS	bb%	ct%	h%	Eye	xBA	G	L	F	PX	hr/f	SX	SBO	RC/G	RAR	R$
Pos	79	04 aaa	149	14	38	2	15	4	257			287	373	660	4	84	30	0.26	0				79		84	23%	3.54	-7.4	$3
Age	34	05 KC	545	75	156	17	86	10	286	315	273	344	455	799	8	80	33	0.44	281	42	24	34	110	12%	108	7%	5.36	9.8	$20
Bats	Right	06 KC	527	77	151	15	81	6	287	236	308	358	457	816	10	82	33	0.62	275	44	18	38	113	9%	75	6%	5.70	7.8	$17
Health	A	07 KC	366	44	94	6	62	12	257	317	217	303	347	650	6	81	30	0.34	228	44	17	39	61	5%	95	14%	3.41	-17.6	$10
PT/Exp	B	08 OAK	402	48	98	13	59	4	244	295	211	291	386	677	6	84	26	0.42	251	42	17	42	84	9%	77	6%	3.75	-13.2	$9
Consist	C	1st Half	251	32	60	6	43	3	239			279	363	642	5	84	26	0.35	247	42	17	41	74	7%	92	7%	3.32	-11.5	$6
LIMA Plan	D	2nd Half	151	16	38	7	16	1	252			311	424	735	8	83	26	0.52	253	41	16	43	100	13%	33	5%	4.45	-1.8	$4
+/- Score	-3	09 Proj	325	39	84	9	47	5	258			311	395	706	7	82	29	0.44	252	43	17	40	86	9%	73	9%	4.14	-7.7	$9

Rising FB trend without PX punch to back it up. BA may rebound a bit, but most glaring deficiency is production vs RHP: .601 OPS in 2008; .529 in 2007. Potential limited value in a platoon situation.

Bruce,Jay

			AB	R	H	HR	RBI	SB	Avg	vL	vR	OB	Slg	OPS	bb%	ct%	h%	Eye	xBA	G	L	F	PX	hr/f	SX	SBO	RC/G	RAR	R$
Pos	98	04	0	0	0	0	0	0	0							0			0						0				
Age	22	05	0	0	0	0	0	0	0							0			0						0				
Bats	Left	06	0	0	0	0	0	0	0							0			0						0				
Health	A	07 a/a	253	36	81	15	39	3	322			376	600	976	8	79	36	0.41	0				177		73	10%	7.51	15.9	$12
PT/Exp	F	08 CIN	* 597	91	168	30	82	11	281	190	286	329	487	817	7	75	33	0.29	274	45	21	34	131	20%	95	12%	5.47	4.7	$25
Consist	F	1st Half	306	46	97	13	45	9	316			364	510	874	7	77	37	0.33	282	46	23	31	122	18%	109	15%	6.22	8.6	$15
LIMA Plan	C+	2nd Half	291	45	71	17	37	2	244			293	464	757	6	74	27	0.26	270	44	20	36	141	22%	72	8%	4.65	-4.8	$9
+/- Score	6	09 Proj	571	85	157	32	81	9	275			327	511	839	7	77	31	0.33	290	45	21	35	149	21%	87	12%	5.76	11.6	$22

21-52-.254 in 413 AB at CIN. Can he put it together at 22? PRO: 14 HR in Aug/Sep after Jun/Jul drought; MLB xBA (.272) CON: ct%, struggles vs LHP are significant holes. Still, one day: UP: 40 HR, .300 BA

Bruntlett,Eric

			AB	R	H	HR	RBI	SB	Avg	vL	vR	OB	Slg	OPS	bb%	ct%	h%	Eye	xBA	G	L	F	PX	hr/f	SX	SBO	RC/G	RAR	R$
Pos	765	04 aaa	332	38	73	5	28	11	219			276	313	589	7	83	25	0.45	0				56		115	19%	2.81	-24.7	$5
Age	31	05 HOU	109	19	24	4	14	7	220	295	125	286	413	699	8	77	25	0.40	264	31	28	41	122	12%	172	39%	4.11	-4.2	$4
Bats	Right	06 HOU	* 192	21	47	1	16	5	245	350	241	341	313	653	13	81	30	0.78	230	41	20	38	52	2%	57	13%	3.90	-7.9	$3
Health	A	07 HOU	* 365	36	77	1	28	14	210	237	253	286	263	549	10	82	26	0.58	226	46	19	35	37	1%	101	21%	2.46	-33.5	$3
PT/Exp	F	08 PHI	212	37	46	2	15	9	217	254	199	288	297	585	9	83	25	0.60	251	47	20	33	55	3%	128	20%	2.90	-16.6	$4
Consist	B	1st Half	134	27	32	2	12	8	239			301	321	622	8	87	26	0.67	255	48	20	32	47	5%	150	24%	3.35	-8.4	$4
LIMA Plan	F	2nd Half	78	10	14	0	3	1	179			264	256	521	10	78	23	0.53	243	44	21	34	71	0%	71	12%	2.09	-8.5	($0)
+/- Score	38	09 Proj	86	12	19	1	6	4	221			297	288	585	10	81	27	0.58	238	44	21	35	51	2%	86	22%	2.89	-6.7	$1

AB increased substantially due to Rollins injury; shield thy eyes from the results. xBA says he's underperforming; h% history removes any waning optimism. Only MLB player to slug under .300 in the past 2 seasons.

Buck,John

			AB	R	H	HR	RBI	SB	Avg	vL	vR	OB	Slg	OPS	bb%	ct%	h%	Eye	xBA	G	L	F	PX	hr/f	SX	SBO	RC/G	RAR	R$
Pos	2	04 2TM	* 465	61	118	22	58	1	254	222	241	300	437	737	6	77	29	0.28	248	45	16	39	113	16%	38	3%	4.37	4.2	$12
Age	28	05 KC	401	40	97	12	47	2	242	310	214	283	389	672	5	77	29	0.24	242	44	17	40	103	10%	51	5%	3.60	-5.1	$7
Bats	Right	06 KC	371	37	91	11	50	0	245	246	245	295	396	691	7	77	29	0.31	253	45	20	35	101	11%	32	2%	3.91	-5.5	$6
Health	A	07 KC	347	41	77	18	48	0	222	189	231	295	429	724	9	73	25	0.39	244	43	13	44	142	16%	23	1%	4.39	1.1	$7
PT/Exp	C	08 KC	370	48	83	9	48	0	224	236	219	297	365	661	9	74	28	0.40	234	43	16	41	106	8%	43	3%	3.69	-5.7	$5
Consist	B	1st Half	196	26	49	3	23	0	250			323	367	690	10	78	31	0.49	231	42	15	43	92	5%	37	6%	4.14	-0.3	$3
LIMA Plan	D	2nd Half	174	22	34	6	25	0	195			267	362	629	9	70	24	0.32	236	44	17	39	124	13%	59	0%	3.18	-5.5	$2
+/- Score	15	09 Proj	384	46	87	13	51	0	227			293	391	683	9	74	27	0.36	240	43	16	40	115	12%	40	2%	3.88	-4.3	$6

Improved 1H ct% and Eye to no measurable result; hacked his way to a few more 2H HR. While a 20-HR power spike is still possible, low ct% indicates that a .250 BA is a stretch.

Buck,Travis

			AB	R	H	HR	RBI	SB	Avg	vL	vR	OB	Slg	OPS	bb%	ct%	h%	Eye	xBA	G	L	F	PX	hr/f	SX	SBO	RC/G	RAR	R$
Pos	9	04	0	0	0	0	0	0	0							0			0						0				
Age	25	05	0	0	0	0	0	0	0							0			0						0				
Bats	Left	06 aa	212	27	58	3	19	8	274			330	425	755	8	85	31	0.56	0				105		102	18%	4.95	-1.6	$6
Health	C	07 OAK	285	41	82	7	34	4	288	323	277	373	474	847	12	77	35	0.59	274	44	19	37	131	9%	107	6%	6.34	6.7	$9
PT/Exp	F	08 OAK	* 324	37	76	8	37	4	235	196	239	299	370	668	8	80	27	0.46	240	46	14	41	89	8%	79	6%	3.76	-15.6	$6
Consist	D	1st Half	102	12	30	1	8	2	292			358	386	744	9	87	33	0.78	0				61		85	6%	4.89	-1.3	$3
LIMA Plan	D+	2nd Half	222	25	47	7	30	2	210			271	362	633	8	77	24	0.37	241	46	14	41	103	10%	72	6%	3.22	-14.8	$3
+/- Score	2	09 Proj	411	52	108	9	45	7	263			334	414	748	10	80	31	0.53	260	45	17	38	103	7%	98	7%	4.87	-6.1	$10

7-25-.226 in 155 AB at OAK. Minor injuries, 24% MLB h% contributed to disappointing follow-up. Strong Sept finish (4 HR in 49 AB) and impressive plate skills history piques our interest. Ct% above 80% is key.

Burke,Chris

			AB	R	H	HR	RBI	SB	Avg	vL	vR	OB	Slg	OPS	bb%	ct%	h%	Eye	xBA	G	L	F	PX	hr/f	SX	SBO	RC/G	RAR	R$
Pos	7	04 aaa	483	74	138	13	41	29	286			343	447	790	8	88	30	0.71	0				94		128	35%	5.30	1.5	$20
Age	29	05 HOU	* 408	60	104	7	34	18	254	265	239	304	384	688	7	82	29	0.40	251	38	19	42	87	5%	137	24%	3.98	-16.5	$12
Bats	Right	06 HOU	366	58	101	9	40	11	276	327	257	326	418	744	7	79	33	0.35	252	36	23	41	95	8%	102	13%	4.62	-6.6	$12
Health	A	07 HOU	* 385	49	85	8	33	12	222	292	197	279	344	622	7	85	24	0.51	242	38	17	45	77	5%	107	20%	3.26	-25.0	$6
PT/Exp	D	08 ARI	165	20	32	2	12	5	194	209	177	307	273	580	14	80	23	0.82	215	38	18	44	52	3%	96	10%	2.95	-12.9	$1
Consist	B	1st Half	104	10	18	0	7	3	173			289	202	491	14	85	20	1.06	196	35	17	48	25	0%	65	9%	2.09	-11.2	($0)
LIMA Plan	F	2nd Half	61	10	14	2	5	2	230			338	393	731	14	72	29	0.56	244	44	20	36	107	13%	121	11%	4.82	-1.1	$2
+/- Score	17	09 Proj	94	13	21	2	8	3	223			306	349	655	11	80	26	0.60	239	39	19	42	80	6%	112	15%	3.73	-4.7	$2

Impressed ARI with a .361/.429/.705 spring, but then reminded us of the March-stat minefield. A full pantry of routine fly balls. When one's full-season OPS is less than some hitters' SLG, you know there are issues.

Burke,Jamie

			AB	R	H	HR	RBI	SB	Avg	vL	vR	OB	Slg	OPS	bb%	ct%	h%	Eye	xBA	G	L	F	PX	hr/f	SX	SBO	RC/G	RAR	R$
Pos	2	04 CHW	* 254	31	66	2	24	0	260			307	335	642	6	89	29	0.63	0				51		36	0%	3.59	-5.5	$3
Age	37	05 aaa	351	37	77	8	38	1	218			270	344	614	7	87	23	0.54	0				80		49	5%	3.17	-8.0	$4
Bats	Right	06 aaa	370	39	93	9	41	0	251			287	379	666	5	89	26	0.45	0				75		36	0%	3.69	-7.4	$6
Health	A	07 SEA	113	19	34	1	12	0	301	280	307	342	398	740	6	85	35	0.41	280	38	28	34	74	3%	52	3%	4.59	0.9	$3
PT/Exp	F	08 SEA	92	10	24	1	8	0	261	341	196	299	326	625	5	92	27	0.71	239	53	14	33	41	4%	39	4%	3.39	-2.2	$1
Consist	C	1st Half	49	4	10	1	3	0	204			278	286	563	9	92	20	1.25	224	42	16	42	45	5%	17	0%	2.93	-1.9	$0
LIMA Plan	F	2nd Half	43	6	14	0	5	0	326			326	372	698	0	93	35	0.00	257	65	13	23	37	0%	58	8%	3.83	-0.4	$1
+/- Score	-45	09 Proj	66	8	17	1	7	0	258			302	368	670	6	87	28	0.49	288	38	28	34	75	6%	44	3%	3.80	-0.9	$1

Read nothing into .341 BA vs LHP; it was accumulated in all of 41 AB. Rostering either of these back-to-back Burkes will beseige your batting totals, bequeath blanks, and bestir bewilderment.

Burrell,Pat

			AB	R	H	HR	RBI	SB	Avg	vL	vR	OB	Slg	OPS	bb%	ct%	h%	Eye	xBA	G	L	F	PX	hr/f	SX	SBO	RC/G	RAR	R$
Pos	7	04 PHI	448	66	115	24	84	2	257	271	253	367	455	822	15	71	31	0.60	242	35	20	45	130	17%	43	1%	6.00	7.3	$16
Age	32	05 PHI	562	78	158	32	117	0	281	318	269	389	504	892	15	72	34	0.62	267	31	24	45	153	18%	27	0%	7.00	26.3	$24
Bats	Right	06 PHI	462	80	119	29	95	0	258	290	244	388	502	890	18	72	30	0.75	262	31	21	48	158	18%	32	0%	7.03	24.0	$18
Health	A	07 PHI	472	77	121	30	97	0	256	255	257	401	502	903	19	75	28	0.95	265	31	18	51	158	17%	18	0%	7.21	25.5	$18
PT/Exp	A	08 PHI	536	74	134	33	86	0	250	279	238	370	507	877	16	75	28	0.75	282	34	20	45	169	18%	41	0%	6.73	20.7	$18
Consist	A	1st Half	266	44	72	19	49	0	271			412	571	984	19	75	29	0.96	303	35	21	45	197	21%	47	0%	8.32	22.0	$12
LIMA Plan	B	2nd Half	270	30	62	14	37	0	230			325	444	769	12	74	26	0.55	262	34	20	46	142	15%	29	0%	5.13	-2.4	$6
+/- Score	24	09 Proj	509	75	129	31	92	0	253			377	498	875	17	74	28	0.76	270	33	20	47	160	17%	40	0%	6.75	20.4	$18

Timing is everything. For 526 AB from Jul 07-Jun 08, he hit .285-41-114 -- a difference-making "season." But a loss of timing (and patience) spun him into a deep 2H slump. Upside window closing, though PX still shines.

Burriss,Emmanuel

			AB	R	H	HR	RBI	SB	Avg	vL	vR	OB	Slg	OPS	bb%	ct%	h%	Eye	xBA	G	L	F	PX	hr/f	SX	SBO	RC/G	RAR	R$
Pos	64	04	0	0	0	0	0	0	0							0			0						0				
Age	24	05	0	0	0	0	0	0	0							0			0						0				
Bats	Both	06	0	0	0	0	0	0	0							0			0						0				
Health	A	07	0	0	0	0	0	0	0							0			0						0				
PT/Exp	F	08 SF	* 302	41	83	1	23	15	274	292	278	329	320	649	8	90	30	0.86	264	65	14	21	28	2%	110	22%	3.78	-7.6	$9
Consist	F	1st Half	162	19	43	0	12	8	264			302	319	621	5	91	29	0.59	268	62	15	23	34	0%	123	27%	3.36	-6.1	$4
LIMA Plan	C	2nd Half	140	22	40	1	11	7	286			359	321	680	10	90	31	1.14	253	67	14	19	21	4%	85	19%	4.24	-1.6	$5
+/- Score	6	09 Proj	422	59	113	2	32	21	268			328	311	640	8	90	29	0.92	262	65	14	21	27	2%	107	22%	3.70	-9.9	$12

1-18-13-.283 in 240 AB at SF. PRO: 2H improvement in bb% and OBA, excellent ct% CON: No power, just 62 AB in minors above A-ball. Speed has value, but temper 2009 expectations.

BRENT HERSHEY

Buscher,Brian

Buscher,Brian			AB	R	H	HR	RBI	SB	Avg	vL	vR	OB	Slg	OPS	bb%	ct%	h%	Eye	xBA	G	L	F	PX	hr/f	SX	SBO	RC/G	RAR	R$
Pos	5	04	0	0	0	0	0	0	0							0			0						0				
Age	28	05 aa	215	15	43	1	18	4	199			255	252	507	7	85	23	0.51	0				37		70	13%	1.94	-18.5	$0
Bats	Left	06 aa	467	40	109	6	45	5	233			288	330	618	7	82	27	0.43	0				62		66	7%	3.15	-29.8	$4
Health	A	07 MIN	* 461	55	118	13	58	4	256	200	250	320	394	714	9	87	27	0.74	262	43	16	40	85	8%	59	4%	4.43	-6.0	$10
PT/Exp	D	08 MIN	* 403	50	112	9	70	1	277	205	316	332	394	727	8	85	31	0.54	276	33	28	39	76	7%	32	4%	4.46	-4.9	$11
Consist	B	1st Half	243	33	68	6	38	1	279			327	407	733	7	90	29	0.70	321	35	35	31	77	9%	42	6%	4.56	-2.3	$7
LIMA Plan	D	2nd Half	160	17	44	3	32	0	275			341	375	716	9	77	34	0.43	239	33	25	42	73	6%	25	2%	4.37	-2.3	$4
+/- Score	-26	09 Proj	322	35	83	7	47	2	258			317	371	688	8	84	29	0.53	261	35	25	40	74	6%	50	5%	4.04	-8.0	$7

4-47-.294 in 218 AB at MIN. Managed to retain some small amount of relevance by boosting LD%, which led to xBA gain. That level will be hard to sustain, and he also has to prove he can hit LH to have any 2009 value.

Butler,Billy

Butler,Billy			AB	R	H	HR	RBI	SB	Avg	vL	vR	OB	Slg	OPS	bb%	ct%	h%	Eye	xBA	G	L	F	PX	hr/f	SX	SBO	RC/G	RAR	R$
Pos	03	04	0	0	0	0	0	0	0							0			0						0				
Age	23	05 aa	112	12	33	3	15	0	295			328	462	789	5	89	31	0.47	0				107		22	0%	5.07	-3.0	$3
Bats	Right	06 aa	477	67	147	11	79	1	308			354	447	801	7	90	33	0.71	0				84		55	1%	5.34	-14.0	$16
Health	A	07 KC	* 532	72	150	18	92	1	282	340	272	360	457	817	11	85	31	0.79	292	47	21	33	110	12%	56	1%	5.73	-7.7	$17
PT/Exp	C	08 KC	* 544	60	154	15	66	0	283	340	244	338	421	759	8	88	30	0.71	264	49	17	35	84	9%	26	1%	4.89	-0.7	$14
Consist	B	1st Half	293	28	84	5	29	0	287			355	403	758	10	89	31	0.94	262	51	16	33	75	6%	33	1%	5.06	1.1	$6
LIMA Plan	C	2nd Half	251	32	70	10	37	0	279			317	442	759	5	88	28	0.47	271	47	17	36	94	12%	27	0%	4.66	-1.9	$8
+/- Score	-12	09 Proj	582	72	167	20	85	0	287			342	449	791	8	88	30	0.68	281	48	18	34	98	11%	34	1%	5.23	-5.3	$17

11-55-.275 in 443 AB at KC. PRO: PX and hr/f rose in 2H, ct% rebounded to MLE level. CON: PX still below average, and high GB% saps power. Plenty of long-term potential, but temper expectations for 2009.

Bynum,Freddie

Bynum,Freddie			AB	R	H	HR	RBI	SB	Avg	vL	vR	OB	Slg	OPS	bb%	ct%	h%	Eye	xBA	G	L	F	PX	hr/f	SX	SBO	RC/G	RAR	R$
Pos	6	04 a/a	523	62	124	2	37	30	237			283	304	587	6	81	29	0.33	0				47		130	33%	2.71	-25.5	$11
Age	29	05 aaa	378	44	90	2	31	18	238			292	320	612	7	83	28	0.44	0				55		133	28%	3.13	-13.2	$8
Bats	Left	06 CHC	136	20	35	4	12	8	257	130	283	303	456	759	6	68	35	0.20	253	45	25	30	127	15%	143	40%	5.13	3.2	$5
Health	D	07 BAL	96	21	25	2	11	8	260	263	260	276	448	723	2	69	36	0.07	245	42	15	44	150	7%	210	60%	4.46	0.5	$4
PT/Exp	F	08 BAL	* 262	27	51	1	21	8	194	118	189	253	257	510	7	73	26	0.30	194	42	17	41	44	1%	125	21%	1.62	-22.9	$1
Consist	D	1st Half	134	15	30	1	9	3	221			267	304	571	6	76	29	0.26	208	42	16	42	59	2%	110	22%	2.42	-8.1	$1
LIMA Plan	F	2nd Half	128	12	21	0	13	5	166			239	207	446	9	71	23	0.33	0	44	22	33	28	0%	129	21%	0.73	-15.2	$0
+/- Score	6	09 Proj	33	4	7	0	3	1	212			267	332	599	7	74	28	0.29	234	44	22	34	76	4%	131	30%	2.86	-1.6	$0

0-8-.179 in 112 AB at BAL. Horrible OBA, ct% and Eye mean one thing - he's not bad as a pinch-runner. Ask yourself how desperate for SBs am I really?" and then pass.

Byrd,Marlon

Byrd,Marlon			AB	R	H	HR	RBI	SB	Avg	vL	vR	OB	Slg	OPS	bb%	ct%	h%	Eye	xBA	G	L	F	PX	hr/f	SX	SBO	RC/G	RAR	R$
Pos	897	04 PHI	* 498	58	112	7	46	4	225	213	232	269	325	594	6	83	26	0.35	252	58	14	28	65	6%	79	9%	2.81	-28.3	$5
Age	31	05 2NL	* 329	38	94	8	38	8	287	326	228	338	434	772	7	82	33	0.44	268	38	22	40	100	7%	92	11%	5.01	4.2	$11
Bats	Right	06 WAS	* 352	44	79	10	42	6	223	188	242	293	361	654	9	78	26	0.44	251	45	21	34	87	11%	71	11%	3.54	-9.8	$6
Health	B	07 TEX	* 590	78	169	14	89	7	286	327	300	328	432	761	6	79	34	0.30	263	47	20	33	94	9%	105	7%	4.79	4.4	$18
PT/Exp	C	08 TEX	403	70	120	10	53	7	298	277	308	370	462	831	10	85	33	0.74	293	46	21	33	106	9%	105	7%	5.92	6.4	$15
Consist	C	1st Half	143	21	35	3	13	2	245			321	385	705	10	78	29	0.52	256	47	19	35	93	8%	102	8%	4.34	-4.3	$3
LIMA Plan	C	2nd Half	260	49	85	7	40	5	327			397	504	900	10	88	35	0.97	312	46	23	32	112	10%	100	7%	6.73	9.6	$12
+/- Score	4	09 Proj	485	72	135	12	63	8	278			340	430	770	9	82	32	0.51	275	46	21	33	98	9%	100	8%	5.06	1.4	$15

In 2007, it was a huge 1H but lackluster 2H. This year, it was a monster 2H. Difference is that 2008 saw career-highs in bb%, ct% and Eye. Figured out how to hit RHers too.
UP: .320 BA.

Byrnes,Eric

Byrnes,Eric			AB	R	H	HR	RBI	SB	Avg	vL	vR	OB	Slg	OPS	bb%	ct%	h%	Eye	xBA	G	L	F	PX	hr/f	SX	SBO	RC/G	RAR	R$
Pos	7	04 OAK	569	91	161	20	73	17	283	344	260	337	467	804	7	80	32	0.41	258	34	18	47	117	9%	122	12%	5.37	7.0	$21
Age	33	05 2TM	412	49	93	10	40	7	226	263	205	282	371	653	7	83	25	0.45	250	32	20	48	96	6%	102	10%	3.58	-18.3	$7
Bats	Right	06 ARI	562	82	150	26	79	25	267	323	244	309	482	791	6	84	28	0.39	281	38	18	44	124	12%	120	24%	5.06	-3.1	$23
Health	F	07 ARI	626	103	179	21	83	50	286	248	297	346	460	806	8	84	31	0.58	260	35	19	46	101	9%	148	32%	5.43	1.3	$32
PT/Exp	B	08 ARI	206	28	43	6	23	4	209	258	188	266	369	635	7	83	23	0.44	264	39	19	42	104	8%	98	21%	3.34	-13.6	$3
Consist	C	1st Half	206	28	43	6	23	4	209			266	369	635	7	83	23	0.44	264	39	19	42	104	8%	98	21%	3.34	-13.6	$3
LIMA Plan	C+	2nd Half	0	0	0	0	0	0	0																				
+/- Score	17	09 Proj	585	84	155	20	72	19	265			317	441	758	7	83	29	0.45	265	37	19	45	108	9%	116	18%	4.79	-10.1	$20

Sore hamstrings hurt him all year, and a torn hamstring knocked him out for good in June. BPIs down, but 23% hit rate is a primary culprit. Won't see 50 SB again, but still offers power/speed blend if healthy.

Cabrera,Asdrubal

Cabrera,Asdrubal			AB	R	H	HR	RBI	SB	Avg	vL	vR	OB	Slg	OPS	bb%	ct%	h%	Eye	xBA	G	L	F	PX	hr/f	SX	SBO	RC/G	RAR	R$
Pos	46	04	0	0	0	0	0	0	0							0			0						0				
Age	23	05	0	0	0	0	0	0	0							0			0						0				
Bats	Both	06 aaa	393	58	106	5	39	13	269			332	375	706	9	80	33	0.47	0				76		88	22%	4.31	-0.6	$10
Health	A	07 CLE	* 565	108	167	9	75	23	295	340	259	365	423	788	10	87	33	0.86	276	44	20	36	84	5%	122	18%	5.44	22.9	$23
PT/Exp	C	08 CLE	* 493	71	135	10	59	6	274	349	230	344	394	738	10	80	33	0.52	257	46	21	34	85	8%	67	8%	4.71	-2.6	$13
Consist	B	1st Half	238	30	57	2	20	3	239			314	315	630	10	79	30	0.52	232	44	20	35	56	3%	71	9%	3.38	-10.9	$3
LIMA Plan	C	2nd Half	255	41	78	8	39	3	306			372	467	839	10	80	36	0.53	278	46	21	32	111	12%	55	8%	5.93	7.3	$10
+/- Score	-15	09 Proj	461	75	126	12	57	7	273			343	418	761	10	82	31	0.60	274	45	21	34	96	9%	78	10%	5.00	7.1	$14

6-47-.259 in 352 AB at CLE. PRO: Big 2H, maintained high bb%, hr/f spike. CON: BA vs RH, SX drop, ct% regression. Developing as a hitter, but the SB decline chops his value.

Cabrera,Jolbert

Cabrera,Jolbert			AB	R	H	HR	RBI	SB	Avg	vL	vR	OB	Slg	OPS	bb%	ct%	h%	Eye	xBA	G	L	F	PX	hr/f	SX	SBO	RC/G	RAR	R$
Pos	7	04 SEA	359	38	97	6	47	10	270			301	384	686	4	81	32	0.23	0				76		99	15%	3.78	-12.1	$9
Age	36	05	0	0	0	0	0	0	0							0			0						0				
Bats	Right	06 JPN	342	40	83	5	49	5	243			283	354	637	5	86	27	0.39	0				73		90	9%	3.38	-18.8	$6
Health	B	07 aa	200	12	36	3	12	0	179			198	273	471	2	84	20	0.16	0				63		43	5%	1.23	-25.8	($2)
PT/Exp	F	08 CIN	* 330	35	77	6	32	5	232	238	260	270	369	639	5	80	27	0.26	267	47	21	32	92	8%	102	13%	3.27	-21.7	$5
Consist	F	1st Half	233	19	55	3	22	3	234			270	359	629	5	82	27	0.27	0	54	23	23	84	8%	87	15%	3.18	-16.0	$3
LIMA Plan	F	2nd Half	97	16	22	3	10	2	227			272	392	664	6	74	28	0.24	260	46	21	33	113	12%	126	11%	3.54	-5.5	$2
+/- Score	7	09 Proj	100	11	22	2	10	1	220			255	348	604	5	81	25	0.24	262	46	21	33	83	7%	94	11%	2.81	-7.9	$1

3-12-.252 in 115 AB at CIN.
Career notes of interest:
- Played every position but P
- 1.000 career postseason BA
- Older brother of O.Cabrera
- Shot in backside during 2001 carjacking attempt.

Cabrera,Melky

Cabrera,Melky			AB	R	H	HR	RBI	SB	Avg	vL	vR	OB	Slg	OPS	bb%	ct%	h%	Eye	xBA	G	L	F	PX	hr/f	SX	SBO	RC/G	RAR	R$
Pos	8	04	0	0	0	0	0	0	0							0			0						0				
Age	24	05 a/a	523	63	133	12	68	12	255			297	371	669	6	86	28	0.44	0				72		100	11%	3.71	-11.0	$14
Bats	Both	06 NYY	* 582	93	175	11	73	15	301	286	278	372	423	795	10	89	33	0.98	273	49	17	33	73	7%	99	11%	5.50	13.7	$20
Health	A	07 NYY	545	66	149	8	73	13	273	250	282	327	391	717	7	88	30	0.63	281	51	20	29	71	6%	112	12%	4.46	-1.1	$14
PT/Exp	B	08 NYY	414	42	103	8	37	9	249	213	265	298	341	639	7	86	27	0.50	249	46	19	35	55	6%	79	10%	3.39	-24.0	$8
Consist	C	1st Half	283	27	69	7	32	6	244			310	350	660	9	86	26	0.68	253	46	19	36	64	8%	60	9%	3.74	-13.6	$6
LIMA Plan	D	2nd Half	131	15	34	1	5	3	260			271	321	591	2	86	29	0.11	239	48	18	34	37	3%	101	13%	2.59	-10.6	$2
+/- Score	-1	09 Proj	301	36	80	5	30	7	266			320	364	683	7	87	29	0.60	260	49	19	33	59	6%	90	11%	4.01	-8.3	$7

I never understood what the Yankees saw in this guy. His BPIs were never much more than average. Yankees always go for greatness; there was never greatness here, just mediocrity. And now less.

Cabrera,Miguel

Cabrera,Miguel			AB	R	H	HR	RBI	SB	Avg	vL	vR	OB	Slg	OPS	bb%	ct%	h%	Eye	xBA	G	L	F	PX	hr/f	SX	SBO	RC/G	RAR	R$
Pos	3	04 FLA	603	101	177	33	112	5	294	262	302	365	512	878	10	75	34	0.46	275	45	19	35	138	20%	70	4%	6.43	8.1	$27
Age	26	05 FLA	613	106	198	33	116	1	323	304	329	387	561	948	9	80	36	0.51	305	38	24	37	154	18%	59	1%	7.22	26.3	$32
Bats	Right	06 FLA	576	112	195	26	114	9	339	321	344	424	568	992	13	81	38	0.80	306	40	24	35	144	16%	74	7%	8.02	30.6	$32
Health	A	07 FLA	588	91	188	34	119	2	320	364	309	400	565	965	12	78	36	0.62	292	40	21	39	153	19%	50	2%	7.59	23.0	$29
PT/Exp	A	08 DET	616	85	180	37	127	1	292	311	286	351	537	889	8	80	32	0.44	294	41	20	39	153	19%	47	1%	6.36	18.6	$27
Consist	B	1st Half	303	37	85	11	48	1	281			351	459	810	10	80	32	0.54	266	42	18	40	118	11%	50	1%	5.57	2.5	$9
LIMA Plan	D	2nd Half	313	48	95	26	79	0	304			351	613	965	7	79	31	0.35	320	40	21	38	187	28%	35	0%	7.13	15.9	$18
+/- Score	7	09 Proj	599	93	190	40	124	1	317			385	589	974	10	79	34	0.53	307	41	21	38	169	22%	40	1%	7.51	36.1	$30

Took a while to get used to new ballpark, but 2H outburst keeps expectations high. H% was well below his three-year average, so expect a return to .300+ BA. 2H PX surge bodes well for '09.
UP: .325 BA, 45 HR.

SCOTT MONROE

Cabrera,Orlando			AB	R	H	HR	RBI	SB	Avg	vL	vR	OB	Slg	OPS	bb%	ct%	h%	Eye	xBA	G	L	F	PX	hr/f	SX	SBO	RC/G	RAR	R$
Pos	6	04 2TM	621	75	163	10	62	17	262	295	249	307	382	689	6	91	27	0.74	273	44	18	38	72	5%	104	14%	4.14	-2.8	$15
Age	34	05 ANA	540	70	139	8	57	21	257	242	266	306	365	671	7	91	27	0.76	267	41	19	39	67	4%	123	17%	3.96	-9.5	$15
Bats	Right	06 LAA	607	95	171	9	72	27	282	243	297	337	404	741	8	90	30	0.88	264	39	17	43	79	4%	114	18%	4.82	7.0	$20
Health	A	07 LAA	638	101	192	8	86	20	301	308	299	346	397	743	6	90	33	0.69	261	43	18	39	64	4%	100	13%	4.71	7.4	$23
PT/Exp	A	08 CHW	661	93	186	8	57	19	281	273	284	338	371	708	8	89	31	0.79	272	46	21	33	59	4%	90	13%	4.40	1.3	$18
Consist	A	1st Half	339	51	93	6	32	12	274			328	375	703	7	88	30	0.69	265	48	18	34	65	6%	93	14%	4.26	-0.7	$10
LIMA Plan	C+	2nd Half	322	42	93	2	25	7	289			348	366	714	8	90	32	0.91	279	43	25	32	54	2%	77	11%	4.55	2.0	$8
+/- Score	-26	09 Proj	616	89	171	7	64	15	278			331	368	699	7	90	30	0.79	266	44	20	36	61	3%	91	11%	4.30	-0.9	$16

PX and SX beginning to show typical mid-30s decline, but huge AB totals sustain his value. However, at this age, 600+ AB only gets tougher to reach.
DN: Less than 400 AB, 10 SB

Cairo,Miguel			AB	R	H	HR	RBI	SB	Avg	vL	vR	OB	Slg	OPS	bb%	ct%	h%	Eye	xBA	G	L	F	PX	hr/f	SX	SBO	RC/G	RAR	R$
Pos	3	04 NYY	360	48	105	6	42	11	292	336	267	325	417	742	5	86	32	0.37	267	44	20	36	73	5%	128	15%	4.54	-4.5	$11
Age	34	05 NYM	327	31	82	2	19	13	251	191	273	292	324	616	5	91	27	0.61	269	44	22	34	53	2%	88	20%	3.30	-22.4	$6
Bats	Right	06 NYY	222	28	53	0	30	13	239	279	221	281	320	601	6	86	28	0.42	257	53	16	31	55	0%	148	27%	3.05	-15.8	$5
Health	B	07 2TM	174	20	44	0	15	10	253	254	252	297	328	625	6	86	29	0.46	227	43	14	43	53	0%	129	27%	3.34	-12.2	$4
PT/Exp	F	08 SEA	221	34	55	0	23	5	249	267	237	305	330	636	8	86	29	0.56	265	49	20	31	62	0%	116	12%	3.56	-11.3	$4
Consist	A	1st Half	68	9	14	0	7	2	206			289	235	525	11	88	23	1.00	226	52	15	33	24	0%	75	15%	2.49	-6.0	$1
LIMA Plan	F	2nd Half	153	25	41	0	16	3	268			313	373	685	6	84	32	0.42	279	47	23	30	79	0%	119	11%	4.07	-5.3	$3
+/- Score	-7	09 Proj	172	23	43	0	18	7	250			301	335	636	7	86	29	0.53	256	48	18	35	60	0%	126	19%	3.53	-8.9	$4

Can still run a bit, but that is all he brings to the table. It's a testament to how bad things were in SEA that he somehow got 221 AB, most of them at 1B.

Callaspo,Alberto			AB	R	H	HR	RBI	SB	Avg	vL	vR	OB	Slg	OPS	bb%	ct%	h%	Eye	xBA	G	L	F	PX	hr/f	SX	SBO	RC/G	RAR	R$
Pos	4	04 aa	550	62	139	4	39	12	253			301	325	626	6	96	26	1.81	0				45		70	19%	3.69	-10.9	$9
Age	26	05 a/a	557	60	147	8	59	8	264			299	357	656	5	96	26	1.27	0				56		57	17%	3.85	-8.3	$12
Bats	Both	06 ARI	* 532	74	162	6	59	6	305	278	208	362	427	789	8	95	31	1.78	242	46	8	46	63	3%	94	8%	5.50	13.4	$16
Health	B	07 ARI	* 370	48	100	5	31	2	271	219	214	329	380	709	8	92	28	1.11	285	47	21	32	68	4%	60	5%	4.53	-1.9	$7
PT/Exp	D	08 KC	213	21	65	0	16	2	305	333	291	362	371	733	8	93	33	1.36	289	47	26	28	40	0%	77	4%	4.87	-0.1	$5
Consist	B	1st Half	100	8	29	0	4	1	290			349	330	679	8	91	32	1.00	273	53	24	23	24	0%	64	6%	4.18	-2.0	$1
LIMA Plan	B	2nd Half	113	13	36	0	12	1	319			374	407	781	8	96	33	2.00	302	41	28	31	54	0%	83	3%	5.47	1.7	$3
+/- Score	-12	09 Proj	493	57	144	3	42	5	292			348	381	729	8	94	31	1.37	295	46	25	29	54	2%	83	6%	4.80	4.6	$10

The elite ct% and Eye levels look attractive, but the paltry PX is a killer, and he isn't fast enough to beat out grounders. With league-average power or speed, we'd have something here. For now, just empty BA.

Cameron,Mike			AB	R	H	HR	RBI	SB	Avg	vL	vR	OB	Slg	OPS	bb%	ct%	h%	Eye	xBA	G	L	F	PX	hr/f	SX	SBO	RC/G	RAR	R$
Pos	8	04 NYM	493	76	114	30	76	22	231	216	235	311	479	790	10	71	26	0.40	253	31	16	53	167	16%	108	25%	5.36	10.8	$20
Age	36	05 NYM	308	47	84	12	39	13	273	311	261	335	477	813	9	72	34	0.34	271	42	21	38	151	14%	126	18%	5.71	10.1	$13
Bats	Right	06 SD	552	88	148	22	83	25	268	252	273	352	482	833	11	74	32	0.50	255	38	17	45	137	12%	134	22%	6.08	26.5	$23
Health	B	07 SD	571	88	138	21	78	18	242	294	222	321	431	752	11	72	30	0.42	245	37	19	44	131	12%	122	16%	4.96	7.5	$17
PT/Exp	A	08 MIL	444	69	108	25	70	17	243	282	231	325	477	803	11	68	30	0.38	255	33	22	46	169	18%	108	20%	5.71	12.9	$18
Consist	B	1st Half	180	27	39	12	28	6	217			299	461	760	10	66	25	0.34	243	34	16	50	177	20%	81	18%	5.06	1.8	$6
LIMA Plan	B+	2nd Half	264	42	69	13	42	11	261			343	489	832	11	70	33	0.41	264	32	25	43	164	16%	115	21%	6.13	10.9	$12
+/- Score	-17	09 Proj	500	78	125	24	75	16	250			330	469	799	11	70	31	0.40	253	35	20	45	153	15%	114	17%	5.61	14.7	$19

Looked rusty returning from April suspension, but that was just a h% blip. 2H was right in line with prior years. PX and FB say power output should remain stable, and 2H SX says he can still run, too.

Cano,Robinson			AB	R	H	HR	RBI	SB	Avg	vL	vR	OB	Slg	OPS	bb%	ct%	h%	Eye	xBA	G	L	F	PX	hr/f	SX	SBO	RC/G	RAR	R$
Pos	4	04 a/a	508	58	135	12	66	2	267			316	413	729	7	89	28	0.67	0				83		71	7%	4.57	3.3	$11
Age	26	05 NYY	* 630	95	189	17	83	1	299	270	305	322	466	788	3	88	32	0.27	303	50	21	29	103	11%	76	3%	4.95	14.3	$21
Bats	Left	06 NYY	482	62	165	15	78	5	342	287	363	366	525	891	4	89	36	0.33	314	52	20	28	112	12%	66	6%	6.10	24.8	$20
Health	A	07 NYY	617	93	189	19	97	4	306	328	296	348	488	835	6	86	33	0.46	299	52	17	31	112	12%	85	6%	5.66	28.2	$23
PT/Exp	A	08 NYY	597	70	162	14	72	2	271	292	263	302	410	712	4	89	29	0.40	285	47	19	33	86	8%	55	4%	4.18	-12.1	$14
Consist	B	1st Half	302	32	73	6	33	1	242			275	358	633	4	91	25	0.54	275	50	18	33	73	7%	41	6%	3.40	-13.5	$4
LIMA Plan	C	2nd Half	295	38	89	8	39	1	302			329	464	793	4	87	33	0.31	292	45	21	34	100	9%	73	3%	5.04	1.2	$9
+/- Score	18	09 Proj	601	78	180	16	83	3	300			332	459	790	5	88	32	0.40	294	49	19	32	98	10%	65	5%	5.06	9.8	$19

A dreadful April (.151) ruined his full year totals; 2H in line with prior levels. But there's no growth to be found here, even as he enters peak years. Should rebound toward 2007 levels, but no further.. yet.

Cantu,Jorge			AB	R	H	HR	RBI	SB	Avg	vL	vR	OB	Slg	OPS	bb%	ct%	h%	Eye	xBA	G	L	F	PX	hr/f	SX	SBO	RC/G	RAR	R$
Pos	53	04 TAM	* 541	76	157	20	89	3	290	373	270	320	505	825	4	82	32	0.25	304	46	20	34	140	13%	79	3%	5.45	8.2	$18
Age	27	05 TAM	598	73	171	28	117	1	286	256	296	308	497	805	3	86	29	0.23	305	42	21	37	128	15%	44	1%	5.03	8.9	$22
Bats	Right	06 TAM	413	40	103	14	62	1	249	233	256	294	404	698	6	78	29	0.29	250	42	20	38	97	11%	50	2%	3.93	-13.1	$8
Health	A	07 2TM	* 300	33	77	4	33	0	255	232	283	308	374	682	7	81	31	0.39	262	45	22	34	89	5%	42	0%	3.94	-11.4	$4
PT/Exp	C	08 FLA	628	92	174	29	95	6	277	293	272	320	481	801	6	82	30	0.36	281	34	21	45	128	13%	67	6%	5.17	-3.5	$24
Consist	B	1st Half	321	47	88	14	47	2	274			323	467	790	7	81	30	0.38	268	39	17	44	124	12%	52	5%	5.09	-2.6	$11
LIMA Plan	C	2nd Half	307	45	86	15	48	4	280			318	495	813	5	84	29	0.34	294	30	25	45	133	13%	71	6%	5.26	-1.0	$12
+/- Score	21	09 Proj	564	72	152	20	81	3	270			313	447	759	6	82	30	0.34	273	37	21	42	114	11%	60	3%	4.71	-11.1	$17

Other than more fly balls and more AB, this breakout was composed of skills that he already owned. Should be sustainable, but as 2005-06 shows, the success/failure line for this skill set is thin.

Carlin,Luke			AB	R	H	HR	RBI	SB	Avg	vL	vR	OB	Slg	OPS	bb%	ct%	h%	Eye	xBA	G	L	F	PX	hr/f	SX	SBO	RC/G	RAR	R$
Pos	2	04	0	0	0	0	0	0	0							0			0						0				
Age	28	05 aa	230	19	49	1	20	3	215			304	264	568	11	82	26	0.72	0				36		59	8%	2.78	-8.1	$1
Bats	Both	06 aaa	249	21	54	3	22	0	219			321	310	631	13	82	26	0.85	0				61		30	0%	3.64	-5.6	$1
Health	A	07 aa	300	27	50	0	13	0	168			260	229	490	11	72	23	0.45	0				55		54	4%	1.48	-28.4	($4)
PT/Exp	F	08 SD	* 182	23	35	4	22	0	192	167	145	293	297	590	13	64	27	0.40	191	52	13	35	80	10%	57	0%	2.75	-8.4	$1
Consist	D	1st Half	96	14	20	2	11	0	207			337	334	671	16	62	31	0.52	209	48	18	35	108	9%	73	0%	4.25	0.1	$1
LIMA Plan	F	2nd Half	86	9	15	2	11	0	176			240	255	495	8	66	23	0.25	151	60	5	35	51	11%	31	0%	1.09	-8.7	$0
+/- Score	-0	09 Proj	62	6	12	1	6	0	194			286	267	553	11	71	26	0.45	185	53	12	35	56	5%	35	2%	2.23	-4.0	($0)

1-6-.149 in 94 AB at SD. Fairly patient at the plate, at least until pitchers realize that there is little danger to throwing him fastballs down the middle. No reason to have his name on your draft materials.

Carroll,Jamey			AB	R	H	HR	RBI	SB	Avg	vL	vR	OB	Slg	OPS	bb%	ct%	h%	Eye	xBA	G	L	F	PX	hr/f	SX	SBO	RC/G	RAR	R$
Pos	45	04 MON	219	36	63	0	16	5	288	250	310	378	370	748	13	90	32	1.52	285	48	23	29	57	0%	103	8%	5.31	4.3	$6
Age	35	05 WAS	303	44	76	0	22	3	251	293	235	326	284	610	10	82	31	0.62	255	53	26	21	27	0%	76	7%	3.23	-12.1	$4
Bats	Right	06 COL	463	84	139	5	36	10	300	359	283	376	404	780	11	86	34	0.85	275	49	23	29	64	4%	95	14%	5.39	10.3	$15
Health	A	07 COL	227	45	51	2	22	6	225	262	194	310	300	609	11	85	26	0.82	260	44	25	32	50	3%	113	12%	3.35	-9.4	$4
PT/Exp	C	08 CLE	347	60	96	1	36	7	277	261	284	341	346	687	9	81	34	0.52	260	45	27	27	49	1%	117	9%	4.12	-7.7	$9
Consist	C	1st Half	170	30	50	0	16	6	294			355	365	720	9	82	36	0.52	258	40	30	30	47	0%	136	12%	4.53	-1.7	$5
LIMA Plan	D	2nd Half	177	30	46	1	20	1	260			328	328	656	9	81	32	0.53	259	51	25	25	50	3%	80	5%	3.72	-6.1	$4
+/- Score	-27	09 Proj	225	40	60	1	22	5	267			340	341	681	10	83	32	0.67	263	46	25	28	51	2%	109	10%	4.13	-2.3	$5

Classic backup IF who hits the ball on the ground to take advantage of his speed, and swipes the occasional bag. Unfortunately, speed is a skill of the young, and he's no longer young.

Casey,Sean			AB	R	H	HR	RBI	SB	Avg	vL	vR	OB	Slg	OPS	bb%	ct%	h%	Eye	xBA	G	L	F	PX	hr/f	SX	SBO	RC/G	RAR	R$
Pos	3	04 CIN	571	101	185	24	99	2	324	306	332	374	534	909	7	94	32	1.28	330	43	23	34	115	13%	74	1%	6.57	9.3	$27
Age	34	05 CIN	529	75	165	9	58	2	312	335	298	369	423	793	8	91	33	1.00	284	52	19	29	73	6%	53	1%	5.40	-2.9	$18
Bats	Left	06 2TM	397	47	108	8	59	0	272	287	266	328	388	716	8	89	29	0.77	278	44	23	33	71	7%	28	1%	4.45	-14.3	$9
Health	C	07 DET	453	40	134	4	54	2	296	365	285	352	393	745	8	91	32	0.93	276	46	21	33	68	3%	40	3%	4.88	-4.7	$10
PT/Exp	C	08 BOS	199	14	64	0	17	1	322	324	321	375	392	767	8	87	37	0.68	278	38	28	34	59	0%	27	1%	5.10	-0.9	$4
Consist	A	1st Half	106	7	38	0	8	1	358			409	453	862	8	93	38	1.29	322	39	30	30	74	0%	27	3%	6.25	2.6	$3
LIMA Plan	F	2nd Half	93	7	26	0	9	0	280			337	323	659	8	81	35	0.44	226	36	24	40	39	0%	16	0%	3.69	-4.1	$1
+/- Score	-41	09 Proj	193	18	54	2	21	1	280			337	367	703	8	88	31	0.72	271	42	24	34	63	3%	31	2%	4.35	-5.0	$3

Still makes good contact, but with no power or speed, that's a marginal skill at best. H% history and xBA say that BA won't revisit .300 level, either.

RAY MURPHY

Cash,Kevin

			AB	R	H	HR	RBI	SB	Avg	vL	vR	OB	Slg	OPS	bb%	ct%	h%	Eye	xBA	G	L	F	PX	hr/f	SX	SBO	RC/G	RAR	R$
Pos	2	04 TOR	181	18	35	4	21	0	193			236	309	545	5	67	26	0.17	0				92		33	0%	1.89	-14.0	$0
Age	31	05 aaa	143	16	32	6	18	0	226			270	392	662	6	77	25	0.26	0				110		28	0%	3.42	-2.1	$3
Bats	Right	06 aaa	240	15	38	2	18	1	159			225	225	450	8	69	22	0.27	0				53		48	6%	0.65	-29.8	($3)
Health	A	07 aaa	176	18	27	5	20	0	155			234	290	524	9	69	19	0.33	0				100		29	0%	1.65	-15.8	($1)
PT/Exp	F	08 BOS	142	11	32	3	15	0	225	361	179	313	338	651	11	65	33	0.36	199	50	18	32	97	10%	11	0%	3.69	-2.2	$1
Consist	D	1st Half	79	5	19	1	9	0	241			318	342	660	10	67	35	0.35	216	50	22	28	93	7%	9	0%	3.82	-0.9	$1
LIMA Plan	F	2nd Half	63	6	13	2	6	0	206			306	333	639	12	62	30	0.38	179	50	13	38	103	14%	15	0%	3.51	-1.3	$0
+/- Score	-58	09 Proj	**126**	**11**	**24**	**3**	**13**	**0**	**190**			**270**	**302**	**573**	**10**	**67**	**26**	**0.33**	**202**	**50**	**17**	**33**	**89**	**11%**	**24**	**1%**	**2.40**	**-7.4**	**$0**

Rising bb% can't offset poor ct%, average power and too many GBs. One of many backup catchers who can hurt you with increased playing time. Unrosterable in any format.

Casilla,Alexi

			AB	R	H	HR	RBI	SB	Avg	vL	vR	OB	Slg	OPS	bb%	ct%	h%	Eye	xBA	G	L	F	PX	hr/f	SX	SBO	RC/G	RAR	R$
Pos	4	04	0	0	0	0	0	0	0							0			0						0				
Age	24	05	0	0	0	0	0	0	0							0			0						0				
Bats	Both	06 aa	170	26	48	1	12	18	282			348	371	718	9	88	32	0.85	0				59		134	42%	4.63	1.3	$7
Health	A	07 MIN *	509	67	126	3	29	35	248	274	181	302	308	611	7	84	29	0.50	260	62	16	22	43	3%	118	34%	3.13	-13.5	$13
PT/Exp	D	08 MIN *	481	67	126	7	52	10	262	264	289	325	343	668	8	87	29	0.72	245	52	15	34	52	5%	73	10%	3.90	-13.9	$12
Consist	C	1st Half	248	33	66	4	32	7	267			335	359	695	9	86	30	0.76	255	53	16	31	61	6%	69	14%	4.25	-4.7	$7
LIMA Plan	D+	2nd Half	233	34	60	3	20	3	258			313	326	640	8	88	28	0.68	235	51	14	35	44	4%	69	6%	3.54	-9.2	$5
+/- Score	-14	09 Proj	**418**	**58**	**109**	**4**	**34**	**17**	**261**			**320**	**334**	**654**	**8**	**86**	**29**	**0.64**	**248**	**54**	**15**	**31**	**49**	**4%**	**98**	**19%**	**3.72**	**-9.3**	**$10**

7-50-.281 in 385 AB at MIN. Slowed by thumb injury after July. Parlayed GB and turf into 35% h% and .314 BA at home, but lack of pop makes repeat unlikely. The upside? SB should increase with SBO.

Castillo,Jose

			AB	R	H	HR	RBI	SB	Avg	vL	vR	OB	Slg	OPS	bb%	ct%	h%	Eye	xBA	G	L	F	PX	hr/f	SX	SBO	RC/G	RAR	R$
Pos	5	04 PIT	383	44	98	8	39	3	256	267	253	298	368	666	6	76	32	0.25	246	59	16	24	75	11%	75	5%	3.55	-17.0	$7
Age	28	05 PIT	370	49	99	11	53	2	268	258	271	310	416	727	6	84	29	0.39	282	46	23	31	90	11%	76	5%	4.34	-4.7	$11
Bats	Right	06 PIT	518	54	131	14	65	6	253	259	251	296	382	679	6	81	29	0.33	253	46	19	34	81	10%	51	8%	3.72	-27.1	$11
Health	A	07 PIT	221	18	54	0	24	0	244	246	244	264	335	599	3	78	31	0.13	250	57	18	25	78	0%	41	0%	2.72	-18.9	$1
PT/Exp	C	08 2NL	426	46	105	6	37	2	246	238	250	291	376	667	6	81	29	0.33	275	51	21	28	91	6%	77	4%	3.71	-21.0	$6
Consist	B	1st Half	290	35	76	6	27	1	262			314	421	735	7	83	30	0.45	291	52	20	28	106	9%	72	4%	4.60	-6.5	$6
LIMA Plan	F	2nd Half	136	11	29	0	10	1	213			241	279	521	4	76	28	0.16	239	49	23	29	56	0%	77	4%	1.70	-15.4	$0
+/- Score	38	09 Proj	**272**	**26**	**66**	**3**	**27**	**1**	**243**			**277**	**352**	**629**	**5**	**79**	**30**	**0.23**	**260**	**51**	**20**	**28**	**80**	**5%**	**72**	**4%**	**3.15**	**-18.3**	**$3**

Returned to earth in 2H after short-lived power-and-patience spike. Only the inattentive or delusional held on through August. There's still nothing to recommend here.

Castillo,Luis

			AB	R	H	HR	RBI	SB	Avg	vL	vR	OB	Slg	OPS	bb%	ct%	h%	Eye	xBA	G	L	F	PX	hr/f	SX	SBO	RC/G	RAR	R$
Pos	4	04 FLA	564	91	164	2	47	21	291	308	285	374	348	722	12	88	33	1.10	272	65	17	19	32	2%	131	11%	4.81	3.1	$18
Age	33	05 FLA	439	72	132	4	30	10	301	423	259	391	374	764	13	93	32	2.03	305	63	22	15	41	6%	96	10%	5.47	11.2	$14
Bats	Both	06 MIN	584	84	173	3	49	25	296	256	316	358	370	728	9	90	33	0.97	283	61	18	21	44	3%	117	18%	4.74	10.2	$18
Health	C	07 2TM	548	91	165	1	38	19	301	296	303	363	359	722	9	92	33	1.18	283	67	15	18	37	1%	115	13%	4.73	5.8	$17
PT/Exp	B	08 NYM	298	46	73	3	28	17	245	211	257	353	305	659	14	88	27	1.43	272	66	16	18	36	6%	108	17%	4.21	-5.0	$9
Consist	A	1st Half	245	42	64	3	26	13	261			365	331	696	14	91	28	1.90	283	65	16	19	39	7%	112	16%	4.71	-0.4	$9
LIMA Plan	D	2nd Half	53	4	9	0	2	4	170			302	189	490	16	74	23	0.71	210	74	13	13	19	0%	71	22%	1.62	-5.4	$0
+/- Score	9	09 Proj	**303**	**41**	**84**	**1**	**21**	**16**	**277**			**366**	**330**	**696**	**12**	**86**	**32**	**0.99**	**264**	**67**	**16**	**17**	**34**	**3%**	**109**	**16%**	**4.48**	**-2.0**	**$9**

Ongoing leg issues were chipping at pop, xBA. Still, DL time and BA crash weren't expected. Other skills remain intact, but even with a h% rebound, this old 33-year old may never see 500 PA again.

Casto,Kory

			AB	R	H	HR	RBI	SB	Avg	vL	vR	OB	Slg	OPS	bb%	ct%	h%	Eye	xBA	G	L	F	PX	hr/f	SX	SBO	RC/G	RAR	R$
Pos	3	04	0	0	0	0	0	0	0							0			0						0				
Age	27	05	0	0	0	0	0	0	0							0			0						0				
Bats	Left	06 aa	489	72	114	16	68	5	233			326	394	720	12	79	26	0.66	0				97		83	7%	4.56	-17.1	$10
Health	A	07 aaa	462	51	98	9	53	4	212			289	322	610	10	75	26	0.43	278	45	34	21	78	12%	69	7%	3.02	-38.6	$4
PT/Exp	D	08 WAS *	293	30	68	7	36	2	232	48	239	312	350	662	10	79	27	0.54	273	48	27	25	82	11%	39	5%	3.75	-17.6	$5
Consist	C	1st Half	138	13	32	3	20	1	232			308	335	643	10	84	26	0.70	264	46	23	31	66	8%	36	5%	3.61	-8.9	$2
LIMA Plan	F	2nd Half	155	17	36	4	16	1	233			315	363	678	11	74	29	0.46	272	49	28	23	97	14%	39	5%	3.95	-8.4	$2
+/- Score	-3	09 Proj	**157**	**18**	**38**	**4**	**19**	**1**	**242**			**321**	**356**	**677**	**10**	**77**	**29**	**0.51**	**269**	**48**	**28**	**24**	**79**	**12%**	**42**	**5%**	**3.91**	**-9.2**	**$3**

2-16-.214 in 163 AB at WAS. Patience, LD% are intriguing but GB rate stunts power and and ct% caps BA. Unlikely to help unless one of these changes. Age keeps him barely watchable for now.

Castro,Juan

			AB	R	H	HR	RBI	SB	Avg	vL	vR	OB	Slg	OPS	bb%	ct%	h%	Eye	xBA	G	L	F	PX	hr/f	SX	SBO	RC/G	RAR	R$
Pos	6	04 CIN	299	36	73	5	26	1	244	238	247	278	378	656	4	83	28	0.27	254	45	16	40	90	5%	80	2%	3.50	-5.6	$4
Age	36	05 MIN	272	27	70	5	33	0	257	247	262	281	386	667	3	86	29	0.23	275	50	19	31	87	7%	47	2%	3.58	-7.8	$5
Bats	Right	06 2TM	251	18	63	3	28	1	251	268	244	282	351	633	4	86	28	0.31	265	49	21	29	59	5%	65	5%	3.25	-8.4	$3
Health	A	07 CIN	89	5	16	0	5	0	180	226	155	215	236	451	4	76	24	0.19	199	39	17	43	52	0%	21	0%	0.83	-10.4	($1)
PT/Exp	F	08 2TM *	213	23	44	3	18	0	207	185	196	259	286	545	7	84	23	0.44	217	49	13	38	54	4%	35	0%	2.28	-14.6	$1
Consist	D	1st Half	33	5	9	1	2	0	258			314	386	700	8	93	26	1.15	0	30	10	60	75	5%	43	0%	4.35	-0.1	$1
LIMA Plan	F	2nd Half	180	18	36	2	16	0	197			249	268	517	6	82	23	0.39	211	50	13	36	49	4%	33	0%	1.87	-14.8	$0
+/- Score	-0	09 Proj	**200**	**19**	**47**	**3**	**21**	**0**	**235**			**270**	**340**	**610**	**5**	**84**	**27**	**0.30**	**253**	**49**	**17**	**33**	**69**	**5%**	**57**	**2%**	**2.96**	**-8.8**	**$2**

2-16-.192 in 161 AB at CIN and BAL. It's possible that he doesn't have the worst skill set on this page. But his age makes him the worst gamble for an upside surprise. Don't even think about it.

Castro,Ramon

			AB	R	H	HR	RBI	SB	Avg	vL	vR	OB	Slg	OPS	bb%	ct%	h%	Eye	xBA	G	L	F	PX	hr/f	SX	SBO	RC/G	RAR	R$
Pos	2	04 FLA *	312	31	56	4	28	4	179	143	134	254	279	532	9	81	21	0.52	188	32	11	58	61	3%	100	13%	2.18	-16.7	($0)
Age	33	05 NYM *	339	43	76	13	59	2	223	290	236	293	412	705	9	76	26	0.41	259	36	19	45	133	11%	61	3%	4.19	4.2	$8
Bats	Right	06 NYM	126	13	30	4	12	0	238	269	230	319	389	708	11	68	32	0.38	227	36	22	42	112	11%	17	0%	4.40	0.2	$2
Health	F	07 NYM	144	24	41	11	31	0	285	276	287	331	556	887	6	73	32	0.26	271	36	18	46	171	23%	30	0%	6.34	7.7	$7
PT/Exp	F	08 NYM	143	15	35	7	24	0	245	277	218	308	441	748	8	76	27	0.38	271	36	24	40	128	16%	15	0%	4.64	1.8	$4
Consist	D	1st Half	55	7	14	2	8	0	255			339	418	757	11	75	31	0.50	250	46	20	34	114	14%	23	0%	4.98	1.2	$1
LIMA Plan	F	2nd Half	88	8	21	5	16	0	239			287	455	742	6	77	25	0.30	289	29	26	44	135	17%	7	0%	4.41	0.5	$2
+/- Score	0	09 Proj	**156**	**19**	**41**	**8**	**26**	**0**	**263**			**324**	**466**	**790**	**8**	**74**	**31**	**0.35**	**262**	**36**	**21**	**42**	**134**	**16%**	**26**	**1%**	**5.21**	**4.4**	**$5**

Once again unable to take full advantage of opportunity due to lack of durability. Remains a reasonable #2 catching choice with good power and poor BA. But age is now increasing the risk factor here.

Catalanotto,Frank

			AB	R	H	HR	RBI	SB	Avg	vL	vR	OB	Slg	OPS	bb%	ct%	h%	Eye	xBA	G	L	F	PX	hr/f	SX	SBO	RC/G	RAR	R$
Pos	370	04 TOR	249	27	73	1	26	1	293	227	307	338	390	728	6	87	33	0.52	289	44	27	29	70	2%	58	1%	4.56	-3.0	$5
Age	35	05 TOR	419	56	126	8	59	0	301	290	302	357	451	809	8	87	33	0.70	289	45	21	35	96	6%	64	2%	5.56	5.4	$13
Bats	Left	06 TOR	437	56	131	7	56	1	300	237	306	374	439	814	11	92	32	1.41	290	48	19	34	88	5%	46	3%	5.86	5.3	$11
Health	B	07 TEX	331	52	86	11	44	2	260	231	261	318	444	762	8	89	27	0.76	309	51	19	30	108	12%	93	4%	4.97	-2.8	$9
PT/Exp	C	08 TEX	248	28	68	2	21	1	274	167	280	328	399	728	7	88	30	0.69	288	53	18	30	92	3%	56	3%	4.67	-4.3	$4
Consist	B	1st Half	168	20	47	2	10	1	280			349	399	748	10	90	30	1.06	288	56	18	27	85	5%	41	4%	5.04	-1.1	$3
LIMA Plan	D	2nd Half	80	8	21	0	11	0	262			280	400	680	2	85	31	0.17	281	46	17	36	107	0%	67	0%	3.85	-3.3	$1
+/- Score	-10	09 Proj	**256**	**32**	**70**	**4**	**30**	**1**	**273**			**324**	**418**	**742**	**7**	**88**	**30**	**0.63**	**293**	**49**	**19**	**32**	**98**	**5%**	**68**	**3%**	**4.77**	**-3.7**	**$5**

BA rebounded thanks to h%, but not back to 2003-06 levels. Slow erosion in LD%, severe platoon status reaffirmed by by only 15 PA vs. LH. Still useful, but age and declining AB should give you pause.

Cedeno,Ronny

			AB	R	H	HR	RBI	SB	Avg	vL	vR	OB	Slg	OPS	bb%	ct%	h%	Eye	xBA	G	L	F	PX	hr/f	SX	SBO	RC/G	RAR	R$
Pos	46	04 aa	384	34	96	5	42	9	250			291	349	640	5	82	29	0.32	0				64		83	22%	3.32	-12.0	$7
Age	26	05 CHC *	325	48	105	8	35	10	323	256	341	365	454	819	6	89	34	0.63	291	61	14	25	79	12%	91	14%	5.48	8.1	$15
Bats	Right	06 CHC	534	51	131	6	41	8	245	230	251	269	339	608	3	80	30	0.16	227	47	16	37	58	4%	96	14%	2.76	-29.6	$7
Health	A	07 CHC *	361	48	106	13	42	7	294	176	225	343	451	794	7	84	32	0.45	263	33	23	44	92	9%	76	12%	5.16	4.7	$13
PT/Exp	C	08 CHC	216	36	58	2	28	4	269	257	282	325	352	677	8	81	32	0.44	249	52	18	30	64	4%	83	8%	3.88	-5.5	$6
Consist	D	1st Half	127	21	35	1	20	3	276			343	362	705	9	80	34	0.50	241	54	15	31	70	3%	78	10%	4.33	-1.6	$4
LIMA Plan	F	2nd Half	89	15	23	1	8	1	258			298	337	635	5	83	30	0.33	260	50	22	28	56	5%	77	4%	3.25	-3.9	$2
+/- Score	2	09 Proj	**164**	**23**	**45**	**3**	**18**	**3**	**274**			**320**	**387**	**707**	**6**	**82**	**32**	**0.37**	**259**	**49**	**19**	**32**	**74**	**7%**	**89**	**10%**	**4.15**	**-2.6**	**$5**

Made better contact in 2H while being plagued by lower h%. But even better contact and a h% north of 30% can't hide the lack of power and speed here. The best thing about this profile is his age.

JOCK THOMPSON

Chavez,Endy

			AB	R	H	HR	RBI	SB	Avg	vL	vR	OB	Slg	OPS	bb%	ct%	h%	Eye	xBA	G	L	F	PX	hr/f	SX	SBO	RC/G	RAR	R$
Pos	97	04 MON	* 567	72	157	5	39	36	277	241	290	319	369	688	6	92	29	0.78	279	57	15	28	52	3%	143	29%	4.15	-18.8	$19
Age	31	05 2NL	* 203	27	42	1	14	6	207	381	179	257	285	542	6	91	23	0.71	288	57	21	23	46	2%	137	19%	2.57	-17.2	$2
Bats	Left	06 NYM	353	48	108	4	42	12	306	333	298	350	431	781	6	88	34	0.55	295	55	20	25	76	5%	120	15%	5.15	3.7	$13
Health	C	07 NYM	150	20	43	1	17	5	287	276	289	327	380	707	6	89	32	0.56	284	60	17	23	57	3%	111	17%	4.29	-2.5	$4
PT/Exp	D	08 NYM	270	30	72	1	12	6	267	194	278	310	330	640	6	92	29	0.77	270	53	19	28	40	1%	99	9%	3.63	-12.2	$5
Consist	B	1st Half	157	16	39	1	6	4	248			302	306	608	7	93	26	1.09	263	47	20	32	38	2%	67	11%	3.38	-8.4	$2
LIMA Plan	F	2nd Half	113	14	33	0	6	2	292			322	363	685	4	90	32	0.45	278	61	17	22	42	0%	112	6%	3.99	-3.8	$3
+/- Score	-11	09 Proj	231	29	64	1	18	6	277			318	362	680	6	90	30	0.62	280	57	18	25	52	2%	110	11%	4.03	-6.8	$5

Surface stats are in a three-year swoon, and the skills show why. 2nd half SX feels like a rebound, but it's being skewed by two triples in a small AB sample. Minus speed, all those ground balls just become ground outs.

Chavez,Eric

			AB	R	H	HR	RBI	SB	Avg	vL	vR	OB	Slg	OPS	bb%	ct%	h%	Eye	xBA	G	L	F	PX	hr/f	SX	SBO	RC/G	RAR	R$
Pos	5	04 OAK	475	87	131	29	77	6	276	306	257	396	501	898	17	79	29	0.96	272	41	18	42	131	19%	57	5%	6.91	27.3	$20
Age	31	05 OAK	625	92	168	27	101	6	269	260	271	331	466	796	8	79	30	0.45	271	39	18	43	130	13%	77	4%	5.29	14.2	$22
Bats	Left	06 OAK	485	74	117	22	72	3	241	197	257	353	435	788	15	79	26	0.84	260	39	18	44	118	13%	68	2%	5.50	7.1	$12
Health	F	07 OAK	341	43	82	15	46	4	240	234	244	309	446	755	9	78	27	0.45	264	36	17	46	136	12%	78	8%	4.82	-0.5	$8
PT/Exp	D	08 OAK	89	10	22	2	14	0	247	333	215	295	393	688	6	80	29	0.33	252	42	17	41	108	7%	28	0%	3.93	-2.5	$2
Consist	B	1st Half	86	10	22	2	14	0	256			297	407	704	5	80	30	0.29	258	42	17	41	111	7%	30	0%	4.08	-2.0	$2
LIMA Plan	D	2nd Half	3	0	0	0	0	0	0			250	0	250	25	67	0	1.00	0	50	0	50	0	0%		0%	-2.42	-0.9	$0
+/- Score	-23	09 Proj	220	31	56	8	34	1	255			330	433	763	10	79	29	0.54	261	39	17	43	119	10%	68	3%	5.00	0.8	$6

Ct% is the only skill that wasn't at a five-year low in 2008. He could still have a big year left in him, but if you spend more than a buck or two on that chance, you're ignoring the reality, which includes yet another surgery.

Chavez,Raul

			AB	R	H	HR	RBI	SB	Avg	vL	vR	OB	Slg	OPS	bb%	ct%	h%	Eye	xBA	G	L	F	PX	hr/f	SX	SBO	RC/G	RAR	R$
Pos	2	04 HOU	162	9	34	0	23	0	210	139	230	256	259	515	6	77	27	0.26	212	52	19	29	45	0%	23	3%	1.71	-10.6	$0
Age	36	05 HOU	* 218	12	40	2	16	1	185	133	188	213	256	468	3	83	22	0.20	204	44	12	43	52	3%	38	3%	1.17	-18.2	($1)
Bats	Right	06 aa	196	12	34	1	14	0	171			203	229	431	4	87	19	0.30	0				39		23	0%	0.97	-21.7	($2)
Health	A	07 aaa	290	23	54	4	25	1	186			211	264	474	3	86	20	0.23	0				52		47	2%	1.37	-27.7	($1)
PT/Exp	F	08 PIT	* 201	19	51	3	19	0	255	240	264	278	345	623	3	88	28	0.27	262	41	23	36	57	4%	42	0%	3.10	-6.5	$3
Consist	C	1st Half	148	14	35	3	18	0	238			261	353	614	3	88	25	0.26	278	35	26	39	71	5%	48	0%	3.01	-5.3	$2
LIMA Plan	F	2nd Half	53	5	16	0	1	0	302			327	321	648	4	87	35	0.29	218	48	20	33	16	0%	25	0%	3.36	-1.2	$1
+/- Score	-31	09 Proj	135	11	31	1	10	0	230			256	292	548	3	86	26	0.26	240	46	20	34	43	3%	32	1%	2.22	-8.2	$1

1-10-.259 in 116 AB at PIT. Last season was worth more in Roto dollars than every other season in his career combined. I'd like to see A-Rod or Pujols pull that off.

Choo,Shin-Soo

			AB	R	H	HR	RBI	SB	Avg	vL	vR	OB	Slg	OPS	bb%	ct%	h%	Eye	xBA	G	L	F	PX	hr/f	SX	SBO	RC/G	RAR	R$
Pos	97	04 aa	517	80	149	13	76	36	288			356	416	771	9	83	33	0.60	0				72		141	27%	5.09	1.3	$25
Age	26	05 aaa	444	61	106	9	45	16	239		91	332	356	688	12	80	28	0.70	0	57	7	36	78	7%	102	20%	4.22	-10.4	$11
Bats	Left	06 2AL	* 532	84	153	14	63	27	288	278	281	358	444	801	10	78	35	0.50	294	56	24	20	102	17%	126	22%	5.53	-2.0	$21
Health	C	07 aaa	208	29	49	2	23	9	233			297	324	620	8	83	27	0.53	0				64		111	22%	3.29	-12.1	$4
PT/Exp	D	08 CLE	* 359	69	107	15	69	5	299	286	317	382	523	905	12	74	37	0.53	289	41	23	36	161	15%	91	10%	7.08	17.4	$17
Consist	F	1st Half	117	16	30	3	19	2	258			355	417	772	13	75	32	0.60	260	43	20	38	124	9%	51	13%	5.37	0.0	$3
LIMA Plan	B+	2nd Half	242	53	77	12	50	3	318			396	574	970	11	74	39	0.49	300	41	24	36	180	19%	105	8%	7.92	16.9	$13
+/- Score	-18	09 Proj	500	83	137	17	76	15	274			351	461	813	11	77	33	0.52	278	43	23	35	129	13%	110	17%	5.72	5.0	$19

14-66-.309 in 317 AB at CLE. PX breakout was pumped up by 28 doubles; other than that, he's owned these skills before, most notably hr/f. If SBO returns and 2H is for real... UP: .300 BA, 25 HR, 20 SB

Church,Ryan

			AB	R	H	HR	RBI	SB	Avg	vL	vR	OB	Slg	OPS	bb%	ct%	h%	Eye	xBA	G	L	F	PX	hr/f	SX	SBO	RC/G	RAR	R$
Pos	9	04 aaa	347	54	107	14	58	0	307			374	537	911	10	86	33	0.78	0				135		73	1%	6.78	16.9	$14
Age	30	05 WAS	268	41	77	9	42	3	287	367	277	346	466	812	8	74	36	0.34	274	46	24	30	125	15%	102	7%	5.64	3.0	$10
Bats	Left	06 WAS	* 390	47	91	17	60	10	232	265	279	316	425	741	11	72	28	0.44	246	39	18	43	130	14%	79	12%	4.76	-0.2	$11
Health	C	07 WAS	470	57	128	15	70	3	272	229	287	341	464	805	9	77	32	0.46	284	43	22	35	138	12%	53	4%	5.58	9.4	$13
PT/Exp	C	08 NYM	319	54	88	12	49	2	276	264	282	344	439	783	9	74	34	0.40	262	45	24	31	110	16%	69	5%	5.23	0.4	$12
Consist	B	1st Half	187	35	57	10	35	1	305			366	519	885	9	76	36	0.40	285	40	26	34	135	21%	73	4%	6.43	6.4	$9
LIMA Plan	D+	2nd Half	132	19	31	2	14	1	235			313	326	639	10	71	32	0.39	227	54	19	27	73	8%	56	8%	3.41	-7.2	$2
+/- Score	-29	09 Proj	442	64	122	17	64	4	276			346	455	802	10	75	34	0.42	269	45	22	32	124	16%	62	6%	5.51	5.8	$15

Pair of concussions ruined his season. Second one happened on May 20; you can see the impact in his 1H/2H splits. If he gets a clean bill of health, those 1st half skills are repeatable, giving him $20 potential.

Cintron,Alex

			AB	R	H	HR	RBI	SB	Avg	vL	vR	OB	Slg	OPS	bb%	ct%	h%	Eye	xBA	G	L	F	PX	hr/f	SX	SBO	RC/G	RAR	R$
Pos	6	04 ARI	564	56	148	4	49	3	262	295	250	301	363	664	5	90	29	0.53	261	45	18	37	63	2%	82	4%	3.81	-5.2	$8
Age	30	05 ARI	330	36	90	8	48	1	273	301	267	298	415	713	4	90	28	0.36	293	43	22	34	86	8%	61	4%	4.17	2.0	$9
Bats	Both	06 CHW	288	35	82	5	41	10	285	274	288	309	392	701	3	88	31	0.29	274	46	23	31	60	6%	115	18%	3.97	-3.6	$9
Health	B	07 CHW	185	23	45	2	19	2	243	238	244	278	324	603	5	81	29	0.26	230	43	19	39	56	3%	84	7%	2.79	-8.3	$3
PT/Exp	F	08 BAL	* 208	19	55	3	17	0	264	250	301	298	341	640	5	87	29	0.36	258	49	22	29	47	5%	41	4%	3.32	-6.1	$3
Consist	B	1st Half	135	12	34	3	14	0	249			269	353	622	3	85	28	0.18	274	51	24	25	61	9%	55	3%	2.95	-5.5	$2
LIMA Plan	F	2nd Half	73	7	21	0	3	0	293			349	320	669	8	90	33	0.83	235	47	20	32	22	0%	30	4%	3.99	-0.7	$1
+/- Score	-27	09 Proj	123	13	33	1	11	1	268			305	350	655	5	86	30	0.39	253	46	21	33	50	4%	72	6%	3.54	-2.9	$2

1-10-.286 in 133 AB at BAL. Last four years represent his peak age seasons, yet they look like those of a player nearing retirement. Maybe he should take a hint.

Clark,Tony

			AB	R	H	HR	RBI	SB	Avg	vL	vR	OB	Slg	OPS	bb%	ct%	h%	Eye	xBA	G	L	F	PX	hr/f	SX	SBO	RC/G	RAR	R$
Pos	3	04 NYY	253	37	56	16	49	0	221	196	236	294	458	752	9	64	28	0.28	235	52	12	36	173	27%	31	0%	5.04	0.4	$7
Age	36	05 ARI	349	47	106	30	87	0	304	313	299	370	636	1007	10	75	33	0.42	324	43	22	34	215	33%	35	0%	8.04	23.2	$20
Bats	Both	06 ARI	132	13	26	6	16	0	197	125	213	269	364	633	9	70	23	0.33	231	38	22	40	109	16%	16	0%	3.11	-12.0	$1
Health	B	07 ARI	221	31	55	17	51	0	249	219	254	314	511	825	9	73	26	0.36	273	49	17	34	157	31%	39	0%	5.58	-3.6	$9
PT/Exp	F	08 2NL	151	12	34	3	24	0	225	280	198	357	318	675	17	64	33	0.56	184	51	26	24	77	13%	0	0%	4.23	-6.9	$2
Consist	D	1st Half	81	5	20	1	11	0	247			384	321	705	18	63	38	0.60	229	43	33	24	67	8%	4	0%	4.82	-2.2	$1
LIMA Plan	F	2nd Half	70	7	14	2	13	0	200			325	314	640	16	64	28	0.52	198	59	17	24	88	19%	15	0%	3.54	-4.8	$1
+/- Score	-50	09 Proj	96	10	22	4	17	0	229			328	394	722	13	68	29	0.45	229	49	21	30	115	22%	14	0%	4.58	-3.7	$2

Another victim of Petco Park? Petco: .160 BA, 69 PX, 58% ct Other: .257 BA, 81 PX, 66% ct Not really. More likely just a victim of age and slowing bat speed. And not even moving to Coors Field would cure that.

Clement,Jeff

			AB	R	H	HR	RBI	SB	Avg	vL	vR	OB	Slg	OPS	bb%	ct%	h%	Eye	xBA	G	L	F	PX	hr/f	SX	SBO	RC/G	RAR	R$
Pos	20	04	0	0	0	0	0	0	0							0			0						0				
Age	25	05	0	0	0	0	0	0	0							0			0						0				
Bats	Left	06 aaa	304	26	72	5	36	0	237			284	342	626	6	82	27	0.36	0				69		38	3%	3.18	-11.0	$3
Health	A	07 aa	455	62	107	16	66	0	236			315	420	734	10	81	26	0.61	0				120		44	0%	4.67	4.3	$9
PT/Exp	F	08 SEA	* 375	48	95	15	56	0	253	289	209	330	448	778	10	76	29	0.48	265	41	18	40	135	13%	35	1%	5.21	11.2	$10
Consist	C	1st Half	249	38	62	12	39	0	249			348	478	826	13	78	27	0.69	287	39	20	41	153	16%	41	0%	5.94	12.8	$7
LIMA Plan	D	2nd Half	126	10	33	3	17	0	262			290	389	679	4	73	34	0.15	224	42	17	40	97	8%	23	4%	3.65	-2.0	$2
+/- Score	11	09 Proj	486	56	120	16	68	0	247			310	409	718	8	78	29	0.42	253	42	18	40	111	10%	34	1%	4.35	1.5	$10

5-23-.227 in 203 AB at SEA. Minor league skills did not carry over to the majors. Even when he hit .325 in Aug, xBA was only .233. That said, he's still young enough, and his MLEs are good enough, to justify a second look.

Cora,Alex

			AB	R	H	HR	RBI	SB	Avg	vL	vR	OB	Slg	OPS	bb%	ct%	h%	Eye	xBA	G	L	F	PX	hr/f	SX	SBO	RC/G	RAR	R$
Pos	6	04 LA	405	47	107	10	47	3	264	239	267	341	380	721	10	90	27	1.15	255	46	17	37	59	7%	70	5%	4.67	6.4	$9
Age	33	05 2AL	250	25	58	3	24	7	232	281	227	264	332	596	4	88	25	0.37	267	52	17	30	57	4%	121	17%	2.91	-12.5	$4
Bats	Left	06 BOS	235	31	56	1	18	6	238	333	219	295	298	593	7	88	27	0.66	243	51	16	32	37	2%	108	12%	3.06	-9.6	$3
Health	B	07 BOS	207	30	51	3	18	1	246	179	257	271	386	658	3	89	27	0.30	278	43	20	37	81	4%	115	5%	3.60	-4.2	$3
PT/Exp	F	08 BOS	152	14	41	0	9	1	270	286	266	339	349	688	10	91	29	1.23	281	42	25	33	53	0%	71	4%	4.44	0.5	$2
Consist	B	1st Half	51	3	14	0	4	0	275			339	353	692	9	88	31	0.83	298	27	31	42	65	0%	10	0%	4.36	0.0	$1
LIMA Plan	F	2nd Half	101	11	27	0	5	1	267			339	347	686	10	93	29	1.57	285	49	23	28	47	0%	89	6%	4.50	0.5	$1
+/- Score	-16	09 Proj	130	14	33	1	10	1	254			309	349	658	7	90	28	0.78	272	44	22	34	58	2%	90	6%	3.90	-1.7	$2

Hasn't owned LD% this good since 2001. Still, if he can repackage it with the elite ct% and a dash of his former speed, he could surprise with a .300 BA. But low AB makes even that a remote possibility.

BRANDON KRUSE

Coste,Chris

			AB	R	H	HR	RBI	SB	Avg	vL	vR	OB	Slg	OPS	bb%	ct%	h%	Eye	xBA	G	L	F	PX	hr/f	SX	SBO	RC/G	RAR	R$
Pos	2	04 aaa	262	25	63	2	20	2	240			280	337	617	5	87	27	0.42	0				68		64	8%	3.20	-6.9	$2
Age	36	05 aaa	499	50	116	15	59	2	233			273	368	641	5	86	24	0.39	0				81		40	6%	3.31	-9.0	$8
Bats	Right	06 PHI	*345	36	88	9	45	1	256	288	345	293	394	688	5	82	29	0.30	288	40	29	31	89	10%	35	2%	3.82	-5.2	$7
Health	A	07 PHI	*327	29	74	9	49	0	228	405	228	258	341	600	4	85	24	0.28	233	43	17	40	66	8%	22	0%	2.74	-16.8	$4
PT/Exp	D	08 PHI	274	28	72	9	36	0	263	296	249	303	423	727	6	81	29	0.31	273	38	23	39	106	10%	24	2%	4.29	0.7	$7
Consist	C	1st Half	138	16	43	7	20	0	312			354	543	897	6	84	33	0.41	307	33	23	44	145	14%	15	0%	6.31	7.8	$6
LIMA Plan	F	2nd Half	136	12	29	2	16	0	213			252	301	553	5	79	26	0.24	240	44	22	34	64	6%	35	4%	2.13	-8.8	$1
+/- Score	-20	09 Proj	233	23	57	6	31	0	245			282	378	660	5	83	27	0.30	262	40	22	37	85	9%	30	2%	3.47	-5.3	$4

1H success, 2H collapse - so much can happen in small sample sizes. Has just 601 career MLB AB at age 36, and marginal MLEs before that, so we can't read much into anything he does, really.

Counsell,Craig

			AB	R	H	HR	RBI	SB	Avg	vL	vR	OB	Slg	OPS	bb%	ct%	h%	Eye	xBA	G	L	F	PX	hr/f	SX	SBO	RC/G	RAR	R$
Pos	56	04 MIL	476	60	116	2	24	17	244	184	254	327	317	644	11	82	30	0.67	249	47	23	30	50	2%	120	14%	3.72	-19.2	$8
Age	38	05 ARI	578	85	148	9	42	26	256	269	253	345	375	720	12	88	28	1.13	286	49	20	31	77	6%	123	18%	4.79	0.2	$17
Bats	Left	06 ARI	372	56	95	4	30	15	255	256	255	313	347	659	8	87	28	0.66	263	48	20	31	53	4%	118	22%	3.81	-18.7	$9
Health	B	07 MIL	282	31	62	3	24	4	220	157	234	319	309	627	13	83	25	0.87	232	46	15	38	58	3%	77	7%	3.61	-17.4	$2
PT/Exp	D	08 MIL	248	31	56	1	14	3	226	190	229	347	302	649	16	83	27	1.10	259	47	23	30	59	2%	69	5%	4.07	-9.8	$2
Consist	A	1st Half	120	16	29	1	8	2	242			331	342	673	12	83	28	0.80	283	50	26	24	70	4%	86	8%	4.15	-4.4	$2
LIMA Plan	D	2nd Half	128	15	27	0	6	1	211			361	266	626	19	83	25	1.36	236	44	21	35	48	0%	40	2%	3.95	-5.6	$0
+/- Score	-2	09 Proj	212	27	49	1	14	4	231			335	309	644	14	84	27	0.97	250	47	20	33	54	3%	77	8%	3.89	-9.8	$2

Dwindling AB, dwindling skills both say that the end is near. Now that he's stopped running, there's been no reason to own him for two straight seasons. We'll go ahead and pencil him in for a third right now.

Crawford,Carl

			AB	R	H	HR	RBI	SB	Avg	vL	vR	OB	Slg	OPS	bb%	ct%	h%	Eye	xBA	G	L	F	PX	hr/f	SX	SBO	RC/G	RAR	R$
Pos	7	04 TAM	626	104	185	11	55	59	296	295	296	333	450	783	5	87	33	0.43	283	48	20	33	82	6%	180	45%	5.10	2.8	$31
Age	27	05 TAM	644	101	194	15	81	46	301	244	326	329	469	798	4	87	33	0.32	289	45	20	35	97	8%	172	34%	5.15	7.7	$32
Bats	Left	06 TAM	600	89	183	18	77	58	305	288	311	345	482	827	6	86	33	0.44	292	52	18	30	92	12%	168	40%	5.55	6.2	$33
Health	B	07 TAM	584	93	184	11	80	50	315	318	314	351	466	816	5	81	38	0.29	277	48	20	32	101	7%	160	38%	5.46	6.8	$31
PT/Exp	A	08 TAM	443	69	121	8	57	25	273	248	285	319	400	719	6	86	30	0.50	276	49	21	30	69	7%	156	26%	4.38	-6.1	$17
Consist	B	1st Half	321	54	88	8	44	20	274			321	405	726	6	86	30	0.48	272	49	19	32	72	9%	149	29%	4.39	-4.3	$14
LIMA Plan	B	2nd Half	122	15	33	0	13	5	270			315	385	701	6	89	31	0.57	287	47	25	28	61	0%	133	19%	4.34	-1.8	$3
+/- Score	11	09 Proj	589	88	171	12	73	44	290			331	441	772	6	85	32	0.42	286	48	21	30	85	8%	163	33%	4.96	0.3	$26

Hamstring and finger injuries ended his four-year run of $30 seasons. But other than PX and SBO, both likely affected by the injuries, his skills remained intact, making him a good bet to start a new $30 streak in 2009.

Crede,Joe

			AB	R	H	HR	RBI	SB	Avg	vL	vR	OB	Slg	OPS	bb%	ct%	h%	Eye	xBA	G	L	F	PX	hr/f	SX	SBO	RC/G	RAR	R$
Pos	5	04 CHW	490	67	117	21	69	1	239	256	230	288	418	707	6	83	25	0.42	253	34	16	49	105	10%	44	3%	4.07	-12.3	$11
Age	31	05 CHW	432	54	109	22	62	1	252	277	246	293	454	747	5	85	25	0.38	277	36	18	45	119	13%	38	2%	4.47	-0.4	$12
Bats	Right	06 CHW	544	76	154	30	94	0	283	273	288	318	506	824	5	89	27	0.48	285	31	18	51	121	12%	28	2%	5.34	5.1	$19
Health	F	07 CHW	167	13	36	4	22	0	216	206	218	260	317	577	6	86	23	0.42	211	32	15	53	61	5%	23	3%	2.60	-11.7	$1
PT/Exp	C	08 CHW	335	41	83	17	55	0	248	122	289	310	460	769	8	87	24	0.67	266	32	14	54	123	11%	32	4%	4.94	0.6	$9
Consist	F	1st Half	257	35	69	15	46	0	268			338	502	840	10	86	26	0.75	268	32	12	56	136	12%	23	5%	5.80	6.9	$9
LIMA Plan	D	2nd Half	78	6	14	2	9	0	179			210	321	530	4	88	18	0.33	259	31	21	48	79	6%	58	0%	2.14	-6.9	$0
+/- Score	13	09 Proj	415	43	103	17	60	0	248			291	423	715	6	87	25	0.47	258	32	17	51	100	9%	41	2%	4.19	-8.4	$9

Back problems did him in again, and leave lingering questions about his future. PX, hr/f tell the story: Plus power when he's healthy, no power when he's not ('07 and 2H of '08). Don't go betting heavy on health.

Crisp,Coco

			AB	R	H	HR	RBI	SB	Avg	vL	vR	OB	Slg	OPS	bb%	ct%	h%	Eye	xBA	G	L	F	PX	hr/f	SX	SBO	RC/G	RAR	R$
Pos	8	04 CLE	491	78	146	15	71	20	297	311	290	345	446	791	7	86	32	0.52	283	50	19	31	86	11%	103	23%	5.16	6.3	$21
Age	29	05 CLE	594	86	178	16	69	15	300	252	325	348	465	813	7	86	33	0.54	294	46	20	34	106	9%	105	13%	5.47	19.7	$22
Bats	Both	06 BOS	413	58	109	8	36	22	264	277	259	315	385	700	7	84	30	0.46	257	48	16	36	77	6%	125	24%	4.14	-6.3	$12
Health	B	07 BOS	526	85	141	6	60	28	268	270	267	332	382	714	9	84	31	0.60	258	47	17	36	75	4%	146	23%	4.47	-1.0	$17
PT/Exp	B	08 BOS	361	55	102	7	41	20	283	295	278	346	407	753	9	84	32	0.59	256	41	20	39	80	6%	119	25%	4.88	-4.9	$14
Consist	A	1st Half	196	24	53	5	22	12	270			313	434	746	6	84	30	0.39	269	37	20	44	105	7%	124	33%	4.63	-4.1	$7
LIMA Plan	C	2nd Half	165	31	49	2	19	8	297			383	376	759	12	83	35	0.82	241	46	19	34	51	4%	106	19%	5.15	-0.9	$7
+/- Score	-18	09 Proj	319	50	89	6	36	16	279			342	400	742	9	84	32	0.60	259	45	18	37	78	6%	126	23%	4.76	-1.8	$12

This is not a skill set suited for full-time AB, particularly in sim leagues. Three years of consistent mediocrity in BOS, as highlighted by xBA and RAR. But SBs will continue to keep him Rotisserily viable.

Crosby,Bobby

			AB	R	H	HR	RBI	SB	Avg	vL	vR	OB	Slg	OPS	bb%	ct%	h%	Eye	xBA	G	L	F	PX	hr/f	SX	SBO	RC/G	RAR	R$
Pos	6	04 OAK	545	70	130	22	64	7	239	194	254	312	426	737	10	74	28	0.41	257	45	17	38	127	14%	73	8%	4.65	3.1	$12
Age	29	05 OAK	333	66	92	9	38	0	276	314	260	345	456	802	10	84	31	0.65	301	54	18	28	118	12%	86	0%	5.53	9.1	$10
Bats	Right	06 OAK	358	42	82	9	40	8	229	185	242	299	338	637	9	79	27	0.47	236	47	18	35	69	9%	75	9%	3.34	-11.6	$6
Health	F	07 OAK	349	40	79	8	31	10	226	222	228	274	341	615	6	82	25	0.37	261	48	20	32	77	9%	84	15%	3.01	-13.6	$6
PT/Exp	B	08 OAK	559	66	133	7	61	7	238	222	244	299	349	648	8	83	28	0.51	253	48	16	36	82	4%	71	7%	3.61	-12.1	$9
Consist	A	1st Half	323	40	83	4	37	5	257			316	375	691	8	83	30	0.50	265	47	18	35	90	4%	64	10%	4.13	-1.9	$7
LIMA Plan	D	2nd Half	236	26	50	3	24	2	212			276	314	590	8	83	24	0.53	236	50	12	38	72	4%	73	4%	2.91	-10.4	$2
+/- Score	24	09 Proj	359	43	83	7	37	6	231			292	350	642	8	82	27	0.47	254	48	17	35	82	7%	82	9%	3.46	-9.7	$6

So maybe it wasn't the injuries after all. A full season of health resulted in... yet another lousy performance. There's nothing to like in these skills, no signs of life. A's appear ready to move on. Follow their lead.

Cruz,Nelson

			AB	R	H	HR	RBI	SB	Avg	vL	vR	OB	Slg	OPS	bb%	ct%	h%	Eye	xBA	G	L	F	PX	hr/f	SX	SBO	RC/G	RAR	R$
Pos	9	04 a/a	275	43	74	12	36	6	268			319	451	770	7	77	31	0.32	0				116		91	14%	4.88	-0.9	$9
Age	28	05 a/a	455	57	111	20	60	14	244			313	438	752	9	76	28	0.42	0				134		73	21%	4.77	-2.8	$15
Bats	Right	06 2TM	*501	75	133	25	87	16	265	217	226	327	465	792	8	75	31	0.36	249	46	12	42	126	16%	91	18%	5.23	0.3	$20
Health	A	07 TEX	*469	57	117	21	66	3	249	212	245	303	441	743	7	74	29	0.30	246	38	16	46	129	13%	63	8%	4.58	-12.9	$12
PT/Exp	C	08 TEX	*498	86	143	34	95	20	287	419	298	357	551	908	10	79	30	0.52	302	40	22	38	160	23%	98	21%	6.66	18.6	$27
Consist	C	1st Half	268	50	76	18	48	12	282			360	548	908	11	80	29	0.60	0				159		110	24%	6.71	10.5	$15
LIMA Plan	C+	2nd Half	230	33	67	16	46	7	291			354	553	907	9	78	31	0.44	299	40	22	38	161	23%	83	18%	6.61	8.2	$12
+/- Score	2	09 Proj	512	76	139	29	87	14	271			334	500	834	9	77	30	0.41	274	40	18	42	144	18%	86	17%	5.74	5.4	$22

7-26-.330 in 115 AB at TEX. Biggest season of his career comes, of course, at age 27. Skill history still creates doubts about BA, and '08 hr/f looks like an outlier, but he finally appears ready to deliver in the majors.

Cuddyer,Michael

			AB	R	H	HR	RBI	SB	Avg	vL	vR	OB	Slg	OPS	bb%	ct%	h%	Eye	xBA	G	L	F	PX	hr/f	SX	SBO	RC/G	RAR	R$
Pos	9	04 MIN	339	49	89	12	45	5	263	293	245	335	440	775	10	78	30	0.50	259	39	19	42	116	11%	75	11%	5.14	4.4	$10
Age	30	05 MIN	422	55	111	12	42	3	263	280	260	328	422	750	9	78	31	0.44	271	53	18	29	109	13%	72	6%	4.81	1.4	$10
Bats	Right	06 MIN	557	102	158	24	109	6	284	297	276	355	504	860	10	77	33	0.48	286	44	21	35	145	16%	110	4%	6.28	9.7	$22
Health	D	07 MIN	547	87	151	16	81	5	276	308	263	352	433	785	10	80	32	0.60	266	45	19	36	102	10%	98	3%	5.32	-2.7	$17
PT/Exp	B	08 MIN	249	30	62	3	36	5	249	250	249	318	369	687	9	84	29	0.63	267	46	21	33	78	4%	113	9%	4.18	-8.7	$5
Consist	C	1st Half	234	30	59	3	35	5	252			314	376	690	8	84	29	0.57	268	46	20	34	79	4%	118	10%	4.16	-8.3	$6
LIMA Plan	C+	2nd Half	15	0	3	0	1	0	200			368	267	635	21	80	25	1.33	0	50	25	25	61	0%		0%	4.08	-0.6	$0
+/- Score	29	09 Proj	476	71	127	14	72	6	267			336	438	773	9	80	31	0.52	275	46	20	35	111	11%	104	7%	5.13	-3.4	$14

Injury-marred season pulls him further away from '06 value, and forces us to accept what he is: an average-skilled player at a generally deep position. SX, SBO do bear watching, as they could yield double-digit steals.

Cunningham,Aaron

			AB	R	H	HR	RBI	SB	Avg	vL	vR	OB	Slg	OPS	bb%	ct%	h%	Eye	xBA	G	L	F	PX	hr/f	SX	SBO	RC/G	RAR	R$
Pos	7	04	0	0	0	0	0	0	0							0			0						0				
Age	23	05	0	0	0	0	0	0	0							0			0						0				
Bats	Right	06	0	0	0	0	0	0	0							0			0						0				
Health	A	07 aa	118	21	32	5	17	1	271			328	517	845	8	81	30	0.45	0				148		112	15%	5.93	2.6	$4
PT/Exp	F	08 OAK	*506	75	143	13	65	15	283	208	268	340	435	775	8	79	34	0.42	231	34	14	52	102	6%	112	15%	5.08	3.3	$18
Consist	B	1st Half	209	22	50	4	17	6	239			296	349	646	8	78	29	0.38	0				76		85	19%	3.42	-9.2	$4
LIMA Plan	D	2nd Half	297	53	93	9	48	9	313			370	495	865	8	80	37	0.45	246	34	14	52	119	7%	126	13%	6.23	11.2	$14
+/- Score	-16	09 Proj	161	26	42	5	22	3	261			319	457	777	8	80	30	0.43	256	33	17	50	124	8%	123	16%	5.12	0.8	$5

1-14-.250 in 80 AB at OAK. Promising power/speed combo, though high FB%, low LD% and subpar ct% is a bad mix for BA. Age, struggles in majors (.222 xBA) suggest more time in AAA is in order. Tuck him away.

BRANDON KRUSE

Cust,Jack

			AB	R	H	HR	RBI	SB	Avg	vL	vR	OB	Slg	OPS	bb%	ct%	h%	Eye	xBA	G	L	F	PX	hr/f	SX	SBO	RC/G	RAR	R$
Pos	70	04 aaa	344	48	73	16	48	4	213			327	394	721	15	68	26	0.53	0				124		75	4%	4.63	-5.9	$7
Age	30	05 aaa	476	71	105	15	56	2	220			353	367	720	17	74	27	0.80	0				105		46	4%	4.76	-4.0	$8
Bats	Left	06 aaa	441	71	103	19	57	0	233			384	405	789	20	76	26	1.02	0				109		20	2%	5.73	6.9	$9
Health	A	07 OAK	* 475	73	119	32	96	0	250	218	273	400	507	906	20	58	35	0.60	252	42	23	35	214	34%	27	1%	8.25	45.1	$17
PT/Exp	C	08 OAK	485	79	113	35	80	0	233	235	229	376	489	864	19	59	31	0.56	245	40	21	39	204	31%	19	0%	7.33	36.1	$16
Consist	D	1st Half	244	39	57	13	39	0	234			385	426	811	20	63	31	0.66	228	44	20	36	147	24%	21	0%	6.32	10.8	$7
LIMA Plan	C+	2nd Half	241	40	56	22	41	0	232			366	552	918	17	56	30	0.48	263	35	22	43	270	38%	16	0%	8.55	26.8	$9
+/- Score	6	09 Proj	484	77	114	32	80	0	236			379	475	854	19	62	31	0.61	249	40	22	38	184	28%	22	1%	6.96	29.3	$15

There are no comps for his skill set. A PX over 200 with this ridiculous strikeout rate? Seems impossible to sustain... unless he keeps hitting 1/3 of his FB out. Can't rule that out, but it seems unlikely, doesn't it?

Damon,Johnny

			AB	R	H	HR	RBI	SB	Avg	vL	vR	OB	Slg	OPS	bb%	ct%	h%	Eye	xBA	G	L	F	PX	hr/f	SX	SBO	RC/G	RAR	R$
Pos	780	04 BOS	627	126	192	20	94	20	306	278	319	381	477	858	11	89	32	1.07	293	49	17	34	95	11%	125	14%	6.24	22.6	$29
Age	35	05 BOS	624	117	197	10	75	18	316	327	310	369	439	808	8	89	34	0.77	288	45	23	32	77	6%	136	10%	5.53	13.6	$26
Bats	Left	06 NYY	593	115	169	24	80	25	285	297	280	358	482	840	10	86	30	0.79	287	41	19	40	113	12%	124	20%	5.93	12.8	$26
Health	A	07 NYY	533	93	144	12	63	27	270	281	266	351	396	746	11	85	30	0.84	271	48	18	33	81	8%	121	18%	4.93	-1.6	$20
PT/Exp	A	08 NYY	555	95	168	17	71	29	303	258	321	375	461	836	10	85	33	0.78	285	44	22	34	95	11%	125	20%	5.92	16.6	$26
Consist	B	1st Half	298	46	94	6	35	13	315			386	463	849	10	85	35	0.77	287	46	21	33	96	7%	109	19%	6.14	10.6	$13
LIMA Plan	B	2nd Half	257	49	74	11	36	16	288			362	459	822	10	85	30	0.79	283	41	24	36	94	14%	130	21%	5.67	6.0	$14
+/- Score	-32	09 Proj	533	96	155	17	69	26	291			365	447	812	10	86	31	0.81	282	44	21	35	94	10%	126	19%	5.64	10.5	$24

Healthy and consistent, with very few signs of skill erosion. At 35, that's hitting the jackpot, even if you're not a ballplayer. xBA says don't pay for a repeat of .300 BA; other than that, looks set for yet another $20 season.

Davis,Chris

			AB	R	H	HR	RBI	SB	Avg	vL	vR	OB	Slg	OPS	bb%	ct%	h%	Eye	xBA	G	L	F	PX	hr/f	SX	SBO	RC/G	RAR	R$
Pos	35	04	0	0	0	0	0	0	0							0			0						0				
Age	23	05	0	0	0	0	0	0	0							0			0						0				
Bats	Left	06	0	0	0	0	0	0	0							0			0						0				
Health	A	07 aa	109	18	30	11	21	0	275			342	642	984	9	80	25	0.50	0				218		19	0%	7.42	5.4	$5
PT/Exp	F	08 TEX	* 592	104	174	36	112	6	294	279	287	339	557	896	6	76	34	0.28	300	35	25	40	176	20%	88	7%	6.49	20.1	$28
Consist	B	1st Half	309	56	94	21	61	5	304			348	579	928	6	80	32	0.34	0	29	29	43	171	20%	89	8%	6.70	12.1	$17
LIMA Plan	C+	2nd Half	283	48	80	15	51	1	283			328	534	861	6	71	35	0.23	285	35	25	40	183	19%	81	5%	6.29	8.2	$12
+/- Score	16	09 Proj	551	94	157	36	104	3	285			338	556	894	7	77	31	0.34	306	35	25	40	176	21%	69	4%	6.46	18.6	$25

17-55-.285 in 295 AB at TEX. Mammoth power and strong LD% give him more BA potential than you'd expect from a hitter with his ct% issues. That's a huge plus from a guy who already offers this... UP: 45 HR.

Davis,Rajai

			AB	R	H	HR	RBI	SB	Avg	vL	vR	OB	Slg	OPS	bb%	ct%	h%	Eye	xBA	G	L	F	PX	hr/f	SX	SBO	RC/G	RAR	R$
Pos	8	04	0	0	0	0	0	0	0							0			0						0				
Age	28	05 aa	499	62	121	3	26	34	242			287	310	597	6	88	27	0.52	0				46		133	35%	3.02	-21.3	$13
Bats	Right	06 aaa	385	50	107	2	20	44	278			323	345	668	6	85	32	0.46	0				47		127	50%	3.77	-8.9	$16
Health	A	07 2NL	* 401	55	108	4	32	43	269	299	258	329	372	701	8	87	30	0.69	252	43	17	40	66	3%	144	51%	4.35	-2.2	$17
PT/Exp	D	08 2TM	218	31	54	3	20	30	248	232	250	278	358	635	4	82	29	0.23	259	48	22	30	62	6%	191	72%	3.19	-12.4	$11
Consist	B	1st Half	94	12	20	1	8	15	213			237	287	524	3	81	25	0.17	239	47	21	32	45	4%	185	95%	1.75	-9.9	$4
LIMA Plan	D+	2nd Half	124	19	34	2	12	15	274			308	411	719	5	82	32	0.27	274	49	23	28	75	7%	178	58%	4.26	-2.9	$7
+/- Score	24	09 Proj	231	32	60	2	18	27	260			301	361	662	6	84	30	0.37	261	47	21	32	60	4%	170	58%	3.65	-8.0	$10

Poor OBA forces him to crank up SBO to keep up the SB pace. Elite speed skills are making it work, but he's just about maxed out the approach. Needs more AB or bb%, xBA growth; won't likely get either.

DeJesus,David

			AB	R	H	HR	RBI	SB	Avg	vL	vR	OB	Slg	OPS	bb%	ct%	h%	Eye	xBA	G	L	F	PX	hr/f	SX	SBO	RC/G	RAR	R$
Pos	789	04 KC	* 560	89	163	12	52	14	291	224	309	349	429	778	8	87	32	0.67	275	50	17	33	81	8%	102	19%	5.16	3.6	$18
Age	29	05 KC	461	69	135	9	56	5	293	270	303	352	445	797	8	84	34	0.55	286	45	22	32	100	7%	99	8%	5.41	9.0	$14
Bats	Left	06 KC	491	83	145	8	56	6	295	307	291	352	446	798	8	86	33	0.61	296	49	22	29	95	7%	113	7%	5.45	3.7	$14
Health	A	07 KC	605	101	157	7	58	10	260	240	267	330	372	702	10	86	29	0.77	263	46	19	36	71	4%	120	8%	4.42	-10.9	$13
PT/Exp	A	08 KC	518	70	159	12	73	11	307	302	310	363	452	815	8	86	34	0.65	295	46	25	29	87	9%	101	12%	5.58	10.6	$19
Consist	C	1st Half	256	36	81	8	41	6	316			371	480	851	8	88	33	0.73	303	44	25	31	94	11%	94	14%	5.95	7.7	$11
LIMA Plan	C+	2nd Half	262	34	78	4	32	5	298			357	424	780	8	84	34	0.59	287	48	25	27	79	7%	100	10%	5.22	2.7	$8
+/- Score	-23	09 Proj	563	89	169	13	78	10	300			360	453	812	9	86	33	0.66	291	47	22	31	92	9%	109	10%	5.58	10.0	$20

Won't lead the way to victory in any one category, but these across-the-board contributions do add up. So while this is probably as good as it gets, $20 hitters don't grow on trees, even in the outfield.

Delgado,Carlos

			AB	R	H	HR	RBI	SB	Avg	vL	vR	OB	Slg	OPS	bb%	ct%	h%	Eye	xBA	G	L	F	PX	hr/f	SX	SBO	RC/G	RAR	R$
Pos	3	04 TOR	458	74	123	32	99	0	269	271	267	364	535	899	13	75	29	0.60	284	36	21	43	167	22%	24	1%	6.82	24.1	$19
Age	36	05 FLA	521	81	157	33	115	0	301	229	327	386	582	968	12	77	34	0.60	313	40	23	37	186	22%	47	0%	7.71	30.1	$27
Bats	Left	06 NYM	524	89	139	38	114	0	265	226	282	356	548	904	12	77	28	0.62	291	42	18	40	168	23%	40	0%	6.78	11.8	$22
Health	A	07 NYM	538	71	139	24	87	4	258	267	254	324	448	772	9	78	29	0.44	259	39	18	43	122	13%	56	3%	4.98	-18.0	$16
PT/Exp	A	08 NYM	598	96	162	38	115	1	271	267	273	349	518	868	11	79	28	0.58	306	42	25	34	152	24%	42	1%	6.21	8.3	$26
Consist	D	1st Half	298	39	68	14	45	1	228			301	419	720	9	78	25	0.48	269	44	19	37	119	16%	58	1%	4.34	-12.5	$7
LIMA Plan	C	2nd Half	300	57	94	24	70	0	313			396	617	1013	12	80	32	0.69	342	39	30	31	183	32%	30	1%	8.03	18.6	$18
+/- Score	1	09 Proj	562	89	151	35	100	1	269			348	512	860	11	78	29	0.56	293	40	22	37	149	21%	51	1%	6.13	4.2	$22

Nearly waived in 1st half, MVP talk in the 2nd. Overall, 2008 makes 2007 look like an aberration. Still, if you remove that season, there remain declines in OPS, PX and RC/G. That seems about right.

Dellucci,David

			AB	R	H	HR	RBI	SB	Avg	vL	vR	OB	Slg	OPS	bb%	ct%	h%	Eye	xBA	G	L	F	PX	hr/f	SX	SBO	RC/G	RAR	R$
Pos	70	04 TEX	335	59	80	17	61	9	239	107	254	332	436	768	12	73	28	0.53	247	40	17	43	124	16%	98	14%	5.11	1.7	$12
Age	35	05 TEX	435	97	109	29	65	5	251	242	254	362	513	875	15	72	28	0.63	273	41	16	43	170	22%	113	6%	6.68	25.3	$18
Bats	Left	06 PHI	264	41	77	13	39	1	292	200	299	360	530	890	10	77	34	0.45	270	37	19	44	142	15%	84	5%	6.62	10.2	$10
Health	C	07 CLE	178	25	41	4	20	2	230	167	240	297	382	679	9	78	28	0.43	260	43	20	37	106	8%	97	7%	3.95	-5.9	$3
PT/Exp	D	08 CLE	336	41	80	11	47	3	238		251	289	405	694	7	77	28	0.32	252	41	17	42	113	10%	80	7%	3.95	-9.1	$7
Consist	C	1st Half	193	23	43	7	26	2	223			286	389	674	8	76	26	0.37	241	40	15	45	116	11%	53	7%	3.73	-6.6	$4
LIMA Plan	D	2nd Half	143	18	37	4	21	1	259			293	427	720	5	79	30	0.23	265	43	19	38	110	9%	92	7%	4.22	-2.7	$4
+/- Score	3	09 Proj	225	31	56	7	31	2	249			309	410	719	8	77	30	0.38	252	41	18	40	108	10%	87	7%	4.36	-3.9	$5

Two years of faded PX, hr/f and inconsistent fly ball rates tell us that his power is on the wane, and steadily declining Eye makes it unlikely to bounce back. Without plus power, he doesn't have much to offer.

Denorfia,Chris

			AB	R	H	HR	RBI	SB	Avg	vL	vR	OB	Slg	OPS	bb%	ct%	h%	Eye	xBA	G	L	F	PX	hr/f	SX	SBO	RC/G	RAR	R$
Pos	7	04 aa	221	26	48	6	23	4	219			298	348	646	10	82	24	0.63	0				79		77	10%	3.60	-10.9	$3
Age	28	05 CIN	* 549	76	145	17	69	11	264	273	259	324	422	746	8	84	29	0.55	285	66	10	24	98	15%	98	12%	4.71	-10.1	$17
Bats	Right	06 CIN	* 418	57	133	8	49	15	318	317	262	380	437	817	9	85	36	0.69	280	59	17	24	75	9%	88	12%	5.66	4.6	$17
Health	C	07 OAK	0	0	0	0	0	0	0							0			0						0				
PT/Exp	F	08 OAK	* 251	33	62	2	22	6	247	241	333	287	331	617	5	83	29	0.33	272	61	18	20	62	4%	92	17%	3.08	-13.4	$4
Consist	F	1st Half	66	9	16	0	6	2	237			301	267	568	8	77	31	0.40	235	68	18	15	29	0%	76	10%	2.48	-4.7	$1
LIMA Plan	F	2nd Half	185	24	46	2	16	4	251			281	353	634	4	85	28	0.29	0	40	20	40	73	3%	89	20%	3.28	-8.8	$3
+/- Score	1	09 Proj	130	17	34	2	13	3	262			316	360	676	7	83	30	0.48	273	62	17	20	70	9%	71	13%	3.87	-4.1	$3

1-9-.290 in 62 AB at OAK. First season after torn elbow ligament gets derailed by back injury. Note that MLB xBA was only .250. 2006 skills still offer hope, but he's running out of time and fresh starts.

DeRosa,Mark

			AB	R	H	HR	RBI	SB	Avg	vL	vR	OB	Slg	OPS	bb%	ct%	h%	Eye	xBA	G	L	F	PX	hr/f	SX	SBO	RC/G	RAR	R$
Pos	4975	04 ATL	309	33	74	3	31	1	239	233	242	292	320	613	7	83	28	0.43	245	48	20	32	58	4%	41	5%	3.10	-14.1	$3
Age	34	05 TEX	148	26	36	8	20	1	243	322	188	317	439	756	10	76	27	0.46	267	47	19	35	123	21%	60	3%	4.76	2.8	$5
Bats	Right	06 TEX	520	78	154	13	74	4	296	342	278	351	456	807	8	80	35	0.43	286	49	23	29	109	11%	70	6%	5.48	19.7	$16
Health	A	07 CHC	502	64	147	10	72	1	293	283	297	366	420	786	10	81	34	0.62	260	42	22	36	84	7%	50	2%	5.37	9.4	$14
PT/Exp	A	08 CHC	505	103	144	21	87	6	285	310	275	371	481	852	12	79	33	0.65	280	40	22	38	126	14%	104	4%	6.22	20.5	$23
Consist	A	1st Half	264	49	78	10	45	3	295			382	462	844	12	78	35	0.64	269	43	22	35	110	14%	67	3%	6.13	9.9	$12
LIMA Plan	C+	2nd Half	241	54	66	11	42	3	274			359	502	861	12	80	30	0.67	290	37	23	41	143	14%	124	4%	6.31	10.6	$11
+/- Score	9	09 Proj	501	87	140	15	78	3	279			356	439	794	11	80	32	0.59	271	42	22	36	104	10%	81	3%	5.45	10.5	$17

Reversed three years of power skill decline and posted career year at age 33. That sentence serves as both a statement of facts and a list of reasons why you shouldn't go expecting an encore in 2009.

BRANDON KRUSE

DeWitt,Blake

		Yr	AB	R	H	HR	RBI	SB	Avg	vL	vR	OB	Slg	OPS	bb%	ct%	h%	Eye	xBA	G	L	F	PX	hr/f	SX	SBO	RC/G	RAR	R$
Pos	54	04	0	0	0	0	0	0	0							0			0						0				
Age	23	05	0	0	0	0	0	0	0							0			0						0				
Bats	Left	06 aa	104	6	18	1	6	0	173			225	212	437	6	80	21	0.33	0				23		26	4%	0.75	-15.3	($1)
Health	A	07 aa	178	17	45	5	17	0	253			277	416	693	3	88	26	0.27	0				101		48	3%	3.89	-7.1	$3
PT/Exp	F	08 LA	* 479	58	126	12	66	4	264	286	257	337	386	723	10	83	30	0.66	257	47	19	34	74	9%	77	3%	4.54	-11.5	$12
Consist	D	1st Half	234	31	62	5	32	2	265			333	393	726	9	81	31	0.53	0				83		85	3%	4.55	-5.5	$6
LIMA Plan	C	2nd Half	245	27	64	7	34	2	263			341	380	721	11	86	28	0.82	256	47	19	34	66	10%	58	2%	4.55	-5.8	$6
+/- Score	12	09 Proj	585	59	147	14	65	3	251			305	375	679	7	84	28	0.49	260	47	19	34	75	8%	64	4%	3.88	-26.4	$11

9-52-.264 in 368 AB at LA. Got everyone excited after a 5-HR, .322 May, but it was mostly downhill from there. If there's skill growth here, it's only from non-existent to subpar. At 23, there's time. Maybe.

Diaz,Matt

		Yr	AB	R	H	HR	RBI	SB	Avg	vL	vR	OB	Slg	OPS	bb%	ct%	h%	Eye	xBA	G	L	F	PX	hr/f	SX	SBO	RC/G	RAR	R$
Pos	7	04 aaa	503	68	147	16	78	13	293			323	484	807	4	83	33	0.25	0				123		109	16%	5.25	0.8	$19
Age	31	05 KC	* 374	44	103	10	51	8	276	370	143	303	436	739	4	83	31	0.23	289	51	20	29	101	11%	106	15%	4.40	-3.5	$11
Bats	Right	06 ATL	297	37	97	7	32	5	327	295	358	351	475	825	4	84	37	0.22	288	50	24	27	87	11%	92	12%	5.39	1.1	$11
Health	F	07 ATL	358	44	121	12	45	4	338	356	318	366	497	864	4	82	39	0.25	277	46	21	34	101	12%	55	4%	5.82	4.3	$15
PT/Exp	D	08 ATL	* 173	13	40	3	18	4	231	319	159	253	295	548	3	77	28	0.13	239	52	25	24	39	10%	59	15%	1.83	-19.0	$2
Consist	F	1st Half	132	9	33	2	14	4	250			267	311	577	2	76	32	0.09	238	52	25	23	40	9%	58	19%	2.18	-12.9	$3
LIMA Plan	F	2nd Half	41	4	7	1	4	0	171			209	244	453	5	80	19	0.25	0	67	0	33	38	9%	37	0%	0.83	-6.1	($0)
+/- Score	-17	09 Proj	203	22	57	5	24	3	281			305	407	713	3	81	33	0.18	272	49	23	27	81	11%	76	11%	4.00	-8.0	$6

2-14-.244 in 135 AB at ATL. Torn PCL ended his season, but skills had collapsed long before that. Flatlined vs. RHP (.159 BA, 67% ct, 17 PX). At 31, the odds of him becoming an everyday player are remote.

Dickerson,Chris

		Yr	AB	R	H	HR	RBI	SB	Avg	vL	vR	OB	Slg	OPS	bb%	ct%	h%	Eye	xBA	G	L	F	PX	hr/f	SX	SBO	RC/G	RAR	R$
Pos	7	04	0	0	0	0	0	0	0							0			0						0				
Age	27	05	0	0	0	0	0	0	0							0			0						0				
Bats	Left	06 aa	389	58	85	11	43	19	217			316	376	692	13	68	29	0.44	0				116		131	23%	4.29	-11.2	$9
Health	A	07 a/a	468	57	108	12	46	25	231			304	355	659	9	69	31	0.33	0				87		118	25%	3.64	-22.5	$12
PT/Exp	D	08 CIN	* 451	69	115	15	55	24	254	286	309	339	435	774	11	72	32	0.46	240	37	18	45	125	10%	138	27%	5.32	-1.4	$17
Consist	C	1st Half	220	29	47	3	20	13	213			298	305	604	11	75	27	0.48	0				62		133	31%	3.01	-17.0	$5
LIMA Plan	C	2nd Half	231	40	68	12	34	11	294			377	559	936	12	69	37	0.43	273	37	18	45	189	17%	137	23%	7.71	15.0	$13
+/- Score	9	09 Proj	370	53	90	12	42	19	243			325	408	733	11	70	32	0.40	227	37	18	45	116	10%	131	26%	4.76	-7.0	$12

6-15-.304 in 102 AB at CIN. PRO: That 2nd half! That power/speed combo! CON: That 1st half. That ct% and xBA. Erratic power history. Already 27. 102 great AB in the majors doesn't make him a star.

Dillon,Joe

		Yr	AB	R	H	HR	RBI	SB	Avg	vL	vR	OB	Slg	OPS	bb%	ct%	h%	Eye	xBA	G	L	F	PX	hr/f	SX	SBO	RC/G	RAR	R$
Pos	4	04 a/a	520	76	121	21	73	9	232			286	437	723	7	79	26	0.35	0				128		113	14%	4.33	-0.2	$13
Age	33	05 aaa	386	57	101	15	47	7	263			331	432	763	9	85	27	0.70	330	50	32	18	100	26%	88	8%	4.94	6.7	$13
Bats	Right	06 JPN	87	9	16	1	7	0	182			238	294	532	7	82	21	0.40	0				65		85	0%	2.11	-6.3	($0)
Health	A	07 MIL	* 395	67	111	16	68	5	280	556	276	356	504	860	11	88	29	0.96	362	44	37	19	132	24%	96	5%	6.23	17.2	$15
PT/Exp	F	08 MIL	* 246	36	49	4	21	2	200	357	128	293	297	590	12	80	23	0.66	242	37	24	39	64	6%	76	5%	2.94	-14.2	$2
Consist	F	1st Half	89	15	18	1	6	2	203			319	285	604	15	73	27	0.62	216	37	22	41	69	3%	75	7%	3.14	-4.5	$1
LIMA Plan	F	2nd Half	157	21	31	4	16	0	198			278	304	582	10	84	21	0.70	0	38	31	31	62	9%	66	4%	2.86	-9.6	$1
+/- Score	28	09 Proj	31	5	7	1	4	0	226			309	377	686	11	82	25	0.68	289	39	27	33	100	11%	59	7%	4.13	-0.5	$1

1-6-.213 in 75 AB at MIL. LH-masher (career 1.089 OPS vs. LH) has never been able to get more than a cup of coffee in majors. Just once, you'd think he could get a bagel or even a lousy piece of toast.

Dobbs,Greg

		Yr	AB	R	H	HR	RBI	SB	Avg	vL	vR	OB	Slg	OPS	bb%	ct%	h%	Eye	xBA	G	L	F	PX	hr/f	SX	SBO	RC/G	RAR	R$
Pos	5	04 SEA	* 511	45	120	11	59	7	235			256	354	610	3	86	26	0.20	0				68		88	14%	2.86	-32.1	$7
Age	30	05 SEA	* 332	29	86	3	37	5	260			303	336	639	6	86	29	0.45	248	35	24	42	53	2%	66	8%	3.42	-10.4	$6
Bats	Left	06 SEA	* 406	51	110	7	47	11	270			321	385	706	7	85	30	0.51	281	52	22	26	70	8%	99	16%	4.23	-9.2	$10
Health	A	07 PHI	324	45	88	10	55	3	272	214	277	331	451	782	8	79	32	0.43	254	38	16	46	115	9%	98	4%	5.18	-3.9	$10
PT/Exp	D	08 PHI	226	30	68	9	40	3	301	111	309	333	491	824	5	82	33	0.28	279	30	25	45	119	11%	74	7%	5.39	0.2	$10
Consist	B	1st Half	109	12	35	2	18	2	321			357	440	797	5	78	40	0.25	241	33	24	43	81	5%	81	9%	5.21	-0.5	$4
LIMA Plan	D	2nd Half	117	18	33	7	22	1	282			311	538	850	4	86	28	0.31	317	29	25	47	152	15%	57	5%	5.59	0.7	$5
+/- Score	-47	09 Proj	231	30	65	8	37	3	281			323	460	783	6	83	31	0.36	270	33	22	45	110	9%	91	8%	5.01	-2.6	$8

OPS, RC/G highlight five years of improved performance, but his value has plateaued thanks to declining AB. That leaves him as just another replacement level hitter with more value in the real world than here.

Doumit,Ryan

		Yr	AB	R	H	HR	RBI	SB	Avg	vL	vR	OB	Slg	OPS	bb%	ct%	h%	Eye	xBA	G	L	F	PX	hr/f	SX	SBO	RC/G	RAR	R$
Pos	2	04 aa	221	24	51	8	26	0	233			286	421	707	7	83	25	0.43	0				123		31	2%	4.19	0.8	$3
Age	28	05 PIT	* 396	56	110	15	62	3	278	296	243	317	455	772	5	81	31	0.31	276	51	16	33	114	14%	64	9%	4.82	11.7	$14
Bats	Both	06 PIT	* 171	18	38	6	24	0	222	208	208	292	397	689	9	73	27	0.37	243	46	17	38	118	13%	44	0%	4.01	-1.7	$2
Health	F	07 PIT	* 305	44	87	12	47	4	286	246	282	346	487	833	8	77	34	0.40	277	42	21	38	136	13%	77	9%	5.85	12.4	$11
PT/Exp	D	08 PIT	431	71	137	15	69	2	318	330	314	352	501	854	5	87	34	0.42	307	41	23	35	116	11%	55	4%	5.77	18.1	$19
Consist	B	1st Half	160	35	55	10	25	0	344			386	619	1005	6	87	35	0.52	327	40	19	41	164	18%	46	0%	7.50	13.5	$10
LIMA Plan	D+	2nd Half	271	36	82	5	44	2	303			332	432	764	4	87	33	0.35	296	42	26	32	88	7%	54	6%	4.75	4.1	$10
+/- Score	-8	09 Proj	448	66	135	16	74	2	301			348	489	837	7	84	33	0.45	293	42	21	36	118	12%	59	4%	5.68	17.8	$18

Growth in ct%, LD% and xBA has turned him into near-elite catching option. Last remaining obstacles are health/stamina; if 2H drops were only caused by fatigue from career-high AB, then '09 could be best year yet.

Drew,J.D.

		Yr	AB	R	H	HR	RBI	SB	Avg	vL	vR	OB	Slg	OPS	bb%	ct%	h%	Eye	xBA	G	L	F	PX	hr/f	SX	SBO	RC/G	RAR	R$
Pos	9	04 ATL	518	118	158	31	93	12	305	287	313	434	569	1003	19	78	34	1.02	294	43	19	38	158	20%	126	7%	8.52	46.0	$30
Age	33	05 LA	252	48	72	15	36	1	286	235	304	406	520	926	17	80	30	1.02	284	46	15	39	142	19%	57	2%	7.30	14.6	$11
Bats	Left	06 LA	494	84	140	20	100	2	283	244	296	393	498	891	15	79	33	0.84	281	45	19	36	133	14%	76	3%	6.94	30.4	$19
Health	C	07 BOS	466	84	126	11	64	4	270	224	286	376	423	799	14	79	32	0.79	261	46	18	37	107	8%	89	4%	5.77	3.7	$13
PT/Exp	B	08 BOS	368	79	103	19	64	4	280	284	279	407	519	926	18	78	31	0.99	290	42	18	40	153	17%	99	4%	7.47	22.0	$16
Consist	C	1st Half	241	58	73	16	49	2	303			413	577	989	16	78	33	0.87	302	43	18	40	170	21%	90	3%	8.10	18.1	$14
LIMA Plan	B+	2nd Half	127	21	30	3	15	2	236			398	409	807	21	78	28	1.21	266	41	20	40	120	8%	97	4%	6.23	3.3	$3
+/- Score	11	09 Proj	435	82	118	18	68	5	271			396	480	877	17	78	31	0.96	280	43	18	38	136	14%	95	4%	6.85	18.5	$16

$30 skills trapped in a body made of crackers. Eye, PX, hr/f and xBA all show that injuries haven't robbed him of his talent, but no matter how tempting the upside might be, you can't bid full value.

Drew,Stephen

		Yr	AB	R	H	HR	RBI	SB	Avg	vL	vR	OB	Slg	OPS	bb%	ct%	h%	Eye	xBA	G	L	F	PX	hr/f	SX	SBO	RC/G	RAR	R$
Pos	6	04	0	0	0	0	0	0	0							0			0						0				
Age	26	05 aa	101	10	20	3	10	2	198			277	327	604	10	74	24	0.42	0				90		54	21%	2.85	-4.6	$1
Bats	Left	06 ARI	* 551	69	154	16	62	4	279	350	308	328	452	780	7	81	31	0.45	275	36	24	40	98	9%	89	6%	5.07	11.2	$15
Health	A	07 ARI	543	60	129	12	60	9	238	246	235	313	370	684	10	82	27	0.60	238	38	16	46	85	6%	96	6%	4.07	-6.1	$9
PT/Exp	A	08 ARI	611	91	178	21	67	3	291	267	300	336	502	838	6	82	33	0.38	287	35	23	43	132	10%	102	4%	5.76	19.3	$20
Consist	C	1st Half	293	44	76	11	29	2	259			298	464	762	5	83	28	0.32	280	36	21	43	123	10%	109	5%	4.74	0.9	$8
LIMA Plan	C+	2nd Half	318	47	102	10	38	1	321			370	538	908	7	81	37	0.42	295	34	24	42	141	9%	90	4%	6.71	17.8	$13
+/- Score	-1	09 Proj	614	90	172	23	78	2	280			336	482	817	8	83	31	0.49	281	36	21	43	121	11%	80	4%	5.54	18.5	$19

Sophomore slump yields junior jump. PX growth and resurgent LD% drove this breakout, and both got even stronger in 2H. A repeat seems like the safest bet, but don't rule out further growth. A star in the making.

Dukes,Elijah

		Yr	AB	R	H	HR	RBI	SB	Avg	vL	vR	OB	Slg	OPS	bb%	ct%	h%	Eye	xBA	G	L	F	PX	hr/f	SX	SBO	RC/G	RAR	R$
Pos	9	04	0	0	0	0	0	0	0							0			0						0				
Age	24	05 aa	443	61	114	14	61	16	257			315	413	728	8	84	28	0.54	0				93		113	24%	4.47	-6.8	$15
Bats	Right	06 aaa	283	57	82	9	49	8	289			383	471	854	13	85	31	1.00	0				103		122	13%	6.34	9.0	$13
Health	C	07 TAM	184	27	35	10	21	2	190	260	164	313	391	705	15	76	19	0.75	236	42	11	48	118	15%	79	11%	4.32	-7.1	$3
PT/Exp	F	08 WAS	* 323	55	83	14	49	14	257	231	278	368	455	824	15	70	33	0.58	258	47	18	35	143	18%	107	19%	6.18	9.6	$14
Consist	D	1st Half	177	24	44	4	20	10	247			353	377	730	14	70	33	0.54	233	47	20	33	93	10%	124	20%	4.88	-1.6	$6
LIMA Plan	C+	2nd Half	146	31	39	10	29	4	268			386	550	936	16	69	32	0.63	289	47	16	37	204	27%	70	18%	7.76	11.2	$8
+/- Score	-2	09 Proj	390	67	96	18	59	12	246			353	448	801	14	72	29	0.60	252	45	15	40	134	16%	103	16%	5.72	7.8	$14

13-44-.264 in 275 AB at WAS. Been trading ct% for power, and you can't really argue with the results. But with only two partial pro seasons under his belt, has that trade-off really been tested? UP: 30 HR. DN: .225 BA.

BRANDON KRUSE

Duncan,Chris

Duncan,Chris		AB	R	H	HR	RBI	SB	Avg	vL	vR	OB	Slg	OPS	bb%	ct%	h%	Eye	xBA	G	L	F	PX	hr/f	SX	SBO	RC/G	RAR	R$
Pos 73	04 aa	387	47	98	13	52	7	253			342	406	748	12	79	29	0.65	0				99		54	10%	4.90	-3.3	$10
Age 27	05 aaa	430	45	100	16	58	1	233			314	395	709	11	80	25	0.61	0				104		33	4%	4.32	-9.3	$8
Bats Left	* 06 STL	461	81	128	28	71	1	277	170	318	351	519	870	10	75	31	0.45	280	44	21	35	148	23%	63	2%	6.34	14.4	$18
Health C	07 STL	375	51	97	21	70	2	259	213	271	353	480	833	13	67	33	0.45	248	40	18	42	160	20%	36	3%	6.25	9.8	$13
PT/Exp C	08 STL	222	26	55	6	27	2	248	147	266	348	365	713	13	77	30	0.65	243	42	23	36	79	10%	42	4%	4.49	-6.1	$5
Consist B	1st Half	185	22	44	5	21	2	238			341	357	698	14	77	28	0.67	243	40	23	37	80	10%	45	5%	4.31	-6.2	$4
LIMA Plan F	2nd Half	37	4	11	1	6	0	297			381	405	786	12	76	37	0.56	232	50	21	29	71	12%	15	0%	5.39	-0.0	$1
+/- Score -1	09 Proj	**62**	**8**	**16**	**3**	**9**	**0**	**258**			**346**	**436**	**783**	**12**	**75**	**30**	**0.54**	**259**	**44**	**21**	**36**	**118**	**16%**	**38**	**4%**	**5.31**	**-0.1**	**$2**

Doctors called herniated disc in his neck "career threatening," and surgery to fix it was first of its kind for any pro athlete. So there are some questions about his future. Still, age and power skills make him worth a flyer.

Dunn,Adam

Dunn,Adam		AB	R	H	HR	RBI	SB	Avg	vL	vR	OB	Slg	OPS	bb%	ct%	h%	Eye	xBA	G	L	F	PX	hr/f	SX	SBO	RC/G	RAR	R$
Pos 79	04 CIN	568	105	151	46	102	6	266	256	271	383	569	952	16	66	32	0.55	272	33	19	48	215	26%	62	4%	8.14	44.3	$27
Age 29	05 CIN	543	107	134	40	101	4	247	199	273	377	540	917	17	69	28	0.68	282	36	17	47	209	23%	77	4%	7.50	34.8	$24
Bats Left	06 CIN	561	99	131	40	92	7	234	270	215	361	490	851	17	65	28	0.58	251	28	24	49	176	22%	66	4%	6.63	23.3	$20
Health A	07 CIN	522	101	138	40	106	9	264	239	278	384	554	937	16	68	31	0.61	273	35	19	47	197	24%	87	6%	7.76	36.4	$26
PT/Exp A	08 2NL	517	79	122	40	100	2	236	195	253	382	513	894	19	68	26	0.74	267	36	18	46	190	25%	31	2%	7.19	27.4	$20
Consist B	1st Half	253	42	56	20	48	1	221			382	502	884	21	65	25	0.75	258	36	16	48	201	25%	29	2%	7.22	13.9	$9
LIMA Plan B+	2nd Half	264	37	66	20	52	1	250			381	523	904	17	71	27	0.74	275	36	19	45	180	24%	26	1%	7.16	13.5	$11
+/- Score 2	09 Proj	**531**	**90**	**131**	**41**	**101**	**5**	**247**			**379**	**532**	**911**	**18**	**68**	**28**	**0.67**	**270**	**34**	**19**	**47**	**194**	**25%**	**60**	**3%**	**7.41**	**32.0**	**$23**

So... what are the odds that he hits 40 HRs yet again? In truth, pretty remote. Still, this is a consistent, durable skill set, though admittedly one that has more value in sim formats than traditional roto.

Duran,German

Duran,German		AB	R	H	HR	RBI	SB	Avg	vL	vR	OB	Slg	OPS	bb%	ct%	h%	Eye	xBA	G	L	F	PX	hr/f	SX	SBO	RC/G	RAR	R$
Pos 5	04	0	0	0	0	0	0	0							0			0						0				
Age 24	05	0	0	0	0	0	0	0							0			0						0				
Bats Right	06	0	0	0	0	0	0	0							0			0						0				
Health A	07 aa	480	67	132	19	69	9	275			315	475	790	6	86	28	0.43	0				118		100	10%	5.07	-2.4	$16
PT/Exp F	08 TEX *	220	31	49	4	20	1	224	271	192	262	351	613	5	82	26	0.28	241	39	18	43	80	5%	104	5%	2.97	-12.9	$3
Consist F	1st Half	149	20	30	4	13	1	204			249	336	584	6	81	23	0.31	238	42	17	42	77	8%	104	3%	2.58	-10.7	$1
LIMA Plan F	2nd Half	71	11	19	0	8	0	266			291	383	674	3	83	32	0.21	248	35	20	45	85	0%	110	7%	3.75	-2.3	$1
+/- Score 15	09 Proj	**167**	**24**	**42**	**4**	**19**	**1**	**251**			**287**	**406**	**693**	**5**	**84**	**28**	**0.31**	**261**	**37**	**19**	**44**	**97**	**6%**	**101**	**8%**	**3.95**	**-4.6**	**$4**

3-16-.231 in 143 AB at TEX. Skill regression in both Triple-A and the majors says he was in over his head. His '07 power-speed-ct% combo offers some potential, though it looks like a utility role may be in his future.

Durham,Ray

Durham,Ray		AB	R	H	HR	RBI	SB	Avg	vL	vR	OB	Slg	OPS	bb%	ct%	h%	Eye	xBA	G	L	F	PX	hr/f	SX	SBO	RC/G	RAR	R$
Pos 4	04 SF	471	95	133	17	65	10	282	333	263	360	484	844	11	87	29	0.95	288	44	16	40	112	10%	136	10%	6.08	19.7	$19
Age 37	05 SF	497	67	144	12	62	6	290	290	292	352	429	781	9	88	31	0.81	292	47	21	32	90	9%	61	6%	5.24	9.5	$16
Bats Both	06 SF	498	79	146	26	93	7	293	341	277	359	538	897	9	88	29	0.84	309	46	17	37	130	16%	102	7%	6.51	26.6	$22
Health A	07 SF	464	56	101	11	71	10	218	200	224	298	343	641	10	84	24	0.71	241	45	13	41	77	7%	89	10%	3.59	-15.9	$8
PT/Exp B	08 2NL	370	64	107	6	45	8	289	238	303	378	432	811	13	81	35	0.74	272	41	21	38	110	5%	75	10%	5.86	11.4	$13
Consist F	1st Half	221	35	64	2	25	5	290			377	403	780	12	81	35	0.72	270	46	22	32	91	4%	74	8%	5.48	4.4	$7
LIMA Plan D	2nd Half	149	29	43	4	20	3	289			380	477	857	13	81	34	0.76	278	35	18	46	138	7%	71	13%	6.43	7.1	$6
+/- Score -36	09 Proj	**248**	**40**	**67**	**5**	**35**	**4**	**270**			**352**	**411**	**763**	**11**	**83**	**31**	**0.75**	**264**	**43**	**18**	**40**	**97**	**6%**	**82**	**8%**	**5.18**	**3.4**	**$7**

PX rebound was caused by doubles, not HR. His hr/f trend confirms there's nothing to see here, and that 2006 is still a fluke. Now speed and ct% are fading as well, meaning BA and SB could be the next to go.

Dye,Jermaine

Dye,Jermaine		AB	R	H	HR	RBI	SB	Avg	vL	vR	OB	Slg	OPS	bb%	ct%	h%	Eye	xBA	G	L	F	PX	hr/f	SX	SBO	RC/G	RAR	R$
Pos 9	04 OAK	532	87	141	23	80	4	265	280	259	327	464	791	8	76	31	0.38	258	39	18	43	127	13%	91	4%	5.27	8.8	$17
Age 35	05 CHW	529	74	145	31	86	11	274	252	278	324	512	836	7	81	29	0.39	295	38	21	41	145	18%	86	12%	5.60	13.8	$22
Bats Right	06 CHW	539	103	170	44	120	7	315	337	305	383	622	1004	10	78	33	0.50	307	39	20	40	179	26%	84	6%	7.86	32.1	$31
Health A	07 CHW	508	68	129	28	78	2	254	292	241	315	486	801	8	79	27	0.42	282	35	19	46	152	15%	42	3%	5.29	-3.2	$15
PT/Exp A	08 CHW	590	96	172	34	96	3	292	285	294	341	541	881	7	82	31	0.42	305	35	22	43	154	16%	67	4%	6.17	13.3	$25
Consist D	1st Half	295	50	90	18	50	3	305			353	556	909	7	81	33	0.39	301	35	23	42	155	18%	72	7%	6.51	9.3	$14
LIMA Plan C+	2nd Half	295	46	82	16	46	0	278			328	525	853	7	84	28	0.47	308	34	22	44	153	15%	47	0%	5.85	4.1	$11
+/- Score 1	09 Proj	**581**	**92**	**164**	**35**	**98**	**4**	**282**			**338**	**533**	**871**	**8**	**81**	**30**	**0.43**	**297**	**36**	**21**	**44**	**156**	**17%**	**69**	**4%**	**6.11**	**12.0**	**$24**

Three of the last four seasons (we're looking at you, 2006 anomaly) look very similar in terms of skills. Add in good health and no signs of age-related decline, and you've got a good idea what to expect in '09.

Easley,Damion

Easley,Damion		AB	R	H	HR	RBI	SB	Avg	vL	vR	OB	Slg	OPS	bb%	ct%	h%	Eye	xBA	G	L	F	PX	hr/f	SX	SBO	RC/G	RAR	R$
Pos 4	04 FLA	223	26	53	9	43	4	238	149	294	312	457	769	10	84	25	0.67	295	41	18	41	138	12%	77	11%	5.10	3.3	$6
Age 39	05 FLA	267	37	64	9	30	4	240	333	218	307	419	727	9	82	26	0.55	289	40	23	37	119	11%	87	8%	4.52	-0.3	$7
Bats Right	06 ARI	189	24	44	9	28	1	233	245	217	310	418	728	10	84	23	0.70	261	45	15	40	99	14%	57	4%	4.50	-0.6	$4
Health A	07 NYM	193	24	54	10	26	0	280	371	202	344	466	811	9	82	30	0.54	249	40	16	44	106	14%	21	2%	5.39	3.8	$6
PT/Exp D	08 NYM	316	33	85	6	44	0	269	287	260	310	370	681	6	88	29	0.50	262	47	21	33	58	7%	45	0%	3.88	-8.0	$7
Consist C	1st Half	136	14	35	2	14	0	257			308	353	661	7	87	28	0.56	245	43	18	38	64	4%	25	0%	3.74	-4.1	$2
LIMA Plan F	2nd Half	180	19	50	4	30	0	278			312	383	695	5	89	29	0.45	275	49	23	28	54	9%	54	0%	3.99	-4.0	$5
+/- Score -30	09 Proj	**227**	**23**	**58**	**6**	**32**	**0**	**256**			**311**	**373**	**684**	**7**	**85**	**28**	**0.55**	**251**	**44**	**19**	**37**	**69**	**8%**	**40**	**1%**	**3.96**	**-5.0**	**$5**

Looks like he stuck around one year too long (he should've read the 2008 Forecaster). Can still put the bat on the ball, but the power has faded. So he's just a punch-and-Judy singles hitter, and where's the glory in that?

Eckstein,David

Eckstein,David		AB	R	H	HR	RBI	SB	Avg	vL	vR	OB	Slg	OPS	bb%	ct%	h%	Eye	xBA	G	L	F	PX	hr/f	SX	SBO	RC/G	RAR	R$
Pos 6	04 ANA	566	92	156	2	35	16	276	279	274	326	332	658	7	91	30	0.86	267	50	21	30	38	1%	104	12%	3.87	-9.7	$13
Age 34	05 STL	630	90	185	8	61	11	294	262	306	353	395	748	8	93	31	1.32	290	46	23	31	59	4%	100	9%	5.00	18.4	$19
Bats Right	06 STL	500	68	146	2	23	7	292	280	298	333	344	677	6	92	32	0.76	266	49	22	29	34	1%	67	8%	4.00	-5.0	$10
Health C	07 STL	434	58	134	3	31	10	309	298	314	345	382	727	5	95	32	1.09	274	41	22	37	49	2%	82	8%	4.59	1.7	$13
PT/Exp C	08 2TM	324	32	86	2	27	2	265	313	246	330	349	678	9	90	29	0.97	275	51	20	28	61	2%	42	3%	4.20	-2.6	$5
Consist A	1st Half	191	22	53	1	18	2	277			346	356	702	9	92	30	1.25	280	55	19	26	57	2%	49	5%	4.56	0.4	$4
LIMA Plan F	2nd Half	133	10	33	1	9	0	248			306	338	644	8	88	28	0.69	263	46	21	33	67	3%	16	0%	3.68	-3.1	$1
+/- Score -7	09 Proj	**279**	**27**	**76**	**2**	**20**	**2**	**272**			**324**	**349**	**673**	**7**	**91**	**29**	**0.90**	**272**	**47**	**21**	**32**	**54**	**2%**	**46**	**5%**	**4.06**	**-2.8**	**$4**

Return of walks and ground balls would've been valuable if he still had any speed skills. Now all that's left is an empty BA, and maybe not even that, if 2nd half ct% and xBA are any indication. DN: .250 BA.

Edmonds,Jim

Edmonds,Jim		AB	R	H	HR	RBI	SB	Avg	vL	vR	OB	Slg	OPS	bb%	ct%	h%	Eye	xBA	G	L	F	PX	hr/f	SX	SBO	RC/G	RAR	R$
Pos 8	04 STL	498	102	150	42	111	8	301	330	293	419	643	1062	17	70	35	0.67	303	34	21	45	231	27%	89	7%	9.54	67.3	$31
Age 38	05 STL	467	88	123	29	89	5	263	296	251	384	533	917	16	70	31	0.65	281	35	19	47	198	19%	65	7%	7.49	40.1	$21
Bats Left	06 STL	350	52	90	19	70	4	257	156	295	355	471	826	13	71	31	0.52	252	35	20	44	142	17%	55	4%	6.00	15.9	$13
Health B	07 STL	365	39	92	12	53	0	252	198	268	328	403	730	10	79	29	0.55	244	36	19	44	93	9%	37	2%	4.57	0.4	$8
PT/Exp C	08 2NL	340	53	80	20	55	2	235	146	250	342	479	821	14	76	25	0.67	276	37	18	45	157	17%	68	4%	5.86	11.5	$11
Consist C	1st Half	190	18	45	8	28	2	237			322	416	738	11	78	26	0.57	254	32	21	47	112	12%	55	6%	4.68	-0.3	$4
LIMA Plan D	2nd Half	150	35	35	12	27	0	233			365	560	925	17	73	23	0.78	307	44	14	43	217	26%	74	2%	7.39	12.1	$6
+/- Score 27	09 Proj	**242**	**38**	**61**	**12**	**41**	**1**	**252**			**353**	**462**	**815**	**14**	**75**	**29**	**0.63**	**261**	**37**	**18**	**45**	**138**	**14%**	**63**	**3%**	**5.83**	**8.6**	**$8**

Keys to this stunning rebound:
- Leaving Petco (.363 OPS)
- Discontinued post-concussion medication after trade to Cubs
- Only 14% of AB vs. LHers.

198 PX, 23% hr/f with Chicago. Watch where he lands.

Ellis,Mark

Ellis,Mark		AB	R	H	HR	RBI	SB	Avg	vL	vR	OB	Slg	OPS	bb%	ct%	h%	Eye	xBA	G	L	F	PX	hr/f	SX	SBO	RC/G	RAR	R$
Pos 4	04 OAK	0	0	0	0	0	0	0							0			0						0				
Age 31	05 OAK	434	76	137	13	52	1	316	313	318	379	477	856	9	88	34	0.86	285	47	18	35	93	10%	78	3%	6.10	23.1	$17
Bats Right	06 OAK	441	64	110	11	52	4	249	278	242	312	385	697	8	83	28	0.53	254	39	19	42	87	7%	82	4%	4.15	0.3	$9
Health C	07 OAK	583	84	161	19	76	9	276	313	263	327	441	768	7	84	30	0.47	254	32	18	50	104	8%	89	9%	4.90	15.9	$18
PT/Exp B	08 OAK	442	55	103	12	41	14	233	176	256	315	373	688	11	85	25	0.82	253	34	20	46	85	7%	108	13%	4.22	-9.0	$10
Consist B	1st Half	278	43	70	8	29	9	252			344	410	754	12	87	27	1.05	259	33	18	49	97	7%	106	13%	5.12	1.9	$8
LIMA Plan B	2nd Half	164	12	33	4	12	5	201			264	311	575	8	83	22	0.50	244	35	24	42	64	7%	82	13%	2.62	-11.7	$1
+/- Score 25	09 Proj	**511**	**66**	**132**	**18**	**54**	**14**	**258**			**323**	**424**	**748**	**9**	**84**	**28**	**0.62**	**264**	**35**	**20**	**45**	**99**	**9%**	**100**	**12%**	**4.74**	**4.0**	**$15**

Shoulder injury ruined 2H, but...
- Note SX and SBO trend
- 1H Eye, FB% could be building blocks for power rebound
- 20-point BA/xBA variance

Likely undervalued for 2009, but don't ignore the injury history.

BRANDON KRUSE

Ellsbury,Jacoby

Ellsbury,Jacoby			AB	R	H	HR	RBI	SB	Avg	vL	vR	OB	Sig	OPS	bb%	ct%	h%	Eye	xBA	G	L	F	PX	hr/f	SX	SBO	RC/G	RAR	R$
Pos	879	04	0	0	0	0	0	0	0							0			0						0				
Age	25	05	0	0	0	0	0	0	0							0			0						0				
Bats	Left	06 aa	198	25	57	3	16	14	289			358	407	765	10	89	32	0.94	0				70		113	35%	5.17	3.7	$7
Health	A	07 BOS	* 552	89	172	5	53	44	312	346	356	358	418	776	7	89	35	0.63	285	52	19	29	70	4%	143	31%	5.12	9.0	$25
PT/Exp	C	08 BOS	554	98	155	9	47	50	280	295	275	329	394	723	7	86	31	0.51	279	52	20	28	69	7%	161	39%	4.44	-14.7	$25
Consist	A	1st Half	269	54	72	5	24	34	268			341	383	724	10	85	30	0.75	275	48	23	29	66	8%	177	45%	4.63	-5.7	$15
LIMA Plan	C+	2nd Half	285	44	83	4	23	16	291			318	404	721	4	86	33	0.28	280	55	18	27	72	6%	134	32%	4.23	-9.2	$11
+/- Score	19	09 Proj	**558**	**90**	**164**	**7**	**49**	**40**	**294**			**343**	**404**	**747**	**7**	**87**	**33**	**0.58**	**282**	**52**	**20**	**28**	**69**	**5%**	**140**	**31%**	**4.75**	**-3.2**	**$23**

Lack of power may have led pitchers to start throwing more strikes (see 2nd half bb%). You can see the impact on 2H OBA and SBO. How he adjusts is crucial, as this is the difference between a $20 and $30 season.

Encarnacion,Edwin

Encarnacion,Edwin			AB	R	H	HR	RBI	SB	Avg	vL	vR	OB	Sig	OPS	bb%	ct%	h%	Eye	xBA	G	L	F	PX	hr/f	SX	SBO	RC/G	RAR	R$
Pos	5	04 aa	469	65	123	13	67	15	262			328	418	746	9	85	28	0.66	0				100		90	15%	4.80	-2.5	$15
Age	26	05 CIN	* 501	63	134	23	77	9	268	246	234	331	479	810	9	80	30	0.47	299	41	24	35	142	16%	70	9%	5.47	10.0	$18
Bats	Right	06 CIN	406	60	112	15	72	6	276	248	287	342	473	815	9	81	31	0.53	285	41	21	37	127	12%	72	9%	5.62	1.5	$14
Health	A	07 CIN	* 548	77	163	19	82	9	297	284	291	345	456	801	7	84	33	0.44	260	38	19	43	97	10%	78	6%	5.25	-5.5	$21
PT/Exp	B	08 CIN	506	75	127	26	68	1	251	292	235	332	466	798	11	80	27	0.60	264	34	16	50	135	13%	51	1%	5.39	0.3	$15
Consist	A	1st Half	262	44	65	13	32	1	248			330	462	792	11	81	26	0.63	261	35	14	50	133	12%	67	1%	5.33	-0.3	$8
LIMA Plan	C	2nd Half	244	31	62	13	36	0	254			333	471	805	11	79	27	0.57	266	34	18	49	137	14%	19	0%	5.46	0.6	$7
+/- Score	21	09 Proj	**467**	**66**	**125**	**20**	**69**	**2**	**268**			**336**	**465**	**801**	**9**	**81**	**29**	**0.54**	**269**	**37**	**18**	**45**	**124**	**12%**	**59**	**3%**	**5.39**	**-0.2**	**$15**

7% FB surge led to career-high HR total, but it's killing his BA potential. And that, in turn, is hurting his RBI totals. And both of those things are limiting his overall value. He's got a real BPI butterfly effect going on.

Erstad,Darin

Erstad,Darin			AB	R	H	HR	RBI	SB	Avg	vL	vR	OB	Sig	OPS	bb%	ct%	h%	Eye	xBA	G	L	F	PX	hr/f	SX	SBO	RC/G	RAR	R$
Pos	78	04 ANA	495	79	146	7	69	16	295	253	316	344	400	744	7	85	34	0.50	273	57	16	27	70	6%	114	12%	4.68	-3.6	$18
Age	34	05 ANA	609	86	166	7	66	10	273	232	291	325	371	696	7	82	32	0.43	264	48	22	30	71	5%	100	8%	4.10	-10.8	$15
Bats	Left	06 LAA	95	8	21	0	5	1	221	192	232	267	326	594	6	81	27	0.33	240	51	12	37	82	0%	82	11%	2.91	-6.7	($0)
Health	F	07 CHW	* 357	36	82	4	34	7	231	157	282	295	306	601	8	83	27	0.55	244	53	17	30	52	4%	75	9%	3.03	-21.8	$4
PT/Exp	F	08 HOU	322	49	89	4	31	2	276	243	286	307	363	670	4	79	34	0.21	264	51	25	24	65	7%	63	6%	3.55	-17.3	$8
Consist	A	1st Half	109	18	33	2	14	1	303			350	450	800	7	82	36	0.40	309	47	30	24	110	9%	62	10%	5.36	-0.2	$4
LIMA Plan	F	2nd Half	213	31	56	2	17	1	263			283	319	602	3	77	33	0.13	240	53	23	24	42	5%	66	4%	2.58	-17.6	$4
+/- Score	-53	09 Proj	**230**	**32**	**59**	**3**	**24**	**3**	**257**			**302**	**342**	**643**	**6**	**80**	**31**	**0.32**	**256**	**51**	**22**	**27**	**62**	**6%**	**70**	**8%**	**3.34**	**-13.8**	**$5**

Five years of lackluster skills culminate in a miserable 2H. LD% is the only thing standing between him and BA oblivion. Yet the Astros liked this season enough to sign up for another one. Don't be like the Astros.

Escobar,Yunel

Escobar,Yunel			AB	R	H	HR	RBI	SB	Avg	vL	vR	OB	Sig	OPS	bb%	ct%	h%	Eye	xBA	G	L	F	PX	hr/f	SX	SBO	RC/G	RAR	R$
Pos	6	04	0	0	0	0	0	0	0							0			0						0				
Age	26	05	0	0	0	0	0	0	0							0			0						0				
Bats	Right	06 aa	428	51	107	2	43	7	249			337	322	658	12	82	30	0.73	0				51		78	11%	3.93	-5.9	$6
Health	A	07 ATL	* 499	72	161	7	54	11	323	355	303	373	443	816	7	86	36	0.58	295	56	21	23	81	7%	83	11%	5.58	15.2	$18
PT/Exp	C	08 ATL	514	71	148	10	60	2	288	262	299	361	401	762	10	88	31	0.95	275	58	17	25	69	9%	51	4%	5.12	7.1	$15
Consist	C	1st Half	294	44	87	6	30	2	296			373	398	771	11	86	33	0.90	275	59	19	22	61	11%	58	6%	5.21	4.8	$9
LIMA Plan	D+	2nd Half	220	27	61	4	30	0	277			346	405	750	9	90	29	1.05	275	57	14	29	80	7%	45	2%	5.01	2.4	$6
+/- Score	-5	09 Proj	**476**	**64**	**139**	**7**	**54**	**5**	**292**			**358**	**403**	**761**	**9**	**87**	**32**	**0.78**	**278**	**57**	**18**	**25**	**72**	**7%**	**68**	**7%**	**5.06**	**7.7**	**$14**

Ct% growth has been great but his value is going to stall unless he can start hitting 'em out or stealing some bases. Given his bb% and SBO history, steals seem to be the likeliest path.

Ethier,Andre

Ethier,Andre			AB	R	H	HR	RBI	SB	Avg	vL	vR	OB	Sig	OPS	bb%	ct%	h%	Eye	xBA	G	L	F	PX	hr/f	SX	SBO	RC/G	RAR	R$
Pos	97	04	0	0	0	0	0	0	0							0			0						0				
Age	27	05 a/a	516	81	145	14	64	1	281			332	424	756	7	85	31	0.52	0				91		58	4%	4.78	-2.8	$16
Bats	Left	06 LA	* 482	62	148	12	64	7	307	351	298	366	469	835	9	81	36	0.50	267	41	22	37	95	8%	98	9%	5.87	14.6	$17
Health	A	07 LA	447	50	127	13	64	0	284	279	286	351	452	803	9	85	31	0.68	275	46	18	36	106	10%	30	3%	5.50	7.8	$12
PT/Exp	B	08 LA	525	90	160	20	77	6	305	243	326	375	510	885	10	83	34	0.67	311	41	27	32	129	14%	95	6%	6.51	19.1	$23
Consist	B	1st Half	255	35	69	7	32	2	271			331	424	754	8	85	30	0.61	284	40	23	37	101	9%	54	4%	4.86	-2.5	$7
LIMA Plan	B	2nd Half	270	55	91	13	45	4	337			415	593	1008	12	81	38	0.72	333	43	30	27	157	22%	116	7%	8.13	20.9	$16
+/- Score	10	09 Proj	**570**	**96**	**171**	**26**	**97**	**5**	**300**			**367**	**526**	**892**	**10**	**83**	**32**	**0.63**	**311**	**43**	**24**	**33**	**135**	**17%**	**89**	**6%**	**6.51**	**23.0**	**$25**

Best part of 2H breakout? It featured some growth vs. LHers:
1H - 76% ct, 0.31 Eye, 65 PX
2H - 86% ct, 1.00 Eye, 99 PX
Also has terrific growth trends in PX, hr/f and xBA. With peak age, 2009 looks very promising.

Evans,Nick

Evans,Nick			AB	R	H	HR	RBI	SB	Avg	vL	vR	OB	Sig	OPS	bb%	ct%	h%	Eye	xBA	G	L	F	PX	hr/f	SX	SBO	RC/G	RAR	R$
Pos	7	04	0	0	0	0	0	0	0							0			0						0				
Age	23	05	0	0	0	0	0	0	0							0			0						0				
Bats	Right	06	0	0	0	0	0	0	0							0			0						0				
Health	A	07	0	0	0	0	0	0	0							0			0						0				
PT/Exp	F	08 NYM	* 405	62	111	13	54	2	274	319	135	323	462	784	7	81	31	0.37	290	44	23	33	121	12%	98	3%	5.12	-3.5	$13
Consist	F	1st Half	288	43	78	11	44	2	271			323	476	798	7	80	30	0.39	0	57	14	29	126	17%	107	4%	5.29	-1.1	$10
LIMA Plan	F	2nd Half	117	19	33	2	10	0	282			323	427	750	6	82	33	0.33	287	41	25	34	109	6%	46	0%	4.70	-2.4	$3
+/- Score	9	09 Proj	**295**	**46**	**82**	**8**	**33**	**1**	**278**			**323**	**446**	**769**	**6**	**81**	**32**	**0.36**	**287**	**42**	**24**	**34**	**114**	**9%**	**79**	**2%**	**4.93**	**-3.8**	**$8**

2-9-.257 in 109 AB at NYM. Made jump from Double-A to majors with aplomb, but BA vs. RH, 2H PX and hr/f drops say he's still a work in progress. SX inflated by 7 triples in 296 AB in minors; speed ain't his game.

Everett,Adam

Everett,Adam			AB	R	H	HR	RBI	SB	Avg	vL	vR	OB	Sig	OPS	bb%	ct%	h%	Eye	xBA	G	L	F	PX	hr/f	SX	SBO	RC/G	RAR	R$
Pos	6	04 HOU	384	66	105	8	31	13	273	235	282	304	385	690	4	85	30	0.30	234	41	15	45	66	5%	134	15%	3.84	-3.2	$12
Age	32	05 HOU	549	58	136	11	54	21	248	227	255	282	364	646	5	81	29	0.25	243	39	19	42	79	6%	107	23%	3.30	-10.9	$14
Bats	Right	06 HOU	514	52	123	6	59	9	239	250	237	286	352	639	6	86	27	0.48	250	37	20	43	69	3%	95	13%	3.48	-13.7	$8
Health	F	07 HOU	220	18	51	2	15	4	232	214	238	278	318	596	6	86	26	0.45	242	45	17	38	58	3%	70	12%	2.95	-10.1	$2
PT/Exp	D	08 MIN	127	19	27	2	20	0	213	310	184	281	323	603	9	88	23	0.80	239	39	15	46	68	4%	71	0%	3.26	-4.2	$2
Consist	A	1st Half	74	9	14	1	7	0	189			241	324	565	6	88	20	0.56	254	41	14	45	87	3%	79	0%	2.74	-3.7	$0
LIMA Plan	F	2nd Half	53	10	13	1	13	0	245			333	321	654	12	89	26	1.17	219	37	16	47	43	5%	49	0%	3.95	-0.6	$2
+/- Score	13	09 Proj	**194**	**25**	**45**	**3**	**26**	**2**	**232**			**291**	**332**	**623**	**8**	**87**	**25**	**0.63**	**240**	**40**	**17**	**44**	**64**	**4%**	**83**	**6%**	**3.36**	**-5.8**	**$3**

You have to be pretty awful to combine an Eye this good with an xBA this bad. Glove may keep him employed in real life, but in this version of the game, there's no reason to own him anymore.

Fahey,Brandon

Fahey,Brandon			AB	R	H	HR	RBI	SB	Avg	vL	vR	OB	Sig	OPS	bb%	ct%	h%	Eye	xBA	G	L	F	PX	hr/f	SX	SBO	RC/G	RAR	R$
Pos	6	04 aa	208	17	44	1	13	3	210			265	261	526	7	88	23	0.63	0				32		73	8%	2.28	-13.1	$0
Age	28	05 aa	500	58	133	3	43	15	266			320	333	653	7	86	31	0.57	0				46		99	15%	3.68	-8.5	$11
Bats	Left	06 BAL	* 319	44	77	2	26	7	241	190	244	312	307	618	9	83	28	0.62	259	56	21	23	41	3%	102	14%	3.32	-10.6	$4
Health	A	07 aaa	343	35	76	2	26	12	221			282	294	576	8	87	25	0.66	0				41		121	18%	2.88	-15.9	$4
PT/Exp	F	08 BAL	* 328	28	70	1	30	1	213	200	235	257	280	537	6	80	27	0.29	230	45	20	35	53	1%	56	8%	2.05	-23.4	$0
Consist	B	1st Half	176	13	39	1	18	1	223			272	270	542	6	81	27	0.36	211	50	17	33	36	2%	32	12%	2.14	-12.1	$1
LIMA Plan	F	2nd Half	152	15	31	0	12	0	201			239	292	531	5	77	26	0.22	240	43	21	36	73	0%	79	0%	1.96	-11.3	($0)
+/- Score	-7	09 Proj	**65**	**7**	**14**	**0**	**5**	**1**	**215**			**268**	**304**	**572**	**7**	**82**	**26**	**0.41**	**255**	**49**	**21**	**30**	**60**	**2%**	**98**	**12%**	**2.67**	**-3.4**	**$0**

0-12-.226 in 106 AB at BAL. Looks like he and Everett are engaged in a spirited battle for the title of least valuable hitter on this page. Judging by RC/G and RAR, Fahey wins, but really, we all lose.

Feliz,Pedro

Feliz,Pedro			AB	R	H	HR	RBI	SB	Avg	vL	vR	OB	Sig	OPS	bb%	ct%	h%	Eye	xBA	G	L	F	PX	hr/f	SX	SBO	RC/G	RAR	R$
Pos	5	04 SF	503	72	139	22	84	5	276	291	269	308	485	793	4	83	30	0.27	286	47	15	37	125	14%	89	7%	5.01	-0.8	$18
Age	34	05 SF	569	69	142	20	81	0	250	271	245	297	422	718	6	82	27	0.37	267	44	17	39	108	11%	55	2%	4.24	-9.0	$14
Bats	Right	06 SF	603	75	147	22	98	1	244	212	253	283	428	711	5	81	27	0.29	261	40	16	43	110	10%	69	2%	4.10	-25.0	$14
Health	B	07 SF	557	61	141	20	72	2	253	257	252	290	418	708	5	87	26	0.41	265	43	15	42	95	10%	53	3%	4.10	-24.7	$12
PT/Exp	A	08 PHI	425	43	106	14	58	0	249	288	231	303	402	706	7	87	26	0.61	263	47	16	37	89	10%	34	0%	4.22	-14.4	$9
Consist	A	1st Half	273	28	71	9	39	0	260			311	421	732	7	90	26	0.74	276	47	16	37	93	10%	34	0%	4.56	-6.4	$7
LIMA Plan	D	2nd Half	152	15	35	5	19	0	230			291	368	659	8	82	25	0.48	243	45	17	39	79	10%	44	0%	3.59	-8.2	$2
+/- Score	-13	09 Proj	**394**	**43**	**97**	**13**	**54**	**0**	**246**			**293**	**399**	**692**	**6**	**85**	**26**	**0.45**	**258**	**44**	**16**	**40**	**90**	**10%**	**48**	**1%**	**3.97**	**-16.7**	**$8**

xBA, RC/G histories show that his mediocrity hasn't changed in four years. But it took fading power to finally get him a ticket to the World Series at 33. Life's funny that way.

BRANDON KRUSE

Fielder,Prince

Fielder,Prince			AB	R	H	HR	RBI	SB	Avg	vL	vR	OB	Slg	OPS	bb%	ct%	h%	Eye	xBA	G	L	F	PX	hr/f	SX	SBO	RC/G	RAR	R$
Pos	3	04 aa	497	72	139	25	81	12	279			364	496	860	12	83	29	0.76	0				129		73	13%	6.22	10.7	$20
Age	24	05 MIL	* 437	58	123	25	80	7	281	500	281	351	510	860	10	81	30	0.58	332	37	35	28	142	25%	49	11%	6.06	5.8	$19
Bats	Left	06 MIL	569	82	154	28	81	7	271	247	280	339	483	822	9	78	30	0.47	273	42	18	39	132	16%	70	6%	5.66	-5.6	$19
Health	A	07 MIL	573	109	165	50	119	2	288	261	301	385	618	1002	14	79	29	0.74	315	35	19	46	196	24%	53	2%	8.01	30.2	$31
PT/Exp	A	08 MIL	588	86	162	34	102	3	276	239	295	366	507	873	13	77	30	0.63	278	41	19	40	146	19%	55	3%	6.44	11.9	$24
Consist	D	1st Half	298	47	81	16	43	1	272			356	487	843	12	80	29	0.64	274	42	18	41	131	17%	57	1%	5.98	2.1	$11
LIMA Plan	B	2nd Half	290	39	81	18	59	2	279			376	528	904	13	75	32	0.62	282	40	20	40	161	21%	47	4%	6.95	10.1	$13
+/- Score	4	09 Proj	**553**	**86**	**154**	**39**	**115**	**4**	**278**			**367**	**555**	**922**	**12**	**78**	**29**	**0.63**	**297**	**39**	**19**	**41**	**169**	**22%**	**58**	**4%**	**6.99**	**17.6**	**$26**

HR output lost some meat, but who knows if it was his diet. 50 HR may have just been the product of favorable hr/f + FB. hr/f can be fickle, so for now, his upside is between '07 and '08. At age 24, that's not bad.

Fields,Josh

Fields,Josh			AB	R	H	HR	RBI	SB	Avg	vL	vR	OB	Slg	OPS	bb%	ct%	h%	Eye	xBA	G	L	F	PX	hr/f	SX	SBO	RC/G	RAR	R$
Pos	5	04	0	0	0	0	0	0	0							0			0						0				
Age	26	05 aa	474	55	98	14	57	5	207			267	338	605	8	73	25	0.31	0				95		60	12%	2.79	-27.8	$7
Bats	Right	06 aaa	482	82	140	21	66	26	290	167	143	362	500	862	10	72	36	0.41	0	58	8	33	143	18%	126	22%	6.42	15.9	$23
Health	A	07 CHW	* 578	79	145	34	100	8	251	321	213	333	481	814	11	69	31	0.39	255	41	17	43	166	20%	60	9%	5.82	16.3	$20
PT/Exp	D	08 CHW	* 308	37	65	9	31	7	212	273	95	290	361	651	10	65	29	0.32	227	67	7	27	118	18%	95	11%	3.62	-12.1	$5
Consist	C	1st Half	175	23	39	8	22	3	220			285	414	699	8	70	27	0.30					135		104	8%	4.12	-4.0	$4
LIMA Plan	D	2nd Half	133	14	27	2	10	4	200			296	292	588	12	59	32	0.33	184	67	7	27	92	9%	64	16%	2.88	-8.5	$1
+/- Score	-7	09 Proj	**368**	**48**	**85**	**14**	**45**	**9**	**231**			**310**	**398**	**708**	**10**	**67**	**31**	**0.35**	**230**	**48**	**14**	**38**	**128**	**14%**	**86**	**13%**	**4.40**	**-5.3**	**$9**

0-2-.156 in 32 AB at CHW. A lost season, due in large part to a strained knee. We know he owns elite power, but we'll never see it unless he improves ct% and BA vs RHers.

Figgins,Chone

Figgins,Chone			AB	R	H	HR	RBI	SB	Avg	vL	vR	OB	Slg	OPS	bb%	ct%	h%	Eye	xBA	G	L	F	PX	hr/f	SX	SBO	RC/G	RAR	R$
Pos	5	04 ANA	577	83	171	5	60	34	296	314	289	351	419	771	8	84	35	0.52	254	37	25	39	69	3%	150	27%	5.12	3.5	$22
Age	31	05 ANA	642	113	186	8	57	62	290	244	313	354	397	751	9	84	33	0.63	255	41	22	37	66	4%	162	38%	4.92	7.7	$32
Bats	Both	06 LAA	604	93	161	9	62	52	267	233	280	338	376	714	10	83	31	0.65	253	44	21	36	65	5%	151	37%	4.48	-9.6	$24
Health	C	07 LAA	442	81	146	3	58	41	330	326	331	400	432	832	10	82	40	0.63	277	47	26	26	72	3%	147	32%	6.00	13.7	$25
PT/Exp	A	08 LAA	453	72	125	1	22	34	276	272	277	363	318	681	12	82	33	0.78	242	46	24	30	33	1%	109	27%	4.21	-9.0	$15
Consist	D	1st Half	184	26	54	0	9	14	293			393	332	724	14	81	36	0.86	250	56	23	22	34	0%	85	25%	4.86	-0.1	$7
LIMA Plan	C+	2nd Half	269	46	71	1	13	20	264			342	309	651	11	83	31	0.71	235	40	25	35	32	1%	120	30%	3.77	-9.0	$9
+/- Score	-33	09 Proj	**437**	**72**	**122**	**2**	**36**	**39**	**279**			**358**	**348**	**705**	**11**	**83**	**34**	**0.70**	**252**	**45**	**24**	**31**	**48**	**2%**	**139**	**33%**	**4.47**	**-5.3**	**$18**

Charged out of the gates, then nagging injuries got in the way: hamstring, toe, knee, elbow. He's not a .300+ BA guy; that was h% induced. But base skills remain strong, so 40 SB could return with better durability.

Flores,Jesus

Flores,Jesus			AB	R	H	HR	RBI	SB	Avg	vL	vR	OB	Slg	OPS	bb%	ct%	h%	Eye	xBA	G	L	F	PX	hr/f	SX	SBO	RC/G	RAR	R$
Pos	2	04	0	0	0	0	0	0	0							0			0						0				
Age	24	05	0	0	0	0	0	0	0							0			0						0				
Bats	Right	06	0	0	0	0	0	0	0							0			0						0				
Health	A	07 WAS	180	21	44	4	25	0	244	270	220	299	361	660	7	73	31	0.29	225	50	17	34	86	9%	34	2%	3.55	-4.7	$3
PT/Exp	F	08 WAS	* 360	30	85	9	65	0	236	308	238	279	374	654	6	74	30	0.23	251	37	25	38	103	9%	35	1%	3.41	-8.6	$7
Consist	A	1st Half	207	19	50	5	35	0	241			307	395	702	9	72	31	0.35	265	38	27	36	124	9%	22	2%	4.26	0.3	$4
LIMA Plan	D	2nd Half	153	11	35	4	30	0	229			239	346	585	1	75	28	0.05	234	37	24	39	75	9%	42	0%	2.25	-9.1	$3
+/- Score	13	09 Proj	**416**	**39**	**99**	**9**	**54**	**0**	**238**			**280**	**358**	**638**	**6**	**74**	**30**	**0.22**	**235**	**42**	**21**	**36**	**88**	**8%**	**35**	**2%**	**3.19**	**-13.1**	**$6**

8-59-.256 in 301 AB at WAS. Was deadly with runners on, which inflated his RBI. Can't hit RHers. Poor skill foundation. At age 24, he has time to refine his approach. Just don't expect it to happen soon.

Floyd,Cliff

Floyd,Cliff			AB	R	H	HR	RBI	SB	Avg	vL	vR	OB	Slg	OPS	bb%	ct%	h%	Eye	xBA	G	L	F	PX	hr/f	SX	SBO	RC/G	RAR	R$
Pos	0	04 NYM	396	55	103	18	63	11	260	239	269	339	462	801	11	74	31	0.46	262	43	18	40	138	16%	74	14%	5.53	2.6	$15
Age	36	05 NYM	550	85	150	34	98	12	273	224	290	347	505	853	10	82	28	0.64	287	41	18	42	135	18%	94	9%	5.97	-0.9	$26
Bats	Left	06 NYM	332	45	81	11	44	6	244	179	266	305	407	711	8	83	27	0.50	262	42	18	40	99	10%	85	8%	4.27	-21.3	$8
Health	C	07 CHC	282	40	80	9	45	0	284	303	281	363	422	785	11	83	31	0.74	250	46	17	37	81	10%	40	0%	5.31	-7.4	$9
PT/Exp	D	08 TAM	246	32	66	11	39	1	268	100	275	343	455	798	10	76	31	0.48	274	51	20	29	125	20%	37	1%	5.41	3.4	$8
Consist	B	1st Half	102	14	26	6	15	1	255			339	471	810	11	75	29	0.50	266	53	16	32	139	25%	40	3%	5.56	1.9	$3
LIMA Plan	D	2nd Half	144	18	40	5	24	0	278			346	444	790	9	78	33	0.47	276	50	23	27	116	16%	22	0%	5.31	1.6	$4
+/- Score	-46	09 Proj	**337**	**46**	**88**	**9**	**53**	**2**	**261**			**336**	**394**	**730**	**10**	**79**	**31**	**0.54**	**255**	**47**	**19**	**34**	**90**	**10%**	**64**	**3%**	**4.61**	**-9.3**	**$9**

Has neither the durability nor approach vs. LHers to play every day. And despite lofty PX, GB% trend means double-digit HR will continue to be a reach. If power goes, BA will follow suit. Bid cautiously.

Fontenot,Mike

Fontenot,Mike			AB	R	H	HR	RBI	SB	Avg	vL	vR	OB	Slg	OPS	bb%	ct%	h%	Eye	xBA	G	L	F	PX	hr/f	SX	SBO	RC/G	RAR	R$
Pos	4	04 aaa	524	65	132	8	44	12	252			310	372	682	8	81	30	0.45	0				77		110	15%	3.97	-5.9	$10
Age	28	05 aaa	375	45	87	5	30	2	232			315	348	664	11	84	27	0.74	0				76		87	4%	3.98	-4.2	$4
Bats	Left	06 aaa	362	49	98	8	32	5	271			348	418	766	11	83	31	0.70	0				96		76	8%	5.15	8.3	$8
Health	A	07 CHC	* 445	64	120	8	53	7	269	212	297	319	409	728	7	83	31	0.43	270	47	19	34	88	6%	110	11%	4.50	-2.6	$12
PT/Exp	D	08 CHC	243	42	74	9	40	2	305	333	302	390	514	904	12	79	36	0.67	295	38	24	38	146	12%	71	3%	6.96	14.5	$11
Consist	D	1st Half	115	22	29	4	15	2	252			323	443	766	9	80	28	0.52	285	42	20	38	133	11%	83	7%	5.04	0.9	$4
LIMA Plan	C	2nd Half	128	20	45	5	25	0	352			447	578	1025	15	78	42	0.79	306	34	28	38	157	13%	51	0%	8.71	12.8	$7
+/- Score	-10	09 Proj	**309**	**47**	**89**	**11**	**42**	**3**	**288**			**363**	**478**	**841**	**11**	**81**	**33**	**0.62**	**288**	**39**	**24**	**37**	**124**	**11%**	**82**	**6%**	**6.03**	**11.5**	**$11**

Looked more like A-Rod than a utility MI in 2H. Credit most of that to an inflated h%. Elite PX came out of nowhere, but it was nice all year long. Good base skill support means 2nd half is worth speculating on.

Francisco,Ben

Francisco,Ben			AB	R	H	HR	RBI	SB	Avg	vL	vR	OB	Slg	OPS	bb%	ct%	h%	Eye	xBA	G	L	F	PX	hr/f	SX	SBO	RC/G	RAR	R$
Pos	79	04 aa	497	60	113	12	60	18	227			288	362	650	8	85	25	0.55	0				83		107	21%	3.59	-24.4	$11
Age	27	05 a/a	330	39	91	5	39	12	276			319	400	719	6	85	31	0.41	0				81		119	20%	4.35	-6.5	$10
Bats	Right	06 aaa	515	76	134	14	56	24	260			318	416	734	8	86	28	0.63	0				93		123	22%	4.62	-9.0	$17
Health	A	07 CLE	* 439	61	126	13	56	19	287	286	273	340	452	792	8	82	33	0.45	281	47	19	35	112	10%	91	26%	5.24	2.6	$17
PT/Exp	C	08 CLE	* 539	72	137	16	60	7	255	269	265	318	411	730	9	79	30	0.45	249	34	18	48	109	8%	70	7%	4.52	-5.3	$13
Consist	B	1st Half	288	36	74	7	34	6	258			322	402	724	9	79	31	0.45	241	35	17	48	102	6%	80	12%	4.48	-3.1	$7
LIMA Plan	C+	2nd Half	251	36	63	9	26	1	251			314	422	736	8	79	28	0.44	257	34	19	47	117	10%	49	2%	4.56	-2.1	$6
+/- Score	-8	09 Proj	**515**	**71**	**135**	**18**	**59**	**10**	**262**			**321**	**434**	**756**	**8**	**82**	**29**	**0.47**	**261**	**35**	**19**	**47**	**113**	**9%**	**78**	**12%**	**4.79**	**-2.3**	**$15**

15-54-.266 in 447 AB at CLE. A marginal full-timer. Decent power, but not much else. Lack of a green light hurt his wheels, so SB could return. If 2H PX growth continues:
UP: 20 HR, 20 SB

Francoeur,Jeff

Francoeur,Jeff			AB	R	H	HR	RBI	SB	Avg	vL	vR	OB	Slg	OPS	bb%	ct%	h%	Eye	xBA	G	L	F	PX	hr/f	SX	SBO	RC/G	RAR	R$
Pos	9	04 aa	76	7	13	2	8	1	171			171	263	434	0	79	19	0.00	0				53		10	10%	0.34	-11.5	$0
Age	25	05 ATL	* 592	76	161	25	99	14	272	403	268	306	483	789	5	79	31	0.23	284	40	19	41	144	13%	96	17%	5.02	-3.9	$23
Bats	Right	06 ATL	651	83	169	29	103	1	260	292	248	285	449	733	3	80	29	0.17	264	45	18	37	107	15%	60	5%	4.20	-11.0	$18
Health	A	07 ATL	642	84	188	19	105	5	293	317	281	336	444	780	6	80	34	0.33	261	43	19	37	101	10%	55	4%	4.99	2.0	$22
PT/Exp	A	08 ATL	599	70	143	11	71	0	239	210	251	285	359	644	6	81	28	0.35	258	45	21	34	82	7%	54	1%	3.39	-32.2	$9
Consist	C	1st Half	322	39	77	8	41	0	239			284	385	669	6	82	27	0.34	269	43	21	35	96	9%	57	1%	3.67	-14.7	$6
LIMA Plan	D+	2nd Half	277	31	66	3	30	0	238			287	329	616	6	81	28	0.37	246	47	20	33	65	4%	48	0%	3.07	-17.5	$3
+/- Score	33	09 Proj	**496**	**61**	**128**	**13**	**69**	**2**	**258**			**300**	**402**	**702**	**6**	**81**	**30**	**0.31**	**262**	**45**	**20**	**36**	**95**	**9%**	**64**	**4%**	**4.02**	**-15.1**	**$12**

Three reasons why he hasn't reached bottom...
- Continued PX drop
- FB decline
- 2H was even worse

SX trend says '05 SB are a distant memory. Bid cautiously.

Frandsen,Kevin

Frandsen,Kevin			AB	R	H	HR	RBI	SB	Avg	vL	vR	OB	Slg	OPS	bb%	ct%	h%	Eye	xBA	G	L	F	PX	hr/f	SX	SBO	RC/G	RAR	R$
Pos	4	04	0	0	0	0	0	0	0							0			0						0				
Age	26	05 a/a	218	31	61	3	26	6	280			296	394	690	2	93	29	0.33	0				77		89	23%	3.95	-2.5	$7
Bats	Right	06 SF	* 386	47	99	4	30	5	256	200	217	279	368	647	3	90	28	0.32	259	48	13	39	71	3%	80	14%	3.49	-12.7	$6
Health	F	07 SF	* 331	36	94	6	36	7	282	262	274	337	392	729	8	91	30	0.92	290	53	21	26	66	7%	65	12%	4.65	-0.5	$9
PT/Exp	F	08 SF	1	0	0	0	0	0	0			0	0	0	0	100	0		0	100	0	0	0					-0.3	$0
Consist	F	1st Half	0	0	0	0	0	0	0																				
LIMA Plan	D	2nd Half	1	0	0	0	0	0	0											100	0	0							
+/- Score		09 Proj	**335**	**42**	**92**	**5**	**35**	**2**	**275**			**306**	**389**	**695**	**4**	**92**	**29**	**0.55**	**291**	**52**	**19**	**28**	**73**	**5%**	**59**	**10%**	**4.11**	**-5.9**	**$8**

A ruptured Achilles cost him the year. Showed signs he could be a regular in '07, so don't write him off. The problem is his upside; PX and SX history says it is limited, even if scouts like him.

STEPHEN NICKRAND

Freel,Ryan		Year	AB	R	H	HR	RBI	SB	Avg	vL	vR	OB	Slg	OPS	bb%	ct%	h%	Eye	xBA	G	L	F	PX	hr/f	SX	SBO	RC/G	RAR	R$
Pos	8	04 CIN	505	74	140	3	28	37	277	235	290	362	368	730	12	83	33	0.76	258	50	20	29	58	2%	150	27%	4.84	2.8	$18
Age	33	05 CIN	369	69	100	4	21	36	271	302	263	360	371	731	12	84	31	0.86	285	53	24	24	68	5%	149	37%	4.86	3.3	$17
Bats	Right	06 CIN	454	67	123	8	27	37	271	303	261	352	399	751	11	78	33	0.58	255	44	21	35	89	6%	114	34%	4.99	7.4	$17
Health	F	07 CIN	277	44	68	3	16	15	245	143	315	292	347	638	6	83	29	0.38	254	49	18	33	66	4%	141	34%	3.38	-9.8	$7
PT/Exp	D	08 CIN	131	17	39	0	10	6	298	339	261	338	359	697	6	86	35	0.44	270	56	20	24	51	0%	82	26%	4.12	-2.3	$4
Consist	C	1st Half	131	17	39	0	10	6	298			338	359	697	6	86	35	0.44	270	56	20	24	51	0%	82	26%	4.12	-2.3	$4
LIMA Plan	D	2nd Half	0	0	0	0	0	0	0							0			0										
+/- Score	-49	09 Proj	**251**	**38**	**69**	**2**	**16**	**12**	**275**			**338**	**373**	**711**	**9**	**83**	**32**	**0.56**	**266**	**51**	**20**	**29**	**68**	**4%**	**114**	**25%**	**4.42**	**-1.6**	**$8**

AB trend tells the whole story. Brittle utility types in their mid-30s aren't likely to become durable again. Torn hamstring means he could come out of gates slow in '09. No longer a premium SB source.

Fukudome,Kosuke		Year	AB	R	H	HR	RBI	SB	Avg	vL	vR	OB	Slg	OPS	bb%	ct%	h%	Eye	xBA	G	L	F	PX	hr/f	SX	SBO	RC/G	RAR	R$
Pos	9	04 JPN	404	59	90	14	79	7	224			292	428	719	9	78	25	0.44	0				120		132	12%	4.44	-6.9	$11
Age	32	05 JPN	612	99	158	17	100	12	257			338	434	772	11	80	30	0.62	0				115		126	10%	5.23	4.6	$20
Bats	Left	06 JPN	578	114	162	19	101	10	281			349	485	834	10	85	30	0.69	0				123		133	8%	5.91	11.4	$22
Health	B	07 JPN	269	62	74	8	47	5	274			398	441	839	17	77	33	0.89	0				123		74	7%	6.43	9.6	$11
PT/Exp	B	08 CHC	501	79	129	10	58	12	257	276	251	361	379	740	14	79	31	0.78	259	51	19	30	83	8%	97	9%	4.97	-3.2	$14
Consist	B	1st Half	284	55	84	6	34	7	296			405	430	834	15	81	35	0.95	272	51	20	29	90	9%	100	9%	6.27	8.6	$12
LIMA Plan	B+	2nd Half	217	24	45	4	24	5	207			301	313	614	12	77	25	0.59	241	50	18	32	73	7%	87	10%	3.20	-13.5	$3
+/- Score	-20	09 Proj	**520**	**91**	**143**	**15**	**75**	**11**	**275**			**372**	**439**	**810**	**13**	**79**	**32**	**0.74**	**275**	**51**	**19**	**31**	**108**	**12%**	**102**	**8%**	**5.82**	**11.4**	**$19**

CON:
- Tanked in 2nd half
- 0 HR in 127 AB vs. LHers

PRO:
- Decent power/speed combo
- Good base skills
- Imports take a year to adjust

Furcal,Rafael		Year	AB	R	H	HR	RBI	SB	Avg	vL	vR	OB	Slg	OPS	bb%	ct%	h%	Eye	xBA	G	L	F	PX	hr/f	SX	SBO	RC/G	RAR	R$
Pos	6	04 ATL	563	103	157	14	59	29	279	276	280	346	414	760	9	87	30	0.82	273	50	16	34	76	8%	139	20%	5.01	14.3	$23
Age	31	05 ATL	616	100	175	12	58	46	284	288	280	350	429	778	9	87	31	0.79	296	47	24	30	86	8%	163	31%	5.27	23.1	$29
Bats	Both	06 LA	654	113	196	15	63	37	300	324	293	370	445	815	10	85	33	0.74	284	50	21	29	83	9%	133	23%	5.70	24.8	$28
Health	F	07 LA	581	87	157	6	47	25	270	313	254	333	355	688	9	88	30	0.81	263	50	19	32	52	4%	116	17%	4.21	-4.0	$16
PT/Exp	B	08 LA	143	34	51	5	16	8	357	365	352	436	573	1009	12	88	38	1.18	324	49	19	32	130	12%	136	21%	8.11	13.0	$10
Consist	F	1st Half	134	34	49	5	16	8	366			444	597	1041	12	89	39	1.27	330	49	18	33	138	13%	142	20%	8.48	13.1	$10
LIMA Plan	B+	2nd Half	9	0	2	0	0	0	222			300	222	522	10	78	29	0.50	0	43	43	14	0	0%	26	33%	1.94	-0.8	$0
+/- Score	-21	09 Proj	**570**	**109**	**176**	**17**	**57**	**35**	**309**			**380**	**482**	**862**	**10**	**87**	**33**	**0.91**	**300**	**49**	**19**	**31**	**101**	**11%**	**143**	**24%**	**6.26**	**28.0**	**$29**

Was on his way to a career year before a bad back got in the way. Stable base skills, prior durability make full rebound likely if healthy. And if 1st half PX wasn't a fluke...
UP: 20 HR, 40 SB

Garciaparra,Nomar		Year	AB	R	H	HR	RBI	SB	Avg	vL	vR	OB	Slg	OPS	bb%	ct%	h%	Eye	xBA	G	L	F	PX	hr/f	SX	SBO	RC/G	RAR	R$
Pos	6	04 2TM	326	55	103	10	44	4	316	240	329	365	494	859	7	91	33	0.83	297	34	24	42	101	8%	97	5%	6.02	15.1	$13
Age	35	05 CHC	230	28	65	9	30	0	283	281	285	318	452	770	5	90	28	0.50	305	40	25	35	99	13%	26	0%	4.80	5.5	$7
Bats	Right	06 LA	469	82	142	20	93	3	303	341	294	360	505	865	8	94	29	1.40	306	38	20	42	107	11%	76	2%	6.15	23.0	$21
Health	F	07 LA	431	39	122	7	59	3	283	213	303	331	371	702	7	90	30	0.76	254	43	19	37	53	5%	40	3%	4.26	-2.3	$10
PT/Exp	C	08 LA	163	24	43	8	28	1	264	339	224	326	466	792	8	93	24	1.36	298	40	18	43	109	12%	48	5%	5.33	3.3	$6
Consist	C	1st Half	31	6	7	1	5	1	226			314	323	637	11	97	21	4.00	297	43	27	30	42	11%	82	10%	4.01	-0.6	$1
LIMA Plan	C	2nd Half	132	18	36	7	23	0	273			329	500	829	8	92	25	1.10	298	39	15	46	126	12%	32	3%	5.66	3.9	$5
+/- Score	12	09 Proj	**325**	**45**	**91**	**13**	**53**	**1**	**280**			**332**	**461**	**792**	**7**	**92**	**27**	**0.93**	**294**	**39**	**20**	**41**	**101**	**10%**	**55**	**3%**	**5.26**	**7.1**	**$11**

2H shows he still has some pop and base skills remain good, but he needs to be a DH somewhere. Don't bet on durability improving in his mid-30s. Bid if he moves to the AL; otherwise, he's end-game filler only.

Gardner,Brett		Year	AB	R	H	HR	RBI	SB	Avg	vL	vR	OB	Slg	OPS	bb%	ct%	h%	Eye	xBA	G	L	F	PX	hr/f	SX	SBO	RC/G	RAR	R$
Pos	8	04	0	0	0	0	0	0	0							0			0						0				
Age	25	05	0	0	0	0	0	0	0							0			0						0				
Bats	Left	06 aa	217	39	55	0	13	26	255			330	291	620	10	81	31	0.60	0				23		161	42%	3.34	-7.9	$9
Health	A	07 a/a	384	75	100	1	24	36	260			343	341	684	11	80	32	0.64	0				56		169	34%	4.23	-3.4	$15
PT/Exp	F	08 NYY	* 468	75	117	3	43	44	251	125	252	343	338	681	12	78	32	0.64	229	48	17	35	58	2%	163	35%	4.19	-16.4	$18
Consist	A	1st Half	285	50	71	3	24	30	247			359	350	709	15	77	31	0.76	0				67		161	38%	4.67	-6.0	$12
LIMA Plan	D	2nd Half	183	26	47	0	19	14	256			314	321	635	8	80	32	0.43	225	48	17	35	44	0%	153	30%	3.42	-10.5	$6
+/- Score	-5	09 Proj	**125**	**21**	**32**	**0**	**10**	**12**	**256**			**336**	**329**	**665**	**11**	**80**	**32**	**0.60**	**227**	**48**	**17**	**35**	**48**	**1%**	**158**	**35%**	**3.93**	**-3.8**	**$5**

0-16-.228 in 127 AB at NYY. Elite speed potential, but was overmatched by MLB pitching. Knows how to take a walk, so there's hope. But he'll need some luck to get a consistent 30% SBO in bigs.

Garko,Ryan		Year	AB	R	H	HR	RBI	SB	Avg	vL	vR	OB	Slg	OPS	bb%	ct%	h%	Eye	xBA	G	L	F	PX	hr/f	SX	SBO	RC/G	RAR	R$
Pos	3	04 a/a	192	25	57	4	34	1	297			341	438	779	6	86	33	0.48	0				93		48	2%	5.06	-2.2	$6
Age	28	05 aaa	452	58	119	13	59	1	263			315	409	724	7	84	29	0.46	0				93		52	4%	4.38	-12.8	$11
Bats	Right	06 CLE	* 549	69	137	20	100	4	250	333	281	321	413	734	9	81	28	0.56	254	42	17	41	102	11%	43	6%	4.58	-13.7	$14
Health	A	07 CLE	484	62	140	21	61	0	289	310	281	336	483	819	7	81	32	0.36	270	38	19	44	125	12%	34	1%	5.45	2.5	$15
PT/Exp	B	08 CLE	495	61	135	14	90	0	273	315	259	333	404	737	8	83	31	0.52	251	39	20	41	83	8%	35	0%	4.59	-9.7	$14
Consist	B	1st Half	260	30	63	6	39	0	242			309	346	655	9	83	27	0.58	238	40	20	41	66	7%	26	0%	3.64	-12.6	$5
LIMA Plan	C	2nd Half	235	31	72	8	51	0	306			361	468	829	8	82	35	0.47	264	38	21	42	103	10%	39	0%	5.66	2.5	$9
+/- Score	-17	09 Proj	**516**	**65**	**144**	**20**	**90**	**1**	**279**			**336**	**453**	**789**	**8**	**82**	**31**	**0.47**	**267**	**38**	**20**	**42**	**109**	**11%**	**41**	**1%**	**5.15**	**-1.7**	**$17**

FB and PX pointed to HR burst in '08, but that didn't happen. A low hr/f deserves part of the blame. Looked better in 2H, so don't write him off yet.
If he rebounds against RHers:
UP: 30 HR

Gathright,Joey		Year	AB	R	H	HR	RBI	SB	Avg	vL	vR	OB	Slg	OPS	bb%	ct%	h%	Eye	xBA	G	L	F	PX	hr/f	SX	SBO	RC/G	RAR	R$
Pos	8	04 a/a	362	51	112	0	14	39	309			357	356	714	7	81	38	0.39	0				36		128	48%	4.30	-4.0	$17
Age	28	05 TAM	* 429	62	114	1	26	42	266	353	269	315	336	651	7	83	32	0.42	282	72	15	13	47	2%	160	46%	3.59	-9.0	$16
Bats	Left	06 2AL	383	59	91	1	41	22	238	232	239	313	292	605	10	80	29	0.56	256	67	16	17	38	2%	129	26%	3.13	-18.1	$9
Health	A	07 KC	* 451	61	132	0	37	27	292	282	312	367	341	707	11	87	34	0.90	292	65	23	12	36	0%	102	26%	4.56	0.4	$15
PT/Exp	C	08 KC	279	41	71	0	22	21	254	250	256	304	272	577	7	86	30	0.50	242	68	13	19	12	0%	129	29%	2.72	-21.9	$8
Consist	D	1st Half	214	29	52	0	15	18	243			286	262	548	6	86	28	0.42	242	66	14	20	12	0%	131	35%	2.33	-19.7	$6
LIMA Plan	F	2nd Half	65	12	19	0	7	3	292			361	308	669	10	86	34	0.78	231	76	8	16	13	0%	88	12%	3.99	-2.5	$2
+/- Score	0	09 Proj	**255**	**39**	**68**	**0**	**22**	**16**	**267**			**332**	**300**	**631**	**9**	**85**	**31**	**0.65**	**254**	**70**	**14**	**17**	**24**	**0%**	**117**	**25%**	**3.48**	**-11.1**	**$8**

OBA has been higher than his Slg for three years. PX and GB confirm that dubious feat will continue. We know he's a burner, but SX hasn't been elite for four years. Don't overvalue his raw speed.

German,Esteban		Year	AB	R	H	HR	RBI	SB	Avg	vL	vR	OB	Slg	OPS	bb%	ct%	h%	Eye	xBA	G	L	F	PX	hr/f	SX	SBO	RC/G	RAR	R$
Pos	74	04 OAK	* 291	34	80	2	28	14	275	167	271	317	344	661	6	88	31	0.50	268	67	13	20	40	4%	124	20%	3.71	-10.3	$8
Age	31	05 aaa	489	68	128	4	46	29	262			323	348	671	8	89	29	0.81	0				56		132	26%	4.03	-14.4	$16
Bats	Right	06 KC	279	44	91	3	34	7	326	347	311	411	459	869	13	82	39	0.82	284	58	18	24	86	6%	113	10%	6.62	10.8	$10
Health	A	07 KC	348	49	92	4	37	11	264	277	255	345	376	722	11	83	31	0.72	270	52	20	27	71	5%	116	16%	4.68	-3.7	$9
PT/Exp	D	08 KC	216	30	53	0	22	7	245	255	236	303	338	641	8	81	30	0.43	268	53	22	26	71	0%	127	19%	3.55	-8.5	$4
Consist	D	1st Half	71	7	12	0	6	2	169			213	197	411	5	76	22	0.24	232	60	21	19	27	0%	84	21%	0.28	-10.7	($0)
LIMA Plan	F	2nd Half	145	23	41	0	16	5	283			346	407	753	9	83	34	0.56	285	50	22	28	91	0%	134	18%	5.05	0.8	$4
+/- Score	25	09 Proj	**191**	**27**	**50**	**1**	**20**	**6**	**262**			**329**	**361**	**690**	**9**	**82**	**32**	**0.55**	**270**	**54**	**20**	**25**	**68**	**3%**	**124**	**17%**	**4.20**	**-4.2**	**$4**

2H SX spike and previous bb% suggest he could net 20 SB if given the chance. That won't happen unless he shows some pop. And BA won't bounce back if pop is gone. It's a domino effect.

Gerut,Jody		Year	AB	R	H	HR	RBI	SB	Avg	vL	vR	OB	Slg	OPS	bb%	ct%	h%	Eye	xBA	G	L	F	PX	hr/f	SX	SBO	RC/G	RAR	R$
Pos	8	04 CLE	481	72	121	11	51	13	252	208	271	327	405	733	10	88	27	0.92	276	46	16	38	91	7%	115	15%	4.80	1.3	$12
Age	31	05 2TM	* 218	23	61	3	20	1	278	103	284	352	399	750	10	88	31	0.93	280	50	19	31	83	5%	51	3%	5.04	3.9	$4
Bats	Left	06	0	0	0	0	0	0	0							0			0						0				
Health	F	07	0	0	0	0	0	0	0							0			0						0				
PT/Exp	F	08 SD	* 435	62	122	17	56	9	280	308	293	337	476	813	8	85	29	0.59	289	47	17	36	113	13%	108	12%	5.47	9.1	$16
Consist	F	1st Half	281	39	74	7	29	8	262			330	413	743	9	84	29	0.63	273	51	16	33	93	9%	104	15%	4.77	0.2	$8
LIMA Plan	B	2nd Half	154	23	48	10	27	1	312			350	591	941	6	88	30	0.47	320	43	18	39	147	19%	93	5%	6.69	8.2	$8
+/- Score	-10	09 Proj	**416**	**55**	**117**	**19**	**65**	**5**	**281**			**343**	**500**	**843**	**9**	**87**	**29**	**0.72**	**304**	**47**	**18**	**35**	**123**	**15%**	**89**	**8%**	**5.86**	**14.6**	**$15**

14-43-.296 in 328 AB at SD. Two reasons not to write off an early-30s breakout...
- PX and FB gains in 2H
- Can hit both LH/RHers now

He could be following a Luis Gonzalez career path.

STEPHEN NICKRAND

Giambi,Jason

			AB	R	H	HR	RBI	SB	Avg	vL	vR	OB	Slg	OPS	bb%	ct%	h%	Eye	xBA	G	L	F	PX	hr/f	SX	SBO	RC/G	RAR	R$
Pos	30	04 NYY	264	33	55	12	40	0	208	263	185	328	379	707	15	77	23	0.76	207	41	9	50	104	12%	22	1%	4.39	-4.9	$4
Age	38	05 NYY	417	74	113	32	87	0	271	261	276	421	535	956	21	74	29	0.99	272	33	19	48	167	22%	18	0%	7.92	33.7	$19
Bats	Left	06 NYY	446	92	113	37	113	2	253	213	270	401	558	959	20	76	25	1.04	286	30	16	53	185	20%	48	1%	7.84	31.6	$21
Health	C	07 NYY	254	31	60	14	39	1	236	239	235	340	433	773	14	74	26	0.61	235	30	16	53	127	14%	29	1%	5.18	-0.6	$6
PT/Exp	B	08 NYY	458	68	113	32	96	2	247	231	253	354	502	856	14	76	26	0.68	270	33	17	50	160	18%	46	2%	6.25	13.3	$18
Consist	D	1st Half	228	41	60	17	46	2	263			373	548	921	15	81	26	0.93	296	32	18	51	169	18%	67	4%	7.05	11.8	$10
LIMA Plan	C	2nd Half	230	27	53	15	50	0	230			335	457	791	14	70	26	0.53	240	34	17	49	150	19%	10	0%	5.44	1.2	$7
+/- Score	-4	09 Proj	432	64	105	26	81	1	243			358	462	820	15	75	27	0.71	250	32	16	51	140	16%	36	1%	5.87	7.7	$14

Injury risk will only get worse in upper 30s, but he's a 30 HR lock if healthy. BA will remain a liability if 2H ct% dip continues. Otherwise, base skills are holding strong. At age 38, expect a decline, but not major.

Giles,Brian

			AB	R	H	HR	RBI	SB	Avg	vL	vR	OB	Slg	OPS	bb%	ct%	h%	Eye	xBA	G	L	F	PX	hr/f	SX	SBO	RC/G	RAR	R$
Pos	9	04 SD	609	97	173	23	94	10	284	237	309	375	475	850	13	87	30	1.11	279	37	20	44	106	10%	106	7%	6.24	16.3	$24
Age	38	05 SD	545	92	164	15	83	13	301	289	306	426	483	909	18	88	32	1.86	299	37	24	39	110	8%	111	8%	7.35	31.8	$24
Bats	Left	06 SD	604	87	159	14	83	9	263	217	282	371	397	769	15	90	27	1.73	264	40	18	43	79	6%	63	6%	5.53	13.4	$16
Health	B	07 SD	483	72	131	13	51	4	271	241	286	356	416	773	12	87	29	1.05	269	40	19	40	87	8%	60	7%	5.31	6.0	$12
PT/Exp	A	08 SD	559	81	171	12	63	2	306	301	309	399	456	856	13	91	32	1.67	294	42	21	37	93	6%	63	2%	6.48	19.7	$18
Consist	B	1st Half	302	37	93	5	29	1	308			405	447	852	14	89	33	1.48	287	44	21	35	88	5%	58	3%	6.47	10.6	$9
LIMA Plan	B+	2nd Half	257	44	78	7	34	1	304			393	467	860	13	93	31	2.00	301	39	22	40	98	7%	62	1%	6.49	9.1	$10
+/- Score	-25	09 Proj	507	77	147	11	61	1	290			385	430	814	13	90	31	1.49	279	40	20	39	86	6%	53	2%	5.98	13.1	$15

Revived BA due to improved approach vs. LHers. Few handle the plate better, so he can keep .300 BA if PX doesn't nosedive again. But with FB dip, that's no sure thing. Hope for .300 BA, pay for .285.

Glaus,Troy

			AB	R	H	HR	RBI	SB	Avg	vL	vR	OB	Slg	OPS	bb%	ct%	h%	Eye	xBA	G	L	F	PX	hr/f	SX	SBO	RC/G	RAR	R$
Pos	5	04 ANA	207	47	52	18	42	2	251	242	255	349	575	924	13	75	25	0.60	298	39	16	45	196	26%	88	9%	7.07	13.4	$10
Age	32	05 ARI	538	78	139	37	97	4	258	244	263	359	522	881	14	73	29	0.58	276	37	17	46	177	20%	54	4%	6.66	29.5	$22
Bats	Right	06 TOR	540	105	136	38	104	3	252	292	238	355	513	868	14	75	27	0.64	270	34	17	49	162	19%	55	3%	6.40	22.1	$21
Health	C	07 TOR	385	60	101	20	62	0	262	361	235	363	473	836	14	74	31	0.60	261	34	21	45	142	16%	35	1%	6.11	13.9	$12
PT/Exp	A	08 STL	544	69	147	27	99	0	270	221	290	371	483	854	14	81	29	0.84	276	38	19	43	133	14%	26	1%	6.28	14.1	$19
Consist	A	1st Half	287	32	76	11	50	0	265			364	453	817	14	83	29	0.90	272	38	18	44	120	11%	31	1%	5.87	4.1	$8
LIMA Plan	C+	2nd Half	257	37	71	16	49	0	276			378	518	895	14	79	29	0.78	281	38	19	43	149	18%	17	0%	6.76	10.1	$11
+/- Score	-10	09 Proj	543	78	144	26	98	0	265			366	470	836	14	77	30	0.70	262	36	19	45	131	14%	31	1%	6.07	10.4	$19

Reasons for optimism...
- 2nd half PX rebound
- Big ct% gain

On the other hand...
- Weakening overall hr/f trend
- Continued PX and FB erosion

It's a wash - if he stays healthy.

Gload,Ross

			AB	R	H	HR	RBI	SB	Avg	vL	vR	OB	Slg	OPS	bb%	ct%	h%	Eye	xBA	G	L	F	PX	hr/f	SX	SBO	RC/G	RAR	R$
Pos	3	04 CHW	234	28	75	7	44	0	321	425	299	374	479	853	8	84	36	0.54	288	39	25	35	100	10%	22	4%	5.96	6.2	$9
Age	33	05 aaa	236	34	73	13	34	0	308			353	555	909	6	86	32	0.50	0				149		44	2%	6.45	7.1	$10
Bats	Left	06 CHW	156	22	51	3	18	6	327	308	333	352	462	813	4	90	35	0.40	300	51	21	27	76	8%	121	14%	5.29	-0.5	$6
Health	B	07 KC	320	37	92	7	51	2	288	388	269	321	441	762	5	88	31	0.41	294	50	19	31	97	8%	74	5%	4.79	-4.2	$9
PT/Exp	D	08 KC	388	46	106	3	37	3	273	263	277	314	348	662	6	90	30	0.59	270	46	22	32	51	3%	60	7%	3.77	-16.8	$7
Consist	B	1st Half	190	24	50	1	16	1	263			303	332	635	5	89	29	0.55	265	50	20	30	50	2%	51	8%	3.47	-10.1	$3
LIMA Plan	F	2nd Half	198	22	56	2	21	2	283			324	364	687	6	90	31	0.63	273	42	24	34	51	3%	65	5%	4.06	-6.8	$4
+/- Score	-16	09 Proj	265	32	75	4	32	3	283			321	405	725	5	89	30	0.51	287	47	22	31	76	6%	82	7%	4.43	-6.3	$7

How can this guy get 400 AB? Any power he once had seems gone, even if aberrant hr/f rebounds some. Only hope is to mine for BA. A hit rate normalization could give him a .300+ BA again. Lots of "ifs."

Gomes,Jonny

			AB	R	H	HR	RBI	SB	Avg	vL	vR	OB	Slg	OPS	bb%	ct%	h%	Eye	xBA	G	L	F	PX	hr/f	SX	SBO	RC/G	RAR	R$
Pos	09	04 aaa	390	63	89	20	67	7	228			306	451	758	10	69	27	0.37	0				158		89	15%	5.00	-3.6	$12
Age	28	05 TAM *	510	86	141	30	87	14	276	287	280	354	524	877	11	71	33	0.42	263	29	23	48	166	17%	118	14%	6.62	8.8	$24
Bats	Right	06 TAM	385	53	83	20	59	1	216	297	187	323	431	754	14	70	25	0.53	238	29	17	54	149	14%	44	6%	5.04	-16.7	$8
Health	A	07 TAM *	391	54	97	18	56	16	247	313	218	326	451	777	10	64	34	0.32	227	26	21	53	163	14%	105	21%	5.58	-7.7	$14
PT/Exp	D	08 TAM *	261	37	50	10	32	8	190	182	182	258	364	622	8	71	23	0.32	215	34	10	56	127	9%	112	20%	3.05	-15.8	$5
Consist	D	1st Half	108	17	22	6	15	5	204			265	417	682	8	74	22	0.32	238	40	10	51	132	15%	134	29%	3.71	-4.2	$3
LIMA Plan	F	2nd Half	153	20	28	4	17	3	180			254	327	580	9	69	24	0.31	186	18	11	71	123	5%	81	14%	2.55	-11.8	$1
+/- Score	52	09 Proj	63	9	13	3	9	2	206			285	384	669	10	69	25	0.35	219	30	16	54	130	12%	72	17%	3.73	-3.6	$1

8-21-.182 in 154 AB at TAM. Can barely crack both a 70% ct% and the Mendoza Line vs. RHers, and even bombed vs. lefties. At age 28, time is running out. He's not close to becoming a full-timer again.

Gomez,Carlos

			AB	R	H	HR	RBI	SB	Avg	vL	vR	OB	Slg	OPS	bb%	ct%	h%	Eye	xBA	G	L	F	PX	hr/f	SX	SBO	RC/G	RAR	R$
Pos	8	04	0	0	0	0	0	0	0							0			0						0				
Age	23	05	0	0	0	0	0	0	0							0			0						0				
Bats	Right	06 aa	430	54	122	6	48	42	283			326	410	736	6	80	34	0.31	0				84		148	46%	4.54	-0.2	$19
Health	B	07 NYM *	265	34	65	4	23	26	245	254	212	301	336	637	7	83	28	0.46	233	45	16	39	58	5%	124	48%	3.37	-9.5	$9
PT/Exp	D	08 MIN	577	79	149	7	59	33	258	270	254	289	360	650	4	75	33	0.18	224	44	17	39	73	4%	150	32%	3.32	-34.9	$18
Consist	B	1st Half	332	46	88	5	29	21	265			291	373	664	3	75	34	0.14	221	42	17	41	76	5%	149	37%	3.46	-18.6	$11
LIMA Plan	D+	2nd Half	245	33	61	2	30	12	249			287	343	630	5	76	32	0.22	227	46	17	37	69	3%	143	26%	3.14	-16.2	$7
+/- Score	-13	09 Proj	453	60	111	6	46	25	245			288	346	634	6	79	30	0.28	232	45	17	38	70	4%	132	32%	3.21	-24.1	$12

Big SB totals are sexy, but that's the only good thing here. Base skills were bad all year. He's just 23, so we can't be too critical but if he's not careful he'll end up on the Esix Snead List. (NOO!!! Not the Snead List!!)

Gomez,Chris

			AB	R	H	HR	RBI	SB	Avg	vL	vR	OB	Slg	OPS	bb%	ct%	h%	Eye	xBA	G	L	F	PX	hr/f	SX	SBO	RC/G	RAR	R$
Pos	5	04 TOR	341	41	96	3	37	3	282	300	274	336	346	682	8	88	31	0.68	264	45	25	30	40	3%	63	5%	4.05	-8.3	$7
Age	37	05 BAL	219	27	61	1	18	2	279	317	243	358	342	700	11	92	30	1.59	272	52	20	28	46	2%	49	4%	4.64	0.9	$4
Bats	Right	06 BAL	132	14	45	2	17	1	341	333	345	374	439	813	5	92	36	0.64	280	51	21	28	61	6%	36	7%	5.38	1.3	$5
Health	B	07 2AL	222	21	66	1	21	1	297	292	301	328	374	701	4	88	33	0.38	279	51	23	25	55	2%	50	5%	4.10	-4.8	$4
PT/Exp	F	08 PIT	183	26	50	1	20	0	273	226	298	321	333	655	7	84	32	0.43	234	44	20	36	46	2%	41	0%	3.59	-9.3	$4
Consist	B	1st Half	107	18	34	0	13	0	318			348	355	703	4	90	35	0.45	257	42	25	33	30	0%	48	0%	4.13	-3.5	$3
LIMA Plan	F	2nd Half	76	8	16	1	7	0	211			286	303	588	10	75	27	0.42	201	48	12	40	73	4%	28	0%	2.75	-6.2	$0
+/- Score	-40	09 Proj	65	8	16	1	7	0	246			296	316	612	7	85	28	0.48	248	48	20	32	50	3%	46	3%	3.13	-4.4	$1

Used to give quality AB vs. LHers. Now, all he's got is his glove and versatility. xBA trend confirms days of .270+ BA are over. Without that, his fanalytic value is nil, even in the deepest of leagues.

Gonzalez,Adrian

			AB	R	H	HR	RBI	SB	Avg	vL	vR	OB	Slg	OPS	bb%	ct%	h%	Eye	xBA	G	L	F	PX	hr/f	SX	SBO	RC/G	RAR	R$
Pos	3	04 TEX *	499	55	144	13	77	1	289		286	334	435	769	6	88	31	0.58	265	34	20	46	87	6%	48	2%	4.93	-0.8	$14
Age	26	05 TEX *	478	60	133	20	63	0	278	71	243	325	458	783	6	86	29	0.49	279	39	20	41	105	12%	40	0%	5.00	-1.3	$14
Bats	Left	06 SD	570	83	173	24	82	0	304	312	301	362	500	862	8	80	34	0.46	286	44	23	33	122	16%	35	1%	6.10	1.5	$21
Health	A	07 SD	646	101	182	30	100	0	282	263	290	347	502	849	9	78	32	0.46	277	37	19	44	143	14%	49	0%	6.02	-2.1	$23
PT/Exp	A	08 SD	616	103	172	36	119	0	279	213	320	357	510	866	11	77	31	0.52	283	43	20	37	146	21%	35	0%	6.26	9.2	$27
Consist	A	1st Half	330	51	95	21	68	0	288			353	530	883	9	79	31	0.47	283	40	19	41	146	20%	40	0%	6.31	5.3	$15
LIMA Plan	D+	2nd Half	286	52	77	15	51	0	269			361	486	847	13	75	31	0.57	282	47	22	31	146	22%	35	0%	6.18	3.7	$11
+/- Score	-10	09 Proj	600	95	170	30	102	0	283			353	496	849	10	79	32	0.50	281	42	21	37	135	17%	37	0%	6.01	2.2	$23

PRO:
- PX trend, hr/f spike

CON:
- ct% slowly eroding
- Getting worse vs. LHers
- 2nd half FB%

For profit, buy 2007, not 2008.

Gonzalez,Alberto

			AB	R	H	HR	RBI	SB	Avg	vL	vR	OB	Slg	OPS	bb%	ct%	h%	Eye	xBA	G	L	F	PX	hr/f	SX	SBO	RC/G	RAR	R$
Pos	6	04	0	0	0	0	0	0	0							0			0						0				
Age	26	05	0	0	0	0	0	0	0							0			0						0				
Bats	Right	06 a/a	449	58	122	5	43	4	272			322	363	685	7	92	29	0.94	0				53		84	4%	4.17	-2.7	$9
Health	A	07 a/a	493	58	120	1	48	12	244			289	338	627	6	87	28	0.49	0				63		119	15%	3.42	-14.2	$7
PT/Exp	D	08 2TM *	322	33	74	5	34	3	230	219	275	275	328	603	6	86	25	0.44	285	44	28	29	68	6%	52	8%	2.99	-14.6	$4
Consist	B	1st Half	138	12	31	0	14	3	222			295	257	552	9	84	26	0.66	230	51	19	30	30	0%	55	9%	2.57	-8.1	$1
LIMA Plan	F	2nd Half	184	21	43	5	19	0	235			259	381	641	3	87	25	0.24	330	36	36	27	95	11%	45	6%	3.27	-6.8	$3
+/- Score	26	09 Proj	99	11	24	1	10	1	242			287	343	631	6	87	27	0.49	289	43	28	29	65	4%	89	10%	3.40	-3.0	$1

1-10-.257 in 101 AB at NYY and WAS. Only thing worth speculating on is SB. He could give you 10 if he gets 400 AB. But if he gets 400 AB he'll likely be on a bad team that won't let him steal. Hail Yossarian!

STEPHEN NICKRAND

Gonzalez,Alex

			AB	R	H	HR	RBI	SB	Avg	vL	vR	OB	Slg	OPS	bb%	ct%	h%	Eye	xBA	G	L	F	PX	hr/f	SX	SBO	RC/G	RAR	R$
Pos	6	04 FLA	561	67	130	23	79	3	232	278	220	267	419	686	5	78	26	0.21	242	33	16	51	118	10%	79	4%	3.71	-7.1	$12
Age	32	05 FLA	435	45	115	5	45	5	264	216	277	313	368	681	7	81	32	0.38	236	37	18	45	80	3%	57	7%	3.90	-0.8	$9
Bats	Right	06 BOS	388	48	99	9	50	1	255	278	244	295	397	692	5	83	29	0.33	256	37	20	43	91	6%	68	1%	3.93	-5.4	$7
Health	F	07 CIN	393	55	107	16	55	0	272	234	287	314	468	782	6	81	30	0.32	278	34	22	44	125	12%	43	1%	4.97	5.9	$11
PT/Exp	D	08 CIN	0	0	0	0	0	0	0																				
Consist	C	1st Half	0	0	0	0	0	0	0																				
LIMA Plan	D	2nd Half	0	0	0	0	0	0	0																				
+/- Score		09 Proj	396	48	103	11	50	2	260			303	412	715	6	81	30	0.32	254	36	19	45	102	7%	60	4%	4.20	-3.3	$9

Sidelined by microfracture knee surgery. Before injury, PX spike conjured memories of 20+ HR ability. But at age 32, prudent move is to pay for 2006 and hope for a few more HR. Base skills are just too weak.

Gonzalez,Carlos

			AB	R	H	HR	RBI	SB	Avg	vL	vR	OB	Slg	OPS	bb%	ct%	h%	Eye	xBA	G	L	F	PX	hr/f	SX	SBO	RC/G	RAR	R$
Pos	89	04	0	0	0	0	0	0	0							0			0						0				
Age	23	05	0	0	0	0	0	0	0							0			0						0				
Bats	Left	06	0	0	0	0	0	0	0							0			0						0				
Health	A	07 aa	500	60	136	16	71	8	272			316	454	770	6	82	30	0.36	0				119		78	13%	4.89	5.2	$15
PT/Exp	F	08 OAK *	475	49	115	7	48	5	242	188	263	280	358	638	5	77	30	0.23	249	49	18	33	88	6%	76	7%	3.23	-30.1	$7
Consist	D	1st Half	261	29	67	5	32	3	257			297	402	699	5	82	30	0.33	279	44	21	35	104	7%	74	7%	4.07	-9.8	$5
LIMA Plan	D	2nd Half	214	20	48	2	16	2	224			259	304	563	4	71	30	0.16	214	53	16	31	64	4%	74	7%	2.16	-20.9	$1
+/- Score	13	09 Proj	336	36	79	5	33	4	235			276	357	633	5	78	29	0.26	255	50	17	32	90	6%	83	10%	3.21	-17.8	$4

4-26-.242 in 302 AB at OAK. MLB debut was a flop. Marginal power and speed, GB hitter, can't hit LHers, 2H fade. Reason for optimism? He's still young. That's it. There's talent here, but it'll be a wait.

Gonzalez,Edgar

			AB	R	H	HR	RBI	SB	Avg	vL	vR	OB	Slg	OPS	bb%	ct%	h%	Eye	xBA	G	L	F	PX	hr/f	SX	SBO	RC/G	RAR	R$
Pos	4	04 aa	392	43	97	7	41	4	246			293	371	664	6	79	29	0.32	0				84		87	7%	3.63	-8.3	$6
Age	30	05 a/a	384	35	82	5	36	3	213			268	322	589	7	81	25	0.38	0				79		61	14%	2.78	-19.0	$3
Bats	Right	06 a/a	353	42	108	9	54	9	306			378	450	829	10	82	35	0.63	0				89		85	13%	5.87	14.9	$13
Health	A	07 aa	459	40	94	5	33	9	204			255	289	545	6	84	23	0.42	0				60		83	13%	2.30	-29.7	$2
PT/Exp	D	08 SD *	407	46	107	10	42	1	263	283	268	319	372	690	8	78	32	0.38	236	47	19	33	74	9%	27	7%	3.94	-10.0	$8
Consist	F	1st Half	205	21	58	6	23	0	282			339	416	755	8	81	33	0.45	259	43	22	35	89	9%	20	7%	4.78	0.0	$5
LIMA Plan	F	2nd Half	202	25	49	4	19	1	243			298	327	625	7	75	30	0.32	217	50	18	32	57	8%	46	7%	3.05	-10.5	$3
+/- Score	-45	09 Proj	162	17	40	3	16	2	247			304	348	652	8	80	29	0.41	241	48	19	33	69	7%	48	10%	3.50	-5.9	$3

7-33-.274 in 325 AB at SD. Short on time? For these marginal utility types, scan their PX and SX history to see if there's anything to mine for. See triple digits? Anywhere? See how quick that was? Next.

Gonzalez,Luis

			AB	R	H	HR	RBI	SB	Avg	vL	vR	OB	Slg	OPS	bb%	ct%	h%	Eye	xBA	G	L	F	PX	hr/f	SX	SBO	RC/G	RAR	R$
Pos	79	04 ARI	379	69	98	17	48	2	259	244	266	371	493	865	15	85	27	1.17	285	36	16	48	137	11%	91	3%	6.55	12.4	$12
Age	41	05 ARI	579	90	157	24	79	4	271	269	272	358	459	817	12	84	29	0.87	284	38	20	42	118	12%	59	3%	5.74	6.7	$20
Bats	Left	06 ARI	586	93	159	15	73	0	271	259	277	348	444	792	11	90	28	1.19	291	40	19	41	105	7%	44	1%	5.55	5.1	$15
Health	B	07 LA	464	70	129	15	68	6	278	317	267	356	433	789	11	88	29	1.00	274	42	19	39	89	9%	77	6%	5.41	0.7	$15
PT/Exp	B	08 FLA	341	30	89	8	47	1	261	239	267	340	413	754	11	87	28	0.95	275	41	19	40	99	7%	33	3%	5.07	-3.5	$7
Consist	A	1st Half	222	20	60	5	29	1	270			355	405	760	12	87	29	1.00	267	42	19	39	85	7%	40	4%	5.17	-1.6	$5
LIMA Plan	D	2nd Half	119	10	29	3	18	0	244			313	429	742	9	88	25	0.86	286	41	17	42	125	7%	13	0%	4.89	-1.9	$2
+/- Score	-18	09 Proj	246	30	63	5	34	0	256			335	402	737	11	88	27	0.98	273	41	18	41	95	6%	46	2%	4.91	-3.4	$5

He could milk one more season with these solid base skills. Problem is, his power has eroded and will now be taking BA with it. If he does return for one last season, expect RAR trend to continue.

Gordon,Alex

			AB	R	H	HR	RBI	SB	Avg	vL	vR	OB	Slg	OPS	bb%	ct%	h%	Eye	xBA	G	L	F	PX	hr/f	SX	SBO	RC/G	RAR	R$
Pos	5	04	0	0	0	0	0	0	0							0			0						0				
Age	25	05	0	0	0	0	0	0	0							0			0						0				
Bats	Left	06 aa	486	87	139	20	79	17	286			361	490	851	10	83	31	0.67	0				127		104	15%	6.09	11.6	$21
Health	A	07 KC	543	60	134	15	60	14	247	217	258	300	411	710	7	75	30	0.30	249	37	19	44	120	8%	100	15%	4.24	-10.2	$12
PT/Exp	B	08 KC	493	72	128	16	59	9	260	234	273	347	432	779	12	76	31	0.55	252	31	21	48	125	9%	82	8%	5.34	6.7	$14
Consist	C	1st Half	308	47	80	10	40	2	260			339	422	761	11	76	31	0.49	251	32	22	46	118	9%	50	5%	5.04	1.4	$8
LIMA Plan	B	2nd Half	185	25	48	6	19	7	259			360	449	808	14	76	31	0.64	256	30	20	50	138	9%	96	13%	5.85	5.2	$6
+/- Score	-6	09 Proj	503	69	136	23	85	11	270			345	488	833	10	76	31	0.48	271	33	20	46	148	13%	84	10%	5.91	14.9	$19

Why a breakout may be closer than it seems...
- 2nd half PX, FB spikes
- bb% gains

He actually had a 140+ PX in 2 of last 3 months. Get ready.
UP: 30 HR

Gotay,Ruben

			AB	R	H	HR	RBI	SB	Avg	vL	vR	OB	Slg	OPS	bb%	ct%	h%	Eye	xBA	G	L	F	PX	hr/f	SX	SBO	RC/G	RAR	R$
Pos	5	04 KC *	556	78	154	10	74	8	277			340	408	748	9	85	31	0.65	0				79		93	12%	4.86	-0.8	$15
Age	26	05 KC *	392	48	87	7	40	2	222			279	339	618	7	85	25	0.52	238	38	16	46	78	5%	71	7%	3.23	-15.4	$4
Bats	Both	06 aaa	491	55	119	10	55	9	242			287	367	654	6	84	27	0.38	0				79		81	14%	3.53	-25.6	$9
Health	A	07 NYM *	272	35	74	6	34	4	272	194	318	339	409	748	9	80	32	0.50	277	46	24	29	95	9%	67	10%	4.82	-6.2	$7
PT/Exp	F	08 ATL	102	10	24	2	8	1	235	154	263	322	343	665	11	69	32	0.41	224	42	23	35	88	8%	39	7%	3.84	-4.7	$1
Consist	C	1st Half	69	5	14	1	4	1	203			304	275	579	13	68	28	0.45	204	46	22	33	58	7%	36	10%	2.61	-6.1	$0
LIMA Plan	F	2nd Half	33	5	10	1	4	0	303			361	485	846	8	70	41	0.30	266	35	26	39	149	11%	32	0%	6.32	0.9	$1
+/- Score	-45	09 Proj	64	7	15	1	6	1	234			304	336	640	9	79	28	0.46	242	44	21	35	72	7%	50	11%	3.41	-3.9	$1

He's been below replacement level for five years while better skilled players toil in the upper minors. Marginal power, eroding speed give little hope for either in '09. 2nd half PX was a sample size mirage. Stay away.

Granderson,Curtis

			AB	R	H	HR	RBI	SB	Avg	vL	vR	OB	Slg	OPS	bb%	ct%	h%	Eye	xBA	G	L	F	PX	hr/f	SX	SBO	RC/G	RAR	R$
Pos	8	04 aa	462	75	122	16	79	12	265			354	433	787	12	82	29	0.78	0				93		118	14%	5.42	10.1	$17
Age	28	05 DET *	607	87	167	20	77	20	275	364	257	332	488	820	8	75	34	0.34	273	48	17	35	137	12%	137	19%	5.77	26.2	$22
Bats	Left	06 DET	596	90	155	19	68	8	260	218	274	334	438	772	10	71	34	0.38	246	39	22	39	122	12%	116	8%	5.28	10.8	$15
Health	A	07 DET	612	122	185	23	74	26	302	160	337	357	552	909	8	77	36	0.37	279	34	21	45	158	11%	165	18%	6.89	39.6	$29
PT/Exp	A	08 DET	553	112	155	22	66	12	280	259	288	362	494	856	11	80	32	0.64	276	40	19	41	128	12%	137	10%	6.26	14.3	$22
Consist	C	1st Half	229	44	69	9	28	6	301			352	498	850	7	82	34	0.44	271	40	18	42	116	11%	132	16%	5.89	3.5	$10
LIMA Plan	B+	2nd Half	324	68	86	13	38	6	265			369	491	859	14	78	30	0.76	280	41	20	39	137	13%	136	6%	6.49	10.6	$12
+/- Score	4	09 Proj	598	118	166	25	73	21	278			351	507	858	10	78	32	0.50	276	38	20	41	141	13%	153	15%	6.25	22.2	$25

Remains a top-flight OF. Lack of green light cut his SB; his wheels are fine. So is his power. And he made huge gains vs. LHers. If 2H HR and green light align, watch out.
UP: 30 HR, 30 SB

Greene,Khalil

			AB	R	H	HR	RBI	SB	Avg	vL	vR	OB	Slg	OPS	bb%	ct%	h%	Eye	xBA	G	L	F	PX	hr/f	SX	SBO	RC/G	RAR	R$
Pos	6	04 SD	484	67	132	15	65	4	273	291	266	345	446	791	10	81	31	0.56	257	36	18	45	110	8%	86	4%	5.37	17.2	$14
Age	29	05 SD	436	51	109	15	70	5	250	200	267	291	431	722	5	79	29	0.27	267	33	22	44	124	10%	92	6%	4.25	3.7	$12
Bats	Right	06 SD	412	56	101	15	55	5	245	271	237	310	427	738	9	79	28	0.45	256	35	19	46	115	10%	83	6%	4.60	3.0	$10
Health	D	07 SD	611	89	155	27	97	4	254	268	249	291	468	759	5	79	28	0.25	270	35	18	47	139	12%	90	4%	4.66	3.7	$18
PT/Exp	B	08 SD	389	30	83	10	35	5	213	188	222	255	339	595	5	74	26	0.22	221	32	21	48	86	7%	75	8%	2.58	-24.6	$4
Consist	C	1st Half	309	26	71	8	32	5	230			274	356	630	6	75	28	0.25	220	29	21	49	84	7%	82	9%	3.07	-14.6	$5
LIMA Plan	C	2nd Half	80	4	12	2	3	0	150			181	275	456	4	71	18	0.13	211	42	18	40	95	9%	10	0%	0.62	-10.7	($1
+/- Score	-2	09 Proj	581	59	146	18	62	4	251			293	407	700	6	76	30	0.24	241	36	19	45	107	9%	69	4%	3.98	-8.7	$12

Lost season ended with self-inflicted broken hand. He owns good power skills, but '07 is the outlier here. Mediocre BPIs, ct% erosion rule out big rebound. Pay for 2005-6 production.

Griffey Jr.,Ken

			AB	R	H	HR	RBI	SB	Avg	vL	vR	OB	Slg	OPS	bb%	ct%	h%	Eye	xBA	G	L	F	PX	hr/f	SX	SBO	RC/G	RAR	R$
Pos	98	04 CIN	300	49	76	20	60	1	253	198	286	349	513	862	13	78	26	0.66	278	37	16	47	160	18%	42	1%	6.27	8.6	$12
Age	39	05 CIN	491	85	148	35	92	0	301	278	314	371	576	947	10	81	31	0.58	308	34	22	44	168	20%	29	1%	7.09	24.9	$26
Bats	Left	06 CIN	428	62	108	27	72	0	252	204	278	315	486	801	8	82	25	0.50	268	42	15	43	130	18%	25	0%	5.21	5.5	$14
Health	B	07 CIN	528	78	146	30	93	6	277	236	300	377	496	873	14	81	29	0.86	265	35	16	49	128	14%	63	4%	6.46	23.7	$21
PT/Exp	B	08 2TM	486	66	120	18	71	0	247	202	272	350	422	772	14	82	27	0.87	269	38	20	42	112	11%	34	1%	5.30	0.3	$12
Consist	C	1st Half	274	36	65	10	36	0	237			347	398	745	14	82	26	0.94	250	39	17	44	102	10%	25	1%	4.99	-2.4	$6
LIMA Plan	C	2nd Half	212	30	55	8	35	0	259			354	453	807	13	81	29	0.78	289	36	24	40	127	12%	45	0%	5.70	2.6	$6
+/- Score	2	09 Proj	459	66	118	18	75	0	257			350	431	781	13	81	28	0.77	261	37	19	44	109	11%	42	1%	5.34	1.6	$13

Why '08 is his new baseline...
- PX trend
- Progressive FB erosion
- Can't hit LHers anymore

Solid control of plate will extend career, but without 20+ HR pop, it won't help you much.

STEPHEN NICKRAND

Gross,Gabe

			AB	R	H	HR	RBI	SB	Avg	vL	vR	OB	Slg	OPS	bb%	ct%	h%	Eye	xBA	G	L	F	PX	hr/f	SX	SBO	RC/G	RAR	R$
Pos	9	04 aaa	377	44	106	8	46	3	281			358	430	788	11	82	33	0.66	0				102		47	8%	5.43	4.7	$10
Age	29	05 TOR	* 482	62	130	6	44	12	270	91	272	341	391	732	10	82	32	0.59	240	30	21	49	88	3%	104	11%	4.74	0.5	$12
Bats	Left	06 MIL	208	42	57	9	38	1	274	95	294	381	476	857	15	71	35	0.60	259	34	23	42	143	14%	52	1%	6.61	10.9	$8
Health	A	07 MIL	* 259	39	67	11	33	5	258	91	244	351	470	822	13	80	28	0.74	279	39	20	41	128	13%	108	8%	5.87	7.5	$8
PT/Exp	D	08 2TM	345	46	82	13	40	4	238	191	249	334	414	749	13	76	28	0.61	249	41	17	43	115	12%	83	6%	4.93	-3.6	$8
Consist	B	1st Half	170	20	40	6	22	2	235			343	406	749	14	74	29	0.62	236	39	15	46	119	11%	65	8%	5.04	-1.2	$4
LIMA Plan	D+	2nd Half	175	26	42	7	18	2	240			325	423	748	11	79	27	0.59	261	42	18	40	112	13%	93	4%	4.83	-2.3	$4
+/- Score	1	09 Proj	**306**	**46**	**77**	**12**	**39**	**4**	**252**			**346**	**440**	**785**	**13**	**77**	**29**	**0.63**	**261**	**39**	**19**	**42**	**122**	**12%**	**94**	**6%**	**5.43**	**1.9**	**$8**

Still has a 20 HR season in his bat. Posted a 129+ PX in three separate months. But until he can start to hit LHers a little, he won't be a full-timer again. At age 29, time is running out. Keep paying for 10-15 HR.

Grudzielanek,Mark

			AB	R	H	HR	RBI	SB	Avg	vL	vR	OB	Slg	OPS	bb%	ct%	h%	Eye	xBA	G	L	F	PX	hr/f	SX	SBO	RC/G	RAR	R$
Pos	4	04 CHC	257	32	79	6	23	1	307	220	349	346	432	777	6	88	33	0.47	280	41	24	34	73	8%	56	3%	4.95	2.4	$8
Age	38	05 STL	528	64	155	8	59	8	294	296	288	327	407	734	5	85	33	0.32	283	48	24	28	77	6%	85	10%	4.42	-2.1	$16
Bats	Right	06 KC	548	85	163	7	52	3	297	277	305	332	409	740	5	87	33	0.41	293	52	23	25	71	6%	88	3%	4.55	6.5	$14
Health	D	07 KC	453	70	137	6	51	1	302	321	294	336	426	762	5	87	34	0.38	281	49	19	31	85	5%	69	3%	4.80	10.0	$13
PT/Exp	B	08 KC	331	36	99	3	24	2	299	395	265	337	399	736	5	88	33	0.46	285	46	24	30	74	3%	45	3%	4.55	-3.1	$7
Consist	A	1st Half	244	30	75	2	15	2	307			355	406	761	7	89	34	0.67	288	49	23	28	72	3%	49	4%	4.96	0.5	$6
LIMA Plan	D	2nd Half	87	6	24	1	9	0	276			284	379	663	1	84	32	0.07	285	35	29	36	78	4%	16	0%	3.38	-3.7	$1
+/- Score	-37	09 Proj	**441**	**53**	**126**	**5**	**42**	**2**	**286**			**315**	**395**	**710**	**4**	**86**	**32**	**0.32**	**283**	**45**	**24**	**31**	**77**	**5%**	**58**	**3%**	**4.15**	**-4.0**	**$9**

Carbon copy of previous years before ankle injury cost him final two months. He'll give you an empty .300 BA, but that's all you're buying here anyway. Given recent injury and age, don't buy 400+ AB either.

Guerrero,Vladimir

			AB	R	H	HR	RBI	SB	Avg	vL	vR	OB	Slg	OPS	bb%	ct%	h%	Eye	xBA	G	L	F	PX	hr/f	SX	SBO	RC/G	RAR	R$
Pos	90	04 ANA	612	124	206	39	126	15	337	342	335	389	598	987	8	88	33	0.70	322	42	20	38	142	19%	107	10%	7.35	42.5	$37
Age	33	05 ANA	520	95	165	32	108	13	317	313	319	389	565	954	10	91	30	1.27	322	44	17	39	135	18%	100	9%	7.17	34.5	$31
Bats	Right	06 LAA	607	92	200	33	116	15	329	401	307	381	552	932	8	89	33	0.74	306	44	19	37	121	16%	76	11%	6.73	17.4	$32
Health	A	07 LAA	574	89	186	27	125	2	324	321	325	398	547	945	11	89	33	1.15	308	48	16	36	133	15%	38	3%	7.19	25.9	$28
PT/Exp	A	08 LAA	541	85	164	27	91	5	303	286	309	363	521	884	9	86	31	0.66	301	47	17	36	128	16%	74	5%	6.30	14.0	$24
Consist	B	1st Half	283	41	80	13	43	1	283			341	484	825	8	84	30	0.56	289	45	19	36	119	15%	65	3%	5.58	1.8	$10
LIMA Plan	C+	2nd Half	258	44	84	14	48	4	326			387	562	949	9	88	33	0.81	313	49	15	36	137	17%	74	8%	7.07	11.8	$14
+/- Score	-5	09 Proj	**540**	**87**	**171**	**26**	**103**	**4**	**317**			**379**	**531**	**910**	**9**	**88**	**32**	**0.82**	**302**	**47**	**17**	**36**	**125**	**15%**	**62**	**4%**	**6.64**	**18.5**	**$25**

Early signs of a new baseline...
- Gradual ct%, FB erosion
- No longer owns LHers
- More frequent aches and pains

Skill foundation remains solid, but he's not elite anymore. Pay for a .300 BA, not 30 HR.

Guillen,Carlos

			AB	R	H	HR	RBI	SB	Avg	vL	vR	OB	Slg	OPS	bb%	ct%	h%	Eye	xBA	G	L	F	PX	hr/f	SX	SBO	RC/G	RAR	R$
Pos	53	04 DET	522	97	166	20	97	12	318	269	348	380	542	922	9	83	35	0.60	300	41	22	37	132	12%	134	11%	6.91	28.3	$25
Age	33	05 DET	334	48	107	5	23	2	320	368	306	366	434	800	7	87	36	0.53	274	44	23	33	70	5%	82	5%	5.33	7.5	$10
Bats	Both	06 DET	543	100	174	19	85	20	320	291	332	399	519	918	12	84	35	0.82	291	42	20	38	122	11%	114	16%	7.01	29.7	$26
Health	B	07 DET	564	86	167	21	102	13	296	302	295	359	502	860	9	84	32	0.59	287	39	20	41	126	11%	112	13%	6.14	20.2	$24
PT/Exp	A	08 DET	420	68	120	10	54	9	286	287	285	375	436	811	13	84	32	0.90	281	45	20	35	100	8%	92	9%	5.80	11.0	$14
Consist	B	1st Half	281	38	82	7	42	6	292			372	448	821	11	85	32	0.88	285	43	20	36	104	8%	77	9%	5.86	7.7	$10
LIMA Plan	B	2nd Half	139	30	38	3	12	3	273			380	410	790	15	81	32	0.92	272	48	20	32	92	8%	102	8%	5.67	3.2	$4
+/- Score	-12	09 Proj	**465**	**81**	**137**	**13**	**64**	**7**	**295**			**375**	**467**	**842**	**11**	**83**	**33**	**0.78**	**283**	**43**	**20**	**36**	**109**	**9%**	**99**	**8%**	**6.10**	**16.0**	**$17**

Second straight year that injuries crept in late. Little skills erosion, so he should bounce back. But durability won't, especially in his mid-30s. Without that, '06-'07 levels will become a distant memory.

Guillen,Jose

			AB	R	H	HR	RBI	SB	Avg	vL	vR	OB	Slg	OPS	bb%	ct%	h%	Eye	xBA	G	L	F	PX	hr/f	SX	SBO	RC/G	RAR	R$
Pos	970	04 ANA	565	88	166	27	104	5	294	299	292	337	497	835	6	84	31	0.40	289	47	18	34	116	17%	80	6%	5.56	13.5	$23
Age	32	05 WAS	551	81	156	24	76	1	283	215	303	321	479	800	5	81	31	0.30	291	44	22	34	124	16%	61	2%	5.14	-1.8	$20
Bats	Right	06 WAS	241	28	52	9	40	1	216	200	221	262	398	660	6	80	23	0.31	252	41	14	45	113	10%	61	2%	3.50	-9.4	$4
Health	B	07 SEA	593	84	172	23	99	5	290	362	268	336	460	796	6	80	33	0.35	266	48	16	36	108	14%	75	4%	5.16	-5.6	$21
PT/Exp	B	08 KC	598	66	158	20	97	2	264	305	248	291	438	730	4	82	29	0.22	279	47	18	35	116	12%	49	3%	4.24	-19.3	$16
Consist	C	1st Half	324	38	91	13	61	1	281			300	488	788	3	81	31	0.15	295	47	19	34	141	14%	42	2%	4.88	-4.4	$11
LIMA Plan	C	2nd Half	274	28	67	7	36	1	245			281	380	661	5	84	27	0.31	259	47	17	36	87	9%	54	3%	3.52	-15.0	$5
+/- Score	-4	09 Proj	**565**	**69**	**149**	**17**	**90**	**3**	**264**			**301**	**420**	**721**	**5**	**82**	**30**	**0.29**	**265**	**46**	**17**	**37**	**102**	**10%**	**67**	**3%**	**4.21**	**-19.0**	**$15**

PROS:
- Owns LHers, power is good

CONS:
- Mediocre vs. RHers
- 2H collapse
- Bad and whiny teammate

DN: 15 HR, part-time job

Gutierrez,Franklin

			AB	R	H	HR	RBI	SB	Avg	vL	vR	OB	Slg	OPS	bb%	ct%	h%	Eye	xBA	G	L	F	PX	hr/f	SX	SBO	RC/G	RAR	R$
Pos	9	04 a/a	289	36	77	4	33	5	265			313	400	712	6	75	34	0.28	0				105		83	14%	4.30	-5.9	$7
Age	26	05 a/a	450	65	104	8	40	13	231			278	358	635	6	83	26	0.38	0				88		114	21%	3.33	-22.7	$9
Bats	Right	06 CLE	* 485	81	129	9	44	12	266	262	277	336	396	732	10	77	33	0.46	262	43	23	34	97	7%	83	15%	4.66	-14.3	$12
Health	A	07 CLE	* 400	66	113	16	50	14	283	330	232	329	463	792	7	76	34	0.29	253	43	15	42	120	13%	108	19%	5.17	-3.8	$16
PT/Exp	C	08 CLE	399	54	99	8	41	9	248	252	246	296	383	679	6	78	30	0.31	247	42	17	41	98	6%	103	13%	3.81	-18.4	$9
Consist	B	1st Half	194	24	44	3	18	4	227			265	335	600	5	77	28	0.23	222	35	18	47	79	4%	98	15%	2.72	-15.7	$3
LIMA Plan	D+	2nd Half	205	30	55	5	23	5	268			324	429	754	8	79	32	0.40	269	49	15	36	116	9%	98	12%	4.83	-3.2	$6
+/- Score	15	09 Proj	**354**	**53**	**92**	**11**	**38**	**9**	**260**			**311**	**422**	**733**	**7**	**78**	**31**	**0.34**	**257**	**44**	**17**	**40**	**113**	**10%**	**93**	**16%**	**4.48**	**-9.3**	**$10**

Ups and downs continue. Had a 115+ PX in July and Aug, but as a GB hitter, consistent HR stroke isn't there. Can run, but it won't matter if his bb% drop continues. 2H gives hope, but don't expect age 26 breakout.

Guzman,Cristian

			AB	R	H	HR	RBI	SB	Avg	vL	vR	OB	Slg	OPS	bb%	ct%	h%	Eye	xBA	G	L	F	PX	hr/f	SX	SBO	RC/G	RAR	R$
Pos	6	04 MIN	576	84	158	8	46	10	274	326	250	310	384	694	5	89	30	0.47	280	57	16	27	67	6%	104	10%	4.06	-6.6	$13
Age	31	05 WAS	456	39	100	4	31	7	219	161	242	260	314	573	5	83	26	0.33	270	56	20	24	62	4%	106	11%	2.58	-19.4	$3
Bats	Both	06 WAS	0	0	0	0	0	0	0							0			0						0				
Health	F	07 WAS	174	31	57	2	14	2	328	357	318	381	466	846	8	88	36	0.71	293	60	17	23	72	6%	114	3%	6.02	7.2	$6
PT/Exp	D	08 WAS	579	77	183	9	55	6	316	354	299	342	440	783	4	90	34	0.40	305	53	23	25	77	7%	84	7%	4.98	5.5	$19
Consist	C	1st Half	357	48	112	5	27	3	314			340	434	774	4	93	33	0.54	301	55	18	26	76	6%	76	6%	4.93	2.9	$11
LIMA Plan	C	2nd Half	222	29	71	4	28	3	320			346	450	797	4	86	36	0.29	308	48	29	22	79	9%	99	8%	5.09	2.8	$8
+/- Score	-55	09 Proj	**484**	**67**	**146**	**7**	**44**	**6**	**302**			**338**	**426**	**763**	**5**	**88**	**33**	**0.44**	**296**	**55**	**21**	**24**	**73**	**7%**	**112**	**7%**	**4.85**	**4.9**	**$14**

Finally was healthy enough to post a .300 BA in a full season. xBA confirms it was for real. SX history bodes well for more SB if SBO cooperates. Problem is, guys with durability issues seldom become durable in 30s.

Hafner,Travis

			AB	R	H	HR	RBI	SB	Avg	vL	vR	OB	Slg	OPS	bb%	ct%	h%	Eye	xBA	G	L	F	PX	hr/f	SX	SBO	RC/G	RAR	R$
Pos	0	04 CLE	482	96	150	28	109	3	311	244	344	396	583	979	12	77	36	0.61	295	38	19	44	175	17%	82	3%	7.90	34.1	$25
Age	31	05 CLE	486	94	148	33	108	0	305	269	319	402	595	996	14	75	35	0.64	310	43	20	37	201	25%	30	0%	8.26	29.6	$26
Bats	Left	06 CLE	454	100	140	42	117	0	308	321	300	433	659	1092	18	76	33	0.90	323	39	21	40	216	30%	37	0%	9.57	38.7	$28
Health	D	07 CLE	545	80	145	24	100	1	266	274	261	382	451	833	16	79	30	0.89	267	48	17	35	118	16%	44	1%	6.14	-1.6	$18
PT/Exp	B	08 CLE	198	21	39	5	24	1	197	220	189	293	323	617	12	72	25	0.49	246	42	25	33	96	11%	38	4%	3.14	-11.3	$1
Consist	F	1st Half	157	19	34	4	22	1	217			317	350	667	13	72	28	0.52	250	41	25	34	103	11%	42	5%	3.88	-5.1	$2
LIMA Plan	C+	2nd Half	41	2	5	1	2	0	122			200	220	420	9	73	14	0.36	221	47	23	30	67	11%	6	0%	0.30	-6.5	($1)
+/- Score	40	09 Proj	**413**	**70**	**112**	**18**	**82**	**1**	**271**			**379**	**472**	**851**	**15**	**75**	**32**	**0.70**	**273**	**42**	**21**	**37**	**139**	**16%**	**50**	**2%**	**6.41**	**10.1**	**$15**

Offseason shoulder surgery puts start of '09 in doubt. His swift decline clearly has been injury related, but it's unclear if the surgery will fix things. Until we know, use '07 as your baseline.

Hairston,Jerry

			AB	R	H	HR	RBI	SB	Avg	vL	vR	OB	Slg	OPS	bb%	ct%	h%	Eye	xBA	G	L	F	PX	hr/f	SX	SBO	RC/G	RAR	R$
Pos	67	04 BAL	287	43	87	2	24	13	303	316	296	367	397	764	9	90	33	1.00	265	37	23	40	64	2%	100	22%	5.18	5.9	$10
Age	32	05 CHC	380	51	99	4	30	8	261	255	263	316	368	685	8	88	29	0.67	279	43	22	34	75	4%	92	17%	4.13	2.0	$8
Bats	Right	06 2TM	170	25	35	0	10	5	206	153	245	262	253	515	7	80	26	0.38	207	42	17	41	36	0%	119	17%	1.87	-13.5	$1
Health	D	07 TEX	159	22	30	3	16	5	189	228	150	241	289	530	6	85	20	0.46	217	35	14	52	66	4%	100	19%	2.13	-11.0	$2
PT/Exp	F	08 CIN	* 340	55	110	9	48	16	324	345	316	371	502	873	7	87	35	0.57	296	32	27	41	113	7%	121	21%	6.18	14.2	$18
Consist	F	1st Half	215	30	70	5	25	13	326			358	508	866	5	87	36	0.38	320	36	31	33	122	7%	123	30%	6.00	8.0	$11
LIMA Plan	D	2nd Half	125	25	40	4	22	3	322			391	492	883	10	87	34	0.89	264	26	23	51	98	8%	106	10%	6.45	6.1	$7
+/- Score	-35	09 Proj	**259**	**41**	**72**	**5**	**31**	**9**	**278**			**332**	**405**	**737**	**8**	**86**	**31**	**0.57**	**253**	**34**	**21**	**45**	**81**	**5%**	**105**	**17%**	**4.63**	**1.1**	**$9**

6-36-.326 in 261 AB at CIN. BA was completely driven by inflated hit rate. At 32, injury history won't suddenly go away. Will give you 15-20 SB in 400 AB; the AB will be the tricky part due to his health.

STEPHEN NICKRAND

Hairston,Scott

			AB	R	H	HR	RBI	SB	Avg	vL	vR	OB	Slg	OPS	bb%	ct%	h%	Eye	xBA	G	L	F	PX	hr/f	SX	SBO	RC/G	RAR	R$
Pos	87	04 ARI	* 454	59	116	17	43	3	256	307	223	300	458	758	6	78	30	0.28	260	38	19	44	123	11%	99	10%	4.76	1.5	$11
Age	28	05 ARI	* 229	31	59	12	28	2	259	182		305	471	776	6	85	26	0.43	0	29	7	64	119	9%	87	4%	4.85	2.0	$7
Bats	Right	06 aaa	396	64	116	20	63	2	292	375	429	358	510	868	9	83	31	0.62	0	50	30	20	126	31%	62	2%	6.15	17.6	$16
Health	D	07 2NL	263	37	64	11	36	2	243	235	247	311	452	764	9	79	27	0.47	260	34	15	50	134	10%	79	3%	4.95	3.3	$7
PT/Exp	D	08 SD	326	42	81	17	31	3	248	280	224	308	479	786	8	74	28	0.33	258	38	14	48	151	15%	88	6%	5.19	4.3	$9
Consist	B	1st Half	223	26	52	9	20	2	233			282	422	703	6	74	27	0.26	240	38	14	48	125	11%	82	7%	4.04	-4.8	$4
LIMA Plan	C	2nd Half	103	16	29	8	11	1	282			362	602	964	11	74	31	0.48	297	38	13	49	209	22%	76	4%	7.67	8.5	$5
+/- Score	17	09 Proj	392	56	107	21	47	3	273			337	512	849	9	77	30	0.43	269	36	15	49	151	14%	83	4%	5.98	15.1	$14

We could ignore the 8 HR in 103 AB in 2H as a sample size fluke, but his BPIs see growth. Injuries, trouble with RHP relegate him to a platoon role but 2006's MLEs say there's more potential here. Speculate.

Hall,Bill

			AB	R	H	HR	RBI	SB	Avg	vL	vR	OB	Slg	OPS	bb%	ct%	h%	Eye	xBA	G	L	F	PX	hr/f	SX	SBO	RC/G	RAR	R$
Pos	5	04 MIL	394	44	95	10	55	13	241	190	256	278	383	661	5	70	32	0.17	232	43	20	37	104	10%	116	23%	3.53	-18.4	$10
Age	29	05 MIL	501	69	146	17	62	18	291	328	277	343	495	838	7	79	34	0.38	295	43	23	34	138	12%	124	20%	5.83	14.9	$21
Bats	Right	06 MIL	537	101	145	35	85	8	270	300	261	347	553	900	11	70	32	0.39	273	33	19	48	192	19%	92	13%	7.01	23.9	$23
Health	A	07 MIL	452	59	115	14	63	4	254	270	247	315	425	740	8	72	33	0.31	254	36	23	41	131	10%	50	8%	4.72	-11.9	$11
PT/Exp	B	08 MIL	404	50	91	15	55	5	225	306	174	290	396	686	8	69	29	0.30	241	39	21	40	127	13%	66	12%	3.96	-17.6	$9
Consist	D	1st Half	236	23	50	10	28	3	212			268	386	653	7	72	25	0.27	237	44	16	40	122	15%	45	17%	3.37	-15.0	$4
LIMA Plan	C	2nd Half	168	27	41	5	27	2	244			321	411	732	10	66	34	0.33	240	30	29	41	135	11%	91	7%	4.86	-2.5	$5
+/- Score	-4	09 Proj	425	60	105	16	61	6	247			312	436	748	9	70	32	0.32	252	36	22	41	140	13%	82	11%	4.87	-6.8	$12

What happened against RHP? Answer: a 22% hit rate, which should regress IF given chance to play vs. RHP. But since 2006 outlier, his plunging Eye and SX trump moderate power, making him below replacement level.

Hall,Toby

			AB	R	H	HR	RBI	SB	Avg	vL	vR	OB	Slg	OPS	bb%	ct%	h%	Eye	xBA	G	L	F	PX	hr/f	SX	SBO	RC/G	RAR	R$
Pos	2	04 TAM	404	35	103	8	60	0	255	294	242	297	366	663	6	90	27	0.59	238	40	15	44	67	5%	20	2%	3.75	-6.9	$7
Age	33	05 TAM	432	28	124	5	48	0	287	302	281	313	368	681	4	91	31	0.41	251	41	21	39	54	3%	12	0%	3.84	-2.2	$8
Bats	Right	06 2TM	278	17	72	8	31	0	259	292	248	285	406	691	3	92	26	0.45	215	37	16	47	84	7%	0	4%	3.96	-3.4	$4
Health	B	07 CHW	116	8	24	0	3	0	207	288	141	227	241	468	3	90	23	0.25	217	41	17	41	28	0%	27	0%	1.46	-10.2	($1)
PT/Exp	F	08 CHW	127	7	33	2	7	0	260	377	176	293	331	624	5	85	29	0.32	282	28	28	44	44	4%	0	0%	3.06	-4.2	$1
Consist	F	1st Half	64	4	19	1	4	0	297			328	391	719	4	89	32	0.43	293	28	30	42	61	4%	8	0%	4.26	0.1	$1
LIMA Plan	F	2nd Half	63	3	14	1	3	0	222			258	270	527	5	81	26	0.25	222	27	25	47	25	4%	6	0%	1.77	-4.7	($0)
+/- Score	-19	09 Proj	135	8	33	2	8	0	244			274	315	589	4	87	27	0.32	237	34	22	44	45	4%	16	1%	2.72	-6.1	$1

Decent platoon hitter against southpaws, but you can see the skills erosion. Unless your league allows you to micro-manage down to every at bat, the only value here is as a stop-gap injury replacement.

Hamilton,Josh

			AB	R	H	HR	RBI	SB	Avg	vL	vR	OB	Slg	OPS	bb%	ct%	h%	Eye	xBA	G	L	F	PX	hr/f	SX	SBO	RC/G	RAR	R$
Pos	89	04	0	0	0	0	0	0	0							0			0						0				
Age	27	05	0	0	0	0	0	0	0							0			0						0				
Bats	Left	06	0	0	0	0	0	0	0							0			0						0				
Health	B	07 CIN	* 338	60	100	23	54	6	295	222	314	364	563	927	10	78	32	0.50	307	45	22	33	161	26%	88	10%	6.93	22.7	$17
PT/Exp	D	08 TEX	624	98	190	32	130	9	304	288	313	369	530	900	9	80	34	0.51	300	46	21	33	141	20%	100	5%	6.60	21.3	$30
Consist	A	1st Half	327	52	102	19	80	3	312			368	563	931	8	82	33	0.49	317	45	23	32	151	22%	86	3%	6.84	13.2	$17
LIMA Plan	B	2nd Half	297	46	88	13	50	6	296			370	495	865	11	77	35	0.52	279	46	20	34	129	17%	92	8%	6.31	7.9	$13
+/- Score	-2	09 Proj	614	101	184	35	113	10	300			367	539	906	10	79	33	0.51	301	45	21	33	148	22%	94	7%	6.69	29.5	$29

Do three lost years mean he is still in growth phase? Learned how to make contact against LHP, supporting .300 BA. Now learning to condition himself for endurance to avoid another 2H fade, so... UP: 40 HR.

Hanigan,Ryan

			AB	R	H	HR	RBI	SB	Avg	vL	vR	OB	Slg	OPS	bb%	ct%	h%	Eye	xBA	G	L	F	PX	hr/f	SX	SBO	RC/G	RAR	R$
Pos	2	04	0	0	0	0	0	0	0							0			0						0				
Age	28	05 aa	330	31	84	3	21	3	254			324	311	635	9	89	28	0.93	0				39		46	3%	3.66	-2.4	$4
Bats	Right	06 a/a	139	16	29	0	13	0	207			310	220	530	13	81	26	0.78	0				11		31	0%	2.32	-8.9	($0)
Health	A	07 a/a	324	35	73	3	27	0	226			312	311	624	11	86	25	0.91	0				58		36	2%	3.57	-7.8	$2
PT/Exp	F	08 CIN	* 357	35	94	6	34	1	264	237	298	318	348	667	7	87	29	0.63	263	51	21	28	54	6%	35	1%	3.82	-4.0	$6
Consist	B	1st Half	176	17	42	3	16	1	240			296	320	616	7	84	27	0.50	0				53		39	2%	3.14	-5.6	$2
LIMA Plan	F	2nd Half	181	19	52	3	18	0	288			340	375	715	7	91	31	0.85	268	51	21	28	54	6%	21	0%	4.45	1.2	$4
+/- Score	1	09 Proj	254	26	64	3	22	0	252			322	321	643	9	87	28	0.77	253	51	21	28	45	5%	32	1%	3.67	-4.3	$3

2-9-.271 in 89 AB at CIN. Small signs of growth here. Decent contact rate usually means he won't kill your BA, but miniscule PX means his batted balls are going nowhere. Decent $1 catcher? Barely.

Hannahan,Jack

			AB	R	H	HR	RBI	SB	Avg	vL	vR	OB	Slg	OPS	bb%	ct%	h%	Eye	xBA	G	L	F	PX	hr/f	SX	SBO	RC/G	RAR	R$
Pos	5	04 aa	374	40	86	6	32	6	229			306	325	631	10	86	25	0.79	0				61		70	8%	3.56	-16.3	$4
Age	29	05 a/a	257	25	56	3	24	5	218			282	296	578	8	78	27	0.40	0				60		62	12%	2.59	-16.4	$2
Bats	Left	06 aaa	415	53	107	8	56	8	257			344	369	714	12	74	33	0.51	0				84		59	10%	4.51	-9.1	$10
Health	A	07 OAK	* 480	65	128	13	79	6	267	400	239	380	416	796	15	74	34	0.69	251	37	23	39	111	10%	55	6%	5.79	12.8	$14
PT/Exp	C	08 OAK	441	49	96	10	48	2	218	204	223	304	347	651	11	70	29	0.41	228	37	21	42	106	8%	46	2%	3.63	-16.9	$5
Consist	D	1st Half	224	25	49	3	25	1	219			322	330	652	13	71	29	0.53	228	38	21	41	97	5%	40	2%	3.78	-7.6	$2
LIMA Plan	F	2nd Half	217	24	47	7	23	1	217			286	364	650	9	68	28	0.30	228	36	21	43	115	11%	42	2%	3.48	-9.4	$3
+/- Score	2	09 Proj	212	25	50	5	26	2	236			326	363	689	12	72	30	0.49	233	37	21	42	98	8%	47	5%	4.16	-4.6	$4

How low can ct% go? Dared to open up swing even more in 2H, which proceeded to kill OB and net all of four more HR. Bottom line... players with a .218 BA rarely get 441 AB, and when they do, it's usually once.

Hardy,J.J.

			AB	R	H	HR	RBI	SB	Avg	vL	vR	OB	Slg	OPS	bb%	ct%	h%	Eye	xBA	G	L	F	PX	hr/f	SX	SBO	RC/G	RAR	R$
Pos	6	04 aaa	101	15	27	4	18	0	270			320	489	808	7	93	26	1.10	0				125		34	0%	5.48	3.4	$3
Age	26	05 MIL	372	46	92	9	50	0	247	245	240	327	384	711	11	87	26	0.92	276	44	20	35	88	8%	38	0%	4.54	6.3	$8
Bats	Right	06 MIL	128	13	31	5	14	1	242	294	223	297	398	696	7	82	26	0.45	260	47	19	34	90	14%	36	6%	3.96	-1.5	$2
Health	C	07 MIL	592	89	164	26	80	2	277	316	264	323	463	786	6	88	28	0.55	278	41	17	42	105	12%	50	3%	5.03	9.8	$19
PT/Exp	B	08 MIL	569	78	161	24	74	2	283	304	276	343	478	821	8	83	31	0.53	279	48	15	36	118	14%	68	2%	5.58	15.2	$19
Consist	B	1st Half	256	30	68	6	27	1	266			338	402	740	10	85	29	0.74	253	50	13	37	91	7%	39	1%	4.80	1.2	$6
LIMA Plan	C+	2nd Half	313	48	93	18	47	1	297			347	540	887	7	81	32	0.40	295	47	17	35	141	20%	81	2%	6.26	14.1	$14
+/- Score	1	09 Proj	550	80	151	28	83	2	275			330	488	818	8	85	28	0.53	289	46	17	37	123	16%	59	3%	5.45	15.1	$20

Big 2H doesn't necessarily mean growth; he did just the reverse last year. But overall, we rely on the big picture, and those trends are up. Now at "age 26 with experience" year, can envision... UP: .290, 30 HR.

Harris,Brendan

			AB	R	H	HR	RBI	SB	Avg	vL	vR	OB	Slg	OPS	bb%	ct%	h%	Eye	xBA	G	L	F	PX	hr/f	SX	SBO	RC/G	RAR	R$
Pos	645	04 MON	* 436	55	114	14	47	0	261			297	431	728	5	87	27	0.39	0				103		42	4%	4.35	2.8	$10
Age	28	05 aaa	470	49	106	9	58	7	225			270	331	601	6	88	24	0.51	0				64		78	12%	3.01	-18.2	$7
Bats	Right	06 CIN	* 409	55	110	11	54	4	269			329	421	750	8	80	31	0.44	219	37	9	54	101	6%	65	5%	4.79	5.0	$11
Health	A	07 TAM	521	72	149	12	59	4	286	345	264	339	434	773	7	82	33	0.44	274	43	21	35	102	8%	79	4%	5.04	10.9	$14
PT/Exp	B	08 MIN	434	57	115	7	49	1	265	265	265	326	394	720	8	77	33	0.40	255	53	16	30	96	7%	68	2%	4.45	1.5	$9
Consist	A	1st Half	265	34	66	4	22	1	249			304	351	655	7	76	31	0.33	233	52	16	32	76	6%	63	3%	3.53	-6.3	$4
LIMA Plan	F	2nd Half	169	23	49	3	27	0	290			358	462	820	10	80	35	0.53	287	55	17	28	126	8%	63	0%	5.84	7.1	$5
+/- Score	-16	09 Proj	248	33	68	5	31	1	274			332	425	757	8	80	32	0.44	271	50	18	32	105	8%	72	3%	4.90	3.9	$6

This is what end-game gambles look like: middling skills, doubles power, but tantalizing stretches inflate value. Rising GB% limits power. Defense is suspect, so regular playing time is a question. Take a pass.

Harris,Willie

			AB	R	H	HR	RBI	SB	Avg	vL	vR	OB	Slg	OPS	bb%	ct%	h%	Eye	xBA	G	L	F	PX	hr/f	SX	SBO	RC/G	RAR	R$
Pos	7	04 CHW	409	68	107	2	27	19	262	181	279	343	323	666	11	81	32	0.65	241	51	20	29	43	2%	119	19%	3.95	-12.0	$11
Age	30	05 CHW	* 230	33	56	2	16	18	242	286	252	317	335	652	10	79	30	0.53	251	52	19	30	68	4%	139	34%	3.70	-7.2	$7
Bats	Left	06 BOS	* 263	45	51	7	16	15	193			273	307	580	10	75	23	0.44	243	68	9	24	74	14%	133	33%	2.58	-22.3	$5
Health	A	07 ATL	* 402	70	111	3	37	22	277	191	283	351	408	760	10	81	34	0.60	259	42	21	37	88	2%	144	30%	5.16	-2.3	$14
PT/Exp	D	08 WAS	367	58	92	13	43	13	251	240	255	341	417	757	12	82	27	0.76	265	43	18	38	98	11%	123	14%	5.03	-4.2	$12
Consist	C	1st Half	109	22	23	4	10	6	211			328	385	713	15	75	24	0.70	239	34	22	44	106	11%	156	18%	4.56	-2.9	$3
LIMA Plan	D	2nd Half	258	36	69	9	33	7	267			346	430	776	11	85	29	0.79	273	47	17	36	95	11%	94	13%	5.21	-1.6	$9
+/- Score	0	09 Proj	248	41	66	6	24	12	266			349	407	756	11	80	31	0.64	254	44	19	37	88	8%	126	21%	5.03	-2.5	$9

Late-blooming power looks fluky, fueled by huge hr/f jump. Owns the OB skills and speed but so far the elusive combo of OB, PT, and green light have not meshed. If they ever do... UP: 30 SB

MICHAEL ROY

Hart,Corey

			AB	R	H	HR	RBI	SB	Avg	vL	vR	OB	Slg	OPS	bb%	ct%	h%	Eye	xBA	G	L	F	PX	hr/f	SX	SBO	RC/G	RAR	R$
Pos	9	04 aaa	441	59	119	14	59	15	269			322	450	772	7	84	30	0.48	0				109		117	22%	5.01	0.2	$15
Age	27	05 MIL	*486	73	126	15	59	25	259	211	184	318	440	759	8	84	28	0.54	313	54	22	24	112	15%	146	29%	4.89	-5.2	$19
Bats	Right	06 MIL	*337	47	94	13	50	14	279	304	272	332	474	806	7	75	34	0.32	258	42	17	41	128	12%	105	29%	5.47	6.9	$14
Health	A	07 MIL	505	86	149	24	81	23	295	331	278	342	539	881	7	80	33	0.36	282	37	17	46	147	13%	146	25%	6.26	19.6	$25
PT/Exp	B	08 MIL	612	76	164	20	91	23	268	281	263	299	459	758	4	82	30	0.25	281	40	19	40	123	10%	124	25%	4.65	-9.6	$23
Consist	C	1st Half	309	40	89	14	51	10	288			323	511	834	5	82	31	0.29	296	41	20	39	138	14%	109	19%	5.55	3.1	$14
LIMA Plan	B	2nd Half	303	36	75	6	40	13	248			274	406	680	4	82	28	0.20	266	39	18	42	109	6%	131	32%	3.74	-13.2	$9
+/- Score	17	09 Proj	595	83	163	25	98	25	274			314	493	808	6	81	30	0.31	283	40	18	42	137	12%	128	27%	5.30	4.2	$26

Took him 100+ more AB to hit 4 fewer HR than '07. Overrated? Nah, just unlucky with 2H hr/f. Once that rebounds, he regains 30 HR upside. And 1H xBA says that .300 is possible, especially if he gets some h% help.

Hawpe,Brad

			AB	R	H	HR	RBI	SB	Avg	vL	vR	OB	Slg	OPS	bb%	ct%	h%	Eye	xBA	G	L	F	PX	hr/f	SX	SBO	RC/G	RAR	R$
Pos	9	04 COL	*450	54	126	28	66	3	280	154	261	332	524	856	7	79	30	0.38	304	53	21	26	142	30%	59	6%	5.88	7.5	$17
Age	29	05 COL	305	38	80	9	47	2	262	250	264	353	403	757	12	77	31	0.61	249	52	17	32	90	12%	76	4%	5.04	-1.9	$9
Bats	Left	06 COL	499	67	146	22	84	5	293	232	302	384	515	899	13	75	35	0.60	279	42	22	36	142	16%	77	6%	6.98	31.0	$19
Health	B	07 COL	516	80	150	29	116	0	291	214	315	387	539	926	14	73	35	0.59	278	36	21	43	165	18%	48	1%	7.37	35.9	$23
PT/Exp	A	08 COL	488	69	138	25	85	2	283	282	283	379	498	877	13	73	34	0.57	267	38	23	39	144	18%	58	2%	6.73	21.2	$19
Consist	B	1st Half	219	28	57	11	34	0	260			370	475	845	15	76	30	0.72	267	40	19	40	136	16%	46	0%	6.26	6.8	$7
LIMA Plan	C+	2nd Half	269	41	81	14	51	2	301			388	517	904	12	70	39	0.47	267	36	26	38	152	19%	55	4%	7.17	14.8	$13
+/- Score	-22	09 Proj	518	79	143	26	101	2	276			370	498	868	13	74	33	0.56	272	39	22	39	146	18%	67	3%	6.55	22.2	$21

Year-over-year, has nice, stable skill set, with a BA that outdoes xBA thanks to LD%-driven h%. 2H shows upside and risk: he's a potential .300-30 hitter if he can avoid the temptation to swing for the fences all the time.

Headley,Chase

			AB	R	H	HR	RBI	SB	Avg	vL	vR	OB	Slg	OPS	bb%	ct%	h%	Eye	xBA	G	L	F	PX	hr/f	SX	SBO	RC/G	RAR	R$
Pos	7	04	0	0	0	0	0	0	0							0			0						0				
Age	24	05	0	0	0	0	0	0	0							0			0						0				
Bats	Both	06	0	0	0	0	0	0	0							0			0						0				
Health	A	07 aa	451	73	130	17	69	1	288	167	250	382	495	877	13	74	36	0.58	0	36	21	43	145	12%	69	1%	6.75	19.6	$16
PT/Exp	F	08 SD	*590	74	155	19	71	4	263	276	265	326	432	758	9	72	34	0.33	258	38	25	37	125	12%	75	3%	4.98	-7.5	$16
Consist	D	1st Half	312	46	79	13	38	0	254			309	449	758	7	75	30	0.32	0				137		51	0%	4.83	-5.4	$8
LIMA Plan	C+	2nd Half	278	28	76	6	33	4	273			344	414	758	10	69	38	0.34	238	38	25	37	112	8%	81	6%	5.17	-2.0	$7
+/- Score	6	09 Proj	537	74	147	18	71	3	274			350	455	805	10	72	35	0.43	262	38	25	37	130	12%	81	3%	5.71	5.1	$16

9-38-.269 in 331 AB with SD.
PRO:
- Power is legit
CON:
- Still struggling to make contact
- Less than 300 AB at Triple-A
High-upside work in progress.

Helms,Wes

			AB	R	H	HR	RBI	SB	Avg	vL	vR	OB	Slg	OPS	bb%	ct%	h%	Eye	xBA	G	L	F	PX	hr/f	SX	SBO	RC/G	RAR	R$
Pos	53	04 MIL	278	25	74	4	29	0	266	306	248	325	367	691	8	78	33	0.39	226	43	18	39	71	5%	37	1%	4.04	-8.2	$4
Age	32	05 MIL	168	18	50	4	24	0	298	305	294	352	458	810	8	82	34	0.47	270	44	18	38	111	8%	46	2%	5.51	3.4	$5
Bats	Right	06 FLA	240	30	79	10	47	0	329	336	323	383	575	958	8	77	39	0.38	299	38	26	36	155	15%	66	6%	7.48	12.9	$11
Health	A	07 PHI	280	21	69	5	39	0	246	282	221	294	368	662	6	78	30	0.31	239	39	20	41	90	6%	14	0%	3.59	-16.7	$4
PT/Exp	D	08 FLA	251	28	61	5	31	0	243	258	234	291	347	638	6	74	31	0.26	225	42	20	38	77	7%	30	0%	3.20	-16.1	$4
Consist	F	1st Half	144	18	35	4	21	0	243			288	382	670	6	69	33	0.20	231	39	22	39	109	10%	34	0%	3.67	-7.3	$3
LIMA Plan	F	2nd Half	107	10	26	1	10	0	243			296	299	595	7	81	29	0.40	214	45	19	36	39	3%	24	0%	2.80	-8.2	$1
+/- Score	-22	09 Proj	130	13	31	3	17	0	238			291	355	646	7	77	29	0.32	239	41	21	38	84	7%	30	1%	3.37	-7.9	$2

PX, xBA, Eye all in freefall. hr/f shows his general lack of pop, and he can't even hit lefties any more. But hey, at least he's eligible at both corner positions. Not that you'd want him there.

Helton,Todd

			AB	R	H	HR	RBI	SB	Avg	vL	vR	OB	Slg	OPS	bb%	ct%	h%	Eye	xBA	G	L	F	PX	hr/f	SX	SBO	RC/G	RAR	R$
Pos	3	04 COL	547	115	190	32	96	3	347	320	360	470	620	1090	19	87	36	1.76	322	35	21	44	158	15%	68	1%	9.42	48.5	$33
Age	35	05 COL	509	92	163	20	79	3	320	245	351	437	534	972	17	84	35	1.33	305	33	24	42	140	11%	69	1%	8.01	32.7	$24
Bats	Left	06 COL	546	94	165	15	81	3	302	326	295	402	476	878	14	88	32	1.42	291	35	24	41	102	8%	76	3%	6.74	11.2	$20
Health	D	07 COL	557	86	178	17	91	0	320	285	334	437	494	931	17	87	35	1.57	299	40	24	36	109	10%	34	0%	7.53	20.8	$22
PT/Exp	A	08 COL	299	39	79	7	29	0	264	246	270	389	388	777	17	83	30	1.22	264	38	23	38	82	7%	20	0%	5.61	-1.0	$6
Consist	C	1st Half	292	37	78	7	29	0	267			389	394	782	17	84	30	1.21	264	38	23	39	84	7%	19	0%	5.66	-0.6	$6
LIMA Plan	C+	2nd Half	7	2	1	0	0	0	143			400	143	543	30	71	20	1.50	0	40	40	20	0	0%	53	0%	2.61	-0.7	$0
+/- Score	-20	09 Proj	368	59	107	10	52	0	291			407	449	856	16	86	32	1.39	285	37	23	40	102	8%	38	0%	6.60	7.4	$12

Finally had surgery for long-standing back problems. Hitters seldom recover their power in these cases, making more than 10 HR a gift. On plus side, Eye still superb, so .300 BA possible, but let others absorb that risk.

Hermida,Jeremy

			AB	R	H	HR	RBI	SB	Avg	vL	vR	OB	Slg	OPS	bb%	ct%	h%	Eye	xBA	G	L	F	PX	hr/f	SX	SBO	RC/G	RAR	R$
Pos	9	04	0	0	0	0	0	0	0							0			0						0				
Age	25	05 FLA	*427	77	115	19	67	22	269	200	306	415	480	895	20	78	31	1.12	275	31	24	45	142	13%	114	14%	7.20	24.0	$21
Bats	Left	06 FLA	307	37	77	5	28	4	251	219	261	324	368	692	10	77	31	0.47	246	45	20	35	84	6%	72	6%	4.15	-5.6	$5
Health	C	07 FLA	429	54	127	18	63	3	296	292	297	366	501	867	10	76	36	0.45	277	44	21	35	141	16%	45	6%	6.37	17.9	$15
PT/Exp	B	08 FLA	502	74	125	17	61	6	249	240	252	315	406	721	9	73	31	0.35	243	46	18	36	109	13%	99	5%	4.41	-11.5	$14
Consist	F	1st Half	288	45	78	8	38	2	271			331	427	758	8	74	34	0.35	248	44	18	38	112	10%	88	3%	4.93	-2.1	$9
LIMA Plan	C+	2nd Half	214	29	47	9	23	4	220			292	379	671	9	71	27	0.35	236	49	17	34	104	18%	89	9%	3.68	-9.9	$5
+/- Score	15	09 Proj	502	70	130	18	63	8	259			336	427	763	10	74	32	0.45	255	46	19	36	115	13%	83	7%	5.04	-0.2	$15

2H h% drop brutalized his BA; he's better than .220. However, needs to reverse declining ct% if he wants to see bright side of .260. And he hits too many GB to expect repeat of 140+ PX. Work to do.

Hernandez,Anderson

			AB	R	H	HR	RBI	SB	Avg	vL	vR	OB	Slg	OPS	bb%	ct%	h%	Eye	xBA	G	L	F	PX	hr/f	SX	SBO	RC/G	RAR	R$
Pos	4	04 aa	394	56	97	4	25	15	246			284	332	617	5	81	30	0.28	0				57		128	23%	3.00	-16.0	$8
Age	26	05 a/a	526	65	151	7	44	28	287			323	373	696	5	84	33	0.33	0				55		107	32%	3.95	-6.1	$19
Bats	Both	06 NYM	*480	47	110	1	25	15	229	211	128	261	277	539	4	84	27	0.27	218	49	15	36	30	1%	107	18%	2.09	-36.9	$4
Health	A	07 aa	554	67	143	4	33	12	259			291	334	625	4	87	29	0.35	0				51		94	16%	3.20	-18.9	$9
PT/Exp	C	08 WAS	*560	56	108	4	45	8	193	366	300	247	269	515	7	84	22	0.44	266	39	30	31	51	3%	93	14%	1.97	-50.6	$1
Consist	C	1st Half	329	31	50	3	17	8	151			202	226	427	6	83	17	0.36	0				53		99	23%	0.83	-43.8	($2)
LIMA Plan	F	2nd Half	231	25	58	1	28	1	251			309	330	639	8	85	29	0.56	269	39	30	31	48	2%	85	7%	3.55	-8.4	$3
+/- Score	54	09 Proj	203	22	50	1	16	4	246			289	324	613	6	85	29	0.39	264	41	27	32	51	2%	96	15%	3.10	-9.9	$3

0-17-.333 in 81 AB at WAS. Defensive specialist: all glove, no bat. 50%+ GB% in 2000+ minor league AB gives hope he might eek out some SB using decent speed, but sub-.300 OB makes us shrug and move on.

Hernandez,Luis

			AB	R	H	HR	RBI	SB	Avg	vL	vR	OB	Slg	OPS	bb%	ct%	h%	Eye	xBA	G	L	F	PX	hr/f	SX	SBO	RC/G	RAR	R$
Pos	6	04	0	0	0	0	0	0	0							0			0						0				
Age	24	05 aa	415	41	92	2	28	4	222			284	282	566	8	88	25	0.73	0				37		80	9%	2.80	-18.8	$2
Bats	Both	06 a/a	453	40	112	2	33	4	247			279	307	586	4	89	28	0.38	0				37		68	8%	2.80	-21.4	$4
Health	A	07 BAL	*466	47	110	1	43	7	236	300	286	263	294	557	4	88	27	0.29	263	51	22	27	39	1%	89	13%	2.42	-26.6	$4
PT/Exp	D	08 BAL	*284	23	52	0	12	4	182	200	250	220	206	425	5	88	21	0.40	239	57	17	26	20	0%	67	10%	1.01	-30.5	($2)
Consist	D	1st Half	144	16	31	0	4	4	212			253	226	479	5	87	24	0.41	231	57	17	26	11	0%	81	13%	1.55	-12.5	$0
LIMA Plan	F	2nd Half	140	8	21	0	8	0	151			184	185	370	4	90	17	0.39	0				28		35	4%	0.48	-18.1	($3)
+/- Score	41	09 Proj	105	9	25	0	7	1	238			273	272	544	5	88	27	0.40	242	55	19	26	26	1%	50	9%	2.33	-6.4	$1

0-3-.241 in 79 AB at BAL. Named Opening Day SS by Orioles, but couldn't hold onto the job. RAR tells the story why. <Totally irrelevant fact> He is the only player born in Quibor, Venezuela. </End irrelevance>

Hernandez,Ramon

			AB	R	H	HR	RBI	SB	Avg	vL	vR	OB	Slg	OPS	bb%	ct%	h%	Eye	xBA	G	L	F	PX	hr/f	SX	SBO	RC/G	RAR	R$
Pos	2	04 SD	384	45	106	18	63	1	276	310	264	337	477	813	8	88	27	0.78	297	47	19	34	113	16%	33	1%	5.48	18.2	$13
Age	32	05 SD	369	36	107	12	58	1	290	238	304	323	450	773	5	89	30	0.45	295	46	21	33	93	11%	53	1%	4.84	10.8	$12
Bats	Right	06 BAL	501	66	138	23	91	1	275	291	270	333	479	812	8	84	29	0.54	286	44	19	38	119	14%	53	1%	5.42	14.4	$16
Health	C	07 BAL	364	40	94	9	62	1	258	250	261	325	382	707	9	84	29	0.61	248	49	16	35	81	8%	29	4%	4.30	0.1	$8
PT/Exp	B	08 BAL	467	49	120	15	65	0	257	283	245	305	407	711	6	87	27	0.51	276	47	20	33	91	11%	31	0%	4.22	0.4	$10
Consist	B	1st Half	230	22	55	7	29	0	239			286	387	673	6	87	25	0.50	277	44	21	35	89	10%	34	0%	3.78	-2.8	$4
LIMA Plan	D+	2nd Half	237	27	65	8	36	0	274			323	426	749	7	86	29	0.52	272	50	19	31	93	12%	22	0%	4.65	3.1	$7
+/- Score	4	09 Proj	487	54	129	16	76	1	265			319	420	739	7	86	28	0.55	274	47	19	34	94	11%	38	1%	4.57	4.6	$12

2005: Hand surgery
2006: Healthy productive year
2007: Groin contusion
2008: Wrist inflammation
Odds of an '06 repeat are slim, but you can't turn your back on moderately productive CA talent.

JOSHUA RANDALL

Hill,Aaron

		AB	R	H	HR	RBI	SB	Avg	vL	vR	OB	Slg	OPS	bb%	ct%	h%	Eye	xBA	G	L	F	PX	hr/f	SX	SBO	RC/G	RAR	R$
Pos 4	04 aa	480	75	134	11	77	3	279			360	417	777	11	88	30	1.03	0				84		70	3%	5.36	13.9	$15
Age 27	05 TOR	* 517	67	143	7	55	4	277	298	269	325	398	723	7	89	30	0.67	284	43	22	36	81	4%	83	4%	4.54	6.0	$12
Bats Right	06 TOR	546	70	159	6	50	5	291	298	288	342	386	728	7	88	32	0.64	261	46	19	35	61	4%	80	4%	4.57	6.9	$12
Health F	07 TOR	608	87	177	17	78	4	291	317	283	336	459	795	6	83	33	0.40	282	40	21	39	114	9%	69	5%	5.21	20.7	$18
PT/Exp B	08 TOR	205	19	54	2	20	4	263	286	258	317	361	678	7	85	30	0.52	237	35	17	47	73	2%	55	11%	3.95	-5.6	$4
Consist B	1st Half	205	19	54	2	20	4	263			317	361	678	7	85	30	0.52	237	35	17	47	73	2%	55	11%	3.95	-5.6	$4
LIMA Plan D+	2nd Half	0	0	0	0	0	0	0							0			0										
+/- Score -12	**09 Proj**	**491**	**61**	**134**	**16**	**54**	**3**	**273**			**326**	**442**	**768**	**7**	**86**	**29**	**0.58**	**281**	**41**	**19**	**40**	**105**	**9%**	**57**	**4%**	**4.96**	**6.8**	**$12**

Lost 4 months to concussion, leaving us only a small '08 sample. FB swing (though not 47% worth) just requires decent hr/f to bring back the power. All is contingent on health. He's a high-risk, high-reward pick now.

Hinske,Eric

		AB	R	H	HR	RBI	SB	Avg	vL	vR	OB	Slg	OPS	bb%	ct%	h%	Eye	xBA	G	L	F	PX	hr/f	SX	SBO	RC/G	RAR	R$
Pos 970	04 TOR	570	66	140	15	69	12	246	268	236	311	375	686	9	81	28	0.50	245	43	18	39	79	8%	86	13%	3.98	-12.3	$12
Age 31	05 TOR	477	79	125	15	68	8	262	172	281	327	430	757	9	75	32	0.38	258	41	20	39	122	11%	99	10%	4.91	3.0	$15
Bats Left	06 2AL	277	43	75	13	34	2	271	167	293	353	487	840	11	71	34	0.44	254	40	16	43	148	15%	77	5%	6.18	4.2	$8
Health A	07 BOS	186	25	38	6	21	3	204	200	205	308	398	706	13	71	25	0.52	244	45	11	44	142	10%	112	7%	4.49	-5.9	$3
PT/Exp D	08 TAM	381	59	94	20	60	10	247	143	262	329	465	794	11	77	27	0.53	276	39	20	41	142	17%	87	13%	5.37	0.1	$14
Consist C	1st Half	212	34	56	13	44	7	264			353	528	881	12	79	28	0.66	303	39	20	41	168	19%	93	16%	6.50	7.1	$10
LIMA Plan D	2nd Half	169	25	38	7	16	3	225			299	385	684	10	74	26	0.41	243	39	20	41	107	14%	68	9%	3.87	-7.7	$4
+/- Score -0	**09 Proj**	**280**	**41**	**66**	**12**	**36**	**5**	**236**			**321**	**435**	**756**	**11**	**74**	**28**	**0.49**	**259**	**41**	**17**	**42**	**136**	**14%**	**94**	**10%**	**4.96**	**-3.5**	**$7**

Got the playing time, plus boost from hr/f, et voilà! Uncertain role and extreme splits make him unsuited as every day player, so any follow up again depends on finding AB. 2005 with a bit more power is good skills benchmark.

Hoffpauir,Micah

		AB	R	H	HR	RBI	SB	Avg	vL	vR	OB	Slg	OPS	bb%	ct%	h%	Eye	xBA	G	L	F	PX	hr/f	SX	SBO	RC/G	RAR	R$
Pos 7	04 a/a	343	46	89	9	60	1	260			307	410	717	6	84	29	0.43	0				89		78	7%	4.30	-9.0	$9
Age 29	05 a/a	413	38	90	4	37	2	219			272	283	555	7	86	25	0.53	0				41		65	2%	2.50	-32.1	$2
Bats Left	06 a/a	393	55	94	21	71	1	238			321	451	772	11	75	27	0.49	0				132		55	3%	5.07	-1.7	$11
Health A	07 aaa	310	39	76	12	51	2	246			285	428	713	5	89	24	0.48	0				107		50	4%	4.18	-9.3	$8
PT/Exp F	08 CHC	* 363	56	109	20	76	3	302	273	355	334	575	909	5	82	32	0.27	346	22	41	37	177	19%	73	4%	6.41	9.8	$18
Consist D	1st Half	124	20	35	5	20	1	283			299	509	808	2	80	32	0.11	310	13	39	48	155	11%	71	5%	5.11	-1.1	$5
LIMA Plan D	2nd Half	239	36	74	15	55	2	311			351	610	961	6	83	32	0.36	372	31	42	27	187	28%	65	4%	7.06	10.6	$13
+/- Score 26	**09 Proj**	**207**	**29**	**56**	**10**	**38**	**1**	**271**			**312**	**499**	**812**	**6**	**83**	**29**	**0.36**	**328**	**21**	**41**	**38**	**142**	**15%**	**71**	**4%**	**5.32**	**-0.3**	**$8**

2-8-.342 in 73 AB at CHC
Bull Durham prospect profiles as slugger, but low bb% limits upside. Has nothing left to prove in minors, though at his age, won't get many chances. Good reserve round pick.

Holliday,Matt

		AB	R	H	HR	RBI	SB	Avg	vL	vR	OB	Slg	OPS	bb%	ct%	h%	Eye	xBA	G	L	F	PX	hr/f	SX	SBO	RC/G	RAR	R$
Pos 7	04 COL	400	65	116	14	57	3	290	237	307	341	488	829	7	79	34	0.36	284	50	17	32	131	14%	86	6%	5.71	3.1	$15
Age 29	05 COL	479	68	147	19	87	14	307	324	302	355	505	861	7	84	34	0.46	299	48	21	31	118	15%	125	13%	5.98	8.4	$24
Bats Right	06 COL	602	119	196	34	114	10	326	327	325	374	586	961	7	82	35	0.43	313	45	21	34	153	20%	104	9%	7.19	31.2	$33
Health B	07 COL	636	120	216	36	137	11	340	301	351	399	607	1006	9	80	38	0.50	313	44	20	36	166	20%	101	8%	7.92	42.5	$38
PT/Exp A	08 COL	539	107	173	25	88	28	321	293	329	403	538	941	12	81	36	0.71	303	46	22	33	139	18%	121	16%	7.30	27.1	$34
Consist B	1st Half	262	43	87	10	39	9	332			407	538	945	11	82	38	0.69	310	48	23	29	133	16%	104	11%	7.33	13.2	$14
LIMA Plan D+	2nd Half	277	64	86	15	49	19	310			399	538	937	13	80	34	0.73	296	43	20	36	145	19%	116	21%	7.27	13.9	$19
+/- Score -9	**09 Proj**	**597**	**116**	**188**	**29**	**108**	**17**	**315**			**385**	**546**	**931**	**10**	**81**	**35**	**0.59**	**304**	**45**	**21**	**34**	**145**	**18%**	**116**	**11%**	**7.05**	**27.1**	**$33**

PRO:
- Rising bb%
- SBO triggered SB bonanza

CON:
- Relatively low FB%
- xBA questions .320+ BAs

He's peaked; don't expect more.

Holm,Stephen

		AB	R	H	HR	RBI	SB	Avg	vL	vR	OB	Slg	OPS	bb%	ct%	h%	Eye	xBA	G	L	F	PX	hr/f	SX	SBO	RC/G	RAR	R$
Pos 2	04	0	0	0	0	0	0	0							0			0						0				
Age 29	05	0	0	0	0	0	0	0							0			0						0				
Bats Right	06	0	0	0	0	0	0	0							0			0						0				
Health A	07 aa	254	24	51	6	19	2	203			282	314	596	10	85	22	0.73	0				70		40	4%	3.07	-10.3	$1
PT/Exp F	08 SF	* 150	17	40	1	17	0	267	235	269	353	373	726	12	81	32	0.71	282	47	26	26	87	3%	29	2%	4.80	2.6	$3
Consist D	1st Half	70	8	15	1	5	0	214			295	357	652	10	79	26	0.53	273	48	20	31	115	6%	43	7%	3.74	-1.0	$0
LIMA Plan F	2nd Half	80	9	25	0	12	0	312			402	387	790	13	84	37	0.92	0	43	50	7	65	0%	21	0%	5.69	3.2	$2
+/- Score 7	**09 Proj**	**62**	**7**	**15**	**1**	**6**	**0**	**242**			**327**	**345**	**671**	**11**	**83**	**28**	**0.73**	**267**	**46**	**24**	**30**	**75**	**5%**	**34**	**3%**	**4.05**	**-0.4**	**$1**

1-6-.262 in 84 AB at SF
After seven seasons in minors, mostly at Single-A, finally got a taste of the big leagues. We can try to say something nice, like that his Eye and PX give hope, but it's not our job to be nice.

Howard,Ryan

		AB	R	H	HR	RBI	SB	Avg	vL	vR	OB	Slg	OPS	bb%	ct%	h%	Eye	xBA	G	L	F	PX	hr/f	SX	SBO	RC/G	RAR	R$
Pos 3	04 a/a	485	75	119	35	105	1	246			315	516	831	9	68	28	0.32	0				182		47	3%	5.93	6.7	$19
Age 29	05 PHI	* 522	82	160	36	106	0	307	148	320	381	584	965	11	71	37	0.41	304	44	27	29	193	33%	43	1%	7.84	31.9	$27
Bats Left	06 PHI	581	104	182	58	149	0	313	279	331	421	659	1080	16	69	36	0.60	298	42	22	36	220	40%	24	0%	9.69	57.7	$36
Health A	07 PHI	529	94	142	47	136	1	268	225	297	392	584	976	17	62	34	0.54	277	31	24	44	233	32%	31	1%	8.78	40.2	$27
PT/Exp A	08 PHI	610	105	153	48	146	1	251	224	268	339	543	881	12	67	29	0.41	284	41	22	36	200	32%	68	1%	6.80	19.2	$29
Consist C	1st Half	311	51	67	20	68	1	215			309	460	769	12	63	27	0.37	254	44	20	37	180	28%	79	1%	5.37	-3.4	$10
LIMA Plan B	2nd Half	299	54	86	28	78	0	288			370	629	999	12	72	31	0.46	315	40	24	36	219	36%	56	1%	8.16	20.4	$18
+/- Score 40	**09 Proj**	**576**	**100**	**156**	**49**	**141**	**1**	**271**			**368**	**580**	**949**	**13**	**67**	**32**	**0.47**	**288**	**39**	**23**	**38**	**212**	**33%**	**50**	**1%**	**7.86**	**32.8**	**$30**

xBA paints optimistic picture, but without mid-30s h% and low-20s LD% his BA won't cooperate. Sub-40% FB% also means he's dependent on huge hr/f to generate all those HR. He's not doomed, just vulnerable.

Hudson,Orlando

		AB	R	H	HR	RBI	SB	Avg	vL	vR	OB	Slg	OPS	bb%	ct%	h%	Eye	xBA	G	L	F	PX	hr/f	SX	SBO	RC/G	RAR	R$
Pos 4	04 TOR	489	73	132	12	58	7	270	262	272	339	438	777	9	80	32	0.52	276	48	20	32	107	9%	112	8%	5.22	16.1	$13
Age 31	05 TOR	461	62	125	10	63	7	271	227	288	316	412	728	6	86	30	0.46	290	52	20	28	88	9%	108	7%	4.45	4.2	$13
Bats Both	06 ARI	579	87	166	15	67	9	287	338	270	355	454	809	10	87	31	0.78	289	49	19	32	95	9%	100	9%	5.62	16.8	$18
Health C	07 ARI	517	69	152	10	63	10	294	281	298	378	441	819	12	83	34	0.80	283	52	20	28	90	8%	110	7%	5.90	17.3	$16
PT/Exp A	08 ARI	407	54	124	8	41	4	305	269	321	367	450	817	9	85	34	0.65	294	48	23	29	96	8%	82	4%	5.68	10.1	$13
Consist A	1st Half	279	35	81	7	35	2	290			351	455	806	9	85	32	0.60	292	44	23	33	105	9%	81	4%	5.51	5.8	$9
LIMA Plan C	2nd Half	128	19	43	1	6	2	336			401	437	839	10	85	39	0.74	296	58	23	19	78	5%	58	4%	6.04	4.2	$5
+/- Score -25	**09 Proj**	**491**	**69**	**138**	**8**	**49**	**3**	**281**			**352**	**416**	**768**	**10**	**85**	**32**	**0.71**	**288**	**52**	**21**	**27**	**88**	**7%**	**83**	**3%**	**5.17**	**6.4**	**$12**

Broken wrist ended his season in August. Such injuries can wreck power, what little he has. That hurts BA despite high GB and LD. Tweaks to hammy, ankle call SX into question too. Don't ignore his health rating.

Huff,Aubrey

		AB	R	H	HR	RBI	SB	Avg	vL	vR	OB	Slg	OPS	bb%	ct%	h%	Eye	xBA	G	L	F	PX	hr/f	SX	SBO	RC/G	RAR	R$
Pos 053	04 TAM	600	92	178	29	104	5	297	304	293	357	493	850	9	88	30	0.76	291	46	18	36	106	15%	77	3%	5.88	9.7	$24
Age 32	05 TAM	575	70	150	22	92	8	261	254	262	319	428	747	8	85	28	0.56	270	48	15	37	100	12%	69	10%	4.66	-23.0	$18
Bats Left	06 2TM	454	57	121	21	66	0	267	233	278	339	469	808	10	86	27	0.78	287	45	19	36	114	15%	35	0%	5.51	-12.0	$13
Health A	07 BAL	550	68	154	15	72	1	280	305	272	338	442	780	8	84	31	0.55	270	46	16	38	103	9%	64	1%	5.14	-17.1	$14
PT/Exp A	08 BAL	598	96	182	32	108	4	304	270	321	361	552	913	8	85	31	0.60	310	41	17	42	152	15%	76	3%	6.62	27.6	$27
Consist B	1st Half	303	46	83	14	46	2	274			341	498	840	9	84	29	0.65	299	41	18	41	142	13%	68	3%	5.87	8.1	$11
LIMA Plan C+	2nd Half	295	50	99	18	62	2	336			382	607	988	7	86	34	0.54	320	41	17	42	162	17%	67	3%	7.37	18.8	$17
+/- Score 2	**09 Proj**	**587**	**85**	**172**	**28**	**102**	**3**	**293**			**351**	**513**	**865**	**8**	**85**	**31**	**0.61**	**297**	**43**	**17**	**39**	**133**	**14%**	**69**	**2%**	**6.08**	**8.5**	**$23**

Signs he'll hit 30 HR again:
- Mid-teens hr/f is his norm
- Rising FB% trend

Signs he won't:
- Atypical '08 PX driven by 2Bs
- High GB% prior to 2008
- Sept. fade (.395 Slg, 91 PX)

Hundley,Nicholas

		AB	R	H	HR	RBI	SB	Avg	vL	vR	OB	Slg	OPS	bb%	ct%	h%	Eye	xBA	G	L	F	PX	hr/f	SX	SBO	RC/G	RAR	R$
Pos 2	04	0	0	0	0	0	0	0							0			0						0				
Age 25	05	0	0	0	0	0	0	0							0			0						0				
Bats Right	06	0	0	0	0	0	0	0							0			0						0				
Health A	07 aa	373	47	79	17	61	0	211			281	402	683	9	80	22	0.48	0				118		39	2%	3.87	-5.7	$7
PT/Exp F	08 SD	* 422	47	89	13	55	0	212	224	243	254	353	607	5	78	24	0.26	234	39	17	44	92	9%	43	0%	2.76	-19.0	$6
Consist C	1st Half	220	26	40	8	30	0	184			230	338	567	6	81	19	0.32	0				94		40	0%	2.31	-13.3	$2
LIMA Plan F	2nd Half	202	21	49	5	25	0	242			281	370	651	5	74	30	0.21	221	39	17	44	90	8%	47	0%	3.33	-5.3	$3
+/- Score 20	**09 Proj**	**228**	**26**	**49**	**8**	**33**	**0**	**215**			**268**	**377**	**645**	**7**	**78**	**24**	**0.33**	**244**	**39**	**17**	**44**	**103**	**11%**	**54**	**1%**	**3.30**	**-6.6**	**$3**

5-24-.237 in 198 AB at SD
2nd half surge would be more encouraging if 1st half wasn't so subterranean. When you have your last CA spot open and you need a $1 filler, think back to this chart and say... Henry Blanco.

JOSHUA RANDALL

Hunter,Torii			AB	R	H	HR	RBI	SB	Avg	vL	vR	OB	Slg	OPS	bb%	ct%	h%	Eye	xBA	G	L	F	PX	hr/f	SX	SBO	RC/G	RAR	R$
Pos	8	04 MIN	520	79	141	23	81	21	271	255	278	323	475	798	7	81	30	0.40	281	48	15	37	129	15%	96	23%	5.23	7.9	$21
Age	33	05 MIN	372	63	100	14	56	23	269	283	263	330	452	782	8	83	29	0.52	282	49	14	36	118	13%	119	32%	5.13	9.2	$17
Bats	Right	06 MIN	557	86	155	31	98	12	278	319	262	332	490	822	7	81	30	0.42	277	45	18	37	121	18%	88	12%	5.46	12.7	$23
Health	B	07 MIN	600	94	172	28	107	18	287	314	276	331	505	836	6	83	31	0.40	297	49	14	37	140	15%	88	20%	5.62	18.8	$27
PT/Exp	A	08 LAA	551	85	153	21	78	19	278	304	268	338	466	804	8	80	31	0.46	285	46	19	35	125	14%	105	17%	5.41	0.9	$22
Consist	A	1st Half	298	40	81	9	37	9	272			318	446	764	6	81	31	0.34	277	48	16	35	118	11%	105	17%	4.84	-4.4	$10
LIMA Plan	C+	2nd Half	253	45	72	12	41	10	285			360	490	851	11	80	31	0.60	294	44	22	34	133	17%	89	16%	6.06	5.1	$12
+/- Score	-2	09 Proj	580	92	165	26	93	20	284			341	485	826	8	81	31	0.46	287	47	17	36	128	15%	92	17%	5.60	10.7	$25

Slight declines in FB% and hr/f have cost him 10 HR in two years. But that's fairly mild, and the only real sign of age in his skills. He's been a $20 earner four of the last five years; health willing, he should do it again.

Hu,Chin-Lung			AB	R	H	HR	RBI	SB	Avg	vL	vR	OB	Slg	OPS	bb%	ct%	h%	Eye	xBA	G	L	F	PX	hr/f	SX	SBO	RC/G	RAR	R$
Pos	64	04	0	0	0	0	0	0	0							0			0						0				
Age	25	05	0	0	0	0	0	0	0							0			0						0				
Bats	Right	06 aa	488	68	116	5	33	11	238			303	311	615	9	87	26	0.74	0				47		92	12%	3.34	-15.5	$7
Health	A	07 a/a	517	73	147	12	50	13	285			320	432	751	5	91	30	0.58	0				89		96	17%	4.72	5.1	$16
PT/Exp	D	08 LA	* 272	32	60	1	21	4	222	158	186	267	286	553	6	85	26	0.42	243	61	12	27	39	2%	120	6%	2.44	-18.1	$2
Consist	D	1st Half	118	14	19	0	7	1	160			226	211	437	8	80	20	0.43	224	62	12	26	30	0%	117	4%	0.96	-14.3	($1)
LIMA Plan	F	2nd Half	154	18	41	1	14	3	269			300	344	644	4	89	30	0.41	0	43	14	43	44	2%	107	7%	3.48	-5.1	$3
+/- Score	18	09 Proj	287	37	71	3	24	6	247			291	344	635	6	88	27	0.51	274	61	15	24	58	5%	108	11%	3.44	-9.0	$5

0-9-.181 in 116 AB at LA. A season he'd like to forget, but don't write him off just yet. Ct%, SX still showed signs of life, and GB% could be put to good use. On the radar last year, now he's under, and that's to your benefit.

Iannetta,Chris			AB	R	H	HR	RBI	SB	Avg	vL	vR	OB	Slg	OPS	bb%	ct%	h%	Eye	xBA	G	L	F	PX	hr/f	SX	SBO	RC/G	RAR	R$
Pos	2	04	0	0	0	0	0	0	0							0			0						0				
Age	26	05 aa	60	6	12	1	9	0	200			284	283	567	10	72	26	0.41	0				64		25	0%	2.39	-2.9	$0
Bats	Right	06 COL	* 384	59	118	14	47	1	307	231	266	386	495	880	11	85	33	0.88	309	52	23	25	108	17%	59	2%	6.51	22.7	$14
Health	A	07 COL	* 251	29	57	5	33	0	228	204	223	322	354	676	12	75	29	0.55	226	41	18	41	85	6%	62	0%	4.03	-3.0	$3
PT/Exp	D	08 COL	333	50	88	18	65	0	264	275	261	370	505	875	14	72	31	0.61	277	38	21	41	166	18%	47	0%	6.75	24.4	$13
Consist	F	1st Half	141	19	40	7	27	0	284			365	525	890	11	71	35	0.44	270	34	20	47	175	15%	50	0%	6.93	10.8	$6
LIMA Plan	C+	2nd Half	192	31	48	11	38	0	250			374	490	863	17	73	28	0.75	283	41	23	37	160	21%	44	0%	6.61	13.6	$7
+/- Score	8	09 Proj	412	62	109	19	73	0	265			362	478	839	13	75	31	0.61	270	39	20	40	140	15%	54	0%	6.15	22.7	$14

2007 FB% jump pays off in 2008 power. Traded ct% to get here; perhaps '07 struggles were a transition period. Breakout was not Coors-aided (175 PX home, 160 PX away). With full-time AB, could be a Top 5 catcher.

Ibanez,Raul			AB	R	H	HR	RBI	SB	Avg	vL	vR	OB	Slg	OPS	bb%	ct%	h%	Eye	xBA	G	L	F	PX	hr/f	SX	SBO	RC/G	RAR	R$
Pos	7	04 SEA	481	67	146	16	62	1	304	295	307	352	472	824	7	85	33	0.50	283	44	21	35	102	11%	47	2%	5.55	8.1	$16
Age	36	05 SEA	614	92	172	20	89	9	280	274	283	355	436	791	10	84	31	0.72	281	46	21	34	98	12%	82	7%	5.37	11.3	$21
Bats	Left	06 SEA	626	103	181	33	123	2	289	243	308	356	516	872	9	82	31	0.57	288	42	19	39	132	17%	65	3%	6.22	18.4	$25
Health	A	07 SEA	573	80	167	21	105	0	291	256	305	351	480	831	8	83	32	0.55	277	42	18	40	118	11%	56	0%	5.74	11.2	$20
PT/Exp	A	08 SEA	635	85	186	23	110	2	293	305	288	358	479	836	9	83	32	0.58	279	41	19	40	120	11%	52	3%	5.85	17.8	$23
Consist	A	1st Half	316	35	87	9	50	1	275			344	437	781	9	86	30	0.75	283	38	21	40	104	8%	39	3%	5.25	3.6	$9
LIMA Plan	C+	2nd Half	319	50	99	14	60	1	310			371	520	892	9	79	36	0.47	277	43	16	40	137	14%	63	3%	6.53	14.6	$14
+/- Score	-23	09 Proj	583	83	166	21	93	1	285			349	469	818	9	82	32	0.56	277	42	19	39	117	11%	56	2%	5.62	11.1	$19

The epitome of consistency and health. But this was 2nd straight year with 1H PX near 100 and single-digit hr/f. And 2H ct% drop was steep. At his age, little things add up, and could subtract from R$.

Iguchi,Tadahito			AB	R	H	HR	RBI	SB	Avg	vL	vR	OB	Slg	OPS	bb%	ct%	h%	Eye	xBA	G	L	F	PX	hr/f	SX	SBO	RC/G	RAR	R$
Pos	4	04 JPN	510	94	158	14	87	16	311			358	474	832	7	83	35	0.44	0				102		117	15%	5.68	18.7	$24
Age	34	05 CHW	511	74	142	15	71	15	278	274	279	339	438	777	8	78	33	0.41	274	48	22	30	106	13%	118	14%	5.13	14.6	$18
Bats	Right	06 CHW	555	97	156	18	67	11	281	252	298	350	422	772	10	80	32	0.54	253	51	16	34	88	12%	80	9%	5.05	14.7	$18
Health	C	07 2TM	465	67	124	9	43	14	267	266	267	347	400	747	11	81	31	0.65	260	43	20	37	89	6%	114	11%	4.93	7.8	$12
PT/Exp	C	08 2NL	310	29	72	2	24	8	232	190	247	292	306	598	8	76	30	0.35	222	49	17	34	60	2%	90	11%	2.84	-18.1	$4
Consist	C	1st Half	239	25	62	2	20	8	259			324	343	668	9	77	33	0.43	230	46	18	36	64	3%	91	13%	3.80	-6.7	$5
LIMA Plan	F	2nd Half	71	4	10	0	4	0	141			176	183	359	4	70	20	0.14	177	58	12	30	43	0%	29	0%	-0.65	-13.0	($2)
+/- Score	-10	09 Proj	193	22	45	3	17	4	233			294	338	632	8	77	29	0.37	237	50	17	34	76	6%	90	10%	3.28	-8.3	$3

Perfect storm of age, injury and Petco Park drove his skills and production to new lows. Should be able to bounce back a little, but RC/G shows that BPIs were already fading. His days as a starter are likely over.

Infante,Omar			AB	R	H	HR	RBI	SB	Avg	vL	vR	OB	Slg	OPS	bb%	ct%	h%	Eye	xBA	G	L	F	PX	hr/f	SX	SBO	RC/G	RAR	R$
Pos	756	04 DET	503	69	133	16	55	13	264	277	257	319	449	768	7	78	31	0.36	249	35	18	46	114	9%	130	17%	4.97	0.5	$14
Age	27	05 DET	406	36	90	9	43	8	222	178	236	251	367	618	4	82	25	0.22	242	33	16	51	101	5%	101	12%	2.98	-21.6	$6
Bats	Right	06 DET	224	35	62	4	25	3	277	286	273	319	415	735	6	80	33	0.31	242	38	19	43	86	5%	122	9%	4.50	-4.4	$6
Health	B	07 DET	* 204	27	58	2	21	5	284	281	265	326	362	688	6	85	33	0.42	227	33	21	47	53	2%	94	10%	3.96	-6.2	$5
PT/Exp	F	08 ATL	317	45	93	3	40	0	293	325	273	339	416	756	6	86	33	0.50	290	33	30	37	85	3%	70	1%	4.87	-4.9	$9
Consist	B	1st Half	103	11	29	1	11	0	282			351	427	778	10	87	31	0.85	300	35	31	34	86	3%	72	0%	5.39	-0.1	$2
LIMA Plan	D	2nd Half	214	34	64	2	29	0	299			333	411	745	5	86	34	0.35	288	32	30	38	85	3%	49	2%	4.61	-4.8	$7
+/- Score	-8	09 Proj	328	45	91	4	38	3	277			323	401	724	6	84	32	0.43	264	34	25	41	81	4%	99	6%	4.44	-8.7	$8

Huge jump in xBA was all about sky-high LD%, which will be very difficult to sustain. And speed disappeared despite best OBA since 2002. Big downside risk here; keep xBA history burned into memory and don't overbid.

Inge,Brandon			AB	R	H	HR	RBI	SB	Avg	vL	vR	OB	Slg	OPS	bb%	ct%	h%	Eye	xBA	G	L	F	PX	hr/f	SX	SBO	RC/G	RAR	R$
Pos	25	04 DET	408	43	117	13	64	5	287	327	258	339	453	792	7	82	32	0.44	259	44	17	39	93	10%	91	8%	5.21	10.1	$13
Age	31	05 DET	616	75	161	16	72	7	261	288	257	330	419	749	9	77	32	0.45	247	40	18	42	105	8%	98	8%	4.84	14.8	$15
Bats	Right	06 DET	542	83	137	27	83	7	253	243	256	308	463	771	7	76	28	0.34	255	40	14	46	133	14%	85	9%	4.90	7.8	$17
Health	A	07 DET	508	64	120	14	71	9	236	333	209	301	376	677	8	70	31	0.31	232	37	22	41	105	10%	93	9%	3.85	-6.7	$11
PT/Exp	B	08 DET	347	41	71	11	51	4	205	232	196	292	369	661	11	73	25	0.46	231	37	16	46	113	9%	93	8%	3.72	-5.1	$5
Consist	B	1st Half	144	19	31	6	23	1	215			307	417	723	12	69	27	0.42	239	41	15	45	144	14%	89	6%	4.64	2.0	$3
LIMA Plan	D	2nd Half	203	22	40	5	28	3	197			282	335	617	11	76	23	0.49	226	35	17	48	94	7%	90	10%	3.15	-6.7	$2
+/- Score	24	09 Proj	222	28	51	7	32	3	230			303	396	699	10	74	28	0.40	238	38	18	44	115	10%	86	9%	4.17	-0.5	$5

Miguel Cabrera signing shoved him to the bench after off '07 and he never really recovered, even with occasional regular PT. BA is plummeting, xBA is flat and the more he swings for the fences, the worse it gets.

Inglett,Joe			AB	R	H	HR	RBI	SB	Avg	vL	vR	OB	Slg	OPS	bb%	ct%	h%	Eye	xBA	G	L	F	PX	hr/f	SX	SBO	RC/G	RAR	R$
Pos	47	04 aa	266	37	66	1	15	3	249			307	343	651	8	89	28	0.79	0				61		97	11%	3.85	-4.0	$3
Age	30	05 aaa	322	41	86	1	29	10	268			295	360	655	4	89	30	0.36	0				60		127	21%	3.62	-6.9	$8
Bats	Left	06 CLE	* 422	59	122	5	39	13	288	217	292	341	390	731	7	83	34	0.47	270	47	24	29	67	4%	112	14%	4.56	5.2	$12
Health	A	07 aaa	392	35	82	3	45	5	209			270	293	562	8	85	24	0.54	0				52		86	20%	2.63	-21.7	$2
PT/Exp	D	08 TOR	* 398	54	120	4	44	10	301	276	298	355	416	771	8	87	34	0.65	292	49	25	26	68	4%	123	11%	5.12	2.5	$13
Consist	F	1st Half	165	21	53	3	21	3	320			387	470	857	10	90	35	1.05	314	55	24	22	81	9%	98	10%	6.26	6.2	$6
LIMA Plan	D	2nd Half	233	33	67	1	23	7	288			331	378	708	6	85	33	0.44	276	46	26	28	58	2%	131	12%	4.27	-4.0	$7
+/- Score	-8	09 Proj	357	45	97	2	37	8	272			326	364	690	7	86	31	0.57	280	49	25	26	58	2%	113	14%	4.15	-3.3	$8

3-39-.297 in 344 AB at TOR. Was his season fact or fluke? FACT: Owned all of these skills before, just never in same year. FLUKE: 2H slumps in Eye, xBA, made it just a great half-season. VERDICT: Feels a little flukish.

Ishikawa,Travis			AB	R	H	HR	RBI	SB	Avg	vL	vR	OB	Slg	OPS	bb%	ct%	h%	Eye	xBA	G	L	F	PX	hr/f	SX	SBO	RC/G	RAR	R$
Pos	3	04	0	0	0	0	0	0	0							0			0						0				
Age	25	05	0	0	0	0	0	0	0							0			0						0				
Bats	Left	06 aa	298	33	67	10	42	0	225			306	391	697	10	70	29	0.38	0				112		67	0%	4.22	-13.5	$4
Health	A	07 aa	173	13	31	2	13	1	181			240	242	481	7	76	23	0.32	0				39		60	2%	1.24	-24.8	($1)
PT/Exp	F	08 SF	* 500	70	131	21	94	9	263		280	329	471	800	9	80	29	0.49	302	56	18	26	138	20%	83	13%	5.40	-4.8	$19
Consist	F	1st Half	266	31	69	8	47	8	258			335	413	749	10	81	29	0.62	0				104		83	16%	4.88	-6.7	$9
LIMA Plan	F	2nd Half	234	39	63	13	47	1	268			321	537	858	7	78	29	0.36	322	56	18	26	179	28%	69	6%	6.02	2.0	$10
+/- Score	57	09 Proj	247	29	67	11	35	2	271			332	463	795	8	77	31	0.39	275	54	18	28	124	20%	58	6%	5.28	-4.2	$8

3-15-.274 in 95 AB at SF. Monster 2nd half, but he'll need to hit a lot more FB to sustain the power (41% FB in minors last year suggests he can). Still needs to prove himself vs. LH. Keep an eye on him this spring.

BRANDON KRUSE

Iwamura,Akinori			AB	R	H	HR	RBI	SB	Avg	vL	vR	OB	Slg	OPS	bb%	ct%	h%	Eye	xBA	G	L	F	PX	hr/f	SX	SBO	RC/G	RAR	R$
Pos	4	04 JPN	533	97	149	27	100	7	280			349	464	813	10	69	36	0.34	0				123		74	7%	5.72	20.8	$23
Age	30	05 JPN	548	81	163	18	99	5	298			357	475	832	8	75	37	0.37	0				122		99	5%	5.90	23.7	$22
Bats	Left	06 JPN	546	82	158	19	75	7	290			357	456	813	9	78	34	0.47	0				104		94	4%	5.59	18.7	$19
Health	A	07 TAM	491	82	140	7	34	12	285	323	268	361	411	772	11	77	36	0.51	248	46	20	34	84	6%	123	13%	5.27	17.9	$14
PT/Exp	A	08 TAM	627	91	172	6	48	8	274	260	280	347	380	727	10	79	34	0.53	248	47	20	33	73	4%	102	7%	4.66	-4.1	$13
Consist	A	1st Half	323	46	89	5	23	5	276			345	375	719	10	80	33	0.54	240	45	19	36	67	5%	85	7%	4.48	-3.8	$8
LIMA Plan	C+	2nd Half	304	45	83	1	25	3	273			350	385	735	11	78	35	0.53	254	48	21	30	80	1%	104	7%	4.87	-0.2	$6
+/- Score	-20	09 Proj	598	92	158	10	57	9	264			338	392	730	10	77	33	0.49	252	47	20	33	86	7%	114	8%	4.68	3.6	$14

Typically, imports take a year to adjust and then rebound close to their numbers in Japan. Not only was there no rebound, his BPIs eroded further... and in 627 AB! There are remnants of skill here, but be careful bidding.

Izturis,Cesar			AB	R	H	HR	RBI	SB	Avg	vL	vR	OB	Slg	OPS	bb%	ct%	h%	Eye	xBA	G	L	F	PX	hr/f	SX	SBO	RC/G	RAR	R$
Pos	6	04 LA	670	90	193	4	62	25	288	269	295	331	381	712	6	90	32	0.61	275	49	21	31	56	2%	129	18%	4.38	4.8	$21
Age	29	05 LA	444	48	114	2	31	8	257	303	242	296	322	618	5	89	29	0.49	273	52	22	26	46	2%	81	14%	3.24	-9.5	$7
Bats	Both	06 2NL	252	21	61	1	20	1	240	206	253	296	308	603	7	94	25	1.23	256	52	16	31	43	1%	44	8%	3.41	-7.3	$1
Health	D	07 2NL	314	31	81	0	16	3	258	186	285	300	315	616	6	94	27	1.00	279	49	23	28	39	0%	69	7%	3.46	-9.1	$3
PT/Exp	D	08 STL	414	50	109	1	24	24	263	304	237	312	309	621	7	94	28	1.12	266	47	22	31	27	1%	120	24%	3.53	-13.4	$11
Consist	A	1st Half	195	21	47	1	12	6	241			302	313	615	8	95	25	1.70	276	47	21	32	42	2%	102	17%	3.64	-5.9	$3
LIMA Plan	D	2nd Half	219	29	62	0	12	18	283			320	306	626	5	93	31	0.75	256	46	24	31	14	0%	125	30%	3.43	-7.5	$8
+/- Score	12	09 Proj	380	42	99	1	23	14	261			307	312	618	6	93	28	0.98	269	48	22	30	33	1%	98	18%	3.47	-11.4	$7

STL gave him the green light, and the result was a nice profit for his owners. Of course, SB is about all he brings to the party, so value going forward remains tied to both the tenuous health of his legs and his Mgr's whim.

Izturis,Maicer			AB	R	H	HR	RBI	SB	Avg	vL	vR	OB	Slg	OPS	bb%	ct%	h%	Eye	xBA	G	L	F	PX	hr/f	SX	SBO	RC/G	RAR	R$
Pos	64	04 aaa	376	50	116	2	28	11	309			378	383	761	10	94	32	1.91	0				48		71	19%	5.30	10.8	$12
Age	28	05 ANA *	222	25	59	1	16	12	265	191	268	331	369	700	9	89	29	0.91	271	45	20	35	66	1%	128	28%	4.48	-0.6	$6
Bats	Both	06 LAA	352	64	103	5	44	14	293	247	307	362	412	773	10	90	31	1.09	285	49	19	32	73	5%	119	18%	5.31	9.0	$13
Health	F	07 LAA	336	47	97	6	51	7	289	280	291	352	405	757	9	88	31	0.85	264	45	17	38	73	5%	92	8%	5.00	6.7	$11
PT/Exp	C	08 LAA	290	44	78	3	37	11	269	258	272	329	362	691	8	91	29	0.96	287	49	23	29	59	4%	114	15%	4.30	-0.2	$9
Consist	B	1st Half	211	32	56	3	27	9	265			326	346	672	8	91	28	1.06	292	54	23	24	50	7%	92	17%	4.07	-1.6	$7
LIMA Plan	C+	2nd Half	79	12	22	0	10	2	278			337	405	742	8	89	31	0.78	271	35	23	42	83	0%	124	10%	4.95	1.4	$2
+/- Score	15	09 Proj	351	53	99	5	45	11	282			345	409	754	9	90	30	0.93	282	45	20	35	77	5%	115	14%	5.01	6.6	$11

Numbers never quite recovered from unlucky Apr (.206 BA, .296 xBA). Stats matched skills after that, but torn thumb ligament shut him down early. Still has higher-upside skills, but may be earning dreaded "utilityman" tag.

Jackson,Conor			AB	R	H	HR	RBI	SB	Avg	vL	vR	OB	Slg	OPS	bb%	ct%	h%	Eye	xBA	G	L	F	PX	hr/f	SX	SBO	RC/G	RAR	R$
Pos	73	04 aa	226	24	62	5	27	2	274			331	416	747	8	88	29	0.73	0				83		66	10%	4.81	-2.5	$5
Age	26	05 ARI *	418	54	123	8	59	2	294	258	157	387	455	841	13	92	31	1.91	277	44	12	44	105	5%	52	4%	6.35	11.8	$13
Bats	Right	06 ARI	485	75	141	15	79	1	291	296	288	362	441	803	10	85	32	0.74	265	38	21	41	89	9%	52	1%	5.50	3.4	$16
Health	A	07 ARI	415	56	118	15	60	2	284	320	270	365	467	833	11	88	29	1.06	287	38	20	43	110	10%	47	3%	5.96	7.1	$13
PT/Exp	B	08 ARI	540	87	162	12	75	10	300	315	295	369	446	815	10	89	32	0.97	282	40	22	38	87	7%	109	7%	5.73	4.7	$21
Consist	A	1st Half	253	46	78	7	41	6	308			390	478	869	12	91	32	1.48	288	41	20	39	92	8%	128	8%	6.49	7.4	$12
LIMA Plan	B	2nd Half	287	41	84	5	34	4	293			349	418	767	8	87	32	0.66	277	39	23	38	83	5%	81	6%	5.05	-3.0	$9
+/- Score	12	09 Proj	535	84	157	19	81	6	293			365	478	843	10	88	31	0.94	291	39	21	40	107	10%	88	5%	6.00	9.3	$21

Came back to earth after a huge start, but there's still a lot to like in this skill set. Top-shelf Eye means reliable BA & OB, and while power spike was delayed, he's entering age 26 season. Breakout sleeper? Hm.

Jacobs,Mike			AB	R	H	HR	RBI	SB	Avg	vL	vR	OB	Slg	OPS	bb%	ct%	h%	Eye	xBA	G	L	F	PX	hr/f	SX	SBO	RC/G	RAR	R$
Pos	3	04 aaa	96	7	16	1	5	0	167			231	219	450	8	67	24	0.25	0				41		23	0%	0.54	-15.5	($1)
Age	28	05 NYM *	533	67	148	30	91	1	277	400	305	322	522	843	6	81	29	0.34	309	41	23	37	156	19%	41	3%	5.68	1.2	$21
Bats	Left	06 FLA	469	54	123	20	77	3	262	182	281	327	473	800	9	78	30	0.43	277	40	20	40	138	14%	55	3%	5.41	-8.1	$14
Health	B	07 FLA	426	57	113	17	54	1	265	290	257	315	458	773	7	76	31	0.31	255	36	18	46	128	11%	57	3%	4.96	-14.5	$11
PT/Exp	B	08 FLA	477	67	118	32	93	1	247	218	257	300	514	814	7	75	26	0.30	280	35	18	47	171	19%	61	1%	5.41	-4.5	$18
Consist	A	1st Half	248	31	58	18	47	1	234			266	512	779	4	74	24	0.17	276	35	15	50	179	20%	61	3%	4.80	-6.9	$9
LIMA Plan	C+	2nd Half	229	36	60	14	46	0	262			335	515	850	10	76	29	0.45	284	35	20	45	164	18%	49	0%	6.03	2.0	$9
+/- Score	29	09 Proj	454	72	123	30	88	1	271			325	541	866	7	76	29	0.34	288	36	19	45	171	19%	64	2%	6.09	2.8	$19

Profile of a PX spike: maintained elevated FB% while swapping a little contact for extra *oomph*. BA will be the next to arrive, and xBA consistently shows he's not just an all-or-nothing slugger. UP: .285 BA, 35 HR

Jenkins,Geoff			AB	R	H	HR	RBI	SB	Avg	vL	vR	OB	Slg	OPS	bb%	ct%	h%	Eye	xBA	G	L	F	PX	hr/f	SX	SBO	RC/G	RAR	R$
Pos	9	04 MIL	621	89	164	27	93	3	264	215	281	315	472	787	7	75	31	0.30	270	44	19	37	134	16%	93	3%	5.16	-2.3	$20
Age	34	05 MIL	538	87	157	25	86	0	292	261	307	359	513	872	9	74	35	0.41	295	40	27	34	159	19%	43	0%	6.44	17.7	$22
Bats	Left	06 MIL	484	62	131	17	70	4	271	133	306	346	434	780	10	73	34	0.43	254	44	22	34	110	14%	59	3%	5.28	7.1	$14
Health	A	07 MIL	420	45	107	21	64	2	255	215	262	308	471	779	7	72	30	0.28	268	41	21	37	147	18%	51	4%	5.09	2.6	$11
PT/Exp	C	08 PHI	293	27	72	9	29	1	246	130	256	303	392	695	8	77	29	0.35	253	44	21	35	102	11%	30	3%	4.00	-10.4	$5
Consist	B	1st Half	209	22	50	6	21	1	239			290	378	668	7	78	28	0.32	245	39	20	41	96	9%	42	2%	3.61	-9.8	$3
LIMA Plan	F	2nd Half	84	5	22	3	8	0	262			333	429	762	10	75	32	0.43	264	56	23	20	117	23%	9	4%	4.98	-0.5	$2
+/- Score	-7	09 Proj	252	25	65	7	31	0	258			320	402	722	8	75	32	0.36	253	46	22	32	102	11%	41	3%	4.43	-4.6	$5

We *have* seen this before; check out how much '08 looks like '06, skills-wise. Picked it up a little before hip injury, but BPIs overall are falling fast. Looming PT challenge is the straw that makes him too risky to roster.

Jeter,Derek			AB	R	H	HR	RBI	SB	Avg	vL	vR	OB	Slg	OPS	bb%	ct%	h%	Eye	xBA	G	L	F	PX	hr/f	SX	SBO	RC/G	RAR	R$
Pos	6	04 NYY	643	111	188	23	78	23	292	314	285	340	471	811	7	85	32	0.46	293	49	19	32	109	13%	111	16%	5.38	16.5	$26
Age	34	05 NYY	654	122	202	19	70	14	309	317	305	382	450	831	11	82	35	0.66	289	60	19	21	86	17%	108	8%	5.87	23.4	$27
Bats	Right	06 NYY	623	118	214	14	97	34	343	390	328	409	483	892	10	84	39	0.68	306	59	22	18	90	15%	125	17%	6.61	35.7	$34
Health	A	07 NYY	639	102	206	12	73	15	322	317	324	377	452	829	8	84	37	0.56	291	56	20	24	87	9%	93	11%	5.75	25.2	$25
PT/Exp	A	08 NYY	596	88	179	11	69	11	300	302	300	356	408	764	8	86	34	0.61	278	58	18	24	68	9%	91	8%	4.96	10.4	$20
Consist	B	1st Half	307	47	86	4	35	5	280			330	388	718	7	88	31	0.62	286	62	16	23	68	7%	104	8%	4.45	1.0	$8
LIMA Plan	C+	2nd Half	289	41	93	7	34	6	322			384	429	813	9	83	37	0.60	267	55	20	25	67	12%	60	9%	5.54	9.4	$11
+/- Score	-11	09 Proj	586	93	170	12	71	10	290			350	413	764	8	85	33	0.60	285	57	19	23	79	11%	93	9%	4.98	10.4	$19

Aug-Sept rush made season respectable, but skills continue their decline. He still does a lot well, just not as well as he used to nor as well as some would lead you to believe. And no, "clutch" is not a roto category.

Johjima,Kenji			AB	R	H	HR	RBI	SB	Avg	vL	vR	OB	Slg	OPS	bb%	ct%	h%	Eye	xBA	G	L	F	PX	hr/f	SX	SBO	RC/G	RAR	R$
Pos	2	04 JPN	498	89	134	22	89	5	269			323	456	779	7	91	26	0.93	0				99		83	8%	5.09	14.8	$19
Age	32	05 JPN	411	68	118	14	56	3	288			331	477	808	6	93	28	0.88	0				102		100	7%	5.41	17.5	$15
Bats	Right	06 SEA	506	61	147	18	76	3	291	263	298	317	451	768	4	91	29	0.43	287	45	19	36	88	11%	56	3%	4.73	4.6	$15
Health	A	07 SEA	485	52	139	14	61	0	287	327	276	308	433	741	3	92	29	0.37	288	46	20	34	88	9%	24	2%	4.43	1.9	$12
PT/Exp	B	08 SEA	379	29	86	7	39	2	227	205	237	264	332	596	5	91	23	0.58	277	45	21	34	66	6%	42	3%	3.02	-13.4	$3
Consist	B	1st Half	218	16	50	3	20	2	229			260	317	576	4	91	24	0.45	264	48	19	33	56	5%	46	4%	2.75	-9.5	$2
LIMA Plan	D	2nd Half	161	13	36	4	19	0	224			269	354	623	6	92	22	0.77	293	42	24	34	79	8%	17	0%	3.40	-3.9	$2
+/- Score	36	09 Proj	415	42	115	11	51	1	277			310	415	725	5	91	28	0.56	289	45	21	34	81	9%	46	2%	4.37	1.5	$10

The bad news: With his contract, SEA is stuck with him. The good news: Age, xBA, h% and history all point to a rebound. Brings little else, but it means a potential draft-day bargain.

Johnson,Kelly			AB	R	H	HR	RBI	SB	Avg	vL	vR	OB	Slg	OPS	bb%	ct%	h%	Eye	xBA	G	L	F	PX	hr/f	SX	SBO	RC/G	RAR	R$
Pos	4	04 aa	479	62	125	14	45	8	261			323	424	747	8	82	29	0.50	0				105		74	15%	4.75	5.7	$12
Age	27	05 ATL *	445	77	114	16	59	8	256	257	236	357	438	795	14	79	29	0.74	288	44	26	30	117	15%	115	7%	5.61	13.7	$15
Bats	Left	06 aaa *	39	3	12	1	7	1	308			400	487	887	13	85	34	1.00	0				121		32	8%	6.81	2.6	$2
Health	D	07 ATL	521	91	144	16	68	9	276	272	278	372	457	828	13	78	33	0.68	261	43	19	39	113	10%	116	8%	6.07	20.6	$18
PT/Exp	C	08 ATL	547	86	157	12	69	11	287	333	270	349	446	795	9	79	34	0.46	274	39	25	36	110	8%	111	11%	5.42	10.1	$19
Consist	B	1st Half	280	44	79	7	35	7	282			358	450	808	11	80	33	0.59	274	37	23	40	117	8%	103	11%	5.67	7.2	$10
LIMA Plan	B	2nd Half	267	42	78	5	34	4	292			339	442	781	7	79	36	0.33	274	41	26	33	102	7%	113	11%	5.15	2.8	$9
+/- Score	-4	09 Proj	538	87	149	16	67	10	277			351	455	807	10	79	32	0.54	276	41	23	36	115	11%	111	10%	5.62	14.1	$18

Two steps forward, two steps back. The bb% dip isn't troubling yet, barring a repeat. Nothing really jumps out, but overall skills just hint at... more. At age 27, it could happen fast. More upside than down in this projection.

ROD TRUESDELL

Johnson,Nick			AB	R	H	HR	RBI	SB	Avg	vL	vR	OB	Slg	OPS	bb%	ct%	h%	Eye	xBA	G	L	F	PX	hr/f	SX	SBO	RC/G	RAR	R$
Pos	3	04 MON	251	35	63	7	33	6	251	323	228	354	398	752	14	77	30	0.69	259	47	20	33	103	11%	65	11%	5.08	-6.5	$7
Age	30	05 WAS	453	66	131	15	74	3	289	328	277	396	479	875	15	81	33	0.92	289	44	21	35	129	12%	59	7%	6.73	14.6	$17
Bats	Left	06 WAS	500	100	145	23	77	10	290	303	285	418	520	938	18	80	32	1.11	302	42	22	36	148	16%	69	7%	7.65	23.1	$22
Health	F	07 WAS	0	0	0	0	0	0	0							0			0						0				
PT/Exp	D	08 WAS	109	15	24	5	20	0	220	167	247	401	431	833	23	77	24	1.32	285	38	24	39	144	15%	14	0%	6.49	2.5	$3
Consist	C	1st Half	109	15	24	5	20	0	220			401	431	833	23	77	24	1.32	285	38	24	39	144	15%	14	0%	6.49	2.5	$3
LIMA Plan	D+	2nd Half	0	0	0	0	0	0	0							0			0										
+/- Score	6	09 Proj	230	35	65	9	37	0	283			411	486	897	18	79	32	1.04	287	42	22	36	136	14%	40	3%	7.16	8.4	$8

It's Nick's Anatomy, Season 9! After thumb ('01), knee, wrist ('02), hand, back ('03), back, cheek ('04), heel ('05), hand, leg ('06), leg ('07), and wrist woes, you'll thrill to all-new injuries. See what part Nick hurts next!

Johnson,Reed			AB	R	H	HR	RBI	SB	Avg	vL	vR	OB	Slg	OPS	bb%	ct%	h%	Eye	xBA	G	L	F	PX	hr/f	SX	SBO	RC/G	RAR	R$
Pos	87	04 TOR	537	68	145	10	61	6	270	301	255	306	380	686	5	82	31	0.29	264	55	19	26	71	9%	83	7%	3.81	-14.0	$12
Age	32	05 TOR	398	55	107	8	58	5	269	279	262	307	412	719	5	79	32	0.27	278	51	22	27	95	9%	110	12%	4.27	-0.2	$11
Bats	Right	06 TOR	461	86	147	12	49	8	319	323	316	364	479	844	7	82	37	0.41	282	47	20	33	105	10%	101	8%	5.83	14.4	$18
Health	C	07 TOR	275	31	65	2	14	4	236	325	202	278	320	598	5	80	29	0.29	238	47	19	34	62	3%	91	9%	2.80	-14.4	$2
PT/Exp	C	08 CHC	333	52	101	6	50	5	303	333	280	341	420	761	5	80	37	0.28	261	41	24	35	86	7%	67	12%	4.76	0.2	$13
Consist	F	1st Half	181	31	49	3	31	4	271			320	387	706	7	85	31	0.46	266	40	22	38	81	5%	83	17%	4.22	-2.8	$6
LIMA Plan	D	2nd Half	152	21	52	3	19	1	342			367	461	828	4	74	45	0.15	256	43	27	30	92	9%	47	7%	5.61	3.5	$6
+/- Score	-50	09 Proj	331	48	91	6	38	5	275			314	389	703	5	79	33	0.27	257	45	22	33	81	6%	79	10%	4.04	-5.6	$9

Rebounded from disk woes, but not as much as it looks; that 2H h% won't repeat. Limited value in a platoon role, but short hits off lefties is all he does well. Worse, back problems have a way of lingering. High risk, low upside.

Jones,Adam			AB	R	H	HR	RBI	SB	Avg	vL	vR	OB	Slg	OPS	bb%	ct%	h%	Eye	xBA	G	L	F	PX	hr/f	SX	SBO	RC/G	RAR	R$
Pos	8	04	0	0	0	0	0	0	0							0			0						0				
Age	23	05 aa	228	32	65	6	19	8	286			349	428	777	9	81	33	0.51	0				89		107	18%	5.11	4.5	$8
Bats	Right	06 SEA *	454	71	124	16	66	15	273	235	211	317	441	758	6	81	31	0.34	291	44	27	29	102	15%	111	19%	4.69	0.3	$16
Health	A	07 SEA *	485	81	136	23	77	9	280	310	194	330	499	829	7	75	33	0.30	282	34	27	39	145	16%	104	15%	5.69	16.3	$19
PT/Exp	C	08 BAL	480	61	129	9	57	10	269	256	275	304	398	701	5	77	33	0.22	246	47	18	35	86	7%	124	11%	4.01	-18.6	$13
Consist	C	1st Half	287	31	78	4	29	7	272			310	387	697	5	76	35	0.23	233	45	17	38	84	5%	106	13%	4.00	-11.1	$7
LIMA Plan	C+	2nd Half	193	30	51	5	28	3	264			294	415	708	4	80	31	0.21	265	50	19	31	89	10%	129	9%	4.02	-7.5	$6
+/- Score	8	09 Proj	514	76	140	16	69	12	272			314	432	747	6	78	32	0.28	264	47	19	34	102	12%	115	14%	4.57	-5.7	$17

You can see him figuring some things out along the way... note 2H ct%, xBA, hr/f. Eventually, the talent flashed in MLEs will surface, but those 2H gains aren't enough to show it happening in '09. But eventually.

Jones,Andruw			AB	R	H	HR	RBI	SB	Avg	vL	vR	OB	Slg	OPS	bb%	ct%	h%	Eye	xBA	G	L	F	PX	hr/f	SX	SBO	RC/G	RAR	R$
Pos	8	04 ATL	570	85	149	29	91	6	261	265	260	343	488	831	11	74	30	0.48	272	48	16	36	147	19%	78	8%	5.94	21.6	$20
Age	32	05 ATL	586	95	154	51	128	5	263	254	265	335	575	910	10	81	24	0.57	313	42	16	42	180	26%	73	6%	6.56	34.1	$30
Bats	Right	06 ATL	565	107	148	41	129	4	262	260	263	355	531	886	13	78	27	0.65	288	39	19	42	158	22%	59	3%	6.54	34.4	$26
Health	C	07 ATL	572	83	127	26	94	5	222	225	221	307	413	719	11	76	25	0.51	251	39	17	44	122	14%	74	5%	4.41	-2.1	$14
PT/Exp	B	08 LA	209	21	33	3	14	0	158	178	147	254	249	503	11	64	23	0.36	183	48	13	39	77	6%	55	2%	1.42	-23.0	($2)
Consist	F	1st Half	133	18	22	2	7	0	165			275	271	545	13	66	23	0.44	192	43	13	44	86	5%	70	0%	2.15	-11.3	($1)
LIMA Plan	D	2nd Half	76	3	11	1	7	0	145			217	211	427	8	59	23	0.23	156	58	13	29	60	8%	18	7%	0.09	-12.0	($1)
+/- Score	14	09 Proj	437	52	101	16	58	0	231			314	385	699	11	69	30	0.40	220	45	16	39	110	13%	35	2%	4.22	-5.4	$8

Will he bounce back? Well, can he get back in shape, fix his swing, and get healthy? Sure he can, he's not old. But will he? Who knows? He IS going for a new contract. The range: UP: 2007 DN: Andruw who?

Jones,Brandon			AB	R	H	HR	RBI	SB	Avg	vL	vR	OB	Slg	OPS	bb%	ct%	h%	Eye	xBA	G	L	F	PX	hr/f	SX	SBO	RC/G	RAR	R$
Pos	7	04	0	0	0	0	0	0	0							0			0						0				
Age	25	05	0	0	0	0	0	0	0							0			0						0				
Bats	Left	06 aa	176	17	46	7	24	4	261			319	466	785	8	79	30	0.41	0				121		101	14%	5.17	-0.2	$5
Health	A	07 a/a	554	75	152	17	93	15	274			339	444	783	9	79	32	0.46	0	58	17	25	112	16%	100	15%	5.22	0.3	$19
PT/Exp	D	08 ATL *	462	52	110	8	59	9	237	267	267	306	363	669	9	79	28	0.47	267	44	24	33	92	6%	78	13%	3.85	-22.1	$9
Consist	B	1st Half	244	28	59	3	24	3	242			300	366	667	8	76	31	0.34	0				100		73	10%	3.77	-12.1	$4
LIMA Plan	C	2nd Half	218	23	51	5	35	6	232			311	361	672	10	84	26	0.70	275	44	24	33	84	8%	77	17%	3.99	-9.6	$5
+/- Score	15	09 Proj	414	48	112	11	61	10	271			336	423	758	9	80	32	0.48	274	45	23	32	101	10%	87	14%	4.93	-5.5	$13

.267-1-17 in 116 AB at ATL. Another toolsy, touted OF, but so far these skills don't shout upside, and he's not a pup. Give the scouts the benefit of the doubt for now; that said, little here even hints at a '09 surge.

Jones,Chipper			AB	R	H	HR	RBI	SB	Avg	vL	vR	OB	Slg	OPS	bb%	ct%	h%	Eye	xBA	G	L	F	PX	hr/f	SX	SBO	RC/G	RAR	R$
Pos	5	04 ATL	472	69	117	30	96	2	248	268	238	362	485	847	15	80	25	0.88	277	46	15	39	137	21%	51	1%	6.16	15.3	$17
Age	37	05 ATL	358	66	106	21	72	5	296	254	303	414	556	970	17	84	30	1.29	329	42	23	35	162	20%	62	5%	7.84	30.3	$19
Bats	Both	06 ATL	411	87	133	26	86	6	324	293	332	411	596	1007	13	82	34	0.84	307	41	19	40	156	19%	93	5%	8.07	28.2	$24
Health	D	07 ATL	513	108	173	29	102	5	337	274	378	429	604	1033	14	85	35	1.09	323	44	19	37	157	18%	87	3%	8.42	37.6	$30
PT/Exp	B	08 ATL	439	82	160	22	75	4	364	394	349	473	574	1047	17	86	39	1.48	311	43	24	33	121	18%	64	2%	8.78	37.3	$27
Consist	A	1st Half	254	48	100	16	46	2	394			487	630	1117	15	87	41	1.44	324	40	26	34	130	21%	43	2%	9.38	24.2	$18
LIMA Plan	B	2nd Half	185	34	60	6	29	2	324			454	497	951	19	84	36	1.52	295	47	22	31	109	12%	70	2%	7.90	12.4	$9
+/- Score	-75	09 Proj	383	74	122	18	71	2	319			426	535	961	16	85	34	1.22	304	44	21	35	128	16%	69	2%	7.72	23.7	$19

Still so much to love, and yet the signs of decline loom, notably lowest PX in a decade, more nagging injuries. BA will regress with h%, but others will bid up. This may finally be the year to let others overspend on him.

Jones,Jacque			AB	R	H	HR	RBI	SB	Avg	vL	vR	OB	Slg	OPS	bb%	ct%	h%	Eye	xBA	G	L	F	PX	hr/f	SX	SBO	RC/G	RAR	R$
Pos	7	04 MIN	555	69	141	24	80	13	254	245	258	304	427	731	7	79	28	0.34	263	57	13	30	104	18%	77	17%	4.34	-10.0	$17
Age	34	05 MIN	523	74	130	23	73	13	249	201	268	315	438	753	9	77	28	0.43	281	59	15	26	120	22%	110	13%	4.76	0.6	$17
Bats	Left	06 CHC	533	73	152	27	81	9	285	234	303	329	499	828	6	78	32	0.30	293	56	19	26	131	25%	80	8%	5.53	4.2	$21
Health	A	07 CHC	453	52	129	5	66	6	285	295	283	335	400	734	7	85	33	0.49	284	58	19	23	81	6%	72	7%	4.61	-9.6	$12
PT/Exp	C	08 2TM	116	15	17	1	7	0	147		168	238	207	445	11	78	18	0.54	206	55	12	33	38	3%	86	4%	0.99	-16.2	($1)
Consist	F	1st Half	116	15	17	1	7	0	147			238	207	445	11	78	18	0.54	206	55	12	33	38	3%	86	4%	0.99	-16.2	($1)
LIMA Plan	F	2nd Half	0	0	0	0	0	0	0							0			0										
+/- Score	59	09 Proj	64	8	15	1	8	1	234			297	320	617	8	79	28	0.43	237	57	16	28	63	6%	60	8%	3.11	-4.0	$1

There is no way he was going to maintain those PX levels with that G/F profile. Unaided. Anyway, now he's a GB hitter with no speed, and that's a fast way out of a ML job. Obviously.

Joyce,Matthew			AB	R	H	HR	RBI	SB	Avg	vL	vR	OB	Slg	OPS	bb%	ct%	h%	Eye	xBA	G	L	F	PX	hr/f	SX	SBO	RC/G	RAR	R$
Pos	79	04	0	0	0	0	0	0	0							0			0						0				
Age	24	05	0	0	0	0	0	0	0							0			0						0				
Bats	Left	06	0	0	0	0	0	0	0							0			0						0				
Health	A	07 aa	456	57	108	15	66	4	236			308	408	717	9	73	29	0.39	0				124		70	9%	4.43	-10.7	$9
PT/Exp	F	08 DET *	442	69	108	23	67	2	244	227	255	323	482	805	10	73	28	0.43	266	35	17	47	162	15%	82	7%	5.60	9.9	$13
Consist	C	1st Half	254	39	59	16	45	2	232			302	489	790	9	75	25	0.39	257	36	9	55	164	15%	91	9%	5.23	3.0	$8
LIMA Plan	D	2nd Half	188	30	49	7	22	0	261			350	473	824	12	71	33	0.48	262	35	20	45	159	12%	71	4%	6.10	6.9	$5
+/- Score	21	09 Proj	251	36	65	11	36	1	259			335	478	813	10	73	31	0.42	261	35	18	47	154	13%	71	7%	5.74	5.9	$7

.252-12-33 in 242 AB at DET. Intriguing power growth. PX and hr/f held their own at DET, a strong sign. Shaky ct% keeps ceiling on power output and BA, but with a larger opportunity: UP: 30 HR

Kapler,Gabe			AB	R	H	HR	RBI	SB	Avg	vL	vR	OB	Slg	OPS	bb%	ct%	h%	Eye	xBA	G	L	F	PX	hr/f	SX	SBO	RC/G	RAR	R$
Pos	8	04 BOS	290	51	79	6	33	5	272	317	238	308	390	698	5	83	31	0.31	254	49	16	34	74	7%	103	12%	3.95	-6.4	$8
Age	33	05 BOS	97	15	24	1	9	1	247	314	210	270	351	621	3	85	28	0.20	267	54	16	30	78	4%	81	5%	3.03	-3.6	$2
Bats	Right	06 BOS *	155	23	38	2	14	1	245	265	242	313	359	672	9	86	27	0.73	253	47	14	38	76	4%	77	5%	4.04	-2.9	$2
Health	A	07	0	0	0	0	0	0	0							0			0						0				
PT/Exp	F	08 MIL	229	36	69	8	38	3	301	354	272	339	498	837	5	83	34	0.33	291	46	18	36	125	12%	98	7%	5.64	5.7	$10
Consist	F	1st Half	123	21	38	5	23	3	309			351	504	855	6	84	34	0.40	286	44	18	38	117	13%	103	9%	5.84	3.7	$6
LIMA Plan	F	2nd Half	106	15	31	3	15	0	292			324	491	815	5	82	33	0.26	295	48	17	35	135	10%	76	5%	5.40	2.0	$4
+/- Score	-77	09 Proj	243	37	69	6	31	1	284			331	443	774	7	84	32	0.44	274	47	16	37	102	8%	80	5%	5.00	2.5	$7

Kudos to MIL GM Doug Melvin for giving this former A-ball field manager a 4th OF job. Believe it or not, best PX of his entire ML career. Terrorized LHers to 1001 OPS tune. A repeat? Skills say so; history says not so fast.

ROD TRUESDELL

Kearns,Austin			AB	R	H	HR	RBI	SB	Avg	vL	vR	OB	Slg	OPS	bb%	ct%	h%	Eye	xBA	G	L	F	PX	hr/f	SX	SBO	RC/G	RAR	R$
Pos	9	04 CIN	* 300	43	72	11	44	4	240	213	235	335	423	759	13	70	31	0.48	238	49	12	39	128	13%	95	7%	5.17	-1.0	$8
Age	28	05 CIN	* 498	81	127	24	84	0	254	233	240	331	483	813	10	73	30	0.43	294	49	23	29	166	23%	46	0%	5.72	6.8	$17
Bats	Right	06 2NL	537	86	142	24	86	9	264	336	236	356	467	823	12	75	31	0.56	264	42	19	39	132	15%	78	8%	5.91	17.8	$19
Health	D	07 WAS	587	84	156	16	74	2	266	292	258	345	411	756	11	82	30	0.67	267	45	20	35	95	10%	47	2%	4.98	1.7	$14
PT/Exp	B	08 WAS	313	40	68	7	32	2	217	153	241	296	316	612	10	80	25	0.56	244	47	21	32	64	9%	51	5%	3.10	-20.2	$4
Consist	C	1st Half	150	14	28	3	16	1	187			274	267	540	11	81	21	0.62	221	50	17	33	49	8%	39	8%	2.25	-14.3	$0
LIMA Plan	D+	2nd Half	163	26	40	4	16	1	245			317	362	679	9	79	29	0.50	262	43	25	32	78	10%	60	2%	3.90	-6.2	$3
+/- Score	22	09 Proj	**496**	**70**	**130**	**16**	**61**	**2**	**262**			**341**	**414**	**755**	**11**	**79**	**30**	**0.56**	**261**	**45**	**21**	**34**	**98**	**12%**	**49**	**3%**	**4.91**	**-2.2**	**$13**

Power numbers crashed while other skills held up, so it seems likely the elbow was hurting all year. Adding old pop to new ct% baseline could mean that power spike comes now. So monitor health, but looks like a bargain.

Kemp,Matt			AB	R	H	HR	RBI	SB	Avg	vL	vR	OB	Slg	OPS	bb%	ct%	h%	Eye	xBA	G	L	F	PX	hr/f	SX	SBO	RC/G	RAR	R$
Pos	89	04	0	0	0	0	0	0	0							0			0						0				
Age	24	05	0	0	0	0	0	0	0							0			0						0				
Bats	Right	06 LA	* 535	93	157	16	84	28	293	229	264	343	464	806	7	79	34	0.36	272	40	24	36	107	10%	134	24%	5.40	14.5	$25
Health	A	07 LA	* 453	73	147	14	58	18	324	390	318	359	505	863	5	80	38	0.28	272	45	17	37	113	10%	132	20%	5.99	17.9	$22
PT/Exp	B	08 LA	606	93	176	18	76	35	290	369	260	340	459	799	7	75	36	0.30	269	45	23	32	119	12%	133	29%	5.40	11.4	$28
Consist	B	1st Half	282	38	80	7	43	16	284			331	436	767	7	71	38	0.25	260	45	25	30	116	12%	122	27%	5.07	2.6	$13
LIMA Plan	C+	2nd Half	324	55	96	11	33	19	296			349	478	827	7	78	35	0.36	277	45	21	34	121	13%	132	30%	5.70	8.8	$16
+/- Score	-14	09 Proj	**590**	**95**	**167**	**21**	**87**	**30**	**283**			**329**	**471**	**800**	**6**	**78**	**33**	**0.31**	**278**	**45**	**21**	**34**	**122**	**13%**	**139**	**27%**	**5.29**	**11.3**	**$27**

As if the SB and overall solid numbers aren't yummy enough, note the 2H skills gains across the board. Struggled a bit vs. RHP, but past splits are less severe. Regression to the mean there takes him to star status.

Kendall,Jason			AB	R	H	HR	RBI	SB	Avg	vL	vR	OB	Slg	OPS	bb%	ct%	h%	Eye	xBA	G	L	F	PX	hr/f	SX	SBO	RC/G	RAR	R$
Pos	2	04 PIT	574	86	183	3	51	11	319	291	325	383	390	774	9	93	34	1.46	276	51	20	29	49	2%	67	9%	5.35	24.1	$19
Age	34	05 OAK	601	70	163	0	53	8	271	293	264	327	321	648	8	94	29	1.28	277	53	21	26	38	0%	72	6%	3.92	-1.8	$11
Bats	Right	06 OAK	552	76	163	1	50	11	295	331	285	357	342	699	9	90	33	0.98	273	50	24	26	35	1%	72	8%	4.41	0.1	$13
Health	A	07 2TM	466	45	113	3	41	3	242	198	259	290	309	599	6	91	26	0.74	248	44	19	38	45	2%	53	6%	3.17	-16.7	$4
PT/Exp	A	08 MIL	516	46	127	2	49	8	246	250	245	313	324	636	9	91	27	1.11	259	46	18	37	54	1%	75	8%	3.80	-6.4	$7
Consist	B	1st Half	249	22	68	1	24	5	273			335	357	692	8	92	29	1.21	266	48	17	35	56	1%	81	9%	4.42	1.5	$5
LIMA Plan	D	2nd Half	267	24	59	1	25	3	221			293	292	585	9	90	24	1.04	251	44	18	38	53	1%	53	6%	3.20	-8.3	$2
+/- Score	14	09 Proj	**436**	**35**	**108**	**1**	**40**	**3**	**248**			**309**	**308**	**617**	**8**	**91**	**27**	**1.01**	**253**	**46**	**19**	**34**	**44**	**1%**	**47**	**5%**	**3.53**	**-9.3**	**$4**

Another late-career CA power spike... sorry, can't even write that with a straight face. If you can afford the low per-AB output he'll grind out a few $$ value. Open with $1, then let whoever interrupts the crickets have him.

Kendrick,Howie			AB	R	H	HR	RBI	SB	Avg	vL	vR	OB	Slg	OPS	bb%	ct%	h%	Eye	xBA	G	L	F	PX	hr/f	SX	SBO	RC/G	RAR	R$
Pos	4	04	0	0	0	0	0	0	0							0			0						0				
Age	25	05 aa	190	27	57	5	33	9	300			318	484	802	3	92	31	0.31	0				117		118	37%	5.14	4.3	$9
Bats	Right	06 LAA	* 557	70	171	14	79	15	307	264	295	329	476	804	3	85	34	0.22	289	52	15	33	107	9%	109	15%	5.14	15.6	$20
Health	F	07 LAA	* 388	63	122	8	49	6	315	325	322	332	451	783	3	82	37	0.14	273	54	16	30	94	8%	95	10%	4.83	8.8	$14
PT/Exp	C	08 LAA	340	43	104	3	37	11	306	300	308	330	421	750	3	83	36	0.21	283	54	20	26	86	4%	103	18%	4.57	-3.0	$11
Consist	A	1st Half	141	13	43	0	15	3	305			319	411	731	2	83	37	0.13	278	56	18	26	87	0%	83	19%	4.32	-2.3	$4
LIMA Plan	D+	2nd Half	199	30	61	3	22	8	307			337	427	764	4	83	36	0.26	285	52	22	26	85	7%	114	17%	4.74	-0.8	$8
+/- Score	-0	09 Proj	**373**	**51**	**115**	**6**	**46**	**9**	**308**			**330**	**442**	**772**	**3**	**84**	**35**	**0.20**	**286**	**54**	**18**	**28**	**94**	**7%**	**98**	**15%**	**4.77**	**3.0**	**$13**

Skills remain stagnant at best, and he can't stay on the field -- which may not be independent events. Another empty .300 BA will inflate perceived value. The tools are there, but the injury-prone label is sticking.

Kennedy,Adam			AB	R	H	HR	RBI	SB	Avg	vL	vR	OB	Slg	OPS	bb%	ct%	h%	Eye	xBA	G	L	F	PX	hr/f	SX	SBO	RC/G	RAR	R$
Pos	4	04 ANA	468	70	130	10	48	15	278	250	286	336	406	742	8	80	33	0.45	246	40	21	39	79	7%	125	15%	4.67	7.9	$14
Age	33	05 ANA	416	49	125	2	37	19	300	296	302	346	370	716	7	85	35	0.45	255	41	24	35	55	2%	90	18%	4.34	2.5	$14
Bats	Left	06 LAA	451	50	123	4	55	16	273	193	291	331	384	714	8	84	32	0.54	274	41	27	32	72	3%	113	21%	4.44	4.3	$11
Health	C	07 STL	279	27	61	3	18	6	219	122	235	276	290	566	7	88	24	0.67	236	43	17	40	44	3%	81	11%	2.73	-17.0	$2
PT/Exp	C	08 STL	339	42	95	2	36	7	280	270	283	322	372	694	6	87	32	0.49	274	43	25	32	60	2%	114	9%	4.12	-6.2	$9
Consist	D	1st Half	193	19	51	1	20	4	264			317	326	644	7	85	30	0.54	252	44	24	33	43	2%	81	9%	3.55	-6.8	$4
LIMA Plan	D	2nd Half	146	23	44	1	16	3	301			329	432	760	4	90	33	0.40	301	43	26	31	81	2%	134	8%	4.83	0.2	$5
+/- Score	-8	09 Proj	**393**	**48**	**106**	**3**	**38**	**10**	**270**			**316**	**364**	**680**	**6**	**87**	**30**	**0.52**	**266**	**42**	**23**	**34**	**60**	**3%**	**109**	**12%**	**3.97**	**-8.3**	**$9**

Hit rate returned to normal, and with it most of his per-AB value. But he's spending a LOT of time on the bench. A return to more playing time could bump him back to double-digit steals.

Kent,Jeff			AB	R	H	HR	RBI	SB	Avg	vL	vR	OB	Slg	OPS	bb%	ct%	h%	Eye	xBA	G	L	F	PX	hr/f	SX	SBO	RC/G	RAR	R$
Pos	4	04 HOU	540	96	156	27	107	7	289	284	290	348	531	880	8	82	31	0.51	289	36	20	44	141	14%	121	7%	6.29	25.6	$25
Age	41	05 LA	553	100	160	29	105	6	289	306	285	371	512	883	12	85	30	0.85	291	31	21	48	136	13%	69	5%	6.46	29.5	$27
Bats	Right	06 LA	407	61	119	14	68	1	292	347	275	377	477	853	12	83	32	0.80	276	34	23	43	111	10%	57	2%	6.24	18.6	$14
Health	B	07 LA	494	78	149	20	79	1	302	299	302	374	500	874	10	88	31	0.93	285	38	18	45	118	10%	43	3%	6.35	22.5	$19
PT/Exp	B	08 LA	440	42	123	12	59	0	280	288	276	318	418	736	5	88	30	0.48	282	40	23	37	84	8%	29	1%	4.48	-3.6	$11
Consist	B	1st Half	249	26	64	8	34	0	257			291	406	697	5	88	27	0.39	275	42	20	37	86	10%	38	0%	3.95	-5.9	$6
LIMA Plan	D+	2nd Half	191	16	59	4	25	0	309			353	435	787	6	89	33	0.62	294	38	26	36	81	7%	17	2%	5.16	2.0	$6
+/- Score	-31	09 Proj	**436**	**55**	**124**	**10**	**56**	**0**	**284**			**343**	**423**	**766**	**8**	**87**	**31**	**0.68**	**273**	**38**	**22**	**40**	**87**	**7%**	**36**	**2%**	**5.01**	**3.7**	**$12**

When a 25-year-old's season is ruined by injury, we expect the rebound. But this 40-year-old's knee is almost shot, and back trouble is always dicey. And do they explain the bb% collapse? This rebound may not come.

Keppinger,Jeff			AB	R	H	HR	RBI	SB	Avg	vL	vR	OB	Slg	OPS	bb%	ct%	h%	Eye	xBA	G	L	F	PX	hr/f	SX	SBO	RC/G	RAR	R$
Pos	6	04 a/a	389	47	113	1	31	10	292			340	357	696	7	95	30	1.61	0				42		83	15%	4.42	1.4	$10
Age	29	05 aaa	255	34	78	3	25	4	307			340	412	752	5	96	31	1.16	0				63		94	7%	4.84	4.1	$8
Bats	Right	06 KC	* 510	67	152	6	50	0	298	222	303	354	378	732	8	93	31	1.25	273	58	19	23	48	5%	31	2%	4.77	5.1	$11
Health	B	07 CIN	* 469	66	155	7	47	3	331	362	320	387	450	837	8	95	34	1.67	297	47	21	32	71	5%	66	3%	5.97	18.8	$16
PT/Exp	C	08 CIN	459	45	122	3	43	3	266	360	225	311	346	657	6	95	28	1.25	289	51	21	28	52	2%	65	3%	3.95	-9.1	$8
Consist	D	1st Half	175	19	56	3	22	2	320			377	434	811	8	95	32	2.00	302	54	20	26	66	7%	65	3%	5.70	5.0	$6
LIMA Plan	D	2nd Half	284	26	66	0	21	1	232			268	292	561	5	94	25	0.88	279	49	22	29	43	0%	55	3%	2.85	-15.3	$1
+/- Score	22	09 Proj	**242**	**28**	**70**	**2**	**23**	**2**	**289**			**339**	**380**	**719**	**7**	**95**	**30**	**1.37**	**290**	**50**	**21**	**29**	**56**	**4%**	**62**	**4%**	**4.63**	**1.0**	**$6**

On his way to another .300+ BA before fracturing kneecap. Never the same after, although xBA shows some bad luck. Super ct% means Avg will rebound. Again pegged for utility role, but that can change. Great end-gamer.

Kinsler,Ian			AB	R	H	HR	RBI	SB	Avg	vL	vR	OB	Slg	OPS	bb%	ct%	h%	Eye	xBA	G	L	F	PX	hr/f	SX	SBO	RC/G	RAR	R$
Pos	4	04 aa	271	42	78	8	37	6	288			352	454	806	9	85	31	0.68	0				106		71	13%	5.51	9.0	$10
Age	26	05 aaa	526	71	127	18	64	13	241			291	395	687	7	88	24	0.61	0				91		89	16%	3.98	-5.7	$14
Bats	Right	06 TEX	423	65	121	14	55	11	286	271	292	348	454	802	9	85	31	0.63	270	35	21	44	103	9%	89	13%	5.40	15.4	$15
Health	D	07 TEX	483	96	127	20	61	23	263	339	239	347	441	788	11	83	28	0.75	262	35	20	46	108	11%	125	17%	5.34	18.8	$20
PT/Exp	B	08 TEX	518	102	165	18	71	26	319	281	332	373	517	890	8	87	34	0.67	296	32	24	43	124	9%	138	19%	6.42	21.3	$28
Consist	B	1st Half	346	72	111	13	50	20	321			372	532	903	7	87	34	0.61	291	33	22	46	128	9%	153	22%	6.53	15.2	$20
LIMA Plan	B+	2nd Half	172	30	54	5	21	6	314			376	488	864	9	88	34	0.81	311	32	29	39	115	9%	84	14%	6.20	6.1	$8
+/- Score	-6	09 Proj	**541**	**108**	**164**	**24**	**95**	**27**	**303**			**367**	**511**	**878**	**9**	**86**	**32**	**0.71**	**294**	**33**	**24**	**43**	**126**	**12%**	**126**	**19%**	**6.29**	**27.1**	**$30**

August sports hernia was all that prevented a $40 breakout. Has had injury issues before, so can't ink in full season value yet. But there's not a stat here that isn't skills-supported. A healthy year could be scary-good.

Konerko,Paul			AB	R	H	HR	RBI	SB	Avg	vL	vR	OB	Slg	OPS	bb%	ct%	h%	Eye	xBA	G	L	F	PX	hr/f	SX	SBO	RC/G	RAR	R$
Pos	3	04 CHW	563	84	156	41	117	1	277	288	273	356	535	891	11	81	28	0.64	284	42	17	41	144	22%	33	1%	6.42	22.8	$24
Age	33	05 CHW	575	98	163	40	100	0	283	261	289	372	534	906	12	81	29	0.74	303	33	25	42	148	20%	26	0%	6.71	26.1	$26
Bats	Right	06 CHW	566	97	177	35	113	1	313	318	310	379	551	930	10	82	33	0.58	297	33	25	42	139	18%	41	1%	6.88	22.2	$27
Health	B	07 CHW	549	71	142	31	90	0	259	296	244	351	490	841	12	81	27	0.76	280	38	17	45	145	16%	17	1%	5.99	11.7	$17
PT/Exp	A	08 CHW	438	59	105	22	62	2	240	236	241	338	438	776	13	82	25	0.81	283	41	22	37	119	16%	52	2%	5.23	-0.6	$12
Consist	B	1st Half	228	27	49	8	30	1	215			317	368	685	13	81	23	0.79	265	45	20	35	95	12%	52	2%	4.16	-7.8	$3
LIMA Plan	C+	2nd Half	210	32	56	14	32	1	267			361	514	875	13	82	26	0.84	303	36	23	41	146	20%	37	2%	6.37	6.6	$8
+/- Score	32	09 Proj	**553**	**79**	**150**	**32**	**90**	**1**	**271**			**360**	**493**	**853**	**12**	**82**	**28**	**0.75**	**287**	**38**	**21**	**41**	**133**	**17%**	**36**	**1%**	**6.10**	**13.1**	**$20**

Nagging injuries ruined power skills that were already trending down. Returned to form in all areas in Aug-Sept. Stable Eye and sturdier past both say he should rebound well. Still, his salad days are behind him.

ROD TRUESDELL

Kotchman,Casey

			AB	R	H	HR	RBI	SB	Avg	vL	vR	OB	Slg	OPS	bb%	ct%	h%	Eye	xBA	G	L	F	PX	hr/f	SX	SBO	RC/G	RAR	R$
Pos	3	04 a/a	313	42	108	6	46	0	346			383	507	889	6	92	36	0.79	0				103		28	0%	6.31	6.8	$13
Age	26	05 ANA	* 489	63	128	14	66	1	263	250	277	327	408	735	9	91	27	1.02	305	55	21	24	86	13%	43	4%	4.74	-5.0	$12
Bats	Left	06 LAA	79	6	12	1	6	0	152	214	138	221	215	436	8	84	17	0.54	218	67	11	23	40	7%	37	6%	1.04	-11.7	($1)
Health	C	07 LAA	443	64	131	11	68	2	296	315	292	371	467	838	11	90	31	1.23	300	51	16	33	109	8%	58	5%	6.09	10.2	$14
PT/Exp	C	08 2TM	525	65	143	14	74	2	272	303	261	319	410	729	6	93	27	0.92	292	53	18	30	80	10%	51	2%	4.57	-13.9	$14
Consist	F	1st Half	287	35	83	8	38	2	289			329	429	758	6	94	29	1.06	294	54	16	30	80	10%	51	3%	4.86	-5.1	$9
LIMA Plan	C+	2nd Half	238	30	60	6	36	0	252			307	387	694	7	90	26	0.83	290	51	20	29	79	10%	50	2%	4.21	-9.0	$5
+/- Score	10	09 Proj	548	72	161	14	80	2	294			349	444	794	8	91	30	0.99	294	54	17	29	90	10%	51	3%	5.37	-3.0	$17

Good thing: Ct% better than ever, meaning BA will rebound. Less-good thing: Still too many GB for a slow 1B. Family health issues certainly a distraction; even so, there's no power spike coming with this G/F ratio.

Kotsay,Mark

			AB	R	H	HR	RBI	SB	Avg	vL	vR	OB	Slg	OPS	bb%	ct%	h%	Eye	xBA	G	L	F	PX	hr/f	SX	SBO	RC/G	RAR	R$
Pos	8	04 OAK	606	78	190	15	63	8	314	336	239	371	459	829	8	88	34	0.79	276	38	21	41	86	7%	71	7%	5.76	17.3	$20
Age	33	05 OAK	582	75	163	15	82	5	280	324	261	326	421	747	6	91	29	0.78	301	40	25	35	86	8%	58	7%	4.75	7.9	$17
Bats	Left	06 OAK	502	57	138	7	59	6	275	265	278	333	386	720	8	89	30	0.80	269	46	19	35	70	4%	77	6%	4.56	-1.4	$10
Health	F	07 OAK	* 243	21	50	1	21	2	207	130	238	276	280	556	9	91	22	1.08	241	45	15	41	54	1%	50	6%	2.90	-12.4	$0
PT/Exp	C	08 2TM	402	45	111	6	49	2	276	250	288	329	403	732	7	89	30	0.71	281	42	22	36	80	5%	68	6%	4.67	-4.3	$9
Consist	D	1st Half	170	23	50	4	21	2	294			344	435	780	7	91	31	0.81	293	42	23	34	80	8%	89	6%	5.16	0.5	$6
LIMA Plan	F	2nd Half	232	22	61	2	28	0	263			319	379	698	8	88	29	0.66	273	41	21	37	80	3%	50	5%	4.31	-5.0	$4
+/- Score	-10	09 Proj	290	31	78	4	33	2	269			326	384	710	8	90	29	0.81	272	43	20	37	74	4%	64	6%	4.46	-2.8	$6

Continues to deal with his balky back, which means this is as good as we can hope for. Skills relatively constant for years now. Don't take that as any sort of endorsement: "mediocre and oft-injured" isn't on my draft list.

Kouzmanoff,Kevin

			AB	R	H	HR	RBI	SB	Avg	vL	vR	OB	Slg	OPS	bb%	ct%	h%	Eye	xBA	G	L	F	PX	hr/f	SX	SBO	RC/G	RAR	R$
Pos	5	04 aa	24	3	4	1	5	0	167			231	333	564	8	75	18	0.33	0				107		41	0%	2.21	-2.2	$0
Age	27	05	0	0	0	0	0	0	0							0			0						0				
Bats	Right	06 CLE	* 402	65	129	20	78	4	321	167	227	376	546	922	8	85	34	0.61	295	59	9	32	132	18%	61	7%	6.71	18.5	$19
Health	A	07 SD	484	57	133	18	74	1	275	356	240	320	457	776	6	81	31	0.34	267	41	18	41	116	11%	50	1%	4.93	-9.3	$14
PT/Exp	B	08 SD	624	71	162	23	84	0	260	237	269	286	433	719	4	78	30	0.17	263	40	22	39	112	12%	52	0%	4.07	-23.6	$16
Consist	C	1st Half	313	36	85	11	36	0	272			296	435	731	3	78	32	0.16	257	38	22	40	101	11%	57	0%	4.20	-10.4	$8
LIMA Plan	C	2nd Half	311	35	77	12	48	0	248			276	431	706	4	77	29	0.17	268	41	21	38	123	13%	43	0%	3.93	-13.2	$8
+/- Score	4	09 Proj	583	71	157	23	89	0	269			307	455	762	5	80	30	0.27	271	41	20	39	118	13%	50	1%	4.70	-11.8	$17

PRO:
- Career-high HR

CON:
- Miniscule, dwindling Eye
- Disturbing RAR, OPS trends
- Needed lots of AB for the HR

The "cons" put the "pro" at risk.

Kubel,Jason

			AB	R	H	HR	RBI	SB	Avg	vL	vR	OB	Slg	OPS	bb%	ct%	h%	Eye	xBA	G	L	F	PX	hr/f	SX	SBO	RC/G	RAR	R$
Pos	09	04 a/a	488	85	162	18	89	14	332			393	547	940	9	89	35	0.91	0				127		107	14%	7.07	23.0	$26
Age	26	05 MIN	0	0	0	0	0	0	0							0			0						0				
Bats	Left	06 MIN	* 340	41	86	12	48	4	253	243	240	302	415	717	7	80	29	0.35	272	49	21	31	99	14%	83	5%	4.21	-22.1	$8
Health	C	07 MIN	418	49	114	13	65	5	273	236	280	338	450	787	9	81	31	0.52	287	43	22	35	121	11%	79	5%	5.28	-11.5	$12
PT/Exp	C	08 MIN	463	74	126	20	78	0	272	232	283	339	471	810	9	80	30	0.52	274	40	20	41	122	13%	69	1%	5.50	7.6	$16
Consist	B	1st Half	247	41	65	12	42	0	263			328	466	794	9	81	28	0.52	265	42	16	42	116	14%	79	2%	5.24	2.2	$8
LIMA Plan	C	2nd Half	216	33	61	8	36	0	282			351	477	828	10	79	33	0.51	284	37	24	39	128	12%	60	0%	5.82	5.4	$7
+/- Score	2	09 Proj	442	64	122	19	72	0	276			340	479	819	9	81	30	0.51	286	41	21	38	126	14%	63	1%	5.60	0.6	$14

Baby steps, but in the right direction. FB trend with steady hr/f hint at a bigger power spike coming. Splits say platoon role is actually good for his owners. Expect more baby steps, but: UP: .290 BA, 27 HR

LaHair,Bryan

			AB	R	H	HR	RBI	SB	Avg	vL	vR	OB	Slg	OPS	bb%	ct%	h%	Eye	xBA	G	L	F	PX	hr/f	SX	SBO	RC/G	RAR	R$
Pos	3	04	0	0	0	0	0	0	0							0			0						0				
Age	26	05	0	0	0	0	0	0	0							0			0						0				
Bats	Left	06 a/a	424	52	121	15	67	3	285			353	441	794	9	78	34	0.46	0				100		49	2%	5.33	-4.6	$13
Health	A	07 aa	552	65	131	10	67	0	238			291	367	658	7	78	29	0.34	0				98		37	1%	3.59	-34.8	$7
PT/Exp	D	08 SEA	* 452	45	103	11	50	1	227	91	281	302	364	666	10	73	28	0.41	240	43	20	38	102	9%	38	3%	3.75	-20.9	$6
Consist	B	1st Half	287	26	61	8	35	1	213			292	370	662	10	74	26	0.44	0				115		44	3%	3.70	-13.9	$3
LIMA Plan	F	2nd Half	165	19	42	3	16	0	252			321	353	674	9	72	33	0.36	219	43	20	38	80	7%	30	2%	3.85	-6.9	$2
+/- Score	6	09 Proj	146	16	35	3	17	0	240			306	369	675	9	75	30	0.38	242	43	20	38	98	8%	35	2%	3.83	-6.3	$2

3-10-.250 in 136 AB at SEA. Got a brief audition in the wake of SEA's shipwreck, but did little to impress, nor to offset his prior body of work. A marginal prospect at best. All but family members can safely tune away.

Laird,Gerald

			AB	R	H	HR	RBI	SB	Avg	vL	vR	OB	Slg	OPS	bb%	ct%	h%	Eye	xBA	G	L	F	PX	hr/f	SX	SBO	RC/G	RAR	R$
Pos	2	04 TEX	147	20	33	1	16	0	224	317	189	283	286	569	8	76	29	0.34	214	44	19	36	48	2%	51	3%	2.43	-8.6	$1
Age	29	05 TEX	* 321	43	86	14	42	8	269			315	457	772	6	85	28	0.44	265	39	15	45	108	11%	104	14%	4.86	7.8	$11
Bats	Right	06 TEX	243	46	72	7	22	3	296	400	241	329	473	803	5	78	36	0.22	257	34	19	46	124	8%	99	7%	5.27	5.8	$8
Health	B	07 TEX	407	48	91	9	47	6	224	239	218	277	349	626	7	75	28	0.29	201	33	12	55	89	5%	94	9%	3.10	-14.9	$6
PT/Exp	C	08 TEX	344	54	95	6	41	2	276	245	288	322	398	720	6	82	32	0.37	258	38	22	41	90	5%	57	7%	4.32	1.3	$9
Consist	D	1st Half	183	32	56	4	25	1	306			349	437	786	6	83	35	0.38	260	43	18	38	92	7%	58	6%	5.08	4.5	$7
LIMA Plan	D	2nd Half	161	22	39	2	16	1	242			291	354	645	6	81	29	0.35	256	32	25	43	87	4%	59	8%	3.44	-3.6	$2
+/- Score	-22	09 Proj	356	52	92	7	40	1	258			305	387	692	6	79	31	0.32	241	36	19	45	92	6%	63	5%	3.96	-3.0	$7

One year, he'll get stronger and turn some of those FB into HR. It's warning track power now, speed skills are gone, and xBA is his true level. The competition is on his heels; needs a change of address to get AB.

Lamb,Mike

			AB	R	H	HR	RBI	SB	Avg	vL	vR	OB	Slg	OPS	bb%	ct%	h%	Eye	xBA	G	L	F	PX	hr/f	SX	SBO	RC/G	RAR	R$
Pos	5	04 HOU	278	38	80	14	58	1	288	349	277	359	511	870	10	77	33	0.49	284	44	22	34	135	19%	70	3%	6.33	9.9	$12
Age	33	05 HOU	322	41	76	12	53	1	236	182	243	285	419	704	6	80	26	0.34	274	42	22	36	111	13%	94	3%	4.06	-6.9	$8
Bats	Left	06 HOU	381	70	117	12	45	2	307	211	324	365	475	840	8	86	33	0.64	276	40	20	39	97	9%	75	5%	5.86	3.8	$14
Health	A	07 HOU	311	45	90	11	40	0	289	362	277	363	453	816	10	86	31	0.80	267	43	18	39	94	11%	46	0%	5.67	0.5	$10
PT/Exp	D	08 2TM	247	22	58	1	32	0	235	67	258	284	320	604	6	87	27	0.52	239	39	19	43	57	1%	64	2%	3.13	-14.8	$2
Consist	C	1st Half	197	17	44	1	26	0	223			271	299	571	6	86	25	0.48	223	37	17	46	50	1%	61	2%	2.71	-14.6	$1
LIMA Plan	D	2nd Half	50	5	14	0	6	0	280			333	400	733	7	88	32	0.67	297	45	25	30	82	0%	74	0%	4.78	-0.5	$1
+/- Score	0	09 Proj	216	27	59	5	28	0	273			332	427	760	8	86	30	0.62	277	42	21	37	93	7%	74	2%	4.95	-1.2	$5

Little other than a hidden injury can explain hr/f collapse (98 FB, one HR!). MIN already on the hook for '09 salary, so someone will give him a shot. With health and the right venue, he could rebound. Reserve round fodder.

Langerhans,Ryan

			AB	R	H	HR	RBI	SB	Avg	vL	vR	OB	Slg	OPS	bb%	ct%	h%	Eye	xBA	G	L	F	PX	hr/f	SX	SBO	RC/G	RAR	R$
Pos	7	04 aaa	456	91	126	18	63	4	276			363	471	834	12	79	32	0.65	0				125		79	10%	6.01	10.9	$17
Age	29	05 ATL	326	48	87	8	42	0	267	298	261	342	426	768	10	77	33	0.49	276	40	26	33	114	10%	66	2%	5.16	-1.7	$9
Bats	Left	06 ATL	315	46	76	7	28	1	241	308	232	345	378	723	14	71	32	0.55	232	41	21	38	96	8%	72	3%	4.76	-4.6	$5
Health	A	07 2TM	* 261	37	47	7	25	4	181	219	157	275	314	590	11	63	26	0.35	197	44	13	43	105	10%	102	8%	2.74	-20.7	$2
PT/Exp	D	08 WAS	* 324	47	79	5	36	11	243	217	239	351	367	718	14	73	32	0.62	250	44	25	31	93	6%	121	13%	4.75	-6.5	$8
Consist	F	1st Half	205	27	49	2	24	10	240			333	321	654	12	75	31	0.55	269	48	33	19	64	6%	108	18%	3.77	-10.2	$5
LIMA Plan	D	2nd Half	119	20	30	3	12	1	249			381	445	826	18	70	33	0.71	262	42	22	36	144	10%	98	4%	6.50	3.8	$3
+/- Score	18	09 Proj	181	27	43	4	19	3	238			342	382	725	14	70	32	0.54	236	43	20	37	107	9%	102	8%	4.81	-3.1	$4

3-12-.234 in 111 AB at WAS. A few signs of skills life, although even those just returned him to being decent. If he was 22 with this kind of 2H PX spike, we'd be interested. But at 29, what we see is his peak flying by.

Larish,Jeff

			AB	R	H	HR	RBI	SB	Avg	vL	vR	OB	Slg	OPS	bb%	ct%	h%	Eye	xBA	G	L	F	PX	hr/f	SX	SBO	RC/G	RAR	R$
Pos	5	04	0	0	0	0	0	0	0							0			0						0				
Age	26	05	0	0	0	0	0	0	0							0			0						0				
Bats	Left	06	0	0	0	0	0	0	0							0			0						0				
Health	A	07 aa	454	66	109	25	93	5	241			354	460	815	15	76	26	0.74	0				139		68	5%	5.82	7.8	$15
PT/Exp	F	08 DET	* 488	51	109	18	67	2	223	250	260	292	388	680	9	74	27	0.37	247	44	19	37	114	13%	48	4%	3.84	-15.6	$8
Consist	D	1st Half	256	28	57	13	46	0	222			302	429	731	10	74	25	0.44	253	52	14	34	137	20%	33	2%	4.52	-2.8	$6
LIMA Plan	F	2nd Half	232	23	52	5	21	2	224			280	343	623	7	74	28	0.29	235	39	22	39	89	7%	61	8%	3.08	-12.9	$2
+/- Score	19	09 Proj	124	15	29	5	20	1	234			319	408	727	11	75	27	0.49	253	43	19	38	118	15%	38	5%	4.53	-1.3	$3

2-16-.260 in 104 AB at DET. Hit 14 HR by mid-May, just nine after that. Then didn't impress in stint with DET. It all means his prospect status is fading. Best guess: he peaks in 2 seasons, has HR value for a year or two.

ROD TRUESDELL

LaRoche,Adam

		Year	AB	R	H	HR	RBI	SB	Avg	vL	vR	OB	Slg	OPS	bb%	ct%	h%	Eye	xBA	G	L	F	PX	hr/f	SX	SBO	RC/G	RAR	R$
Pos	3	04 ATL	324	45	90	13	45	0	278	250	280	333	488	821	8	76	33	0.35	278	46	19	35	145	15%	45	0%	5.67	-2.6	$10
Age	29	05 ATL	451	53	117	20	78	0	259	191	269	318	455	773	8	81	28	0.45	283	44	21	34	127	16%	21	2%	4.95	-8.5	$14
Bats	Left	06 ATL	492	89	140	32	90	0	285	241	297	356	561	917	10	74	33	0.43	292	38	21	41	180	21%	41	2%	7.02	14.1	$21
Health	A	07 PIT	563	71	153	21	88	1	272	299	262	344	458	802	10	77	32	0.47	264	36	21	44	130	11%	31	1%	5.51	-9.9	$16
PT/Exp	A	08 PIT	492	66	133	25	85	1	270	241	282	342	500	842	10	75	31	0.44	277	37	20	43	154	16%	57	2%	6.02	4.1	$18
Consist	C	1st Half	274	32	63	8	34	1	230			306	376	682	10	76	28	0.45	247	39	21	40	101	10%	56	1%	3.95	-14.8	$5
LIMA Plan	C+	2nd Half	218	34	70	17	51	0	321			388	656	1044	10	75	36	0.44	315	34	19	46	220	22%	57	2%	8.65	17.1	$13
+/- Score	4	09 Proj	506	72	139	27	90	1	275			345	513	858	10	76	32	0.44	282	37	20	42	159	16%	45	2%	6.21	4.8	$19

Crazy fluctuations from month to month, and annually from 1H to 2H. You just have to ride it all out. In the end, the PX rebound was solid and looks to be sustainable. But we feel for you weekly H2H gamers.

LaRoche,Andy

		Year	AB	R	H	HR	RBI	SB	Avg	vL	vR	OB	Slg	OPS	bb%	ct%	h%	Eye	xBA	G	L	F	PX	hr/f	SX	SBO	RC/G	RAR	R$
Pos	5	04	0	0	0	0	0	0	0							0			0						0				
Age	25	05 aa	223	33	53	7	34	2	238			312	377	688	10	80	27	0.55	0				91		59	7%	4.03	-4.1	$6
Bats	Right	06 a/a	432	66	122	17	69	8	282			363	461	824	11	87	29	0.96	0				102		71	10%	5.81	7.0	$16
Health	B	07 LA	* 358	60	92	16	48	4	258	200	235	351	455	806	13	83	27	0.83	279	41	19	40	119	14%	66	6%	5.62	0.1	$11
PT/Exp	D	08 2NL	* 368	47	73	9	40	4	198	143	175	302	293	595	13	85	21	1.00	238	49	16	35	56	8%	61	4%	3.19	-25.4	$4
Consist	C	1st Half	168	31	40	5	21	2	237			366	345	710	17	88	24	1.70	250	35	22	43	59	7%	60	4%	4.86	-2.6	$4
LIMA Plan	C	2nd Half	200	16	33	4	19	2	164			244	249	493	10	82	18	0.60	226	52	15	34	52	7%	48	4%	1.70	-24.1	($1)
+/- Score	26	09 Proj	462	65	111	15	58	5	240			332	375	707	12	84	26	0.86	255	48	16	36	81	11%	59	6%	4.43	-13.5	$11

5-18-.166 in 223 AB at PIT. So, maybe he kept using the wrong "A. Laroche" bat. Kept insisting it was bad luck, and hey, h% says he was right, to a point. Past skills say to bet "rebound" -- if you feel lucky.

LaRue,Jason

		Year	AB	R	H	HR	RBI	SB	Avg	vL	vR	OB	Slg	OPS	bb%	ct%	h%	Eye	xBA	G	L	F	PX	hr/f	SX	SBO	RC/G	RAR	R$
Pos	2	04 CIN	390	46	98	14	55	0	251	274	244	298	431	729	6	72	31	0.24	251	43	19	38	126	13%	49	2%	4.44	7.2	$9
Age	35	05 CIN	361	38	94	14	60	0	260	257	262	336	452	787	10	72	33	0.41	265	42	23	36	145	15%	16	0%	5.42	17.1	$10
Bats	Right	06 CIN	191	22	37	8	21	1	194	235	179	294	346	639	12	73	22	0.53	234	44	20	36	94	16%	37	2%	3.34	-6.0	$2
Health	B	07 KC	169	14	25	4	13	1	148	160	143	226	272	498	9	61	21	0.26	203	48	17	35	114	11%	42	3%	1.27	-17.0	($2)
PT/Exp	F	08 STL	164	17	35	4	21	0	213	196	220	279	348	627	8	88	22	0.75	259	39	18	43	80	6%	46	0%	3.46	-3.8	$2
Consist	F	1st Half	87	11	21	3	11	0	241			327	402	729	11	91	24	1.38	270	33	20	47	85	8%	60	0%	4.82	1.6	$2
LIMA Plan	F	2nd Half	77	6	14	1	10	0	182			222	286	508	5	84	20	0.33	241	46	16	38	75	4%	27	0%	1.83	-5.9	($0)
+/- Score	42	09 Proj	123	12	25	3	14	0	203			273	332	605	9	77	24	0.41	235	42	18	39	89	9%	32	1%	2.89	-5.2	$1

CON:
- 2006
- 2007
- 2008

PRO:
- One less player you need to worry about on your draft list.

Lee,Carlos

		Year	AB	R	H	HR	RBI	SB	Avg	vL	vR	OB	Slg	OPS	bb%	ct%	h%	Eye	xBA	G	L	F	PX	hr/f	SX	SBO	RC/G	RAR	R$
Pos	7	04 CHW	591	103	180	31	99	11	305	308	303	363	525	887	8	85	31	0.63	284	33	20	47	126	13%	76	10%	6.30	22.2	$27
Age	32	05 MIL	618	85	164	32	114	13	265	261	267	327	487	814	8	86	26	0.66	294	34	20	46	134	13%	76	11%	5.47	2.4	$26
Bats	Right	06 2TM	624	102	187	37	116	19	300	313	296	359	540	899	9	90	29	0.89	311	40	20	40	128	16%	95	12%	6.42	20.8	$31
Health	B	07 HOU	627	93	190	32	119	10	303	338	292	357	528	885	8	90	30	0.84	297	38	16	46	126	12%	67	9%	6.26	15.6	$29
PT/Exp	A	08 HOU	436	61	137	28	100	4	314	330	309	368	569	937	8	89	30	0.76	317	35	21	44	142	17%	49	4%	6.77	15.9	$24
Consist	A	1st Half	309	40	86	18	62	4	278			326	528	854	7	89	27	0.63	316	35	21	44	144	15%	56	7%	5.81	3.4	$14
LIMA Plan	D+	2nd Half	127	21	51	10	38	0	402			465	669	1134	11	89	40	1.07	319	35	23	42	137	21%	15	0%	9.08	10.9	$11
+/- Score	-25	09 Proj	608	93	188	38	125	8	309			368	553	922	9	89	30	0.85	308	36	20	44	133	16%	61	6%	6.65	21.1	$32

On his way to career season before broken pinkie. But only skills change was hr/f, and that was within a normal range of variance (& no boost from HOU park). Bid expecting not the full '08, but '06-'07 with fewer SB.

Lee,Derrek

		Year	AB	R	H	HR	RBI	SB	Avg	vL	vR	OB	Slg	OPS	bb%	ct%	h%	Eye	xBA	G	L	F	PX	hr/f	SX	SBO	RC/G	RAR	R$
Pos	3	04 CHC	605	90	168	32	98	12	278	306	271	351	504	855	10	79	31	0.53	282	41	19	40	141	17%	75	10%	6.09	2.4	$25
Age	33	05 CHC	594	120	199	46	107	15	335	333	339	418	662	1080	13	82	35	0.78	340	39	22	39	202	24%	104	10%	8.91	51.7	$41
Bats	Right	06 CHC	175	30	50	8	30	8	286	292	283	375	474	849	13	77	33	0.61	263	41	20	38	118	16%	75	21%	6.19	1.0	$8
Health	C	07 CHC	567	91	180	22	82	6	317	339	312	393	513	907	11	80	37	0.62	282	41	21	38	129	13%	60	6%	6.86	11.3	$24
PT/Exp	B	08 CHC	623	93	181	20	90	8	291	306	286	363	462	825	10	81	33	0.60	283	45	21	34	113	12%	88	5%	5.81	1.3	$23
Consist	B	1st Half	333	56	97	15	51	4	291			360	498	859	10	83	31	0.63	297	47	20	34	126	16%	82	6%	6.11	3.6	$14
LIMA Plan	C	2nd Half	290	37	84	5	39	4	290			366	421	787	11	79	35	0.56	267	43	24	34	97	7%	76	4%	5.44	-2.3	$9
+/- Score	10	09 Proj	592	92	176	22	89	6	297			374	483	858	11	80	34	0.61	280	43	21	36	122	13%	68	6%	6.24	6.1	$23

He's obviously not the '05 Lee. But is he even the '07 Lee? 2H hr/f very out of character, and should revert. But FB trending down even during 1H HR streak. Taken all together, projection shows his new, non-2005 level.

Lewis,Fred

		Year	AB	R	H	HR	RBI	SB	Avg	vL	vR	OB	Slg	OPS	bb%	ct%	h%	Eye	xBA	G	L	F	PX	hr/f	SX	SBO	RC/G	RAR	R$
Pos	7	04	0	0	0	0	0	0	0							0			0						0				
Age	28	05 aa	508	62	121	5	38	24	238			311	340	651	10	78	29	0.49	0				73		128	27%	3.68	-21.3	$11
Bats	Left	06 aaa	439	64	106	9	43	14	241			320	379	698	10	82	28	0.64	0				80		130	20%	4.31	-12.2	$10
Health	A	07 SF	* 328	57	85	8	42	11	259	276	289	327	413	739	9	80	30	0.50	266	55	15	30	92	10%	145	14%	4.71	-6.2	$11
PT/Exp	D	08 SF	468	81	132	9	40	21	282	270	285	353	440	793	10	74	37	0.41	263	54	18	28	109	9%	150	20%	5.58	2.1	$18
Consist	B	1st Half	277	51	78	6	23	13	282			360	458	819	11	74	36	0.47	274	54	18	28	122	11%	146	23%	5.98	4.5	$11
LIMA Plan	C+	2nd Half	191	30	54	3	17	8	283			341	414	755	8	73	37	0.33	248	54	19	28	90	8%	144	16%	4.98	-2.4	$7
+/- Score	-19	09 Proj	494	80	131	10	48	23	265			334	410	745	9	77	33	0.45	263	54	18	28	94	9%	150	21%	4.84	-7.8	$17

Seems to want to be a slugger (ct% trend). Milked a little PX out of the deal, but to what end? Legs are his meal ticket. Hit rate shows BA at risk if he doesn't wise up. Should exploit GB ways, hit it, and RUN, Lewis, RUN!

Lillibridge,Brent

		Year	AB	R	H	HR	RBI	SB	Avg	vL	vR	OB	Slg	OPS	bb%	ct%	h%	Eye	xBA	G	L	F	PX	hr/f	SX	SBO	RC/G	RAR	R$
Pos	6	04	0	0	0	0	0	0	0							0			0						0				
Age	25	05	0	0	0	0	0	0	0							0			0						0				
Bats	Right	06	0	0	0	0	0	0	0							0			0						0				
Health	A	07 a/a	525	67	135	11	50	36	257			302	371	673	6	79	31	0.30	0				75		126	36%	3.68	-10.8	$17
PT/Exp	F	08 ATL	* 435	46	83	4	39	21	190	171	222	241	291	532	6	76	24	0.28	211	45	11	44	73	3%	145	35%	1.96	-37.7	$5
Consist	D	1st Half	230	18	40	1	13	13	172			220	226	446	6	75	23	0.24	0	64	7	29	43	2%	112	42%	0.73	-30.0	$1
LIMA Plan	F	2nd Half	205	28	43	3	26	8	210			265	364	629	7	77	26	0.32	232	39	12	49	106	4%	154	26%	3.30	-8.6	$4
+/- Score	18	09 Proj	197	23	45	4	24	11	228			277	352	629	6	77	28	0.29	219	44	11	45	83	5%	131	33%	3.15	-8.1	$5

1-8-.200 in 80 AB at ATL. Skills collapse at higher levels not a good sign for this one-time hot prospect. Super SX, but as always, you can't steal first. Still youngish; lure of big SB from SS will keep us watching from afar.

Lind,Adam

		Year	AB	R	H	HR	RBI	SB	Avg	vL	vR	OB	Slg	OPS	bb%	ct%	h%	Eye	xBA	G	L	F	PX	hr/f	SX	SBO	RC/G	RAR	R$
Pos	7	04	0	0	0	0	0	0	0							0			0						0				
Age	25	05	0	0	0	0	0	0	0							0			0						0				
Bats	Left	06 TOR	* 517	66	171	26	91	3	331	444	353	389	559	948	9	79	38	0.44	278	35	19	46	148	14%	39	3%	7.21	27.6	$23
Health	A	07 TOR	* 464	51	118	17	70	1	254	194	251	297	420	717	6	78	29	0.28	259	45	19	37	109	13%	46	3%	4.15	-12.1	$11
PT/Exp	C	08 TOR	* 515	69	148	15	83	3	288	253	294	330	458	788	6	82	33	0.34	285	51	19	30	110	12%	88	3%	5.11	3.7	$17
Consist	F	1st Half	228	24	62	8	48	1	274			330	461	790	8	82	31	0.45	275	68	6	26	123	16%	61	3%	5.23	2.5	$7
LIMA Plan	C	2nd Half	287	45	86	7	35	2	300			330	456	786	4	82	35	0.25	281	49	21	31	101	10%	104	3%	5.00	1.2	$10
+/- Score	18	09 Proj	521	65	148	19	82	2	284			328	468	796	6	80	32	0.33	279	48	19	33	119	14%	69	3%	5.18	3.5	$17

9-40-.282 in 326 AB at TOR. Infamous Shandler Tout Wars pick finally got the call, and put up tantalizing BPI's. Solid, but not quite "put all together." But owns '06 skills -- and they could arrive now. More likely, 2010.

Lo Duca,Paul

		Year	AB	R	H	HR	RBI	SB	Avg	vL	vR	OB	Slg	OPS	bb%	ct%	h%	Eye	xBA	G	L	F	PX	hr/f	SX	SBO	RC/G	RAR	R$
Pos	2	04 2NL	535	68	153	13	80	4	286	314	276	331	421	752	6	91	30	0.73	282	44	20	36	78	7%	64	6%	4.78	14.8	$16
Age	37	05 FLA	445	45	126	6	57	4	283	314	277	334	380	714	7	93	29	1.10	294	45	24	30	61	5%	57	5%	4.52	9.2	$11
Bats	Right	06 NYM	512	80	163	5	49	3	318	336	311	349	428	777	4	93	34	0.63	289	45	21	34	71	3%	70	2%	5.02	9.4	$16
Health	C	07 NYM	445	46	121	9	54	2	272	341	245	309	378	687	5	93	28	0.73	291	48	23	29	60	8%	54	2%	4.04	-5.0	$9
PT/Exp	C	08 2NL	173	16	42	0	15	1	243	254	237	303	295	598	8	94	26	1.36	267	45	22	33	40	0%	43	2%	3.42	-4.1	$1
Consist	B	1st Half	72	7	15	0	4	0	208			269	264	533	8	94	22	1.50	241	50	15	35	42	0%	32	0%	2.76	-3.2	($0)
LIMA Plan	F	2nd Half	101	9	27	0	11	1	267			327	317	644	8	93	29	1.29	282	42	27	31	38	0%	42	3%	3.89	-0.9	$2
+/- Score	5	09 Proj	98	10	27	2	10	1	276			323	382	706	7	93	28	1.02	286	46	22	32	64	6%	38	2%	4.37	0.4	$2

Year-long hand problems were certainly a big part of the BPI skid, but he's been in decline for a while. Elite ct% still means BA upside, but with dwindling AB, benefit will be small. Now JA$G (Just Another $1 Guy).

ROD TRUESDELL

Loney,James

			AB	R	H	HR	RBI	SB	Avg	vL	vR	OB	Slg	OPS	bb%	ct%	h%	Eye	xBA	G	L	F	PX	hr/f	SX	SBO	RC/G	RAR	R$
Pos	3	04 aa	395	37	88	4	34	5	223			295	303	598	9	83	26	0.60	0				54		59	11%	3.04	-29.8	$3
Age	24	05 aa	500	59	121	9	51	0	242			306	350	656	8	86	27	0.65	0				71		37	4%	3.74	-24.2	$7
Bats	Left	06 LA	* 468	73	156	10	74	8	333	350	268	379	503	882	7	92	35	0.96	286	49	12	39	96	6%	96	11%	6.32	4.0	$21
Health	A	07 LA	* 577	63	170	16	93	2	295	319	336	350	455	805	8	84	33	0.54	279	42	22	36	98	9%	61	2%	5.41	-11.5	$18
PT/Exp	B	08 LA	595	66	172	13	90	7	289	249	305	339	434	773	7	86	32	0.53	282	44	22	34	90	7%	84	7%	5.03	-11.8	$19
Consist	B	1st Half	301	38	91	6	41	3	302			360	449	808	8	86	34	0.64	278	46	19	35	91	7%	88	7%	5.54	-1.6	$10
LIMA Plan	C	2nd Half	294	28	81	7	49	4	276			317	418	736	6	85	30	0.42	287	41	25	33	90	8%	78	7%	4.50	-10.4	$9
+/- Score	-1	09 Proj	**585**	**67**	**170**	**13**	**88**	**6**	**291**			**342**	**436**	**778**	**7**	**86**	**32**	**0.56**	**282**	**43**	**22**	**35**	**90**	**8%**	**75**	**6%**	**5.09**	**-12.9**	**$18**

Sept fade kept him from hitting .300 on the year, but high ct%, LD provide a solid BA base. PX is now well-established, and combined with consistent GB bias, trumps any optimism for age-related HR growth.

Longoria,Evan

			AB	R	H	HR	RBI	SB	Avg	vL	vR	OB	Slg	OPS	bb%	ct%	h%	Eye	xBA	G	L	F	PX	hr/f	SX	SBO	RC/G	RAR	R$
Pos	5	04	0	0	0	0	0	0	0							0			0						0				
Age	23	05	0	0	0	0	0	0	0							0			0						0				
Bats	Right	06 aa	105	15	27	6	20	2	257			264	476	740	1	80	27	0.05	0				128		78	18%	4.08	-3.6	$4
Health	A	07 a/a	485	91	142	25	90	4	292			382	507	889	13	80	32	0.73	0				134		65	3%	6.63	18.7	$22
PT/Exp	D	08 TAM	448	67	122	27	85	7	272	242	284	340	531	871	9	73	32	0.38	285	39	20	42	180	20%	91	6%	6.42	19.7	$19
Consist	C	1st Half	262	41	70	15	47	4	267			347	523	870	11	74	31	0.46	288	37	21	43	179	18%	79	6%	6.47	11.9	$11
LIMA Plan	C+	2nd Half	186	26	52	12	38	3	280			330	543	873	7	72	33	0.26	282	42	18	40	181	22%	82	7%	6.35	7.7	$9
+/- Score	30	09 Proj	**529**	**85**	**147**	**32**	**101**	**7**	**278**			**342**	**526**	**868**	**9**	**76**	**31**	**0.41**	**286**	**40**	**19**	**41**	**161**	**20%**	**81**	**6%**	**6.20**	**19.8**	**$23**

Spectacular debut - now what? Hard to believe, but there's room for improvement. Low ct% and BA vs LHP held back BA. Needs to show he can repeat hr/f, but power output will sustain over a full season of ABs.

Lopez,Felipe

			AB	R	H	HR	RBI	SB	Avg	vL	vR	OB	Slg	OPS	bb%	ct%	h%	Eye	xBA	G	L	F	PX	hr/f	SX	SBO	RC/G	RAR	R$
Pos	4	04 CIN	* 557	75	135	15	66	3	242	292	226	299	384	683	7	75	30	0.33	240	44	18	38	96	9%	72	6%	3.87	-12.5	$11
Age	28	05 CIN	580	97	169	23	85	15	291	244	312	355	486	841	9	81	33	0.51	301	54	20	27	124	18%	115	13%	5.89	21.8	$26
Bats	Both	06 2NL	617	98	169	11	52	44	274	246	285	358	381	739	12	80	33	0.64	252	50	19	30	69	7%	118	27%	4.83	4.2	$24
Health	A	07 WAS	603	70	148	9	50	24	245	269	235	306	352	658	8	82	29	0.49	259	50	20	30	67	6%	113	20%	3.68	-18.5	$13
PT/Exp	A	08 2NL	481	64	136	6	46	8	283	306	270	342	387	728	8	83	33	0.52	261	50	19	31	73	5%	76	11%	4.57	-2.8	$13
Consist	C	1st Half	256	25	62	2	20	4	242			314	324	639	10	82	29	0.60	241	47	18	35	63	3%	51	11%	3.57	-9.3	$3
LIMA Plan	D+	2nd Half	225	39	74	4	26	4	329			373	458	831	7	84	38	0.43	282	53	20	27	84	8%	99	11%	5.68	5.5	$10
+/- Score	-11	09 Proj	**480**	**67**	**133**	**8**	**47**	**10**	**277**			**338**	**392**	**730**	**8**	**82**	**33**	**0.51**	**263**	**51**	**19**	**30**	**76**	**7%**	**87**	**12%**	**4.58**	**-1.8**	**$13**

Regained prior BA levels, can power or speed follow? 2005 hr/f was outlier, double-digit HRs won't return. SX and SBO trends, plus poor SB success (< 50% '07-08) say he's lost a step at 28. Hey, it happens.

Lopez,Jose

			AB	R	H	HR	RBI	SB	Avg	vL	vR	OB	Slg	OPS	bb%	ct%	h%	Eye	xBA	G	L	F	PX	hr/f	SX	SBO	RC/G	RAR	R$
Pos	4	04 SEA	* 482	66	130	17	60	5	270	214	238	304	440	744	5	89	27	0.44	291	42	21	38	99	11%	66	8%	4.52	6.2	$13
Age	25	05 SEA	* 372	44	103	6	54	6	277	273	235	303	430	733	4	88	30	0.30	289	41	19	40	110	5%	67	17%	4.43	3.2	$10
Bats	Right	06 SEA	603	78	170	10	79	5	282	331	265	312	405	716	4	87	31	0.33	268	49	18	33	72	6%	100	5%	4.21	1.5	$15
Health	A	07 SEA	524	58	132	11	62	2	252	244	254	279	355	634	4	88	27	0.31	249	46	17	37	61	6%	58	4%	3.22	-12.1	$9
PT/Exp	A	08 SEA	644	80	191	17	89	6	297	298	296	325	443	767	4	87	31	0.40	289	44	20	36	91	8%	64	6%	4.77	-2.1	$21
Consist	C	1st Half	395	47	115	6	45	3	290			313	394	707	3	90	31	0.34	277	46	21	34	66	5%	67	4%	4.09	-8.9	$10
LIMA Plan	C	2nd Half	249	33	76	11	44	3	307			343	520	863	5	88	31	0.49	312	42	20	38	130	13%	52	8%	5.87	6.7	$11
+/- Score	-3	09 Proj	**613**	**76**	**173**	**19**	**90**	**5**	**282**			**312**	**442**	**754**	**4**	**88**	**29**	**0.38**	**286**	**45**	**19**	**36**	**96**	**10%**	**65**	**6%**	**4.60**	**2.3**	**$19**

Nice growth season, but can he maintain it? Rise in FB%, hr/f drove 2H power surge. High ct% will keep his BA solid. There's more here, if he can hold those 2nd half FB gains...
UP: 20-25 HR, .300 BA

Loretta,Mark

			AB	R	H	HR	RBI	SB	Avg	vL	vR	OB	Slg	OPS	bb%	ct%	h%	Eye	xBA	G	L	F	PX	hr/f	SX	SBO	RC/G	RAR	R$
Pos	4	04 SD	620	108	208	16	76	5	335	352	329	392	495	887	9	93	34	1.29	300	40	22	38	94	7%	72	4%	6.47	30.3	$27
Age	37	05 SD	404	54	113	3	38	8	280	309	269	352	347	698	10	92	30	1.32	281	40	28	32	44	3%	80	9%	4.52	-0.5	$11
Bats	Right	06 BOS	635	75	181	5	59	4	285	274	290	336	361	697	7	90	31	0.78	272	35	27	38	51	2%	56	3%	4.27	2.6	$12
Health	B	07 HOU	460	52	132	4	41	1	287	317	278	349	372	721	9	91	31	1.07	266	41	22	36	54	3%	46	2%	4.67	-0.3	$9
PT/Exp	B	08 HOU	261	27	73	4	38	0	280	330	250	352	383	735	10	89	30	0.97	286	37	27	36	69	5%	20	0%	4.83	0.4	$6
Consist	A	1st Half	139	12	36	3	21	0	259			327	381	708	9	87	28	0.78	291	34	28	38	79	7%	14	0%	4.41	-1.5	$3
LIMA Plan	F	2nd Half	122	15	37	1	17	0	303			380	385	765	11	90	33	1.25	281	39	26	34	57	3%	25	0%	5.29	1.7	$4
+/- Score	-27	09 Proj	**258**	**30**	**74**	**3**	**31**	**1**	**287**			**353**	**376**	**730**	**9**	**90**	**31**	**1.02**	**277**	**38**	**26**	**36**	**59**	**4%**	**36**	**2%**	**4.76**	**0.4**	**$6**

Father Time has not been kind to this skill set. Only good plate control remains, and that lacks value without accompanying power or speed. A suitable in-season stop-gap, but no reason to go here on draft day.

Lowell,Mike

			AB	R	H	HR	RBI	SB	Avg	vL	vR	OB	Slg	OPS	bb%	ct%	h%	Eye	xBA	G	L	F	PX	hr/f	SX	SBO	RC/G	RAR	R$
Pos	5	04 FLA	598	87	175	27	85	5	293	344	279	361	505	866	10	87	30	0.83	286	32	19	49	124	11%	64	4%	6.19	18.8	$23
Age	35	05 FLA	500	56	118	8	58	4	236	308	222	300	360	660	8	88	25	0.79	262	32	21	47	84	4%	75	3%	3.91	-13.0	$8
Bats	Right	06 BOS	573	79	163	20	80	2	284	241	302	339	475	813	8	89	29	0.77	302	38	22	41	114	10%	48	3%	5.53	8.4	$17
Health	B	07 BOS	589	79	191	21	120	3	324	323	325	380	501	881	8	88	34	0.75	277	36	18	46	107	9%	55	3%	6.29	22.2	$25
PT/Exp	A	08 BOS	419	58	115	17	73	2	274	318	263	335	461	795	8	85	29	0.62	280	32	21	47	116	10%	43	4%	5.28	4.8	$14
Consist	B	1st Half	247	38	75	12	47	1	304			363	526	889	9	87	31	0.74	301	31	21	48	135	12%	41	3%	6.37	10.1	$11
LIMA Plan	D+	2nd Half	172	20	40	5	26	1	233			294	366	660	8	83	26	0.50	249	35	20	45	86	8%	44	5%	3.64	-6.5	$3
+/- Score	-18	09 Proj	**482**	**64**	**135**	**17**	**81**	**1**	**280**			**339**	**455**	**795**	**8**	**86**	**30**	**0.66**	**277**	**34**	**20**	**46**	**108**	**9%**	**48**	**3%**	**5.30**	**5.7**	**$15**

Injuries slowed him in 2nd half, leading to hip surgery. Pre-injury, 1H skills were stable, with no sign of mid-30s decline. Question is whether his health accelerates the inevitable decline. Bid cautiously.

Lowrie,Jed

			AB	R	H	HR	RBI	SB	Avg	vL	vR	OB	Slg	OPS	bb%	ct%	h%	Eye	xBA	G	L	F	PX	hr/f	SX	SBO	RC/G	RAR	R$
Pos	65	04	0	0	0	0	0	0	0							0			0						0				
Age	25	05	0	0	0	0	0	0	0							0			0						0				
Bats	Both	06	0	0	0	0	0	0	0							0			0						0				
Health	A	07 a/a	497	71	143	10	60	4	288			371	471	842	12	84	33	0.85	0				126		77	6%	6.22	25.9	$14
PT/Exp	F	08 BOS	* 458	62	116	6	72	2	253	338	222	340	395	734	12	77	32	0.57	259	32	25	43	111	4%	81	2%	4.88	7.3	$10
Consist	C	1st Half	206	31	56	5	30	1	273			349	423	772	10	81	32	0.63	287	47	24	29	104	10%	68	2%	5.21	5.2	$6
LIMA Plan	B	2nd Half	252	31	60	1	42	1	237			332	371	704	12	74	32	0.54	247	28	25	46	116	1%	84	1%	4.60	2.0	$4
+/- Score	6	09 Proj	**503**	**69**	**134**	**8**	**72**	**3**	**266**			**352**	**426**	**778**	**12**	**80**	**32**	**0.66**	**273**	**31**	**25**	**44**	**118**	**4%**	**80**	**3%**	**5.44**	**15.8**	**$12**

2-46-.258 in 260 AB at BOS. Can take a BB, but fine AA ct% didn't translate to the majors in first try. Mix MLE ct% with MLB LD%, and BA will be an asset. 2H wrist woes likely explain poor hr/f, so there's more upside.

Ludwick,Ryan

			AB	R	H	HR	RBI	SB	Avg	vL	vR	OB	Slg	OPS	bb%	ct%	h%	Eye	xBA	G	L	F	PX	hr/f	SX	SBO	RC/G	RAR	R$
Pos	97	04 CLE	* 242	24	52	8	29	0	217			259	387	646	5	72	27	0.20	0				124		24	0%	3.27	-10.6	$3
Age	30	05 CLE	* 229	27	38	7	16	0	168			233	303	536	8	77	19	0.37	191	32	7	61	89	6%	61	5%	1.95	-20.8	($0)
Bats	Right	06 aaa	508	71	118	23	70	2	233			291	434	725	8	68	30	0.25	0				145		63	7%	4.51	-10.9	$11
Health	A	07 STL	* 409	59	105	19	75	5	257	221	298	311	459	770	7	77	29	0.34	259	37	16	47	134	13%	57	10%	4.90	0.2	$14
PT/Exp	C	08 STL	538	104	161	37	113	4	299	266	316	372	591	963	10	73	35	0.42	296	27	26	47	198	20%	81	6%	7.69	37.4	$30
Consist	D	1st Half	256	51	73	16	56	4	285			362	574	937	11	75	32	0.48	301	26	28	46	196	18%	105	8%	7.32	15.4	$14
LIMA Plan	C+	2nd Half	282	53	88	21	57	0	312			380	606	987	10	71	37	0.38	292	29	25	47	201	23%	47	4%	8.07	22.2	$16
+/- Score	-39	09 Proj	**575**	**94**	**155**	**32**	**104**	**4**	**270**			**333**	**511**	**845**	**9**	**73**	**32**	**0.36**	**274**	**30**	**23**	**47**	**164**	**16%**	**66**	**6%**	**6.02**	**16.1**	**$23**

If we knew where to look... Turns out 156 PX in 2H 2007 foretold this breakout. Likely LD regression, poor ct% now put the BA at risk. G/L/F and hr/f say the power is real; pay for that, but not the BA.

Lugo,Julio

			AB	R	H	HR	RBI	SB	Avg	vL	vR	OB	Slg	OPS	bb%	ct%	h%	Eye	xBA	G	L	F	PX	hr/f	SX	SBO	RC/G	RAR	R$
Pos	6	04 TAM	581	83	160	7	75	21	275	300	267	337	396	733	9	82	33	0.51	264	49	18	33	84	5%	121	16%	4.67	3.4	$18
Age	33	05 TAM	616	89	182	6	57	39	295	306	291	359	403	762	9	88	33	0.85	282	49	20	31	71	4%	131	26%	5.11	9.6	$24
Bats	Right	06 2TM	435	69	121	12	37	24	278	263	284	338	421	758	8	83	31	0.51	268	47	20	34	87	10%	114	27%	4.86	6.0	$16
Health	D	07 BOS	570	71	135	8	73	33	237	226	241	296	349	645	8	86	26	0.59	262	46	17	37	78	4%	120	28%	3.62	-11.6	$15
PT/Exp	B	08 BOS	261	27	70	1	22	12	268	283	264	353	330	682	12	80	33	0.67	247	60	18	23	51	2%	72	18%	4.18	-1.2	$6
Consist	B	1st Half	234	23	63	1	18	11	269			355	338	692	12	81	33	0.69	250	58	18	24	57	2%	72	18%	4.33	-0.0	$6
LIMA Plan	D	2nd Half	27	4	7	0	4	1	259			333	259	593	10	78	33	0.50	219	76	14	10	0	0%	72	20%	2.84	-1.2	$1
+/- Score	-38	09 Proj	**313**	**41**	**80**	**4**	**30**	**21**	**256**			**325**	**360**	**685**	**9**	**83**	**29**	**0.62**	**264**	**50**	**18**	**31**	**74**	**5%**	**110**	**29%**	**4.12**	**-2.1**	**$10**

Lost 2H to quad injury, but he was sidelined with a sore back as early as spring training, so this looks like a total injury-marred season. The problem: At 33, with two off-years, the young footsteps start gaining.

DAVE ADLER

Maier,Mitch

			AB	R	H	HR	RBI	SB	Avg	vL	vR	OB	Slg	OPS	bb%	ct%	h%	Eye	xBA	G	L	F	PX	hr/f	SX	SBO	RC/G	RAR	R$
Pos	8	04	0	0	0	0	0	0	0							0			0						0				
Age	26	05 aa	322	40	68	5	35	7	211			236	334	571	3	89	22	0.30	0				76		131	20%	2.63	-18.1	$4
Bats	Left	06 aa	543	70	140	10	68	10	257			297	385	681	5	86	28	0.40	0				78		91	19%	3.89	-10.9	$12
Health	A	07 aa	544	58	127	10	48	5	233			268	349	617	5	85	26	0.32	0				73		83	6%	3.06	-24.2	$6
PT/Exp	D	08 KC	* 436	54	122	6	41	9	279	273	293	320	387	707	6	87	31	0.46	280	48	22	30	71	6%	86	12%	4.20	-14.4	$11
Consist	B	1st Half	258	30	68	5	25	5	264			296	382	678	4	91	28	0.50	0				77		67	13%	3.88	-11.1	$6
LIMA Plan	F	2nd Half	178	24	54	2	16	5	301			352	396	747	7	82	36	0.43	258	48	22	30	63	4%	102	12%	4.73	-3.1	$5
+/- Score	-7	09 Proj	166	20	43	3	16	3	259			298	371	670	5	86	29	0.39	277	48	22	30	74	6%	86	13%	3.74	-6.0	$3

0-9-.286 in 91 AB at KC. Nothing much here on the skills scale, but did take a huge step up in the 2nd half with an OBA significantly north of .300. Can we draw conclusions from a 178 AB sample? Probably not.

Markakis,Nick

			AB	R	H	HR	RBI	SB	Avg	vL	vR	OB	Slg	OPS	bb%	ct%	h%	Eye	xBA	G	L	F	PX	hr/f	SX	SBO	RC/G	RAR	R$
Pos	9	04	0	0	0	0	0	0	0							0			0						0				
Age	25	05 aa	120	19	39	3	28	0	325			413	533	946	13	78	40	0.69	0				158		65	3%	7.68	8.7	$6
Bats	Left	06 BAL	491	72	143	16	62	2	291	286	293	348	448	796	8	85	32	0.60	285	51	20	29	92	13%	67	1%	5.29	-5.0	$15
Health	A	07 BAL	637	97	191	23	112	18	300	274	311	361	485	846	9	82	33	0.54	284	45	18	37	120	12%	98	13%	5.94	7.8	$28
PT/Exp	A	08 BAL	599	106	182	20	88	10	304	297	310	403	487	890	14	81	35	0.87	292	46	21	33	126	12%	67	8%	6.86	24.9	$25
Consist	B	1st Half	307	48	88	12	40	8	287			390	469	859	14	78	33	0.78	282	43	23	34	125	15%	63	11%	6.46	9.6	$12
LIMA Plan	B	2nd Half	292	58	94	8	48	2	322			416	507	923	14	84	36	1.00	302	49	19	32	128	10%	65	5%	7.27	15.0	$13
+/- Score	7	09 Proj	587	98	179	24	105	9	305			387	513	900	12	82	34	0.74	300	47	20	34	136	15%	76	8%	6.78	22.8	$26

Decline in counting stats hides the fact that skills improved. Still in growth phase, so more improvement is likely. All we ask for are a few more fly balls. If he complies... UP: 30 HR

Marte,Andy

			AB	R	H	HR	RBI	SB	Avg	vL	vR	OB	Slg	OPS	bb%	ct%	h%	Eye	xBA	G	L	F	PX	hr/f	SX	SBO	RC/G	RAR	R$
Pos	5	04 aa	387	48	101	21	64	1	260			352	499	851	12	78	29	0.63	0				152		38	2%	6.19	13.6	$12
Age	25	05 ATL	* 446	53	117	20	76	0	262	174	118	362	468	830	14	82	28	0.88	258	35	13	52	130	10%	32	3%	5.99	15.9	$14
Bats	Right	06 CLE	* 521	69	128	19	69	1	246	227	225	310	433	742	8	78	28	0.42	256	34	17	48	125	9%	54	1%	4.66	-5.3	$11
Health	A	07 CLE	* 409	44	97	14	60	0	237	278	154	274	396	671	5	84	25	0.32	252	29	19	52	99	8%	35	0%	3.60	-15.5	$7
PT/Exp	D	08 CLE	235	21	52	3	17	1	221	293	198	265	315	580	6	78	27	0.27	209	34	16	49	69	3%	54	6%	2.51	-17.2	$1
Consist	C	1st Half	55	3	7	0	0	1	127			158	145	303	4	73	18	0.13	142	25	15	60	18	0%	68	25%	-1.37	-12.0	($1)
LIMA Plan	F	2nd Half	180	18	45	3	17	0	250			297	367	664	6	79	30	0.32	229	37	17	46	83	5%	50	2%	3.62	-6.7	$2
+/- Score	-7	09 Proj	243	24	61	6	25	1	251			299	380	679	6	79	30	0.32	224	32	16	51	87	6%	51	4%	3.77	-8.0	$4

Forget first impressions; he's running out of time to make ANY impression. Eye, PX, hr/f all heading the wrong way; can't hit RHP. 2nd half BA, PX are a glimmer of hope, but he needs to produce now.

Martinez,Victor

			AB	R	H	HR	RBI	SB	Avg	vL	vR	OB	Slg	OPS	bb%	ct%	h%	Eye	xBA	G	L	F	PX	hr/f	SX	SBO	RC/G	RAR	R$
Pos	2	04 CLE	520	77	147	23	108	0	283	282	283	357	492	849	10	87	29	0.87	284	40	16	44	123	12%	38	1%	6.05	25.2	$19
Age	30	05 CLE	547	73	167	20	80	0	305	274	320	377	475	852	10	86	33	0.81	286	48	21	32	106	13%	22	1%	6.08	30.8	$20
Bats	Both	06 CLE	572	82	181	16	93	0	316	290	332	392	465	857	11	86	35	0.91	280	44	22	34	92	9%	25	0%	6.23	27.9	$20
Health	C	07 CLE	562	78	169	25	114	0	301	289	307	370	505	876	10	86	31	0.82	297	42	20	38	126	13%	22	0%	6.31	31.2	$22
PT/Exp	B	08 CLE	266	30	74	2	35	0	278	339	260	338	365	703	8	88	31	0.75	266	45	22	33	64	3%	26	0%	4.37	1.4	$5
Consist	C	1st Half	198	17	55	0	21	0	278			332	333	665	7	88	31	0.70	259	47	23	30	46	0%	20	0%	3.92	-1.5	$3
LIMA Plan	C	2nd Half	68	13	19	2	14	0	279			355	456	811	11	87	30	0.89	285	38	18	43	118	8%	44	0%	5.70	2.9	$3
+/- Score	5	09 Proj	505	73	149	16	89	0	295			364	463	827	10	87	31	0.83	286	42	20	37	106	10%	29	0%	5.80	21.6	$17

Elbow problems plagued him all year, so let's give him a mulligan. Looked healthy in 57 Sept ABs (2 HR, .288). Even with the power outage, BPIs remain solid. Expect a return to the top of the AL catcher list.

Martin,Russell

			AB	R	H	HR	RBI	SB	Avg	vL	vR	OB	Slg	OPS	bb%	ct%	h%	Eye	xBA	G	L	F	PX	hr/f	SX	SBO	RC/G	RAR	R$
Pos	2	04	0	0	0	0	0	0	0							0			0						0				
Age	26	05 aa	405	67	108	7	48	12	267			361	358	719	13	86	30	1.05	0				57		87	14%	4.74	10.0	$13
Bats	Right	06 LA	* 489	76	136	10	72	10	278	366	265	351	425	776	10	87	31	0.83	290	50	20	30	90	8%	92	12%	5.30	13.5	$16
Health	A	07 LA	540	87	158	19	87	21	293	357	273	371	469	839	11	84	32	0.75	283	48	18	34	108	12%	100	18%	5.99	24.0	$24
PT/Exp	A	08 LA	553	87	155	13	69	18	280	253	291	381	396	777	14	85	31	1.08	271	51	19	30	73	9%	79	12%	5.46	19.7	$21
Consist	B	1st Half	280	41	86	8	37	7	307			403	443	846	14	86	33	1.15	283	51	20	28	84	12%	59	10%	6.26	15.9	$12
LIMA Plan	C+	2nd Half	273	46	69	5	32	11	253			358	348	706	14	84	29	1.02	256	51	18	31	62	7%	90	13%	4.61	3.2	$9
+/- Score	-11	09 Proj	476	76	130	12	65	13	273			365	402	767	13	85	30	0.95	273	50	19	31	81	9%	84	12%	5.25	13.9	$16

No matter how you cut it, 550 AB is a TON of playing time for a demanding position like CA. Workload may have caught up to him in 2nd half; xBA, PX, hr/f all took a hit. Never overbid these guys.

Mather,Joe

			AB	R	H	HR	RBI	SB	Avg	vL	vR	OB	Slg	OPS	bb%	ct%	h%	Eye	xBA	G	L	F	PX	hr/f	SX	SBO	RC/G	RAR	R$
Pos	7	04	0	0	0	0	0	0	0							0			0						0				
Age	26	05	0	0	0	0	0	0	0							0			0						0				
Bats	Right	06	0	0	0	0	0	0	0							0			0						0				
Health	A	07 aa	487	59	104	22	57	7	213			270	392	662	7	85	21	0.52	0				104		84	7%	3.62	-23.8	$9
PT/Exp	F	08 STL	* 344	53	83	19	48	7	240	219	261	310	464	774	9	82	24	0.56	279	30	22	48	134	14%	86	11%	4.99	-4.4	$12
Consist	C	1st Half	216	34	53	11	30	5	246			325	460	785	10	84	25	0.74	287	33	22	44	125	14%	85	12%	5.23	-1.2	$7
LIMA Plan	D	2nd Half	128	20	30	8	19	2	231			285	470	755	7	78	24	0.34	276	29	21	49	151	16%	69	8%	4.61	-3.1	$4
+/- Score	25	09 Proj	258	36	61	13	34	4	236			298	444	741	8	82	24	0.49	272	30	21	49	123	13%	70	8%	4.53	-6.6	$7

8-18-.241 in 133 AB at STL. Flyball hitter with good power and decent contact, but a terrible hit rate. That translates into lots of HRs and a middling BA. As his OBA sinks below .300, his value will rapidly fade.

Mathis,Jeff

			AB	R	H	HR	RBI	SB	Avg	vL	vR	OB	Slg	OPS	bb%	ct%	h%	Eye	xBA	G	L	F	PX	hr/f	SX	SBO	RC/G	RAR	R$
Pos	2	04 aa	432	46	87	10	45	2	201			268	331	599	8	81	23	0.47	0				83		70	3%	2.91	-15.7	$3
Age	26	05 aaa	427	59	105	16	56	3	246			296	420	717	7	86	25	0.52	0				105		76	8%	4.29	4.9	$11
Bats	Right	06 LAA	* 439	57	106	6	41	2	241	133	150	285	364	650	6	83	28	0.37	216	29	12	59	85	3%	75	3%	3.52	-11.6	$5
Health	A	07 LAA	* 421	57	90	8	45	3	214	242	203	265	332	597	6	78	26	0.32	225	42	13	45	87	5%	77	6%	2.77	-19.8	$4
PT/Exp	D	08 LAA	283	35	55	9	42	2	194	224	184	272	318	590	10	68	25	0.33	184	36	11	53	90	9%	52	6%	2.58	-14.5	$4
Consist	B	1st Half	131	17	28	5	19	1	214			299	359	658	11	69	27	0.40	201	39	12	49	102	11%	47	6%	3.58	-2.5	$2
LIMA Plan	F	2nd Half	152	18	27	4	23	1	178			247	283	530	8	67	23	0.28	169	33	11	56	79	7%	56	6%	1.69	-12.4	$1
+/- Score	-22	09 Proj	221	28	46	6	28	1	208			271	329	600	8	74	25	0.34	201	36	12	52	87	7%	56	5%	2.76	-10.3	$3

PRO: High FB, rising hr/f, walks.
CON: Plummeting ct%
Pick your poison. As a backup catcher, he'll thrill you with an occasional HR, but his BA will absolutely kill you.

Matsui,Hideki

			AB	R	H	HR	RBI	SB	Avg	vL	vR	OB	Slg	OPS	bb%	ct%	h%	Eye	xBA	G	L	F	PX	hr/f	SX	SBO	RC/G	RAR	R$
Pos	07	04 NYY	584	109	174	31	108	3	298	265	314	390	522	912	13	82	32	0.85	289	41	19	39	131	16%	75	2%	6.93	26.2	$26
Age	34	05 NYY	629	108	192	23	116	2	305	354	278	368	496	865	9	88	32	0.81	296	47	16	36	117	12%	64	2%	6.18	2.7	$26
Bats	Left	06 NYY	172	32	52	8	29	1	302	226	336	397	494	891	14	87	31	1.17	275	39	17	44	108	12%	49	2%	6.70	1.3	$7
Health	F	07 NYY	547	100	156	25	103	4	285	274	290	369	488	857	12	87	29	1.00	289	43	17	40	117	13%	83	3%	6.21	-0.4	$22
PT/Exp	C	08 NYY	337	43	99	9	45	0	294	315	284	365	424	790	10	86	32	0.81	261	47	19	34	82	9%	23	0%	5.36	4.1	$10
Consist	B	1st Half	251	37	81	7	34	0	323			397	458	855	11	88	35	1.03	270	47	19	34	83	9%	26	0%	6.20	8.4	$9
LIMA Plan	C	2nd Half	86	6	18	2	11	0	209			269	326	594	8	80	24	0.41	230	48	17	35	79	8%	12	0%	2.78	-5.7	$0
+/- Score	-43	09 Proj	501	71	142	18	78	1	283			359	446	805	11	85	31	0.78	269	45	18	38	99	11%	43	1%	5.53	-0.4	$16

Knee injury played a major role in the power drop; wasn't the same after he returned. Consistent plate approach means the BA should be safe. Rebound likely, but age and injury history limit future PT.

Matsui,Kaz

			AB	R	H	HR	RBI	SB	Avg	vL	vR	OB	Slg	OPS	bb%	ct%	h%	Eye	xBA	G	L	F	PX	hr/f	SX	SBO	RC/G	RAR	R$
Pos	4	04 NYM	460	65	125	7	44	14	272	306	262	330	396	726	8	79	33	0.41	270	48	23	29	89	7%	107	14%	4.51	-1.3	$13
Age	33	05 NYM	267	31	68	3	24	6	255	279	246	292	352	644	5	84	29	0.33	270	51	22	27	60	5%	123	11%	3.39	-9.2	$5
Bats	Both	06 2NL	* 370	56	98	6	40	13	266	119	299	309	375	684	6	82	31	0.35	258	48	20	31	69	6%	121	15%	3.87	-7.8	$11
Health	F	07 COL	410	84	118	4	37	32	288	271	291	342	405	747	8	83	34	0.49	264	45	21	34	77	3%	169	31%	4.81	1.3	$18
PT/Exp	C	08 HOU	375	58	110	6	33	20	293	291	294	357	427	783	9	86	33	0.70	281	46	21	34	89	6%	124	22%	5.31	5.8	$15
Consist	B	1st Half	225	31	61	1	18	15	271			339	342	681	9	84	32	0.62	234	45	16	39	57	1%	101	26%	4.09	-4.4	$8
LIMA Plan	C	2nd Half	150	27	49	5	15	5	327			384	553	937	9	89	34	0.88	345	47	26	27	133	14%	131	17%	7.04	9.2	$8
+/- Score	-14	09 Proj	387	65	110	6	36	15	284			341	418	758	8	85	32	0.56	282	46	22	32	86	5%	134	17%	4.95	2.7	$13

As players age, the best way to maintain their value is to work the count more for better pitches. His slowly rising bb% and ct% show a maturing hitter who will likely stay employed even with all his DL stints.

DAVE ADLER

Matthews Jr.,Gary

			AB	R	H	HR	RBI	SB	Avg	vL	vR	OB	Slg	OPS	bb%	ct%	h%	Eye	xBA	G	L	F	PX	hr/f	SX	SBO	RC/G	RAR	R$
Pos	978	04 TEX	* 428	60	117	18	60	8	273	244	289	348	474	822	10	79	31	0.55	290	45	24	31	123	17%	100	8%	5.74	12.8	$14
Age	34	05 TEX	475	72	121	17	55	9	255	241	260	322	436	758	9	81	28	0.52	283	51	17	32	114	14%	116	9%	4.88	2.5	$14
Bats	Both	06 TEX	620	102	194	19	79	10	313	314	313	372	495	867	9	84	35	0.59	296	51	19	30	112	12%	97	9%	6.21	9.3	$23
Health	A	07 LAA	516	79	130	18	72	18	252	175	275	324	419	743	10	80	28	0.54	264	51	13	36	107	12%	110	16%	4.71	-12.1	$17
PT/Exp	A	08 LAA	426	53	103	8	46	8	242	285	223	314	357	671	10	78	29	0.47	251	59	14	27	79	9%	94	9%	3.85	-19.3	$8
Consist	C	1st Half	282	31	68	7	33	6	241			316	365	682	10	76	29	0.46	246	60	14	27	83	12%	86	10%	3.95	-12.0	$6
LIMA Plan	D+	2nd Half	144	22	35	1	13	2	243			310	340	650	9	81	29	0.52	260	58	15	26	73	3%	95	8%	3.68	-7.2	$2
+/- Score	-14	09 Proj	408	59	100	9	48	6	245			315	379	694	9	80	29	0.52	262	55	15	30	90	9%	94	8%	4.16	-14.8	$9

The slide continues. As youth fades in the rear-view mirror, odds of a rebound decrease, and the large contract looks worse and worse.

But he gets an "A" in Health.

Mauer,Joe

			AB	R	H	HR	RBI	SB	Avg	vL	vR	OB	Slg	OPS	bb%	ct%	h%	Eye	xBA	G	L	F	PX	hr/f	SX	SBO	RC/G	RAR	R$
Pos	2	04 MIN	107	18	33	6	17	1	308	182	365	373	570	943	9	87	31	0.79	321	46	18	36	146	18%	81	3%	7.04	7.9	$5
Age	26	05 MIN	489	61	144	9	55	13	294	232	323	373	411	784	11	87	32	0.95	296	52	24	24	75	9%	93	8%	5.42	19.0	$16
Bats	Left	06 MIN	521	86	181	13	84	8	347	331	356	433	507	940	13	90	37	1.46	318	49	25	26	94	11%	86	5%	7.38	40.0	$24
Health	B	07 MIN	406	62	119	7	60	7	293	283	299	380	426	806	12	87	32	1.12	292	55	18	28	87	7%	94	6%	5.80	17.1	$13
PT/Exp	A	08 MIN	536	98	176	9	85	1	328	361	312	419	451	871	14	91	35	1.68	298	49	23	28	76	7%	67	1%	6.66	34.9	$21
Consist	C	1st Half	269	50	87	3	34	0	323			415	446	861	14	92	34	1.91	302	49	22	30	84	4%	53	1%	6.61	17.3	$10
LIMA Plan	A	2nd Half	267	48	89	6	51	1	333			424	457	881	14	90	36	1.50	293	50	23	27	69	9%	75	1%	6.71	17.6	$12
+/- Score	-17	09 Proj	519	88	166	11	82	3	320			407	457	864	13	89	34	1.37	300	51	22	28	84	8%	76	2%	6.50	31.4	$20

This is going to sound like heresy, but aside from a bunch of extra walks, isn't this the same offensive skill set as Placido Polanco? Yet Mauer will get drafted in the 1st 5 rounds, and Placido? 10th if he's lucky.

Maybin,Cameron

			AB	R	H	HR	RBI	SB	Avg	vL	vR	OB	Slg	OPS	bb%	ct%	h%	Eye	xBA	G	L	F	PX	hr/f	SX	SBO	RC/G	RAR	R$
Pos	8	04	0	0	0	0	0	0	0							0			0						0				
Age	22	05	0	0	0	0	0	0	0							0			0						0				
Bats	Right	06	0	0	0	0	0	0	0							0			0						0				
Health	A	07 DET	* 69	17	14	4	10	5	203		200	298	436	733	12	61	26	0.35	244	54	4	43	191	22%	138	33%	4.97	0.9	$3
PT/Exp	F	08 FLA	* 422	70	115	11	43	22	272	375	542	358	423	782	12	72	35	0.48	273	50	29	21	101	17%	144	22%	5.46	9.0	$17
Consist	A	1st Half	290	45	71	10	30	14	244			330	421	752	11	72	30	0.46	0				117		141	25%	4.99	2.2	$10
LIMA Plan	C	2nd Half	132	24	44	1	13	8	335			420	427	847	13	73	45	0.54	256	50	29	21	66	5%	134	18%	6.49	6.2	$7
+/- Score	-2	09 Proj	303	52	81	6	31	17	267			357	395	752	12	73	35	0.51	266	50	29	21	87	12%	148	22%	5.10	4.2	$11

0-2-.500 in 32 AB at FLA. Still a work in progress. Five-tool talent has plenty of speed. High GB% is curtailing power for now, but he's still growing. Low ct% will be a drag on his BA for the short term.

McAnulty,Paul

			AB	R	H	HR	RBI	SB	Avg	vL	vR	OB	Slg	OPS	bb%	ct%	h%	Eye	xBA	G	L	F	PX	hr/f	SX	SBO	RC/G	RAR	R$
Pos	7	04	0	0	0	0	0	0	0							0			0						0				
Age	28	05 a/a	449	52	113	11	54	4	253			316	393	709	8	82	29	0.51	0				95		69	5%	4.31	-9.5	$10
Bats	Left	06 aaa	478	58	124	12	60	1	259			327	410	737	9	86	28	0.74	0				90		57	3%	4.75	-6.5	$10
Health	A	07 SD	* 273	24	56	4	29	0	205			273	296	569	9	78	25	0.42	288	43	37	20	62	11%	39	3%	2.47	-24.8	$1
PT/Exp	D	08 SD	* 316	35	77	12	52	0	242		215	351	425	776	14	75	29	0.66	251	41	18	41	124	12%	40	0%	5.39	-0.3	$8
Consist	F	1st Half	131	9	27	3	12	0	206			338	344	681	17	70	27	0.67	220	41	17	42	104	8%	35	0%	4.25	-4.8	$0
LIMA Plan	F	2nd Half	185	26	50	9	40	0	268			361	482	843	13	78	30	0.66	0	50	50	0	138		42	0%	6.12	3.7	$7
+/- Score	12	09 Proj	31	3	7	1	4	0	226			315	378	693	12	78	26	0.59	258	41	21	38	106	10%	29	2%	4.20	-1.1	$0

3-13-.207 in 135 AB at SD. The good news... Increased plate patience translated into more power and productivity. The bad news... He's 28, he batted .207 in SD, so nobody cares about the good news.

McCann,Brian

			AB	R	H	HR	RBI	SB	Avg	vL	vR	OB	Slg	OPS	bb%	ct%	h%	Eye	xBA	G	L	F	PX	hr/f	SX	SBO	RC/G	RAR	R$
Pos	2	04	0	0	0	0	0	0	0							0			0						0				
Age	25	05 ATL	* 346	43	90	10	46	3	260	344	259	337	408	744	10	86	28	0.82	283	42	23	35	92	10%	55	7%	4.86	10.9	$9
Bats	Left	06 ATL	442	61	147	24	93	2	333	266	351	389	572	962	8	88	34	0.76	310	35	22	43	135	14%	38	2%	7.16	32.6	$23
Health	A	07 ATL	504	51	136	18	92	0	270	264	273	317	452	770	6	85	29	0.47	276	39	19	43	115	10%	18	1%	4.90	6.8	$14
PT/Exp	B	08 ATL	509	68	153	23	87	5	301	299	301	371	523	894	10	87	31	0.89	306	37	20	43	135	12%	67	3%	6.55	32.7	$22
Consist	A	1st Half	278	35	82	14	45	1	295			359	536	895	9	86	30	0.74	306	40	18	43	146	14%	48	1%	6.50	17.6	$11
LIMA Plan	B	2nd Half	231	33	71	9	42	4	307			385	506	891	11	89	32	1.12	306	33	24	43	122	10%	61	6%	6.62	15.1	$11
+/- Score	23	09 Proj	509	64	150	21	90	4	295			359	500	859	9	87	31	0.77	298	37	21	42	124	11%	58	3%	6.10	26.2	$20

Rebounded from sophomore slump with growth across the board. Power slumped in Aug and Sept, so perhaps he was wearing down. 2H rise in Eye and LD shows that he hasn't peaked yet; bid full value.

McDonald,John

			AB	R	H	HR	RBI	SB	Avg	vL	vR	OB	Slg	OPS	bb%	ct%	h%	Eye	xBA	G	L	F	PX	hr/f	SX	SBO	RC/G	RAR	R$
Pos	6	04 CLE	93	17	19	2	7	0	204	200	220	237	344	581	4	88	21	0.36	253	43	13	44	81	6%	111	0%	2.74	-5.0	$1
Age	34	05 2AL	166	18	46	0	16	6	277	298	253	322	325	647	6	86	32	0.46	259	55	21	24	36	0%	98	14%	3.55	-4.8	$4
Bats	Right	06 TOR	260	35	58	3	23	7	223	230	220	268	308	576	6	84	25	0.39	243	48	18	34	49	4%	128	15%	2.63	-14.3	$3
Health	D	07 TOR	327	32	82	1	31	7	251	329	223	275	333	608	3	85	29	0.23	257	40	23	37	62	1%	95	13%	2.95	-13.0	$5
PT/Exp	D	08 TOR	186	21	39	1	18	3	210	250	184	250	269	519	5	87	24	0.40	222	42	15	43	44	1%	75	10%	2.03	-13.4	$1
Consist	B	1st Half	39	3	7	0	1	2	179			238	205	443	7	79	23	0.38	198	39	19	42	24	0%	75	33%	0.92	-4.4	($0)
LIMA Plan	F	2nd Half	147	18	32	1	17	1	218			253	286	539	5	88	24	0.41	228	43	15	43	49	2%	65	3%	2.30	-9.1	$1
+/- Score	-8	09 Proj	143	17	34	1	14	3	238			276	314	589	5	86	27	0.37	245	46	18	36	51	2%	100	11%	2.81	-6.6	$2

John McDonald has an arm, E-I-E-I-O. Unfortunately, he has no bat, E-I-E-I-O.

That's it. Move on.

McLouth,Nate

			AB	R	H	HR	RBI	SB	Avg	vL	vR	OB	Slg	OPS	bb%	ct%	h%	Eye	xBA	G	L	F	PX	hr/f	SX	SBO	RC/G	RAR	R$
Pos	8	04 aa	515	76	153	6	59	25	297			345	414	759	7	91	32	0.81	0				76		116	23%	4.98	4.3	$20
Age	27	05 PIT	* 506	68	133	9	42	28	263	100	292	307	374	680	6	88	29	0.52	273	52	16	31	70	6%	121	29%	3.92	-9.7	$17
Bats	Left	06 PIT	270	50	63	7	16	10	233	260	227	281	385	666	6	78	27	0.31	264	39	25	35	99	9%	141	20%	3.63	-6.6	$6
Health	A	07 PIT	329	62	85	13	38	22	258	269	256	337	459	796	11	77	30	0.51	245	31	16	53	132	10%	147	26%	5.47	9.1	$14
PT/Exp	C	08 PIT	597	113	165	26	94	23	276	261	282	347	497	845	10	84	29	0.70	287	35	19	47	137	11%	134	17%	5.98	21.2	$28
Consist	C	1st Half	318	59	89	15	52	9	280			346	522	868	9	86	29	0.71	295	35	17	49	146	11%	121	16%	6.21	13.4	$15
LIMA Plan	B+	2nd Half	279	54	76	11	42	14	272			349	470	819	11	83	30	0.69	278	34	21	45	126	11%	129	18%	5.72	7.8	$14
+/- Score	13	09 Proj	581	107	164	28	103	20	282			349	511	859	9	82	30	0.56	283	35	19	46	140	13%	127	15%	6.09	24.1	$28

Reasons for 2008 breakout:
- He sustained '07's skill gains
- He got more at bats

Nothing magic here. If you pro-rate his '07 HR to 597 AB, you get 24. Now the fun starts... UP: 30 HR, 30 SB.

Mench,Kevin

			AB	R	H	HR	RBI	SB	Avg	vL	vR	OB	Slg	OPS	bb%	ct%	h%	Eye	xBA	G	L	F	PX	hr/f	SX	SBO	RC/G	RAR	R$
Pos	7	04 TEX	438	69	122	26	71	0	279	319	259	329	539	868	7	86	28	0.52	299	36	17	46	146	15%	58	0%	6.00	13.1	$16
Age	31	05 TEX	557	71	147	25	73	4	264	296	257	325	469	793	8	88	26	0.74	287	38	17	45	120	11%	67	5%	5.27	8.8	$17
Bats	Right	06 2TM	446	45	120	13	68	1	269	303	257	311	419	730	6	87	29	0.46	267	42	18	39	88	9%	49	1%	4.41	-10.2	$10
Health	A	07 MIL	288	39	77	8	37	3	267	314	212	306	441	747	5	93	27	0.76	291	42	17	41	98	7%	92	6%	4.74	-5.1	$8
PT/Exp	D	08 TOR	* 299	36	70	3	32	2	233	237	256	290	356	646	7	85	26	0.55	298	45	27	27	85	5%	88	3%	3.65	-10.8	$4
Consist	B	1st Half	198	24	44	3	21	1	220			274	353	627	7	90	23	0.73	273	41	19	40	79	5%	89	2%	3.49	-8.2	$2
LIMA Plan	F	2nd Half	101	12	26	0	11	1	258			322	362	684	9	76	34	0.40	318	51	39	10	100	0%	52	4%	4.13	-2.1	$2
+/- Score	43	09 Proj	130	16	33	3	16	1	254			305	406	712	7	86	28	0.52	288	43	22	35	101	7%	75	4%	4.35	-2.3	$3

0-10-.243 in 115 AB at TOR. I hate to cast aspersions, and please don't consider this a witch hunt, but isn't it too coincidental that a former HR hitter's power would go MIA at his peak power age?

Metcalf,Travis

			AB	R	H	HR	RBI	SB	Avg	vL	vR	OB	Slg	OPS	bb%	ct%	h%	Eye	xBA	G	L	F	PX	hr/f	SX	SBO	RC/G	RAR	R$
Pos	5	04	0	0	0	0	0	0	0							0			0						0				
Age	26	05	0	0	0	0	0	0	0							0			0						0				
Bats	Right	06 aa	425	41	85	7	29	8	199			262	288	550	8	77	24	0.37	0				59		80	16%	2.19	-41.8	$1
Health	B	07 TEX	* 422	56	96	10	52	2	227	237	265	284	377	661	7	77	27	0.35	253	39	19	42	111	8%	62	4%	3.62	-16.1	$6
PT/Exp	D	08 TEX	* 321	37	68	10	41	0	212	162	368	250	352	602	5	81	23	0.26	238	40	16	44	89	8%	49	2%	2.73	-21.4	$4
Consist	C	1st Half	147	10	26	2	14	0	175			200	263	463	3	79	21	0.15	0	67	0	33	61	5%	60	4%	0.95	-18.8	($1)
LIMA Plan	F	2nd Half	174	27	42	8	27	0	244			290	428	718	6	83	25	0.38	264	36	18	46	112	12%	41	0%	4.16	-3.7	$5
+/- Score	22	09 Proj	131	16	32	4	15	1	244			291	379	670	6	79	28	0.32	241	39	18	43	92	8%	45	4%	3.63	-4.9	$2

6-14-.232 in 56 AB at TEX. Decent power at A-ball (37 HR in '04/'05), but hasn't translated to upper levels. 2nd half output is a good sign, but it's a small sign, and at age 26, we need to see big signs.

DAVE ADLER

Michaels,Jason			AB	R	H	HR	RBI	SB	Avg	vL	vR	OB	Slg	OPS	bb%	ct%	h%	Eye	xBA	G	L	F	PX	hr/f	SX	SBO	RC/G	RAR	R$
Pos	97	04 PHI	299	44	82	10	40	2	274	286	270	364	415	778	12	73	34	0.53	232	40	20	40	95	12%	45	4%	5.33	0.4	$9
Age	32	05 PHI	289	54	88	4	31	3	304	323	289	396	415	812	13	84	35	0.98	270	41	25	35	75	5%	87	5%	5.89	5.2	$10
Bats	Right	06 CLE	494	77	132	9	55	9	267	291	252	326	391	717	8	80	32	0.43	256	40	23	38	87	6%	88	11%	4.37	-18.5	$12
Health	A	07 CLE	267	43	72	7	39	3	270	287	252	321	397	718	7	81	31	0.40	236	37	17	46	82	7%	78	10%	4.27	-9.6	$8
PT/Exp	C	08 2TM	286	28	64	8	53	2	224	187	241	291	360	651	9	77	26	0.42	239	38	19	43	92	8%	57	4%	3.49	-15.6	$5
Consist	A	1st Half	148	14	34	3	31	1	230			274	351	625	6	76	28	0.26	236	37	20	43	92	6%	44	6%	3.06	-10.0	$3
LIMA Plan	F	2nd Half	138	14	30	5	22	1	217			308	370	677	12	78	24	0.60	241	39	18	42	92	11%	60	3%	3.93	-5.7	$2
+/- Score	1	09 Proj	**187**	**24**	**43**	**5**	**29**	**2**	**230**			**298**	**368**	**666**	**9**	**79**	**27**	**0.46**	**245**	**38**	**19**	**42**	**91**	**8%**	**76**	**7%**	**3.73**	**-8.5**	**$4**

.800 OPS vs LHP in 2007, .509 in 2008. Low h%, but bigger problem was declining ct% and xBA. He's already a part time player, but if he can't hit LHers any more, then there's no reason to keep giving him ABs.

Mientkiewicz,Doug			AB	R	H	HR	RBI	SB	Avg	vL	vR	OB	Slg	OPS	bb%	ct%	h%	Eye	xBA	G	L	F	PX	hr/f	SX	SBO	RC/G	RAR	R$
Pos	35	04 2AL	391	47	93	6	35	2	238	220	246	321	350	672	11	86	26	0.86	253	43	18	39	74	5%	53	5%	4.10	-10.5	$4
Age	34	05 NYM	275	36	66	11	29	0	240	214	245	319	407	726	10	86	24	0.82	268	49	16	35	100	13%	30	1%	4.59	-8.4	$6
Bats	Left	06 KC	314	37	89	4	43	3	283	274	286	355	411	766	10	84	33	0.70	270	41	22	37	88	4%	74	3%	5.18	-2.1	$7
Health	F	07 NYY	166	26	46	5	24	0	277	231	286	341	440	780	9	86	30	0.70	293	36	24	39	106	9%	35	0%	5.19	-0.3	$5
PT/Exp	D	08 PIT	285	37	79	2	30	0	277	250	283	374	379	753	13	90	30	1.57	274	39	22	38	69	2%	46	0%	5.36	-3.0	$6
Consist	A	1st Half	136	22	36	1	13	0	265			371	346	717	14	89	29	1.53	251	36	21	43	58	2%	36	0%	4.96	-3.0	$3
LIMA Plan	D	2nd Half	149	15	43	1	17	0	289			376	409	786	12	91	31	1.62	294	43	24	34	78	2%	53	0%	5.72	-0.1	$3
+/- Score	-7	09 Proj	**186**	**25**	**51**	**3**	**22**	**0**	**274**			**357**	**402**	**759**	**11**	**88**	**30**	**1.06**	**279**	**40**	**22**	**38**	**83**	**5%**	**55**	**1%**	**5.21**	**-3.5**	**$4**

Random facts:
- Six teams in 5 years
- 3 years of consistent RC/G
- Caught the last out of the 2004 World Series.
- Undraftable in most fantasy formats

Miles,Aaron			AB	R	H	HR	RBI	SB	Avg	vL	vR	OB	Slg	OPS	bb%	ct%	h%	Eye	xBA	G	L	F	PX	hr/f	SX	SBO	RC/G	RAR	R$
Pos	46	04 COL	* 576	80	168	6	52	13	292	267	301	327	365	691	5	90	32	0.54	264	55	17	28	43	4%	97	13%	4.03	-9.5	$17
Age	32	05 COL	* 356	41	97	2	29	5	271	234	292	287	344	631	2	89	30	0.20	282	54	23	23	45	3%	105	8%	3.18	-14.1	$7
Bats	Both	06 STL	426	48	112	2	30	2	263	291	256	323	347	671	8	90	29	0.90	280	55	20	25	51	2%	78	2%	4.09	-6.3	$5
Health	A	07 STL	414	55	120	2	32	2	290	286	292	330	348	678	6	90	32	0.63	257	54	18	28	39	2%	62	2%	3.96	-8.6	$8
PT/Exp	C	08 STL	379	49	120	4	31	3	317	315	317	356	398	754	6	90	34	0.62	280	54	21	25	51	5%	70	5%	4.78	0.1	$12
Consist	A	1st Half	192	21	63	1	13	1	328			368	380	748	6	92	35	0.75	271	54	22	24	36	2%	36	4%	4.74	-0.1	$6
LIMA Plan	F	2nd Half	187	28	57	3	18	2	305			343	417	761	6	89	33	0.52	286	54	20	26	66	7%	92	5%	4.82	0.2	$6
+/- Score	-40	09 Proj	**264**	**34**	**75**	**2**	**21**	**2**	**284**			**326**	**367**	**693**	**6**	**90**	**31**	**0.62**	**277**	**54**	**20**	**26**	**51**	**4%**	**80**	**5%**	**4.13**	**-4.3**	**$6**

Have you ever seen a more consistent contact rate? Every 9 times he puts the ball into play, you know a strikeout is coming next. (Does Vegas know about this?) There's BPI growth here, but at 32, '08 could be his peak.

Millar,Kevin			AB	R	H	HR	RBI	SB	Avg	vL	vR	OB	Slg	OPS	bb%	ct%	h%	Eye	xBA	G	L	F	PX	hr/f	SX	SBO	RC/G	RAR	R$
Pos	3	04 BOS	513	75	152	18	74	1	296	299	297	367	472	838	10	82	33	0.62	258	36	17	47	112	9%	38	1%	5.92	13.2	$17
Age	37	05 BOS	449	57	122	9	50	0	272	246	283	350	399	749	11	84	31	0.73	250	34	20	46	87	5%	37	1%	4.94	-1.9	$10
Bats	Right	06 BAL	430	64	117	15	64	1	272	244	283	360	437	797	12	83	30	0.80	270	35	22	42	103	10%	38	1%	5.53	1.4	$12
Health	A	07 BAL	476	63	121	17	63	1	254	250	256	357	420	777	14	80	28	0.81	251	29	20	51	109	9%	41	1%	5.36	1.4	$11
PT/Exp	B	08 BAL	535	73	126	20	72	0	236	238	232	325	394	719	12	83	25	0.76	251	30	19	51	99	9%	28	1%	4.53	-11.9	$11
Consist	B	1st Half	286	41	69	11	44	0	241			338	395	734	13	84	25	0.91	243	32	17	51	92	9%	29	1%	4.76	-4.3	$7
LIMA Plan	D	2nd Half	249	32	57	9	28	0	229			309	394	703	10	81	25	0.62	260	27	22	51	108	9%	27	0%	4.25	-7.6	$4
+/- Score	-3	09 Proj	**409**	**56**	**102**	**15**	**54**	**0**	**249**			**339**	**410**	**749**	**12**	**82**	**27**	**0.75**	**255**	**31**	**20**	**49**	**103**	**9%**	**32**	**1%**	**4.91**	**-4.3**	**$9**

Other than the BA drop, '08 was a virtual mirror image of '07. In fact, skills have remained the same for years. Rising HR trend due to increased PT; that won't continue. "Cowboy Up" is likely to fall from the saddle.

Milledge,Lastings			AB	R	H	HR	RBI	SB	Avg	vL	vR	OB	Slg	OPS	bb%	ct%	h%	Eye	xBA	G	L	F	PX	hr/f	SX	SBO	RC/G	RAR	R$
Pos	8	04	0	0	0	0	0	0	0							0			0						0				
Age	24	05 aa	193	27	61	3	20	9	316			354	446	800	6	81	38	0.32	0				99		86	29%	5.28	4.7	$9
Bats	Right	06 NYM	* 473	70	130	11	61	15	275	241	241	355	429	783	11	79	33	0.60	268	44	22	34	99	8%	102	20%	5.39	13.2	$15
Health	A	07 NYM	* 246	41	71	10	40	8	289	317	250	330	472	801	6	78	34	0.27	282	47	24	29	113	18%	117	16%	5.21	4.7	$11
PT/Exp	C	08 WAS	523	65	140	14	61	24	268	258	272	317	402	719	7	82	31	0.40	263	45	20	35	85	9%	104	24%	4.28	-7.1	$19
Consist	B	1st Half	302	35	74	7	32	13	245			296	368	664	7	83	28	0.42	258	46	18	36	82	8%	88	23%	3.65	-9.9	$8
LIMA Plan	C	2nd Half	221	30	66	7	29	11	299			346	448	794	7	80	35	0.36	268	44	23	33	91	12%	112	25%	5.17	2.7	$10
+/- Score	19	09 Proj	**553**	**78**	**157**	**19**	**72**	**23**	**284**			**334**	**453**	**787**	**7**	**80**	**33**	**0.38**	**277**	**45**	**22**	**33**	**106**	**13%**	**111**	**23%**	**5.12**	**7.8**	**$23**

Arrived as a speedster - ran often and racked up the SBs. Will the power follow? FB% rise helps, and the 2H hr/f is a good sign. Still young, so there's room for growth; the seeds of a breakout are here.

Molina,Bengie			AB	R	H	HR	RBI	SB	Avg	vL	vR	OB	Slg	OPS	bb%	ct%	h%	Eye	xBA	G	L	F	PX	hr/f	SX	SBO	RC/G	RAR	R$
Pos	2	04 ANA	337	36	93	10	54	0	276	252	286	313	404	716	5	90	28	0.51	252	48	16	36	71	9%	25	1%	4.23	-1.0	$8
Age	34	05 ANA	410	45	121	15	69	0	295	393	253	339	446	785	6	90	30	0.66	277	41	21	38	86	11%	18	2%	5.05	11.7	$14
Bats	Right	06 TOR	433	44	123	19	57	1	284	358	246	314	467	781	4	89	28	0.40	296	39	23	38	99	13%	37	2%	4.84	5.3	$12
Health	A	07 SF	497	38	137	19	81	0	276	271	277	297	433	729	3	89	28	0.28	264	37	19	44	85	10%	18	0%	4.20	-3.3	$13
PT/Exp	B	08 SF	530	47	155	16	95	0	292	297	291	317	445	762	3	93	29	0.50	270	35	18	47	90	7%	15	0%	4.72	7.4	$17
Consist	B	1st Half	273	26	84	6	49	0	308			335	440	774	4	93	31	0.61	273	33	20	47	81	5%	18	0%	4.91	5.2	$9
LIMA Plan	D+	2nd Half	257	21	71	10	46	0	276			298	451	749	3	92	27	0.40	265	38	15	47	99	9%	10	0%	4.51	2.2	$8
+/- Score	-15	09 Proj	**492**	**44**	**140**	**17**	**82**	**0**	**285**			**310**	**442**	**752**	**4**	**91**	**28**	**0.42**	**271**	**37**	**19**	**44**	**89**	**9%**	**17**	**0%**	**4.55**	**4.2**	**$15**

Two ships passing in the night - falling hr/f, rising FB%. The end result is consistent HR totals. Rarely walks, but with elite ct%, high BA is a cinch. Consistent production behind the plate - always a good thing.

Molina,Jose			AB	R	H	HR	RBI	SB	Avg	vL	vR	OB	Slg	OPS	bb%	ct%	h%	Eye	xBA	G	L	F	PX	hr/f	SX	SBO	RC/G	RAR	R$
Pos	2	04 ANA	203	26	53	3	25	4	261	339	229	296	374	670	5	74	34	0.19	226	48	15	37	80	5%	113	10%	3.62	-4.2	$5
Age	33	05 ANA	184	14	42	6	25	2	228	306	186	279	348	627	7	78	26	0.32	243	50	20	30	74	14%	39	4%	3.01	-5.6	$3
Bats	Right	06 LAA	225	18	54	4	22	1	240	218	254	269	369	638	4	78	29	0.18	245	42	18	39	96	6%	38	2%	3.18	-8.3	$2
Health	A	07 2AL	191	18	49	1	19	2	257	360	220	276	340	616	3	77	33	0.12	250	48	23	29	73	2%	55	8%	2.84	-8.1	$2
PT/Exp	F	08 NYY	268	32	58	3	18	0	216	188	230	250	313	563	4	81	26	0.23	248	48	19	33	75	4%	44	0%	2.32	-15.4	$1
Consist	A	1st Half	145	13	33	0	10	0	228			253	317	571	3	83	28	0.20	254	54	17	29	79	0%	32	0%	2.50	-7.4	$0
LIMA Plan	F	2nd Half	123	19	25	3	8	0	203			246	309	555	5	78	24	0.26	237	40	22	39	70	8%	58	0%	2.11	-8.0	$1
+/- Score	17	09 Proj	**168**	**18**	**39**	**2**	**14**	**1**	**232**			**263**	**333**	**596**	**4**	**79**	**28**	**0.20**	**245**	**46**	**20**	**34**	**77**	**5%**	**53**	**3%**	**2.65**	**-8.1**	**$2**

The Molina brother without the ct%-gene. Injuries gave him PT, but he didn't do much with it. No speed to take advantage of the GBs. Low PX and hr/f, so there won't be a lot of HRs. xBA says it all - consistent mediocrity.

Molina,Yadier			AB	R	H	HR	RBI	SB	Avg	vL	vR	OB	Slg	OPS	bb%	ct%	h%	Eye	xBA	G	L	F	PX	hr/f	SX	SBO	RC/G	RAR	R$
Pos	2	04 STL	* 264	28	72	3	27	0	273	250	272	340	352	692	9	89	30	0.90	250	46	20	34	52	4%	26	1%	4.30	3.7	$5
Age	26	05 STL	385	36	97	8	49	2	252	299	231	294	358	653	6	92	26	0.77	274	51	18	31	62	7%	48	5%	3.70	-1.1	$7
Bats	Right	06 STL	417	29	90	6	49	1	216	213	217	262	321	583	6	90	23	0.63	257	42	18	39	67	4%	26	4%	2.94	-18.0	$2
Health	B	07 STL	353	30	97	6	40	1	275	288	269	339	368	707	9	88	30	0.79	248	46	19	35	58	6%	25	2%	4.38	-0.5	$7
PT/Exp	C	08 STL	444	37	135	7	56	0	304	323	296	351	392	743	7	93	31	1.10	264	46	21	33	53	5%	13	1%	4.77	6.9	$12
Consist	B	1st Half	237	18	70	4	26	0	295			353	384	737	8	95	30	1.75	262	47	20	33	51	5%	13	1%	4.85	4.2	$6
LIMA Plan	D	2nd Half	207	19	65	3	30	0	314			349	401	750	5	92	33	0.65	270	45	22	33	54	5%	21	2%	4.69	2.7	$6
+/- Score	-31	09 Proj	**423**	**36**	**119**	**7**	**52**	**1**	**281**			**331**	**373**	**705**	**7**	**91**	**30**	**0.84**	**260**	**46**	**20**	**34**	**57**	**5%**	**20**	**2%**	**4.33**	**1.0**	**$9**

Great ct% but mostly all singles. Unlike brothers, he's willing to take a walk. Low hr/f and FB% limit power upside. He's got age on his side, so some growth wouldn't be a surprise.

Monroe,Craig			AB	R	H	HR	RBI	SB	Avg	vL	vR	OB	Slg	OPS	bb%	ct%	h%	Eye	xBA	G	L	F	PX	hr/f	SX	SBO	RC/G	RAR	R$
Pos	0	04 DET	447	65	131	18	72	3	293	256	314	329	488	824	6	82	32	0.37	277	46	16	38	117	13%	76	6%	5.49	2.3	$16
Age	32	05 DET	567	69	157	20	89	8	277	303	270	325	446	771	7	83	30	0.42	285	49	19	32	106	13%	83	8%	4.88	-16.1	$19
Bats	Right	06 DET	541	89	138	28	92	2	255	271	249	303	482	785	6	77	28	0.29	272	38	18	44	146	15%	73	4%	5.04	-22.0	$17
Health	A	07 2TM	392	53	86	12	59	0	219	271	194	268	370	638	6	73	27	0.24	226	36	16	48	111	9%	41	5%	3.19	-37.0	$6
PT/Exp	C	08 MIN	163	22	33	8	29	0	202	138	276	274	405	679	9	71	23	0.33	249	44	16	40	146	17%	40	3%	3.79	-5.8	$3
Consist	C	1st Half	130	17	27	7	23	0	208			264	423	687	7	71	24	0.26	252	42	16	41	153	18%	31	0%	3.82	-4.5	$3
LIMA Plan	F	2nd Half	33	5	6	1	6	0	182			308	333	641	15	70	23	0.60	232	52	13	35	119	12%	53	11%	3.57	-1.5	$0
+/- Score	4	09 Proj	**93**	**13**	**22**	**4**	**15**	**0**	**237**			**287**	**424**	**711**	**7**	**72**	**28**	**0.26**	**248**	**41**	**17**	**41**	**132**	**15%**	**49**	**4%**	**4.14**	**-4.0**	**$2**

Skill slide mirrors drop in ct%. Used to be money vs LHP, but that's not the case any more (.449 OPS). He can still put them over the fence occasionally, but he's unlikely to get enough PT to make a difference.

DAVE ADLER

Montanez,Luis			AB	R	H	HR	RBI	SB	Avg	vL	vR	OB	Slg	OPS	bb%	ct%	h%	Eye	xBA	G	L	F	PX	hr/f	SX	SBO	RC/G	RAR	R$
Pos	7	04	0	0	0	0	0	0	0							0			0						0				
Age	27	05 aa	153	17	37	2	13	0	241			290	342	633	7	87	27	0.54	0				67		61	5%	3.43	-7.4	$2
Bats	Right	06 a/a	386	46	102	11	53	5	264			319	405	723	7	81	30	0.43	0				91		54	9%	4.37	-9.5	$10
Health	A	07 a/a	333	44	86	9	32	4	257			314	368	682	8	86	28	0.59	0				66		53	9%	3.93	-12.5	$7
PT/Exp	D	08 BAL	* 567	92	163	25	92	3	287	283	305	327	494	821	6	86	30	0.43	291	47	14	38	121	13%	76	6%	5.40	8.8	$22
Consist	B	1st Half	326	46	87	14	46	3	268			307	460	767	5	87	27	0.45	0				114		66	8%	4.78	-0.7	$10
LIMA Plan	F	2nd Half	241	46	75	11	46	0	313			353	541	894	6	85	33	0.41	296	47	14	38	132	14%	91	3%	6.27	9.3	$11
+/- Score	22	09 Proj	159	23	44	7	22	1	277			324	480	804	7	85	28	0.48	283	47	14	38	118	14%	68	7%	5.24	1.3	$5

3-14-.293 in 116 AB at BAL. Tore the cover off the ball at AA en route to Eastern League triple crown. But at 27, he's past the age where teams will plan their future around him. Could have a few good years. A few.

Montero,Miguel			AB	R	H	HR	RBI	SB	Avg	vL	vR	OB	Slg	OPS	bb%	ct%	h%	Eye	xBA	G	L	F	PX	hr/f	SX	SBO	RC/G	RAR	R$
Pos	2	04	0	0	0	0	0	0	0							0			0						0				
Age	25	05 aa	108	10	24	2	10	1	225			264	323	588	5	81	26	0.28	0				53		97	4%	2.60	-4.3	$1
Bats	Left	06 a/a	439	38	118	15	66	1	269	333	231	338	426	764	9	87	28	0.81	0	38	15	46	91	9%	13	5%	5.02	8.2	$10
Health	A	07 ARI	214	30	48	10	37	0	224	286	218	291	397	688	9	84	22	0.57	243	39	14	47	97	12%	32	0%	3.93	-3.3	$5
PT/Exp	F	08 ARI	184	24	47	5	18	0	255	286	250	325	435	760	9	73	32	0.39	263	36	22	41	138	9%	49	0%	5.07	4.6	$4
Consist	C	1st Half	81	8	20	0	5	0	247			337	333	670	12	72	34	0.48	229	36	24	41	87	0%	23	0%	4.08	-0.3	$1
LIMA Plan	F	2nd Half	103	16	27	5	13	0	262			315	515	830	7	75	31	0.31	291	37	21	42	176	15%	71	0%	5.79	4.7	$3
+/- Score	10	09 Proj	224	28	56	7	28	0	250			315	421	736	9	79	29	0.44	256	37	19	44	113	10%	54	1%	4.59	2.3	$5

Slow out of the box due to broken finger. Ct% plummeted; high h% was only thing to save BA. He's shown that he can put up decent power numbers. With regular playing time... UP: 20 HR.

Morales,Kendry			AB	R	H	HR	RBI	SB	Avg	vL	vR	OB	Slg	OPS	bb%	ct%	h%	Eye	xBA	G	L	F	PX	hr/f	SX	SBO	RC/G	RAR	R$
Pos	9	04	0	0	0	0	0	0	0							0			0						0				
Age	25	05 aa	281	36	75	13	42	2	267			299	445	744	4	88	26	0.38	0				100		55	3%	4.41	-4.6	$9
Bats	Both	06 LAA	* 453	53	119	14	63	1	263	229	235	306	413	718	6	87	28	0.47	266	52	15	34	86	11%	46	6%	4.28	-18.4	$10
Health	A	07 LAA	* 374	48	113	8	47	0	302	241	311	335	445	779	5	87	33	0.37	252	47	11	42	96	6%	40	3%	4.95	-5.7	$11
PT/Exp	D	08 LAA	* 378	44	107	14	60	1	283	214	213	317	446	764	5	88	29	0.42	259	41	15	44	96	10%	29	5%	4.70	-7.1	$12
Consist	A	1st Half	189	18	53	6	29	1	279			313	418	730	5	89	29	0.47	0				83		32	6%	4.37	-5.4	$5
LIMA Plan	C	2nd Half	189	26	54	9	31	0	288			322	475	797	5	87	29	0.38	267	41	15	44	110	12%	34	4%	5.04	-1.7	$7
+/- Score	-11	09 Proj	533	65	151	18	78	1	283			318	444	762	5	87	30	0.41	260	46	14	41	96	10%	36	4%	4.70	-10.2	$16

3-8-.213 in 61 AB at LAA. Has shown he can hit for BA at AAA; now it's time to do it in the bigs. High ct% says it'll be there soon. With league-average power, HR totals won't be huge, but enough to justify full-time AB.

Mora,Melvin			AB	R	H	HR	RBI	SB	Avg	vL	vR	OB	Slg	OPS	bb%	ct%	h%	Eye	xBA	G	L	F	PX	hr/f	SX	SBO	RC/G	RAR	R$
Pos	5	04 BAL	550	111	187	27	104	11	340	303	352	411	562	973	11	83	37	0.69	296	40	21	39	135	15%	75	9%	7.54	38.0	$31
Age	37	05 BAL	593	86	168	27	88	7	283	234	304	339	474	813	8	81	31	0.45	267	37	18	45	119	13%	66	7%	5.41	15.3	$22
Bats	Right	06 BAL	624	96	171	16	83	11	274	253	282	332	391	723	8	84	30	0.55	249	39	20	41	71	7%	87	7%	4.41	-10.7	$18
Health	B	07 BAL	467	67	128	14	58	9	274	254	280	340	418	758	9	82	31	0.57	256	40	19	42	93	9%	80	9%	4.89	0.2	$14
PT/Exp	A	08 BAL	513	77	146	23	104	3	285	314	272	333	483	816	7	86	29	0.53	298	42	21	37	117	14%	59	8%	5.40	7.7	$21
Consist	A	1st Half	288	35	66	10	39	2	229			284	389	673	7	84	24	0.48	270	43	19	38	98	11%	60	13%	3.76	-10.0	$6
LIMA Plan	C	2nd Half	225	42	80	13	65	1	356			396	604	1000	6	89	36	0.63	333	40	24	36	141	18%	62	3%	7.39	14.4	$15
+/- Score	-13	09 Proj	517	76	142	21	89	2	275			330	454	784	8	85	29	0.56	282	40	21	39	108	12%	52	5%	5.09	3.2	$17

The odds of a 37 year-old repeating a late career surge, especially given that the surge occurred in little more than 2 months, is virtually nil. When bidding hits $20, you should have dropped out $5 ago.

Morgan,Nyjer			AB	R	H	HR	RBI	SB	Avg	vL	vR	OB	Slg	OPS	bb%	ct%	h%	Eye	xBA	G	L	F	PX	hr/f	SX	SBO	RC/G	RAR	R$
Pos	7	04	0	0	0	0	0	0	0							0			0						0				
Age	28	05	0	0	0	0	0	0	0							0			0						0				
Bats	Left	06 aa	219	31	56	1	8	17	254			294	322	615	5	87	29	0.42	0				37		149	46%	3.16	-14.0	$6
Health	A	07 PIT	* 271	37	71	1	14	25	262	259	313	310	332	642	7	83	31	0.41	246	57	16	27	41	2%	152	45%	3.46	-15.6	$9
PT/Exp	F	08 PIT	* 482	67	127	1	33	42	264	240	304	297	331	628	5	84	31	0.30	270	50	25	26	51	1%	144	45%	3.21	-31.9	$17
Consist	A	1st Half	193	20	38	0	10	16	195			224	233	457	4	82	24	0.21	250	67	15	19	29	0%	136	60%	1.05	-27.8	$3
LIMA Plan	F	2nd Half	289	47	89	1	23	26	309			345	396	742	5	85	36	0.37	282	44	28	28	65	1%	142	38%	4.60	-6.6	$14
+/- Score	-1	09 Proj	132	18	35	0	8	12	265			305	327	631	5	84	31	0.36	258	53	21	26	43	1%	135	44%	3.28	-8.4	$5

0-7-.294, 9 SB in 160 AB at PIT. Did well after Aug callup (.347); gets a leg-up on '09 PT. Needs to increase bb% to get OBA to a reasonable level. If he wins a regular job, SX and SBO lead to... UP: 40 SB.

Morneau,Justin			AB	R	H	HR	RBI	SB	Avg	vL	vR	OB	Slg	OPS	bb%	ct%	h%	Eye	xBA	G	L	F	PX	hr/f	SX	SBO	RC/G	RAR	R$
Pos	3	04 MIN	* 568	83	157	36	112	1	276	240	283	341	537	878	9	83	28	0.58	291	38	16	46	152	17%	34	1%	6.22	19.9	$22
Age	27	05 MIN	490	62	117	22	79	0	239	205	254	301	437	738	8	81	25	0.47	271	42	18	41	121	14%	56	2%	4.54	-8.0	$12
Bats	Left	06 MIN	592	97	190	34	130	3	321	315	325	377	559	936	8	84	34	0.57	305	36	24	41	137	17%	49	4%	6.85	22.8	$29
Health	A	07 MIN	590	84	160	31	111	1	271	228	294	343	492	834	10	85	28	0.70	289	45	16	39	130	16%	53	1%	5.77	8.6	$21
PT/Exp	A	08 MIN	623	97	187	23	129	0	300	284	310	376	499	875	11	86	32	0.89	298	43	19	38	124	11%	48	1%	6.43	19.9	$25
Consist	B	1st Half	321	44	99	12	63	0	308			369	483	852	9	84	34	0.60	277	46	19	35	103	13%	55	1%	5.98	6.2	$13
LIMA Plan	C+	2nd Half	302	53	88	11	66	0	291			383	517	900	13	89	30	1.36	321	41	19	40	145	10%	43	0%	6.90	13.7	$12
+/- Score	2	09 Proj	597	92	174	27	121	1	291			364	509	872	10	85	30	0.78	299	42	19	39	132	14%	54	1%	6.30	17.2	$24

A drop in hr/f hurt HR totals, but he was no less productive overall. 2nd half PX was more in line with recent past, so HRs should return in '09.

Moss,Brandon			AB	R	H	HR	RBI	SB	Avg	vL	vR	OB	Slg	OPS	bb%	ct%	h%	Eye	xBA	G	L	F	PX	hr/f	SX	SBO	RC/G	RAR	R$
Pos	79	04	0	0	0	0	0	0	0							0			0						0				
Age	25	05 aa	500	74	127	13	53	5	254			314	406	720	8	78	30	0.40	0				106		89	6%	4.40	-9.3	$12
Bats	Left	06 aa	508	66	138	11	72	7	271			336	416	752	9	81	32	0.51	0				99		75	9%	4.88	-4.9	$13
Health	A	07 aaa	493	59	136	13	70	3	276			347	452	800	10	73	35	0.41	0				140		46	6%	5.65	6.4	$13
PT/Exp	D	08 2TM	* 399	42	98	14	58	3	247	267	239	305	437	742	8	72	31	0.30	261	44	20	36	134	13%	87	6%	4.73	-4.9	$9
Consist	B	1st Half	197	25	52	7	29	2	262			315	451	766	7	73	33	0.28	276	41	28	31	132	15%	96	6%	5.03	-0.6	$6
LIMA Plan	D	2nd Half	202	17	47	7	29	1	232			294	424	718	8	72	29	0.31	256	45	18	37	136	13%	73	5%	4.43	-4.3	$4
+/- Score	28	09 Proj	343	39	88	10	48	3	257			320	432	752	8	74	32	0.36	262	44	20	36	126	11%	75	6%	4.88	-2.8	$8

8-34-.246 in 236 AB at BOS and PIT.
PRO: Above average power
CON: Struggles to make contact; coming off Sept. knee surgery.
If healthy, could be a sleeper power source.

Murphy,Daniel			AB	R	H	HR	RBI	SB	Avg	vL	vR	OB	Slg	OPS	bb%	ct%	h%	Eye	xBA	G	L	F	PX	hr/f	SX	SBO	RC/G	RAR	R$
Pos	7	04	0	0	0	0	0	0	0							0			0						0				
Age	24	05	0	0	0	0	0	0	0							0			0						0				
Bats	Left	06	0	0	0	0	0	0	0							0			0						0				
Health	A	07 aa	361	48	98	11	56	12	271			333	432	765	8	89	28	0.84	0				97		84	18%	5.03	-1.8	$12
PT/Exp	F	08 NYM	* 492	72	139	13	73	12	283	400	306	350	443	793	9	86	31	0.76	322	41	33	25	100	12%	96	14%	5.42	-0.1	$18
Consist	A	1st Half	243	32	70	7	39	7	286			335	436	770	7	90	30	0.69	0				89		90	13%	4.98	-3.0	$10
LIMA Plan	C	2nd Half	249	40	69	6	34	5	279			365	450	814	12	83	32	0.80	317	41	33	25	112	11%	97	14%	5.84	3.1	$9
+/- Score	26	09 Proj	340	48	94	9	51	9	276			343	438	781	9	87	30	0.79	325	41	33	25	99	12%	92	16%	5.27	-1.1	$12

2-17.313 in 131 AB at NYM. 39% hit rate in majors. While he's got good ct%, he's not a .300 hitter. A good end-game power-speed combo for those who like across-the-board contributors.

Murphy,David			AB	R	H	HR	RBI	SB	Avg	vL	vR	OB	Slg	OPS	bb%	ct%	h%	Eye	xBA	G	L	F	PX	hr/f	SX	SBO	RC/G	RAR	R$
Pos	97	04	0	0	0	0	0	0	0							0			0						0				
Age	27	05 aa	480	59	123	12	63	11	257			311	394	705	7	85	28	0.52	0				87		92	14%	4.22	-10.8	$13
Bats	Left	06 a/a	490	59	127	10	61	6	259			327	422	749	9	85	29	0.67	0				106		80	9%	4.93	-4.1	$10
Health	B	07 2AL	* 512	56	137	10	51	7	267	409	325	318	405	723	7	85	30	0.49	288	42	26	32	89	7%	95	7%	4.45	-15.6	$10
PT/Exp	C	08 TEX	415	64	114	15	74	7	275	258	282	325	465	790	7	83	30	0.44	282	42	18	40	121	11%	102	9%	5.17	-2.3	$15
Consist	B	1st Half	315	44	85	10	52	5	270			313	451	764	6	82	30	0.35	274	41	17	42	120	9%	95	10%	4.82	-4.9	$10
LIMA Plan	C+	2nd Half	100	20	29	5	22	2	290			360	510	870	10	87	29	0.85	307	45	20	36	124	16%	103	7%	6.23	2.4	$5
+/- Score	12	09 Proj	451	66	127	16	70	7	282			339	469	808	8	85	30	0.57	289	43	19	37	114	11%	100	8%	5.45	0.9	$16

Was tearing it up before knee injury ended season in early August. Got the most he could out of a middling skill set, with help from lineup and ballpark. Average hr/f and FB% mean PX will likely come down.

DAVE ADLER

Murphy,Donnie			AB	R	H	HR	RBI	SB	Avg	vL	vR	OB	Slg	OPS	bb%	ct%	h%	Eye	xBA	G	L	F	PX	hr/f	SX	SBO	RC/G	RAR	R$
Pos	5	04	0	0	0	0	0	0	0							0			0						0				
Age	26	05 aa	214	25	58	7	24	1	271			304	430	733	4	89	28	0.42	0				93		59	4%	4.39	-1.5	$6
Bats	Right	06 aa	366	43	77	9	34	5	209			240	347	587	4	86	22	0.29	0				85		86	15%	2.70	-29.3	$3
Health	B	07 OAK	* 293	46	76	8	39	4	261	279	187	315	434	749	7	75	32	0.32	256	35	19	46	133	8%	86	9%	4.78	-0.7	$8
PT/Exp	F	08 OAK	* 244	28	50	11	33	3	205	196	175	256	389	645	6	70	25	0.22	250	38	23	39	132	16%	80	9%	3.26	-12.4	$4
Consist	D	1st Half	89	10	16	4	10	2	177			244	330	574	8	64	23	0.24	220	43	22	35	113	20%	63	11%	2.26	-7.5	$1
LIMA Plan	F	2nd Half	155	18	34	7	23	1	221			263	423	686	5	73	26	0.21	265	30	26	44	142	13%	74	7%	3.78	-5.2	$3
+/- Score	33	09 Proj	122	15	30	5	15	1	246			292	433	725	6	75	29	0.26	263	37	22	42	128	14%	54	8%	4.28	-2.2	$3

3-13-.184 in 103 AB at OAK. Elbow injury shortened season; four-year plunge in ct% calls for a shorter swing. Power is real and will extend his fanalytic shelf-life, but MLB transition has proven tough (.607 career OPS).

Murton,Matt			AB	R	H	HR	RBI	SB	Avg	vL	vR	OB	Slg	OPS	bb%	ct%	h%	Eye	xBA	G	L	F	PX	hr/f	SX	SBO	RC/G	RAR	R$
Pos	7	04	0	0	0	0	0	0	0							0			0						0				
Age	27	05 CHC	* 487	60	150	15	54	17	308	380	246	364	459	823	8	86	33	0.65	291	62	14	24	87	15%	104	15%	5.61	3.7	$20
Bats	Right	06 CHC	455	70	135	13	62	5	297	301	295	360	444	804	9	86	32	0.73	289	58	18	24	84	14%	79	5%	5.47	2.8	$16
Health	A	07 CHC	* 386	58	107	13	43	2	278	319	257	345	456	801	9	86	30	0.71	281	47	16	37	109	11%	61	2%	5.44	0.9	$11
PT/Exp	C	08 2TM	* 391	35	86	1	28	5	220	125	217	277	292	568	7	89	25	0.70	266	60	16	25	53	1%	69	9%	2.86	-27.6	$2
Consist	C	1st Half	222	20	54	1	16	3	243			308	313	620	9	90	27	0.96	274	67	15	19	49	2%	63	7%	3.55	-10.6	$2
LIMA Plan	F	2nd Half	169	15	32	0	12	2	189			235	264	499	6	87	22	0.45	259	53	17	30	58	0%	80	12%	1.92	-17.5	($1)
+/- Score	56	09 Proj	207	24	54	3	20	2	261			319	379	698	8	87	29	0.66	273	54	17	29	76	7%	68	7%	4.25	-5.5	$4

0-8-.186 in 70 AB at CHC and OAK. Unfortunate h% and hr/f% contributed to the 2008 wreckage, but G/L/F rate history extinguishes power hopes. Steady and solid plate skills provide current limited value.

Nady,Xavier			AB	R	H	HR	RBI	SB	Avg	vL	vR	OB	Slg	OPS	bb%	ct%	h%	Eye	xBA	G	L	F	PX	hr/f	SX	SBO	RC/G	RAR	R$
Pos	97	04 SD	* 368	50	102	19	66	2	277	344	178	320	492	812	6	87	27	0.49	313	58	17	25	119	24%	62	2%	5.27	-0.2	$14
Age	30	05 SD	326	40	85	13	43	2	261	323	220	307	439	746	6	79	29	0.33	271	44	20	36	112	14%	75	4%	4.54	-6.7	$9
Bats	Right	06 2NL	468	57	131	17	63	3	280	336	263	323	453	776	6	82	31	0.35	266	46	17	37	106	12%	52	5%	4.91	1.9	$14
Health	A	07 PIT	431	55	120	20	72	3	278	295	274	315	476	791	5	77	32	0.23	267	39	21	40	127	15%	60	4%	5.03	1.9	$15
PT/Exp	B	08 2TM	555	76	169	25	97	2	305	262	317	350	510	860	7	81	34	0.38	300	41	25	34	131	16%	52	2%	5.93	10.0	$23
Consist	B	1st Half	257	37	81	10	49	1	315			371	514	885	8	82	35	0.50	307	39	27	35	132	14%	41	1%	6.38	7.6	$11
LIMA Plan	D+	2nd Half	298	39	88	15	48	1	295			331	507	838	5	81	32	0.28	295	43	23	34	130	18%	52	3%	5.54	2.2	$12
+/- Score	-13	09 Proj	531	80	154	24	97	3	290			332	488	820	6	80	32	0.32	286	42	22	36	125	15%	63	3%	5.41	2.9	$21

First 500-AB season nets career year. Is it repeatable?
PRO: Rising PX and hr/f; better lineup in NY.
CON: Unsustainable LD% spike; Eye ratio suspect.
Could ditto 2008, but DN: 2007.

Napoli,Mike			AB	R	H	HR	RBI	SB	Avg	vL	vR	OB	Slg	OPS	bb%	ct%	h%	Eye	xBA	G	L	F	PX	hr/f	SX	SBO	RC/G	RAR	R$
Pos	2	04	0	0	0	0	0	0	0							0			0						0				
Age	27	05 aa	439	71	87	22	74	9	199			299	398	697	13	75	21	0.57	0				131		89	13%	4.14	3.3	$12
Bats	Right	06 LAA	* 346	57	78	18	51	3	225	185	241	337	434	770	14	65	29	0.48	222	34	14	52	155	15%	50	7%	5.47	11.3	$9
Health	C	07 LAA	219	40	54	10	34	5	247	291	232	345	443	788	13	71	30	0.52	246	36	19	46	139	14%	94	11%	5.52	8.0	$7
PT/Exp	D	08 LAA	227	39	62	20	49	7	273	286	270	370	586	956	13	69	31	0.50	276	31	17	52	209	24%	83	15%	7.80	23.8	$13
Consist	C	1st Half	137	17	29	12	29	4	212			299	489	788	11	68	21	0.39	240	28	11	60	181	21%	51	16%	5.23	4.5	$5
LIMA Plan	C+	2nd Half	90	22	33	8	20	3	367			472	733	1206	17	71	45	0.69	325	35	24	41	251	31%	103	14%	11.52	17.0	$8
+/- Score	-5	09 Proj	301	56	81	21	56	7	269			371	531	902	14	70	32	0.54	265	33	18	48	179	20%	83	12%	7.11	25.1	$14

FB history, rising PX, hr/f and xBA validate power spike. If ct% even reached the high-70s, he'd be a dangerous player. As is, catching demands and health risk temper expectations. But with 400 AB... UP: 30 HR

Navarro,Dioner			AB	R	H	HR	RBI	SB	Avg	vL	vR	OB	Slg	OPS	bb%	ct%	h%	Eye	xBA	G	L	F	PX	hr/f	SX	SBO	RC/G	RAR	R$
Pos	2	04 a/a	391	46	101	3	42	2	259			332	349	681	10	88	29	0.89	0				59		73	2%	4.22	1.8	$6
Age	25	05 LA	* 417	43	103	7	35	1	247	435	248	322	346	668	10	91	26	1.31	275	45	22	33	61	6%	29	4%	4.14	4.4	$6
Bats	Both	06 2TM	* 308	30	74	6	29	3	241	286	245	315	336	651	10	82	28	0.59	240	35	24	41	60	6%	47	4%	3.62	-6.9	$4
Health	B	07 TAM	388	46	88	9	44	3	227	226	227	287	356	643	8	83	25	0.49	248	42	17	41	84	7%	76	4%	3.47	-9.6	$5
PT/Exp	C	08 TAM	427	43	126	7	54	0	295	257	308	347	407	755	7	89	32	0.69	282	46	23	30	76	6%	17	3%	4.87	8.2	$11
Consist	B	1st Half	208	23	65	4	31	0	313			364	438	802	8	89	34	0.74	287	48	22	30	83	7%	23	5%	5.42	7.0	$7
LIMA Plan	D	2nd Half	219	20	61	3	23	0	279			331	379	710	7	88	31	0.65	282	45	25	30	69	5%	22	2%	4.35	1.0	$4
+/- Score	-21	09 Proj	414	43	112	8	47	0	271			329	390	719	8	86	30	0.63	269	43	22	35	77	7%	31	2%	4.45	2.5	$8

H% is an outlier given previous levels and makes BA repeat unlikely. Would like to see more indication of power growth by now; more FB is a place to start. Still just 25, and without a strong RHP/LHP split, so there's time.

Newhan,David			AB	R	H	HR	RBI	SB	Avg	vL	vR	OB	Slg	OPS	bb%	ct%	h%	Eye	xBA	G	L	F	PX	hr/f	SX	SBO	RC/G	RAR	R$
Pos	4	04 BAL	* 635	105	188	15	80	18	296	297	316	343	454	796	7	81	35	0.38	271	49	18	33	95	9%	150	11%	5.28	21.0	$23
Age	35	05 BAL	218	31	44	5	21	9	202	250	194	275	312	587	9	79	23	0.49	253	53	17	29	75	10%	100	21%	2.74	-9.6	$4
Bats	Left	06 BAL	131	14	33	4	18	4	252	182	266	290	374	664	5	83	28	0.32	249	50	17	34	71	11%	67	19%	3.49	-2.5	$3
Health	C	07 aa	173	16	38	4	18	4	218			269	340	609	6	81	25	0.36	0				78		85	21%	2.96	-7.6	$2
PT/Exp	F	08 HOU	* 302	36	72	8	35	6	239	286	258	273	387	660	5	81	27	0.25	273	51	18	30	94	11%	107	14%	3.47	-11.8	$7
Consist	B	1st Half	209	26	48	6	25	5	230			260	377	637	4	84	25	0.26	0	63	13	25	92	13%	98	20%	3.20	-10.1	$5
LIMA Plan	F	2nd Half	93	10	24	2	10	1	258			303	409	712	6	73	33	0.24	250	50	19	31	101	10%	98	5%	4.27	-1.4	$2
+/- Score	6	09 Proj	99	11	24	2	11	2	242			286	375	661	6	80	28	0.30	257	50	18	32	83	10%	98	14%	3.53	-3.5	$2

2-12-.260 in 104 AB at HOU. League-average PX and SX would seem to have value off the bench. But age, declining Eye and starter/sub splits (.308 BA as a starter; .179 as a sub/PH) make us dubious.

Nieves,Wil			AB	R	H	HR	RBI	SB	Avg	vL	vR	OB	Slg	OPS	bb%	ct%	h%	Eye	xBA	G	L	F	PX	hr/f	SX	SBO	RC/G	RAR	R$
Pos	2	04 aaa	421	42	101	7	37	2	239			254	350	604	2	88	26	0.17	0				65		71	12%	2.85	-15.7	$5
Age	31	05 aaa	380	34	91	3	29	1	240			258	318	576	2	91	26	0.27	0				52		59	2%	2.68	-13.9	$3
Bats	Right	06 aaa	321	24	71	5	28	2	221			255	298	553	4	91	23	0.49	0				45		40	4%	2.49	-18.6	$1
Health	A	07 NYY	* 151	11	30	1	14	1	199			234	265	499	4	86	22	0.33	311	52	35	13	44	6%	63	3%	1.75	-12.1	($0)
PT/Exp	F	08 WAS	* 201	18	50	1	22	1	250	304	242	301	324	625	7	83	30	0.42	252	54	20	26	55	2%	57	3%	3.26	-5.6	$2
Consist	C	1st Half	104	12	24	1	12	1	233			286	299	585	7	81	28	0.39	222	61	12	27	48	4%	52	3%	2.69	-4.8	$1
LIMA Plan	F	2nd Half	97	6	26	0	10	0	268			317	351	668	7	85	32	0.47	277	49	26	26	62	0%	52	4%	3.86	-1.0	$1
+/- Score	-17	09 Proj	132	10	31	1	13	1	235			276	316	592	5	86	27	0.40	275	53	24	24	54	3%	62	4%	2.87	-5.5	$1

1-20-.261 in 176 AB at WAS. Sustained bb% gain throughout 2008 merely lifted him from unrosterable to just shy of replacement level. But GB and anemic PX history indicate the chance of relevance is bleak.

Norton,Greg			AB	R	H	HR	RBI	SB	Avg	vL	vR	OB	Slg	OPS	bb%	ct%	h%	Eye	xBA	G	L	F	PX	hr/f	SX	SBO	RC/G	RAR	R$
Pos	7	04 DET	* 270	30	46	5	15	1	170	182	167	253	256	509	10	75	21	0.45	196	40	15	45	54	6%	64	3%	1.65	-29.0	($1)
Age	36	05 aaa	323	41	77	14	41	0	240			309	426	735	9	82	25	0.55	0				115		38	2%	4.55	-4.7	$8
Bats	Both	06 TAM	294	47	87	17	45	1	296	283	299	371	520	891	11	77	34	0.51	270	38	19	42	140	18%	32	7%	6.59	11.7	$12
Health	B	07 TAM	202	25	49	4	23	1	243	174	251	360	347	706	15	73	31	0.67	225	33	24	43	80	6%	35	3%	4.55	-2.9	$3
PT/Exp	D	08 2TM	187	29	49	7	35	0	262	192	289	373	439	811	15	76	31	0.75	279	45	24	30	123	16%	27	0%	5.88	4.0	$6
Consist	D	1st Half	113	13	27	2	16	0	239			333	372	705	12	76	30	0.59	280	48	28	24	106	10%	24	0%	4.47	-2.3	$2
LIMA Plan	F	2nd Half	74	16	22	5	19	0	297			429	541	969	19	77	33	1.00	281	42	19	39	150	23%	30	0%	7.98	5.8	$4
+/- Score	-23	09 Proj	150	23	39	7	25	0	260			367	455	822	14	76	30	0.70	270	40	22	37	129	17%	34	2%	5.94	3.4	$5

Power rebounded, but attribute 2H surge to uncharacteristic hr/f. Maintained good plate skills, and for two years has connected with authority (LD%). Best used as situational/PH: OPS vs RHP, .841; vs. LHP, .735.

Ochoa,Ivan			AB	R	H	HR	RBI	SB	Avg	vL	vR	OB	Slg	OPS	bb%	ct%	h%	Eye	xBA	G	L	F	PX	hr/f	SX	SBO	RC/G	RAR	R$
Pos	6	04	0	0	0	0	0	0	0							0			0						0				
Age	26	05 aa	419	39	100	2	26	14	239			283	301	584	6	83	28	0.36	0				41		101	26%	2.69	-20.4	$6
Bats	Both	06 a/a	374	53	86	1	28	22	230			303	281	583	9	83	28	0.60	0				35		130	24%	2.89	-17.1	$8
Health	A	07 aa	179	17	46	2	16	7	255			285	361	646	4	85	29	0.29	0				70		106	21%	3.41	-5.1	$4
PT/Exp	F	08 SF	* 412	52	106	5	29	17	257	244	173	311	349	660	7	79	31	0.38	237	60	11	30	65	5%	108	26%	3.63	-12.5	$10
Consist	A	1st Half	272	42	78	5	27	15	287			348	397	745	9	81	34	0.50	0				70		124	31%	4.75	0.9	$11
LIMA Plan	F	2nd Half	140	10	28	0	2	2	198			236	255	491	5	75	26	0.20	207	60	11	30	55	0%	56	11%	1.33	-14.7	($1)
+/- Score	-15	09 Proj	197	21	47	1	13	7	239			285	315	601	6	81	29	0.34	233	60	11	30	56	3%	100	22%	2.88	-9.7	$3

0-3-.200 in 120 AB in SF. Raised expectations with .318/.399/.445 three-month run at Triple-A, but was severely overmatched upon recall. Any future value will be derived from SB, though SBO and SX were down in 2H. Wait.

BRENT HERSHEY

Ojeda,Augie

			AB	R	H	HR	RBI	SB	Avg	vL	vR	OB	Slg	OPS	bb%	ct%	h%	Eye	xBA	G	L	F	PX	hr/f	SX	SBO	RC/G	RAR	R$
Pos	456	04 MIN	* 386	54	87	4	23	6	226			300	303	604	10	91	24	1.17	0				50		71	12%	3.43	-7.8	$4
Age	34	05 aaa	310	32	58	2	25	3	186			247	247	494	8	90	20	0.78	0				44		62	7%	2.04	-23.0	($0)
Bats	Both	06 aaa	306	33	65	3	21	4	212			300	274	574	11	87	23	1.00	0				38		68	5%	3.02	-12.7	$1
Health	A	07 ARI	* 210	27	51	1	22	2	244	250	292	314	310	624	9	88	27	0.82	248	43	21	36	41	2%	86	3%	3.53	-7.3	$3
PT/Exp	F	08 ARI	231	27	56	0	17	0	242	250	240	319	299	618	10	90	27	1.08	254	50	20	31	38	0%	56	0%	3.61	-8.0	$2
Consist	A	1st Half	94	10	29	0	14	0	309			375	394	769	10	89	35	1.00	288	55	23	22	52	0%	72	0%	5.30	1.3	$3
LIMA Plan	F	2nd Half	137	17	27	0	3	0	197			281	234	515	10	90	22	1.14	228	46	18	37	29	0%	40	0%	2.46	-10.0	($1)
+/- Score	-17	09 Proj	126	15	30	0	10	1	238			314	304	617	10	89	27	0.99	256	48	20	32	43	1%	71	2%	3.55	-4.4	$1

Exhibit A on the value of the entire profile. Outfitted with appropriate blinders, bb%, ct% and Eye ratio look pretty good. But when one's SLG has not exceeded OBA since 2004, it's time to change lanes. Quickly.

Olivo,Miguel

			AB	R	H	HR	RBI	SB	Avg	vL	vR	OB	Slg	OPS	bb%	ct%	h%	Eye	xBA	G	L	F	PX	hr/f	SX	SBO	RC/G	RAR	R$
Pos	20	04 2AL	301	46	70	13	40	7	233	322	196	280	439	719	6	72	28	0.24	254	47	14	39	134	16%	132	22%	4.29	-0.4	$8
Age	30	05 2TM	* 300	36	68	11	43	7	225	284	188	247	381	628	3	72	28	0.11	244	47	18	35	109	15%	103	17%	2.87	-9.5	$7
Bats	Right	06 FLA	430	52	113	16	58	2	263	273	258	278	440	717	2	76	31	0.09	255	42	19	39	112	13%	70	6%	3.99	-4.4	$11
Health	A	07 FLA	452	43	107	16	60	3	237	295	221	260	405	665	3	73	29	0.11	239	43	17	40	112	12%	75	6%	3.39	-14.1	$8
PT/Exp	C	08 KC	306	29	78	12	41	7	255	262	251	272	444	716	2	73	31	0.09	255	38	17	44	140	12%	73	14%	4.04	-1.3	$8
Consist	B	1st Half	180	17	47	9	28	2	261			285	494	779	3	72	32	0.12	273	40	18	42	174	16%	44	7%	4.97	4.1	$5
LIMA Plan	F	2nd Half	126	12	31	3	13	5	246			252	373	625	1	75	30	0.03	226	36	17	47	94	7%	85	23%	2.77	-5.3	$3
+/- Score	2	09 Proj	239	25	59	8	31	4	247			265	420	685	2	74	30	0.09	248	41	17	42	123	11%	88	13%	3.64	-4.3	$6

Took power to new levels in 1H, then griped about 2H PT when production waned. Rising FB, solid hr/f and PX history say HR spike possible; xBA, bb% reveal little BA hope. UP: 400 AB, 20 HR. DN: 200 AB, malcontent.

Ordonez,Magglio

			AB	R	H	HR	RBI	SB	Avg	vL	vR	OB	Slg	OPS	bb%	ct%	h%	Eye	xBA	G	L	F	PX	hr/f	SX	SBO	RC/G	RAR	R$
Pos	9	04 CHW	202	32	59	9	37	0	292	339	273	344	485	829	7	89	29	0.73	284	49	15	36	100	14%	69	4%	5.61	5.1	$8
Age	35	05 DET	305	38	92	8	46	0	302	308	300	364	436	800	9	89	32	0.86	284	44	23	34	84	9%	23	0%	5.45	6.2	$10
Bats	Right	06 DET	593	82	177	24	104	1	298	294	300	348	477	825	7	85	32	0.52	273	45	18	38	104	13%	35	3%	5.53	-2.2	$21
Health	C	07 DET	595	117	216	28	139	4	363	410	351	435	595	1030	11	87	39	0.96	316	42	19	39	146	14%	57	2%	8.22	40.5	$36
PT/Exp	A	08 DET	561	72	178	21	103	1	317	328	314	376	494	870	9	86	34	0.70	288	44	20	36	107	12%	36	3%	6.17	12.4	$23
Consist	F	1st Half	300	42	92	12	50	0	307			373	490	863	10	87	32	0.80	285	43	19	38	112	12%	24	2%	6.16	6.6	$12
LIMA Plan	C	2nd Half	261	30	86	9	53	1	330			379	498	878	7	86	36	0.58	290	45	22	33	100	12%	50	5%	6.19	5.8	$11
+/- Score	-33	09 Proj	538	79	165	20	100	0	307			368	491	859	9	87	32	0.72	290	44	20	37	112	12%	39	2%	6.07	10.3	$21

Made up for mid-season DL stint with scorching Sept (5 HR, 25 RBI). Best non-'07 season since '03; stable skills indicate this could be his mid-30s plateau. That does mean that 30-HR are a thing of the past, though.

Ortiz,David

			AB	R	H	HR	RBI	SB	Avg	vL	vR	OB	Slg	OPS	bb%	ct%	h%	Eye	xBA	G	L	F	PX	hr/f	SX	SBO	RC/G	RAR	R$
Pos	0	04 BOS	582	94	175	41	139	0	301	250	326	381	603	984	11	77	33	0.56	304	35	20	46	189	20%	43	0%	7.83	40.3	$29
Age	33	05 BOS	601	119	180	47	148	1	300	300	297	401	604	1005	15	79	32	0.82	316	31	23	46	189	21%	51	1%	8.13	34.8	$34
Bats	Left	06 BOS	558	115	160	54	137	1	287	278	292	412	636	1048	18	79	27	1.02	315	36	17	47	200	26%	51	1%	8.76	36.3	$31
Health	C	07 BOS	549	116	182	35	117	3	332	308	343	444	621	1065	17	81	36	1.08	317	38	17	45	188	17%	59	2%	9.09	41.2	$32
PT/Exp	A	08 BOS	416	74	110	23	89	1	264	221	279	370	507	878	14	82	27	0.95	295	37	19	45	152	15%	53	1%	6.58	19.8	$17
Consist	C	1st Half	210	36	53	13	43	0	252			354	486	840	14	82	25	0.89	278	39	16	45	138	17%	29	0%	5.99	6.5	$8
LIMA Plan	B+	2nd Half	206	38	57	10	46	1	277			387	529	916	15	82	30	1.00	308	34	21	45	166	13%	67	2%	7.19	13.2	$9
+/- Score	18	09 Proj	533	102	154	35	118	2	289			399	564	963	15	81	30	0.96	306	36	18	45	172	18%	55	1%	7.68	31.6	$26

Sept statements that wrist is "not OK" contradict a 6-HR, .336 xBA month. Assuming health, expect a rebound to near pre-2008 levels, though keep an eye on L/R splits and eroding hr/f.

Ortmeier,Dan

			AB	R	H	HR	RBI	SB	Avg	vL	vR	OB	Slg	OPS	bb%	ct%	h%	Eye	xBA	G	L	F	PX	hr/f	SX	SBO	RC/G	RAR	R$
Pos	7	04	0	0	0	0	0	0	0							0			0						0				
Age	27	05 aa	503	68	120	14	64	29	238			291	385	677	7	80	27	0.37	0				92		139	35%	3.78	-19.5	$17
Bats	Both	06 a/a	429	45	94	7	36	12	219			265	328	593	6	84	25	0.38	0				69		101	25%	2.82	-32.5	$5
Health	B	07 SF	* 462	48	108	13	55	13	233	257	310	274	387	661	5	78	27	0.26	260	53	14	32	99	11%	115	17%	3.50	-26.1	$9
PT/Exp	F	08 SF	* 161	14	31	1	12	5	193	238	182	244	267	511	6	73	26	0.26	222	65	11	24	66	4%	75	28%	1.59	-20.1	$1
Consist	C	1st Half	64	4	14	0	5	2	219			296	313	608	10	72	30	0.39	231	65	11	24	94	0%	54	27%	3.14	-4.6	$0
LIMA Plan	F	2nd Half	97	10	17	1	7	3	175			208	237	445	4	74	23	0.16	0				48		92	29%	0.58	-15.6	$0
+/- Score	-0	09 Proj	113	11	25	2	10	4	221			268	338	606	6	77	27	0.28	248	62	12	26	82	8%	103	25%	2.87	-8.9	$2

0-5-.219 in 64 AB in SF. A May X-ray revealed a broken finger he didn't know he had; was out for 2 mos. Gave up switch-hitting in April, returned to it in Aug. Rocky season for anyone, let alone a sub-100 PX infielder.

Overbay,Lyle

			AB	R	H	HR	RBI	SB	Avg	vL	vR	OB	Slg	OPS	bb%	ct%	h%	Eye	xBA	G	L	F	PX	hr/f	SX	SBO	RC/G	RAR	R$
Pos	3	04 MIL	583	83	175	16	88	2	300	298	301	386	479	864	12	78	36	0.63	286	45	23	31	128	11%	48	2%	6.51	8.9	$20
Age	32	05 MIL	537	80	148	19	72	1	276	270	278	367	449	816	13	82	31	0.80	292	51	21	27	114	16%	51	1%	5.81	3.2	$17
Bats	Left	06 TOR	581	82	181	22	92	5	312	284	322	371	508	879	9	83	34	0.57	302	46	22	32	124	14%	56	5%	6.32	14.2	$22
Health	B	07 TOR	425	49	102	10	44	2	240	287	224	316	391	706	10	82	27	0.60	282	49	21	31	105	9%	66	2%	4.37	-11.3	$6
PT/Exp	A	08 TOR	544	74	147	15	69	1	270	215	291	358	419	777	12	79	32	0.64	269	44	23	33	103	11%	47	2%	5.31	0.6	$14
Consist	C	1st Half	273	37	72	6	33	1	264			372	396	767	15	79	32	0.81	260	50	20	30	90	9%	58	3%	5.36	0.7	$6
LIMA Plan	C	2nd Half	271	37	75	9	36	0	277			342	443	785	9	79	32	0.47	279	38	26	36	116	12%	27	0%	5.23	-0.3	$8
+/- Score	-17	09 Proj	518	69	141	15	66	1	272			350	435	785	11	80	31	0.61	280	45	22	32	110	11%	48	1%	5.34	1.1	$13

Can he revisit 2006 or is wrist injury too much to overcome? PRO: 2H gain--FB, hr/f, and PX. CON: 2H expense--bb%, Eye; struggled vLHP all year. At 32, needs a perfect season to be much over replacement level.

Ozuna,Pablo

			AB	R	H	HR	RBI	SB	Avg	vL	vR	OB	Slg	OPS	bb%	ct%	h%	Eye	xBA	G	L	F	PX	hr/f	SX	SBO	RC/G	RAR	R$
Pos	4	04 aaa	472	58	114	5	57	23	242			269	324	593	3	91	26	0.39	0				51		120	35%	2.91	-20.8	$12
Age	34	05 CHW	203	27	56	0	11	14	276	306	248	300	330	630	3	87	32	0.27	287	73	15	12	37	0%	137	39%	3.22	-5.5	$6
Bats	Right	06 CHW	189	25	62	2	17	6	328	322	348	352	444	796	4	92	35	0.44	287	49	19	32	71	4%	101	23%	5.15	5.4	$7
Health	D	07 CHW	78	9	19	0	3	3	244	256	231	272	282	554	4	88	28	0.33	223	51	13	37	32	0%	84	16%	2.41	-3.7	$1
PT/Exp	F	08 2TM	96	11	25	1	9	1	260	387	200	283	344	627	3	92	28	0.38	269	57	16	28	47	4%	89	17%	3.26	-4.5	$2
Consist	D	1st Half	61	3	17	0	6	0	279			302	311	613	3	95	29	0.67	234	52	17	31	25	0%	22	6%	3.26	-2.8	$1
LIMA Plan	F	2nd Half	35	8	8	1	3	1	229			250	400	650	3	86	24	0.20	309	66	14	21	91	16%	195	50%	3.35	-1.7	$1
+/- Score	-17	09 Proj	101	11	28	0	9	4	277			302	347	649	3	91	30	0.39	275	59	17	24	44	2%	104	25%	3.53	-3.1	$3

With enough AB, ct% should produce a passable BA (more than can be said for many utility IF). And for a 34-year old, his SX score is holding up well. But with that Eye ratio and PX, plate appearances will be scarce.

Pagan,Angel

			AB	R	H	HR	RBI	SB	Avg	vL	vR	OB	Slg	OPS	bb%	ct%	h%	Eye	xBA	G	L	F	PX	hr/f	SX	SBO	RC/G	RAR	R$
Pos	7	04 a/a	494	72	129	3	55	28	261			315	360	676	7	82	31	0.43	0				66		153	27%	3.92	-18.6	$15
Age	27	05 aaa	509	57	124	6	32	23	244			297	338	635	7	81	29	0.41	0				61		121	29%	3.35	-26.4	$11
Bats	Both	06 CHC	170	28	42	5	18	4	247	196	272	308	394	702	8	84	27	0.54	260	51	15	34	81	10%	112	14%	4.18	-5.4	$4
Health	F	07 CHC	* 264	34	62	7	28	8	237	236	289	283	391	674	6	80	27	0.33	244	36	18	46	96	7%	126	18%	3.74	-12.9	$6
PT/Exp	F	08 NYM	91	12	25	0	13	4	275	250	294	353	374	727	11	80	34	0.61	247	36	23	41	79	0%	115	14%	4.79	-1.6	$3
Consist	B	1st Half	91	12	25	0	13	4	275			353	374	727	11	80	34	0.61	247	36	23	41	79	0%	115	14%	4.79	-1.6	$3
LIMA Plan	F	2nd Half	0	0	0	0	0	0	0																				
+/- Score	-10	09 Proj	133	18	34	2	15	4	256			317	383	700	8	81	30	0.48	250	42	19	39	82	5%	118	15%	4.23	-4.5	$3

Season cut short in May by torn labrum suffered while diving into the stands after a foul ball; had surgery in July. Sustained gains in bb% could provide SB opps, but first has to establish health and win a role.

Patterson,Corey

			AB	R	H	HR	RBI	SB	Avg	vL	vR	OB	Slg	OPS	bb%	ct%	h%	Eye	xBA	G	L	F	PX	hr/f	SX	SBO	RC/G	RAR	R$
Pos	8	04 CHC	631	91	168	24	72	32	266	289	258	315	452	767	7	73	33	0.27	250	40	19	41	123	13%	139	27%	4.93	5.2	$25
Age	29	05 CHC	* 542	60	121	17	44	20	223	169	231	264	362	626	5	74	27	0.22	239	46	18	36	92	12%	115	23%	2.95	-26.9	$12
Bats	Left	06 BAL	463	75	128	16	53	45	276	207	301	308	443	751	4	80	32	0.22	256	39	21	40	99	11%	166	50%	4.51	-2.1	$23
Health	A	07 BAL	461	65	124	8	45	37	269	310	251	301	386	687	4	86	30	0.32	253	44	21	35	78	5%	132	42%	3.86	-9.0	$18
PT/Exp	C	08 CIN	366	46	75	10	34	14	205	188	209	238	344	582	4	84	22	0.28	259	46	15	38	85	8%	123	37%	2.58	-25.4	$7
Consist	B	1st Half	190	25	36	6	16	10	189			222	342	564	4	88	19	0.35	262	43	14	43	89	8%	141	54%	2.48	-14.1	$4
LIMA Plan	C	2nd Half	176	21	39	4	18	4	222			255	347	602	4	81	25	0.24	255	50	17	33	81	9%	98	24%	2.74	-11.0	$3
+/- Score	37	09 Proj	411	55	103	11	41	16	251			284	392	676	4	83	28	0.27	256	45	17	39	88	8%	119	28%	3.66	-12.0	$12

Oh, the benefits that come with #1 prospect hype. MLB GMs (and some of your competitors) will look at double-digit HR and SB and fill a roster spot. You see declining SX, below-avg power, awful Eye and think "ABs at risk."

BRENT HERSHEY

Patterson,Eric			AB	R	H	HR	RBI	SB	Avg	vL	vR	OB	Slg	OPS	bb%	ct%	h%	Eye	xBA	G	L	F	PX	hr/f	SX	SBO	RC/G	RAR	R$
Pos	4	04	0	0	0	0	0	0	0							0			0						0				
Age	26	05	0	0	0	0	0	0	0							0			0						0				
Bats	Left	06 a/a	508	79	137	11	59	46	270			339	411	750	9	81	32	0.54	0				85		159	39%	4.87	7.7	$23
Health	A	07 aa	516	75	135	12	52	19	261			317	401	718	7	85	29	0.55	0				85		116	21%	4.40	0.7	$15
PT/Exp	D	08 2TM	*445	54	108	8	50	24	242	217	187	294	361	656	7	79	29	0.35	237	39	18	43	84	5%	130	26%	3.55	-17.0	$13
Consist	B	1st Half	225	25	61	6	27	10	270			308	417	725	5	78	32	0.25	247	38	19	42	100	8%	115	20%	4.31	-3.4	$7
LIMA Plan	D	2nd Half	220	29	47	2	23	15	214			281	304	585	9	80	26	0.46	228	40	18	43	69	3%	128	31%	2.80	-13.9	$5
+/- Score	-1	09 Proj	226	31	57	4	24	12	252			310	381	690	8	82	29	0.45	245	39	18	43	84	6%	127	27%	4.05	-3.7	$7

1-15-.188, 10 SB in 133 AB at CHC and OAK. Flashed power/speed combo in 1H at AAA; will need to improve ct% at MLB level (73%) to repeat. For now, speed skills are ready.
UP: 350 AB, 20 SB.

Paulino,Ronny			AB	R	H	HR	RBI	SB	Avg	vL	vR	OB	Slg	OPS	bb%	ct%	h%	Eye	xBA	G	L	F	PX	hr/f	SX	SBO	RC/G	RAR	R$
Pos	2	04 aa	369	43	93	12	48	2	252			298	410	709	6	87	26	0.50	0				93		56	5%	4.20	1.4	$8
Age	28	05 a/a	436	54	115	14	46	5	265			312	412	724	6	87	28	0.51	0				89		79	4%	4.36	5.8	$11
Bats	Right	06 PIT	*471	39	144	6	59	1	306	339	300	356	390	747	7	82	36	0.42	247	47	23	31	58	5%	25	1%	4.68	4.4	$12
Health	A	07 PIT	457	56	120	11	55	2	263	407	218	312	389	702	7	83	30	0.42	252	47	17	36	83	8%	44	3%	4.09	-4.5	$10
PT/Exp	C	08 PIT	*229	21	54	5	32	0	235	235	202	299	377	676	8	76	29	0.39	250	43	19	38	107	7%	38	3%	3.88	-2.3	$3
Consist	A	1st Half	149	16	38	5	26	0	252			315	434	749	8	81	28	0.48	279	42	20	38	123	10%	48	3%	4.78	2.5	$4
LIMA Plan	F	2nd Half	80	5	16	0	6	0	204			269	271	541	8	68	30	0.29	0	60	0	40	71	0%	25	5%	2.06	-5.4	($0)
+/- Score	19	09 Proj	65	6	16	1	8	0	246			303	360	663	8	78	30	0.37	246	45	20	34	84	6%	33	3%	3.65	-1.1	$1

2-18-.212 in 118 AB at PIT. After some modest skills gains in the 1H, ankle injury derailed 2008. Problems vRHP have worsened; replacement-level upside only a possibility if MLB team takes a chance. And the stars align.

Payton,Jay			AB	R	H	HR	RBI	SB	Avg	vL	vR	OB	Slg	OPS	bb%	ct%	h%	Eye	xBA	G	L	F	PX	hr/f	SX	SBO	RC/G	RAR	R$
Pos	78	04 SD	458	57	119	8	55	2	260	283	248	323	367	690	9	88	28	0.77	245	43	16	41	61	5%	78	2%	4.20	-16.5	$9
Age	36	05 2AL	408	62	109	18	63	0	267	283	258	308	444	751	6	88	27	0.51	285	42	19	38	98	13%	50	1%	4.59	-1.5	$13
Bats	Right	06 OAK	557	78	165	10	59	8	296	296	296	323	418	741	4	91	31	0.42	286	45	22	34	73	6%	94	8%	4.52	-10.3	$15
Health	B	07 BAL	434	48	111	7	58	5	256	285	244	292	376	667	5	90	27	0.52	277	50	17	33	72	5%	91	7%	3.80	-15.8	$8
PT/Exp	B	08 BAL	340	41	82	7	41	8	241	248	240	291	344	635	7	84	27	0.45	250	45	19	36	62	7%	100	10%	3.32	-15.5	$7
Consist	B	1st Half	157	18	40	6	30	3	255			295	395	690	5	82	28	0.32	246	45	16	39	82	12%	61	8%	3.77	-5.0	$5
LIMA Plan	F	2nd Half	183	23	42	1	11	5	230			288	301	588	8	86	26	0.60	253	45	22	33	45	2%	111	13%	2.98	-10.4	$2
+/- Score	-6	09 Proj	231	28	59	4	28	3	255			299	369	668	6	87	28	0.49	264	46	19	35	67	6%	88	7%	3.75	-8.1	$5

The four-year slippery slope: OPS, xBA, PX all trending south. Speed skills holding up OK, but do you want to spend auction cash on a 36-year old needing AB and SB opps to justify a roster spot? Not with that OBA.

Pearce,Steven			AB	R	H	HR	RBI	SB	Avg	vL	vR	OB	Slg	OPS	bb%	ct%	h%	Eye	xBA	G	L	F	PX	hr/f	SX	SBO	RC/G	RAR	R$
Pos	9	04	0	0	0	0	0	0	0							0			0						0				
Age	26	05	0	0	0	0	0	0	0							0			0						0				
Bats	Right	06	0	0	0	0	0	0	0							0			0						0				
Health	A	07 PIT	*480	74	141	15	78	12	293	429	259	342	482	823	7	87	31	0.57	308	48	20	32	117	11%	102	12%	5.59	9.6	$19
PT/Exp	D	08 PIT	*495	45	113	13	64	11	229	321	222	274	378	652	6	82	26	0.34	252	38	17	45	100	7%	80	15%	3.44	-26.4	$10
Consist	F	1st Half	298	27	70	8	41	5	233			272	391	664	5	86	25	0.39					103		56	15%	3.63	-14.2	$6
LIMA Plan	D	2nd Half	197	17	44	5	23	7	223			276	358	633	7	75	27	0.30	228	38	17	45	94	7%	95	16%	3.19	-12.0	$4
+/- Score	7	09 Proj	328	38	83	9	46	8	253			301	412	713	6	83	28	0.39	263	40	17	42	104	8%	86	14%	4.22	-8.1	$9

4-15-.248 in 109 AB at PIT. Hit all 4 HR in final three weeks. MLB contact (80%), xBA (.262) indicate ready skills, and has some speed to boot. Just needs an opportunity.
UP: 400 AB, 18 HR, 15 SB.

Pedroia,Dustin			AB	R	H	HR	RBI	SB	Avg	vL	vR	OB	Slg	OPS	bb%	ct%	h%	Eye	xBA	G	L	F	PX	hr/f	SX	SBO	RC/G	RAR	R$
Pos	4	04	0	0	0	0	0	0	0							0			0						0				
Age	25	05 a/a	453	63	125	10	52	7	276			343	415	758	9	92	28	1.35	0				85		84	8%	5.12	10.1	$13
Bats	Right	06 BOS	*512	56	145	7	53	1	283	162	212	349	404	754	9	94	29	1.68	301	48	23	30	75	5%	39	4%	5.16	15.1	$10
Health	A	07 BOS	520	86	165	8	50	7	317	348	303	374	442	816	8	92	33	1.12	284	43	18	38	83	4%	80	5%	5.70	23.8	$17
PT/Exp	A	08 BOS	653	118	213	17	83	20	326	313	331	374	493	867	7	92	34	0.96	310	43	21	36	104	8%	112	11%	6.14	21.7	$30
Consist	A	1st Half	343	54	104	8	37	9	303			343	440	784	6	91	32	0.68	296	44	22	34	87	7%	92	10%	5.10	2.0	$13
LIMA Plan	D+	2nd Half	310	64	109	9	46	11	352			407	552	959	9	93	36	1.38	326	42	20	38	123	8%	117	13%	7.27	18.8	$18
+/- Score	7	09 Proj	634	105	210	19	84	23	331			385	504	890	8	92	34	1.17	310	43	20	37	105	9%	106	13%	6.45	33.0	$31

Growth in power and speed arrived sooner than expected and vaulted him into the 2B elite. Across-the-board growth 1H-to-2H hints at more upside. Ct%/Eye combo legitimates BA title. One worth paying for.

Pena,Carlos			AB	R	H	HR	RBI	SB	Avg	vL	vR	OB	Slg	OPS	bb%	ct%	h%	Eye	xBA	G	L	F	PX	hr/f	SX	SBO	RC/G	RAR	R$
Pos	3	04 DET	481	89	116	27	82	7	241	245	240	338	472	810	13	70	29	0.48	251	40	16	44	153	18%	112	6%	5.80	11.7	$17
Age	30	05 DET	*517	73	131	28	82	3	254	146	255	342	462	804	12	70	31	0.45	247	38	18	45	146	17%	47	5%	5.66	8.7	$17
Bats	Left	06 BOS	*451	66	112	21	68	4	249	273	273	339	433	772	12	76	28	0.57	258	48	17	35	115	18%	58	3%	5.13	-3.8	$12
Health	A	07 TAM	490	99	138	46	121	1	282	271	286	406	627	1033	17	71	30	0.73	308	37	18	45	233	30%	46	1%	8.96	51.0	$28
PT/Exp	B	08 TAM	490	76	121	31	102	1	247	190	280	370	494	864	16	66	31	0.58	250	32	18	50	181	19%	49	1%	6.86	23.1	$18
Consist	F	1st Half	223	28	51	11	37	0	229			325	426	751	13	67	29	0.43	225	36	15	49	143	15%	39	0%	5.05	-1.5	$5
LIMA Plan	C+	2nd Half	267	48	70	20	65	1	262			405	551	955	19	66	32	0.70	269	28	20	51	213	22%	52	2%	8.36	24.0	$13
+/- Score	3	09 Proj	497	83	128	34	103	2	258			374	521	895	16	69	30	0.60	265	34	18	48	182	21%	59	2%	7.12	26.9	$20

Big 2H salvaged season, though disappointed those expecting 2007 repeat. Sustained bb% but not hr/f rate; continued ct% drop is especially troublesome. The skinny: Pay for a .250-ish hitter with some serious thump.

Pena,Tony			AB	R	H	HR	RBI	SB	Avg	vL	vR	OB	Slg	OPS	bb%	ct%	h%	Eye	xBA	G	L	F	PX	hr/f	SX	SBO	RC/G	RAR	R$
Pos	6	04 aa	495	56	113	10	29	21	229			250	327	577	3	81	27	0.14	0				64		99	36%	2.32	-30.6	$9
Age	28	05 aaa	485	41	109	4	35	15	225			251	309	560	3	79	28	0.17	0				63		95	32%	2.21	-31.5	$6
Bats	Right	06 ATL	*344	48	91	2	25	11	265			293	340	633	4	81	32	0.22	259	53	22	25	50	3%	122	16%	3.16	-12.0	$8
Health	A	07 KC	509	58	136	2	47	5	267	271	266	281	356	637	2	85	31	0.13	270	57	19	25	60	2%	100	10%	3.18	-16.5	$8
PT/Exp	D	08 KC	225	22	38	1	14	3	169	243	135	190	209	399	3	78	21	0.12	214	55	16	29	28	2%	99	11%	0.10	-31.2	($1)
Consist	D	1st Half	169	15	26	0	8	3	154			178	189	368	3	79	20	0.14	220	53	18	29	27	0%	108	15%	-0.22	-25.7	($2)
LIMA Plan	F	2nd Half	56	7	12	1	6	0	214			228	268	496	2	77	26	0.08	187	60	9	30	30	8%	52	0%	1.10	-5.6	$0
+/- Score	28	09 Proj	68	8	15	1	6	1	221			240	276	516	2	80	27	0.13	225	57	15	28	40	4%	72	11%	1.57	-5.8	$1

Speed the only positive here. When you consistently sport an OPS in the low .600s, a mid-teens Eye ratio and a 60ish PX, it still sometimes takes a 21% h% before you lose your job. Whatta gig.

Pena,Wily Mo			AB	R	H	HR	RBI	SB	Avg	vL	vR	OB	Slg	OPS	bb%	ct%	h%	Eye	xBA	G	L	F	PX	hr/f	SX	SBO	RC/G	RAR	R$
Pos	7	04 CIN	336	45	87	26	66	5	259	302	244	304	527	831	6	68	30	0.20	269	50	16	33	174	34%	72	10%	5.79	3.4	$15
Age	27	05 CIN	311	42	79	19	51	2	254	291	234	299	492	791	6	63	34	0.17	259	48	20	32	189	31%	50	5%	5.63	2.7	$11
Bats	Right	06 BOS	276	36	83	11	42	0	301	260	326	348	489	837	7	67	41	0.22	242	40	21	39	137	15%	57	1%	6.16	7.5	$9
Health	F	07 2TM	289	42	73	13	39	2	253	330	203	305	439	745	7	67	33	0.23	248	48	20	32	136	21%	69	4%	4.76	-3.7	$8
PT/Exp	D	08 WAS	195	10	40	2	10	0	205	241	179	244	267	511	5	75	26	0.21	217	54	21	25	47	5%	17	2%	1.50	-24.0	($1)
Consist	F	1st Half	174	10	38	2	10	0	218			261	287	548	5	76	28	0.24	225	53	22	26	52	6%	18	3%	2.02	-18.2	($0)
LIMA Plan	F	2nd Half	21	0	2	0	0	0	95			95	95	190	0	71	13	0.00	117	67	13	20	0	0%	3	0%	-3.10	-6.3	($1)
+/- Score	33	09 Proj	262	29	67	10	33	1	256			302	427	729	6	69	33	0.22	247	48	21	32	122	18%	56	4%	4.47	-7.0	$6

April oblique injury and shoulder surgery in July contributed to lost season. PX history has tantalized, but still seeks opportunity. Health and PT a prerequisite; more FB, 70% ct would be icing. High risk/reward.

Pence,Hunter			AB	R	H	HR	RBI	SB	Avg	vL	vR	OB	Slg	OPS	bb%	ct%	h%	Eye	xBA	G	L	F	PX	hr/f	SX	SBO	RC/G	RAR	R$
Pos	9	04	0	0	0	0	0	0	0							0			0						0				
Age	26	05	0	0	0	0	0	0	0							0			0						0				
Bats	Right	06 aa	523	81	133	24	79	15	254			317	471	788	8	82	27	0.51	0				124		126	16%	5.19	-0.3	$18
Health	A	07 HOU	*551	70	174	20	86	13	315	354	314	354	531	885	6	80	36	0.31	299	49	19	32	135	14%	116	13%	6.31	21.5	$24
PT/Exp	B	08 HOU	595	78	160	25	83	11	269	250	275	315	466	781	6	79	30	0.32	276	52	14	34	125	15%	88	15%	4.98	-3.6	$21
Consist	C	1st Half	304	37	81	10	40	5	266			310	438	747	6	79	31	0.30	263	47	16	37	113	11%	83	16%	4.58	-5.5	$9
LIMA Plan	C+	2nd Half	291	41	79	15	43	6	271			321	495	815	7	79	30	0.35	289	57	12	31	138	21%	91	15%	5.40	1.8	$12
+/- Score	-1	09 Proj	608	87	172	30	100	10	283			329	516	846	6	80	31	0.35	293	48	16	35	142	18%	99	13%	5.78	12.7	$25

Wild month-to-month swings (2 mos of sub-.700 OPS, 2 mos of .900+) characterized season, but nice foundation overall. PX and hr/f primed for a party if/when all those GB turn into LD and FB. Get on the guest list.

BRENT HERSHEY

Pennington,Cliff

			AB	R	H	HR	RBI	SB	Avg	vL	vR	OB	Slg	OPS	bb%	ct%	h%	Eye	xBA	G	L	F	PX	hr/f	SX	SBO	RC/G	RAR	R$
Pos	4	04	0	0	0	0	0	0	0							0			0						0				
Age	24	05	0	0	0	0	0	0	0							0			0						0				
Bats	Both	06	0	0	0	0	0	0	0							0			0						0				
Health	A	07 aa	271	34	60	2	17	7	222			302	294	595	10	89	24	1.08	0				48		90	11%	3.32	-8.6	$3
PT/Exp	F	08 OAK	*539	80	126	1	34	27	233	289	213	334	284	617	13	87	27	1.14	216	36	19	46	36	0%	116	19%	3.65	-20.4	$11
Consist	A	1st Half	315	47	69	1	19	16	219			315	280	596	12	88	25	1.15	0				40		121	22%	3.40	-14.7	$5
LIMA Plan	D	2nd Half	224	33	57	0	15	11	253			359	288	647	14	85	30	1.14	209	36	19	46	30	0%	87	15%	4.01	-5.8	$5
+/- Score	-1	09 Proj	215	30	50	1	14	9	233			326	290	616	12	88	26	1.12	222	36	19	46	40	1%	100	15%	3.61	-5.7	$3

0-9-.242 in 99 AB at OAK. An exception to the tenet that strong Eye and ct% yields a high BA. 2008 AAA line (.297 BA/ .426 OB; 236 AB) offers a bit of hope; any improvement would provide potential SB value.

Peralta,Jhonny

			AB	R	H	HR	RBI	SB	Avg	vL	vR	OB	Slg	OPS	bb%	ct%	h%	Eye	xBA	G	L	F	PX	hr/f	SX	SBO	RC/G	RAR	R$
Pos	6	04 aaa	556	88	166	12	69	6	298			349	440	789	7	82	35	0.44	0				97		77	7%	5.22	14.3	$18
Age	26	05 CLE	504	82	147	24	78	0	292	305	288	365	520	885	10	75	35	0.45	285	46	19	35	158	18%	59	1%	6.65	29.4	$19
Bats	Right	06 CLE	569	84	146	13	68	0	257	267	252	323	385	708	9	73	33	0.37	236	48	19	34	91	9%	57	1%	4.30	-1.9	$11
Health	A	07 CLE	574	87	155	21	72	4	270	275	269	340	430	770	10	75	33	0.42	252	47	19	35	111	14%	60	5%	5.07	13.0	$17
PT/Exp	A	08 CLE	605	104	167	23	89	3	276	247	285	329	473	802	7	79	32	0.38	284	44	20	36	132	13%	90	3%	5.35	17.5	$21
Consist	B	1st Half	296	47	76	12	35	2	257			306	453	759	7	79	29	0.33	279	44	18	37	132	14%	81	3%	4.75	3.6	$8
LIMA Plan	C+	2nd Half	309	57	91	11	54	1	294			351	492	843	8	80	34	0.43	289	43	22	35	131	13%	85	2%	5.92	13.6	$12
+/- Score	38	09 Proj	609	99	168	21	85	3	276			336	451	787	8	77	33	0.40	269	45	20	35	119	13%	75	3%	5.23	15.4	$19

Now, 2005's 18% hr/f, 35% h% seen as borderline outliers. In the three seasons since, PX, xBA ct% all trending up, while hr/f relatively stable. With this many AB at 26, is a power spike in the offing? UP: 30 HR, 100 RBI

Phillips,Brandon

			AB	R	H	HR	RBI	SB	Avg	vL	vR	OB	Slg	OPS	bb%	ct%	h%	Eye	xBA	G	L	F	PX	hr/f	SX	SBO	RC/G	RAR	R$
Pos	4	04 CLE	*543	65	141	6	39	11	260	167	188	306	361	667	6	91	28	0.71	269	35	24	41	65	3%	80	20%	3.91	-2.9	$10
Age	27	05 aaa	459	60	102	10	35	5	222			270	340	610	6	85	24	0.42	0				76		78	11%	3.02	-18.8	$6
Bats	Right	06 CIN	536	65	148	17	75	25	276	299	268	320	427	748	6	84	30	0.40	271	46	19	35	90	11%	102	20%	4.58	-0.2	$20
Health	A	07 CIN	650	107	187	30	94	32	288	341	262	322	485	807	5	83	31	0.30	285	47	18	35	111	16%	133	25%	5.15	8.3	$31
PT/Exp	A	08 CIN	559	80	146	21	78	23	261	296	247	309	442	751	7	83	28	0.42	281	50	16	34	105	13%	128	25%	4.65	-2.0	$22
Consist	B	1st Half	323	48	90	13	47	16	279			325	480	805	6	83	30	0.41	289	49	17	35	117	14%	145	24%	5.28	4.8	$15
LIMA Plan	C+	2nd Half	236	32	56	8	31	7	237			289	390	678	7	83	25	0.44	270	52	16	32	88	13%	107	25%	3.79	-7.2	$7
+/- Score	19	09 Proj	526	85	144	23	75	21	274			318	464	782	6	84	29	0.40	286	49	17	34	109	15%	121	23%	4.94	3.6	$23

2007 is the outlier; fueled by 100 more AB and hr/f uptick. 2008 repeated skills from '06 (RC/G). Solid 20/20 potential, but G/L/F caps his power for now. As BA rebounds, ample SBO and SX could drive SB spike.

Pierre,Juan

			AB	R	H	HR	RBI	SB	Avg	vL	vR	OB	Slg	OPS	bb%	ct%	h%	Eye	xBA	G	L	F	PX	hr/f	SX	SBO	RC/G	RAR	R$
Pos	7	04 FLA	678	100	221	3	49	45	326	305	334	368	407	775	6	95	34	1.29	299	56	21	23	43	2%	138	30%	5.19	-4.8	$30
Age	31	05 FLA	656	96	181	2	47	57	276	284	267	319	354	672	6	93	29	0.91	309	55	25	20	43	2%	170	39%	4.05	-24.9	$27
Bats	Left	06 CHC	699	87	204	3	40	58	292	293	291	323	388	711	4	95	31	0.84	305	55	21	24	52	2%	147	41%	4.40	-17.1	$26
Health	B	07 LA	668	96	196	0	41	64	293	274	301	327	353	680	5	94	31	0.89	285	53	21	26	36	0%	147	40%	4.08	-24.5	$27
PT/Exp	A	08 LA	375	44	106	1	28	40	283	346	257	322	328	650	6	94	30	0.92	289	53	24	23	28	1%	126	45%	3.76	-18.3	$16
Consist	A	1st Half	274	30	76	0	24	35	277			320	318	637	6	94	30	1.00	286	53	23	24	28	0%	126	51%	3.66	-14.1	$13
LIMA Plan	D+	2nd Half	101	14	30	1	4	5	297			330	356	687	5	93	31	0.71	296	55	26	20	29	5%	112	31%	4.02	-4.2	$3
+/- Score	-17	09 Proj	299	40	87	1	18	25	291			327	353	680	5	94	31	0.86	293	54	23	23	36	2%	135	39%	4.05	-11.5	$12

Lowest AB total since 2000, but speed remained a roto game-changer. Likely to get dinged up more as he ages--his DL trip was a career first. SX starting to wane, but batting profile still consistent. PT=SB.

Pierzynski,A.J.

			AB	R	H	HR	RBI	SB	Avg	vL	vR	OB	Slg	OPS	bb%	ct%	h%	Eye	xBA	G	L	F	PX	hr/f	SX	SBO	RC/G	RAR	R$
Pos	2	04 SF	471	45	128	11	77	0	272	227	283	300	410	710	4	94	27	0.70	287	47	19	35	78	7%	39	1%	4.27	6.2	$11
Age	32	05 CHW	460	61	118	18	56	0	257	230	262	292	420	711	5	85	27	0.34	285	46	22	32	98	14%	35	2%	4.05	0.5	$11
Bats	Left	06 CHW	509	65	150	16	64	1	295	270	304	324	436	760	4	86	32	0.31	279	44	23	33	84	11%	43	1%	4.60	2.7	$14
Health	A	07 CHW	472	54	124	14	50	1	263	252	266	300	403	702	5	86	28	0.38	262	43	18	39	88	9%	37	2%	4.02	-3.7	$10
PT/Exp	B	08 CHW	534	66	150	13	60	1	281	286	279	306	416	721	3	87	30	0.27	266	44	18	38	86	7%	50	1%	4.18	-0.2	$13
Consist	A	1st Half	274	36	81	5	30	1	296			328	423	751	5	89	32	0.43	272	45	17	38	83	5%	63	1%	4.65	3.5	$7
LIMA Plan	C	2nd Half	260	30	69	8	30	0	265			282	408	690	2	84	29	0.15	259	43	18	39	90	9%	31	0%	3.66	-3.9	$6
+/- Score	-3	09 Proj	505	61	134	12	54	1	265			294	391	685	4	86	29	0.30	263	44	19	37	80	8%	43	1%	3.78	-6.8	$10

4 reasons to be cautious:
- Career-high AB total
- Lowest Eye ratio since 2002
- Mediocre xBA two yrs running
- hr/f in steep decline

Steady ct% a plus; if that slips... DN: .250, single-digit HR

Pie,Felix

			AB	R	H	HR	RBI	SB	Avg	vL	vR	OB	Slg	OPS	bb%	ct%	h%	Eye	xBA	G	L	F	PX	hr/f	SX	SBO	RC/G	RAR	R$
Pos	8	04	0	0	0	0	0	0	0							0			0						0				
Age	24	05 aa	240	39	71	12	23	13	298			341	538	879	6	81	33	0.34	0				152		133	42%	6.19	12.4	$12
Bats	Left	06 aaa	559	78	165	17	57	18	295			350	468	818	8	81	34	0.44	0				107		107	20%	5.60	16.7	$20
Health	A	07 CHC	*406	69	115	10	57	16	283	111	241	333	436	769	7	81	33	0.39	271	48	20	32	92	9%	137	22%	4.94	4.8	$16
PT/Exp	D	08 CHC	*418	51	104	9	51	11	249	91	264	290	381	671	5	83	28	0.33	262	49	17	34	83	8%	106	21%	3.68	-13.4	$11
Consist	B	1st Half	198	21	40	4	24	5	204			242	319	561	5	80	24	0.25	243	45	18	38	76	7%	101	19%	2.26	-15.5	$3
LIMA Plan	D	2nd Half	220	30	64	5	28	6	290			332	437	769	6	85	32	0.42	0	62	15	23	90	11%	110	22%	4.91	1.1	$8
+/- Score	6	09 Proj	263	37	72	7	32	9	274			319	428	747	6	82	31	0.37	274	49	19	32	96	10%	115	23%	4.63	0.0	$9

1-10-.241 in 83 AB in CHC. Never fully recovered from 1H h%, but 2H plate skills are aligned with MLEs. Still owns impressive 2005 (PX and SX) and 2007 (SX) BPI. Overdue for clear MLB opportunity.

Podsednik,Scott

			AB	R	H	HR	RBI	SB	Avg	vL	vR	OB	Slg	OPS	bb%	ct%	h%	Eye	xBA	G	L	F	PX	hr/f	SX	SBO	RC/G	RAR	R$
Pos	8	04 MIL	645	86	157	12	39	70	243	224	249	306	363	669	8	84	27	0.55	255	48	17	35	71	6%	162	49%	3.85	-15.8	$26
Age	33	05 CHW	507	80	147	0	25	59	290	330	284	350	349	699	8	85	34	0.63	271	56	20	23	49	0%	129	50%	4.31	0.5	$24
Bats	Left	06 CHW	524	86	137	3	45	40	261	216	278	330	353	684	9	82	32	0.56	263	49	23	28	63	2%	146	38%	4.12	-8.6	$18
Health	D	07 CHW	*287	40	70	3	16	14	244	279	229	296	363	659	7	82	29	0.41	275	53	19	28	83	4%	135	32%	3.69	-7.4	$6
PT/Exp	D	08 COL	162	22	41	1	15	12	253	167	264	320	333	654	9	83	30	0.57	272	51	24	24	58	3%	121	34%	3.73	-4.9	$5
Consist	A	1st Half	103	13	23	1	13	8	223			304	301	605	10	84	26	0.75	259	56	18	26	48	4%	129	30%	3.25	-4.7	$3
LIMA Plan	F	2nd Half	59	9	18	0	2	4	305			349	390	739	6	80	38	0.33	295	43	36	21	77	0%	94	41%	4.65	-0.2	$2
+/- Score	-9	09 Proj	161	23	43	1	11	11	267			325	360	686	8	82	32	0.48	275	50	25	26	69	3%	121	37%	4.07	-2.7	$5

Plate skills stable, and xBA still calls for a small BA rebound. But at 33, the future is a backup OF -- for as long as his legs hold up. On that front, one look at the SX trend tells you much of what you need to know.

Polanco,Placido

			AB	R	H	HR	RBI	SB	Avg	vL	vR	OB	Slg	OPS	bb%	ct%	h%	Eye	xBA	G	L	F	PX	hr/f	SX	SBO	RC/G	RAR	R$
Pos	4	04 PHI	503	74	150	17	55	7	298	327	287	334	441	775	5	92	30	0.69	303	48	23	29	77	13%	69	8%	4.91	4.3	$18
Age	33	05 2TM	501	84	166	9	56	4	331	348	324	373	447	820	6	95	34	1.32	323	48	27	25	69	8%	78	4%	5.60	16.6	$20
Bats	Right	06 DET	461	58	136	4	52	1	295	272	305	320	364	685	4	94	31	0.63	278	51	21	28	42	3%	53	2%	3.98	-1.8	$10
Health	B	07 DET	587	105	200	9	67	7	341	326	345	380	458	838	6	95	35	1.23	307	45	24	31	72	5%	87	5%	5.79	27.4	$23
PT/Exp	A	08 DET	580	90	178	8	58	7	307	321	301	346	417	764	6	93	32	0.81	282	47	19	35	69	4%	93	5%	4.95	0.9	$18
Consist	C	1st Half	286	42	92	3	29	2	322			364	420	784	6	92	34	0.86	285	49	20	31	64	4%	67	2%	5.20	2.4	$9
LIMA Plan	C	2nd Half	294	48	86	5	29	5	293			329	415	744	5	93	30	0.76	278	44	17	38	74	5%	102	8%	4.70	-1.5	$9
+/- Score	-2	09 Proj	629	99	197	9	67	7	313			350	423	773	5	94	32	0.88	291	47	21	32	67	5%	88	5%	5.04	9.6	$20

Rare is the player you can count on for BA. Top-shelf ct% and repeatedly bettering xBA is the basis here. FB climbing, but poor PX and hr/f history mitigates any additional power hope. Be content w/ consistency.

Posada,Jorge

			AB	R	H	HR	RBI	SB	Avg	vL	vR	OB	Slg	OPS	bb%	ct%	h%	Eye	xBA	G	L	F	PX	hr/f	SX	SBO	RC/G	RAR	R$
Pos	2	04 NYY	449	72	122	21	81	1	272	275	270	391	481	872	16	80	30	0.96	279	52	17	31	133	19%	29	3%	6.68	30.4	$15
Age	37	05 NYY	474	67	124	19	71	1	262	281	246	352	430	782	12	80	29	0.70	259	43	17	39	108	13%	39	1%	5.30	17.6	$14
Bats	Both	06 NYY	465	65	129	23	93	3	277	263	284	365	492	857	12	79	31	0.66	276	38	20	42	132	15%	63	2%	6.24	24.1	$17
Health	F	07 NYY	506	91	171	20	90	2	338	331	341	422	543	966	13	81	39	0.76	296	40	22	37	140	13%	58	1%	7.70	44.9	$24
PT/Exp	C	08 NYY	168	18	45	3	22	0	268	255	274	359	411	770	13	77	33	0.63	256	40	21	40	108	6%	38	0%	5.34	5.5	$3
Consist	D	1st Half	126	13	36	3	20	0	286			366	460	827	11	81	33	0.67	277	36	21	43	124	7%	40	0%	5.96	6.3	$3
LIMA Plan	C	2nd Half	42	5	9	0	2	0	214			340	262	602	16	67	32	0.57	188	54	18	29	52	0%	27	0%	3.16	-1.3	($0)
+/- Score	-19	09 Proj	455	63	127	16	79	0	279			369	468	837	12	80	32	0.72	277	40	20	40	126	11%	44	0%	6.08	23.6	$14

Shoulder woes defined his year, led to DL trip and July surgery. Most plate skills held up, a good sign given his age. Best-case is return to (non-h%-aided) '05-'06 level, but recovery, health are keys. Slow start candidate.

BRENT HERSHEY

Prado,Martin

			AB	R	H	HR	RBI	SB	Avg	vL	vR	OB	Slg	OPS	bb%	ct%	h%	Eye	xBA	G	L	F	PX	hr/f	SX	SBO	RC/G	RAR	R$
Pos	5	04	0	0	0	0	0	0	0							0			0						0				
Age	25	05 aa	143	15	37	1	10	3	259			329	336	665	9	90	28	1.00	0				50		76	14%	4.06	-2.5	$2
Bats	Right	06 ATL	* 459	48	124	4	45	4	270	310	154	315	349	664	6	85	31	0.44	228	49	14	37	49	3%	65	6%	3.70	-23.8	$8
Health	B	07 aaa	395	55	119	4	37	5	301			351	397	748	7	90	33	0.79	0				63		73	7%	4.84	-4.4	$11
PT/Exp	D	08 ATL	228	36	73	2	33	3	320	283	349	378	461	838	8	87	36	0.72	289	42	23	35	93	3%	110	6%	5.99	3.8	$9
Consist	C	1st Half	39	10	11	0	6	1	282			391	462	853	15	92	31	2.33	252	43	3	54	100	0%	137	8%	6.81	1.6	$2
LIMA Plan	D	2nd Half	189	26	62	2	27	2	328			374	460	835	7	86	37	0.54	298	41	27	31	91	4%	84	5%	5.81	2.2	$7
+/- Score	-1	09 Proj	**325**	**39**	**94**	**3**	**35**	**4**	**289**			**339**	**385**	**724**	**7**	**87**	**32**	**0.59**	**245**	**43**	**16**	**41**	**64**	**3%**	**74**	**7%**	**4.52**	**-8.1**	**$8**

Became a valuable bench player and opened the door for more AB in 2009. OPS, bb%, PX and SX are all trending in the right direction. xBA says that he's not really a .300 hitter yet, but at only 25, there's still time.

Pujols,Albert

			AB	R	H	HR	RBI	SB	Avg	vL	vR	OB	Slg	OPS	bb%	ct%	h%	Eye	xBA	G	L	F	PX	hr/f	SX	SBO	RC/G	RAR	R$
Pos	3	04 STL	592	133	196	46	123	5	331	379	319	414	657	1071	12	91	30	1.62	350	41	17	41	174	21%	74	6%	8.58	41.4	$38
Age	29	05 STL	591	129	195	41	117	16	330	300	340	424	609	1034	14	89	32	1.49	336	42	20	38	156	21%	106	9%	8.30	42.2	$41
Bats	Right	06 STL	535	119	177	49	137	7	331	336	329	429	671	1100	15	91	29	1.84	341	37	18	45	170	23%	67	5%	8.98	42.0	$38
Health	A	07 STL	565	99	185	32	103	2	327	367	313	428	568	996	15	90	32	1.71	311	42	19	39	133	16%	32	4%	7.98	28.1	$29
PT/Exp	A	08 STL	524	100	187	37	116	7	357	411	333	463	653	1116	17	90	35	1.93	350	40	22	37	167	21%	53	5%	9.43	49.4	$37
Consist	C	1st Half	241	43	86	17	47	2	357			478	635	1113	19	90	35	2.24	335	47	19	34	153	23%	35	3%	9.55	23.4	$16
LIMA Plan	C	2nd Half	283	57	101	20	69	5	357			450	668	1118	15	90	35	1.66	359	35	25	40	179	20%	59	7%	9.32	25.9	$21
+/- Score	-17	09 Proj	**563**	**110**	**193**	**40**	**122**	**7**	**343**			**444**	**634**	**1078**	**15**	**90**	**33**	**1.80**	**340**	**40**	**21**	**39**	**160**	**20%**	**57**	**5%**	**8.90**	**44.4**	**$37**

Threats of a premature shut-down depressed his draft value, but he rewarded those who stuck by him with a career-high OPS. Off-season elbow surgery should remove his only lingering question mark.

Punto,Nick

			AB	R	H	HR	RBI	SB	Avg	vL	vR	OB	Slg	OPS	bb%	ct%	h%	Eye	xBA	G	L	F	PX	hr/f	SX	SBO	RC/G	RAR	R$
Pos	64	04 MIN	91	17	23	2	12	6	253	250	254	340	319	658	12	79	30	0.63	225	32	29	39	34	7%	105	18%	3.70	-2.0	$4
Age	31	05 MIN	394	45	94	4	26	13	239	210	246	302	335	637	8	78	30	0.42	254	51	21	28	69	5%	113	20%	3.41	-13.9	$7
Bats	Both	06 MIN	459	73	133	1	45	17	290	331	267	356	373	728	9	85	34	0.69	264	46	24	30	53	1%	133	15%	4.72	4.0	$13
Health	C	07 MIN	472	53	99	1	25	16	210	175	226	292	271	563	10	81	26	0.61	224	51	15	35	46	1%	106	17%	2.67	-24.1	$3
PT/Exp	B	08 MIN	338	43	96	2	28	15	284	302	274	346	382	728	9	83	34	0.56	256	45	21	35	69	2%	117	20%	4.64	3.0	$10
Consist	F	1st Half	65	7	17	0	8	4	262			333	354	687	10	85	31	0.70	263	55	16	29	66	0%	117	26%	4.29	-0.1	$2
LIMA Plan	D+	2nd Half	273	36	79	2	20	11	289			349	388	737	8	83	34	0.53	254	42	22	36	69	2%	114	19%	4.72	3.1	$8
+/- Score	-27	09 Proj	**417**	**52**	**109**	**2**	**34**	**17**	**261**			**330**	**348**	**678**	**9**	**83**	**31**	**0.59**	**251**	**48**	**19**	**33**	**61**	**2%**	**120**	**19%**	**4.07**	**-3.4**	**$9**

Rebound year similar to 2006's breakout season. But don't be fooled by BA, as h% and xBA indicate he's more apt to hit .260 than .280. Speed is for real and 20+ SB are in reach, but don't expect much else.

Quentin,Carlos

			AB	R	H	HR	RBI	SB	Avg	vL	vR	OB	Slg	OPS	bb%	ct%	h%	Eye	xBA	G	L	F	PX	hr/f	SX	SBO	RC/G	RAR	R$
Pos	7	04 aa	210	29	68	5	28	0	324			366	486	852	6	92	34	0.82	0				101		34	14%	5.92	4.3	$8
Age	26	05 aaa	452	68	121	16	62	6	268			345	445	789	10	89	27	1.08	0				104		91	5%	5.43	5.2	$15
Bats	Right	06 ARI	* 484	74	127	16	72	5	262	171	280	331	469	800	9	86	28	0.72	296	46	16	38	125	10%	99	4%	5.51	3.6	$14
Health	B	07 ARI	* 344	52	83	9	52	2	242	172	230	294	400	694	7	80	28	0.37	260	43	16	41	110	8%	69	7%	4.03	-13.8	$7
PT/Exp	C	08 CHW	480	96	138	36	100	7	288	246	303	374	571	944	12	83	28	0.83	309	41	15	43	164	21%	78	7%	7.14	30.9	$26
Consist	F	1st Half	285	54	81	19	61	5	284			374	537	911	13	84	28	0.89	290	41	14	45	144	18%	78	9%	6.79	15.7	$15
LIMA Plan	B	2nd Half	195	42	57	17	39	2	292			373	621	993	11	83	28	0.74	334	42	18	40	194	26%	64	4%	7.66	15.2	$11
+/- Score	-6	09 Proj	**505**	**90**	**143**	**27**	**89**	**5**	**283**			**354**	**521**	**875**	**10**	**84**	**29**	**0.67**	**297**	**42**	**16**	**42**	**145**	**15%**	**78**	**6%**	**6.29**	**19.2**	**$21**

Legit breakout season. BA can go even higher according to xBA and gains in bb% and ct%. HRs maxed out with high hr/f (thanks to "The Cell"). Expect a slight dropoff in power in 2009, especially given wrist concerns.

Quinlan,Robb

			AB	R	H	HR	RBI	SB	Avg	vL	vR	OB	Slg	OPS	bb%	ct%	h%	Eye	xBA	G	L	F	PX	hr/f	SX	SBO	RC/G	RAR	R$
Pos	53	04 ANA	* 268	33	81	6	34	4	302	390	317	360	459	819	8	86	33	0.65	296	47	22	31	101	8%	71	8%	5.65	5.5	$8
Age	32	05 ANA	134	17	31	5	14	0	231	289	137	270	403	672	5	81	25	0.27	277	51	18	30	114	15%	45	4%	3.58	-3.7	$2
Bats	Right	06 LAA	234	28	75	9	32	2	321	326	313	340	491	832	3	88	34	0.25	288	53	17	30	95	14%	60	5%	5.32	1.9	$9
Health	B	07 LAA	178	21	44	3	21	3	247	269	203	302	348	650	7	85	28	0.52	241	48	14	38	69	5%	60	11%	3.58	-6.9	$3
PT/Exp	F	08 LAA	164	15	43	1	11	4	262	282	244	320	311	631	8	83	31	0.50	221	48	18	34	26	2%	90	11%	3.35	-7.4	$3
Consist	B	1st Half	89	9	24	1	6	1	270			330	315	645	8	80	33	0.44	193	54	13	33	28	4%	42	7%	3.41	-3.8	$1
LIMA Plan	F	2nd Half	75	6	19	0	5	3	253			309	307	615	7	87	29	0.60	241	42	25	34	22	0%	110	17%	3.30	-3.5	$1
+/- Score	-21	09 Proj	**196**	**20**	**50**	**3**	**19**	**4**	**255**			**306**	**352**	**657**	**7**	**85**	**29**	**0.48**	**249**	**48**	**18**	**34**	**58**	**5%**	**89**	**11%**	**3.64**	**-7.2**	**$4**

The Good: LD% and SX both increased.
The Bad: PX and xBA both sunk to new lows; problems vRHP. Will continue to provide negative RAR production in MLB, but hopefully not in your lineup.

Quintanilla,Omar

			AB	R	H	HR	RBI	SB	Avg	vL	vR	OB	Slg	OPS	bb%	ct%	h%	Eye	xBA	G	L	F	PX	hr/f	SX	SBO	RC/G	RAR	R$
Pos	46	04	0	0	0	0	0	0	0							0			0						0				
Age	27	05 COL	* 474	59	123	4	30	3	259	67	239	299	338	637	5	90	28	0.57	277	42	26	32	48	3%	80	6%	3.49	-14.9	$7
Bats	Left	06 COL	* 342	39	85	3	25	4	249	250	167	298	360	657	7	86	28	0.51	279	52	20	28	73	4%	84	8%	3.74	-8.7	$4
Health	A	07 COL	* 418	47	112	3	37	2	269	100	250	315	373	688	6	83	32	0.40	303	55	29	16	77	5%	66	3%	4.03	-8.0	$6
PT/Exp	D	08 COL	* 283	40	70	3	21	2	248	209	246	309	352	662	8	81	30	0.47	266	52	20	28	81	5%	64	3%	3.76	-8.4	$4
Consist	A	1st Half	212	30	58	2	16	2	275			323	381	704	7	85	32	0.46	287	48	25	27	81	4%	64	3%	4.23	-3.2	$5
LIMA Plan	F	2nd Half	71	10	12	1	5	0	169			272	268	539	12	70	22	0.48	208	60	10	29	83	7%	44	0%	2.10	-6.2	($0)
+/- Score	0	09 Proj	**64**	**8**	**15**	**1**	**5**	**0**	**234**			**297**	**326**	**623**	**8**	**81**	**28**	**0.46**	**249**	**55**	**17**	**28**	**70**	**4%**	**51**	**3%**	**3.27**	**-2.8**	**$1**

2-15-.238 in 210 AB at COL. Epitome of a good-field, no-hit middle infielder. Anemic in both PX and SX, and ct% has now dropped for three straight years. No power, no speed, and poor contact...three strikes, yer out.

Quintero,Humberto

			AB	R	H	HR	RBI	SB	Avg	vL	vR	OB	Slg	OPS	bb%	ct%	h%	Eye	xBA	G	L	F	PX	hr/f	SX	SBO	RC/G	RAR	R$
Pos	2	04 SD	* 331	37	89	6	35	0	270			293	396	689	3	91	28	0.35	0				80		34	3%	3.92	1.1	$6
Age	29	05 HOU	* 254	23	56	6	31	1	220			244	346	590	3	84	24	0.21	286	61	20	18	82	16%	44	4%	2.60	-9.3	$3
Bats	Right	06 HOU	* 313	33	82	3	31	3	262			298	366	664	5	86	30	0.36	316	61	28	11	69	10%	77	4%	3.68	-6.0	$5
Health	A	07 HOU	* 230	17	55	3	16	0	240			254	336	590	2	85	27	0.12	302	55	30	15	63	11%	40	4%	2.57	-12.9	$1
PT/Exp	F	08 HOU	* 298	25	61	4	24	0	205	273	215	230	277	507	3	84	23	0.20	222	59	12	29	46	5%	43	3%	1.64	-24.1	$0
Consist	C	1st Half	159	12	31	2	12	0	193			210	259	469	2	88	21	0.17	248	61	15	24	39	5%	58	6%	1.31	-14.8	($1)
LIMA Plan	F	2nd Half	139	13	31	2	12	0	220			252	298	550	4	80	26	0.21	206	58	11	31	54	6%	30	0%	2.07	-9.1	$1
+/- Score	20	09 Proj	**237**	**21**	**54**	**3**	**20**	**0**	**228**			**252**	**319**	**571**	**3**	**84**	**26**	**0.21**	**247**	**58**	**15**	**27**	**59**	**6%**	**52**	**3%**	**2.42**	**-13.2**	**$1**

2-12-.226 in 168 AB at HOU. 2008 AB set a new career high in his 6th season in MLB. At 29, isn't it time for that late-career batting surge? He did have a 7-game hitting streak in August, so that might have been it.

Quiroz,Guillermo

			AB	R	H	HR	RBI	SB	Avg	vL	vR	OB	Slg	OPS	bb%	ct%	h%	Eye	xBA	G	L	F	PX	hr/f	SX	SBO	RC/G	RAR	R$
Pos	2	04 aaa	255	28	59	7	28	0	231			300	408	707	9	83	25	0.59	0				115		40	0%	4.35	2.1	$3
Age	27	05 TOR	* 119	12	24	5	20	0	202	95	333	258	361	619	7	71	24	0.26	184	62	0	38	110	15%	22	0%	2.87	-4.3	$2
Bats	Right	06 a/a	202	17	49	5	32	0	240			285	360	645	6	79	28	0.30	0				79		18	0%	3.30	-6.5	$3
Health	B	07 aa	259	17	59	5	25	1	226			259	330	589	4	82	26	0.24	0				73		29	2%	2.62	-13.7	$1
PT/Exp	F	08 BAL	134	12	25	2	14	0	187	200	183	253	269	522	8	75	23	0.35	203	50	15	35	62	6%	26	0%	1.77	-10.3	($0)
Consist	B	1st Half	75	10	16	2	8	0	213			280	320	600	9	80	24	0.47	211	48	12	40	67	8%	37	0%	2.85	-3.1	$1
LIMA Plan	F	2nd Half	59	2	9	0	6	0	153			219	203	422	8	68	22	0.26	188	53	20	28	55	0%	8	0%	0.28	-7.7	($1)
+/- Score	13	09 Proj	**130**	**10**	**27**	**2**	**15**	**0**	**208**			**262**	**304**	**566**	**7**	**76**	**26**	**0.31**	**218**	**51**	**16**	**33**	**72**	**7%**	**24**	**0%**	**2.33**	**-7.7**	**$0**

Once upon a time, his MLEs showed power potential. But that was way back when Doug Glanville still roamed CF and before Rafael Palmeiro defiantly pointed his finger. Now? Not so much.

Rabelo,Mike

			AB	R	H	HR	RBI	SB	Avg	vL	vR	OB	Slg	OPS	bb%	ct%	h%	Eye	xBA	G	L	F	PX	hr/f	SX	SBO	RC/G	RAR	R$
Pos	2	04	0	0	0	0	0	0	0							0			0						0				
Age	29	05 aa	282	24	61	2	19	0	217			253	290	543	5	87	24	0.37	0				52		44	2%	2.31	-13.9	$0
Bats	Both	06 a/a	350	42	82	7	42	3	234			285	360	645	7	79	28	0.34	0				86		68	6%	3.40	-10.4	$5
Health	A	07 DET	168	14	43	1	18	0	256	276	252	282	357	639	3	76	33	0.15	266	52	27	22	79	4%	62	0%	3.21	-5.3	$2
PT/Exp	F	08 FLA	109	9	22	3	10	0	202	222	198	256	294	550	7	77	23	0.32	221	49	20	31	54	12%	27	4%	2.03	-7.5	$0
Consist	B	1st Half	109	9	22	3	10	0	202			256	294	550	7	77	23	0.32	221	49	20	31	54	12%	27	4%	2.03	-7.5	$0
LIMA Plan	F	2nd Half	0	0	0	0	0	0	0																				
+/- Score	1	09 Proj	**80**	**8**	**18**	**1**	**8**	**0**	**225**			**270**	**315**	**585**	**6**	**79**	**27**	**0.29**	**247**	**50**	**22**	**27**	**62**	**8%**	**39**	**3%**	**2.55**	**-4.1**	**$1**

According to both RC/G and RAR, he is the least crappy catcher from among the trio of crappy catchers on this page. So he's got that going for him.

SCOTT MONROE

Raburn,Ryan			AB	R	H	HR	RBI	SB	Avg	vL	vR	OB	Slg	OPS	bb%	ct%	h%	Eye	xBA	G	L	F	PX	hr/f	SX	SBO	RC/G	RAR	R$
Pos	79	04 aa	395	59	99	13	54	4	251			319	428	747	9	75	30	0.40	0				119		108	4%	4.81	-4.4	$10
Age	28	05 aaa	466	53	109	16	57	7	234			294	399	694	8	81	26	0.44	0				101		99	9%	4.02	-14.3	$10
Bats	Right	06 aaa	451	62	116	18	73	15	257			328	454	782	10	75	30	0.43	0				127		118	16%	5.25	0.5	$15
Health	A	07 DET	* 453	81	125	19	84	14	277	259	338	353	489	842	11	78	32	0.54	281	41	19	39	141	13%	122	14%	6.05	13.2	$20
PT/Exp	D	08 DET	182	26	43	4	20	3	236	238	235	298	368	666	8	73	30	0.33	231	47	14	39	99	8%	92	9%	3.71	-6.3	$4
Consist	D	1st Half	79	14	17	3	9	1	215			287	405	692	9	73	25	0.38	253	41	14	45	142	12%	76	6%	4.06	-1.9	$2
LIMA Plan	F	2nd Half	103	12	26	1	11	2	252			306	340	646	7	73	34	0.29	215	52	14	34	66	4%	96	11%	3.43	-4.3	$2
+/- Score	-25	09 Proj	159	24	40	5	22	4	252			319	411	729	9	75	31	0.39	248	46	15	39	111	10%	97	11%	4.55	-1.9	$4

Unable to build on recent power and patience gains. Over-aggressive approach hurt ct% and BA as GBs surged. Likely to rebound a tad, but at his age, opportunities will be few, with little room for error.

Ramirez,Alexei			AB	R	H	HR	RBI	SB	Avg	vL	vR	OB	Slg	OPS	bb%	ct%	h%	Eye	xBA	G	L	F	PX	hr/f	SX	SBO	RC/G	RAR	R$
Pos	4	04 Cuba	360	59	96	11	46	7	267			313	442	754	6	84	29	0.42	0				105		126	11%	4.73	4.0	$11
Age	27	05 Cuba	331	50	100	14	46	8	302			347	492	840	6	89	31	0.62	0				108		99	11%	5.68	12.2	$15
Bats	Right	06 Cuba	212	28	58	7	30	3	274			345	420	764	10	92	27	1.44	0				75		67	8%	5.15	4.8	$6
Health	A	07 Cuba	340	51	114	20	68	7	335			418	562	979	12	89	33	1.30	0				121		62	8%	7.58	29.0	$19
PT/Exp	C	08 CHW	480	65	139	21	77	13	290	312	281	315	475	790	4	87	30	0.30	288	47	17	37	106	14%	88	20%	4.89	0.0	$20
Consist	F	1st Half	187	22	55	5	24	3	294			316	439	755	3	87	32	0.25	270	47	16	38	93	8%	58	11%	4.53	-1.9	$6
LIMA Plan	C	2nd Half	293	43	84	16	53	10	287			315	498	813	4	87	28	0.32	298	47	17	36	114	17%	102	25%	5.12	2.0	$14
+/- Score	10	09 Proj	516	73	149	23	85	12	289			339	476	815	7	88	29	0.65	290	47	17	37	104	14%	82	13%	5.40	13.6	$21

Fine first year given prior experience. Free-swinger with with unique contact; power, speed improved with more AB. Exploited the Cell for 13 HR. Skill consolidation likely. Pay for good but streaky production.

Ramirez,Aramis			AB	R	H	HR	RBI	SB	Avg	vL	vR	OB	Slg	OPS	bb%	ct%	h%	Eye	xBA	G	L	F	PX	hr/f	SX	SBO	RC/G	RAR	R$
Pos	5	04 CHC	547	99	174	36	103	0	318	267	328	374	578	952	8	89	31	0.79	319	34	23	43	139	17%	37	1%	6.96	28.0	$29
Age	30	05 CHC	463	72	140	31	92	0	302	355	284	351	568	919	7	87	29	0.58	320	39	20	41	153	19%	28	1%	6.52	22.1	$23
Bats	Right	06 CHC	594	93	173	38	119	2	291	261	301	346	561	907	8	89	27	0.79	309	35	18	47	141	15%	66	2%	6.46	16.1	$27
Health	A	07 CHC	506	72	157	26	101	0	310	395	286	364	549	914	8	87	32	0.65	299	39	18	44	136	13%	47	0%	6.60	13.6	$22
PT/Exp	A	08 CHC	554	97	160	27	111	2	289	239	305	373	518	891	12	83	31	0.79	291	31	20	48	145	12%	56	2%	6.62	19.5	$25
Consist	A	1st Half	291	54	84	14	55	1	289			378	502	880	13	82	31	0.79	285	33	21	46	135	13%	47	2%	6.54	9.5	$13
LIMA Plan	C+	2nd Half	263	43	76	13	56	1	289			366	536	902	11	84	30	0.78	299	30	19	51	155	11%	58	3%	6.72	9.9	$12
+/- Score	-1	09 Proj	547	89	162	30	110	1	296			364	545	909	10	86	30	0.74	302	34	19	47	146	14%	54	2%	6.65	19.0	$25

Identical 1H-2H bottom lines accompanied by mid-year BA slide. Seemingly traded off between ct% and bb%, but remained healthy, hiked FB%. Solid BPI and stable power hint at return to 30 HR level.

Ramirez,Hanley			AB	R	H	HR	RBI	SB	Avg	vL	vR	OB	Slg	OPS	bb%	ct%	h%	Eye	xBA	G	L	F	PX	hr/f	SX	SBO	RC/G	RAR	R$
Pos	6	04 aa	129	23	39	4	13	11	301			344	472	816	6	84	33	0.42	0				101		140	39%	5.41	4.1	$7
Age	25	05 aa	461	57	119	5	45	22	258			308	360	668	7	89	28	0.65	0				64		122	29%	3.90	-5.0	$13
Bats	Right	06 FLA	633	119	185	17	59	51	292	307	288	350	480	830	8	80	34	0.44	280	44	21	35	118	10%	164	40%	5.83	26.6	$31
Health	A	07 FLA	639	125	212	29	81	51	332	399	312	382	562	944	8	85	36	0.55	298	40	18	42	137	13%	141	36%	6.98	43.8	$41
PT/Exp	A	08 FLA	589	125	177	33	67	35	301	258	313	395	540	935	14	79	33	0.75	295	46	17	37	148	19%	126	24%	7.29	44.2	$35
Consist	B	1st Half	321	70	95	19	36	20	296			377	536	913	12	77	33	0.56	289	47	19	34	147	22%	144	25%	6.94	20.9	$19
LIMA Plan	D+	2nd Half	268	55	82	14	31	15	306			415	545	960	16	82	33	1.06	301	45	16	39	149	16%	102	23%	7.71	23.3	$16
+/- Score	-21	09 Proj	584	115	179	31	86	30	307			381	551	933	11	82	33	0.67	299	43	18	40	147	16%	125	25%	7.07	42.3	$34

Mending from labrum surgery, hr/f spike trumped 31% FB% in Apr-May. Ct%, FBs returned but bb% hike unmined due to SBO drop. Skills in transition could shift his contributions in HR/SB. But 30+ HR are a lock.

Ramirez,Manny			AB	R	H	HR	RBI	SB	Avg	vL	vR	OB	Slg	OPS	bb%	ct%	h%	Eye	xBA	G	L	F	PX	hr/f	SX	SBO	RC/G	RAR	R$
Pos	70	04 BOS	568	108	175	43	130	2	308	306	309	395	613	1008	13	78	33	0.66	302	41	15	43	188	22%	38	4%	8.13	49.6	$31
Age	36	05 BOS	554	112	162	45	144	1	292	236	313	382	594	976	13	79	30	0.67	319	37	24	39	185	27%	56	1%	7.63	44.8	$32
Bats	Right	06 BOS	449	79	144	35	102	0	321	326	319	444	619	1064	18	77	35	0.98	306	36	22	42	181	24%	26	1%	9.19	48.1	$24
Health	A	07 BOS	483	84	143	20	88	0	296	344	279	386	493	879	13	81	33	0.77	284	38	22	41	129	13%	40	0%	6.58	20.5	$19
PT/Exp	A	08 2TM	552	102	183	37	121	3	332	308	339	423	601	1024	14	78	37	0.70	306	38	23	39	173	22%	61	2%	8.45	47.9	$33
Consist	F	1st Half	290	48	83	16	52	1	286			369	514	883	12	76	33	0.54	274	40	19	41	149	18%	58	1%	6.59	11.8	$12
LIMA Plan	C+	2nd Half	262	54	100	21	69	2	382			479	698	1178	16	80	42	0.92	341	36	28	36	197	28%	45	2%	10.41	33.5	$21
+/- Score	-35	09 Proj	527	92	161	30	105	1	306			404	548	952	14	79	34	0.78	297	37	23	40	154	18%	44	1%	7.56	34.5	$25

Slowed in 1H by hamstring issues, began stunning return to $30 before the trade. 2H h% played role, but PX came all the way back, skills look vintage. Downside risk in age, legs, moods - See 2006-7 AB.

Ramirez,Max			AB	R	H	HR	RBI	SB	Avg	vL	vR	OB	Slg	OPS	bb%	ct%	h%	Eye	xBA	G	L	F	PX	hr/f	SX	SBO	RC/G	RAR	R$
Pos	2	04	0	0	0	0	0	0	0							0			0						0				
Age	24	05	0	0	0	0	0	0	0							0			0						0				
Bats	Right	06	0	0	0	0	0	0	0							0			0						0				
Health	A	07	0	0	0	0	0	0	0							0			0						0				
PT/Exp	F	08 TEX	* 326	49	94	18	52	2	289	71	281	361	515	876	10	78	32	0.52	266	33	17	50	141	14%	66	4%	6.34	19.7	$13
Consist	F	1st Half	253	40	79	15	41	2	314			385	562	948	10	79	35	0.57	0	22	22	56	154	13%	71	5%	7.25	21.1	$12
LIMA Plan	F	2nd Half	73	9	15	3	11	0	203			272	352	625	9	75	23	0.38	216	38	14	48	95	11%	29	0%	3.02	-2.7	$1
+/- Score	0	09 Proj	159	22	39	8	25	0	245			316	426	742	9	77	27	0.45	237	37	15	48	114	13%	39	2%	4.59	1.6	$4

2-9-.217 in 46 AB at TEX. Part of TEX talent glut at CA, he may not remain at that position. Plus patience, budding power both seen in .928 OPS over 1500 minor league AB. Elite upside, could help this year.

Redmond,Mike			AB	R	H	HR	RBI	SB	Avg	vL	vR	OB	Slg	OPS	bb%	ct%	h%	Eye	xBA	G	L	F	PX	hr/f	SX	SBO	RC/G	RAR	R$
Pos	2	04 FLA	246	19	63	2	25	1	256	179	279	296	341	638	5	89	28	0.50	266	47	21	32	60	3%	36	2%	3.47	-2.5	$3
Age	38	05 MIN	148	17	46	1	26	0	311	345	289	338	392	730	4	91	34	0.43	288	53	24	23	59	3%	30	0%	4.41	1.6	$5
Bats	Right	06 MIN	179	20	61	0	23	0	341	443	275	355	413	769	2	90	38	0.22	291	46	27	27	57	0%	29	0%	4.73	1.5	$5
Health	A	07 MIN	272	23	80	1	38	0	294	330	277	338	353	691	6	92	32	0.78	251	44	21	35	43	1%	18	0%	4.18	-0.8	$5
PT/Exp	F	08 MIN	129	14	37	0	12	0	287	277	297	313	333	647	4	91	31	0.45	287	47	28	25	37	0%	31	0%	3.54	-2.4	$2
Consist	B	1st Half	56	6	16	0	4	0	286			333	357	690	7	89	32	0.67	302	39	31	29	58	0%	27	0%	4.20	0.0	$1
LIMA Plan	F	2nd Half	73	8	21	0	8	0	288			297	315	612	1	93	31	0.20	276	53	25	22	21	0%	35	0%	3.03	-2.4	$1
+/- Score	-10	09 Proj	168	17	47	0	19	0	280			309	338	647	4	91	31	0.48	279	47	25	28	45	1%	31	0%	3.57	-3.2	$3

Career part-timer, now at age 37, as part-time as ever. Value resides solely in LD% and ct%; potential BA leverage is minimized by AB. Unlikely to hurt your BA, but won't increase your HR total.

Reed,Jeremy			AB	R	H	HR	RBI	SB	Avg	vL	vR	OB	Slg	OPS	bb%	ct%	h%	Eye	xBA	G	L	F	PX	hr/f	SX	SBO	RC/G	RAR	R$
Pos	8	04 aaa	509	74	132	11	64	22	259			333	385	718	10	90	27	1.10	0				69		121	21%	4.65	-0.5	$16
Age	27	05 SEA	488	61	124	3	45	12	254	200	269	321	352	673	9	85	29	0.65	264	49	19	33	73	2%	90	17%	4.04	-3.5	$9
Bats	Left	06 SEA	212	27	46	6	17	2	217		243	256	377	633	5	85	23	0.35	261	51	13	37	83	9%	115	13%	3.26	-9.3	$2
Health	B	07 aa	563	70	132	10	47	10	235			282	349	631	6	86	26	0.47	0				74		86	15%	3.34	-20.5	$8
PT/Exp	D	08 SEA	* 435	49	119	7	46	7	274	115	285	322	390	712	7	88	30	0.60	287	52	20	28	77	6%	74	9%	4.35	-12.5	$10
Consist	B	1st Half	228	26	66	7	24	5	291			347	432	779	8	90	30	0.84	300	53	21	26	83	12%	70	9%	5.15	-1.3	$7
LIMA Plan	D	2nd Half	207	23	53	0	22	2	256			294	343	637	5	86	30	0.39	274	51	20	29	69	0%	72	9%	3.45	-11.6	$3
+/- Score	-21	09 Proj	398	48	105	6	39	6	264			310	381	691	6	87	29	0.52	275	51	18	31	75	6%	87	11%	4.08	-10.3	$8

2-31-.269 in 286 AB at SEA. Showed little in MLB return. Sub-par power, little patience, average speed at best - and not enough LD contact to compensate. SEA may allow more chances; you shouldn't.

Renteria,Edgar			AB	R	H	HR	RBI	SB	Avg	vL	vR	OB	Slg	OPS	bb%	ct%	h%	Eye	xBA	G	L	F	PX	hr/f	SX	SBO	RC/G	RAR	R$
Pos	6	04 STL	586	84	168	10	72	17	287	366	264	331	401	732	6	87	32	0.50	281	47	22	31	75	6%	83	18%	4.51	6.4	$20
Age	33	05 BOS	623	100	172	8	70	9	276	326	253	335	385	720	8	84	32	0.55	278	47	24	29	76	5%	99	7%	4.48	-1.4	$17
Bats	Right	06 ATL	598	100	175	14	70	17	293	333	281	359	436	796	9	85	33	0.70	288	47	22	31	90	9%	97	13%	5.43	18.0	$22
Health	B	07 ATL	494	87	164	12	57	11	332	349	323	389	470	859	9	84	38	0.60	284	46	23	31	89	9%	91	8%	6.09	21.3	$22
PT/Exp	A	08 DET	503	69	136	10	55	6	270	366	239	320	382	702	7	87	29	0.58	276	46	22	32	69	7%	81	6%	4.19	-2.0	$12
Consist	C	1st Half	277	38	75	5	32	2	271			324	350	675	7	87	30	0.63	263	48	23	29	45	7%	67	5%	3.88	-3.6	$7
LIMA Plan	C+	2nd Half	226	31	61	5	23	4	270			315	420	736	6	87	29	0.52	291	43	21	36	99	7%	87	9%	4.58	1.6	$6
+/- Score	-9	09 Proj	517	79	150	11	58	9	290			344	420	764	8	86	32	0.59	283	46	22	32	84	8%	89	8%	4.95	8.7	$16

The vagaries of Luck. BA dove 60+ points with expected h% regression, while xBA, GLF barely moved. BPI stability, history say BA and SB will get a bounce. BPIs and age say a big bounce is unlikely.

JOCK THOMPSON

Reyes,Argenis			AB	R	H	HR	RBI	SB	Avg	vL	vR	OB	Slg	OPS	bb%	ct%	h%	Eye	xBA	G	L	F	PX	hr/f	SX	SBO	RC/G	RAR	R$
Pos	4	04	0	0	0	0	0	0	0							0			0						0				
Age	26	05	0	0	0	0	0	0	0							0			0						0				
Bats	Both	06	0	0	0	0	0	0	0							0			0						0				
Health	A	07 aa	467	52	108	2	25	22	231			261	291	552	4	88	26	0.34	0				42		114	28%	2.40	-28.0	$7
PT/Exp	F	08 NYM	* 421	45	97	1	20	12	230	167	233	278	263	541	6	85	27	0.45	293	62	29	9	24	3%	90	16%	2.26	-32.5	$4
Consist	A	1st Half	291	29	68	0	17	10	234			290	269	559	7	86	27	0.56	0				27		86	19%	2.59	-19.5	$4
LIMA Plan	F	2nd Half	130	17	29	1	3	2	220			248	250	499	4	84	26	0.23	283	62	29	9	18	10%	80	9%	1.52	-13.0	$1
+/- Score	36	09 Proj	67	8	15	0	3	2	224			260	266	526	5	86	26	0.35	299	62	29	9	31	5%	81	20%	2.04	-5.5	$1

1-3-.218 in 110 AB at NYM. Decent contact, mediocre patience, little power. GB%, nine HR in 2700+ minor league AB speak to his slappiness. And not enough speed to be intriguing. Pass.

Reyes,Jose			AB	R	H	HR	RBI	SB	Avg	vL	vR	OB	Slg	OPS	bb%	ct%	h%	Eye	xBA	G	L	F	PX	hr/f	SX	SBO	RC/G	RAR	R$
Pos	6	04 NYM	220	33	56	2	14	19	255	326	237	271	373	644	2	86	29	0.16	265	43	19	38	80	3%	176	51%	3.32	-5.3	$8
Age	25	05 NYM	696	99	190	7	58	60	273	288	269	300	386	687	4	89	30	0.35	272	47	20	33	63	3%	182	44%	3.93	-0.5	$29
Bats	Both	06 NYM	647	122	194	19	81	64	300	330	288	353	487	840	8	87	32	0.65	294	45	21	34	98	10%	168	45%	5.85	27.4	$37
Health	A	07 NYM	681	119	191	12	57	78	280	318	266	354	421	775	10	89	30	0.99	269	42	18	40	81	5%	164	48%	5.33	17.6	$35
PT/Exp	A	08 NYM	688	113	204	16	68	56	297	280	303	358	475	833	9	88	32	0.80	302	44	23	33	100	8%	163	36%	5.90	24.8	$35
Consist	B	1st Half	339	60	99	9	34	28	292			357	478	834	9	87	32	0.76	301	45	22	33	107	9%	164	38%	5.91	12.5	$18
LIMA Plan	C	2nd Half	349	53	105	7	34	28	301			360	473	832	8	89	32	0.86	303	43	25	32	93	7%	157	34%	5.89	12.4	$17
+/- Score	3	09 Proj	678	114	197	19	65	63	291			350	475	824	8	88	31	0.77	297	44	22	35	101	9%	168	42%	5.73	24.3	$36

BA rebounded thanks to h% nudge and a few more LD. SB declined due to minor hammy woes and SBO dip but he's a good bet to surpass 60 again. An elite, stable skill set at pre-peak age. Pay full value.

Reynolds,Mark			AB	R	H	HR	RBI	SB	Avg	vL	vR	OB	Slg	OPS	bb%	ct%	h%	Eye	xBA	G	L	F	PX	hr/f	SX	SBO	RC/G	RAR	R$
Pos	5	04	0	0	0	0	0	0	0							0			0						0				
Age	25	05	0	0	0	0	0	0	0							0			0						0				
Bats	Right	06 aa	114	20	30	8	18	0	264			322	528	849	8	70	31	0.29	0				177		48	4%	6.08	2.8	$4
Health	A	07 ARI	* 500	84	139	23	79	3	278	278	279	347	495	842	10	69	36	0.34	250	36	20	44	153	15%	92	4%	6.29	9.7	$18
PT/Exp	C	08 ARI	539	87	129	28	97	11	239	279	226	320	458	778	11	62	33	0.31	235	36	19	45	172	19%	109	10%	5.67	4.8	$20
Consist	A	1st Half	275	55	71	17	52	5	258			338	509	847	11	64	34	0.33	252	35	20	44	188	22%	118	7%	6.58	9.7	$13
LIMA Plan	B+	2nd Half	264	32	58	11	45	6	220			302	405	707	11	60	32	0.30	217	36	18	46	156	15%	86	13%	4.68	-5.7	$7
+/- Score	18	09 Proj	509	82	130	26	86	8	255			329	475	804	10	65	34	0.32	243	36	19	45	164	17%	100	8%	5.85	6.7	$19

PRO: Big-time power with SB bonus, still in growth stages. CON: Set MLB whiff mark, ct% in danger zone, streakiness may cost him AB - see 2H dip. Will help if he holds job - and if you can compensate for BA.

Riggans,Shawn			AB	R	H	HR	RBI	SB	Avg	vL	vR	OB	Slg	OPS	bb%	ct%	h%	Eye	xBA	G	L	F	PX	hr/f	SX	SBO	RC/G	RAR	R$
Pos	2	04	0	0	0	0	0	0	0							0			0						0				
Age	28	05 aa	310	30	77	5	40	1	250			293	354	647	6	79	30	0.29	0				77		35	4%	3.35	-5.1	$5
Bats	Right	06 aaa	417	39	111	10	49	2	265			306	400	706	5	79	31	0.28	0				89		56	4%	4.07	-3.7	$8
Health	A	07 aaa	121	10	30	4	14	0	251			274	432	706	3	75	31	0.12	0				129		56	14%	3.98	-1.4	$2
PT/Exp	F	08 TAM	135	21	30	6	24	0	222	233	213	286	407	693	8	78	24	0.40	260	47	16	37	122	15%	42	0%	3.94	-1.0	$3
Consist	A	1st Half	73	11	20	4	15	0	274			321	479	800	6	79	30	0.33	275	48	18	33	126	21%	31	0%	5.12	1.9	$3
LIMA Plan	F	2nd Half	62	10	10	2	9	0	161			246	323	569	10	76	18	0.47	241	45	13	43	117	10%	56	0%	2.47	-3.5	$0
+/- Score	42	09 Proj	131	16	32	4	19	0	244			293	406	700	6	77	29	0.30	248	46	15	39	113	11%	39	4%	4.00	-1.0	$3

Improving power limited by GB%. Sub-par ct% makes BA a liability. Patience appears to be on the up-tick, which would have to continue for this profile to become even mildly interesting.

Rios,Alex			AB	R	H	HR	RBI	SB	Avg	vL	vR	OB	Slg	OPS	bb%	ct%	h%	Eye	xBA	G	L	F	PX	hr/f	SX	SBO	RC/G	RAR	R$
Pos	98	04 TOR	* 611	67	168	4	47	17	275	287	286	318	376	695	6	82	33	0.36	274	57	20	23	68	3%	125	13%	4.07	-11.0	$13
Age	28	05 TOR	481	71	126	10	59	14	262	249	271	303	397	700	6	79	31	0.28	263	49	19	31	90	8%	129	20%	4.02	-9.8	$14
Bats	Right	06 TOR	450	68	136	17	82	15	302	295	305	353	516	868	7	80	35	0.39	282	37	22	42	134	11%	123	18%	6.18	6.5	$20
Health	A	07 TOR	643	114	191	24	85	17	297	345	283	352	498	850	8	84	32	0.53	283	36	20	44	125	10%	125	12%	5.94	7.9	$27
PT/Exp	A	08 TOR	635	91	185	15	79	32	291	289	292	337	461	799	6	82	33	0.39	280	41	21	38	113	7%	134	25%	5.32	-0.8	$26
Consist	A	1st Half	328	45	92	4	30	16	280			337	399	736	8	78	35	0.38	261	48	21	31	92	5%	112	23%	4.66	-6.6	$11
LIMA Plan	B	2nd Half	307	46	93	11	49	16	303			337	528	865	5	87	32	0.41	299	34	21	45	134	9%	150	28%	5.96	5.1	$15
+/- Score	-2	09 Proj	621	95	182	19	85	25	293			340	483	823	7	83	33	0.42	283	39	21	40	121	9%	135	20%	5.59	3.8	$26

Sharp 1H GB% spike sapped power. Three years of uneven 1H-2H performance put upside breakout in doubt. SBO rise, BA / xBA stability are pluses. Still, with consistent 1H-2H: UP: 30 HR, 30 SB.

Rivas,Luis			AB	R	H	HR	RBI	SB	Avg	vL	vR	OB	Slg	OPS	bb%	ct%	h%	Eye	xBA	G	L	F	PX	hr/f	SX	SBO	RC/G	RAR	R$
Pos	64	04 MIN	336	44	86	10	34	15	256	291	240	284	432	715	4	84	28	0.25	271	46	15	40	102	9%	151	25%	4.13	-3.3	$10
Age	29	05 MIN	* 274	35	66	3	28	7	241	260	244	282	337	620	5	88	26	0.49	294	55	22	23	66	5%	102	14%	3.26	-10.7	$5
Bats	Right	06 aaa	229	18	45	2	21	2	195			224	257	481	4	85	22	0.25	0				39		69	7%	1.44	-21.4	($0)
Health	A	07 aaa	410	47	91	8	34	10	222			284	331	615	8	84	25	0.54	0				68		83	18%	3.17	-15.4	$6
PT/Exp	F	08 PIT	206	25	45	3	20	3	218	288	195	265	311	576	6	87	24	0.48	252	51	16	33	53	5%	101	11%	2.71	-12.3	$2
Consist	C	1st Half	104	10	24	3	15	2	231			266	365	631	5	88	24	0.42	267	55	13	32	73	10%	87	14%	3.26	-4.4	$2
LIMA Plan	F	2nd Half	102	15	21	0	5	1	206			264	255	519	7	85	24	0.53	234	48	19	34	33	0%	107	8%	2.13	-8.1	$0
+/- Score	17	09 Proj	99	12	22	1	9	2	222			269	315	585	6	86	25	0.45	249	50	16	33	54	5%	97	12%	2.78	-5.2	$1

Definition of "Never", courtesy of Dictionary.com:
1) Not ever; at no time
2) Not at all; absolutely not.
3) Never mind; don't bother.

Words of wisdom.

Rivera,Juan			AB	R	H	HR	RBI	SB	Avg	vL	vR	OB	Slg	OPS	bb%	ct%	h%	Eye	xBA	G	L	F	PX	hr/f	SX	SBO	RC/G	RAR	R$
Pos	7	04 MON	394	49	121	12	49	6	307	276	328	362	464	827	8	89	32	0.76	295	49	20	31	93	11%	70	7%	5.67	2.5	$14
Age	30	05 ANA	350	46	95	15	59	1	271	252	286	316	454	771	6	87	27	0.52	282	46	17	37	106	13%	43	12%	4.85	1.4	$11
Bats	Right	06 LAA	448	65	139	23	85	0	310	351	293	358	525	882	7	87	32	0.56	287	51	16	33	121	18%	23	3%	6.13	11.7	$18
Health	F	07 LAA	* 104	6	23	2	19	0	224	276	286	247	341	588	3	90	23	0.30	241	44	15	41	77	5%	10	0%	2.78	-7.1	$1
PT/Exp	D	08 LAA	256	31	63	12	45	1	246	233	253	290	438	728	6	87	24	0.48	265	37	14	48	111	11%	40	4%	4.33	-4.0	$7
Consist	F	1st Half	62	6	11	0	3	0	177			227	226	453	6	82	22	0.36	195	39	14	47	43	0%	40	0%	1.16	-7.4	($1)
LIMA Plan	D+	2nd Half	194	25	52	12	42	1	268			311	505	816	6	89	25	0.55	287	37	14	49	132	14%	38	5%	5.28	2.4	$8
+/- Score	27	09 Proj	463	50	123	16	76	1	266			306	424	730	5	87	28	0.45	259	42	15	43	95	9%	31	3%	4.37	-7.8	$12

2009 Mystery Man...
PRO: Power, FB%, ct% all surged with regular 2H AB.
CON: Poor bb%, selectivity endanger LD% and PROs.
If CONs are just part of injury rust... UP: 2006 redux

Rivera,Mike			AB	R	H	HR	RBI	SB	Avg	vL	vR	OB	Slg	OPS	bb%	ct%	h%	Eye	xBA	G	L	F	PX	hr/f	SX	SBO	RC/G	RAR	R$
Pos	2	04 aaa	210	12	35	4	18	1	168			207	270	477	5	79	19	0.23	0				63		65	6%	1.19	-19.8	($2)
Age	32	05 aaa	213	23	47	11	29	2	222			245	432	676	3	86	21	0.21	0				121		69	9%	3.53	-2.4	$5
Bats	Right	06 MIL	* 355	40	91	14	61	3	257	226	279	298	429	727	6	83	28	0.33	244	38	14	48	103	10%	43	7%	4.26	-0.8	$10
Health	A	07 aaa	349	29	62	15	48	4	178			222	346	568	5	79	18	0.27	0				103		42	17%	2.23	-24.4	$3
PT/Exp	F	08 MIL	62	8	19	1	14	2	306	176	356	368	435	803	9	84	35	0.60	282	44	23	33	94	6%	63	11%	5.51	2.2	$3
Consist	F	1st Half	40	7	13	1	8	1	325			341	450	791	2	83	38	0.14	261	42	21	36	82	8%	77	9%	4.86	0.7	$2
LIMA Plan	F	2nd Half	22	1	6	0	6	1	273			407	409	816	19	86	32	1.67	318	47	26	26	114	0%	34	13%	6.46	1.4	$1
+/- Score	-55	09 Proj	134	13	32	6	18	1	239			272	409	681	4	82	25	0.26	242	38	14	48	102	11%	39	8%	3.63	-2.5	$3

In limited exposure, flashed little of the power promised in previous seasons. 2008 profile is a small sample, h%-driven mirage that would be be exposed with extended AB. Not that this matters much.

Roberts,Brian			AB	R	H	HR	RBI	SB	Avg	vL	vR	OB	Slg	OPS	bb%	ct%	h%	Eye	xBA	G	L	F	PX	hr/f	SX	SBO	RC/G	RAR	R$
Pos	4	04 BAL	641	107	175	4	53	29	273	215	299	346	376	721	10	85	32	0.75	259	39	21	39	75	2%	112	22%	4.68	11.3	$19
Age	31	05 BAL	561	92	176	18	73	27	314	273	332	387	515	902	11	85	34	0.81	307	35	27	37	128	10%	125	21%	6.78	41.0	$28
Bats	Both	06 BAL	563	85	161	10	55	36	286	235	308	350	410	760	9	88	31	0.83	277	44	21	35	77	6%	126	25%	5.04	14.8	$21
Health	A	07 BAL	621	103	180	12	57	50	290	268	299	379	432	810	13	84	33	0.90	258	36	20	45	95	5%	132	27%	5.83	32.2	$28
PT/Exp	A	08 BAL	614	107	181	9	57	40	295	313	289	379	448	827	12	83	34	0.80	285	40	24	36	107	5%	144	26%	6.05	20.1	$26
Consist	B	1st Half	319	49	94	5	30	21	295			373	480	853	11	82	35	0.70	288	34	26	40	128	5%	145	30%	6.36	13.4	$13
LIMA Plan	B	2nd Half	295	58	87	4	27	19	295			385	414	798	13	84	34	0.91	280	47	22	31	85	5%	122	21%	5.71	6.8	$13
+/- Score	2	09 Proj	610	104	178	9	58	41	292			374	427	801	12	84	33	0.84	274	40	22	38	93	5%	131	25%	5.68	20.9	$26

Traded FB for LD and GB, resulting in fewer HR, more 2B, and BA up-tick. BPIs - notably SX and bb% - say he's aging well. Remains a reliable skill set and top-shelf SB source from an MI slot.

JOCK THOMPSON

Roberts,Dave

			AB	R	H	HR	RBI	SB	Avg	vL	vR	OB	Slg	OPS	bb%	ct%	h%	Eye	xBA	G	L	F	PX	hr/f	SX	SBO	RC/G	RAR	R$
Pos	7	04 2TM	319	64	81	4	35	38	254	179	270	333	379	713	11	85	29	0.79	261	50	16	35	72	4%	198	44%	4.60	-5.6	$16
Age	36	05 SD	411	65	113	8	38	23	275	258	278	358	428	786	11	86	31	0.90	295	50	22	28	89	8%	146	27%	5.50	1.9	$16
Bats	Left	06 SD	499	80	146	2	44	49	293	292	293	358	393	751	9	88	33	0.84	281	56	19	25	54	2%	164	34%	5.04	-3.0	$23
Health	F	07 SF	396	61	103	2	23	31	260	156	285	331	364	695	10	83	31	0.64	260	48	21	32	64	2%	162	31%	4.32	-12.1	$13
PT/Exp	C	08 SF	107	18	24	0	9	5	224		229	346	280	627	16	83	27	1.11	236	50	19	31	32	0%	134	20%	3.81	-5.4	$2
Consist	B	1st Half	17	0	2	0	1	0	118			167	118	284	6	76	15	0.25	0	58	17	25	0	0%	26	33%	-1.36	-4.3	($1)
LIMA Plan	D+	2nd Half	90	18	22	0	8	5	244			376	311	687	17	84	29	1.36	243	49	20	32	38	0%	140	19%	4.70	-2.0	$3
+/- Score	-4	09 Proj	**294**	**51**	**78**	**2**	**25**	**18**	**265**			**355**	**365**	**721**	**12**	**85**	**31**	**0.95**	**265**	**51**	**19**	**29**	**57**	**2%**	**152**	**23%**	**4.81**	**-4.9**	**$10**

Sidelined by torn meniscus in late April, flashed previous skill levels after August return. But speed is only remaining value. Struggling vs. LHP at decline age, only part-time ABs beckon. Buy only the SB.

Rodriguez,Alex

			AB	R	H	HR	RBI	SB	Avg	vL	vR	OB	Slg	OPS	bb%	ct%	h%	Eye	xBA	G	L	F	PX	hr/f	SX	SBO	RC/G	RAR	R$
Pos	5	04 NYY	601	112	172	36	106	28	286	311	279	370	512	883	12	78	31	0.61	274	46	16	39	132	20%	117	17%	6.48	26.6	$32
Age	33	05 NYY	605	124	194	48	130	21	321	300	330	409	610	1019	13	77	35	0.65	302	45	16	40	179	26%	94	13%	8.29	61.9	$41
Bats	Right	06 NYY	572	113	166	35	121	15	290	294	289	387	523	909	14	76	33	0.65	273	42	18	40	143	20%	93	10%	6.99	31.9	$29
Health	A	07 NYY	583	143	183	54	156	24	314	272	327	410	645	1055	14	79	32	0.79	323	41	17	42	199	28%	98	15%	8.64	59.8	$45
PT/Exp	A	08 NYY	510	104	154	35	103	18	302	263	316	381	573	953	11	77	33	0.56	300	42	18	40	175	22%	94	14%	7.39	35.4	$31
Consist	C	1st Half	233	45	75	16	44	11	322			399	601	1000	11	80	35	0.64	312	39	20	41	177	21%	89	17%	7.92	18.9	$15
LIMA Plan	D+	2nd Half	277	59	79	19	59	7	285			365	549	914	11	75	32	0.50	290	44	17	39	174	24%	85	11%	6.94	16.2	$16
+/- Score	-4	09 Proj	**560**	**119**	**164**	**41**	**123**	**20**	**293**			**381**	**571**	**952**	**12**	**77**	**31**	**0.63**	**300**	**42**	**17**	**40**	**174**	**24%**	**95**	**14%**	**7.39**	**39.3**	**$34**

Quad strain zapped May. Less selectivity cut ct% and drove GB in 2H. Impatient approach hurt all year. BA, xBA and SB remain erratic with floors still intact. Power remains Elite; that's what you're paying for.

Rodriguez,Ivan

			AB	R	H	HR	RBI	SB	Avg	vL	vR	OB	Slg	OPS	bb%	ct%	h%	Eye	xBA	G	L	F	PX	hr/f	SX	SBO	RC/G	RAR	R$
Pos	2	04 DET	527	72	176	19	86	7	334	343	330	382	510	892	7	83	38	0.45	285	45	22	33	108	13%	71	7%	6.38	28.5	$23
Age	37	05 DET	504	71	139	14	50	7	276	294	271	291	444	736	2	82	31	0.12	292	48	22	30	111	11%	112	10%	4.26	3.4	$14
Bats	Right	06 DET	547	74	164	13	69	8	300	340	284	332	437	769	5	84	34	0.30	282	50	21	28	83	10%	96	8%	4.77	5.5	$17
Health	A	07 DET	502	50	141	11	63	2	281	302	274	294	420	714	2	81	33	0.09	273	52	19	28	96	10%	60	4%	3.97	-4.6	$11
PT/Exp	B	08 2AL	398	44	110	7	35	10	276	289	272	316	394	710	5	83	32	0.34	282	56	20	24	78	9%	103	11%	4.17	-0.3	$10
Consist	B	1st Half	238	28	66	3	25	6	277			320	403	724	6	83	32	0.37	291	55	22	23	86	7%	112	10%	4.41	1.5	$6
LIMA Plan	D	2nd Half	160	16	44	4	10	4	275			310	381	691	5	84	31	0.31	261	58	17	25	65	12%	60	12%	3.81	-1.7	$4
+/- Score	-4	09 Proj	**335**	**38**	**95**	**7**	**35**	**6**	**284**			**314**	**413**	**727**	**4**	**83**	**32**	**0.25**	**278**	**54**	**20**	**27**	**84**	**10%**	**85**	**9%**	**4.25**	**0.1**	**$9**

Power metrics continued to to dive, though they've likely hit bottom now. Ct% and bb% perked up slightly, but there's little upside from here. At age 37, only LD% is keeping him near replacement level.

Rodriguez,Luis

			AB	R	H	HR	RBI	SB	Avg	vL	vR	OB	Slg	OPS	bb%	ct%	h%	Eye	xBA	G	L	F	PX	hr/f	SX	SBO	RC/G	RAR	R$
Pos	6	04 aaa	486	56	116	4	40	3	239			300	326	626	8	90	26	0.89	0				59		56	4%	3.57	-10.6	$5
Age	28	05 MIN	* 305	34	79	3	34	2	260	233	276	328	358	686	9	88	29	0.84	265	43	21	36	66	3%	62	6%	4.25	-2.8	$5
Bats	Both	06 MIN	115	11	27	2	6	0	235	250	231	318	322	640	11	86	26	0.88	239	46	19	34	53	6%	19	0%	3.68	-2.5	$1
Health	A	07 MIN	155	18	34	2	12	1	219	226	218	275	303	579	7	91	23	0.86	248	54	13	34	49	4%	72	3%	2.99	-6.2	$1
PT/Exp	F	08 SD	* 298	30	81	1	18	1	273	238	309	319	344	663	6	94	29	1.23	274	49	19	31	47	1%	59	2%	4.03	-5.1	$4
Consist	B	1st Half	91	8	22	1	6	0	242			296	329	625	7	96	24	2.07	0				49		47	0%	3.74	-2.4	$1
LIMA Plan	F	2nd Half	207	22	59	0	12	1	286			329	351	680	6	94	31	1.02	270	49	19	31	46	0%	58	3%	4.16	-2.7	$4
+/- Score	9	09 Proj	**97**	**10**	**24**	**1**	**7**	**0**	**247**			**304**	**335**	**640**	**8**	**92**	**26**	**1.01**	**263**	**50**	**17**	**33**	**52**	**3%**	**69**	**2%**	**3.74**	**-2.1**	**$1**

0-12-.281 in 202 AB at SD. Career .712 OPS in minors, .686 OPS in 647 MLB AB. Without a PX or SX better than 76 in any season, we will anoint him our Poster Boy for Empty Contact.

Rodriguez,Sean

			AB	R	H	HR	RBI	SB	Avg	vL	vR	OB	Slg	OPS	bb%	ct%	h%	Eye	xBA	G	L	F	PX	hr/f	SX	SBO	RC/G	RAR	R$
Pos	4	04	0	0	0	0	0	0	0							0			0						0				
Age	24	05	0	0	0	0	0	0	0							0			0						0				
Bats	Right	06	0	0	0	0	0	0	0							0			0						0				
Health	A	07 aa	508	76	120	15	66	14	236			302	386	688	9	77	28	0.40	0				104		92	19%	3.97	-5.9	$13
PT/Exp	F	08 LAA	* 415	75	103	20	53	6	247	178	213	311	461	772	8	77	28	0.41	262	41	12	47	141	13%	103	8%	4.99	1.2	$13
Consist	C	1st Half	181	31	40	8	22	4	223			313	402	716	12	78	25	0.59	258	56	10	34	117	16%	77	10%	4.39	-2.8	$5
LIMA Plan	F	2nd Half	234	44	62	12	32	2	266			310	506	815	6	77	30	0.28	265	33	13	54	159	12%	106	6%	5.43	3.7	$8
+/- Score	17	09 Proj	**128**	**22**	**31**	**5**	**17**	**2**	**242**			**306**	**426**	**732**	**8**	**77**	**28**	**0.40**	**246**	**41**	**12**	**47**	**125**	**11%**	**77**	**13%**	**4.49**	**0.1**	**$4**

3-10-.203 in 167 AB at LAA. Power came fast in 2H, as suggested by 120 PX in 102 MLB AB. Ct% and pitch selection need improvement, but he has time. Intriguing MI profile, might be a year away.

Rolen,Scott

			AB	R	H	HR	RBI	SB	Avg	vL	vR	OB	Slg	OPS	bb%	ct%	h%	Eye	xBA	G	L	F	PX	hr/f	SX	SBO	RC/G	RAR	R$
Pos	5	04 STL	500	109	157	34	124	4	314	371	302	400	598	998	13	82	33	0.78	298	30	21	49	164	17%	92	4%	7.93	38.9	$31
Age	34	05 STL	196	28	46	5	28	1	235	237	234	321	383	704	11	86	25	0.89	274	35	23	42	95	7%	70	6%	4.47	-1.9	$4
Bats	Right	06 STL	521	94	154	22	95	7	296	259	310	364	518	882	10	87	31	0.81	294	33	20	48	133	10%	77	8%	6.42	13.6	$23
Health	D	07 STL	392	55	104	8	58	5	265	204	287	329	398	727	9	86	29	0.66	260	38	20	43	85	6%	81	7%	4.59	-11.6	$10
PT/Exp	B	08 TOR	408	58	107	11	50	5	262	250	266	337	431	768	10	83	29	0.65	272	36	21	44	113	7%	94	5%	5.14	3.1	$11
Consist	C	1st Half	215	26	62	6	26	4	288			360	474	834	10	85	32	0.73	289	32	24	44	122	7%	89	7%	5.95	6.4	$7
LIMA Plan	C+	2nd Half	193	32	45	5	24	1	233			312	383	695	10	80	27	0.58	252	40	17	43	102	8%	80	2%	4.21	-3.9	$4
+/- Score	-8	09 Proj	**442**	**68**	**117**	**15**	**64**	**3**	**265**			**337**	**446**	**783**	**10**	**84**	**29**	**0.68**	**276**	**36**	**20**	**44**	**116**	**9%**	**70**	**4%**	**5.27**	**5.0**	**$13**

Pain from surgically-repaired shoulder limited power and AB resulting in another lost year. Skills not completely shot; PX, FB% nurture slim hopes. With just moderately better health... UP: 20 HR.

Rollins,Jimmy

			AB	R	H	HR	RBI	SB	Avg	vL	vR	OB	Slg	OPS	bb%	ct%	h%	Eye	xBA	G	L	F	PX	hr/f	SX	SBO	RC/G	RAR	R$
Pos	6	04 PHI	657	119	190	14	73	30	289	303	285	346	455	801	8	89	31	0.78	292	43	21	36	96	7%	157	22%	5.49	25.3	$27
Age	30	05 PHI	677	115	196	12	54	41	290	278	292	336	431	767	6	90	31	0.66	297	44	24	32	85	6%	166	26%	5.01	20.0	$29
Bats	Both	06 PHI	689	127	191	25	83	36	277	277	277	332	478	810	8	88	28	0.71	299	44	19	37	111	11%	149	24%	5.49	22.2	$30
Health	A	07 PHI	716	139	212	30	94	41	296	321	286	341	531	872	6	88	30	0.58	294	36	20	44	124	11%	169	27%	6.10	33.1	$37
PT/Exp	A	08 PHI	556	76	154	11	59	47	277	288	272	345	437	782	9	90	29	1.05	311	45	24	31	95	7%	156	32%	5.40	12.3	$25
Consist	B	1st Half	239	34	63	6	28	17	264			323	431	754	8	90	27	0.88	314	42	26	32	102	9%	139	29%	4.96	2.3	$10
LIMA Plan	C	2nd Half	317	42	91	5	31	30	287			362	442	803	10	90	31	1.19	308	48	23	30	90	6%	159	34%	5.73	9.9	$15
+/- Score	18	09 Proj	**633**	**103**	**184**	**17**	**72**	**44**	**291**			**349**	**475**	**824**	**8**	**89**	**30**	**0.84**	**303**	**43**	**22**	**35**	**104**	**9%**	**162**	**28%**	**5.74**	**22.2**	**$30**

Sprained ankle cut into ABs. FB, hr/f plunge cut into HRs. Power should reverse course with better health, but forget 2007 HR outlier. Speed is his primary tool; the SBO and LD up-ticks make it lethal.

Romero,Alex

			AB	R	H	HR	RBI	SB	Avg	vL	vR	OB	Slg	OPS	bb%	ct%	h%	Eye	xBA	G	L	F	PX	hr/f	SX	SBO	RC/G	RAR	R$
Pos	9	04	0	0	0	0	0	0	0							0			0						0				
Age	25	05 aa	509	56	141	12	66	10	277			319	415	733	6	88	30	0.51	0				87		72	17%	4.50	-7.1	$15
Bats	Left	06 a/a	403	47	102	5	41	20	253			319	352	671	9	90	27	0.93	0				59		110	25%	4.08	-13.7	$10
Health	A	07 aa	533	66	148	5	52	10	278			317	378	695	5	92	30	0.67	0				63		89	15%	4.19	-15.5	$12
PT/Exp	F	08 ARI	* 308	36	82	4	27	7	265	174	241	294	381	675	4	88	29	0.33	273	47	19	34	72	4%	112	14%	3.78	-12.6	$7
Consist	A	1st Half	186	22	52	3	15	3	281			312	397	709	4	89	30	0.42	267	38	22	41	71	4%	89	12%	4.20	-5.3	$5
LIMA Plan	F	2nd Half	122	14	30	1	12	4	242			266	357	623	3	86	27	0.23	274	51	18	31	74	3%	135	17%	3.14	-7.4	$2
+/- Score	12	09 Proj	**104**	**12**	**27**	**1**	**10**	**3**	**260**			**297**	**372**	**670**	**5**	**89**	**28**	**0.48**	**276**	**49**	**18**	**32**	**71**	**4%**	**102**	**17%**	**3.82**	**-3.8**	**$2**

1-12-.230 in 135 AB at ARI. See Luis Rodriguez. A little younger, a little more speed, and not enough of either to be interesting.

Ross,Cody

			AB	R	H	HR	RBI	SB	Avg	vL	vR	OB	Slg	OPS	bb%	ct%	h%	Eye	xBA	G	L	F	PX	hr/f	SX	SBO	RC/G	RAR	R$
Pos	89	04 aaa	238	30	52	10	34	1	218			256	408	664	5	87	21	0.39	0				107		71	3%	3.58	-8.1	$4
Age	28	05 aaa	388	49	78	14	40	3	201			258	353	611	7	83	21	0.45	0				92		71	8%	2.99	-17.5	$5
Bats	Right	06 2NL	* 319	45	78	16	52	1	244	245	216	317	447	764	10	76	27	0.45	258	36	21	43	122	15%	59	5%	4.91	4.5	$9
Health	C	07 FLA	173	35	58	12	39	2	335	385	306	404	653	1057	10	78	37	0.53	332	41	21	38	211	23%	59	4%	8.71	18.9	$11
PT/Exp	D	08 FLA	461	59	120	22	73	6	260	285	249	310	488	798	7	75	30	0.28	273	36	21	43	152	15%	101	7%	5.30	7.5	$16
Consist	F	1st Half	190	21	43	13	32	4	226			279	484	764	7	79	22	0.36	276	35	15	50	152	17%	78	11%	4.67	-0.4	$6
LIMA Plan	C	2nd Half	271	38	77	9	41	2	284			331	491	822	7	72	37	0.25	271	37	25	38	152	12%	100	5%	5.83	8.3	$9
+/- Score	21	09 Proj	**354**	**53**	**96**	**19**	**61**	**4**	**271**			**329**	**510**	**840**	**8**	**77**	**31**	**0.37**	**286**	**37**	**21**	**42**	**156**	**16%**	**80**	**6%**	**5.84**	**12.3**	**$14**

PRO: Confirmed legit power, sustained good LD%.
CON: Patience regressed, ct% trending down, continued 1H-2H streakiness.
Reliable pop, but 72% ct% vs. RHP will cut into playing time.

JOCK THOMPSON

Ross,Dave			AB	R	H	HR	RBI	SB	Avg	vL	vR	OB	Slg	OPS	bb%	ct%	h%	Eye	xBA	G	L	F	PX	hr/f	SX	SBO	RC/G	RAR	R$
Pos	2	04 LA	165	13	28	5	15	0	170	125	198	239	291	530	8	62	23	0.24	172	33	15	52	87	9%	42	0%	1.68	-11.5	($1)
Age	32	05 2NL	125	11	30	3	15	0	240	200	253	275	392	667	5	78	29	0.21	237	38	15	47	108	7%	52	0%	3.56	-0.9	$2
Bats	Right	06 CIN	247	37	63	21	52	0	255	316	228	352	579	931	13	70	28	0.49	281	32	17	51	211	24%	34	0%	7.44	22.4	$10
Health	B	07 CIN	311	32	63	17	39	0	203	248	175	273	399	671	9	70	23	0.33	233	34	19	48	129	16%	14	0%	3.61	-7.9	$4
PT/Exp	D	08 2TM	142	18	32	3	13	0	225	206	241	368	352	720	18	73	29	0.82	245	38	25	37	100	8%	25	2%	4.88	3.0	$2
Consist	F	1st Half	86	7	21	1	7	0	244			363	337	700	16	74	32	0.73	220	37	21	43	77	4%	18	3%	4.54	0.9	$1
LIMA Plan	F	2nd Half	56	11	11	2	6	0	196			375	375	750	22	70	24	0.94	277	41	31	28	140	18%	35	0%	5.36	2.1	$1
+/- Score	-6	09 Proj	124	16	30	5	15	0	242			353	425	777	15	71	30	0.59	250	36	22	42	132	14%	25	1%	5.45	4.4	$3

Power was slow to return after back issues shelved him for most of March and April. LD uptick still positive, but poor ct% still calls the tune. Extreme BA killer with patience, power, and now a questionable role.

Rowand,Aaron			AB	R	H	HR	RBI	SB	Avg	vL	vR	OB	Slg	OPS	bb%	ct%	h%	Eye	xBA	G	L	F	PX	hr/f	SX	SBO	RC/G	RAR	R$
Pos	8	04 CHW	487	94	151	24	69	17	310	302	315	350	544	894	6	81	34	0.33	302	46	19	35	145	17%	120	19%	6.32	21.5	$25
Age	31	05 CHW	578	77	156	13	69	16	270	303	259	308	407	715	5	80	32	0.28	275	52	21	28	92	10%	119	15%	4.18	-1.7	$17
Bats	Right	06 PHI	405	59	106	12	47	10	262	222	275	293	425	718	4	81	30	0.24	276	44	22	34	101	11%	110	16%	4.15	-3.5	$12
Health	B	07 PHI	612	105	189	27	89	6	309	315	306	358	515	873	7	81	35	0.39	287	43	20	38	133	15%	65	5%	6.15	27.0	$26
PT/Exp	A	08 SF	549	57	149	13	70	2	271	286	266	325	410	735	7	77	33	0.35	254	49	19	32	102	10%	31	4%	4.55	-2.9	$13
Consist	D	1st Half	287	38	85	8	44	1	296			344	463	808	7	79	35	0.34	280	48	21	31	121	11%	39	5%	5.43	5.6	$10
LIMA Plan	C	2nd Half	262	19	64	5	26	1	244			305	351	656	8	75	31	0.35	224	50	17	33	80	8%	25	3%	3.55	-9.3	$3
+/- Score	-33	09 Proj	555	72	149	15	71	3	268			318	417	735	7	79	32	0.34	263	47	20	34	103	10%	58	5%	4.50	-2.1	$14

We're not in Philly or The Cell anymore. .256/.328/.386 home numbers confirm worst fears. FB decline also hurt power. Poor ct%, h% dip ruined 2H. Speed is no longer a plus, rebound upside is unexciting.

Ruggiano,Justin			AB	R	H	HR	RBI	SB	Avg	vL	vR	OB	Slg	OPS	bb%	ct%	h%	Eye	xBA	G	L	F	PX	hr/f	SX	SBO	RC/G	RAR	R$
Pos	7	04	0	0	0	0	0	0	0							0			0						0				
Age	27	05 aa	156	18	46	5	22	7	292			345	441	787	7	70	39	0.27	0				109		96	23%	5.34	1.4	$7
Bats	Right	06 aa	400	72	103	11	68	13	257			355	447	801	13	72	33	0.55	0				135		129	19%	5.84	7.5	$14
Health	A	07 aaa	482	73	141	19	69	25	292			360	472	832	10	69	39	0.35	0				133		103	25%	6.12	12.7	$22
PT/Exp	D	08 TAM	* 333	47	82	10	47	18	247	174	233	291	407	697	6	71	32	0.21	256	41	27	33	120	13%	131	30%	4.03	-8.2	$12
Consist	C	1st Half	185	30	49	5	26	11	267			316	409	725	7	73	34	0.26	256	40	28	32	100	11%	142	27%	4.40	-2.4	$8
LIMA Plan	D	2nd Half	148	17	33	6	21	7	221			258	404	662	5	67	29	0.16	259	42	25	33	147	17%	91	34%	3.55	-6.0	$4
+/- Score	14	09 Proj	111	16	29	4	16	5	261			319	443	762	8	70	34	0.29	263	41	26	33	135	15%	119	27%	5.07	0.4	$4

2-7-.197 in 76 AB at TAM. Playable LD power and good speed. But contact has always been a stumbling block, and patience remains in question. Both will limit his AB unless they improve.

Ruiz,Carlos			AB	R	H	HR	RBI	SB	Avg	vL	vR	OB	Slg	OPS	bb%	ct%	h%	Eye	xBA	G	L	F	PX	hr/f	SX	SBO	RC/G	RAR	R$
Pos	2	04 aa	349	33	77	12	37	6	222			256	361	617	4	89	22	0.44	0				74		72	16%	3.10	-10.5	$5
Age	30	05 aaa	339	37	89	4	30	3	263			307	401	707	6	89	29	0.56	0				85		99	11%	4.34	4.4	$6
Bats	Right	06 PHI	* 437	58	126	20	76	4	289	263	260	354	488	842	9	85	30	0.68	291	47	19	34	113	16%	53	5%	5.85	18.5	$17
Health	A	07 PHI	374	42	97	6	54	6	259	189	282	334	396	730	10	87	29	0.86	278	46	18	36	91	5%	81	7%	4.79	3.9	$8
PT/Exp	C	08 PHI	320	47	70	4	31	1	219	212	220	313	300	613	12	88	24	1.16	255	54	17	29	54	5%	49	3%	3.55	-6.5	$3
Consist	C	1st Half	172	22	37	2	20	0	215			286	291	576	9	86	24	0.71	238	53	16	31	51	4%	38	0%	2.87	-7.1	$1
LIMA Plan	D	2nd Half	148	25	33	2	11	1	223			343	311	654	15	91	23	1.93	272	55	18	27	57	6%	54	6%	4.31	0.5	$2
+/- Score	25	09 Proj	374	50	91	7	44	3	243			325	363	689	11	88	26	1.00	273	52	17	31	76	7%	64	6%	4.33	1.0	$7

Traded FB for GB, resulting in disappointing power plunge. Noticeably bad in HR-friendly home venue (.179/.286/.262). His h% will rebound, and ct%, bb% allow hope. But prior optimism is pretty much gone.

Ryan,Brendan			AB	R	H	HR	RBI	SB	Avg	vL	vR	OB	Slg	OPS	bb%	ct%	h%	Eye	xBA	G	L	F	PX	hr/f	SX	SBO	RC/G	RAR	R$
Pos	64	04	0	0	0	0	0	0	0							0			0						0				
Age	27	05 aa	154	20	35	1	7	4	227			277	302	579	6	91	24	0.74	0				50		110	11%	2.97	-6.0	$2
Bats	Right	06 a/a	69	9	15	1	8	1	217			250	275	525	4	86	24	0.30	0				32		76	13%	1.92	-5.3	$1
Health	A	07 STL	* 501	71	120	5	23	20	240	354	238	288	311	599	6	89	26	0.63	252	47	19	34	42	3%	118	20%	3.09	-20.6	$9
PT/Exp	F	08 STL	197	30	48	0	10	7	244	261	229	300	289	590	8	84	29	0.52	247	52	19	28	39	0%	97	16%	2.92	-10.1	$4
Consist	B	1st Half	134	21	37	0	7	5	276			322	328	650	6	84	33	0.43	254	48	22	29	45	0%	92	18%	3.57	-4.1	$4
LIMA Plan	F	2nd Half	63	9	11	0	3	2	175			257	206	463	10	84	21	0.70	229	60	13	26	27	0%	91	13%	1.54	-6.3	$0
+/- Score	-6	09 Proj	111	16	25	0	5	4	225			283	274	557	7	87	26	0.62	247	54	17	29	36	2%	91	16%	2.61	-6.4	$1

Slap-hitter supreme. Unless once-excellent ct% rebounds, SBO gets a hike, and bb% continues upward climb, he'll have trouble staying in the majors. His best shot is off the bench vs. LHP. Avoid.

Salazar,Jeff			AB	R	H	HR	RBI	SB	Avg	vL	vR	OB	Slg	OPS	bb%	ct%	h%	Eye	xBA	G	L	F	PX	hr/f	SX	SBO	RC/G	RAR	R$
Pos	7	04 aa	224	33	48	1	15	9	212			300	299	599	11	88	24	1.09	0				57		122	19%	3.43	-12.4	$3
Age	28	05 a/a	497	59	117	8	40	11	236			308	353	661	9	85	26	0.71	0				77		89	18%	3.89	-17.6	$8
Bats	Left	06 COL	* 381	59	96	8	37	11	252		294	331	390	721	10	84	28	0.73	242	32	21	47	79	5%	120	15%	4.62	-7.2	$9
Health	A	07 ARI	* 494	68	124	9	59	14	252	300	274	321	402	724	9	85	28	0.71	272	35	24	41	93	5%	125	15%	4.65	-10.4	$12
PT/Exp	D	08 ARI	128	17	27	2	12	0	211	300	203	322	344	666	14	68	29	0.51	203	37	16	47	95	5%	88	5%	4.04	-5.6	$1
Consist	A	1st Half	97	10	20	2	10	0	206			313	340	653	13	69	28	0.50	204	34	15	51	102	6%	65	7%	3.76	-5.1	$1
LIMA Plan	F	2nd Half	31	7	7	0	2	0	226			351	355	706	16	65	35	0.55	200	45	20	35	72	0%	107	0%	4.98	-0.4	$0
+/- Score	-25	09 Proj	98	13	23	2	10	2	235			319	359	678	11	80	28	0.63	227	34	17	49	82	4%	90	13%	4.08	-3.9	$2

Power has never been this RHP killer's strong suite. But he opted for more patience and FBs in limited AB. Contact and BA were the first two casualties. Even with a reversion, an MLB job could be the third.

Salazar,Oscar			AB	R	H	HR	RBI	SB	Avg	vL	vR	OB	Slg	OPS	bb%	ct%	h%	Eye	xBA	G	L	F	PX	hr/f	SX	SBO	RC/G	RAR	R$
Pos	3	04 aa	163	13	28	4	16	2	171			209	283	492	5	81	18	0.25	0				68		55	10%	1.37	-21.9	($0)
Age	30	05 MEX	264	35	65	5	30	2	246			323	348	672	10	87	27	0.86	0				63		67	5%	4.04	-10.3	$5
Bats	Right	06 VNZ	229	36	60	7	42	1	262			324	419	743	8	87	27	0.72	0				88		77	5%	4.75	-6.5	$7
Health	A	07 aa	532	47	105	14	61	2	197			222	330	551	3	84	21	0.20	0				84		51	6%	2.15	-59.7	$3
PT/Exp	D	08 BAL	* 527	66	132	15	76	6	250	211	349	308	409	716	8	87	26	0.65	280	40	19	40	100	8%	71	7%	4.41	-13.4	$13
Consist	F	1st Half	272	30	66	8	38	4	243			281	397	678	5	89	25	0.48	253	50	6	44	96	8%	66	9%	3.85	-11.5	$6
LIMA Plan	F	2nd Half	255	35	66	7	38	2	258			334	422	756	10	86	28	0.79	285	38	23	39	103	8%	72	5%	5.01	-2.0	$7
+/- Score	10	09 Proj	163	20	42	5	23	1	258			308	409	717	7	86	28	0.52	273	39	21	40	93	8%	67	6%	4.34	-4.4	$4

5-15-.284 in 81 AB at BAL. Career minor leaguer made the most of Sept playing time. Improving power, decent ct%. But age and BPI limits say best shot may be as utility player off the bench.

Saltalamacchia,J			AB	R	H	HR	RBI	SB	Avg	vL	vR	OB	Slg	OPS	bb%	ct%	h%	Eye	xBA	G	L	F	PX	hr/f	SX	SBO	RC/G	RAR	R$
Pos	2	04	0	0	0	0	0	0	0							0			0						0				
Age	24	05	0	0	0	0	0	0	0							0			0						0				
Bats	Both	06 aa	313	29	69	8	38	0	220			335	358	693	15	78	26	0.78	0				91		30	1%	4.36	-0.2	$3
Health	A	07 2TM	* 389	55	105	16	44	2	270	226	290	322	450	772	7	77	31	0.33	256	44	17	39	118	14%	62	2%	4.92	6.3	$11
PT/Exp	F	08 TEX	* 253	35	64	5	36	0	252	158	311	345	381	726	12	66	36	0.42	229	31	27	42	112	7%	51	3%	4.91	5.4	$5
Consist	A	1st Half	176	23	40	5	26	0	226			328	366	695	13	69	30	0.49	216	33	19	47	106	9%	55	2%	4.31	0.7	$3
LIMA Plan	D	2nd Half	77	12	24	0	10	0	312			384	416	799	10	60	52	0.29	242	28	40	32	127	0%	44	4%	6.59	5.1	$2
+/- Score	-31	09 Proj	362	49	96	9	46	0	265			342	409	751	11	70	36	0.39	248	36	26	38	114	9%	45	2%	5.04	8.4	$8

3-26-.252 in 198 AB at TEX. 2H h%-fueled surge aborted by strained right arm in early Sept. Flashed patience, LD power while struggling with ct% and LHP. Bright future, but note short-term +/- risk.

Sanchez,Freddy			AB	R	H	HR	RBI	SB	Avg	vL	vR	OB	Slg	OPS	bb%	ct%	h%	Eye	xBA	G	L	F	PX	hr/f	SX	SBO	RC/G	RAR	R$
Pos	4	04 PIT	* 144	10	32	1	11	3	222		176	263	306	569	5	90	24	0.53	263	63	13	25	53	3%	78	13%	2.75	-8.3	$1
Age	31	05 PIT	453	54	132	5	35	2	291	326	278	331	400	731	6	92	31	0.75	294	46	23	31	68	4%	73	3%	4.60	0.5	$11
Bats	Right	06 PIT	582	85	200	6	85	3	344	442	316	377	473	849	5	91	37	0.60	305	37	28	36	85	3%	60	3%	5.85	18.8	$23
Health	B	07 PIT	602	77	183	11	81	0	304	364	282	339	442	781	5	87	33	0.42	280	39	22	38	88	5%	49	1%	5.02	5.2	$17
PT/Exp	A	08 PIT	569	75	154	9	52	0	271	289	266	297	371	667	4	89	29	0.33	282	45	24	30	62	6%	56	1%	3.64	-18.4	$12
Consist	C	1st Half	326	36	76	5	32	0	233			260	319	579	4	88	25	0.30	269	43	25	33	55	5%	40	1%	2.62	-21.2	$4
LIMA Plan	C	2nd Half	243	39	78	4	20	0	321			345	440	786	4	91	34	0.39	299	48	24	28	72	7%	68	0%	4.98	1.4	$8
+/- Score	-3	09 Proj	569	76	162	9	61	0	285			316	400	716	4	89	31	0.42	287	43	24	33	73	5%	59	1%	4.27	-7.1	$14

1H dominated by unlucky h%, recovery from 2007 shoulder surgery - not necessarily in order. Healthy now, GB%, Eye say previous power is likely a ceiling. BA drives value, but you could do worse at 2B

JOCK THOMPSON

Sandoval,Pablo

			AB	R	H	HR	RBI	SB	Avg	vL	vR	OB	Slg	OPS	bb%	ct%	h%	Eye	xBA	G	L	F	PX	hr/f	SX	SBO	RC/G	RAR	R$
Pos	3	04	0	0	0	0	0	0	0							0			0						0				
Age	22	05	0	0	0	0	0	0	0							0			0						0				
Bats	Both	06	0	0	0	0	0	0	0							0			0						0				
Health	A	07	0	0	0	0	0	0	0							0			0						0				
PT/Exp	F	08 SF	* 320	50	105	9	57	0	328	237	383	350	491	841	3	90	34	0.35	319	45	26	29	99	11%	51	1%	5.54	-1.7	$14
Consist	F	1st Half	19	2	5	0	1	0	263			300	316	616	5	84	31	0.33					45		32	0%	3.08	-1.5	$0
LIMA Plan	D+	2nd Half	301	48	100	9	56	0	332			354	502	855	3	91	34	0.36	323	45	26	29	102	11%	51	1%	5.68	-0.4	$14
+/- Score	3	09 Proj	**415**	**73**	**122**	**14**	**85**	**0**	**294**			**319**	**482**	**801**	**4**	**90**	**30**	**0.36**	**328**	**45**	**26**	**29**	**113**	**13%**	**66**	**2%**	**5.12**	**-8.7**	**$17**

3-24-.345 in 145 AB at SF...
...after 20-96-.350 at AA-A+.
PRO: Excellent hard contact, budding power, MLB debut.
CON: Patience, just 175 minor league AB above A-ball.
The question is when.

Santiago,Ramon

			AB	R	H	HR	RBI	SB	Avg	vL	vR	OB	Slg	OPS	bb%	ct%	h%	Eye	xBA	G	L	F	PX	hr/f	SX	SBO	RC/G	RAR	R$
Pos	64	04 SEA	* 282	37	48	1	22	7	169			233	218	451	8	90	19	0.81	0				29		114	23%	1.58	-27.2	($0)
Age	29	05 aaa	441	54	93	8	40	15	211			265	315	579	7	88	23	0.59	0				64		108	23%	2.82	-20.1	$7
Bats	Both	06 DET	* 163	20	37	1	14	3	227			267	294	562	5	80	28	0.27	235	58	15	27	47	3%	97	11%	2.32	-10.4	$1
Health	B	07 DET	* 432	44	104	3	33	10	240	300	281	265	329	595	3	84	28	0.22	261	39	26	35	61	2%	105	21%	2.75	-20.3	$5
PT/Exp	F	08 DET	124	30	35	4	18	1	282	320	273	390	460	850	15	86	30	1.29	297	44	23	33	102	11%	112	2%	6.41	7.3	$5
Consist	F	1st Half	36	10	13	1	11	0	361			465	611	1076	16	97	35	7.00	358	42	21	36	141	8%	98	0%	9.22	4.4	$2
LIMA Plan	F	2nd Half	88	20	22	3	7	1	250			359	398	757	15	82	28	0.94	273	44	24	31	84	13%	106	3%	5.15	2.1	$2
+/- Score	2	09 Proj	**262**	**40**	**68**	**4**	**21**	**8**	**260**			**320**	**357**	**677**	**8**	**83**	**30**	**0.53**	**257**	**45**	**22**	**33**	**61**	**6%**	**110**	**15%**	**3.92**	**-3.3**	**$6**

Notable across-the-board BPI spike, all suspect due to the sample size. Hikes in xBA, bb% are interesting if SBO returns. With an increased role, he could be a defensible end-game flyer.

Schierholtz,Nate

			AB	R	H	HR	RBI	SB	Avg	vL	vR	OB	Slg	OPS	bb%	ct%	h%	Eye	xBA	G	L	F	PX	hr/f	SX	SBO	RC/G	RAR	R$
Pos	9	04	0	0	0	0	0	0	0							0			0						0				
Age	25	05	0	0	0	0	0	0	0							0			0						0				
Bats	Left	06 aa	470	56	127	14	55	8	270			310	445	755	5	83	30	0.33	0				103		108	10%	4.68	-7.3	$12
Health	A	07 SF	* 523	63	156	12	65	11	299	500	266	319	463	782	3	87	33	0.23	271	44	15	41	97	6%	114	14%	4.89	0.1	$17
PT/Exp	D	08 SF	* 425	65	125	14	67	8	294	333	315	326	503	828	5	87	31	0.38	337	46	30	24	121	16%	128	12%	5.51	3.8	$17
Consist	A	1st Half	276	37	72	9	43	8	261			300	452	752	5	86	28	0.41	0				107		136	16%	4.69	-4.1	$9
LIMA Plan	D	2nd Half	149	27	53	6	24	0	354			375	596	971	3	89	37	0.30	362	46	30	24	146	18%	85	6%	6.99	6.9	$8
+/- Score	45	09 Proj	**240**	**34**	**70**	**6**	**34**	**4**	**292**			**319**	**474**	**793**	**4**	**87**	**32**	**0.30**	**313**	**46**	**25**	**29**	**109**	**10%**	**114**	**12%**	**5.08**	**0.2**	**$8**

1-5-.320 in 75 AB at SF.
PRO: Good hard contact, set personal HR best in AAA (18).
CON: Pitch selection and now FB% depressing MLB HRs.
His age and raw power give him some end-game value.

Schneider,Brian

			AB	R	H	HR	RBI	SB	Avg	vL	vR	OB	Slg	OPS	bb%	ct%	h%	Eye	xBA	G	L	F	PX	hr/f	SX	SBO	RC/G	RAR	R$
Pos	2	04 MON	436	40	112	12	49	0	257	244	260	322	399	721	9	86	28	0.67	272	49	20	32	83	10%	42	1%	4.49	8.7	$8
Age	32	05 WAS	369	38	99	10	44	1	268	265	269	322	409	731	7	87	29	0.60	281	47	21	33	88	10%	46	1%	4.53	7.8	$9
Bats	Left	06 WAS	410	30	105	4	55	2	256	271	251	319	329	648	8	84	30	0.57	250	47	23	30	50	4%	28	3%	3.62	-8.7	$6
Health	A	07 WAS	408	33	96	6	54	0	235	212	244	328	336	663	12	86	26	1.00	236	48	15	36	66	5%	23	0%	4.08	-4.3	$4
PT/Exp	C	08 NYM	335	30	86	9	38	0	257	187	277	340	367	707	11	84	28	0.79	274	53	26	21	66	15%	12	0%	4.39	1.7	$6
Consist	A	1st Half	180	13	46	2	16	0	256			333	306	639	10	84	29	0.75	254	55	26	19	31	7%	11	0%	3.59	-3.3	$2
LIMA Plan	D	2nd Half	155	17	40	7	22	0	258			347	439	785	12	84	27	0.84	297	51	25	24	107	23%	13	0%	5.32	5.0	$4
+/- Score	-25	09 Proj	**361**	**32**	**94**	**9**	**45**	**0**	**260**			**340**	**373**	**713**	**11**	**85**	**29**	**0.79**	**263**	**50**	**22**	**28**	**70**	**10%**	**19**	**1%**	**4.48**	**2.5**	**$7**

Held most of last year's BPI gains and then some, ending up with a slightly better bottom line. Still a good end-game pick, but AB now threatened by increasing futility vs. LHP: 52 AB, only one XBH.

Schumaker,Skip

			AB	R	H	HR	RBI	SB	Avg	vL	vR	OB	Slg	OPS	bb%	ct%	h%	Eye	xBA	G	L	F	PX	hr/f	SX	SBO	RC/G	RAR	R$
Pos	879	04 aa	516	62	140	3	34	15	271			333	350	683	9	90	30	0.90	0				52		89	20%	4.22	-7.0	$11
Age	29	05 aaa	440	51	111	4	26	10	252			290	340	630	5	90	27	0.55	0				59		97	13%	3.41	-13.1	$7
Bats	Left	06 aaa	369	42	104	3	23	10	281			319	350	668	5	88	31	0.46	0				42		94	13%	3.75	-8.4	$8
Health	A	07 STL	* 409	42	111	6	40	3	272	375	327	317	385	702	6	86	30	0.48	274	54	19	27	73	6%	53	7%	4.18	-4.2	$8
PT/Exp	C	08 STL	540	87	163	8	46	8	302	168	340	358	406	763	8	89	33	0.78	299	58	22	20	62	8%	108	6%	5.02	4.2	$18
Consist	B	1st Half	280	53	84	6	30	6	300			364	439	803	9	88	33	0.80	303	55	21	24	84	10%	121	7%	5.52	6.0	$11
LIMA Plan	D+	2nd Half	260	34	79	2	16	2	304			351	369	720	7	90	33	0.76	290	62	22	16	38	5%	75	5%	4.49	-1.8	$7
+/- Score	-6	09 Proj	**391**	**51**	**114**	**5**	**31**	**6**	**292**			**340**	**387**	**728**	**7**	**88**	**32**	**0.64**	**291**	**58**	**21**	**21**	**59**	**7%**	**88**	**8%**	**4.54**	**-1.0**	**$10**

Maximized upside from all-contact, no-power game and 36% h% vs. RHP in first full MLB season. Barring a dramatic improvement vs. LHP, he's unlikely to repeat BA or AB total in 2009.

Scott,Luke

			AB	R	H	HR	RBI	SB	Avg	vL	vR	OB	Slg	OPS	bb%	ct%	h%	Eye	xBA	G	L	F	PX	hr/f	SX	SBO	RC/G	RAR	R$
Pos	70	04 aa	208	31	49	14	44	0	236			312	500	812	10	81	23	0.59	0				155		33	4%	5.45	1.6	$7
Age	30	05 HOU	* 478	56	110	23	67	3	230	286	178	287	446	733	7	79	24	0.39	261	43	11	46	134	13%	82	6%	4.44	-13.1	$12
Bats	Left	06 HOU	* 532	79	153	26	85	7	287	240	366	369	517	887	11	81	31	0.68	291	36	24	40	133	15%	95	5%	6.58	19.9	$21
Health	A	07 HOU	369	49	94	18	64	3	255	271	252	348	504	852	13	74	30	0.56	284	41	19	40	167	16%	88	4%	6.36	10.9	$12
PT/Exp	B	08 BAL	476	67	122	23	65	2	256	215	269	331	471	801	10	79	28	0.52	272	39	17	44	139	14%	56	3%	5.43	8.1	$14
Consist	B	1st Half	235	35	66	14	32	2	281			355	532	887	10	79	30	0.54	284	39	15	46	160	17%	65	5%	6.49	10.9	$9
LIMA Plan	B	2nd Half	241	32	56	9	33	0	232			307	411	718	10	78	26	0.50	261	39	19	42	119	11%	48	2%	4.40	-3.3	$5
+/- Score	-7	09 Proj	**509**	**71**	**135**	**25**	**78**	**3**	**265**			**344**	**489**	**833**	**11**	**78**	**30**	**0.55**	**278**	**39**	**18**	**42**	**144**	**15%**	**73**	**4%**	**5.89**	**14.0**	**$16**

2H h% and dip in FBs derailed terrific season, but end result still wasn't awful. Excellent power, relatively stable BPIs, peak age bode well for 2009. Struggles in extended AB vs. LHP limit breakout potential.

Scutaro,Marco

			AB	R	H	HR	RBI	SB	Avg	vL	vR	OB	Slg	OPS	bb%	ct%	h%	Eye	xBA	G	L	F	PX	hr/f	SX	SBO	RC/G	RAR	R$
Pos	645	04 OAK	455	50	124	7	43	0	273	276	271	297	393	691	3	87	30	0.28	270	43	20	36	80	5%	41	0%	3.89	-7.4	$8
Age	33	05 OAK	381	48	94	9	37	5	247	171	262	312	391	703	9	87	26	0.75	282	43	21	36	90	7%	89	7%	4.34	-2.4	$8
Bats	Right	06 OAK	365	52	97	5	41	5	266	218	279	354	397	751	12	82	31	0.76	262	44	21	36	84	5%	111	5%	5.11	7.3	$8
Health	A	07 OAK	338	49	88	7	41	2	260	309	245	330	361	691	9	88	28	0.88	253	39	20	41	62	6%	53	3%	4.23	-0.6	$7
PT/Exp	B	08 TOR	517	76	138	7	60	7	267	268	267	340	356	696	10	87	29	0.88	264	43	23	35	59	4%	76	5%	4.34	0.2	$12
Consist	A	1st Half	236	33	61	2	27	5	258			345	318	662	12	86	29	0.94	256	40	27	33	38	3%	82	8%	4.02	-2.1	$5
LIMA Plan	D	2nd Half	281	43	77	5	33	2	274			336	388	723	8	89	30	0.81	271	45	19	36	76	6%	61	2%	4.59	2.1	$7
+/- Score	-17	09 Proj	**380**	**54**	**101**	**6**	**44**	**4**	**266**			**336**	**367**	**703**	**10**	**87**	**29**	**0.81**	**262**	**42**	**21**	**37**	**65**	**5%**	**73**	**4%**	**4.39**	**0.5**	**$9**

Came away with first 500 AB season of career thanks to injuries. But an established .260 hitter with little power or speed isn't likely to get a shot at a repeat. Unlikely to either help or sink you.

Sexson,Richie

			AB	R	H	HR	RBI	SB	Avg	vL	vR	OB	Slg	OPS	bb%	ct%	h%	Eye	xBA	G	L	F	PX	hr/f	SX	SBO	RC/G	RAR	R$
Pos	3	04 ARI	90	20	21	9	23	0	233	222	236	337	578	914	13	77	20	0.67	311	48	14	38	201	35%	44	0%	6.81	2.3	$5
Age	34	05 SEA	558	99	147	39	121	1	263	333	244	365	541	906	14	70	31	0.53	286	40	19	41	197	25%	48	1%	7.16	33.5	$25
Bats	Right	06 SEA	591	75	156	34	107	1	264	204	282	336	504	840	10	74	30	0.42	272	42	18	40	160	19%	28	1%	5.97	9.4	$19
Health	B	07 SEA	434	58	89	21	63	1	205	238	195	289	399	687	11	77	22	0.51	259	47	15	38	127	17%	42	1%	3.95	-17.7	$8
PT/Exp	B	08 2AL	280	29	62	12	36	1	221	325	178	325	382	707	13	69	27	0.50	229	47	18	35	113	18%	28	1%	4.36	-7.8	$5
Consist	C	1st Half	226	24	51	9	26	0	226			316	376	693	12	67	29	0.41	220	46	19	34	109	17%	16	0%	4.14	-7.7	$4
LIMA Plan	F	2nd Half	54	5	11	3	10	1	204			358	407	766	19	78	21	1.08	253	49	14	37	126	19%	25	5%	5.32	0.1	$1
+/- Score	-22	09 Proj	**212**	**25**	**47**	**9**	**35**	**1**	**222**			**328**	**398**	**725**	**14**	**74**	**26**	**0.61**	**246**	**46**	**16**	**37**	**120**	**15%**	**38**	**2%**	**4.61**	**-4.3**	**$4**

Fourth consecutive season of PX and xBA erosion, this time due to ct% plunge and more struggles vs. RHP. His best shot now - a job vs. LHP and fewer AB - is worth little in our game.

Shealy,Ryan

			AB	R	H	HR	RBI	SB	Avg	vL	vR	OB	Slg	OPS	bb%	ct%	h%	Eye	xBA	G	L	F	PX	hr/f	SX	SBO	RC/G	RAR	R$
Pos	3	04 aa	469	68	134	27	77	1	286			350	532	881	9	77	32	0.42	0				154		60	1%	6.40	12.2	$18
Age	29	05 COL	* 498	65	143	21	69	4	286	125	373	336	484	820	7	86	30	0.52	314	45	25	30	121	16%	70	3%	5.47	-1.8	$18
Bats	Right	06 2TM	* 424	58	112	19	76	1	264	185	311	312	472	784	6	81	28	0.37	270	37	18	45	125	12%	61	2%	5.01	-8.6	$13
Health	C	07 KC	* 294	28	61	7	38	0	208	125	258	267	319	586	7	72	26	0.29	217	35	21	44	82	7%	23	0%	2.52	-25.0	$2
PT/Exp	D	08 KC	* 473	52	114	22	68	0	241	273	325	309	428	736	9	77	27	0.43	244	35	17	48	120	13%	18	1%	4.50	-10.8	$11
Consist	F	1st Half	203	17	42	8	21	0	208			267	360	627	7	79	22	0.39	0				96		19	2%	3.09	-13.8	$2
LIMA Plan	D	2nd Half	270	34	72	15	48	0	266			339	478	818	10	75	30	0.45	252	35	17	48	139	15%	18	0%	5.62	2.7	$9
+/- Score	-9	09 Proj	**450**	**51**	**109**	**19**	**66**	**0**	**242**			**304**	**414**	**718**	**8**	**77**	**28**	**0.38**	**248**	**36**	**19**	**45**	**113**	**12%**	**27**	**1%**	**4.26**	**-13.5**	**$10**

7-20-.301 in 70 AB at KC.
PRO: Power rebound, FB%, 33 MLB AB vs. LHP, and age.
CON: Mediocre BPIs accompanying PX.
Upside as low-BA HR source is likely now or never.

JOCK THOMPSON

Sheffield,Gary			AB	R	H	HR	RBI	SB	Avg	vL	vR	OB	Slg	OPS	bb%	ct%	h%	Eye	xBA	G	L	F	PX	hr/f	SX	SBO	RC/G	RAR	R$
Pos	0	04 NYY	573	117	166	36	121	5	290	314	282	388	534	922	14	86	29	1.11	295	42	17	41	134	18%	60	6%	7.01	27.7	$28
Age	40	05 NYY	584	104	170	34	123	10	291	359	266	375	512	887	12	87	29	1.03	296	42	17	41	125	16%	75	6%	6.47	7.3	$29
Bats	Right	06 NYY	151	22	45	6	25	5	298	344	286	354	450	804	8	89	30	0.81	269	49	15	37	81	12%	73	13%	5.34	-4.6	$6
Health	F	07 DET	494	107	131	25	75	22	265	245	271	372	462	834	15	86	27	1.18	278	41	17	42	112	14%	110	16%	6.04	-2.9	$23
PT/Exp	C	08 DET	418	52	94	19	57	9	225	239	220	319	400	719	12	80	24	0.70	251	43	14	43	107	13%	66	9%	4.46	-6.0	$11
Consist	C	1st Half	164	22	37	5	16	3	226			332	366	697	14	78	26	0.72	239	46	14	40	96	10%	60	6%	4.32	-3.0	$3
LIMA Plan	C+	2nd Half	254	30	57	14	41	6	224			311	421	732	11	81	22	0.68	258	41	14	45	115	15%	58	12%	4.54	-3.0	$7
+/- Score	1	09 Proj	408	64	98	18	62	6	240			333	414	747	12	84	25	0.84	261	43	15	42	102	13%	67	8%	4.86	-8.6	$12

Age and injuries have sapped once-formidable skill set. 2H HR surge a result of opening up swing to the detriment of bb% and ct%. Better health could produce bigger up-tick, but this is nothing to bet on.

Shelton,Chris			AB	R	H	HR	RBI	SB	Avg	vL	vR	OB	Slg	OPS	bb%	ct%	h%	Eye	xBA	G	L	F	PX	hr/f	SX	SBO	RC/G	RAR	R$
Pos	3	04 DET	*108	10	28	1	9	0	259			365	315	680	14	73	35	0.62	0				42		16	0%	4.16	-2.6	$1
Age	28	05 DET	*569	92	170	25	94	0	300	277	303	362	510	872	9	80	34	0.48	293	38	24	38	138	14%	50	1%	6.27	18.6	$23
Bats	Right	06 DET	*482	68	129	19	60	2	268	276	273	337	454	791	9	71	34	0.36	233	33	20	48	124	12%	83	3%	5.47	0.7	$13
Health	A	07 aaa	498	66	119	11	57	4	238			336	364	700	13	73	30	0.55	0				94		60	4%	4.36	-20.0	$9
PT/Exp	D	08 TEX	*353	40	91	10	46	1	256	184	250	329	415	744	10	77	31	0.47	268	27	29	44	112	8%	56	1%	4.78	-5.0	$8
Consist	B	1st Half	145	18	34	4	23	1	236			334	372	707	13	69	32	0.47	240	27	29	44	111	9%	43	2%	4.49	-3.4	$3
LIMA Plan	F	2nd Half	208	22	56	6	23	0	271			325	444	769	7	83	30	0.47	0				113		49	0%	4.98	-1.7	$5
+/- Score	8	09 Proj	107	13	27	3	13	0	252			332	412	744	11	75	31	0.48	253	33	24	42	111	9%	66	2%	4.84	-1.3	$2

2-11-.216 in 97 AB at TEX. Once a streaky, low-BA HR source, his power appears to be declining prematurely. LD%, bb% are solid, but without better contact, his career is in now in jeopardy.

Shoppach,Kelly			AB	R	H	HR	RBI	SB	Avg	vL	vR	OB	Slg	OPS	bb%	ct%	h%	Eye	xBA	G	L	F	PX	hr/f	SX	SBO	RC/G	RAR	R$
Pos	2	04 aaa	399	50	85	17	52	0	213			280	404	683	8	73	25	0.34	0				132		30	0%	3.86	-2.6	$6
Age	29	05 aaa	370	46	84	19	57	0	227			294	423	716	9	76	25	0.39	0				127		24	0%	4.22	3.5	$9
Bats	Right	06 CLE	*188	18	46	6	25	0	247	314	213	298	409	708	7	63	36	0.20	211	43	15	42	137	12%	23	2%	4.51	0.6	$3
Health	A	07 CLE	161	26	42	7	30	0	261	265	260	308	472	780	6	65	36	0.20	249	46	15	39	176	17%	41	0%	5.45	5.4	$5
PT/Exp	F	08 CLE	352	67	92	21	55	0	261	304	246	330	517	847	9	62	36	0.27	260	38	19	43	213	22%	43	0%	6.72	25.8	$13
Consist	C	1st Half	133	20	33	5	17	0	248			291	444	734	6	65	35	0.17	237	38	16	46	168	13%	42	0%	4.80	2.4	$3
LIMA Plan	D+	2nd Half	219	47	59	16	38	0	269			352	562	914	11	61	37	0.33	272	38	20	41	242	29%	44	0%	7.93	23.5	$10
+/- Score	-7	09 Proj	382	62	97	19	60	0	254			314	476	790	8	64	34	0.24	248	41	17	42	181	19%	40	0%	5.66	15.9	$12

Maximized legit power and abysmal ct% via significant reduction in GBs and improved patience. ABs inherited via injury made it a career year. Even with BA risk, a good HR source from the CA slot.

Sizemore,Grady			AB	R	H	HR	RBI	SB	Avg	vL	vR	OB	Slg	OPS	bb%	ct%	h%	Eye	xBA	G	L	F	PX	hr/f	SX	SBO	RC/G	RAR	R$
Pos	8	04 CLE	*556	74	142	10	65	15	255	178	280	315	381	696	8	84	29	0.53	255	47	16	37	77	6%	111	19%	4.17	-9.1	$13
Age	26	05 CLE	640	111	185	22	81	22	289	245	308	342	484	827	8	79	34	0.39	292	44	24	31	125	14%	145	19%	5.70	25.8	$27
Bats	Left	06 CLE	655	134	190	28	76	22	290	214	329	366	533	898	11	77	34	0.51	275	33	20	47	158	12%	152	16%	6.86	40.6	$28
Health	A	07 CLE	628	118	174	24	78	33	277	284	274	377	462	839	14	75	33	0.65	250	33	21	47	125	11%	124	20%	6.22	30.7	$28
PT/Exp	A	08 CLE	634	101	170	33	90	38	268	224	286	366	502	868	13	79	29	0.75	281	35	19	46	147	14%	127	23%	6.44	20.1	$30
Consist	A	1st Half	319	51	84	19	45	19	263			358	517	875	13	80	27	0.75	284	34	18	48	155	15%	124	23%	6.46	10.3	$16
LIMA Plan	B+	2nd Half	315	50	86	14	45	19	273			374	486	860	14	79	31	0.76	279	36	21	43	140	13%	116	22%	6.43	9.8	$15
+/- Score	15	09 Proj	612	106	168	29	91	31	275			366	498	863	13	78	31	0.66	274	35	20	45	143	13%	131	21%	6.39	25.4	$29

Reversed ct% slide, held FB gains, made the best of SBO hike - and generated a 30-30 season. BA should rebound some with h%, but you're really paying for the elite power-and-speed combination.

Smith,Seth			AB	R	H	HR	RBI	SB	Avg	vL	vR	OB	Slg	OPS	bb%	ct%	h%	Eye	xBA	G	L	F	PX	hr/f	SX	SBO	RC/G	RAR	R$
Pos	9	04	0	0	0	0	0	0	0							0			0						0				
Age	26	05	0	0	0	0	0	0	0							0			0						0				
Bats	Left	06 aa	524	61	146	13	55	3	279			329	452	781	7	90	29	0.74	0				104		65	6%	5.19	-0.4	$12
Health	A	07 aa	451	50	124	14	61	5	275			320	447	767	6	86	30	0.47	0				104		83	8%	4.89	-3.9	$12
PT/Exp	D	08 COL	*356	50	94	11	50	8	265		289	348	421	769	11	84	29	0.80	282	45	21	34	98	11%	89	8%	5.17	-0.2	$12
Consist	A	1st Half	269	38	73	7	36	8	270			351	412	762	11	85	29	0.83	274	52	16	32	88	10%	98	10%	5.10	-0.7	$9
LIMA Plan	F	2nd Half	87	12	22	4	14	0	248			339	451	790	12	81	26	0.73	296	41	24	35	131	16%	24	0%	5.41	0.6	$2
+/- Score	21	09 Proj	141	18	40	5	19	2	284			348	461	810	9	85	31	0.66	294	42	23	35	108	11%	72	5%	5.54	1.9	$5

4-15-.259 in 108 AB at COL. Career .300 hitter in minors hinting at improved patience. GB rate is limiting his power, but age and athleticism buy him time. An end-game pick at best, for now.

Snider,Travis			AB	R	H	HR	RBI	SB	Avg	vL	vR	OB	Slg	OPS	bb%	ct%	h%	Eye	xBA	G	L	F	PX	hr/f	SX	SBO	RC/G	RAR	R$
Pos	7	04	0	0	0	0	0	0	0							0			0						0				
Age	21	05	0	0	0	0	0	0	0							0			0						0				
Bats	Left	06	0	0	0	0	0	0	0							0			0						0				
Health	A	07	0	0	0	0	0	0	0							0			0						0				
PT/Exp	F	08 TOR	*499	74	135	21	87	2	271	286	305	340	458	799	9	72	34	0.38	292	37	35	29	137	20%	47	2%	5.50	9.3	$17
Consist	F	1st Half	238	33	61	10	37	1	255			323	428	751	9	71	32	0.35	0				122		44	3%	4.80	-0.4	$7
LIMA Plan	D+	2nd Half	261	41	75	10	50	1	286			356	485	842	10	73	35	0.41	303	37	35	29	150	19%	44	3%	6.13	9.4	$10
+/- Score	27	09 Proj	380	57	98	11	67	2	258			329	407	736	10	73	33	0.39	280	37	35	29	114	13%	51	2%	4.70	-2.7	$10

2-13-.301 in 73 AB at TOR. Excellent prospect put skills on on display in small MLB sample size. Power, xBA are intriguing. Age, ct%, and only 424 minor league AB above A-ball point to risk.

Snyder,Chris			AB	R	H	HR	RBI	SB	Avg	vL	vR	OB	Slg	OPS	bb%	ct%	h%	Eye	xBA	G	L	F	PX	hr/f	SX	SBO	RC/G	RAR	R$
Pos	2	04 ARI	*442	57	114	16	55	2	258	250	234	331	446	776	10	85	27	0.72	286	38	21	42	118	10%	45	3%	5.18	17.7	$11
Age	28	05 ARI	326	24	66	6	28	0	202	260	185	290	301	590	11	73	26	0.46	220	51	19	29	75	9%	16	1%	2.76	-10.5	$0
Bats	Right	06 ARI	184	19	51	6	32	0	277	246	294	354	424	778	11	79	32	0.56	254	45	22	33	93	13%	14	0%	5.20	4.5	$5
Health	A	07 ARI	326	37	82	13	47	0	252	316	215	333	433	766	11	79	28	0.60	248	40	15	45	117	11%	19	1%	5.05	5.9	$7
PT/Exp	D	08 ARI	334	47	79	16	64	0	237	250	231	346	452	798	14	70	29	0.55	254	38	18	44	158	16%	38	0%	5.76	15.5	$10
Consist	A	1st Half	191	22	47	7	33	0	246			336	440	776	12	72	31	0.49	262	41	21	39	143	13%	39	0%	5.37	6.5	$5
LIMA Plan	D+	2nd Half	143	25	32	9	31	0	224			358	469	827	17	66	27	0.63	245	34	15	51	180	19%	28	0%	6.29	9.1	$5
+/- Score	15	09 Proj	396	51	99	19	68	0	250			347	457	804	13	74	29	0.57	255	40	18	42	141	16%	22	0%	5.66	16.5	$12

Continued strong PX surge, tying career-high HR in 100 fewer AB. Improved patience, sustained FB% bode well, but ct% issues kill his BA. 20 HR upside if he can exploit home field (only 9 HR in two years.)

Soriano,Alfonso			AB	R	H	HR	RBI	SB	Avg	vL	vR	OB	Slg	OPS	bb%	ct%	h%	Eye	xBA	G	L	F	PX	hr/f	SX	SBO	RC/G	RAR	R$
Pos	7	04 TEX	613	77	170	28	91	18	277	266	284	314	480	794	5	80	31	0.27	259	33	19	48	121	12%	108	17%	5.05	1.9	$23
Age	33	05 TEX	637	102	171	36	104	30	268	257	272	304	512	816	5	80	28	0.26	287	34	19	47	155	15%	133	26%	5.29	10.4	$31
Bats	Right	06 WAS	647	119	179	46	95	41	277	293	271	345	560	904	9	75	30	0.42	277	29	20	51	175	18%	113	37%	6.70	27.6	$36
Health	C	07 CHC	579	97	173	33	70	19	299	254	311	334	560	894	5	78	34	0.24	286	34	20	46	166	16%	120	20%	6.35	15.9	$27
PT/Exp	A	08 CHC	453	76	127	29	75	19	280	351	252	343	532	875	9	77	31	0.42	282	29	23	48	160	17%	96	19%	6.23	10.5	$24
Consist	A	1st Half	212	36	60	15	40	7	283			330	547	878	7	78	30	0.33	289	30	23	47	162	19%	87	16%	6.08	4.0	$12
LIMA Plan	B	2nd Half	241	40	67	14	35	12	278			353	519	872	10	76	31	0.49	278	28	23	49	159	16%	92	22%	6.35	6.4	$12
+/- Score	-23	09 Proj	550	92	156	34	82	24	284			338	539	878	8	77	31	0.36	281	31	21	48	162	17%	112	23%	6.24	13.5	$28

Only injuries (strained calf, broken hand) slowed another fine season. In spite of creeping age and health risk, skill set is one of the most stable around. Pay for elite power-and-speed combination.

Soto,Geovany			AB	R	H	HR	RBI	SB	Avg	vL	vR	OB	Slg	OPS	bb%	ct%	h%	Eye	xBA	G	L	F	PX	hr/f	SX	SBO	RC/G	RAR	R$
Pos	2	04 aa	332	41	81	8	41	1	244			318	358	676	10	80	28	0.55	0				73		39	3%	3.91	-1.6	$6
Age	26	05 aaa	288	24	66	3	32	0	230			323	306	630	12	80	28	0.69	0				58		18	1%	3.50	-3.6	$2
Bats	Right	06 aaa	367	32	93	6	37	0	253			323	360	683	9	80	30	0.52	189	60	5	35	75	6%	18	1%	4.02	-3.8	$4
Health	A	07 CHC	*439	73	143	26	95	0	325	444	333	390	588	978	10	78	37	0.48	305	41	22	37	170	21%	45	0%	7.68	37.8	$23
PT/Exp	C	08 CHC	494	66	141	23	86	0	285	312	276	365	504	869	11	76	34	0.51	276	38	21	41	150	15%	36	1%	6.45	31.1	$19
Consist	F	1st Half	271	30	77	13	47	0	284			374	517	891	13	74	34	0.56	280	38	21	42	164	16%	26	0%	6.87	20.2	$10
LIMA Plan	D+	2nd Half	223	36	64	10	39	0	287			354	489	842	9	77	33	0.45	272	38	21	41	132	14%	56	2%	5.95	10.9	$9
+/- Score	2	09 Proj	471	64	131	20	79	0	278			352	474	826	10	77	32	0.50	270	38	21	41	130	13%	35	1%	5.80	20.8	$16

Year-long consistency at most demanding position marked excellent rookie year. Power and patience are legit, ct% is cushioned by LD%. Moderate consolidation is likely; pay for the projections.

JOCK THOMPSON

Span,Denard

Span,Denard			AB	R	H	HR	RBI	SB	Avg	vL	vR	OB	Slg	OPS	bb%	ct%	h%	Eye	xBA	G	L	F	PX	hr/f	SX	SBO	RC/G	RAR	R$
Pos	9	04	0	0	0	0	0	0	0							0			0						0				
Age	25	05 aa	263	40	71	0	22	9	270			319	323	642	7	86	31	0.53	0				32		127	23%	3.56	-11.2	$7
Bats	Left	06 aa	536	75	146	2	42	23	272			319	332	651	6	86	32	0.48	0				37		122	22%	3.60	-25.4	$14
Health	A	07 aaa	487	58	127	3	54	25	261			313	345	658	7	81	32	0.40	0				57		120	29%	3.65	-22.6	$13
PT/Exp	D	08 MIN	* 503	96	148	8	59	30	294	283	299	381	424	805	12	81	35	0.75	295	54	26	20	85	9%	141	26%	5.76	5.7	$23
Consist	C	1st Half	191	30	56	2	15	15	294			370	389	759	11	79	36	0.59	280	67	19	15	72	9%	113	37%	5.10	-1.5	$8
LIMA Plan	C+	2nd Half	312	66	92	6	44	15	295			387	446	833	13	83	34	0.87	304	53	26	21	92	11%	145	20%	6.15	7.0	$14
+/- Score	21	09 Proj	570	92	160	6	60	30	281			349	381	730	10	82	33	0.60	286	54	26	20	65	6%	133	26%	4.67	-11.7	$20

6-47-.293 in 347 AB at MIN. Improved patience and better pitch selection resulted in 2H LD spike and fine rookie year. No real power to speak of, but SX and 72% SB success rate say pay for the speed.

Spilborghs,Ryan

Spilborghs,Ryan			AB	R	H	HR	RBI	SB	Avg	vL	vR	OB	Slg	OPS	bb%	ct%	h%	Eye	xBA	G	L	F	PX	hr/f	SX	SBO	RC/G	RAR	R$
Pos	79	04	0	0	0	0	0	0	0							0			0						0				
Age	29	05 a/a	478	63	134	7	51	11	281			337	429	766	8	85	32	0.55	0				103		108	15%	5.06	0.4	$14
Bats	Right	06 COL	* 436	62	129	8	46	11	295	323	267	348	422	770	7	85	33	0.53	279	51	21	29	78	7%	103	11%	5.01	-2.9	$14
Health	B	07 COL	* 388	57	109	14	62	6	282	356	271	349	452	801	9	84	31	0.63	289	50	21	30	101	15%	81	9%	5.40	0.5	$14
PT/Exp	D	08 COL	233	38	73	6	36	7	313	326	306	410	468	877	14	82	36	0.93	295	55	21	24	100	13%	96	12%	6.70	8.3	$11
Consist	B	1st Half	160	24	47	4	26	6	294			405	450	855	16	83	34	1.07	295	57	20	23	98	13%	102	13%	6.55	5.1	$7
LIMA Plan	F	2nd Half	73	14	26	2	10	1	356			420	507	927	10	82	41	0.62	293	52	23	25	102	13%	58	11%	7.01	3.1	$4
+/- Score	-20	09 Proj	188	30	55	5	26	4	293			366	441	807	10	83	33	0.69	290	52	21	26	95	12%	85	12%	5.60	1.2	$7

Classic tweener, improved game via better patience and pitch selection. But his ABs aren't apt to increase without more speed or power. And he's hit GBs for too long to bet on the latter developing now.

Stairs,Matt

Stairs,Matt			AB	R	H	HR	RBI	SB	Avg	vL	vR	OB	Slg	OPS	bb%	ct%	h%	Eye	xBA	G	L	F	PX	hr/f	SX	SBO	RC/G	RAR	R$
Pos	0	04 KC	439	48	117	18	66	1	267	223	278	340	451	791	10	79	30	0.53	254	50	13	37	112	14%	55	1%	5.32	0.2	$11
Age	41	05 KC	396	55	109	13	66	1	275	259	278	371	444	815	13	83	31	0.87	269	40	19	42	111	10%	42	2%	5.84	-2.1	$12
Bats	Left	06 2AL	348	42	86	13	51	0	247	217	252	325	420	744	10	75	29	0.47	245	43	17	39	117	13%	22	0%	4.76	-17.1	$7
Health	A	07 TOR	357	58	103	21	64	2	289	289	288	367	549	916	11	82	30	0.67	305	40	18	42	166	17%	55	3%	6.86	6.2	$15
PT/Exp	C	08 2TM	337	46	85	13	49	1	252	235	254	335	409	745	11	73	31	0.47	243	43	20	37	105	14%	53	2%	4.78	-1.4	$9
Consist	F	1st Half	210	31	55	8	28	1	262			335	414	749	10	77	31	0.47	251	45	20	35	99	14%	45	3%	4.75	-1.1	$6
LIMA Plan	F	2nd Half	127	15	30	5	21	0	236			336	402	737	13	68	31	0.46	227	38	21	41	116	14%	48	0%	4.88	-0.2	$3
+/- Score	-37	09 Proj	217	30	54	7	34	1	249			334	411	745	11	75	30	0.52	248	42	19	40	110	11%	57	2%	4.84	-4.6	$5

A repeat of 2006 after 2007 surge. Stayed patient after 1H power dive, but all-or-nothing 2H approach in fewer AB hints at future. Still viable as a LH bat off the bench, but age and xBA suggest end is near.

Stewart,Ian

Stewart,Ian			AB	R	H	HR	RBI	SB	Avg	vL	vR	OB	Slg	OPS	bb%	ct%	h%	Eye	xBA	G	L	F	PX	hr/f	SX	SBO	RC/G	RAR	R$
Pos	5	04	0	0	0	0	0	0	0							0			0						0				
Age	24	05	0	0	0	0	0	0	0							0			0						0				
Bats	Left	06 aa	462	58	118	9	55	2	255			312	424	736	8	84	29	0.51	0				109		80	11%	4.69	-7.8	$8
Health	A	07 COL	* 457	63	130	14	63	9	284	100	242	346	442	788	9	81	33	0.48	269	46	19	35	101	11%	85	8%	5.24	-4.8	$15
PT/Exp	C	08 COL	* 523	79	133	24	81	6	254	370	231	323	471	794	9	73	30	0.39	267	31	25	44	147	14%	103	8%	5.42	0.8	$18
Consist	A	1st Half	251	39	60	14	38	4	239			297	490	787	8	76	26	0.34	259	22	22	56	155	13%	121	14%	5.16	-1.6	$8
LIMA Plan	C	2nd Half	272	40	73	10	43	2	267			346	454	800	11	71	34	0.42	260	33	26	41	139	12%	65	4%	5.66	2.3	$9
+/- Score	19	09 Proj	446	63	119	16	64	6	267			332	454	786	9	77	31	0.43	268	33	25	42	124	11%	91	8%	5.27	-1.8	$14

10-41-.259 in 266 AB at COL.
PRO: Spikes in FB, LD, PX; Coors Field.
CON: Plunge in ct%, struggles vs. RHP (.231 BA) and on the road (.234 BA).
You're paying for the power.

Stewart,Shannon

Stewart,Shannon			AB	R	H	HR	RBI	SB	Avg	vL	vR	OB	Slg	OPS	bb%	ct%	h%	Eye	xBA	G	L	F	PX	hr/f	SX	SBO	RC/G	RAR	R$
Pos	7	04 MIN	378	46	115	11	47	6	304	257	325	381	447	828	11	88	32	1.07	278	42	22	37	80	9%	72	7%	5.90	10.0	$13
Age	35	05 MIN	551	69	151	10	56	7	274	244	283	316	388	705	6	87	30	0.47	268	46	20	35	73	6%	83	8%	4.16	-8.8	$13
Bats	Right	06 MIN	174	21	51	2	21	3	293	288	295	346	368	714	7	89	32	0.74	231	48	14	39	43	3%	78	7%	4.41	-3.7	$5
Health	F	07 OAK	576	79	167	12	48	11	290	269	298	343	394	738	8	90	31	0.78	272	45	21	34	62	7%	78	8%	4.67	-6.0	$16
PT/Exp	D	08 TOR	175	14	42	1	14	3	240	286	222	325	303	628	11	90	26	1.22	269	52	22	26	36	2%	75	7%	3.75	-5.8	$2
Consist	B	1st Half	175	14	42	1	14	3	240			325	303	628	11	90	26	1.22	269	52	22	26	36	2%	75	7%	3.75	-5.8	$2
LIMA Plan	F	2nd Half	0	0	0	0	0	0	0																				
+/- Score	16	09 Proj	68	8	17	1	7	1	250			316	323	638	9	89	27	0.87	251	48	19	33	44	5%	52	8%	3.63	-2.7	$1

Contact is his only remaining skill now in decline phase. Speed and power have been absent too long to reappear, even with improved health. Which - like another 500 AB season - is just too improbable.

Suzuki,Ichiro

Suzuki,Ichiro			AB	R	H	HR	RBI	SB	Avg	vL	vR	OB	Slg	OPS	bb%	ct%	h%	Eye	xBA	G	L	F	PX	hr/f	SX	SBO	RC/G	RAR	R$
Pos	98	04 SEA	704	101	262	8	60	36	372	404	359	413	455	868	7	91	40	0.78	294	64	18	18	47	7%	109	17%	6.07	24.3	$35
Age	35	05 SEA	679	111	206	15	68	33	303	352	284	349	436	785	7	90	32	0.73	304	54	21	24	71	10%	150	20%	5.17	8.9	$29
Bats	Left	06 SEA	695	110	224	9	49	45	322	352	312	367	416	783	7	90	35	0.69	279	51	22	28	50	5%	150	20%	5.15	-9.6	$30
Health	A	07 SEA	678	111	238	6	68	37	351	331	358	395	431	825	7	89	39	0.64	280	56	20	24	48	4%	127	18%	5.62	2.2	$33
PT/Exp	A	08 SEA	686	103	213	6	42	43	310	287	321	358	386	745	7	91	34	0.78	286	57	20	23	44	4%	139	20%	4.77	-11.0	$27
Consist	B	1st Half	341	57	100	3	21	33	293			350	370	720	8	89	32	0.81	284	58	20	22	46	4%	148	31%	4.55	-7.7	$16
LIMA Plan	C	2nd Half	345	46	113	3	21	10	328			366	403	769	6	92	35	0.75	285	57	20	23	42	4%	108	10%	4.98	-3.5	$12
+/- Score	-18	09 Proj	653	100	208	7	49	32	319			364	401	765	7	90	35	0.72	285	56	20	24	48	5%	131	17%	4.97	-7.2	$25

BA drop was expected along with h% regression. Hamstring issues slowed 2H SBO, but he played through to put up eighth consecutive 200 hit season. He's aging well, almost imperceptibly.

Suzuki,Kurt

Suzuki,Kurt			AB	R	H	HR	RBI	SB	Avg	vL	vR	OB	Slg	OPS	bb%	ct%	h%	Eye	xBA	G	L	F	PX	hr/f	SX	SBO	RC/G	RAR	R$
Pos	2	04	0	0	0	0	0	0	0							0			0						0				
Age	25	05	0	0	0	0	0	0	0							0			0						0				
Bats	Right	06 aa	376	52	94	6	45	4	250			333	366	699	11	89	27	1.10	0				74		68	6%	4.51	1.5	$7
Health	A	07 OAK	* 424	53	105	9	61	0	249	151	281	315	363	679	9	83	28	0.57	232	39	16	45	78	6%	29	0%	3.95	-4.2	$8
PT/Exp	C	08 OAK	534	54	149	7	42	2	279	246	291	335	369	704	8	87	31	0.65	250	45	19	36	60	4%	37	3%	4.29	1.6	$10
Consist	A	1st Half	272	32	78	3	26	2	287			340	375	715	7	86	32	0.59	244	41	19	40	60	3%	60	5%	4.40	1.6	$6
LIMA Plan	D+	2nd Half	262	22	71	4	16	0	271			330	363	692	8	88	30	0.72	250	50	19	31	60	6%	18	1%	4.18	-0.1	$4
+/- Score	-32	09 Proj	543	62	143	9	57	2	263			327	368	695	9	86	29	0.68	251	45	18	37	69	5%	42	2%	4.23	-0.3	$10

Sub-par power metrics dipped further in first full MLB season behind the plate. Made good, consistent contact throughout the year, but only position, age, and opportunity keep this skill set relevant for now.

Sweeney,Mike

Sweeney,Mike			AB	R	H	HR	RBI	SB	Avg	vL	vR	OB	Slg	OPS	bb%	ct%	h%	Eye	xBA	G	L	F	PX	hr/f	SX	SBO	RC/G	RAR	R$
Pos	0	04 KC	411	56	118	22	79	3	287	221	312	340	504	844	7	89	28	0.75	282	37	15	47	117	13%	47	5%	5.74	5.1	$16
Age	35	05 KC	470	63	141	21	83	3	300	279	308	346	517	863	7	87	31	0.54	294	36	17	47	136	11%	54	3%	5.96	-0.8	$19
Bats	Right	06 KC	217	23	56	8	33	2	258	266	255	343	438	781	11	78	30	0.58	262	35	21	44	121	11%	40	3%	5.29	-7.2	$5
Health	F	07 KC	* 265	26	69	7	38	0	260	301	242	305	404	709	6	89	27	0.59	270	35	20	45	88	7%	34	0%	4.25	-15.3	$5
PT/Exp	F	08 OAK	126	13	36	2	12	0	286	321	260	323	397	720	5	95	29	1.17	263	42	17	41	70	4%	23	0%	4.52	-1.4	$3
Consist	B	1st Half	120	13	35	2	12	0	292			331	400	731	6	95	29	1.17	261	43	17	41	67	4%	24	0%	4.63	-1.0	$3
LIMA Plan	F	2nd Half	6	0	1	0	0	0	167			167	333	500	0	100	17		0	33	17	50	122	0%			2.40	-0.5	($0)
+/- Score	-23	09 Proj	65	7	17	2	9	0	262			316	418	734	7	88	27	0.66	269	38	18	44	96	8%	34	2%	4.58	-1.8	$2

No sign of power or patience for two years. Durability left the station long ago. All that remains is empty contact, and at his age, any turnaround is likely to be short-lived. Avoid.

Sweeney,Ryan

Sweeney,Ryan			AB	R	H	HR	RBI	SB	Avg	vL	vR	OB	Slg	OPS	bb%	ct%	h%	Eye	xBA	G	L	F	PX	hr/f	SX	SBO	RC/G	RAR	R$
Pos	98	04	0	0	0	0	0	0	0							0			0						0				
Age	24	05 aa	426	54	120	1	39	4	281			327	348	675	6	90	31	0.72	0				47		68	9%	4.02	-11.8	$9
Bats	Left	06 CHW	* 484	65	150	15	75	7	310			357	469	825	7	86	34	0.52	353	50	39	11	94	35%	66	10%	5.55	-1.5	$18
Health	A	07 CHW	* 442	52	116	13	50	7	263			339	397	737	10	85	29	0.77	317	60	28	13	84	27%	61	10%	4.74	-9.9	$11
PT/Exp	C	08 OAK	* 421	57	122	6	49	9	289	216	307	354	393	747	9	83	34	0.59	259	45	21	34	72	5%	96	7%	4.83	-6.2	$13
Consist	A	1st Half	208	32	63	3	30	6	302			360	421	781	8	85	35	0.59	278	48	22	30	79	6%	112	9%	5.23	-0.8	$8
LIMA Plan	D+	2nd Half	213	25	59	3	19	3	277			347	366	714	10	82	33	0.59	241	42	21	38	64	5%	53	6%	4.43	-5.6	$5
+/- Score	52	09 Proj	383	49	109	8	45	7	285			348	405	753	9	85	32	0.63	270	45	22	33	77	8%	70	9%	4.86	-5.6	$11

5-45-.285 in 384 AB at OAK. No power from LD stroke, FB spike, though 2H hand injuries factored in. One xBH in 88 AB vs. LHP is troublesome. Minus pop, he must hike bb%, SBO to be a force. He has time.

JOCK THOMPSON

Swisher,Nick

			AB	R	H	HR	RBI	SB	Avg	vL	vR	OB	Slg	OPS	bb%	ct%	h%	Eye	xBA	G	L	F	PX	hr/f	SX	SBO	RC/G	RAR	R$
Pos	83	04 aaa	443	83	105	23	70	2	237			350	456	806	15	81	25	0.90	0				132		59	5%	5.71	13.8	$14
Age	28	05 OAK	* 485	69	117	21	75	0	241	197	248	321	447	768	11	76	28	0.49	271	38	19	43	144	13%	39	2%	5.09	11.7	$12
Bats	Both	06 OAK	556	106	141	35	95	1	254	291	241	364	493	857	15	73	29	0.64	259	33	19	48	152	18%	55	2%	6.42	28.7	$20
Health	A	07 OAK	539	84	141	22	78	3	262	291	250	377	455	832	16	76	31	0.76	258	37	18	46	136	12%	53	3%	6.19	26.0	$16
PT/Exp	A	08 CHW	497	86	109	24	69	3	219	197	227	330	410	740	14	73	25	0.61	250	35	21	45	129	15%	63	4%	4.82	-8.2	$12
Consist	B	1st Half	276	48	66	11	37	1	239			352	417	769	15	77	27	0.76	265	33	24	43	117	12%	59	3%	5.27	-0.6	$7
LIMA Plan	C+	2nd Half	221	38	43	13	32	2	195			302	403	705	13	67	22	0.47	233	37	16	47	146	18%	61	5%	4.26	-7.6	$5
+/- Score	21	09 Proj	475	81	118	24	70	3	248			356	451	808	14	73	29	0.63	253	36	19	45	137	15%	57	3%	5.76	11.3	$15

Surprisingly tough year in a friendly park.
GOOD: PX and patience intact, h% & xBA point to BA rebound.
BAD: A .250 BA still hurts, 2H ct% is a warning sign.
A weapon in OBP leagues.

Tatis,Fernando

			AB	R	H	HR	RBI	SB	Avg	vL	vR	OB	Slg	OPS	bb%	ct%	h%	Eye	xBA	G	L	F	PX	hr/f	SX	SBO	RC/G	RAR	R$
Pos	79	04	0	0	0	0	0	0	0							0			0						0				
Age	34	05	0	0	0	0	0	0	0							0			0						0				
Bats	Right	06 BAL	* 382	47	100	8	41	7	260	286	214	329	387	716	9	80	31	0.51	236	44	15	41	83	7%	88	8%	4.41	-8.5	$8
Health	A	07 aa	120	13	22	9	22	0	184			258	432	690	9	81	15	0.53	0				141		11	0%	3.85	-5.2	$2
PT/Exp	F	08 NYM	* 393	46	103	20	69	3	262	311	287	332	468	800	9	79	29	0.50	295	42	26	32	128	19%	56	3%	5.34	-0.9	$13
Consist	C	1st Half	207	18	44	10	32	2	213			263	381	643	6	79	23	0.31	280	56	23	21	102	28%	40	5%	3.18	-14.3	$4
LIMA Plan	D	2nd Half	186	28	59	10	37	1	317			404	565	968	13	80	35	0.73	313	36	27	37	157	18%	56	2%	7.67	11.2	$10
+/- Score	-42	09 Proj	267	31	68	14	46	2	255			326	471	797	10	80	27	0.54	295	41	25	34	130	19%	53	3%	5.30	-0.6	$9

11-47-.297 in 273 AB at NYM. Reached double-digit MLB HR for first time since 2002. Well-supported by the skills, and still owns past power skills (34 HR in '99). Odds of a repeat are not zero; could disappear too.

Taveras,Willy

			AB	R	H	HR	RBI	SB	Avg	vL	vR	OB	Slg	OPS	bb%	ct%	h%	Eye	xBA	G	L	F	PX	hr/f	SX	SBO	RC/G	RAR	R$
Pos	8	04 aa	409	62	126	2	22	45	308			355	357	712	7	85	36	0.50	0				33		128	41%	4.29	-4.5	$21
Age	27	05 HOU	592	82	172	3	29	34	291	233	311	319	341	661	4	83	35	0.24	244	55	19	26	33	2%	134	25%	3.46	-18.6	$20
Bats	Right	06 HOU	529	83	147	1	30	33	278	254	285	321	338	660	6	83	33	0.39	248	56	18	27	40	1%	137	27%	3.64	-12.2	$16
Health	A	07 COL	372	64	119	2	24	33	320	371	304	356	382	738	5	85	37	0.38	244	52	17	32	41	2%	134	34%	4.50	-0.3	$18
PT/Exp	B	08 COL	479	64	120	1	26	68	251	266	245	303	296	599	7	84	30	0.46	245	52	20	28	34	1%	152	54%	2.96	-25.5	$22
Consist	C	1st Half	271	39	68	1	17	36	251			295	306	601	6	83	30	0.38	250	51	20	28	41	2%	155	55%	2.92	-14.7	$12
LIMA Plan	D+	2nd Half	208	25	52	0	9	32	250			313	284	596	8	84	30	0.56	238	52	20	28	25	0%	142	54%	3.01	-10.8	$9
+/- Score	18	09 Proj	393	57	109	1	20	44	277			324	327	651	6	84	33	0.43	244	52	19	29	35	1%	146	43%	3.55	-12.4	$17

Has figured out how to optimally exploit his one skill: hits ball on ground, runs at almost every opportunity. H%-fueled BA drop should reverse, but lack of any other discernible skill raises playing time questions.

Teagarden,Taylor

			AB	R	H	HR	RBI	SB	Avg	vL	vR	OB	Slg	OPS	bb%	ct%	h%	Eye	xBA	G	L	F	PX	hr/f	SX	SBO	RC/G	RAR	R$
Pos	2	04	0	0	0	0	0	0	0							0			0						0				
Age	25	05	0	0	0	0	0	0	0							0			0						0				
Bats	Right	06	0	0	0	0	0	0	0							0			0						0				
Health	A	07 aa	102	16	27	6	14	0	266			318	466	784	7	68	34	0.24	0				137		31	0%	5.22	2.5	$3
PT/Exp	F	08 TEX	* 293	34	59	13	33	1	202	91	389	278	382	660	10	71	24	0.37	239	25	25	50	122	12%	62	3%	3.56	-5.8	$4
Consist	D	1st Half	192	19	36	6	14	1	190			277	325	602	11	75	22	0.47	0				86		71	4%	2.88	-8.0	$1
LIMA Plan	F	2nd Half	101	15	23	7	19	0	225			281	490	771	7	65	27	0.22	268	25	25	50	203	21%	31	0%	5.20	3.1	$3
+/- Score	29	09 Proj	193	26	47	9	27	0	244			304	412	716	8	68	31	0.28	232	25	25	50	120	13%	38	1%	4.33	0.5	$5

6-17-.319 in 47 AB at TEX. Hot Sept. puts him on many radar screens. Is he ready?
PRO: Power/patience profile.
CON: Sketchy ct%, only 350 AB in high minors.
Intriguing, but a year away.

Teahen,Mark

			AB	R	H	HR	RBI	SB	Avg	vL	vR	OB	Slg	OPS	bb%	ct%	h%	Eye	xBA	G	L	F	PX	hr/f	SX	SBO	RC/G	RAR	R$
Pos	97	04 a/a	512	55	140	12	58	0	273			333	422	756	8	81	32	0.48	0				100		43	1%	4.89	-1.6	$11
Age	27	05 KC	* 474	63	116	7	58	7	245	200	263	310	371	682	9	76	31	0.39	273	53	23	24	96	8%	105	8%	3.99	-10.0	$9
Bats	Left	06 KC	* 472	83	141	20	82	10	298	274	296	374	527	900	11	80	34	0.60	289	49	16	35	136	15%	136	7%	6.78	14.6	$20
Health	A	07 KC	544	78	155	7	60	13	285	255	297	351	410	761	9	77	36	0.43	260	50	21	29	90	6%	120	11%	5.06	-6.8	$15
PT/Exp	B	08 KC	572	66	146	15	59	4	255	262	252	311	402	713	7	77	31	0.35	264	49	21	31	101	11%	73	5%	4.26	-18.5	$12
Consist	C	1st Half	296	34	76	8	27	2	257			329	409	738	10	79	30	0.52	267	51	19	30	97	11%	80	5%	4.71	-5.7	$6
LIMA Plan	C+	2nd Half	276	32	70	7	32	2	254			290	395	685	5	75	31	0.20	260	46	22	32	107	11%	53	5%	3.77	-12.9	$6
+/- Score	-14	09 Proj	501	66	135	12	59	7	269			329	421	750	8	77	33	0.39	268	49	20	31	104	10%	100	7%	4.79	-8.4	$13

Hopes of reclaiming 2006's power are all but extinguished; simply hits too many grounders. What's left is an average skill set. Return of lost SB would add value, but beyond age there is little cause for optimism.

Teixeira,Mark

			AB	R	H	HR	RBI	SB	Avg	vL	vR	OB	Slg	OPS	bb%	ct%	h%	Eye	xBA	G	L	F	PX	hr/f	SX	SBO	RC/G	RAR	R$
Pos	3	04 TEX	549	102	154	38	112	4	281	313	267	360	557	917	11	79	29	0.58	302	40	21	40	166	22%	78	3%	6.87	29.1	$25
Age	29	05 TEX	644	112	194	43	144	4	301	292	301	372	575	946	10	81	32	0.58	314	40	21	38	168	22%	81	2%	7.14	36.1	$34
Bats	Both	06 TEX	628	99	177	33	110	2	282	302	275	371	514	885	12	80	31	0.70	288	39	20	41	146	16%	51	1%	6.61	21.0	$23
Health	A	07 2TM	494	86	151	30	105	0	306	357	282	394	563	957	13	77	34	0.64	293	39	20	41	165	19%	40	0%	7.56	25.1	$24
PT/Exp	A	08 2TM	574	102	177	33	121	2	308	303	311	408	552	961	14	84	32	1.04	312	43	21	36	149	19%	46	1%	7.58	32.3	$29
Consist	A	1st Half	301	47	83	16	62	0	276			375	495	870	14	82	29	0.87	287	45	19	36	136	18%	24	0%	6.45	8.1	$12
LIMA Plan	B	2nd Half	273	55	94	17	59	2	344			444	615	1059	15	86	35	1.29	333	40	23	37	163	20%	50	2%	8.78	23.0	$17
+/- Score	4	09 Proj	589	104	180	35	122	2	306			399	558	957	13	81	33	0.83	306	41	21	38	156	19%	51	1%	7.50	30.9	$29

Quietly consolidated already-impressive skill set: ct% and xBA jumped, improved vs RHP. 1H GB% blip put a temporary drag on power. AAA reliability with the possibilty of a step forward. UP: 40 HR, .320 BA.

Tejada,Miguel

			AB	R	H	HR	RBI	SB	Avg	vL	vR	OB	Slg	OPS	bb%	ct%	h%	Eye	xBA	G	L	F	PX	hr/f	SX	SBO	RC/G	RAR	R$
Pos	6	04 BAL	653	107	203	34	150	4	311	327	306	358	534	893	7	89	31	0.66	312	47	19	34	122	17%	71	3%	6.26	31.8	$31
Age	32	05 BAL	654	89	199	26	98	5	304	293	309	344	515	860	6	87	32	0.48	315	48	19	33	129	14%	85	4%	5.90	23.9	$25
Bats	Right	06 BAL	648	99	214	24	100	6	330	335	329	375	498	873	7	88	35	0.58	305	51	22	27	98	16%	61	4%	6.06	28.1	$27
Health	B	07 BAL	514	72	152	18	81	2	296	323	287	348	442	789	7	89	30	0.75	279	52	17	31	82	13%	49	2%	5.17	12.6	$18
PT/Exp	A	08 HOU	632	92	179	13	66	7	283	282	284	309	415	724	4	89	30	0.33	297	48	23	29	82	8%	84	9%	4.28	-6.4	$18
Consist	B	1st Half	327	57	95	10	43	6	291			324	456	779	5	88	31	0.40	307	44	26	31	99	11%	106	11%	4.92	2.7	$13
LIMA Plan	C	2nd Half	305	35	84	3	23	1	275			294	370	664	3	90	30	0.25	282	52	21	27	64	4%	55	7%	3.60	-9.1	$6
+/- Score	25	09 Proj	536	76	153	12	70	4	285			322	414	737	5	89	30	0.48	289	50	21	29	78	9%	74	6%	4.50	0.2	$16

Temporarily reversed his career trajectory in 1H, then went back to pounding balls in the ground. 2H PX & hr/f collapses suggest that he's not just going downhill, he's picking up speed. More problems than B-12 can fix.

Thames,Marcus

			AB	R	H	HR	RBI	SB	Avg	vL	vR	OB	Slg	OPS	bb%	ct%	h%	Eye	xBA	G	L	F	PX	hr/f	SX	SBO	RC/G	RAR	R$
Pos	7	04 DET	* 399	72	107	29	83	4	268	284	226	339	564	903	10	80	27	0.54	304	33	19	48	176	19%	75	7%	6.58	18.9	$18
Age	32	05 DET	* 364	54	95	24	63	4	262	212	186	341	522	863	11	75	29	0.47	256	27	14	59	165	15%	89	5%	6.25	16.2	$14
Bats	Right	06 DET	348	61	89	26	60	1	256	238	266	327	549	876	10	74	27	0.40	268	26	15	59	185	17%	72	3%	6.38	12.3	$13
Health	A	07 DET	269	37	65	18	54	2	242	310	209	277	498	775	5	73	26	0.18	273	38	16	46	173	20%	54	7%	4.80	-1.9	$9
PT/Exp	D	08 DET	316	50	76	25	56	0	241	234	245	294	516	810	7	70	26	0.25	265	32	17	51	184	22%	34	5%	5.42	5.4	$12
Consist	C	1st Half	148	28	41	15	33	0	277			340	622	961	9	75	27	0.38	301	32	15	52	212	26%	37	3%	7.24	10.1	$8
LIMA Plan	D+	2nd Half	168	22	35	10	23	0	208			253	423	675	6	65	25	0.17	234	32	19	49	156	19%	42	7%	3.66	-6.3	$3
+/- Score	-17	09 Proj	298	46	72	22	54	1	242			295	507	802	7	72	26	0.27	266	33	16	51	177	20%	44	5%	5.29	3.1	$11

Combination of borderline ct% and part-time role will lead to erratic results. The power is now well-established, so too is the BA risk. Punishes LHPs, so more AB won't necessarily be a good thing. Pay for 300 AB.

Theriot,Ryan

			AB	R	H	HR	RBI	SB	Avg	vL	vR	OB	Slg	OPS	bb%	ct%	h%	Eye	xBA	G	L	F	PX	hr/f	SX	SBO	RC/G	RAR	R$
Pos	6	04	0	0	0	0	0	0	0							0			0						0				
Age	29	05 aa	445	41	113	1	43	19	253			309	324	632	7	91	28	0.93	0				50		99	24%	3.67	-8.0	$9
Bats	Right	06 CHC	* 414	71	122	3	35	26	294	346	317	358	399	756	9	88	33	0.81	296	50	27	24	62	3%	148	23%	5.06	8.2	$16
Health	A	07 CHC	537	80	143	3	45	28	266	286	260	328	346	674	8	91	29	0.98	278	49	21	30	54	2%	121	20%	4.14	-4.8	$15
PT/Exp	B	08 CHC	580	85	178	1	38	22	307	305	308	384	359	743	11	90	34	1.26	284	57	23	20	34	1%	97	15%	5.07	7.2	$19
Consist	B	1st Half	297	46	93	1	22	13	313			391	370	761	11	91	34	1.41	289	57	23	20	39	2%	88	18%	5.30	5.6	$11
LIMA Plan	B	2nd Half	283	39	85	0	16	9	300			377	346	724	11	89	34	1.13	278	56	24	20	29	0%	101	13%	4.82	1.5	$8
+/- Score	-35	09 Proj	568	82	164	2	43	25	289			358	355	713	10	90	32	1.07	283	54	23	24	44	2%	109	18%	4.65	2.6	$18

PRO: Stable plate control and OBA are ideal for a SB guy.
CON: SX, SBO declines, drop in SB success (2008: 63%, previously 87%) raise questions about his speedster status. Pay for a repeat only.

RAY MURPHY

Thomas,Clete

			AB	R	H	HR	RBI	SB	Avg	vL	vR	OB	Slg	OPS	bb%	ct%	h%	Eye	xBA	G	L	F	PX	hr/f	SX	SBO	RC/G	RAR	R$
Pos	7	04	0	0	0	0	0	0	0							0			0						0				
Age	25	05	0	0	0	0	0	0	0							0			0						0				
Bats	Left	06	0	0	0	0	0	0	0							0			0						0				
Health	A	07 aa	528	91	138	7	49	16	261			331	373	704	9	80	32	0.52	0				77		122	18%	4.33	-13.7	$14
PT/Exp	F	08 DET *	407	43	95	8	45	25	234	368	268	310	366	676	10	75	29	0.44	238	40	19	41	97	6%	109	36%	3.94	-11.5	$11
Consist	A	1st Half	232	27	59	5	26	14	253			319	383	702	9	77	31	0.41	262	44	24	32	95	8%	103	31%	4.21	-4.4	$7
LIMA Plan	F	2nd Half	175	15	37	3	19	11	210			299	342	641	11	73	27	0.48	180	29	4	67	100	3%	108	42%	3.56	-7.4	$3
+/- Score	6	09 Proj	131	17	32	2	14	6	244			319	361	681	10	77	30	0.47	222	38	16	46	84	5%	105	28%	4.02	-3.7	$3

1-9-.284 in 116 AB at DET. Give him a pass on 2H decline; he was playing with a torn elbow ligament. TJ surgery in Sept., will likely start 2009 on DL. Speed and patience are promising, now needs to regain MLE ct%.

Thomas,Frank

			AB	R	H	HR	RBI	SB	Avg	vL	vR	OB	Slg	OPS	bb%	ct%	h%	Eye	xBA	G	L	F	PX	hr/f	SX	SBO	RC/G	RAR	R$
Pos	0	04 CHW	240	53	65	18	49	0	271	200	289	424	563	987	21	76	28	1.12	287	28	18	53	181	18%	31	2%	8.34	21.1	$11
Age	40	05 CHW *	147	21	29	13	29	0	199	281	192	290	489	779	11	74	17	0.48	281	25	21	55	179	22%	19	0%	4.99	-4.8	$4
Bats	Right	06 OAK	466	77	126	39	114	0	270	245	278	378	545	923	15	83	25	1.00	282	24	19	57	145	18%	19	0%	6.96	7.0	$22
Health	F	07 TOR	531	63	147	26	95	0	277	336	259	373	480	853	13	82	29	0.86	262	30	17	53	127	11%	13	0%	6.21	-0.5	$18
PT/Exp	B	08 2AL	246	27	59	8	30	0	240	205	254	344	374	718	14	77	28	0.68	220	28	19	53	85	8%	31	0%	4.55	-2.8	$4
Consist	C	1st Half	151	19	39	7	27	0	258			367	444	811	15	78	29	0.79	240	28	18	55	113	11%	40	0%	5.77	3.7	$5
LIMA Plan	F	2nd Half	95	8	20	1	3	0	211			306	263	569	12	75	27	0.54	191	28	21	51	39	3%	17	0%	2.54	-7.0	($0)
+/- Score	0	09 Proj	211	26	55	10	31	0	261			362	430	792	14	79	29	0.74	239	28	19	53	104	11%	18	0%	5.46	-0.6	$6

Once-stellar skill set is withering away. Latest casualties are ct% and trademark power. Still hits plenty of FB, but they are increasingly harmless. Two lengthy DL stints for quad issues speak to non-existent durability.

Thome,Jim

			AB	R	H	HR	RBI	SB	Avg	vL	vR	OB	Slg	OPS	bb%	ct%	h%	Eye	xBA	G	L	F	PX	hr/f	SX	SBO	RC/G	RAR	R$
Pos	0	04 PHI	508	97	139	42	105	0	274	239	294	397	581	978	17	72	30	0.72	286	38	18	45	198	26%	33	1%	8.17	41.7	$25
Age	38	05 PHI	193	26	40	7	30	0	207	164	233	357	352	709	19	69	26	0.76	222	45	18	37	105	14%	21	0%	4.62	-8.4	$3
Bats	Left	06 CHW	490	108	141	42	109	0	288	236	321	415	598	1013	18	70	33	0.73	287	37	20	43	204	28%	30	0%	8.80	32.4	$26
Health	C	07 CHW	432	79	119	35	96	0	275	196	315	406	563	969	18	69	32	0.71	276	43	18	39	197	30%	21	1%	8.22	24.3	$21
PT/Exp	A	08 CHW	503	93	123	34	90	1	245	233	249	360	503	863	15	71	28	0.62	275	40	18	42	180	23%	43	1%	6.57	24.4	$19
Consist	C	1st Half	242	43	56	16	43	1	231			350	488	837	15	70	26	0.60	270	40	17	43	181	22%	45	1%	6.24	9.5	$8
LIMA Plan	C+	2nd Half	261	50	67	18	47	0	257			370	517	887	15	72	29	0.64	278	40	19	41	178	24%	31	0%	6.87	14.7	$11
+/- Score	0	09 Proj	467	88	126	31	92	0	270			391	521	912	17	70	32	0.67	268	40	19	41	173	23%	33	0%	7.36	24.1	$20

While definitely in the decline phase, so far it's been a gentle fade. xBA and h% say BA plunge should correct. PX now in three-year decline, and hr/f starting to follow. But power skills are still elite, and that's what you pay for.

Tolbert,Matt

			AB	R	H	HR	RBI	SB	Avg	vL	vR	OB	Slg	OPS	bb%	ct%	h%	Eye	xBA	G	L	F	PX	hr/f	SX	SBO	RC/G	RAR	R$
Pos	5	04	0	0	0	0	0	0	0							0			0						0				
Age	27	05	0	0	0	0	0	0	0							0			0						0				
Bats	Both	06 aa	248	29	58	3	31	5	234			308	333	641	10	82	27	0.60	0				69		85	9%	3.60	-12.4	$4
Health	D	07 aaa	417	63	118	6	51	11	283			336	408	744	7	86	32	0.58	0				78		124	12%	4.77	-5.6	$13
PT/Exp	F	08 MIN	113	18	32	0	6	7	283	306	273	325	389	714	6	83	34	0.37	276	41	30	30	70	0%	156	27%	4.37	-1.6	$4
Consist	B	1st Half	83	13	22	0	3	4	265			307	337	644	6	82	32	0.33	269	43	28	29	64	0%	99	24%	3.45	-3.5	$2
LIMA Plan	D	2nd Half	30	5	10	0	3	3	333			375	533	908	6	87	38	0.50	300	35	35	31	84	0%	148	33%	6.81	1.5	$2
+/- Score	4	09 Proj	323	45	86	3	30	15	266			323	365	688	8	83	31	0.50	277	43	28	29	72	3%	119	20%	4.09	-7.4	$9

Made big-league club out of spring training and started hot before tearing thumb ligament, which cost him the summer. Has speed skills that will play, but will need to improve OBA to maximize his value.

Torrealba,Yorvit

			AB	R	H	HR	RBI	SB	Avg	vL	vR	OB	Slg	OPS	bb%	ct%	h%	Eye	xBA	G	L	F	PX	hr/f	SX	SBO	RC/G	RAR	R$
Pos	2	04 SF	172	19	39	6	23	2	227	286	170	296	407	703	9	82	24	0.55	270	59	10	31	102	14%	98	5%	4.23	2.2	$3
Age	30	05 2TM	201	32	47	3	15	1	234	314	209	290	338	629	7	75	30	0.32	242	60	14	26	84	8%	69	2%	3.19	-4.3	$3
Bats	Right	06 COL *	259	23	61	7	44	4	234	246	247	273	407	680	5	79	27	0.25	277	63	13	25	112	14%	85	15%	3.76	-4.6	$5
Health	C	07 COL	396	47	101	8	47	2	255	264	252	314	376	690	8	82	30	0.47	260	53	18	29	81	8%	56	3%	4.04	-4.6	$7
PT/Exp	D	08 COL	236	19	58	6	31	0	246	279	234	282	394	676	5	81	28	0.27	258	50	17	33	103	10%	21	9%	3.69	-3.7	$4
Consist	A	1st Half	163	9	41	3	20	0	252			282	387	669	4	84	28	0.27	268	50	19	30	96	7%	17	13%	3.64	-2.8	$2
LIMA Plan	D	2nd Half	73	10	17	3	11	0	233			282	411	693	6	75	27	0.28	238	50	11	39	121	14%	36	0%	3.87	-0.7	$2
+/- Score	-9	09 Proj	305	33	74	8	41	1	243			290	394	685	6	79	28	0.33	259	53	15	32	102	11%	56	5%	3.84	-3.6	$6

Started out with the lead CA job in COL, but fell into backup role. Has decent pop for the end-game, but GB tendency reduces chances of a late career power spike. Nothing more than a roster filler.

Towles,J.R.

			AB	R	H	HR	RBI	SB	Avg	vL	vR	OB	Slg	OPS	bb%	ct%	h%	Eye	xBA	G	L	F	PX	hr/f	SX	SBO	RC/G	RAR	R$
Pos	2	04	0	0	0	0	0	0	0							0			0						0				
Age	25	05	0	0	0	0	0	0	0							0			0						0				
Bats	Right	06	0	0	0	0	0	0	0							0			0						0				
Health	A	07 HOU *	299	52	88	11	54	9	293	333	387	347	466	813	8	87	31	0.64	283	34	24	42	99	10%	94	22%	5.46	8.9	$13
PT/Exp	F	08 HOU *	314	30	62	10	36	3	198	222	118	259	335	594	8	79	22	0.39	220	41	11	48	86	8%	61	10%	2.72	-15.0	$3
Consist	F	1st Half	176	20	31	8	22	2	178			258	351	609	10	79	18	0.50	226	40	9	51	107	11%	54	5%	2.93	-7.2	$2
LIMA Plan	D	2nd Half	138	11	31	2	14	1	223			260	314	574	5	80	27	0.25	244	44	22	33	60	5%	65	16%	2.42	-7.8	$1
+/- Score	12	09 Proj	376	47	90	11	52	6	239			293	384	677	7	83	26	0.44	242	40	15	45	87	8%	80	17%	3.79	-5.2	$9

4-16-.137 in 146 AB at HOU. Drop in ct% and complete lack of LD earned him an early trip back to the minors, where he righted himself. Potential is here for a power/speed blend, but may need more time to emerge.

Tracy,Chad

			AB	R	H	HR	RBI	SB	Avg	vL	vR	OB	Slg	OPS	bb%	ct%	h%	Eye	xBA	G	L	F	PX	hr/f	SX	SBO	RC/G	RAR	R$
Pos	3	04 ARI *	521	51	150	10	62	4	288	215	305	351	418	770	9	87	31	0.77	260	36	20	44	81	5%	60	4%	5.14	-11.9	$13
Age	28	05 ARI	503	73	155	27	72	3	308	236	324	353	553	906	7	84	32	0.45	310	33	24	42	147	15%	77	3%	6.43	11.4	$23
Bats	Left	06 ARI	597	91	168	20	80	5	281	231	304	341	451	792	8	78	33	0.42	259	36	21	43	112	10%	63	4%	5.27	-12.3	$19
Health	D	07 ARI	227	30	60	7	35	0	264	174	287	348	454	801	11	81	30	0.67	268	37	18	45	125	8%	53	0%	5.61	-3.4	$6
PT/Exp	C	08 ARI *	322	29	85	8	43	0	265	243	271	302	395	696	5	84	30	0.32	264	29	24	47	85	6%	18	0%	3.93	-16.7	$7
Consist	C	1st Half	130	10	32	4	15	0	249			281	370	651	4	87	26	0.34	236	25	19	55	69	6%	11	0%	3.36	-9.1	$2
LIMA Plan	D+	2nd Half	192	19	53	4	28	0	276			315	411	727	5	82	32	0.31	274	30	26	43	97	6%	22	0%	4.35	-7.5	$5
+/- Score	-7	09 Proj	417	47	113	17	63	0	271			324	463	787	7	82	29	0.45	278	33	22	45	120	11%	33	0%	5.12	-9.0	$12

8-39.267 in 273 AB at ARI. Off-season knee surgery held him out until May. High FB% and low PX yielded many cans o' corn. 2H PX uptick gives some hope for rebound, and rumored move back to 3B could help PT

Treanor,Matt

			AB	R	H	HR	RBI	SB	Avg	vL	vR	OB	Slg	OPS	bb%	ct%	h%	Eye	xBA	G	L	F	PX	hr/f	SX	SBO	RC/G	RAR	R$
Pos	2	04 FLA *	253	27	52	5	25	1	206	182	250	282	300	583	10	81	23	0.57	270	56	24	20	60	12%	44	2%	2.77	-8.2	$1
Age	33	05 FLA	134	10	27	0	13	0	201	120	215	287	261	548	11	79	25	0.57	224	49	19	32	55	0%	20	0%	2.44	-5.6	($0)
Bats	Right	06 FLA	157	12	36	2	14	0	229	268	216	313	318	631	11	78	28	0.56	220	44	18	38	59	4%	42	2%	3.42	-4.4	$1
Health	B	07 FLA	171	16	46	4	19	0	269	245	280	342	392	734	10	83	30	0.66	265	42	24	34	75	8%	34	0%	4.68	1.2	$3
PT/Exp	F	08 FLA	206	18	49	2	23	1	238	197	255	299	301	600	8	74	31	0.34	221	55	20	25	50	5%	38	2%	2.81	-8.6	$2
Consist	D	1st Half	166	15	40	1	14	1	241			292	301	593	7	73	32	0.27	222	55	20	25	52	3%	43	2%	2.68	-7.6	$2
LIMA Plan	F	2nd Half	40	3	9	1	9	0	225			326	300	626	13	78	27	0.67	206	53	20	27	41	12%	8	0%	3.30	-1.1	$1
+/- Score	-34	09 Proj	100	9	23	1	9	0	230			301	305	606	9	78	28	0.47	228	48	20	32	55	5%	28	1%	3.01	-3.7	$1

Married to Olympic beach volley-baller Misty May, teammates (predictably) call him "Mr. May". Sure enough, he notched 11 of his 23 RBI that month. Go figure.

Tulowitzki,Troy

			AB	R	H	HR	RBI	SB	Avg	vL	vR	OB	Slg	OPS	bb%	ct%	h%	Eye	xBA	G	L	F	PX	hr/f	SX	SBO	RC/G	RAR	R$
Pos	6	04	0	0	0	0	0	0	0							0			0						0				
Age	24	05	0	0	0	0	0	0	0							0			0						0				
Bats	Right	06 COL *	519	73	139	12	53	8	268	150	263	326	410	737	8	85	29	0.59	286	49	21	30	89	9%	78	10%	4.65	4.4	$13
Health	C	07 COL	609	104	177	24	99	7	291	333	278	351	479	831	9	79	34	0.44	270	42	20	38	119	13%	91	8%	5.76	22.5	$24
PT/Exp	B	08 COL	377	48	99	8	46	1	263	330	242	330	401	731	9	85	29	0.68	272	42	20	37	90	7%	53	7%	4.66	0.4	$9
Consist	C	1st Half	137	12	22	2	14	1	161			228	270	498	8	84	18	0.55	258	47	18	35	78	5%	52	13%	1.85	-12.8	($1)
LIMA Plan	C	2nd Half	240	36	77	6	32	0	321			387	475	862	10	86	35	0.76	279	40	22	39	96	8%	54	5%	6.24	10.5	$9
+/- Score	17	09 Proj	607	87	169	22	91	5	278			341	460	802	9	83	31	0.56	281	42	20	37	112	12%	71	8%	5.40	16.0	$20

April slump and May quad injury ruined 1H, but 2H skills snapped back to rookie levels. Strong Sept. (.330 BA, 126 PX) further signaled his full recovery. Bid on a return to 2007 performance.

RAY MURPHY

Uggla,Dan			AB	R	H	HR	RBI	SB	Avg	vL	vR	OB	Slg	OPS	bb%	ct%	h%	Eye	xBA	G	L	F	PX	hr/f	SX	SBO	RC/G	RAR	R$
Pos	4	04 aa	294	20	65	3	21	7	220			249	301	549	4	86	25	0.28	0				51		77	25%	2.27	-19.3	$2
Age	29	05 aa	495	62	124	16	61	11	251			305	420	725	7	82	28	0.44	0				110		90	17%	4.40	0.8	$14
Bats	Right	06 FLA	611	105	172	27	90	6	282	307	273	334	480	813	7	80	31	0.39	261	41	17	42	113	13%	95	8%	5.42	14.4	$23
Health	A	07 FLA	632	113	155	31	88	2	245	245	245	319	479	798	10	74	29	0.41	262	34	16	51	162	13%	78	2%	5.48	14.6	$19
PT/Exp	A	08 FLA	531	97	138	32	92	5	260	191	283	354	514	868	13	68	32	0.45	261	36	16	48	189	18%	68	7%	6.74	30.8	$22
Consist	B	1st Half	287	57	83	23	58	4	289			370	620	991	11	68	35	0.41	293	34	14	52	240	23%	83	7%	8.41	29.2	$17
LIMA Plan	B	2nd Half	244	40	55	9	34	1	225			335	389	724	14	67	30	0.50	225	39	18	43	127	13%	45	7%	4.75	-0.2	$6
+/- Score	-16	09 Proj	563	95	142	27	84	5	252			331	468	799	11	73	30	0.43	253	36	16	47	149	14%	73	7%	5.53	13.8	$19

After his All Star Game debacle we warned of the psychological fallout. Sure enough, he went into an immediate slump. ct% plummet and hr/f spike were harbingers of doom anyway. DN: Less than 25 HR, .240s BA

Upton,B.J.			AB	R	H	HR	RBI	SB	Avg	vL	vR	OB	Slg	OPS	bb%	ct%	h%	Eye	xBA	G	L	F	PX	hr/f	SX	SBO	RC/G	RAR	R$
Pos	8	04 TAM	* 527	104	159	16	63	24	302	410	163	385	469	853	12	75	38	0.55	262	56	13	31	113	13%	125	18%	6.36	24.3	$24
Age	24	05 aaa	536	75	147	13	56	35	275			349	425	773	10	84	31	0.72	0				96		118	34%	5.21	12.5	$22
Bats	Right	06 TAM	* 573	90	148	8	50	56	258	298	227	345	357	702	12	79	31	0.63	254	54	19	27	65	7%	135	41%	4.38	-5.0	$23
Health	A	07 TAM	474	86	142	24	82	22	300	281	306	384	508	892	12	68	40	0.42	255	43	20	38	156	20%	95	19%	7.13	34.7	$25
PT/Exp	A	08 TAM	531	85	145	9	67	44	273	269	275	385	401	786	15	75	35	0.72	256	51	19	31	101	7%	111	31%	5.72	5.8	$24
Consist	F	1st Half	292	52	83	6	41	23	284			401	421	822	16	76	36	0.81	261	49	20	31	100	9%	116	29%	6.21	7.4	$14
LIMA Plan	B	2nd Half	239	33	62	3	26	21	259			366	377	742	14	73	34	0.63	250	53	18	30	101	6%	96	34%	5.10	-1.8	$9
+/- Score	15	09 Proj	545	89	153	17	70	40	281			377	442	819	13	74	35	0.59	261	49	19	32	116	13%	110	30%	5.99	16.5	$26

Shoulder injury sapped power, at least until Oct. Nice gains in controlling strike zone bode well for future monster years. But when? Looming shoulder surgery darkens 2009 outlook, but a 2H breakout is entirely possible.

Upton,Justin			AB	R	H	HR	RBI	SB	Avg	vL	vR	OB	Slg	OPS	bb%	ct%	h%	Eye	xBA	G	L	F	PX	hr/f	SX	SBO	RC/G	RAR	R$
Pos	9	04	0	0	0	0	0	0	0							0			0						0				
Age	21	05	0	0	0	0	0	0	0							0			0						0				
Bats	Right	06	0	0	0	0	0	0	0							0			0						0				
Health	B	07 ARI	* 399	59	111	15	57	10	278	200	230	350	486	836	10	81	31	0.58	264	36	16	48	127	9%	114	17%	5.95	12.4	$15
PT/Exp	F	08 ARI	356	52	89	15	42	1	250	253	249	349	463	812	13	66	34	0.45	246	37	21	42	157	15%	83	5%	6.15	10.2	$9
Consist	A	1st Half	254	38	60	9	29	1	236			349	417	766	15	64	33	0.48	228	40	20	40	136	14%	87	6%	5.59	3.1	$6
LIMA Plan	B+	2nd Half	102	14	29	6	13	0	284			348	578	927	9	71	35	0.33	291	31	23	46	206	18%	71	0%	7.37	6.2	$4
+/- Score	15	09 Proj	517	75	139	23	67	6	269			348	500	848	11	73	33	0.45	266	35	21	44	155	14%	100	9%	6.28	18.4	$17

2nd half sample is small, but tantalizing. More contact, fewer GBs, elite PX. Can he carry into 2009? That's a lot to ask from a 21-yr old, but those levels do represent his upside, We may just have to wait for it. Invest.

Uribe,Juan			AB	R	H	HR	RBI	SB	Avg	vL	vR	OB	Slg	OPS	bb%	ct%	h%	Eye	xBA	G	L	F	PX	hr/f	SX	SBO	RC/G	RAR	R$
Pos	54	04 CHW	502	82	142	23	74	9	283	264	293	326	506	832	6	81	31	0.33	276	38	18	45	133	13%	107	18%	5.59	9.9	$19
Age	30	05 CHW	481	58	121	16	71	4	252	311	234	301	412	713	7	84	27	0.44	265	38	19	42	98	9%	68	9%	4.21	-4.2	$12
Bats	Right	06 CHW	463	53	109	21	71	1	235	224	244	256	441	697	3	82	24	0.16	271	38	17	45	123	12%	58	3%	3.76	-17.4	$10
Health	A	07 CHW	513	55	120	20	68	1	234	257	225	282	394	675	6	78	26	0.30	230	35	15	50	101	10%	39	9%	3.62	-19.6	$9
PT/Exp	B	08 CHW	324	38	80	7	40	1	247	254	245	295	386	681	6	80	29	0.34	252	34	20	45	99	6%	55	6%	3.84	-10.1	$6
Consist	A	1st Half	135	16	29	3	17	0	215			264	341	605	6	82	24	0.38	245	32	20	48	87	6%	36	0%	2.92	-8.2	$1
LIMA Plan	D	2nd Half	189	22	51	4	23	1	270			317	418	735	6	79	32	0.33	257	36	21	43	108	6%	61	9%	4.53	-1.9	$4
+/- Score	2	09 Proj	438	51	107	14	58	1	244			288	404	692	6	80	28	0.31	252	36	18	46	105	8%	52	6%	3.90	-12.9	$8

More LD and reverting h% helped BA recover in the 2nd half. However, recovery to mediocrity is no big deal. Still has 20-HR potential if he gets the PT, which is now more of a longshot. Bat is sim game killer.

Utley,Chase			AB	R	H	HR	RBI	SB	Avg	vL	vR	OB	Slg	OPS	bb%	ct%	h%	Eye	xBA	G	L	F	PX	hr/f	SX	SBO	RC/G	RAR	R$
Pos	4	04 PHI	* 390	55	102	18	78	7	262	200	279	314	462	776	7	83	27	0.45	291	44	22	34	114	16%	97	11%	4.94	3.7	$15
Age	30	05 PHI	543	93	158	28	105	16	291	220	313	371	540	911	11	80	32	0.63	299	35	23	42	159	15%	125	12%	6.89	35.4	$29
Bats	Left	06 PHI	658	131	203	32	102	15	309	301	312	369	527	896	9	80	35	0.48	275	37	20	43	131	14%	111	10%	6.53	34.8	$32
Health	A	07 PHI	530	104	176	22	103	9	332	318	340	390	566	956	9	83	37	0.56	300	38	20	42	147	12%	112	7%	7.27	35,8	$29
PT/Exp	A	08 PHI	607	113	177	33	104	14	292	277	301	359	535	895	10	83	31	0.62	302	33	24	42	147	15%	117	10%	6.51	29.4	$31
Consist	B	1st Half	313	60	93	23	65	7	297			370	610	980	10	84	29	0.71	323	30	23	47	183	19%	114	9%	7.51	23.6	$19
LIMA Plan	D+	2nd Half	294	53	84	10	39	7	286			348	456	804	9	82	32	0.53	283	37	26	37	109	11%	101	11%	5.42	5.4	$12
+/- Score	14	09 Proj	605	113	183	29	105	13	302			366	529	895	9	82	33	0.56	294	36	22	42	139	14%	114	9%	6.52	30.1	$30

Skill set is remarkably stable, it was good health that drove this return to peak performance. Relative 2H power outage is of some concern, reduces chances of a run at 40 HR. A return to .300 is a much better bet.

Valentin,Javier			AB	R	H	HR	RBI	SB	Avg	vL	vR	OB	Slg	OPS	bb%	ct%	h%	Eye	xBA	G	L	F	PX	hr/f	SX	SBO	RC/G	RAR	R$
Pos	2	04 CIN	202	18	47	6	20	0	233	109	269	292	381	673	8	82	26	0.47	259	35	22	43	91	9%	37	0%	3.80	-0.1	$2
Age	33	05 CIN	221	36	62	14	50	0	281	184	298	367	520	887	12	83	28	0.81	302	34	23	43	141	18%	26	0%	6.47	16.7	$11
Bats	Both	06 CIN	186	24	50	8	27	0	269	111	286	317	441	757	7	84	28	0.45	269	33	23	43	92	12%	44	0%	4.67	1.7	$5
Health	A	07 CIN	243	19	67	2	34	0	276	290	274	328	387	715	7	90	30	0.76	260	40	19	42	80	2%	15	0%	4.52	0.6	$4
PT/Exp	F	08 CIN	129	10	33	4	18	0	256	182	271	329	411	740	10	79	30	0.52	192	41	16	44	106	9%	0	0%	4.69	1.8	$3
Consist	A	1st Half	64	4	14	0	6	0	219			275	281	557	7	83	26	0.45	182	43	9	48	54	0%	17	0%	2.50	-3.3	($0)
LIMA Plan	F	2nd Half	65	6	19	4	12	0	292			378	538	917	12	75	33	0.56	278	39	22	39	162	21%	1	0%	7.04	5.1	$3
+/- Score	-49	09 Proj	223	20	55	10	33	0	247			314	445	758	9	83	26	0.56	270	39	19	43	122	13%	10	0%	4.83	3.9	$5

2H looks like classic mid-30s power spike for CA. Too bad it was wasted over only 65 AB. Not a bad choice for a $1 2nd CA in an NL-only league. Heck, if he gets back over the 200 AB level: UP: See 2005.

Varitek,Jason			AB	R	H	HR	RBI	SB	Avg	vL	vR	OB	Slg	OPS	bb%	ct%	h%	Eye	xBA	G	L	F	PX	hr/f	SX	SBO	RC/G	RAR	R$
Pos	2	04 BOS	467	68	139	19	76	10	298	350	273	380	488	868	12	73	37	0.49	261	42	21	37	132	15%	78	9%	6.56	29.0	$19
Age	37	05 BOS	470	70	132	22	70	2	281	320	267	365	489	854	12	75	33	0.53	285	45	23	32	144	20%	57	1%	6.27	29.8	$17
Bats	Both	06 BOS	365	46	87	12	55	1	238	229	244	324	400	724	11	76	28	0.53	247	45	17	38	106	11%	55	3%	4.55	1.6	$7
Health	B	07 BOS	435	57	111	17	68	1	255	264	252	360	421	780	14	72	32	0.58	236	42	18	40	112	14%	51	2%	5.45	14.8	$11
PT/Exp	B	08 BOS	423	37	93	13	43	0	220	284	201	305	359	665	11	71	28	0.43	205	42	14	45	104	10%	14	1%	3.74	-5.9	$4
Consist	C	1st Half	225	17	50	7	26	0	222			297	373	671	10	73	27	0.39	208	46	12	41	112	10%	9	0%	3.78	-2.8	$2
LIMA Plan	D	2nd Half	198	20	43	6	17	0	217			314	343	658	12	69	28	0.46	198	36	15	48	93	9%	21	2%	3.68	-3.1	$2
+/- Score	-22	09 Proj	343	38	82	12	43	1	239			330	392	722	12	72	30	0.49	228	42	16	42	107	11%	42	2%	4.56	3.3	$6

The late-30s are a cruel time for a catcher. In this case, ct% is slipping, and LD% shows that the quality of contact is also in decline. 4-year xBA trend tells the tale...Do you want to own the next data point in that line?

Vazquez,Ramon			AB	R	H	HR	RBI	SB	Avg	vL	vR	OB	Slg	OPS	bb%	ct%	h%	Eye	xBA	G	L	F	PX	hr/f	SX	SBO	RC/G	RAR	R$
Pos	56	04 SD	* 299	40	72	7	39	3	241	143	248	322	398	720	11	84	27	0.73	294	53	21	26	99	11%	91	5%	4.63	-3.9	$6
Age	32	05 2AL	* 169	18	34	0	9	1	201	250	203	250	254	504	6	80	25	0.32	236	53	19	28	43	0%	79	5%	1.70	-15.0	($0)
Bats	Left	06 CLE	* 166	29	36	2	18	2	217	286	200	323	289	612	14	72	29	0.55	190	40	17	43	50	4%	95	5%	3.17	-9.5	$2
Health	A	07 TEX	* 432	58	91	9	36	3	212	184	246	283	344	626	9	76	26	0.42	248	43	21	36	91	8%	98	4%	3.23	-21.9	$4
PT/Exp	D	08 TEX	300	44	87	6	40	0	290	188	310	370	430	800	11	78	36	0.58	281	46	27	26	98	10%	66	1%	5.63	6.3	$9
Consist	C	1st Half	181	31	58	5	28	0	320			394	508	902	11	80	38	0.61	300	47	25	28	125	12%	81	2%	6.88	9.7	$7
LIMA Plan	F	2nd Half	119	13	29	1	12	0	244			333	311	644	12	75	32	0.53	256	46	31	23	55	5%	24	0%	3.60	-4.5	$1
+/- Score	-46	09 Proj	281	39	67	5	30	1	238			321	348	669	11	76	30	0.52	254	45	25	30	78	7%	74	3%	3.90	-8.3	$4

Rode a h% and hr/f-fueled hot streak to good results in 1H, then turned back into a pumpkin. LH-hitting utility IF are rare, so he probably has some career left. That doesn't mean you need to be along for the ride.

Velez,Eugenio			AB	R	H	HR	RBI	SB	Avg	vL	vR	OB	Slg	OPS	bb%	ct%	h%	Eye	xBA	G	L	F	PX	hr/f	SX	SBO	RC/G	RAR	R$
Pos	4	04	0	0	0	0	0	0	0							0			0						0				
Age	26	05	0	0	0	0	0	0	0							0			0						0				
Bats	Both	06	0	0	0	0	0	0	0							0			0						0				
Health	A	07 aa	394	45	97	1	19	41	247			284	322	606	5	84	29	0.33	0				48		156	61%	3.00	-16.7	$12
PT/Exp	F	08 SF	* 446	52	118	5	42	26	265	235	268	308	398	706	6	84	31	0.39	283	59	15	26	85	5%	144	39%	4.25	-7.0	$14
Consist	C	1st Half	267	28	64	2	18	17	238			286	367	653	6	83	28	0.41	281	61	14	25	82	3%	145	51%	3.66	-9.4	$6
LIMA Plan	C	2nd Half	179	24	54	3	24	9	304			340	446	786	5	85	34	0.37	288	58	15	27	89	7%	134	25%	5.10	1.6	$8
+/- Score	15	09 Proj	421	50	111	3	35	31	264			303	376	680	5	84	31	0.37	273	58	15	27	70	4%	153	45%	3.89	-10.4	$14

1-30-.262 with 15 SB in 275 AB at SF. Looked overmatched in 1H stint in SF (.207 BA), golden in 2H recall (.305 BA); but BPI were identical. Elite SX, decent ct%, GB tendency, pos. flexibility point to an emerging SB force.

RAY MURPHY

Venable,William

		AB	R	H	HR	RBI	SB	Avg	vL	vR	OB	Slg	OPS	bb%	ct%	h%	Eye	xBA	G	L	F	PX	hr/f	SX	SBO	RC/G	RAR	R$
Pos 8	04	0	0	0	0	0	0	0							0			0						0				
Age 26	05	0	0	0	0	0	0	0							0			0						0				
Bats Left	06	0	0	0	0	0	0	0							0			0						0				
Health A	07 aa	515	56	123	7	58	18	238			284	314	598	6	84	27	0.40	0				48		106	15%	2.86	-25.8	$10
PT/Exp F	08 SD	* 552	72	135	12	57	7	245	324	237	305	374	679	8	78	29	0.39	239	49	13	37	86	8%	96	7%	3.87	-14.4	$11
Consist C	1st Half	218	28	57	4	32	3	263			311	384	694	6	78	32	0.31	0				84		95	7%	4.01	-4.6	$6
LIMA Plan F	2nd Half	334	44	78	9	25	4	233			302	368	670	9	78	27	0.45	239	49	13	37	87	9%	91	8%	3.77	-9.8	$6
+/- Score -0	09 Proj	246	30	60	5	27	5	244			298	356	654	7	80	29	0.39	235	49	13	37	72	6%	98	11%	3.54	-8.0	$5

2-10-.264 in 110 AB at SD. Uninspiring production in PCL predictably didn't translate to Petco's pitcher haven. Profiles as a 4th OF mainly due to lack of a "calling card" skill.

Victorino,Shane

		AB	R	H	HR	RBI	SB	Avg	vL	vR	OB	Slg	OPS	bb%	ct%	h%	Eye	xBA	G	L	F	PX	hr/f	SX	SBO	RC/G	RAR	R$
Pos 8	04 a/a	493	77	121	15	50	13	245			280	389	670	5	83	27	0.29	0				82		119	22%	3.58	-16.5	$13
Age 28	05 aaa	494	73	138	16	55	13	279			332	468	800	7	88	29	0.68	0				102		126	19%	5.37	13.6	$18
Bats Both	06 PHI	415	70	119	6	46	4	287	273	293	326	414	740	5	87	32	0.44	272	45	21	34	72	5%	117	6%	4.60	1.9	$12
Health A	07 PHI	456	78	128	12	46	37	281	291	276	335	423	758	8	86	30	0.60	271	47	17	36	85	8%	140	32%	4.85	4.2	$21
PT/Exp B	08 PHI	570	102	167	14	58	36	293	282	298	345	447	792	7	88	31	0.65	284	45	19	36	90	8%	154	29%	5.28	8.8	$27
Consist A	1st Half	265	50	72	2	18	20	272			341	370	711	10	88	30	0.90	261	44	19	37	63	2%	152	30%	4.58	-1.2	$11
LIMA Plan B	2nd Half	305	52	95	12	40	16	311			348	515	863	5	88	33	0.45	304	46	20	35	114	13%	144	29%	5.88	9.7	$17
+/- Score 7	09 Proj	569	98	163	16	60	36	286			335	450	785	7	87	31	0.57	284	46	19	36	93	9%	155	30%	5.14	8.2	$26

2nd straight year of elite SX and SBO cements him as SB force. 2H power spike tantalizes, but flat full-year PX, hr/f trends say that's a mirage. Still, with good ct% and double-digit HR pop, not just a one-trick speedster.

Vidro,Jose

		AB	R	H	HR	RBI	SB	Avg	vL	vR	OB	Slg	OPS	bb%	ct%	h%	Eye	xBA	G	L	F	PX	hr/f	SX	SBO	RC/G	RAR	R$
Pos 0	04 MON	416	51	121	14	60	3	291	267	306	366	450	815	11	89	30	1.11	292	51	19	30	92	12%	45	3%	5.71	4.8	$14
Age 34	05 WAS	309	38	85	7	32	0	275	258	280	341	424	765	9	90	29	1.03	309	44	25	31	92	8%	47	0%	5.15	-7.6	$7
Bats Both	06 WAS	463	52	134	7	47	1	289	323	276	347	395	742	8	90	31	0.85	276	46	22	32	65	5%	45	1%	4.81	-20.9	$10
Health B	07 SEA	548	78	172	6	59	0	314	328	309	385	394	779	10	90	34	1.11	260	51	19	30	54	4%	29	0%	5.36	-12.9	$15
PT/Exp B	08 SEA	308	28	72	7	45	2	234	229	236	276	338	614	6	88	25	0.50	263	48	19	32	62	8%	43	4%	3.11	-16.9	$5
Consist C	1st Half	227	22	50	5	35	1	220			272	326	598	7	86	24	0.52	255	46	19	35	66	7%	40	4%	2.94	-13.9	$3
LIMA Plan F	2nd Half	81	6	22	2	10	1	272			289	370	660	2	94	27	0.40	279	54	20	26	53	10%	35	5%	3.55	-3.2	$2
+/- Score 16	09 Proj	65	7	18	1	8	0	277			326	382	708	7	90	29	0.75	274	50	20	30	65	7%	35	2%	4.33	-2.3	$1

Textbook display of the vagaries of h%: 07-08 BPI are identical, but h% flux created 80-pt BA gap. SEA realized they'd used up all of his good luck, so they released him in August. G'bye! G'bye!

Vizquel,Omar

		AB	R	H	HR	RBI	SB	Avg	vL	vR	OB	Slg	OPS	bb%	ct%	h%	Eye	xBA	G	L	F	PX	hr/f	SX	SBO	RC/G	RAR	R$
Pos 6	04 CLE	567	82	165	7	59	19	291	258	308	356	388	744	9	89	32	0.92	266	43	21	36	60	4%	108	14%	4.89	6.9	$18
Age 42	05 SF	568	66	154	3	45	24	271	253	279	337	350	687	9	90	30	0.97	275	44	24	32	53	2%	106	19%	4.30	5.7	$15
Bats Both	06 SF	579	88	171	4	58	24	295	340	281	357	389	746	9	91	32	1.10	262	40	22	38	51	2%	132	16%	4.99	10.2	$19
Health B	07 SF	513	54	126	4	51	14	246	243	247	305	316	621	8	91	26	0.92	242	41	18	40	43	2%	91	14%	3.50	-14.7	$9
PT/Exp B	08 SF	266	24	59	0	23	5	222	121	250	286	267	553	8	89	25	0.83	241	42	21	37	34	0%	74	13%	2.74	-15.7	$2
Consist C	1st Half	122	11	19	0	8	2	156			237	180	417	10	89	18	0.93	195	49	10	41	20	0%	65	7%	1.23	-13.7	($1)
LIMA Plan F	2nd Half	144	13	40	0	15	3	278			329	340	669	7	90	31	0.73	278	36	30	34	45	0%	71	16%	3.99	-2.7	$3
+/- Score -25	09 Proj	220	24	53	1	21	3	241			304	303	606	8	90	26	0.89	250	41	21	38	41	1%	68	10%	3.35	-7.6	$3

Skills said he lost it in 2007, but he had to come back and confirm it. Note correlation between SX and h%: as speed fades, can't leg out hits anymore. Had laser eye surgery in Oct.; needs fountain of youth.

Votto,Joey

		AB	R	H	HR	RBI	SB	Avg	vL	vR	OB	Slg	OPS	bb%	ct%	h%	Eye	xBA	G	L	F	PX	hr/f	SX	SBO	RC/G	RAR	R$
Pos 3	04	0	0	0	0	0	0	0							0			0						0				
Age 25	05	0	0	0	0	0	0	0							0			0						0				
Bats Left	06 aa	508	78	152	21	71	22	300			383	517	901	12	79	34	0.65	0				143		93	19%	6.86	16.3	$23
Health A	07 CIN	* 580	77	165	26	99	16	284	269	345	359	469	828	10	81	32	0.59	269	28	26	46	112	12%	65	15%	5.74	-6.5	$24
PT/Exp B	08 CIN	526	69	156	24	84	7	297	292	299	368	506	873	10	81	33	0.58	303	44	25	31	131	18%	69	8%	6.33	8.8	$22
Consist B	1st Half	268	34	75	12	38	4	280			346	478	823	9	78	32	0.47	297	44	27	30	131	19%	50	10%	5.67	-0.5	$10
LIMA Plan C	2nd Half	258	35	81	12	46	3	314			390	535	925	11	83	34	0.73	309	45	24	32	132	18%	78	6%	7.00	8.9	$12
+/- Score 4	09 Proj	546	74	166	25	104	9	304			377	506	884	11	81	34	0.61	297	43	25	32	126	17%	67	10%	6.49	9.3	$25

PRO: Across the board 2nd half growth, handled both LH & RH. CON: GB% will slow power growth, despite solid PX & hr/f. xBA says pay for BA now, but wait a bit longer 30+ HRs.

Ward,Daryle

		AB	R	H	HR	RBI	SB	Avg	vL	vR	OB	Slg	OPS	bb%	ct%	h%	Eye	xBA	G	L	F	PX	hr/f	SX	SBO	RC/G	RAR	R$
Pos 3	04 PIT	* 387	50	95	21	71	0	245	296	238	293	478	771	6	83	25	0.41	279	38	16	47	134	14%	47	0%	4.82	-13.0	$12
Age 33	05 PIT	407	46	106	12	63	0	260	200	281	322	405	727	8	85	28	0.62	269	40	21	39	91	9%	34	2%	4.52	-12.9	$10
Bats Left	06 2NL	130	17	40	7	26	0	308	59	345	379	546	925	10	79	34	0.56	286	36	21	43	149	16%	21	3%	7.00	3.6	$6
Health B	07 CHC	110	16	36	3	19	0	327	250	333	439	527	967	17	79	39	0.96	291	40	22	39	149	9%	19	0%	8.11	5.7	$5
PT/Exp F	08 CHC	102	8	22	4	17	0	216	200	217	322	402	724	14	76	24	0.67	233	37	19	44	130	12%	0	0%	4.64	-3.4	$2
Consist F	1st Half	38	3	11	1	8	0	289			438	421	859	21	79	34	1.25	266	47	27	27	90	13%	3	0%	6.84	1.2	$1
LIMA Plan F	2nd Half	64	5	11	3	9	0	172			243	391	633	9	75	18	0.38	248	31	14	55	154	11%	8	0%	3.21	-5.2	$0
+/- Score 8	09 Proj	121	14	31	5	20	0	256			333	467	801	10	79	28	0.56	275	36	19	45	142	12%	23	1%	5.48	-1.4	$3

Small sample sizes lead to wide production swings, but skills are actually quite stable. There's plus power and decent BA ability here if he ever finds more regular playing time. But at 33, that isn't at all likely.

Weeks,Rickie

		AB	R	H	HR	RBI	SB	Avg	vL	vR	OB	Slg	OPS	bb%	ct%	h%	Eye	xBA	G	L	F	PX	hr/f	SX	SBO	RC/G	RAR	R$
Pos 4	04 aa	479	66	121	8	41	11	253			327	397	724	10	78	31	0.50	0				101		105	18%	4.62	4.0	$10
Age 26	05 MIL	* 563	88	143	22	78	23	254	229	244	327	446	773	10	76	30	0.45	278	49	20	31	124	17%	151	18%	5.12	9.3	$22
Bats Right	06 MIL	359	73	100	8	34	19	279	271	280	334	404	738	8	74	36	0.33	241	46	20	33	83	9%	141	23%	4.62	0.2	$14
Health C	07 MIL	409	87	96	16	36	25	235	258	225	357	433	790	16	72	29	0.67	249	42	17	41	133	13%	157	21%	5.72	12.6	$15
PT/Exp B	08 MIL	475	89	111	14	46	19	234	250	227	327	398	725	12	76	28	0.57	249	46	15	39	107	10%	151	18%	4.66	-1.6	$15
Consist C	1st Half	261	48	56	7	22	11	215			305	364	669	12	79	25	0.61	252	50	13	37	96	9%	143	21%	3.91	-7.0	$7
LIMA Plan B+	2nd Half	214	41	55	7	24	8	257			354	439	793	13	72	32	0.54	244	40	18	42	122	11%	143	15%	5.66	5.6	$8
+/- Score 35	09 Proj	473	91	121	18	46	27	256			348	446	794	12	74	31	0.55	256	44	17	39	124	13%	156	22%	5.58	12.2	$19

The whole is less than the sum of the component skills: power, speed, patience should create something better than this. Ct%, BA vs RH, his undoing; teased in 1H with improvement. Still huge upside, too young to dismiss.

Wells,Vernon

		AB	R	H	HR	RBI	SB	Avg	vL	vR	OB	Slg	OPS	bb%	ct%	h%	Eye	xBA	G	L	F	PX	hr/f	SX	SBO	RC/G	RAR	R$
Pos 8	04 TOR	536	82	146	23	67	9	272	287	267	336	472	808	9	85	29	0.61	287	45	17	38	118	13%	93	8%	5.44	11.2	$18
Age 30	05 TOR	620	78	167	28	97	8	269	347	243	321	463	784	7	86	27	0.55	286	41	19	40	113	13%	82	7%	5.04	13.6	$21
Bats Right	06 TOR	611	91	185	32	106	17	303	333	292	359	542	901	8	85	31	0.60	302	42	18	40	136	15%	105	13%	6.48	30.7	$28
Health C	07 TOR	584	85	143	16	80	10	245	311	226	303	402	706	8	85	27	0.55	264	39	17	44	101	7%	103	10%	4.26	-4.7	$14
PT/Exp A	08 TOR	427	63	128	20	78	4	300	333	290	344	496	841	6	89	30	0.63	299	47	17	36	111	15%	66	5%	5.65	3.6	$18
Consist D	1st Half	225	33	64	8	36	2	284			326	444	771	6	87	30	0.47	279	48	18	35	94	12%	70	7%	4.84	-3.2	$8
LIMA Plan C+	2nd Half	202	30	64	12	42	2	317			364	554	919	7	92	30	0.94	319	46	17	37	130	17%	49	4%	6.52	6.3	$10
+/- Score -31	09 Proj	571	84	168	25	96	8	294			345	491	836	7	87	30	0.62	292	44	17	39	115	13%	82	7%	5.67	11.3	$23

Hamstring, back injuries cut into playing time but not production. 2007 now looks like a clear outlier, raising our expectations once more. If health cooperates and GB spike reverses, then: UP: 2006, minus the SB.

Werth,Jayson

		AB	R	H	HR	RBI	SB	Avg	vL	vR	OB	Slg	OPS	bb%	ct%	h%	Eye	xBA	G	L	F	PX	hr/f	SX	SBO	RC/G	RAR	R$
Pos 987	04 LA	* 341	66	93	20	63	6	273	290	249	342	510	852	10	72	33	0.37	261	32	25	43	150	19%	126	8%	6.19	8.8	$16
Age 29	05 LA	* 386	52	94	9	50	15	242	239	237	338	379	717	13	68	34	0.44	226	41	20	39	111	9%	109	15%	4.70	-6.4	$11
Bats Right	06	0	0	0	0	0	0	0							0			0						0				
Health C	07 PHI	255	43	76	8	49	7	298	375	257	401	459	860	15	71	39	0.60	254	40	27	33	109	13%	109	8%	6.71	12.9	$11
PT/Exp D	08 PHI	418	73	114	24	67	20	273	303	255	360	498	858	12	72	33	0.48	266	39	23	38	147	21%	130	16%	6.37	14.1	$22
Consist A	1st Half	178	28	47	11	32	8	264			348	494	843	11	74	30	0.50	277	44	21	35	144	24%	107	17%	6.01	4.3	$9
LIMA Plan B	2nd Half	240	45	67	13	35	12	279			369	500	869	12	70	35	0.47	257	36	24	40	150	19%	130	16%	6.66	10.0	$13
+/- Score 5	09 Proj	516	87	142	26	85	22	275			366	482	848	13	71	34	0.49	259	39	24	37	138	19%	125	14%	6.34	18.9	$25

He's always had this in him, note how 2008 skills are carbon copy of 2004 MLEs. As PT increased, improved vs RHP (1H :.700 OPS, 2H .825 OPS), suggesting this is not a peak. With regular AB... UP: 30 HR, 30 SB

RAY MURPHY

Wigginton,Ty			AB	R	H	HR	RBI	SB	Avg	vL	vR	OB	Slg	OPS	bb%	ct%	h%	Eye	xBA	G	L	F	PX	hr/f	SX	SBO	RC/G	RAR	R$
Pos	57	04 2NL	494	63	129	17	66	7	261	222	272	323	433	756	8	83	28	0.55	278	45	19	36	105	11%	85	6%	4.83	-3.3	$14
Age	31	05 PIT	* 435	58	109	17	62	6	251	247	268	322	428	750	9	83	27	0.63	287	42	22	36	111	13%	66	11%	4.80	0.2	$13
Bats	Right	06 TAM	444	55	122	24	79	4	275	316	260	324	498	821	7	78	30	0.33	277	40	19	41	138	17%	55	7%	5.46	5.8	$15
Health	B	07 2TM	547	71	152	22	67	3	278	284	276	328	459	787	7	79	32	0.36	265	44	18	38	119	13%	41	5%	5.09	-2.4	$16
PT/Exp	B	08 HOU	386	50	110	23	58	4	285	340	265	340	526	866	8	82	30	0.46	292	45	16	39	144	19%	50	10%	5.99	6.9	$16
Consist	B	1st Half	166	18	45	5	13	4	271			349	440	789	11	83	30	0.69	277	46	17	36	115	10%	54	13%	5.40	0.2	$5
LIMA Plan	C	2nd Half	220	32	65	18	45	0	295			332	591	923	5	82	29	0.30	304	44	15	41	166	25%	45	8%	6.43	6.6	$11
+/- Score	-8	09 Proj	514	67	143	27	76	5	278			331	496	827	7	81	30	0.42	281	44	17	39	132	17%	52	8%	5.54	2.0	$19

Fractured thumb in April sapped 1H power; should 2H rebound raise expectations? PRO: ct% uptick, FB% rose in Aug/Sept to drive PX spike. CON: No history to support 2H hr/f spike. 30 HR possible, but don't pay for them.

Wilkerson,Brad			AB	R	H	HR	RBI	SB	Avg	vL	vR	OB	Slg	OPS	bb%	ct%	h%	Eye	xBA	G	L	F	PX	hr/f	SX	SBO	RC/G	RAR	R$
Pos	97	04 MON	573	112	146	32	67	13	255	278	245	371	497	869	16	73	29	0.70	269	31	21	47	162	16%	94	11%	6.66	23.3	$22
Age	31	05 WAS	565	76	140	11	57	8	248	296	228	345	405	750	13	74	32	0.57	249	31	24	45	120	6%	96	11%	5.14	-1.9	$12
Bats	Left	06 TEX	320	56	71	15	44	3	222	190	230	303	422	724	10	64	30	0.32	219	35	15	50	149	15%	100	7%	4.73	-9.1	$7
Health	C	07 TEX	338	54	79	20	62	4	234	258	224	320	467	788	11	68	28	0.40	255	39	17	45	168	19%	77	6%	5.45	-0.5	$11
PT/Exp	D	08 2AL	264	21	58	4	28	3	220	214	221	311	326	637	12	74	28	0.51	221	47	16	37	78	5%	59	11%	3.49	-15.5	$2
Consist	C	1st Half	181	15	42	3	19	3	232			332	331	663	13	72	31	0.53	214	46	17	37	80	6%	36	14%	3.87	-8.4	$2
LIMA Plan	D	2nd Half	83	6	16	1	9	0	193			264	313	577	9	80	23	0.47	229	49	13	38	75	4%	66	0%	2.73	-6.9	($0)
+/- Score	-7	09 Proj	258	31	59	10	34	2	229			314	419	733	11	72	28	0.45	246	43	16	42	129	13%	84	7%	4.68	-5.5	$5

Attractive PX trend crashed to earth, injuries (hamstring, back, shoulder) could be factor. At this point, 2006-07 represent best-case scenario: good pop balanced against low BA. That's only if another opportunity arises.

Willingham,Josh			AB	R	H	HR	RBI	SB	Avg	vL	vR	OB	Slg	OPS	bb%	ct%	h%	Eye	xBA	G	L	F	PX	hr/f	SX	SBO	RC/G	RAR	R$
Pos	7	04 aa	338	60	75	15	57	5	221			356	413	769	17	75	25	0.85	0				126		60	7%	5.36	1.8	$9
Age	30	05 aaa	219	39	57	12	37	4	261			360	492	852	13	81	27	0.82	0				140		99	7%	6.22	7.6	$9
Bats	Right	06 FLA	502	62	139	26	74	2	277	299	269	347	496	843	10	78	31	0.50	267	43	16	41	132	16%	51	1%	5.92	9.6	$17
Health	C	07 FLA	521	75	138	21	89	8	265	218	281	348	463	810	11	77	31	0.54	264	36	21	43	130	12%	97	6%	5.68	4.8	$18
PT/Exp	B	08 FLA	351	54	89	15	51	3	254	242	258	343	470	813	12	77	29	0.59	272	39	19	42	140	13%	99	5%	5.77	3.6	$11
Consist	A	1st Half	112	22	35	8	20	2	313			384	607	991	10	80	33	0.59	316	46	19	36	168	25%	114	6%	7.72	7.0	$7
LIMA Plan	B+	2nd Half	239	32	54	7	31	1	226			325	406	731	13	75	27	0.58	252	36	19	45	126	9%	81	5%	4.79	-4.6	$4
+/- Score	22	09 Proj	508	77	133	23	79	5	262			348	478	826	12	77	30	0.58	273	40	19	42	138	14%	95	5%	5.88	7.5	$17

Back issues DL'd him in May; power suffered until Sept. surge. Net result was stable skill set, but small-sample gains vs LHP are promising and suggest that we may not have seen his peak. UP: 30 HR.

Willits,Reggie			AB	R	H	HR	RBI	SB	Avg	vL	vR	OB	Slg	OPS	bb%	ct%	h%	Eye	xBA	G	L	F	PX	hr/f	SX	SBO	RC/G	RAR	R$
Pos	79	04	0	0	0	0	0	0	0							0			0						0				
Age	27	05 aa	487	55	124	1	34	29	254			308	310	618	7	87	29	0.59	0				41		114	33%	3.31	-25.6	$12
Bats	Both	06 LAA	* 397	78	113	2	33	28	285			391	352	743	15	88	32	1.41	294	39	35	26	45	2%	109	30%	5.25	0.9	$15
Health	A	07 LAA	430	74	126	0	34	27	293	333	276	391	344	735	14	81	36	0.83	246	49	23	28	44	0%	105	20%	5.00	-0.5	$15
PT/Exp	D	08 LAA	* 145	26	33	0	10	3	226	200	193	338	278	616	15	78	29	0.78	207	44	16	40	43	0%	95	9%	3.46	-6.2	$2
Consist	B	1st Half	97	13	22	0	6	2	224			331	292	623	14	77	29	0.69	207	49	12	39	56	0%	92	9%	3.52	-4.0	$1
LIMA Plan	D	2nd Half	48	13	11	0	4	1	229			351	250	601	16	81	28	1.00	203	40	20	40	19	0%	94	11%	3.38	-2.2	$1
+/- Score	-2	09 Proj	282	46	74	1	21	15	262			360	329	689	13	83	32	0.89	244	48	19	32	50	1%	112	23%	4.42	-4.4	$8

0-7-.194 in 108 AB at LAA. Profile of speed/patience held up in reduced role. Pedestrian SX is trumped by OBA/SBO combo. This is a SB contributor if he ever gets off the bench. UP: See 2007.

Wilson,Jack			AB	R	H	HR	RBI	SB	Avg	vL	vR	OB	Slg	OPS	bb%	ct%	h%	Eye	xBA	G	L	F	PX	hr/f	SX	SBO	RC/G	RAR	R$
Pos	6	04 PIT	652	82	201	11	59	8	308	261	318	335	459	793	4	89	33	0.37	286	45	20	36	87	5%	113	7%	5.12	17.7	$20
Age	31	05 PIT	587	60	151	8	52	7	257	255	256	294	363	657	5	90	27	0.53	269	48	18	34	62	4%	100	7%	3.69	-4.6	$11
Bats	Right	06 PIT	543	70	148	8	35	4	273	301	262	314	370	684	6	88	30	0.51	275	47	23	30	61	6%	60	5%	3.96	-6.3	$10
Health	B	07 PIT	477	67	141	12	56	2	296	320	289	348	440	788	7	90	31	0.83	274	39	19	42	86	7%	54	5%	5.25	10.7	$14
PT/Exp	B	08 PIT	305	24	83	1	22	2	272	228	282	302	348	649	4	91	30	0.48	266	41	22	37	54	1%	50	5%	3.61	-9.0	$4
Consist	C	1st Half	125	9	39	0	10	2	312			344	352	696	5	91	34	0.55	278	38	29	32	32	0%	44	5%	4.10	-1.8	$3
LIMA Plan	D	2nd Half	180	15	44	1	12	0	244			273	344	617	4	91	26	0.44	261	43	17	40	69	2%	53	6%	3.27	-7.4	$1
+/- Score	-6	09 Proj	498	52	139	6	42	3	279			316	380	697	5	90	30	0.57	270	42	21	37	65	4%	60	5%	4.15	-4.8	$10

2008 was repeatedly interrupted by injuries, but the story hasn't changed. Puts the ball in play consistently, and weakly. Hr/f plunge was likely injury-related and should revert; but not enough to make him an asset.

Winn,Randy			AB	R	H	HR	RBI	SB	Avg	vL	vR	OB	Slg	OPS	bb%	ct%	h%	Eye	xBA	G	L	F	PX	hr/f	SX	SBO	RC/G	RAR	R$
Pos	9	04 SEA	626	84	179	14	81	21	286	257	299	342	427	768	8	84	32	0.54	279	53	18	29	85	9%	116	16%	5.00	5.4	$21
Age	34	05 2TM	617	85	189	20	63	19	306	269	317	356	499	856	7	85	33	0.53	314	50	21	29	123	13%	107	18%	5.99	17.4	$25
Bats	Both	06 SF	573	82	150	11	56	10	262	219	278	319	396	715	8	89	28	0.76	278	50	17	33	79	6%	92	12%	4.48	-4.9	$13
Health	A	07 SF	593	73	178	14	65	15	300	351	277	349	445	794	7	86	33	0.52	286	51	19	31	94	9%	80	11%	5.24	6.0	$20
PT/Exp	A	08 SF	598	84	183	10	64	25	306	289	313	368	426	795	9	85	35	0.67	280	51	19	30	81	7%	111	14%	5.41	3.6	$24
Consist	A	1st Half	296	44	87	5	34	12	294			367	426	792	10	86	33	0.83	283	51	18	32	90	6%	106	14%	5.50	2.5	$12
LIMA Plan	C+	2nd Half	302	40	96	5	30	13	318			370	427	797	8	84	36	0.53	275	51	21	28	73	7%	103	14%	5.33	1.1	$13
+/- Score	-20	09 Proj	580	78	166	10	62	16	286			343	410	753	8	86	32	0.61	279	51	19	30	81	6%	104	12%	4.87	-3.0	$18

Surprising speed spike drives his value, but speed is a skill of the young, and will be a tough repeat. Steady GB bias and sub-par PX limit power; stable xBA shows true BA ability. As speed declines, value will evaporate.

Wise,Dewayne			AB	R	H	HR	RBI	SB	Avg	vL	vR	OB	Slg	OPS	bb%	ct%	h%	Eye	xBA	G	L	F	PX	hr/f	SX	SBO	RC/G	RAR	R$
Pos	78	04 ATL	162	24	37	6	17	6	228			269	444	713	5	83	24	0.32	0				123		157	26%	4.20	-6.1	$4
Age	31	05 aaa	375	35	80	6	37	18	213			251	314	565	5	82	24	0.29	0				60		135	33%	2.39	-31.4	$7
Bats	Left	06 CIN	* 242	34	58	6	24	6	240			278	395	673	5	80	28	0.26	320	72	22	6	102	49%	110	16%	3.68	-11.5	$5
Health	A	07 aaa	207	27	44	6	16	6	211			235	382	617	3	73	26	0.12	0				113		150	26%	2.82	-15.4	$3
PT/Exp	F	08 CHW	* 320	49	80	14	35	20	251	154	268	306	450	755	7	80	28	0.38	272	35	23	42	122	13%	139	37%	4.72	-1.3	$13
Consist	C	1st Half	221	34	57	9	20	14	260			319	456	775	8	81	29	0.45	293	35	30	35	122	14%	137	39%	5.03	1.2	$9
LIMA Plan	D	2nd Half	99	15	23	5	15	6	232			276	434	711	6	77	25	0.26	258	36	21	43	123	15%	140	30%	4.02	-2.5	$4
+/- Score	39	09 Proj	199	28	51	7	22	9	256			296	443	738	5	78	30	0.25	264	38	22	40	116	12%	141	27%	4.44	-3.0	$7

6-18-.348 with 9 SB in 129 AB at CHW. Speed has long been his strength, but power is recent development that adds intrigue. Age will reduce opportunity, but he's a multi-category contributor as an end-gamer or a pickup.

Wood,Brandon			AB	R	H	HR	RBI	SB	Avg	vL	vR	OB	Slg	OPS	bb%	ct%	h%	Eye	xBA	G	L	F	PX	hr/f	SX	SBO	RC/G	RAR	R$
Pos	56	04	0	0	0	0	0	0	0							0			0						0				
Age	24	05 aaa	19	1	5	0	1	0	263			263	421	684	0	58	45	0.00	0				133		54	0%	4.70	0.0	$0
Bats	Right	06 aa	453	55	107	18	61	14	236			297	446	743	8	76	27	0.35	0				143		103	20%	4.67	-8.0	$12
Health	A	07 LAA	* 470	68	116	21	73	9	247			306	440	746	8	74	29	0.33	255	52	10	38	134	16%	90	9%	4.65	-3.1	$14
PT/Exp	C	08 LAA	* 545	81	135	30	83	9	247	94	229	300	457	757	7	76	28	0.31	249	36	14	50	135	14%	79	12%	4.67	-3.4	$18
Consist	A	1st Half	261	34	53	11	31	3	203			238	380	618	4	74	23	0.17	236	40	14	47	120	12%	88	14%	2.79	-17.3	$4
LIMA Plan	C	2nd Half	284	46	82	19	51	6	288			355	527	882	9	78	31	0.46	262	34	14	52	148	16%	63	11%	6.32	11.6	$14
+/- Score	13	09 Proj	420	60	105	21	64	8	250			307	456	763	8	75	28	0.33	250	38	13	48	136	14%	84	12%	4.82	-0.7	$14

5-13-.200 in 150 AB at LAA. Across-the-board 2H skills growth hints that this long-time prospect may be putting it all together. Power unquestioned, BA dubious, move back to SS would enhance value.

Wright,David			AB	R	H	HR	RBI	SB	Avg	vL	vR	OB	Slg	OPS	bb%	ct%	h%	Eye	xBA	G	L	F	PX	hr/f	SX	SBO	RC/G	RAR	R$
Pos	5	04 NYM	* 600	97	188	31	91	26	313	309	288	378	557	934	9	85	33	0.69	301	35	20	46	146	13%	90	23%	6.97	31.7	$33
Age	26	05 NYM	575	99	176	27	102	17	306	336	300	383	523	907	11	80	34	0.64	303	39	25	35	143	17%	86	13%	6.82	32.4	$31
Bats	Right	06 NYM	582	96	181	26	116	20	311	285	321	381	531	912	10	81	35	0.58	277	36	19	44	133	13%	110	14%	6.85	21.6	$30
Health	A	07 NYM	604	113	196	30	107	34	325	361	311	415	546	962	13	81	36	0.82	297	39	23	38	139	16%	99	18%	7.62	32.6	$37
PT/Exp	A	08 NYM	626	115	189	33	124	15	302	382	275	393	534	927	13	81	33	0.80	303	36	26	38	145	17%	92	10%	7.14	30.6	$34
Consist	B	1st Half	315	48	89	15	64	8	283			379	492	871	13	82	30	0.86	289	38	22	40	129	14%	78	12%	6.47	10.0	$15
LIMA Plan	D+	2nd Half	311	67	100	18	60	7	322			407	576	983	13	80	35	0.74	316	35	29	36	160	20%	97	8%	7.82	20.4	$19
+/- Score	1	09 Proj	604	111	188	36	114	16	311			397	565	962	12	81	34	0.75	308	37	24	39	155	19%	92	11%	7.51	34.8	$34

Skill set elite and stable, with the exception of speed: SX was always marginal, and SBO% dip may be a health-preserving decision. H% dip aside, LD% rise suggests next BA move will be upward. A true stud.

RAY MURPHY

Youkilis,Kevin

Youkilis,Kevin			AB	R	H	HR	RBI	SB	Avg	vL	vR	OB	Slg	OPS	bb%	ct%	h%	Eye	xBA	G	L	F	PX	hr/f	SX	SBO	RC/G	RAR	R$
Pos	35	04 BOS	* 365	58	92	9	50	2	252	250	265	342	389	731	12	82	29	0.75	254	37	21	42	91	7%	56	3%	4.76	-2.5	$8
Age	30	05 BOS	* 231	33	66	7	29	1	284	300	265	390	474	865	15	82	32	0.96	303	32	28	40	133	9%	49	5%	6.61	10.1	$7
Bats	Right	06 BOS	569	100	159	13	72	5	279	270	283	379	429	808	14	79	33	0.76	257	31	24	45	104	6%	79	4%	5.85	6.9	$16
Health	A	07 BOS	528	85	152	16	83	4	288	290	287	379	453	831	13	80	33	0.73	262	34	21	45	113	8%	68	3%	6.04	11.5	$18
PT/Exp	A	08 BOS	538	91	168	29	115	3	312	288	318	383	569	952	10	80	35	0.57	302	34	22	44	166	15%	66	5%	7.34	30.5	$27
Consist	B	1st Half	285	48	89	13	50	3	312			374	540	914	9	80	35	0.50	290	38	19	43	149	13%	81	6%	6.80	11.9	$13
LIMA Plan	C+	2nd Half	253	43	79	16	65	0	312			394	601	995	12	79	34	0.65	317	29	25	45	185	18%	56	4%	7.95	18.6	$14
+/- Score	-16	09 Proj	533	89	161	22	98	3	302			385	514	899	12	80	34	0.68	284	33	23	44	140	12%	64	4%	6.82	22.8	$22

Breakout season, but can he build on it? The arguments: PRO: PX growth; solid FB%; high xBA. CON: High hr/f and h% uptick probably not sustainable. Legit BA, but HR may drop.

Young,Chris

Young,Chris			AB	R	H	HR	RBI	SB	Avg	vL	vR	OB	Slg	OPS	bb%	ct%	h%	Eye	xBA	G	L	F	PX	hr/f	SX	SBO	RC/G	RAR	R$
Pos	8	04	0	0	0	0	0	0	0							0			0						0				
Age	25	05 aa	462	78	115	24	61	25	249			330	489	819	11	78	27	0.54	0				161		126	29%	5.72	18.1	$20
Bats	Right	06 ARI	* 472	67	114	18	66	14	241	360	178	307	440	747	9	86	25	0.66	294	42	20	37	116	12%	99	20%	4.78	4.9	$14
Health	A	07 ARI	569	85	135	32	68	27	237	246	234	291	467	758	7	75	26	0.30	258	37	15	48	146	15%	122	29%	4.71	3.2	$21
PT/Exp	A	08 ARI	625	85	155	22	85	14	248	285	236	316	443	759	9	74	30	0.38	258	38	19	43	137	11%	119	13%	4.99	4.6	$19
Consist	A	1st Half	329	48	76	13	43	4	231			301	426	727	9	75	27	0.40	259	38	19	44	134	12%	92	8%	4.49	-2.5	$8
LIMA Plan	B	2nd Half	296	37	79	9	42	10	267			332	463	795	9	72	34	0.35	256	38	20	42	142	10%	128	18%	5.57	7.2	$10
+/- Score	9	09 Proj	576	82	142	26	81	20	247			312	465	776	9	76	28	0.39	266	38	18	45	143	13%	119	20%	5.10	8.1	$20

Not much change in skills from 2007. Stagnant ct% and trouble vs RHP means he is at best a .250s hitter. SBO drop is situational but SX is still solid so SBs could bounce back.

Young,Delmon

Young,Delmon			AB	R	H	HR	RBI	SB	Avg	vL	vR	OB	Slg	OPS	bb%	ct%	h%	Eye	xBA	G	L	F	PX	hr/f	SX	SBO	RC/G	RAR	R$
Pos	7	04	0	0	0	0	0	0	0							0			0						0				
Age	23	05 a/a	558	75	163	21	81	28	292			321	463	784	4	88	30	0.35	0				96		120	32%	4.90	-2.2	$26
Bats	Right	06 TAM	* 468	68	152	11	71	25	325	379	299	348	485	834	3	83	38	0.20	299	47	26	27	102	10%	136	26%	5.51	4.1	$22
Health	A	07 TAM	645	65	186	13	93	10	288	299	285	316	408	724	4	80	34	0.20	262	46	21	33	86	8%	63	8%	4.19	-15.4	$18
PT/Exp	B	08 MIN	575	80	167	10	69	14	290	300	286	331	405	736	6	82	34	0.33	265	55	17	28	77	8%	106	12%	4.48	-6.1	$18
Consist	B	1st Half	292	39	82	2	28	9	281			327	377	704	6	83	33	0.39	272	59	19	23	65	4%	120	16%	4.19	-5.5	$8
LIMA Plan	C	2nd Half	283	41	85	8	41	5	300			336	435	770	5	81	35	0.28	257	52	15	33	89	11%	72	8%	4.77	-0.6	$11
+/- Score	-4	09 Proj	577	75	165	13	78	16	286			319	416	736	5	82	33	0.27	271	51	19	30	86	9%	103	15%	4.39	-9.1	$19

Not much overall growth, but there were a few positive signs. PRO: bb%/ct%/Eye increased; SX upswing boosted value. CON: PX drop/GB% spike saps power; xBA reveals inflated BA. Breakout not imminent.

Young,Delwyn

Young,Delwyn			AB	R	H	HR	RBI	SB	Avg	vL	vR	OB	Slg	OPS	bb%	ct%	h%	Eye	xBA	G	L	F	PX	hr/f	SX	SBO	RC/G	RAR	R$
Pos	8	04	0	0	0	0	0	0	0							0			0						0				
Age	26	05 a/a	526	54	133	15	55	1	253			285	394	679	4	84	28	0.28	0				92		31	4%	3.68	-11.5	$10
Bats	Both	06 aaa	532	58	124	14	75	2	233			277	378	654	6	85	25	0.39	0				92		40	7%	3.52	-16.6	$8
Health	B	07 LA	* 524	85	147	16	77	4	281	333	421	322	470	791	6	80	33	0.30	273	34	21	45	129	8%	87	6%	5.18	9.7	$17
PT/Exp	D	08 LA	126	10	31	1	7	0	246	231	253	321	341	663	10	73	33	0.41	217	50	17	33	84	3%	16	0%	3.82	-3.4	$1
Consist	D	1st Half	80	5	23	1	4	0	288			352	400	752	9	78	36	0.44	248	52	23	26	90	6%	7	0%	4.92	0.4	$1
LIMA Plan	F	2nd Half	46	5	8	0	3	0	174			269	239	508	12	65	27	0.38	158	47	7	47	72	0%	35	0%	1.64	-4.6	($0)
+/- Score	-44	09 Proj	79	8	21	2	9	0	266			314	411	725	7	81	31	0.38	283	51	22	27	102	11%	36	4%	4.40	-0.5	$2

Pretty much a lost season, as he rotted on the LA bench. 2nd half issues exacerbated by a strained oblique. He's entering his age 27 year, and has only 165 MLB AB. Time is running out on that "prospect" tag.

Young,Dmitri

Young,Dmitri			AB	R	H	HR	RBI	SB	Avg	vL	vR	OB	Slg	OPS	bb%	ct%	h%	Eye	xBA	G	L	F	PX	hr/f	SX	SBO	RC/G	RAR	R$
Pos	3	04 DET	389	72	106	18	60	0	272	248	286	329	481	810	8	82	29	0.46	289	46	20	34	124	16%	69	1%	5.40	4.6	$13
Age	35	05 DET	469	61	127	21	72	1	271	277	269	313	471	784	6	79	30	0.29	285	47	20	33	129	18%	67	1%	4.99	-1.3	$15
Bats	Both	06 DET	172	19	43	7	23	1	250	136	267	295	407	702	6	77	29	0.28	241	52	14	34	91	16%	59	5%	3.93	-7.6	$4
Health	F	07 WAS	460	57	147	13	74	0	320	301	327	379	491	870	9	84	36	0.59	287	43	22	36	114	9%	30	0%	6.27	1.7	$17
PT/Exp	D	08 WAS	150	15	42	4	10	0	280	318	264	393	400	793	16	81	32	1.00	235	58	17	25	77	13%	11	0%	5.70	-0.1	$3
Consist	C	1st Half	124	12	33	4	9	0	266			364	395	759	13	81	30	0.83	235	60	17	24	79	17%	11	0%	5.09	-2.3	$2
LIMA Plan	F	2nd Half	26	3	9	0	1	0	346			514	423	937	26	81	43	1.80	206	48	19	33	69	0%	1	0%	8.37	1.8	$1
+/- Score	-47	09 Proj	223	27	61	8	28	0	274			338	438	776	9	81	31	0.50	267	51	18	31	101	15%	49	1%	5.06	-5.2	$6

Is now 35, and could not stay on the field due to three separate DL stints. BPIs show that the batting skills are still there, but staying healthy will be his biggest obstacle.

Young,Michael

Young,Michael			AB	R	H	HR	RBI	SB	Avg	vL	vR	OB	Slg	OPS	bb%	ct%	h%	Eye	xBA	G	L	F	PX	hr/f	SX	SBO	RC/G	RAR	R$
Pos	6	04 TEX	693	115	216	22	100	12	312	330	307	355	481	835	6	87	33	0.52	286	38	25	38	93	10%	120	8%	5.65	22.3	$28
Age	32	05 TEX	668	114	221	24	91	5	331	340	327	384	513	898	8	86	36	0.64	313	45	26	29	111	14%	87	3%	6.47	33.6	$30
Bats	Right	06 TEX	691	93	217	14	103	7	314	295	320	359	459	817	6	86	35	0.50	303	48	25	27	94	9%	76	5%	5.52	20.7	$23
Health	A	07 TEX	639	80	201	9	94	13	315	309	316	362	418	779	7	83	37	0.44	287	48	27	24	74	7%	77	8%	5.07	13.5	$22
PT/Exp	A	08 TEX	645	102	183	12	82	10	284	305	276	340	402	742	8	83	33	0.50	274	47	23	31	80	7%	98	5%	4.67	6.2	$20
Consist	A	1st Half	340	57	97	7	43	5	285			340	418	757	8	85	33	0.55	277	44	21	35	89	7%	92	5%	4.87	5.1	$11
LIMA Plan	C	2nd Half	305	45	86	5	39	5	282			340	384	724	8	81	33	0.47	270	50	24	26	70	8%	90	5%	4.45	1.1	$9
+/- Score	8	09 Proj	616	90	180	11	80	10	292			344	409	754	7	84	34	0.49	282	47	25	28	80	7%	94	6%	4.80	7.7	$19

Has been undergoing a slow fade since 2005 peak. PX and SX both rebounded slightly, but BA finished under .300, with xBA in support. Lots of value tied to playing time, but that will be tougher to sustain as he ages.

Zaun,Gregg

Zaun,Gregg			AB	R	H	HR	RBI	SB	Avg	vL	vR	OB	Slg	OPS	bb%	ct%	h%	Eye	xBA	G	L	F	PX	hr/f	SX	SBO	RC/G	RAR	R$
Pos	2	04 TOR	338	46	91	6	36	0	269	272	268	358	393	752	12	82	31	0.77	272	45	24	32	87	7%	29	2%	5.07	7.2	$7
Age	38	05 TOR	434	61	109	11	61	2	251	278	241	359	373	732	14	84	28	1.04	257	46	19	35	77	9%	49	3%	4.91	11.5	$10
Bats	Both	06 TOR	290	39	79	12	40	0	272	373	251	363	462	825	12	86	28	0.98	281	38	20	42	113	11%	23	2%	5.88	12.2	$8
Health	C	07 TOR	331	43	80	10	52	0	242	290	229	343	411	754	13	83	26	0.93	270	42	17	41	113	9%	33	0%	5.13	8.3	$7
PT/Exp	D	08 TOR	245	29	58	6	30	2	237	163	255	339	359	698	13	84	26	1.00	244	44	15	40	79	7%	43	4%	4.47	2.0	$4
Consist	B	1st Half	151	19	39	5	16	2	258			364	404	768	14	88	27	1.39	258	43	15	42	86	9%	43	6%	5.37	5.2	$4
LIMA Plan	F	2nd Half	94	10	19	1	14	0	202			299	287	586	12	79	25	0.65	218	46	16	38	67	4%	26	0%	2.93	-3.7	$0
+/- Score	-15	09 Proj	183	23	44	5	25	1	240			339	378	717	13	83	27	0.89	254	43	17	40	92	8%	34	2%	4.65	2.2	$3

Could be finally nearing the end of the road at age 38. Still offers decent skills, but odds are they are going to be less valuable as he fights for playing time and Father Time.

Zimmerman,Ryan

Zimmerman,Ryan			AB	R	H	HR	RBI	SB	Avg	vL	vR	OB	Slg	OPS	bb%	ct%	h%	Eye	xBA	G	L	F	PX	hr/f	SX	SBO	RC/G	RAR	R$
Pos	5	04	0	0	0	0	0	0	0							0			0						0				
Age	24	05 WAS	* 291	39	90	7	32	1	309	400	395	343	481	824	5	86	34	0.38	358	43	38	19	120	15%	41	10%	5.50	5.9	$10
Bats	Right	06 WAS	614	84	176	20	110	11	287	280	289	351	471	822	9	80	33	0.51	282	42	22	36	119	11%	78	11%	5.71	3.8	$23
Health	B	07 WAS	653	99	174	24	91	4	266	374	235	329	458	787	9	81	30	0.49	274	44	17	40	121	11%	85	3%	5.22	-7.3	$19
PT/Exp	A	08 WAS	428	51	121	14	51	1	283	333	259	331	442	773	7	83	31	0.44	275	46	20	34	100	12%	45	2%	4.92	-5.4	$12
Consist	A	1st Half	206	24	53	8	27	0	257			288	427	716	4	82	28	0.24	264	45	18	37	107	13%	27	0%	4.04	-8.0	$5
LIMA Plan	C	2nd Half	222	27	68	6	24	1	306			369	455	824	9	85	34	0.67	284	47	21	31	94	10%	50	3%	5.71	2.1	$7
+/- Score	-13	09 Proj	583	77	166	19	77	3	285			339	456	794	8	83	32	0.47	280	45	20	35	109	11%	61	4%	5.25	-2.6	$18

Ct%, LD and BA all improved despite his shoulder injury, which is a positive sign. If his shoulder is healthy, then value could spike.

UP: 25 HR, .300 BA.

Zobrist,Ben

Zobrist,Ben			AB	R	H	HR	RBI	SB	Avg	vL	vR	OB	Slg	OPS	bb%	ct%	h%	Eye	xBA	G	L	F	PX	hr/f	SX	SBO	RC/G	RAR	R$
Pos	6	04	0	0	0	0	0	0	0							0			0						0				
Age	27	05	0	0	0	0	0	0	0							0			0						0				
Bats	Both	06 TAM	* 567	68	150	5	48	12	265	212	229	340	372	712	10	86	30	0.82	276	47	22	30	67	3%	103	13%	4.58	2.9	$10
Health	C	07 TAM	* 319	47	72	8	29	10	226	182	147	320	358	677	12	81	26	0.74	257	43	20	37	85	8%	101	14%	4.08	-2.0	$6
PT/Exp	D	08 TAM	* 269	44	70	15	41	6	260	269	242	350	491	840	12	79	28	0.66	276	44	13	42	141	17%	96	9%	5.99	13.0	$11
Consist	C	1st Half	53	7	11	3	4	2	200			254	419	672	7	78	20	0.32	254	30	15	55	141	13%	79	33%	3.58	-1.3	$1
LIMA Plan	D	2nd Half	216	37	59	12	37	4	275			372	508	880	13	80	30	0.75	280	46	13	41	141	17%	96	6%	6.56	13.7	$9
+/- Score	-0	09 Proj	258	38	67	10	34	7	260			342	438	780	11	81	29	0.65	262	42	16	42	111	11%	96	13%	5.25	6.8	$8

12-30-.253 in 198 AB at TAM. PX spike caused by increased FB%, but should come down some as hr/f is unsustainable. Sacrificed LD%, but xBA says BA can still climb. Skill growth could lead to a bigger role.

SCOTT MONROE

The Pitchers

QUALIFICATION: All pitchers who had at least 40 IP in the majors in 2008, and some with fewer than 40 IP have been included. The decision point is "potential impact in 2009." Those who may have a role but have battled injuries for several years are often not included, though an injury status update appears on page 183. All of these players will appear on Baseball HQ as roles become clearer.

THROWS: Right (RH) or left (LH). **ROLE:** Starters (projected 18+ batters faced per game) or Relievers (less than 18 BF/G). Each pitcher's current **AGE** is shown.

TYPE evaluates the extent to which a pitcher allows the ball to be put into play and his ground ball or flyball tendency. CON (contact) represents pitchers who allow the ball to be put into play a great deal. PWR (power) represents those with high strikeout and/or walk totals who keep the ball out of play. GB are those who have a ground ball rate more than 50%; xGB are those who have a GB rate more than 55%. FB are those who have a fly ball rate more than 40%; xFB are those who have a FB rate more than 45%.

RELIABILITY GRADES: An analysis of each player's forecast risk, on an A-F scale. High grades go to pitchers who have accumulated few disabled list days (Health), have a history of substantial and regular major league playing time (PT/Exp) and have displayed consistent performance over the past three years, using xERA (Consist).

LIMA PLAN GRADE: Rating that evaluates how well that pitcher would be a good fit for a team employing the LIMA Plan. Best grades will go to pitchers who have excellent base skills and had a 2008 Roto value less than $20. Lowest grades will go to poor skills and values more than $20.

+/- SCORE: A score that measures the probability that a pitcher's 2009 performance will exceed or fall short of 2008's numbers. Two types of variables are tracked: 1) Multi-year trends in BPV, and 2) Outlying 2008 levels for h%, s%, xERA, hr/f and LH/RH variance. Positive scores indicate both rebounds and potential breakouts. Negative scores indicate both corrections and breakdowns.

PLAYER STAT LINES: The past five years' statistics represent the total accumulated in the majors as well as in Triple-A, Double-A ball and various foreign leagues during each year. All non-major league stats used have been converted to a major league equivalent (MLE) performance level. Minor league levels below AA are not included.

Nearly all baseball publications separate a player's statistical experiences in the major leagues from the minor leagues and outside leagues. While this may be appropriate for the sake of official record-keeping, it is not an accurate snapshot of a player's complete performance for the year.

Bill James has proven that minor league statistics (converted to MLEs), at Double-A level or above, provide as accurate a record of a player's performance as Major League statistics. Other researchers have also devised conversion factors for foreign leagues. Since these are accurate barometers, we include them in the pool of historical data.

TEAM DESIGNATIONS: An asterisk (*) appearing with a team name means that major league equivalent Triple-A and/or Double-A numbers are included in that year's stat line. A designation of "a/a" means the stats were accumulated at both levels that year. Other designations: JPN (Japan), MEX (Mexico), KOR (Korea), CUB (Cuba), VNZ (Venezuela) and ind (independent league). All these stats are converted to major league equivalents.

The designation "2TM" appears whenever a player was on more than one major league team, crossing leagues, in a season. "2AL" and "2NL" represent more than one team in the same league. Complete season stats are presented for players who crossed leagues during the season.

SABERMETRIC CATEGORIES: Descriptions of all the categories appear in the glossary. The decimal point has been suppressed on several categories to conserve space.

- Platoon data (vL, vR) and Ball-in-play data (G/L/F) are for major league performance only.
- The xERA2 and new BPV formulas are used when G/L/F data is available. The old formulas are used otherwise.

2009 FORECASTS: It is far too early to be making definitive projections for 2009, especially on playing time. Focus on the skill levels and trends, then consult Baseball HQ for playing time revisions as players change teams and roles become finalized. A free projections update will also be available online in March.

Forecasts are computed from a player's trends over the past five years. Adjustments were made for leading indicators and variances between skill and statistical output. After reviewing the leading indicators, you might opt to make further adjustments.

Although each year's numbers include all playing time at the Double-A level or above, the 2009 forecast only represents potential playing time at the major league level, and again is highly preliminary.

CAPSULE COMMENTARIES provide a brief analysis of each player's BPIs and the potential impact on performance in 2009. For those who played only a portion of 2008 in the Majors, and whose isolated MLB stats are significantly different from their full-season total, their MLB stats are listed here. Note that these commentaries generally look at performance related issues only. Playing time expectations may impact these analyses, so you will have to adjust accordingly. Upside (UP) and downside (DN) statistical potential appears for some players. These are less grounded in hard data and more speculative of skills potential.

DO-IT-YOURSELF ANALYSIS: Here are some data points you can look at in doing your own player analysis:

- Variance between vLH and vRH opposition batting avg
- Variance in 2008 hr/f rate from 10%
- Variance in 2008 hit rate (h%) from 30%
- Variance in 2008 strand rate (s%) to tolerances (65% - 80%)
- Variance between ERA and xERA each year
- Growth or decline in Base Performance Value (BPV)
- Spikes in innings pitched

Aardsma,David

		Yr	Tm	W	L	Sv	IP	K	ERA	WHIP	OBA	vL	vR	BF/G	H%	S%	xERA	G	L	F	Ctl	Dom	Cmd	hr/f	hr/9	RAR	BPV	R$
RH	Reliever	04	aaa	6	4	11	55	47	2.96	1.28	227			5.3	29%	75%	2.77				4.0	7.7	**1.9**		0.2	9.4	91	$11
Age	27	05	aa	10	3	2	96	62	4.34	1.52	287			10.2	33%	71%	4.49				3.5	5.8	**1.7**		0.5	-0.4	53	$7
Type	Pwr	06	CHC *	5	3	8	89	81	4.24	1.38	239	190	225	5.2	29%	72%	4.47	37	19	44	4.4	8.2	**1.8**	9%	1.0	2.7	42	$10
Health	B	07	CHW *	5	3	15	67	76	6.17	1.49	273			5.6	33%	63%	3.23	37	42	21	3.9	10.1	**2.6**	36%	1.9	-13.9	92	$9
PT/Exp	D	08	BOS	4	2	0	49	49	5.54	1.72	263	289	250	4.8	34%	68%	4.83	44	18	38	6.5	9.1	**1.4**	8%	0.7	-7.2	10	$1
Consist	C	1st Half		2	2	0	37	40	2.92	1.38	206			4.7	29%	78%	4.14	45	17	38	5.8	9.7	**1.7**	3%	0.2	6.5	40	$4
LIMA Plan	B+	2nd Half		2	0	0	12	9	13.84	2.82	400			5.2	44%	50%	7.27	43	19	38	8.5	6.9	**0.8**	17%	2.3	-13.7	-83	($3)
+/- Score	25	09	Proj	**3**	**2**	**0**	**44**	**42**	**4.14**	**1.40**	**241**			**5.5**	**30%**	**72%**	**4.08**	**41**	**24**	**35**	**4.6**	**8.7**	**1.9**	**10%**	**0.8**	**1.8**	**53**	**$4**

Two DL stints in 2H derailed his season. 1H xERA gives a good idea what to expect. There's a decent reliever here. Dom is a solid building block. But chronic Ctl problems raise the risk level.

Accardo,Jeremy

		Yr	Tm	W	L	Sv	IP	K	ERA	WHIP	OBA	vL	vR	BF/G	H%	S%	xERA	G	L	F	Ctl	Dom	Cmd	hr/f	hr/9	RAR	BPV	R$
RH	Reliever	04	a/a	3	0	7	42	38	1.71	1.07	228			5.1	30%	82%	2.11				2.1	8.1	**3.8**		0.0	13.6	138	$9
Age	27	05	SF *	4	5	7	73	59	3.45	1.19	234	182	265	4.9	29%	71%	4.03	39	23	38	3.0	7.3	**2.5**	5%	0.5	7.1	68	$10
Type	Pwr	06	2TM	2	4	3	69	54	5.35	1.39	281	241	307	4.6	33%	62%	3.98	42	25	32	2.6	7.0	**2.7**	10%	0.9	-7.0	77	$4
Health	F	07	TOR	4	4	30	67	57	2.14	1.11	212	161	250	4.2	26%	83%	3.53	49	20	30	3.2	7.6	**2.4**	7%	0.5	19.6	78	$21
PT/Exp	C	08	TOR	0	3	4	12	5	6.59	1.54	302	300	300	3.4	32%	56%	5.34	46	15	39	2.9	3.7	**1.3**	6%	0.7	-3.4	10	$1
Consist	C	1st Half		0	3	4	12	5	6.59	1.54	302			3.4	32%	56%	5.34	46	15	39	2.9	3.7	**1.3**	6%	0.7	-3.4	10	$1
LIMA Plan	A	2nd Half		0	0	0	0	0	0.00	0.00																		
+/- Score	54	09	Proj	**3**	**3**	**5**	**58**	**48**	**3.57**	**1.19**	**238**			**4.7**	**29%**	**70%**	**3.79**	**45**	**21**	**35**	**2.8**	**7.4**	**2.7**	**5%**	**0.5**	**4.6**	**81**	**$8**

Missed most of year with arm problems. Don't expect encore of 2006 or 07; ERA difference was due to S% swing. 2005-07 xERA tells the story - he's a solid LIMA reliever who can chalk up saves if called upon.

Aceves,Alfredo

		Yr	Tm	W	L	Sv	IP	K	ERA	WHIP	OBA	vL	vR	BF/G	H%	S%	xERA	G	L	F	Ctl	Dom	Cmd	hr/f	hr/9	RAR	BPV	R$
RH	Starter	04		0	0	0	0	0	0.00	0.00																		
Age	26	05	MEX	9	8	0	145	95	4.78	1.44	281			28.7	32%	68%	4.56				3.0	5.9	**1.9**		0.9	-8.5	49	$7
Type	Con FB	06	MEX	8	5	0	124	90	4.86	1.28	271			27.4	31%	64%	4.26				2.1	6.5	**3.1**		1.2	-5.2	70	$10
Health	A	07	MEX	11	5	0	106	65	4.33	1.32	254			25.0	29%	67%	3.74				3.2	5.5	**1.7**		0.7	1.7	53	$10
PT/Exp	C	08	NYY *	5	5	0	123	78	3.66	1.27	265	238	213	22.4	29%	76%	4.38	42	17	41	2.3	5.7	**2.5**	10%	1.2	10.4	61	$10
Consist	B	1st Half		2	2	0	50	26	2.80	1.13	262			29.0	28%	79%					1.2	4.7	**3.9**		0.8	9.5	89	$6
LIMA Plan	C+	2nd Half		3	3	0	73	52	4.25	1.36	266			19.6	29%	74%	4.43	42	17	41	3.0	6.4	**2.1**	13%	1.5	0.9	53	$5
+/- Score	-1	09	Proj	**4**	**3**	**0**	**66**	**42**	**4.09**	**1.30**	**265**			**25.3**	**29%**	**72%**	**4.49**	**42**	**17**	**41**	**2.6**	**5.7**	**2.2**	**9%**	**1.1**	**-0.5**	**53**	**$5**

1-0, 2.40 ERA in 30 IP at NYY. Mexican League to Yankee Stadium in one year. Ctl bodes well for future success, but low Dom, gopheritis limit his ceiling. Contact flyball pitchers are just dangerous, anywhere.

Acosta,Manny

		Yr	Tm	W	L	Sv	IP	K	ERA	WHIP	OBA	vL	vR	BF/G	H%	S%	xERA	G	L	F	Ctl	Dom	Cmd	hr/f	hr/9	RAR	BPV	R$
RH	Reliever	04		0	0	0	0	0	0.00	0.00																		
Age	28	05		0	0	0	0	0	0.00	0.00																		
Type	Pwr GB	06	a/a	1	6	21	60	48	4.89	1.86	255			5.6	30%	75%	5.28				8.1	7.1	**0.9**		0.9	-2.8	37	$6
Health	B	07	ATL *	10	4	12	82	69	2.69	1.47	229	250	93	5.9	29%	81%	4.19	61	11	29	5.7	7.5	**1.3**	3%	0.2	17.6	20	$14
PT/Exp	D	08	ATL	3	5	3	53	31	3.57	1.40	243	280	218	5.0	26%	79%	4.45	53	19	28	4.4	5.3	**1.2**	15%	1.2	4.6	7	$5
Consist	B	1st Half		3	5	3	40	23	4.69	1.54	260			4.7	27%	75%	4.78	54	17	29	4.9	5.1	**1.0**	18%	1.6	-2.1	-9	$2
LIMA Plan	C	2nd Half		0	0	0	13	8	0.00	0.94	183			6.1	22%	100%	3.46	53	25	22	2.8	5.7	**2.0**	0%	0.0	6.7	56	$2
+/- Score	-39	09	Proj	**3**	**4**	**0**	**44**	**32**	**4.34**	**1.52**	**251**			**5.2**	**28%**	**74%**	**4.32**	**54**	**20**	**26**	**5.2**	**6.6**	**1.3**	**15%**	**1.0**	**0.1**	**12**	**$2**

A bunch of saves at AAA, but poor Cmd will keep him from save opps in majors. S% has helped ERA the past two years; there's a correction coming. Man cannot live by high GB% alone. At least most men.

Adams,Mike

		Yr	Tm	W	L	Sv	IP	K	ERA	WHIP	OBA	vL	vR	BF/G	H%	S%	xERA	G	L	F	Ctl	Dom	Cmd	hr/f	hr/9	RAR	BPV	R$
RH	Reliever	04	MIL *	4	4	0	84	69	3.36	1.13	245	241	252	6.1	29%	73%	3.81	40	18	42	1.9	7.4	**3.8**	8%	0.9	9.4	99	$9
Age	30	05	MIL *	3	5	3	49	51	5.36	1.48	269			5.5	34%	64%	4.00	39	22	39	4.0	9.4	**2.4**	10%	0.9	-6.8	79	$3
Type	Pwr	06	aaa	1	3	2	60	39	4.84	1.68	311			5.8	36%	70%	5.24				3.7	5.9	**1.6**		0.5	-2.4	47	$1
Health	F	07		0	0	0	0	0	0.00	0.00																		
PT/Exp	F	08	SD *	5	4	0	80	84	3.65	1.43	267	228	190	5.2	35%	76%	3.84	42	18	40	3.6	9.5	**2.6**	8%	0.8	6.0	94	$7
Consist	C	1st Half		4	1	0	39	39	4.92	1.84	317			6.6	40%	73%	4.90	32	27	42	4.8	9.0	**1.9**	6%	0.7	-3.1	41	$1
LIMA Plan	B+	2nd Half		1	3	0	41	45	2.44	1.03	213			4.2	28%	82%	3.00	49	13	39	2.4	10.0	**4.1**	10%	0.9	9.2	140	$6
+/- Score	16	09	Proj	**2**	**3**	**13**	**44**	**41**	**4.14**	**1.43**	**273**			**5.4**	**34%**	**72%**	**4.04**	**42**	**18**	**40**	**3.3**	**8.5**	**2.6**	**8%**	**0.8**	**1.6**	**84**	**$7**

2-3, 2.48 ERA in 65 IP at SD. LIMA-worthy results after being out of the majors for a couple of years. Another PETCO groupie (1.31 ERA vs 3.77 on the road). Will miss start of 2009 after shoulder surgery.

Affeldt,Jeremy

		Yr	Tm	W	L	Sv	IP	K	ERA	WHIP	OBA	vL	vR	BF/G	H%	S%	xERA	G	L	F	Ctl	Dom	Cmd	hr/f	hr/9	RAR	BPV	R$
LH	Reliever	04	KC	3	4	13	76	49	4.97	1.62	298	271	312	9.1	34%	69%	4.79	46	21	33	3.8	5.8	**1.5**	7%	0.7	-5.0	26	$6
Age	29	05	KC	0	2	0	49	39	5.30	1.73	288	263	283	4.7	35%	68%	4.47	53	22	25	5.3	7.1	**1.3**	8%	0.5	-5.7	16	($1)
Type	Pwr GB	06	2TM	8	8	1	97	48	6.21	1.62	271	212	289	8.2	28%	63%	5.38	50	17	33	5.1	4.4	**0.9**	12%	1.2	-20.2	-30	$1
Health	B	07	COL	4	3	0	59	46	3.51	1.36	220	250	211	3.4	27%	74%	4.33	53	14	33	5.0	7.0	**1.4**	6%	0.5	6.7	21	$6
PT/Exp	C	08	CIN	1	1	0	78	80	3.33	1.32	261	269	255	4.5	33%	79%	3.10	54	18	28	2.9	9.2	**3.2**	15%	1.0	9.0	120	$6
Consist	C	1st Half		1	0	0	41	41	4.17	1.46	276			4.2	33%	77%	3.49	52	18	31	3.5	9.0	**2.6**	19%	1.5	0.5	97	$2
LIMA Plan	B	2nd Half		0	1	0	37	39	2.41	1.15	244			4.9	33%	80%	2.67	58	18	24	2.2	9.4	**4.3**	8%	0.5	8.5	146	$4
+/- Score	35	09	Proj	**2**	**2**	**0**	**58**	**52**	**3.57**	**1.36**	**255**			**4.6**	**31%**	**76%**	**3.63**	**53**	**17**	**30**	**3.6**	**8.1**	**2.3**	**10%**	**0.8**	**5.1**	**80**	**$4**

Got BBs under control, and the results followed. When hr/f normalized in 2H, he was pretty much lights out. Has emerged as a decent LIMA option; BA splits say he can be more than just a lefty-on-lefty specialist.

Albers,Matt

		Yr	Tm	W	L	Sv	IP	K	ERA	WHIP	OBA	vL	vR	BF/G	H%	S%	xERA	G	L	F	Ctl	Dom	Cmd	hr/f	hr/9	RAR	BPV	R$
RH	Reliever	04		0	0	0	0	0	0.00	0.00																		
Age	26	05		0	0	0	0	0	0.00	0.00																		
Type	GB	06	HOU *	12	5	0	156	113	3.23	1.38	258	333	267	24.9	31%	77%	4.28	43	26	30	3.6	6.5	**1.8**	5%	0.5	24.2	41	$15
Health	D	07	HOU *	6	14	0	164	105	5.43	1.59	288	280	298	18.5	31%	69%	4.77	48	17	35	4.0	5.8	**1.4**	13%	1.4	-20.4	22	$1
PT/Exp	D	08	BAL	3	3	0	49	26	3.49	1.33	237	163	312	7.4	26%	75%	4.71	53	12	34	4.0	4.8	**1.2**	7%	0.7	5.2	8	$4
Consist	A	1st Half		3	3	0	49	26	3.49	1.33	237			7.4	26%	75%	4.71	53	12	34	4.0	4.8	**1.2**	7%	0.7	5.2	8	$4
LIMA Plan	C+	2nd Half		0	0	0	0	0	0.00	0.00																		
+/- Score	-60	09	Proj	**5**	**5**	**0**	**87**	**55**	**4.14**	**1.41**	**260**			**13.0**	**29%**	**72%**	**4.54**	**51**	**15**	**34**	**3.8**	**5.7**	**1.5**	**8%**	**0.8**	**-1.2**	**28**	**$6**

Torn labrum ended season; chose rehab, so should start 2009 on time. If healthy, could get rotation spot but Cmd trend argues against it. Splits (.475 OPS v. RH, .825 vs LH) argue for a specialty bullpen role.

Arredondo,Jose

		Yr	Tm	W	L	Sv	IP	K	ERA	WHIP	OBA	vL	vR	BF/G	H%	S%	xERA	G	L	F	Ctl	Dom	Cmd	hr/f	hr/9	RAR	BPV	R$
RH	Reliever	04		0	0	0	0	0	0.00	0.00																		
Age	25	05		0	0	0	0	0	0.00	0.00																		
Type	Pwr GB	06	aa	2	3	0	60	41	6.58	1.71	328			25.3	37%	61%	6.11				3.0	6.1	**2.1**		1.0	-15.3	38	($2)
Health	A	07	aa	0	1	10	28	24	3.31	1.29	215			4.7	26%	76%	3.11				4.6	7.8	**1.7**		0.7	4.0	74	$6
PT/Exp	F	08	LAA *	11	3	10	78	67	1.88	1.06	205	148	236	4.6	25%	86%	3.41	51	17	31	3.0	7.8	**2.6**	8%	0.6	23.8	87	$19
Consist	D	1st Half		3	1	10	36	31	2.05	0.91	207			4.3	25%	83%	2.75	58	15	27	1.5	7.8	**5.0**	12%	0.8	10.3	135	$10
LIMA Plan	C+	2nd Half		8	2	0	42	36	1.73	1.20	203			4.9	26%	88%	3.91	48	19	33	4.3	7.8	**1.8**	5%	0.4	13.5	50	$9
+/- Score	-46	09	Proj	**7**	**3**	**15**	**73**	**57**	**3.72**	**1.34**	**260**			**7.2**	**31%**	**74%**	**3.87**	**51**	**18**	**32**	**3.1**	**7.1**	**2.3**	**9%**	**0.7**	**5.0**	**72**	**$13**

10-2, 1.62 ERA in 61 IP at LAA. Vulture watch! H%, S% fed this sterling ERA, but it wasn't all luck. With high GB% and Cmd, he's got the profile to close, if the opportunity arises.

Arroyo,Bronson

		Yr	Tm	W	L	Sv	IP	K	ERA	WHIP	OBA	vL	vR	BF/G	H%	S%	xERA	G	L	F	Ctl	Dom	Cmd	hr/f	hr/9	RAR	BPV	R$
RH	Starter	04	BOS	10	9	0	178	142	4.04	1.22	254	269	227	23.1	30%	69%	3.94	41	20	39	2.4	7.2	**3.0**	8%	0.9	8.6	84	$16
Age	32	05	BOS	14	10	0	205	100	4.52	1.30	269	286	234	24.7	29%	67%	4.97	38	18	44	2.4	4.4	**1.9**	7%	1.0	-3.7	31	$14
Type		06	CIN	14	11	0	240	184	3.30	1.19	247	282	206	28.2	28%	78%	4.05	38	21	41	2.4	6.9	**2.9**	11%	1.2	35.3	76	$26
Health	A	07	CIN	9	15	0	211	156	4.23	1.40	281	274	285	26.8	32%	73%	4.55	35	21	44	2.7	6.7	**2.5**	10%	1.2	5.1	61	$12
PT/Exp	A	08	CIN	15	11	0	200	163	4.77	1.44	280	314	254	25.6	32%	70%	4.13	41	23	36	3.1	7.3	**2.4**	13%	1.3	-12.3	69	$12
Consist	A	1st Half		5	7	0	93	88	6.19	1.67	314			23.7	37%	66%	4.27	36	26	38	3.4	8.5	**2.5**	16%	1.7	-22.1	76	($0)
LIMA Plan	C+	2nd Half		10	4	0	107	75	3.53	1.23	247			27.8	28%	74%	3.99	47	20	33	2.8	6.3	**2.3**	10%	0.9	9.7	63	$12
+/- Score	24	09	Proj	**13**	**11**	**0**	**203**	**155**	**4.26**	**1.36**	**271**			**26.3**	**31%**	**72%**	**4.25**	**40**	**22**	**39**	**2.8**	**6.9**	**2.5**	**11%**	**1.2**	**2.2**	**66**	**$14**

1H/2H ERA swing; xERA says the skills weren't that different. Old problems vs LH resurfaced; but he's fixed that before. AAA reliability, mostly dominant (50% PQS DOM) with the occasional clunker (18% PQS DIS).

DAVE ADLER

Ayala,Luis	Yr	Tm	W	L	Sv	IP	K	ERA	WHIP	OBA	vL	vR	BF/G	H%	S%	xERA	G	L	F	Ctl	Dom	Cmd	hr/f	hr/9	RAR	BPV	R$
RH Reliever	04	MON	6	12	2	90	63	2.70	1.19	266	246	282	4.6	31%	79%	3.36	54	19	26	1.5	6.3	**4.2**	8%	0.6	17.4	105	$11
Age 31	05	WAS	8	7	1	71	40	2.66	1.25	273	350	230	4.4	30%	83%	4.21	43	23	34	1.8	5.1	**2.9**	9%	0.9	13.9	64	$10
Type Con	06	WAS	0	0	0	0	0	0.00	0.00																		
Health F	07	WAS	2	2	1	42	28	3.19	1.30	265	243	286	4.1	29%	80%	4.45	39	21	40	2.6	6.0	**2.3**	9%	1.1	6.4	55	$4
PT/Exp D	08	2NL	2	10	9	76	50	5.71	1.45	287	285	288	4.1	32%	61%	4.31	46	22	32	2.9	5.9	**2.1**	11%	1.1	-13.4	54	$3
Consist A	1st Half		1	4	0	43	28	5.48	1.43	268			4.2	30%	63%	4.68	41	22	37	3.6	5.9	**1.6**	10%	1.1	-6.4	29	$0
LIMA Plan B	2nd Half		1	6	9	33	22	6.00	1.48	311			3.9	35%	60%	3.85	51	22	27	1.9	6.0	**3.1**	13%	1.1	-7.0	85	$3
+/- Score 41	09	Proj	**4**	**8**	**5**	**73**	**47**	**4.34**	**1.37**	**281**			**4.1**	**31%**	**70%**	**4.18**	**45**	**22**	**33**	**2.4**	**5.8**	**2.5**	**10%**	**1.0**	**1.4**	**65**	**$6**

TJ surgery in '06; still struggling but three reasons for optimism:
1. Return of high GB%
2. S% says ERA will rebound
3. 122 BPV and 6 saves in Sept.
Might see save opps, but won't thrive with marginal skills.

Backe,Brandon	Yr	Tm	W	L	Sv	IP	K	ERA	WHIP	OBA	vL	vR	BF/G	H%	S%	xERA	G	L	F	Ctl	Dom	Cmd	hr/f	hr/9	RAR	BPV	R$
RH Starter	04	HOU	* 11	8	0	131	114	3.84	1.48	276	347	253	11.1	32%	78%	4.29	40	21	39	3.6	7.8	**2.2**	12%	1.2	6.8	61	$10
Age 31	05	HOU	10	8	0	149	97	4.77	1.46	264	260	266	25.1	29%	70%	4.87	42	20	38	4.0	5.9	**1.4**	10%	1.1	-9.6	16	$7
Type FB	06	HOU	3	2	0	43	19	3.77	1.42	262	317	205	23.3	28%	75%	5.60	36	20	44	3.8	4.0	**1.1**	6%	0.8	3.8	-16	$3
Health F	07	HOU	* 7	3	0	59	30	5.52	1.76	312	245	250	25.0	32%	74%	5.90	42	11	46	4.3	4.6	**1.1**	12%	1.8	-7.9	-15	$1
PT/Exp C	08	HOU	9	14	0	167	127	6.05	1.67	301	304	301	24.7	33%	69%	4.95	38	21	41	4.2	6.9	**1.6**	16%	1.9	-36.5	27	($1)
Consist B	1st Half		5	8	0	95	67	5.12	1.61	289			25.3	31%	74%	5.08	37	20	42	4.2	6.3	**1.5**	15%	1.9	-9.9	17	$1
LIMA Plan F	2nd Half		4	6	0	72	60	7.28	1.76	315			24.0	35%	62%	4.77	39	21	39	4.1	7.5	**1.8**	17%	2.0	-26.6	41	($3)
+/- Score 18	09	Proj	**9**	**12**	**0**	**145**	**96**	**5.28**	**1.65**	**297**			**22.8**	**32%**	**73%**	**5.20**	**39**	**19**	**42**	**4.1**	**6.0**	**1.5**	**13%**	**1.7**	**-15.4**	**13**	**$2**

It's been three years since TJ surgery and another two since he's exhibited any sign of draftable skill. At 31, he's now at the age when pitchers tend to display their peak skills and no sign of a turnaround.

Badenhop,Burke	Yr	Tm	W	L	Sv	IP	K	ERA	WHIP	OBA	vL	vR	BF/G	H%	S%	xERA	G	L	F	Ctl	Dom	Cmd	hr/f	hr/9	RAR	BPV	R$
RH Reliever	04		0	0	0	0	0	0.00	0.00																		
Age 26	05		0	0	0	0	0	0.00	0.00																		
Type GB	06		0	0	0	0	0	0.00	0.00																		
Health D	07	aa	2	0	0	18	10	2.50	0.94	191			23.2	20%	80%	2.31				2.5	5.0	**2.0**		1.0	4.4	59	$3
PT/Exp F	08	FLA	* 3	3	0	53	38	5.39	1.57	294	298	281	17.1	33%	67%	4.04	54	20	26	3.5	6.4	**1.8**	16%	1.2	-7.4	51	$1
Consist D	1st Half		3	3	0	53	38	5.39	1.57	294			17.1	33%	67%	4.04	54	20	26	3.5	6.4	**1.8**	16%	1.2	-7.4	51	$1
LIMA Plan B	2nd Half		0	0	0	0	0	0.00	0.00																		
+/- Score 52	09	Proj	**2**	**2**	**0**	**29**	**21**	**4.66**	**1.52**	**288**			**16.1**	**32%**	**73%**	**3.92**	**54**	**20**	**26**	**3.4**	**6.5**	**1.9**	**17%**	**1.2**	**1.5**	**58**	**$1**

2-3, 6.08 ERA in 47 IP at FLA. Fine Ctl in minors; didn't match it before 2H shoulder woes. Building blocks are here. Keeps the ball on the ground, hr/f won't always be this unkind. A work in progress.

Baek,Cha Seung	Yr	Tm	W	L	Sv	IP	K	ERA	WHIP	OBA	vL	vR	BF/G	H%	S%	xERA	G	L	F	Ctl	Dom	Cmd	hr/f	hr/9	RAR	BPV	R$
RH Starter	04	aaa	5	4	0	72	52	4.74	1.62	314			23.4	36%	72%	5.54				3.0	6.5	**2.2**		0.9	-3.5	51	$2
Age 28	05	aaa	8	8	0	112	65	7.05	1.73	334			21.7	36%	61%	6.74				2.8	5.2	**1.8**		1.5	-38.0	12	($3)
Type Con FB	06	SEA	* 16	5	0	181	113	3.62	1.28	260	211	206	25.4	28%	77%	4.44	43	17	40	2.6	5.6	**2.2**	11%	1.2	21.0	52	$20
Health C	07	SEA	* 5	4	0	104	62	4.98	1.52	309	267	305	23.2	35%	67%	5.00	34	24	42	2.4	5.4	**2.3**	5%	0.6	-6.1	45	$3
PT/Exp C	08	2TM	6	10	0	141	92	4.79	1.34	269	280	256	18.8	30%	67%	4.52	41	19	40	2.7	5.9	**2.1**	10%	1.1	-8.4	50	$7
Consist B	1st Half		1	4	0	60	37	5.43	1.37	269			16.0	30%	61%	4.66	42	18	40	3.0	5.6	**1.9**	9%	1.1	-8.3	39	$1
LIMA Plan C	2nd Half		5	6	0	81	55	4.32	1.32	268			21.5	30%	71%	4.41	39	20	40	2.5	6.1	**2.4**	11%	1.2	-0.1	58	$6
+/- Score 3	09	Proj	**7**	**7**	**0**	**131**	**83**	**4.76**	**1.41**	**284**			**20.9**	**31%**	**68%**	**4.68**	**38**	**21**	**41**	**2.6**	**5.7**	**2.2**	**9%**	**1.0**	**-4.8**	**49**	**$6**

Avoids the free passes, but doesn't do much else to set himself apart. 33/38 DOM/DIS - as Forrest Gump said, he's "like a box of chocolates". 2H Cmd and Dom show growth, but it's not enough to merit a pickup.

Baez,Danys	Yr	Tm	W	L	Sv	IP	K	ERA	WHIP	OBA	vL	vR	BF/G	H%	S%	xERA	G	L	F	Ctl	Dom	Cmd	hr/f	hr/9	RAR	BPV	R$
RH Reliever	04	TAM	4	4	30	68	52	3.57	1.31	238	252	223	4.6	28%	75%	4.53	42	16	43	3.8	6.9	**1.8**	7%	0.8	7.2	40	$17
Age 31	05	TAM	5	4	41	72	51	2.87	1.33	245	268	215	4.6	28%	82%	4.29	47	20	33	3.7	6.4	**1.7**	10%	0.9	13.3	38	$21
Type	06	2NL	5	6	9	59	39	4.56	1.30	264	295	244	4.4	31%	64%	4.58	40	17	43	2.6	5.9	**2.3**	4%	0.5	-0.5	55	$8
Health F	07	BAL	0	6	3	50	29	6.44	1.57	261	346	200	4.3	27%	61%	5.03	51	17	32	5.2	5.2	**1.0**	15%	1.4	-12.0	-17	($0)
PT/Exp D	08	BAL	0	0	0	0	0	0.00	0.00																		
Consist A	1st Half		0	0	0	0	0	0.00	0.00																		
LIMA Plan	2nd Half		0	0	0	0	0	0.00	0.00																		
+/- Score	09	Proj	**1**	**2**	**0**	**29**	**19**	**4.66**	**1.41**	**255**			**4.5**	**28%**	**68%**	**4.68**	**46**	**18**	**36**	**4.0**	**5.9**	**1.5**	**9%**	**0.9**	**-0.9**	**21**	**$1**

TJ surgery late 2007, so he's a risk to start the season. Well suited to be a rightly specialist. 96 saves from '03-'05, but with underwhelming BPV, will more than likely toil anonymously in middle relief.

Bailey,Homer	Yr	Tm	W	L	Sv	IP	K	ERA	WHIP	OBA	vL	vR	BF/G	H%	S%	xERA	G	L	F	Ctl	Dom	Cmd	hr/f	hr/9	RAR	BPV	R$
RH Starter	04		0	0	0	0	0	0.00	0.00																		
Age 23	05		0	0	0	0	0	0.00	0.00																		
Type Pwr	06	aa	7	1	0	68	68	2.02	1.25	230			21.8	31%	83%	2.62				3.7	9.0	**2.5**		0.1	21.0	111	$12
Health A	07	CIN	* 10	5	0	112	83	4.51	1.37	232	284	233	22.9	27%	67%	4.55	47	18	35	4.6	6.6	**1.4**	6%	0.6	-1.1	19	$9
PT/Exp D	08	CIN	* 4	13	0	147	106	6.14	1.70	312	305	423	25.2	35%	65%	4.61	43	25	31	3.8	6.5	**1.7**	13%	1.2	-34.0	36	($4)
Consist B	1st Half		4	9	0	94	64	5.65	1.62	291			25.0	32%	68%	5.14	37	22	41	4.2	6.2	**1.5**	12%	1.5	-15.9	13	($0)
LIMA Plan C+	2nd Half		0	4	0	54	42	7.00	1.83	345			25.6	41%	60%	4.20	47	27	26	3.1	7.1	**2.3**	10%	0.8	-18.1	69	($4)
+/- Score 36	09	Proj	**5**	**5**	**0**	**88**	**69**	**4.60**	**1.39**	**260**			**23.7**	**31%**	**68%**	**4.09**	**46**	**23**	**31**	**3.6**	**7.1**	**2.0**	**10%**	**0.8**	**2.7**	**54**	**$5**

0-6, 7.93 ERA in 36 IP at CIN. He owns the skills, and even showed modest 2H growth, but H%, S%, and hr/f conspired against him. I owned him at $4 and would have to protect him in 2009 for $7... and did it.

Baker,Scott	Yr	Tm	W	L	Sv	IP	K	ERA	WHIP	OBA	vL	vR	BF/G	H%	S%	xERA	G	L	F	Ctl	Dom	Cmd	hr/f	hr/9	RAR	BPV	R$
RH Starter	04	a/a	6	6	0	124	96	4.42	1.26	266			27.3	32%	63%	3.43				2.1	7.0	**3.3**		0.4	-1.2	102	$9
Age 27	05	MIN	* 8	11	0	187	125	3.60	1.23	263	221	257	24.3	29%	74%	4.25	40	19	41	2.0	6.0	**3.0**	9%	1.0	17.8	73	$17
Type FB	06	MIN	* 10	12	0	167	119	5.19	1.54	310	349	299	26.6	35%	68%	4.86	34	19	47	2.4	6.4	**2.6**	8%	1.2	-13.0	62	$7
Health B	07	MIN	* 12	11	1	186	134	4.39	1.29	282	323	257	25.3	32%	68%	4.28	35	22	43	1.7	6.5	**3.9**	7%	0.9	2.6	85	$16
PT/Exp B	08	MIN	11	4	0	172	141	3.45	1.18	249	263	230	25.2	29%	75%	4.10	33	21	46	2.2	7.4	**3.4**	9%	1.0	19.1	84	$20
Consist A	1st Half		4	2	0	63	52	3.57	1.21	265			23.6	30%	77%	3.79	36	25	40	1.7	7.4	**4.3**	13%	1.4	6.0	101	$7
LIMA Plan C	2nd Half		7	2	0	109	89	3.38	1.16	239			26.2	28%	74%	4.29	31	19	50	2.5	7.3	**3.0**	6%	0.8	13.1	75	$13
+/- Score 3	09	Proj	**14**	**7**	**0**	**203**	**162**	**3.77**	**1.22**	**260**			**25.5**	**30%**	**72%**	**4.15**	**34**	**21**	**45**	**2.1**	**7.2**	**3.4**	**8%**	**1.0**	**6.9**	**85**	**$22**

xERA trend confirms growth; he's approaching ace status. HRs due to high FB% are his occasional undoing. But that's the only blemish here. He's the real deal, bid with confidence.

Balester,Collin	Yr	Tm	W	L	Sv	IP	K	ERA	WHIP	OBA	vL	vR	BF/G	H%	S%	xERA	G	L	F	Ctl	Dom	Cmd	hr/f	hr/9	RAR	BPV	R$
RH Starter	04		0	0	0	0	0	0.00	0.00																		
Age 22	05		0	0	0	0	0	0.00	0.00																		
Type	06		0	0	0	0	0	0.00	0.00																		
Health A	07	a/a	4	10	0	150	103	4.45	1.40	280			24.0	32%	68%	4.30				2.7	6.2	**2.3**		0.7	0.2	63	$7
PT/Exp D	08	WAS	* 12	10	0	158	107	4.85	1.41	280	278	298	22.8	31%	69%	4.50	40	22	39	2.8	6.1	**2.2**	12%	1.3	-11.2	52	$9
Consist A	1st Half		9	3	0	78	57	4.17	1.32	271			22.1	30%	73%					2.4	6.5	**2.7**		1.3	1.0	57	$8
LIMA Plan C+	2nd Half		3	7	0	80	50	5.51	1.50	290			23.6	31%	66%	4.80	40	22	39	3.1	5.6	**1.8**	12%	1.3	-12.3	34	$1
+/- Score 29	09	Proj	**6**	**8**	**0**	**120**	**81**	**4.73**	**1.41**	**281**			**23.6**	**31%**	**68%**	**4.52**	**40**	**22**	**39**	**2.8**	**6.1**	**2.2**	**9%**	**1.1**	**-2.6**	**52**	**$5**

3-7, 5.51 ERA in 80 IP at WAS. Struggled in first exposure to the bigs, but there are signs of life here. The problem: a 22 year-old in a losing organization could get lots of bad MLB innings on the road to success.

Balfour,Grant	Yr	Tm	W	L	Sv	IP	K	ERA	WHIP	OBA	vL	vR	BF/G	H%	S%	xERA	G	L	F	Ctl	Dom	Cmd	hr/f	hr/9	RAR	BPV	R$
RH Reliever	04	MIN	4	1	0	39	42	4.37	1.43	241	183	276	4.7	31%	71%	4.24	35	22	44	4.8	9.7	**2.0**	9%	0.9	0.3	56	$4
Age 31	05		0	0	0	0	0	0.00	0.00																		
Type Pwr FB	06		0	0	0	0	0	0.00	0.00																		
Health F	07	2TM	* 2	3	7	68	81	4.57	1.55	255			5.3	36%	70%	3.48	42	36	22	5.2	10.7	**2.0**	11%	0.6	-0.9	71	$6
PT/Exp F	08	TAM	* 7	2	12	82	113	1.23	0.86	131	120	159	4.7	21%	89%	2.99	29	19	52	3.9	12.4	**3.2**	5%	0.5	31.4	126	$24
Consist A	1st Half		3	0	9	39	53	0.73	0.75	97			5.4	16%	93%	2.70	41	14	45	4.0	12.3	**3.1**	4%	0.3	17.2	133	$13
LIMA Plan B+	2nd Half		4	2	3	43	60	1.67	0.95	159			4.2	25%	87%	3.12	25	21	54	3.8	12.6	**3.3**	7%	0.6	14.2	128	$11
+/- Score -92	09	Proj	**4**	**2**	**5**	**58**	**74**	**3.26**	**1.22**	**204**			**4.9**	**30%**	**75%**	**3.50**	**33**	**24**	**43**	**4.5**	**11.5**	**2.6**	**7%**	**0.6**	**6.6**	**96**	**$10**

6-2, 1.54 ERA in 58 IP at TAM. Hit the luck trifecta with H%, S%, and hr/f. But Dom and BPV say there's skill too. Past health woes raise the risk. Sleeper for saves, but regardless of role use xERA to set expectations.

DAVE ADLER

Banks,Josh

		Yr	Tm	W	L	Sv	IP	K	ERA	WHIP	OBA	vL	vR	BF/G	H%	S%	xERA	G	L	F	Ctl	Dom	Cmd	hr/f	hr/9	RAR	BPV	R$
RH	Starter	04	aa	6	6	0	91	66	7.41	1.57	304			22.7	32%	56%	6.48				3.1	6.5	2.1		2.2	-34.5	13	($1)
Age	26	05	aa	8	12	0	162	124	5.95	1.37	314			25.7	35%	59%	5.44				0.7	6.9	10.0		1.5	-33.0	200	$5
Type	Con FB	06	aaa	10	11	0	170	109	7.14	1.49	318			25.9	32%	57%	6.75				1.6	5.8	3.6		2.5	-55.0	28	$0
Health	A	07	aaa	12	10	0	169	85	5.97	1.49	323			27.6	34%	63%	5.98				1.3	4.5	3.4		1.5	-31.4	43	$4
PT/Exp	D	08	SD *	4	9	0	132	69	5.56	1.58	304	293	287	20.5	33%	66%	5.36	36	22	42	3.2	4.7	1.5	8%	1.0	-21.0	14	($1)
Consist	B	1st Half		3	5	0	80	45	5.02	1.43	295			19.3	33%	65%	4.73	38	25	38	2.3	5.1	2.2	6%	0.7	-7.4	46	$2
LIMA Plan	C	2nd Half		1	4	0	53	24	6.37	1.81	317			22.6	33%	67%	6.24	36	20	45	4.5	4.1	0.9	10%	1.5	-13.6	-34	($4)
+/- Score	-1	09	Proj	2	3	0	40	22	5.70	1.57	314			22.2	33%	66%	5.13	36	21	43	2.5	5.0	2.0	10%	1.4	-3.8	37	$0

3-6, 4.75 ERA in 85 IP at SD. Threw 22 shutout innings upon recall in May, but found it rough going after (6.39 ERA). Falling Dom, OBA and xERA history all agree that initial success was beginner's luck.

Bannister,Brian

		Yr	Tm	W	L	Sv	IP	K	ERA	WHIP	OBA	vL	vR	BF/G	H%	S%	xERA	G	L	F	Ctl	Dom	Cmd	hr/f	hr/9	RAR	BPV	R$
RH	Starter	04	aa	3	3	0	44	23	4.84	1.57	293			24.7	33%	68%	4.68				3.6	4.8	1.3		0.4	-2.7	40	$1
Age	28	05	a/a	13	5	0	154	115	3.19	1.29	266			25.0	31%	77%	3.77				2.4	6.7	2.8		0.7	21.2	81	$17
Type	Con FB	06	NYM *	5	4	0	68	40	4.78	1.52	285	286	185	21.6	31%	71%	5.25	40	15	45	3.6	5.3	1.5	9%	1.2	-2.5	16	$3
Health	C	07	KC *	13	10	0	185	87	3.84	1.22	254	281	219	24.7	27%	71%	4.74	41	19	40	2.4	4.2	1.8	8%	1.0	15.2	32	$18
PT/Exp	C	08	KC	9	16	0	183	113	5.76	1.49	294	313	274	25.2	32%	64%	4.84	37	22	41	2.9	5.6	1.9	12%	1.4	-31.9	39	$4
Consist	A	1st Half		7	7	0	103	57	4.88	1.36	276			26.0	30%	66%	4.74	40	21	39	2.6	5.0	1.9	9%	1.0	-6.8	37	$6
LIMA Plan	C+	2nd Half		2	9	0	79	56	6.91	1.66	317			24.3	34%	62%	4.96	34	23	43	3.2	6.3	2.0	15%	1.9	-25.1	41	($3)
+/- Score	17	09	Proj	6	12	0	133	79	5.01	1.45	286			24.2	31%	68%	4.88	38	21	41	2.9	5.3	1.8	10%	1.3	-7.5	34	$5

Rise in Dom brings base skills to the cusp of relevance, but little else encourages optimism. Struggles with runners on base (.940 Opp OPS in '08) a concern, and history says that he'll keep getting into those jams regularly.

Bass,Brian

		Yr	Tm	W	L	Sv	IP	K	ERA	WHIP	OBA	vL	vR	BF/G	H%	S%	xERA	G	L	F	Ctl	Dom	Cmd	hr/f	hr/9	RAR	BPV	R$
RH	Reliever	04	aa	0	4	0	36	17	10.72	2.44	393			19.3	41%	55%	9.64				5.5	4.2	0.8		1.5	-28.4	-27	($9)
Age	27	05	aa	12	8	0	165	86	5.40	1.50	300			27.0	33%	63%	4.76				2.6	4.7	1.8		0.6	-22.3	42	$5
Type	Con xGB	06	a/a	5	6	0	59	24	7.08	1.85	350			21.7	36%	62%	7.07				3.0	3.7	1.2		1.3	-18.6	-5	($2)
Health	A	07	aaa	7	3	1	103	64	5.11	1.44	294			12.1	33%	65%	4.79				2.4	5.6	2.4		0.9	-8.3	53	$5
PT/Exp	D	08	2AL	4	4	1	89	45	4.84	1.44	280	240	310	8.0	29%	69%	4.20	58	17	25	3.1	4.5	1.5	16%	1.2	-5.4	33	$3
Consist	C	1st Half		3	2	1	52	24	4.50	1.48	290			7.9	29%	75%	4.40	56	16	28	2.9	4.2	1.4	18%	1.6	-1.0	30	$2
LIMA Plan	C+	2nd Half		1	2	0	37	21	5.31	1.39	265			8.0	29%	61%	3.92	60	19	21	3.4	5.1	1.5	11%	0.7	-4.4	38	$1
+/- Score	17	09	Proj	5	5	0	96	51	4.78	1.50	291			10.6	31%	70%	4.14	58	18	24	3.1	4.8	1.5	14%	1.0	3.3	39	$3

Traded to BAL from MIN in Sept and given four starts. Showed limited potential in 19 IP sample (4.19 ERA, 6.1 Dom, 1.9 Cmd), and GB profile a plus. BPI history, though, serves as a reality check. Longshot at best.

Batista,Miguel

		Yr	Tm	W	L	Sv	IP	K	ERA	WHIP	OBA	vL	vR	BF/G	H%	S%	xERA	G	L	F	Ctl	Dom	Cmd	hr/f	hr/9	RAR	BPV	R$
RH	Reliever	04	TOR	10	13	5	198	104	4.81	1.52	269	264	285	23.2	29%	70%	4.81	52	18	29	4.4	4.7	1.1	11%	1.0	-9.3	-2	$7
Age	38	05	TOR	5	8	31	74	54	4.12	1.44	277	256	282	4.6	31%	74%	4.23	48	19	33	3.3	6.5	2.0	12%	1.1	2.3	55	$15
Type	Pwr	06	ARI	11	8	0	206	110	4.59	1.53	284	321	257	27.0	31%	71%	4.63	52	20	28	3.7	4.8	1.3	9%	0.8	-2.5	17	$7
Health	A	07	SEA	16	11	0	193	133	4.29	1.52	277	295	258	26.0	32%	73%	4.85	44	17	39	4.0	6.2	1.6	7%	0.8	5.1	27	$13
PT/Exp	A	08	SEA	4	14	1	115	73	6.26	1.86	294	293	298	12.5	32%	69%	5.67	46	20	34	6.2	5.7	0.9	14%	1.5	-27.1	-40	($4)
Consist	B	1st Half		3	10	1	72	46	6.53	1.97	306			17.5	34%	68%	5.94	45	21	35	6.5	5.8	0.9	12%	1.3	-19.3	-50	($4)
LIMA Plan	F	2nd Half		1	4	0	43	27	5.82	1.69	274			8.3	28%	70%	5.24	48	19	33	5.6	5.6	1.0	19%	1.9	-7.9	-25	($1)
+/- Score	-15	09	Proj	5	8	0	91	57	5.24	1.66	282			9.9	31%	71%	5.12	47	19	34	4.9	5.6	1.1	13%	1.3	-7.8	-7	$1

Though h%, s% and hr/f should revert and produce a minor ERA improvement, at 38, Cmd issue will be an ongoing problem. Less destructive in relief (4.56 ERA; 6.70 as SP) is the nicest thing we can say.

Bautista,Denny

		Yr	Tm	W	L	Sv	IP	K	ERA	WHIP	OBA	vL	vR	BF/G	H%	S%	xERA	G	L	F	Ctl	Dom	Cmd	hr/f	hr/9	RAR	BPV	R$
RH	Reliever	04	aa	7	8	0	144	119	5.39	1.63	292			25.2	35%	67%	5.07				4.2	7.4	1.8		0.7	-18.6	56	$2
Age	28	05	KC	2	2	0	35	23	5.88	1.51	266	288	220	22.3	31%	59%	4.00	64	13	23	4.3	5.9	1.4	8%	0.5	-6.6	31	$1
Type	Pwr FB	06	2TM *	3	12	0	121	79	7.90	2.02	336	272	294	21.4	38%	59%	5.44	49	19	32	5.3	5.9	1.1	8%	0.8	-50.6	-10	($11)
Health	D	07	COL *	5	3	0	73	54	5.80	1.90	322			5.9	39%	67%	5.82	30	27	42	5.1	6.7	1.3	1%	0.1	-12.3	-8	($1)
PT/Exp	D	08	2TM	4	4	0	60	44	5.22	1.71	264	279	275	5.5	30%	70%	5.88	37	17	46	6.3	6.6	1.0	7%	0.9	-6.8	-36	$1
Consist	A	1st Half		0	1	0	20	10	3.20	1.52	224			5.1	25%	79%	6.94	31	8	61	6.4	4.6	0.7	3%	0.5	2.7	-82	$1
LIMA Plan	C	2nd Half		4	3	0	41	34	6.21	1.80	282			5.6	33%	66%	5.37	40	21	39	6.2	7.5	1.2	10%	1.1	-9.5	-14	$0
+/- Score	-38	09	Proj	3	4	3	58	41	5.74	1.78	291			6.8	34%	67%	5.67	41	17	42	5.6	6.4	1.1	5%	0.6	-9.2	-17	$0

Surprise winner of DET setup job in March (12 K, 3 BB). Unsurprisingly, walked 12 batters in first 12 April innings, en route to another lost season. Five years, 433 IP, 6.17 ERA, -94.9 RAR. Yet still employed.

Beam,T.J.

		Yr	Tm	W	L	Sv	IP	K	ERA	WHIP	OBA	vL	vR	BF/G	H%	S%	xERA	G	L	F	Ctl	Dom	Cmd	hr/f	hr/9	RAR	BPV	R$
RH	Reliever	04		0	0	0	0	0	0.00	0.00																		
Age	28	05		0	0	0	0	0	0.00	0.00																		
Type	xFB	06	a/a	6	0	4	73	53	1.78	1.17	212			8.1	26%	85%	2.37				3.7	6.5	1.8		0.3	24.8	81	$13
Health	A	07	aaa	4	3	3	47	36	5.03	1.56	322			7.3	37%	71%	6.03				2.0	6.9	3.4		1.4	-3.3	62	$3
PT/Exp	D	08	PIT *	4	3	6	89	51	4.53	1.50	276	310	210	6.3	30%	71%	5.59	36	13	51	3.8	5.2	1.4	6%	0.9	-2.9	5	$5
Consist	F	1st Half		2	2	4	44	28	3.81	1.48	267			6.7	30%	75%	5.98	23	15	62	4.1	5.8	1.4	4%	0.7	2.5	-6	$3
LIMA Plan	C+	2nd Half		2	1	2	45	23	5.25	1.51	284			6.0	30%	67%	5.64	38	13	50	3.5	4.6	1.3	7%	1.1	-5.4	4	$1
+/- Score	-44	09	Proj	4	2	0	65	42	4.60	1.47	286			6.7	32%	70%	5.14	38	13	50	3.1	5.9	1.9	7%	1.0	-6.3	38	$3

2-2, 4.14 ERA in 46 IP at PIT. MLB numbers helped by 26% hit rate; 14 BPV better reflects MLB struggle. Some success in minors (3.09 ERA, 2.9 Cmd) gives a bit of hope for an adjustment.

Beckett,Josh

		Yr	Tm	W	L	Sv	IP	K	ERA	WHIP	OBA	vL	vR	BF/G	H%	S%	xERA	G	L	F	Ctl	Dom	Cmd	hr/f	hr/9	RAR	BPV	R$
RH	Starter	04	FLA	9	9	0	156	152	3.80	1.22	237	281	192	24.9	30%	71%	3.57	46	17	37	3.1	8.8	2.8	10%	0.9	8.8	98	$16
Age	28	05	FLA	15	8	0	178	166	3.38	1.18	233	217	252	25.2	29%	73%	3.61	43	22	36	2.9	8.4	2.9	8%	0.7	18.9	92	$22
Type	Pwr	06	BOS	16	11	0	204	158	5.02	1.30	249	251	238	26.1	27%	66%	4.10	45	17	38	3.3	7.0	2.1	16%	1.6	-11.8	60	$18
Health	C	07	BOS	20	7	0	201	194	3.27	1.14	250	255	235	27.2	32%	74%	3.26	47	16	37	1.8	8.7	4.9	8%	0.8	30.5	133	$31
PT/Exp	A	08	BOS	12	10	0	174	172	4.03	1.19	260	260	252	26.5	33%	68%	3.25	41	25	34	1.8	8.9	5.1	11%	0.9	6.9	131	$20
Consist	A	1st Half		7	5	0	101	101	3.65	1.12	246			27.2	31%	71%	3.27	40	22	38	1.8	9.0	5.1	11%	1.1	8.6	132	$13
LIMA Plan	C+	2nd Half		5	5	0	73	71	4.54	1.28	279			25.7	35%	65%	3.21	42	29	29	1.7	8.7	5.1	10%	0.7	-1.8	131	$7
+/- Score	47	09	Proj	14	10	0	183	173	3.69	1.21	256			26.0	32%	72%	3.40	44	22	35	2.1	8.5	4.0	11%	0.9	23.1	118	$23

A stiff back, bouts with arm numbness and strained oblique yielded... perhaps his best BPI season. The risk isn't poor results, but reduced IP. ERA will improve even if skills regress, but health remains crucial.

Bedard,Erik

		Yr	Tm	W	L	Sv	IP	K	ERA	WHIP	OBA	vL	vR	BF/G	H%	S%	xERA	G	L	F	Ctl	Dom	Cmd	hr/f	hr/9	RAR	BPV	R$
LH	Starter	04	BAL	6	10	0	137	121	4.60	1.60	278	277	269	23.0	34%	72%	4.80	38	19	42	4.7	7.9	1.7	7%	0.9	-2.8	33	$5
Age	30	05	BAL	6	8	0	141	125	4.02	1.39	259	252	263	25.3	32%	72%	4.15	40	23	37	3.6	8.0	2.2	7%	0.6	6.2	63	$11
Type	Pwr	06	BAL	15	11	0	196	171	3.76	1.35	262	200	272	25.4	32%	73%	3.69	49	21	30	3.2	7.8	2.5	9%	0.7	19.2	83	$21
Health	F	07	BAL	13	5	0	182	221	3.16	1.09	216	229	208	26.1	29%	75%	2.81	48	17	35	2.8	10.9	3.9	13%	0.9	30.1	146	$29
PT/Exp	A	08	SEA	6	4	0	81	72	3.67	1.32	235	253	224	22.9	28%	76%	4.31	40	17	43	4.1	8.0	1.9	9%	1.0	6.8	51	$9
Consist	C	1st Half		5	4	0	76	66	3.79	1.30	233			22.9	28%	74%	4.32	40	17	43	4.0	7.8	1.9	9%	0.9	5.2	50	$8
LIMA Plan	B	2nd Half		1	0	0	5	6	1.80	1.60	262			22.6	33%	100%	4.19	38	15	46	5.4	10.8	2.0	17%	1.8	1.6	65	$1
+/- Score	-9	09	Proj	10	8	0	160	150	3.78	1.31	245			24.1	30%	73%	3.94	43	18	39	3.6	8.5	2.4	9%	0.8	9.5	77	$16

Injured shoulder in April; didn't tell team until July. More walks and fewer GB were the effects; most other BPI stable. Surgery less intrusive then anticipated and a March return likely. Could start slow, but expect rebound.

Beimel,Joe

		Yr	Tm	W	L	Sv	IP	K	ERA	WHIP	OBA	vL	vR	BF/G	H%	S%	xERA	G	L	F	Ctl	Dom	Cmd	hr/f	hr/9	RAR	BPV	R$
LH	Reliever	04	aaa	2	4	2	62	37	8.71	2.02	361			6.3	39%	58%	8.28				3.8	5.4	1.4		1.8	-33.4	-10	($7)
Age	32	05	aaa	1	2	0	52	29	4.08	1.61	301			4.9	34%	74%	4.82				3.5	5.0	1.4		0.4	1.5	43	$1
Type		06	LA *	5	1	2	83	37	2.73	1.26	252	234	277	4.8	27%	81%	4.37	57	11	32	2.8	4.0	1.5	8%	0.8	18.0	33	$9
Health	A	07	LA	4	2	1	67	39	3.88	1.29	249	188	294	3.4	29%	67%	4.53	48	18	35	3.2	5.2	1.6	1%	0.1	4.5	33	$6
PT/Exp	D	08	LA	5	1	0	49	32	2.02	1.45	266	278	263	3.0	32%	85%	4.66	47	19	34	3.9	5.9	1.5	0%	0.0	13.6	27	$6
Consist	A	1st Half		3	0	0	25	18	1.08	1.40	262			2.9	32%	91%	4.04	56	16	29	3.6	6.5	1.8	0%	0.0	9.8	53	$4
LIMA Plan	D+	2nd Half		2	1	0	24	14	3.00	1.50	270			3.1	32%	78%	5.29	39	22	39	4.1	5.2	1.3	0%	0.0	3.8	0	$2
+/- Score	-99	09	Proj	3	2	0	54	31	4.04	1.42	267			3.5	30%	72%	4.69	48	18	34	3.5	5.2	1.5	7%	0.7	-2.3	24	$3

Continues to out-pitch BPI, in part by 103-game no-HR streak. Low usage keeps fantasy impact negligible should this craziness continue. It won't. Doubling his ERA isn't even going out on much of a limb.

BRENT HERSHEY

Belisle,Matt

		Yr	Tm	W	L	Sv	IP	K	ERA	WHIP	OBA	vL	vR	BF/G	H%	S%	xERA	G	L	F	Ctl	Dom	Cmd	hr/f	hr/9	RAR	BPV	R$
RH	Reliever	04	aaa	9	11	0	162	89	5.88	1.60	316			26.2	34%	64%	5.66				2.7	4.9	1.8		1.0	-30.8	30	($0)
Age	28	05	CIN	4	8	1	85	59	4.44	1.49	296	331	273	6.3	33%	73%	3.89	52	21	26	2.7	6.2	2.3	15%	1.2	-2.0	68	$4
Type	Con	06	CIN	2	0	0	40	26	3.60	1.55	276	240	295	6.0	30%	81%	4.80	48	17	35	4.3	5.9	1.4	11%	1.1	4.4	16	$2
Health	C	07	CIN	8	9	0	178	125	5.32	1.44	297	298	303	25.8	33%	66%	4.23	42	22	36	2.2	6.3	2.9	12%	1.3	-19.6	75	$6
PT/Exp	C	08	CIN *	7	5	4	77	36	6.13	1.73	345	296	419	10.8	38%	63%	4.49	51	26	23	2.2	4.2	1.9	8%	0.6	-17.6	45	$1
Consist	A	1st Half		6	4	0	60	28	6.62	1.75	358			14.7	39%	61%	4.38	51	26	23	1.6	4.2	2.6	9%	0.8	-17.3	60	($1)
LIMA Plan	C+	2nd Half		1	1	4	17	9	4.39	1.67	296			5.5	34%	71%					4.4	4.5	1.0		0.0	-0.2	45	$2
+/- Score	36	09	Proj	4	3	0	65	37	4.88	1.52	295			8.7	33%	68%	4.59	48	21	31	3.1	5.2	1.7	7%	0.7	-2.0	36	$2

1-4, 7.28 ERA in 30 IP at CIN. A SP in CIN, spent balance as reliever in AAA, where results a bit better (4.26 ERA, 2.4 Cmd). Aug knee surgery complicates matters. Marginal Dom history makes a step forward unlikely.

Bell,Heath

		Yr	Tm	W	L	Sv	IP	K	ERA	WHIP	OBA	vL	vR	BF/G	H%	S%	xERA	G	L	F	Ctl	Dom	Cmd	hr/f	hr/9	RAR	BPV	R$
RH	Reliever	04	a/a	3	1	16	57	50	4.34	1.49	263			5.5	32%	71%	4.29				4.3	7.9	1.8		0.7	0.0	67	$8
Age	31	05	NYM	1	3	0	46	43	5.65	1.49	301	303	288	4.9	38%	61%	3.69	45	24	31	2.5	8.4	3.3	7%	0.6	-8.0	105	$0
Type	Pwr	06	NYM *	3	3	12	72	79	3.59	1.49	301	308	348	6.1	39%	78%	2.95	51	26	23	2.5	9.8	4.0	15%	0.9	8.0	139	$10
Health	A	07	SD	6	4	2	94	102	2.02	0.96	185	216	157	4.5	26%	79%	2.50	59	19	23	2.9	9.8	3.4	6%	0.3	27.8	135	$18
PT/Exp	C	08	SD	6	6	0	78	71	3.58	1.21	231	207	254	4.3	29%	71%	3.68	46	20	35	3.2	8.2	2.5	7%	0.6	6.7	84	$9
Consist	B	1st Half		6	3	0	46	36	2.17	1.01	204			4.3	25%	80%	3.62	48	17	36	2.6	7.1	2.8	4%	0.4	11.9	84	$9
LIMA Plan	A	2nd Half		0	3	0	32	35	5.57	1.49	266			4.4	35%	62%	3.75	43	24	33	4.2	9.8	2.3	10%	0.8	-5.2	83	$0
+/- Score	0	09	Proj	4	5	13	73	74	3.70	1.26	243			4.7	32%	71%	3.32	49	21	30	3.2	9.1	2.8	8%	0.6	9.2	104	$12

Is he Hoffman's successor? PRO: Three seasons of closer-worthy BPV; strong Dom and GB tendency. CON: 2H Ctl, overall regression raises issue of '07 IP spike. Still has potential saves upside.

Bennett,Jeff

		Yr	Tm	W	L	Sv	IP	K	ERA	WHIP	OBA	vL	vR	BF/G	H%	S%	xERA	G	L	F	Ctl	Dom	Cmd	hr/f	hr/9	RAR	BPV	R$
RH	Reliever	04	MIL	1	5	0	71	45	4.81	1.46	280	291	268	5.2	30%	72%	4.65	45	16	38	3.3	5.7	1.7	13%	1.5	-4.8	37	$1
Age	28	05	aaa	2	3	12	62	49	3.22	1.15	213			5.2	25%	75%	2.94				3.5	7.0	2.0		0.9	8.3	70	$10
Type	xGB	06		0	0	0	0	0	0.00	0.00																		
Health	F	07	ATL *	5	6	1	108	52	4.82	1.74	310			11.2	34%	73%	4.52	56	26	18	4.3	4.4	1.0	14%	0.8	-5.3	-3	$0
PT/Exp	D	08	ATL	3	7	3	97	68	3.70	1.37	239	269	228	5.8	28%	73%	3.70	64	15	21	4.3	6.3	1.4	8%	0.5	6.8	38	$7
Consist	B	1st Half		1	4	2	58	44	4.19	1.45	252			6.7	29%	72%	4.01	58	16	26	4.5	6.8	1.5	11%	0.8	0.6	37	$3
LIMA Plan	C	2nd Half		2	3	1	39	24	2.98	1.25	219			4.8	26%	73%	3.11	73	15	13	4.1	5.5	1.3	0%	0.0	6.3	38	$4
+/- Score	-23	09	Proj	3	5	0	83	53	3.90	1.43	259			6.2	30%	73%	3.95	61	16	23	4.0	5.7	1.4	10%	0.7	4.0	34	$4

Improved GB rate drove sub-4 ERA and helped make up for Ctl issues. Has found a home in bullpen -- pummelled for a 6.48 ERA in 4 spot starts. Poor bet to improve unless he suddenly regains 2.0 Cmd level.

Benoit,Joaquin

		Yr	Tm	W	L	Sv	IP	K	ERA	WHIP	OBA	vL	vR	BF/G	H%	S%	xERA	G	L	F	Ctl	Dom	Cmd	hr/f	hr/9	RAR	BPV	R$
RH	Reliever	04	TEX	3	5	0	103	95	5.68	1.40	280	249	311	15.9	32%	63%	4.19	34	19	47	2.7	8.3	3.1	13%	1.7	-15.8	88	$4
Age	31	05	TEX	4	4	0	87	78	3.72	1.23	220	227	196	11.3	26%	72%	4.39	33	19	48	3.9	8.1	2.1	8%	0.9	6.9	50	$9
Type	Pwr xFB	06	TEX	1	1	0	79	85	4.89	1.34	233	191	245	6.0	31%	62%	4.04	37	19	44	4.3	9.7	2.2	5%	0.6	-3.2	73	$5
Health	C	07	TEX	7	4	6	82	87	2.85	1.17	227	172	268	4.8	30%	78%	3.51	37	24	39	3.1	9.5	3.1	7%	0.7	16.7	104	$15
PT/Exp	C	08	TEX	3	2	1	45	43	5.00	1.67	240	184	282	4.7	29%	72%	5.77	27	17	56	7.0	8.6	1.2	9%	1.2	-3.6	-29	$2
Consist	C	1st Half		3	2	1	34	28	5.82	1.71	256			4.8	29%	68%	6.12	24	20	55	6.6	7.4	1.1	9%	1.3	-6.2	-43	$1
LIMA Plan	C+	2nd Half		0	0	0	11	15	2.45	1.55	184			4.5	27%	88%	4.70	38	4	58	8.2	12.3	1.5	7%	0.8	2.6	16	$1
+/- Score	-40	09	Proj	3	2	3	58	55	4.50	1.40	241			6.0	30%	69%	4.61	34	17	49	4.5	8.5	1.9	8%	0.9	-1.3	44	$5

A "tired arm" surfaced in early March; season-long shoulder soreness followed. Rangers grew tired of all the walks and FB. Has shown skills, but repeated health woes (DL in 2006 -- shoulder) elevate risk.

Bergmann,Jason

		Yr	Tm	W	L	Sv	IP	K	ERA	WHIP	OBA	vL	vR	BF/G	H%	S%	xERA	G	L	F	Ctl	Dom	Cmd	hr/f	hr/9	RAR	BPV	R$
RH	Starter	04		0	0	0	0	0	0.00	0.00																		
Age	27	05	a/a	5	2	7	74	66	2.31	1.12	212			7.3	26%	84%	2.80				3.3	8.0	2.4		0.9	18.2	87	$13
Type	xFB	06	WAS *	8	4	4	124	105	5.38	1.54	289	255	353	10.1	34%	67%	4.68	32	24	45	3.5	7.6	2.2	10%	1.2	-13.6	53	$6
Health	B	07	WAS *	8	7	0	139	103	4.02	1.23	238	263	200	22.2	27%	71%	4.64	33	16	50	3.1	6.7	2.1	9%	1.2	7.0	48	$13
PT/Exp	D	08	WAS *	4	13	0	169	118	4.94	1.43	277	309	243	21.0	30%	69%	4.90	30	24	46	3.1	6.3	2.0	11%	1.4	-14.0	37	$4
Consist	A	1st Half		3	7	0	97	77	4.25	1.34	275			24.3	31%	73%	4.59	29	20	51	2.5	7.2	2.9	9%	1.3	0.2	69	$5
LIMA Plan	C+	2nd Half		1	6	0	72	41	5.87	1.54	280			17.8	29%	65%	5.42	31	27	42	4.0	5.1	1.3	13%	1.6	-14.3	-7	($2)
+/- Score	-6	09	Proj	4	5	0	87	64	4.66	1.39	266			15.6	30%	70%	4.80	32	22	47	3.3	6.6	2.0	10%	1.3	-5.0	39	$4

2-11, 5.09 ERA in 140 IP at WAS. Did escalating workload contribute to hefty 1H/2H BPV swing? Same happened in 2007 (1H BPV, 85; 2H, 38). There's upside here (again), but FB, stamina issues still unresolved.

Betancourt,Rafael

		Yr	Tm	W	L	Sv	IP	K	ERA	WHIP	OBA	vL	vR	BF/G	H%	S%	xERA	G	L	F	Ctl	Dom	Cmd	hr/f	hr/9	RAR	BPV	R$
RH	Reliever	04	CLE	5	6	4	66	76	3.94	1.34	276	272	264	4.2	37%	73%	3.50	38	19	44	2.4	10.3	4.2	9%	1.0	4.0	136	$9
Age	34	05	CLE	4	3	1	67	73	2.81	1.10	231	264	204	5.0	31%	77%	3.42	33	22	44	2.3	9.8	4.3	6%	0.7	12.9	126	$11
Type	Pwr xFB	06	CLE	3	4	3	56	48	3.84	1.12	247	221	254	4.5	29%	70%	4.12	23	25	51	1.8	7.7	4.4	8%	1.1	5.0	92	$8
Health	B	07	CLE	5	1	3	79	80	1.48	0.76	186	241	147	4.3	25%	84%	3.28	27	20	54	1.0	9.1	8.9	4%	0.5	29.6	141	$19
PT/Exp	C	08	CLE	3	4	4	71	64	5.07	1.42	275	252	295	4.5	32%	68%	4.52	29	21	50	3.2	8.1	2.6	10%	1.4	-6.3	67	$5
Consist	C	1st Half		2	4	4	37	37	6.13	1.55	303			4.4	36%	64%	4.33	30	21	50	2.9	9.1	3.1	13%	1.7	-8.1	92	$2
LIMA Plan	A	2nd Half		1	0	0	34	27	3.94	1.28	243			4.5	28%	73%	4.72	28	22	50	3.4	7.1	2.1	8%	1.0	1.7	41	$3
+/- Score	17	09	Proj	3	2	3	58	54	3.72	1.17	245			4.5	30%	72%	4.03	28	22	50	2.3	8.4	3.6	9%	1.1	2.8	94	$8

The case for the value of hr/f. In years where it is less than 7%, the result is a sub-3.00 ERA. When closer to the 10% norm, ERA hovers around 4.00. The more FB, the higher the risk. Here, it likely keeps SVs at bay.

Bierd,Randor

		Yr	Tm	W	L	Sv	IP	K	ERA	WHIP	OBA	vL	vR	BF/G	H%	S%	xERA	G	L	F	Ctl	Dom	Cmd	hr/f	hr/9	RAR	BPV	R$
RH	Reliever	04		0	0	0	0	0	0.00	0.00																		
Age	25	05	aa	1	3	0	22	9	7.77	1.82	333			26.1	35%	57%	6.68				3.7	3.7	1.0		1.2	-9.4	-5	($2)
Type	Pwr	06		0	0	0	0	0	0.00	0.00																		
Health	C	07	aa	3	2	1	45	44	4.72	1.09	235			6.7	31%	53%	2.44				2.1	8.7	4.2		0.2	-1.4	143	$5
PT/Exp	F	08	BAL	0	2	0	37	25	4.90	1.83	317	333	301	6.0	36%	73%	5.29	43	22	36	4.7	6.1	1.3	7%	0.7	-2.5	5	($1)
Consist	F	1st Half		0	1	0	13	5	2.03	1.35	257			6.3	27%	88%	4.97	49	19	32	3.4	3.4	1.0	7%	0.7	3.8	-4	$1
LIMA Plan	D	2nd Half		0	1	0	23	20	6.54	2.09	347			5.9	42%	68%	5.45	39	23	38	5.4	7.7	1.4	7%	0.8	-6.3	10	($2)
+/- Score	0	09	Proj	1	2	0	43	34	4.81	1.51	275			6.0	33%	68%	4.49	43	22	35	4.0	7.1	1.8	6%	0.6	-0.4	42	$1

Rule 5 pick from DET, TJS in '05; spent '06 rehabbing in A-ball. Shoulder injury cost him nearly 3 mos in '08. Dom history points to possible future bullpen role, though much seasoning still required.

Billingsley,Chad

		Yr	Tm	W	L	Sv	IP	K	ERA	WHIP	OBA	vL	vR	BF/G	H%	S%	xERA	G	L	F	Ctl	Dom	Cmd	hr/f	hr/9	RAR	BPV	R$
RH	Starter	04	aa	4	1	0	42	42	3.26	1.31	224			22.3	30%	74%	2.85				4.5	9.0	2.0		0.2	5.6	100	$6
Age	24	05	aa	13	6	0	146	136	3.64	1.16	229			21.3	29%	70%	2.99				2.9	8.4	2.9		0.7	12.0	98	$19
Type	Pwr	06	LA *	13	7	0	160	128	3.79	1.47	247	328	213	22.7	29%	76%	4.53	48	16	36	4.9	7.2	1.5	8%	0.8	13.7	25	$13
Health	A	07	LA	12	5	0	147	141	3.31	1.33	240	277	210	14.5	30%	78%	3.99	41	20	39	3.9	8.6	2.2	10%	0.9	20.3	69	$17
PT/Exp	B	08	LA	16	10	0	201	201	3.14	1.34	249	274	225	24.4	32%	78%	3.51	49	20	31	3.6	9.0	2.5	8%	0.6	28.0	92	$22
Consist	B	1st Half		7	7	0	96	102	3.38	1.34	237			22.7	31%	76%	3.58	49	18	33	4.2	9.6	2.3	8%	0.7	10.6	85	$10
LIMA Plan	D+	2nd Half		9	3	0	105	99	2.92	1.33	260			26.2	33%	80%	3.45	49	22	29	3.0	8.5	2.8	8%	0.6	17.4	99	$12
+/- Score	20	09	Proj	17	8	0	203	193	3.28	1.34	245			20.6	31%	77%	3.81	46	20	34	3.8	8.6	2.2	8%	0.7	13.3	75	$22

As solid a profile as one could want from a 24-yr old starter. Consistent growth in all areas reduces risk; 2H skills spike a great sign. Borderline Ctl is the only real qualm. It's a small one. UP: 20 W, sub-3.00 ERA, Cy.

Blackburn,Nick

		Yr	Tm	W	L	Sv	IP	K	ERA	WHIP	OBA	vL	vR	BF/G	H%	S%	xERA	G	L	F	Ctl	Dom	Cmd	hr/f	hr/9	RAR	BPV	R$
RH	Starter	04		0	0	0	0	0	0.00	0.00																		
Age	27	05	a/a	2	4	0	63	30	3.14	1.21	262			26.0	29%	74%	3.30				1.9	4.3	2.3		0.4	9.0	64	$5
Type	Con	06	aa	7	8	0	132	66	6.38	1.70	327			20.3	35%	62%	6.03				2.9	4.5	1.5		1.0	-30.3	18	($2)
Health	A	07	a/a	10	4	0	148	58	3.26	1.26	282			24.8	30%	75%	3.88				1.3	3.5	2.6		0.6	22.0	57	$14
PT/Exp	C	08	MIN	11	11	0	193	96	4.05	1.36	291	295	289	25.1	31%	73%	4.46	45	21	34	1.8	4.5	2.5	10%	1.1	7.1	54	$12
Consist	C	1st Half		6	4	0	98	54	4.05	1.36	300			26.1	33%	73%	4.25	45	21	34	1.4	5.0	3.6	9%	1.0	3.5	75	$7
LIMA Plan	D+	2nd Half		5	7	0	96	42	4.05	1.36	282			24.1	29%	74%	4.67	45	21	34	2.3	4.0	1.8	11%	1.1	3.5	33	$6
+/- Score	6	09	Proj	9	10	0	174	80	4.34	1.37	291			24.1	31%	71%	4.57	45	21	34	1.9	4.1	2.2	10%	1.0	-3.2	46	$10

1H/2H results a carbon copy, but skills tell a different story. Even soft-tossers feel effects of long season; recent IP spikes could be the key. Induces GB and has maintained Cmd, but everybody gets hits. Caution.

BRENT HERSHEY

Blanton,Joe				W	L	Sv	IP	K	ERA	WHIP	OBA	vL	vR	BF/G	H%	S%	xERA	G	L	F	Ctl	Dom	Cmd	hr/f	hr/9	RAR	BPV	R$
RH	Starter	04	aaa	11	8	0	176	121	4.40	1.39	299			27.1	35%	69%	4.54				1.7	6.2	3.7		0.7	-1.1	89	$11
Age	28	05	OAK	12	12	0	201	116	3.54	1.22	239	228	246	25.2	26%	75%	4.45	46	17	38	3.0	5.2	1.7	10%	1.0	20.7	36	$19
Type	Con	06	OAK	16	12	0	194	107	4.82	1.54	306	314	304	27.1	34%	69%	4.87	43	20	37	2.7	5.0	1.8	7%	0.8	-6.3	38	$10
Health	A	07	OAK	14	10	0	230	140	3.95	1.22	270	291	248	28.0	31%	68%	3.93	47	21	32	1.6	5.5	3.5	7%	0.6	15.7	81	$22
PT/Exp	A	08	2TM	9	12	0	198	111	4.69	1.40	275	256	286	25.9	30%	68%	4.65	44	20	35	3.0	5.1	1.7	9%	1.0	-9.3	32	$8
Consist	B	1st Half		4	11	0	114	55	4.97	1.43	288			27.5	31%	66%	4.71	47	19	34	2.6	4.3	1.7	9%	0.9	-9.4	33	$3
LIMA Plan	C	2nd Half		5	1	0	84	56	4.30	1.36	255			23.9	28%	71%	4.58	40	23	37	3.5	6.0	1.7	10%	1.1	0.1	31	$5
+/- Score	-2	09	Proj	11	9	0	189	112	4.39	1.36	275			26.0	30%	69%	4.46	44	20	35	2.6	5.3	2.0	8%	0.9	-2.0	48	$12

Workhorse defined: averaged 205 IP over past four seasons. '05, '06 and '08 skills are remarkably similar -- but amazingly flat. 2007 was his (short-lived) shot at the Derby, and now it's back to the fields.

Blevins,Jerry				W	L	Sv	IP	K	ERA	WHIP	OBA	vL	vR	BF/G	H%	S%	xERA	G	L	F	Ctl	Dom	Cmd	hr/f	hr/9	RAR	BPV	R$
LH	Reliever	04		0	0	0	0	0	0.00	0.00																		
Age	25	05		0	0	0	0	0	0.00	0.00																		
Type	Pwr	06		0	0	0	0	0	0.00	0.00																		
Health	A	07	aa	4	5	4	54	57	2.81	1.17	249			5.4	33%	77%	3.10				2.1	9.5	4.5		0.5	11.0	141	$10
PT/Exp	F	08	OAK *	3	5	10	70	63	3.11	1.25	259	193	256	4.5	32%	77%	3.72	43	18	38	2.4	8.1	3.4	7%	0.7	10.7	103	$11
Consist	B	1st Half		2	1	10	31	27	2.89	1.25	282			4.8	34%	81%					1.3	7.8	6.1		1.0	5.6	144	$7
LIMA Plan	A	2nd Half		1	4	0	39	36	3.28	1.25	239			4.4	31%	74%	3.85	43	18	38	3.3	8.3	2.5	5%	0.5	5.1	83	$4
+/- Score	18	09	Proj	4	4	0	58	56	3.41	1.22	255			4.8	32%	74%	3.54	43	18	38	2.3	8.7	3.7	8%	0.8	6.3	115	$7

1-3, 3.11 ERA in 38 IP at OAK. Deadly against LH (.482 OPS), but showed enough overall to warrant a mention in post-Street conversation. Closer experience in AAA, 100+ BPV stuff a plus. He's worthy in any role.

Boggs,Mitch				W	L	Sv	IP	K	ERA	WHIP	OBA	vL	vR	BF/G	H%	S%	xERA	G	L	F	Ctl	Dom	Cmd	hr/f	hr/9	RAR	BPV	R$
RH	Starter	04		0	0	0	0	0	0.00	0.00																		
Age	25	05		0	0	0	0	0	0.00	0.00																		
Type	GB	06		0	0	0	0	0	0.00	0.00																		
Health	A	07	aa	11	7	0	152	100	4.45	1.65	307			26.7	35%	75%	5.53				3.6	5.9	1.6		0.9	0.2	36	$6
PT/Exp	D	08	STL *	12	5	0	159	79	4.68	1.44	267	321	283	23.9	28%	69%	4.66	52	19	29	3.7	4.4	1.2	10%	0.9	-8.0	9	$7
Consist	B	1st Half		8	1	0	94	46	3.88	1.32	253			23.4	28%	71%	4.62	50	18	32	3.3	4.4	1.3	6%	0.6	4.5	19	$8
LIMA Plan	C	2nd Half		4	4	0	65	32	5.82	1.62	286			24.7	30%	66%	4.67	56	20	24	4.4	4.5	1.0	17%	1.3	-12.5	-5	($0)
+/- Score	-16	09	Proj	2	1	0	30	16	4.88	1.53	284			26.2	31%	69%	4.52	54	19	27	3.7	4.9	1.3	11%	0.9	-0.7	21	$1

3-2, 7.41 ERA in 34 IP at STL. Didn't fool anyone in the majors, though minor-league skills more in line with history (5.8 Dom, 1.8 Cmd). Outside of small-sample GB rate, little hope for improvement.

*

Bonderman,Jeremy				W	L	Sv	IP	K	ERA	WHIP	OBA	vL	vR	BF/G	H%	S%	xERA	G	L	F	Ctl	Dom	Cmd	hr/f	hr/9	RAR	BPV	R$
RH	Starter	04	DET	11	13	0	184	168	4.89	1.31	245	255	223	23.6	29%	65%	3.73	48	18	34	3.6	8.2	2.3	14%	1.2	-10.4	78	$14
Age	26	05	DET	14	13	0	189	145	4.57	1.35	272	287	249	27.9	31%	68%	3.94	48	19	33	2.7	6.9	2.5	11%	1.0	-4.7	77	$15
Type	Pwr	06	DET	14	8	0	214	202	4.08	1.30	262	284	235	26.6	33%	70%	3.47	48	20	32	2.7	8.5	3.2	9%	0.8	12.6	106	$23
Health	F	07	DET	11	9	0	174	145	5.01	1.38	282	268	291	26.8	33%	66%	3.80	48	18	34	2.5	7.5	3.0	12%	1.2	-10.8	94	$12
PT/Exp	A	08	DET	3	4	0	71	44	4.29	1.56	272	291	255	26.6	30%	75%	5.04	47	16	37	4.5	5.6	1.2	10%	1.1	0.5	3	$3
Consist	B	1st Half		3	4	0	71	44	4.29	1.56	272			26.6	30%	75%	5.04	47	16	37	4.5	5.6	1.2	10%	1.1	0.5	3	$3
LIMA Plan	B	2nd Half		0	0	0	0	0	0.00	0.00																		
+/- Score	-17	09	Proj	9	8	0	149	118	4.47	1.40	268			26.8	31%	70%	4.09	48	18	35	3.3	7.1	2.1	11%	1.0	6.1	64	$11

June surgery to remove a rib responsible for a blood clot clouds future, though DET optimistic about a spring return. Elite pre-injury skills, youth on his side, but don't leave home w/o March news/noise detector.

Bonser,Boof				W	L	Sv	IP	K	ERA	WHIP	OBA	vL	vR	BF/G	H%	S%	xERA	G	L	F	Ctl	Dom	Cmd	hr/f	hr/9	RAR	BPV	R$
RH	Reliever	04	a/a	13	10	0	161	136	5.31	1.56	297			25.8	35%	69%	5.57				3.4	7.6	2.3		1.3	-19.2	49	$7
Age	27	05	aaa	11	9	0	160	147	4.89	1.47	280			25.1	33%	70%	4.99				3.3	8.3	2.5		1.3	-11.6	62	$9
Type	Pwr	06	MIN *	13	10	0	186	154	4.21	1.37	266	251	280	25.0	31%	72%	4.30	42	15	43	3.1	7.4	2.4	9%	1.1	8.1	69	$17
Health	A	07	MIN	8	12	0	173	136	5.10	1.53	290	349	214	24.8	33%	70%	4.37	45	17	38	3.4	7.1	2.1	13%	1.4	-12.7	59	$7
PT/Exp	B	08	MIN	3	7	0	118	97	5.93	1.48	294	315	260	11.1	34%	61%	4.23	41	20	39	2.7	7.4	2.7	11%	1.2	-23.2	78	$2
Consist	A	1st Half		3	6	0	78	57	6.23	1.51	299			17.3	34%	59%	4.56	39	21	40	2.8	6.6	2.4	9%	1.0	-18.1	61	$0
LIMA Plan	B+	2nd Half		0	1	0	40	40	5.36	1.41	284			6.5	34%	66%	3.62	44	20	37	2.7	8.9	3.3	16%	1.6	-5.0	110	$1
+/- Score	68	09	Proj	7	5	0	123	104	4.63	1.43	279			16.6	33%	70%	4.11	43	19	38	3.0	7.6	2.5	11%	1.2	4.7	77	$8

Unfortunate h%/s%, 2H hr/f obscures solid growth season. Aired it out in 2H move to relief, but upside is real regardless of the role. One to place on your end-game short list.
UP: SP role, sub-4.00 ERA

Borowski,Joe				W	L	Sv	IP	K	ERA	WHIP	OBA	vL	vR	BF/G	H%	S%	xERA	G	L	F	Ctl	Dom	Cmd	hr/f	hr/9	RAR	BPV	R$
RH	Reliever	04	CHC	2	4	9	21	17	8.10	1.99	312	344	281	4.7	36%	59%	6.07	33	21	46	6.4	7.3	1.1	9%	1.3	-10.0	-31	$1
Age	38	05	2TM	1	5	0	46	27	4.49	1.08	226	192	244	4.3	23%	64%	4.03	47	17	36	2.3	5.3	2.3	16%	1.6	-1.1	56	$3
Type	Pwr xFB	06	FLA	3	3	36	69	64	3.77	1.39	244	167	291	4.1	30%	75%	4.63	33	18	50	4.3	8.3	1.9	7%	0.9	6.1	44	$18
Health	D	07	CLE	4	5	45	66	58	5.07	1.43	294	293	286	4.1	35%	67%	4.24	34	21	45	2.3	7.9	3.4	10%	1.2	-4.6	92	$19
PT/Exp	B	08	CLE	1	3	6	17	9	7.54	1.92	338	333	333	4.5	34%	64%	6.39	23	27	50	4.3	4.9	1.1	13%	2.2	-6.6	-28	$1
Consist	C	1st Half		1	2	6	16	8	6.75	1.81	318			4.5	33%	65%	6.52	23	25	52	4.5	4.5	1.0	10%	1.7	-4.7	-39	$1
LIMA Plan	C+	2nd Half		0	1	0	1	1	17.98	3.00	515			5.9	52%	50%	3.90	25	50	25	0.0	9.0		83%	9.0	-1.7	165	($0)
+/- Score	13	09	Proj	1	1	0	15	11	4.97	1.52	281			4.3	32%	70%	5.01	32	21	47	3.7	6.8	1.8	9%	1.2	-1.1	32	$1

From Opening-Day stopper to April DL resident to August free agent, it was quite a fall. Got hammered again by h%/s% duo, though good luck can't help age and skills decline. Days as a closer are over.

Boyer,Blaine				W	L	Sv	IP	K	ERA	WHIP	OBA	vL	vR	BF/G	H%	S%	xERA	G	L	F	Ctl	Dom	Cmd	hr/f	hr/9	RAR	BPV	R$
RH	Reliever	04		0	0	0	0	0	0.00	0.00											0.0	0.0						
Age	27	05	ATL *	6	6	0	85	66	5.04	1.67	307	298	200	6.9	37%	69%	4.57	48	17	35	3.8	7.0	1.8	5%	0.5	-8.3	49	$2
Type	Pwr	06	ATL	0	0	0	0	0	0.00	0.00				2.8		40%		67	0	33	45.0	0.0	0.0	0%	0.0	0.1	-999	
Health	A	07	aaa	4	3	2	73	51	5.71	2.02	310			17.2	37%	69%	5.78				6.7	6.3	0.9		0.1	-11.3	47	($2)
PT/Exp	D	08	ATL	2	6	1	72	67	5.88	1.36	264	271	256	4.1	32%	58%	3.80	46	16	38	3.1	8.4	2.7	13%	1.3	-14.3	90	$2
Consist	D	1st Half		2	5	1	45	39	3.62	1.19	232			4.3	29%	70%	3.81	45	16	38	3.0	7.9	2.6	6%	0.6	3.6	83	$5
LIMA Plan	B	2nd Half		0	1	0	27	28	9.56	1.65	313			3.8	36%	42%	3.79	47	16	36	3.3	9.2	2.8	23%	2.3	-17.8	102	($3)
+/- Score	96	09	Proj	2	3	3	58	49	4.66	1.43	265			5.7	32%	69%	4.18	47	17	37	3.7	7.6	2.0	9%	0.9	1.2	61	$3

First look: 2H implosion, usage pattern points to a boatload of risk. Second look: 2H h%, s%, hr/f rates as one of the most unlucky combos we've seen. Steady skills throughout; LIMA material if given the chance.

Braden,Dallas				W	L	Sv	IP	K	ERA	WHIP	OBA	vL	vR	BF/G	H%	S%	xERA	G	L	F	Ctl	Dom	Cmd	hr/f	hr/9	RAR	BPV	R$
LH	Reliever	04		0	0	0	0	0	0.00	0.00																		
Age	25	05	aa	9	5	0	97	61	4.08	1.45	289			26.5	33%	71%	4.32				2.8	5.7	2.0		0.5	2.7	60	$7
Type	FB	06	aa	0	0	0	3	2	18.00	3.00	515			17.8	55%	38%	15.50				0.0	6.0			3.0	-5.0	-102	($1)
Health	A	07	OAK *	4	11	0	148	125	5.13	1.39	275	214	324	19.3	33%	64%	4.35	37	18	45	2.9	7.6	2.7	8%	0.9	-11.4	75	$7
PT/Exp	D	08	OAK *	8	5	0	125	82	3.58	1.37	277	319	272	17.8	31%	78%	4.66	38	18	44	2.6	5.9	2.3	8%	1.1	11.8	53	$11
Consist	F	1st Half		4	0	0	58	47	3.32	1.49	294			15.1	35%	79%	4.63	32	24	45	2.8	7.3	2.6	5%	0.7	7.4	65	$5
LIMA Plan	C+	2nd Half		4	5	0	67	35	3.81	1.27	261			21.5	27%	76%	4.76	40	17	43	2.4	4.8	2.0	11%	1.4	4.4	38	$6
+/- Score	-10	09	Proj	6	6	0	108	77	4.08	1.33	269			21.9	31%	72%	4.52	38	18	44	2.7	6.4	2.4	8%	1.0	-1.3	60	$9

5-4, 4.14 ERA in 72 IP at OAK. Started the season with a three-month pass on the Sacramento shuttle, but held his own (3.97 ERA) in 10 OAK starts. Potential, but Dom (5.1 in OAK) and 2H plunge say "not yet."

Bradford,Chad				W	L	Sv	IP	K	ERA	WHIP	OBA	vL	vR	BF/G	H%	S%	xERA	G	L	F	Ctl	Dom	Cmd	hr/f	hr/9	RAR	BPV	R$
RH	Reliever	04	OAK	5	7	1	59	34	4.42	1.27	235	298	211	3.6	26%	66%	3.89	61	16	23	3.7	5.2	1.4	12%	0.8	0.1	33	$5
Age	34	05	BOS	2	1	0	23	10	3.90	1.43	308	409	282	3.2	34%	72%	3.19	65	23	12	1.6	3.9	2.5	10%	0.4	1.4	71	$2
Type	Con xGB	06	NYM	4	2	2	62	45	2.90	1.16	252	250	256	3.6	31%	73%	3.02	63	16	21	1.9	6.5	3.5	3%	0.1	12.1	108	$9
Health	B	07	BAL	4	7	2	65	29	3.34	1.44	297	321	282	3.6	33%	75%	4.03	62	15	23	2.2	4.0	1.8	2%	0.1	9.3	53	$6
PT/Exp	C	08	2AL	4	3	0	59	17	2.12	1.25	261	313	255	3.6	27%	85%	3.71	67	18	16	2.3	2.6	1.1	9%	0.5	16.3	29	$7
Consist	B	1st Half		3	3	0	31	11	2.64	1.34	282			3.6	30%	82%	3.67	66	17	17	2.1	3.2	1.6	11%	0.6	6.5	46	$3
LIMA Plan	C	2nd Half		1	0	0	29	6	1.57	1.15	237			3.6	24%	88%	3.74	67	18	15	2.5	1.9	0.8	7%	0.3	9.8	11	$3
+/- Score	-79	09	Proj	3	5	0	58	23	3.57	1.31	272			3.7	29%	73%	3.73	65	17	18	2.3	3.6	1.5	8%	0.5	5.0	44	$4

All hail the groundball! Cmd, though, is in full-throttle freefall (see 2H) and now further limits his margin of error. LHers feasted again; is it a sign of things to come? xERA is steady, but degree of difficulty rising.

BRENT HERSHEY

Bray,Bill		Yr	Tm	W	L	Sv	IP	K	ERA	WHIP	OBA	vL	vR	BF/G	H%	S%	xERA	G	L	F	Ctl	Dom	Cmd	hr/f	hr/9	RAR	BPV	R$
LH	Reliever	04		0	0	0	0	0	0.00	0.00																		
Age	25	05		0	0	0	0	0	0.00	0.00																		
Type	Pwr	06	2NL *	7	3	7	81	77	4.42	1.39	273	333	252	5.1	33%	71%	3.62	44	25	31	3.0	8.5	**2.9**	13%	1.1	0.7	94	$10
Health	C	07	CIN *	4	5	1	33	39	5.95	1.50	293	158	342	4.0	40%	58%	3.62	37	23	40	3.0	10.5	**3.5**	5%	0.5	-6.2	125	$3
PT/Exp	D	08	CIN *	2	2	1	56	67	3.06	1.54	265	260	274	3.5	36%	83%	3.87	35	27	37	4.7	10.7	**2.3**	9%	0.8	8.4	81	$5
Consist	A	1st Half		2	0	1	33	36	3.01	1.46	238			3.8	32%	80%	4.12	36	28	36	5.2	9.8	**1.9**	6%	0.5	5.1	50	$3
LIMA Plan	A	2nd Half		0	2	0	23	31	3.13	1.65	302			3.1	42%	86%	3.52	34	27	39	3.9	12.1	**3.1**	13%	1.2	3.2	125	$1
+/- Score	14	09 Proj		**3**	**4**	**0**	**44**	**51**	**3.52**	**1.29**	**237**			**3.5**	**32%**	**75%**	**3.46**	**37**	**26**	**37**	**3.7**	**10.6**	**2.8**	**10%**	**0.8**	**4.7**	**104**	**$5**

2-2, 2.87 ERA in 47 IP at CIN. Late start due to bum shoulder. Ctl still spotty, LD% shows he gets hit hard. But pieces in the box for next step: h% correction coming, proven Dom, 2H skills spike. Will they be assembled?

Breslow,Craig		Yr	Tm	W	L	Sv	IP	K	ERA	WHIP	OBA	vL	vR	BF/G	H%	S%	xERA	G	L	F	Ctl	Dom	Cmd	hr/f	hr/9	RAR	BPV	R$
LH	Reliever	04		0	0	0	0	0	0.00	0.00																		
Age	28	05	SD *	2	2	0	77	62	3.04	1.30	243			5.3	30%	77%	4.06	46	20	34	3.6	7.3	**2.0**	5%	0.5	11.4	58	$6
Type	Pwr FB	06	BOS *	7	3	7	79	77	3.86	1.35	252			6.5	33%	71%	4.11	31	29	40	3.6	8.8	**2.4**	5%	0.5	6.8	70	$12
Health	A	07	aaa	2	3	1	68	59	5.84	1.72	318			6.4	38%	66%	5.92				3.6	7.8	**2.2**		1.0	-11.6	54	($0)
PT/Exp	D	08	2AL	0	2	1	47	39	1.91	1.13	204	183	221	3.9	26%	83%	4.14	42	17	42	3.6	7.5	**2.1**	2%	0.2	14.1	56	$6
Consist	D	1st Half		0	0	0	19	18	1.42	1.05	195			4.2	25%	89%	3.77	43	12	45	3.3	8.5	**2.6**	5%	0.5	6.9	85	$3
LIMA Plan	C+	2nd Half		0	2	1	28	21	2.25	1.18	210			3.7	27%	79%	4.41	41	20	39	3.9	6.7	**1.8**	0%	0.0	7.2	36	$3
+/- Score	-72	09 Proj		**1**	**2**	**0**	**44**	**37**	**3.72**	**1.36**	**251**			**4.9**	**31%**	**73%**	**4.33**	**41**	**18**	**41**	**3.7**	**7.7**	**2.1**	**6%**	**0.6**	**0.5**	**56**	**$3**

Bounced from BOS to CLE to MIN in first full MLB season. Consistent Cmd history pointed to potential success, though favorable h%, hr/f combined to overstate. Useful for now, but expect ERA/WHIP regression.

Brocail,Doug		Yr	Tm	W	L	Sv	IP	K	ERA	WHIP	OBA	vL	vR	BF/G	H%	S%	xERA	G	L	F	Ctl	Dom	Cmd	hr/f	hr/9	RAR	BPV	R$
RH	Reliever	04	TEX *	6	2	1	72	59	4.36	1.44	282	190	320	5.7	35%	68%	3.63	55	19	26	3.0	7.4	**2.5**	5%	0.4	0.6	84	$6
Age	42	05	TEX	5	3	1	73	61	5.54	1.70	304	346	267	5.5	38%	65%	4.26	49	23	27	4.2	7.5	**1.8**	3%	0.2	-10.5	50	$2
Type	Pwr	06	SD	2	2	0	28	19	4.82	1.25	255	280	228	4.7	30%	59%	4.17	40	26	33	2.6	6.1	**2.4**	3%	0.3	-1.2	59	$2
Health	F	07	SD	5	1	0	77	43	3.05	1.17	234	182	268	4.7	25%	78%	4.53	42	18	40	2.8	5.0	**1.8**	8%	0.9	13.0	35	$9
PT/Exp	D	08	HOU	7	5	2	69	64	3.93	1.22	245	305	200	4.0	30%	71%	3.78	41	17	42	2.8	8.4	**3.0**	10%	1.0	2.9	96	$9
Consist	B	1st Half		4	3	2	41	35	3.05	1.07	231			3.8	28%	73%	3.82	36	20	44	2.0	7.6	**3.9**	6%	0.7	6.2	98	$7
LIMA Plan	C+	2nd Half		3	2	0	27	29	5.26	1.46	266			4.1	32%	69%	3.69	49	14	37	3.9	9.5	**2.4**	18%	1.6	-3.3	92	$2
+/- Score	-19	09 Proj		**4**	**4**	**3**	**58**	**45**	**4.38**	**1.37**	**260**			**4.6**	**30%**	**71%**	**4.27**	**43**	**19**	**38**	**3.4**	**7.0**	**2.0**	**11%**	**1.1**	**0.5**	**55**	**$5**

Resurrected strikeout rate fueled best skills season since 1999. xERA holding steady, but he's 42 years old and FB rate is riding a five-year escalator. Odds stacked against a repeat.

Brown,Andrew		Yr	Tm	W	L	Sv	IP	K	ERA	WHIP	OBA	vL	vR	BF/G	H%	S%	xERA	G	L	F	Ctl	Dom	Cmd	hr/f	hr/9	RAR	BPV	R$
RH	Reliever	04	a/a	5	10	0	122	110	4.86	1.42	255			20.4	31%	67%	4.23				4.1	8.1	**2.0**		1.0	-7.8	66	$6
Age	28	05	aaa	4	2	4	69	71	3.51	1.05	220			5.6	28%	69%	2.65				2.3	9.2	**3.9**		0.8	6.8	126	$11
Type	Pwr xFB	06	CLE *	5	4	5	72	54	3.40	1.58	250	286	95	6.8	29%	80%	5.44	39	18	43	5.8	6.7	**1.2**	5%	0.6	10.3	-19	$7
Health	D	07	OAK *	5	6	4	82	80	4.33	1.39	259	242	247	5.0	33%	69%	4.06	41	19	41	3.6	8.7	**2.4**	6%	0.6	1.8	78	$9
PT/Exp	D	08	OAK	1	0	0	35	28	3.09	1.26	189	183	190	4.7	22%	78%	5.03	35	15	50	5.4	7.2	**1.3**	6%	0.8	5.4	-3	$3
Consist	C	1st Half		1	0	0	28	24	2.23	1.10	184			4.5	22%	83%	4.41	34	17	49	4.1	7.6	**1.8**	6%	0.6	7.4	38	$4
LIMA Plan	C+	2nd Half		0	0	0	7	4	6.72	1.94	209			5.4	21%	67%	8.33	40	5	55	10.7	5.4	**0.5**	9%	1.3	-2.0	-175	($1)
+/- Score	-67	09 Proj		**4**	**3**	**0**	**69**	**58**	**4.20**	**1.37**	**243**			**5.9**	**29%**	**71%**	**4.71**	**39**	**12**	**49**	**4.2**	**7.6**	**1.8**	**7%**	**0.9**	**-2.4**	**40**	**$6**

Three reasons to be cautious, even if he's healthy in March:
1. '08 results from h%, not skill
2. Shoulder injury wiped out 2H
3. FB% entered the danger zone
Bring up his name, talk up the ERA, and don't bid a penny.

Broxton,Jonathan		Yr	Tm	W	L	Sv	IP	K	ERA	WHIP	OBA	vL	vR	BF/G	H%	S%	xERA	G	L	F	Ctl	Dom	Cmd	hr/f	hr/9	RAR	BPV	R$
RH	Reliever	04		0	0	0	0	0	0.00	0.00																		
Age	24	05	aa	5	3	5	96	90	3.27	1.16	234			11.9	30%	71%	2.73				2.7	8.4	**3.1**		0.4	12.2	113	$13
Type	Pwr	06	LA *	5	1	8	87	113	2.27	1.18	213	244	196	4.5	31%	84%	3.13	39	20	40	3.7	11.6	**3.1**	9%	0.7	23.8	127	$16
Health	A	07	LA	4	4	2	82	99	2.85	1.15	230	200	247	4.0	32%	77%	2.73	49	22	29	2.7	10.9	**4.0**	10%	0.7	15.9	148	$12
PT/Exp	C	08	LA	3	5	14	69	88	3.13	1.17	217	270	181	4.0	33%	72%	2.91	45	23	32	3.5	11.5	**3.3**	4%	0.3	9.7	134	$13
Consist	A	1st Half		2	2	0	34	43	3.47	1.22	228			4.1	33%	72%	2.93	43	26	32	3.5	11.5	**3.3**	8%	0.5	3.3	134	$4
LIMA Plan	B+	2nd Half		1	3	14	35	45	2.80	1.13	207			4.0	32%	73%	2.89	46	21	33	3.6	11.5	**3.2**	0%	0.0	6.4	134	$9
+/- Score	23	09 Proj		**4**	**3**	**18**	**74**	**90**	**2.94**	**1.14**	**216**			**4.4**	**31%**	**75%**	**2.92**	**46**	**22**	**32**	**3.3**	**11.0**	**3.3**	**7%**	**0.5**	**12.9**	**133**	**$16**

Leading candidate to receive a $10+ spike come 2009. Skills consistency uncanny for 24-yr old. Closers do routinely (and inexplicably) fail, but this profile minimizes risk. If Torre hands him the ball, saves will follow.

Bruney,Brian		Yr	Tm	W	L	Sv	IP	K	ERA	WHIP	OBA	vL	vR	BF/G	H%	S%	xERA	G	L	F	Ctl	Dom	Cmd	hr/f	hr/9	RAR	BPV	R$
RH	Reliever	04	ARI *	5	5	5	69	75	2.87	1.20	163	214	172	4.7	23%	76%	4.19	33	26	41	5.9	9.8	**1.7**	5%	0.4	11.9	28	$11
Age	27	05	ARI	1	3	12	46	51	7.43	1.98	302	280	314	4.8	39%	62%	4.90	41	22	37	6.8	10.0	**1.5**	12%	1.2	-18.1	14	$0
Type	Pwr xFB	06	NYY *	2	3	3	37	48	4.84	1.69	245	115	229	5.0	34%	74%	4.54	35	18	47	7.0	11.6	**1.7**	12%	1.2	-1.3	32	$3
Health	D	07	NYY	3	2	0	50	39	4.68	1.62	238	303	209	3.9	28%	72%	6.00	31	17	52	6.7	7.0	**1.1**	7%	0.9	-1.1	-45	$2
PT/Exp	D	08	NYY	3	0	1	34	33	1.84	0.99	157	106	183	4.2	20%	84%	3.80	43	14	44	4.2	8.7	**2.1**	6%	0.5	10.6	63	$7
Consist	D	1st Half		1	0	1	11	12	1.59	1.15	180			5.1	20%	100%	3.91	41	10	48	4.8	9.6	**2.0**	15%	1.6	3.8	62	$2
LIMA Plan	C	2nd Half		2	0	0	23	21	1.96	0.91	145			3.8	20%	76%	3.75	43	16	41	3.9	8.2	**2.1**	0%	0.0	6.8	63	$5
+/- Score	-91	09 Proj		**3**	**2**	**0**	**54**	**53**	**3.83**	**1.35**	**220**			**4.3**	**28%**	**74%**	**4.44**	**38**	**16**	**46**	**5.0**	**8.8**	**1.8**	**8%**	**0.8**	**-0.1**	**40**	**$5**

Out 3 months with torn ligament in foot. Limited sample, but easing up on pitches worked. Unlikely to visit the underside of 3.00 ERA again soon (thank you, h%/s%), but at least now there's hope. Sustainability is the key.

Buchholz,Clay		Yr	Tm	W	L	Sv	IP	K	ERA	WHIP	OBA	vL	vR	BF/G	H%	S%	xERA	G	L	F	Ctl	Dom	Cmd	hr/f	hr/9	RAR	BPV	R$
RH	Starter	04		0	0	0	0	0	0.00	0.00																		
Age	24	05		0	0	0	0	0	0.00	0.00																		
Type	Pwr	06	aa	9	4	0	103	70	4.62	1.65	307			22.4	34%	75%	5.80				3.6	6.1	**1.7**		1.2	-1.3	28	$5
Health	A	07	BOS *	11	6	0	148	168	2.92	1.10	219	217	133	21.2	30%	75%	3.06	38	29	33	2.8	10.2	**3.7**	8%	0.6	28.9	125	$24
PT/Exp	D	08	BOS *	7	11	0	134	122	5.14	1.52	276	293	305	22.1	34%	67%	3.98	48	21	31	4.0	8.2	**2.1**	11%	0.9	-13.1	66	$6
Consist	D	1st Half		6	4	0	81	75	3.91	1.48	270			22.1	34%	74%	3.89	47	22	31	3.9	8.4	**2.1**	7%	0.6	4.3	71	$7
LIMA Plan	B	2nd Half		1	7	0	54	47	6.97	1.58	286			22.0	33%	57%	4.11	48	20	32	4.1	8.0	**1.9**	17%	1.5	-17.4	58	($1)
+/- Score	52	09 Proj		**10**	**9**	**0**	**145**	**138**	**4.28**	**1.37**	**258**			**21.5**	**32%**	**70%**	**3.68**	**47**	**21**	**32**	**3.5**	**8.6**	**2.4**	**11%**	**0.9**	**13.2**	**83**	**$13**

2-9, 6.75 ERA in 76 IP at BOS. Curse of the no-no? Outside of Ctl, BPI held up fine and he was dominant in minors as Sox fiddled w/ his mechanics (2.30 ERA, 3.4 Cmd). Still big upside; buy now if others are impatient.

Buchholz,Taylor		Yr	Tm	W	L	Sv	IP	K	ERA	WHIP	OBA	vL	vR	BF/G	H%	S%	xERA	G	L	F	Ctl	Dom	Cmd	hr/f	hr/9	RAR	BPV	R$
RH	Reliever	04	aaa	6	7	0	98	62	6.15	1.51	303			21.7	32%	62%	5.75				2.6	5.7	**2.2**		1.6	-21.9	28	$1
Age	27	05	aaa	6	0	0	74	36	5.46	1.46	286			17.1	29%	67%	5.47				2.9	4.4	**1.5**		1.7	-10.6	4	$2
Type	FB	06	HOU *	7	13	0	157	108	5.85	1.34	265	249	248	23.1	29%	58%	4.35	44	18	38	2.9	6.2	**2.1**	12%	1.3	-26.3	54	$5
Health	A	07	COL	6	5	0	94	61	4.23	1.33	284	268	306	9.7	32%	69%	4.27	44	17	38	1.9	5.9	**3.1**	7%	0.8	2.3	76	$7
PT/Exp	C	08	COL	6	6	1	66	56	2.17	0.95	194	198	180	4.1	23%	81%	3.72	36	21	43	2.4	7.6	**3.1**	7%	0.7	17.2	85	$12
Consist	A	1st Half		2	2	1	40	30	1.36	0.76	158			4.2	20%	80%	3.40	44	20	36	2.0	6.8	**3.3**	0%	0.0	14.3	90	$8
LIMA Plan	C+	2nd Half		4	4	0	27	26	3.38	1.24	242			4.0	28%	82%	4.15	25	23	52	3.0	8.8	**2.9**	13%	1.7	2.9	79	$4
+/- Score	-31	09 Proj		**7**	**7**	**18**	**79**	**60**	**3.78**	**1.27**	**261**			**5.9**	**30%**	**74%**	**4.22**	**39**	**19**	**42**	**2.5**	**6.9**	**2.7**	**9%**	**1.0**	**1.1**	**72**	**$14**

Yet another hit rate-aided ERA, though three-year growth curve impressive. 1H h%, 2H hr/f% skewed results but maturation evident. If shoulder is OK (two bouts w/ stiffness in '08), a good setup reliever waiting for a shot.

Buehrle,Mark		Yr	Tm	W	L	Sv	IP	K	ERA	WHIP	OBA	vL	vR	BF/G	H%	S%	xERA	G	L	F	Ctl	Dom	Cmd	hr/f	hr/9	RAR	BPV	R$
LH	Starter	04	CHW	16	10	0	245	165	3.89	1.26	271	271	267	29.2	30%	73%	3.81	49	19	32	1.9	6.1	**3.2**	13%	1.2	16.3	85	$22
Age	30	05	CHW	16	8	0	236	149	3.12	1.19	265	271	260	29.4	30%	76%	3.86	46	21	33	1.5	5.7	**3.7**	8%	0.8	36.3	85	$27
Type	Con	06	CHW	12	13	0	204	98	4.99	1.45	300	238	322	27.8	31%	70%	4.72	44	19	37	2.1	4.3	**2.0**	13%	1.6	-10.8	43	$9
Health	A	07	CHW	10	9	0	201	115	3.63	1.26	268	314	258	28.0	29%	74%	4.39	43	18	39	2.0	5.1	**2.6**	9%	1.0	21.8	60	$18
PT/Exp	A	08	CHW	15	12	0	219	140	3.79	1.34	280	293	277	27.4	31%	74%	4.00	50	19	31	2.1	5.8	**2.7**	10%	0.9	15.1	74	$19
Consist	A	1st Half		6	6	0	112	62	3.79	1.30	269			27.7	30%	72%	4.21	50	18	32	2.3	5.0	**2.1**	8%	0.7	7.7	55	$9
LIMA Plan	C	2nd Half		9	6	0	107	78	3.79	1.37	291			27.0	33%	76%	3.79	49	19	31	1.9	6.6	**3.4**	12%	1.1	7.4	93	$10
+/- Score	8	09 Proj		**14**	**11**	**0**	**218**	**133**	**3.97**	**1.32**	**280**			**28.0**	**31%**	**73%**	**4.16**	**47**	**19**	**34**	**2.0**	**5.5**	**2.7**	**11%**	**1.1**	**7.2**	**69**	**$18**

Pulled a 2H Dom rabbit out of his hat to ward off implosion concerns. BPI rosterability has fluctuated through his career, but if the recent trend holds, he could see more success. Can we count on it? xERA is dubious.

BRENT HERSHEY

Burnett,A.J.

Burnett,A.J.		Yr	Tm	W	L	Sv	IP	K	ERA	WHIP	OBA	vL	vR	BF/G	H%	S%	xERA	G	L	F	Ctl	Dom	Cmd	hr/f	hr/9	RAR	BPV	R$
RH	Starter	04	FLA	7	6	0	120	113	3.68	1.17	232	247	211	24.5	29%	69%	3.36	50	17	33	2.9	8.5	**3.0**	8%	0.7	8.7	104	$13
Age	32	05	FLA	12	12	0	209	198	3.44	1.26	238	226	249	27.3	31%	73%	3.07	58	19	22	3.4	8.5	**2.5**	9%	0.5	20.6	98	$21
Type	Pwr GB	06	TOR	10	8	0	135	118	3.99	1.31	266	261	267	27.2	32%	72%	3.47	50	20	29	2.6	7.9	**3.0**	12%	0.9	9.4	100	$15
Health	D	07	TOR	10	8	0	166	176	3.75	1.19	219	200	231	27.2	27%	74%	3.07	55	15	30	3.6	9.6	**2.7**	18%	1.2	15.5	108	$21
PT/Exp	A	08	TOR	18	10	0	221	231	4.07	1.34	253	262	231	26.9	33%	71%	3.43	49	19	32	3.5	9.4	**2.7**	10%	0.8	7.7	101	$23
Consist	A	1st Half		8	7	0	106	108	4.74	1.48	258			26.0	34%	67%	3.80	48	22	30	4.5	9.1	**2.0**	8%	0.6	-5.2	69	$8
LIMA Plan	C+	2nd Half		10	3	0	115	123	3.44	1.22	248			28.0	32%	75%	3.12	49	17	34	2.6	9.6	**3.7**	12%	0.9	12.8	131	$16
+/- Score	31	09	Proj	**13**	**9**	**0**	**183**	**186**	**3.89**	**1.27**	**244**			**27.4**	**31%**	**71%**	**3.30**	**51**	**18**	**31**	**3.2**	**9.1**	**2.8**	**11%**	**0.8**	**25.4**	**106**	**$21**

Avoided DL and saw career-high in GS and IP. Was this by chance, or did push for new deal have any influence? Strong and stable skill set, just needs to stay healthy. He remains one of the bigger risk/reward options.

Burnett,Sean

Burnett,Sean		Yr	Tm	W	L	Sv	IP	K	ERA	WHIP	OBA	vL	vR	BF/G	H%	S%	xERA	G	L	F	Ctl	Dom	Cmd	hr/f	hr/9	RAR	BPV	R$
LH	Reliever	04	PIT *	6	10	0	118	52	5.33	1.60	306	324	293	23.2	32%	68%	4.76	56	14	30	3.2	4.0	**1.2**	11%	1.1	-15.6	19	($0)
Age	26	05	PIT	0	0	0	0	0	0.00	0.00											0.0	0.0						
Type	Pwr GB	06	aaa	8	11	0	120	39	7.27	1.81	332			22.7	34%	60%	6.58				3.7	2.9	**0.8**		1.2	-40.7	-13	($6)
Health	C	07	aaa	4	5	0	70	23	5.99	2.11	348			23.5	37%	71%	7.09				5.4	3.0	**0.6**		0.6	-13.2	-2	($5)
PT/Exp	D	08	PIT *	2	2	3	74	53	3.94	1.51	248	171	328	4.7	28%	77%	4.76	48	19	33	5.3	6.5	**1.2**	11%	1.0	3.0	1	$4
Consist	C	1st Half		1	1	3	40	29	3.66	1.61	249			6.1	28%	81%	5.18	48	15	37	6.1	6.6	**1.1**	12%	1.2	3.0	-21	$2
LIMA Plan	C	2nd Half		1	1	0	34	24	4.27	1.39	246			3.6	28%	70%	4.35	48	22	30	4.3	6.4	**1.5**	10%	0.8	-0.0	26	$1
+/- Score	-43	09	Proj	**3**	**3**	**0**	**58**	**39**	**4.81**	**1.66**	**288**			**7.6**	**33%**	**72%**	**4.78**	**51**	**18**	**31**	**4.7**	**6.1**	**1.3**	**10%**	**0.9**	**-3.1**	**12**	**$1**

1-1, 4.76 ERA in 56 IP at PIT. Completed long road back to MLB. Transitioned from SP to RP, but lots of kinks in skill set. Effectiveness against LH is a good sign, but needs to sustain 2H Ctl gains to stick in majors.

Burres,Brian

Burres,Brian		Yr	Tm	W	L	Sv	IP	K	ERA	WHIP	OBA	vL	vR	BF/G	H%	S%	xERA	G	L	F	Ctl	Dom	Cmd	hr/f	hr/9	RAR	BPV	R$
LH	Starter	04		0	0	0	0	0	0.00	0.00																		
Age	28	05	aa	9	6	0	128	85	5.25	1.67	300			22.6	34%	69%	5.42				4.1	5.9	**1.4**		0.9	-14.9	34	$2
Type	FB	06	aaa	10	6	0	139	98	5.43	1.64	298			24.4	33%	69%	5.62				3.9	6.3	**1.6**		1.2	-15.6	30	$4
Health	A	07	BAL	6	8	0	121	96	5.95	1.70	291	306	281	15.1	34%	66%	5.11	38	22	40	4.9	7.1	**1.5**	9%	1.0	-21.6	12	$0
PT/Exp	C	08	BAL	7	10	0	130	63	6.04	1.66	311	321	306	19.2	33%	65%	5.54	36	24	40	3.5	4.4	**1.3**	9%	1.2	-27.0	-1	($1)
Consist	A	1st Half		6	5	0	87	42	5.09	1.55	298			22.8	31%	70%	5.24	39	22	39	3.1	4.4	**1.4**	10%	1.2	-7.9	11	$2
LIMA Plan	F	2nd Half		1	5	0	43	21	7.95	1.88	335			14.8	36%	57%	6.15	31	27	41	4.2	4.4	**1.1**	7%	1.0	-19.1	-25	($4)
+/- Score	-6	09	Proj	**6**	**8**	**0**	**110**	**67**	**5.42**	**1.62**	**291**			**17.1**	**32%**	**68%**	**5.34**	**36**	**24**	**40**	**4.1**	**5.5**	**1.3**	**9%**	**1.1**	**-12.4**	**2**	**$2**

The Bad News:
- OBA over .300 vs LH and RH
- GB% down, LD% up; esp. 2H
- Severe drop in Dom
- Problems stranding runners

The Good News:
- Uh... he's left-handed?

Burton,Jared

Burton,Jared		Yr	Tm	W	L	Sv	IP	K	ERA	WHIP	OBA	vL	vR	BF/G	H%	S%	xERA	G	L	F	Ctl	Dom	Cmd	hr/f	hr/9	RAR	BPV	R$
RH	Reliever	04		0	0	0	0	0	0.00	0.00																		
Age	27	05		0	0	0	0	0	0.00	0.00																		
Type	Pwr	06	aa	6	5	1	74	50	5.27	1.58	296			6.3	34%	67%	5.17				3.5	6.1	**1.7**		0.9	-6.8	41	$3
Health	C	07	CIN *	5	3	1	62	49	3.35	1.41	242	130	219	4.4	30%	75%	4.69	45	15	40	4.6	7.0	**1.5**	3%	0.3	8.2	25	$6
PT/Exp	D	08	CIN	5	1	0	59	58	3.22	1.38	253	247	250	4.7	32%	80%	3.72	51	14	36	3.8	8.9	**2.3**	10%	0.9	7.6	85	$6
Consist	B	1st Half		4	1	0	43	46	2.29	1.27	251			4.8	33%	85%	3.25	53	12	35	2.9	9.6	**3.3**	7%	0.6	10.6	124	$6
LIMA Plan	C+	2nd Half		1	0	0	15	12	5.84	1.69	257			4.4	28%	70%	5.27	44	18	38	6.4	7.0	**1.1**	17%	1.8	-3.0	-25	($0)
+/- Score	9	09	Proj	**3**	**3**	**0**	**54**	**49**	**4.00**	**1.43**	**258**			**4.6**	**32%**	**74%**	**4.11**	**47**	**15**	**38**	**4.0**	**8.2**	**2.0**	**9%**	**0.8**	**1.5**	**64**	**$4**

A strained lat kept him on the DL almost two months, and likely affected him upon his 2H return. Overall, solid growth year due to: G/F trending up, Cmd jump/Dom increase, and xERA downward trend. Saves potential.

Bush,David

Bush,David		Yr	Tm	W	L	Sv	IP	K	ERA	WHIP	OBA	vL	vR	BF/G	H%	S%	xERA	G	L	F	Ctl	Dom	Cmd	hr/f	hr/9	RAR	BPV	R$
RH	Starter	04	TOR *	11	10	0	196	141	4.45	1.36	286	289	206	26.3	33%	69%	4.33	42	16	42	2.1	6.5	**3.1**	7%	0.9	-0.3	79	$13
Age	29	05	TOR *	7	13	0	191	110	4.77	1.33	287	269	269	23.9	31%	67%	4.23	46	19	35	1.8	5.2	**2.9**	12%	1.3	-9.4	69	$9
Type	Con	06	MIL	12	11	0	210	166	4.41	1.14	253	258	246	25.1	29%	64%	3.49	47	19	34	1.6	7.1	**4.4**	12%	1.1	1.9	109	$20
Health	A	07	MIL	12	10	0	186	134	5.12	1.40	292	246	324	24.4	33%	66%	4.18	43	19	38	2.1	6.5	**3.0**	12%	1.3	-16.0	80	$10
PT/Exp	A	08	MIL	9	10	0	185	109	4.18	1.14	238	244	224	24.2	25%	69%	4.35	41	18	41	2.3	5.3	**2.3**	12%	1.4	2.0	51	$15
Consist	A	1st Half		4	8	0	91	46	5.06	1.28	260			23.8	26%	64%	4.91	40	15	45	2.6	4.6	**1.8**	11%	1.5	-8.8	31	$4
LIMA Plan	C+	2nd Half		5	2	0	94	63	3.34	1.01	215			24.7	23%	74%	3.82	42	21	37	2.1	6.0	**2.9**	14%	1.3	10.8	72	$11
+/- Score	-5	09	Proj	**10**	**10**	**0**	**189**	**125**	**4.20**	**1.24**	**262**			**24.5**	**28%**	**70%**	**4.15**	**43**	**18**	**39**	**2.1**	**6.0**	**2.8**	**12%**	**1.3**	**4.5**	**72**	**$14**

Same old S% and hr/9 issues in 1H, but in 2H he halted rising FB and falling Dom trends, plus started stranding some runners. 2H h% definitely helped, and HR problems remain, but 2H xERA and Cmd renew interest. A little.

Byrdak,Tim

Byrdak,Tim		Yr	Tm	W	L	Sv	IP	K	ERA	WHIP	OBA	vL	vR	BF/G	H%	S%	xERA	G	L	F	Ctl	Dom	Cmd	hr/f	hr/9	RAR	BPV	R$
LH	Reliever	04	aaa	5	1	2	72	52	5.83	1.96	353			6.6	41%	71%	7.15				3.7	6.5	**1.7**		1.0	-13.2	31	($1)
Age	35	05	BAL *	3	3	12	64	67	3.30	1.43	234	214	300	3.6	30%	80%	3.73	51	19	30	5.1	9.4	**1.8**	12%	0.9	8.6	59	$10
Type	Pwr	06	BAL	1	0	0	7	2	12.86	3.14	415			2.7	40%	60%	8.93	52	26	23	10.3	2.6	**0.3**	28%	2.6	-7.2	-202	($2)
Health	B	07	DET	3	0	1	45	49	3.20	1.42	230			5.0	31%	79%	3.55	41	38	21	5.2	9.8	**1.9**	12%	0.6	7.2	55	$6
PT/Exp	D	08	HOU *	2	1	0	62	55	3.97	1.34	236	135	289	4.0	27%	76%	4.18	43	19	39	4.2	7.9	**1.9**	15%	1.4	2.3	50	$4
Consist	F	1st Half		2	0	0	31	21	2.44	1.38	230			4.0	26%	86%	5.06	39	21	39	4.9	5.9	**1.2**	8%	0.9	7.1	-8	$3
LIMA Plan	B	2nd Half		0	1	0	31	34	5.52	1.29	243			4.1	28%	64%	3.40	45	17	38	3.5	9.9	**2.8**	23%	2.0	-4.8	107	$1
+/- Score	-23	09	Proj	**3**	**1**	**0**	**58**	**56**	**4.03**	**1.41**	**248**			**4.3**	**31%**	**74%**	**3.83**	**45**	**25**	**30**	**4.3**	**8.7**	**2.0**	**12%**	**0.9**	**3.7**	**62**	**$4**

2-1, 3.90 ERA in 55 IP at HOU. The argument for making him exclusively situational:

	BA	OPS	Cmd
vLH	.135	.469	3.3
vRH	.289	1.005	0.9

Byrd,Paul

Byrd,Paul		Yr	Tm	W	L	Sv	IP	K	ERA	WHIP	OBA	vL	vR	BF/G	H%	S%	xERA	G	L	F	Ctl	Dom	Cmd	hr/f	hr/9	RAR	BPV	R$
RH	Starter	04	ATL *	9	8	0	126	85	4.43	1.30	281	329	219	24.2	31%	71%	4.45	36	18	46	1.8	6.1	**3.4**	11%	1.4	-2.5	75	$9
Age	38	05	ANA	12	11	0	204	102	3.75	1.20	273	306	234	27.1	29%	72%	4.53	38	20	42	1.2	4.5	**3.6**	8%	1.0	15.7	63	$18
Type	Con FB	06	CLE	10	9	0	179	88	4.88	1.51	315	369	256	25.6	33%	71%	4.84	39	24	37	1.9	4.4	**2.3**	11%	1.3	-7.1	45	$7
Health	A	07	CLE	15	8	0	192	88	4.59	1.39	306	322	280	26.7	32%	70%	4.79	38	21	41	1.3	4.1	**3.1**	10%	1.3	-1.9	55	$13
PT/Exp	A	08	2AL	11	12	0	180	82	4.60	1.32	287	317	255	25.5	29%	71%	4.83	36	23	42	1.7	4.1	**2.4**	12%	1.6	-5.6	42	$11
Consist	A	1st Half		3	9	0	91	35	5.26	1.29	289			23.9	27%	67%	4.82	37	21	42	1.3	3.5	**2.7**	15%	2.1	-10.2	43	$3
LIMA Plan	D+	2nd Half		8	3	0	89	47	3.93	1.35	284			27.3	31%	74%	4.84	35	24	41	2.1	4.7	**2.2**	8%	1.0	4.6	41	$8
+/- Score	-25	09	Proj	**12**	**9**	**0**	**174**	**82**	**4.67**	**1.37**	**294**			**25.7**	**30%**	**70%**	**4.84**	**37**	**22**	**41**	**1.8**	**4.3**	**2.4**	**10%**	**1.3**	**-8.9**	**44**	**$10**

Consistently mediocre, as skills have not changed appreciably in the last four years. Biggest issues are still his inability to get LHers out, and minimizing HR. Depending on where h% falls: UP: 2005. DN: 2006

Cabrera,Daniel

Cabrera,Daniel		Yr	Tm	W	L	Sv	IP	K	ERA	WHIP	OBA	vL	vR	BF/G	H%	S%	xERA	G	L	F	Ctl	Dom	Cmd	hr/f	hr/9	RAR	BPV	R$
RH	Starter	04	BAL *	12	9	1	174	104	4.75	1.50	243	249	270	23.3	27%	69%	5.45	43	17	40	5.3	5.4	**1.0**	7%	0.8	-6.9	-26	$8
Age	27	05	BAL	10	13	0	161	157	4.53	1.43	241	285	174	24.2	30%	69%	3.80	53	18	30	4.9	8.8	**1.8**	11%	0.8	-3.1	57	$12
Type	Pwr	06	BAL	9	10	0	148	157	4.74	1.58	238	231	251	25.6	31%	70%	4.53	41	22	37	6.3	9.5	**1.5**	8%	0.7	-3.4	20	$10
Health	B	07	BAL	9	18	0	204	166	5.55	1.54	264	294	236	26.8	31%	65%	4.64	50	16	35	4.8	7.3	**1.5**	12%	1.1	-26.3	31	$6
PT/Exp	B	08	BAL	8	11	0	183	96	5.26	1.64	283	308	259	26.9	30%	70%	5.23	48	20	32	4.7	4.7	**1.0**	12%	1.2	-20.6	-17	$1
Consist	A	1st Half		5	4	0	109	64	4.53	1.41	258			27.8	28%	71%	4.43	53	17	30	3.9	5.3	**1.4**	13%	1.2	-2.4	21	$5
LIMA Plan	C	2nd Half		3	7	0	74	32	6.35	1.98	318			25.8	33%	70%	6.49	42	23	36	6.0	3.9	**0.7**	11%	1.3	-18.2	-71	($5)
+/- Score	-14	09	Proj	**8**	**13**	**0**	**174**	**114**	**5.14**	**1.60**	**274**			**26.2**	**30%**	**70%**	**4.99**	**46**	**19**	**34**	**4.8**	**5.9**	**1.2**	**11%**	**1.1**	**-12.1**	**0**	**$4**

5 reasons to avoid on draft day:
1. OBA and BA v LH trend
2. xERA spike
3. Dom freefall
4. Was Sept. injury really only an elbow strain, or is there more?
5. Enough with the masochism

Cabrera,Fernando

Cabrera,Fernando		Yr	Tm	W	L	Sv	IP	K	ERA	WHIP	OBA	vL	vR	BF/G	H%	S%	xERA	G	L	F	Ctl	Dom	Cmd	hr/f	hr/9	RAR	BPV	R$
RH	Reliever	04	aaa	4	3	5	75	83	3.77	1.30	213			7.2	28%	73%	3.32				4.8	10.0	**2.1**		0.9	5.3	88	$9
Age	27	05	CLE *	8	2	3	81	88	1.33	1.03	213	196	224	7.1	29%	90%	3.17	35	29	36	2.4	9.7	**4.0**	5%	0.4	30.5	123	$18
Type	Pwr xFB	06	CLE	3	3	0	60	71	5.23	1.41	238	235	248	5.1	29%	68%	3.89	33	23	43	4.8	10.6	**2.2**	18%	1.8	-5.0	73	$5
Health	D	07	2AL	1	2	1	44	48	7.21	1.85	289	319	267	6.3	35%	64%	5.08	31	22	47	6.4	9.9	**1.5**	15%	1.9	-14.6	15	($1)
PT/Exp	D	08	BAL *	2	1	0	41	42	3.93	1.66	276	304	269	5.7	32%	85%	5.06	24	24	52	5.3	9.1	**1.7**	14%	2.0	2.1	23	$2
Consist	B	1st Half		0	0	0	14	12	0.66	1.54	239			5.2	31%	95%					5.9	7.5	**1.3**		0.0	6.4	79	$1
LIMA Plan	C+	2nd Half		2	1	0	27	30	5.60	1.72	294			6.0	33%	79%	4.74	24	23	52	4.9	9.9	**2.0**	22%	3.0	-4.2	47	$1
+/- Score	-39	09	Proj	**3**	**2**	**0**	**45**	**48**	**4.85**	**1.53**	**255**			**6.0**	**32%**	**72%**	**4.50**	**30**	**23**	**47**	**5.1**	**9.7**	**1.9**	**12%**	**1.4**	**-0.4**	**46**	**$3**

2-1, 5.40 ERA in 28 IP at BAL. Look at Ctl, Dom, hr/9: he's the "three true outcomes" of pitchers. What would happen if he faced Jack Cust? All the fielders could probably go home.

SCOTT MONROE

Cain,Matt

			W	L	Sv	IP	K	ERA	WHIP	OBA	vL	vR	BF/G	H%	S%	xERA	G	L	F	Ctl	Dom	Cmd	hr/f	hr/9	RAR	BPV	R$
RH	Starter	04 aa	6	4	0	86	64	3.99	1.38	250			24.7	29%	72%	3.85				4.0	6.7	1.7		0.7	3.8	60	$7
Age	24	05 SF	*12	6	0	191	201	3.35	1.06	192	160	143	23.1	24%	72%	3.89	29	18	53	3.5	9.5	2.7	8%	0.9	21.2	83	$25
Type	Pwr FB	06 SF	13	12	0	190	179	4.16	1.28	226	217	227	25.0	28%	69%	4.34	36	16	48	4.1	8.5	2.1	7%	0.9	7.6	55	$18
Health	A	07 SF	7	16	0	200	163	3.65	1.26	235	248	224	26.1	28%	72%	4.39	39	16	45	3.6	7.3	2.1	5%	0.6	19.3	53	$17
PT/Exp	A	08 SF	8	14	0	218	186	3.76	1.36	251	268	235	27.4	30%	74%	4.51	33	23	44	3.8	7.7	2.0	7%	0.8	13.6	48	$14
Consist	A	1st Half	4	6	0	105	97	4.44	1.36	250			26.5	30%	69%	4.42	31	22	47	3.8	8.3	2.2	9%	1.0	-2.3	57	$6
LIMA Plan	C+	2nd Half	4	8	0	112	89	3.12	1.37	252			28.4	30%	78%	4.60	35	23	42	3.8	7.1	1.9	5%	0.6	15.9	40	$8
+/- Score	4	09 Proj	10	12	0	203	174	3.77	1.31	241			26.0	29%	73%	4.41	35	20	45	3.7	7.7	2.1	8%	0.9	-1.6	53	$17

Development seems stagnant, though still time for growth. 2H Dom decline, LD spike might both be irrelevant. Those are offset by solid skills foundation. Low wins will hold bidding back. BPIs worthy of 15 wins easy.

Campillo,Jorge

			W	L	Sv	IP	K	ERA	WHIP	OBA	vL	vR	BF/G	H%	S%	xERA	G	L	F	Ctl	Dom	Cmd	hr/f	hr/9	RAR	BPV	R$
RH	Starter	04	0	0	0	0	0	0.00	0.00																		
Age	30	05 aaa	4	1	0	66	37	3.15	1.37	277			23.6	31%	79%	4.19				2.6	5.0	2.0		0.7	9.4	49	$5
Type	Con FB	06 SEA	0	0	0	2	1	17.14	1.90	403			10.1	45%	0%	4.28	40	40	20	0.0	4.3		0%	0.0	-3.3	95	($1)
Health	A	07 SEA	*9	6	0	162	76	4.91	1.87	347			26.8	37%	75%	6.65	26	17	57	3.4	4.2	1.2	5%	0.9	-8.2	-11	($1)
PT/Exp	C	08 ATL	8	7	0	159	107	3.91	1.24	261	249	274	16.9	29%	71%	4.23	38	23	39	2.2	6.1	2.8	9%	1.0	7.0	67	$12
Consist	F	1st Half	3	2	0	67	53	2.54	1.03	231			12.1	28%	77%	3.73	37	23	40	1.6	7.1	4.4	5%	0.5	14.4	99	$9
LIMA Plan	D+	2nd Half	5	5	0	91	54	4.92	1.39	282			23.2	30%	68%	4.63	39	23	38	2.6	5.3	2.1	12%	1.4	-7.4	44	$4
+/- Score	-12	09 Proj	7	5	0	139	86	4.35	1.42	284			25.0	31%	72%	4.72	37	22	40	2.7	5.6	2.1	9%	1.0	-6.5	44	$7

Made a good first impression, although 2H is a more accurate snapshot of his potential value as a SP. As a contact pitcher, his margin for error is thin, so odds of a repeat are low.

Camp,Shawn

			W	L	Sv	IP	K	ERA	WHIP	OBA	vL	vR	BF/G	H%	S%	xERA	G	L	F	Ctl	Dom	Cmd	hr/f	hr/9	RAR	BPV	R$
RH	Reliever	04 KC	*3	3	3	88	68	4.59	1.45	297	287	283	6.8	34%	72%	3.55	58	15	27	2.3	6.9	3.0	15%	1.2	-1.7	98	$5
Age	33	05 KC	*4	10	1	116	62	5.26	1.62	319	407	274	10.6	35%	68%	4.45	57	14	29	2.7	4.8	1.8	10%	0.9	-12.8	47	$0
Type	Pwr xGB	06 TAM	7	4	4	75	53	4.68	1.49	305	370	284	4.4	35%	71%	3.62	57	18	24	2.3	6.4	2.8	15%	1.1	-1.1	88	$7
Health	A	07 TAM	0	3	0	40	36	7.20	2.03	358			4.0	42%	66%	3.88	57	21	22	4.1	8.1	2.0	23%	1.6	-13.3	72	($3)
PT/Exp	D	08 TOR	*4	1	4	49	41	3.29	1.14	246	356	204	4.3	31%	71%	3.19	54	19	27	2.0	7.6	3.8	5%	0.4	6.5	114	$8
Consist	A	1st Half	2	1	4	34	28	2.67	0.90	217			4.2	27%	72%	2.88	51	19	29	1.1	7.6	7.1	7%	0.5	7.0	137	$7
LIMA Plan	A	2nd Half	2	0	0	16	13	4.62	1.67	302			4.5	38%	69%	3.95	57	18	24	4.0	7.5	1.9	0%	0.0	-0.5	61	$1
+/- Score	-4	09 Proj	3	2	0	44	35	4.34	1.45	281			4.3	33%	71%	3.58	56	19	25	3.1	7.2	2.3	12%	0.8	4.5	81	$3

3-1, 4.12 ERA in 39 IP at TOR. Did what he needed to do to be successful - got RHers out, kept ball on ground, and avoided walks. xERA shows there is value here, as long as he keeps channeling Chad Bradford.

Capps,Matt

			W	L	Sv	IP	K	ERA	WHIP	OBA	vL	vR	BF/G	H%	S%	xERA	G	L	F	Ctl	Dom	Cmd	hr/f	hr/9	RAR	BPV	R$
RH	Reliever	04	0	0	0	0	0	0.00	0.00																		
Age	25	05 aa	0	2	7	24	23	3.75	1.29	293			4.8	37%	72%	4.21				1.1	8.6	7.7		0.8	1.6	187	$4
Type	Con xFB	06 PIT	9	1	1	80	56	3.82	1.16	264	250	275	3.8	29%	73%	3.90	41	20	40	1.3	6.3	4.7	12%	1.3	6.6	95	$11
Health	B	07 PIT	4	7	18	79	64	2.28	1.01	223	281	181	4.1	27%	80%	4.04	31	19	50	1.8	7.3	4.0	4%	0.6	20.9	91	$18
PT/Exp	B	08 PIT	2	3	21	54	39	3.02	0.97	237	222	245	4.3	27%	72%	3.85	31	23	46	0.8	6.5	7.8	7%	0.8	8.3	104	$14
Consist	A	1st Half	1	3	17	39	28	2.98	1.04	245			4.3	27%	78%	4.06	30	23	48	1.1	6.4	5.6	9%	1.1	6.3	93	$10
LIMA Plan	B	2nd Half	1	0	4	14	11	3.12	0.76	213			4.1	27%	55%	3.30	34	24	41	0.0	6.9		0%	0.0	2.0	136	$4
+/- Score	2	09 Proj	5	4	38	73	53	3.35	1.08	247			4.1	28%	74%	4.01	33	21	45	1.4	6.6	4.8	9%	1.1	3.0	93	$22

Had 2 walks on Opening Day, then just 3 more all year. Mix in a solid Dom rate, and Cmd is first class. Came back strong in 2H after 2 months on DL, so no lingering concerns. All he needs to join the elite is more Sv Opps.

Capuano,Chris

			W	L	Sv	IP	K	ERA	WHIP	OBA	vL	vR	BF/G	H%	S%	xERA	G	L	F	Ctl	Dom	Cmd	hr/f	hr/9	RAR	BPV	R$
LH	Reliever	04 MIL	6	8	0	88	80	5.01	1.45	268	207	282	22.7	30%	72%	4.30	38	19	43	3.8	8.2	2.2	16%	1.8	-8.1	61	$5
Age	30	05 MIL	18	12	0	219	176	3.99	1.38	256	201	270	26.9	29%	76%	4.47	38	21	41	3.7	7.2	1.9	12%	1.3	7.0	45	$18
Type	Pwr FB	06 MIL	11	12	0	221	174	4.03	1.25	269	273	264	27.1	31%	72%	3.94	40	20	40	1.9	7.1	3.7	11%	1.2	12.5	94	$19
Health	F	07 MIL	5	12	0	150	132	5.10	1.49	287	259	293	22.8	34%	68%	4.16	43	18	39	3.2	7.9	2.4	11%	1.2	-12.5	76	$5
PT/Exp	B	08 MIL	0	0	0	0	0	0.00	0.00																		
Consist	A	1st Half	0	0	0	0	0	0.00	0.00																		
LIMA Plan		2nd Half	0	0	0	0	0	0.00	0.00																		
+/- Score		09 Proj	4	4	0	66	55	4.64	1.42	273			26.1	31%	71%	4.29	40	20	40	3.3	7.5	2.3	12%	1.4	0.4	64	$4

Had second Tommy John surgery of career in May, so not likely to see action in 2009 before June. Speculative pick for 2nd half and beyond.

Carlson,Jesse

			W	L	Sv	IP	K	ERA	WHIP	OBA	vL	vR	BF/G	H%	S%	xERA	G	L	F	Ctl	Dom	Cmd	hr/f	hr/9	RAR	BPV	R$
LH	Reliever	04 aa	5	1	1	55	42	6.23	1.59	301			6.1	35%	61%	5.40				3.4	6.8	2.0		1.0	-12.8	48	$1
Age	28	05 a/a	4	3	5	57	50	3.91	1.39	291			4.1	34%	77%	4.97				2.1	8.0	3.8		1.3	2.8	85	$7
Type	Pwr xFB	06 a/a	6	5	3	69	41	5.77	1.69	323			6.0	35%	68%	6.28				3.2	5.3	1.7		1.4	-10.6	17	$2
Health	A	07 aa	8	2	6	70	60	6.94	1.75	341			5.6	41%	59%	6.18				2.7	7.7	2.9		0.7	-21.4	72	$3
PT/Exp	D	08 TOR	7	2	2	60	55	2.25	1.03	195	205	186	3.4	23%	84%	3.86	34	21	45	3.2	8.3	2.6	9%	0.9	15.5	76	$12
Consist	C	1st Half	1	1	1	27	29	1.69	1.16	210			3.0	27%	93%	3.76	33	21	46	3.7	9.8	2.6	10%	1.0	8.8	87	$5
LIMA Plan	C+	2nd Half	6	1	1	33	26	2.70	0.93	183			3.9	21%	75%	3.94	35	20	44	2.7	7.0	2.6	8%	0.8	6.8	67	$8
+/- Score	-47	09 Proj	6	2	0	58	52	3.88	1.33	262			4.3	31%	74%	4.20	34	21	45	2.9	8.1	2.7	9%	1.1	1.6	78	$7

Jumped from AA with skills intact. Double-helping of good fortune (H% and S%) partly responsible for low ERA, but Cmd played a part too. Potential to make a good LIMA pick, but short track record raises risk.

Carlyle,Buddy

			W	L	Sv	IP	K	ERA	WHIP	OBA	vL	vR	BF/G	H%	S%	xERA	G	L	F	Ctl	Dom	Cmd	hr/f	hr/9	RAR	BPV	R$
RH	Reliever	04 a/a	12	6	0	144	105	4.10	1.37	295			22.9	34%	73%	4.79				1.7	6.6	3.8		1.0	4.4	84	$12
Age	31	05 LA	*1	2	2	62	55	5.10	1.41	272			8.9	32%	67%	4.72	26	19	55	3.2	8.0	2.5	9%	1.3	-6.5	62	$2
Type	Pwr FB	06 aaa	3	1	0	28	18	2.14	0.91	193			8.3	21%	81%	1.92				2.1	5.8	2.7		0.7	8.2	86	$6
Health	A	07 ATL	*13	9	0	155	118	4.74	1.36	278	343	229	21.4	31%	70%	4.45	32	23	44	2.5	6.8	2.7	12%	1.5	-6.1	66	$12
PT/Exp	D	08 ATL	2	0	0	63	59	3.59	1.24	227	247	215	5.8	29%	73%	3.84	44	19	37	3.7	8.5	2.3	8%	0.7	5.3	73	$5
Consist	D	1st Half	0	0	0	18	16	2.00	1.33	204			5.1	27%	83%	5.00	32	19	49	5.5	8.0	1.5	0%	0.0	5.0	5	$2
LIMA Plan	B	2nd Half	2	0	0	45	43	4.23	1.21	236			6.2	29%	67%	3.40	48	19	33	3.0	8.7	2.9	12%	1.0	0.2	101	$4
+/- Score	-8	09 Proj	3	2	0	73	62	3.85	1.31	252			6.5	30%	74%	4.19	38	20	42	3.2	7.7	2.4	9%	1.0	1.3	67	$6

Handled bullpen transition well. Three reasons for optimism:
1. FB pitcher turned to GB in 2H.
2. Increased Dom as RP.
3. Very tough on RH batters.
10.45 ERA on 0 days rest was a key flaw. Good $1staff-filler.

Carmona,Fausto

			W	L	Sv	IP	K	ERA	WHIP	OBA	vL	vR	BF/G	H%	S%	xERA	G	L	F	Ctl	Dom	Cmd	hr/f	hr/9	RAR	BPV	R$
RH	Starter	04 a/a	5	9	0	93	62	5.01	1.52	312			25.8	37%	64%	4.68				2.1	6.0	2.8		0.3	-7.7	80	$3
Age	25	05 a/a	13	9	0	173	97	3.86	1.25	272			26.7	30%	70%	3.84				1.7	5.0	2.9		0.7	9.5	69	$15
Type	xGB	06 CLE	*2	13	0	102	85	5.75	1.55	294	299	298	10.4	35%	63%	3.69	60	13	27	3.4	7.5	2.2	12%	1.0	-15.0	80	$2
Health	C	07 CLE	19	8	0	215	137	3.06	1.21	247	275	216	27.7	28%	77%	3.34	64	14	22	2.6	5.7	2.2	11%	0.7	38.4	77	$27
PT/Exp	B	08 CLE	8	7	0	121	58	5.44	1.62	270	303	230	24.9	30%	65%	4.68	63	15	22	5.2	4.3	0.8	8%	0.5	-16.3	-22	$1
Consist	B	1st Half	4	2	0	58	23	3.10	1.59	248			26.1	27%	79%	4.76	67	15	18	5.9	3.6	0.6	3%	0.2	8.9	-50	$3
LIMA Plan	C+	2nd Half	4	5	0	63	35	7.61	1.66	289			23.9	32%	52%	4.56	60	15	25	4.6	5.0	1.1	11%	0.9	-25.2	5	($2)
+/- Score	-4	09 Proj	14	10	0	183	113	3.98	1.43	267			26.5	30%	73%	3.86	63	14	23	3.6	5.6	1.5	10%	0.6	12.7	43	$14

Cmd problems and 2H S% killed value. Workload spike from 2007 had a negative impact. Must get Ctl down and Dom up for return to prominence. Sept levels (3.6 Ctl, 5.5 Dom) suggest a significant rebound is possible.

Carpenter,Chris

			W	L	Sv	IP	K	ERA	WHIP	OBA	vL	vR	BF/G	H%	S%	xERA	G	L	F	Ctl	Dom	Cmd	hr/f	hr/9	RAR	BPV	R$
RH	Reliever	04 STL	15	5	0	182	152	3.46	1.14	248	268	226	26.4	29%	75%	3.21	52	18	29	1.9	7.5	4.0	15%	1.2	18.0	115	$22
Age	34	05 STL	21	5	0	241	213	2.84	1.06	231	264	199	29.1	28%	76%	2.94	55	19	26	1.9	7.9	4.2	10%	0.7	41.9	124	$35
Type	Con GB	06 STL	15	8	0	221	184	3.09	1.07	237	266	210	27.6	28%	75%	3.10	53	18	28	1.7	7.5	4.3	12%	0.9	38.1	119	$30
Health	F	07 STL	0	1	0	6	3	7.50	1.67	347	375	300	27.5	39%	50%	2.93	65	26	9	1.5	4.5	3.0	0%	0.0	-2.3	84	($0)
PT/Exp	C	08 STL	0	1	0	15	7	1.76	1.31	271	158	351	16.2	31%	85%	4.21	51	24	24	2.4	4.1	1.8	0%	0.0	4.7	40	$1
Consist	B	1st Half	0	0	0	0	0	0.00	0.00																		
LIMA Plan	B	2nd Half	0	1	0	15	7	1.77	1.31	271			16.2	31%	85%	4.21	51	24	24	2.4	4.1	1.8	0%	0.0	4.7	40	$1
+/- Score		09 Proj	5	3	0	82	50	3.87	1.26	258			22.7	29%	70%	3.74	54	22	24	2.5	5.5	2.2	10%	0.7	6.0	62	$7

2009 outlook is completely up in the air due to nerve problem in right shoulder. At his age, an uncertain reward does not look like enough to justify the certain risk. Still, your reserve list is made for risks like these.

SCOTT MONROE

Carrasco,D.J.			W	L	Sv	IP	K	ERA	WHIP	OBA	vL	vR	BF/G	H%	S%	xERA	G	L	F	Ctl	Dom	Cmd	hr/f	hr/9	RAR	BPV	R$
RH	Reliever	04 KC *	4	3	3	91	63	4.64	1.64	313	323	259	6.7	36%	73%	4.22	57	13	29	3.3	6.2	**1.9**	9%	0.8	-2.3	59	$3
Age	32	05 KC *	9	10	0	141	66	4.36	1.55	282	286	292	19.7	30%	73%	4.66	54	22	24	3.9	4.2	**1.1**	10%	0.8	0.2	1	$5
Type	GB	06 JPN	0	3	0	10	9	15.30	3.20	438			20.4	50%	52%	13.58				9.0	8.1	**0.9**		2.7	-13.3	-46	($4)
Health	A	07 aaa	5	14	0	137	64	12.10	2.88	444			23.4	46%	57%	12.21				5.6	4.2	**0.7**		1.9	-129.1	-49	($38)
PT/Exp	D	08 CHW *	3	1	1	64	51	4.10	1.27	244	186	244	6.8	30%	66%	3.71	51	21	28	3.2	7.2	**2.2**	4%	0.3	2.0	71	$6
Consist	F	1st Half	0	1	1	17	17	4.96	1.65	313			15.7	41%	67%					3.3	8.9	**2.7**		0.0	-1.3	103	$0
LIMA Plan	B	2nd Half	3	0	0	47	34	3.78	1.13	215			5.5	26%	65%	3.71	51	21	28	3.2	6.6	**2.0**	5%	0.4	3.3	60	$5
+/- Score	-9	09 Proj	**2**	**3**	**0**	**58**	**41**	**4.66**	**1.40**	**262**			**6.1**	**30%**	**67%**	**3.98**	**54**	**19**	**27**	**3.6**	**6.4**	**1.8**	**10%**	**0.8**	**3.2**	**50**	**$3**

1-0, 3.96 ERA in 38 IP at CHW. Transitioned to relief role with decent results. The question is can he sustain it? History says no, but role change is a wildcard. Let's go with "no" until he does it again.

Casilla,Santiago			W	L	Sv	IP	K	ERA	WHIP	OBA	vL	vR	BF/G	H%	S%	xERA	G	L	F	Ctl	Dom	Cmd	hr/f	hr/9	RAR	BPV	R$
RH	Reliever	04	0	0	0	0	0	0.00	0.00																		
Age	28	05	0	0	0	0	0	0.00	0.00																		
Type	Pwr FB	06 OAK *	2	0	4	35	29	4.10	1.14	227	400		5.3	28%	63%	3.33	40	40	20	2.8	7.4	**2.6**	10%	0.5	2.0	76	$5
Health	B	07 OAK *	5	2	5	75	73	4.75	1.38	235	212	230	4.7	29%	66%	4.62	33	16	51	4.7	8.8	**1.9**	7%	0.9	-2.3	43	$8
PT/Exp	D	08 OAK	2	1	2	50	43	3.94	1.59	297	308	291	4.4	36%	77%	4.34	43	20	36	3.6	7.7	**2.2**	9%	0.9	2.6	63	$3
Consist	B	1st Half	2	0	1	21	23	2.54	1.08	240			3.5	30%	85%	3.04	46	14	40	1.7	9.7	**5.8**	13%	1.3	4.8	153	$4
LIMA Plan	B	2nd Half	0	1	1	29	20	4.97	1.97	334			5.2	39%	75%	5.47	42	24	34	5.0	6.2	**1.3**	6%	0.6	-2.2	-2	($1)
+/- Score	10	09 Proj	**3**	**1**	**0**	**58**	**51**	**4.34**	**1.41**	**258**			**4.7**	**31%**	**71%**	**4.32**	**41**	**19**	**41**	**3.9**	**7.9**	**2.0**	**9%**	**0.9**	**0.7**	**56**	**$4**

Two years in a row he's had an excellent 1H followed by an awfu 2H. Trend towards GB will help minimize HR, but erratic Cmd limits short-term upside. 1H peak shows closer potential, but still a ways from harnessing that.

Chacon,Shawn			W	L	Sv	IP	K	ERA	WHIP	OBA	vL	vR	BF/G	H%	S%	xERA	G	L	F	Ctl	Dom	Cmd	hr/f	hr/9	RAR	BPV	R$
RH	Starter	04 COL	1	9	35	63	52	7.13	1.95	285	236	326	4.7	32%	66%	6.30	33	19	48	7.4	7.4	**1.0**	13%	1.7	-22.3	-56	$6
Age	31	05 2TM	8	10	0	151	79	3.45	1.33	240	232	252	23.8	26%	76%	5.10	40	21	39	3.9	4.7	**1.2**	7%	0.8	15.9	-3	$11
Type	FB	06 2TM	7	6	0	109	62	6.36	1.72	287	305	274	19.4	29%	67%	6.15	33	18	50	5.2	5.1	**1.0**	13%	1.9	-24.7	-38	($1)
Health	B	07 PIT	5	4	1	96	79	3.94	1.49	260	317	236	6.6	31%	75%	4.58	44	17	39	4.5	7.4	**1.6**	8%	0.8	5.8	34	$6
PT/Exp	C	08 HOU	2	3	0	86	53	5.04	1.51	267	270	270	25.3	28%	72%	5.32	37	18	45	4.3	5.6	**1.3**	13%	1.7	-8.1	-1	$1
Consist	C	1st Half	2	3	0	86	53	5.04	1.51	267			25.3	28%	72%	5.32	37	18	45	4.3	5.6	**1.3**	13%	1.7	-8.1	-1	$1
LIMA Plan	C	2nd Half	0	0	0	0	0	0.00	0.00																		
+/- Score	-28	09 Proj	**1**	**1**	**0**	**15**	**9**	**4.97**	**1.59**	**281**			**6.5**	**31%**	**71%**	**5.45**	**37**	**18**	**45**	**4.3**	**5.6**	**1.3**	**9%**	**1.2**	**-2.0**	**-2**	**$0**

May have thrown his last pitch after altercation with HOU GM Ed Wade in June. His picture is now in the dictionary under the entry for "career-limiting move".

Chamberlain,Joba			W	L	Sv	IP	K	ERA	WHIP	OBA	vL	vR	BF/G	H%	S%	xERA	G	L	F	Ctl	Dom	Cmd	hr/f	hr/9	RAR	BPV	R$
RH	Reliever	04	0	0	0	0	0	0.00	0.00																		
Age	23	05	0	0	0	0	0	0.00	0.00																		
Type	Pwr	06	0	0	0	0	0	0.00	0.00																		
Health	A	07 NYY *	7	2	1	72	104	2.62	1.11	219	132	156	9.7	34%	80%	2.68	37	22	41	2.9	13.0	**4.5**	9%	0.7	16.8	171	$15
PT/Exp	D	08 NYY	4	3	0	100	118	2.60	1.26	235	247	219	10.0	33%	80%	3.10	52	14	34	3.5	10.6	**3.0**	6%	0.4	21.6	126	$13
Consist	A	1st Half	2	2	0	49	56	2.03	1.27	217			8.2	31%	85%	3.45	52	11	38	4.4	10.3	**2.3**	4%	0.4	13.9	96	$7
LIMA Plan	B+	2nd Half	2	1	0	52	62	3.14	1.24	252			12.6	36%	75%	2.80	52	17	31	2.6	10.8	**4.1**	7%	0.5	7.7	154	$6
+/- Score	25	09 Proj	**12**	**6**	**0**	**199**	**236**	**3.12**	**1.12**	**214**			**25.1**	**30%**	**74%**	**2.94**	**50**	**16**	**35**	**3.2**	**10.7**	**3.4**	**8%**	**0.6**	**36.4**	**134**	**$29**

SP or RP, does it matter?

	Ctl	Dom	Cmd	OBA
SP:	3.4	10.2	3.0	.245
RP:	3.6	11.3	3.1	.211

Apparently not much, as he has elite skills either way. 4.7 Cmd after DL stint, so bid confidently.

Chico,Matt			W	L	Sv	IP	K	ERA	WHIP	OBA	vL	vR	BF/G	H%	S%	xERA	G	L	F	Ctl	Dom	Cmd	hr/f	hr/9	RAR	BPV	R$
LH	Starter	04 aa	3	7	0	62	55	6.68	2.03	342			21.9	41%	68%	7.31				5.1	8.0	**1.6**		1.2	-17.9	33	($4)
Age	25	05 aa	1	7	0	53	32	7.30	1.91	365			25.6	39%	64%	7.89				2.5	5.4	**2.1**		1.7	-19.6	8	($5)
Type	FB	06 aa	9	2	0	103	62	3.24	1.36	271			25.9	30%	80%	4.31				2.8	5.4	**1.9**		1.0	16.2	44	$11
Health	F	07 WAS *	8	10	0	178	100	4.60	1.53	278	273	283	24.0	29%	74%	5.56	33	20	47	4.0	5.1	**1.3**	10%	1.4	-3.8	-5	$5
PT/Exp	D	08 WAS	0	6	0	48	31	6.19	1.67	318	351	312	20.0	34%	67%	4.96	37	23	39	3.2	5.8	**1.8**	15%	1.9	-11.4	34	($2)
Consist	B	1st Half	0	6	0	48	31	6.19	1.67	318			20.0	34%	67%	4.96	37	23	39	3.2	5.8	**1.8**	15%	1.9	-11.4	34	($2)
LIMA Plan	D	2nd Half	0	0	0	0	0	0.00	0.00																		
+/- Score	32	09 Proj	**2**	**4**	**0**	**44**	**28**	**5.38**	**1.63**	**310**			**22.0**	**34%**	**70%**	**5.12**	**36**	**22**	**42**	**3.3**	**5.8**	**1.8**	**11%**	**1.4**	**-4.2**	**29**	**$0**

Underwent TJ surgery in July, will miss at least the first half of the 2009 season. Unless he gets the same procedure as the kid in "Little Big League", don't expect him to be worth owning when he gets back.

Chulk,Vinnie			W	L	Sv	IP	K	ERA	WHIP	OBA	vL	vR	BF/G	H%	S%	xERA	G	L	F	Ctl	Dom	Cmd	hr/f	hr/9	RAR	BPV	R$
RH	Reliever	04 TOR *	4	5	4	84	65	4.29	1.56	278	308	228	5.8	31%	76%	4.77	40	20	39	4.3	7.0	**1.6**	12%	1.3	1.5	28	$5
Age	30	05 TOR	0	1	0	72	39	3.88	1.31	251	283	231	4.9	26%	74%	4.79	42	19	39	3.3	4.9	**1.5**	10%	1.1	4.4	20	$3
Type	FB	06 2TM *	4	5	1	78	78	4.45	1.37	244	206	282	5.0	30%	71%	3.92	43	18	39	4.1	9.0	**2.2**	14%	1.3	0.7	72	$7
Health	C	07 SF	5	4	0	53	41	3.57	1.26	262	290	250	3.9	32%	72%	4.49	31	21	48	2.4	7.0	**2.9**	4%	0.5	5.6	70	$6
PT/Exp	D	08 SF	0	3	0	32	16	4.83	1.29	270	233	274	4.9	27%	69%	4.88	38	16	46	2.3	4.5	**2.0**	12%	1.7	-2.2	37	$1
Consist	A	1st Half	0	3	0	32	16	4.83	1.29	270			4.9	27%	69%	4.88	38	16	46	2.3	4.5	**2.0**	12%	1.7	-2.2	37	$1
LIMA Plan	B	2nd Half	0	0	0	0	0	0.00	0.00																		
+/- Score	-10	09 Proj	**1**	**3**	**0**	**40**	**28**	**4.33**	**1.32**	**264**			**4.8**	**30%**	**70%**	**4.49**	**38**	**18**	**43**	**2.7**	**6.4**	**2.3**	**9%**	**1.1**	**-0.7**	**57**	**$2**

Dom rate all over the map in last several seasons, only has value if he gets it back to '06-'07 levels. Elevated FBs mean HR issues are here to stay. May not get many more chances to straighten things out.

Colome,Jesus			W	L	Sv	IP	K	ERA	WHIP	OBA	vL	vR	BF/G	H%	S%	xERA	G	L	F	Ctl	Dom	Cmd	hr/f	hr/9	RAR	BPV	R$
RH	Reliever	04 TAM *	4	3	5	71	55	3.66	1.32	230	245	163	5.9	28%	72%	4.91	33	20	47	4.3	6.9	**1.6**	4%	0.5	6.8	20	$8
Age	31	05 TAM	2	3	0	45	28	4.59	1.60	298	291	276	5.7	32%	75%	4.89	42	21	36	3.6	5.6	**1.6**	13%	1.4	-1.2	24	$1
Type	Pwr FB	06 a/a	3	1	0	38	19	5.57	1.95	326			6.6	34%	74%	7.01				5.3	4.4	**0.8**		1.4	-4.9	-8	($1)
Health	C	07 WAS	5	1	1	66	43	3.82	1.38	256	311	218	4.7	29%	74%	5.04	36	19	45	3.7	5.9	**1.6**	6%	0.8	4.9	20	$6
PT/Exp	D	08 WAS	2	2	0	71	55	4.31	1.41	234	226	241	5.0	27%	70%	4.96	32	27	41	4.9	7.0	**1.4**	7%	0.8	-0.3	2	$3
Consist	C	1st Half	2	1	0	40	37	5.85	1.65	271			5.9	35%	62%	4.91	32	30	38	5.4	8.3	**1.5**	2%	0.2	-7.8	15	($0)
LIMA Plan	C	2nd Half	0	1	0	31	18	2.32	1.10	179			4.2	17%	90%	5.01	32	23	45	4.4	5.2	**1.2**	12%	1.5	7.4	-14	$3
+/- Score	-53	09 Proj	**3**	**2**	**0**	**73**	**49**	**4.72**	**1.50**	**266**			**5.1**	**29%**	**71%**	**5.16**	**35**	**23**	**42**	**4.3**	**6.1**	**1.4**	**9%**	**1.1**	**-7.4**	**5**	**$2**

Even cherry-picking his best Ctl and Dom, he would still be under a 2.0 Cmd. He simply doesn't strike out enough batters to overcome his bb%. Throw in the high FB%, and you have a lot of 3-run HRs.

Colon,Bartolo			W	L	Sv	IP	K	ERA	WHIP	OBA	vL	vR	BF/G	H%	S%	xERA	G	L	F	Ctl	Dom	Cmd	hr/f	hr/9	RAR	BPV	R$
RH	Starter	04 ANA	18	12	0	208	158	5.02	1.37	268	273	256	26.3	29%	69%	4.49	39	17	45	3.1	6.8	**2.2**	13%	1.6	-15.0	57	$15
Age	35	05 ANA	21	8	0	222	157	3.48	1.16	255	250	258	27.5	29%	74%	3.92	44	17	39	1.7	6.4	**3.7**	10%	1.1	24.3	89	$28
Type	Con	06 LAA	1	5	0	56	31	5.13	1.46	310	354	261	24.6	32%	70%	4.52	41	22	37	1.8	5.0	**2.8**	15%	1.8	-4.0	61	$1
Health	F	07 LAA	6	8	0	99	76	6.34	1.62	320	313	325	23.7	36%	62%	4.51	42	18	40	2.6	6.9	**2.6**	11%	1.4	-22.5	73	$1
PT/Exp	C	08 BOS *	7	3	0	70	44	3.53	1.26	268	309	253	18.4	30%	75%	4.35	40	21	39	2.1	5.7	**2.7**	8%	0.9	7.1	63	$8
Consist	A	1st Half	6	2	0	47	35	3.07	1.16	251			21.3	29%	78%	4.00	38	21	40	1.9	6.6	**3.4**	9%	1.0	7.4	83	$7
LIMA Plan	B	2nd Half	1	1	0	23	10	4.45	1.48	300			14.6	32%	71%	4.92	48	17	35	2.4	3.7	**1.5**	7%	0.8	-0.3	27	$1
+/- Score	-24	09 Proj	**3**	**2**	**0**	**40**	**24**	**4.78**	**1.42**	**292**			**19.0**	**32%**	**69%**	**4.56**	**42**	**20**	**39**	**2.3**	**5.5**	**2.4**	**10%**	**1.1**	**-0.7**	**56**	**$2**

4-2, 3.92 ERA in 39 IP at BOS. PRO: Improved xERA; Ctl trending back in right direction. CON: Dom drop; injury risk. Quit on his team rather than go to pen, another "career-limiting move". End of the line is near.

Condrey,Clay			W	L	Sv	IP	K	ERA	WHIP	OBA	vL	vR	BF/G	H%	S%	xERA	G	L	F	Ctl	Dom	Cmd	hr/f	hr/9	RAR	BPV	R$
RH	Reliever	04 aaa	9	9	0	155	58	6.31	1.78	352			27.0	36%	66%	7.02				2.2	3.3	**1.5**		1.3	-37.5	-3	($5)
Age	33	05 aaa	7	8	0	132	57	5.32	1.71	344			24.5	36%	71%	6.51				2.1	3.9	**1.9**		1.1	-16.5	15	($1)
Type	Con GB	06 PHI *	6	4	6	79	37	3.28	1.52	296			5.9	32%	79%	4.76	48	23	29	3.0	4.2	**1.4**	6%	0.6	11.8	19	$8
Health	A	07 PHI *	6	0	3	72	36	4.55	1.48	296	299	302	6.5	33%	68%	4.58	46	25	28	2.7	4.4	**1.7**	6%	0.5	-1.1	33	$5
PT/Exp	D	08 PHI	3	4	1	69	34	3.26	1.51	304	320	288	5.5	33%	81%	4.34	54	19	27	2.5	4.4	**1.8**	9%	0.8	8.6	45	$4
Consist	A	1st Half	1	1	1	33	18	4.36	1.48	306			6.1	33%	73%	4.30	52	18	31	2.2	4.9	**2.3**	11%	1.1	-0.4	59	$1
LIMA Plan	C+	2nd Half	2	3	0	36	16	2.25	1.53	302			5.0	33%	87%	4.37	57	19	24	2.7	4.0	**1.5**	6%	0.5	9.0	32	$3
+/- Score	-29	09 Proj	**4**	**3**	**0**	**58**	**28**	**4.19**	**1.52**	**303**			**6.3**	**32%**	**74%**	**4.46**	**52**	**21**	**27**	**2.6**	**4.3**	**1.6**	**11%**	**0.9**	**-0.8**	**37**	**$3**

ERA benefitted from high S%, especially in 2H. Not fooling hitters much at all, his only savings grace is a high GB. But low Dom rate means he has no margin of error, so with any bad hr/f luck, he's toast.

SCOTT MONROE

Contreras,Jose

		Yr	Tm	W	L	Sv	IP	K	ERA	WHIP	OBA	vL	vR	BF/G	H%	S%	xERA	G	L	F	Ctl	Dom	Cmd	hr/f	hr/9	RAR	BPV	R$
RH	Starter	04	2AL	13	9	0	170	150	5.50	1.47	257	251	254	24.1	29%	67%	4.37	44	16	40	4.4	7.9	1.8	16%	1.6	-22.5	45	$9
Age	37	05	CHW	15	7	0	204	154	3.61	1.23	235	231	233	26.5	27%	74%	4.08	44	20	36	3.3	6.8	2.1	11%	1.0	19.1	55	$22
Type		06	CHW	13	9	0	196	134	4.27	1.27	260	267	248	27.4	29%	68%	4.24	45	16	39	2.5	6.2	2.4	8%	0.9	6.9	65	$18
Health	D	07	CHW	10	17	0	189	113	5.57	1.56	303	333	270	26.4	33%	65%	4.75	45	19	36	3.0	5.4	1.8	9%	1.0	-24.9	40	$4
PT/Exp	A	08	CHW	7	6	0	121	70	4.54	1.36	276	286	258	25.9	30%	68%	4.17	51	19	30	2.6	5.2	2.0	10%	0.9	-2.8	52	$7
Consist	B	1st Half		7	6	0	104	59	3.99	1.24	257			27.0	28%	70%	3.93	54	18	28	2.4	5.1	2.1	11%	0.9	4.5	58	$9
LIMA Plan	C	2nd Half		0	0	0	17	11	7.80	2.08	373			21.6	42%	62%	5.57	39	24	38	3.6	5.7	1.6	8%	1.0	-7.4	22	($2)
+/- Score	-18	09	Proj	1	1	0	29	19	5.59	1.59	306			26.1	34%	65%	4.68	44	20	36	3.1	5.9	1.9	9%	0.9	-0.9	45	$0

Enhanced his ground-ball approach to take a step back into fantasy relevance, but blew out his Achilles in August. Will miss most of 2009. Career very much in jeopardy.

Cook,Aaron

		Yr	Tm	W	L	Sv	IP	K	ERA	WHIP	OBA	vL	vR	BF/G	H%	S%	xERA	G	L	F	Ctl	Dom	Cmd	hr/f	hr/9	RAR	BPV	R$
RH	Starter	04	COL *	9	5	0	142	61	3.92	1.37	271	267	324	26.5	29%	71%	4.32	58	16	26	2.9	3.9	1.3	6%	0.5	5.9	27	$8
Age	30	05	COL	7	2	0	83	24	3.68	1.41	301	313	281	27.7	31%	76%	3.96	62	20	19	1.7	2.6	1.5	14%	0.9	5.8	40	$5
Type	Con xGB	06	COL	9	15	0	212	92	4.24	1.40	288	314	258	28.6	31%	70%	4.13	58	18	24	2.3	3.9	1.7	10%	0.7	6.4	43	$10
Health	D	07	COL	8	7	0	166	61	4.12	1.34	275	263	295	28.3	29%	71%	4.20	58	19	24	2.4	3.3	1.4	11%	0.8	6.3	31	$9
PT/Exp	A	08	COL	16	9	0	211	96	3.96	1.34	284	297	276	28.2	31%	70%	4.01	56	20	24	2.0	4.1	2.0	7%	0.6	8.1	52	$15
Consist	A	1st Half		10	5	0	116	55	3.64	1.32	276			29.0	29%	75%	4.10	55	18	27	2.2	4.3	2.0	10%	0.9	9.1	51	$10
LIMA Plan	D+	2nd Half		6	4	0	95	41	4.36	1.38	293			27.2	32%	66%	3.89	57	24	20	1.9	3.9	2.1	3%	0.2	-1.0	54	$5
+/- Score	-8	09	Proj	12	9	0	189	79	4.06	1.36	284			27.8	30%	70%	4.07	57	20	23	2.2	3.8	1.7	9%	0.6	6.3	44	$11

Uses one skill (GB%) to produce incredibly consistent results (see xERA trend). Very low PQS DIS% (6%) speaks to his ability to keep his team, and you, in every game with a chance at a W. That's H2H gold.

Corcoran,Roy

		Yr	Tm	W	L	Sv	IP	K	ERA	WHIP	OBA	vL	vR	BF/G	H%	S%	xERA	G	L	F	Ctl	Dom	Cmd	hr/f	hr/9	RAR	BPV	R$
RH	Reliever	04	aaa	5	1	5	44	29	3.67	1.52	261			6.5	32%	73%	3.70				4.7	5.9	1.3		0.0	3.6	65	$5
Age	29	05	aaa	4	4	3	67	47	4.87	1.52	269			5.8	31%	68%	4.52				4.3	6.2	1.4		0.8	-4.7	44	$3
Type	Pwr xGB	06	a/a	2	6	27	59	59	2.03	1.45	214			5.3	29%	86%	2.97				6.1	8.9	1.5		0.2	18.2	91	$16
Health	A	07	aa	4	4	15	61	40	4.98	2.05	329			5.7	39%	74%	6.22				6.0	5.9	1.0		0.2	-3.9	40	$4
PT/Exp	D	08	SEA *	6	2	7	87	47	3.86	1.57	255	258	221	6.0	29%	74%	4.32	69	10	20	5.4	4.9	0.9	4%	0.2	5.2	-11	$7
Consist	F	1st Half		0	0	4	32	20	4.79	1.94	276			5.1	32%	74%	5.26	71	5	24	7.8	5.6	0.7	5%	0.3	-1.8	-63	($0)
LIMA Plan	C	2nd Half		6	2	3	54	27	3.31	1.34	242			6.8	28%	74%	3.85	69	12	19	4.0	4.5	1.1	3%	0.2	7.0	20	$7
+/- Score	-44	09	Proj	4	3	0	58	38	4.66	1.60	272			5.7	32%	70%	3.97	70	10	20	5.0	5.9	1.2	8%	0.5	3.2	20	$2

6-2, 3.22 ERA in 73 IP at SEA. Another case where high GB% covers a lot of ills. But unlike Cook (above), BBs increase the degree of difficulty. As hr/f normalizes, danger level rises.

Cordero,Chad

		Yr	Tm	W	L	Sv	IP	K	ERA	WHIP	OBA	vL	vR	BF/G	H%	S%	xERA	G	L	F	Ctl	Dom	Cmd	hr/f	hr/9	RAR	BPV	R$
RH	Reliever	04	MON	7	3	14	82	83	2.96	1.35	227	243	205	5.1	29%	82%	4.53	29	20	51	4.7	9.1	1.9	7%	0.9	13.2	43	$14
Age	27	05	WAS	2	4	47	74	61	1.82	0.97	208	186	205	3.9	24%	90%	3.87	35	16	49	2.1	7.4	3.6	9%	1.1	22.2	91	$26
Type	Pwr FB	06	WAS	7	4	29	73	69	3.20	1.11	223	219	212	4.3	25%	81%	3.91	35	13	52	2.7	8.5	3.1	13%	1.6	11.6	93	$21
Health	F	07	WAS	3	3	37	75	62	3.36	1.39	262	221	295	4.3	31%	79%	4.45	38	19	43	3.5	7.4	2.1	8%	1.0	9.9	56	$18
PT/Exp	B	08	WAS	0	0	0	4	5	2.09	2.09	331	250	429	3.6	46%	89%	4.62	50	14	36	6.3	10.5	1.7	0%	0.0	1.2	47	$0
Consist	A	1st Half		0	0	0	4	5	2.09	2.09	331			3.6	46%	89%	4.62	50	14	36	6.3	10.5	1.7	0%	0.0	1.2	47	$0
LIMA Plan	B+	2nd Half		0	0	0	0	0	0.00	0.00																		
+/- Score	-78	09	Proj	2	2	8	40	35	3.83	1.33	257			4.4	30%	75%	4.19	40	16	44	3.2	7.9	2.5	10%	1.1	0.8	75	$6

Arm problems ended season almost before it started; had July surgery for torn bicep tendon and torn labrum. Recovery timeline murky, skills were only borderline closer-worthy when healthy. Pass.

Cordero,Francisco

		Yr	Tm	W	L	Sv	IP	K	ERA	WHIP	OBA	vL	vR	BF/G	H%	S%	xERA	G	L	F	Ctl	Dom	Cmd	hr/f	hr/9	RAR	BPV	R$
RH	Reliever	04	TEX	3	4	49	71	79	2.15	1.29	230	235	216	4.5	33%	82%	3.70	42	18	40	4.0	10.0	2.5	1%	0.1	20.1	91	$26
Age	34	05	TEX	3	1	37	69	79	3.39	1.32	239	250	214	4.2	33%	76%	3.53	43	19	38	3.9	10.3	2.6	7%	0.7	8.3	101	$19
Type	Pwr	06	2TM	10	5	22	75	84	3.72	1.34	246	286	219	4.2	33%	74%	3.65	40	21	39	3.8	10.1	2.6	9%	0.8	7.5	96	$18
Health	A	07	MIL	0	4	44	63	86	2.99	1.11	226	225	212	3.9	34%	74%	2.80	41	17	42	2.6	12.2	4.8	7%	0.6	11.2	170	$22
PT/Exp	A	08	CIN	5	4	34	70	78	3.33	1.41	235	212	252	4.2	31%	78%	3.88	41	22	37	4.9	10.0	2.1	9%	0.8	8.2	67	$19
Consist	B	1st Half		3	1	15	36	40	2.52	1.20	179			4.2	24%	83%	3.81	41	18	40	5.3	10.1	1.9	9%	0.8	7.7	58	$11
LIMA Plan	C+	2nd Half		2	3	19	35	38	4.16	1.62	286			4.2	38%	75%	3.96	40	26	34	4.4	9.9	2.2	9%	0.8	0.5	77	$8
+/- Score	-3	09	Proj	4	4	38	73	80	3.72	1.30	233			4.1	31%	73%	3.65	41	21	38	4.0	9.9	2.5	8%	0.7	6.2	90	$20

Gave back all of 2007's skill gains (and then some), but managed to hold closer role. Troubling Ctl spike drove BPV dip, and will raise your anxiety level. But saves could be secure in rocky NL picture.

Corey,Bryan

		Yr	Tm	W	L	Sv	IP	K	ERA	WHIP	OBA	vL	vR	BF/G	H%	S%	xERA	G	L	F	Ctl	Dom	Cmd	hr/f	hr/9	RAR	BPV	R$
RH	Reliever	04		0	0	0	0	0	0.00	0.00																		
Age	35	05	aaa	3	6	0	60	38	7.58	1.72	330			6.3	36%	56%	6.53				3.0	5.7	1.9		1.4	-24.2	21	($3)
Type	Con	06	BOS *	3	1	15	76	59	3.47	1.34	262			5.4	32%	74%	4.21	40	24	35	3.1	6.9	2.2	5%	0.5	10.2	60	$12
Health	A	07	BOS *	7	8	3	78	60	4.88	1.35	265			4.9	31%	64%	2.72	60	30	10	3.0	7.0	2.3	31%	0.9	-3.6	82	$8
PT/Exp	D	08	2TM *	1	3	2	56	29	5.63	1.46	301	274	309	4.4	31%	64%	4.79	42	20	39	2.3	4.7	2.1	12%	1.4	-9.1	43	$1
Consist	D	1st Half		1	1	1	35	18	4.59	1.31	278			4.3	30%	65%	4.62	41	22	37	2.1	4.5	2.2	7%	0.8	-1.2	45	$2
LIMA Plan	B	2nd Half		0	2	1	21	11	7.39	1.72	337			4.6	33%	63%	5.08	43	16	41	2.6	4.9	1.9	19%	2.6	-7.9	39	($1)
+/- Score	13	09	Proj	1	1	0	15	9	4.97	1.45	294			4.9	32%	68%	4.53	43	20	37	2.5	5.6	2.3	11%	1.2	-0.3	54	$1

1-3, 6.80 ERA in 45 IP at BOS and SD. Soft-skilled journeyman got a Golden Ticket (trade to SD in May) and couldn't capitalize. At 35, that was probably his last chance to stick. It's a tough business.

Cormier,Lance

		Yr	Tm	W	L	Sv	IP	K	ERA	WHIP	OBA	vL	vR	BF/G	H%	S%	xERA	G	L	F	Ctl	Dom	Cmd	hr/f	hr/9	RAR	BPV	R$
RH	Reliever	04	ARI *	6	10	0	158	109	4.38	1.59	302	387	297	20.4	34%	74%	4.40	48	21	31	3.3	6.2	1.9	10%	0.9	-2.3	49	$4
Age	28	05	ARI	7	3	0	79	63	5.12	1.63	278	300	273	5.4	33%	69%	4.40	50	23	27	4.9	7.2	1.5	10%	0.8	-8.5	25	$3
Type	GB	06	ATL *	8	8	0	127	66	5.23	1.77	323	271	351	15.7	35%	71%	5.01	50	21	29	3.8	4.7	1.2	10%	0.9	-11.7	8	($0)
Health	A	07	ATL *	7	9	0	106	55	6.10	1.73	323			22.3	33%	69%	4.81	51	19	30	3.4	4.7	1.4	20%	1.9	-21.8	20	($1)
PT/Exp	D	08	BAL *	4	4	1	92	57	3.33	1.46	266	240	308	7.3	31%	77%	4.10	57	21	22	3.9	5.6	1.4	6%	0.4	11.5	29	$7
Consist	A	1st Half		2	3	1	47	30	1.77	1.26	216			7.8	26%	86%	3.88	58	20	22	4.3	5.9	1.4	3%	0.2	14.8	25	$6
LIMA Plan	C+	2nd Half		2	1	0	46	27	4.92	1.66	310			7.0	35%	70%	4.29	56	21	23	3.5	5.3	1.5	8%	0.6	-3.2	34	$0
+/- Score	-36	09	Proj	4	4	0	77	45	4.47	1.54	285			8.5	32%	72%	4.35	54	21	25	3.8	5.3	1.4	11%	0.8	0.7	26	$3

3-3, 3.89 in 74 IP at BAL. The third guy on this page who uses GBs to mask otherwise-ugly skills. Ctl is again the key; he's neither Corcoran-bad nor Cook-good. Struggles with RH hitters are the fatal flaw.

Corpas,Manny

		Yr	Tm	W	L	Sv	IP	K	ERA	WHIP	OBA	vL	vR	BF/G	H%	S%	xERA	G	L	F	Ctl	Dom	Cmd	hr/f	hr/9	RAR	BPV	R$
RH	Reliever	04		0	0	0	0	0	0.00	0.00																		
Age	26	05		0	0	0	0	0	0.00	0.00																		
Type	GB	06	COL *	3	3	19	77	63	2.22	1.06	238	281	290	4.0	29%	81%	3.43	45	20	34	1.6	7.3	4.5	5%	0.5	21.6	112	$17
Health	A	07	COL	4	2	19	78	58	2.08	1.06	223	234	214	4.0	26%	84%	3.31	57	14	28	2.3	6.7	2.9	9%	0.7	22.6	94	$18
PT/Exp	C	08	COL	3	4	4	80	50	4.52	1.46	293	285	308	4.6	33%	70%	4.11	50	23	28	2.6	5.6	2.2	9%	0.8	-2.4	59	$4
Consist	A	1st Half		1	3	4	40	25	5.63	1.58	290			4.9	32%	66%	4.29	55	19	26	3.8	5.6	1.5	15%	1.1	-6.7	31	$1
LIMA Plan	B+	2nd Half		2	1	0	40	25	3.40	1.33	296			4.3	34%	75%	3.93	44	27	30	1.4	5.7	4.2	5%	0.5	4.3	87	$3
+/- Score	28	09	Proj	2	2	20	54	37	3.53	1.25	260			4.3	30%	74%	3.72	51	20	29	2.4	6.2	2.6	10%	0.8	4.1	78	$11

Victimized by a few too many BB and HR in 1H, but largely righted the ship in 2H. Dom trend says all isn't well, and raises warning flags about his ability to close even if he gets the role back.

Correia,Kevin

		Yr	Tm	W	L	Sv	IP	K	ERA	WHIP	OBA	vL	vR	BF/G	H%	S%	xERA	G	L	F	Ctl	Dom	Cmd	hr/f	hr/9	RAR	BPV	R$
RH	Starter	04	aaa	3	7	0	105	59	4.54	1.46	292			15.9	32%	69%	4.70				2.7	5.1	1.9		0.8	-2.5	44	$3
Age	28	05	SF *	5	7	7	104	74	5.21	1.57	277	311	242	10.0	30%	71%	5.01	37	24	39	4.4	6.4	1.4	13%	1.5	-12.4	10	$4
Type		06	SF	2	0	0	69	57	3.51	1.24	247	275	218	6.0	30%	73%	4.27	34	22	44	2.9	7.4	2.6	6%	0.7	8.3	68	$6
Health	B	07	SF	4	7	0	102	80	3.45	1.32	247	217	257	7.3	29%	76%	4.30	45	15	40	3.5	7.1	2.0	7%	0.8	12.2	55	$9
PT/Exp	C	08	SF *	4	8	0	122	76	5.74	1.63	307	307	312	20.6	34%	66%	5.00	38	25	37	3.5	5.6	1.6	10%	1.2	-22.1	24	($2)
Consist	A	1st Half		2	5	0	53	36	4.35	1.36	262			22.8	29%	70%	4.62	36	24	40	3.2	6.1	1.9	9%	1.1	-0.5	38	$3
LIMA Plan	C+	2nd Half		2	3	0	69	40	6.81	1.85	338			19.3	37%	64%	5.33	39	25	35	3.7	5.2	1.4	11%	1.3	-21.5	13	($5)
+/- Score	14	09	Proj	2	3	0	62	42	4.79	1.45	277			5.4	31%	70%	4.69	39	22	39	3.3	6.1	1.8	10%	1.2	-2.7	37	$2

No good news in BPI trends here: Ctl and Dom getting worse; both accelerated in wrong direction in 2H. Returned to bullpen in Sept. with disastrous results, but that may be his best hope for positive value.

RAY MURPHY

Cotts,Neal

Cotts,Neal		Yr	W	L	Sv	IP	K	ERA	WHIP	OBA	vL	vR	BF/G	H%	S%	xERA	G	L	F	Ctl	Dom	Cmd	hr/f	hr/9	RAR	BPV	R$
LH Reliever		04 CHW	4	4	0	65	58	5.67	1.40	249	269	231	5.0	28%	64%	4.05	44	20	35	4.1	8.0	**1.9**	20%	1.8	-9.9	55	$3
Age	29	05 CHW	4	0	0	60	58	1.95	1.11	183	206	155	3.5	25%	82%	3.75	46	18	36	4.3	8.7	**2.0**	2%	0.1	18.0	63	$10
Type	Pwr FB	06 CHW	1	2	1	54	43	5.17	1.63	296	263	314	3.5	32%	75%	4.57	42	21	37	4.0	7.2	**1.8**	19%	2.0	-4.1	41	$1
Health	A	07 CHC *	2	3	0	67	47	6.73	1.82	285			7.9	33%	63%	5.80	44	15	42	6.2	6.4	**1.0**	8%	0.9	-19.0	-32	($3)
PT/Exp	D	08 CHC *	2	2	3	63	65	3.70	1.51	281	269	263	4.0	36%	79%	4.08	37	21	42	3.7	9.4	**2.6**	9%	1.0	4.4	85	$5
Consist	C	1st Half	2	1	3	38	35	3.04	1.61	280			5.0	36%	82%	4.19	46	23	31	4.7	8.5	**1.8**	6%	0.5	5.7	51	$3
LIMA Plan	B	2nd Half	0	1	0	25	30	4.68	1.36	284			3.1	36%	72%	3.40	33	21	46	2.2	10.8	**5.0**	16%	1.8	-1.3	147	$1
+/- Score	15	09 Proj	2	2	0	64	60	4.36	1.53	274			4.3	33%	74%	4.40	39	20	41	4.2	8.4	2.0	10%	1.1	-0.4	55	$2

0-2, 4.29 ERA in 35 IP at CHC. PRO: Elite Dom, made gains vs. RH hitters. CON: Ctl a long-time bugaboo, hr/f problems resurfaced in 2H. Due for some h% help, but expect continued volatility.

Crain,Jesse

Crain,Jesse		Yr	W	L	Sv	IP	K	ERA	WHIP	OBA	vL	vR	BF/G	H%	S%	xERA	G	L	F	Ctl	Dom	Cmd	hr/f	hr/9	RAR	BPV	R$
RH Reliever		04 aaa	3	2	19	50	57	3.05	1.20	233			5.0	31%	78%	3.30				3.0	10.2	**3.4**		0.9	8.0	113	$13
Age	27	05 MIN	12	5	1	79	25	2.73	1.14	215	194	225	4.3	22%	79%	5.08	46	16	37	3.3	2.8	**0.9**	6%	0.7	16.1	-13	$13
Type		06 MIN	4	5	1	76	60	3.54	1.27	235	259	263	4.7	32%	74%	3.28	55	21	24	2.1	7.1	**3.3**	11%	0.7	9.5	103	$9
Health	D	07 MIN	1	2	0	16	10	5.52	1.41	292	269	308	3.9	29%	68%	4.28	48	14	38	2.2	5.5	**2.5**	19%	2.2	-2.0	66	$1
PT/Exp	D	08 MIN	5	4	0	63	50	3.59	1.37	260	250	261	4.1	31%	76%	4.44	41	17	42	3.4	7.2	**2.1**	8%	0.9	5.9	55	$6
Consist	B	1st Half	3	2	0	33	26	2.97	1.41	260			4.5	30%	84%	4.61	40	17	43	3.8	7.0	**1.9**	9%	1.1	5.6	42	$4
LIMA Plan	B	2nd Half	2	2	0	29	24	4.29	1.33	259			3.7	31%	68%	4.25	41	17	41	3.1	7.3	**2.4**	6%	0.6	0.2	69	$3
+/- Score	-9	09 Proj	5	4	0	58	46	3.72	1.31	262			4.3	31%	74%	4.03	45	17	38	2.8	7.1	2.6	9%	0.9	2.8	77	$6

Wasn't quite the same in return from shoulder surgery, but close. 2006 GB% may have been an outlier, leaving a still-LIMA worthy skill set. 2H Ctl dip further evidence of shoulder strength. Not far from another 100 BPV.

Cruz,Juan

Cruz,Juan		Yr	W	L	Sv	IP	K	ERA	WHIP	OBA	vL	vR	BF/G	H%	S%	xERA	G	L	F	Ctl	Dom	Cmd	hr/f	hr/9	RAR	BPV	R$
RH Reliever		04 ATL	6	2	0	72	70	2.75	1.24	225	239	214	6.0	28%	82%	3.68	45	20	35	3.8	8.8	**2.3**	10%	0.9	13.4	79	$10
Age	30	05 OAK *	5	4	0	107	111	4.03	1.32	235	283	296	11.1	31%	70%	3.67	45	19	35	4.0	9.3	**2.3**	9%	0.8	4.5	82	$10
Type	Pwr xFB	06 ARI	5	6	0	94	88	4.20	1.35	231	263	199	13.0	29%	69%	4.18	40	23	37	4.5	8.4	**1.9**	7%	0.7	3.3	48	$8
Health	C	07 ARI	6	1	0	61	87	3.10	1.26	207	269	143	4.8	31%	80%	3.28	35	19	47	4.7	12.8	**2.7**	12%	1.0	10.0	116	$10
PT/Exp	C	08 ARI	4	0	0	52	71	2.61	1.26	189	159	221	3.8	28%	83%	3.83	27	16	57	5.4	12.4	**2.3**	8%	0.9	10.6	82	$8
Consist	B	1st Half	2	0	0	30	44	3.33	1.38	177			3.6	27%	79%	4.14	25	12	63	7.0	13.3	**1.9**	8%	0.9	3.4	54	$3
LIMA Plan	B+	2nd Half	2	0	0	22	27	1.64	1.09	205			4.0	29%	91%	3.45	29	20	51	3.3	11.0	**3.4**	8%	0.8	7.1	118	$4
+/- Score	-34	09 Proj	5	1	0	69	84	3.42	1.26	215			4.8	29%	77%	3.70	33	19	48	4.3	11.0	2.5	10%	1.1	5.4	93	$9

Another reliever with elite Dom garbled by Ctl problems. In this case, xFB profile raises the risk. xERA history smooths some of the volatility and gives a nice range of expectations. Deep sleeper for Svs in right situation.

Cueto,Johnny

Cueto,Johnny		Yr	W	L	Sv	IP	K	ERA	WHIP	OBA	vL	vR	BF/G	H%	S%	xERA	G	L	F	Ctl	Dom	Cmd	hr/f	hr/9	RAR	BPV	R$
RH Starter		04	0	0	0	0	0	0.00	0.00																		
Age	23	05	0	0	0	0	0	0.00	0.00																		
Type	Pwr FB	06	0	0	0	0	0	0.00	0.00																		
Health	A	07 a/a	8	4	0	83	88	3.41	1.15	261			24.1	33%	74%	3.69				1.3	9.6	**7.1**		1.0	10.8	179	$13
PT/Exp	C	08 CIN	9	14	0	174	158	4.81	1.41	266	249	275	24.3	31%	71%	4.16	39	21	41	3.5	8.2	**2.3**	14%	1.5	-11.6	69	$9
Consist	A	1st Half	6	8	0	98	83	4.68	1.36	258			24.7	29%	71%	4.22	38	22	41	3.4	7.6	**2.2**	15%	1.7	-5.0	61	$6
LIMA Plan	A	2nd Half	3	6	0	76	75	4.97	1.49	277			23.9	34%	70%	4.08	40	20	40	3.7	8.9	**2.4**	12%	1.3	-6.6	79	$3
+/- Score	49	09 Proj	14	12	0	199	195	4.12	1.27	256			25.2	31%	72%	3.69	39	21	40	2.7	8.8	3.3	12%	1.2	16.0	104	$19

So much to like here. Exciting Dom, tolerable Ctl, gained strength in 2H. Hr/f was the Achilles' heel, especially at home (1.8 hr/9). Solve that, and everything falls into place. UP: 18 Wins, 3.50 ERA

Danks,John

Danks,John		Yr	W	L	Sv	IP	K	ERA	WHIP	OBA	vL	vR	BF/G	H%	S%	xERA	G	L	F	Ctl	Dom	Cmd	hr/f	hr/9	RAR	BPV	R$
LH Starter		04	0	0	0	0	0	0.00	0.00																		
Age	24	05 aa	4	10	0	98	77	6.82	1.67	322			25.0	37%	60%	6.25				3.0	7.0	**2.4**		1.4	-30.4	41	($3)
Type	Pwr	06 a/a	9	9	0	140	140	5.69	1.59	296			23.4	35%	69%	6.05				3.6	9.0	**2.5**		1.9	-20.3	45	$5
Health	A	07 CHW	6	13	0	139	109	5.50	1.54	290	281	292	23.8	32%	69%	4.79	35	19	46	3.5	7.1	**2.0**	14%	1.8	-17.1	45	$4
PT/Exp	B	08 CHW	12	9	0	195	159	3.32	1.23	249	264	240	24.5	30%	75%	3.84	43	22	35	2.6	7.3	**2.8**	7%	0.7	24.6	82	$22
Consist	C	1st Half	5	4	0	93	69	2.62	1.23	248			24.0	29%	81%	3.91	48	19	34	2.7	6.7	**2.5**	6%	0.6	19.7	73	$11
LIMA Plan	D+	2nd Half	7	5	0	102	90	3.96	1.22	250			24.9	30%	69%	3.78	38	25	37	2.6	7.9	**3.1**	8%	0.8	4.9	90	$11
+/- Score	7	09 Proj	14	10	0	189	158	3.92	1.32	264			23.5	31%	74%	4.08	39	21	40	2.8	7.5	2.7	10%	1.1	8.1	78	$19

Added cut fastball to repertoire, which seemed to drive this breakout. Improved Cmd, reduced FBs, 50 pt reduction in BA vs. RH batters all create a profile for sustained success.

Davies,Kyle

Davies,Kyle		Yr	W	L	Sv	IP	K	ERA	WHIP	OBA	vL	vR	BF/G	H%	S%	xERA	G	L	F	Ctl	Dom	Cmd	hr/f	hr/9	RAR	BPV	R$
RH Starter		04 a/a	4	2	0	67	70	3.33	1.09	208			22.4	25%	76%	3.11				3.2	9.5	**3.0**		1.3	8.4	94	$9
Age	25	05 ATL *	12	8	0	160	119	4.57	1.57	274	264	295	21.2	32%	72%	5.13	34	25	41	4.6	6.7	**1.5**	7%	0.8	-6.3	9	$7
Type	FB	06 ATL	3	7	0	63	51	8.42	1.95	336	333	331	21.9	37%	59%	5.19	37	24	39	4.7	7.3	**1.5**	17%	2.0	-30.6	19	($5)
Health	C	07 2TM	7	15	0	136	99	6.09	1.65	288	275	293	22.2	32%	66%	5.13	39	21	41	4.6	6.6	**1.4**	12%	1.5	-27.3	10	$0
PT/Exp	C	08 KC *	15	9	0	170	101	3.70	1.46	275	251	300	23.3	31%	76%	5.02	39	22	40	3.5	5.3	**1.5**	6%	0.8	13.7	18	$14
Consist	A	1st Half	9	3	0	89	45	3.14	1.53	280			24.6	31%	80%	5.24	39	28	34	3.9	4.5	**1.2**	5%	0.6	13.2	-7	$8
LIMA Plan	C	2nd Half	6	6	0	82	56	4.30	1.38	270			22.0	30%	71%	4.66	39	19	42	3.1	6.2	**2.0**	8%	1.0	0.5	44	$6
+/- Score	-43	09 Proj	12	13	0	174	122	4.86	1.51	279			22.0	31%	70%	4.83	38	22	40	3.7	6.3	1.7	10%	1.2	-8.8	29	$9

9-7, 4.06 ERA in 113 IP at KC. Others look at BPV on bad KC team and move along. But you see 2H skill surge that nearly hit all LIMA filters, plus 3.4 Cmd in Sept., and put him on your end-game watch list. But just watch.

Davis,Doug

Davis,Doug		Yr	W	L	Sv	IP	K	ERA	WHIP	OBA	vL	vR	BF/G	H%	S%	xERA	G	L	F	Ctl	Dom	Cmd	hr/f	hr/9	RAR	BPV	R$
LH Starter		04 MIL	12	12	0	215	168	3.26	1.28	243	259	244	26.6	29%	75%	4.02	47	19	34	3.3	7.0	**2.1**	6%	0.6	26.5	61	$20
Age	33	05 MIL	11	11	0	222	208	3.85	1.30	238	259	228	26.8	29%	74%	3.85	44	20	36	3.8	8.4	**2.2**	12%	1.1	10.9	72	$19
Type	Pwr	06 MIL	11	11	0	203	159	4.92	1.52	265	307	253	26.5	31%	68%	4.61	44	20	36	4.5	7.0	**1.6**	9%	0.8	-10.8	27	$8
Health	B	07 ARI	13	12	0	193	144	4.25	1.59	280	252	290	26.3	32%	75%	4.62	47	19	34	4.4	6.7	**1.5**	10%	1.0	4.2	26	$10
PT/Exp	A	08 ARI	6	8	0	146	112	4.32	1.53	280	321	269	25.0	33%	73%	4.34	47	22	31	3.9	6.9	**1.8**	9%	0.8	-0.8	43	$5
Consist	A	1st Half	3	3	0	57	47	3.79	1.54	265			25.4	33%	75%	4.37	46	24	30	4.7	7.4	**1.6**	6%	0.5	3.4	30	$3
LIMA Plan	C	2nd Half	3	5	0	89	65	4.65	1.53	289			24.7	33%	71%	4.31	47	21	32	3.4	6.6	**1.9**	11%	1.0	-4.2	51	$2
+/- Score	-14	09 Proj	8	9	0	160	123	4.29	1.52	273			26.2	32%	73%	4.41	46	21	33	4.1	6.9	1.7	10%	0.9	-1.3	38	$7

Another typical season, until you factor in the thyroid cancer. Returned after six weeks with his usual stuff. Great comeback on his part; no reason to expect anything different going forward.

Davis,Jason

Davis,Jason		Yr	W	L	Sv	IP	K	ERA	WHIP	OBA	vL	vR	BF/G	H%	S%	xERA	G	L	F	Ctl	Dom	Cmd	hr/f	hr/9	RAR	BPV	R$
RH Starter		04 CLE *	5	9	0	168	105	4.77	1.62	301	305	317	21.8	34%	72%	4.57	52	18	30	3.7	5.6	**1.5**	10%	0.9	-6.9	31	$2
Age	29	05 CLE *	12	7	0	135	98	4.76	1.50	290	193	333	22.1	34%	69%	4.04	49	23	28	3.1	6.5	**2.1**	10%	0.8	-6.4	62	$9
Type		06 CLE	3	2	1	55	37	3.76	1.47	301	316	294	6.2	36%	73%	4.18	49	20	32	2.3	6.0	**2.6**	2%	0.2	5.4	74	$4
Health	A	07 2AL	2	0	0	37	19	5.84	1.81	287			7.3	31%	68%	5.87	49	18	33	6.1	4.6	**0.8**	9%	1.0	-6.1	-54	($1)
PT/Exp	D	08 PIT *	8	13	0	150	59	6.52	1.85	323	342	241	20.5	35%	62%	5.38	52	24	24	4.5	3.5	**0.8**	5%	0.4	-41.7	-29	($8)
Consist	C	1st Half	4	8	0	81	32	7.90	2.14	351			25.7	38%	60%					5.5	3.5	**0.6**		0.4	-36.3	7	($10)
LIMA Plan	F	2nd Half	4	5	0	69	27	4.90	1.51	286			16.0	31%	66%	4.73	52	24	24	3.4	3.5	**1.0**	6%	0.4	-5.3	2	$1
+/- Score	1	09 Proj	2	2	0	43	21	5.23	1.67	296			11.0	32%	69%	5.19	50	20	30	4.4	4.4	1.0	9%	0.8	-4.5	-12	($0)

2-4, 5.29 ERA in 34 IP at PIT. Stunning loss of Dom and, in turn, Cmd since '06 peak. Has tried starting, relieving, keeping score, sitting home... it doesn't matter. Young enough to find his old stuff... somewhere.

de la Rosa,Jorge

de la Rosa,Jorge		Yr	W	L	Sv	IP	K	ERA	WHIP	OBA	vL	vR	BF/G	H%	S%	xERA	G	L	F	Ctl	Dom	Cmd	hr/f	hr/9	RAR	BPV	R$
LH Starter		04 MIL *	5	9	0	109	78	5.45	1.54	279			19.5	32%	65%	4.78				4.0	6.4	**1.6**		0.9	-16.0	44	$1
Age	28	05 MIL	2	2	0	42	42	4.49	2.04	288	321	273	5.5	38%	76%	5.24	49	23	28	8.1	9.0	**1.1**	3%	0.2	-1.3	-31	($1)
Type	Pwr	06 2TM *	8	7	0	109	85	5.72	1.66	286	250	269	14.7	33%	67%	4.95	41	20	39	4.7	7.0	**1.5**	11%	1.2	-16.1	17	$3
Health	C	07 KC	8	12	0	130	82	5.82	1.64	304	234	321	22.8	33%	67%	5.07	41	20	39	3.7	5.7	**1.5**	12%	1.4	-21.0	22	$2
PT/Exp	C	08 COL *	13	8	0	152	145	4.56	1.47	263	289	253	20.9	33%	70%	4.02	46	20	34	4.2	8.6	**2.1**	9%	0.8	-5.4	65	$11
Consist	B	1st Half	5	4	0	70	68	5.38	1.52	286			19.5	35%	66%	3.96	46	16	37	3.5	8.7	**2.5**	12%	1.2	-9.6	85	$3
LIMA Plan	C+	2nd Half	8	4	0	82	77	3.86	1.43	243			22.2	31%	73%	4.10	45	22	33	4.7	8.5	**1.8**	5%	0.4	4.2	48	$8
+/- Score	15	09 Proj	12	10	0	160	138	4.74	1.50	272			22.8	33%	70%	4.29	44	21	36	4.1	7.8	1.9	10%	1.0	1.1	52	$9

10-8, 4.92 in 130 IP at COL. Had a winning formula for thin-air success in 1H, but luck stats did him in. Then couldn't sustain Ctl in 2H. GB/Dom combo is intriguing, but until Ctl improves he's "one skill away".

RAY MURPHY

Delcarmen,Manny			W	L	Sv	IP	K	ERA	WHIP	OBA	vL	vR	BF/G	H%	S%	xERA	G	L	F	Ctl	Dom	Cmd	hr/f	hr/9	RAR	BPV	R$
RH	Reliever	04	0	0	0	0	0	0.00	0.00																		
Age	27	05 a/a	7	5	5	59	62	3.20	1.44	248			5.7	33%	78%	3.68				4.6	9.5	2.1		0.5	8.0	92	$9
Type	Pwr	06 BOS *	2	1	0	70	62	4.62	1.44	283	319	302	5.1	36%	66%	3.80	45	26	30	3.0	8.0	2.7	3%	0.3	-0.6	86	$4
Health	A	07 BOS *	3	2	1	73	73	3.10	1.29	232	167	194	4.8	30%	77%	3.84	45	17	38	4.0	8.9	2.3	7%	0.6	12.7	77	$9
PT/Exp	D	08 BOS	1	2	2	74	72	3.27	1.12	208	190	218	4.1	27%	72%	3.41	52	13	35	3.4	8.7	2.6	7%	0.6	9.9	95	$9
Consist	A	1st Half	0	2	0	34	33	3.97	1.24	244			3.9	31%	69%	3.21	57	12	31	2.9	8.7	3.0	10%	0.8	1.6	113	$3
LIMA Plan	A	2nd Half	1	0	2	40	39	2.68	1.02	174			4.3	23%	74%	3.57	47	14	39	3.8	8.7	2.3	5%	0.4	8.3	79	$6
+/- Score	11	09 Proj	2	2	3	58	56	3.41	1.22	227			4.5	29%	72%	3.62	49	16	35	3.6	8.7	2.4	5%	0.5	5.7	87	$7

Fine Dom / GLF profile out of the pen. Consistent value for past two years with nothing scary on horizon. Legit closer candidate if his Cmd improves just a tad. That's what good LIMA picks are made of.

Dempster,Ryan			W	L	Sv	IP	K	ERA	WHIP	OBA	vL	vR	BF/G	H%	S%	xERA	G	L	F	Ctl	Dom	Cmd	hr/f	hr/9	RAR	BPV	R$
RH	Starter	04 CHC *	2	2	2	41	34	4.37	1.55	251	222	200	6.4	31%	71%	4.38	52	21	28	5.5	7.4	1.4	6%	0.4	-0.5	16	$2
Age	32	05 CHC	5	3	33	92	89	3.13	1.43	242	278	216	6.4	32%	78%	3.44	58	21	21	4.8	8.7	1.8	7%	0.4	12.7	63	$19
Type	Pwr	06 CHC	1	9	24	75	67	4.80	1.51	267	310	226	4.5	33%	68%	4.00	52	18	30	4.3	8.0	1.9	7%	0.6	-2.9	58	$10
Health	A	07 CHC	2	7	28	67	55	4.72	1.33	239	259	224	4.3	28%	67%	4.03	47	20	32	4.0	7.4	1.8	13%	1.1	-2.4	49	$13
PT/Exp	A	08 CHC	17	6	0	207	187	2.96	1.21	230	243	213	25.9	29%	77%	3.58	48	20	32	3.3	8.1	2.5	8%	0.6	33.4	83	$26
Consist	A	1st Half	9	3	0	105	86	3.26	1.18	219			25.3	26%	75%	3.65	51	19	30	3.5	7.4	2.1	11%	0.9	13.1	67	$13
LIMA Plan	D+	2nd Half	8	3	0	102	101	2.65	1.24	241			26.4	32%	79%	3.51	45	21	34	3.1	8.9	2.9	4%	0.4	20.3	100	$13
+/- Score	-13	09 Proj	13	11	0	203	180	3.72	1.32	241			26.1	29%	74%	3.79	49	20	31	3.8	8.0	2.1	10%	0.8	13.7	67	$18

Improbable career year as SP after 3 years in pen, fueled by improved Ctl and Cmd hike. Neither level supports sub-3.00 ERA, and nothing in his past says they're sustainable. He'll be good again, but not this good.

Devine,Joey			W	L	Sv	IP	K	ERA	WHIP	OBA	vL	vR	BF/G	H%	S%	xERA	G	L	F	Ctl	Dom	Cmd	hr/f	hr/9	RAR	BPV	R$
RH	Reliever	04	0	0	0	0	0	0.00	0.00																		
Age	25	05 ATL *	1	2	5	26	28	5.88	1.96	297			5.3	36%	74%	6.91				6.9	9.7	1.4		1.7	-5.3	31	$1
Type	Pwr FB	06 ATL *	2	0	0	17	28	5.26	1.64	212	333	286	4.6	35%	69%	4.08	13	38	50	7.9	14.7	1.9	12%	1.1	-1.6	43	$1
Health	C	07 ATL *	6	4	20	65	72	2.27	1.30	235	300	211	4.6	33%	83%	3.34	57	9	35	3.9	9.9	2.5	4%	0.3	17.4	107	$17
PT/Exp	D	08 OAK	6	1	1	46	49	0.59	0.83	151	197	120	4.1	22%	92%	3.22	39	18	43	3.0	9.6	3.3	0%	0.0	21.2	111	$13
Consist	A	1st Half	3	0	0	22	28	1.23	1.05	205			4.8	32%	87%	2.87	41	22	37	2.9	11.5	4.0	0%	0.0	8.5	148	$5
LIMA Plan	B+	2nd Half	3	1	1	24	21	0.00	0.63	95			3.5	13%	100%	3.56	37	15	48	3.0	8.0	2.6	0%	0.0	12.7	76	$7
+/- Score	******	09 Proj	8	3	18	68	73	3.04	1.09	204			4.3	27%	74%	3.49	40	17	43	3.3	9.7	2.9	7%	0.7	7.8	103	$18

Solid Ctl all year, stinginess with HR speaks to his stuff. 60-day DL stint (elbow) tells us that health remains a red flag. But he looks like the best closer-in-waiting around. Skills AND opportunity.

Dickey,R.A.			W	L	Sv	IP	K	ERA	WHIP	OBA	vL	vR	BF/G	H%	S%	xERA	G	L	F	Ctl	Dom	Cmd	hr/f	hr/9	RAR	BPV	R$
RH	Starter	04 TEX *	7	8	1	117	64	5.30	1.61	319	281	343	18.3	34%	70%	4.87	45	18	37	2.6	4.9	1.9	11%	1.3	-12.6	41	$2
Age	34	05 TEX *	2	8	0	150	78	7.30	1.80	335	200	297	25.3	36%	59%	5.00	52	17	31	3.4	4.7	1.4	11%	1.1	-54.3	21	($11)
Type	Con	06 aaa	9	8	1	131	50	7.87	1.77	327			28.0	32%	57%	7.06				3.6	3.5	1.0		1.9	-54.2	-26	($7)
Health	B	07 aaa	13	6	0	169	103	4.99	1.56	291			24.4	32%	70%	5.32				3.6	5.5	1.5		1.2	-10.9	26	$7
PT/Exp	D	08 SEA *	7	13	0	162	81	5.00	1.61	304	260	306	18.8	33%	70%	5.14	46	17	36	3.4	4.5	1.3	8%	1.0	-13.0	15	$2
Consist	B	1st Half	4	9	0	97	55	4.52	1.61	321			21.9	36%	71%	4.32	52	22	27	2.5	5.1	2.1	6%	0.5	-2.1	56	$2
LIMA Plan	C	2nd Half	3	4	0	65	26	5.71	1.61	278			15.4	27%	68%	6.01	43	14	43	4.7	3.6	0.8	12%	1.7	-10.9	-42	($1)
+/- Score	-29	09 Proj	2	3	0	44	22	5.17	1.63	302			5.0	32%	71%	5.28	46	17	38	3.7	4.6	1.2	10%	1.2	-4.6	5	$0

5-8, 5.21 ERA in 112 IP at SEA. Rubber-armed knuckleballer, cannon fodder as swingman in starts for beleaguered rotation. Again better in pen (2.00 ERA in 36 IP), but role change offers only slim hope.

Dolsi,Freddy			W	L	Sv	IP	K	ERA	WHIP	OBA	vL	vR	BF/G	H%	S%	xERA	G	L	F	Ctl	Dom	Cmd	hr/f	hr/9	RAR	BPV	R$
RH	Reliever	04	0	0	0	0	0	0.00	0.00																		
Age	26	05	0	0	0	0	0	0.00	0.00																		
Type	Pwr GB	06	0	0	0	0	0	0.00	0.00																		
Health	A	07	0	0	0	0	0	0.00	0.00																		
PT/Exp	F	08 DET *	1	5	5	60	36	3.47	1.52	256	364	215	5.4	29%	77%	4.75	51	22	27	5.0	5.4	1.1	6%	0.5	6.5	-7	$4
Consist	F	1st Half	1	2	4	26	14	3.08	1.38	245			5.1	28%	77%	4.57	50	24	26	4.1	4.8	1.1	5%	0.3	4.1	2	$3
LIMA Plan	C	2nd Half	0	3	1	33	22	3.77	1.64	265			5.6	31%	77%	4.89	53	20	28	5.6	6.0	1.1	7%	0.5	2.4	-14	$1
+/- Score	-51	09 Proj	0	2	0	29	18	4.34	1.55	262			5.4	30%	72%	4.71	51	22	27	5.0	5.6	1.1	8%	0.6	-1.0	-4	$0

1-5, 3.96 ERA in 48 IP at DET. GB%, hr/9 suggest potential, but poor Cmd, Ctl stand in the way. Split issues - 5.57 road ERA, .979 OPS vs. LH - say avoid chasing growing pains. Plenty of risk, too little reward.

Dotel,Octavio			W	L	Sv	IP	K	ERA	WHIP	OBA	vL	vR	BF/G	H%	S%	xERA	G	L	F	Ctl	Dom	Cmd	hr/f	hr/9	RAR	BPV	R$
RH	Reliever	04 2TM	6	6	36	85	122	3.70	1.19	221	245	188	4.5	32%	75%	3.19	28	19	54	3.5	12.9	3.7	13%	1.4	6.7	144	$24
Age	35	05 OAK	1	2	7	15	16	3.58	1.39	190	269	107	4.3	23%	79%	4.89	24	26	50	6.6	9.5	1.5	11%	1.2	1.5	-4	$4
Type	Pwr xFB	06 NYY	0	0	0	10	7	10.80	2.90	390	333	414	4.2	43%	63%	8.61	37	20	44	9.9	6.3	0.6	12%	1.8	-7.7	-139	($3)
Health	F	07 2TM	2	1	11	31	41	4.10	1.34	251	265	225	4.0	35%	73%	3.29	38	16	46	3.5	12.0	3.4	12%	1.2	1.4	137	$7
PT/Exp	D	08 CHW	4	4	1	67	92	3.76	1.21	216	240	194	3.8	29%	77%	3.11	38	16	46	3.9	12.4	3.2	18%	1.6	4.8	133	$9
Consist	F	1st Half	3	4	0	38	53	3.10	1.35	231			4.2	34%	81%	3.40	34	19	47	4.5	12.7	2.8	10%	1.0	5.8	118	$5
LIMA Plan	A	2nd Half	1	0	1	29	39	4.61	1.02	195			3.4	22%	68%	2.74	43	12	45	3.1	12.0	3.9	28%	2.5	-0.9	154	$4
+/- Score	37	09 Proj	3	2	3	44	58	3.93	1.22	227			3.9	32%	72%	3.18	38	17	46	3.5	12.0	3.4	13%	1.2	6.7	137	$7

Peaking again 2+ years off of TJS, marked by 2H Ctl / Cmd gains. Avoided DL, beatings at the Cell even with chronic gopheritis, but unlikely to do both again. Still a possibility to inherit save opportunities.

Downs,Scott			W	L	Sv	IP	K	ERA	WHIP	OBA	vL	vR	BF/G	H%	S%	xERA	G	L	F	Ctl	Dom	Cmd	hr/f	hr/9	RAR	BPV	R$
LH	Reliever	04 MON *	13	12	0	198	90	4.68	1.52	311	286	315	25.9	32%	73%	4.46	53	18	29	2.3	4.1	1.8	13%	1.3	-10.2	44	$6
Age	33	05 TOR *	6	6	0	133	104	4.82	1.38	281	234	262	17.3	32%	68%	3.43	54	22	24	2.5	7.1	2.8	18%	1.2	-7.4	91	$7
Type	Pwr xGB	06 TOR	6	2	1	77	61	4.09	1.34	252	232	258	5.6	29%	72%	3.64	56	18	26	3.5	7.1	2.0	15%	1.1	4.4	67	$8
Health	A	07 TOR	4	2	1	58	57	2.17	1.22	223	209	238	3.0	29%	84%	3.02	60	18	22	3.7	8.8	2.4	9%	0.5	16.7	97	$9
PT/Exp	C	08 TOR	0	3	5	71	57	1.78	1.15	213	194	226	4.4	26%	86%	3.13	66	12	22	3.4	7.3	2.1	7%	0.4	22.4	81	$10
Consist	A	1st Half	0	1	5	38	34	1.19	1.17	214			4.3	28%	91%	3.16	63	11	26	3.6	8.1	2.3	4%	0.2	14.7	91	$7
LIMA Plan	B	2nd Half	0	2	0	33	23	2.45	1.12	212			4.4	25%	80%	3.08	68	13	19	3.3	6.3	1.9	11%	0.5	7.7	71	$4
+/- Score	-56	09 Proj	3	3	5	83	68	3.36	1.28	243			5.9	29%	75%	3.27	62	15	23	3.4	7.4	2.2	11%	0.7	11.8	82	$10

Two years of great bottom line numbers across the board. No split issues; only Cmd, xERA suggest pullback from here. But who's complaining? Sept talk of 2009 rotation spot hints at more exposure.

Duchscherer,Justin			W	L	Sv	IP	K	ERA	WHIP	OBA	vL	vR	BF/G	H%	S%	xERA	G	L	F	Ctl	Dom	Cmd	hr/f	hr/9	RAR	BPV	R$
RH	Starter	04 OAK	7	6	0	96	59	3.28	1.22	239	247	235	7.5	25%	79%	4.48	43	17	40	3.0	5.5	1.8	11%	1.2	13.7	39	$10
Age	31	05 OAK	7	4	5	85	85	2.22	1.01	218	225	208	5.2	28%	82%	3.14	44	19	37	2.0	9.0	4.5	9%	0.7	22.6	130	$17
Type		06 OAK	2	1	9	55	51	2.93	1.11	250	248	241	4.2	31%	75%	3.41	37	26	38	1.5	8.3	5.7	7%	0.7	11.1	125	$11
Health	F	07 OAK	3	3	0	16	13	4.97	1.60	281	400	176	4.3	31%	74%	4.52	47	17	36	4.4	7.2	1.6	16%	1.7	-0.9	35	$2
PT/Exp	C	08 OAK	10	8	0	142	95	2.54	1.00	211	227	188	25.2	24%	78%	3.93	41	20	39	2.2	6.0	2.8	7%	0.7	31.6	70	$22
Consist	B	1st Half	8	5	0	85	55	1.91	0.92	198			25.1	23%	81%	3.84	41	23	37	2.0	5.8	2.9	4%	0.4	25.6	69	$16
LIMA Plan	C	2nd Half	2	3	0	57	40	3.49	1.11	231			25.4	25%	73%	4.06	42	16	41	2.4	6.3	2.7	10%	1.1	6.0	70	$6
+/- Score	-44	09 Proj	9	6	0	145	109	3.35	1.14	243			25.6	28%	74%	3.86	43	19	38	2.1	6.8	3.2	9%	0.9	10.2	85	$18

Elite Cmd was up to SP role, but health was not. Chronic hip problem finally shelved him in mid-August. Superior skills, but expect more of the same, i.e. enjoy the early numbers, don't pay for increased IP.

Duke,Zach			W	L	Sv	IP	K	ERA	WHIP	OBA	vL	vR	BF/G	H%	S%	xERA	G	L	F	Ctl	Dom	Cmd	hr/f	hr/9	RAR	BPV	R$
LH	Starter	04 aa	5	1	0	51	30	1.94	1.08	242			22.7	28%	83%	2.66				1.6	5.3	3.3		0.4	15.2	98	$8
Age	26	05 PIT *	20	5	0	192	117	2.49	1.21	260	150	273	26.5	30%	81%	3.78	48	26	26	2.0	5.5	2.7	7%	0.5	41.6	70	$26
Type	Con	06 PIT	10	15	0	215	117	4.48	1.50	296	264	310	28.0	33%	71%	4.43	51	20	29	2.8	4.9	1.7	8%	0.7	0.3	40	$8
Health	C	07 PIT	3	8	0	107	41	5.54	1.73	347	341	363	25.0	36%	70%	4.89	51	20	29	2.1	3.4	1.6	11%	1.2	-14.7	34	($3)
PT/Exp	A	08 PIT	5	14	0	185	87	4.82	1.50	306	279	308	26.4	33%	69%	4.60	48	21	31	2.3	4.2	1.9	9%	0.9	-12.5	41	$2
Consist	A	1st Half	4	5	0	97	36	3.99	1.49	301			26.8	32%	73%	4.83	50	20	29	2.5	3.3	1.3	5%	0.5	3.4	21	$3
LIMA Plan	C+	2nd Half	1	9	0	88	51	5.73	1.50	311			25.9	33%	64%	4.36	46	21	33	2.0	5.2	2.6	14%	1.4	-15.8	62	($1)
+/- Score	8	09 Proj	6	13	0	174	89	4.60	1.46	301			25.4	32%	70%	4.40	49	21	30	2.2	4.6	2.1	10%	1.0	-1.3	50	$5

Good GB%, Elite Ctl doesn't trump sub-standard Dom, lofty h%. Manages HRs, but .831 OPS vs. RH is revealing. And it's not like he dominates LHs. Consistency here isn't a good thing.

JOCK THOMPSON

Dumatrait,Phil

	Yr	Tm	W	L	Sv	IP	K	ERA	WHIP	OBA	vL	vR	BF/G	H%	S%	xERA	G	L	F	Ctl	Dom	Cmd	hr/f	hr/9	RAR	BPV	R$
LH Reliever	04		0	0	0	0	0	0.00	0.00																		
Age 27	05	aa	4	12	0	127	81	3.57	1.56	265			23.8	31%	76%	4.11				4.9	5.7	1.2		0.3	11.4	52	$5
Type	06	a/a	8	11	0	137	82	6.22	1.80	321			24.9	35%	67%	6.49				4.2	5.4	1.3		1.3	-28.7	10	($3)
Health F	07	CIN	* 10	10	0	143	72	6.04	1.70	306	471	443	23.6	32%	66%	5.77	35	23	42	4.1	4.5	1.1	9%	1.2	-28.5	-15	($1)
PT/Exp D	08	PIT	3	4	0	79	52	5.26	1.58	270	206	288	16.8	31%	67%	5.02	42	24	34	4.8	5.9	1.2	8%	0.8	-9.6	-2	$0
Consist B	1st Half		3	4	0	75	51	4.66	1.50	256			16.6	29%	69%	4.89	45	20	35	4.8	6.1	1.3	7%	0.7	-3.6	4	$2
LIMA Plan C+	2nd Half		0	0	0	3	1	18.52	3.23	484			20.9	48%	40%	7.88	6	76	18	5.3	2.6	0.5	32%	2.6	-6.0	-111	($2)
+/- Score -15	09	Proj	**3**	**4**	**0**	**58**	**35**	**5.28**	**1.66**	**291**			**19.0**	**32%**	**69%**	**5.22**	**44**	**20**	**36**	**4.5**	**5.4**	**1.2**	**9%**	**0.9**	**-6.3**	**-2**	**$0**

Lefthanded and consistent, but that's most of the good news. Dom and GB gains offset by ongoing Ctl and arm issues that have dogged his career. Surgery for bursitis ended season in July. Avoid.

Durbin,Chad

	Yr	Tm	W	L	Sv	IP	K	ERA	WHIP	OBA	vL	vR	BF/G	H%	S%	xERA	G	L	F	Ctl	Dom	Cmd	hr/f	hr/9	RAR	BPV	R$
RH Reliever	04	ARI	* 9	10	0	112	81	5.51	1.63	294			15.5	33%	69%	5.67				4.1	6.5	1.6		1.4	-17.2	27	$2
Age 31	05	aaa	4	5	0	115	82	5.93	1.53	287			19.7	31%	65%	5.58				3.5	6.4	1.8		1.6	-23.0	24	$0
Type	06	aaa	11	8	0	185	120	4.34	1.44	292			28.8	33%	72%	4.80				2.5	5.8	2.4		1.0	4.1	52	$12
Health A	07	DET	8	7	1	128	66	4.72	1.43	270	281	255	15.4	28%	71%	5.04	44	16	40	3.5	4.7	1.3	12%	1.5	-3.4	12	$7
PT/Exp C	08	PHI	5	4	1	88	63	2.87	1.32	247	311	214	5.2	29%	79%	4.29	46	21	34	3.6	6.5	1.8	6%	0.5	15.1	43	$9
Consist A	1st Half		2	1	0	44	30	1.44	1.26	240			5.9	29%	89%	4.39	42	22	36	3.3	6.2	1.9	2%	0.2	15.2	43	$5
LIMA Plan C	2nd Half		3	3	1	44	33	4.30	1.39	253			4.7	29%	70%	4.17	49	20	31	3.9	6.7	1.7	10%	0.8	-0.1	44	$3
+/- Score -53	09	Proj	**3**	**3**	**0**	**58**	**38**	**4.03**	**1.40**	**265**			**8.1**	**30%**	**73%**	**4.54**	**45**	**18**	**36**	**3.4**	**5.9**	**1.7**	**9%**	**0.9**	**-1.4**	**37**	**$3**

Found calling out of pen. Put up fine bottom line in tough park thanks to fortunate S%, hr/f in 1H. xERA trend is a positive, but Cmd suggests little upside and plenty of downside from here. Avoid.

Eaton,Adam

	Yr	Tm	W	L	Sv	IP	K	ERA	WHIP	OBA	vL	vR	BF/G	H%	S%	xERA	G	L	F	Ctl	Dom	Cmd	hr/f	hr/9	RAR	BPV	R$
RH Starter	04	SD	10	14	0	199	153	4.61	1.29	267	260	272	25.4	30%	68%	4.18	40	18	42	2.4	6.9	2.9	11%	1.3	-8.6	79	$13
Age 31	05	SD	11	5	0	128	100	4.28	1.44	279	309	255	23.3	33%	72%	4.25	41	24	35	3.1	7.0	2.3	10%	1.0	-0.6	62	$9
Type	06	TEX	7	4	0	65	43	5.12	1.57	299	320	279	22.4	32%	71%	4.84	37	24	38	3.3	6.0	1.8	13%	1.5	-4.5	33	$4
Health D	07	PHI	10	10	0	162	97	6.29	1.63	296	321	284	24.5	31%	64%	5.29	39	19	42	4.0	5.4	1.4	13%	1.7	-37.2	8	($0)
PT/Exp B	08	PHI	4	8	0	107	57	5.80	1.64	303	318	300	23.2	32%	66%	5.16	42	23	35	3.7	4.8	1.3	11%	1.3	-20.2	6	($2)
Consist A	1st Half		2	6	0	93	49	4.85	1.47	281			25.4	30%	69%	4.93	41	23	36	3.3	4.8	1.4	11%	1.2	-6.7	16	$1
LIMA Plan D	2nd Half		2	2	0	14	8	11.96	2.73	418			16.2	45%	56%	6.72	45	25	30	6.3	5.0	0.8	16%	1.9	-13.6	-56	($3)
+/- Score -11	09	Proj	**4**	**4**	**0**	**65**	**41**	**5.16**	**1.50**	**286**			**23.8**	**31%**	**68%**	**4.71**	**41**	**23**	**36**	**3.3**	**5.7**	**1.7**	**12%**	**1.3**	**-2.9**	**32**	**$2**

Poor Cmd, ongoing gopheritis regardless of venue, with GB% capped in low 40%s. Unable to overcome plunging Dom, finally optioned to AAA in July. Unlikely to get any worse, but how could it? Seriously avoid.

Embree,Alan

	Yr	Tm	W	L	Sv	IP	K	ERA	WHIP	OBA	vL	vR	BF/G	H%	S%	xERA	G	L	F	Ctl	Dom	Cmd	hr/f	hr/9	RAR	BPV	R$
LH Reliever	04	BOS	2	2	0	53	37	4.07	1.15	250	240	247	3.0	28%	69%	3.99	38	24	38	1.9	6.3	3.4	11%	1.2	2.4	78	$5
Age 39	05	2AL	2	5	1	52	38	7.62	1.46	297	320	278	3.4	32%	48%	4.23	40	23	36	2.4	6.6	2.7	16%	1.7	-20.8	71	($1)
Type Pwr FB	06	SD	4	3	0	52	53	3.28	1.25	254	240	258	3.0	33%	75%	3.47	43	20	37	2.6	9.2	3.5	8%	0.7	7.7	116	$7
Health A	07	OAK	1	2	17	68	51	3.97	1.26	259	205	278	4.2	31%	69%	4.44	34	20	45	2.5	6.8	2.7	5%	0.7	4.5	66	$11
PT/Exp C	08	OAK	2	5	0	62	57	4.96	1.44	253	232	265	3.8	30%	68%	4.36	45	12	44	4.4	8.3	1.9	10%	1.2	-4.7	54	$3
Consist B	1st Half		1	2	0	33	33	3.85	1.25	245			3.6	31%	71%	3.79	43	11	46	3.0	9.1	3.0	7%	0.8	2.0	103	$3
LIMA Plan C+	2nd Half		1	3	0	29	24	6.21	1.66	262			4.1	29%	65%	5.07	46	13	41	5.9	7.4	1.3	14%	1.6	-6.7	-1	($0)
+/- Score -6	09	Proj	**2**	**4**	**0**	**58**	**48**	**4.66**	**1.47**	**258**			**3.8**	**30%**	**71%**	**4.62**	**41**	**17**	**42**	**4.3**	**7.4**	**1.7**	**11%**	**1.2**	**-1.4**	**36**	**$3**

Age, expanded role vs. RH, and newfound FB level are taking their toll. Solid Dom, but Ctl -- 5.1 vs. RHB -- was shot from mid-May on. LIMA value hinges on his ability to resolve Ctl issues and limit gopheritis.

Escobar,Kelvim

	Yr	Tm	W	L	Sv	IP	K	ERA	WHIP	OBA	vL	vR	BF/G	H%	S%	xERA	G	L	F	Ctl	Dom	Cmd	hr/f	hr/9	RAR	BPV	R$
RH Reliever	04	ANA	11	12	0	208	191	3.94	1.29	247	252	236	26.5	30%	72%	3.93	43	17	40	3.3	8.3	2.5	9%	0.9	12.7	81	$19
Age 33	05	ANA	3	2	1	59	63	3.04	1.11	212	278	138	14.9	28%	74%	3.31	47	15	38	3.2	9.6	3.0	7%	0.6	9.7	111	$9
Type Pwr	06	LAA	11	14	0	189	147	3.62	1.28	265	258	270	26.5	31%	74%	3.93	45	19	36	2.4	7.0	2.9	8%	0.8	21.9	84	$20
Health F	07	LAA	18	7	0	196	160	3.40	1.27	248	264	233	27.3	30%	73%	4.06	44	17	39	3.0	7.4	2.4	5%	0.5	26.6	72	$25
PT/Exp B	08	LAA	0	0	0	0	0	0.00	0.00																		
Consist A	1st Half		0	0	0	0	0	0.00	0.00																		
LIMA Plan	2nd Half		0	0	0	0	0	0.00	0.00																		
+/- Score	09	Proj	**4**	**2**	**15**	**54**	**46**	**3.83**	**1.28**	**247**			**5.5**	**30%**	**72%**	**3.96**	**45**	**17**	**38**	**3.2**	**7.7**	**2.4**	**8%**	**0.8**	**3.1**	**75**	**$11**

Surgery for torn labrum ended season in late July. The good news is that his rotator cuff wasn't involved, making a July '09 return likely. With both BPIs and the experience, a closer role could be his for the taking.

Estes,Shawn

	Yr	Tm	W	L	Sv	IP	K	ERA	WHIP	OBA	vL	vR	BF/G	H%	S%	xERA	G	L	F	Ctl	Dom	Cmd	hr/f	hr/9	RAR	BPV	R$
LH Starter	04	COL	15	8	0	202	117	5.84	1.62	281	280	294	27.0	30%	66%	4.94	52	17	31	4.7	5.2	1.1	14%	1.3	-39.2	-3	$2
Age 36	05	ARI	7	8	0	123	63	4.82	1.44	275	259	284	25.6	29%	69%	4.44	51	22	27	3.3	4.6	1.4	13%	1.1	-8.8	23	$4
Type Con xGB	06	SD	0	1	0	6	4	4.50	1.33	228			25.5	28%	63%	3.57	74	5	21	4.5	6.0	1.3	0%	0.0	-0.0	38	$0
Health F	07	aa	0	1	0	7	3	14.91	2.98	468			10.5	45%	53%	15.56				4.5	3.2	0.7		4.5	-9.2	-138	($3)
PT/Exp F	08	SD	* 7	5	0	88	40	4.76	1.56	303	195	311	23.2	32%	71%	4.51	54	21	25	3.0	4.1	1.4	12%	1.0	-5.4	24	$3
Consist F	1st Half		5	3	0	58	32	4.11	1.35	268			22.6	29%	71%	4.12	57	15	28	2.8	4.9	1.7	10%	0.9	1.2	47	$4
LIMA Plan C	2nd Half		2	2	0	30	8	6.07	1.99	362			24.2	37%	71%	5.38	52	26	22	3.5	2.6	0.7	15%	1.2	-6.5	-19	($2)
+/- Score -23	09	Proj	**5**	**4**	**0**	**70**	**32**	**5.14**	**1.61**	**303**			**24.4**	**32%**	**70%**	**4.51**	**59**	**17**	**24**	**3.5**	**4.1**	**1.2**	**15%**	**1.2**	**-1.5**	**17**	**$1**

2-3, 4.85 ERA in 44 IP at SD. 35-year old FA's only asset is his GB rate. As his historical hr/9, hr/f suggest, it isn't really all that. And as his ERA past suggests, it isn't enough. Cmd alone tells you to avoid.

Eveland,Dana

	Yr	Tm	W	L	Sv	IP	K	ERA	WHIP	OBA	vL	vR	BF/G	H%	S%	xERA	G	L	F	Ctl	Dom	Cmd	hr/f	hr/9	RAR	BPV	R$
LH Starter	04		0	0	0	0	0	0.00	0.00																		
Age 25	05	MIL	* 11	5	1	140	108	3.79	1.44	270			13.6	33%	73%	3.88	51	25	25	3.6	6.9	1.9	6%	0.4	7.9	57	$11
Type Pwr	06	MIL	* 6	8	0	132	135	4.43	1.35	243			19.4	32%	67%	3.55	44	27	29	3.9	9.2	2.3	9%	0.6	1.0	81	$10
Health B	07	aaa	2	0	0	33	16	4.64	1.76	301			11.9	34%	72%	5.13	55	20	25	4.9	4.4	0.9	3%	0.3	-0.7	-21	$0
PT/Exp C	08	OAK	9	9	0	168	118	4.34	1.48	266	248	275	25.5	31%	70%	4.39	49	22	29	4.1	6.3	1.5	7%	0.5	0.2	29	$9
Consist C	1st Half		6	5	0	97	65	3.34	1.35	237			25.9	28%	74%	4.51	48	20	32	4.3	6.0	1.4	3%	0.3	12.1	19	$9
LIMA Plan C	2nd Half		3	4	0	71	53	5.70	1.66	303			25.0	35%	66%	4.23	50	25	25	3.9	6.7	1.7	12%	0.9	-11.9	43	$0
+/- Score -16	09	Proj	**8**	**6**	**0**	**149**	**106**	**4.59**	**1.52**	**272**			**24.5**	**32%**	**70%**	**4.36**	**49**	**23**	**28**	**4.2**	**6.4**	**1.5**	**8%**	**0.7**	**1.2**	**28**	**$7**

Poor Ctl, conditioning held him under 6 IP in most starts and still biggest hurdles in future. Good Dom and GB% have no margin for error or bad luck as seen in 2H. Back-of-rotation filler unless something changes.

Eyre,Scott

	Yr	Tm	W	L	Sv	IP	K	ERA	WHIP	OBA	vL	vR	BF/G	H%	S%	xERA	G	L	F	Ctl	Dom	Cmd	hr/f	hr/9	RAR	BPV	R$
LH Reliever	04	SF	2	2	1	52	49	4.14	1.34	226	200	240	2.7	26%	74%	4.36	41	13	46	4.7	8.4	1.8	12%	1.4	0.8	45	$4
Age 36	05	SF	2	2	0	68	65	2.64	1.09	200	182	213	3.2	26%	76%	3.84	38	18	43	3.4	8.6	2.5	4%	0.4	13.5	78	$9
Type Pwr FB	06	CHC	1	3	0	61	73	3.39	1.49	261	273	261	3.6	33%	85%	3.63	42	20	38	4.4	10.8	2.4	18%	1.6	8.3	94	$4
Health D	07	CHC	2	1	0	52	45	4.13	1.80	286	253	317	4.5	35%	77%	5.28	39	24	38	6.0	7.7	1.3	5%	0.5	1.9	-6	$1
PT/Exp D	08	2NL	5	0	0	26	32	4.20	1.17	241	220	267	2.8	34%	64%	3.10	35	23	42	2.5	11.2	4.6	8%	0.7	0.2	149	$5
Consist D	1st Half		2	0	0	11	14	4.91	1.45	279			2.7	39%	67%	3.60	27	30	43	3.3	11.5	3.5	8%	0.8	-0.9	122	$1
LIMA Plan A	2nd Half		3	0	0	15	18	3.67	0.95	210			2.8	30%	62%	2.72	43	17	40	1.8	11.0	6.0	7%	0.6	1.1	170	$3
+/- Score 16	09	Proj	**4**	**1**	**0**	**44**	**47**	**3.93**	**1.31**	**241**			**3.3**	**32%**	**72%**	**3.74**	**38**	**22**	**40**	**3.7**	**9.7**	**2.6**	**9%**	**0.8**	**3.2**	**90**	**$5**

Health (elbow, groin) limited IP and role to more of a LH specialist, in which Dom, Ctl thrived. Biggest issue remains inconsistency, though 2007 is looking like big outlier. LIMA worthy, but with plenty of risk.

Farnsworth,Kyle

	Yr	Tm	W	L	Sv	IP	K	ERA	WHIP	OBA	vL	vR	BF/G	H%	S%	xERA	G	L	F	Ctl	Dom	Cmd	hr/f	hr/9	RAR	BPV	R$
RH Reliever	04	CHC	4	5	0	66	78	4.76	1.51	264	267	255	4.1	34%	72%	3.85	40	19	41	4.5	10.6	2.4	14%	1.4	-4.1	87	$4
Age 33	05	2TM	1	1	16	70	87	2.19	1.01	182	198	165	3.8	26%	82%	2.91	43	21	36	3.5	11.2	3.2	9%	0.6	18.3	128	$16
Type Pwr xFB	06	NYY	3	6	6	66	75	4.36	1.36	250	215	264	3.9	33%	71%	3.81	34	22	44	3.8	10.2	2.7	11%	1.1	1.6	93	$8
Health A	07	NYY	2	1	0	60	48	4.80	1.45	262	273	242	4.1	30%	71%	5.02	30	19	51	4.1	7.2	1.8	10%	1.4	-2.2	29	$3
PT/Exp C	08	2AL	2	3	1	60	61	4.48	1.53	292	275	318	4.4	34%	81%	4.15	35	19	46	3.3	9.1	2.8	18%	2.2	-1.0	88	$3
Consist C	1st Half		1	2	1	36	34	4.00	1.44	278			4.5	30%	86%	4.06	41	14	44	3.3	8.5	2.6	21%	2.5	1.5	84	$3
LIMA Plan B+	2nd Half		1	1	0	24	27	5.18	1.65	311			4.3	39%	74%	4.26	27	24	49	3.3	10.0	3.0	14%	1.9	-2.5	95	$1
+/- Score 32	09	Proj	**2**	**3**	**0**	**58**	**59**	**4.34**	**1.43**	**268**			**4.1**	**33%**	**73%**	**4.21**	**33**	**20**	**47**	**3.0**	**9.2**	**2.0**	**10%**	**1.2**	**1.6**	**70**	**$1**

Extreme FBer whose ongoing gopheritis often kills bottom line. Worse-than-usual hr/f offset by better Ctl. Dominance keeps door ajar for possibility of a return to 2005, but odds are getting slimmer each year.

JOCK THOMPSON

Feierabend,Ryan

Feierabend,Ryan		Yr	Tm	W	L	Sv	IP	K	ERA	WHIP	OBA	vL	vR	BF/G	H%	S%	xERA	G	L	F	Ctl	Dom	Cmd	hr/f	hr/9	RAR	BPV	R$
LH	Starter	04		0	0	0	0	0	0.00	0.00																		
Age	23	05		0	0	0	0	0	0.00	0.00																		
Type	Con FB	06	aa	9	12	0	153	114	5.64	1.60	300			24.7	34%	66%	5.43				3.5	6.7	**1.9**		1.1	-21.2	42	$4
Health	A	07	SEA *	7	10	0	157	90	5.72	1.77	331			23.1	36%	69%	5.62	35	21	45	3.3	5.1	**1.6**	7%	1.1	-23.5	16	($2)
PT/Exp	D	08	SEA *	8	5	0	115	68	4.20	1.40	289	386	339	23.6	32%	72%	4.70	38	22	40	2.3	5.3	**2.3**	8%	1.0	2.0	49	$8
Consist	B	1st Half		4	1	0	46	29	2.42	1.17	250			23.5	29%	82%					2.0	5.7	**2.8**		0.6	10.9	80	$7
LIMA Plan	C+	2nd Half		4	4	0	69	39	5.40	1.56	312			23.7	34%	67%	4.98	38	22	40	2.5	5.1	**2.0**	9%	1.2	-8.9	39	$1
+/- Score	-8	09	Proj	**6**	**6**	**0**	**108**	**66**	**4.75**	**1.49**	**302**			**22.7**	**33%**	**70%**	**4.82**	**37**	**22**	**41**	**2.4**	**5.5**	**2.3**	**9%**	**1.1**	**-5.3**	**49**	**$5**

1-4, 7.71 ERA in 40 IP at SEA. In marginal skill set, only Ctl is solid and trending in right direction. LD and h% history say this contact pitcher is very hittable. Has time, unlikely to take advantage of it.

Feldman,Scott

Feldman,Scott		Yr	Tm	W	L	Sv	IP	K	ERA	WHIP	OBA	vL	vR	BF/G	H%	S%	xERA	G	L	F	Ctl	Dom	Cmd	hr/f	hr/9	RAR	BPV	R$
RH	Starter	04		0	0	0	0	0	0.00	0.00																		
Age	26	05	aa	1	2	14	61	35	3.10	1.21	229			5.5	26%	76%	3.02				3.4	5.2	**1.5**		0.6	9.1	54	$9
Type		06	TEX *	2	4	4	68	52	3.57	1.26	259	280	259	4.8	30%	76%	3.22	59	19	22	2.5	6.8	**2.7**	18%	1.1	8.3	93	$8
Health	A	07	TEX *	2	3	2	69	39	5.87	1.79	288			6.5	32%	66%	5.11	59	15	26	5.8	5.1	**0.9**	7%	0.5	-11.6	-29	($1)
PT/Exp	D	08	TEX *	8	8	0	164	77	5.33	1.42	274	291	269	23.7	28%	64%	5.01	44	19	37	3.2	4.2	**1.3**	11%	1.2	-19.8	11	$5
Consist	B	1st Half		4	3	0	90	42	4.57	1.29	256			23.7	27%	66%	4.81	45	18	37	2.9	4.2	**1.4**	9%	1.0	-2.4	19	$5
LIMA Plan	C	2nd Half		4	5	0	73	35	6.26	1.58	296			23.6	30%	63%	5.26	42	21	37	3.6	4.3	**1.2**	13%	1.5	-17.3	1	($1)
+/- Score	-10	09	Proj	**3**	**4**	**0**	**87**	**48**	**5.07**	**1.49**	**275**			**9.1**	**30%**	**68%**	**4.77**	**49**	**19**	**32**	**3.8**	**5.0**	**1.3**	**11%**	**1.0**	**-3.8**	**13**	**$2**

6-8, 5.29 ERA in 151 IP at TEX. Poor Dom trending south. Poor Cmd, poor outlook. Will likely move to the pen where he has a 5.05 ERA over past 3 years. It's so much better than the 5.18 ERA he has as a starter.

Feliciano,Pedro

Feliciano,Pedro		Yr	Tm	W	L	Sv	IP	K	ERA	WHIP	OBA	vL	vR	BF/G	H%	S%	xERA	G	L	F	Ctl	Dom	Cmd	hr/f	hr/9	RAR	BPV	R$
LH	Reliever	04	NYM *	5	4	2	53	34	6.79	1.62	280			4.5	31%	58%	5.26				4.8	5.8	**1.2**		1.2	-16.5	24	$0
Age	32	05	JPN	3	2	0	37	38	4.83	1.31	236			4.2	26%	71%	4.64				3.9	9.2	**2.4**		2.0	-2.4	52	$3
Type	Pwr GB	06	NYM	7	2	0	60	54	2.10	1.26	248	231	266	3.9	31%	86%	3.49	49	21	29	3.0	8.1	**2.7**	8%	0.6	17.7	92	$10
Health	A	07	NYM	2	2	2	64	61	3.09	1.22	207	168	221	3.4	27%	75%	3.43	56	17	27	4.4	8.6	**2.0**	7%	0.4	10.5	70	$7
PT/Exp	C	08	NYM	3	4	2	53	50	4.05	1.56	275	210	357	2.8	33%	78%	3.78	53	19	27	4.4	8.4	**1.9**	16%	1.2	1.4	65	$3
Consist	A	1st Half		0	2	0	32	30	2.79	1.39	254			3.2	31%	85%	3.58	56	14	30	3.9	8.4	**2.1**	15%	1.1	5.9	79	$2
LIMA Plan	B+	2nd Half		3	2	2	21	20	6.00	1.81	305			2.3	37%	69%	4.09	49	27	24	5.1	8.6	**1.7**	19%	1.3	-4.5	43	$1
+/- Score	21	09	Proj	**4**	**3**	**0**	**48**	**45**	**3.94**	**1.46**	**258**			**3.0**	**32%**	**74%**	**3.70**	**53**	**20**	**27**	**4.3**	**8.4**	**2.0**	**11%**	**0.8**	**3.8**	**66**	**$4**

His hr/f spiked as Ctl trend continued to deteriorate:
2006: 4.7 Ctl vs. RH batters
2007: 5.0 Ctl vs. RH batters
2008: 6.7 Ctl vs. RH batters
Dom, GB% solid, but rebound hinges on fixing his problems.

Figueroa,Nelson

Figueroa,Nelson		Yr	Tm	W	L	Sv	IP	K	ERA	WHIP	OBA	vL	vR	BF/G	H%	S%	xERA	G	L	F	Ctl	Dom	Cmd	hr/f	hr/9	RAR	BPV	R$
RH	Starter	04	PIT *	12	11	0	180	108	5.39	1.59	320	357	266	23.2	35%	69%	4.48	46	21	33	2.4	5.4	**2.3**	13%	1.3	-25.2	57	$3
Age	34	05		0	0	0	0	0	0.00	0.00																		
Type		06	aaa	3	5	0	76	35	5.48	1.50	297			21.0	30%	67%	5.51				2.7	4.2	**1.5**		1.5	-9.0	8	$1
Health	C	07	MEX	8	6	0	153	84	4.46	1.39	286			34.8	31%	70%	4.61				2.3	4.9	**2.1**		0.9	-0.0	43	$8
PT/Exp	C	08	NYM *	7	10	0	159	107	5.65	1.71	316	371	200	20.4	35%	68%	5.02	41	21	39	3.6	6.1	**1.7**	10%	1.2	-26.9	31	($2)
Consist	B	1st Half		5	5	0	90	60	4.68	1.53	274			21.0	31%	70%	5.11	40	19	41	4.2	6.0	**1.4**	7%	0.8	-4.5	12	$3
LIMA Plan	C+	2nd Half		2	5	0	69	48	6.92	1.94	365			19.6	40%	67%	4.31	48	29	24	2.9	6.3	**2.2**	21%	1.7	-22.4	61	($5)
+/- Score	-7	09	Proj	**1**	**2**	**0**	**29**	**18**	**4.97**	**1.59**	**306**			**11.9**	**33%**	**71%**	**4.75**	**43**	**21**	**36**	**3.1**	**5.6**	**1.8**	**11%**	**1.2**	**-1.5**	**38**	**$0**

3-3, 4.57 ERA in 45 IP at NYM. Journeyman picked up handful of starts through mid-May due to injuries, then returned to AAA until Sept. Brief history says he's best used in relief - and best left off your roster.

Flores,Randy

Flores,Randy		Yr	Tm	W	L	Sv	IP	K	ERA	WHIP	OBA	vL	vR	BF/G	H%	S%	xERA	G	L	F	Ctl	Dom	Cmd	hr/f	hr/9	RAR	BPV	R$
LH	Reliever	04	STL *	6	7	2	136	86	4.10	1.43	276			13.2	31%	72%	4.23				3.2	5.7	**1.8**		0.7	2.7	51	$7
Age	33	05	STL	3	1	1	41	43	3.50	1.21	242	173	304	3.4	30%	76%	3.34	43	22	35	2.8	9.4	**3.3**	13%	1.1	3.8	113	$5
Type	Pwr	06	STL	1	1	0	41	40	5.68	1.72	297	258	329	2.9	37%	68%	4.61	39	22	39	4.8	8.7	**1.8**	10%	1.1	-6.1	45	($0)
Health	B	07	STL	3	0	1	55	47	4.25	1.56	314	326	299	3.5	39%	71%	4.19	41	23	37	2.5	7.7	**3.1**	3%	0.3	1.2	91	$3
PT/Exp	D	08	STL	1	0	1	26	17	5.25	2.10	319	314	316	3.0	37%	75%	5.94	51	19	31	7.0	6.0	**0.9**	7%	0.7	-3.1	-53	($1)
Consist	C	1st Half		1	0	1	19	14	5.13	1.92	278			2.9	33%	72%	5.92	51	13	37	7.5	6.5	**0.9**	4%	0.5	-2.0	-55	($0)
LIMA Plan	D	2nd Half		0	0	0	6	3	5.62	2.66	419			3.2	44%	81%	5.92	50	32	18	5.6	4.2	**0.8**	20%	1.4	-1.1	-48	($1)
+/- Score	-19	09	Proj	**2**	**1**	**0**	**44**	**35**	**4.76**	**1.59**	**281**			**3.3**	**33%**	**71%**	**4.36**	**46**	**24**	**30**	**4.3**	**7.2**	**1.7**	**10%**	**0.8**	**-0.1**	**37**	**$1**

More volatility, this time to the downside and marked by DL time, a demotion to AAA, and year-ending shoulder surgery. There's nothing here worth chasing into 2009. It's all risk, numbers and trends to avoid.

Floyd,Gavin

Floyd,Gavin		Yr	Tm	W	L	Sv	IP	K	ERA	WHIP	OBA	vL	vR	BF/G	H%	S%	xERA	G	L	F	Ctl	Dom	Cmd	hr/f	hr/9	RAR	BPV	R$
RH	Starter	04	a/a	7	9	0	149	104	3.16	1.26	243			25.0	29%	75%	3.24				3.2	6.3	**1.9**		0.5	21.8	71	$14
Age	26	05	PHI *	7	11	0	163	103	7.33	1.67	297	283	283	24.1	33%	55%	5.26	42	19	39	4.2	5.7	**1.3**	8%	1.0	-62.0	7	($7)
Type		06	PHI *	11	7	0	169	105	6.81	1.74	317	306	323	28.1	34%	62%	5.19	39	24	37	3.9	5.6	**1.4**	13%	1.5	-48.5	13	($4)
Health	A	07	CHW *	8	8	0	176	134	4.70	1.44	285	314	286	23.3	32%	72%	4.35	42	17	41	2.8	6.8	**2.4**	13%	1.5	-4.2	67	$10
PT/Exp	B	08	CHW	17	8	0	206	145	3.84	1.26	246	259	226	26.1	27%	75%	4.33	41	19	40	3.1	6.3	**2.1**	12%	1.3	12.9	51	$21
Consist	A	1st Half		9	4	0	102	67	3.45	1.14	216			25.8	23%	76%	4.46	41	15	44	3.3	5.9	**1.8**	11%	1.3	11.2	38	$13
LIMA Plan	F	2nd Half		8	4	0	105	78	4.22	1.38	273			26.4	31%	74%	4.19	41	23	36	2.8	6.7	**2.4**	13%	1.3	1.7	63	$9
+/- Score	-0	09	Proj	**13**	**9**	**0**	**203**	**143**	**4.52**	**1.40**	**272**			**25.8**	**30%**	**72%**	**4.49**	**41**	**20**	**39**	**3.1**	**6.3**	**2.0**	**12%**	**1.3**	**-1.6**	**48**	**$14**

PRO: 42%/12% DOM/DIS, consolidated 2007 skill gains in 2H, good bottom line, age. CON: Marginal Cmd, ugly hr/9 and hr/f, odds of h% up-tick. Unlikely to repeat - particularly that 24% h% at The Cell...

Fogg,Josh

Fogg,Josh		Yr	Tm	W	L	Sv	IP	K	ERA	WHIP	OBA	vL	vR	BF/G	H%	S%	xERA	G	L	F	Ctl	Dom	Cmd	hr/f	hr/9	RAR	BPV	R$
RH	Reliever	04	PIT	11	10	0	178	82	4.65	1.45	278	282	285	24.3	30%	69%	4.94	48	18	34	3.3	4.1	**1.2**	8%	0.9	-8.5	10	$7
Age	32	05	PIT	6	11	0	169	85	5.06	1.47	291	340	249	21.8	30%	69%	4.97	41	21	38	2.8	4.5	**1.6**	12%	1.4	-16.9	24	$2
Type	Con FB	06	COL	11	9	0	172	93	5.49	1.55	298	309	291	24.8	32%	67%	4.98	43	20	37	3.1	4.9	**1.6**	11%	1.3	-21.4	23	$4
Health	C	07	COL	10	9	0	166	94	4.94	1.53	293	279	305	24.6	31%	70%	5.05	40	20	40	3.2	5.1	**1.6**	10%	1.2	-10.6	23	$5
PT/Exp	B	08	CIN	2	7	0	78	45	7.59	1.58	305	299	305	16.0	31%	54%	5.14	38	19	43	3.1	5.2	**1.7**	15%	2.0	-32.0	25	($4)
Consist	A	1st Half		1	2	0	28	17	9.86	1.73	328			12.0	34%	43%	5.38	38	16	47	3.2	5.4	**1.7**	15%	2.2	-19.5	27	($3)
LIMA Plan	F	2nd Half		1	5	0	50	28	6.30	1.50	291			20.1	30%	62%	5.01	38	21	41	3.1	5.0	**1.6**	14%	1.8	-12.5	24	($1)
+/- Score	85	09	Proj	**2**	**4**	**0**	**58**	**32**	**5.28**	**1.55**	**300**			**18.5**	**31%**	**70%**	**5.10**	**40**	**19**	**41**	**3.1**	**5.0**	**1.6**	**12%**	**1.6**	**-5.4**	**23**	**$0**

Dom, Cmd have always been unacceptable, but FB trend makes gopheritis even redder flag. Incendiary combination that even venue change won't help. Unrosterable in any format except Fantasy Masochism.

Fossum,Casey

Fossum,Casey		Yr	Tm	W	L	Sv	IP	K	ERA	WHIP	OBA	vL	vR	BF/G	H%	S%	xERA	G	L	F	Ctl	Dom	Cmd	hr/f	hr/9	RAR	BPV	R$
LH	Reliever	04	ARI *	6	16	0	161	134	5.98	1.60	293	257	316	22.8	33%	67%	4.49	41	21	38	3.9	7.5	**1.9**	16%	1.7	-34.1	49	($0)
Age	31	05	TAM	8	12	0	162	128	4.94	1.42	271	234	278	19.5	31%	67%	4.37	39	22	39	3.3	7.1	**2.1**	11%	1.2	-11.3	55	$8
Type		06	TAM	6	6	0	130	88	5.33	1.53	271	271	263	23.1	30%	67%	4.68	46	21	33	4.4	6.1	**1.4**	13%	1.2	-12.4	16	$4
Health	A	07	TAM	5	8	0	76	53	7.70	1.79	337	320	336	8.9	37%	59%	4.61	45	23	32	3.2	6.3	**2.0**	17%	1.8	-29.9	49	($3)
PT/Exp	C	08	DET *	6	1	0	87	66	4.05	1.24	223	243	310	8.7	26%	69%	4.27	45	19	37	3.9	6.8	**1.7**	9%	0.9	3.2	39	$9
Consist	A	1st Half		4	0	0	52	43	3.69	1.15	204			11.1	24%	69%	3.09	62	19	19	3.8	7.4	**1.9**	16%	0.8	4.2	70	$7
LIMA Plan	C+	2nd Half		2	1	0	35	23	4.59	1.39	249			6.6	27%	69%	4.87	41	19	40	4.1	5.9	**1.4**	9%	1.0	-1.1	15	$2
+/- Score	-32	09	Proj	**3**	**2**	**0**	**44**	**31**	**4.76**	**1.47**	**273**			**9.6**	**31%**	**69%**	**4.53**	**44**	**21**	**35**	**3.7**	**6.4**	**1.7**	**10%**	**1.0**	**-0.6**	**37**	**$2**

3-1, 5.66 ERA in 41 IP at DET. Best bottom line in a while, but Ctl isn't improving, and hr/f, hr/9 are good bets to regress.
Career OPS vs. RH: .845
2008 OPS vs. RH: .920
Future as LH specialist?

Foulke,Keith

Foulke,Keith		Yr	Tm	W	L	Sv	IP	K	ERA	WHIP	OBA	vL	vR	BF/G	H%	S%	xERA	G	L	F	Ctl	Dom	Cmd	hr/f	hr/9	RAR	BPV	R$
RH	Reliever	04	BOS	5	3	32	83	79	2.17	0.94	212	185	232	4.4	26%	83%	3.52	34	16	49	1.6	8.6	**5.3**	7%	0.9	23.2	122	$25
Age	36	05	BOS	5	5	15	45	34	5.97	1.57	294	255	333	4.7	32%	65%	5.34	26	19	55	3.6	6.8	**1.9**	10%	1.6	-8.9	30	$7
Type	xFB	06	BOS	3	1	0	49	36	4.39	1.20	273	301	236	4.6	30%	70%	4.51	24	20	56	1.3	6.6	**5.1**	10%	1.6	1.0	86	$5
Health	F	07		0	0	0	0	0	0.00	0.00																		
PT/Exp	D	08	OAK	0	3	1	31	23	4.06	1.32	243	200	279	4.2	25%	79%	4.94	31	16	53	3.8	6.7	**1.8**	14%	2.0	1.1	27	$2
Consist	A	1st Half		0	2	1	26	20	3.15	1.21	216			4.2	24%	79%	4.61	34	18	48	3.9	7.0	**1.8**	9%	1.1	3.8	34	$3
LIMA Plan	C+	2nd Half		0	1	0	5	3	8.49	1.89	349			4.2	25%	83%	6.41	19	10	71	3.4	5.1	**1.5**	28%	6.8	-2.7	-3	($1)
+/- Score	-44	09	Proj	**3**	**4**	**0**	**54**	**40**	**4.50**	**1.39**	**265**			**4.7**	**29%**	**73%**	**4.98**	**29**	**18**	**53**	**3.3**	**6.7**	**2.0**	**10%**	**1.5**	**-3.7**	**37**	**$4**

Limited by injuries (leg, neck, shoulder) after missing all of 2007 (elbow and knees). Ctl, hr/9, hr/f are all suffering from from rust, age. And even IF he were healthy, hr/9 will hurt. Warning - Flammable Page.

JOCK THOMPSON

Francisco,Frank

			W	L	Sv	IP	K	ERA	WHIP	OBA	vL	vR	BF/G	H%	S%	xERA	G	L	F	Ctl	Dom	Cmd	hr/f	hr/9	RAR	BPV	R$
RH Reliever	04	TEX *	6	5	6	68	84	3.30	1.23	186	247	165	4.7	27%	75%	4.05	28	19	54	5.3	11.1	2.1	6%	0.7	9.5	63	$12
Age 29	05	TEX	0	0	0	0	0	0.00	0.00											0.0	0.0						
Type Pwr xFB	06	TEX *	0	1	0	22	25	3.26	1.22	243		444	4.4	31%	79%	3.13	50	13	38	2.9	10.2	3.6	14%	1.2	3.5	134	$2
Health F	07	TEX	1	1	0	59	49	4.55	1.60	254	221	286	4.5	31%	71%	5.30	35	22	43	5.8	7.4	1.3	4%	0.5	-0.3	-9	$2
PT/Exp D	08	TEX	3	5	5	63	83	3.13	1.15	208	193	207	4.4	30%	77%	3.30	33	19	48	3.7	11.8	3.2	10%	1.0	9.5	123	$11
Consist F	1st Half		1	2	0	32	40	3.66	1.41	237			5.1	33%	76%	3.75	37	19	43	4.8	11.3	2.4	9%	0.8	2.7	89	$3
LIMA Plan B+	2nd Half		2	3	5	31	43	2.59	0.89	177			3.9	25%	79%	2.88	27	19	54	2.6	12.4	4.8	11%	1.2	6.8	158	$8
+/- Score 15	09	Proj	3	4	25	73	82	3.60	1.24	221			4.4	29%	73%	3.82	34	19	47	4.0	10.2	2.6	8%	0.9	5.4	88	$17

Eye-opening gains in second full season off TJ surgery. Ctl improvement neutralized FB% hike, which - mixed with home venue - is biggest red flag. If he consolidates Cmd growth... UP: 35 saves.

Francis,Jeff

			W	L	Sv	IP	K	ERA	WHIP	OBA	vL	vR	BF/G	H%	S%	xERA	G	L	F	Ctl	Dom	Cmd	hr/f	hr/9	RAR	BPV	R$
LH Starter	04	a/a	16	3	0	154	164	2.80	1.00	225			25.2	29%	77%	2.80				1.6	9.6	5.9		1.0	29.3	161	$27
Age 28	05	COL	14	12	0	183	128	5.70	1.63	306	285	317	25.2	34%	67%	4.81	40	22	38	3.4	6.3	1.8	11%	1.3	-32.8	39	$3
Type	06	COL	13	11	0	199	117	4.16	1.29	250	241	252	26.2	28%	69%	4.53	45	19	36	3.1	5.3	1.7	8%	0.8	8.0	34	$16
Health B	07	COL	17	9	0	215	165	4.22	1.38	278	242	289	27.2	32%	72%	4.13	44	18	37	2.6	6.9	2.6	10%	1.0	5.4	75	$18
PT/Exp A	08	COL	4	10	0	144	94	5.01	1.48	288	248	295	26.4	31%	69%	4.55	44	20	36	3.1	5.9	1.9	12%	1.3	-13.1	45	$2
Consist A	1st Half		3	7	0	100	67	5.67	1.55	290			26.3	31%	67%	4.74	43	20	38	3.6	6.0	1.7	14%	1.5	-17.3	32	($0)
LIMA Plan B	2nd Half		1	3	0	44	27	3.50	1.33	284			26.5	32%	76%	4.11	45	22	33	1.9	5.6	3.0	8%	0.8	4.1	73	$3
+/- Score 17	09	Proj	9	10	0	174	119	4.51	1.41	278			26.8	31%	70%	4.38	44	20	36	3.0	6.2	2.1	10%	1.0	-0.9	53	$9

Shut down in mid-Sept as a "precaution" after missing July due to inflamed shoulder. 1H struggles, Cmd and Dom dips are worrisome in light of DL time. Ability to build on 2007 seems to be in doubt.

Franklin,Ryan

			W	L	Sv	IP	K	ERA	WHIP	OBA	vL	vR	BF/G	H%	S%	xERA	G	L	F	Ctl	Dom	Cmd	hr/f	hr/9	RAR	BPV	R$
RH Reliever	04	SEA	4	16	0	200	104	4.90	1.42	284	275	297	27.2	29%	70%	5.16	35	20	45	2.7	4.7	1.7	11%	1.5	-11.6	23	$4
Age 36	05	SEA	8	15	0	190	93	5.11	1.44	283	266	295	25.9	29%	67%	5.10	42	16	42	2.9	4.4	1.5	10%	1.5	-17.3	20	$5
Type Con	06	2NL	6	7	0	77	43	4.55	1.54	283	265	294	5.2	30%	75%	4.91	47	18	35	3.9	5.0	1.3	14%	1.5	-0.6	11	$4
Health A	07	STL	4	4	1	80	44	3.04	1.01	237	238	231	4.6	25%	74%	3.77	48	18	34	1.2	5.0	4.0	9%	0.9	13.7	82	$10
PT/Exp C	08	STL	6	6	17	79	51	3.55	1.47	279	268	285	4.7	31%	80%	4.72	43	19	38	3.4	5.8	1.7	10%	1.1	7.0	33	$12
Consist C	1st Half		2	2	11	38	26	2.82	1.44	260			4.3	30%	83%	4.86	42	18	40	4.0	6.1	1.5	6%	0.7	6.9	22	$7
LIMA Plan D+	2nd Half		4	4	6	40	25	4.23	1.51	296			5.1	32%	78%	4.60	44	21	36	2.9	5.6	1.9	14%	1.6	0.2	44	$5
+/- Score -31	09	Proj	4	4	3	58	34	4.03	1.40	278			5.2	30%	75%	4.57	44	19	37	2.8	5.3	1.9	11%	1.2	-1.7	42	$5

Season marked by anticipated Ctl and H% regression from 2007 outlier. Improved Dom, FB levels account for recent serviceability, but most BPIs remain marginal and trendless. Age now adding to the risk.

Frasor,Jason

			W	L	Sv	IP	K	ERA	WHIP	OBA	vL	vR	BF/G	H%	S%	xERA	G	L	F	Ctl	Dom	Cmd	hr/f	hr/9	RAR	BPV	R$
RH Reliever	04	TOR	4	6	17	68	54	4.10	1.47	250	232	274	4.7	30%	72%	4.54	47	19	35	4.8	7.1	1.5	6%	0.5	2.8	25	$10
Age 31	05	TOR	3	5	1	74	62	3.27	1.28	243	236	257	4.7	29%	78%	3.77	50	18	32	3.4	7.5	2.2	12%	1.0	10.0	71	$8
Type Pwr	06	TOR *	6	3	1	70	81	4.50	1.49	265	211	262	4.5	34%	73%	3.59	43	23	34	4.2	10.4	2.5	16%	1.3	0.5	94	$7
Health A	07	TOR	1	5	3	57	59	4.58	1.23	226	245	200	4.6	30%	61%	3.54	45	19	36	3.6	9.3	2.6	6%	0.5	-0.5	93	$6
PT/Exp D	08	TOR	1	2	0	47	42	4.19	1.44	213	266	174	4.2	26%	72%	4.80	38	24	38	6.1	8.0	1.3	8%	0.8	0.9	-4	$3
Consist B	1st Half		1	1	0	25	23	3.60	1.48	230			3.9	29%	77%	4.66	38	25	37	5.8	8.3	1.4	8%	0.7	2.3	10	$2
LIMA Plan C+	2nd Half		0	1	0	22	19	4.84	1.39	193			4.6	23%	66%	4.96	39	23	39	6.5	7.7	1.2	9%	0.8	-1.4	-20	$1
+/- Score -45	09	Proj	2	3	0	58	55	4.19	1.41	238			4.5	29%	72%	4.22	42	22	36	4.8	8.5	1.8	10%	0.9	1.5	43	$4

Reduced role and IP partly to blame for Ctl collapse, but GB trend is now also an issue. BPIs still hint at promise, but he might need scenery change to realize it. For now, there seems to be little upside here.

Fuentes,Brian

			W	L	Sv	IP	K	ERA	WHIP	OBA	vL	vR	BF/G	H%	S%	xERA	G	L	F	Ctl	Dom	Cmd	hr/f	hr/9	RAR	BPV	R$
LH Reliever	04	COL	2	4	0	44	48	5.70	1.47	270	213	300	4.1	35%	62%	4.06	34	23	44	3.9	9.8	2.5	9%	1.0	-7.8	83	$1
Age 33	05	COL	2	5	31	74	91	2.91	1.26	220	167	236	4.0	31%	79%	3.33	38	26	36	4.1	11.1	2.7	9%	0.7	12.2	103	$18
Type Pwr xFB	06	COL	3	4	30	65	73	3.46	1.17	214	186	217	4.0	28%	75%	3.73	35	16	50	3.6	10.1	2.8	10%	1.1	8.3	97	$18
Health B	07	COL	3	5	20	61	56	3.08	1.13	210	204	207	3.9	25%	76%	3.95	36	21	43	3.4	8.2	2.4	9%	0.9	10.2	71	$14
PT/Exp B	08	COL	1	5	30	63	82	2.73	1.10	210	184	211	3.8	32%	76%	3.15	33	22	46	3.2	11.8	3.7	5%	0.4	11.9	137	$19
Consist B	1st Half		1	4	13	32	28	3.94	1.38	268			3.8	34%	70%	4.24	38	22	41	3.1	7.9	2.5	3%	0.3	1.3	74	$6
LIMA Plan B	2nd Half		0	1	17	31	54	1.47	0.81	139			3.7	27%	87%	2.19	24	22	55	3.2	15.8	4.9	8%	0.6	10.6	199	$12
+/- Score -3	09	Proj	3	4	38	69	83	2.89	1.12	209			3.8	29%	77%	3.39	34	21	46	3.4	10.9	3.2	8%	0.8	8.0	116	$22

Re-seized closer role, finished with across-the-board career numbers. Ctl, GB%, hr/9 all trending positively into free agency. Sub-2 ERA on the road in '07-08 says that a new home could be HUGE plus.

Gabbard,Kason

			W	L	Sv	IP	K	ERA	WHIP	OBA	vL	vR	BF/G	H%	S%	xERA	G	L	F	Ctl	Dom	Cmd	hr/f	hr/9	RAR	BPV	R$
LH Starter	04	aa	3	6	0	53	30	7.47	1.77	316			17.8	35%	56%	5.95				4.2	5.1	1.2		0.8	-20.5	22	($3)
Age 27	05	aa	9	11	0	132	80	6.18	1.69	295			22.6	33%	63%	5.30				4.6	5.4	1.2		0.8	-30.5	30	($1)
Type Pwr xGB	06	BOS *	11	12	0	150	113	4.98	1.49	265			22.8	31%	67%	3.92	58	18	24	4.2	6.8	1.6	14%	0.9	-7.9	43	$9
Health D	07	2AL *	13	3	0	156	109	4.57	1.38	252	236	230	23.2	28%	69%	4.09	55	16	30	3.9	6.3	1.6	13%	1.1	-1.3	42	$13
PT/Exp D	08	TEX *	2	4	0	72	46	5.03	1.86	299	233	307	23.0	34%	74%	4.63	65	13	22	5.9	5.7	1.0	14%	0.9	-6.1	-12	($2)
Consist A	1st Half		2	4	0	72	46	5.03	1.86	299			23.0	34%	74%	4.63	65	13	22	5.9	5.7	1.0	14%	0.9	-6.1	-12	($2)
LIMA Plan C	2nd Half		0	0	0	0	0	0.00	0.00																		
+/- Score 6	09	Proj	3	4	0	58	39	5.12	1.64	284			22.0	32%	70%	4.24	61	15	24	4.7	6.1	1.3	13%	0.9	1.3	22	$1

2-3, 4.82 ERA in 56 IP at TEX. GB-and-Dom combination still a tease. More injuries, with elbow inflammation ending his season in late July. And Ctl, hr/f won't get better unless his health does. We're skeptical.

Gagne,Eric

			W	L	Sv	IP	K	ERA	WHIP	OBA	vL	vR	BF/G	H%	S%	xERA	G	L	F	Ctl	Dom	Cmd	hr/f	hr/9	RAR	BPV	R$
RH Reliever	04	LA	7	3	45	82	114	2.19	0.91	186	233	129	4.5	29%	79%	2.47	42	18	40	2.4	12.5	5.2	7%	0.5	21.0	180	$30
Age 33	05	LA	1	0	8	13	22	2.75	0.99	213	217	185	3.7	35%	82%	1.80	52	11	37	2.1	15.1	7.3	22%	1.4	2.4	246	$5
Type Pwr	06	LA	0	0	1	2	3	0.00	0.50	0			3.4	0%		2.64	33	0	67	4.5	13.5	3.0	0%		1.1	133	$1
Health F	07	2AL	4	2	16	52	51	3.81	1.35	250	224	265	4.1	32%	72%	3.98	39	22	39	3.6	8.8	2.4	5%	0.5	4.5	77	$11
PT/Exp D	08	MIL	4	3	10	46	38	5.44	1.47	261	241	275	4.1	27%	70%	4.50	37	24	39	4.3	7.4	1.7	20%	2.1	-6.7	33	$6
Consist B	1st Half		1	2	10	19	18	6.99	2.02	297			4.8	33%	71%	5.35	40	28	32	7.5	8.4	1.1	27%	2.5	-6.5	-32	$2
LIMA Plan C+	2nd Half		3	1	0	27	20	4.33	1.07	232			3.6	23%	70%	3.96	35	20	45	2.0	6.7	3.3	17%	2.0	-0.2	79	$3
+/- Score 22	09	Proj	3	3	3	44	37	4.34	1.36	251			4.1	30%	70%	4.25	40	21	39	3.7	7.7	2.1	10%	1.0	0.5	55	$4

Lost six weeks to injury again, this time his pitching shoulder. Progressed slowly in 2H return but flashed solid skills in final six weeks. Only good health would return good value. We're skeptical.

Galarraga,Armando

			W	L	Sv	IP	K	ERA	WHIP	OBA	vL	vR	BF/G	H%	S%	xERA	G	L	F	Ctl	Dom	Cmd	hr/f	hr/9	RAR	BPV	R$
RH Starter	04		0	0	0	0	0	0.00	0.00																		
Age 27	05	aa	3	3	0	71	47	6.13	1.46	299			26.0	33%	59%	5.29				2.3	5.9	2.5		1.3	-16.0	44	$0
Type	06	aa	1	6	0	41	31	7.63	2.05	379			22.7	43%	64%	8.41				3.0	6.9	2.3		1.6	-15.7	20	($4)
Health A	07	aa	11	8	0	152	104	5.98	1.68	308			25.9	34%	66%	5.95				3.8	6.1	1.6		1.2	-28.5	26	$1
PT/Exp C	08	DET	13	7	0	179	126	3.73	1.19	232	267	174	24.5	25%	75%	4.20	44	17	40	3.1	6.3	2.1	13%	1.4	13.7	53	$19
Consist F	1st Half		7	2	0	82	55	3.40	1.15	217			23.8	24%	74%	4.23	45	17	38	3.3	6.0	1.8	10%	1.0	9.6	43	$10
LIMA Plan D+	2nd Half		6	5	0	97	71	4.00	1.23	244			25.1	25%	76%	4.18	42	17	41	2.9	6.6	2.3	16%	1.8	4.1	61	$9
+/- Score -15	09	Proj	11	10	0	174	123	4.86	1.47	284			24.6	31%	71%	4.55	43	17	40	3.2	6.4	2.0	12%	1.4	-2.7	51	$9

Where did this come from??? Skills showed growth, but he shook far more out of marginal Cmd and h%-from-nowhere than could be expected. 32% PQS-DOM also says that it's not change you can believe in.

Gallagher,Sean

			W	L	Sv	IP	K	ERA	WHIP	OBA	vL	vR	BF/G	H%	S%	xERA	G	L	F	Ctl	Dom	Cmd	hr/f	hr/9	RAR	BPV	R$
RH Starter	04		0	0	0	0	0	0.00	0.00																		
Age 23	05		0	0	0	0	0	0.00	0.00																		
Type Pwr FB	06	aa	7	5	0	86	84	4.28	1.81	280			27.2	36%	77%	5.17				6.5	8.8	1.4		0.6	2.5	62	$4
Health A	07	CHC *	10	3	1	116	81	4.50	1.47	269			18.8	31%	69%	5.01	39	16	45	3.9	6.3	1.6	5%	0.6	-1.1	26	$8
PT/Exp D	08	2TM *	7	9	0	144	129	4.80	1.44	257	266	259	22.5	31%	68%	4.51	36	22	43	4.2	8.0	1.9	8%	0.9	-8.8	46	$7
Consist A	1st Half		5	5	0	83	73	4.03	1.28	248			21.7	30%	70%	3.95	44	17	40	3.2	7.9	2.5	9%	0.9	2.9	80	$8
LIMA Plan C	2nd Half		2	4	0	62	56	5.84	1.66	269			23.5	33%	65%	5.21	28	26	45	5.6	8.2	1.5	9%	1.1	-11.7	4	($0)
+/- Score 9	09	Proj	6	4	0	87	73	4.76	1.52	262			21.4	31%	70%	4.90	34	23	44	4.7	7.6	1.6	8%	0.9	-5.6	22	$5

5-7, 5.15 ERA in 115 IP at CHC and OAK. Dom, hr/9 speak to his stuff, but until Ctl improves and BPIs stabilize, he's more likely to hurt than help. Someone to watch in March, but likely a year away.

JOCK THOMPSON

Gallardo,Yovani

		Yr	W	L	Sv	IP	K	ERA	WHIP	OBA	vL	vR	BF/G	H%	S%	xERA	G	L	F	Ctl	Dom	Cmd	hr/f	hr/9	RAR	BPV	R$
RH Starter		04	0	0	0	0	0	0.00	0.00																		
Age	23	05	0	0	0	0	0	0.00	0.00																		
Type	Pwr FB	06 aa	5	2	0	77	80	2.22	1.15	214			24.1	29%	81%	2.36				3.4	9.3	2.7		0.3	21.8	115	$12
Health	F	07 MIL	* 17	8	0	188	211	3.56	1.19	232	247	244	23.4	32%	71%	3.37	38	24	38	3.1	10.1	3.3	7%	0.6	20.1	115	$26
PT/Exp	D	08 MIL	* 0	1	0	39	37	3.33	1.42	280	324	204	24.3	34%	81%	4.21	40	12	48	2.9	8.4	2.9	9%	1.1	4.5	91	$2
Consist	B	1st Half	0	1	0	35	30	3.46	1.44	287			25.6	34%	79%	4.32	41	14	45	2.8	7.6	2.8	8%	1.0	3.5	82	$2
LIMA Plan	B	2nd Half	0	0	0	4	7	2.25	1.25	210			16.7	32%	100%	2.98	29	0	71	4.5	15.7	3.5	19%	2.2	1.0	169	$1
+/- Score	13	09 Proj	12	6	0	178	176	3.50	1.23	240			24.6	30%	74%	3.77	40	18	42	3.1	8.9	2.9	8%	0.9	12.6	95	$20

Knee injury in May cost him the season, except for a final-week cameo. Skill set is elite, knee should not present any further problems. Expect workload to be closely monitored in 2009. Meet the new MIL ace.

Garcia,Freddy

		Yr	W	L	Sv	IP	K	ERA	WHIP	OBA	vL	vR	BF/G	H%	S%	xERA	G	L	F	Ctl	Dom	Cmd	hr/f	hr/9	RAR	BPV	R$
RH Starter		04 2AL	13	11	0	210	184	3.81	1.22	245	236	248	28.0	29%	71%	3.82	43	17	40	2.7	7.9	2.9	9%	0.9	16.0	89	$21
Age	32	05 CHW	14	8	0	228	146	3.87	1.25	259	268	249	28.8	29%	72%	3.93	49	21	31	2.4	5.8	2.4	12%	1.0	14.2	67	$20
Type		06 CHW	17	9	0	216	135	4.54	1.28	272	262	271	27.5	29%	68%	4.35	41	18	41	2.0	5.6	2.8	11%	1.3	0.5	66	$20
Health	D	07 PHI	1	5	0	58	50	5.90	1.60	312	292	339	23.9	35%	68%	4.28	36	27	38	2.9	7.8	2.6	17%	1.9	-10.5	74	($0)
PT/Exp	C	08 DET	1	1	0	15	12	4.20	1.13	206	100	265	20.3	21%	71%	4.19	40	14	45	3.6	7.2	2.0	16%	1.8	0.3	51	$2
Consist	A	1st Half	0	0	0	0	0	0.00	0.00																		
LIMA Plan	C+	2nd Half	1	1	0	15	12	4.20	1.13	206			20.3	21%	71%	4.19	40	14	45	3.6	7.2	2.0	16%	1.8	0.3	51	$2
+/- Score	-20	09 Proj	7	8	0	145	107	4.59	1.45	276			27.5	31%	72%	4.52	41	19	40	3.4	6.6	2.0	12%	1.3	-1.7	48	$8

September cameo served as an audition for a 2009 job as he returns from shoulder surgery. Skill set was stable and attractive pre-surgery, age doesn't preclude a strong recovery. A gamble with upside.

Garland,Jon

		Yr	W	L	Sv	IP	K	ERA	WHIP	OBA	vL	vR	BF/G	H%	S%	xERA	G	L	F	Ctl	Dom	Cmd	hr/f	hr/9	RAR	BPV	R$
RH Starter		04 CHW	12	11	0	217	113	4.89	1.38	267	269	277	27.4	27%	68%	4.79	46	17	38	3.2	4.7	1.5	12%	1.4	-12.4	23	$10
Age	29	05 CHW	18	10	0	221	115	3.50	1.17	254	267	242	28.3	27%	74%	4.08	47	21	32	1.9	4.7	2.4	11%	1.1	23.7	58	$24
Type	Con	06 CHW	18	7	0	211	112	4.52	1.36	293	290	297	27.4	31%	69%	4.53	42	20	38	1.7	4.8	2.7	9%	1.1	1.0	59	$17
Health	A	07 CHW	10	13	0	208	98	4.23	1.33	272	259	281	27.6	29%	69%	4.85	39	23	38	2.5	4.2	1.7	7%	0.8	7.0	27	$13
PT/Exp	A	08 LAA	14	8	0	197	90	4.90	1.50	299	300	307	27.2	32%	69%	4.56	50	22	28	2.7	4.1	1.5	12%	1.1	-13.3	29	$7
Consist	A	1st Half	7	5	0	108	47	3.99	1.44	280			27.8	29%	74%	4.65	49	23	28	3.1	3.9	1.3	11%	0.9	4.8	15	$6
LIMA Plan	C	2nd Half	7	3	0	88	43	6.01	1.58	321			26.5	34%	63%	4.46	50	22	28	2.2	4.4	2.0	13%	1.2	-18.1	47	$1
+/- Score	-1	09 Proj	13	10	0	203	98	4.57	1.43	291			27.6	31%	70%	4.61	46	22	32	2.4	4.3	1.8	10%	1.1	-4.7	36	$11

ERA swelled to highest level since 2004 on the strength of a few more hits and HR. Such is the life of a low-DOM pitcher; they live and die on the vagaries of what happens after contact. 2006 best shows his true level.

Garza,Matt

		Yr	W	L	Sv	IP	K	ERA	WHIP	OBA	vL	vR	BF/G	H%	S%	xERA	G	L	F	Ctl	Dom	Cmd	hr/f	hr/9	RAR	BPV	R$
RH Starter		04	0	0	0	0	0	0.00	0.00																		
Age	25	05	0	0	0	0	0	0.00	0.00																		
Type		06 MIN	* 12	9	0	141	123	4.15	1.30	255	245	356	23.8	31%	68%	4.12	35	25	40	3.0	7.8	2.6	6%	0.6	7.2	73	$16
Health	A	07 MIN	* 9	13	0	175	144	4.53	1.59	300	314	276	24.7	36%	72%	4.38	48	15	38	3.4	7.4	2.1	7%	0.7	-0.4	66	$8
PT/Exp	B	08 TAM	11	9	0	185	128	3.70	1.24	246	244	245	25.6	28%	73%	4.32	42	18	40	2.9	6.2	2.2	8%	0.9	14.7	54	$18
Consist	A	1st Half	6	4	0	84	55	3.76	1.21	234			24.7	26%	72%	4.37	44	17	39	3.1	5.9	1.9	9%	1.0	6.0	44	$9
LIMA Plan	D+	2nd Half	5	5	0	101	73	3.65	1.27	256			26.4	29%	74%	4.29	40	20	40	2.7	6.5	2.4	8%	0.9	8.6	63	$9
+/- Score	-5	09 Proj	14	10	0	203	155	3.96	1.37	268			24.8	31%	74%	4.32	42	18	39	3.1	6.9	2.2	9%	0.9	2.6	62	$18

Altered his approach to favor better Ctl over Dom, but real catalyst for breakout was h% swing. 2H uptick in Dom and Cmd shows formula for continued success. Set expectations at that level.

Gaudin,Chad

		Yr	W	L	Sv	IP	K	ERA	WHIP	OBA	vL	vR	BF/G	H%	S%	xERA	G	L	F	Ctl	Dom	Cmd	hr/f	hr/9	RAR	BPV	R$
RH Reliever		04 TAM	* 2	5	2	90	80	5.00	1.54	299	403	301	9.3	36%	70%	4.35	36	23	41	3.1	8.0	2.6	10%	1.1	-6.3	75	$3
Age	26	05 TOR	* 10	11	0	163	117	4.64	1.36	285	481	462	24.9	32%	68%	3.97	40	29	31	2.2	6.5	3.0	12%	1.0	-5.4	76	$11
Type	Pwr	06 OAK	* 7	2	2	88	58	2.45	1.31	210	253	201	6.3	25%	81%	5.20	39	16	45	5.0	5.9	1.2	3%	0.3	22.9	-11	$12
Health	A	07 OAK	11	13	0	199	154	4.43	1.53	267	282	250	26.1	31%	73%	4.31	51	19	30	4.5	7.0	1.5	12%	0.9	2.0	32	$11
PT/Exp	B	08 2TM	9	5	0	90	71	4.40	1.32	266	273	258	7.6	31%	69%	4.19	39	21	40	2.7	7.1	2.6	10%	1.1	-1.0	72	$9
Consist	B	1st Half	5	3	0	60	43	3.58	1.28	261			11.0	30%	75%	4.20	42	19	38	2.5	6.4	2.5	8%	0.9	5.4	67	$6
LIMA Plan	C+	2nd Half	4	2	0	30	28	6.06	1.41	276			4.8	33%	59%	4.16	33	24	44	3.0	8.5	2.8	13%	1.5	-6.4	81	$2
+/- Score	17	09 Proj	6	4	0	65	51	4.05	1.35	263			7.1	30%	73%	4.21	41	21	39	3.1	7.1	2.3	11%	1.1	1.4	64	$6

Transitioned to bullpen work in May, ensuing results were rocky. Back issues may have been root cause, though. Ctl gains combined with 2H/bullpen Dom show the raw elements of a good relief arm.

Geary,Geoff

		Yr	W	L	Sv	IP	K	ERA	WHIP	OBA	vL	vR	BF/G	H%	S%	xERA	G	L	F	Ctl	Dom	Cmd	hr/f	hr/9	RAR	BPV	R$
RH Reliever		04 PHI	* 2	2	8	67	48	4.55	1.61	286	322	261	6.4	32%	75%	5.15	39	17	44	4.3	6.4	1.5	9%	1.2	-2.4	17	$3
Age	32	05 PHI	2	1	0	58	42	3.72	1.29	248	192	294	6.1	29%	73%	4.13	44	23	32	3.3	6.5	2.0	9%	0.8	3.7	51	$4
Type		06 PHI	7	1	1	91	60	2.96	1.35	286	348	249	4.8	33%	79%	3.95	50	19	31	2.0	5.9	3.0	6%	0.6	17.1	81	$10
Health	A	07 PHI	* 5	3	0	92	55	4.14	1.44	291	248	309	5.7	32%	72%	4.32	49	19	32	2.5	5.4	2.1	8%	0.8	3.2	55	$5
PT/Exp	C	08 HOU	2	3	0	64	45	2.53	1.14	200	220	182	4.7	24%	79%	4.46	44	15	41	3.9	6.3	1.6	4%	0.4	13.7	29	$7
Consist	A	1st Half	1	1	0	28	24	3.18	1.34	224			4.5	28%	76%	4.22	49	16	34	4.8	7.6	1.6	4%	0.3	3.8	36	$2
LIMA Plan	C	2nd Half	1	2	0	36	21	2.02	0.98	179			5.0	20%	82%	4.60	39	14	46	3.3	5.3	1.6	4%	0.5	9.9	24	$5
+/- Score	-77	09 Proj	3	2	0	68	45	3.97	1.35	259			5.2	29%	72%	4.49	46	17	37	3.3	6.0	1.8	8%	0.8	-1.2	41	$4

Others see the sexy ERA and primary setup role behind volatile Valverde and think, "saves sleeper". You see ridiculous 2H h% and declining Cmd trend, and think, "That's $4 saved I can spend on lunch."

Germano,Justin

		Yr	W	L	Sv	IP	K	ERA	WHIP	OBA	vL	vR	BF/G	H%	S%	xERA	G	L	F	Ctl	Dom	Cmd	hr/f	hr/9	RAR	BPV	R$
RH Starter		04 SD	* 12	8	0	176	116	4.19	1.32	276			23.4	31%	70%	4.10				2.2	5.9	2.6		0.8	1.5	66	$13
Age	26	05 aaa	10	8	0	161	116	3.97	1.36	288			25.5	33%	73%	4.47				2.0	6.5	3.3		0.9	6.7	79	$12
Type	Con	06 aaa	10	6	0	155	77	5.11	1.50	321			27.4	34%	68%	5.52				1.5	4.5	3.1		1.1	-11.2	49	$6
Health	A	07 SD	* 11	10	0	165	93	4.02	1.24	258	244	272	22.2	28%	69%	4.20	49	17	33	2.4	5.1	2.2	8%	0.8	8.3	55	$14
PT/Exp	D	08 SD	* 2	12	0	142	67	6.66	1.72	336	268	330	22.7	35%	62%	4.95	49	18	33	2.7	4.2	1.6	12%	1.3	-41.8	32	($8)
Consist	C	1st Half	2	7	0	82	40	5.84	1.65	323			20.8	33%	68%	4.81	49	18	33	2.7	4.4	1.6	15%	1.6	-15.9	33	($2)
LIMA Plan	C+	2nd Half	0	5	0	60	27	7.78	1.83	353			25.8	38%	56%					2.6	4.1	1.6		0.9	-25.9	16	($6)
+/- Score	53	09 Proj	1	3	0	40	20	4.78	1.42	292			24.5	31%	69%	4.47	49	18	33	2.3	4.6	2.0	11%	1.1	-0.6	48	$1

0-3, 5.98 ERA in 44 IP at SD. Another low-Dom GB artist, but GB rate isn't high enough to mask otherwise delinquent skills. Capable of eating innings, but there's no upside here, even if he gets back to Petco.

Giese,Dan

		Yr	W	L	Sv	IP	K	ERA	WHIP	OBA	vL	vR	BF/G	H%	S%	xERA	G	L	F	Ctl	Dom	Cmd	hr/f	hr/9	RAR	BPV	R$
RH Reliever		04 aaa	12	5	3	83	46	3.19	1.09	234			6.2	25%	73%	3.01				2.1	4.9	2.4		0.8	11.8	64	$14
Age	31	05 aaa	3	4	2	38	22	7.13	1.64	364			6.7	37%	64%	8.24				0.3	5.3	20.8		2.8	-13.2	366	($0)
Type	xFB	06 a/a	3	4	1	72	41	4.88	1.86	353			7.2	37%	80%	7.67				2.9	5.1	1.8		1.8	-3.2	-3	($1)
Health	A	07 aa	3	1	2	73	46	4.75	1.64	339			7.1	39%	70%	5.52				1.8	5.6	3.2		0.4	-2.6	77	$2
PT/Exp	D	08 NYY	* 5	5	0	102	70	3.07	1.19	243	209	260	12.7	29%	74%	4.72	31	18	51	2.5	6.1	2.4	3%	0.4	16.1	51	$11
Consist	C	1st Half	5	5	0	78	53	2.87	1.15	238			16.7	28%	75%	4.46	36	18	46	2.4	6.1	2.5	3%	0.4	14.2	59	$10
LIMA Plan	C+	2nd Half	0	0	0	24	17	3.70	1.32	259			7.4	30%	73%	5.06	27	19	54	3.0	6.3	2.1	5%	0.7	1.9	38	$1
+/- Score	-46	09 Proj	1	2	0	29	19	4.66	1.38	281			7.8	30%	71%	5.04	28	18	53	2.5	5.9	2.4	10%	1.6	-2.2	45	$1

1-3, 3.53 ERA in 43 IP at NYY. Finally stuck in majors for a summer after 10 yrs in minors. Bled every possible drop of success from pedestrian skill set. It won't last, but "he'll always have the summer of '08".

Glavine,Tom

		Yr	W	L	Sv	IP	K	ERA	WHIP	OBA	vL	vR	BF/G	H%	S%	xERA	G	L	F	Ctl	Dom	Cmd	hr/f	hr/9	RAR	BPV	R$
LH Starter		04 NYM	11	14	0	212	109	3.61	1.29	254	242	255	27.1	27%	74%	4.33	51	19	30	3.0	4.6	1.6	10%	0.8	17.1	32	$15
Age	43	05 NYM	13	13	0	211	105	3.54	1.36	276	323	267	27.4	30%	74%	4.49	47	23	30	2.6	4.5	1.7	6%	0.5	18.4	35	$15
Type		06 NYM	15	7	0	198	131	3.82	1.33	266	200	287	26.3	30%	74%	4.20	44	23	32	2.8	6.0	2.1	11%	1.0	16.3	53	$18
Health	F	07 NYM	13	8	0	200	89	4.45	1.41	279	326	266	25.5	29%	71%	5.02	42	21	37	2.9	4.0	1.4	9%	1.0	-0.6	14	$10
PT/Exp	A	08 ATL	2	4	0	63	37	5.55	1.64	273	290	287	22.2	28%	70%	5.16	47	21	31	5.3	5.3	1.0	17%	1.6	-10.0	-22	($1)
Consist	A	1st Half	2	3	0	59	34	4.86	1.57	264			22.2	28%	73%	5.02	48	21	31	5.0	5.2	1.0	15%	1.4	-4.3	-16	$0
LIMA Plan	F	2nd Half	0	1	0	4	3	15.75	2.75	383			22.7	38%	44%	7.59	33	25	42	9.0	6.7	0.8	31%	4.5	-5.7	-110	($2)
+/- Score	-32	09 Proj	3	3	0	58	34	4.81	1.55	281			25.9	31%	71%	4.85	46	22	32	4.0	5.3	1.3	11%	1.1	-3.7	10	$1

Are August elbow/shoulder surgeries the end of the line? If so, final tallies are 305 Wins, 3.54 ERA and .600 Win%. We'll see you in Cooperstown in 2013, Tom. (If he's not done, stay far, far away.)

RAY MURPHY

Glover,Gary

		Yr	Tm	W	L	Sv	IP	K	ERA	WHIP	OBA	vL	vR	BF/G	H%	S%	xERA	G	L	F	Ctl	Dom	Cmd	hr/f	hr/9	RAR	BPV	R$
RH	Reliever	04	MIL	* 8	7	0	105	43	6.26	1.77	335	273	257	13.3	34%	67%	6.85				3.2	3.7	1.2		1.5	-25.8	-12	($3)
Age	32	05	MIL	* 11	8	1	156	118	4.29	1.46	288	256	318	21.4	33%	74%	4.27	42	22	37	2.8	6.8	2.4	11%	1.1	-0.8	67	$10
Type	FB	06	JPN	5	7	0	96	60	6.17	1.69	331			22.2	35%	69%	7.04				2.7	5.6	2.1		2.0	-19.6	6	($1)
Health	B	07	TAM	6	5	2	77	51	4.89	1.47	285	286	290	5.1	31%	71%	5.02	38	14	48	3.1	5.9	1.9	10%	1.4	-3.7	38	$5
PT/Exp	C	08	2AL	2	3	0	54	37	5.30	1.58	295	304	279	5.2	33%	68%	4.99	39	20	41	3.6	6.1	1.7	9%	1.2	-6.4	29	$1
Consist	C	1st Half		0	2	0	30	19	3.33	1.52	270			5.3	32%	77%	5.31	38	19	43	4.2	5.8	1.4	2%	0.3	3.7	5	$1
LIMA Plan	C+	2nd Half		2	1	0	25	18	7.68	1.67	322			5.1	34%	57%	4.62	40	21	39	2.9	6.6	2.3	18%	2.2	-10.1	58	($1)
+/- Score	-5	09	Proj	2	2	0	29	19	4.97	1.48	288			6.1	32%	69%	4.87	39	18	43	3.1	5.9	1.9	10%	1.2	-1.6	39	$1

Found some Cmd in 2H, but gopheritis obscured those gains. 2008 looks a lot better if you remove 10 ER allowed over 3 days in July. Unfortunately, MLB is opposed to time travel and manipulating history.

Gobble,Jimmy

		Yr	Tm	W	L	Sv	IP	K	ERA	WHIP	OBA	vL	vR	BF/G	H%	S%	xERA	G	L	F	Ctl	Dom	Cmd	hr/f	hr/9	RAR	BPV	R$
LH	Reliever	04	KC	* 11	9	0	167	61	5.39	1.43	284	317	255	25.0	28%	66%	5.48	38	18	44	2.7	3.3	1.2	11%	1.6	-19.7	1	$5
Age	27	05	KC	* 3	8	0	111	77	6.39	1.74	316	304	294	13.0	35%	65%	5.23	40	18	42	4.0	6.2	1.6	10%	1.3	-27.7	23	($4)
Type	Pwr xFB	06	KC	4	6	2	84	80	5.14	1.48	286	255	294	6.2	35%	68%	4.07	38	22	40	3.1	8.6	2.8	12%	1.3	-6.1	86	$5
Health	B	07	KC	4	1	1	54	50	3.02	1.47	270	241	319	3.2	33%	84%	4.43	35	21	44	3.9	8.4	2.2	9%	1.0	9.9	60	$6
PT/Exp	D	08	KC	0	2	1	32	27	8.80	1.96	304	200	382	4.0	35%	54%	6.21	28	19	53	6.5	7.7	1.2	9%	1.4	-17.4	-32	($3)
Consist	C	1st Half		0	2	1	20	17	7.31	1.73	284			3.5	33%	58%	5.79	24	19	57	5.5	7.8	1.4	9%	1.4	-7.2	-6	($1)
LIMA Plan	D+	2nd Half		0	0	0	12	10	11.25	2.33	334			4.8	39%	50%	6.96	35	19	47	8.2	7.5	0.9	11%	1.5	-10.2	-75	($3)
+/- Score	78	09	Proj	2	4	0	58	52	4.50	1.53	288			4.9	34%	74%	4.62	33	20	47	3.6	8.1	2.3	10%	1.2	-1.4	60	$3

Showed promise in '06-07 but was another victim of a bad day: 10 ER in 1 IP on 7/21. We are opposed to MLB's resistance to history manipulation so we are going to ignore 7/21. We are: Pro Mulligans, Pro Asterisks

Gonzalez,Edgar

		Yr	Tm	W	L	Sv	IP	K	ERA	WHIP	OBA	vL	vR	BF/G	H%	S%	xERA	G	L	F	Ctl	Dom	Cmd	hr/f	hr/9	RAR	BPV	R$
RH	Reliever	04	aaa	5	5	0	94	67	4.79	1.26	268			26.2	30%	65%	4.36				2.0	6.4	3.2		1.3	-5.2	68	$6
Age	26	05	aaa	1	5	0	160	100	4.50	1.36	289			25.3	32%	69%	4.61				1.9	5.6	3.0		1.0	-3.9	63	$5
Type	FB	06	ARI	* 6	12	0	180	122	4.49	1.33	286	259	288	21.9	32%	68%	4.54	38	15	47	1.7	6.1	3.5	7%	0.9	-0.1	78	$10
Health	D	07	ARI	8	4	0	102	62	5.03	1.35	277	313	237	13.6	29%	68%	4.48	45	15	40	2.5	5.5	2.2	13%	1.6	-7.6	54	$6
PT/Exp	C	08	ARI	1	3	0	48	32	6.00	1.65	300	259	336	12.9	33%	66%	5.20	38	20	43	3.9	6.0	1.5	12%	1.5	-10.2	17	($1)
Consist	A	1st Half		1	3	0	48	32	6.00	1.65	300			12.9	33%	66%	5.20	38	20	43	3.9	6.0	1.5	12%	1.5	-10.2	17	($1)
LIMA Plan	D+	2nd Half		0	0	0	0	0	0.00	0.00																		
+/- Score	10	09	Proj	2	3	0	64	42	4.68	1.34	272			7.5	30%	68%	4.52	40	18	42	2.6	6.0	2.3	10%	1.3	-1.4	56	$3

Strained elbow ended his year in July. Excellent Cmd history in minors (career 3.1 Cmd), has not yet carried over to majors. At 26, needs either a change of scenery or permanent move to pen to get off Triple-A shuttle.

Gonzalez,Gio

		Yr	Tm	W	L	Sv	IP	K	ERA	WHIP	OBA	vL	vR	BF/G	H%	S%	xERA	G	L	F	Ctl	Dom	Cmd	hr/f	hr/9	RAR	BPV	R$
LH	Starter	04		0	0	0	0	0	0.00	0.00																		
Age	23	05		0	0	0	0	0	0.00	0.00																		
Type	Pwr	06	aa	7	12	0	154	139	6.36	1.64	281			26.0	32%	65%	6.01				4.8	8.1	1.7		1.9	-35.0	25	$1
Health	A	07	aa	9	7	0	150	165	4.44	1.35	251			23.7	33%	69%	3.94				3.7	9.9	2.7		0.9	0.4	94	$13
PT/Exp	D	08	OAK	* 9	11	0	157	140	5.27	1.46	251	194	260	20.8	30%	66%	4.45	42	18	40	4.6	8.0	1.7	11%	1.2	-17.8	39	$8
Consist	C	1st Half		4	6	0	87	75	5.64	1.61	285			23.2	34%	66%					4.4	7.7	1.8		1.1	-13.9	49	$1
LIMA Plan	C	2nd Half		5	5	0	70	65	4.80	1.27	204			18.3	24%	66%	4.20	42	18	40	5.0	8.4	1.7	14%	1.3	-3.9	37	$6
+/- Score	24	09	Proj	8	9	0	139	135	4.73	1.40	249			22.3	31%	69%	4.10	42	18	40	4.2	8.7	2.1	11%	1.1	5.5	64	$10

1-4, 7.68 ERA in 34 IP at OAK. Regressed in 1H in minors, then righted self in July to earn callup, and got torched in majors. MLB Dom (9.0) shows caliber of his stuff, but more polish clearly needed. Good long-term play.

Gonzalez,Mike

		Yr	Tm	W	L	Sv	IP	K	ERA	WHIP	OBA	vL	vR	BF/G	H%	S%	xERA	G	L	F	Ctl	Dom	Cmd	hr/f	hr/9	RAR	BPV	R$
LH	Reliever	04	PIT	* 5	2	3	63	83	1.14	0.95	205	213	194	4.0	32%	90%	2.29	50	19	31	2.0	11.8	5.9	5%	0.3	24.3	188	$14
Age	30	05	PIT	1	3	5	50	58	2.70	1.32	199	156	223	4.2	28%	80%	3.47	53	18	30	5.6	10.4	1.9	6%	0.4	9.5	68	$6
Type	Pwr	06	PIT	3	4	24	54	64	2.17	1.35	216	163	227	4.3	32%	83%	3.79	37	27	36	5.2	10.7	2.1	2%	0.2	15.5	67	$16
Health	F	07	ATL	2	0	2	17	13	1.59	1.35	238	333	189	4.0	30%	87%	4.73	39	20	41	4.2	6.9	1.6	0%	0.0	6.0	26	$3
PT/Exp	D	08	ATL	* 1	3	15	45	52	3.47	1.31	257	259	196	4.2	34%	79%	3.61	31	25	44	3.1	10.5	3.4	11%	1.2	4.4	114	$9
Consist	C	1st Half		1	0	3	15	12	1.95	1.52	337			5.1	40%	90%	4.64	31	15	54	0.8	7.2	9.6	4%	0.6	4.3	118	$3
LIMA Plan	B	2nd Half		0	3	12	30	40	4.24	1.21	208			3.8	28%	71%	3.23	31	26	43	4.2	12.1	2.9	18%	1.5	0.1	113	$7
+/- Score	14	09	Proj	3	4	25	73	85	3.10	1.23	224			4.2	30%	78%	3.45	37	23	40	3.7	10.6	2.8	10%	0.9	7.9	104	$17

0-3, 4.28 ERA with 14 Sv in 34 IP at ATL. Returned in June with vintage skills, reclaimed closer role. FB% trend means HR problems will continue, but overall a solid and closer-worthy skill set.

Gordon,Tom

		Yr	Tm	W	L	Sv	IP	K	ERA	WHIP	OBA	vL	vR	BF/G	H%	S%	xERA	G	L	F	Ctl	Dom	Cmd	hr/f	hr/9	RAR	BPV	R$
RH	Reliever	04	NYY	9	4	4	89	96	2.22	0.89	182	185	174	4.2	25%	77%	2.91	47	16	38	2.3	9.7	4.2	6%	0.5	24.3	136	$20
Age	41	05	NYY	5	4	2	80	69	2.58	1.10	207	187	217	4.1	24%	81%	3.55	53	12	35	3.3	7.7	2.4	10%	0.9	17.7	83	$13
Type	Pwr	06	PHI	3	4	34	59	68	3.35	1.27	241	185	277	4.2	31%	80%	3.11	45	23	31	3.4	10.4	3.1	19%	1.4	8.3	119	$19
Health	F	07	PHI	3	2	6	40	32	4.73	1.33	262	310	222	3.9	29%	70%	3.87	49	16	35	2.9	7.2	2.5	16%	1.6	-1.5	78	$5
PT/Exp	C	08	PHI	5	4	2	30	26	5.15	1.62	270	246	266	4.0	33%	69%	4.94	40	17	43	5.2	7.9	1.5	8%	0.9	-3.2	21	$3
Consist	B	1st Half		5	4	1	28	26	5.20	1.66	277			4.1	34%	70%	4.92	39	16	45	5.2	8.4	1.6	8%	1.0	-3.2	28	$3
LIMA Plan	C+	2nd Half		0	0	1	2	0	4.50	1.00	151			2.6	15%	50%	4.82	57	29	14	4.5	0.0	0.0	0%	0.0	-0.1	-86	$0
+/- Score	-28	09	Proj	2	3	0	29	24	4.74	1.44	251			4.1	30%	68%	4.40	45	17	38	4.4	7.6	1.7	9%	0.9	-0.2	40	$2

Two saves in 2008 give him 158 for his career. Now at 41, all skills trending in the wrong direction, facing off-season elbow surgery. A 159th save would be an upset.

Gorzelanny,Tom

		Yr	Tm	W	L	Sv	IP	K	ERA	WHIP	OBA	vL	vR	BF/G	H%	S%	xERA	G	L	F	Ctl	Dom	Cmd	hr/f	hr/9	RAR	BPV	R$
LH	Starter	04		0	0	0	0	0	0.00	0.00																		
Age	26	05	aa	8	5	0	129	102	3.88	1.36	264			24.0	32%	71%	3.68				3.1	7.1	2.3		0.4	6.8	80	$11
Type	FB	06	PIT	* 8	10	0	160	120	3.53	1.20	227	239	223	24.5	27%	70%	3.97	49	18	33	3.4	6.7	2.0	5%	0.4	18.8	57	$16
Health	B	07	PIT	14	10	0	202	135	3.88	1.40	273	217	284	27.2	31%	74%	4.60	42	18	40	3.0	6.0	2.0	7%	0.8	13.5	47	$15
PT/Exp	B	08	PIT	* 9	10	0	140	91	5.74	1.65	284	261	299	22.9	31%	67%	5.46	40	16	44	4.8	5.9	1.2	10%	1.4	-25.5	-5	$0
Consist	B	1st Half		6	6	0	83	49	6.18	1.75	273			24.2	29%	67%	6.02	43	14	43	6.2	5.3	0.9	12%	1.5	-19.6	-50	($2)
LIMA Plan	C	2nd Half		3	4	0	57	42	5.10	1.51	299			21.1	34%	68%	4.90	31	21	48	2.8	6.7	2.4	8%	1.1	-5.9	54	$2
+/- Score	-9	09	Proj	9	11	0	161	112	4.65	1.44	274			23.3	31%	70%	4.69	41	18	41	3.4	6.3	1.9	10%	1.2	-6.9	41	$8

6-9, 6.66 ERA in 105 IP at PIT. Atrocious sophomore year, although he righted himself a bit in 2H (mostly in AAA). Whispers of conditioning and dedication issues. Borderline skills to begin with, small margin for rebound.

Grabow,John

		Yr	Tm	W	L	Sv	IP	K	ERA	WHIP	OBA	vL	vR	BF/G	H%	S%	xERA	G	L	F	Ctl	Dom	Cmd	hr/f	hr/9	RAR	BPV	R$
LH	Reliever	04	PIT	2	5	1	61	64	5.15	1.78	319	327	319	4.2	40%	73%	3.85	48	23	29	4.1	9.4	2.3	15%	1.2	-6.7	84	$0
Age	30	05	PIT	2	3	0	52	42	4.85	1.37	239	219	250	3.5	28%	66%	4.18	47	20	33	4.3	7.3	1.7	12%	1.0	-3.9	39	$2
Type	Pwr	06	PIT	4	2	0	69	66	4.16	1.42	258	275	251	4.2	32%	73%	3.81	49	18	34	3.9	8.6	2.2	11%	0.9	2.8	76	$5
Health	A	07	PIT	3	2	1	52	42	4.53	1.45	278	238	303	3.6	33%	71%	4.01	50	17	33	3.3	7.3	2.2	11%	1.0	-0.6	70	$3
PT/Exp	C	08	PIT	6	3	4	76	62	2.84	1.28	219	239	207	4.3	25%	83%	4.43	40	20	41	4.4	7.3	1.7	10%	1.1	13.4	31	$10
Consist	A	1st Half		4	2	0	39	29	3.66	1.35	255			4.4	28%	79%	4.52	36	24	40	3.4	6.6	1.9	12%	1.4	2.9	40	$4
LIMA Plan	D+	2nd Half		2	1	4	37	33	1.96	1.20	175			4.2	21%	88%	4.31	45	14	41	5.4	8.1	1.5	8%	0.7	10.5	23	$6
+/- Score	-58	09	Proj	4	2	5	58	50	4.03	1.40	248			4.0	30%	73%	4.22	45	18	37	4.2	7.8	1.9	10%	0.9	0.9	50	$6

Stellar 2H was driven by as lucky a h%/s% combo as you'll ever see. Amid the ERA surge, he managed to lose his GB bias and regained his sub-2.0 Cmd. Many questions in PIT pen, but he's not the answer.

Green,Sean

		Yr	Tm	W	L	Sv	IP	K	ERA	WHIP	OBA	vL	vR	BF/G	H%	S%	xERA	G	L	F	Ctl	Dom	Cmd	hr/f	hr/9	RAR	BPV	R$
RH	Reliever	04	aa	4	3	2	77	38	4.93	1.57	288			6.7	31%	70%	5.19				3.9	4.4	1.1		1.0	-5.6	17	$2
Age	30	05	a/a	4	3	15	73	51	4.37	1.53	253			6.0	30%	70%	3.84				5.2	6.3	1.2		0.3	-0.6	60	$8
Type	Pwr xGB	06	SEA	0	0	0	32	15	4.50	1.47	274			5.9	30%	69%	4.42	58	19	24	3.7	4.2	1.2	8%	0.6	0.2	13	$1
Health	A	07	SEA	* 7	3	1	85	60	3.73	1.64	285	329	286	5.2	34%	76%	4.06	61	19	20	4.7	6.4	1.4	4%	0.2	8.2	28	$6
PT/Exp	D	08	SEA	4	5	1	79	62	4.67	1.47	264	299	233	4.8	32%	66%	3.51	63	17	20	4.1	7.1	1.7	6%	0.3	-3.2	58	$4
Consist	A	1st Half		1	2	0	43	41	3.33	1.36	247			4.6	31%	77%	3.06	62	18	19	3.9	8.5	2.2	13%	0.6	5.5	87	$4
LIMA Plan	C+	2nd Half		3	3	1	36	21	6.30	1.60	284			5.0	33%	56%	4.11	64	16	20	4.3	5.3	1.2	0%	0.0	-8.6	22	$1
+/- Score	8	09	Proj	4	3	0	73	51	4.34	1.49	268			5.2	32%	70%	3.77	62	18	20	4.1	6.3	1.5	9%	0.5	5.8	43	$4

Eye-popping GB rate mixes with erratic but tempting Ctl/Dom; all were working in 1H. Possibility of bigger role? L/R split (vs RH: .583 OPS, vs LH: 827 OPS) says middle relief specialist is his optimal use.

RAY MURPHY

Gregg,Kevin

		Yr	Tm	W	L	Sv	IP	K	ERA	WHIP	OBA	vL	vR	BF/G	H%	S%	xERA	G	L	F	Ctl	Dom	Cmd	hr/f	hr/9	RAR	BPV	R$
RH	Reliever	04	ANA	5	2	1	87	84	4.23	1.31	259	260	250	6.7	33%	68%	3.74	44	18	38	2.9	8.7	**3.0**	6%	0.6	2.2	100	$8
Age	30	05	ANA *	4	3	0	98	81	4.65	1.50	282	267	279	10.9	33%	70%	4.13	48	19	33	3.5	7.4	**2.1**	10%	0.9	-3.3	64	$4
Type	Pwr FB	06	LAA	3	4	0	78	71	4.15	1.40	285	298	268	10.5	34%	74%	4.17	36	18	46	2.4	8.2	**3.4**	9%	1.2	3.9	96	$6
Health	A	07	FLA	0	5	32	84	87	3.54	1.23	210	162	247	4.7	27%	73%	4.34	29	16	55	4.3	9.3	**2.2**	6%	0.8	9.2	59	$18
PT/Exp	B	08	FLA	7	8	29	69	58	3.41	1.28	208	181	222	4.0	26%	73%	4.30	45	20	35	4.8	7.6	**1.6**	5%	0.4	7.3	29	$18
Consist	A	1st Half		6	2	14	39	32	2.33	1.29	186			4.4	24%	82%	4.47	46	22	32	5.8	7.4	**1.3**	3%	0.2	9.3	1	$11
LIMA Plan	C	2nd Half		1	6	15	30	26	4.80	1.27	235			3.6	29%	61%	4.07	43	17	39	3.6	7.8	**2.2**	6%	0.6	-2.0	65	$7
+/- Score	-24	09	Proj	4	7	18	73	64	3.97	1.31	236			4.9	29%	72%	4.29	39	18	42	4.0	7.9	2.0	8%	0.9	0.4	53	$12

Warning signs abound: BPV and Cmd show stark downward trends, highlighting Ctl/Dom erosion. Reinvented himself as a GB artist, but it was h% that propped him up. Lost closer role in Sept., not likely to get it back.

Greinke,Zack

		Yr	Tm	W	L	Sv	IP	K	ERA	WHIP	OBA	vL	vR	BF/G	H%	S%	xERA	G	L	F	Ctl	Dom	Cmd	hr/f	hr/9	RAR	BPV	R$
RH	Starter	04	KC *	9	12	0	173	118	3.85	1.19	262	251	262	23.7	28%	74%	4.25	35	20	45	1.7	6.1	**3.6**	12%	1.5	12.4	77	$16
Age	25	05	KC	5	17	0	183	114	5.80	1.56	311	340	279	24.9	34%	64%	4.75	39	23	37	2.6	5.6	**2.2**	10%	1.1	-32.3	48	($0)
Type	Pwr	06	KC *	9	3	0	111	87	4.69	1.23	260	400	200	22.0	30%	63%	3.75	35	35	30	2.2	7.0	**3.2**	11%	0.9	-1.8	81	$12
Health	A	07	KC	7	7	1	122	106	3.69	1.30	262	266	263	9.9	32%	74%	4.23	32	22	46	2.7	7.8	**2.9**	7%	0.9	12.3	79	$13
PT/Exp	B	08	KC	13	10	0	202	183	3.47	1.28	261	287	232	26.5	32%	76%	3.75	43	19	38	2.5	8.1	**3.3**	9%	0.9	21.9	100	$22
Consist	A	1st Half		7	4	0	111	89	3.65	1.27	255			27.4	29%	77%	4.10	42	16	42	2.8	7.2	**2.6**	12%	1.3	9.6	76	$11
LIMA Plan	C+	2nd Half		6	6	0	91	94	3.25	1.28	270			25.6	36%	75%	3.33	43	23	34	2.2	9.3	**4.3**	6%	0.5	12.3	129	$11
+/- Score	25	09	Proj	14	10	0	203	182	3.50	1.26	260			26.5	32%	75%	3.82	39	21	40	2.4	8.1	3.4	9%	0.9	15.1	97	$23

Finally all the way back from 2006 absence, nudged his skills to a new level. Spike in GB% particularly encouraging. 2H Cmd spike says best is yet to come, eases burnout concerns. UP: sub-3.00 ERA.

Grilli,Jason

		Yr	Tm	W	L	Sv	IP	K	ERA	WHIP	OBA	vL	vR	BF/G	H%	S%	xERA	G	L	F	Ctl	Dom	Cmd	hr/f	hr/9	RAR	BPV	R$
RH	Reliever	04	CHW *	11	12	0	197	108	6.66	1.69	312	292	296	27.6	32%	64%	5.46	40	17	43	3.7	4.9	**1.3**	14%	1.9	-54.3	6	($4)
Age	32	05	aaa	1	9	0	160	86	5.38	1.63	308			27.0	33%	69%	5.76				3.3	4.9	**1.5**		1.2	-21.2	17	($3)
Type	Pwr	06	DET	2	3	0	62	31	4.21	1.39	259	292	249	5.2	28%	71%	5.00	47	15	38	3.6	4.5	**1.2**	8%	0.9	2.7	8	$3
Health	A	07	DET	5	3	0	80	62	4.74	1.42	265	237	275	6.1	32%	66%	4.44	45	16	39	3.6	7.0	**1.9**	5%	0.6	-2.3	51	$5
PT/Exp	C	08	2TM	3	3	1	75	69	3.00	1.40	241	237	242	5.4	31%	78%	4.20	42	23	34	4.6	8.3	**1.8**	3%	0.2	12.1	46	$7
Consist	A	1st Half		2	1	0	38	36	2.84	1.34	224			5.6	30%	78%	4.13	47	16	38	4.7	8.5	**1.8**	3%	0.2	6.9	50	$4
LIMA Plan	C	2nd Half		1	2	1	37	33	3.16	1.46	257			5.2	33%	77%	4.26	39	30	32	4.4	8.0	**1.8**	3%	0.2	5.2	43	$3
+/- Score	-41	09	Proj	3	3	0	64	53	4.11	1.43	257			6.0	31%	72%	4.34	43	20	36	4.1	7.5	1.8	7%	0.7	0.3	46	$4

Breakout or fluke?
Breakout: Dom trends up, gains vs RH hitters.
Fluke: LD spike didn't hurt bottom line, unsustainable hr/f (especially for Coors in 2H).
Without 2.0 Cmd, repeat unlikely.

Guardado,Eddie

		Yr	Tm	W	L	Sv	IP	K	ERA	WHIP	OBA	vL	vR	BF/G	H%	S%	xERA	G	L	F	Ctl	Dom	Cmd	hr/f	hr/9	RAR	BPV	R$
LH	Reliever	04	SEA	2	2	18	45	45	2.79	1.00	196	109	228	4.3	22%	84%	3.82	28	17	55	2.8	9.0	**3.2**	13%	1.6	9.1	92	$13
Age	38	05	SEA	2	3	36	56	48	2.73	1.19	247	231	242	4.0	29%	83%	4.05	35	19	46	2.4	7.7	**3.2**	9%	1.1	11.4	87	$18
Type	xFB	06	2TM	1	3	13	37	39	3.89	1.54	297	239	324	3.8	34%	87%	4.28	33	14	54	3.2	9.5	**3.0**	17%	2.4	2.9	96	$7
Health	F	07	CIN	0	0	0	14	8	7.23	1.46	293	333	273	4.0	31%	50%	5.27	23	29	48	2.6	5.3	**2.0**	9%	1.3	-4.7	25	($1)
PT/Exp	D	08	2AL	4	4	4	56	33	4.16	1.23	240	210	268	3.6	27%	66%	5.24	25	22	53	3.0	5.3	**1.7**	4%	0.6	1.3	16	$6
Consist	B	1st Half		1	1	1	28	17	3.18	0.95	184			3.3	20%	68%	4.78	28	18	54	2.9	5.4	**1.9**	5%	0.6	4.1	26	$4
LIMA Plan	D+	2nd Half		3	3	3	28	16	5.14	1.50	288			3.9	32%	65%	5.70	22	26	52	3.2	5.1	**1.6**	4%	0.6	-2.7	6	$3
+/- Score	-79	09	Proj	3	4	0	58	35	4.97	1.50	291			3.9	31%	71%	5.45	26	23	51	3.1	5.4	1.8	9%	1.4	-7.3	18	$2

Seems to have left his Dom on the operating table during '06 TJ surgery. Still tough on LHers, but save opps are gone for good, as are his LIMA qualifications.

Guerrier,Matt

		Yr	Tm	W	L	Sv	IP	K	ERA	WHIP	OBA	vL	vR	BF/G	H%	S%	xERA	G	L	F	Ctl	Dom	Cmd	hr/f	hr/9	RAR	BPV	R$
RH	Reliever	04	aaa	5	10	0	144	83	3.93	1.28	280			25.2	31%	72%	4.27				1.7	5.2	**3.1**		1.0	7.3	67	$9
Age	30	05	MIN	0	3	0	71	46	3.41	1.33	261	279	247	7.0	30%	76%	4.30	47	19	34	3.0	5.8	**1.9**	8%	0.8	8.4	48	$4
Type	Pwr	06	MIN	1	0	1	69	37	3.38	1.43	286	333	256	7.7	30%	81%	4.71	45	18	37	2.7	4.8	**1.8**	10%	1.2	10.0	36	$4
Health	A	07	MIN	2	4	1	88	68	2.35	1.05	222	264	187	4.8	26%	83%	3.60	47	16	36	2.1	7.0	**3.2**	10%	0.9	23.4	93	$13
PT/Exp	C	08	MIN	6	9	1	76	59	5.19	1.59	281	282	272	4.5	32%	71%	4.57	47	18	35	4.4	7.0	**1.6**	14%	1.4	-7.9	32	$3
Consist	C	1st Half		4	3	1	44	29	3.27	1.43	253			4.9	29%	80%	4.72	47	17	36	4.3	5.9	**1.4**	8%	0.8	5.8	16	$5
LIMA Plan	B	2nd Half		2	6	0	32	30	7.80	1.80	316			4.1	36%	60%	4.36	46	19	35	4.5	8.4	**1.9**	22%	2.2	-13.8	54	($1)
+/- Score	20	09	Proj	4	7	0	78	60	4.27	1.42	272			4.8	31%	73%	4.21	47	18	36	3.3	6.9	2.1	12%	1.2	2.0	59	$5

Mix a few more walks with a h% reversal and an unfortunate hr/f, and suddenly your ERA starts with a 5 instead of a 2. Ctl problems spiked in Aug/Sep, burnout a possible cause. Good candidate for a partial rebound.

Guthrie,Jeremy

		Yr	Tm	W	L	Sv	IP	K	ERA	WHIP	OBA	vL	vR	BF/G	H%	S%	xERA	G	L	F	Ctl	Dom	Cmd	hr/f	hr/9	RAR	BPV	R$
RH	Starter	04	a/a	9	10	0	149	85	5.46	1.72	314			25.6	34%	69%	5.89				3.9	5.1	**1.3**		1.0	-20.6	22	($0)
Age	30	05	aaa	12	10	0	136	84	5.39	1.57	301			24.4	34%	66%	5.19				3.2	5.6	**1.7**		0.9	-18.2	38	$4
Type		06	CLE *	9	5	0	142	88	4.61	1.55	275			21.2	32%	70%	4.73	50	19	31	4.3	5.6	**1.3**	6%	0.5	-1.0	13	$7
Health	A	07	BAL	7	5	0	175	123	3.70	1.21	250	255	243	22.6	28%	74%	4.09	42	19	38	2.4	6.3	**2.6**	11%	1.2	17.5	69	$17
PT/Exp	A	08	BAL	10	12	0	191	120	3.63	1.23	247	241	243	26.4	27%	75%	4.32	44	18	38	2.7	5.7	**2.1**	11%	1.1	16.8	50	$17
Consist	A	1st Half		4	7	0	116	74	3.50	1.20	243			26.5	26%	76%	4.26	42	20	38	2.6	5.8	**2.2**	11%	1.2	12.1	52	$10
LIMA Plan	D	2nd Half		6	5	0	75	46	3.84	1.27	251			26.2	27%	73%	4.41	46	15	38	2.9	5.5	**1.9**	10%	1.1	4.7	46	$7
+/- Score	-17	09	Proj	9	12	0	189	121	4.11	1.34	265			24.3	29%	72%	4.45	44	18	38	2.9	5.8	2.0	10%	1.1	-0.6	49	$13

Others will see the ERA/WHIP stability and consider 2008 a repeat of 2007 breakout. But you see erosion in skill set and wonder whether a double-digit bid is wise. Possibly not. DN: 4.50 ERA.

Halladay,Roy

		Yr	Tm	W	L	Sv	IP	K	ERA	WHIP	OBA	vL	vR	BF/G	H%	S%	xERA	G	L	F	Ctl	Dom	Cmd	hr/f	hr/9	RAR	BPV	R$
RH	Starter	04	TOR	8	8	0	133	95	4.20	1.35	272	285	258	27.0	31%	70%	3.60	60	13	27	2.6	6.4	**2.4**	11%	0.9	3.9	82	$10
Age	32	05	TOR	12	4	0	141	108	2.42	0.96	229	217	235	28.9	27%	78%	2.69	61	18	21	1.1	6.9	**6.0**	13%	0.7	34.0	132	$24
Type	Con GB	06	TOR	16	5	0	220	132	3.19	1.10	251	259	244	27.6	28%	74%	3.23	57	21	22	1.4	5.4	**3.9**	12%	0.8	37.1	95	$29
Health	C	07	TOR	16	7	0	225	139	3.72	1.24	267	265	270	30.3	30%	71%	3.79	53	18	29	1.9	5.6	**2.9**	7%	0.6	22.0	79	$23
PT/Exp	A	08	TOR	20	11	0	246	206	2.78	1.05	241	243	230	28.7	29%	76%	2.98	54	19	27	1.4	7.5	**5.3**	9%	0.7	47.5	129	$37
Consist	B	1st Half		9	6	0	130	106	2.90	1.04	242			28.7	29%	74%	2.91	55	20	25	1.3	7.3	**5.6**	10%	0.6	23.2	130	$19
LIMA Plan	C	2nd Half		11	5	0	116	100	2.64	1.06	240			28.8	29%	78%	3.06	52	19	29	1.6	7.8	**5.0**	9%	0.7	24.3	128	$19
+/- Score	12	09	Proj	17	8	0	218	161	3.10	1.12	251			29.3	29%	74%	3.25	55	19	27	1.6	6.7	4.1	9%	0.7	31.6	109	$29

Best Dom since 2001 drove this surge. Combination of recent durability and desirable Dom/GB makes this a relatively safe SP investment. But "safe" is relative when it comes to SPs, so if bidding hits $30, drop out.

Hamels,Cole

		Yr	Tm	W	L	Sv	IP	K	ERA	WHIP	OBA	vL	vR	BF/G	H%	S%	xERA	G	L	F	Ctl	Dom	Cmd	hr/f	hr/9	RAR	BPV	R$
LH	Starter	04		0	0	0	0	0	0.00	0.00																		
Age	25	05	aa	2	0	0	19	18	2.84	1.32	183			26.8	22%	83%	3.04				6.2	8.5	**1.4**		0.9	3.4	70	$3
Type		06	PHI *	11	8	0	155	177	3.59	1.15	228	207	244	24.3	30%	73%	3.34	39	18	43	2.8	10.2	**3.6**	11%	1.1	17.1	125	$21
Health	B	07	PHI	15	5	0	183	177	3.39	1.12	240	247	236	26.5	29%	76%	3.38	42	19	39	2.1	8.7	**4.1**	13%	1.2	23.5	119	$25
PT/Exp	A	08	PHI	14	10	0	227	196	3.09	1.08	231	262	215	27.6	27%	77%	3.59	40	22	39	2.1	7.8	**3.7**	11%	1.1	33.1	101	$28
Consist	A	1st Half		8	5	0	120	103	3.38	1.03	216			27.9	25%	72%	3.63	39	22	40	2.3	7.7	**3.3**	11%	1.1	13.3	93	$16
LIMA Plan	C+	2nd Half		6	5	0	107	93	2.77	1.14	248			27.2	29%	82%	3.56	41	22	38	1.8	7.8	**4.2**	11%	1.1	19.9	109	$13
+/- Score	20	09	Proj	15	7	0	209	186	3.41	1.12	241			26.3	28%	75%	3.55	40	20	39	2.0	8.0	4.0	12%	1.2	20.4	109	$26

We knew the skills were there, he answered questions about durability in a big way. But is he out of the woods? 40-inning IP spike plus post-season work raise the burnout risk. But that is the only blemish here.

Hammel,Jason

		Yr	Tm	W	L	Sv	IP	K	ERA	WHIP	OBA	vL	vR	BF/G	H%	S%	xERA	G	L	F	Ctl	Dom	Cmd	hr/f	hr/9	RAR	BPV	R$
RH	Reliever	04		0	0	0	0	0	0.00	0.00																		
Age	26	05	a/a	11	4	0	136	106	3.38	1.32	260			26.2	31%	76%	3.81				2.9	7.0	**2.4**		0.7	15.6	74	$14
Type		06	TAM *	5	15	0	171	132	6.10	1.62	311	372	299	23.5	36%	62%	4.51	44	19	38	3.1	6.9	**2.2**	9%	1.0	-32.5	63	$1
Health	A	07	TAM *	7	10	0	161	129	5.50	1.52	278	310	277	19.3	33%	64%	4.73	41	16	43	3.9	7.2	**1.8**	7%	0.9	-19.7	43	$5
PT/Exp	C	08	TAM	4	4	2	78	44	4.60	1.51	273	281	265	8.7	29%	73%	4.80	47	21	32	4.0	5.1	**1.3**	13%	1.3	-2.4	7	$4
Consist	A	1st Half		3	3	0	47	27	4.98	1.62	289			14.2	31%	72%	4.96	47	21	32	4.2	5.2	**1.2**	14%	1.3	-3.7	4	$1
LIMA Plan	C+	2nd Half		1	1	2	31	17	4.03	1.34	247			5.3	26%	74%	4.57	47	22	31	3.7	4.9	**1.3**	13%	1.2	1.2	12	$2
+/- Score	-11	09	Proj	4	5	0	87	57	4.66	1.47	273			9.6	30%	70%	4.62	45	20	35	3.7	5.9	1.6	10%	1.0	-2.2	29	$4

Continues to struggle to bring his MLE skills to the majors. Cmd hasn't touched 2.0 level in bigs, and trending the wrong way. Time isn't quite up yet, but no sign that a step forward is imminent.

RAY MURPHY

Hampson,Justin	Yr	Tm	W	L	Sv	IP	K	ERA	WHIP	OBA	vL	vR	BF/G	H%	S%	xERA	G	L	F	Ctl	Dom	Cmd	hr/f	hr/9	RAR	BPV	R$
LH Reliever	04	aa	10	9	0	170	83	5.40	1.78	328			29.6	33%	76%	7.24				3.6	4.4	**1.2**		2.0	-22.2	-19	($2)
Age 28	05	aaa	5	13	0	144	79	6.37	1.67	306			24.5	33%	63%	5.88				3.8	4.9	**1.3**		1.3	-36.7	13	($4)
Type FB	06	COL *	9	4	0	133	88	4.65	1.56	304			16.6	34%	73%	4.90	33	27	40	2.9	5.9	**2.0**	9%	1.1	-2.6	39	$6
Health C	07	SD *	3	4	0	66	42	3.19	1.38	260	213	255	5.8	30%	78%	4.62	47	15	38	3.5	5.8	**1.6**	6%	0.6	10.0	34	$5
PT/Exp D	08	SD	2	1	0	31	19	2.93	1.34	264	250	302	3.7	31%	78%	4.88	39	16	45	2.9	5.6	**1.9**	2%	0.3	5.1	38	$3
Consist A	1st Half		0	1	0	9	8	7.24	1.72	346			4.0	42%	57%	4.83	31	14	55	2.1	8.3	**4.0**	6%	1.0	-3.2	102	($1)
LIMA Plan C+	2nd Half		2	0	0	22	11	1.23	1.18	225			3.6	26%	88%	4.87	43	17	40	3.3	4.5	**1.4**	0%	0.0	8.3	13	$3
+/- Score -41	09	Proj	**3**	**2**	**0**	**44**	**25**	**4.09**	**1.43**	**275**			**7.4**	**30%**	**74%**	**5.07**	**41**	**16**	**43**	**3.3**	**5.1**	**1.6**	**8%**	**1.0**	**-3.9**	**22**	**$3**

Shoulder tendinitis delayed the start of his season. No reason to think he's capable of more than lefty specialist role. Sub-par Dom and Cmd, struggles vs RH hitters. Hr/f corrections will push his ERA toward historical xERA.

Hampton,Mike	Yr	Tm	W	L	Sv	IP	K	ERA	WHIP	OBA	vL	vR	BF/G	H%	S%	xERA	G	L	F	Ctl	Dom	Cmd	hr/f	hr/9	RAR	BPV	R$
LH Starter	04	ATL	13	9	0	172	87	4.29	1.53	290	253	300	26.4	31%	73%	4.56	52	21	27	3.4	4.5	**1.3**	9%	0.8	-0.6	20	$8
Age 36	05	ATL	5	3	0	69	27	3.52	1.33	275	338	263	24.5	29%	75%	4.53	51	20	29	2.3	3.5	**1.5**	7%	0.7	6.2	29	$5
Type Con GB	06	ATL	0	0	0	0	0	0.00	0.00																		
Health F	07	ATL	0	0	0	0	0	0.00	0.00																		
PT/Exp F	08	ATL *	3	5	0	91	49	4.65	1.45	278	339	267	23.4	30%	71%	4.28	53	22	26	3.3	4.8	**1.5**	15%	1.2	-4.2	30	$2
Consist F	1st Half		0	1	0	6	5	1.55	1.73	300			14.2	37%	90%					4.7	7.0	**1.5**		0.0	2.0	69	$0
LIMA Plan C	2nd Half		3	4	0	85	44	4.87	1.43	277			24.6	29%	69%	4.27	53	22	26	3.2	4.7	**1.5**	16%	1.3	-6.3	30	$2
+/- Score -10	09	Proj	**7**	**9**	**0**	**137**	**68**	**4.40**	**1.45**	**281**			**25.0**	**30%**	**71%**	**4.45**	**52**	**21**	**27**	**3.2**	**4.5**	**1.4**	**11%**	**0.9**	**-1.9**	**25**	**$5**

3-4, 4.85 ERA in 78 IP at ATL. Good news: Came off two-year shutdown with old skills intact. Bad news: That skill set was terrible. GB bias will limit the downside, but there is no upside here, even if healthy.

Hanrahan,Joel	Yr	Tm	W	L	Sv	IP	K	ERA	WHIP	OBA	vL	vR	BF/G	H%	S%	xERA	G	L	F	Ctl	Dom	Cmd	hr/f	hr/9	RAR	BPV	R$
RH Reliever	04	aaa	7	7	0	119	83	4.38	1.58	268			21.4	29%	76%	5.21				4.9	6.3	**1.3**		1.4	-0.6	25	$5
Age 27	05	aa	9	8	0	111	82	5.26	1.64	291			22.1	33%	71%	5.64				4.3	6.7	**1.5**		1.3	-13.1	29	$3
Type Pwr	06	a/a	11	5	0	140	91	4.32	1.57	260			24.2	29%	74%	4.51				5.2	5.9	**1.1**		0.8	3.4	37	$8
Health A	07	WAS *	10	7	0	126	101	5.24	1.67	276	267	305	21.5	31%	72%	5.38	31	25	44	5.4	7.2	**1.3**	12%	1.4	-12.6	-6	$4
PT/Exp C	08	WAS	6	3	9	84	93	3.95	1.36	235	228	237	5.2	31%	74%	3.70	43	22	36	4.5	9.9	**2.2**	12%	1.0	3.3	78	$11
Consist C	1st Half		5	2	0	51	59	4.26	1.42	231			5.8	31%	72%	3.88	41	20	39	5.1	10.5	**2.0**	10%	0.9	0.1	68	$5
LIMA Plan C+	2nd Half		1	1	9	34	34	3.48	1.28	240			4.6	30%	77%	3.45	45	23	32	3.5	9.1	**2.6**	14%	1.1	3.3	93	$6
+/- Score 16	09	Proj	**4**	**4**	**28**	**73**	**71**	**4.10**	**1.41**	**255**			**6.5**	**32%**	**73%**	**3.99**	**40**	**23**	**37**	**4.0**	**8.8**	**2.2**	**11%**	**1.0**	**3.2**	**70**	**$15**

Ended year as WAS closer. Can he hold the job? PRO: Elite Dom, GB tendency, rising Cmd continued in 2H. CON: Long-term Ctl problems and gopheritis mean volatility. Pay for saves, expect agita.

Hansen,Craig	Yr	Tm	W	L	Sv	IP	K	ERA	WHIP	OBA	vL	vR	BF/G	H%	S%	xERA	G	L	F	Ctl	Dom	Cmd	hr/f	hr/9	RAR	BPV	R$
RH Reliever	04		0	0	0	0	0	0.00	0.00											0.0	0.0						
Age 25	05	BOS *	0	0	1	13	11	2.08	1.46	304	600	333	4.7	37%	89%	4.02	50	8	42	2.1	7.6	**3.7**	6%	0.7	3.7	109	$1
Type Pwr GB	06	BOS *	4	4	0	85	63	4.76	1.51	271	344	276	6.6	32%	67%	4.62	44	22	35	4.1	6.7	**1.6**	5%	0.5	-2.2	30	$4
Health A	07	aaa	3	1	3	51	41	5.28	2.04	327			6.3	40%	73%	6.29				6.0	7.2	**1.2**		0.4	-5.2	48	($0)
PT/Exp D	08	2TM *	3	7	3	64	50	5.18	1.56	216	230	225	4.7	26%	65%	4.91	57	12	31	7.0	7.0	**1.0**	5%	0.4	-6.9	-28	$2
Consist D	1st Half		2	2	1	40	35	3.58	1.17	204			4.8	26%	69%	3.71	58	7	36	4.0	7.8	**1.9**	5%	0.4	3.6	68	$5
LIMA Plan C	2nd Half		1	5	2	24	15	7.84	2.20	236			4.6	27%	62%	7.74	56	18	26	11.9	5.6	**0.5**	5%	0.4	-10.5	-186	($2)
+/- Score -26	09	Proj	**1**	**2**	**0**	**29**	**23**	**5.28**	**1.59**	**248**			**5.0**	**30%**	**66%**	**4.68**	**53**	**16**	**31**	**5.9**	**7.1**	**1.2**	**8%**	**0.6**	**-1.1**	**0**	**$0**

Ctl trend shows you all you need to know. In 2005, he threw hard and around the plate, and walked few. By the end of 2008, he was still throwing hard, but around 25 miles outside of Pittsburgh, walking everyone.

Happ,J.A.	Yr	Tm	W	L	Sv	IP	K	ERA	WHIP	OBA	vL	vR	BF/G	H%	S%	xERA	G	L	F	Ctl	Dom	Cmd	hr/f	hr/9	RAR	BPV	R$
LH Starter	04		0	0	0	0	0	0.00	0.00																		
Age 26	05		0	0	0	0	0	0.00	0.00																		
Type Pwr FB	06	a/a	7	2	0	80	71	3.70	1.35	252			26.3	32%	72%	3.47				3.6	8.0	**2.2**		0.4	8.1	86	$9
Health A	07	aaa	4	6	0	118	100	6.40	1.72	293			22.8	35%	63%	5.70				5.0	7.6	**1.5**		1.1	-28.2	40	($2)
PT/Exp D	08	PHI *	9	7	0	167	153	4.52	1.39	261	209	247	22.5	31%	71%	4.30	31	27	43	3.5	8.2	**2.3**	11%	1.2	-5.1	62	$10
Consist D	1st Half		5	6	0	101	87	4.67	1.47	275			26.1	32%	72%					3.6	7.7	**2.2**		1.3	-5.0	51	$4
LIMA Plan C	2nd Half		4	1	0	66	66	4.28	1.27	240			18.3	30%	68%	3.97	31	27	43	3.5	9.0	**2.6**	9%	1.0	-0.1	78	$6
+/- Score 17	09	Proj	**10**	**7**	**0**	**148**	**138**	**4.27**	**1.39**	**261**			**24.5**	**32%**	**72%**	**4.26**	**31**	**27**	**43**	**3.5**	**8.4**	**2.4**	**10%**	**1.1**	**1.4**	**65**	**$11**

1-0, 3.69 ERA in 32 IP at PHI. Regained prospect status by making 2007 look like an outlier. 2H Cmd, BPV spike say he's ready now, and opportunity likely coming soon. Expect HR issues in PHI, but a worthy investment.

Harang,Aaron	Yr	Tm	W	L	Sv	IP	K	ERA	WHIP	OBA	vL	vR	BF/G	H%	S%	xERA	G	L	F	Ctl	Dom	Cmd	hr/f	hr/9	RAR	BPV	R$
RH Starter	04	CIN	10	9	0	161	125	4.86	1.43	280	262	292	25.0	31%	70%	4.26	42	19	38	3.0	7.0	**2.4**	13%	1.5	-11.9	66	$8
Age 31	05	CIN	11	13	0	211	163	3.84	1.27	267	253	279	27.6	31%	72%	4.04	39	22	39	2.2	6.9	**3.2**	9%	0.9	10.7	83	$17
Type FB	06	CIN	16	11	0	234	216	3.77	1.27	268	267	270	27.3	33%	74%	3.72	39	22	40	2.2	8.3	**3.9**	10%	1.1	20.8	108	$24
Health B	07	CIN	16	6	0	232	218	3.73	1.14	246	237	246	27.7	30%	71%	3.56	40	18	42	2.0	8.5	**4.2**	10%	1.1	19.9	116	$27
PT/Exp A	08	CIN	6	17	0	184	153	4.79	1.38	283	298	274	26.4	32%	71%	4.25	34	22	44	2.4	7.5	**3.1**	14%	1.7	-11.7	81	$8
Consist A	1st Half		3	10	0	119	102	4.47	1.35	284			26.7	33%	71%	4.06	33	24	43	2.0	7.7	**3.8**	12%	1.4	-3.0	95	$6
LIMA Plan B	2nd Half		3	7	0	66	51	5.35	1.45	280			26.1	29%	72%	4.59	36	18	46	3.2	7.0	**2.2**	18%	2.3	-8.7	54	$2
+/- Score 39	09	Proj	**11**	**14**	**0**	**203**	**164**	**4.21**	**1.32**	**266**			**26.9**	**30%**	**72%**	**4.22**	**37**	**20**	**43**	**2.7**	**7.3**	**2.7**	**11%**	**1.3**	**3.0**	**74**	**$15**

Is he Dusty's latest victim? 5/25 relief outing on 2 days rest ruined his year: 6.00 June ERA, DL'd early July. Pitched better after return, but Dom was still off. Multiple years of heavy workload; full recovery unlikely.

Harden,Rich	Yr	Tm	W	L	Sv	IP	K	ERA	WHIP	OBA	vL	vR	BF/G	H%	S%	xERA	G	L	F	Ctl	Dom	Cmd	hr/f	hr/9	RAR	BPV	R$
RH Starter	04	OAK	11	7	0	189	167	4.00	1.33	243	254	227	26.0	30%	71%	4.07	45	18	37	3.9	7.9	**2.1**	8%	0.8	10.2	62	$16
Age 27	05	OAK	10	5	0	128	121	2.53	1.06	205	179	221	23.2	26%	78%	3.35	43	26	31	3.0	8.5	**2.8**	7%	0.5	29.1	93	$21
Type Pwr FB	06	OAK	4	0	0	46	49	4.29	1.23	192	176	211	21.3	24%	67%	3.67	43	24	32	5.1	9.5	**1.9**	14%	1.0	1.6	57	$6
Health F	07	OAK	1	2	0	26	27	2.45	1.13	199	292	98	14.9	25%	85%	3.65	39	19	42	3.9	9.5	**2.5**	11%	1.1	6.5	83	$4
PT/Exp C	08	2TM	10	2	0	148	181	2.07	1.06	187	200	167	23.6	26%	84%	3.46	30	21	49	3.7	11.0	**3.0**	7%	0.7	40.9	106	$26
Consist A	1st Half		5	0	0	67	83	2.15	1.09	199			24.4	28%	84%	3.56	29	16	55	3.5	11.1	**3.2**	6%	0.7	17.8	114	$12
LIMA Plan C	2nd Half		5	2	0	81	98	2.00	1.04	177			22.9	25%	85%	3.38	31	25	44	3.9	10.9	**2.8**	8%	0.7	23.0	100	$14
+/- Score -38	09	Proj	**11**	**4**	**0**	**145**	**160**	**3.17**	**1.16**	**204**			**23.7**	**27%**	**75%**	**3.65**	**36**	**21**	**43**	**3.9**	**9.9**	**2.5**	**9%**	**0.8**	**13.0**	**87**	**$21**

Finally brought together skills and health, but not out of the woods. Workload was carefully monitored, "minor" off-season shoulder surgery a possibility. Chronically injured players don't suddenly get healthy. Beware.

Haren,Dan	Yr	Tm	W	L	Sv	IP	K	ERA	WHIP	OBA	vL	vR	BF/G	H%	S%	xERA	G	L	F	Ctl	Dom	Cmd	hr/f	hr/9	RAR	BPV	R$
RH Starter	04	STL *	14	7	0	174	164	4.34	1.35	277	190	330	21.2	34%	71%	3.72	45	16	39	2.4	8.5	**3.5**	10%	1.1	-1.8	110	$15
Age 28	05	OAK	14	12	0	217	163	3.73	1.22	257	252	258	26.4	29%	73%	3.66	48	20	32	2.2	6.8	**3.1**	12%	1.1	17.1	88	$22
Type	06	OAK	14	13	0	223	176	4.12	1.21	263	246	268	27.1	30%	70%	3.66	45	19	36	1.8	7.1	**3.9**	13%	1.3	12.1	102	$24
Health A	07	OAK	15	9	0	223	192	3.07	1.21	254	230	264	27.0	30%	79%	3.68	44	17	38	2.2	7.8	**3.5**	10%	1.0	39.4	102	$28
PT/Exp A	08	ARI	16	8	0	216	206	3.33	1.13	251	241	253	26.5	31%	73%	3.23	44	21	35	1.7	8.6	**5.2**	9%	0.8	25.0	132	$27
Consist A	1st Half		8	4	0	111	96	2.85	0.97	220			25.3	27%	74%	3.31	44	19	38	1.5	7.8	**5.1**	9%	0.8	19.5	120	$17
LIMA Plan C+	2nd Half		8	4	0	105	110	3.85	1.30	281			27.8	36%	72%	3.13	45	24	31	1.8	9.4	**5.2**	9%	0.8	5.5	144	$11
+/- Score 30	09	Proj	**15**	**9**	**0**	**218**	**197**	**3.64**	**1.20**	**259**			**26.4**	**31%**	**73%**	**3.46**	**45**	**20**	**35**	**2.0**	**8.2**	**4.1**	**10%**	**1.0**	**23.7**	**116**	**$24**

Transitioned back to NL without difficulty, elite-caliber skills, highly desirable Dom/GB profile, AAA reliability. BPV trend says we may not have seen his best work yet. If so...
UP: 20 W, sub-3.00 ERA, Cy.

Harrison,Matt	Yr	Tm	W	L	Sv	IP	K	ERA	WHIP	OBA	vL	vR	BF/G	H%	S%	xERA	G	L	F	Ctl	Dom	Cmd	hr/f	hr/9	RAR	BPV	R$
LH Starter	04		0	0	0	0	0	0.00	0.00																		
Age 23	05		0	0	0	0	0	0.00	0.00																		
Type Con	06	aa	3	4	0	77	48	5.14	1.57	319			26.6	36%	68%	5.40				2.2	5.6	**2.5**		0.8	-5.9	53	$1
Health A	07	aa	5	7	0	116	67	4.34	1.49	296			25.6	33%	70%	4.63				2.7	5.2	**1.9**		0.5	1.8	51	$5
PT/Exp D	08	TEX *	15	6	0	168	88	4.73	1.55	298	310	297	25.0	32%	71%	5.07	40	23	36	3.2	4.7	**1.5**	9%	1.0	-7.9	17	$8
Consist B	1st Half		6	3	0	78	42	4.16	1.52	297			24.7	33%	73%					3.0	4.8	**1.6**		0.7	1.8	37	$4
LIMA Plan C	2nd Half		9	3	0	90	46	5.22	1.58	300			25.2	32%	69%	5.14	40	23	36	3.3	4.6	**1.4**	10%	1.2	-9.7	11	$4
+/- Score -4	09	Proj	**8**	**9**	**0**	**145**	**81**	**4.66**	**1.46**	**289**			**25.4**	**31%**	**70%**	**4.80**	**40**	**23**	**36**	**2.9**	**5.0**	**1.8**	**9%**	**1.0**	**-6.8**	**32**	**$7**

9-3, 5.49 ERA in 84 IP at TEX. Steadied himself after rough 1st month in majors (July ERA: 7.40), but lack of Dom says he's a long way from contributing. He's got time, but no need to let him develop on your roster.

RAY MURPHY

Hawkins,LaTroy			W	L	Sv	IP	K	ERA	WHIP	OBA	vL	vR	BF/G	H%	S%	xERA	G	L	F	Ctl	Dom	Cmd	hr/f	hr/9	RAR	BPV	R$
RH	Reliever	04 CHC	5	4	25	82	69	2.63	1.05	237	230	236	4.2	28%	82%	3.58	38	21	41	1.5	7.6	**4.9**	10%	1.1	16.5	111	$19
Age	36	05 2NL	2	8	6	56	43	3.85	1.46	268	228	297	3.7	31%	77%	4.51	44	17	39	3.9	6.9	**1.8**	10%	1.1	2.7	42	$5
Type	GB	06 BAL	3	2	0	60	27	4.49	1.46	301	323	285	4.4	33%	69%	4.85	44	21	35	2.2	4.0	**1.8**	5%	0.6	0.5	34	$3
Health	B	07 COL	2	5	0	55	29	3.42	1.23	250	237	266	3.7	27%	76%	3.56	63	16	21	2.6	4.7	**1.8**	16%	1.0	6.9	56	$5
PT/Exp	D	08 2TM	3	1	1	62	48	3.92	1.21	233	293	189	4.5	28%	67%	4.04	46	17	37	3.2	7.0	**2.2**	5%	0.4	3.0	63	$6
Consist	B	1st Half	1	1	0	34	18	6.03	1.52	271			5.6	30%	59%	5.26	43	20	37	4.2	4.7	**1.1**	7%	0.8	-7.3	-7	($0)
LIMA Plan	C+	2nd Half	2	0	1	28	30	1.30	0.83	179			3.5	26%	83%	2.75	51	13	36	1.9	9.7	**5.0**	0%	0.0	10.3	152	$6
+/- Score	-29	09 Proj	**3**	**3**	**0**	**64**	**43**	**3.97**	**1.32**	**260**			**4.1**	**30%**	**72%**	**4.10**	**50**	**17**	**32**	**3.0**	**6.1**	**2.0**	**9%**	**0.9**	**2.2**	**58**	**$5**

Remarkable 2H skill recovery in HOU injects life into career that appeared near end. History says he can be serviceable if he has either the GB or Dom, but had never shown both together. Expect one or the other in 2009.

Heilman,Aaron			W	L	Sv	IP	K	ERA	WHIP	OBA	vL	vR	BF/G	H%	S%	xERA	G	L	F	Ctl	Dom	Cmd	hr/f	hr/9	RAR	BPV	R$
RH	Reliever	04 NYM *	8	13	0	179	125	5.52	1.64	295	232	286	26.3	33%	68%	4.45	51	20	29	4.1	6.3	**1.5**	13%	1.1	-27.9	31	$0
Age	30	05 NYM	5	3	5	108	106	3.17	1.15	222	208	236	8.3	29%	73%	3.32	46	24	31	3.1	8.8	**2.9**	7%	0.5	14.4	100	$14
Type	Pwr	06 NYM	4	5	0	87	73	3.62	1.16	229	231	231	4.8	28%	69%	3.83	45	17	38	2.9	7.6	**2.6**	5%	0.5	9.3	81	$9
Health	A	07 NYM	7	7	1	86	63	3.03	1.07	229	234	218	4.2	26%	75%	3.68	45	21	34	2.1	6.6	**3.2**	9%	0.8	14.8	85	$13
PT/Exp	C	08 NYM	3	8	3	76	80	5.21	1.59	259	308	222	4.4	33%	69%	4.25	41	24	35	5.4	9.5	**1.7**	14%	1.2	-8.8	42	$3
Consist	A	1st Half	0	3	0	42	45	4.68	1.42	265			4.6	34%	69%	3.72	43	20	38	3.6	9.6	**2.6**	11%	1.1	-2.1	95	$1
LIMA Plan	B+	2nd Half	3	5	3	34	35	5.88	1.81	252			4.2	31%	70%	5.05	39	29	32	7.7	9.3	**1.2**	17%	1.3	-6.7	-24	$1
+/- Score	26	09 Proj	**5**	**6**	**3**	**73**	**67**	**3.85**	**1.34**	**247**			**4.6**	**30%**	**74%**	**3.89**	**43**	**23**	**35**	**3.7**	**8.3**	**2.2**	**11%**	**1.0**	**4.0**	**70**	**$8**

Jacked up his Dom at expense of Ctl; knee tendinitis may have been root cause. 1H skills were some of his best, but unclear whether he can regain those levels. There is a rebound in here, but '07 likely out of reach.

Hendrickson,Mark			W	L	Sv	IP	K	ERA	WHIP	OBA	vL	vR	BF/G	H%	S%	xERA	G	L	F	Ctl	Dom	Cmd	hr/f	hr/9	RAR	BPV	R$
LH	Reliever	04 TAM	10	15	0	183	87	4.82	1.40	290	291	295	24.7	31%	67%	4.69	46	19	36	2.3	4.3	**1.9**	9%	1.0	-8.7	40	$7
Age	34	05 TAM	11	8	0	178	89	5.91	1.55	311	258	328	25.7	33%	63%	4.67	46	22	32	2.5	4.5	**1.8**	12%	1.2	-33.8	38	$2
Type		06 2TM	6	15	0	164	99	4.22	1.43	272	287	264	23.0	30%	72%	4.65	48	16	36	3.4	5.4	**1.6**	9%	0.9	6.1	32	$8
Health	A	07 LA	4	8	0	123	92	5.21	1.39	291	258	300	13.6	33%	64%	3.94	44	23	33	2.1	6.7	**3.2**	12%	1.1	-11.8	86	$4
PT/Exp	A	08 FLA	7	8	0	134	81	5.45	1.47	282	248	296	16.3	31%	64%	4.66	44	20	35	3.2	5.5	**1.7**	11%	1.1	-19.5	33	$3
Consist	B	1st Half	7	6	0	91	56	5.93	1.56	288			24.0	31%	64%	4.79	47	18	35	3.8	5.5	**1.5**	12%	1.3	-18.7	23	$1
LIMA Plan	B	2nd Half	0	2	0	43	25	4.43	1.26	268			9.4	30%	66%	4.40	38	25	37	2.1	5.3	**2.5**	8%	0.8	-0.8	54	$1
+/- Score	5	09 Proj	**3**	**3**	**0**	**58**	**38**	**4.03**	**1.33**	**268**			**5.2**	**30%**	**73%**	**4.26**	**44**	**21**	**35**	**2.6**	**5.9**	**2.2**	**11%**	**1.1**	**0.6**	**57**	**$4**

2nd straight year with dramatic start/relief splits:

Year	SP ERA	RP ERA
2007	6.24	3.03
2008	6.13	3.69

Doesn't it seem like MLB teams should be aware of this stuff?

Hensley,Clay			W	L	Sv	IP	K	ERA	WHIP	OBA	vL	vR	BF/G	H%	S%	xERA	G	L	F	Ctl	Dom	Cmd	hr/f	hr/9	RAR	BPV	R$
RH	Reliever	04 aa	11	10	0	159	95	5.66	1.65	319			26.9	36%	66%	5.71				3.0	5.4	**1.8**		0.9	-25.8	36	$1
Age	29	05 SD *	3	3	0	137	91	2.62	1.00	205	275	103	13.8	24%	74%	3.33	59	16	25	2.5	6.0	**2.4**	6%	0.4	27.6	78	$16
Type	GB	06 SD	11	12	0	187	122	3.71	1.34	248	263	239	21.5	28%	74%	4.16	54	17	30	3.7	5.9	**1.6**	9%	0.7	18.0	39	$15
Health	F	07 SD *	3	10	0	121	65	8.68	2.34	378	287	324	24.5	41%	63%	6.37	49	15	36	5.6	4.8	**0.9**	11%	1.4	-63.5	-38	($19)
PT/Exp	C	08 SD *	2	3	0	87	48	5.55	1.71	295	288	221	8.4	32%	69%	5.18	51	18	31	4.8	4.9	**1.0**	11%	1.0	-13.8	-12	($3)
Consist	D	1st Half	1	1	0	36	17	4.67	1.78	321			12.1	34%	76%					4.0	4.3	**1.1**		1.0	-1.8	9	($1)
LIMA Plan	F	2nd Half	1	2	0	51	31	6.18	1.67	275			6.9	30%	63%	5.15	51	18	31	5.4	5.4	**1.0**	11%	1.1	-12.0	-19	($2)
+/- Score	-17	09 Proj	**2**	**3**	**0**	**54**	**30**	**5.50**	**1.70**	**296**			**8.1**	**32%**	**69%**	**5.06**	**53**	**17**	**31**	**4.7**	**5.0**	**1.1**	**11%**	**1.0**	**-4.8**	**-5**	**($1)**

1-2, 5.31 ERA in 39 IP at SD. A case study in the power and limits of the GB skill. When GBs work in conjunction with Ctl/Cmd (see 2005, even 2006), good things happen. But once Cmd approaches 1.0, GBs can't help.

Herges,Matt			W	L	Sv	IP	K	ERA	WHIP	OBA	vL	vR	BF/G	H%	S%	xERA	G	L	F	Ctl	Dom	Cmd	hr/f	hr/9	RAR	BPV	R$
RH	Reliever	04 SF	4	5	23	65	39	5.25	1.71	329	366	318	4.3	36%	71%	5.01	44	18	39	2.9	5.4	**1.9**	9%	1.1	-8.0	40	$7
Age	39	05 2NL *	2	3	0	58	35	3.88	1.71	320	256	333	5.0	34%	83%	5.17	39	22	39	3.4	5.4	**1.6**	12%	1.6	2.6	23	$1
Type		06 FLA	2	3	0	71	36	4.31	1.72	319	300	340	5.0	35%	75%	5.11	47	22	31	3.5	4.6	**1.3**	6%	0.6	1.6	11	$0
Health	A	07 COL *	7	2	1	84	55	2.60	1.13	224	216	184	5.1	25%	81%	4.18	46	15	38	2.9	5.9	**2.0**	8%	0.8	18.8	53	$12
PT/Exp	D	08 COL	3	4	0	64	46	5.04	1.60	303	280	326	5.0	35%	68%	4.63	40	26	34	3.4	6.4	**1.9**	7%	0.7	-6.1	43	$1
Consist	B	1st Half	2	3	0	41	29	3.32	1.35	263			4.8	31%	75%	4.31	43	22	35	3.1	6.4	**2.1**	5%	0.4	4.8	53	$3
LIMA Plan	C+	2nd Half	1	1	0	24	17	8.01	2.03	363			5.3	41%	60%	5.19	34	33	32	3.8	6.5	**1.7**	11%	1.1	-10.9	26	($3)
+/- Score	-12	09 Proj	**2**	**2**	**0**	**44**	**29**	**4.70**	**1.50**	**283**			**5.0**	**32%**	**70%**	**4.64**	**41**	**25**	**34**	**3.5**	**5.9**	**1.7**	**10%**	**1.0**	**-1.6**	**32**	**$1**

Textbook example of sample-size problems that plague RPs. Combined 2007-08 h% falls right around 30%. xERA, BPV show those years were similar, luck caused wide ERA variance. Lesson done. Career too maybe.

Hernandez,Felix			W	L	Sv	IP	K	ERA	WHIP	OBA	vL	vR	BF/G	H%	S%	xERA	G	L	F	Ctl	Dom	Cmd	hr/f	hr/9	RAR	BPV	R$
RH	Starter	04 aa	5	1	0	57	62	3.56	1.16	226			23.3	31%	68%	2.67				3.0	9.8	**3.2**		0.4	5.5	124	$8
Age	23	05 SEA *	13	8	0	172	187	2.35	1.04	194	164	224	22.0	27%	78%	2.36	67	14	19	3.3	9.8	**3.0**	10%	0.4	42.8	133	$30
Type	Pwr xGB	06 SEA	12	14	0	191	176	4.52	1.34	266	281	241	26.2	32%	69%	3.14	58	18	25	2.8	8.3	**2.9**	17%	1.1	0.8	109	$18
Health	B	07 SEA	14	7	0	190	165	3.93	1.38	280	299	262	27.3	34%	74%	3.12	61	16	23	2.5	7.8	**3.1**	15%	0.9	13.6	112	$19
PT/Exp	A	08 SEA	9	11	0	201	175	3.45	1.39	259	275	242	27.9	32%	77%	3.72	52	18	29	3.6	7.8	**2.2**	10%	0.8	22.1	75	$17
Consist	A	1st Half	6	5	0	108	93	2.83	1.25	242			28.1	30%	80%	3.59	51	18	30	3.2	7.8	**2.4**	9%	0.7	20.2	83	$13
LIMA Plan	B	2nd Half	3	6	0	93	82	4.17	1.54	279			27.6	34%	75%	3.88	53	19	28	4.1	8.0	**2.0**	11%	0.9	2.0	64	$4
+/- Score	27	09 Proj	**12**	**11**	**0**	**203**	**183**	**3.33**	**1.30**	**254**			**26.7**	**31%**	**76%**	**3.29**	**56**	**18**	**26**	**3.0**	**8.1**	**2.7**	**11%**	**0.8**	**28.4**	**99**	**$22**

Slight loss of Ctl a concern, but Dom/GB combination more than covers the occasional BB. Overdue for some h% help, SEA IF defense perhaps betraying him. It's coming, it's coming...
UP: Sub-3.00 ERA, rejoicing

Hernandez,Livan			W	L	Sv	IP	K	ERA	WHIP	OBA	vL	vR	BF/G	H%	S%	xERA	G	L	F	Ctl	Dom	Cmd	hr/f	hr/9	RAR	BPV	R$
RH	Starter	04 MON	11	15	0	255	186	3.60	1.24	246	258	238	30.3	28%	74%	4.04	46	19	35	2.9	6.6	**2.2**	10%	0.9	20.8	63	$21
Age	34	05 WAS	15	10	0	246	147	3.99	1.43	279	290	278	30.6	31%	74%	4.65	40	26	34	3.1	5.4	**1.8**	9%	0.9	7.9	31	$14
Type	Con	06 2NL	13	13	0	216	128	4.83	1.50	288	302	275	28.1	31%	71%	5.13	37	20	44	3.3	5.3	**1.6**	9%	1.2	-9.2	23	$9
Health	A	07 ARI	11	11	0	204	90	4.93	1.60	300	295	320	28.0	30%	73%	5.55	38	21	41	3.5	4.0	**1.1**	11%	1.5	-12.8	-6	$3
PT/Exp	A	08 2TM	13	11	0	180	67	6.05	1.67	336	340	344	26.6	34%	65%	5.16	44	22	34	2.2	3.4	**1.6**	11%	1.3	-38.7	25	($2)
Consist	A	1st Half	8	5	0	110	39	5.22	1.60	335			27.7	35%	69%	5.06	44	22	34	1.6	3.2	**2.0**	9%	1.1	-12.5	35	$1
LIMA Plan	F	2nd Half	5	6	0	70	28	7.36	1.76	337			25.1	34%	59%	5.33	46	20	34	3.0	3.6	**1.2**	13%	1.5	-26.3	9	($4)
+/- Score	-1	09 Proj	**9**	**9**	**0**	**149**	**63**	**5.01**	**1.54**	**302**			**26.6**	**31%**	**71%**	**5.21**	**42**	**21**	**37**	**2.9**	**3.8**	**1.3**	**11%**	**1.3**	**-15.3**	**10**	**$3**

ERA jumped over 6.00, but xERA says this has been the same bad pitcher for several years. Still only 34; Roger Clemens was still pitching for BOS at that age and had 11 years yet to go. Fair warning.

Hill,Rich			W	L	Sv	IP	K	ERA	WHIP	OBA	vL	vR	BF/G	H%	S%	xERA	G	L	F	Ctl	Dom	Cmd	hr/f	hr/9	RAR	BPV	R$
LH	Starter	04	0	0	0	0	0	0.00	0.00																		
Age	29	05 a/a	10	4	0	122	152	4.34	1.23	246			24.2	31%	73%	4.36				2.8	11.2	**4.0**		1.8	-0.6	104	$15
Type	Pwr xFB	06 CHC *	13	8	0	199	205	3.34	1.12	222	262	220	25.1	28%	74%	3.86	30	18	52	2.8	9.3	**3.3**	8%	0.9	28.2	99	$26
Health	B	07 CHC	11	8	0	195	183	3.92	1.19	236	191	247	25.1	28%	72%	3.85	36	21	43	2.9	8.4	**2.9**	12%	1.2	12.1	88	$20
PT/Exp	C	08 CHC *	3	4	0	46	37	6.45	2.10	250	154	200	19.1	28%	71%	7.70	33	17	50	10.4	7.2	**0.7**	10%	1.4	-12.3	-141	($3)
Consist	D	1st Half	3	4	0	46	37	6.45	2.10	250			19.1	28%	71%	7.70	33	17	50	10.4	7.2	**0.7**	10%	1.4	-12.3	-141	($3)
LIMA Plan	C	2nd Half	0	0	0	0	0	0.00	0.00																		
+/- Score	-37	09 Proj	**9**	**7**	**0**	**133**	**118**	**4.20**	**1.33**	**244**			**21.7**	**29%**	**72%**	**4.46**	**33**	**19**	**48**	**3.8**	**8.0**	**2.1**	**10%**	**1.2**	**-2.0**	**53**	**$11**

1-0, 4.12 ERA in 20 IP at CHC. Banished to the minors in May, then shelved by arm and back problems. Likely wasn't healthy even before getting sent down. Scheduled to pitch winter ball. Prior skills say worth a flier.

Hill,Shawn			W	L	Sv	IP	K	ERA	WHIP	OBA	vL	vR	BF/G	H%	S%	xERA	G	L	F	Ctl	Dom	Cmd	hr/f	hr/9	RAR	BPV	R$
RH	Starter	04 aa	5	7	0	87	43	4.58	1.50	310			22.7	34%	69%	4.88				2.1	4.4	**2.1**		0.5	-2.5	47	$3
Age	28	05	0	0	0	0	0	0.00	0.00																		
Type	Con	06 WAS *	4	6	0	91	44	3.95	1.36	290			23.0	32%	70%	4.36	50	19	31	1.9	4.3	**2.2**	4%	0.4	6.1	54	$5
Health	F	07 WAS	4	5	0	97	65	3.42	1.14	239	288	189	24.7	27%	73%	3.58	55	17	28	2.3	6.0	**2.6**	11%	0.8	12.0	78	$10
PT/Exp	C	08 WAS	1	5	0	63	39	5.83	1.75	330	294	374	24.7	37%	66%	4.70	46	25	28	3.3	5.5	**1.7**	8%	0.7	-12.2	36	($3)
Consist	B	1st Half	1	5	0	63	39	5.83	1.75	330			24.7	37%	66%	4.70	46	25	28	3.3	5.5	**1.7**	8%	0.7	-12.2	36	($3)
LIMA Plan	D+	2nd Half	0	0	0	0	0	0.00	0.00																		
+/- Score	23	09 Proj	**4**	**8**	**0**	**122**	**73**	**4.15**	**1.42**	**286**			**23.9**	**32%**	**72%**	**4.18**	**50**	**21**	**29**	**2.6**	**5.4**	**2.1**	**9%**	**0.8**	**2.4**	**55**	**$5**

Battled arm problems all year, leading to Sept. elbow surgery. Deserves a health-related mulligan on 2008 skill decline, but make him show he's healthy before expecting a return to prior skill levels.

RAY MURPHY

Hinshaw,Alex

		Yr	W	L	Sv	IP	K	ERA	WHIP	OBA	vL	vR	BF/G	H%	S%	xERA	G	L	F	Ctl	Dom	Cmd	hr/f	hr/9	RAR	BPV	R$
LH	Reliever	04	0	0	0	0	0	0.00	0.00																		
Age	26	05	0	0	0	0	0	0.00	0.00																		
Type	Pwr xFB	06	0	0	0	0	0	0.00	0.00																		
Health	A	07 aa	3	1	0	41	41	2.54	1.13	185			9.8	24%	79%	2.15				4.4	8.9	**2.0**		0.5	9.8	101	$7
PT/Exp	F	08 SF *	2	1	7	55	63	2.64	1.30	196	205	235	3.8	26%	83%	4.36	25	22	53	5.5	10.4	**1.9**	7%	0.8	11.0	42	$9
Consist	F	1st Half	1	1	7	34	42	1.91	0.99	158			4.0	23%	84%	3.62	24	18	58	4.1	11.3	**2.7**	5%	0.5	9.8	94	$8
LIMA Plan	B+	2nd Half	1	0	0	21	21	3.78	1.78	249			3.6	30%	83%	5.81	26	25	49	7.6	8.8	**1.2**	10%	1.3	1.3	-41	$1
+/- Score	-29	09 Proj	2	1	0	44	46	4.14	1.45	232			5.0	29%	75%	4.69	26	23	51	5.4	9.5	1.8	10%	1.2	-1.9	30	$3

2-1, 3.40 ERA in 40 IP at SF. PRO: Excellent Dom, BA splits show he's tough on LH and RH. CON: Ctl went from weak to terrible upon MLB callup, xFB profile means volatility. Draft only with antacid chaser.

Hirsh,Jason

		Yr	W	L	Sv	IP	K	ERA	WHIP	OBA	vL	vR	BF/G	H%	S%	xERA	G	L	F	Ctl	Dom	Cmd	hr/f	hr/9	RAR	BPV	R$
RH	Starter	04	0	0	0	0	0	0.00	0.00																		
Age	27	05 aa	1	8	0	172	133	4.15	1.28	263			24.9	31%	69%	3.82				2.4	6.9	**2.9**		0.8	3.3	80	$9
Type	xFB	06 HOU *	16	6	0	181	129	3.33	1.25	231	211	303	23.6	27%	76%	4.96	30	18	52	3.6	6.4	**1.8**	6%	0.8	26.0	27	$21
Health	F	07 COL	5	7	0	112	75	4.81	1.34	245	236	250	25.2	26%	68%	5.18	30	18	51	3.8	6.0	**1.6**	10%	1.4	-5.3	13	$6
PT/Exp	C	08 COL *	4	4	0	108	44	7.58	2.02	345	450	273	24.2	35%	65%	7.67	19	17	64	4.8	3.7	**0.8**	8%	1.9	-44.0	-67	($11)
Consist	C	1st Half	0	2	0	28	13	7.34	2.08	323			23.5	34%	65%					6.6	4.2	**0.6**		1.1	-10.7	-4	($4)
LIMA Plan	F	2nd Half	4	2	0	80	31	7.66	2.00	352			24.5	35%	65%	7.51	19	17	64	4.2	3.5	**0.8**	9%	2.2	-33.3	-53	($8)
+/- Score	-24	09 Proj	3	4	0	79	47	5.27	1.63	296			23.8	31%	72%	5.86	29	18	53	4.0	5.4	1.3	10%	1.6	-14.7	-5	($0)

0-0, 8.31 ERA in 9 IP at COL. Started year on DL after strained shoulder in March, struggled in minors until Sept callup. Likely wasn't healthy all year, but prior skill levels weren't worth getting excited about, anyway.

Hochevar,Luke

		Yr	W	L	Sv	IP	K	ERA	WHIP	OBA	vL	vR	BF/G	H%	S%	xERA	G	L	F	Ctl	Dom	Cmd	hr/f	hr/9	RAR	BPV	R$
RH	Starter	04	0	0	0	0	0	0.00	0.00																		
Age	25	05	0	0	0	0	0	0.00	0.00																		
Type	Con GB	06	0	0	0	0	0	0.00	0.00																		
Health	B	07 KC *	4	10	0	165	121	6.03	1.59	310	273	208	23.9	35%	64%	3.70	63	10	27	2.9	6.6	**2.3**	18%	1.4	-31.0	83	$0
PT/Exp	D	08 KC *	7	13	0	146	82	5.28	1.44	276	314	244	25.5	30%	64%	4.51	52	17	32	3.3	5.0	**1.5**	9%	0.9	-16.8	31	$4
Consist	B	1st Half	6	6	0	95	58	4.40	1.46	264			26.1	29%	72%	4.50	54	15	31	4.0	5.5	**1.4**	11%	1.0	-0.6	22	$5
LIMA Plan	C+	2nd Half	1	7	0	51	24	6.92	1.42	299			24.4	32%	49%	4.51	48	19	32	2.0	4.3	**2.2**	7%	0.7	-16.1	50	($1)
+/- Score	18	09 Proj	9	12	0	174	111	4.66	1.41	285			24.3	32%	69%	4.15	51	17	32	2.6	5.7	2.2	12%	1.1	6.0	63	$9

6-12, 5.51 ERA in 129 IP at KC. Lock-step fluctuations in Ctl and Dom indicate he's learning how to pitch at the MLB level. Strong GB% is a building block, but subpar Dom, problems with LHers say he's not ready yet.

Hoffman,Trevor

		Yr	W	L	Sv	IP	K	ERA	WHIP	OBA	vL	vR	BF/G	H%	S%	xERA	G	L	F	Ctl	Dom	Cmd	hr/f	hr/9	RAR	BPV	R$
RH	Reliever	04 SD	3	3	40	54	53	2.32	0.92	216	255	161	3.8	27%	80%	3.38	31	22	47	1.3	8.8	**6.6**	7%	0.8	13.0	132	$21
Age	41	05 SD	1	6	43	57	54	2.99	1.12	244	291	179	3.9	31%	74%	3.60	37	21	42	1.9	8.5	**4.5**	4%	0.5	8.9	117	$20
Type	xFB	06 SD	0	2	46	63	50	2.14	0.97	213	194	214	3.8	25%	84%	3.85	32	22	45	1.9	7.1	**3.8**	8%	0.9	18.2	89	$24
Health	A	07 SD	4	5	42	57	44	2.98	1.12	233	299	169	3.8	29%	73%	4.44	31	18	52	2.4	6.9	**2.9**	2%	0.3	10.2	69	$22
PT/Exp	A	08 SD	3	6	30	45	46	3.77	1.04	229	291	165	3.7	27%	72%	3.37	39	14	47	1.8	9.1	**5.1**	14%	1.6	2.8	133	$16
Consist	B	1st Half	1	5	15	27	31	5.00	1.19	255			4.0	31%	65%	3.37	37	12	51	2.0	10.3	**5.2**	17%	2.0	-2.4	147	$7
LIMA Plan	C+	2nd Half	2	1	15	18	15	1.97	0.82	189			3.4	21%	85%	3.35	42	16	42	1.5	7.4	**5.0**	10%	1.0	5.2	113	$9
+/- Score	-6	09 Proj	3	4	29	44	34	3.72	1.15	246			3.8	28%	73%	4.12	36	17	47	2.1	7.0	3.4	10%	1.2	1.2	85	$15

Reports of his demise were premature, as Cmd and BPV rebounds show. The clock is still ticking, but skill set appears capable of lasting another year, as long as his body cooperates. 41 is still 41; hedge your bets.

Howell,J.P.

		Yr	W	L	Sv	IP	K	ERA	WHIP	OBA	vL	vR	BF/G	H%	S%	xERA	G	L	F	Ctl	Dom	Cmd	hr/f	hr/9	RAR	BPV	R$
LH	Reliever	04	0	0	0	0	0	0.00	0.00											0.0	0.0						
Age	26	05 KC *	8	6	0	127	99	5.16	1.48	263	229	271	22.4	31%	65%	3.86	58	19	24	4.3	7.0	**1.6**	12%	0.8	-12.3	45	$6
Type	Pwr GB	06 TAM *	9	8	0	133	103	4.60	1.53	298	400	281	22.8	36%	70%	4.08	45	26	29	3.0	7.0	**2.3**	7%	0.6	-0.7	68	$8
Health	A	07 TAM *	8	14	0	179	177	5.43	1.45	286	296	325	25.2	35%	66%	3.51	46	23	31	2.9	8.9	**3.1**	17%	1.4	-20.4	106	$9
PT/Exp	C	08 TAM	6	1	3	89	92	2.22	1.13	198	188	197	5.7	26%	83%	3.20	54	17	30	3.9	9.3	**2.4**	9%	0.6	23.5	93	$15
Consist	A	1st Half	6	0	2	51	45	3.00	1.14	200			6.9	24%	76%	3.45	56	15	29	3.9	7.9	**2.0**	10%	0.7	8.5	72	$9
LIMA Plan	B	2nd Half	0	1	1	38	47	1.17	1.12	194			4.6	28%	93%	2.89	51	19	30	4.0	11.0	**2.8**	8%	0.5	15.0	119	$7
+/- Score	-12	09 Proj	4	3	5	73	73	3.48	1.28	238			8.7	31%	75%	3.34	52	19	29	3.6	9.1	2.5	10%	0.7	9.7	96	$10

As '07-08 BPVs show, h%, s%, hr/f corrections drove the ERA turnaround. Strong Dom, handles LH and RH batters, works in an unsettled pen. Classic LIMA option with saves or vulture wins upside.

Howry,Bob

		Yr	W	L	Sv	IP	K	ERA	WHIP	OBA	vL	vR	BF/G	H%	S%	xERA	G	L	F	Ctl	Dom	Cmd	hr/f	hr/9	RAR	BPV	R$
RH	Reliever	04 CLE *	5	3	0	68	58	4.09	1.20	247	291	169	5.1	29%	70%	3.94	33	28	40	2.5	7.7	**3.1**	11%	1.2	2.9	81	$7
Age	35	05 CLE	7	4	3	73	48	2.47	0.89	192	186	198	3.5	22%	74%	3.92	40	19	41	2.0	5.9	**3.0**	5%	0.5	17.2	71	$14
Type	xFB	06 CHC	4	5	5	76	71	3.19	1.14	246	247	244	3.7	30%	76%	3.68	38	18	44	2.0	8.4	**4.2**	8%	0.9	12.2	113	$11
Health	A	07 CHC	6	7	8	81	72	3.32	1.17	249	192	283	4.3	30%	75%	4.00	32	20	48	2.1	8.0	**3.8**	7%	0.9	11.1	97	$13
PT/Exp	C	08 CHC	7	5	1	71	59	5.35	1.46	311	328	297	4.3	35%	68%	4.28	35	18	47	1.7	7.5	**4.5**	12%	1.7	-9.4	103	$4
Consist	A	1st Half	2	2	1	39	32	4.65	1.42	310			4.4	36%	71%	4.16	34	22	45	1.4	7.4	**5.3**	11%	1.4	-1.8	108	$2
LIMA Plan	A+	2nd Half	5	3	0	32	27	6.19	1.50	312			4.2	35%	63%	4.42	36	13	50	2.0	7.6	**3.9**	13%	2.0	-7.6	98	$2
+/- Score	43	09 Proj	6	6	5	73	62	3.85	1.23	266			4.1	31%	73%	4.01	35	18	47	1.9	7.7	4.1	10%	1.2	2.9	101	$10

Others see ERA jump in 35-yr old and think "he's done", but you see a superior LIMA guy with skills intact. Depending on where he lands in free agency, could find his way into a closer role by summer.

Hudson,Tim

		Yr	W	L	Sv	IP	K	ERA	WHIP	OBA	vL	vR	BF/G	H%	S%	xERA	G	L	F	Ctl	Dom	Cmd	hr/f	hr/9	RAR	BPV	R$
RH	Starter	04 OAK	12	6	0	188	103	3.54	1.26	268	298	229	29.2	30%	71%	3.65	60	17	23	2.1	4.9	**2.3**	6%	0.4	20.7	70	$16
Age	33	05 ATL	14	9	0	192	115	3.52	1.35	264	285	240	28.3	29%	77%	3.69	59	21	21	3.0	5.4	**1.8**	16%	0.9	17.3	51	$16
Type	Con xGB	06 ATL	13	12	0	218	141	4.87	1.44	276	281	265	27.2	31%	68%	3.88	58	18	24	3.3	5.8	**1.8**	15%	1.0	-10.3	52	$10
Health	D	07 ATL	16	10	0	224	132	3.33	1.22	259	261	261	27.3	30%	72%	3.43	62	17	22	2.1	5.3	**2.5**	6%	0.4	30.3	78	$23
PT/Exp	A	08 ATL	11	7	0	142	85	3.17	1.16	238	255	223	25.2	27%	75%	3.48	59	19	22	2.5	5.4	**2.1**	11%	0.7	19.3	66	$16
Consist	A	1st Half	8	6	0	114	67	3.31	1.21	246			26.2	27%	75%	3.59	58	19	22	2.6	5.3	**2.0**	12%	0.8	13.6	61	$12
LIMA Plan	D	2nd Half	3	1	0	28	18	2.60	0.97	204			21.6	24%	73%	3.04	64	16	20	2.3	5.8	**2.6**	6%	0.3	5.7	86	$5
+/- Score	-7	09 Proj	2	1	0	22	12	4.09	1.32	262			23.3	29%	70%	3.75	61	17	22	2.9	4.9	1.7	13%	0.8	1.6	50	$2

Had TJ surgery in August, expected to miss most of 2009. Has $12M mutual option with Braves for 2010, so it's not a given he will ever pitch for ATL again. This limits his stash appeal as an NL-only keeper.

Hughes,Phil

		Yr	W	L	Sv	IP	K	ERA	WHIP	OBA	vL	vR	BF/G	H%	S%	xERA	G	L	F	Ctl	Dom	Cmd	hr/f	hr/9	RAR	BPV	R$
RH	Starter	04	0	0	0	0	0	0.00	0.00																		
Age	22	05	0	0	0	0	0	0.00	0.00																		
Type	Pwr FB	06 aa	10	3	0	116	120	2.96	1.02	206			21.8	28%	71%	2.05				2.6	9.3	**3.6**		0.4	22.4	132	$20
Health	F	07 NYY *	9	4	0	108	93	3.88	1.18	224	264	210	22.1	27%	68%	4.18	37	18	45	3.3	7.7	**2.3**	6%	0.7	8.4	65	$14
PT/Exp	D	08 NYY *	1	4	0	63	51	6.57	1.71	313	333	299	20.9	37%	61%	4.87	34	27	39	3.9	7.3	**1.9**	7%	0.9	-17.3	39	($2)
Consist	C	1st Half	0	4	0	22	13	9.00	2.14	354			18.5	39%	56%	6.34	33	29	38	5.3	5.3	**1.0**	6%	0.8	-12.6	-37	($3)
LIMA Plan	C+	2nd Half	1	0	0	41	38	5.27	1.49	289			22.6	36%	65%	4.19	38	21	41	3.1	8.3	**2.7**	8%	0.9	-4.7	83	$1
+/- Score	65	09 Proj	7	8	0	149	127	4.59	1.40	264			23.0	32%	69%	4.39	35	24	41	3.5	7.7	2.2	8%	0.9	0.7	57	$10

0-4, 6.62 ERA in 34 IP at NYY. Injury again cost him a big chunk of season, this time fractured rib. 2H skill surge (mostly in minors) serves as reminder of his promise, but needs a healthy year to re-establish himself.

Hurley,Eric

		Yr	W	L	Sv	IP	K	ERA	WHIP	OBA	vL	vR	BF/G	H%	S%	xERA	G	L	F	Ctl	Dom	Cmd	hr/f	hr/9	RAR	BPV	R$
RH	Starter	04	0	0	0	0	0	0.00	0.00																		
Age	23	05	0	0	0	0	0	0.00	0.00																		
Type	xFB	06 aa	3	1	0	37	27	2.68	0.97	193			24.0	21%	81%	2.54				2.7	6.6	**2.5**		1.2	8.4	71	$6
Health	D	07 aa	11	9	0	162	115	5.17	1.33	261			24.6	27%	67%	4.93				3.1	6.4	**2.1**		1.8	-14.1	30	$10
PT/Exp	D	08 TEX *	4	7	0	107	74	5.61	1.56	299	269	267	25.2	32%	69%	5.51	22	22	57	3.3	6.3	**1.9**	11%	1.8	-16.7	24	$1
Consist	C	1st Half	3	6	0	97	72	5.62	1.61	305			25.8	33%	70%	5.45	22	22	57	3.3	6.7	**2.0**	11%	1.8	-15.3	30	$0
LIMA Plan	C	2nd Half	1	1	0	10	2	5.51	1.14	227			19.9	19%	56%	6.10	22	22	56	2.8	1.8	**0.6**	11%	1.8	-1.4	-42	$1
+/- Score	8	09 Proj	6	5	0	102	74	4.88	1.39	272			25.7	30%	70%	5.14	22	22	57	3.0	6.6	2.2	10%	1.6	-9.0	36	$6

1-2, 5.47 ERA in 25 IP at TEX. Shoulder tendinitis shut him down for 2H. Barely-acceptable Cmd leaves little margin for error, xFB profile a poor fit for TEX ballpark. Nothing but downside for short term.

RAY MURPHY

Isringhausen,Jason

Isringhausen,Jason			W	L	Sv	IP	K	ERA	WHIP	OBA	vL	vR	BF/G	H%	S%	xERA	G	L	F	Ctl	Dom	Cmd	hr/f	hr/9	RAR	BPV	R$
RH Reliever	04	STL	4	2	47	75	71	2.88	1.04	206	205	195	4.0	26%	74%	3.41	44	19	37	2.8	8.5	**3.1**	7%	0.6	12.8	101	$25
Age 36	05	STL	1	2	39	59	51	2.14	1.19	205	170	229	3.8	25%	85%	3.67	51	20	29	4.1	7.8	**1.9**	9%	0.6	15.4	58	$19
Type Pwr	06	STL	4	8	33	58	52	3.56	1.46	223	270	187	4.3	25%	83%	4.62	44	18	38	5.9	8.1	**1.4**	16%	1.5	6.6	8	$16
Health D	07	STL	4	0	32	65	54	2.48	1.07	186	196	167	4.1	23%	79%	3.94	45	18	37	3.9	7.4	**1.9**	6%	0.6	15.7	52	$20
PT/Exp B	08	STL	1	5	12	43	36	5.69	1.64	285	186	327	4.6	34%	66%	4.20	51	22	28	4.6	7.6	**1.6**	14%	1.1	-7.5	40	$4
Consist A	1st Half		1	5	11	28	21	5.72	1.63	286			4.6	33%	65%	4.54	47	23	30	4.5	6.7	**1.5**	11%	1.0	-5.1	25	$4
LIMA Plan B	2nd Half		0	0	1	14	15	5.62	1.67	283			4.7	35%	68%	3.53	58	19	23	5.0	9.4	**1.9**	21%	1.2	-2.4	70	$0
+/- Score 20	09	Proj	**2**	**4**	**5**	**44**	**36**	**4.34**	**1.47**	**255**			**4.3**	**30%**	**72%**	**4.21**	**49**	**19**	**31**	**4.6**	**7.4**	**1.6**	**10%**	**0.8**	**0.7**	**39**	**$4**

Skill set, long unworthy of the closer role, finally betrayed him. Surgery to repair torn tendon raises doubts about 2009, but he says he'll be back. Will have to earn any future save opps; skills say that won't happen.

Jackson,Edwin

Jackson,Edwin			W	L	Sv	IP	K	ERA	WHIP	OBA	vL	vR	BF/G	H%	S%	xERA	G	L	F	Ctl	Dom	Cmd	hr/f	hr/9	RAR	BPV	R$
RH Starter	04	aaa	6	4	0	90	66	4.63	1.36	237			20.3	29%	64%	3.22				4.4	6.6	**1.5**		0.3	-3.2	71	$6
Age 25	05	LA *	11	13	0	145	78	5.57	1.53	277	333	236	21.5	29%	65%	5.58	36	19	46	4.0	4.8	**1.2**	9%	1.2	-23.8	-8	$3
Type	06	TAM *	3	7	5	109	83	6.60	1.86	314	233	333	11.6	37%	64%	4.86	52	17	31	5.1	6.8	**1.3**	9%	0.8	-27.5	15	($2)
Health A	07	TAM	5	15	0	161	128	5.76	1.76	300	313	285	23.5	35%	68%	4.90	45	19	36	4.9	7.2	**1.5**	10%	1.1	-24.9	19	($1)
PT/Exp B	08	TAM	14	11	0	183	108	4.42	1.51	278	295	268	25.4	30%	74%	5.12	39	21	40	3.8	5.3	**1.4**	9%	1.1	-1.6	11	$10
Consist A	1st Half		4	6	0	96	60	4.33	1.45	260			26.2	29%	72%	4.97	43	19	39	4.1	5.6	**1.4**	8%	0.8	0.3	10	$5
LIMA Plan D	2nd Half		10	5	0	88	48	4.52	1.56	296			24.5	31%	76%	5.29	35	23	42	3.4	4.9	**1.5**	11%	1.4	-1.9	11	$6
+/- Score -25	09	Proj	**7**	**8**	**0**	**122**	**81**	**4.81**	**1.56**	**283**			**22.7**	**32%**	**71%**	**4.98**	**41**	**20**	**39**	**4.1**	**6.0**	**1.5**	**9%**	**1.0**	**-8.4**	**17**	**$5**

His stuff is far better than these BPI show, but 3-year BPV trend highlights the lack of growth. He's young enough yet to take a big step forward, but if that happens it will be a "Where did THAT come from?" event.

Jackson,Zach

Jackson,Zach			W	L	Sv	IP	K	ERA	WHIP	OBA	vL	vR	BF/G	H%	S%	xERA	G	L	F	Ctl	Dom	Cmd	hr/f	hr/9	RAR	BPV	R$
LH Reliever	04		0	0	0	0	0	0.00	0.00																		
Age 26	05	a/a	8	7	0	101	67	6.05	1.75	332			27.8	38%	64%	5.99				3.1	6.0	**1.9**		0.7	-21.8	43	($1)
Type Con GB	06	aaa	4	6	0	107	52	5.47	1.62	295			27.0	31%	68%	5.48				4.0	4.4	**1.1**		1.2	-12.5	10	($0)
Health A	07	aaa	11	10	0	169	112	5.69	1.68	312			26.8	36%	66%	5.58				3.6	6.0	**1.6**		0.8	-25.6	39	$2
PT/Exp D	08	2TM *	6	9	0	142	79	7.58	1.68	330	348	271	16.0	35%	55%	4.64	52	15	33	2.6	5.0	**1.9**	13%	1.5	-57.5	49	($7)
Consist B	1st Half		1	5	0	59	30	8.49	1.87	351			12.8	37%	54%	4.25	64	14	21	3.1	4.5	**1.5**	19%	1.4	-30.4	41	($7)
LIMA Plan C+	2nd Half		5	4	0	83	49	6.94	1.54	314			19.6	33%	56%	4.39	51	15	34	2.3	5.3	**2.3**	14%	1.5	-27.1	63	($1)
+/- Score 112	09	Proj	**7**	**8**	**0**	**129**	**77**	**4.95**	**1.61**	**313**			**24.4**	**34%**	**72%**	**4.55**	**52**	**15**	**33**	**2.9**	**5.4**	**1.8**	**11%**	**1.2**	**-2.8**	**48**	**$3**

2-3, 5.55 ERA in 58 IP at CLE. Yet another low-Dom, borderline Cmd guy who tries to cover his shortcomings with GBs. Odd reverse split (.872 OPS vs LH) may be key. Fix that and he could improve quickly. A project.

James,Chuck

James,Chuck			W	L	Sv	IP	K	ERA	WHIP	OBA	vL	vR	BF/G	H%	S%	xERA	G	L	F	Ctl	Dom	Cmd	hr/f	hr/9	RAR	BPV	R$
LH Starter	04		0	0	0	0	0	0.00	0.00																		
Age 27	05	a/a	10	4	0	119	117	3.10	1.04	222			21.5	28%	72%	2.55				2.1	8.8	**4.2**		0.7	17.8	131	$19
Type Pwr xFB	06	ATL *	12	4	0	152	113	3.78	1.25	243	297	215	19.9	26%	76%	4.80	28	19	53	3.1	6.7	**2.1**	10%	1.4	13.2	41	$16
Health B	07	ATL	11	10	0	161	116	4.24	1.38	265	252	268	23.1	28%	77%	4.86	31	20	49	3.2	6.5	**2.0**	13%	1.8	3.7	38	$12
PT/Exp C	08	ATL *	7	10	0	116	85	5.06	1.61	278	148	360	22.8	31%	71%	5.57	31	17	52	4.7	6.6	**1.4**	8%	1.2	-11.2	2	$2
Consist A	1st Half		5	5	0	71	49	4.10	1.52	263			22.5	30%	75%	5.56	31	18	51	4.6	6.2	**1.3**	6%	0.9	1.5	-5	$4
LIMA Plan C+	2nd Half		2	5	0	45	36	6.57	1.74	301			23.2	34%	65%	5.64	32	12	56	4.7	7.2	**1.5**	10%	1.6	-12.7	12	($2)
+/- Score -24	09	Proj	**2**	**2**	**0**	**29**	**22**	**4.66**	**1.45**	**268**			**21.1**	**30%**	**71%**	**5.05**	**30**	**19**	**51**	**3.7**	**6.8**	**1.8**	**9%**	**1.2**	**-2.5**	**31**	**$2**

2-5, 9.10 ERA in 30 IP at ATL. Tried to pitch through partial rotator cuff tear, then had rotator cuff/labrum surgery in September. 2009 season now in doubt. Give him a pass on 2008, check back in a year.

Jenks,Bobby

Jenks,Bobby			W	L	Sv	IP	K	ERA	WHIP	OBA	vL	vR	BF/G	H%	S%	xERA	G	L	F	Ctl	Dom	Cmd	hr/f	hr/9	RAR	BPV	R$
RH Reliever	04	aaa	0	1	0	12	12	9.75	2.25	360			20.7	44%	56%	8.47				6.0	9.0	**1.5**		1.5	-8.0	24	($2)
Age 28	05	CHW *	2	3	25	80	89	3.12	1.37	247	105	298	5.1	34%	78%	3.45	45	26	30	4.1	10.0	**2.5**	6%	0.5	12.3	93	$16
Type xGB	06	CHW	3	4	41	69	80	4.03	1.40	253	227	268	4.5	35%	72%	2.87	59	19	22	4.0	10.4	**2.6**	13%	0.7	4.5	115	$20
Health A	07	CHW	3	5	40	65	56	2.77	0.89	197	237	169	3.8	25%	68%	2.99	54	16	31	1.8	7.8	**4.3**	4%	0.3	13.9	123	$24
PT/Exp A	08	CHW	3	1	30	62	38	2.63	1.10	227	219	241	4.4	26%	77%	3.67	58	14	28	2.5	5.5	**2.2**	6%	0.4	13.1	68	$18
Consist A	1st Half		2	0	18	32	19	1.95	1.11	235			4.1	27%	83%	3.29	64	15	21	2.2	5.3	**2.4**	5%	0.3	9.6	77	$11
LIMA Plan C	2nd Half		1	1	12	29	19	3.37	1.09	217			4.7	25%	70%	4.00	51	13	36	2.8	5.8	**2.1**	6%	0.6	3.6	59	$7
+/- Score -21	09	Proj	**3**	**3**	**38**	**68**	**48**	**3.44**	**1.22**	**244**			**4.4**	**28%**	**73%**	**3.70**	**55**	**16**	**29**	**2.8**	**6.4**	**2.3**	**8%**	**0.7**	**6.1**	**73**	**$19**

Outwardly solid year, but ongoing Dom erosion reached critical levels. Monthly Dom trend suggests summer back issues were a cause. Strong GB rate kept him effective, but only an elite closer if Dom returns.

Jimenez,Cesar

Jimenez,Cesar			W	L	Sv	IP	K	ERA	WHIP	OBA	vL	vR	BF/G	H%	S%	xERA	G	L	F	Ctl	Dom	Cmd	hr/f	hr/9	RAR	BPV	R$
LH Reliever	04		0	0	0	0	0	0.00	0.00																		
Age 24	05	a/a	3	5	4	76	64	3.44	1.27	255			6.5	31%	76%	3.73				2.7	7.5	**2.8**		0.9	8.1	82	$8
Type FB	06	a/a	5	12	3	123	71	4.87	1.53	270			20.3	30%	68%	4.38				4.4	5.2	**1.2**		0.6	-5.3	38	$4
Health A	07	aaa	2	1	2	26	20	4.50	1.73	290			7.6	34%	76%	5.60				5.2	6.9	**1.3**		1.0	-0.1	35	$2
PT/Exp D	08	SEA *	1	5	3	72	67	3.80	1.32	267	317	203	5.1	34%	72%	3.99	39	18	43	2.6	8.3	**3.1**	6%	0.6	4.9	95	$6
Consist C	1st Half		1	3	3	38	41	4.15	1.33	283			5.6	37%	70%					2.0	9.6	**4.9**		0.7	0.9	138	$4
LIMA Plan B	2nd Half		0	2	0	34	26	3.41	1.31	249			4.7	30%	74%	4.53	39	18	43	3.4	6.8	**2.0**	5%	0.5	4.0	47	$2
+/- Score 12	09	Proj	**1**	**4**	**0**	**58**	**45**	**4.03**	**1.31**	**258**			**7.0**	**30%**	**71%**	**4.36**	**39**	**18**	**43**	**2.9**	**7.0**	**2.4**	**8%**	**0.9**	**0.5**	**63**	**$4**

0-2, 3.41 ERA in 34 IP at SEA. Missed most of 2007 with fractured left elbow, came back and set AAA on fire in 1H. Needs to carry over health and growth, but BA vs RH says he may not be more than a specialist.

Jimenez,Ubaldo

Jimenez,Ubaldo			W	L	Sv	IP	K	ERA	WHIP	OBA	vL	vR	BF/G	H%	S%	xERA	G	L	F	Ctl	Dom	Cmd	hr/f	hr/9	RAR	BPV	R$
RH Starter	04		0	0	0	0	0	0.00	0.00																		
Age 25	05	aa	2	5	0	63	45	7.43	1.60	283			23.7	28%	59%	6.58				4.4	6.4	**1.5**		2.6	-24.3	-10	($3)
Type Pwr GB	06	a/a	14	4	0	151	128	4.88	1.48	254			25.6	31%	67%	4.09				4.7	7.6	**1.6**		0.7	-6.7	63	$11
Health A	07	COL *	12	9	0	185	145	6.51	1.67	285	244	212	25.0	33%	61%	4.85	46	17	37	4.9	7.0	**1.4**	10%	1.1	-47.6	19	($0)
PT/Exp B	08	COL	12	12	0	199	172	3.99	1.43	245	248	241	25.4	31%	72%	3.94	54	18	28	4.7	7.8	**1.7**	7%	0.5	7.0	47	$13
Consist B	1st Half		2	8	0	94	75	4.71	1.59	271			24.9	33%	69%	4.16	57	17	26	4.9	7.2	**1.5**	7%	0.5	-5.0	33	$1
LIMA Plan D+	2nd Half		10	4	0	105	97	3.34	1.30	221			26.0	28%	75%	3.75	51	19	30	4.5	8.3	**1.9**	7%	0.5	12.0	59	$12
+/- Score -6	09	Proj	**11**	**13**	**0**	**203**	**169**	**4.48**	**1.51**	**259**			**25.0**	**31%**	**72%**	**4.18**	**52**	**18**	**30**	**4.7**	**7.5**	**1.6**	**11%**	**0.9**	**4.0**	**38**	**$10**

A definite step forward, but let's not call it a breakout just yet. Enhanced GB is a big plus for Coors, but still struggling to cross 2.0 Cmd line. Until he does, there is more downside here than upside.

Johnson,Jim

Johnson,Jim			W	L	Sv	IP	K	ERA	WHIP	OBA	vL	vR	BF/G	H%	S%	xERA	G	L	F	Ctl	Dom	Cmd	hr/f	hr/9	RAR	BPV	R$
RH Reliever	04		0	0	0	0	0	0.00	0.00																		
Age 25	05		0	0	0	0	0	0.00	0.00																		
Type xGB	06	aa	13	6	0	156	108	6.30	1.72	320			26.8	36%	63%	5.96				3.5	6.2	**1.8**		1.0	-34.3	35	$1
Health A	07	aaa	6	12	0	148	95	5.72	1.70	326			26.3	36%	66%	6.27				3.0	5.8	**1.9**		1.2	-22.9	28	($1)
PT/Exp D	08	BAL	2	4	1	69	38	2.23	1.19	218	227	212	5.2	26%	79%	4.11	59	14	27	3.7	5.0	**1.4**	0%	0.0	18.0	27	$8
Consist C	1st Half		2	2	1	46	24	1.17	0.95	166			5.4	20%	86%	4.19	53	14	33	3.5	4.7	**1.3**	0%	0.0	18.2	21	$8
LIMA Plan C	2nd Half		0	2	0	22	14	4.42	1.70	307			4.9	36%	71%	3.87	67	15	18	4.0	5.6	**1.4**	0%	0.0	-0.2	38	($0)
+/- Score -71	09	Proj	**2**	**4**	**0**	**64**	**39**	**4.25**	**1.48**	**278**			**6.7**	**32%**	**71%**	**3.93**	**62**	**15**	**23**	**3.5**	**5.5**	**1.6**	**8%**	**0.6**	**3.9**	**44**	**$3**

Yet another example of a flimsy skill set propped up by a huge GB rate. But the secret to his success was HR avoidance (56 FB, 0 HR), which can't sustain. Give him expected 5 HR against, and 2008 looks very ordinary.

Johnson,Josh

Johnson,Josh			W	L	Sv	IP	K	ERA	WHIP	OBA	vL	vR	BF/G	H%	S%	xERA	G	L	F	Ctl	Dom	Cmd	hr/f	hr/9	RAR	BPV	R$
RH Starter	04		0	0	0	0	0	0.00	0.00																		
Age 25	05	FLA *	1	4	0	151	112	4.71	1.56	288			22.5	35%	68%	4.38				3.8	6.7	**1.8**		0.2	-8.6	68	$1
Type Pwr	06	FLA	12	7	0	157	133	3.10	1.30	235	246	227	21.4	28%	79%	4.06	46	19	36	3.9	7.6	**2.0**	9%	0.8	27.0	56	$18
Health F	07	FLA	0	3	0	16	14	7.45	2.42	370	419	361	21.0	45%	68%	5.85	44	22	33	6.9	8.0	**1.2**	5%	0.6	-5.9	-19	($2)
PT/Exp C	08	FLA *	8	2	0	106	89	3.73	1.38	279	288	259	26.9	34%	74%	3.74	48	21	31	2.6	7.5	**2.9**	8%	0.7	7.1	90	$9
Consist D	1st Half		0	1	0	11	6	6.89	1.91	392			26.6	44%	60%					0.9	4.7	**5.4**		0.0	-3.6	118	($1)
LIMA Plan C	2nd Half		8	1	0	95	83	3.36	1.32	263			26.9	32%	77%	3.64	48	21	31	2.8	7.9	**2.8**	9%	0.8	10.7	91	$10
+/- Score 19	09	Proj	**12**	**7**	**0**	**180**	**146**	**3.81**	**1.33**	**256**			**23.1**	**31%**	**72%**	**3.96**	**46**	**21**	**33**	**3.2**	**7.3**	**2.3**	**8%**	**0.7**	**8.4**	**69**	**$16**

7-1, 3.61 ERA in 88 IP at FLA. Triumphant return from 2007 TJ surgery, and ahead of schedule. Ctl gains need to be validated, but reclamation of pre-surgery skills restores him to spot among best young SP.

RAY MURPHY

Johnson,Randy

	Yr	Tm	W	L	Sv	IP	K	ERA	WHIP	OBA	vL	vR	BF/G	H%	S%	xERA	G	L	F	Ctl	Dom	Cmd	hr/f	hr/9	RAR	BPV	R$
LH Starter	04	ARI	16	14	0	245	290	2.61	0.90	204	163	204	26.8	28%	74%	2.63	45	18	37	1.6	10.6	**6.6**	8%	0.7	50.1	171	$41
Age 45	05	NYY	17	8	0	225	211	3.80	1.13	246	185	257	26.8	29%	72%	3.35	45	17	38	1.9	8.4	**4.5**	13%	1.3	16.0	124	$29
Type Pwr FB	06	NYY	17	11	0	205	172	5.00	1.24	251	194	259	25.8	29%	62%	3.99	42	16	43	2.6	7.6	**2.9**	11%	1.2	-11.3	85	$20
Health F	07	ARI	4	3	0	57	72	3.81	1.15	245	182	257	23.1	34%	71%	2.86	40	19	40	2.1	11.4	**5.5**	12%	1.1	4.3	168	$8
PT/Exp A	08	ARI	11	10	0	184	173	3.91	1.24	262	215	267	25.5	32%	73%	3.68	40	18	42	2.2	8.5	**3.9**	11%	1.2	8.1	112	$17
Consist B	1st Half		4	6	0	82	76	4.94	1.44	289			25.5	35%	67%	3.98	41	19	40	2.6	8.3	**3.2**	9%	1.0	-6.8	98	$4
LIMA Plan C+	2nd Half		7	4	0	102	97	3.09	1.08	238			25.5	28%	79%	3.44	40	18	43	1.8	8.6	**4.9**	12%	1.3	14.9	124	$14
+/- Score -2	09	Proj	**9**	**9**	**0**	**145**	**133**	**4.10**	**1.26**	**251**			**25.2**	**30%**	**71%**	**3.84**	**41**	**18**	**41**	**2.8**	**8.3**	**3.0**	**11%**	**1.2**	**9.0**	**92**	**$13**

An astounding return from yet another back surgery. Skill set is long past peak, but more than sufficient for continued success. Win #300 should come by June. Health grade and age are the only negatives in this box.

Jones,Todd

	Yr	Tm	W	L	Sv	IP	K	ERA	WHIP	OBA	vL	vR	BF/G	H%	S%	xERA	G	L	F	Ctl	Dom	Cmd	hr/f	hr/9	RAR	BPV	R$
RH Reliever	04	2NL	11	5	2	82	59	4.17	1.43	266	221	290	4.6	31%	72%	4.59	41	21	38	3.6	6.5	**1.8**	7%	0.8	1.0	38	$9
Age 41	05	FLA	1	5	40	73	62	2.10	1.03	229	211	229	4.2	29%	79%	3.04	53	21	27	1.7	7.6	**4.4**	4%	0.2	19.4	121	$22
Type	06	DET	2	6	37	64	28	3.94	1.27	279	264	284	4.3	30%	69%	4.16	53	18	29	1.5	3.9	**2.5**	6%	0.6	4.9	60	$16
Health C	07	DET	1	4	38	61	33	4.26	1.42	270	265	269	4.2	30%	69%	4.75	46	21	33	3.4	4.8	**1.4**	5%	0.4	1.9	20	$15
PT/Exp B	08	DET	4	1	18	42	14	4.96	1.63	298	289	304	4.2	30%	71%	5.63	43	24	33	3.9	3.0	**0.8**	10%	1.1	-3.2	-29	$7
Consist B	1st Half		3	0	15	32	12	4.78	1.50	285			4.2	30%	69%	5.36	43	22	35	3.4	3.4	**1.0**	7%	0.8	-1.7	-9	$6
LIMA Plan	2nd Half		1	1	3	10	2	5.57	2.06	339			4.4	32%	78%	6.64	44	29	27	5.6	1.9	**0.3**	19%	1.9	-1.5	-95	$1
+/- Score	09	Proj																									

Announced his retirement in September. Ends career with a 3.97 ERA over 1072 IP, with 319 Saves (14th all-time) and over $30M in earnings. Not bad for a guy with a career Cmd below 2.0.

Julio,Jorge

	Yr	Tm	W	L	Sv	IP	K	ERA	WHIP	OBA	vL	vR	BF/G	H%	S%	xERA	G	L	F	Ctl	Dom	Cmd	hr/f	hr/9	RAR	BPV	R$
RH Reliever	04	BAL	2	5	22	69	70	4.57	1.42	233	234	221	4.6	28%	72%	4.31	41	14	45	5.1	9.1	**1.8**	13%	1.4	-1.1	46	$12
Age 30	05	BAL	3	5	0	71	58	5.94	1.40	275	281	257	4.6	30%	62%	4.25	40	18	41	3.0	7.3	**2.4**	16%	1.8	-13.8	68	$2
Type Pwr	06	2NL	2	4	16	66	88	4.23	1.32	218	185	234	4.5	30%	73%	3.29	40	21	39	4.8	12.0	**2.5**	17%	1.4	2.1	105	$11
Health A	07	2NL	0	5	0	62	56	5.23	1.60	280	227	322	4.1	34%	69%	4.04	52	19	30	4.5	8.1	**1.8**	14%	1.2	-6.1	54	($0)
PT/Exp C	08	2TM *	4	2	13	69	69	3.13	1.63	261	255	236	4.8	34%	82%	4.47	46	18	36	5.8	9.0	**1.6**	6%	0.5	10.0	31	$9
Consist B	1st Half		0	1	1	27	20	4.43	1.78	285			5.5	33%	77%	5.68	35	23	42	5.9	6.9	**1.2**	8%	1.0	-0.4	-23	($0)
LIMA Plan B	2nd Half		4	1	12	42	49	2.31	1.54	244			4.5	35%	85%	3.12	69	8	23	5.7	10.4	**1.8**	4%	0.2	10.4	82	$9
+/- Score -39	09	Proj	**2**	**3**	**0**	**64**	**65**	**4.54**	**1.53**	**254**			**4.6**	**32%**	**72%**	**4.10**	**46**	**19**	**35**	**5.1**	**9.2**	**1.8**	**11%**	**1.0**	**2.1**	**52**	**$3**

3-0, 3.60 ERA in 30 IP at CLE/ATL. Reversed recent decline by limiting HR ball for a change. 2H GB spike is only 12 IP, not enough to get excited. Throws hard enough that he'll get more MLB chances, but not from you.

Jurrjens,Jair

	Yr	Tm	W	L	Sv	IP	K	ERA	WHIP	OBA	vL	vR	BF/G	H%	S%	xERA	G	L	F	Ctl	Dom	Cmd	hr/f	hr/9	RAR	BPV	R$
RH Starter	04		0	0	0	0	0	0.00	0.00																		
Age 23	05		0	0	0	0	0	0.00	0.00																		
Type GB	06	aa	4	3	0	67	48	4.22	1.52	300			24.8	34%	75%	5.15				2.8	6.5	**2.3**		1.0	2.5	52	$4
Health A	07	DET *	10	6	0	143	94	4.47	1.42	284	262	167	23.9	32%	69%	4.80	38	18	44	2.7	5.9	**2.2**	6%	0.8	0.6	50	$10
PT/Exp C	08	ATL	13	10	0	188	139	3.68	1.37	261	261	260	26.1	31%	73%	3.88	52	22	27	3.3	6.6	**2.0**	7%	0.5	13.7	59	$15
Consist B	1st Half		8	3	0	98	69	2.94	1.32	250			25.9	30%	78%	3.99	51	21	28	3.4	6.3	**1.9**	6%	0.5	16.1	51	$10
LIMA Plan C	2nd Half		5	7	0	90	70	4.49	1.43	274			26.2	33%	68%	3.77	53	23	25	3.3	7.0	**2.1**	9%	0.6	-2.4	67	$5
+/- Score 6	09	Proj	**12**	**11**	**0**	**203**	**149**	**3.90**	**1.36**	**267**			**24.9**	**31%**	**73%**	**3.90**	**50**	**21**	**29**	**3.0**	**6.6**	**2.2**	**9%**	**0.8**	**11.0**	**66**	**$15**

Things you like to see in a young starting pitcher:
- GB rate over 50%
- Dom trending up, including 2H
- 2H fade not supported by skills
- Handles LH and RH hitters

A worthy investment.

Karstens,Jeff

	Yr	Tm	W	L	Sv	IP	K	ERA	WHIP	OBA	vL	vR	BF/G	H%	S%	xERA	G	L	F	Ctl	Dom	Cmd	hr/f	hr/9	RAR	BPV	R$
RH Starter	04		0	0	0	0	0	0.00	0.00																		
Age 26	05	aa	12	11	0	169	123	4.95	1.54	313			26.9	36%	69%	5.36				2.3	6.6	**2.9**		1.0	-13.5	63	$7
Type Con FB	06	NYY *	13	6	0	189	108	4.33	1.40	277	253	233	24.8	30%	72%	5.26	33	16	51	2.8	5.1	**1.8**	7%	1.1	5.2	28	$14
Health F	07	NYY *	5	4	0	51	31	5.06	1.69	309			16.7	34%	73%	5.87	27	21	52	3.8	5.4	**1.4**	8%	1.3	-3.5	-0	$2
PT/Exp D	08	PIT *	8	10	0	120	68	4.61	1.38	288	265	293	24.5	31%	70%	4.57	42	20	39	2.1	5.1	**2.4**	11%	1.3	-4.9	53	$6
Consist B	1st Half		2	3	0	36	27	5.38	1.37	283			22.2	31%	66%					2.3	6.8	**2.9**		1.8	-5.0	47	$1
LIMA Plan C	2nd Half		6	7	0	83	40	4.27	1.39	291			25.6	31%	72%	4.78	42	20	39	2.1	4.4	**2.1**	9%	1.1	0.0	42	$5
+/- Score 5	09	Proj	**7**	**7**	**0**	**95**	**58**	**4.45**	**1.39**	**285**			**21.5**	**31%**	**72%**	**4.78**	**37**	**19**	**44**	**2.4**	**5.5**	**2.3**	**10%**	**1.3**	**-5.2**	**49**	**$6**

2-6, 4.03 ERA in 51 IP at PIT. Good Ctl is one piece of the puzzle; if he combined it with either 6.0+ Dom or 50%+ GB%, he'd be serviceable. Has shown the Dom in AAA, but running out of chances to bring it to majors.

Kazmir,Scott

	Yr	Tm	W	L	Sv	IP	K	ERA	WHIP	OBA	vL	vR	BF/G	H%	S%	xERA	G	L	F	Ctl	Dom	Cmd	hr/f	hr/9	RAR	BPV	R$
LH Starter	04	aa	3	3	0	51	48	1.85	1.01	184			25.0	25%	80%	1.42				3.4	8.5	**2.5**		0.0	15.7	123	$9
Age 25	05	TAM	10	9	0	186	174	3.77	1.46	247	174	268	25.5	31%	75%	4.38	42	20	38	4.8	8.4	**1.7**	6%	0.6	13.7	41	$15
Type Pwr FB	06	TAM	10	8	0	144	163	3.25	1.28	245	227	242	25.2	32%	78%	3.42	42	19	39	3.2	10.2	**3.1**	10%	0.9	23.3	115	$20
Health C	07	TAM	13	9	0	207	239	3.48	1.38	252	217	263	26.1	34%	77%	3.64	43	16	41	3.9	10.4	**2.7**	8%	0.8	26.1	104	$24
PT/Exp A	08	TAM	12	8	0	152	166	3.49	1.27	223	198	227	23.6	28%	79%	4.02	31	20	49	4.1	9.8	**2.4**	12%	1.4	16.2	74	$19
Consist A	1st Half		7	3	0	67	72	2.28	1.04	196			24.1	26%	82%	3.64	32	20	48	3.2	9.7	**3.0**	6%	0.7	17.1	97	$13
LIMA Plan C+	2nd Half		5	5	0	85	94	4.43	1.44	242			23.3	29%	77%	4.33	30	20	50	4.9	9.9	**2.0**	16%	1.9	-0.9	55	$7
+/- Score 15	09	Proj	**13**	**10**	**0**	**189**	**207**	**3.68**	**1.30**	**234**			**24.9**	**30%**	**75%**	**3.84**	**37**	**19**	**44**	**4.0**	**9.9**	**2.5**	**10%**	**1.1**	**13.5**	**86**	**$22**

Missed April with strained elbow, came back strong but faded late. Ctl and FB trends troubling, impact his ability to pitch deep in games (only one GS > 6.0 IP after 6/11). Skills are still here, but risk is elevated.

Kendrick,Kyle

	Yr	Tm	W	L	Sv	IP	K	ERA	WHIP	OBA	vL	vR	BF/G	H%	S%	xERA	G	L	F	Ctl	Dom	Cmd	hr/f	hr/9	RAR	BPV	R$
RH Starter	04		0	0	0	0	0	0.00	0.00																		
Age 24	05		0	0	0	0	0	0.00	0.00																		
Type Con	06		0	0	0	0	0	0.00	0.00																		
Health A	07	PHI *	14	11	0	202	91	3.88	1.33	283	321	241	26.8	30%	73%	4.45	47	21	32	1.9	4.0	**2.1**	9%	0.9	13.7	45	$15
PT/Exp C	08	PHI	11	9	0	156	68	5.49	1.61	306	334	271	22.8	32%	68%	4.99	44	27	29	3.3	3.9	**1.2**	14%	1.3	-23.5	4	$1
Consist B	1st Half		7	3	0	86	39	4.59	1.44	285			23.5	30%	71%	4.61	47	24	29	2.8	4.1	**1.4**	13%	1.1	-3.4	22	$4
LIMA Plan C	2nd Half		4	6	0	69	29	6.61	1.83	331			22.0	34%	66%	5.47	41	30	29	3.9	3.8	**1.0**	16%	1.6	-20.1	-18	($4)
+/- Score 8	09	Proj	**6**	**5**	**0**	**87**	**39**	**4.97**	**1.54**	**302**			**24.3**	**32%**	**70%**	**4.83**	**44**	**26**	**30**	**2.9**	**4.0**	**1.4**	**12%**	**1.1**	**-5.3**	**17**	**$2**

Pinpoint Ctl and a lot of GBs made him effective in 2007, but both deserted him in sophomore year. His decline only picked up speed as year went on, 2H BPV is a flashing neon "Stay Away" sign. Heed its warning.

Kennedy,Ian

	Yr	Tm	W	L	Sv	IP	K	ERA	WHIP	OBA	vL	vR	BF/G	H%	S%	xERA	G	L	F	Ctl	Dom	Cmd	hr/f	hr/9	RAR	BPV	R$
RH Starter	04		0	0	0	0	0	0.00	0.00																		
Age 24	05		0	0	0	0	0	0.00	0.00																		
Type Pwr xFB	06		0	0	0	0	0	0.00	0.00																		
Health A	07	NYY *	7	2	0	102	91	3.00	1.13	209	161	216	23.0	26%	74%	4.36	26	23	51	3.4	8.0	**2.3**	4%	0.5	19.0	56	$15
PT/Exp D	08	NYY *	5	7	0	109	87	4.89	1.43	266	236	397	20.5	32%	66%	4.71	41	12	48	3.6	7.2	**2.0**	6%	0.8	-7.2	50	$6
Consist A	1st Half		1	3	0	46	33	6.09	1.48	250			18.3	28%	59%	5.29	40	12	48	4.9	6.5	**1.3**	7%	1.0	-9.9	2	$0
LIMA Plan C	2nd Half		4	4	0	63	54	4.01	1.38	277			22.6	34%	72%	4.06	50	7	43	2.7	7.7	**2.8**	6%	0.7	2.6	94	$5
+/- Score -6	09	Proj	**7**	**6**	**0**	**123**	**103**	**4.11**	**1.31**	**245**			**21.6**	**29%**	**71%**	**4.49**	**38**	**14**	**48**	**3.5**	**7.6**	**2.1**	**8%**	**1.0**	**-1.0**	**57**	**$11**

0-4, 8.17 ERA in 40 IP at NYY. Continues to own minor-league hitters (4.2 Cmd in AAA) but got pummeled in majors. Skills should win out in the end, but it may take a change of scenery before that happens.

Kensing,Logan

	Yr	Tm	W	L	Sv	IP	K	ERA	WHIP	OBA	vL	vR	BF/G	H%	S%	xERA	G	L	F	Ctl	Dom	Cmd	hr/f	hr/9	RAR	BPV	R$
RH Reliever	04	FLA	0	3	0	13	7	10.23	2.12	338	320	367	13.3	32%	57%	6.48	43	15	43	6.1	4.8	**0.8**	24%	3.4	-9.7	-59	($3)
Age 26	05	aa	4	1	0	39	29	4.02	1.45	272			24.5	31%	75%	4.50				3.6	6.7	**1.9**		0.9	1.4	52	$3
Type Pwr xFB	06	FLA	1	3	1	37	45	4.60	1.32	222			4.3	29%	70%	3.86	29	24	47	4.6	10.9	**2.4**	14%	1.5	-0.5	78	$3
Health D	07	FLA	3	0	0	13	13	1.35	1.35	227			6.3	31%	89%	4.73	29	20	51	4.7	8.8	**1.9**	0%	0.0	5.0	37	$3
PT/Exp D	08	FLA	3	1	0	55	55	4.23	1.50	243	208	259	5.1	30%	75%	4.76	34	18	48	5.4	9.0	**1.7**	10%	1.1	0.3	28	$3
Consist A	1st Half		3	1	0	39	33	3.72	1.47	232			5.7	27%	79%	5.18	33	18	49	5.6	7.7	**1.4**	9%	1.2	2.6	-2	$3
LIMA Plan C+	2nd Half		0	0	0	17	22	5.42	1.57	266			4.1	38%	67%	3.85	36	18	47	4.9	11.9	**2.4**	10%	1.1	-2.4	97	$0
+/- Score -19	09	Proj	**2**	**2**	**0**	**60**	**56**	**4.54**	**1.43**	**237**			**5.1**	**28%**	**71%**	**4.71**	**33**	**19**	**48**	**5.0**	**8.5**	**1.7**	**10%**	**1.2**	**-2.7**	**29**	**$3**

RPs who give up too many BB and FB are usually tagged as "avoids." But anyone who can also strike out a batter an inning has to remain on the radar. So, keep him on your radar. And avoid him. For now.

RAY MURPHY

Kershaw,Clayton

	Yr	Tm	W	L	Sv	IP	K	ERA	WHIP	OBA	vL	vR	BF/G	H%	S%	xERA	G	L	F	Ctl	Dom	Cmd	hr/f	hr/9	RAR	BPV	R$
LH Starter	04		0	0	0	0	0	0.00	0.00																		
Age 21	05		0	0	0	0	0	0.00	0.00																		
Type Pwr	06		0	0	0	0	0	0.00	0.00																		
Health A	07	aa	1	2	0	24	26	4.88	1.63	228			21.8	26%	76%	5.24				7.1	9.8	**1.4**		1.9	-1.2	40	$1
PT/Exp D	08	LA	* 7	8	0	169	157	3.48	1.30	240	250	269	20.4	30%	74%	3.69	48	21	31	3.7	8.4	**2.2**	8%	0.6	16.4	76	$14
Consist D	1st Half		0	5	0	76	74	3.24	1.35	236			19.1	31%	75%	3.79	49	18	33	4.3	8.8	**2.0**	4%	0.4	9.6	69	$5
LIMA Plan C+	2nd Half		7	3	0	93	83	3.68	1.27	242			21.6	30%	73%	3.62	48	22	31	3.3	8.0	**2.4**	10%	0.8	6.8	81	$10
+/- Score 21	09	Proj	**10**	**8**	**0**	**174**	**161**	**3.78**	**1.27**	**240**			**25.1**	**30%**	**72%**	**3.59**	**48**	**21**	**31**	**3.4**	**8.3**	**2.4**	**10%**	**0.8**	**16.2**	**84**	**$16**

5-5, 4.26 ERA in 108 IP at LA. Given age and inexperience, a remarkable debut. A prospect right out of Central Casting: elite Dom, GB tilt, Ctl settled as year went on. Only injuries can keep him from greatness.

Kobayashi,Masa

	Yr	Tm	W	L	Sv	IP	K	ERA	WHIP	OBA	vL	vR	BF/G	H%	S%	xERA	G	L	F	Ctl	Dom	Cmd	hr/f	hr/9	RAR	BPV	R$
RH Reliever	04	JPN	8	5	20	58	47	4.82	1.35	251			4.9	29%	66%	4.08				3.7	7.3	**2.0**		1.0	-3.4	60	$12
Age 34	05	JPN	2	2	29	45	31	3.23	1.42	293			4.2	31%	88%	5.72				2.2	6.2	**2.8**		2.0	6.0	32	$13
Type Con	06	JPN	6	2	34	54	46	3.31	1.16	257			4.2	30%	76%	3.68				1.7	7.7	**4.6**		1.1	8.0	113	$20
Health A	07	JPN	2	7	27	47	33	4.52	1.53	300			4.3	34%	74%	5.46				2.9	6.3	**2.2**		1.3	-0.3	41	$11
PT/Exp B	08	CLE	4	5	6	56	35	4.52	1.42	293	280	292	4.2	32%	72%	3.98	50	21	28	2.3	5.7	**2.5**	15%	1.3	-1.2	69	$5
Consist D	1st Half		4	3	4	40	26	3.15	1.23	252			4.4	28%	78%	3.86	53	16	31	2.5	5.9	**2.4**	10%	0.9	5.9	70	$7
LIMA Plan B	2nd Half		0	2	2	16	9	8.02	1.91	379			4.0	39%	62%	4.28	45	32	23	1.7	5.2	**3.0**	28%	2.3	-7.1	69	($1)
+/- Score 21	09	Proj	**3**	**6**	**3**	**58**	**37**	**4.34**	**1.41**	**294**			**4.1**	**33%**	**72%**	**3.90**	**48**	**27**	**26**	**2.2**	**5.7**	**2.6**	**14%**	**1.1**	**3.7**	**70**	**$4**

Cmd-and-GB approach worked in 1H, but 2H filled with liners and HR. May have just been 1H overuse that wore him out, but Dom is right at the threshold of minimally-acceptable levels, thus limiting rebound potential.

Kuo,Hong-Chih

	Yr	Tm	W	L	Sv	IP	K	ERA	WHIP	OBA	vL	vR	BF/G	H%	S%	xERA	G	L	F	Ctl	Dom	Cmd	hr/f	hr/9	RAR	BPV	R$
LH Reliever	04		0	0	0	0	0	0.00	0.00																		
Age 27	05	aa	1	2	3	33	49	3.82	1.48	250			5.6	40%	74%	3.86				4.9	13.4	**2.7**		0.5	2.0	126	$4
Type Pwr	06	LA	* 5	8	1	112	123	3.70	1.45	255	241	246	9.6	34%	75%	3.72	44	21	34	4.3	9.9	**2.3**	8%	0.6	10.8	83	$9
Health C	07	LA	* 1	5	0	50	49	6.32	1.61	290	240	296	15.2	36%	60%	4.78	31	20	49	4.2	8.8	**2.1**	7%	0.9	-11.8	54	($1)
PT/Exp D	08	LA	5	3	1	80	96	2.14	1.01	210	202	205	7.5	30%	81%	2.72	46	20	34	2.4	10.8	**4.6**	6%	0.5	21.0	155	$14
Consist D	1st Half		3	1	0	46	55	1.76	1.00	212			10.0	31%	84%	2.59	47	22	30	2.2	10.8	**5.0**	6%	0.4	14.2	161	$8
LIMA Plan B+	2nd Half		2	2	1	34	41	2.65	1.03	207			5.6	30%	76%	2.89	45	17	38	2.6	10.9	**4.1**	7%	0.5	6.8	147	$6
+/- Score 1	09	Proj	**3**	**5**	**3**	**74**	**82**	**3.67**	**1.20**	**230**			**6.3**	**31%**	**71%**	**3.40**	**41**	**19**	**40**	**3.2**	**10.0**	**3.2**	**8%**	**0.7**	**8.5**	**114**	**$9**

Finally blessed with good health, and/or a usage pattern that he could handle. Skills were always there, but future role matters. As a RP, he's a LIMA weapon. As a SP, he's a lengthy DL stint waiting to happen.

Kuroda,Hiroki

	Yr	Tm	W	L	Sv	IP	K	ERA	WHIP	OBA	vL	vR	BF/G	H%	S%	xERA	G	L	F	Ctl	Dom	Cmd	hr/f	hr/9	RAR	BPV	R$
RH Starter	04	JPN	7	9	0	147	131	5.78	1.61	326			31.7	38%	68%	6.50				2.2	8.0	**3.6**		1.7	-26.0	62	$2
Age 34	05	JPN	15	12	0	213	157	3.94	1.17	246			30.0	27%	71%	3.68				2.2	6.6	**3.0**		1.2	9.7	73	$22
Type Con GB	06	JPN	13	6	1	189	137	2.31	1.10	254			29.2	29%	85%	3.35				1.2	6.5	**5.2**		0.9	51.6	125	$28
Health A	07	JPN	12	8	0	180	117	4.41	1.34	271			29.5	28%	74%	4.93				2.6	5.8	**2.2**		1.7	1.2	33	$13
PT/Exp A	08	LA	9	10	0	183	116	3.73	1.22	259	260	246	24.5	30%	70%	3.77	51	20	29	2.1	5.7	**2.8**	8%	0.6	12.2	76	$15
Consist C	1st Half		3	6	0	82	50	4.05	1.35	266			25.1	29%	73%	4.39	46	21	34	3.0	5.5	**1.9**	10%	1.0	2.3	42	$4
LIMA Plan C+	2nd Half		6	4	0	101	66	3.48	1.11	254			23.9	30%	68%	3.28	56	20	24	1.3	5.9	**4.4**	5%	0.4	9.9	104	$11
+/- Score -8	09	Proj	**11**	**9**	**0**	**189**	**121**	**3.92**	**1.27**	**264**			**27.2**	**30%**	**71%**	**3.80**	**52**	**20**	**28**	**2.3**	**5.8**	**2.5**	**11%**	**0.9**	**12.6**	**72**	**$15**

Key takeaway... he got stronger in 2H, something unexpected given the travel demands in LA. Those Cmd/BPV spikes may not fully sustain, but there is room to remain effective while regressing from those levels.

Lackey,John

	Yr	Tm	W	L	Sv	IP	K	ERA	WHIP	OBA	vL	vR	BF/G	H%	S%	xERA	G	L	F	Ctl	Dom	Cmd	hr/f	hr/9	RAR	BPV	R$
RH Starter	04	ANA	14	13	0	198	144	4.68	1.39	278	303	248	25.9	32%	68%	4.34	44	16	40	2.7	6.5	**2.4**	9%	1.0	-6.0	66	$13
Age 30	05	ANA	14	5	0	209	199	3.44	1.33	261	274	241	26.9	33%	75%	3.64	45	23	33	3.1	8.6	**2.8**	7%	0.6	23.9	94	$22
Type	06	LAA	13	11	0	217	190	3.56	1.27	249	263	231	27.6	31%	72%	3.93	43	18	39	3.0	7.9	**2.6**	6%	0.6	26.6	82	$25
Health B	07	LAA	19	9	0	224	179	3.01	1.21	257	280	229	28.0	31%	77%	3.75	45	19	36	2.1	7.2	**3.4**	7%	0.7	41.2	96	$30
PT/Exp A	08	LAA	12	5	0	163	130	3.75	1.23	259	221	301	28.2	29%	76%	3.69	45	20	35	2.2	7.2	**3.3**	15%	1.4	12.1	93	$18
Consist A	1st Half		6	1	0	69	54	1.44	0.89	199			29.1	23%	91%	3.37	45	19	37	1.7	7.1	**4.2**	9%	0.8	24.6	104	$14
LIMA Plan C+	2nd Half		6	4	0	95	76	5.42	1.48	298			27.7	33%	69%	3.93	45	21	34	2.6	7.2	**2.8**	20%	1.9	-12.5	84	$4
+/- Score 27	09	Proj	**15**	**8**	**0**	**203**	**165**	**3.59**	**1.25**	**259**			**28.2**	**30%**	**75%**	**3.77**	**45**	**20**	**36**	**2.3**	**7.3**	**3.1**	**11%**	**1.1**	**16.3**	**91**	**$23**

Strained tricep cost him first six weeks of season, but returned in vintage form. 1H/2H swing was just an expected statistical correction after 1H levels. BPV trend is all you really need to look at. Solid.

Laffey,Aaron

	Yr	Tm	W	L	Sv	IP	K	ERA	WHIP	OBA	vL	vR	BF/G	H%	S%	xERA	G	L	F	Ctl	Dom	Cmd	hr/f	hr/9	RAR	BPV	R$
LH Starter	04		0	0	0	0	0	0.00	0.00																		
Age 24	05		0	0	0	0	0	0.00	0.00																		
Type Con GB	06	aa	8	3	0	112	54	4.34	1.54	305			26.3	33%	73%	5.03				2.7	4.3	**1.6**		0.7	2.6	32	$5
Health A	07	CLE	* 17	6	0	180	115	3.79	1.29	271	322	271	24.5	31%	70%	3.25	62	19	19	2.1	5.7	**2.7**	8%	0.4	15.9	86	$20
PT/Exp D	08	CLE	* 11	9	0	155	85	4.88	1.54	302	244	292	25.6	33%	68%	4.54	51	19	30	2.9	4.9	**1.7**	7%	0.7	-10.2	40	$6
Consist D	1st Half		7	6	0	101	50	3.39	1.27	264			24.9	29%	74%	4.29	51	18	31	2.3	4.5	**1.9**	7%	0.6	12.0	46	$10
LIMA Plan C+	2nd Half		4	3	0	54	35	7.68	2.06	364			26.8	41%	61%	4.86	53	21	26	4.0	5.8	**1.5**	9%	0.8	-22.2	28	($4)
+/- Score 14	09	Proj	**9**	**8**	**0**	**139**	**82**	**4.29**	**1.44**	**287**			**25.2**	**32%**	**71%**	**4.10**	**54**	**19**	**27**	**2.8**	**5.3**	**1.9**	**9%**	**0.7**	**5.5**	**53**	**$9**

5-7, 4.23 ERA in 94 IP at CLE. Had a 2.83 ERA in first 11 starts then colapsed to 8.37 in final 5 outings leading to demotion. Ctl and GB% provide stability and limit downside, but needs one more plus skill.

Lannan,John

	Yr	Tm	W	L	Sv	IP	K	ERA	WHIP	OBA	vL	vR	BF/G	H%	S%	xERA	G	L	F	Ctl	Dom	Cmd	hr/f	hr/9	RAR	BPV	R$
LH Starter	04		0	0	0	0	0	0.00	0.00																		
Age 24	05		0	0	0	0	0	0.00	0.00																		
Type GB	06		0	0	0	0	0	0.00	0.00																		
Health A	07	WAS	* 8	5	0	109	43	3.31	1.38	257	273	273	24.6	28%	76%	5.11	51	14	35	3.6	3.6	**1.0**	5%	0.5	14.9	-5	$9
PT/Exp C	08	WAS	9	15	0	182	117	3.91	1.34	251	259	250	25.0	27%	75%	4.02	54	19	27	3.6	5.8	**1.6**	15%	1.1	8.2	40	$12
Consist C	1st Half		4	9	0	94	56	3.54	1.31	262			24.8	28%	77%	3.97	55	16	29	2.8	5.4	**1.9**	14%	1.1	8.4	55	$7
LIMA Plan D+	2nd Half		5	6	0	88	61	4.30	1.37	239			25.2	26%	72%	4.07	53	23	25	4.4	6.2	**1.4**	17%	1.1	-0.3	24	$5
+/- Score 5	09	Proj	**11**	**12**	**0**	**189**	**124**	**4.11**	**1.41**	**262**			**25.5**	**30%**	**73%**	**4.17**	**53**	**19**	**28**	**3.7**	**5.9**	**1.6**	**11%**	**0.9**	**4.0**	**39**	**$11**

Yet another example of a high GB% drawing good results from a mediocre skill set. Favorable h% definitely helped him along; that and 2H Cmd decline cast doubt about repeatability.

League,Brandon

	Yr	Tm	W	L	Sv	IP	K	ERA	WHIP	OBA	vL	vR	BF/G	H%	S%	xERA	G	L	F	Ctl	Dom	Cmd	hr/f	hr/9	RAR	BPV	R$
RH Reliever	04	aa	6	4	2	104	79	4.93	1.55	283			11.3	34%	66%	4.40				3.9	6.8	**1.8**		0.3	-7.6	66	$4
Age 26	05	TOR	* 5	4	0	98	50	6.57	1.67	314	333	269	11.6	33%	62%	4.22	60	19	21	3.4	4.5	**1.3**	21%	1.4	-26.7	28	($3)
Type xGB	06	TOR	* 4	4	9	96	66	2.80	1.33	275	276	178	6.4	33%	78%	2.75	73	13	14	2.3	6.2	**2.6**	7%	0.3	20.9	99	$13
Health D	07	TOR	0	0	0	12	7	6.15	2.22	365			4.3	41%	72%	5.16	59	18	23	5.4	5.4	**1.0**	10%	0.8	-2.4	-11	($1)
PT/Exp D	08	TOR	* 3	5	3	67	50	3.78	1.45	274	263	200	5.8	32%	75%	3.09	67	19	14	3.5	6.7	**1.9**	17%	0.7	4.7	70	$5
Consist F	1st Half		2	4	2	37	27	5.43	1.67	304			7.7	35%	67%	4.05	56	22	22	3.9	6.5	**1.7**	11%	0.7	-4.9	45	$1
LIMA Plan B	2nd Half		1	1	1	30	23	1.78	1.19	233			4.3	28%	88%	2.69	68	19	13	3.0	6.8	**2.3**	17%	0.6	9.6	89	$4
+/- Score 39	09	Proj	**4**	**4**	**0**	**83**	**58**	**3.58**	**1.36**	**264**			**6.3**	**31%**	**74%**	**3.31**	**64**	**18**	**18**	**3.1**	**6.3**	**2.0**	**11%**	**0.5**	**11.4**	**70**	**$7**

1-2, 2.18 ERA in 33 IP at TOR. Finally combined superb GB% with acceptable Cmd in 2H at TOR, to very good results. Will need to show he can do it over a larger sample, but has the look of an elite LIMA option.

Ledezma,Wil

	Yr	Tm	W	L	Sv	IP	K	ERA	WHIP	OBA	vL	vR	BF/G	H%	S%	xERA	G	L	F	Ctl	Dom	Cmd	hr/f	hr/9	RAR	BPV	R$
LH Reliever	04	DET	* 14	6	0	164	107	3.40	1.25	261	227	285	21.4	30%	74%	4.27	46	14	39	2.3	5.9	**2.5**	5%	0.6	21.0	68	$18
Age 28	05	DET	* 6	7	0	99	66	6.90	1.70	298	352	286	22.9	33%	60%	5.26	43	18	40	4.5	6.0	**1.3**	10%	1.2	-30.9	6	($2)
Type Pwr FB	06	DET	* 7	6	0	131	95	3.45	1.36	263	241	261	15.6	30%	77%	4.74	34	21	46	3.2	6.5	**2.1**	7%	0.8	18.0	44	$13
Health A	07	2TM	3	3	0	59	47	5.62	1.82	295	312	288	6.4	34%	70%	5.48	39	20	41	5.8	7.1	**1.2**	9%	1.1	-8.4	-10	($1)
PT/Exp D	08	2NL	0	2	0	58	53	4.17	1.58	237	255	233	9.4	30%	74%	5.13	37	21	42	6.3	8.2	**1.3**	6%	0.6	0.7	-8	$1
Consist B	1st Half		0	2	0	45	38	5.03	1.63	254			14.5	31%	70%	5.23	37	21	41	6.0	7.7	**1.3**	7%	0.8	-4.2	-10	($1)
LIMA Plan C	2nd Half		0	0	0	14	15	1.32	1.40	173			4.2	26%	89%	4.79	36	18	45	7.3	9.9	**1.4**	0%	0.0	4.9	-4	$1
+/- Score -48	09	Proj	**2**	**2**	**0**	**44**	**33**	**4.97**	**1.56**	**268**			**12.2**	**31%**	**70%**	**5.09**	**38**	**20**	**43**	**4.8**	**6.8**	**1.4**	**9%**	**1.0**	**-4.0**	**10**	**$1**

DET, ATL, ARI, SD (x2) have all taken a look at him since start of 2007. All say "he's got a good arm, let's take a look". Then they actually get that look, and learn why everyone else gave up on him. Ctl trend says it all.

RAY MURPHY

Lee,Cliff

Lee,Cliff		Yr	Tm	W	L	Sv	IP	K	ERA	WHIP	OBA	vL	vR	BF/G	H%	S%	xERA	G	L	F	Ctl	Dom	Cmd	hr/f	hr/9	RAR	BPV	R$
LH	Starter	04	CLE	14	8	0	179	161	5.43	1.50	271	231	277	24.0	31%	67%	4.60	34	21	45	4.1	8.1	2.0	13%	1.5	-22.0	48	$9
Age	30	05	CLE	18	5	0	202	143	3.79	1.22	254	293	237	26.1	29%	72%	4.35	35	21	44	2.3	6.4	2.8	8%	1.0	14.6	66	$23
Type		06	CLE	14	11	0	200	129	4.41	1.41	284	261	282	26.3	31%	73%	4.95	33	19	48	2.6	5.8	2.2	9%	1.3	3.8	45	$15
Health	B	07	CLE	* 7	11	0	143	109	5.73	1.59	283	327	267	22.3	32%	65%	5.29	35	15	50	4.3	6.8	1.6	8%	1.1	-21.6	19	$3
PT/Exp	A	08	CLE	22	3	0	223	170	2.54	1.11	254	272	245	29.0	31%	78%	3.57	46	19	35	1.4	6.9	5.0	5%	0.5	49.8	110	$34
Consist	C	1st Half		11	1	0	104	90	2.34	1.04	239			27.4	30%	79%	3.26	46	19	35	1.4	7.8	5.6	5%	0.4	25.6	127	$19
LIMA Plan	D	2nd Half		11	2	0	120	80	2.71	1.17	266			30.6	31%	78%	3.85	46	19	36	1.4	6.0	4.4	5%	0.5	24.2	95	$17
+/- Score	-16	09	Proj	16	8	0	203	150	3.59	1.28	265			25.8	31%	75%	4.13	43	18	39	2.4	6.7	2.8	8%	0.9	7.4	76	$22

Except for the sudden emphasis on GBs, breakout was really a consolidation of skills he already owned. Late-season Dom dip and big IP spike raise workload concerns, but very good chance he'll repeat to level of xERA.

Lester,Jon

Lester,Jon		Yr	Tm	W	L	Sv	IP	K	ERA	WHIP	OBA	vL	vR	BF/G	H%	S%	xERA	G	L	F	Ctl	Dom	Cmd	hr/f	hr/9	RAR	BPV	R$
LH	Starter	04		0	0	0	0	0	0.00	0.00																		
Age	25	05	aa	1	6	0	148	139	3.40	1.30	244			24.1	31%	75%	3.49				3.5	8.4	2.4		0.7	16.5	87	$11
Type	Pwr	06	BOS	* 10	6	0	127	100	4.39	1.64	283	397	271	22.3	33%	75%	4.93	41	22	38	4.8	7.1	1.5	8%	0.9	2.7	16	$8
Health	C	07	BOS	* 9	5	0	140	97	4.69	1.52	270	231	267	23.1	31%	70%	5.31	34	19	47	4.3	6.2	1.4	7%	0.9	-3.1	8	$7
PT/Exp	B	08	BOS	16	6	0	210	152	3.21	1.27	254	217	273	26.7	30%	76%	3.96	47	21	32	2.8	6.5	2.3	7%	0.6	29.5	66	$23
Consist	B	1st Half		6	3	0	109	68	3.48	1.35	261			25.8	29%	76%	4.35	47	20	32	3.2	5.6	1.7	8%	0.7	11.7	40	$9
LIMA Plan	F	2nd Half		10	3	0	102	84	2.92	1.19	247			27.8	31%	76%	3.56	48	21	31	2.4	7.4	3.1	5%	0.4	17.9	95	$15
+/- Score	-15	09	Proj	12	7	0	183	136	3.98	1.38	261			24.6	30%	73%	4.34	44	21	36	3.5	6.7	1.9	8%	0.8	1.9	48	$15

Altered approach (worked inside more) with success. Flipped G/F ratio and made major Cmd/BPV gains in 2H. But don't ignore workload concerns after 70 IP spike. It could be too good, too much, too soon.

Lewis,Jensen

Lewis,Jensen		Yr	Tm	W	L	Sv	IP	K	ERA	WHIP	OBA	vL	vR	BF/G	H%	S%	xERA	G	L	F	Ctl	Dom	Cmd	hr/f	hr/9	RAR	BPV	R$
RH	Reliever	04		0	0	0	0	0	0.00	0.00																		
Age	24	05		0	0	0	0	0	0.00	0.00																		
Type	Pwr FB	06	aa	1	2	0	39	39	4.83	1.51	299			24.7	38%	69%	4.99				2.8	9.0	3.3		0.9	-1.5	90	$2
Health	A	07	CLE	* 4	1	2	81	89	2.10	1.11	216			5.5	30%	83%	3.65	32	19	48	3.0	9.9	3.3	4%	0.4	24.1	107	$14
PT/Exp	D	08	CLE	* 1	6	14	86	70	4.19	1.44	264	267	264	6.1	31%	74%	4.57	35	25	40	3.9	7.3	1.9	10%	1.0	1.7	41	$8
Consist	C	1st Half		1	4	1	50	37	4.35	1.51	263			7.1	30%	73%	5.06	34	24	42	4.5	6.7	1.5	8%	0.9	0.0	10	$2
LIMA Plan	C+	2nd Half		0	2	13	36	33	3.97	1.35	265			5.0	32%	75%	3.97	37	25	39	3.0	8.2	2.8	12%	1.2	1.7	82	$6
+/- Score	10	09	Proj	1	3	18	58	52	3.88	1.31	252			6.3	30%	74%	4.12	35	24	41	3.3	8.1	2.5	10%	1.1	2.2	70	$10

Stepped into closer role in Aug and BPV skyrocketed. 13 saves without a BS as closer also says he's up to the job. But CLE wants to bring in someone else, which will drive down his spring value. Capitalize.

Lewis,Scott

Lewis,Scott		Yr	Tm	W	L	Sv	IP	K	ERA	WHIP	OBA	vL	vR	BF/G	H%	S%	xERA	G	L	F	Ctl	Dom	Cmd	hr/f	hr/9	RAR	BPV	R$
LH	Starter	04		0	0	0	0	0	0.00	0.00																		
Age	25	05		0	0	0	0	0	0.00	0.00																		
Type	Con xFB	06		0	0	0	0	0	0.00	0.00																		
Health	A	07	aa	7	9	0	134	105	4.73	1.49	301			21.9	35%	69%	5.05				2.5	7.0	2.8		0.9	-4.4	69	$7
PT/Exp	D	08	CLE	* 12	4	0	121	84	3.18	1.17	262	130	254	23.6	30%	75%	4.42	36	12	51	1.5	6.3	4.1	5%	0.7	17.4	86	$16
Consist	B	1st Half		5	3	0	73	59	1.81	1.02	235			24.0	28%	86%					1.4	7.2	5.1		0.6	22.9	140	$13
LIMA Plan	C+	2nd Half		7	1	0	48	26	5.27	1.40	299			23.0	33%	62%	5.15	36	12	51	1.7	4.8	2.8	5%	0.7	-5.5	54	$4
+/- Score	-13	09	Proj	10	8	0	133	88	4.20	1.28	270			23.3	30%	71%	4.70	36	12	51	2.1	6.0	2.8	8%	1.2	-4.6	65	$12

4-0. 2.62 ERA in 24 IP at CLE. Four token starts in Sept may put him in hunt for rotation spot. Cmd numbers say he could have some success, and if he can recapture 2007 Dom...
UP: 13 wins, 3.75 ERA.

Lidge,Brad

Lidge,Brad		Yr	Tm	W	L	Sv	IP	K	ERA	WHIP	OBA	vL	vR	BF/G	H%	S%	xERA	G	L	F	Ctl	Dom	Cmd	hr/f	hr/9	RAR	BPV	R$
RH	Reliever	04	HOU	6	5	29	94	157	1.91	0.92	177	191	155	4.5	31%	85%	2.24	32	21	47	2.9	15.0	5.2	10%	0.8	27.3	203	$28
Age	32	05	HOU	4	4	42	70	103	2.31	1.15	227	244	202	4.1	36%	83%	2.35	47	23	30	2.9	13.2	4.5	11%	0.6	16.8	183	$25
Type	Pwr	06	HOU	1	5	32	75	104	5.28	1.40	246	286	201	4.2	35%	64%	3.00	44	23	33	4.3	12.5	2.9	17%	1.2	-7.3	130	$15
Health	B	07	HOU	5	3	19	67	88	3.36	1.25	222	184	243	4.2	31%	79%	3.22	42	15	43	4.0	11.8	2.9	13%	1.2	8.8	124	$15
PT/Exp	A	08	PHI	2	0	41	69	92	1.95	1.23	204	273	105	4.0	32%	84%	3.01	46	22	32	4.5	11.9	2.6	4%	0.3	19.9	117	$24
Consist	A	1st Half		1	0	19	32	42	0.84	1.06	174			4.0	28%	91%	2.84	46	22	32	4.2	11.8	2.8	0%	0.0	13.5	123	$12
LIMA Plan	C+	2nd Half		1	0	22	37	50	2.90	1.37	228			4.0	34%	80%	3.15	46	21	33	4.8	12.1	2.5	7%	0.5	6.3	111	$11
+/- Score	-41	09	Proj	3	2	45	73	93	3.10	1.20	206			4.0	30%	77%	3.09	44	20	36	4.2	11.5	2.7	10%	0.7	11.2	116	$24

A remarkable turnaround year, except for one little detail: skills were there all along. ERA will return to mortal levels as hr/f finds a midpoint, but that leaves plenty of room for an effective, even elite, closer.

Lieber,Jon

Lieber,Jon		Yr	Tm	W	L	Sv	IP	K	ERA	WHIP	OBA	vL	vR	BF/G	H%	S%	xERA	G	L	F	Ctl	Dom	Cmd	hr/f	hr/9	RAR	BPV	R$
RH	Reliever	04	NYY	14	8	0	176	102	4.34	1.33	303	346	250	27.7	33%	70%	3.90	52	15	33	0.9	5.2	5.7	10%	1.0	2.0	99	$13
Age	39	05	PHI	17	13	0	218	149	4.21	1.21	266	305	223	25.7	29%	70%	3.75	46	22	33	1.7	6.1	3.6	15%	1.4	1.0	89	$20
Type	Con	06	PHI	9	11	0	168	100	4.93	1.31	293	304	278	26.3	31%	66%	4.10	43	22	35	1.3	5.4	4.2	13%	1.4	-9.1	83	$9
Health	F	07	PHI	3	6	0	78	54	4.73	1.45	293	310	278	24.3	34%	68%	4.09	44	28	29	2.5	6.2	2.5	9%	0.8	-2.9	65	$3
PT/Exp	C	08	CHC	2	3	0	47	27	4.05	1.39	309	368	272	7.7	32%	80%	4.34	40	21	39	1.2	5.2	4.5	16%	1.9	1.3	80	$2
Consist	A	1st Half		2	3	0	42	23	3.02	1.34	303			7.7	32%	86%	4.38	39	22	39	1.1	5.0	4.6	12%	1.5	6.4	77	$3
LIMA Plan	B+	2nd Half		0	0	0	5	4	12.60	1.80	362			7.9	33%	33%	4.05	44	17	39	1.8	7.2	4.0	43%	5.4	-5.1	103	($1)
+/- Score	5	09	Proj	5	6	0	87	53	4.14	1.37	290			23.3	32%	73%	4.29	43	21	35	2.0	5.5	2.8	11%	1.1	0.5	67	$5

Foot and arm injuries cost him 2H. On a lesser team, he likely would have spent some time in rotation. Skills say he can still help in that role, although rising BA vs LH is the first sign of his approaching skills demise.

Lilly,Ted

Lilly,Ted		Yr	Tm	W	L	Sv	IP	K	ERA	WHIP	OBA	vL	vR	BF/G	H%	S%	xERA	G	L	F	Ctl	Dom	Cmd	hr/f	hr/9	RAR	BPV	R$
LH	Starter	04	TOR	12	10	0	197	168	4.06	1.32	235	196	238	26.1	27%	73%	4.52	36	18	46	4.1	7.7	1.9	10%	1.2	9.0	42	$17
Age	33	05	TOR	10	11	0	126	96	5.57	1.53	275	336	248	22.4	30%	68%	4.82	37	22	41	4.1	6.9	1.7	14%	1.6	-18.6	26	$5
Type	Pwr xFB	06	TOR	15	13	0	181	160	4.32	1.43	259	202	265	24.7	30%	75%	4.44	38	19	43	4.0	7.9	2.0	12%	1.4	5.3	50	$17
Health	B	07	CHC	15	8	0	207	174	3.83	1.14	237	258	230	24.7	27%	71%	4.11	34	17	49	2.4	7.6	3.2	10%	1.2	15.3	83	$24
PT/Exp	A	08	CHC	17	9	0	205	184	4.09	1.23	245	307	219	25.0	28%	72%	4.01	34	22	44	2.8	8.1	2.9	12%	1.4	4.6	81	$21
Consist	A	1st Half		9	5	0	107	100	4.55	1.30	251			25.0	29%	70%	4.11	33	22	45	3.2	8.4	2.6	13%	1.5	-3.7	76	$9
LIMA Plan	D+	2nd Half		8	4	0	98	84	3.58	1.14	237			24.9	27%	74%	3.91	34	22	43	2.4	7.7	3.2	12%	1.3	8.3	87	$12
+/- Score	8	09	Proj	16	10	0	203	176	4.13	1.27	251			25.0	29%	72%	4.18	35	20	45	3.0	7.8	2.6	11%	1.3	3.9	73	$19

Followed up on 2007 breakout with a carbon copy performance. Fly balls will get him in trouble some days, but one-time enigma has morphed into a highly-skilled stable and consistent SP option.

Lincecum,Tim

Lincecum,Tim		Yr	Tm	W	L	Sv	IP	K	ERA	WHIP	OBA	vL	vR	BF/G	H%	S%	xERA	G	L	F	Ctl	Dom	Cmd	hr/f	hr/9	RAR	BPV	R$
RH	Starter	04		0	0	0	0	0	0.00	0.00																		
Age	24	05		0	0	0	0	0	0.00	0.00																		
Type	Pwr	06		0	0	0	0	0	0.00	0.00																		
Health	A	07	SF	* 11	5	0	177	188	3.35	1.20	214	214	238	25.2	29%	73%	3.52	47	15	38	3.9	9.5	2.5	7%	0.6	23.5	92	$22
PT/Exp	C	08	SF	18	5	0	227	265	2.62	1.17	221	221	221	27.3	31%	78%	3.17	44	21	35	3.3	10.5	3.2	6%	0.4	46.3	121	$33
Consist	A	1st Half		9	1	0	110	114	2.38	1.24	231			26.8	31%	82%	3.50	44	22	34	3.5	9.4	2.7	5%	0.4	25.6	96	$15
LIMA Plan	C	2nd Half		9	4	0	117	151	2.84	1.11	212			27.8	32%	75%	2.87	43	20	37	3.1	11.6	3.7	6%	0.5	20.7	145	$18
+/- Score	19	09	Proj	12	7	0	198	222	3.14	1.18	218			26.1	30%	75%	3.30	45	19	36	3.6	10.1	2.8	7%	0.6	25.3	109	$25

One of the game's best SPs. Huge BPV, elite Dom with decent GB% in support, kicked skills to another level in 2H. Still-improving Ctl, shreds LH and RH hitters. Workload a concern, but this skill set is nearly flawless.

Lincoln,Mike

Lincoln,Mike		Yr	Tm	W	L	Sv	IP	K	ERA	WHIP	OBA	vL	vR	BF/G	H%	S%	xERA	G	L	F	Ctl	Dom	Cmd	hr/f	hr/9	RAR	BPV	R$
RH	Reliever	04	STL	3	2	0	17	14	5.26	0.94	172	130	184	5.1	21%	40%	3.39	57	10	34	3.2	7.4	2.3	7%	0.5	-2.1	82	$3
Age	34	05		0	0	0	0	0	0.00	0.00																		
Type	Pwr GB	06		0	0	0	0	0	0.00	0.00																		
Health	F	07		0	0	0	0	0	0.00	0.00																		
PT/Exp	D	08	CIN	2	5	0	70	57	4.48	1.28	250	225	268	4.6	28%	69%	3.63	52	18	30	3.1	7.3	2.4	16%	1.3	-1.8	79	$4
Consist	F	1st Half		0	2	0	38	31	4.50	1.16	241			5.3	26%	68%	2.98	60	17	23	2.4	7.3	3.1	27%	1.7	-1.1	106	$2
LIMA Plan	B+	2nd Half		2	3	0	32	26	4.46	1.42	260			4.0	31%	70%	4.39	44	18	38	3.9	7.2	1.9	8%	0.8	-0.7	47	$2
+/- Score	24	09	Proj	3	5	0	69	55	4.07	1.34	258			4.5	30%	72%	3.86	53	15	33	3.3	7.2	2.2	10%	0.9	4.1	72	$5

2-5, 4.48 ERA in 70 IP at CIN. Took three years to come back from a pair of TJ surgeries, with skills remarkably in line with pre-injury levels. If he can avoid a third TJ surgery, he makes a nice end-game LIMA pickup.

RAY MURPHY

Lindstrom,Matt

		Yr	Tm	W	L	Sv	IP	K	ERA	WHIP	OBA	vL	vR	BF/G	H%	S%	xERA	G	L	F	Ctl	Dom	Cmd	hr/f	hr/9	RAR	BPV	R$
RH	Reliever	04		0	0	0	0	0	0.00	0.00																		
Age	29	05	aa	2	5	0	73	44	6.43	2.26	341			10.8	37%	74%	8.18				7.3	5.4	0.7		1.5	-19.2	-10	($8)
Type	Pwr	06	aa	2	4	11	40	40	6.18	1.89	341			5.5	43%	66%	6.24				3.9	9.0	2.3		0.5	-8.2	74	$3
Health	A	07	FLA	3	4	0	67	62	3.09	1.30	259	263	255	4.0	34%	75%	3.70	47	16	36	2.8	8.3	3.0	3%	0.3	11.0	99	$7
PT/Exp	D	08	FLA	3	3	5	57	43	3.14	1.45	261	324	214	3.8	32%	77%	4.35	46	23	30	4.1	6.8	1.7	2%	0.2	8.0	36	$6
Consist	D	1st Half		1	1	0	24	19	5.19	1.93	318			3.9	39%	70%	4.90	47	29	24	5.6	7.0	1.3	0%	0.0	-2.7	2	($1)
LIMA Plan	C+	2nd Half		2	2	5	33	24	1.64	1.09	212			3.7	26%	86%	3.96	46	18	36	3.0	6.5	2.2	3%	0.3	10.7	61	$7
+/- Score	-22	09	Proj	3	4	20	58	46	3.88	1.36	248			4.2	29%	73%	4.13	47	21	33	3.9	7.1	1.8	9%	0.8	1.5	49	$11

Closing, but for how long?
- Prone to Ctl, Cmd issues
- Declining Dom rate
- Artificially low hr/f
- Sizable ERA/xERA variance
- 2007 BPV not closer-worthy

These are risky saves to chase.

Linebrink,Scott

		Yr	Tm	W	L	Sv	IP	K	ERA	WHIP	OBA	vL	vR	BF/G	H%	S%	xERA	G	L	F	Ctl	Dom	Cmd	hr/f	hr/9	RAR	BPV	R$
RH	Reliever	04	SD	7	3	0	84	83	2.14	1.04	205	178	236	4.6	26%	85%	3.68	33	21	46	2.8	8.9	3.2	8%	0.9	22.0	96	$14
Age	32	05	SD	8	1	1	73	70	1.84	1.07	210	195	223	4.0	27%	85%	3.62	39	21	41	2.8	8.6	3.0	5%	0.5	21.7	95	$14
Type	FB	06	SD	7	4	2	75	68	3.59	1.22	248	204	294	4.3	30%	75%	3.84	39	19	42	2.6	8.1	3.1	10%	1.1	8.3	93	$10
Health	B	07	2NL	5	6	1	70	50	3.71	1.32	255	215	284	4.2	27%	79%	4.29	42	21	37	3.2	6.4	2.0	15%	1.5	6.2	49	$7
PT/Exp	C	08	CHW	2	2	1	46	40	3.69	1.08	239	200	263	3.7	27%	74%	3.61	39	18	43	1.7	7.8	4.4	14%	1.6	3.7	110	$6
Consist	B	1st Half		2	2	0	33	29	1.36	0.82	184			3.4	22%	92%	3.23	43	16	41	1.6	7.9	4.8	9%	0.8	12.1	119	$7
LIMA Plan	A	2nd Half		0	0	1	13	11	9.47	1.73	348			4.4	36%	50%	4.56	32	21	47	2.0	7.4	3.7	23%	3.4	-8.4	89	($1)
+/- Score	8	09	Proj	5	3	0	58	51	3.26	1.10	234			4.0	28%	75%	3.72	38	20	42	2.2	7.9	3.6	10%	1.1	5.1	100	$9

A strong rebound season, and Cmd and BPV were better than peak years in SD. 2nd half drop caused by shoulder injury and bad luck. As long as shoulder is healthy, looks ready to go back to being a LIMA-worthy pick.

Liriano,Francisco

		Yr	Tm	W	L	Sv	IP	K	ERA	WHIP	OBA	vL	vR	BF/G	H%	S%	xERA	G	L	F	Ctl	Dom	Cmd	hr/f	hr/9	RAR	BPV	R$
LH	Starter	04	aa	3	2	0	39	46	3.94	1.72	313			26.0	42%	79%	5.76				3.9	10.6	2.7		0.9	2.0	86	$2
Age	25	05	MIN *	13	9	0	190	220	3.41	1.12	226	222	221	23.3	31%	71%	2.82	50	19	31	2.7	10.4	3.9	9%	0.6	22.6	143	$27
Type	Pwr	06	MIN	12	3	1	121	144	2.16	1.00	207	202	206	16.9	29%	82%	2.33	55	21	23	2.4	10.7	4.5	13%	0.7	35.8	162	$26
Health	F	07	MIN	0	0	0	0	0	0.00	0.00																		
PT/Exp	C	08	MIN *	16	6	0	194	160	3.85	1.30	256	217	266	24.8	31%	71%	4.14	42	18	40	3.0	7.4	2.5	6%	0.7	11.9	73	$20
Consist	D	1st Half		5	5	0	94	65	5.44	1.53	281			24.7	33%	64%	4.68	43	23	34	3.8	6.2	1.6	7%	0.7	-12.7	29	$2
LIMA Plan	C+	2nd Half		11	1	0	100	95	2.35	1.08	230			24.9	29%	82%	3.50	41	17	41	2.2	8.6	4.0	7%	0.7	24.6	115	$18
+/- Score	4	09	Proj	15	9	0	203	198	3.46	1.20	239			25.3	30%	73%	3.27	49	20	31	2.8	8.8	3.1	9%	0.7	28.9	110	$26

6-4, 3.91 ERA in 76 IP at MIN. Found post-TJ surgery comfort zone in 2nd half, though Dom shows he's not quite all the way back, and rising FB% puts him at risk for HR. Don't pay for the 2006 version just yet.

Litsch,Jesse

		Yr	Tm	W	L	Sv	IP	K	ERA	WHIP	OBA	vL	vR	BF/G	H%	S%	xERA	G	L	F	Ctl	Dom	Cmd	hr/f	hr/9	RAR	BPV	R$
RH	Starter	04		0	0	0	0	0	0.00	0.00																		
Age	24	05		0	0	0	0	0	0.00	0.00																		
Type	Con	06	aa	3	4	0	69	47	7.29	1.74	352			26.8	40%	57%	6.58				1.8	6.1	3.4		1.0	-23.6	61	($3)
Health	A	07	TOR *	15	11	0	187	98	3.42	1.29	264	308	229	24.6	28%	77%	4.43	48	18	34	2.5	4.7	1.8	9%	1.0	25.2	42	$19
PT/Exp	C	08	TOR	13	9	0	176	99	3.58	1.23	264	270	250	25.2	28%	75%	4.06	49	20	32	2.0	5.1	2.5	11%	1.0	16.7	64	$18
Consist	C	1st Half		8	4	0	97	52	3.82	1.21	272			25.0	29%	74%	3.97	49	19	33	1.4	4.8	3.5	13%	1.3	6.3	76	$10
LIMA Plan	D+	2nd Half		5	5	0	79	47	3.29	1.26	254			25.5	28%	76%	4.17	48	21	31	2.7	5.3	2.0	8%	0.7	10.3	49	$8
+/- Score	4	09	Proj	13	12	0	194	111	4.04	1.34	277			25.0	30%	72%	4.23	48	19	32	2.3	5.1	2.3	10%	1.0	4.6	58	$15

xERA shows this wasn't quite the breakout it appeared to be. Dom is below 5.6 tipping point, and shows almost no signs of growth. Likely overvalued in '09, so be prepared to just observe him from the opposing dugout.

Liz,Radhames

		Yr	Tm	W	L	Sv	IP	K	ERA	WHIP	OBA	vL	vR	BF/G	H%	S%	xERA	G	L	F	Ctl	Dom	Cmd	hr/f	hr/9	RAR	BPV	R$
RH	Starter	04		0	0	0	0	0	0.00	0.00																		
Age	25	05		0	0	0	0	0	0.00	0.00																		
Type	Pwr xFB	06	aa	3	1	0	50	48	7.59	2.04	328			24.8	38%	67%	8.01				5.9	8.5	1.4		2.2	-19.0	4	($3)
Health	A	07	BAL *	11	6	0	162	157	4.46	1.48	243	244	275	20.9	30%	72%	5.00	23	25	52	5.2	8.7	1.7	8%	1.0	1.0	18	$13
PT/Exp	D	08	BAL *	9	13	0	171	130	5.49	1.57	279	318	269	24.0	32%	67%	5.14	34	20	46	4.3	6.8	1.6	9%	1.2	-24.1	20	$4
Consist	D	1st Half		3	5	0	84	68	5.09	1.44	262			22.8	31%	66%	5.06	26	22	52	4.0	7.4	1.8	7%	1.0	-7.6	29	$3
LIMA Plan	D+	2nd Half		6	8	0	88	62	5.87	1.68	295			25.2	33%	68%	5.37	36	20	44	4.5	6.3	1.4	11%	1.4	-16.4	6	$1
+/- Score	-8	09	Proj	7	12	0	160	127	4.91	1.49	265			24.3	30%	70%	4.98	33	21	47	4.3	7.2	1.7	10%	1.3	-10.9	24	$7

6-6, 6.72 ERA in 84 IP at BAL. Just as he gets Ctl and FB% heading in the right direction, strikeouts decline. Apparently he's a terrible multi-tasker. Now has 6.77 ERA in 109 MLB IP, with 1.1 Cmd. Pass. Then flee.

Loe,Kameron

		Yr	Tm	W	L	Sv	IP	K	ERA	WHIP	OBA	vL	vR	BF/G	H%	S%	xERA	G	L	F	Ctl	Dom	Cmd	hr/f	hr/9	RAR	BPV	R$
RH	Reliever	04	a/a	12	9	0	157	115	4.24	1.54	311			26.9	36%	74%	5.27				2.4	6.6	2.8		0.9	1.9	65	$9
Age	27	05	TEX *	11	7	1	120	65	3.97	1.37	268	284	223	9.7	29%	74%	3.82	61	16	22	3.0	4.9	1.6	15%	1.0	5.9	46	$11
Type	Con GB	06	TEX	3	6	0	78	34	5.88	1.63	323	313	321	23.7	34%	65%	4.79	51	19	30	2.5	3.9	1.5	11%	1.0	-12.7	31	($1)
Health	B	07	TEX	6	11	0	136	78	5.36	1.60	297	328	262	22.0	33%	67%	4.43	56	18	26	3.7	5.2	1.4	11%	0.9	-14.3	27	$2
PT/Exp	C	08	TEX *	4	5	1	89	42	6.13	1.80	340	400	200	10.5	36%	68%	5.13	50	16	33	3.1	4.3	1.4	11%	1.3	-19.5	21	($3)
Consist	B	1st Half		3	4	0	47	24	6.68	1.99	370			9.9	40%	67%	5.57	41	22	38	3.0	4.7	1.6	8%	1.1	-13.4	23	($3)
LIMA Plan	C+	2nd Half		1	1	1	42	18	5.52	1.59	303			11.2	31%	68%	4.88	55	14	32	3.3	3.8	1.2	14%	1.5	-6.1	13	($0)
+/- Score	7	09	Proj	2	3	0	44	22	5.38	1.61	310			14.1	33%	68%	4.59	54	17	29	3.1	4.6	1.5	11%	1.0	-0.9	30	$0

1-0, 3.23 ERA in 31 IP at TEX. Somehow pitched better in majors than Triple-A, including 2.5 Cmd. But he's just a reliever who can only retire RH. If your league is deep enough to make that valuable, we're impressed.

Logan,Boone

		Yr	Tm	W	L	Sv	IP	K	ERA	WHIP	OBA	vL	vR	BF/G	H%	S%	xERA	G	L	F	Ctl	Dom	Cmd	hr/f	hr/9	RAR	BPV	R$
LH	Reliever	04		0	0	0	0	0	0.00	0.00																		
Age	24	05		0	0	0	0	0	0.00	0.00																		
Type	Pwr	06	CHW *	3	1	12	59	66	5.46	1.49	267			4.4	37%	61%	3.83	44	17	39	4.2	10.1	2.4	5%	0.4	-6.6	91	$7
Health	A	07	CHW	2	1	0	51	35	4.97	1.56	292	221	357	3.3	33%	71%	4.48	51	14	35	3.6	6.2	1.8	12%	1.2	-2.9	45	$1
PT/Exp	D	08	CHW	2	3	0	42	42	5.96	1.68	323	291	351	3.5	39%	67%	3.86	43	23	34	3.0	8.9	3.0	15%	1.5	-8.4	102	$0
Consist	B	1st Half		2	1	0	28	29	2.23	1.10	239			3.4	31%	83%	3.24	41	21	38	1.9	9.2	4.8	7%	0.6	7.4	133	$5
LIMA Plan	A+	2nd Half		0	2	0	14	13	13.50	2.86	448			3.7	50%	54%	5.24	47	25	28	5.1	8.4	1.6	30%	3.2	-15.8	36	($5)
+/- Score	87	09	Proj	2	1	0	40	39	3.87	1.34	259			3.7	33%	73%	3.54	47	20	33	3.2	8.9	2.8	11%	0.9	4.3	99	$4

2nd half implosion undermined terrific season with solid Ctl and Cmd growth. H%, hr/f indicate he's been plagued by bad luck. Let's face it: if a RH pitcher had those 1H skills, we'd be yelling "future closer!" For now, LIMA.

Lohse,Kyle

		Yr	Tm	W	L	Sv	IP	K	ERA	WHIP	OBA	vL	vR	BF/G	H%	S%	xERA	G	L	F	Ctl	Dom	Cmd	hr/f	hr/9	RAR	BPV	R$
RH	Starter	04	MIN	9	13	0	194	111	5.34	1.63	305	290	324	25.2	33%	70%	5.03	45	18	37	3.5	5.1	1.5	11%	1.3	-21.6	20	$1
Age	30	05	MIN	9	13	0	178	86	4.19	1.43	296	291	305	25.0	31%	74%	4.64	44	22	34	2.2	4.3	2.0	10%	1.1	3.9	40	$9
Type	Con	06	2TM *	7	11	0	150	106	5.30	1.48	287	288	304	17.4	33%	65%	4.50	43	20	37	3.1	6.4	2.1	9%	1.0	-14.4	52	$5
Health	A	07	2NL	9	12	0	193	122	4.62	1.37	276	276	282	24.3	31%	68%	4.68	37	22	41	2.7	5.7	2.1	8%	1.0	-4.7	46	$10
PT/Exp	A	08	STL	15	6	0	200	119	3.78	1.30	272	254	285	25.6	30%	73%	4.17	46	22	32	2.2	5.4	2.4	9%	0.8	12.1	61	$17
Consist	A	1st Half		10	2	0	105	50	3.68	1.27	267			24.5	29%	72%	4.39	48	20	32	2.2	4.3	1.9	6%	0.6	7.7	43	$10
LIMA Plan	D+	2nd Half		5	4	0	95	69	3.90	1.33	278			26.8	32%	74%	3.93	43	25	32	2.2	6.6	3.0	11%	1.0	4.4	80	$7
+/- Score	-8	09	Proj	11	9	0	189	119	4.34	1.37	279			23.8	31%	70%	4.39	43	22	35	2.5	5.7	2.2	9%	1.0	-1.1	55	$11

ERA improvement has rapidly outpaced his skill growth, which has been gradual at best. 2H was nice, but are you willing to bet big bucks on one good half-season vs. four and a half mediocre ones? We're not.

Looper,Braden

		Yr	Tm	W	L	Sv	IP	K	ERA	WHIP	OBA	vL	vR	BF/G	H%	S%	xERA	G	L	F	Ctl	Dom	Cmd	hr/f	hr/9	RAR	BPV	R$
RH	Starter	04	NYM	2	5	29	83	60	2.71	1.23	268	311	227	4.9	32%	79%	3.14	62	15	23	1.7	6.5	3.8	8%	0.5	15.9	110	$17
Age	34	05	NYM	4	7	28	59	27	3.96	1.47	281	336	210	4.3	29%	76%	4.64	51	21	27	3.4	4.1	1.2	12%	1.1	2.1	13	$12
Type	Con	06	STL	9	3	0	73	41	3.57	1.31	269	287	272	4.5	31%	72%	4.23	49	20	30	2.5	5.0	2.1	4%	0.4	8.3	52	$9
Health	A	07	STL	12	12	0	175	87	4.94	1.34	271	279	261	24.0	28%	65%	4.71	42	21	36	2.6	4.5	1.7	10%	1.1	-11.0	30	$10
PT/Exp	A	08	STL	12	14	0	199	108	4.16	1.31	278	279	279	25.5	30%	72%	4.19	48	20	32	2.0	4.9	2.4	12%	1.1	2.7	59	$13
Consist	B	1st Half		9	5	0	99	44	4.26	1.40	288			25.2	30%	71%	4.60	48	20	32	2.4	4.0	1.7	9%	0.9	0.1	34	$6
LIMA Plan	C	2nd Half		3	9	0	100	64	4.06	1.22	268			25.8	29%	72%	3.81	48	19	32	1.7	5.8	3.4	14%	1.4	2.6	84	$6
+/- Score	-7	09	Proj	13	14	0	198	109	4.19	1.32	274			24.6	30%	71%	4.26	48	20	32	2.3	5.0	2.2	10%	1.0	2.0	54	$14

PRO: Relocated above-average Dom and elite Cmd in 2nd half.
CON: The three and a half years in between when they were nowhere to be found.
Value him at '07 level; hope he revisits those glory days again.

BRANDON KRUSE

Lopez,Aquilino			W	L	Sv	IP	K	ERA	WHIP	OBA	vL	vR	BF/G	H%	S%	xERA	G	L	F	Ctl	Dom	Cmd	hr/f	hr/9	RAR	BPV	R$
RH	Reliever	04 TOR *	2	7	5	63	38	7.29	1.75	326			5.9	33%	63%	7.48				3.4	5.4	1.6		2.3	-22.2	-13	($2)
Age	34	05 2NL *	5	5	5	81	79	4.92	1.29	274	346	184	6.1	32%	69%	3.61	33	26	40	2.0	8.8	4.4	18%	1.9	-6.7	115	$8
Type	xFB	06 aaa	3	4	2	62	60	5.65	1.53	287			6.7	33%	68%	5.72				3.5	8.7	2.5		1.8	-8.7	47	$3
Health	A	07 DET *	3	5	27	71	55	3.70	1.33	276			5.2	32%	76%	4.15	44	13	43	2.2	7.0	3.1	9%	1.1	7.0	87	$15
PT/Exp	D	08 DET	4	1	0	79	61	3.55	1.37	279	298	265	7.0	32%	78%	4.65	29	22	49	2.5	7.0	2.8	7%	1.0	7.8	65	$7
Consist	C	1st Half	2	1	0	34	24	2.67	1.25	269			6.1	32%	80%	4.43	34	20	46	1.9	6.4	3.4	4%	0.5	7.0	77	$4
LIMA Plan	C+	2nd Half	2	0	0	45	37	4.20	1.47	287			7.9	33%	76%	4.81	26	23	51	3.0	7.4	2.5	10%	1.4	0.8	56	$3
+/- Score	-16	09 Proj	3	3	0	69	55	4.20	1.37	277			6.3	32%	74%	4.52	31	21	48	2.6	7.2	2.8	10%	1.3	-0.8	68	$5

Years of under-the-radar skills finally pay off in most valuable MLB season since 2003. But now xERA says he's overvalued, thanks to high FB% and risk of gopheritis. Can't his skills and surface stats just get along?

Lopez,Javier			W	L	Sv	IP	K	ERA	WHIP	OBA	vL	vR	BF/G	H%	S%	xERA	G	L	F	Ctl	Dom	Cmd	hr/f	hr/9	RAR	BPV	R$
LH	Reliever	04 COL	1	2	0	40	20	7.61	1.77	284	221	350	2.9	32%	53%	5.22	55	23	22	5.8	4.5	0.8	3%	0.2	-16.6	-44	($3)
Age	31	05 2NL *	1	2	4	40	29	6.30	1.80	294			3.2	34%	64%	5.50				5.6	6.5	1.2		0.7	-10.1	39	($1)
Type	xGB	06 BOS *	3	1	17	65	41	2.96	1.56	294	250	208	4.4	34%	82%	3.35	65	22	13	3.5	5.6	1.6	15%	0.6	12.9	51	$10
Health	A	07 BOS *	4	2	0	57	38	3.80	1.55	277	293	176	3.3	33%	75%	4.47	53	20	28	4.3	6.0	1.4	4%	0.3	5.0	23	$4
PT/Exp	D	08 BOS	2	0	0	59	38	2.43	1.35	241	182	311	3.6	27%	84%	3.91	60	18	22	4.1	5.8	1.4	10%	0.6	14.0	31	$6
Consist	B	1st Half	2	0	0	31	17	2.32	1.32	243			3.6	26%	87%	4.27	57	15	28	3.8	4.9	1.3	11%	0.9	7.7	22	$3
LIMA Plan	D+	2nd Half	0	0	0	28	21	2.54	1.38	239			3.7	29%	82%	3.45	62	22	16	4.5	6.7	1.5	8%	0.3	6.3	40	$2
+/- Score	-77	09 Proj	2	1	0	44	28	3.93	1.49	264			3.6	30%	74%	4.12	58	20	22	4.3	5.8	1.3	10%	0.6	1.6	23	$2

Can you spot the factors behind his career-best 2.43 ERA? Sure, a 60% GB rate helps, but the real heroes were H% and S%. His Cmd and BPV histories tell you all you need to know. You can safely ignore him.

Lowe,Derek			W	L	Sv	IP	K	ERA	WHIP	OBA	vL	vR	BF/G	H%	S%	xERA	G	L	F	Ctl	Dom	Cmd	hr/f	hr/9	RAR	BPV	R$
RH	Starter	04 BOS	14	12	0	189	110	5.23	1.60	299	305	293	25.9	33%	67%	3.97	62	17	20	3.5	5.2	1.5	12%	0.8	-18.7	39	$5
Age	35	05 LA	12	15	0	222	146	3.61	1.25	263	296	219	26.5	29%	76%	3.22	64	15	21	2.2	5.9	2.7	19%	1.1	17.5	88	$18
Type	Con xGB	06 LA	16	8	0	218	123	3.63	1.27	264	270	255	26.1	30%	72%	3.22	67	16	17	2.3	5.1	2.2	11%	0.6	23.0	75	$20
Health	A	07 LA	12	14	0	199	147	3.88	1.27	257	271	239	25.3	30%	72%	3.08	65	16	19	2.7	6.6	2.5	17%	0.9	13.3	91	$18
PT/Exp	A	08 LA	14	11	0	211	147	3.24	1.13	246	251	240	25.2	29%	72%	3.17	60	17	23	1.9	6.3	3.3	10%	0.6	26.8	99	$23
Consist	A	1st Half	5	8	0	111	82	3.88	1.27	263			25.9	31%	71%	3.38	58	17	25	2.3	6.6	2.8	12%	0.8	5.3	92	$8
LIMA Plan	C	2nd Half	9	3	0	100	65	2.53	0.98	226			24.3	27%	74%	2.92	62	17	21	1.4	5.9	4.1	7%	0.4	21.4	107	$16
+/- Score	6	09 Proj	13	10	0	193	130	3.50	1.22	258			25.8	30%	73%	3.19	63	16	21	2.2	6.1	2.8	11%	0.7	27.4	91	$19

L.A. was good to him (2005-08):
Home - 2.78 ERA, 3.4 Cmd
Away - 4.28 ERA, 2.3 Cmd
But splits were similar with BOS, so solid home skills may travel just fine to any destination. Still, info worth tucking away.

Lowe,Mark			W	L	Sv	IP	K	ERA	WHIP	OBA	vL	vR	BF/G	H%	S%	xERA	G	L	F	Ctl	Dom	Cmd	hr/f	hr/9	RAR	BPV	R$
RH	Reliever	04	0	0	0	0	0	0.00	0.00																		
Age	25	05	0	0	0	0	0	0.00	0.00																		
Type	Pwr	06 SEA *	1	1	3	32	28	1.98	1.13	225	167	205	5.4	29%	83%	3.54	49	19	33	2.8	7.8	2.8	3%	0.3	10.2	91	$6
Health	D	07 SEA	0	0	0	3	3	6.67	1.85	208			3.2	18%	75%	6.92				10.0	10.0	1.0		3.3	-0.7	-6	($0)
PT/Exp	D	08 SEA	1	5	1	64	55	5.37	1.76	303	354	250	5.2	37%	70%	4.70	45	21	35	4.8	7.8	1.6	9%	0.8	-8.0	33	($0)
Consist	F	1st Half	1	3	1	37	35	4.34	1.64	280			5.1	36%	73%	4.31	46	22	32	4.8	8.4	1.8	6%	0.5	0.0	46	$2
LIMA Plan	D	2nd Half	0	2	0	26	20	6.82	1.93	332			5.3	38%	66%	5.27	43	19	38	4.8	6.8	1.4	11%	1.4	-8.0	15	($2)
+/- Score	10	09 Proj	1	3	0	58	47	4.34	1.52	268			5.3	32%	73%	4.46	45	20	35	4.3	7.3	1.7	10%	0.9	-0.3	37	$2

Elbow injuries have turned him from a promising young reliever to a pitcher to avoid. Miserable 2nd half clouds his future even further. Until he gets Cmd back, act as though 2006 was someone else. Like Sidd Finch.

Lowry,Noah			W	L	Sv	IP	K	ERA	WHIP	OBA	vL	vR	BF/G	H%	S%	xERA	G	L	F	Ctl	Dom	Cmd	hr/f	hr/9	RAR	BPV	R$
LH	Reliever	04 SF *	13	5	0	181	134	3.98	1.35	273	338	238	23.4	32%	72%	4.32	42	17	41	2.6	6.7	2.5	7%	0.8	6.4	69	$14
Age	28	05 SF	13	13	0	204	172	3.79	1.32	251	213	259	26.2	30%	74%	4.15	41	20	39	3.3	7.6	2.3	9%	0.9	11.5	65	$18
Type		06 SF	7	10	0	159	84	4.75	1.40	270	312	262	25.4	28%	69%	5.22	36	18	45	3.2	4.8	1.5	9%	1.2	-5.2	14	$7
Health	F	07 SF	14	8	0	156	87	3.92	1.55	261	216	277	26.8	29%	76%	5.35	45	20	36	5.0	5.0	1.0	7%	0.7	9.7	-22	$10
PT/Exp	B	08 SF	0	0	0	0	0	0.00	0.00																		
Consist	A	1st Half	0	0	0	0	0	0.00	0.00																		
LIMA Plan		2nd Half	0	0	0	0	0	0.00	0.00																		
+/- Score		09 Proj	7	7	0	116	66	4.44	1.42	261			23.9	28%	71%	5.03	41	19	40	3.8	5.1	1.3	9%	1.0	-9.9	9	$6

Wrist surgery and elbow injury took away his season. Given his skill trends, it may have been for the best. We can hope that health will allow him to hit reset, but his issues go way back. Take a flyer, nothing more.

Lyon,Brandon			W	L	Sv	IP	K	ERA	WHIP	OBA	vL	vR	BF/G	H%	S%	xERA	G	L	F	Ctl	Dom	Cmd	hr/f	hr/9	RAR	BPV	R$
RH	Reliever	04 ARI	0	0	0	0	0	0.00	0.00											0.0	0.0						
Age	29	05 ARI	0	2	14	29	17	6.49	1.86	349	317	364	4.3	37%	69%	5.06	42	23	35	3.1	5.3	1.7	16%	1.9	-8.1	32	$2
Type		06 ARI	2	4	0	69	46	3.91	1.30	259	244	270	4.3	29%	72%	4.22	43	24	33	2.9	6.0	2.1	10%	0.9	4.9	51	$5
Health	C	07 ARI	6	4	2	74	40	2.68	1.24	251	233	267	4.2	29%	78%	4.64	43	19	38	2.7	4.9	1.8	2%	0.2	16.0	36	$10
PT/Exp	C	08 ARI	3	5	26	59	44	4.70	1.48	310	278	321	4.3	36%	70%	4.26	40	22	38	2.0	6.7	3.4	9%	1.1	-3.2	85	$11
Consist	A	1st Half	2	2	17	33	26	2.73	1.15	250			4.0	28%	85%	3.88	36	24	41	1.9	7.1	3.7	13%	1.4	6.3	90	$10
LIMA Plan	C+	2nd Half	1	3	9	26	18	7.19	1.90	372			4.7	43%	60%	4.75	44	21	35	2.1	6.2	3.0	6%	0.7	-9.5	77	$1
+/- Score	26	09 Proj	4	5	8	64	45	3.83	1.31	269			4.2	31%	74%	4.15	42	22	36	2.4	6.4	2.6	10%	1.0	1.5	70	$8

CON: xERA saw this ERA slide coming last year, and supported it this year.
PRO: Career-best Cmd, BPV say he's still a viable closer candidate. Except now you can buy him at a discount.

Maddux,Greg			W	L	Sv	IP	K	ERA	WHIP	OBA	vL	vR	BF/G	H%	S%	xERA	G	L	F	Ctl	Dom	Cmd	hr/f	hr/9	RAR	BPV	R$
RH	Starter	04 CHC	16	11	0	212	151	4.03	1.18	267	271	268	26.4	29%	72%	3.41	51	20	29	1.4	6.4	4.6	18%	1.5	6.1	106	$21
Age	43	05 CHC	13	15	0	225	136	4.24	1.22	274	283	270	26.6	30%	69%	3.59	52	22	27	1.4	5.4	3.8	15%	1.2	0.2	89	$17
Type	Con GB	06 2NL	15	14	0	210	117	4.20	1.22	270	254	284	25.6	30%	67%	3.81	51	21	28	1.6	5.0	3.2	10%	0.9	7.4	76	$18
Health	A	07 SD	14	11	0	198	104	4.14	1.24	284	280	289	24.2	31%	67%	3.86	51	20	29	1.1	4.7	4.2	7%	0.6	7.1	84	$16
PT/Exp	A	08 2NL	8	13	0	194	98	4.22	1.21	272	272	271	24.3	29%	67%	3.94	49	21	30	1.4	4.5	3.3	11%	1.0	1.2	72	$12
Consist	A	1st Half	3	6	0	107	53	4.04	1.26	274			24.9	29%	70%	4.04	49	23	28	1.8	4.5	2.5	10%	0.8	3.1	60	$6
LIMA Plan	C+	2nd Half	5	7	0	87	45	4.45	1.14	268			23.5	28%	64%	3.82	49	19	32	0.9	4.7	5.0	12%	1.1	-1.9	86	$7
+/- Score	-8	09 Proj	10	11	0	174	93	4.24	1.21	274			24.8	30%	67%	3.84	50	20	29	1.3	4.8	3.7	11%	0.9	10.8	80	$13

Marvel at the consistency of his ERA and WHIP, then also note the trends in his Dom and xERA. 5.47 ERA outside Petco in '08, but 33% hit rate, 61% strand rate inflated it. Still value here, but you have to tread carefully.

Madrigal,Warner			W	L	Sv	IP	K	ERA	WHIP	OBA	vL	vR	BF/G	H%	S%	xERA	G	L	F	Ctl	Dom	Cmd	hr/f	hr/9	RAR	BPV	R$
RH	Reliever	04	0	0	0	0	0	0.00	0.00																		
Age	25	05	0	0	0	0	0	0.00	0.00																		
Type	Pwr xFB	06	0	0	0	0	0	0.00	0.00																		
Health	A	07	0	0	0	0	0	0.00	0.00																		
PT/Exp	F	08 TEX *	1	2	15	72	57	4.22	1.41	261	323	208	5.0	31%	72%	4.79	33	20	47	3.7	7.1	1.9	7%	0.9	1.2	39	$8
Consist	F	1st Half	1	0	14	36	35	3.68	1.43	261			5.1	33%	76%					3.9	8.8	2.2		0.8	2.9	79	$7
LIMA Plan	C+	2nd Half	0	2	1	36	22	4.75	1.39	262			5.0	29%	67%	5.18	33	20	47	3.5	5.5	1.6	7%	1.0	-1.8	16	$1
+/- Score	-19	09 Proj	1	2	3	58	44	4.34	1.41	262			5.0	30%	72%	4.87	33	20	47	3.7	6.8	1.8	8%	1.1	-3.2	34	$4

0-2, 4.75 ERA in 36 IP at TEX. Former OF converted to pitching in 2006. 1st half of '08 was in minors; 2nd half was in majors; skills didn't quite carry over. But with closing experience, decent upside, he's worth watching.

Madson,Ryan			W	L	Sv	IP	K	ERA	WHIP	OBA	vL	vR	BF/G	H%	S%	xERA	G	L	F	Ctl	Dom	Cmd	hr/f	hr/9	RAR	BPV	R$
RH	Reliever	04 PHI	9	3	1	77	55	2.34	1.13	238	252	227	6.0	28%	83%	3.47	54	18	28	2.2	6.4	2.9	9%	0.7	18.3	87	$13
Age	28	05 PHI	6	5	0	87	79	4.14	1.25	255	292	233	4.7	31%	70%	3.29	48	25	27	2.6	8.2	3.2	16%	1.1	1.2	103	$8
Type		06 PHI	11	9	2	134	99	5.70	1.69	318	306	336	12.4	36%	68%	4.62	43	22	35	3.4	6.6	2.0	12%	1.3	-20.1	50	$3
Health	C	07 PHI	2	2	1	56	43	3.05	1.27	233	170	275	6.2	27%	79%	4.03	47	21	32	3.7	6.9	1.9	10%	0.8	9.5	50	$6
PT/Exp	C	08 PHI	4	2	1	83	67	3.05	1.23	253	268	243	4.5	31%	77%	3.55	51	19	30	2.5	7.3	2.9	8%	0.7	12.5	93	$9
Consist	B	1st Half	1	0	0	43	33	3.16	1.19	240			5.0	29%	75%	3.82	47	20	34	2.7	7.0	2.5	7%	0.6	5.8	76	$4
LIMA Plan	B	2nd Half	3	2	1	40	34	2.92	1.27	267			4.1	33%	79%	3.26	55	18	26	2.2	7.6	3.4	9%	0.7	6.6	110	$5
+/- Score	2	09 Proj	4	3	3	73	58	3.48	1.31	260			5.5	31%	76%	3.75	49	20	31	2.9	7.2	2.5	10%	0.9	5.3	80	$7

Same ERA as '07, but much better skills (and 2nd half was best work yet). With similarly strong relief skills in 2004-05, we probably have enough data to call '07 an anomaly. Good 2nd tier LIMA option.

BRANDON KRUSE

Mahay,Ron		W	L	Sv	IP	K	ERA	WHIP	OBA	vL	vR	BF/G	H%	S%	xERA	G	L	F	Ctl	Dom	Cmd	hr/f	hr/9	RAR	BPV	R$
LH Reliever	04 TEX	3	0	0	67	54	2.55	1.33	241	227	241	4.7	29%	83%	4.42	44	14	42	3.9	7.3	**1.9**	6%	0.7	15.5	47	$7
Age 37	05 TEX *	1	5	1	59	52	7.02	1.73	308	302	322	7.2	36%	62%	4.16	48	23	29	4.3	7.9	**1.9**	20%	1.7	-19.3	54	($2)
Type Pwr	06 TEX	1	3	0	57	56	3.95	1.44	251	240	258	4.0	31%	76%	4.13	41	21	38	4.4	8.8	**2.0**	12%	1.1	4.3	58	$4
Health B	07 2TM *	3	1	1	77	62	3.45	1.51	252	189	242	5.2	30%	78%	4.55	49	17	34	5.0	7.2	**1.4**	7%	0.6	9.6	22	$5
PT/Exp D	08 KC	5	0	0	65	49	3.48	1.39	251	255	250	4.9	29%	77%	4.65	40	19	41	4.0	6.8	**1.7**	8%	0.8	6.9	32	$6
Consist A	1st Half	4	0	0	42	29	2.13	1.28	232			5.1	27%	85%	4.64	43	16	41	3.8	6.2	**1.6**	4%	0.4	11.6	29	$6
LIMA Plan C	2nd Half	1	0	0	22	20	6.03	1.61	284			4.6	33%	66%	4.65	35	25	41	4.4	8.0	**1.8**	14%	1.6	-4.6	38	$0
+/- Score -37	09 Proj	**3**	**1**	**0**	**54**	**42**	**4.21**	**1.46**	**256**			**4.8**	**30%**	**74%**	**4.63**	**41**	**20**	**39**	**4.4**	**7.1**	**1.6**	**10%**	**1.0**	**-1.4**	**29**	**$4**

He's never been able to rein in Ctl problems, and now fading Dom rate and advancing age will only make matters worse. He's been dodging the bullet for years thanks to S%, but xERA shows a 5.00 ERA isn't far off.

Maholm,Paul		W	L	Sv	IP	K	ERA	WHIP	OBA	vL	vR	BF/G	H%	S%	xERA	G	L	F	Ctl	Dom	Cmd	hr/f	hr/9	RAR	BPV	R$
LH Starter	04	0	0	0	0	0	0.00	0.00											0.0	0.0						
Age 26	05 PIT *	10	4	0	158	107	3.30	1.31	258	87	232	23.9	30%	75%	3.74	55	20	25	3.0	6.1	**2.1**	7%	0.5	18.5	63	$14
Type GB	06 PIT	8	10	0	176	117	4.76	1.61	289	233	313	26.6	33%	72%	4.39	53	20	27	4.1	6.0	**1.4**	12%	1.0	-5.8	27	$4
Health A	07 PIT	10	15	0	178	105	5.01	1.42	289	238	305	26.6	31%	67%	4.12	53	17	30	2.5	5.3	**2.1**	12%	1.1	-12.9	60	$7
PT/Exp A	08 PIT	9	9	0	206	139	3.71	1.28	257	183	279	27.9	29%	74%	3.79	54	19	28	2.7	6.1	**2.2**	12%	0.9	14.3	67	$15
Consist A	1st Half	5	5	0	103	65	4.28	1.36	275			27.5	30%	72%	4.16	48	19	32	2.6	5.7	**2.2**	13%	1.2	-0.1	58	$6
LIMA Plan C	2nd Half	4	4	0	103	74	3.14	1.20	238			28.4	28%	75%	3.39	59	18	23	2.9	6.4	**2.2**	10%	0.6	14.4	76	$10
+/- Score 7	09 Proj	**10**	**11**	**0**	**209**	**139**	**3.88**	**1.35**	**269**			**27.0**	**30%**	**74%**	**3.88**	**54**	**18**	**28**	**2.8**	**6.0**	**2.1**	**11%**	**0.9**	**11.8**	**63**	**$14**

This isn't an ace-caliber skill set (Dom and Cmd are just over recommended levels), but when everything breaks right, like it did in the 2nd half, he's got $20 upside. And as PIT pitcher, he's almost always under the radar.

Maine,John		W	L	Sv	IP	K	ERA	WHIP	OBA	vL	vR	BF/G	H%	S%	xERA	G	L	F	Ctl	Dom	Cmd	hr/f	hr/9	RAR	BPV	R$
RH Starter	04 a/a	9	8	0	147	124	4.40	1.47	277			24.0	33%	72%	4.65				3.5	7.6	**2.1**		0.9	-1.1	62	$9
Age 28	05 BAL *	8	14	0	168	121	5.78	1.50	283	227	275	22.5	32%	63%	4.38	46	21	34	3.5	6.5	**1.9**	13%	1.2	-29.2	46	$4
Type Pwr FB	06 NYM *	9	10	0	146	112	4.14	1.31	250	231	191	23.8	29%	71%	4.60	38	15	47	3.3	6.9	**2.1**	8%	1.0	6.2	49	$12
Health C	07 NYM	15	10	0	191	180	3.91	1.27	238	237	234	25.0	29%	73%	4.10	37	18	45	3.5	8.5	**2.4**	10%	1.1	12.1	72	$20
PT/Exp B	08 NYM	10	8	0	140	122	4.18	1.35	236	238	229	23.9	28%	72%	4.31	41	20	39	4.3	7.8	**1.8**	10%	1.0	1.6	43	$11
Consist A	1st Half	8	6	0	98	80	3.86	1.36	248			24.7	29%	73%	4.39	41	19	40	3.9	7.3	**1.9**	8%	0.8	5.0	47	$9
LIMA Plan C	2nd Half	2	2	0	42	42	4.93	1.33	207			22.3	24%	67%	4.13	40	23	37	5.4	9.0	**1.7**	18%	1.5	-3.4	35	$2
+/- Score -2	09 Proj	**12**	**10**	**0**	**181**	**161**	**4.04**	**1.34**	**243**			**24.0**	**29%**	**73%**	**4.22**	**39**	**20**	**41**	**3.9**	**8.0**	**2.1**	**11%**	**1.1**	**2.7**	**57**	**$15**

Bone spur in shoulder may have caused some of the Cmd slide, though 1H skills weren't stellar either. Overall, this looked a lot like 2005-06, making 2007 an outlier. Don't assume he'll just bounce back to that level.

Majewski,Gary		W	L	Sv	IP	K	ERA	WHIP	OBA	vL	vR	BF/G	H%	S%	xERA	G	L	F	Ctl	Dom	Cmd	hr/f	hr/9	RAR	BPV	R$
RH Reliever	04 aaa	4	5	15	57	50	4.09	1.36	251			5.0	32%	68%	3.44				3.8	7.9	**2.1**		0.3	1.8	86	$10
Age 29	05 WAS *	4	4	1	86	50	2.93	1.36	248	236	259	4.7	29%	77%	4.75	46	20	34	3.9	5.2	**1.4**	2%	0.2	14.0	13	$7
Type GB	06 2NL	4	4	0	70	43	4.62	1.54	286	290	279	4.8	32%	70%	4.46	53	19	29	3.7	5.5	**1.5**	8%	0.6	-1.2	30	$3
Health A	07 CIN *	1	5	4	61	35	6.49	1.70	328			4.0	36%	61%	4.66	52	18	31	2.9	5.1	**1.7**	9%	0.9	-15.6	43	($1)
PT/Exp D	08 CIN *	3	1	3	66	45	5.85	1.77	336	348	373	5.3	38%	69%	4.48	50	19	30	3.1	6.1	**2.0**	13%	1.3	-12.9	55	($1)
Consist A	1st Half	2	1	3	39	26	5.10	1.65	328			5.7	37%	70%	4.07	50	25	25	2.4	6.0	**2.4**	12%	1.0	-4.0	69	$1
LIMA Plan B	2nd Half	1	0	0	27	19	6.92	1.94	347			4.7	38%	67%	4.87	51	16	33	4.0	6.3	**1.6**	15%	1.6	-8.9	34	($2)
+/- Score 49	09 Proj	**2**	**2**	**0**	**44**	**30**	**5.11**	**1.59**	**303**			**4.6**	**34%**	**69%**	**4.37**	**50**	**18**	**31**	**3.3**	**6.1**	**1.9**	**11%**	**1.0**	**-0.1**	**51**	**$1**

1-0, 6.53 ERA in 40 IP at CIN. Any skill growth you see in 2008 came in Triple-A; had 1.8 Cmd, 29 BPV and 5.14 xERA in CIN. ERA, WHIP were likely to keep you away, but just in case, we thought we'd erase all doubts.

Manning,Charlie		W	L	Sv	IP	K	ERA	WHIP	OBA	vL	vR	BF/G	H%	S%	xERA	G	L	F	Ctl	Dom	Cmd	hr/f	hr/9	RAR	BPV	R$
LH Reliever	04 a/a	7	6	0	107	81	6.29	1.71	328			12.7	39%	62%	5.85				3.0	6.8	**2.3**		0.7	-25.7	56	($1)
Age 30	05 a/a	5	4	2	82	55	4.62	1.70	277			7.3	32%	73%	5.03				5.6	6.0	**1.1**		0.7	-3.2	36	$2
Type Pwr FB	06 a/a	8	3	1	84	59	4.06	1.44	267			7.5	31%	73%	4.19				3.7	6.3	**1.7**		0.7	4.7	54	$8
Health A	07 a/a	4	2	3	61	48	5.89	1.60	273			6.7	33%	61%	4.53				4.9	7.1	**1.5**		0.5	-10.8	59	$2
PT/Exp D	08 WAS *	1	3	6	69	62	4.12	1.49	233	203	247	4.0	27%	76%	4.87	40	16	44	5.7	8.1	**1.4**	11%	1.2	1.3	9	$4
Consist A	1st Half	0	1	6	43	43	2.87	1.36	220			5.0	29%	81%	4.43	41	11	49	5.1	9.1	**1.8**	6%	0.7	7.4	46	$5
LIMA Plan C	2nd Half	1	2	0	26	19	6.16	1.71	252			3.1	26%	69%	5.78	40	19	42	6.8	6.5	**1.0**	18%	2.1	-6.1	-50	($1)
+/- Score -34	09 Proj	**2**	**2**	**0**	**44**	**35**	**4.76**	**1.56**	**260**			**4.9**	**30%**	**73%**	**5.04**	**40**	**17**	**43**	**5.2**	**7.2**	**1.4**	**11%**	**1.2**	**-3.7**	**8**	**$1**

1-3, 5.14 ERA in 42 IP at WAS. Can't seem to get Ctl and Dom on the same page. Still, could have a future as situational lefty: 9.3 Dom, 2.6 Cmd, .203 BA vs. LH in '08. That has value for MLB teams, but none for yours.

Marcum,Shaun		W	L	Sv	IP	K	ERA	WHIP	OBA	vL	vR	BF/G	H%	S%	xERA	G	L	F	Ctl	Dom	Cmd	hr/f	hr/9	RAR	BPV	R$
RH Starter	04	0	0	0	0	0	0.00	0.00																		
Age 27	05 a/a	13	5	0	157	115	5.50	1.38	298			25.0	33%	64%	5.35				1.7	6.6	**4.0**		1.6	-23.2	70	$9
Type FB	06 TOR *	7	4	0	130	117	4.90	1.48	283	303	256	14.7	33%	71%	4.43	36	18	46	3.3	8.1	**2.4**	12%	1.5	-5.6	70	$8
Health B	07 TOR	12	6	1	159	122	4.13	1.25	249	259	237	17.4	27%	73%	4.17	40	18	42	2.8	6.9	**2.5**	13%	1.5	7.3	68	$17
PT/Exp B	08 TOR	9	7	0	151	123	3.39	1.16	228	244	200	24.7	26%	77%	3.92	43	17	40	3.0	7.3	**2.5**	12%	1.2	17.9	73	$18
Consist A	1st Half	5	4	0	99	86	2.64	1.00	206			25.8	24%	80%	3.49	45	16	39	2.5	7.8	**3.2**	11%	1.0	20.7	98	$15
LIMA Plan D+	2nd Half	4	3	0	53	37	4.79	1.46	267			23.1	28%	73%	4.78	40	20	41	3.9	6.3	**1.6**	15%	1.7	-2.9	25	$3
+/- Score 1	09 Proj	**1**	**1**	**0**	**15**	**11**	**4.34**	**1.31**	**255**			**20.4**	**29%**	**71%**	**4.33**	**41**	**18**	**41**	**3.1**	**6.8**	**2.2**	**11%**	**1.2**	**0.2**	**58**	**$1**

Elbow pain ruined his 2nd half, and now TJ surgery will cost him most, if not all, of 2009. 1st half skills - particularly Cmd and BPV - were those of a budding ace. Full bloom may not happen 'til 2011, if at all.

Marmol,Carlos		W	L	Sv	IP	K	ERA	WHIP	OBA	vL	vR	BF/G	H%	S%	xERA	G	L	F	Ctl	Dom	Cmd	hr/f	hr/9	RAR	BPV	R$
RH Reliever	04	0	0	0	0	0	0.00	0.00																		
Age 26	05 aa	3	4	0	81	62	4.77	1.55	266			25.9	30%	73%	5.16				4.8	6.9	**1.4**		1.4	-4.7	30	$2
Type Pwr xFB	06 CHC *	8	9	0	138	117	5.21	1.59	252	229	263	19.5	30%	68%	5.58	29	18	53	5.8	7.6	**1.3**	7%	1.0	-12.2	-12	$4
Health A	07 CHC *	9	2	1	110	134	2.87	1.14	200	209	146	6.7	28%	77%	3.66	31	16	52	3.9	10.9	**2.8**	6%	0.7	21.1	101	$18
PT/Exp C	08 CHC	2	4	7	87	114	2.68	0.93	140	180	98	4.1	18%	78%	3.27	35	10	55	4.2	11.8	**2.8**	10%	1.0	17.1	110	$16
Consist C	1st Half	1	3	3	47	66	3.06	0.87	131			4.2	18%	69%	3.05	33	8	59	4.0	12.6	**3.1**	10%	1.0	7.0	130	$8
LIMA Plan C+	2nd Half	1	1	4	40	48	2.23	0.99	150			3.9	19%	86%	3.56	36	12	52	4.5	10.7	**2.4**	11%	1.1	10.1	87	$8
+/- Score -11	09 Proj	**3**	**3**	**13**	**73**	**83**	**3.35**	**1.20**	**206**			**6.1**	**27%**	**77%**	**3.93**	**33**	**13**	**54**	**4.2**	**10.3**	**2.4**	**10%**	**1.1**	**3.6**	**83**	**$12**

Closer-caliber skills just waiting for the opportunity. That said, Ctl is still a problem, and we've yet to see the worst of the hr/9 damage that could come from his mega-extreme FB%. Not elite yet, but he's working on it.

Marquis,Jason		W	L	Sv	IP	K	ERA	WHIP	OBA	vL	vR	BF/G	H%	S%	xERA	G	L	F	Ctl	Dom	Cmd	hr/f	hr/9	RAR	BPV	R$
RH Starter	04 STL	15	7	0	201	138	3.71	1.42	275	278	271	27.3	31%	78%	3.85	56	19	26	3.1	6.2	**2.0**	16%	1.2	13.6	60	$15
Age 30	05 STL	13	14	0	207	100	4.13	1.33	261	238	280	26.6	27%	73%	4.44	52	17	31	3.0	4.3	**1.4**	14%	1.3	2.9	28	$13
Type	06 STL	14	16	0	194	96	6.03	1.52	288	288	291	26.1	29%	64%	5.21	43	17	40	3.5	4.5	**1.3**	13%	1.6	-36.9	7	$3
Health A	07 CHC	12	9	0	192	109	4.60	1.39	260	274	242	24.3	28%	69%	4.58	50	17	33	3.6	5.1	**1.4**	11%	1.0	-4.1	23	$11
PT/Exp A	08 CHC	11	9	0	167	91	4.53	1.45	268	244	287	25.2	29%	70%	4.78	48	20	33	3.8	4.9	**1.3**	8%	0.8	-5.3	12	$8
Consist A	1st Half	6	4	0	85	44	4.96	1.52	285			25.3	31%	68%	4.94	46	22	33	3.6	4.6	**1.3**	8%	0.8	-7.2	10	$2
LIMA Plan D+	2nd Half	5	5	0	82	47	4.08	1.37	248			25.0	27%	71%	4.62	50	18	32	4.0	5.2	**1.3**	8%	0.8	2.0	14	$5
+/- Score -33	09 Proj	**10**	**11**	**0**	**174**	**96**	**4.76**	**1.49**	**278**			**25.6**	**30%**	**70%**	**4.78**	**48**	**18**	**33**	**3.6**	**5.0**	**1.4**	**10%**	**1.0**	**-9.4**	**18**	**$6**

Terrible skills, but at least he's consistent, right? Hasn't had a skill worth talking about for four years, and it's starting to eat into his IP. There's no upside here, and his downside is always a repeat of 2006.

Marshall,Sean		W	L	Sv	IP	K	ERA	WHIP	OBA	vL	vR	BF/G	H%	S%	xERA	G	L	F	Ctl	Dom	Cmd	hr/f	hr/9	RAR	BPV	R$
LH Reliever	04 aa	2	2	0	29	19	10.13	2.25	382			25.0	43%	53%	8.44				4.6	5.9	**1.3**		1.0	-20.7	12	($5)
Age 26	05 aa	0	1	0	25	20	4.55	1.14	239			25.4	28%	60%	3.09				2.3	7.2	**3.2**		0.8	-0.7	94	$2
Type	06 CHC *	6	11	0	146	95	5.48	1.55	271	256	273	23.4	29%	67%	4.91	47	17	36	4.6	5.8	**1.3**	12%	1.3	-17.9	7	$2
Health A	07 CHC *	9	8	0	128	79	3.65	1.36	264	203	280	21.8	29%	77%	4.44	48	16	36	3.1	5.6	**1.8**	11%	1.2	12.3	43	$11
PT/Exp D	08 CHC *	4	6	1	97	76	4.01	1.28	255	269	236	9.9	30%	72%	4.19	41	17	42	2.8	7.1	**2.6**	9%	1.1	3.2	72	$7
Consist A	1st Half	1	3	1	52	35	4.53	1.34	269			10.0	30%	69%	4.72	40	11	48	2.8	6.2	**2.2**	8%	1.1	-1.7	54	$2
LIMA Plan C+	2nd Half	3	3	0	45	41	3.40	1.20	240			9.8	29%	76%	3.74	42	19	39	2.8	8.2	**2.9**	10%	1.0	4.8	92	$5
+/- Score 4	09 Proj	**8**	**7**	**0**	**122**	**94**	**3.93**	**1.33**	**263**			**22.4**	**30%**	**74%**	**4.12**	**45**	**17**	**38**	**2.9**	**7.0**	**2.4**	**11%**	**1.1**	**3.2**	**70**	**$10**

3-5, 3.86 ERA in 65 IP at CHC. Spent much of MLB time in pen, but fared better in rotation:
SP - 2.8 Ctl, 8.3 Dom, 3.0 Cmd
RP - 3.8 Ctl, 7.5 Dom, 2.0 Cmd
Rising trends in Cmd, xERA and BPV. As SP, he's a sleeper.

BRANDON KRUSE

Marte,Damaso

	Yr	Tm	W	L	Sv	IP	K	ERA	WHIP	OBA	vL	vR	BF/G	H%	S%	xERA	G	L	F	Ctl	Dom	Cmd	hr/f	hr/9	RAR	BPV	R$
LH Reliever	04	CHW	6	5	6	73	68	3.44	1.23	213	143	263	4.1	25%	78%	4.25	36	17	46	4.2	8.4	**2.0**	11%	1.2	8.9	52	$11
Age 34	05	CHW	3	4	4	45	54	3.79	1.73	261	267	244	3.2	35%	81%	4.43	40	21	39	6.6	10.8	**1.6**	11%	1.0	3.2	35	$4
Type Pwr FB	06	PIT	1	7	0	58	63	3.72	1.41	237	225	258	3.4	31%	75%	4.13	34	25	41	4.8	9.8	**2.0**	8%	0.8	5.5	58	$4
Health A	07	PIT	2	0	0	45	51	2.38	1.10	200	94	271	2.8	28%	79%	3.48	43	13	44	3.6	10.1	**2.8**	4%	0.4	11.4	106	$7
PT/Exp C	08	2TM	5	3	5	65	71	4.02	1.20	221	247	196	3.7	30%	67%	3.74	33	23	44	3.6	9.8	**2.7**	7%	0.7	2.3	91	$9
Consist A	1st Half		4	0	1	40	43	3.17	1.11	228			4.0	30%	73%	3.49	34	21	45	2.5	9.7	**3.9**	7%	0.7	5.5	120	$7
LIMA Plan A	2nd Half		1	3	4	25	28	5.34	1.34	210			3.4	28%	59%	4.19	32	26	42	5.3	10.0	**1.9**	8%	0.7	-3.2	45	$3
+/- Score 4	09	Proj	**3**	**4**	**0**	**58**	**64**	**3.72**	**1.24**	**220**			**3.3**	**29%**	**72%**	**3.79**	**36**	**21**	**43**	**4.0**	**9.9**	**2.5**	**8%**	**0.8**	**4.2**	**84**	**$6**

PRO: Steady Dom rate, another year with strong Cmd, BPV. CON: Ctl issues keep coming back, and are a deadly combo with his FB%. Still meets the LIMA filters, but how confident do you feel after that 2nd half?

Martinez,Pedro

	Yr	Tm	W	L	Sv	IP	K	ERA	WHIP	OBA	vL	vR	BF/G	H%	S%	xERA	G	L	F	Ctl	Dom	Cmd	hr/f	hr/9	RAR	BPV	R$
RH Starter	04	BOS	16	9	0	217	227	3.90	1.17	240	236	240	26.9	30%	70%	3.50	38	19	43	2.5	9.4	**3.7**	10%	1.1	14.3	118	$26
Age 37	05	NYM	15	8	0	217	208	2.82	0.95	206	215	192	27.1	26%	74%	3.43	38	17	45	1.9	8.6	**4.4**	8%	0.8	38.2	119	$33
Type Pwr	06	NYM	9	8	0	132	137	4.49	1.11	225	231	211	23.2	27%	63%	3.52	36	19	44	2.7	9.3	**3.5**	12%	1.3	-0.1	110	$15
Health F	07	NYM	3	1	0	28	32	2.57	1.43	295	319	261	24.4	41%	80%	3.72	31	24	44	2.3	10.3	**4.6**	0%	0.0	6.4	134	$4
PT/Exp C	08	NYM	5	6	0	109	87	5.61	1.57	292	304	282	24.5	33%	68%	4.41	41	24	35	3.6	7.2	**2.0**	16%	1.6	-18.1	50	$1
Consist A	1st Half		2	2	0	30	21	7.13	1.75	330			23.6	37%	59%	4.94	38	24	37	3.3	6.2	**1.9**	10%	1.2	-10.7	40	($1)
LIMA Plan B+	2nd Half		3	4	0	79	66	5.03	1.50	277			24.8	31%	72%	4.20	42	23	34	3.8	7.5	**2.0**	18%	1.7	-7.4	54	$2
+/- Score 31	09	Proj	**9**	**8**	**0**	**146**	**126**	**4.32**	**1.38**	**263**			**25.1**	**31%**	**72%**	**4.20**	**37**	**23**	**40**	**3.3**	**7.8**	**2.3**	**11%**	**1.2**	**2.5**	**65**	**$10**

Signs that the end is near:
- Lowest Dom/Cmd of his career
- Highest hr/9 of his career
- Fastball velocity way down
- xERA trend is disturbing
- The name "Pedro" no longer means "fear" but "Feliciano."

Masset,Nick

	Yr	Tm	W	L	Sv	IP	K	ERA	WHIP	OBA	vL	vR	BF/G	H%	S%	xERA	G	L	F	Ctl	Dom	Cmd	hr/f	hr/9	RAR	BPV	R$
RH Reliever	04		0	0	0	0	0	0.00	0.00																		
Age 27	05	aa	7	12	0	157	88	8.27	1.94	352			26.3	38%	57%	7.52				3.7	5.1	**1.4**		1.5	-76.8	-0	($14)
Type	06	a/a	6	7	3	115	88	5.32	1.75	314			16.8	38%	68%	5.43				4.1	6.9	**1.7**		0.5	-11.4	54	$2
Health A	07	CHW *	2	7	0	84	50	6.75	1.79	325			10.5	35%	63%	5.41	43	17	40	3.8	5.3	**1.4**	9%	1.2	-23.4	12	($4)
PT/Exp D	08	2TM	2	0	1	62	43	3.92	1.56	289	262	316	6.6	33%	78%	4.26	53	20	28	3.8	6.2	**1.7**	12%	1.0	3.0	41	$3
Consist B	1st Half		0	0	1	35	27	3.31	1.50	271			7.1	33%	78%	3.89	55	22	23	4.1	6.9	**1.7**	8%	0.5	4.3	47	$2
LIMA Plan C+	2nd Half		2	0	0	27	16	4.72	1.65	311			6.1	33%	77%	4.71	49	17	34	3.4	5.4	**1.6**	16%	1.7	-1.4	34	$1
+/- Score 1	09	Proj	**3**	**3**	**0**	**69**	**45**	**4.73**	**1.64**	**301**			**8.7**	**34%**	**73%**	**4.65**	**49**	**18**	**32**	**3.8**	**5.9**	**1.6**	**11%**	**1.1**	**-2.3**	**31**	**$1**

Solid GB% plus better luck with S%, hr/f have helped him claw his way to replacement level. But he won't go any further without improved Cmd. And he's given us no reason to believe that skill is in his toolbox.

Masterson,Justin

	Yr	Tm	W	L	Sv	IP	K	ERA	WHIP	OBA	vL	vR	BF/G	H%	S%	xERA	G	L	F	Ctl	Dom	Cmd	hr/f	hr/9	RAR	BPV	R$
RH Reliever	04		0	0	0	0	0	0.00	0.00																		
Age 24	05		0	0	0	0	0	0.00	0.00																		
Type Pwr xGB	06		0	0	0	0	0	0.00	0.00																		
Health A	07	aa	4	3	0	58	43	6.21	1.50	287			25.6	34%	57%	4.69				3.3	6.6	**2.0**		0.7	-12.5	57	$1
PT/Exp D	08	BOS *	8	8	0	136	106	3.79	1.29	236	238	196	11.9	28%	72%	3.76	54	18	27	3.8	7.0	**1.9**	10%	0.7	9.4	57	$13
Consist B	1st Half		6	5	0	92	72	4.30	1.35	238			23.1	28%	69%	4.00	52	20	29	4.2	7.0	**1.7**	10%	0.8	0.5	43	$7
LIMA Plan B	2nd Half		2	3	0	43	34	2.70	1.18	232			5.7	28%	79%	3.36	58	17	26	2.9	7.1	**2.4**	9%	0.6	8.8	84	$5
+/- Score 10	09	Proj	**4**	**4**	**0**	**73**	**57**	**3.85**	**1.35**	**258**			**8.6**	**31%**	**73%**	**3.66**	**56**	**18**	**27**	**3.4**	**7.1**	**2.1**	**10%**	**0.7**	**6.8**	**71**	**$6**

6-5, 3.16 ERA in 88 IP at BOS. Move to pen was a good fit:
SP - 4.7 Ctl, 6.5 Dom, 1.4 Cmd
RP - 3.1 Ctl, 7.6 Dom, 2.4 Cmd
GB%/Dom combo is promising. If he returns to SP, must prove these skills can carry back over.

Matsuzaka,Daisuke

	Yr	Tm	W	L	Sv	IP	K	ERA	WHIP	OBA	vL	vR	BF/G	H%	S%	xERA	G	L	F	Ctl	Dom	Cmd	hr/f	hr/9	RAR	BPV	R$
RH Starter	04	JPN	10	6	0	146	134	3.60	1.29	249			26.7	31%	74%	3.60				3.2	8.3	**2.6**		0.7	13.4	87	$15
Age 28	05	JPN	14	13	0	215	238	2.86	1.14	233			31.2	31%	79%	3.14				2.5	10.0	**3.9**		0.9	38.3	123	$30
Type Pwr FB	06	JPN	17	5	0	186	211	2.64	1.02	220			29.4	29%	80%	2.78				2.0	10.2	**5.0**		1.0	43.2	146	$34
Health A	07	BOS	15	12	0	205	201	4.40	1.32	249	238	253	27.1	31%	70%	4.01	38	18	44	3.5	8.8	**2.5**	10%	1.1	2.7	80	$20
PT/Exp A	08	BOS	18	3	0	168	154	2.90	1.32	213	225	195	24.5	27%	80%	4.50	39	18	43	5.0	8.3	**1.6**	6%	0.6	30.0	29	$23
Consist B	1st Half		9	1	0	70	60	3.21	1.39	212			23.2	26%	78%	5.03	35	18	47	5.7	7.7	**1.4**	6%	0.6	9.8	-1	$9
LIMA Plan D	2nd Half		9	2	0	98	94	2.67	1.28	214			25.6	27%	81%	4.14	41	18	41	4.6	8.7	**1.9**	7%	0.6	20.2	51	$14
+/- Score -46	09	Proj	**14**	**9**	**0**	**189**	**179**	**3.82**	**1.35**	**242**			**26.8**	**30%**	**75%**	**4.22**	**39**	**18**	**43**	**4.1**	**8.5**	**2.1**	**10%**	**1.1**	**4.7**	**61**	**$20**

Lots to be worried about here:
- Three-year slide in most BPIs.
- Huge gap between ERA, xERA
- W-L, ERA make '08 look like '06, but skills were worlds apart.
Will be dangerously overvalued. DN: 10 wins, 4.50 ERA

McCarthy,Brandon

	Yr	Tm	W	L	Sv	IP	K	ERA	WHIP	OBA	vL	vR	BF/G	H%	S%	xERA	G	L	F	Ctl	Dom	Cmd	hr/f	hr/9	RAR	BPV	R$
RH Starter	04	aa	3	1	0	26	25	4.15	1.31	262			27.5	32%	71%	4.12				2.8	8.7	**3.1**		1.0	0.6	89	$3
Age 25	05	CHW *	10	9	0	186	165	4.31	1.19	249	182	276	23.9	28%	70%	3.80	35	23	42	2.3	8.0	**3.5**	14%	1.5	1.5	95	$18
Type xFB	06	CHW	4	7	0	84	69	4.70	1.31	245	197	270	6.7	26%	71%	4.40	38	15	47	3.5	7.4	**2.1**	15%	1.8	-1.5	54	$7
Health F	07	TEX	5	10	0	102	59	4.87	1.56	279	292	263	19.8	31%	69%	5.64	36	17	47	4.2	5.2	**1.2**	6%	0.8	-4.5	-7	$3
PT/Exp C	08	TEX	1	1	0	22	10	4.09	1.27	244	293	195	18.4	25%	72%	5.44	24	30	46	3.3	4.1	**1.3**	9%	1.2	0.7	-12	$1
Consist B	1st Half		0	0	0	0	0	0.00	0.00																		
LIMA Plan C	2nd Half		1	1	0	22	10	4.09	1.27	244			18.4	25%	72%	5.44	24	30	46	3.3	4.1	**1.3**	9%	1.2	0.7	-12	$1
+/- Score -59	09	Proj	**6**	**8**	**0**	**116**	**68**	**4.66**	**1.41**	**268**			**18.6**	**28%**	**71%**	**5.20**	**33**	**21**	**46**	**3.4**	**5.3**	**1.5**	**10%**	**1.4**	**-11.1**	**13**	**$6**

It's getting tougher and tougher to remember the days when he was a prospect, or to keep any faith in a skills rebound. With a FB% this high, no Dom and no Cmd, he might as well just be throwing batting practice.

McClellan,Kyle

	Yr	Tm	W	L	Sv	IP	K	ERA	WHIP	OBA	vL	vR	BF/G	H%	S%	xERA	G	L	F	Ctl	Dom	Cmd	hr/f	hr/9	RAR	BPV	R$
RH Reliever	04		0	0	0	0	0	0.00	0.00																		
Age 24	05		0	0	0	0	0	0.00	0.00																		
Type	06		0	0	0	0	0	0.00	0.00																		
Health D	07	aa	2	0	0	30	25	2.77	1.09	239			5.0	29%	77%	2.88				1.8	7.5	**4.1**		0.6	6.3	119	$4
PT/Exp D	08	STL	2	7	1	76	59	4.04	1.39	270	238	291	4.8	32%	72%	3.94	48	21	31	3.1	7.0	**2.3**	10%	0.8	2.1	69	$4
Consist C	1st Half		0	3	1	44	38	2.66	1.23	266			4.7	32%	82%	3.28	51	20	29	1.8	7.8	**4.2**	10%	0.8	8.7	119	$4
LIMA Plan B+	2nd Half		2	4	0	32	21	5.96	1.61	276			5.0	31%	63%	4.97	46	21	33	4.8	6.0	**1.2**	9%	0.9	-6.6	1	($0)
+/- Score 27	09	Proj	**4**	**5**	**3**	**87**	**68**	**3.83**	**1.31**	**260**			**4.9**	**31%**	**73%**	**3.85**	**48**	**21**	**32**	**2.9**	**7.0**	**2.4**	**10%**	**0.8**	**5.2**	**74**	**$8**

Looked like a future closer until he hit a wall in the 2nd half. Probably wasn't the best idea to have him throw so many IP in second year after TJ surgery. But now you can invest in the upside at a reasonable price.

McClung,Seth

	Yr	Tm	W	L	Sv	IP	K	ERA	WHIP	OBA	vL	vR	BF/G	H%	S%	xERA	G	L	F	Ctl	Dom	Cmd	hr/f	hr/9	RAR	BPV	R$
RH Reliever	04	a/a	3	2	0	27	19	5.00	1.37	240			8.3	26%	67%	4.28				4.3	6.3	**1.5**		1.3	-2.2	36	$2
Age 28	05	TAM *	9	11	0	127	108	6.23	1.54	265	294	197	14.2	30%	62%	4.79	37	21	42	4.7	7.6	**1.6**	13%	1.5	-29.1	24	$3
Type Pwr	06	TAM	6	12	6	103	59	6.29	1.83	292	299	289	12.5	31%	67%	6.25	37	20	43	5.9	5.2	**0.9**	9%	1.2	-22.0	-52	($0)
Health A	07	MIL *	3	6	5	89	92	2.58	1.47	227			6.6	30%	84%	4.05	53	13	34	5.8	9.3	**1.6**	8%	0.6	20.3	42	$10
PT/Exp C	08	MIL	6	6	0	105	87	4.02	1.41	238	251	235	12.3	28%	73%	4.49	44	18	38	4.7	7.4	**1.6**	9%	0.9	3.3	29	$7
Consist C	1st Half		5	3	0	59	46	4.25	1.33	237			14.0	26%	73%	4.48	42	17	41	4.1	7.0	**1.7**	13%	1.4	0.2	35	$5
LIMA Plan D+	2nd Half		1	3	0	46	41	3.72	1.50	240			10.7	31%	74%	4.49	48	18	34	5.5	8.0	**1.5**	2%	0.2	3.1	22	$2
+/- Score -23	09	Proj	**4**	**6**	**0**	**81**	**69**	**4.70**	**1.58**	**261**			**6.6**	**31%**	**72%**	**4.78**	**43**	**18**	**39**	**5.3**	**7.7**	**1.5**	**10%**	**1.0**	**-4.3**	**18**	**$3**

How does a guy with a career 5.55 ERA and these skills keep getting work? 2007 xERA looks nice, but it was skewed by small sample size FB%. Take that away, and it's a sea of lousy BPIs. Stay out of the water.

McGowan,Dustin

	Yr	Tm	W	L	Sv	IP	K	ERA	WHIP	OBA	vL	vR	BF/G	H%	S%	xERA	G	L	F	Ctl	Dom	Cmd	hr/f	hr/9	RAR	BPV	R$
RH Starter	04	aa	2	1	0	31	25	6.10	1.52	255			22.9	28%	63%	5.23				4.9	7.3	**1.5**		1.7	-6.7	26	$1
Age 27	05	TOR *	1	5	0	80	62	5.91	1.54	297	243	301	18.8	33%	66%	4.23	47	17	36	3.2	7.0	**2.2**	18%	1.8	-15.2	65	($0)
Type Pwr	06	TOR *	5	7	1	111	96	6.32	1.76	292	327	283	13.3	35%	64%	4.76	43	26	31	5.4	7.8	**1.4**	10%	0.9	-24.1	14	($0)
Health D	07	TOR *	12	12	0	192	169	3.85	1.23	234	257	198	24.8	29%	69%	3.54	53	16	31	3.3	7.9	**2.4**	8%	0.7	15.4	85	$21
PT/Exp D	08	TOR	6	7	0	111	85	4.37	1.37	268	295	252	25.2	32%	69%	4.30	41	21	38	3.1	6.9	**2.2**	7%	0.7	-0.3	60	$8
Consist B	1st Half		6	6	0	101	78	4.26	1.39	269			25.7	32%	70%	4.35	42	20	38	3.2	6.9	**2.2**	7%	0.7	1.0	58	$7
LIMA Plan C+	2nd Half		0	1	0	10	7	5.40	1.20	262			20.6	30%	55%	3.83	38	31	31	1.8	6.3	**3.5**	10%	0.9	-1.3	80	$0
+/- Score 10	09	Proj	**6**	**7**	**0**	**116**	**93**	**4.58**	**1.38**	**263**			**23.7**	**31%**	**69%**	**4.07**	**43**	**23**	**33**	**3.3**	**7.2**	**2.2**	**11%**	**1.0**	**5.0**	**61**	**$8**

Workload warnings came to pass in the form of shoulder surgery. Declines in Dom, GB% took away his two best skills, and whether that was injury-related or not, it makes the 2009 outlook awfully cloudy.

BRANDON KRUSE

Meche,Gil

Meche,Gil				W	L	Sv	IP	K	ERA	WHIP	OBA	vL	vR	BF/G	H%	S%	xERA	G	L	F	Ctl	Dom	Cmd	hr/f	hr/9	RAR	BPV	R$
RH Starter		04	SEA *	8	10	0	184	140	5.23	1.50	279	269	278	24.7	31%	68%	4.80	37	19	44	3.7	6.8	**1.9**	11%	1.4	-18.1	39	$6
Age	30	05	SEA	10	8	0	143	83	5.09	1.57	275	266	285	22.2	30%	70%	5.40	40	20	40	4.5	5.2	**1.2**	9%	1.1	-12.8	-10	$4
Type	Pwr	06	SEA	11	8	0	186	156	4.50	1.43	258	240	271	25.3	30%	72%	4.36	43	18	38	4.1	7.5	**1.9**	11%	1.2	1.4	47	$14
Health	A	07	KC	9	13	0	216	156	3.67	1.30	264	242	284	26.8	30%	74%	4.04	47	18	35	2.6	6.5	**2.5**	9%	0.9	22.3	72	$19
PT/Exp	A	08	KC	14	11	0	210	183	3.98	1.32	256	238	273	26.2	31%	71%	4.06	39	22	39	3.1	7.8	**2.5**	8%	0.8	9.5	74	$20
Consist	A	1st Half		6	8	0	102	82	4.66	1.32	257			25.5	30%	67%	4.18	40	21	39	3.1	7.2	**2.3**	10%	1.1	-4.0	65	$8
LIMA Plan	C	2nd Half		8	3	0	108	101	3.33	1.31	255			26.9	32%	76%	3.95	38	23	39	3.2	8.4	**2.7**	6%	0.6	13.5	82	$12
+/- Score	6	09	Proj	**14**	**8**	**0**	**203**	**173**	**3.72**	**1.30**	**255**			**26.0**	**30%**	**74%**	**3.99**	**42**	**20**	**38**	**3.0**	**7.7**	**2.5**	**10%**	**1.0**	**10.8**	**76**	**$21**

Reasons to go an extra buck:
- Best Dom of his career
- Back-to-back healthy seasons
- 62%/6% DOM/DIS in PQS
- Dialed skills up a notch in 2H.

Becoming a consistent, reliable investment. KC laughs last?

Mendoza,Luis

Mendoza,Luis				W	L	Sv	IP	K	ERA	WHIP	OBA	vL	vR	BF/G	H%	S%	xERA	G	L	F	Ctl	Dom	Cmd	hr/f	hr/9	RAR	BPV	R$
RH Reliever		04		0	0	0	0	0	0.00	0.00																		
Age	25	05		0	0	0	0	0	0.00	0.00																		
Type	Con GB	06	aa	3	9	0	86	43	9.93	2.15	394			27.3	43%	51%	8.24				2.8	4.5	**1.6**		0.8	-57.5	11	($13)
Health	B	07	aa	15	4	0	148	78	5.26	1.53	298			25.4	32%	66%	5.08				3.0	4.7	**1.6**		0.9	-14.6	30	$7
PT/Exp	D	08	TEX *	5	11	1	99	51	7.81	1.84	345	336	350	13.9	38%	55%	4.95	50	21	29	3.2	4.6	**1.4**	7%	0.7	-42.5	25	($7)
Consist	D	1st Half		3	4	1	43	22	5.87	1.61	324			14.9	37%	60%	4.37	54	20	26	2.4	4.7	**2.0**	2%	0.2	-8.0	53	$1
LIMA Plan	C+	2nd Half		2	7	0	57	29	9.28	2.02	360			13.3	39%	52%	5.34	49	21	29	3.9	4.6	**1.2**	11%	1.1	-34.4	5	($7)
+/- Score	100	09	Proj	**3**	**4**	**0**	**45**	**23**	**5.46**	**1.66**	**320**			**17.0**	**35%**	**68%**	**4.69**	**50**	**21**	**29**	**3.0**	**4.7**	**1.5**	**11%**	**1.0**	**-1.5**	**30**	**$0**

3-8, 8.67 ERA in 63 IP at TEX. GB pitcher in search of another above-average skill. Had a PQS DISaster in 8 of 11 (73%) starts. Fun Fact: Among pitchers with 60+ IP, his .928 opponents OPS ranked 268th out of 269. Ouch.

Meredith,Cla

Meredith,Cla				W	L	Sv	IP	K	ERA	WHIP	OBA	vL	vR	BF/G	H%	S%	xERA	G	L	F	Ctl	Dom	Cmd	hr/f	hr/9	RAR	BPV	R$
RH Reliever		04		0	0	0	0	0	0.00	0.00																		
Age	25	05	a/a	3	5	19	61	46	5.16	1.46	300			5.2	35%	65%	4.89				2.2	6.8	**3.1**		0.9	-6.4	73	$8
Type	xGB	06	SD *	8	1	2	96	70	1.96	0.96	221	281	107	4.8	26%	83%	2.40	69	16	15	1.4	6.5	**4.7**	14%	0.6	29.9	127	$18
Health	A	07	SD	5	6	0	80	59	3.50	1.39	295	286	303	4.3	35%	76%	2.65	72	14	14	1.9	6.7	**3.5**	16%	0.7	9.1	118	$7
PT/Exp	C	08	SD	0	3	0	70	49	4.10	1.47	285	351	258	4.2	33%	73%	3.26	67	16	17	3.1	6.3	**2.0**	15%	0.8	1.5	75	$2
Consist	A	1st Half		0	2	0	40	25	4.24	1.36	275			4.1	31%	71%	3.49	61	19	20	2.7	5.6	**2.1**	15%	0.9	0.1	68	$1
LIMA Plan	A+	2nd Half		0	1	0	30	24	3.90	1.60	299			4.4	36%	76%	2.90	74	12	14	3.6	7.2	**2.0**	15%	0.6	1.4	85	$0
+/- Score	51	09	Proj	**3**	**4**	**0**	**79**	**58**	**3.10**	**1.24**	**263**			**4.3**	**31%**	**76%**	**2.67**	**70**	**14**	**15**	**2.1**	**6.6**	**3.2**	**13%**	**0.6**	**16.1**	**112**	**$7**

With 246 IP over 2006-08, can't help wondering if Ctl slide was brought on by fatigue. Still, GB% and Dom showed life in 2H, and he has yet to reap hr/9 benefits of low FB%. Off year just resets his value to LIMA sleeper level.

Miller,Andrew

Miller,Andrew				W	L	Sv	IP	K	ERA	WHIP	OBA	vL	vR	BF/G	H%	S%	xERA	G	L	F	Ctl	Dom	Cmd	hr/f	hr/9	RAR	BPV	R$
LH Reliever		04		0	0	0	0	0	0.00	0.00																		
Age	23	05		0	0	0	0	0	0.00	0.00																		
Type	Pwr GB	06	DET	0	1	0	10	6	6.24	1.78	219			5.9	26%	61%	5.03	64	24	12	8.9	5.3	**0.6**	0%	0.0	-2.1	-103	($0)
Health	C	07	DET *	7	5	0	100	85	4.67	1.56	275	175	312	23.6	33%	71%	4.18	49	21	30	4.4	7.6	**1.7**	11%	0.9	-2.0	46	$6
PT/Exp	D	08	FLA	6	10	0	107	89	5.87	1.64	284	226	307	16.9	35%	63%	4.55	46	22	33	4.7	7.5	**1.6**	6%	0.6	-21.2	31	$0
Consist	B	1st Half		5	7	0	87	67	5.05	1.59	291			23.2	35%	67%	4.54	45	22	33	3.9	6.9	**1.8**	5%	0.5	-8.4	41	$2
LIMA Plan	C+	2nd Half		1	3	0	20	22	9.45	1.85	252			8.0	33%	46%	4.64	53	19	28	8.1	9.9	**1.2**	13%	0.9	-12.8	-10	($2)
+/- Score	29	09	Proj	**7**	**11**	**0**	**116**	**103**	**4.89**	**1.50**	**255**			**23.3**	**31%**	**68%**	**3.98**	**52**	**21**	**27**	**4.8**	**8.0**	**1.7**	**11%**	**0.8**	**5.2**	**44**	**$5**

Not the first pitcher to have Ctl problems in his formative years, though it would be nice to see at least a little skill growth. Long-term potential is still there, but there's little to suggest it will arrive in 2009.

Miller,Justin

Miller,Justin				W	L	Sv	IP	K	ERA	WHIP	OBA	vL	vR	BF/G	H%	S%	xERA	G	L	F	Ctl	Dom	Cmd	hr/f	hr/9	RAR	BPV	R$
RH Reliever		04	TOR *	4	5	0	97	66	5.74	1.72	303			20.5	33%	70%	6.36				4.4	6.1	**1.4**		1.6	-15.7	13	($1)
Age	31	05	aaa	3	1	2	50	46	3.09	1.27	255			7.5	32%	77%	3.46				2.7	8.2	**3.0**		0.6	7.5	99	$6
Type	Pwr	06	JPN	0	1	0	12	10	13.04	2.64	363			5.6	38%	54%	11.58				9.3	7.8	**0.8**		3.7	-12.6	-65	($4)
Health	A	07	FLA *	5	0	6	76	90	3.41	1.36	248	324	184	4.3	35%	76%	3.63	43	14	43	3.9	10.7	**2.7**	6%	0.6	9.5	108	$10
PT/Exp	D	08	FLA	4	2	0	47	43	4.24	1.41	259	310	224	4.4	32%	71%	4.46	32	24	44	3.9	8.3	**2.2**	7%	0.8	0.2	55	$4
Consist	F	1st Half		2	2	0	38	36	4.23	1.38	255			4.5	31%	71%	4.43	31	21	47	3.8	8.5	**2.3**	8%	0.9	0.2	60	$3
LIMA Plan	B+	2nd Half		2	0	0	8	7	4.29	1.55	275			4.2	35%	69%	4.52	35	35	30	4.3	7.5	**1.8**	0%	0.0	-0.0	32	$1
+/- Score	-10	09	Proj	**4**	**2**	**0**	**69**	**64**	**3.94**	**1.37**	**258**			**6.0**	**32%**	**74%**	**4.11**	**36**	**24**	**40**	**3.5**	**8.4**	**2.4**	**9%**	**0.9**	**2.0**	**70**	**$6**

If we ignore odd '06 stint in JPN, we've got three straight seasons of plus Cmd and BPV work that has likely gone unnoticed by most owners. Those skills have clearly faded a bit, but he's still an underrated LIMA option.

Miller,Trever

Miller,Trever				W	L	Sv	IP	K	ERA	WHIP	OBA	vL	vR	BF/G	H%	S%	xERA	G	L	F	Ctl	Dom	Cmd	hr/f	hr/9	RAR	BPV	R$
LH Reliever		04	TAM	1	1	1	49	43	3.12	1.29	258	214	303	3.4	32%	77%	3.44	53	17	29	2.8	7.9	**2.9**	7%	0.6	7.9	99	$5
Age	35	05	TAM	2	2	0	44	35	4.08	1.68	266	267	289	3.3	31%	77%	5.15	40	25	35	5.9	7.1	**1.2**	9%	0.8	1.6	-13	$2
Type	Pwr FB	06	HOU	2	3	1	50	56	3.05	1.10	229	224	225	2.9	29%	79%	3.45	33	18	49	2.3	10.0	**4.3**	11%	1.3	8.9	128	$7
Health	B	07	HOU	0	0	1	46	46	4.86	1.47	256	209	289	2.7	32%	69%	4.52	34	18	48	4.5	8.9	**2.0**	10%	1.2	-2.5	52	$2
PT/Exp	D	08	TAM	2	0	2	43	44	4.16	1.36	242	209	286	2.7	32%	68%	4.24	32	25	44	4.2	9.1	**2.2**	4%	0.4	1.0	62	$4
Consist	B	1st Half		0	0	0	21	16	3.91	1.40	236			2.6	29%	71%	5.30	32	16	53	4.8	7.0	**1.5**	3%	0.4	1.1	6	$1
LIMA Plan	B+	2nd Half		2	0	2	23	28	4.38	1.33	248			2.9	36%	66%	3.36	32	33	35	3.6	11.1	**3.1**	5%	0.4	-0.1	114	$3
+/- Score	-24	09	Proj	**2**	**1**	**0**	**44**	**45**	**4.14**	**1.36**	**246**			**2.8**	**32%**	**71%**	**4.08**	**34**	**22**	**44**	**3.9**	**9.3**	**2.4**	**8%**	**0.8**	**1.8**	**73**	**$4**

You can set your watch to his 1H/2H splits - this is the third straight year that he's doubled his Cmd rate in the 2nd half. We'd say just think of July 1st as Miller Time, but we don't want to get sued.

Millwood,Kevin

Millwood,Kevin				W	L	Sv	IP	K	ERA	WHIP	OBA	vL	vR	BF/G	H%	S%	xERA	G	L	F	Ctl	Dom	Cmd	hr/f	hr/9	RAR	BPV	R$
RH Starter		04	PHI	9	6	0	141	125	4.85	1.46	280	309	250	24.7	34%	68%	4.11	42	21	37	3.3	8.0	**2.5**	9%	0.9	-10.2	75	$7
Age	34	05	CLE	9	11	0	192	146	2.86	1.22	252	269	227	26.5	29%	81%	3.78	46	21	33	2.4	6.8	**2.8**	10%	0.9	35.8	82	$21
Type		06	TEX	16	12	0	215	157	4.52	1.31	273	285	258	26.7	31%	67%	3.96	45	21	34	2.2	6.6	**3.0**	10%	1.0	1.0	81	$20
Health	C	07	TEX	10	14	0	173	123	5.16	1.62	304	288	311	25.3	35%	69%	4.49	46	21	32	3.5	6.4	**1.8**	10%	1.0	-13.9	46	$5
PT/Exp	A	08	TEX	9	10	0	169	125	5.07	1.59	316	273	354	26.3	37%	69%	4.37	41	25	34	2.6	6.7	**2.6**	9%	1.0	-15.0	68	$5
Consist	A	1st Half		5	4	0	85	60	5.08	1.68	317			26.1	36%	71%	4.57	42	27	31	3.4	6.4	**1.9**	10%	1.0	-7.7	43	$1
LIMA Plan	B+	2nd Half		4	6	0	84	65	5.05	1.51	316			26.5	37%	68%	4.17	39	24	37	1.8	7.0	**3.8**	9%	1.0	-7.3	94	$3
+/- Score	16	09	Proj	**11**	**12**	**0**	**189**	**140**	**4.39**	**1.42**	**288**			**25.5**	**33%**	**71%**	**4.12**	**43**	**23**	**34**	**2.5**	**6.7**	**2.7**	**10%**	**1.0**	**7.1**	**74**	**$13**

Ctl linked to health of his legs. Hamstring put him on DL twice in '07, Ctl shot up. More hammy issues in 1H of '08, Ctl still up. Came off DL in August, 1.3 Ctl rest of season. Still has upside, you just can't pay full price for it.

Miner,Zach

Miner,Zach				W	L	Sv	IP	K	ERA	WHIP	OBA	vL	vR	BF/G	H%	S%	xERA	G	L	F	Ctl	Dom	Cmd	hr/f	hr/9	RAR	BPV	R$
RH Reliever		04	aa	6	10	0	129	96	6.55	1.61	297			21.7	34%	59%	5.49				3.8	6.7	**1.8**		1.1	-35.2	40	($1)
Age	27	05	a/a	5	9	1	140	87	4.88	1.73	305			24.2	34%	72%	5.56				4.5	5.6	**1.2**		0.8	-10.0	31	($0)
Type		06	DET *	13	6	0	144	94	4.44	1.42	271	320	245	17.3	31%	70%	4.38	47	21	32	3.3	5.9	**1.8**	9%	0.8	2.1	41	$12
Health	C	07	DET *	4	8	0	107	63	4.97	1.51	276	207	317	10.1	31%	67%	4.42	56	16	27	3.9	5.3	**1.4**	8%	0.7	-6.1	24	$3
PT/Exp	C	08	DET	8	5	0	118	62	4.27	1.39	262	269	256	11.3	29%	70%	4.83	45	20	35	3.5	4.7	**1.3**	7%	0.8	1.1	14	$8
Consist	A	1st Half		3	3	0	43	23	4.43	1.48	249			6.1	28%	69%	4.98	51	19	30	4.8	4.8	**1.0**	5%	0.4	-0.4	-15	$2
LIMA Plan	D+	2nd Half		5	2	0	75	39	4.18	1.34	269			22.9	29%	71%	4.74	43	20	37	2.7	4.7	**1.7**	8%	1.0	1.5	30	$5
+/- Score	-35	09	Proj	**7**	**10**	**0**	**145**	**81**	**4.59**	**1.46**	**271**			**12.0**	**30%**	**70%**	**4.72**	**48**	**19**	**33**	**3.7**	**5.0**	**1.4**	**9%**	**0.9**	**-5.3**	**18**	**$6**

Skills have been lousy no matter what his role. And now with a fading Dom rate and a sizable ERA/xERA gap, the difference between his surface stats and skills is a trap just waiting for some unsuspecting owner.

Misch,Pat

Misch,Pat				W	L	Sv	IP	K	ERA	WHIP	OBA	vL	vR	BF/G	H%	S%	xERA	G	L	F	Ctl	Dom	Cmd	hr/f	hr/9	RAR	BPV	R$
LH Starter		04	aa	7	6	0	159	101	3.91	1.26	269			25.6	31%	70%	3.82				2.0	5.7	**2.8**		0.7	8.5	73	$11
Age	27	05	a/a	7	11	0	163	92	5.80	1.62	322			26.4	35%	66%	5.95				2.5	5.1	**2.0**		1.2	-30.1	28	($1)
Type	Con	06	a/a	9	6	0	168	110	3.94	1.46	305			26.3	35%	75%	4.92				2.0	5.9	**3.0**		0.8	12.0	67	$11
Health	A	07	SF *	2	9	1	107	81	4.13	1.42	281			8.9	33%	71%	4.15	43	24	33	2.9	6.8	**2.4**	7%	0.6	3.9	67	$5
PT/Exp	D	08	SF *	6	8	0	139	77	7.27	1.76	335	281	270	18.6	35%	61%	5.08	44	19	36	3.1	5.0	**1.6**	16%	1.9	-51.5	29	($8)
Consist	B	1st Half		2	6	0	86	54	6.77	1.72	317			22.2	34%	63%	4.97	43	21	36	3.7	5.7	**1.5**	15%	1.7	-26.6	23	($4)
LIMA Plan	C+	2nd Half		4	2	0	53	23	8.07	1.83	363			14.9	36%	59%	5.44	50	6	44	2.0	3.9	**1.9**	14%	2.2	-25.0	43	($4)
+/- Score	74	09	Proj	**2**	**3**	**0**	**54**	**33**	**4.50**	**1.52**	**302**			**9.2**	**33%**	**73%**	**4.59**	**44**	**21**	**35**	**2.7**	**5.5**	**2.1**	**11%**	**1.2**	**-1.7**	**49**	**$1**

0-3, 5.68 ERA in 52 IP at SF.
CON: Regressed at Triple-A last year, weak Dom history, age
PRO: Good Ctl history, 2.5 Cmd with Giants last year, including 6.5 Dom rate
He's intriguing. Watch his role.

BRANDON KRUSE

Mock,Garrett

		Yr	W	L	Sv	IP	K	ERA	WHIP	OBA	vL	vR	BF/G	H%	S%	xERA	G	L	F	Ctl	Dom	Cmd	hr/f	hr/9	RAR	BPV	R$
RH	Reliever	04	0	0	0	0	0	0.00	0.00																		
Age	26	05	0	0	0	0	0	0.00	0.00																		
Type	Pwr	06 aa	4	12	0	147	104	7.31	1.83	335			25.9	38%	60%	6.74				3.7	6.3	**1.7**		1.3	-50.7	24	($8)
Health	A	07 aa	1	5	0	51	32	7.05	2.10	351			23.3	39%	66%	7.43				5.2	5.7	**1.1**		0.9	-16.3	14	($5)
PT/Exp	D	08 WAS *	7	6	0	145	125	3.56	1.32	262	279	207	13.7	32%	75%	3.90	45	19	36	2.9	7.8	**2.7**	8%	0.7	12.8	83	$12
Consist	F	1st Half	4	4	0	85	61	4.04	1.35	285			24.3	33%	70%	3.42	52	27	21	2.0	6.5	**3.2**	10%	0.6	2.5	92	$5
LIMA Plan	C+	2nd Half	3	2	0	60	64	2.87	1.29	226			8.4	29%	82%	3.87	42	16	43	4.2	9.6	**2.3**	9%	0.9	10.3	78	$7
+/- Score	4	09 Proj	**3**	**5**	**0**	**79**	**62**	**4.70**	**1.52**	**280**			**21.8**	**32%**	**72%**	**4.54**	**43**	**18**	**39**	**3.8**	**7.1**	**1.9**	**10%**	**1.1**	**-1.9**	**47**	**$2**

1-3, 4.17 ERA in 41 IP at WAS. 1H FB% is misleading; it came in just 10 IP. 2.0 Ctl in Triple-A, 5.0 Ctl in majors, so while this was a nice growth year, still has work to do. Sleeper potential as SP, but he'll require patience.

Moehler,Brian

		Yr	W	L	Sv	IP	K	ERA	WHIP	OBA	vL	vR	BF/G	H%	S%	xERA	G	L	F	Ctl	Dom	Cmd	hr/f	hr/9	RAR	BPV	R$
RH	Starter	04 aa	3	9	0	108	42	5.83	1.63	321			24.6	34%	64%	5.75				2.7	3.5	**1.3**		0.9	-19.9	12	($3)
Age	37	05 FLA	6	12	0	158	95	4.55	1.52	308	320	305	19.0	34%	71%	4.41	44	25	31	2.4	5.4	**2.3**	9%	0.9	-6.0	55	$4
Type	Con	06 FLA	7	11	0	122	58	6.57	1.66	323	351	297	19.2	34%	62%	4.96	45	22	33	2.8	4.3	**1.5**	13%	1.4	-31.3	25	($2)
Health	A	07 HOU	1	4	1	60	36	4.07	1.41	285	303	268	6.2	31%	75%	4.18	52	16	32	2.6	5.4	**2.1**	13%	1.2	2.6	59	$3
PT/Exp	B	08 HOU	11	8	0	150	82	4.56	1.35	282	307	255	20.6	30%	69%	4.44	44	21	35	2.2	4.9	**2.3**	11%	1.2	-5.4	52	$9
Consist	B	1st Half	4	3	0	64	40	3.81	1.38	275			18.3	29%	78%	4.43	45	18	37	2.8	5.7	**2.0**	13%	1.4	3.6	49	$4
LIMA Plan	C	2nd Half	7	5	0	86	42	5.11	1.32	287			22.9	30%	63%	4.44	43	23	34	1.7	4.4	**2.6**	10%	1.0	-8.9	54	$5
+/- Score	-10	09 Proj	**6**	**8**	**0**	**120**	**65**	**4.80**	**1.43**	**293**			**20.9**	**31%**	**69%**	**4.50**	**46**	**20**	**34**	**2.4**	**4.9**	**2.0**	**11%**	**1.1**	**-2.4**	**47**	**$4**

Not a good sign when terms like "rotation filler," "inning-eater" & "replacement level" represent your upside.Turns LHers into batting champs, but Ctl keeps him in the game. If that ever goes, this will get ugly fast.

Morales,Franklin

		Yr	W	L	Sv	IP	K	ERA	WHIP	OBA	vL	vR	BF/G	H%	S%	xERA	G	L	F	Ctl	Dom	Cmd	hr/f	hr/9	RAR	BPV	R$
LH	Starter	04	0	0	0	0	0	0.00	0.00																		
Age	23	05	0	0	0	0	0	0.00	0.00																		
Type	Pwr	06	0	0	0	0	0	0.00	0.00																		
Health	A	07 COL *	8	6	0	152	109	4.46	1.48	262	129	273	23.8	30%	71%	4.14	55	19	27	4.3	6.5	**1.5**	11%	0.8	-0.6	34	$8
PT/Exp	D	08 COL *	11	7	0	135	80	6.18	1.76	278	200	295	24.4	30%	66%	6.00	40	20	40	6.0	5.3	**0.9**	9%	1.1	-31.9	-50	($2)
Consist	D	1st Half	6	5	0	76	36	6.71	1.83	288			24.2	31%	63%	6.52	40	20	40	6.2	4.2	**0.7**	8%	0.9	-23.0	-74	($3)
LIMA Plan	C	2nd Half	5	2	0	59	44	5.49	1.66	265			24.6	29%	70%					5.8	6.7	**1.2**		1.4	-8.9	25	$1
+/- Score	-15	09 Proj	**6**	**4**	**0**	**87**	**58**	**5.38**	**1.63**	**271**			**24.8**	**30%**	**68%**	**5.21**	**44**	**20**	**36**	**5.3**	**6.0**	**1.1**	**10%**	**1.0**	**-9.4**	**-12**	**$1**

1-2, 6.39 ERA in 25 IP at COL. Why he lost the strike zone in '08:
- Unexplained myopic spasms
- Using Metric-based strike zone
- Coors Field too close to satellites for his GPS to work.
- He left it with his car keys.

Morrow,Brandon

		Yr	W	L	Sv	IP	K	ERA	WHIP	OBA	vL	vR	BF/G	H%	S%	xERA	G	L	F	Ctl	Dom	Cmd	hr/f	hr/9	RAR	BPV	R$
RH	Reliever	04	0	0	0	0	0	0.00	0.00																		
Age	24	05	0	0	0	0	0	0.00	0.00																		
Type	Pwr xFB	06	0	0	0	0	0	0.00	0.00																		
Health	A	07 SEA	3	4	0	63	66	4.12	1.67	239	278	221	4.8	32%	75%	5.28	35	18	47	7.1	9.4	**1.3**	4%	0.4	3.0	-10	$3
PT/Exp	D	08 SEA *	4	6	10	95	104	3.77	1.21	191	198	149	6.9	24%	73%	4.11	33	16	51	4.9	9.9	**2.0**	11%	1.1	6.7	57	$14
Consist	C	1st Half	0	1	4	30	39	0.59	0.97	159			3.6	23%	100%	3.06	41	16	43	3.9	11.4	**2.9**	7%	0.6	14.1	119	$7
LIMA Plan	D+	2nd Half	4	5	6	65	66	5.27	1.33	205			11.4	24%	63%	4.67	29	17	54	5.4	9.2	**1.7**	11%	1.4	-7.4	27	$7
+/- Score	-17	09 Proj	**8**	**12**	**0**	**174**	**190**	**4.14**	**1.40**	**227**			**24.3**	**29%**	**74%**	**4.34**	**35**	**17**	**48**	**5.2**	**9.8**	**1.9**	**10%**	**1.1**	**1.8**	**50**	**$15**

3-4, 3.34 ERA in 64 IP at SEA. Frankly, if you were SEA, which skill set would you choose: the 1st half (RP) or 2nd half (SP)? Youth, Dom are reasons to give starting another shot, but the pen looks like his true calling.

Morton,Charlie

		Yr	W	L	Sv	IP	K	ERA	WHIP	OBA	vL	vR	BF/G	H%	S%	xERA	G	L	F	Ctl	Dom	Cmd	hr/f	hr/9	RAR	BPV	R$
RH	Starter	04	0	0	0	0	0	0.00	0.00																		
Age	25	05	0	0	0	0	0	0.00	0.00																		
Type	Pwr GB	06	0	0	0	0	0	0.00	0.00																		
Health	A	07 aa	4	6	0	79	55	5.62	1.72	300			9.0	36%	65%	5.08				4.6	6.3	**1.4**		0.4	-11.3	51	($0)
PT/Exp	D	08 ATL *	9	10	0	154	111	4.27	1.34	241	306	245	22.6	29%	68%	4.22	50	18	31	4.0	6.5	**1.6**	6%	0.5	-0.1	38	$10
Consist	B	1st Half	6	3	0	96	74	2.81	1.13	217			24.3	28%	72%	3.77	50	18	32	3.1	6.9	**2.2**	0%	0.0	17.3	69	$12
LIMA Plan	C	2nd Half	3	7	0	58	37	6.71	1.70	279			20.5	30%	62%	5.07	50	19	31	5.5	5.8	**1.1**	15%	1.4	-17.3	-15	($2)
+/- Score	-13	09 Proj	**6**	**9**	**0**	**106**	**75**	**4.95**	**1.56**	**273**			**23.7**	**31%**	**69%**	**4.57**	**50**	**18**	**31**	**4.5**	**6.4**	**1.4**	**10%**	**0.9**	**-3.1**	**21**	**$3**

4-8, 6.15 ERA in 74 IP at ATL. 3.0 Cmd in Triple-A, 1.2 in the majors, that's what did him in. '07 relief BPIs and only 12 starts prior to call-up suggest he was rushed. Seems likely to spend at least part of '09 in minors.

Moseley,Dustin

		Yr	W	L	Sv	IP	K	ERA	WHIP	OBA	vL	vR	BF/G	H%	S%	xERA	G	L	F	Ctl	Dom	Cmd	hr/f	hr/9	RAR	BPV	R$
RH	Starter	04 a/a	5	6	0	119	74	4.54	1.41	271			25.8	30%	70%	4.49				3.3	5.6	**1.7**		1.0	-2.9	41	$5
Age	27	05 aaa	4	6	0	82	32	4.82	1.60	310			21.8	32%	71%	5.52				3.0	3.5	**1.2**		1.0	-5.3	9	$1
Type		06 aaa	13	8	0	149	96	4.95	1.49	294			25.3	33%	68%	5.00				2.9	5.8	**2.0**		1.0	-7.8	42	$9
Health	A	07 LAA	4	3	0	92	50	4.40	1.35	272	224	323	8.5	30%	68%	4.47	48	18	34	2.6	4.9	**1.9**	7%	0.7	1.2	43	$6
PT/Exp	C	08 LAA *	9	14	0	167	100	8.76	1.94	361	366	300	25.3	39%	55%	4.91	48	21	31	3.1	5.4	**1.7**	16%	1.8	-90.7	38	($15)
Consist	A	1st Half	5	7	0	85	52	7.65	1.79	340			24.9	37%	57%	5.03	40	23	37	3.0	5.6	**1.9**	12%	1.4	-34.6	38	($4)
LIMA Plan	C+	2nd Half	4	7	0	82	47	9.92	2.10	381			25.6	40%	54%	4.54	58	18	24	3.3	5.2	**1.6**	25%	2.1	-56.1	41	($12)
+/- Score	133	09 Proj	**3**	**4**	**0**	**58**	**35**	**5.12**	**1.52**	**297**			**23.4**	**32%**	**69%**	**4.48**	**48**	**19**	**33**	**2.9**	**5.4**	**1.8**	**12%**	**1.2**	**-0.4**	**45**	**$2**

2-4, 6.79 ERA in 50 IP at LAA. Zero skill growth in three years, and then bad luck just piled on. Think YOU had a bad year? According to RAR, his lousiness nearly offset the work of Cliff Lee and Roy Halladay combined.

Mota,Guillermo

		Yr	W	L	Sv	IP	K	ERA	WHIP	OBA	vL	vR	BF/G	H%	S%	xERA	G	L	F	Ctl	Dom	Cmd	hr/f	hr/9	RAR	BPV	R$
RH	Reliever	04 2NL	9	8	4	96	85	2.99	1.16	217	196	236	5.0	26%	77%	3.72	47	17	36	3.5	8.0	**2.3**	9%	0.7	15.0	75	$15
Age	35	05 FLA	2	2	2	67	60	4.70	1.45	256	243	262	5.2	32%	67%	4.43	41	19	41	4.3	8.1	**1.9**	6%	0.7	-3.8	48	$3
Type	Pwr	06 2TM	4	3	0	55	46	4.57	1.43	261	252	261	4.6	29%	75%	4.71	34	18	48	3.9	7.5	**1.9**	14%	1.8	-0.3	41	$4
Health	A	07 NYM *	2	3	0	67	52	6.26	1.52	291	235	284	5.0	33%	60%	4.37	44	18	38	3.2	7.1	**2.2**	11%	1.2	-15.0	62	($0)
PT/Exp	D	08 MIL	5	6	1	57	50	4.11	1.40	244	287	216	4.2	29%	74%	4.13	45	22	33	4.4	7.9	**1.8**	13%	1.1	1.2	46	$5
Consist	A	1st Half	2	5	1	31	31	4.06	1.45	249			4.7	31%	76%	4.23	39	21	40	4.6	9.0	**1.9**	12%	1.2	0.8	54	$3
LIMA Plan	C	2nd Half	3	1	0	26	19	4.15	1.35	239			3.8	27%	72%	3.98	51	23	26	4.2	6.6	**1.6**	15%	1.0	0.4	36	$3
+/- Score	-14	09 Proj	**5**	**4**	**0**	**63**	**52**	**4.46**	**1.42**	**257**			**4.5**	**30%**	**72%**	**4.28**	**44**	**20**	**36**	**4.0**	**7.5**	**1.9**	**12%**	**1.2**	**0.5**	**48**	**$4**

xERA has rebounded slightly thanks to decrease in FB%, but the rest of his skills have been stagnant for four years. As a result, sense opps have dried up and so has his value. Feels like he's just running out the clock.

Moyer,Jamie

		Yr	W	L	Sv	IP	K	ERA	WHIP	OBA	vL	vR	BF/G	H%	S%	xERA	G	L	F	Ctl	Dom	Cmd	hr/f	hr/9	RAR	BPV	R$
LH	Starter	04 SEA	7	13	0	202	125	5.21	1.39	276	293	263	25.6	28%	69%	4.71	39	17	43	2.8	5.6	**2.0**	15%	2.0	-19.5	42	$7
Age	46	05 SEA	13	7	0	200	102	4.28	1.39	285	294	278	26.9	30%	72%	4.92	37	22	41	2.3	4.6	**2.0**	8%	1.0	2.4	34	$12
Type		06 2TM	11	14	0	211	108	4.31	1.32	277	251	285	27.1	29%	72%	4.67	40	21	39	2.2	4.6	**2.1**	12%	1.4	5.6	42	$14
Health	A	07 PHI	14	12	0	199	133	5.01	1.45	283	309	279	26.4	31%	69%	4.63	39	21	39	3.0	6.0	**2.0**	12%	1.4	-14.4	45	$10
PT/Exp	A	08 PHI	16	7	0	196	123	3.71	1.33	264	240	270	25.3	29%	75%	4.39	44	21	35	2.8	5.6	**2.0**	9%	0.9	13.5	47	$17
Consist	A	1st Half	7	6	0	100	62	4.13	1.40	282			25.5	31%	75%	4.24	47	21	32	2.6	5.6	**2.1**	13%	1.3	1.8	55	$6
LIMA Plan	D	2nd Half	9	1	0	96	61	3.28	1.26	245			25.1	28%	75%	4.54	40	21	38	3.1	5.7	**1.8**	5%	0.6	11.7	38	$11
+/- Score	-54	09 Proj	**11**	**10**	**0**	**156**	**96**	**4.33**	**1.38**	**270**			**25.8**	**30%**	**72%**	**4.64**	**41**	**21**	**38**	**3.1**	**5.5**	**1.8**	**10%**	**1.1**	**-5.9**	**36**	**$10**

Cmd has been consistent, but fluctuations in Dom, hr/f and S% have caused annual swings in ERA. That means you could get a 2004 just as easily as another 2008. Use xERA as your target, set your bid limit, divide by 46.

Moylan,Peter

		Yr	W	L	Sv	IP	K	ERA	WHIP	OBA	vL	vR	BF/G	H%	S%	xERA	G	L	F	Ctl	Dom	Cmd	hr/f	hr/9	RAR	BPV	R$
RH	Reliever	04	0	0	0	0	0	0.00	0.00																		
Age	30	05	0	0	0	0	0	0.00	0.00																		
Type	Pwr xGB	06 ATL *	1	7	1	71	60	8.33	2.02	323			7.0	39%	57%	4.67	58	17	25	6.1	7.5	**1.2**	11%	0.8	-33.7	8	($7)
Health	F	07 ATL	5	3	1	90	63	1.80	1.07	204	242	184	4.5	24%	87%	3.37	62	13	25	3.1	6.3	**2.0**	9%	0.6	29.2	70	$14
PT/Exp	D	08 ATL	0	1	1	6	5	1.58	1.05	237	273	167	3.2	27%	100%	2.50	67	11	22	1.6	7.9	**5.0**	28%	1.6	1.9	144	$1
Consist	C	1st Half	0	1	1	6	5	1.58	1.05	237			3.2	27%	100%	2.50	67	11	22	1.6	7.9	**5.0**	28%	1.6	1.9	144	$1
LIMA Plan	B+	2nd Half	0	0	0	0	0	0.00	0.00																		
+/- Score	-66	09 Proj	**2**	**3**	**0**	**54**	**41**	**3.50**	**1.35**	**255**			**5.2**	**30%**	**75%**	**3.48**	**64**	**12**	**24**	**3.5**	**6.8**	**2.0**	**10%**	**0.7**	**5.8**	**71**	**$4**

Hmm... any connection between 81 games, 90 IP in 2007 and TJ surgery in 2008? Has shown growth, but relatively small sample size combined with this injury makes it hard to gauge what to expect when he returns.

BRANDON KRUSE

Mujica,Edward

		Yr	Tm	W	L	Sv	IP	K	ERA	WHIP	OBA	vL	vR	BF/G	H%	S%	xERA	G	L	F	Ctl	Dom	Cmd	hr/f	hr/9	RAR	BPV	R$
RH	Reliever	04		0	0	0	0	0	0.00	0.00																		
Age	25	05	aa	2	1	10	34	29	3.43	1.35	299			5.4	37%	75%	4.25				1.3	7.7	**5.8**		0.5	3.7	147	$6
Type	xFB	06	CLE *	4	2	13	69	53	2.21	1.28	275	324	341	6.6	34%	83%	4.75	26	18	55	1.9	6.9	**3.5**	2%	0.3	20.1	75	$14
Health	A	07	CLE *	2	1	14	50	47	6.63	1.39	294			4.9	35%	52%	4.47	26	16	58	2.0	8.4	**4.3**	8%	1.3	-13.2	102	$6
PT/Exp	D	08	CLE *	3	4	4	65	51	6.26	1.58	307	277	318	5.7	36%	60%	4.85	30	23	46	2.9	7.1	**2.4**	7%	1.0	-15.3	57	$2
Consist	A	1st Half		0	3	4	38	31	5.92	1.66	309			6.4	36%	66%	5.29	21	26	52	3.6	7.3	**2.1**	8%	1.2	-7.4	36	$0
LIMA Plan	B+	2nd Half		3	1	0	27	20	6.74	1.46	305			4.9	36%	51%	4.50	35	22	43	2.0	6.7	**3.3**	5%	0.7	-7.9	80	$1
+/- Score	72	09	Proj	**3**	**2**	**0**	**54**	**44**	**4.67**	**1.35**	**283**			**5.4**	**33%**	**68%**	**4.41**	**31**	**21**	**48**	**2.2**	**7.3**	**3.4**	**9%**	**1.2**	**0.1**	**82**	**$4**

3-2, 6.75 ERA in 38 IP at CLE. Must have broken a mirror sometime between 2006 and '07,because that's when his S% plummeted into the abyss. Good skills are buried under all this. A nice LIMA sleeper.

Mussina,Mike

		Yr	Tm	W	L	Sv	IP	K	ERA	WHIP	OBA	vL	vR	BF/G	H%	S%	xERA	G	L	F	Ctl	Dom	Cmd	hr/f	hr/9	RAR	BPV	R$
RH	Starter	04	NYY	12	9	0	164	132	4.60	1.33	278	254	299	25.8	32%	68%	3.85	44	21	36	2.2	7.2	**3.3**	12%	1.2	-3.5	93	$13
Age	40	05	NYY	13	8	0	179	142	4.42	1.37	283	282	286	25.6	33%	71%	3.98	45	18	37	2.4	7.1	**3.0**	11%	1.2	-1.1	88	$14
Type	Con	06	NYY	15	7	0	197	172	3.52	1.11	249	223	258	24.8	30%	72%	3.53	42	17	40	1.6	7.9	**4.9**	10%	1.0	25.3	119	$28
Health	B	07	NYY	11	10	0	152	91	5.15	1.47	305	315	307	23.8	34%	65%	4.54	42	22	36	2.1	5.4	**2.6**	7%	0.8	-12.1	61	$8
PT/Exp	A	08	NYY	20	9	0	200	150	3.37	1.22	275	236	317	24.4	32%	75%	3.48	48	22	30	1.4	6.7	**4.8**	9%	0.8	24.2	110	$25
Consist	C	1st Half		10	6	0	95	58	3.87	1.24	277			23.3	30%	73%	3.90	44	25	32	1.4	5.5	**3.9**	12%	1.1	5.6	82	$11
LIMA Plan	D+	2nd Half		10	3	0	105	92	2.91	1.21	273			25.5	34%	76%	3.09	53	19	28	1.4	7.9	**5.8**	6%	0.4	18.6	136	$15
+/- Score	-4	09	Proj	**14**	**8**	**0**	**164**	**107**	**3.91**	**1.35**	**280**			**24.9**	**31%**	**74%**	**4.13**	**46**	**21**	**33**	**2.3**	**5.9**	**2.6**	**10%**	**1.0**	**6.0**	**69**	**$15**

This was essentially '06 with a little more GB% and a little less Dom, giving hope that this is a repeatable skill set. That's if he comes back. If not, then he will be one of the few that took the George Brett Path to Retirement.

Myers,Brett

		Yr	Tm	W	L	Sv	IP	K	ERA	WHIP	OBA	vL	vR	BF/G	H%	S%	xERA	G	L	F	Ctl	Dom	Cmd	hr/f	hr/9	RAR	BPV	R$
RH	Starter	04	PHI	11	11	0	176	116	5.52	1.47	283	278	293	24.1	30%	66%	4.38	47	19	34	3.2	5.9	**1.9**	16%	1.6	-27.4	46	$5
Age	28	05	PHI	13	8	0	215	208	3.72	1.21	241	241	233	26.1	29%	75%	3.30	46	23	31	2.8	8.7	**3.1**	17%	1.3	13.8	104	$22
Type	Pwr	06	PHI	12	7	0	198	189	3.91	1.30	258	259	254	26.9	31%	75%	3.59	46	18	36	2.9	8.6	**3.0**	14%	1.3	14.1	101	$19
Health	B	07	PHI	5	7	21	69	83	4.32	1.28	239	183	274	5.7	32%	70%	3.14	46	19	35	3.5	10.9	**3.1**	15%	1.3	0.9	124	$14
PT/Exp	B	08	PHI *	11	15	0	210	183	4.46	1.38	267	235	293	27.3	31%	71%	3.77	47	20	32	3.1	7.8	**2.5**	15%	1.3	-4.8	82	$13
Consist	B	1st Half		3	9	0	102	88	5.84	1.56	286			26.8	31%	69%	4.28	44	18	38	3.9	7.8	**2.0**	20%	2.1	-19.7	57	($0)
LIMA Plan	C+	2nd Half		8	6	0	108	95	3.16	1.20	249			27.9	31%	74%	3.25	51	23	26	2.4	7.9	**3.3**	7%	0.5	14.9	106	$13
+/- Score	42	09	Proj	**15**	**9**	**0**	**185**	**178**	**3.76**	**1.26**	**250**			**26.6**	**31%**	**73%**	**3.41**	**48**	**20**	**32**	**2.9**	**8.7**	**3.0**	**12%**	**1.0**	**21.2**	**104**	**$20**

Terrific 2H after demotion to minors. If those skills represent change in approach, this could be big. Especially Ctl and FB%, as BB and HR have long been his downfall. Add in peak age: UP: 18 Wins, 3.25 ERA.

Nathan,Joe

		Yr	Tm	W	L	Sv	IP	K	ERA	WHIP	OBA	vL	vR	BF/G	H%	S%	xERA	G	L	F	Ctl	Dom	Cmd	hr/f	hr/9	RAR	BPV	R$
RH	Reliever	04	MIN	1	2	44	72	89	1.62	0.98	191	212	160	3.9	28%	85%	3.18	35	16	49	2.9	11.1	**3.9**	4%	0.4	25.0	136	$28
Age	34	05	MIN	7	4	43	70	94	2.70	0.97	189	160	206	3.9	28%	75%	2.93	37	12	50	2.8	12.1	**4.3**	7%	0.6	14.4	157	$28
Type	Pwr	06	MIN	7	0	36	68	95	1.59	0.79	165	193	130	4.0	27%	82%	2.42	36	22	42	2.1	12.6	**5.9**	5%	0.4	25.0	183	$29
Health	A	07	MIN	4	2	37	72	77	1.88	1.02	211	221	199	4.2	29%	84%	3.17	40	21	39	2.4	9.7	**4.1**	6%	0.5	23.2	128	$26
PT/Exp	A	08	MIN	1	2	39	68	74	1.33	0.90	184	167	192	3.8	25%	91%	2.79	47	19	33	2.4	9.8	**4.1**	9%	0.7	25.2	138	$25
Consist	B	1st Half		0	0	22	34	37	1.34	0.95	215			3.8	28%	93%	2.59	52	16	32	1.6	9.9	**6.2**	11%	0.8	12.5	164	$13
LIMA Plan	C+	2nd Half		1	2	17	34	37	1.32	0.85	151			3.8	20%	89%	2.99	43	23	35	3.2	9.8	**3.1**	8%	0.5	12.7	111	$12
+/- Score	-78	09	Proj	**3**	**2**	**40**	**73**	**78**	**2.48**	**1.08**	**218**			**4.1**	**29%**	**81%**	**3.19**	**42**	**20**	**38**	**2.6**	**9.7**	**3.7**	**9%**	**0.7**	**11.0**	**124**	**$24**

Dom has declined, but the fact that it slid in conjunction with a big drop in FB% makes this pretty much a wash. Low H%, high S% means ERA is heading up a little; other than that, he's about as elite as closers get.

Nelson,Joe

		Yr	Tm	W	L	Sv	IP	K	ERA	WHIP	OBA	vL	vR	BF/G	H%	S%	xERA	G	L	F	Ctl	Dom	Cmd	hr/f	hr/9	RAR	BPV	R$
RH	Reliever	04	a/a	3	2	13	51	57	4.29	1.71	293			5.8	39%	74%	5.00				4.9	9.9	**2.0**		0.4	0.3	86	$6
Age	34	05	a/a	0	3	7	59	58	5.14	1.65	273			6.1	32%	74%	5.73				5.3	8.8	**1.6**		1.7	-6.1	36	$2
Type	Pwr	06	KC *	3	3	16	76	76	3.72	1.27	219	180	252	4.8	27%	75%	4.09	34	23	43	4.3	9.0	**2.1**	11%	1.1	7.9	58	$13
Health	F	07		0	0	0	0	0	0.00	0.00																		
PT/Exp	D	08	FLA *	4	2	12	79	88	2.30	1.18	224	227	189	4.2	30%	84%	3.38	40	23	38	3.3	10.0	**3.0**	8%	0.7	19.3	109	$15
Consist	B	1st Half		2	1	11	41	45	2.25	1.11	224			4.7	31%	81%	3.13	43	23	35	2.7	9.9	**3.7**	6%	0.5	10.2	127	$10
LIMA Plan	B	2nd Half		2	1	1	38	43	2.35	1.25	223			3.7	29%	86%	3.58	39	23	39	4.0	10.1	**2.5**	11%	0.9	9.1	91	$5
+/- Score	-33	09	Proj	**3**	**2**	**0**	**73**	**77**	**3.60**	**1.34**	**238**			**4.6**	**31%**	**76%**	**3.86**	**38**	**23**	**40**	**4.1**	**9.6**	**2.3**	**11%**	**1.0**	**4.3**	**77**	**$6**

3-1, 2.00 ERA in 54 IP at FLA. Little odd to see skill growth from a 34-year-old who just lost a season to shoulder surgery, but there it is. It's not something you should invest heavily in, but it's certainly worth a flyer.

Neshek,Pat

		Yr	Tm	W	L	Sv	IP	K	ERA	WHIP	OBA	vL	vR	BF/G	H%	S%	xERA	G	L	F	Ctl	Dom	Cmd	hr/f	hr/9	RAR	BPV	R$
RH	Reliever	04	aa	2	1	2	35	32	5.40	1.77	298			6.3	37%	68%	5.35				5.1	8.3	**1.6**		0.5	-4.6	63	$1
Age	28	05	aa	6	4	24	82	75	2.92	1.37	275			6.4	33%	84%	4.47				2.7	8.2	**3.1**		1.1	14.0	80	$17
Type	Pwr xFB	06	MIN *	10	4	14	97	125	2.65	1.02	219	244	140	5.9	29%	84%	3.08	32	14	54	2.1	11.6	**5.5**	13%	1.4	22.8	162	$25
Health	F	07	MIN	7	2	0	70	74	2.94	1.01	182	181	185	3.7	23%	75%	3.78	32	16	52	3.5	9.5	**2.7**	8%	0.9	13.5	87	$13
PT/Exp	D	08	MIN	0	1	0	13	15	4.74	1.20	242	250	233	3.7	31%	64%	3.42	31	28	42	2.7	10.2	**3.8**	14%	1.4	-0.6	118	$1
Consist	B	1st Half		0	1	0	13	15	4.74	1.20	242			3.7	31%	64%	3.42	31	28	42	2.7	10.2	**3.8**	14%	1.4	-0.6	118	$1
LIMA Plan	A	2nd Half		0	0	0	0	0	0.00	0.00																		
+/- Score	61	09	Proj																									

One of the better non-closer skill sets in baseball, however... chose rehab for partially torn elbow ligament, which so often results in TJ surgery anyway. Interesting speculation for 2010.

Nippert,Dustin

		Yr	Tm	W	L	Sv	IP	K	ERA	WHIP	OBA	vL	vR	BF/G	H%	S%	xERA	G	L	F	Ctl	Dom	Cmd	hr/f	hr/9	RAR	BPV	R$
RH	Starter	04	aa	2	5	0	71	65	4.30	1.81	306			24.1	40%	74%	5.06				5.1	8.2	**1.6**		0.0	0.4	77	$0
Age	28	05	aa	8	3	0	117	84	3.07	1.36	258			27.8	31%	77%	3.58				3.4	6.4	**1.9**		0.4	17.8	70	$11
Type	Pwr	06	ARI *	13	10	0	150	123	6.11	1.69	317	333	375	25.7	37%	64%	4.13	56	12	32	3.4	7.4	**2.1**	11%	1.1	-30.0	73	$2
Health	B	07	ARI *	1	4	0	81	74	6.15	1.49	256	238	290	7.8	31%	59%	4.34	38	28	34	4.7	8.2	**1.7**	12%	1.1	-17.3	36	($0)
PT/Exp	D	08	TEX *	9	7	0	135	86	5.98	1.73	320	263	354	19.6	35%	68%	5.23	37	24	39	3.7	5.7	**1.6**	11%	1.4	-27.1	19	($1)
Consist	B	1st Half		7	4	0	72	37	6.84	1.84	343			19.0	36%	64%	5.28	37	31	31	3.3	4.6	**1.4**	13%	1.4	-22.1	10	($2)
LIMA Plan	C+	2nd Half		2	3	0	63	49	5.00	1.62	291			20.4	33%	73%	4.87	37	23	40	4.1	7.0	**1.7**	12%	1.4	-5.1	29	$1
+/- Score	7	09	Proj	**3**	**5**	**0**	**73**	**56**	**5.09**	**1.50**	**279**			**21.4**	**32%**	**68%**	**4.58**	**38**	**25**	**37**	**3.7**	**7.0**	**1.9**	**11%**	**1.1**	**-1.4**	**40**	**$3**

3-5, 6.40 ERA in 71 IP at TEX. CON: xERA, BPV and Cmd all trending down, HR going up. PRO: In 6 MLB starts to end '08, posted 8.2 Dom, 2.2 Cmd. Prime pick for the desperate and reckless. Perhaps a 10% play.

Nolasco,Ricky

		Yr	Tm	W	L	Sv	IP	K	ERA	WHIP	OBA	vL	vR	BF/G	H%	S%	xERA	G	L	F	Ctl	Dom	Cmd	hr/f	hr/9	RAR	BPV	R$
RH	Starter	04	a/a	8	7	0	147	134	5.53	1.57	301			23.6	36%	67%	5.52				3.1	8.2	**2.6**		1.2	-21.6	62	$4
Age	26	05	aa	1	3	0	161	152	3.74	1.41	281			25.8	35%	76%	4.53				2.7	8.5	**3.1**		0.9	11.2	86	$9
Type	FB	06	FLA	11	11	0	140	99	4.82	1.41	285	338	240	17.3	32%	69%	4.46	39	21	40	2.6	6.4	**2.4**	11%	1.3	-5.8	60	$9
Health	D	07	FLA *	1	5	0	39	26	10.18	1.96	361	293	350	19.2	39%	48%	5.44	37	19	44	3.3	6.0	**1.8**	14%	2.1	-28.0	35	($6)
PT/Exp	B	08	FLA	15	8	0	212	186	3.52	1.10	243	238	239	25.1	28%	73%	3.64	39	19	42	1.8	7.9	**4.4**	11%	1.2	19.7	111	$25
Consist	C	1st Half		8	4	0	96	67	4.04	1.31	262			23.8	29%	74%	4.58	34	21	45	2.7	6.3	**2.3**	10%	1.3	2.7	52	$8
LIMA Plan	C	2nd Half		7	4	0	117	119	3.09	0.93	226			26.4	28%	73%	2.93	43	17	40	1.0	9.2	**9.2**	11%	1.1	17.0	159	$17
+/- Score	18	09	Proj	**13**	**9**	**0**	**183**	**151**	**3.98**	**1.26**	**266**			**24.7**	**30%**	**73%**	**3.97**	**39**	**19**	**42**	**2.1**	**7.4**	**3.5**	**12%**	**1.3**	**8.3**	**93**	**$17**

Said he began using new cutter on June 15th, and you can see the results in his 2nd half. At the same time, threw 104 pitches per start over last 20 GS, after elbow issues ended '07 early. UP: $30 season. DN: DL.

Nunez,Leo

		Yr	Tm	W	L	Sv	IP	K	ERA	WHIP	OBA	vL	vR	BF/G	H%	S%	xERA	G	L	F	Ctl	Dom	Cmd	hr/f	hr/9	RAR	BPV	R$
RH	Reliever	04		0	0	0	0	0	0.00	0.00											0.0	0.0						
Age	25	05	KC *	4	2	4	66	44	6.53	1.59	308	374	298	5.6	34%	61%	4.92	37	21	42	3.0	6.0	**2.0**	12%	1.5	-17.6	42	$1
Type	FB	06	KC *	3	4	8	72	55	3.62	1.44	272	211	355	7.0	31%	79%	4.17	41	30	30	3.5	6.9	**2.0**	14%	1.1	8.3	48	$8
Health	D	07	KC *	4	6	0	87	64	3.17	1.11	236	275	248	14.6	26%	78%	4.28	32	19	49	2.1	6.6	**3.1**	10%	1.3	14.3	71	$11
PT/Exp	D	08	KC	4	1	0	48	26	2.98	1.24	248	272	230	4.5	28%	76%	4.87	39	18	43	2.8	4.8	**1.7**	3%	0.4	8.1	29	$6
Consist	A	1st Half		3	1	0	21	14	1.71	0.95	180			3.9	22%	80%	4.11	42	19	39	3.0	6.0	**2.0**	0%	0.0	6.8	47	$5
LIMA Plan	C+	2nd Half		1	0	0	27	12	3.96	1.47	294			5.0	32%	74%	5.46	37	17	45	2.6	4.0	**1.5**	5%	0.7	1.3	15	$1
+/- Score	-52	09	Proj	**4**	**2**	**0**	**59**	**40**	**3.85**	**1.28**	**257**			**6.0**	**29%**	**74%**	**4.53**	**38**	**19**	**43**	**2.8**	**6.2**	**2.2**	**9%**	**1.1**	**-0.8**	**52**	**$6**

Strained lat likely to blame for 2H Dom loss. But 1H looked a lot like 2005-06. And that pitcher walks a tightrope between modest value and a long stay on the waiver wire. ERA/xERA gap means someone will overpay.

BRANDON KRUSE

O'Day,Darren

O'Day,Darren		Yr	Tm	W	L	Sv	IP	K	ERA	WHIP	OBA	vL	vR	BF/G	H%	S%	xERA	G	L	F	Ctl	Dom	Cmd	hr/f	hr/9	RAR	BPV	R$
RH	Reliever	04		0	0	0	0	0	0.00	0.00																		
Age	26	05		0	0	0	0	0	0.00	0.00																		
Type	GB	06		0	0	0	0	0	0.00	0.00																		
Health	A	07	aa	3	4	10	29	18	5.21	1.66	291			4.6	32%	70%	5.40				4.6	5.6	1.2		1.0	-2.7	27	$4
PT/Exp	F	08	LAA *	2	3	7	76	52	4.43	1.41	285	275	290	6.5	33%	68%	3.88	55	17	28	2.6	6.2	2.4	8%	0.6	-0.8	75	$6
Consist	D	1st Half		1	1	4	17	12	4.68	1.43	293			7.4	33%	70%					2.3	6.2	2.6		1.2	-0.7	54	$2
LIMA Plan	B	2nd Half		1	2	3	59	41	4.36	1.40	282			6.2	33%	68%	3.90	55	17	28	2.6	6.2	2.3	6%	0.5	-0.1	73	$4
+/- Score	19	09	Proj	1	2	0	44	29	4.14	1.38	277			6.7	31%	71%	3.90	55	17	28	2.7	6.0	2.2	10%	0.8	2.8	68	$2

0-1, 4.57 ERA in 43 IP at LAA. Torn labrum puts '09 in doubt. As a sidearmer with a 6.0+ Dom and 50%+ GB%, he's got some upside if healthy. He had a 117 BPV in his last 18 IP with LAA. High risk, potentially high reward.

Ohlendorf,Ross

Ohlendorf,Ross		Yr	Tm	W	L	Sv	IP	K	ERA	WHIP	OBA	vL	vR	BF/G	H%	S%	xERA	G	L	F	Ctl	Dom	Cmd	hr/f	hr/9	RAR	BPV	R$
RH	Reliever	04		0	0	0	0	0	0.00	0.00																		
Age	26	05		0	0	0	0	0	0.00	0.00																		
Type		06	a/a	10	8	0	182	111	4.33	1.40	305			28.1	34%	70%	4.75				1.5	5.5	3.7		0.8	4.3	80	$11
Health	A	07	aaa	3	4	0	68	41	6.67	1.93	356			15.0	39%	66%	7.34				3.3	5.4	1.6		1.2	-18.6	14	($4)
PT/Exp	D	08	2TM *	6	8	0	132	98	5.66	1.72	327	370	273	14.5	37%	69%	4.51	43	24	33	3.1	6.7	2.1	12%	1.2	-21.9	58	($1)
Consist	F	1st Half		1	1	0	40	36	6.53	1.73	307			7.4	36%	65%	4.35	47	18	35	4.3	8.1	1.9	16%	1.6	-10.9	55	($1)
LIMA Plan	B	2nd Half		5	7	0	92	62	5.28	1.71	335			25.0	38%	71%	4.58	38	31	31	2.6	6.0	2.3	11%	1.1	-11.0	55	$0
+/- Score	38	09	Proj	3	4	0	77	57	4.82	1.54	301			8.8	34%	71%	4.28	44	22	34	2.9	6.7	2.3	12%	1.2	0.9	63	$2

1-4, 6.46 ERA in 62 IP at NYY and PIT. SP or RP? You pick...

	Ctl	Dom
SP	4.9	5.3
RP	4.3	8.1

And LHers smoke him. Could emerge quickly in short relief.

Ohman,Will

Ohman,Will		Yr	Tm	W	L	Sv	IP	K	ERA	WHIP	OBA	vL	vR	BF/G	H%	S%	xERA	G	L	F	Ctl	Dom	Cmd	hr/f	hr/9	RAR	BPV	R$
LH	Reliever	04	aaa	3	3	0	52	64	4.73	1.70	286			5.3	39%	74%	5.47				5.1	11.0	2.2		1.1	-2.5	76	$2
Age	31	05	CHC *	3	2	1	51	55	3.21	1.22	201	175	231	2.8	24%	81%	3.36	53	15	33	4.6	9.7	2.1	20%	1.4	6.5	81	$6
Type	Pwr	06	CHC	1	1	0	65	74	4.15	1.31	217	158	243	3.5	29%	70%	3.95	34	23	44	4.7	10.2	2.2	9%	0.8	2.7	69	$5
Health	A	07	CHC *	2	4	1	43	39	5.14	1.80	308	236	325	3.1	38%	71%	4.97	41	18	42	4.9	8.2	1.7	5%	0.6	-3.8	34	$0
PT/Exp	D	08	ATL	4	1	1	59	53	3.68	1.24	236	200	256	2.9	30%	70%	3.91	36	29	35	3.4	8.1	2.4	5%	0.5	4.3	70	$6
Consist	C	1st Half		3	0	1	33	30	3.30	1.25	220			3.2	29%	73%	3.94	39	29	32	4.1	8.3	2.0	4%	0.3	3.9	54	$4
LIMA Plan	B	2nd Half		1	1	0	26	23	4.15	1.23	254			2.6	31%	67%	3.87	33	28	38	2.4	8.0	3.3	7%	0.7	0.4	89	$2
+/- Score	-21	09	Proj	3	2	0	58	52	3.88	1.33	255			3.0	31%	73%	4.03	38	24	38	3.3	8.1	2.5	9%	0.9	2.2	73	$5

Why this surge was for real...
- Broke sub-4.0 Ctl barrier
- Dom didn't erode
- Cmd got even better in 2H

Regression of inflated LD can only help too. Just needs chance at bigger role now.

Okajima,Hideki

Okajima,Hideki		Yr	Tm	W	L	Sv	IP	K	ERA	WHIP	OBA	vL	vR	BF/G	H%	S%	xERA	G	L	F	Ctl	Dom	Cmd	hr/f	hr/9	RAR	BPV	R$
LH	Reliever	04	JPN	4	3	5	47	50	3.81	1.28	211			3.7	25%	78%	3.90				4.8	9.6	2.0		1.6	3.1	66	$7
Age	33	05	JPN	1	0	0	53	53	6.54	1.56	283			5.7	31%	67%	6.68				4.0	9.0	2.3		2.8	-14.6	15	($1)
Type	Pwr FB	06	JPN	2	2	4	55	60	2.85	1.21	241			4.1	30%	84%	3.83				2.8	9.8	3.4		1.4	11.4	97	$8
Health	A	07	BOS	3	2	5	69	63	2.22	0.97	204	236	182	4.1	25%	82%	3.41	45	15	41	2.2	8.2	3.7	8%	0.8	19.5	111	$13
PT/Exp	C	08	BOS	3	2	1	62	60	2.61	1.16	219	184	234	4.0	27%	82%	4.02	32	20	48	3.3	8.7	2.6	8%	0.9	13.3	77	$9
Consist	B	1st Half		1	2	1	34	33	3.15	1.37	271			4.3	33%	81%	4.26	33	17	50	2.9	8.7	3.0	8%	1.0	5.1	89	$3
LIMA Plan	B	2nd Half		2	0	0	28	27	1.95	0.90	143			3.5	18%	83%	3.73	32	25	43	3.9	8.8	2.3	7%	0.6	8.2	63	$5
+/- Score	-36	09	Proj	3	2	3	63	59	3.02	1.23	228			4.1	28%	80%	4.05	37	19	44	3.6	8.5	2.4	9%	1.0	2.9	71	$8

PRO:
- Dom stayed strong
- Remains good LIMA guy

CON:
- FB jump
- 2H Ctl, H%

Bid cautiously; heed xERA.

Oliver,Darren

Oliver,Darren		Yr	Tm	W	L	Sv	IP	K	ERA	WHIP	OBA	vL	vR	BF/G	H%	S%	xERA	G	L	F	Ctl	Dom	Cmd	hr/f	hr/9	RAR	BPV	R$
LH	Reliever	04	2NL	3	3	0	72	46	5.98	1.48	297	321	300	11.8	31%	63%	4.73	39	19	42	2.6	5.7	2.2	14%	1.7	-15.3	49	$0
Age	38	05	aaa	1	3	0	31	15	10.93	2.50	441			24.1	46%	56%	11.11				2.4	4.4	1.8		1.8	-25.5	-24	($7)
Type		06	NYM	4	1	0	81	60	3.44	1.12	235	208	244	7.3	25%	77%	3.70	48	17	35	2.3	6.7	2.9	16%	1.4	10.4	83	$9
Health	A	07	LAA	3	1	0	64	51	3.78	1.26	242	289	209	4.4	29%	71%	4.10	48	12	40	3.2	7.1	2.2	7%	0.7	5.8	68	$6
PT/Exp	C	08	LAA	7	1	0	72	48	2.88	1.15	248	229	271	5.4	29%	77%	3.97	47	16	37	2.0	6.0	3.0	6%	0.6	13.1	79	$10
Consist	A	1st Half		2	1	0	36	18	3.22	1.29	281			4.9	31%	76%	4.57	48	12	40	1.7	4.5	2.6	4%	0.5	5.0	60	$3
LIMA Plan	C+	2nd Half		5	0	0	36	30	2.52	1.01	211			6.1	25%	79%	3.38	46	21	33	2.3	7.6	3.3	9%	0.8	8.0	99	$7
+/- Score	-38	09	Proj	4	2	0	68	49	3.84	1.28	265			5.8	30%	73%	4.05	46	16	38	2.4	6.5	2.7	10%	1.1	3.1	77	$6

Remains an effective short reliever due to good Cmd. But age, inflated S% say '07 stats are more likely than '08; xERAs are closer to true level. Still, 60 IP of sub-4.00 ERA will help you in deep leagues.

Olsen,Scott

Olsen,Scott		Yr	Tm	W	L	Sv	IP	K	ERA	WHIP	OBA	vL	vR	BF/G	H%	S%	xERA	G	L	F	Ctl	Dom	Cmd	hr/f	hr/9	RAR	BPV	R$
LH	Starter	04		0	0	0	0	0	0.00	0.00																		
Age	25	05	FLA *	7	5	0	100	106	4.68	1.47	277	333	238	23.1	35%	70%	3.99	41	14	45	3.5	9.5	2.7	9%	1.1	-5.3	96	$6
Type	FB	06	FLA	12	10	0	180	166	4.05	1.30	239	182	255	24.6	29%	73%	3.89	45	18	37	3.7	8.3	2.2	12%	1.1	9.8	71	$17
Health	A	07	FLA	10	15	0	177	133	5.81	1.76	312	331	311	25.1	35%	70%	5.07	38	24	39	4.3	6.8	1.6	13%	1.5	-30.1	21	($1)
PT/Exp	A	08	FLA	8	11	0	202	113	4.19	1.31	255	187	266	25.8	27%	73%	4.88	37	20	42	3.1	5.0	1.6	11%	1.3	1.9	23	$11
Consist	B	1st Half		4	4	0	106	58	3.47	1.25	237			26.1	25%	77%	5.05	36	18	46	3.4	4.9	1.5	9%	1.2	10.5	11	$8
LIMA Plan	D+	2nd Half		4	7	0	95	55	5.00	1.37	275			25.6	29%	68%	4.69	39	22	39	2.7	5.2	1.9	13%	1.5	-8.6	37	$3
+/- Score	-28	09	Proj	10	12	0	189	120	4.73	1.44	277			24.9	30%	71%	4.80	39	21	40	3.2	5.7	1.8	11%	1.3	-10.7	32	$8

Why we can't expect a repeat...
- Dom continues sharp decline
- FB trend = even more HRs
- ERA was helped by low h%

He's still just 25, so he has time to tap into '05-'06 skills again. But it won't likely be in 2009.

Olson,Garrett

Olson,Garrett		Yr	Tm	W	L	Sv	IP	K	ERA	WHIP	OBA	vL	vR	BF/G	H%	S%	xERA	G	L	F	Ctl	Dom	Cmd	hr/f	hr/9	RAR	BPV	R$
LH	Starter	04		0	0	0	0	0	0.00	0.00																		
Age	25	05		0	0	0	0	0	0.00	0.00																		
Type	Pwr	06	aa	6	5	0	84	76	4.71	1.51	286			26.6	36%	69%	4.54				3.4	8.1	2.4		0.6	-2.0	77	$5
Health	A	07	BAL *	10	10	0	160	133	5.11	1.42	260			24.0	30%	66%	4.74	34	17	49	3.8	7.5	2.0	9%	1.2	-11.9	43	$10
PT/Exp	D	08	BAL *	10	12	0	169	117	5.97	1.69	304	310	309	23.6	35%	65%	5.08	42	19	39	4.1	6.2	1.5	8%	1.0	-33.8	21	$0
Consist	A	1st Half		7	4	0	88	65	4.07	1.46	276			22.8	32%	73%	4.69	41	18	42	3.5	6.6	1.9	6%	0.7	3.0	44	$7
LIMA Plan	C	2nd Half		3	8	0	80	52	8.06	1.94	333			24.4	37%	58%	5.55	43	20	37	4.8	5.8	1.2	10%	1.2	-36.8	-4	($7)
+/- Score	19	09	Proj	6	12	0	140	107	5.10	1.51	277			23.8	32%	68%	4.67	41	19	40	3.9	6.9	1.8	10%	1.1	-4.2	39	$5

9-10, 6.65 ERA in 132 IP at BAL. Had a 4.03 ERA on June 1 which, for those who ONLY look at ERA would justify continued work. However, his xERA that day was 4.67 which might make one reconsider another 95 IP.

Osoria,Franquelis

Osoria,Franquelis		Yr	Tm	W	L	Sv	IP	K	ERA	WHIP	OBA	vL	vR	BF/G	H%	S%	xERA	G	L	F	Ctl	Dom	Cmd	hr/f	hr/9	RAR	BPV	R$
RH	Reliever	04	a/a	8	5	5	89	65	3.94	1.18	257			6.6	31%	64%	2.96				1.8	6.6	3.6		0.2	4.4	113	$12
Age	27	05	LA *	6	6	9	84	44	2.78	1.26	268	392	140	5.5	30%	79%	3.49	59	23	18	2.0	4.7	2.3	10%	0.5	15.2	67	$12
Type	Con GB	06	LA *	2	4	2	68	37	5.16	2.06	367			6.1	40%	75%	5.65	47	18	35	3.8	4.8	1.3	6%	0.8	-5.7	8	($3)
Health	A	07	PIT *	2	7	11	83	37	4.02	1.57	300			5.8	32%	75%	4.81	52	19	29	3.3	4.1	1.3	8%	0.7	4.1	15	$5
PT/Exp	D	08	PIT	4	3	0	61	31	6.08	1.63	337	373	312	6.4	35%	65%	4.33	50	22	28	1.8	4.6	2.6	16%	1.5	-13.5	62	($1)
Consist	B	1st Half		3	2	0	52	27	6.02	1.64	337			6.6	36%	65%	4.39	49	22	28	1.9	4.6	2.5	15%	1.4	-11.3	60	($1)
LIMA Plan	D	2nd Half		1	1	0	8	4	6.43	1.55	336			5.4	34%	64%	4.00	52	23	26	1.1	4.3	4.0	24%	2.1	-2.2	78	$0
+/- Score	55	09	Proj	2	2	0	40	21	4.56	1.47	292			6.0	32%	70%	4.32	51	22	27	2.7	4.8	1.8	11%	0.9	0.1	41	$1

As a groundballer with good Cmd, normally he'd be worth following. But it won't matter if he can't crack a 5.0+ Dom. History says that won't happen. Soft-tossing RHers in RP roles come and go. He'll do the same.

Oswalt,Roy

Oswalt,Roy		Yr	Tm	W	L	Sv	IP	K	ERA	WHIP	OBA	vL	vR	BF/G	H%	S%	xERA	G	L	F	Ctl	Dom	Cmd	hr/f	hr/9	RAR	BPV	R$
RH	Starter	04	HOU	20	10	0	237	206	3.49	1.24	259	257	264	27.4	32%	73%	3.69	43	23	35	2.4	7.8	3.3	7%	0.6	22.5	98	$26
Age	31	05	HOU	20	12	0	241	184	2.95	1.21	263	279	247	28.4	31%	78%	3.49	49	22	29	1.8	6.9	3.8	8%	0.7	38.6	102	$29
Type	GB	06	HOU	15	8	0	220	166	2.98	1.17	262	264	262	27.3	31%	77%	3.50	49	20	31	1.6	6.8	4.4	9%	0.7	40.8	107	$27
Health	B	07	HOU	14	7	0	212	154	3.18	1.33	270	272	259	27.3	32%	77%	3.83	53	16	31	2.5	6.5	2.6	7%	0.6	32.5	80	$21
PT/Exp	A	08	HOU	17	10	0	209	165	3.54	1.18	253	262	243	26.7	29%	74%	3.40	50	20	29	2.0	7.1	3.5	13%	1.0	18.9	102	$23
Consist	A	1st Half		7	8	0	115	94	4.61	1.38	289			27.5	33%	71%	3.60	48	22	30	2.1	7.3	3.5	16%	1.4	-4.8	101	$7
LIMA Plan	C+	2nd Half		10	2	0	93	71	2.22	0.93	203			25.7	24%	78%	3.15	54	18	28	1.9	6.8	3.6	7%	0.5	23.7	103	$17
+/- Score	25	09	Proj	17	8	0	218	167	3.23	1.19	253			27.1	30%	75%	3.50	51	19	30	2.1	6.9	3.3	10%	0.8	22.5	97	$25

Remains comfortably among the game's elite SP. Slight ERA spike was the result of a high 1H hr/f. We can't use 2H ERA as our baseline for '09, since that was H% induced. But he's still a premium 3.00 ERA guy.

STEPHEN NICKRAND

Owings,Micah		Yr	Tm	W	L	Sv	IP	K	ERA	WHIP	OBA	vL	vR	BF/G	H%	S%	xERA	G	L	F	Ctl	Dom	Cmd	hr/f	hr/9	RAR	BPV	R$
RH	Starter	04		0	0	0	0	0	0.00	0.00																		
Age	26	05		0	0	0	0	0	0.00	0.00																		
Type	FB	06	a/a	16	2	0	162	112	4.41	1.54	301			26.8	35%	71%	4.80				2.9	6.2	2.1		0.6	2.2	59	$12
Health	A	07	ARI	8	8	0	153	106	4.30	1.28	253	265	240	22.1	28%	70%	4.49	37	20	42	2.9	6.2	2.1	10%	1.2	2.3	48	$11
PT/Exp	B	08	ARI	6	9	0	105	87	5.93	1.38	260	268	242	20.5	30%	58%	4.48	34	23	43	3.5	7.5	2.1	10%	1.2	-21.5	51	$3
Consist	A	1st Half		6	7	0	92	79	5.18	1.35	268			24.5	32%	63%	4.25	33	24	43	2.8	7.7	2.7	10%	1.2	-10.4	73	$5
LIMA Plan	B	2nd Half		0	2	0	13	8	11.34	1.65	201			9.7	20%	26%	6.50	41	19	41	8.5	5.7	0.7	13%	1.4	-11.1	-109	($2)
+/- Score	68	09	Proj	4	4	0	69	51	4.47	1.33	263			24.3	30%	70%	4.41	37	21	42	2.9	6.7	2.3	10%	1.2	-0.6	58	$5

Turned from breakout sleeper to bust. Terrible S% deserves most of blame. If he can keep ball down, he'll bounce back. Some will see a near-6.00 ERA and pass. You'll see a good 1H Dom and Cmd and speculate.

Padilla,Vicente		Yr	Tm	W	L	Sv	IP	K	ERA	WHIP	OBA	vL	vR	BF/G	H%	S%	xERA	G	L	F	Ctl	Dom	Cmd	hr/f	hr/9	RAR	BPV	R$
RH	Starter	04	PHI	7	7	0	115	82	4.54	1.35	268	289	241	24.6	30%	70%	4.26	44	18	38	2.8	6.4	2.3	12%	1.3	-3.9	61	$7
Age	31	05	PHI	9	12	0	147	103	4.71	1.50	260	297	222	24.0	28%	72%	4.61	46	22	32	4.5	6.3	1.4	15%	1.3	-8.5	15	$6
Type	Pwr	06	TEX	15	10	0	200	156	4.50	1.38	268	305	228	26.1	31%	69%	4.12	44	22	34	3.2	7.0	2.2	10%	0.9	1.4	63	$17
Health	D	07	TEX	6	10	0	120	71	5.76	1.63	301	329	271	23.8	33%	66%	4.91	46	21	34	3.7	5.3	1.4	11%	1.2	-18.6	18	$1
PT/Exp	A	08	TEX	14	8	0	171	127	4.74	1.46	277	312	240	25.8	31%	71%	4.46	43	19	38	3.4	6.7	2.0	13%	1.4	-8.2	49	$11
Consist	B	1st Half		10	4	0	105	71	4.13	1.38	262			26.5	28%	77%	4.64	41	18	41	3.4	6.1	1.8	14%	1.6	2.9	36	$9
LIMA Plan	C	2nd Half		4	4	0	66	56	5.70	1.58	300			24.9	36%	64%	4.18	46	21	33	3.4	7.6	2.2	10%	1.0	-11.1	69	$2
+/- Score	-6	09	Proj	12	11	0	174	134	4.60	1.45	274			24.5	31%	71%	4.29	44	20	35	3.5	6.9	2.0	12%	1.1	2.8	54	$12

He has established this as his baseline. Gopheritis is a warning sign given rising FB and hr/9 history. LHers have him for lunch, along with some fava beans and a nice chianti. Maybe a new role is in order?

Papelbon,Jonathan		Yr	Tm	W	L	Sv	IP	K	ERA	WHIP	OBA	vL	vR	BF/G	H%	S%	xERA	G	L	F	Ctl	Dom	Cmd	hr/f	hr/9	RAR	BPV	R$
RH	Reliever	04		0	0	0	0	0	0.00	0.00											0.0	0.0						
Age	28	05	BOS *	9	5	1	148	125	3.11	1.14	233	190	319	15.9	27%	77%	3.90	35	25	40	2.6	7.6	2.9	10%	1.0	23.0	79	$19
Type	Pwr	06	BOS	4	2	35	68	75	0.93	0.78	172	203	128	4.3	24%	92%	2.96	37	17	46	1.7	9.9	5.8	4%	0.4	30.5	147	$28
Health	A	07	BOS	1	3	37	58	84	1.85	0.77	154	104	200	3.6	24%	83%	2.61	29	16	55	2.3	13.0	5.6	8%	0.8	19.1	178	$25
PT/Exp	A	08	BOS	5	4	41	69	77	2.34	0.95	229	235	210	4.0	31%	77%	2.53	49	20	31	1.0	10.0	9.6	7%	0.5	17.2	179	$26
Consist	A	1st Half		3	2	24	36	47	2.00	0.86	198			3.8	29%	82%	2.27	46	19	35	1.5	11.8	7.8	11%	0.8	10.4	195	$16
LIMA Plan	C+	2nd Half		2	2	17	33	30	2.70	1.05	260			4.3	33%	74%	2.82	52	20	28	0.5	8.1	15.0	4%	0.3	6.8	161	$11
+/- Score	18	09	Proj	4	4	45	73	80	2.23	0.94	215			4.4	29%	81%	2.85	43	19	39	1.5	9.9	6.7	9%	0.7	14.1	159	$28

While his BPV didn't budge from 2007-08, he became a different pitcher, and one that could have more long-term success. More GB, more precision, slightly less power... it's a formula that could preserve his arm for... forever.

Park,Chan Ho		Yr	Tm	W	L	Sv	IP	K	ERA	WHIP	OBA	vL	vR	BF/G	H%	S%	xERA	G	L	F	Ctl	Dom	Cmd	hr/f	hr/9	RAR	BPV	R$
RH	Reliever	04	TEX *	4	11	0	125	82	6.17	1.56	303	277	284	25.6	31%	66%	4.64	46	14	40	3.0	5.9	2.0	18%	2.2	-26.9	49	($1)
Age	35	05	2TM	12	8	0	155	113	5.74	1.68	292	305	279	23.8	34%	65%	4.62	50	21	29	4.6	6.6	1.4	7%	0.6	-27.6	21	$2
Type		06	SD	7	7	0	136	96	4.82	1.40	275	266	278	24.5	30%	69%	4.36	44	18	38	2.9	6.3	2.2	12%	1.3	-5.6	57	$7
Health	C	07	aa	6	14	0	135	86	8.38	1.97	365			27.5	38%	61%	8.75				3.1	5.7	1.8		2.4	-65.3	-18	($12)
PT/Exp	C	08	LA	4	4	2	95	79	3.40	1.40	265	301	237	7.6	31%	80%	3.81	51	19	30	3.4	7.5	2.2	14%	1.1	10.2	71	$8
Consist	F	1st Half		3	2	1	54	41	2.51	1.32	252			10.4	28%	88%	3.96	48	20	32	3.4	6.9	2.1	14%	1.2	11.6	59	$6
LIMA Plan	C+	2nd Half		1	2	1	42	38	4.54	1.49	282			5.7	34%	72%	3.61	54	17	28	3.5	8.2	2.4	14%	1.1	-1.4	87	$2
+/- Score	-9	09	Proj	3	4	0	69	52	4.86	1.46	280			10.7	32%	70%	4.11	49	18	33	3.3	6.8	2.1	14%	1.3	1.9	61	$2

In a small sample size, he pitched really well in the 2H. But history says he can't consistently post a 2.0+ Cmd. And LHers still hit him hard, so he'll be exposed with more innings. Expect regression.

Parra,Manny		Yr	Tm	W	L	Sv	IP	K	ERA	WHIP	OBA	vL	vR	BF/G	H%	S%	xERA	G	L	F	Ctl	Dom	Cmd	hr/f	hr/9	RAR	BPV	R$
LH	Starter	04		0	0	0	0	0	0.00	0.00																		
Age	26	05	aa	5	6	0	91	75	4.55	1.58	324			25.6	40%	70%	5.12				2.1	7.4	3.6		0.4	-2.7	98	$4
Type	Pwr GB	06	aa	3	0	0	31	25	4.18	1.36	273			22.2	35%	66%	3.38				2.7	7.3	2.7		0.0	1.3	101	$3
Health	A	07	MIL *	10	5	0	133	119	3.34	1.32	254	174	280	21.6	33%	74%	4.30	33	23	44	3.3	8.1	2.5	2%	0.3	17.8	68	$14
PT/Exp	C	08	MIL	10	8	0	166	147	4.39	1.54	279	233	288	23.1	34%	74%	3.84	52	22	27	4.1	8.0	2.0	13%	1.0	-2.5	63	$8
Consist	B	1st Half		8	2	0	87	68	3.94	1.55	265			24.2	31%	77%	4.48	48	20	32	4.8	7.1	1.5	11%	0.9	3.5	24	$6
LIMA Plan	B+	2nd Half		2	6	0	79	79	4.88	1.54	294			22.1	37%	70%	3.17	55	24	21	3.3	9.0	2.7	18%	1.0	-6.0	106	$2
+/- Score	35	09	Proj	12	8	0	180	161	3.91	1.36	262			23.3	32%	73%	3.55	50	22	27	3.3	8.1	2.5	10%	0.8	17.4	86	$15

Why '09 could be his breakout:
- Electric skills in 2H
- Transformation into GBer
- h%, hr/f masked 2H growth

He's close now. If he finds an out pitch vs. RHers...
UP: 3.25 ERA, 200 K

Parrish,John		Yr	Tm	W	L	Sv	IP	K	ERA	WHIP	OBA	vL	vR	BF/G	H%	S%	xERA	G	L	F	Ctl	Dom	Cmd	hr/f	hr/9	RAR	BPV	R$
LH	Starter	04	BAL	6	3	1	78	71	3.46	1.58	236			6.3	30%	78%	4.00				6.3	8.2	1.3		0.5	9.3	70	$7
Age	31	05	BAL *	1	0	0	26	38	3.12	1.88	262			6.6	40%	85%	3.87	47	26	28	8.0	13.2	1.7	12%	0.7	4.0	46	$2
Type	Pwr	06		0	0	0	0	0	0.00	0.00																		
Health	D	07	2AL	2	2	0	52	41	5.71	1.92	301	293	298	4.8	37%	68%	5.10	54	16	29	6.4	7.1	1.1	4%	0.3	-7.7	-13	($1)
PT/Exp	D	08	TOR *	11	2	0	133	96	4.21	1.62	290	305	279	20.2	33%	76%	5.13	37	22	41	4.2	6.5	1.5	7%	0.9	2.3	17	$7
Consist	A	1st Half		11	1	0	88	72	3.74	1.66	291			25.2	35%	78%	5.75	24	18	59	4.5	7.3	1.6	3%	0.6	6.6	11	$8
LIMA Plan	C	2nd Half		0	1	0	45	24	5.12	1.56	289			14.5	30%	71%	5.24	39	22	39	3.7	4.8	1.3	12%	1.4	-4.3	4	($0)
+/- Score	-38	09	Proj	3	3	0	87	64	5.07	1.64	275			23.4	32%	70%	4.89	46	21	33	5.2	6.6	1.3	9%	0.8	-5.0	4	$1

1-1, 4.04 ERA in 42 IP at TOR. Used to be a guy with a live arm worth following. Now he's another middling SP with poor skills and a history of elbow troubles. He's not rosterable in MLB, let alone in your league.

Pavano,Carl		Yr	Tm	W	L	Sv	IP	K	ERA	WHIP	OBA	vL	vR	BF/G	H%	S%	xERA	G	L	F	Ctl	Dom	Cmd	hr/f	hr/9	RAR	BPV	R$
RH	Starter	04	FLA	18	8	0	222	139	3.00	1.18	253	267	240	29.3	29%	76%	3.91	48	19	32	2.0	5.6	2.8	7%	0.6	34.6	74	$26
Age	33	05	NYY	4	6	0	100	56	4.77	1.47	314	335	294	25.8	33%	72%	4.16	50	19	31	1.6	5.0	3.1	15%	1.5	-4.9	75	$3
Type	Con	06	a/a	2	0	0	17	15	1.59	1.12	250			17.2	33%	84%	2.45				1.6	7.9	5.0		0.0	6.1	158	$3
Health	F	07	NYY	1	0	0	11	4	4.78	1.24	274	208	350	23.5	28%	62%	4.67	46	18	36	1.6	3.2	2.0	7%	0.8	-0.4	38	$1
PT/Exp	F	08	NYY *	5	3	0	48	26	5.40	1.47	295	324	283	21.2	30%	68%	4.95	40	17	42	2.6	4.8	1.9	13%	1.7	-6.3	35	$2
Consist	C	1st Half		0	0	0	0	0	0.00	0.00																		
LIMA Plan	C	2nd Half		5	3	0	48	26	5.40	1.47	295			21.2	30%	68%	4.95	40	17	42	2.6	4.8	1.9	13%	1.7	-6.3	35	$2
+/- Score	-8	09	Proj	8	8	0	125	67	4.61	1.39	284			23.4	30%	70%	4.52	47	18	35	2.4	4.8	2.0	11%	1.2	-1.4	45	$7

4-2, 5.77 ERA in 34 IP at NYY. When NYY signed him to a 4-year deal, I warned HQers:
- Breakout? Marginal 5.6 K rate
- Move to AL will add to his ERA
- NY pressure, park effects

Lots of reasons to be wary...

Peavy,Jake		Yr	Tm	W	L	Sv	IP	K	ERA	WHIP	OBA	vL	vR	BF/G	H%	S%	xERA	G	L	F	Ctl	Dom	Cmd	hr/f	hr/9	RAR	BPV	R$
RH	Starter	04	SD	15	6	0	166	173	2.28	1.20	238	235	238	25.3	31%	84%	3.40	43	20	37	2.9	9.4	3.3	8%	0.7	40.7	112	$25
Age	27	05	SD	13	7	0	203	216	2.88	1.04	221	223	212	26.8	29%	76%	3.04	44	20	35	2.2	9.6	4.3	10%	0.8	34.2	135	$29
Type	Pwr	06	SD	11	14	0	202	215	4.10	1.23	247	242	243	26.2	32%	69%	3.60	38	18	44	2.8	9.6	3.5	10%	1.0	9.7	114	$20
Health	B	07	SD	19	6	0	223	240	2.54	1.06	212	242	174	26.1	29%	78%	3.23	44	17	39	2.7	9.7	3.5	6%	0.5	52.0	122	$37
PT/Exp	A	08	SD	10	11	0	174	166	2.85	1.18	230	263	194	26.4	28%	80%	3.64	41	21	38	3.1	8.6	2.8	10%	0.9	30.4	91	$21
Consist	A	1st Half		5	5	0	81	80	2.90	1.19	240			25.5	30%	80%	3.42	42	23	35	2.7	8.9	3.3	10%	0.9	13.6	108	$10
LIMA Plan	C+	2nd Half		5	6	0	93	86	2.81	1.17	220			27.2	27%	80%	3.83	41	19	40	3.4	8.3	2.5	9%	0.9	16.8	77	$11
+/- Score	5	09	Proj	15	8	0	198	197	3.05	1.18	233			26.1	29%	78%	3.54	42	20	39	2.9	9.0	3.1	10%	1.0	19.4	102	$26

Sore elbow kept him out for nearly a month. Skills held pretty strong, but you have to wonder if three 200+ IP seasons before age 27 are catching up with him. He's still elite, but discount him a little.

Pelfrey,Mike		Yr	Tm	W	L	Sv	IP	K	ERA	WHIP	OBA	vL	vR	BF/G	H%	S%	xERA	G	L	F	Ctl	Dom	Cmd	hr/f	hr/9	RAR	BPV	R$
RH	Starter	04		0	0	0	0	0	0.00	0.00																		
Age	25	05		0	0	0	0	0	0.00	0.00																		
Type	Con	06	NYM *	7	3	0	95	84	4.16	1.57	279	278	326	23.7	35%	73%	4.07	49	23	29	4.3	7.9	1.9	6%	0.5	3.9	55	$6
Health	A	07	NYM *	6	14	0	147	92	5.16	1.60	292	321	279	22.9	33%	68%	4.64	48	23	28	4.0	5.6	1.4	9%	0.7	-13.4	20	$2
PT/Exp	C	08	NYM	13	11	0	201	110	3.72	1.36	270	307	245	26.8	30%	73%	4.35	50	21	30	2.9	4.9	1.7	6%	0.5	13.6	39	$14
Consist	A	1st Half		5	6	0	87	48	4.46	1.65	294			26.4	33%	72%	5.06	47	23	30	4.3	5.0	1.2	4%	0.4	-2.1	-1	$2
LIMA Plan	D+	2nd Half		8	5	0	114	62	3.16	1.14	250			27.2	28%	74%	3.84	52	19	29	1.8	4.9	2.7	7%	0.6	15.6	69	$13
+/- Score	-26	09	Proj	13	10	0	189	108	4.01	1.39	273			24.6	30%	72%	4.31	49	21	29	3.0	5.2	1.7	9%	0.8	0.6	40	$13

Normally you shouldn't bid on a guy with a bad Dom trend. But as a GBer with improving Ctl and good stuff, he might be able to offset some Dom loss. He'll sustain a sub-4.00 ERA if 2H Ctl gains were for real. Be careful.

STEPHEN NICKRAND

Pena,Tony

Pena,Tony		W	L	Sv	IP	K	ERA	WHIP	OBA	vL	vR	BF/G	H%	S%	xERA	G	L	F	Ctl	Dom	Cmd	hr/f	hr/9	RAR	BPV	R$
RH Reliever	04	0	0	0	0	0	0.00	0.00																		
Age 27	05 aa	7	13	0	148	83	5.58	1.59	318			26.7	34%	67%	5.88				2.5	5.1	**2.0**		1.3	-23.2	27	$0
Type	06 ARI *	8	5	14	76	53	3.33	1.22	266			4.8	30%	75%	4.11	39	22	39	1.8	6.2	**3.5**	7%	0.8	10.9	81	$15
Health A	07 ARI	5	4	2	85	63	3.27	1.10	208	245	176	4.6	24%	73%	4.06	48	12	40	3.3	6.6	**2.0**	8%	0.8	12.2	57	$11
PT/Exp C	08 ARI	3	2	3	73	52	4.33	1.33	281	296	267	4.3	33%	67%	3.92	47	20	32	2.1	6.4	**3.1**	7%	0.6	-0.6	84	$5
Consist A	1st Half	1	1	1	38	29	3.08	1.18	246			4.1	30%	73%	3.88	45	19	36	2.4	6.9	**2.9**	2%	0.2	5.6	83	$4
LIMA Plan B+	2nd Half	2	1	2	35	23	5.71	1.50	315			4.5	35%	63%	3.97	50	21	29	1.8	6.0	**3.3**	11%	1.0	-6.1	86	$1
+/- Score 23	09 Proj	**4**	**3**	**3**	**69**	**51**	**3.81**	**1.27**	**269**			**4.9**	**31%**	**73%**	**3.86**	**47**	**17**	**35**	**2.1**	**6.7**	**3.2**	**9%**	**0.9**	**4.1**	**89**	**$7**

A closer in waiting? Hang on. The Cmd is nice and his GB ability limits his risk. But he's gotta do better than a 6.0-ish Dom. And he needs an out pitch vs. LHers. Good LIMA guy, not closer material yet.

Penny,Brad

Penny,Brad		W	L	Sv	IP	K	ERA	WHIP	OBA	vL	vR	BF/G	H%	S%	xERA	G	L	F	Ctl	Dom	Cmd	hr/f	hr/9	RAR	BPV	R$
RH Starter	04 2NL	9	10	0	143	111	3.15	1.22	244	242	243	24.7	29%	77%	4.06	43	19	38	2.8	7.0	**2.5**	7%	0.8	19.7	70	$15
Age 30	05 LA	7	9	0	175	122	3.91	1.29	273	263	276	25.4	31%	72%	3.94	47	20	34	2.1	6.3	**3.0**	9%	0.9	7.3	81	$12
Type Con	06 LA	16	9	0	189	148	4.33	1.38	279	275	283	23.9	33%	70%	4.07	44	20	36	2.6	7.0	**2.7**	9%	0.9	3.6	79	$16
Health D	07 LA	16	4	0	208	135	3.03	1.31	253	229	286	26.6	30%	77%	4.20	49	20	31	3.2	5.8	**1.8**	4%	0.4	35.8	47	$22
PT/Exp A	08 LA	6	9	0	95	51	6.27	1.63	295	328	284	22.7	31%	62%	4.91	49	20	31	4.0	4.8	**1.2**	13%	1.2	-23.4	7	($1)
Consist A	1st Half	5	9	0	86	47	5.88	1.60	295			25.8	32%	63%	4.79	49	21	30	3.8	4.9	**1.3**	10%	0.9	-17.0	14	($0)
LIMA Plan F	2nd Half	1	0	0	9	4	10.00	1.89	302			10.8	25%	54%	6.13	45	16	39	6.0	4.0	**0.7**	32%	4.0	-6.4	-67	($1)
+/- Score 19	09 Proj	**8**	**8**	**0**	**125**	**69**	**4.46**	**1.44**	**274**			**23.7**	**30%**	**71%**	**4.73**	**47**	**19**	**34**	**3.4**	**5.0**	**1.5**	**10%**	**1.0**	**-6.1**	**23**	**$6**

Reaches 200 IP, and voilà, shoulder issues resurface. But don't let injury fears be your primary concern. After all, his skills have been getting worse for years. That's a bad combo. Save your pennies.

Peralta,Joel

Peralta,Joel		W	L	Sv	IP	K	ERA	WHIP	OBA	vL	vR	BF/G	H%	S%	xERA	G	L	F	Ctl	Dom	Cmd	hr/f	hr/9	RAR	BPV	R$
RH Reliever	04 aaa	4	2	1	56	54	5.18	1.56	307			6.4	38%	67%	5.24				2.8	8.7	**3.1**		0.9	-5.8	86	$3
Age 33	05 ANA *	5	1	10	54	47	3.82	1.16	216	273	178	4.7	25%	70%	4.22	34	20	46	3.5	7.8	**2.2**	9%	1.0	3.7	58	$10
Type xFB	06 KC	1	3	1	73	57	4.43	1.24	264	338	234	4.8	30%	68%	4.27	32	22	46	2.1	7.0	**3.4**	10%	1.2	1.2	79	$6
Health A	07 KC	1	3	1	88	66	3.80	1.28	273	248	290	5.9	32%	73%	4.17	36	22	42	1.9	6.8	**3.5**	8%	0.9	7.7	83	$7
PT/Exp C	08 KC *	2	2	2	71	52	4.44	1.27	256	247	294	5.9	27%	73%	4.45	35	17	48	2.7	6.7	**2.5**	15%	1.9	-0.8	61	$5
Consist A	1st Half	1	2	2	42	31	3.41	1.18	247			5.8	26%	81%	4.20	40	13	47	2.4	6.7	**2.8**	14%	1.7	4.9	75	$5
LIMA Plan B	2nd Half	1	0	0	29	21	5.96	1.39	270			6.2	28%	64%	4.76	31	20	48	3.1	6.6	**2.1**	16%	2.2	-5.7	43	$1
+/- Score 4	09 Proj	**2**	**2**	**0**	**78**	**60**	**4.50**	**1.31**	**264**			**5.7**	**30%**	**70%**	**4.42**	**34**	**20**	**46**	**2.7**	**6.9**	**2.6**	**11%**	**1.4**	**0.0**	**65**	**$5**

1-2, 5.98 ERA in 52 IP at KC. Gave back pinpoint control and was bitten by hr/9. A hr/f fix will help some. But as his low h% normalizes, the net result will be more of the same. Even worse if RHers OBA continues.

Percival,Troy

Percival,Troy		W	L	Sv	IP	K	ERA	WHIP	OBA	vL	vR	BF/G	H%	S%	xERA	G	L	F	Ctl	Dom	Cmd	hr/f	hr/9	RAR	BPV	R$
RH Reliever	04 ANA	2	3	33	49	33	2.93	1.26	237	218	244	4.0	25%	84%	4.98	32	16	52	3.5	6.0	**1.7**	9%	1.3	9.1	25	$16
Age 39	05 DET	1	3	8	25	20	5.76	1.20	212	173	250	4.0	19%	61%	4.81	27	14	59	4.0	7.2	**1.8**	17%	2.5	-4.3	28	$4
Type Pwr xFB	06	0	0	0	0	0	0.00	0.00																		
Health F	07 STL *	3	0	0	46	43	1.79	0.97	181	220	136	4.5	23%	85%	4.04	33	12	55	3.1	8.3	**2.7**	5%	0.6	15.0	78	$8
PT/Exp D	08 TAM	2	1	28	46	38	4.53	1.23	184	185	171	3.8	18%	70%	5.36	23	10	67	5.3	7.5	**1.4**	11%	1.8	-1.0	-8	$13
Consist C	1st Half	1	0	19	28	30	3.54	0.96	168			3.8	20%	70%	4.10	19	14	67	3.5	9.6	**2.7**	9%	1.3	2.8	75	$10
LIMA Plan D	2nd Half	1	1	9	18	8	6.10	1.64	207			3.8	16%	71%	7.80	29	5	66	8.1	4.1	**0.5**	14%	2.5	-3.8	-140	$3
+/- Score -74	09 Proj	**2**	**1**	**10**	**29**	**22**	**4.66**	**1.59**	**268**			**4.4**	**29%**	**76%**	**5.84**	**28**	**11**	**61**	**5.0**	**6.8**	**1.4**	**9%**	**1.6**	**-5.1**	**-5**	**$5**

Resurrected career before bad back sidelined him. But it was smoke and mirrors. 28 SV with a negative BPV? Credit a tiny h%. And monstrous FB rates are a ticking time bomb. Don't be around when they detonate.

Perez,Chris

Perez,Chris		W	L	Sv	IP	K	ERA	WHIP	OBA	vL	vR	BF/G	H%	S%	xERA	G	L	F	Ctl	Dom	Cmd	hr/f	hr/9	RAR	BPV	R$
RH Reliever	04	0	0	0	0	0	0.00	0.00																		
Age 23	05	0	0	0	0	0	0.00	0.00																		
Type Pwr FB	06	0	0	0	0	0	0.00	0.00																		
Health A	07 aa	2	1	36	54	68	3.33	1.19	141			4.1	19%	75%	2.16				6.5	11.3	**1.7**		0.8	7.5	106	$19
PT/Exp F	08 STL *	4	4	18	67	74	3.51	1.36	223	220	231	4.3	28%	79%	3.98	39	20	41	5.0	10.0	**2.0**	13%	1.2	6.3	62	$13
Consist D	1st Half	3	1	8	36	35	3.07	1.37	221			4.2	29%	78%	4.13	41	24	35	5.1	9.0	**1.7**	6%	0.5	5.2	42	$7
LIMA Plan C	2nd Half	1	3	10	31	39	4.00	1.36	225			4.3	27%	80%	3.74	37	17	47	4.8	11.1	**2.3**	20%	2.0	1.0	84	$6
+/- Score 21	09 Proj	**3**	**3**	**33**	**73**	**86**	**3.72**	**1.32**	**218**			**4.2**	**29%**	**75%**	**3.78**	**38**	**19**	**43**	**4.8**	**10.7**	**2.2**	**11%**	**1.0**	**5.0**	**78**	**$18**

7 SV, 3.46 ERA in 41 IP at STL. Electric Dom suggests he has closer talent. He also fares well against both LH and RH bats. Ctl remains only real concern, but it's trending the right way. UP: 40 SV

Perez,Odalis

Perez,Odalis		W	L	Sv	IP	K	ERA	WHIP	OBA	vL	vR	BF/G	H%	S%	xERA	G	L	F	Ctl	Dom	Cmd	hr/f	hr/9	RAR	BPV	R$
LH Starter	04 LA	7	6	0	196	128	3.26	1.14	246	270	241	25.7	27%	77%	3.69	52	16	32	2.0	5.9	**2.9**	14%	1.2	24.3	81	$18
Age 31	05 LA	7	8	0	108	74	4.57	1.27	263	256	264	23.8	29%	66%	4.07	44	20	36	2.3	6.2	**2.6**	11%	1.1	-4.4	70	$8
Type	06 2TM	6	8	0	126	81	6.21	1.59	322	336	316	17.8	35%	62%	4.42	44	23	34	2.2	5.8	**2.6**	12%	1.3	-26.3	66	$0
Health D	07 KC	8	11	0	137	64	5.57	1.66	315	301	323	24.2	34%	67%	5.22	45	20	35	3.3	4.2	**1.3**	8%	0.9	-18.1	10	$1
PT/Exp A	08 WAS	7	12	0	160	119	4.34	1.48	288	218	306	23.4	33%	74%	4.21	47	20	34	3.1	6.7	**2.2**	13%	1.2	-1.4	62	$7
Consist B	1st Half	2	5	0	74	51	3.88	1.53	284			23.6	31%	80%	4.57	49	16	36	3.8	6.2	**1.6**	13%	1.3	3.6	36	$2
LIMA Plan C+	2nd Half	5	7	0	85	68	4.74	1.44	291			23.3	34%	70%	3.91	45	23	32	2.5	7.2	**2.8**	13%	1.2	-5.0	84	$4
+/- Score 5	09 Proj	**7**	**11**	**0**	**145**	**100**	**4.28**	**1.41**	**279**			**22.4**	**31%**	**73%**	**4.24**	**46**	**20**	**34**	**2.9**	**6.2**	**2.2**	**11%**	**1.1**	**1.9**	**59**	**$8**

How many of your leaguemates know he has posted a 60+ BPV in four of the last five years? Durability aside, skills are stable and he pitched really well in 2H. Emerging GB ability will help too. HIdden value pick.

Perez,Oliver

Perez,Oliver		W	L	Sv	IP	K	ERA	WHIP	OBA	vL	vR	BF/G	H%	S%	xERA	G	L	F	Ctl	Dom	Cmd	hr/f	hr/9	RAR	BPV	R$
LH Starter	04 PIT	12	10	0	196	239	2.98	1.15	208	220	204	26.6	28%	79%	3.47	37	15	48	3.7	11.0	**3.0**	10%	1.0	30.9	112	$26
Age 27	05 PIT	7	5	0	103	97	5.85	1.67	260	313	255	23.6	29%	70%	5.23	34	17	49	6.1	8.5	**1.4**	16%	2.0	-20.4	-1	$1
Type Pwr xFB	06 2NL *	5	18	0	163	152	7.08	1.71	288	260	300	23.6	33%	61%	5.05	30	23	47	5.1	8.4	**1.7**	14%	1.8	-52.2	22	($5)
Health B	07 NYM	15	10	0	177	174	3.56	1.31	235	206	235	25.8	29%	77%	4.34	33	17	50	4.0	8.8	**2.2**	9%	1.1	18.9	62	$20
PT/Exp A	08 NYM	10	7	0	194	180	4.22	1.40	234	158	258	24.7	28%	73%	4.66	32	22	46	4.9	8.4	**1.7**	10%	1.1	1.2	29	$13
Consist B	1st Half	6	5	0	90	76	4.98	1.47	241			23.3	27%	71%	4.83	35	23	42	5.2	7.6	**1.5**	15%	1.6	-7.9	10	$4
LIMA Plan D+	2nd Half	4	2	0	104	104	3.56	1.34	227			26.0	29%	75%	4.51	29	21	50	4.6	9.0	**2.0**	6%	0.7	9.1	45	$8
+/- Score -23	09 Proj	**13**	**8**	**0**	**199**	**192**	**4.07**	**1.42**	**243**			**24.7**	**29%**	**75%**	**4.58**	**32**	**20**	**48**	**4.7**	**8.7**	**1.9**	**10%**	**1.2**	**-6.0**	**41**	**$15**

The ups and downs continue. Key is Ctl: when it's creeps over 5.0, and that nagging gopheritis hits, things start to look like '05-'06. But 2H recalled 2007. The $20 upside's there, but it's all high risk, high reward.

Perez,Rafael

Perez,Rafael		W	L	Sv	IP	K	ERA	WHIP	OBA	vL	vR	BF/G	H%	S%	xERA	G	L	F	Ctl	Dom	Cmd	hr/f	hr/9	RAR	BPV	R$
LH Reliever	04	0	0	0	0	0	0.00	0.00																		
Age 27	05 aa	4	3	1	66	39	2.10	1.12	249			17.8	28%	85%	3.15				1.7	5.3	**3.1**		0.7	18.0	82	$9
Type Pwr xGB	06 CLE *	4	8	0	106	90	3.65	1.28	246			10.4	31%	71%	3.66	58	9	33	3.2	7.6	**2.4**	5%	0.4	11.9	85	$11
Health A	07 CLE *	4	5	1	107	90	2.97	1.19	252	145	213	8.5	31%	77%	3.37	53	17	30	2.2	7.6	**3.4**	9%	0.7	20.3	107	$13
PT/Exp D	08 CLE	4	4	2	76	86	3.54	1.18	237	222	243	4.3	31%	73%	2.61	57	19	24	2.7	10.1	**3.7**	17%	0.9	7.6	144	$10
Consist B	1st Half	1	1	0	36	36	3.47	1.40	265			4.2	33%	80%	3.38	50	23	27	3.5	8.9	**2.6**	18%	1.2	3.9	95	$3
LIMA Plan B+	2nd Half	3	3	2	40	50	3.60	0.97	210			4.3	30%	64%	1.97	64	14	21	2.0	11.2	**5.6**	15%	0.7	3.7	190	$7
+/- Score 63	09 Proj	**3**	**3**	**10**	**58**	**61**	**3.10**	**1.16**	**238**			**6.1**	**31%**	**75%**	**2.77**	**57**	**18**	**26**	**2.5**	**9.5**	**3.8**	**10%**	**0.6**	**11.8**	**138**	**$11**

As a lefty, his path to close won't be easy. But look at that 2H. An 11.0+ Dom AND a 60% GB? No LH/RH splits either. An inflated hr/f hid how good he was. If opportunity is there... UP: 30 SV

Perkins,Glen

Perkins,Glen		W	L	Sv	IP	K	ERA	WHIP	OBA	vL	vR	BF/G	H%	S%	xERA	G	L	F	Ctl	Dom	Cmd	hr/f	hr/9	RAR	BPV	R$
LH Starter	04	0	0	0	0	0	0.00	0.00																		
Age 26	05 aa	4	4	0	79	58	6.04	1.62	292			25.6	35%	60%	4.78				4.1	6.6	**1.6**		0.5	-16.9	56	($0)
Type FB	06 a/a	4	12	0	121	113	5.50	1.64	294			23.0	36%	68%	5.36				4.2	8.4	**2.0**		1.0	-14.6	57	$2
Health D	07 MIN *	0	2	0	42	27	5.04	1.43	246	250	222	7.9	25%	70%	5.15	39	18	44	4.6	5.8	**1.3**	14%	1.8	-2.7	-3	$1
PT/Exp D	08 MIN *	14	5	0	184	96	4.26	1.48	292	352	288	24.5	31%	76%	5.04	38	22	40	2.8	4.7	**1.6**	11%	1.3	2.0	23	$11
Consist A	1st Half	6	3	0	98	60	4.06	1.52	291			24.1	32%	76%	5.06	35	24	41	3.2	5.5	**1.7**	9%	1.1	3.5	24	$5
LIMA Plan C	2nd Half	8	2	0	86	36	4.48	1.44	293			25.1	29%	74%	5.04	40	21	39	2.4	3.8	**1.6**	13%	1.6	-1.5	21	$5
+/- Score -23	09 Proj	**6**	**8**	**0**	**145**	**87**	**4.84**	**1.46**	**281**			**24.4**	**30%**	**70%**	**4.93**	**39**	**21**	**41**	**3.2**	**5.4**	**1.7**	**11%**	**1.3**	**-9.0**	**27**	**$5**

12-4, 4.41 ERA in 151 IP at MIN. Don't be skewed by the W-L. It came with empty skill support. Dom trend is scary and LH batters own him -- and he's a lefty. This ERA has at least a run and a half of downside.

STEPHEN NICKRAND

Petit,Yusmeiro		Yr	Tm	W	L	Sv	IP	K	ERA	WHIP	OBA	vL	vR	BF/G	H%	S%	xERA	G	L	F	Ctl	Dom	Cmd	hr/f	hr/9	RAR	BPV	R$
RH	Reliever	04	aa	1	1	0	12	15	5.25	1.50	262			26.5	37%	65%	4.31				4.5	11.3	2.5		0.8	-1.3	100	$1
Age	24	05	a/a	9	6	0	132	133	3.65	1.03	234			21.7	28%	70%	3.24				1.5	9.1	6.1		1.3	10.6	152	$18
Type	xFB	06	FLA *	5	7	0	122	88	5.27	1.39	293	381	400	16.5	33%	65%	4.59	29	24	46	2.0	6.5	3.2	10%	1.4	-11.8	70	$5
Health	A	07	ARI *	11	8	0	150	93	4.91	1.40	268	274	250	21.0	28%	70%	5.27	33	15	52	3.4	5.6	1.7	10%	1.6	-9.0	20	$8
PT/Exp	D	08	ARI *	6	8	0	116	100	5.44	1.25	273	231	205	16.2	31%	61%	4.08	33	17	50	1.7	7.8	4.5	12%	1.6	-16.8	104	$6
Consist	B	1st Half		3	4	0	68	62	6.29	1.41	311			17.3	37%	57%	4.05	25	29	46	1.2	8.3	6.7	10%	1.4	-16.8	119	$1
LIMA Plan	C+	2nd Half		3	4	0	49	38	4.26	1.03	213			14.8	21%	69%	4.08	35	14	51	2.4	7.0	2.9	16%	2.0	0.1	74	$5
+/- Score	71	09	Proj	9	9	0	145	113	4.59	1.25	262			23.2	29%	68%	4.39	33	16	51	2.2	7.0	3.1	10%	1.4	-1.0	77	$11

3-5, 4.31 ERA in 56 IP at ARI. This isn't a 5.00+ ERA SP. With the Dom he owns and last year's Cmd, he has the tools of a top-tier arm. Extreme FB% is biggest concern. hr/f correction will help. UP: 3.75 ERA

Pettitte,Andy		Yr	Tm	W	L	Sv	IP	K	ERA	WHIP	OBA	vL	vR	BF/G	H%	S%	xERA	G	L	F	Ctl	Dom	Cmd	hr/f	hr/9	RAR	BPV	R$
LH	Starter	04	HOU	6	4	0	83	79	3.90	1.23	233	290	208	23.0	29%	70%	3.21	53	21	26	3.4	8.6	2.5	14%	0.9	3.7	95	$9
Age	36	05	HOU	17	9	0	222	171	2.39	1.03	231	200	239	26.6	27%	80%	3.18	50	23	27	1.7	6.9	4.2	10%	0.7	50.8	108	$33
Type	GB	06	HOU	14	13	0	214	178	4.20	1.44	283	259	290	25.9	33%	74%	3.72	50	22	29	2.9	7.5	2.5	14%	1.1	7.5	83	$15
Health	B	07	NYY	15	9	0	215	141	4.05	1.43	282	298	282	26.0	32%	72%	4.32	48	19	33	2.9	5.9	2.0	7%	0.7	12.0	54	$16
PT/Exp	A	08	NYY	14	14	0	204	158	4.54	1.41	288	203	325	26.8	34%	69%	3.71	51	20	29	2.4	7.0	2.9	10%	0.8	-4.9	89	$14
Consist	B	1st Half		9	5	0	106	78	3.98	1.34	279			26.6	32%	73%	3.61	53	19	28	2.2	6.6	3.0	13%	1.0	4.8	91	$10
LIMA Plan	B	2nd Half		5	9	0	98	80	5.16	1.49	298			27.0	36%	65%	3.82	50	21	29	2.7	7.4	2.8	8%	0.6	-9.8	88	$4
+/- Score	16	09	Proj	13	12	0	194	149	3.99	1.35	273			25.9	32%	72%	3.77	50	20	30	2.6	6.9	2.6	10%	0.8	15.7	81	$17

Slightly elevated hit rate, trouble vs. RHers resulted in some ERA erosion. Given few obvious skills reasons, both should normalize a bit. If so, as a GBer with a 7.0+ Dom, he's still got the skills and profile to rebound.

Pineiro,Joel		Yr	Tm	W	L	Sv	IP	K	ERA	WHIP	OBA	vL	vR	BF/G	H%	S%	xERA	G	L	F	Ctl	Dom	Cmd	hr/f	hr/9	RAR	BPV	R$
RH	Starter	04	SEA	6	11	0	140	111	4.69	1.33	267	209	316	28.4	30%	69%	4.09	43	17	39	2.8	7.1	2.6	13%	1.3	-4.4	75	$8
Age	30	05	SEA	7	11	0	189	107	5.62	1.48	296	295	305	27.7	32%	63%	4.54	45	22	33	2.7	5.1	1.9	11%	1.1	-29.1	43	$3
Type	Con	06	SEA	8	13	1	165	87	6.37	1.65	310	287	332	18.9	33%	62%	4.82	47	23	29	3.5	4.7	1.4	13%	1.3	-37.0	17	($1)
Health	C	07	2TM	7	5	0	98	60	4.33	1.39	285	250	308	10.0	31%	73%	4.25	49	17	34	2.4	5.5	2.3	13%	1.3	1.6	61	$7
PT/Exp	B	08	STL	7	7	1	149	81	5.14	1.45	300	297	304	25.0	32%	67%	4.24	49	22	30	2.1	4.9	2.3	14%	1.3	-16.0	58	$4
Consist	A	1st Half		2	4	0	71	36	4.33	1.27	271			24.7	29%	68%	4.35	45	21	34	2.0	4.6	2.3	10%	1.0	-0.5	51	$3
LIMA Plan	B	2nd Half		5	3	1	78	45	5.88	1.60	325			25.2	34%	67%	4.13	51	22	26	2.2	5.2	2.4	19%	1.6	-15.5	64	$0
+/- Score	32	09	Proj	9	9	0	165	95	4.64	1.46	299			24.1	32%	71%	4.31	48	21	31	2.3	5.2	2.2	12%	1.1	0.7	56	$7

PROS:
- GBer
- Ctl becoming pinpoint

CONS:
- Sub-5.0 Dom becoming norm
- RHers continue to smoke him

Use 1H as his upside.

Pinto,Renyel		Yr	Tm	W	L	Sv	IP	K	ERA	WHIP	OBA	vL	vR	BF/G	H%	S%	xERA	G	L	F	Ctl	Dom	Cmd	hr/f	hr/9	RAR	BPV	R$
LH	Reliever	04	a/a	12	9	0	151	169	3.58	1.38	230			24.0	31%	76%	3.55				4.8	10.1	2.1		0.7	14.3	92	$16
Age	26	05	a/a	11	5	0	152	129	4.50	1.53	258			24.2	32%	69%	4.02				5.0	7.6	1.5		0.4	-3.6	69	$9
Type	Pwr FB	06	FLA *	8	2	1	124	123	3.40	1.46	234			12.1	30%	78%	4.33	45	16	39	5.4	8.9	1.7	8%	0.7	16.6	39	$12
Health	B	07	FLA	2	4	1	59	56	3.68	1.31	214	210	227	4.4	26%	76%	4.36	37	19	44	4.9	8.6	1.8	10%	1.1	5.4	37	$5
PT/Exp	D	08	FLA	2	5	0	65	56	4.45	1.41	222	264	203	4.2	25%	72%	4.46	46	17	37	5.4	7.8	1.4	14%	1.3	-1.4	18	$3
Consist	A	1st Half		2	3	0	46	42	2.95	1.42	223			4.6	28%	82%	4.31	49	15	36	5.5	8.3	1.5	9%	0.8	7.4	27	$4
LIMA Plan	C	2nd Half		0	2	0	19	14	8.05	1.37	219			3.4	20%	43%	4.78	39	21	39	5.2	6.6	1.3	23%	2.4	-8.9	-4	($1)
+/- Score	-17	09	Proj	2	3	0	44	39	4.76	1.49	246			5.1	29%	70%	4.62	41	19	40	5.2	8.1	1.6	10%	1.0	-1.5	25	$2

This 2H is the most fascinating line I've seen. Only 20% of balls in play fell for hits, but of those who reached base, more than half eventually scored. Plus, nearly one in 4 fly balls went yard. Net = 8.05 ERA

Ponson,Sidney		Yr	Tm	W	L	Sv	IP	K	ERA	WHIP	OBA	vL	vR	BF/G	H%	S%	xERA	G	L	F	Ctl	Dom	Cmd	hr/f	hr/9	RAR	BPV	R$
RH	Starter	04	BAL	11	15	0	215	115	5.31	1.55	304	305	288	29.2	33%	67%	4.61	51	18	32	2.9	4.8	1.7	10%	1.0	-23.3	37	$4
Age	32	05	BAL	7	11	0	130	68	6.23	1.73	325	360	299	26.3	35%	65%	4.70	53	20	27	3.3	4.7	1.4	12%	1.1	-29.8	26	($3)
Type	Con GB	06	2TM	4	5	0	85	48	6.25	1.69	311	304	328	20.6	34%	63%	4.86	51	18	31	3.8	5.1	1.3	11%	1.1	-18.1	18	($1)
Health	A	07	MIN	2	5	0	37	23	7.02	1.91	340	265	410	25.7	36%	66%	4.80	54	17	29	4.1	5.6	1.4	18%	1.7	-11.5	22	($2)
PT/Exp	C	08	2AL *	9	7	0	163	69	5.00	1.66	312	344	269	24.1	33%	71%	4.82	54	19	26	3.5	3.8	1.1	12%	1.0	-13.1	8	$1
Consist	A	1st Half		6	3	0	89	40	3.90	1.67	312			25.5	34%	78%	4.59	59	17	24	3.5	4.0	1.2	10%	0.8	4.9	15	$3
LIMA Plan	C	2nd Half		3	4	0	74	29	6.32	1.65	311			22.5	32%	63%	5.01	51	21	28	3.4	3.5	1.0	14%	1.3	-18.0	0	($2)
+/- Score	-22	09	Proj	4	5	0	73	33	5.34	1.66	308			23.7	32%	69%	4.88	53	19	28	3.6	4.1	1.1	12%	1.1	-4.1	8	$0

8-5, 5.04 ERA in 135 IP at TEX and NYY. What is it about this guy that continues to merit a paycheck? 11 years and only once with an ERA under 4.24. Must be his ability to walk to the mound without falling down.

Price,David		Yr	Tm	W	L	Sv	IP	K	ERA	WHIP	OBA	vL	vR	BF/G	H%	S%	xERA	G	L	F	Ctl	Dom	Cmd	hr/f	hr/9	RAR	BPV	R$
LH	Starter	04		0	0	0	0	0	0.00	0.00																		
Age	23	05		0	0	0	0	0	0.00	0.00																		
Type	Pwr	06		0	0	0	0	0	0.00	0.00																		
Health	A	07		0	0	0	0	0	0.00	0.00																		
PT/Exp	F	08	TAM *	8	1	0	89	74	2.73	1.22	242	158	188	20.5	29%	81%	3.81	50	13	38	2.9	7.5	2.6	8%	0.8	17.8	84	$13
Consist	F	1st Half		1	0	0	6	6	3.09	1.37	196			25.8	27%	75%					6.2	8.7	1.4		0.0	0.9	98	$1
LIMA Plan	C+	2nd Half		7	1	0	83	68	2.70	1.21	245			20.2	29%	82%	3.77	50	13	38	2.7	7.4	2.7	9%	0.9	16.8	88	$12
+/- Score	-5	09	Proj	10	5	0	145	121	3.91	1.41	263			25.1	31%	75%	4.11	50	13	38	3.6	7.5	2.1	10%	1.0	5.5	66	$13

0-0, 1.93 ERA in 14 IP at TAM. SP prospects don't get better than this. On top of having elite stuff, he induces GB well too. Problem is, he's green. Only 75 IP above High-A. Odds are he'll need more seasoning.

Proctor,Scott		Yr	Tm	W	L	Sv	IP	K	ERA	WHIP	OBA	vL	vR	BF/G	H%	S%	xERA	G	L	F	Ctl	Dom	Cmd	hr/f	hr/9	RAR	BPV	R$
RH	Reliever	04	aaa	2	3	4	44	33	3.66	1.44	263			5.5	31%	77%	4.30				3.9	6.8	1.8		0.9	3.7	54	$4
Age	32	05	NYY *	6	1	14	85	77	5.65	1.53	297	300	217	6.0	34%	69%	4.66	30	17	53	3.0	8.1	2.7	13%	2.0	-13.5	72	$8
Type	Pwr xFB	06	NYY	6	4	1	102	89	3.53	1.19	236	204	250	5.1	28%	75%	4.23	33	18	49	2.9	7.8	2.7	8%	1.1	13.0	74	$13
Health	C	07	2TM	5	5	0	86	64	3.65	1.41	243	250	237	4.5	27%	79%	5.40	28	16	55	4.6	6.7	1.5	8%	1.3	8.7	2	$7
PT/Exp	C	08	LA	2	0	0	39	46	6.05	1.68	273	263	260	4.3	35%	67%	4.23	38	21	41	5.6	10.7	1.9	16%	1.6	-8.5	57	$0
Consist	C	1st Half		1	0	0	32	36	6.81	1.83	287			4.6	36%	65%	4.72	35	23	42	6.2	10.2	1.6	16%	1.7	-9.9	29	($1)
LIMA Plan	C+	2nd Half		1	0	0	7	10	2.57	1.00	202			3.4	29%	83%	2.32	50	13	38	2.6	12.9	5.0	18%	1.3	1.5	190	$2
+/- Score	47	09	Proj	1	1	0	29	27	4.66	1.52	268			4.9	32%	73%	4.62	36	17	46	4.3	8.4	1.9	10%	1.2	-1.0	48	$1

Shave 10 years off his age and his Dom alone would make him worth watching. As it stands, he can't find the plate, and he's got big hr/9 issues. Plus offseason elbow surgery clouds '09. Too much risk.

Purcey,David		Yr	Tm	W	L	Sv	IP	K	ERA	WHIP	OBA	vL	vR	BF/G	H%	S%	xERA	G	L	F	Ctl	Dom	Cmd	hr/f	hr/9	RAR	BPV	R$
LH	Starter	04		0	0	0	0	0	0.00	0.00																		
Age	27	05	aa	4	3	0	43	39	4.53	1.65	258			24.6	32%	73%	4.55				6.0	8.1	1.3		0.6	-1.2	61	$2
Type	Pwr xFB	06	a/a	6	12	0	140	106	8.02	2.03	326			24.7	37%	61%	7.24				6.0	6.8	1.1		1.5	-60.4	11	($11)
Health	A	07	aa	3	5	0	62	42	7.42	1.67	329			25.9	38%	53%	5.83				2.6	6.1	2.4		0.8	-22.6	52	($2)
PT/Exp	D	08	TOR *	11	12	0	182	154	4.37	1.40	268	284	261	25.4	32%	71%	4.52	32	23	45	3.3	7.6	2.3	8%	1.0	-0.6	57	$13
Consist	C	1st Half		6	7	0	98	79	4.54	1.47	262			25.2	30%	72%	4.39	35	35	30	4.3	7.3	1.7	14%	1.1	-2.3	29	$6
LIMA Plan	D+	2nd Half		5	5	0	85	75	4.18	1.31	274			25.6	33%	70%	4.18	31	21	47	2.2	8.0	3.6	7%	0.9	1.7	93	$8
+/- Score	7	09	Proj	11	10	0	160	128	4.57	1.45	275			24.9	32%	71%	4.72	32	22	46	3.4	7.2	2.1	9%	1.1	-5.8	48	$11

3-6, 5.54 ERA in 65 IP at TOR. Poor MLB results don't tell the whole story. Huge growth in 2H. As a former 1st round pick, these surging skills are worthy of speculation. If they repeat... UP: 3.75 ERA, 175 K

Putz,J.J.		Yr	Tm	W	L	Sv	IP	K	ERA	WHIP	OBA	vL	vR	BF/G	H%	S%	xERA	G	L	F	Ctl	Dom	Cmd	hr/f	hr/9	RAR	BPV	R$
RH	Reliever	04	SEA	0	3	9	63	47	4.71	1.43	271	234	308	5.1	30%	71%	4.06	52	15	32	3.4	6.7	2.0	16%	1.4	-2.2	59	$5
Age	32	05	SEA	6	5	1	60	45	3.60	1.35	255	321	197	4.0	29%	78%	3.78	55	17	28	3.5	6.8	2.0	16%	1.2	5.7	61	$7
Type	Pwr	06	SEA	4	1	36	78	104	2.30	0.92	211	211	204	4.2	32%	76%	2.22	51	16	33	1.5	12.0	8.0	7%	0.5	21.7	204	$27
Health	C	07	SEA	6	1	40	72	82	1.38	0.70	155	148	158	3.8	21%	89%	2.60	42	17	41	1.6	10.3	6.3	9%	0.8	27.6	161	$32
PT/Exp	B	08	SEA	6	5	15	46	56	3.89	1.60	261	258	253	4.5	36%	77%	4.08	40	20	40	5.4	10.9	2.0	8%	0.8	2.6	67	$10
Consist	B	1st Half		2	3	7	19	23	5.21	2.00	282			4.7	40%	73%	5.40	33	22	44	8.1	10.9	1.4	7%	0.5	-2.0	-10	$3
LIMA Plan	B+	2nd Half		4	2	8	27	33	2.97	1.32	245			4.3	33%	82%	3.28	44	19	37	3.6	10.9	3.0	12%	1.0	4.6	120	$7
+/- Score	18	09	Proj	7	5	25	73	84	3.60	1.26	230			4.3	31%	74%	3.39	43	18	38	3.7	10.4	2.8	10%	0.9	9.3	109	$19

Elbow issue torpedoed his season. Skills were elite again when he was healthy late in year. He's both potential value pick and a big health risk until we know more about his elbow. High risk, high reward.

STEPHEN NICKRAND

Qualls,Chad

		Yr	Tm	W	L	Sv	IP	K	ERA	WHIP	OBA	vL	vR	BF/G	H%	S%	xERA	G	L	F	Ctl	Dom	Cmd	hr/f	hr/9	RAR	BPV	R$
RH	Reliever	04	HOU *	7	6	2	139	82	5.95	1.64	326	264	267	11.1	36%	63%	4.15	58	15	27	2.5	5.3	2.2	9%	0.8	-29.0	65	($1)
Age	30	05	HOU	6	4	0	79	60	3.30	1.21	246	218	275	4.3	29%	75%	3.17	58	21	20	2.6	6.8	2.6	15%	0.8	9.3	88	$9
Type	Pwr xGB	06	HOU	7	3	0	88	56	3.78	1.18	234	229	251	4.5	26%	71%	3.59	60	14	26	2.9	5.7	2.0	14%	1.0	7.7	64	$10
Health	A	07	HOU	6	5	5	83	78	3.05	1.32	265	248	289	4.4	32%	82%	3.24	57	14	29	2.7	8.5	3.1	14%	1.1	14.1	114	$11
PT/Exp	C	08	ARI	4	8	9	74	71	2.81	1.07	227	220	229	3.8	29%	75%	2.71	58	19	23	2.2	8.7	3.9	9%	0.5	13.3	133	$13
Consist	A	1st Half		1	6	1	38	41	3.29	1.17	229			3.9	31%	72%	2.77	56	21	23	3.1	9.6	3.2	9%	0.5	4.6	125	$4
LIMA Plan	B+	2nd Half		3	2	8	35	30	2.29	0.96	225			3.7	28%	78%	2.64	61	16	23	1.3	7.6	6.0	9%	0.5	8.7	142	$9
+/- Score	18	09	Proj	5	5	30	74	69	3.18	1.17	244			4.2	31%	74%	2.91	58	17	25	2.3	8.4	3.6	10%	0.6	12.9	126	$19

Got his chance to close late in year and made the most of it. As a GBer with a rising Dom and no LH/RH splits, he's got the goods of a top-tier one. If he can sustain gains vs. RHers... UP: 40 SV

Ramirez,Edwar

		Yr	Tm	W	L	Sv	IP	K	ERA	WHIP	OBA	vL	vR	BF/G	H%	S%	xERA	G	L	F	Ctl	Dom	Cmd	hr/f	hr/9	RAR	BPV	R$
RH	Reliever	04		0	0	0	0	0	0.00	0.00																		
Age	28	05		0	0	0	0	0	0.00	0.00																		
Type	Pwr xFB	06		0	0	0	0	0	0.00	0.00																		
Health	A	07	NYY *	5	1	8	77	108	3.12	1.30	215			5.9	32%	79%	3.69	35	6	60	4.7	12.5	2.6	7%	0.8	13.2	110	$14
PT/Exp	F	08	NYY *	6	1	1	64	73	3.36	1.11	203	229	195	4.1	27%	74%	3.51	33	22	45	3.5	10.3	2.9	10%	1.0	7.8	101	$11
Consist	A	1st Half		2	0	0	36	38	2.50	1.00	185			4.3	24%	79%	3.75	29	18	53	3.3	9.6	2.9	7%	0.8	8.2	92	$6
LIMA Plan	A	2nd Half		4	1	1	28	35	4.45	1.24	224			3.9	30%	68%	3.24	37	26	37	3.8	11.1	2.9	16%	1.3	-0.4	112	$5
+/- Score	17	09	Proj	4	2	0	58	68	3.57	1.21	220			4.7	29%	75%	3.59	34	20	46	3.7	10.6	2.8	11%	1.1	6.0	102	$8

5-1, 3.90 ERA in 55 IP at NYY. From this small 2-season data sample, here is what stands between him and stardom:
1. A Ctl rate of 3.0
2. A GB rate of 40%
It's close, but time is limited at 28

Ramirez,Horacio

		Yr	Tm	W	L	Sv	IP	K	ERA	WHIP	OBA	vL	vR	BF/G	H%	S%	xERA	G	L	F	Ctl	Dom	Cmd	hr/f	hr/9	RAR	BPV	R$
LH	Reliever	04	ATL	2	4	0	60	31	2.40	1.35	231	220	227	25.6	24%	88%	4.53	54	20	26	4.5	4.6	1.0	14%	1.0	13.8	-6	$5
Age	29	05	ATL	11	9	0	202	80	4.63	1.39	273	267	286	26.4	27%	71%	4.69	48	23	29	3.0	3.6	1.2	15%	1.4	-9.6	10	$8
Type	Con GB	06	ATL	5	5	0	76	37	4.49	1.52	284	286	288	24.2	31%	71%	4.60	54	20	26	3.7	4.4	1.2	9%	0.7	-0.1	12	$3
Health	F	07	SEA	8	7	0	98	40	7.16	1.85	335	330	340	23.4	35%	61%	5.48	48	21	31	3.9	3.7	1.0	11%	1.2	-32.1	-12	($4)
PT/Exp	C	08	2AL *	2	5	0	56	19	3.68	1.36	286	350	258	6.9	30%	73%	4.41	53	22	25	2.0	3.0	1.5	7%	0.6	4.7	30	$3
Consist	B	1st Half		1	1	0	23	8	2.38	1.12	254			15.3	25%	85%	3.33	67	17	17	1.5	3.0	2.0	19%	1.0	5.5	59	$3
LIMA Plan	C	2nd Half		1	4	0	34	11	4.55	1.52	307			5.1	33%	68%	4.75	52	22	26	2.4	2.9	1.2	3%	0.3	-0.9	18	$0
+/- Score	-41	09	Proj	2	2	0	29	11	4.66	1.48	294			10.6	30%	70%	4.69	52	21	27	2.8	3.4	1.2	11%	0.9	-1.0	16	$1

1-4, 4.34 ERA in 37 IP at KC and CHW. Uh-oh, here he goes again, posting a decent ERA in small innings and leading some to think he has value. Look at Dom, look at BA vs LH, look at xERA. Now look someplace else.

Ramirez,Ramon

		Yr	Tm	W	L	Sv	IP	K	ERA	WHIP	OBA	vL	vR	BF/G	H%	S%	xERA	G	L	F	Ctl	Dom	Cmd	hr/f	hr/9	RAR	BPV	R$
RH	Reliever	04	a/a	4	9	0	133	121	6.02	1.49	296			26.7	36%	60%	5.06				2.7	8.2	3.0		1.0	-27.6	78	$2
Age	27	05	a/a	9	9	0	141	107	4.73	1.43	274			20.5	31%	71%	4.91				3.3	6.8	2.1		1.4	-7.5	43	$8
Type	Pwr	06	COL	4	3	0	67	61	3.48	1.26	234	274	194	4.6	29%	74%	4.19	41	14	45	3.6	8.2	2.3	6%	0.7	8.3	68	$7
Health	A	07	COL *	12	3	1	91	83	4.83	1.49	264	240	357	5.9	32%	69%	4.87	31	17	52	4.3	8.2	1.9	7%	1.0	-4.5	41	$9
PT/Exp	D	08	KC	3	2	1	72	70	2.64	1.23	220	300	153	4.2	29%	78%	3.72	46	19	35	3.9	8.8	2.3	3%	0.3	15.1	77	$9
Consist	B	1st Half		0	1	0	40	43	2.68	1.24	225			4.4	32%	76%	3.50	45	21	34	3.8	9.6	2.5	0%	0.0	8.3	94	$4
LIMA Plan	C+	2nd Half		3	1	1	31	27	2.58	1.21	213			3.9	26%	81%	4.01	47	16	37	4.0	7.7	1.9	6%	0.6	6.8	56	$5
+/- Score	-34	09	Proj	4	3	0	69	63	3.55	1.33	240			5.0	30%	75%	4.09	43	17	40	3.9	8.3	2.1	8%	0.8	2.8	64	$7

A top-tier setup guy now that he's out of Coors. Not a terribly high ceiling, but serviceable. Given creaky elbow, he's got injury risk. But you won't lose much on a small investment. Great LIMA stash.

Rasner,Darrell

		Yr	Tm	W	L	Sv	IP	K	ERA	WHIP	OBA	vL	vR	BF/G	H%	S%	xERA	G	L	F	Ctl	Dom	Cmd	hr/f	hr/9	RAR	BPV	R$
RH	Starter	04		0	0	0	0	0	0.00	0.00																		
Age	28	05	aa	6	7	0	150	79	4.17	1.34	288			23.7	32%	69%	4.20				1.8	4.7	2.7		0.6	2.6	63	$8
Type	Con	06	NYY *	7	1	0	78	50	3.82	1.35	287			20.9	32%	73%	4.50	40	18	42	2.0	5.7	2.9	7%	0.8	7.1	68	$8
Health	D	07	NYY *	2	3	0	33	14	3.03	1.38	276	375	212	17.6	28%	83%	5.15	40	20	40	2.8	3.8	1.4	9%	1.1	6.0	12	$3
PT/Exp	D	08	NYY *	9	10	0	144	89	4.50	1.40	279	279	312	21.5	31%	69%	4.68	40	21	39	2.8	5.5	2.0	8%	0.9	-2.8	42	$9
Consist	B	1st Half		8	6	0	88	60	3.29	1.23	262			24.4	30%	74%	4.37	36	22	42	2.1	6.1	2.9	5%	0.6	11.4	68	$11
LIMA Plan	C	2nd Half		1	4	0	56	29	6.39	1.67	303			18.5	32%	63%	5.28	44	21	35	4.0	4.6	1.2	11%	1.3	-14.2	-2	($2)
+/- Score	-18	09	Proj																									

5-10, 5.40 ERA in 113 IP at NYY. A tale of two halves. Problem is, just 25% of first half starts with NYY were PQS-4/5. He needs a 2.0 Cmd just to survive. Maybe he'll find it in Japan.

Rauch,Jon

		Yr	Tm	W	L	Sv	IP	K	ERA	WHIP	OBA	vL	vR	BF/G	H%	S%	xERA	G	L	F	Ctl	Dom	Cmd	hr/f	hr/9	RAR	BPV	R$
RH	Reliever	04	2TM *	11	5	0	122	82	3.91	1.29	257	321	203	18.4	28%	74%	4.62	43	11	47	2.9	6.0	2.1	10%	1.3	6.6	52	$12
Age	30	05	WAS *	3	5	0	51	43	3.53	1.16	234	255	186	9.5	27%	74%	4.33	26	23	51	2.6	7.6	2.9	8%	1.1	4.5	69	$6
Type	Pwr xFB	06	WAS	4	5	2	91	86	3.36	1.25	233	254	216	4.5	28%	79%	4.24	30	21	49	3.6	8.5	2.4	11%	1.3	12.7	65	$10
Health	B	07	WAS	8	4	4	87	71	3.61	1.10	234	208	249	4.0	28%	69%	4.25	33	13	53	2.2	7.3	3.4	5%	0.7	8.8	85	$13
PT/Exp	B	08	2NL	4	8	18	72	66	4.14	1.19	254	268	242	4.0	30%	70%	3.84	31	23	46	2.0	8.3	4.1	12%	1.4	1.1	104	$13
Consist	A	1st Half		4	2	16	42	39	2.55	0.92	217			3.9	27%	77%	3.43	33	22	46	1.3	8.3	6.5	8%	0.9	9.0	126	$13
LIMA Plan	B	2nd Half		0	6	2	29	27	6.43	1.56	303			4.1	34%	64%	4.45	30	24	46	3.1	8.3	2.7	17%	2.1	-7.8	74	($0)
+/- Score	28	09	Proj	5	5	15	64	57	3.69	1.24	254			4.4	30%	76%	4.14	31	20	48	2.6	8.1	3.2	10%	1.3	1.6	86	$12

Became an elite closer in 1H. 2H collapse was H%, S%, and hr/f induced, all of which are correctable. Late year elbow stiffness clouds '09 outlook but BPV trend bodes well, if healthy. A $10 bid could yield $20.

Ray,Chris

		Yr	Tm	W	L	Sv	IP	K	ERA	WHIP	OBA	vL	vR	BF/G	H%	S%	xERA	G	L	F	Ctl	Dom	Cmd	hr/f	hr/9	RAR	BPV	R$
RH	Reliever	04		0	0	0	0	0	0.00	0.00											0.0	0.0						
Age	27	05	BAL *	2	5	18	77	77	2.12	1.05	203	284	174	4.3	25%	87%	3.54	35	23	41	2.9	9.0	3.1	11%	1.1	21.5	95	$18
Type	Pwr FB	06	BAL	4	4	33	66	51	2.73	1.09	195	184	202	4.3	21%	84%	4.41	35	16	48	3.7	7.0	1.9	11%	1.4	14.9	39	$20
Health	F	07	BAL	5	6	16	43	44	4.43	1.24	225	233	212	4.1	28%	67%	3.62	45	18	38	3.8	9.3	2.4	12%	1.1	0.4	87	$11
PT/Exp	C	08	BAL	0	0	0	0	0	0.00	0.00											0.0	0.0						
Consist	B	1st Half		0	0	0	0	0	0.00	0.00											0.0	0.0				0.0	55	
LIMA Plan		2nd Half		0	0	0	0	0	0.00	0.00																		
+/- Score		09	Proj	3	4	15	44	36	3.93	1.26	232			4.3	27%	72%	4.30	39	19	42	3.7	7.4	2.0	10%	1.0	0.7	51	$9

He'll be 18 months post-TJ surgery by the start of spring training. Closer-worthy skills prior to going under knife mean he could bounce back quick. Watch Ctl; it can be a bugaboo for post-TJ guys.

Redding,Tim

		Yr	Tm	W	L	Sv	IP	K	ERA	WHIP	OBA	vL	vR	BF/G	H%	S%	xERA	G	L	F	Ctl	Dom	Cmd	hr/f	hr/9	RAR	BPV	R$
RH	Starter	04	HOU *	6	11	0	128	77	6.11	1.70	308	345	283	18.5	34%	65%	5.21	42	21	37	4.0	5.4	1.4	10%	1.2	-29.2	9	($3)
Age	31	05	2TM *	3	9	0	92	61	7.02	1.70	323			19.4	36%	58%	6.08				3.2	5.9	1.9		1.1	-30.8	32	($4)
Type		06	aaa	12	10	0	187	118	4.91	1.50	292			28.5	31%	72%	5.48				3.1	5.7	1.9		1.6	-9.0	23	$9
Health	A	07	WAS *	12	11	0	173	95	5.54	1.68	315	245	282	24.9	34%	68%	5.34	38	22	39	3.4	4.9	1.5	8%	1.0	-23.7	14	$2
PT/Exp	B	08	WAS	10	11	0	182	120	4.95	1.43	275	277	274	24.0	30%	69%	4.70	40	20	40	3.2	5.9	1.8	11%	1.3	-15.1	38	$7
Consist	A	1st Half		6	3	0	103	65	4.21	1.33	257			24.3	28%	72%	4.68	41	18	41	3.2	5.7	1.8	10%	1.1	0.8	34	$7
LIMA Plan	C	2nd Half		4	8	0	79	55	5.90	1.55	298			23.6	32%	65%	4.72	38	22	39	3.2	6.2	2.0	13%	1.6	-16.0	43	$0
+/- Score	-9	09	Proj	7	8	0	116	73	5.28	1.54	295			23.5	32%	69%	4.90	40	21	39	3.3	5.7	1.7	11%	1.3	-8.0	31	$3

Well, SOMEONE has to pitch on bad teams. Here is just innings upon innings of consistent mediocrity. In fact, 2008 was the high water mark of the past 5 years, which means his BPV almost hit 40. Please don't bid.

Reyes,Anthony

		Yr	Tm	W	L	Sv	IP	K	ERA	WHIP	OBA	vL	vR	BF/G	H%	S%	xERA	G	L	F	Ctl	Dom	Cmd	hr/f	hr/9	RAR	BPV	R$
RH	Reliever	04	aa	6	2	0	74	90	3.28	1.09	246			24.8	35%	69%	2.70				1.6	10.9	6.9		0.4	9.7	206	$11
Age	27	05	STL *	8	7	0	141	132	3.82	1.10	230	125	148	21.0	28%	67%	3.91	35	13	52	2.3	8.4	3.7	7%	0.9	7.4	103	$16
Type	FB	06	STL *	11	9	0	169	143	4.20	1.25	259	278	249	23.5	30%	72%	4.11	35	20	46	2.4	7.6	3.2	12%	1.4	5.9	85	$16
Health	A	07	STL *	3	15	0	144	99	5.49	1.37	259	290	234	22.0	28%	62%	4.80	35	21	44	3.5	6.2	1.8	10%	1.3	-18.9	32	$3
PT/Exp	D	08	2TM *	8	5	1	114	69	3.81	1.50	283	240	267	17.4	31%	78%	4.82	43	21	36	3.5	5.4	1.6	9%	1.0	7.0	25	$7
Consist	A	1st Half		3	3	1	50	33	4.35	1.56	298			13.1	34%	73%	4.84	35	23	42	3.2	6.0	1.9	6%	0.8	-0.2	35	$2
LIMA Plan	C	2nd Half		5	2	0	64	36	3.39	1.45	271			23.4	29%	82%	4.78	46	21	34	3.6	5.0	1.4	12%	1.2	7.2	15	$5
+/- Score	-25	09	Proj	6	8	0	116	72	4.66	1.41	272			22.9	30%	70%	4.84	39	21	41	3.3	5.6	1.7	10%	1.2	-6.6	29	$6

4-2, 2.76 ERA in 49 IP at STL and CLE. Made some surface gains after leaving STL. But his 2.00 ERA in Aug came with a 25 BPV. With this BPV trend and late season elbow issue, there's not much upside here.

STEPHEN NICKRAND

148

Reyes,Dennys

Reyes,Dennys		W	L	Sv	IP	K	ERA	WHIP	OBA	vL	vR	BF/G	H%	S%	xERA	G	L	F	Ctl	Dom	Cmd	hr/f	hr/9	RAR	BPV	R$
LH Reliever	04 KC	4	8	0	108	91	4.75	1.52	272	316	254	12.0	32%	70%	4.12	51	17	32	4.2	7.6	1.8	11%	1.0	-4.2	53	$4
Age 32	05 SD	3	2	0	43	35	5.21	2.06	319	208	359	6.0	38%	74%	4.41	65	17	18	6.7	7.3	1.1	11%	0.6	-5.1	-6	($1)
Type Pwr xGB	06 MIN *	6	0	0	68	59	0.80	1.01	208	148	244	3.8	26%	95%	2.58	69	11	20	2.4	7.8	3.2	8%	0.4	31.6	122	$15
Health B	07 MIN	2	1	0	29	21	3.99	1.88	292	273	364	2.8	35%	78%	4.70	64	13	22	6.5	6.5	1.0	5%	0.3	1.9	-16	$1
PT/Exp D	08 MIN	3	0	0	46	39	2.33	1.19	235	202	276	2.5	28%	84%	3.12	60	17	23	2.9	7.6	2.6	13%	0.8	11.5	95	$7
Consist D	1st Half	2	0	0	24	12	2.28	1.18	239			2.6	27%	81%	3.97	58	15	27	2.7	4.6	1.7	5%	0.4	6.0	46	$3
LIMA Plan B	2nd Half	1	0	0	23	27	2.39	1.19	230			2.5	30%	88%	2.31	62	19	19	3.2	10.8	3.4	28%	1.2	5.5	148	$3
+/- Score -31	09 Proj	2	3	0	58	46	3.41	1.34	248			3.5	30%	76%	3.45	62	16	22	3.7	7.1	1.9	10%	0.6	7.0	68	$5

"Pwr xGB" is the best possible combination but you can see what happens when home plate becomes elusive. When he's on, he's superb. When he's not... Given his recent cycle, 2009 is not looking too good.

Reyes,Jo-Jo

Reyes,Jo-Jo		W	L	Sv	IP	K	ERA	WHIP	OBA	vL	vR	BF/G	H%	S%	xERA	G	L	F	Ctl	Dom	Cmd	hr/f	hr/9	RAR	BPV	R$
LH Starter	04	0	0	0	0	0	0.00	0.00																		
Age 24	05	0	0	0	0	0	0.00	0.00																		
Type Pwr	06	0	0	0	0	0	0.00	0.00																		
Health A	07 ATL *	14	3	0	160	121	4.34	1.48	260	129	317	23.5	30%	73%	4.74	45	15	40	4.4	6.8	1.5	9%	1.0	1.8	25	$11
PT/Exp D	08 ATL *	4	12	0	152	111	5.03	1.56	283	255	313	22.0	32%	70%	4.43	49	19	32	4.0	6.6	1.6	13%	1.2	-14.3	36	$1
Consist A	1st Half	4	7	0	92	78	3.51	1.31	251			23.0	30%	75%	3.67	51	20	29	3.3	7.6	2.3	10%	0.8	8.7	76	$8
LIMA Plan C	2nd Half	0	5	0	60	33	7.39	1.94	328			20.7	34%	64%	5.69	46	19	35	5.1	5.0	1.0	16%	1.8	-23.0	-25	($7)
+/- Score 12	09 Proj	7	9	0	160	123	4.51	1.50	277			22.1	32%	72%	4.36	47	18	34	3.8	6.9	1.8	11%	1.0	-0.4	47	$6

3-11, 5.81 ERA in 113 IP at ATL. A yo-yo season for Jo-Jo. Great start, then 2H skills collapsed. Prior solid Cmd at Triple-A, GB ways bode well, but will struggle until he can solve RHers. More minors time would serve all here.

Reynolds,Greg

Reynolds,Greg		W	L	Sv	IP	K	ERA	WHIP	OBA	vL	vR	BF/G	H%	S%	xERA	G	L	F	Ctl	Dom	Cmd	hr/f	hr/9	RAR	BPV	R$
RH Starter	04	0	0	0	0	0	0.00	0.00																		
Age 23	05	0	0	0	0	0	0.00	0.00																		
Type Con	06	0	0	0	0	0	0.00	0.00																		
Health C	07 aa	4	1	0	50	31	1.97	0.96	216			24.3	25%	82%	2.19				1.6	5.6	3.4		0.5	15.4	101	$9
PT/Exp D	08 COL *	3	11	0	125	53	6.55	1.79	335	344	299	21.8	35%	65%	5.42	45	22	33	3.4	3.8	1.1	11%	1.3	-35.2	1	($8)
Consist F	1st Half	3	8	0	89	32	5.70	1.57	305			23.6	31%	66%	5.16	48	20	32	3.0	3.2	1.0	12%	1.3	-15.8	1	($2)
LIMA Plan C+	2nd Half	0	3	0	36	21	8.68	2.34	401			18.8	44%	63%	6.39	29	29	41	4.1	5.4	1.3	8%	1.3	-19.4	-7	($7)
+/- Score 34	09 Proj	5	7	0	125	73	4.54	1.40	291			20.8	32%	70%	4.48	41	24	36	2.2	5.3	2.4	10%	1.1	-2.1	55	$5

2-8, 8.13 ERA in 62 IP at COL. Minor shoulder surgery in '07, followed by late '08 shoulder problems likely means he was hurt pretty much all year. You won't read that in the papers but you can pretty much deduce it.

Rhodes,Arthur

Rhodes,Arthur		W	L	Sv	IP	K	ERA	WHIP	OBA	vL	vR	BF/G	H%	S%	xERA	G	L	F	Ctl	Dom	Cmd	hr/f	hr/9	RAR	BPV	R$
LH Reliever	04 OAK	3	3	9	38	34	5.18	1.75	299	314	283	4.8	33%	78%	4.89	40	17	43	4.9	8.0	1.6	18%	2.1	-3.5	29	$4
Age 39	05 CLE	3	1	0	43	43	2.09	1.04	214	286	155	3.6	28%	81%	3.32	41	23	36	2.5	9.0	3.6	5%	0.4	12.1	113	$8
Type Pwr FB	06 PHI	0	5	4	45	48	5.38	1.70	269	290	246	3.8	36%	67%	4.78	36	22	41	6.0	9.6	1.6	4%	0.4	-5.0	25	$1
Health F	07 SEA	0	0	0	0	0	0.00	0.00																		
PT/Exp D	08 2TM	4	1	2	35	40	2.04	1.25	220	157	309	2.4	32%	82%	3.94	27	28	45	4.1	10.2	2.5	0%	0.0	9.9	78	$7
Consist B	1st Half	2	0	1	15	17	3.67	1.50	252			2.5	36%	73%	4.04	25	42	33	4.9	10.4	2.1	0%	0.0	1.1	58	$2
LIMA Plan C+	2nd Half	2	1	1	21	23	0.87	1.07	194			2.3	29%	91%	3.86	28	18	54	3.5	10.0	2.9	0%	0.0	8.7	93	$5
+/- Score -76	09 Proj	3	2	3	44	45	3.52	1.33	232			3.3	30%	76%	4.12	33	24	43	4.3	9.3	2.1	8%	0.8	1.4	61	$6

Return from TJ surgery went quite well. Problem is, you're tying up a roster spot with a 40 IP guy who's pushing 40. Sim gamers might micro-manage his sexy Dom trend. Others should prospect elsewhere.

Richard,Clayton

Richard,Clayton		W	L	Sv	IP	K	ERA	WHIP	OBA	vL	vR	BF/G	H%	S%	xERA	G	L	F	Ctl	Dom	Cmd	hr/f	hr/9	RAR	BPV	R$
LH Starter	04	0	0	0	0	0	0.00	0.00																		
Age 25	05	0	0	0	0	0	0.00	0.00																		
Type Con	06	0	0	0	0	0	0.00	0.00																		
Health A	07	0	0	0	0	0	0.00	0.00																		
PT/Exp D	08 CHW *	14	11	0	175	102	4.19	1.27	274	274	320	22.2	31%	67%	3.84	50	23	27	1.8	5.3	2.9	8%	0.6	3.3	74	$16
Consist F	1st Half	10	6	0	109	59	3.38	1.12	251			25.9	28%	69%					1.6	4.9	3.1		0.3	13.0	89	$14
LIMA Plan C+	2nd Half	4	5	0	66	43	5.54	1.51	310			18.2	35%	65%	3.96	50	23	27	2.2	5.9	2.7	13%	1.1	-9.6	75	$2
+/- Score 17	09 Proj	10	9	0	133	81	4.33	1.32	280			24.5	31%	68%	3.85	50	23	27	2.0	5.5	2.8	10%	0.8	9.4	73	$11

2-5, 6.04 ERA in 47 IP at CHW. Control artist didn't miss many MLB bats in his debut. But 2H Cmd shows he has upside, and as a GBer, it may come quick. He has the seeds of something good here. Patience.

Rincon,Juan

Rincon,Juan		W	L	Sv	IP	K	ERA	WHIP	OBA	vL	vR	BF/G	H%	S%	xERA	G	L	F	Ctl	Dom	Cmd	hr/f	hr/9	RAR	BPV	R$
RH Reliever	04 MIN	11	6	2	82	106	2.63	1.02	184	148	206	4.2	27%	76%	2.86	45	16	39	3.5	11.6	3.3	7%	0.5	18.2	138	$18
Age 30	05 MIN	6	6	0	77	84	2.45	1.21	225	218	228	4.2	31%	79%	3.26	48	20	32	3.5	9.8	2.8	3%	0.2	18.2	108	$12
Type	06 MIN	3	1	1	74	65	2.91	1.35	267	222	303	4.2	34%	78%	3.54	51	22	28	2.9	7.9	2.7	3%	0.2	15.0	92	$8
Health A	07 MIN	3	3	0	60	49	5.13	1.56	279	313	236	4.2	32%	70%	4.38	49	16	36	4.2	7.4	1.8	14%	1.4	-4.6	46	$2
PT/Exp C	08 2AL	3	3	0	55	39	5.86	1.65	301	323	279	5.4	34%	66%	4.82	42	22	36	3.9	6.3	1.6	12%	1.3	-10.3	29	$0
Consist B	1st Half	2	2	0	28	20	6.11	1.75	295			5.4	32%	68%	5.54	40	14	46	5.1	6.4	1.3	12%	1.6	-6.1	-5	($0)
LIMA Plan C+	2nd Half	1	1	0	27	19	5.60	1.54	306			5.3	35%	64%	4.10	44	29	27	2.6	6.3	2.4	12%	1.0	-4.2	64	$0
+/- Score 12	09 Proj	2	2	0	44	31	4.91	1.52	283			4.8	32%	69%	4.51	46	21	34	3.7	6.3	1.7	10%	1.0	-0.5	38	$2

Suspended for failing a drug test in May 2005. Since then the plummet into the abyss has been relentless. We could use him as a case study but some people still think this stark trend could have happened anyway.

Riske,David

Riske,David		W	L	Sv	IP	K	ERA	WHIP	OBA	vL	vR	BF/G	H%	S%	xERA	G	L	F	Ctl	Dom	Cmd	hr/f	hr/9	RAR	BPV	R$
RH Reliever	04 CLE	7	3	5	77	78	3.74	1.43	241	224	255	4.7	29%	79%	4.37	36	18	45	4.8	9.1	1.9	12%	1.3	6.6	49	$10
Age 32	05 CLE	3	4	1	72	48	3.12	0.97	213	210	204	4.8	22%	76%	3.78	42	20	38	1.9	6.0	3.2	14%	1.4	11.2	77	$10
Type FB	06 2AL	1	2	0	44	28	3.89	1.30	244	280	224	4.5	26%	75%	4.77	36	22	42	3.5	5.7	1.6	11%	1.2	3.6	23	$3
Health C	07 KC	1	4	4	70	52	2.45	1.26	237	202	265	4.5	27%	86%	4.39	41	17	41	3.5	6.7	1.9	9%	1.0	17.6	46	$9
PT/Exp D	08 MIL	1	2	2	42	27	5.32	1.70	283	359	240	4.3	31%	71%	5.82	29	29	42	5.3	5.7	1.1	10%	1.3	-5.5	-33	($0)
Consist B	1st Half	0	1	1	23	15	5.09	1.48	262			4.8	29%	68%	5.05	33	29	38	4.3	5.9	1.4	11%	1.2	-2.3	1	$0
LIMA Plan F	2nd Half	1	1	1	19	12	5.60	1.97	306			3.9	33%	74%	6.77	24	30	46	6.5	5.6	0.9	10%	1.4	-3.2	-74	($1)
+/- Score -38	09 Proj	2	3	0	64	40	4.82	1.56	278			4.4	30%	72%	5.35	33	25	42	4.3	5.7	1.3	10%	1.3	-7.9	-2	$1

Had bone spur removed from elbow in Sept, which explains 2H collapse. But his BPIs have been pretty lousy since 2005. Not for the riske-averse. [The editors apologize for not removing the bad pun.]

Rivera,Mariano

Rivera,Mariano		W	L	Sv	IP	K	ERA	WHIP	OBA	vL	vR	BF/G	H%	S%	xERA	G	L	F	Ctl	Dom	Cmd	hr/f	hr/9	RAR	BPV	R$
RH Reliever	04 NYY	4	2	53	78	66	1.96	1.09	228	234	215	4.2	29%	83%	3.13	60	11	29	2.3	7.6	3.3	5%	0.3	23.9	113	$30
Age 39	05 NYY	7	4	43	78	80	1.38	0.87	185	177	176	4.2	25%	85%	2.62	57	14	29	2.1	9.2	4.4	4%	0.2	28.8	145	$31
Type Pwr xGB	06 NYY	5	5	34	75	55	1.80	0.96	224	194	248	4.6	27%	83%	3.21	54	16	30	1.3	6.6	5.0	5%	0.4	25.5	115	$25
Health A	07 NYY	3	4	30	71	74	3.16	1.12	253	255	241	4.3	33%	72%	2.76	53	19	29	1.5	9.3	6.2	7%	0.5	11.9	158	$20
PT/Exp A	08 NYY	6	5	39	71	77	1.40	0.66	171	147	183	4.0	23%	84%	2.20	55	15	31	0.8	9.8	12.8	8%	0.5	25.7	188	$30
Consist B	1st Half	2	2	22	36	42	0.74	0.55	142			3.7	20%	94%	2.19	46	17	37	0.7	10.4	14.0	7%	0.5	16.1	192	$17
LIMA Plan C	2nd Half	4	3	17	34	35	2.09	0.78	198			4.2	26%	76%	2.18	62	12	26	0.8	9.2	11.7	9%	0.5	9.6	184	$14
+/- Score -49	09 Proj	5	5	35	73	67	2.73	1.08	236			4.5	30%	77%	2.97	55	15	29	1.9	8.3	4.5	8%	0.6	13.0	133	$23

This is sick. An 11.7 Cmd and 62% GB% in 2H? Nearly 40, he's actually on a growth trend! Sure, that hit rate was a fluke, but he would have been elite anyway. Others will pay top $ for K-Rod; smart $ stays here.

Rivera,Saul

Rivera,Saul		W	L	Sv	IP	K	ERA	WHIP	OBA	vL	vR	BF/G	H%	S%	xERA	G	L	F	Ctl	Dom	Cmd	hr/f	hr/9	RAR	BPV	R$
RH Reliever	04 aa	2	3	4	54	30	7.08	2.23	358			6.3	39%	69%	8.10				5.9	4.9	0.8		1.1	-18.2	-4	($5)
Age 31	05 aa	3	3	9	76	50	3.27	1.53	304			8.5	35%	79%	4.72				2.7	5.9	2.2		0.4	9.7	62	$7
Type Pwr GB	06 WAS *	4	1	2	88	61	3.01	1.52	264	194	290	5.9	31%	81%	4.83	46	19	35	4.6	6.2	1.3	5%	0.5	16.1	12	$7
Health A	07 WAS	4	6	3	93	64	3.68	1.40	251	271	244	4.7	30%	71%	4.46	50	18	32	4.1	6.2	1.5	1%	0.1	8.6	29	$7
PT/Exp C	08 WAS	5	6	0	84	65	3.96	1.49	275	271	284	4.9	34%	72%	3.92	54	21	25	3.8	7.0	1.9	5%	0.3	3.2	56	$5
Consist A	1st Half	3	4	0	50	32	3.60	1.34	242			5.1	28%	72%	4.22	55	16	28	4.0	5.8	1.5	5%	0.4	4.1	30	$4
LIMA Plan B	2nd Half	2	2	0	34	33	4.50	1.71	319			4.6	41%	72%	3.45	52	28	20	3.4	8.7	2.5	5%	0.3	-1.0	95	$1
+/- Score -8	09 Proj	4	4	0	73	56	3.85	1.35	255			4.6	30%	72%	3.86	51	21	28	3.5	7.0	2.0	8%	0.6	4.3	61	$6

He's got the makings of a hidden LIMA gem. Sterling 2H, extreme GBer, nice Ctl trend. An obscene 2H H% kept him hidden. If Cmd growth continues and opportunity is there...
UP: 30 Saves

STEPHEN NICKRAND

Robertson,David

		Yr	W	L	Sv	IP	K	ERA	WHIP	OBA	vL	vR	BF/G	H%	S%	xERA	G	L	F	Ctl	Dom	Cmd	hr/f	hr/9	RAR	BPV	R$
RH	Reliever	04	0	0	0	0	0	0.00	0.00																		
Age	24	05	0	0	0	0	0	0.00	0.00																		
Type	Pwr FB	06	0	0	0	0	0	0.00	0.00																		
Health	A	07	0	0	0	0	0	0.00	0.00																		
PT/Exp	F	08 NYY *	8	0	3	84	101	3.34	1.22	211	259	254	6.3	30%	72%	3.45	43	16	41	4.2	10.9	**2.6**	5%	0.4	10.4	103	$14
Consist	F	1st Half	3	0	3	53	63	2.03	1.09	189			7.1	29%	79%	3.32	38	25	38	3.9	10.7	**2.7**	0%	0.0	15.2	102	$10
LIMA Plan	A	2nd Half	5	0	0	30	38	5.64	1.45	247			5.3	34%	63%	3.64	43	15	42	4.8	11.3	**2.4**	13%	1.2	-4.8	96	$3
+/- Score	17	09 Proj	**4**	**2**	**0**	**49**	**60**	**4.04**	**1.27**	**224**			**5.9**	**31%**	**70%**	**3.40**	**43**	**15**	**42**	**4.0**	**11.0**	**2.7**	**10%**	**0.9**	**6.2**	**110**	**$6**

4-0, 5.34 ERA in 30 IP at NYY Mowed 'em down during brief stint in minors: 77 K in 54 IP at Double-A and Triple-A. Limiting factor is Ctl, and he has yet to show he can corral it. Still, a high-ceiling arm in the making.

Robertson,Nate

		Yr	W	L	Sv	IP	K	ERA	WHIP	OBA	vL	vR	BF/G	H%	S%	xERA	G	L	F	Ctl	Dom	Cmd	hr/f	hr/9	RAR	BPV	R$
LH	Starter	04 DET	12	10	1	196	155	4.91	1.41	275	252	279	25.0	31%	69%	3.90	50	17	33	3.0	7.1	**2.3**	15%	1.4	-11.5	75	$12
Age	31	05 DET	7	16	0	196	122	4.50	1.36	267	244	272	26.2	29%	71%	4.17	49	20	30	3.0	5.6	**1.9**	15%	1.3	-3.0	48	$10
Type		06 DET	13	13	0	208	137	3.85	1.31	260	181	284	27.5	28%	75%	4.17	47	20	33	2.9	5.9	**2.0**	13%	1.3	18.2	53	$19
Health	A	07 DET	9	13	0	178	119	4.76	1.47	284	296	278	26.0	32%	70%	4.58	45	18	37	3.2	6.0	**1.9**	10%	1.1	-5.6	45	$9
PT/Exp	A	08 DET	7	11	0	169	108	6.35	1.66	314	323	311	24.1	34%	63%	4.84	44	19	37	3.3	5.8	**1.7**	12%	1.4	-41.6	37	($2)
Consist	A	1st Half	6	6	0	96	66	5.23	1.52	303			26.7	34%	67%	4.60	41	19	40	2.6	6.2	**2.4**	9%	1.1	-10.5	59	$3
LIMA Plan	F	2nd Half	1	5	0	72	42	7.83	1.85	329			21.6	35%	59%	5.16	49	18	33	4.2	5.2	**1.2**	16%	1.7	-31.1	7	($6)
+/- Score	34	09 Proj	**5**	**8**	**0**	**116**	**72**	**5.28**	**1.56**	**289**			**24.7**	**32%**	**68%**	**4.81**	**46**	**19**	**35**	**3.7**	**5.6**	**1.5**	**11%**	**1.2**	**-5.5**	**24**	**$2**

Bad skills and bad luck are a given. But just wondering... If his 2006 ERA hadn't given false hope (and more people looked at xERA), would he still be accumulating bad innings that we now have to analyze?

Rodney,Fernando

		Yr	W	L	Sv	IP	K	ERA	WHIP	OBA	vL	vR	BF/G	H%	S%	xERA	G	L	F	Ctl	Dom	Cmd	hr/f	hr/9	RAR	BPV	R$
RH	Reliever	04 DET	0	0	0	0	0	0.00	0.00											0.0	0.0						
Age	32	05 DET	2	3	9	44	42	2.86	1.27	239	265	219	4.7	29%	82%	3.64	40	28	31	3.5	8.6	**2.5**	13%	1.0	8.2	79	$8
Type	Pwr	06 DET	7	4	7	71	65	3.54	1.19	203	202	192	4.6	25%	72%	3.57	57	12	31	4.3	8.2	**1.9**	10%	0.8	8.9	66	$13
Health	F	07 DET	2	6	1	51	54	4.26	1.32	243	247	231	4.5	32%	69%	3.55	45	19	35	3.7	9.6	**2.6**	11%	0.9	1.5	95	$5
PT/Exp	C	08 DET	0	6	13	40	49	4.91	1.59	230	256	186	4.8	32%	69%	4.14	40	26	33	6.7	10.9	**1.6**	9%	0.7	-2.8	34	$5
Consist	A	1st Half	0	1	0	4	2	11.25	1.75	210			3.7	18%	33%	8.32	23	8	69	9.0	4.5	**0.5**	12%	2.3	-3.4	-161	($1)
LIMA Plan	B+	2nd Half	0	5	13	36	47	4.21	1.57	232			4.9	34%	73%	3.71	43	29	28	6.4	11.7	**1.8**	8%	0.5	0.6	56	$6
+/- Score	6	09 Proj	**3**	**6**	**18**	**58**	**62**	**3.88**	**1.26**	**227**			**4.7**	**30%**	**71%**	**3.36**	**48**	**21**	**31**	**3.9**	**9.6**	**2.5**	**11%**	**0.8**	**7.6**	**94**	**$12**

Reasons he won't close in 2009:
- TJS in '04; recurring arm problems; 199 DL days since '05
- 2008: 68% Sv%, 60% REff
- History of poor Ctl
- Collapsing GB%

DN: 0 Sv, 4.50+ ERA

Rodriguez,Francisco

		Yr	W	L	Sv	IP	K	ERA	WHIP	OBA	vL	vR	BF/G	H%	S%	xERA	G	L	F	Ctl	Dom	Cmd	hr/f	hr/9	RAR	BPV	R$
RH	Reliever	04 ANA	4	1	12	84	123	1.82	1.00	177	213	127	4.8	30%	82%	2.52	44	19	37	3.5	13.2	**3.7**	3%	0.2	27.0	163	$20
Age	27	05 ANA	2	5	45	67	91	2.68	1.15	192	213	153	4.1	28%	81%	2.92	46	17	38	4.3	12.2	**2.8**	13%	0.9	14.0	128	$25
Type	Pwr	06 LAA	2	3	47	73	98	1.73	1.10	202	215	179	4.2	30%	89%	3.07	39	14	47	3.5	12.1	**3.5**	8%	0.7	25.5	141	$28
Health	A	07 LAA	5	2	40	67	90	2.81	1.25	209	187	217	4.4	32%	78%	3.22	43	17	40	4.5	12.0	**2.6**	5%	0.4	14.1	115	$24
PT/Exp	A	08 LAA	2	3	62	68	77	2.24	1.29	219	227	205	3.8	30%	85%	3.66	42	20	38	4.5	10.1	**2.3**	6%	0.5	17.8	82	$29
Consist	A	1st Half	0	1	32	35	33	2.04	1.19	174			3.8	23%	83%	4.23	42	20	38	5.4	8.4	**1.6**	3%	0.3	10.0	26	$15
LIMA Plan	C	2nd Half	2	2	30	33	44	2.45	1.39	262			3.7	38%	86%	3.11	43	19	37	3.5	12.0	**3.4**	10%	0.8	7.7	142	$14
+/- Score	-29	09 Proj	**3**	**3**	**40**	**73**	**82**	**2.98**	**1.34**	**230**			**4.1**	**31%**	**81%**	**3.72**	**42**	**18**	**40**	**4.5**	**10.2**	**2.3**	**10%**	**0.9**	**6.3**	**83**	**$22**

Set the MLB saves record with the lowest BPV (and only sub-100 level) of his career. Now he'll have to hope for similar opportunities with a vulnerable skill set. xERA trend is scary.
DN: 50% return on investment

Rodriguez,Wandy

		Yr	W	L	Sv	IP	K	ERA	WHIP	OBA	vL	vR	BF/G	H%	S%	xERA	G	L	F	Ctl	Dom	Cmd	hr/f	hr/9	RAR	BPV	R$
LH	Starter	04 aa	11	6	0	142	86	5.98	1.85	334			26.1	37%	69%	6.77				3.9	5.5	**1.4**		1.2	-28.7	14	($2)
Age	30	05 HOU *	14	12	0	177	118	5.42	1.50	279	275	273	23.1	30%	67%	4.46	46	23	31	3.7	6.0	**1.6**	16%	1.4	-25.6	31	$6
Type	Pwr	06 HOU *	11	12	0	161	110	5.97	1.65	294	262	298	21.0	33%	65%	4.82	45	22	33	4.3	6.1	**1.4**	11%	1.1	-29.6	17	$1
Health	B	07 HOU	9	13	0	183	158	4.58	1.32	258	252	254	25.0	31%	68%	4.04	41	19	40	3.1	7.8	**2.5**	10%	1.1	-3.5	77	$13
PT/Exp	B	08 HOU	9	7	0	137	131	3.54	1.31	260	282	248	23.2	32%	76%	3.72	40	23	36	2.9	8.6	**3.0**	10%	0.9	12.4	95	$13
Consist	B	1st Half	3	3	0	59	51	2.58	1.15	237			24.1	29%	81%	3.76	39	22	39	2.4	7.7	**3.2**	8%	0.8	12.4	91	$7
LIMA Plan	B	2nd Half	6	4	0	78	80	4.27	1.44	276			22.7	35%	73%	3.67	42	24	34	3.2	9.2	**2.9**	12%	1.0	0.0	98	$6
+/- Score	21	09 Proj	**13**	**9**	**0**	**180**	**165**	**3.91**	**1.33**	**260**			**23.1**	**32%**	**73%**	**3.81**	**42**	**22**	**36**	**3.0**	**8.3**	**2.8**	**10%**	**1.0**	**11.7**	**88**	**$17**

In past, S% issues kept him from reaching potential; this year it was injuries. Excellent Dom and BPV growth; troubling PQS DIS spike (13% to 32%). With just the good parts happening...
UP: 15 Wins, 3.25 ERA, 175 K

Rogers,Kenny

		Yr	W	L	Sv	IP	K	ERA	WHIP	OBA	vL	vR	BF/G	H%	S%	xERA	G	L	F	Ctl	Dom	Cmd	hr/f	hr/9	RAR	BPV	R$
LH	Starter	04 TEX	18	9	0	213	127	5.07	1.52	300	292	292	27.0	33%	69%	4.67	43	21	35	2.8	5.4	**1.9**	10%	1.1	-16.7	42	$10
Age	44	05 TEX	14	8	0	195	87	3.46	1.32	271	201	291	27.6	29%	75%	4.62	47	20	33	2.4	4.0	**1.6**	7%	0.7	21.9	31	$16
Type	Con	06 DET	17	8	0	204	99	3.84	1.26	253	200	268	25.1	27%	73%	4.38	50	18	32	2.7	4.4	**1.6**	11%	1.0	18.1	33	$21
Health	F	07 DET	3	4	0	63	36	4.43	1.43	268	197	289	24.9	29%	72%	4.49	48	23	29	3.6	5.1	**1.4**	13%	1.1	0.6	22	$3
PT/Exp	A	08 DET	9	13	0	174	82	5.70	1.63	302	293	315	26.3	32%	66%	5.42	41	21	38	3.7	4.2	**1.2**	9%	1.1	-29.0	-3	($0)
Consist	B	1st Half	6	5	0	100	40	4.59	1.55	288			26.3	30%	72%	5.51	44	19	38	3.7	3.6	**1.0**	7%	0.9	-3.0	-13	$3
LIMA Plan	F	2nd Half	3	8	0	74	42	7.20	1.74	320			26.4	34%	59%	5.30	38	24	37	3.7	5.1	**1.4**	12%	1.5	-26.0	10	($4)
+/- Score	-47	09 Proj	**8**	**10**	**0**	**144**	**70**	**5.19**	**1.57**	**290**			**25.9**	**31%**	**69%**	**5.16**	**44**	**22**	**34**	**3.8**	**4.4**	**1.2**	**10%**	**1.1**	**-13.1**	**-0**	**$3**

H% and S% woes made things look worse than they were, but they were still plenty bad. Age is a factor, but it's the degrading Ctl that shows he's reaching the end of the road. That, and all the runs he's giving up.

Romero,J.C.

		Yr	W	L	Sv	IP	K	ERA	WHIP	OBA	vL	vR	BF/G	H%	S%	xERA	G	L	F	Ctl	Dom	Cmd	hr/f	hr/9	RAR	BPV	R$
LH	Reliever	04 MIN	7	4	1	74	69	3.52	1.34	226	261	199	4.3	29%	74%	3.70	56	15	29	4.6	8.4	**1.8**	7%	0.5	8.3	60	$9
Age	32	05 MIN	4	3	0	57	48	3.47	1.56	237	198	268	3.8	28%	81%	4.51	55	14	31	6.2	7.6	**1.2**	12%	0.9	6.3	3	$4
Type	Pwr xGB	06 LAA	1	2	0	48	31	6.74	1.77	296	202	382	3.5	34%	60%	4.82	57	16	27	5.2	5.8	**1.1**	7%	0.6	-12.9	-2	($2)
Health	A	07 2TM	2	2	1	56	42	1.92	1.40	197	208	198	3.3	24%	88%	4.53	60	11	29	6.4	6.7	**1.1**	7%	0.5	17.7	-14	$6
PT/Exp	D	08 PHI	4	4	1	59	52	2.75	1.34	198	102	282	3.1	24%	82%	3.70	62	16	22	5.8	7.9	**1.4**	14%	0.8	11.1	26	$7
Consist	B	1st Half	4	1	0	31	29	1.73	1.41	207			3.6	25%	93%	3.81	62	12	26	6.0	8.3	**1.4**	14%	0.9	9.8	27	$5
LIMA Plan	D+	2nd Half	0	3	1	28	23	3.90	1.26	187			2.7	22%	70%	3.55	61	21	18	5.5	7.5	**1.4**	15%	0.6	1.3	24	$2
+/- Score	-67	09 Proj	**2**	**3**	**0**	**48**	**38**	**3.98**	**1.54**	**239**			**3.3**	**28%**	**75%**	**4.23**	**60**	**15**	**25**	**5.9**	**7.2**	**1.2**	**12%**	**0.8**	**0.6**	**9**	**$2**

PRO: Extreme GB% suggests low H% and LD% aren't just luck
CON: Terrible Ctl; xERAs over 4.00, mostly
Verdict: With these BPIs, there is always a risk of a 2006-like debacle. Why take the chance?

Romo,Sergio

		Yr	W	L	Sv	IP	K	ERA	WHIP	OBA	vL	vR	BF/G	H%	S%	xERA	G	L	F	Ctl	Dom	Cmd	hr/f	hr/9	RAR	BPV	R$
RH	Reliever	04	0	0	0	0	0	0.00	0.00																		
Age	26	05	0	0	0	0	0	0.00	0.00																		
Type	Pwr xFB	06	0	0	0	0	0	0.00	0.00																		
Health	A	07	0	0	0	0	0	0.00	0.00																		
PT/Exp	F	08 SF *	4	4	11	67	61	3.31	0.99	203	83	176	4.7	26%	67%	3.95	33	14	53	2.4	8.2	**3.4**	4%	0.6	7.9	92	$13
Consist	F	1st Half	1	3	11	29	27	5.17	1.30	261			4.7	33%	57%	4.08	50	0	50	2.7	8.2	**3.0**	3%	0.3	-3.2	102	$5
LIMA Plan	B+	2nd Half	3	1	0	38	34	1.89	0.75	153			4.7	18%	80%	3.61	32	15	53	2.2	8.1	**3.7**	6%	0.7	11.1	98	$8
+/- Score	-17	09 Proj	**4**	**4**	**0**	**64**	**58**	**3.97**	**1.21**	**251**			**5.0**	**30%**	**70%**	**4.18**	**32**	**15**	**53**	**2.4**	**8.2**	**3.4**	**7%**	**1.0**	**1.2**	**93**	**$6**

3-1, 2.12 ERA in 34 IP at SF Breezed through Single-A with 8.3+ Dom from '05-'07. Barely pitched above that level, though; so expect growing pains. Prone to FB (47% in minors) which will hurt when hr/f normalizes.

Rosales,Leo

		Yr	W	L	Sv	IP	K	ERA	WHIP	OBA	vL	vR	BF/G	H%	S%	xERA	G	L	F	Ctl	Dom	Cmd	hr/f	hr/9	RAR	BPV	R$
RH	Reliever	04	0	0	0	0	0	0.00	0.00																		
Age	27	05	0	0	0	0	0	0.00	0.00																		
Type		06 aa	5	6	0	61	43	4.58	1.47	285			5.1	32%	71%	4.77				3.1	6.4	**2.0**		1.0	-0.4	50	$4
Health	A	07 aaa	1	1	14	24	21	4.70	1.71	305			4.7	36%	76%	5.98				4.3	7.8	**1.8**		1.3	-0.7	40	$5
PT/Exp	F	08 ARI *	3	3	9	66	39	5.68	1.80	319	286	263	5.6	35%	70%	5.40	45	18	37	4.3	5.3	**1.2**	11%	1.3	-11.5	1	$1
Consist	B	1st Half	2	1	9	40	23	5.95	1.87	336			6.2	36%	72%	5.05	50	19	31	4.0	5.2	**1.3**	16%	1.6	-8.2	13	$1
LIMA Plan	C	2nd Half	1	2	0	26	16	5.27	1.70	292			4.9	33%	69%	5.48	44	18	38	4.9	5.4	**1.1**	6%	0.7	-3.3	-12	($0)
+/- Score	2	09 Proj	**2**	**2**	**0**	**29**	**18**	**4.97**	**1.62**	**294**			**5.3**	**32%**	**72%**	**5.05**	**45**	**18**	**38**	**4.0**	**5.6**	**1.4**	**11%**	**1.2**	**-2.5**	**14**	**$1**

1-1, 4.20 ERA in 30 IP at ARI Was effective closer in minors, but doesn't have the goods to do so in Majors (check that BPV). Rising OBA, falling Cmd show he's overmatched. Running out of time to make an impact.

JOSHUA RANDALL

Rowland-Smith,Ryan

			W	L	Sv	IP	K	ERA	WHIP	OBA	vL	vR	BF/G	H%	S%	xERA	G	L	F	Ctl	Dom	Cmd	hr/f	hr/9	RAR	BPV	R$
LH Reliever		04	0	0	0	0	0	0.00	0.00																		
Age	26	05 aa	6	7	0	122	93	5.16	1.67	305			17.0	36%	68%	5.23				3.9	6.9	**1.8**		0.6	-12.9	54	$1
Type	Pwr FB	06 aa	1	3	4	41	42	3.84	1.63	286			8.1	37%	76%	4.65				4.5	9.1	**2.0**		0.5	3.5	82	$3
Health	A	07 SEA *	4	4	1	80	85	4.29	1.49	262			6.9	34%	72%	4.35	34	21	46	4.4	9.5	**2.2**	6%	0.7	2.2	64	$6
PT/Exp	D	08 SEA *	7	3	2	136	88	3.50	1.36	251	311	224	11.7	28%	78%	4.90	39	19	42	3.8	5.8	**1.5**	8%	1.0	14.3	20	$12
Consist	A	1st Half	2	1	2	41	33	2.65	1.15	207			5.2	25%	80%	4.63	29	20	51	3.8	7.3	**1.9**	5%	0.7	8.5	37	$6
LIMA Plan	D+	2nd Half	5	2	0	96	55	3.86	1.45	269			23.2	29%	77%	4.98	43	19	39	3.8	5.2	**1.4**	10%	1.1	5.8	12	$6
+/- Score	-27	**09 Proj**	**11**	**10**	**0**	**189**	**141**	**4.34**	**1.43**	**262**			**23.4**	**30%**	**72%**	**4.82**	**36**	**19**	**44**	**3.8**	**6.7**	**1.8**	**8%**	**1.0**	**-9.3**	**32**	**$13**

5-3, 3.42 ERA in 118 IP at SEA
CON: Only kept ERA < 4.00 with assist from H% & S%; poor Ctl.
PRO: Great Dom in '06-'07
CON: But as a reliever.
PRO: Impressed SEA as starter
CON: ERA will rise in '09.

Rupe,Josh

			W	L	Sv	IP	K	ERA	WHIP	OBA	vL	vR	BF/G	H%	S%	xERA	G	L	F	Ctl	Dom	Cmd	hr/f	hr/9	RAR	BPV	R$
RH Reliever		04	0	0	0	0	0	0.00	0.00																		
Age	26	05 a/a	10	10	0	158	101	6.20	1.68	314			26.0	34%	65%	6.07				3.5	5.7	**1.6**		1.3	-37.0	22	($1)
Type	GB	06 TEX *	1	2	2	48	20	4.69	1.58	289			6.4	30%	72%	4.33	66	13	21	3.9	3.8	**1.0**	14%	0.9	-0.8	6	$1
Health	A	07 aaa	2	2	0	37	15	6.76	1.80	329			25.0	34%	64%	6.71				3.8	3.7	**1.0**		1.4	-10.5	-8	($2)
PT/Exp	D	08 TEX	3	1	0	89	53	5.14	1.56	270	308	262	8.7	30%	67%	4.97	49	18	33	4.6	5.3	**1.2**	8%	0.8	-8.7	-2	$1
Consist	F	1st Half	3	1	0	45	22	3.42	1.32	250			9.5	28%	72%	4.83	45	21	34	3.4	4.4	**1.3**	2%	0.2	5.1	11	$4
LIMA Plan	C	2nd Half	0	0	0	45	31	6.86	1.79	289			8.1	32%	63%	5.10	53	15	32	5.9	6.3	**1.1**	15%	1.4	-13.8	-15	($3)
+/- Score	-22	**09 Proj**	**3**	**2**	**0**	**73**	**44**	**4.97**	**1.59**	**281**			**8.8**	**31%**	**70%**	**4.61**	**55**	**16**	**29**	**4.3**	**5.5**	**1.3**	**11%**	**1.0**	**-1.7**	**14**	**$1**

Ctl headed in the wrong direction, but at least he kept it under his Dom for a change. Awful for pitches 1-15 (career .971 OPS against); decent for pitches 15+ (.674). Maybe he needs more warm-up time.

Rusch,Glendon

			W	L	Sv	IP	K	ERA	WHIP	OBA	vL	vR	BF/G	H%	S%	xERA	G	L	F	Ctl	Dom	Cmd	hr/f	hr/9	RAR	BPV	R$
LH Reliever		04 CHC *	8	3	2	148	103	3.34	1.23	263	225	265	17.1	31%	74%	4.12	40	23	37	2.1	6.3	**3.0**	6%	0.6	16.8	75	$14
Age	34	05 CHC	9	8	0	145	111	4.53	1.57	300	333	294	14.2	35%	72%	4.51	38	28	35	3.3	6.9	**2.1**	8%	0.9	-5.1	51	$6
Type		06 CHC	3	8	0	66	59	7.49	1.80	316	348	310	12.5	34%	65%	4.85	35	22	43	4.5	8.0	**1.8**	23%	2.9	-24.5	36	($3)
Health	F	07	0	0	0	0	0	0.00	0.00																		
PT/Exp	D	08 2NL *	6	7	0	125	73	5.42	1.57	308	257	296	13.3	34%	67%	4.83	41	23	36	2.8	5.3	**1.9**	9%	1.1	-17.6	38	$1
Consist	A	1st Half	2	5	0	65	34	6.35	1.83	336			15.5	36%	66%	5.57	42	19	39	3.6	4.7	**1.3**	8%	1.1	-16.7	7	($4)
LIMA Plan	C+	2nd Half	4	2	0	59	39	4.39	1.28	273			11.3	30%	68%	4.12	41	24	35	2.0	5.9	**3.0**	10%	1.1	-0.9	72	$4
+/- Score	-1	**09 Proj**	**2**	**3**	**0**	**44**	**26**	**4.97**	**1.52**	**294**			**12.9**	**32%**	**70%**	**4.88**	**39**	**24**	**38**	**3.1**	**5.4**	**1.7**	**11%**	**1.2**	**-2.9**	**30**	**$1**

5-5, 5.16 ERA in 83 IP at COL and SD. Return from blood clot in lung is nice story, but consistent .300+ OBA and high H% tell you all you need to know. Days of him being sleeper roster filler are long gone. Avoid.

Ryan,B.J.

			W	L	Sv	IP	K	ERA	WHIP	OBA	vL	vR	BF/G	H%	S%	xERA	G	L	F	Ctl	Dom	Cmd	hr/f	hr/9	RAR	BPV	R$
LH Reliever		04 BAL	4	6	3	87	122	2.28	1.14	207	94	252	4.6	33%	81%	2.81	41	22	38	3.6	12.6	**3.5**	6%	0.4	23.1	148	$15
Age	33	05 BAL	1	4	36	70	100	2.44	1.14	215	211	206	4.1	34%	80%	2.58	45	21	34	3.3	12.8	**3.8**	8%	0.5	16.7	164	$22
Type	Pwr FB	06 TOR	2	2	38	72	86	1.37	0.86	171	120	182	4.2	25%	86%	2.93	37	20	43	2.5	10.7	**4.3**	4%	0.4	28.3	140	$27
Health	F	07 TOR	0	2	3	4	3	12.56	2.56	366	333	333	4.7	40%	50%	7.68	24	35	41	8.4	6.3	**0.8**	15%	2.1	-4.3	-111	($0)
PT/Exp	B	08 TOR	2	4	32	58	58	2.95	1.28	220	230	211	4.1	28%	79%	4.07	39	19	42	4.3	9.0	**2.1**	6%	0.6	10.0	61	$17
Consist	F	1st Half	1	3	16	28	31	2.25	1.21	202			4.0	27%	84%	3.82	37	20	43	4.5	10.0	**2.2**	7%	0.6	7.2	73	$9
LIMA Plan	B	2nd Half	1	1	16	30	27	3.60	1.33	235			4.1	29%	74%	4.30	40	19	41	4.2	8.1	**1.9**	6%	0.6	2.8	50	$8
+/- Score	-39	**09 Proj**	**2**	**3**	**35**	**58**	**63**	**3.10**	**1.17**	**220**			**4.2**	**29%**	**76%**	**3.52**	**39**	**20**	**41**	**3.4**	**9.8**	**2.9**	**8%**	**0.8**	**6.4**	**101**	**$19**

Pitchers usually take two years to recover completely from TJS, though a little less for RPs. As good as this return is, xERA and BPV concur that it was not as good as it appeared. Bid with just a little bit of caution.

Sabathia,C.C.

			W	L	Sv	IP	K	ERA	WHIP	OBA	vL	vR	BF/G	H%	S%	xERA	G	L	F	Ctl	Dom	Cmd	hr/f	hr/9	RAR	BPV	R$
LH Starter		04 CLE	11	10	0	188	139	4.12	1.32	249	265	248	26.6	29%	71%	4.50	39	20	41	3.4	6.7	**1.9**	9%	1.0	7.3	44	$15
Age	28	05 CLE	15	10	0	196	161	4.04	1.26	251	248	248	26.4	30%	70%	3.64	49	20	31	2.8	7.4	**2.6**	11%	0.9	8.1	84	$20
Type	Pwr	06 CLE	12	11	0	192	172	3.23	1.18	251	271	242	28.1	31%	75%	3.48	45	19	36	2.1	8.1	**3.9**	9%	0.8	31.5	112	$23
Health	A	07 CLE	19	7	0	241	209	3.21	1.14	259	203	275	28.8	32%	74%	3.42	45	18	37	1.4	7.8	**5.6**	8%	0.7	38.5	126	$33
PT/Exp	A	08 2TM	17	10	0	253	251	2.70	1.11	238	205	247	29.2	31%	78%	3.10	47	22	32	2.1	8.9	**4.3**	9%	0.7	50.0	129	$35
Consist	A	1st Half	6	8	0	114	118	3.78	1.24	254			28.0	33%	72%	3.38	43	21	36	2.5	9.3	**3.7**	10%	0.9	7.4	120	$10
LIMA Plan	C	2nd Half	11	2	0	139	133	1.82	1.01	224			30.3	29%	85%	2.87	50	22	28	1.8	8.6	**4.9**	8%	0.5	42.6	136	$25
+/- Score	16	**09 Proj**	**16**	**9**	**0**	**218**	**201**	**3.02**	**1.14**	**246**			**28.5**	**30%**	**77%**	**3.31**	**46**	**20**	**34**	**2.0**	**8.3**	**4.2**	**10%**	**0.8**	**28.8**	**120**	**$29**

Was 0-3 with a 13.50 ERA after four starts and had owners jumping out of windows. Went 17-7, 1.88 ERA over remaining 235 IP. Mega-innings and long outings advise caution but you gotta like that BPV trend.

Sadler,Billy

			W	L	Sv	IP	K	ERA	WHIP	OBA	vL	vR	BF/G	H%	S%	xERA	G	L	F	Ctl	Dom	Cmd	hr/f	hr/9	RAR	BPV	R$
RH Reliever		04 aa	0	3	0	30	19	4.93	1.47	233			7.8	26%	68%	4.07				5.5	5.8	**1.0**		0.9	-2.2	37	$0
Age	27	05 aa	6	5	5	82	63	4.27	1.32	247			7.6	30%	67%	3.39				3.6	6.9	**1.9**		0.5	0.4	73	$8
Type	Pwr FB	06 a/a	6	3	21	55	65	3.26	1.22	182			4.5	26%	73%	2.18				5.3	10.5	**2.0**		0.3	8.6	113	$16
Health	A	07 a/a	3	2	7	54	57	6.68	1.78	249			5.2	31%	63%	5.22				7.6	9.5	**1.2**		1.1	-14.8	54	$2
PT/Exp	D	08 SF *	1	1	1	77	71	3.03	1.46	217	193	228	6.2	27%	81%	5.11	32	21	47	6.1	8.3	**1.4**	6%	0.7	11.8	-6	$5
Consist	D	1st Half	0	1	0	40	38	3.77	1.52	199			5.9	24%	78%	5.75	26	18	56	7.4	8.5	**1.2**	7%	0.9	2.5	-41	$1
LIMA Plan	C	2nd Half	1	0	1	38	33	2.25	1.40	235			6.5	30%	85%	4.42	38	25	36	4.7	8.0	**1.7**	5%	0.5	9.4	32	$4
+/- Score	-68	**09 Proj**	**1**	**3**	**0**	**54**	**49**	**4.71**	**1.53**	**245**			**5.8**	**30%**	**70%**	**4.98**	**33**	**22**	**45**	**5.6**	**8.2**	**1.5**	**7%**	**0.8**	**-4.2**	**10**	**$1**

0-1, 4.06 ERA in 44 IP at SF. Waste of a great Dom due to horrible Ctl. Don't be misled by '08 ERA when past two years' xERA shows downside. 21 Sv season in minors may look enticing; notice it wasn't repeated.

Saito,Takashi

			W	L	Sv	IP	K	ERA	WHIP	OBA	vL	vR	BF/G	H%	S%	xERA	G	L	F	Ctl	Dom	Cmd	hr/f	hr/9	RAR	BPV	R$
RH Reliever		04 JPN	2	5	0	44	39	9.65	1.93	356			13.3	36%	58%	10.02				3.3	8.0	**2.4**		4.1	-28.8	-40	($5)
Age	39	05 JPN	3	4	0	106	98	4.75	1.46	285			22.1	33%	73%	5.41				3.1	8.3	**2.7**		1.7	-5.8	54	$4
Type	Pwr	06 LA	6	2	24	78	107	2.07	0.91	179	229	129	4.2	28%	78%	2.79	36	16	49	2.7	12.3	**4.7**	4%	0.3	23.2	164	$24
Health	B	07 LA	2	1	39	64	78	1.40	0.72	154	186	114	3.7	21%	88%	2.49	46	13	41	1.8	10.9	**6.0**	9%	0.7	24.0	171	$27
PT/Exp	B	08 LA	4	4	18	47	60	2.49	1.19	232	244	209	4.3	35%	78%	2.93	47	17	36	3.1	11.5	**3.8**	2%	0.2	10.3	149	$14
Consist	A	1st Half	3	3	12	34	47	2.40	1.22	240			4.4	38%	80%	2.76	43	20	37	2.9	12.6	**4.3**	3%	0.3	7.8	168	$10
LIMA Plan	B+	2nd Half	1	1	6	13	13	2.71	1.13	210			4.1	29%	73%	3.41	54	11	35	3.4	8.8	**2.6**	0%	0.0	2.6	99	$4
+/- Score	-10	**09 Proj**	**3**	**3**	**28**	**54**	**56**	**3.53**	**1.25**	**238**			**5.3**	**31%**	**74%**	**3.54**	**47**	**14**	**39**	**3.4**	**9.4**	**2.8**	**9%**	**0.8**	**5.3**	**104**	**$15**

Lost 2 months to elbow sprain; arm seemed sound upon return. Excellent BPIs bode well for future success with exception of one data point... his age. You don't often see triple-digit BPVs and pitchers pushing 40.

Samardzija,Jeff

			W	L	Sv	IP	K	ERA	WHIP	OBA	vL	vR	BF/G	H%	S%	xERA	G	L	F	Ctl	Dom	Cmd	hr/f	hr/9	RAR	BPV	R$
RH Reliever		04	0	0	0	0	0	0.00	0.00																		
Age	24	05	0	0	0	0	0	0.00	0.00																		
Type		06	0	0	0	0	0	0.00	0.00																		
Health	A	07 aa	3	3	0	34	17	4.22	1.38	283			24.4	26%	84%	6.14				2.4	4.5	**1.9**		2.6	1.0	-14	$3
PT/Exp	D	08 CHC *	8	6	1	141	95	4.47	1.53	261	167	276	13.1	30%	72%	4.81	46	22	32	4.8	6.1	**1.3**	9%	0.8	-3.4	4	$6
Consist	C	1st Half	4	6	0	88	44	5.38	1.64	272			22.3	29%	67%					5.3	4.5	**0.8**		0.8	-12.0	20	($1)
LIMA Plan	C+	2nd Half	4	0	1	53	51	2.95	1.34	243			7.5	31%	80%	3.74	46	22	32	4.0	8.7	**2.2**	9%	0.7	8.6	74	$6
+/- Score	-29	**09 Proj**	**3**	**2**	**3**	**44**	**29**	**4.34**	**1.45**	**268**			**13.6**	**30%**	**71%**	**4.49**	**46**	**22**	**32**	**3.7**	**6.0**	**1.6**	**9%**	**0.8**	**-0.8**	**31**	**$3**

1-0, 2.28 ERA in 27 IP at CHC. Lightbulb went on in Triple-A, where he K'd 40 in 38 IP; sustained Dom in Majors. Rapid ascent suggests caution - may need more seasoning. A 2010 ETA is the safer bet.

Sampson,Chris

			W	L	Sv	IP	K	ERA	WHIP	OBA	vL	vR	BF/G	H%	S%	xERA	G	L	F	Ctl	Dom	Cmd	hr/f	hr/9	RAR	BPV	R$
RH Reliever		04	0	0	0	0	0	0.00	0.00																		
Age	30	05 aa	4	12	4	150	63	5.28	1.61	339			21.2	36%	68%	6.04				1.4	3.8	**2.6**		1.0	-18.0	35	($0)
Type	Con GB	06 aaa	12	3	4	125	54	3.17	1.19	274			19.0	29%	78%	3.94				1.1	3.9	**3.6**		1.0	20.9	69	$17
Health	B	07 HOU	7	8	0	122	51	4.59	1.38	287	291	292	21.8	29%	72%	4.73	47	17	36	2.2	3.8	**1.7**	13%	1.5	-2.4	33	$6
PT/Exp	C	08 HOU	6	4	0	117	61	4.22	1.20	263	273	261	9.0	29%	65%	3.86	56	15	29	1.8	4.7	**2.7**	7%	0.6	0.7	71	$8
Consist	B	1st Half	3	3	0	66	32	5.16	1.40	297			13.0	32%	63%	4.16	55	18	28	1.9	4.3	**2.3**	8%	0.7	-7.3	60	$2
LIMA Plan	C+	2nd Half	3	1	0	51	29	3.00	0.94	213			6.2	24%	69%	3.47	58	12	30	1.6	5.1	**3.2**	7%	0.5	8.0	86	$7
+/- Score	1	**09 Proj**	**3**	**2**	**0**	**58**	**28**	**4.34**	**1.31**	**278**			**11.7**	**30%**	**69%**	**4.26**	**53**	**15**	**32**	**2.0**	**4.3**	**2.2**	**9%**	**0.9**	**0.6**	**55**	**$3**

Starter or reliever? You decide:

	IP	Ctl	Dom	OBA
as SP	185	2.0	3.8	.283
as RP	88	1.7	5.0	.237

Either way, pinpoint Ctl and high GB% help, but also leave him at mercy of H% and defense.

JOSHUA RANDALL

Sanchez,Anibal		W	L	Sv	IP	K	ERA	WHIP	OBA	vL	vR	BF/G	H%	S%	xERA	G	L	F	Ctl	Dom	Cmd	hr/f	hr/9	RAR	BPV	R$
RH Starter	04	0	0	0	0	0	0.00	0.00																		
Age 25	05 aa	3	5	0	57	54	4.41	1.38	281			22.3	35%	70%	4.46				2.5	8.5	3.4		0.9	-0.8	92	$4
Type Pwr	06 FLA	* 13	9	0	199	155	3.48	1.33	252	229	202	25.7	30%	76%	4.36	45	14	41	3.5	7.0	2.0	7%	0.8	24.8	55	$19
Health F	07 FLA	2	1	0	30	14	4.80	2.07	337	329	357	24.9	36%	78%	6.56	45	15	40	5.7	4.2	0.7	7%	0.9	-1.4	-55	($1)
PT/Exp D	08 FLA	2	5	0	52	50	5.57	1.57	270	340	188	23.2	33%	66%	4.19	40	27	32	4.7	8.7	1.9	14%	1.2	-8.3	48	$1
Consist F	1st Half	0	0	0	0	0	0.00	0.00																		
LIMA Plan B	2nd Half	2	5	0	52	50	5.57	1.57	270			23.2	33%	66%	4.19	40	27	32	4.7	8.7	1.9	14%	1.2	-8.3	48	$1
+/- Score 34	09 Proj	7	8	0	131	114	4.28	1.52	273			24.1	33%	74%	4.36	43	20	37	4.1	7.9	1.9	10%	1.0	-0.3	51	$7

Return from June '07 TJS was predictably bumpy. Amid the bad luck-fueled debacle were a few positive signs: regained Dom, and he closed out Sept with back-to-back PQS DOMs. A good speculative pick.

Sanchez,Duaner		W	L	Sv	IP	K	ERA	WHIP	OBA	vL	vR	BF/G	H%	S%	xERA	G	L	F	Ctl	Dom	Cmd	hr/f	hr/9	RAR	BPV	R$
RH Reliever	04 LA	3	1	0	80	44	3.38	1.35	264	276	260	5.1	28%	79%	4.40	52	16	33	3.0	5.0	1.6	11%	1.0	8.8	37	$5
Age 29	05 LA	4	7	8	82	71	3.73	1.35	245	310	182	4.4	29%	75%	4.09	44	21	35	4.0	7.8	2.0	10%	0.9	5.2	56	$9
Type Pwr	06 NYM	5	1	0	55	44	2.61	1.22	217	276	179	4.7	26%	80%	3.96	52	13	34	3.9	7.2	1.8	6%	0.5	12.7	54	$8
Health F	07 NYM	0	0	0	0	0	0.00	0.00																		
PT/Exp D	08 NYM	5	1	0	58	44	4.32	1.32	247	200	268	3.7	29%	69%	4.09	44	25	31	3.6	6.8	1.9	11%	0.9	-0.4	48	$5
Consist A	1st Half	3	0	0	35	27	3.89	1.12	210			4.3	25%	67%	3.80	48	20	33	3.4	7.0	2.1	9%	0.8	1.6	61	$4
LIMA Plan C+	2nd Half	2	1	0	24	17	4.96	1.61	296			3.2	34%	71%	4.53	39	33	29	3.8	6.5	1.7	13%	1.1	-2.0	30	$1
+/- Score -4	09 Proj	3	3	0	58	44	4.03	1.40	258			4.1	30%	73%	4.21	46	22	32	3.7	6.8	1.8	11%	0.9	0.9	46	$4

Declining Dom a concern, especially in light of his return from July '06 shoulder surgery. He's been mentioned as a closer candidate, but low BPV and .270 OBA with runners on makes that a dubious proposition.

Sanchez,Jonathan		W	L	Sv	IP	K	ERA	WHIP	OBA	vL	vR	BF/G	H%	S%	xERA	G	L	F	Ctl	Dom	Cmd	hr/f	hr/9	RAR	BPV	R$
LH Starter	04	0	0	0	0	0	0.00	0.00																		
Age 26	05	0	0	0	0	0	0.00	0.00																		
Type Pwr	06 SF	* 7	4	2	95	96	3.79	1.22	210	256	248	8.6	28%	67%	4.10	36	20	45	4.3	9.1	2.1	3%	0.3	8.2	62	$12
Health B	07 SF	* 1	5	0	72	84	5.03	1.54	269	197	321	8.3	36%	69%	3.90	39	22	39	4.5	10.5	2.3	11%	1.0	-5.3	83	$2
PT/Exp C	08 SF	9	12	0	158	157	5.01	1.45	257	235	263	23.8	33%	66%	4.08	41	21	37	4.3	8.9	2.1	8%	0.8	-14.5	65	$8
Consist A	1st Half	8	4	0	102	102	3.79	1.34	238			25.6	31%	73%	4.06	39	19	41	4.1	9.0	2.2	7%	0.7	6.0	67	$10
LIMA Plan B	2nd Half	1	8	0	56	55	7.23	1.64	288			21.3	36%	55%	4.11	44	25	31	4.5	8.8	2.0	11%	1.0	-20.5	60	($2)
+/- Score 30	09 Proj	7	13	0	174	178	4.50	1.44	255			12.0	32%	70%	3.99	41	22	37	4.3	9.2	2.1	10%	0.9	7.5	69	$10

Post-June collapse not all due to high H% and low S%:

PQS	DOM	DIS
1H	53%	18%
2H	33%	50%

Huge IP jump, Aug shoulder strain increase his risk profile.

Santana,Ervin		W	L	Sv	IP	K	ERA	WHIP	OBA	vL	vR	BF/G	H%	S%	xERA	G	L	F	Ctl	Dom	Cmd	hr/f	hr/9	RAR	BPV	R$
RH Starter	04 aa	2	1	0	43	41	3.75	1.44	270			23.5	34%	75%	4.16				3.5	8.5	2.4		0.6	3.2	84	$3
Age 26	05 ANA	* 18	9	0	191	140	4.14	1.34	264	261	271	24.7	30%	72%	4.58	37	19	44	3.0	6.6	2.2	8%	1.0	5.5	53	$18
Type Pwr FB	06 LAA	16	8	0	204	141	4.28	1.23	239	254	229	25.7	27%	67%	4.54	38	17	44	3.1	6.2	2.0	8%	0.9	7.0	45	$21
Health A	07 LAA	* 9	15	0	182	152	5.94	1.60	302	284	292	24.9	35%	65%	4.73	36	19	46	3.4	7.5	2.2	11%	1.5	-32.3	57	$4
PT/Exp A	08 LAA	16	7	0	219	214	3.49	1.12	243	240	234	27.6	30%	72%	3.46	39	20	42	1.9	8.8	4.6	9%	0.9	23.1	123	$29
Consist B	1st Half	9	3	0	108	99	3.32	1.07	224			27.0	27%	72%	3.71	37	18	44	2.3	8.2	3.5	8%	0.8	13.7	101	$16
LIMA Plan C+	2nd Half	7	4	0	111	115	3.66	1.17	261			28.3	33%	72%	3.22	40	21	39	1.5	9.3	6.1	11%	1.1	9.4	145	$14
+/- Score 26	09 Proj	17	6	0	203	191	3.41	1.19	252			25.3	31%	76%	3.69	38	19	43	2.1	8.5	4.0	10%	1.1	18.4	111	$27

To the superb numbers you see at the left, add this: PQS DOM / DIS of 75% / 0%. Showed he can tame FB%, too (rate fell every month except Aug). Some regression to mean is likely; regardless, these are elite skills.

Santana,Johan		W	L	Sv	IP	K	ERA	WHIP	OBA	vL	vR	BF/G	H%	S%	xERA	G	L	F	Ctl	Dom	Cmd	hr/f	hr/9	RAR	BPV	R$
LH Starter	04 MIN	20	6	0	228	265	2.61	0.92	195	192	191	25.8	26%	77%	2.92	41	16	43	2.1	10.5	4.9	10%	0.9	51.4	150	$42
Age 30	05 MIN	16	7	0	231	238	2.88	0.97	216	256	200	27.3	28%	74%	3.21	40	17	43	1.8	9.3	5.3	9%	0.9	42.5	137	$38
Type Pwr	06 MIN	19	6	0	233	245	2.78	1.00	220	254	206	26.9	28%	77%	3.09	41	20	40	1.8	9.5	5.2	10%	0.9	51.2	140	$41
Health A	07 MIN	15	13	0	219	235	3.33	1.07	229	197	234	26.5	28%	76%	3.28	38	18	44	2.1	9.7	4.5	13%	1.4	31.8	132	$33
PT/Exp A	08 NYM	16	7	0	234	206	2.54	1.15	238	247	227	28.0	29%	83%	3.62	41	22	36	2.4	7.9	3.3	10%	0.9	50.1	96	$30
Consist A	1st Half	7	7	0	114	103	3.01	1.22	250			27.7	30%	81%	3.51	45	21	34	2.5	8.2	3.2	13%	1.1	17.7	101	$13
LIMA Plan C	2nd Half	9	0	0	121	103	2.09	1.08	225			28.4	28%	84%	3.71	38	23	39	2.3	7.7	3.3	7%	0.7	32.4	92	$18
+/- Score -12	09 Proj	16	7	0	218	202	3.19	1.14	238			27.6	29%	76%	3.58	40	21	39	2.3	8.4	3.6	10%	1.0	20.5	106	$28

Seventh year in a row he's had PQS DOM > 70%. Chinks in the armor are evident, though, as seen in falling Cmd and xERA trend. The days of R$ near $40 aren't coming back; more than 200 Ks could be next to go.

Sarfate,Dennis		W	L	Sv	IP	K	ERA	WHIP	OBA	vL	vR	BF/G	H%	S%	xERA	G	L	F	Ctl	Dom	Cmd	hr/f	hr/9	RAR	BPV	R$
RH Reliever	04 aa	7	12	0	129	93	5.97	1.95	311			22.4	35%	71%	6.65				6.1	6.5	1.1		1.2	-25.9	17	($4)
Age 28	05 a/a	9	10	0	142	102	4.18	1.44	261			23.8	30%	73%	4.30				4.0	6.5	1.6		0.9	2.1	48	$9
Type Pwr FB	06 aaa	10	7	0	125	103	4.87	1.88	299			17.7	36%	74%	5.70				6.1	7.4	1.2		0.7	-5.4	45	$2
Health A	07 aaa	2	7	4	61	60	6.06	2.06	301			6.8	37%	71%	6.58				7.6	8.8	1.2		1.1	-12.1	41	($2)
PT/Exp D	08 BAL	4	3	0	81	88	4.68	1.54	214	198	234	6.2	28%	71%	4.67	41	17	43	6.9	9.8	1.4	9%	0.9	-3.3	9	$5
Consist C	1st Half	4	1	0	36	39	2.98	1.57	203			4.7	27%	82%	4.84	46	14	40	7.7	9.7	1.3	6%	0.5	6.1	-9	$4
LIMA Plan C	2nd Half	0	2	0	44	49	6.08	1.51	223			8.6	28%	61%	4.53	37	19	44	6.3	9.9	1.6	12%	1.2	-9.5	24	$0
+/- Score -23	09 Proj	3	4	0	59	61	4.88	1.64	242			7.7	30%	72%	4.89	41	17	43	6.7	9.3	1.4	10%	1.1	-3.4	5	$2

Had clavicle surgery Sept '08; expected to be ready for Spring Training. Bad as RP (REff 58%), worse as SP (4 GS, 4 PQS 0s). Throwing in the high 90s does no good when batters don't have to swing at your pitches.

Saunders,Joe		W	L	Sv	IP	K	ERA	WHIP	OBA	vL	vR	BF/G	H%	S%	xERA	G	L	F	Ctl	Dom	Cmd	hr/f	hr/9	RAR	BPV	R$
LH Starter	04 aa	4	3	0	39	20	6.66	1.85	344			23.3	37%	65%	6.94				3.3	4.7	1.4		1.2	-11.2	8	($1)
Age 27	05 a/a	10	7	0	160	88	4.00	1.47	290			26.0	32%	73%	4.55				2.8	5.0	1.7		0.6	6.1	44	$9
Type Con	06 LAA	* 17	7	0	205	132	3.48	1.27	254	220	274	25.3	29%	75%	4.12	48	20	32	2.8	5.8	2.1	8%	0.8	27.2	54	$23
Health A	07 LAA	* 12	12	0	193	131	5.78	1.58	313	274	304	27.2	35%	64%	4.43	45	21	34	2.7	6.1	2.3	10%	1.1	-30.5	61	$5
PT/Exp B	08 LAA	17	7	0	198	103	3.41	1.21	251	260	250	26.4	27%	75%	4.46	47	15	38	2.4	4.7	1.9	9%	1.0	22.9	44	$22
Consist A	1st Half	11	4	0	106	53	3.06	1.15	237			27.0	25%	79%	4.44	47	14	39	2.5	4.5	1.8	10%	1.1	16.9	40	$14
LIMA Plan F	2nd Half	6	3	0	92	50	3.82	1.28	266			25.8	29%	72%	4.49	46	17	37	2.3	4.9	2.1	7%	0.8	6.0	48	$8
+/- Score -25	09 Proj	14	11	0	204	114	4.25	1.37	277			26.5	30%	72%	4.54	46	17	36	2.6	5.0	1.9	10%	1.1	-2.9	45	$14

xERA and BPV weren't fooled by this performance. Solid Ctl is commendable, but where'd the Dom go? With higher GB%, we'd be willing to accept lower K/9; instead, his FB% adds more danger. Could implode.

Scherzer,Max		W	L	Sv	IP	K	ERA	WHIP	OBA	vL	vR	BF/G	H%	S%	xERA	G	L	F	Ctl	Dom	Cmd	hr/f	hr/9	RAR	BPV	R$
RH Reliever	04	0	0	0	0	0	0.00	0.00																		
Age 24	05	0	0	0	0	0	0.00	0.00																		
Type Pwr	06	0	0	0	0	0	0.00	0.00																		
Health A	07 aa	4	4	0	73	65	5.20	1.62	272			23.7	34%	67%	4.55				5.1	8.0	1.6		0.5	-6.6	66	$2
PT/Exp D	08 ARI	* 1	5	0	109	133	3.39	1.24	229	319	167	15.6	32%	74%	3.07	42	28	30	3.6	10.9	3.0	10%	0.7	11.8	118	$10
Consist C	1st Half	0	2	0	56	69	3.29	1.16	221			15.3	32%	72%	2.85	43	29	29	3.3	11.1	3.4	8%	0.5	6.8	132	$5
LIMA Plan B	2nd Half	1	3	0	53	63	3.50	1.32	236			16.0	32%	76%	3.31	40	27	32	4.1	10.8	2.7	12%	0.9	5.0	103	$4
+/- Score 32	09 Proj	8	8	0	149	166	3.82	1.30	234			23.2	31%	72%	3.39	41	28	31	3.9	10.1	2.6	10%	0.7	17.4	94	$14

0-4, 3.05 ERA in 56 IP at ARI Ignore the 4 losses; this was an outstanding debut. Lack of stamina may limit him to relief, but you know to draft skills, not roles. Had only 15% LD% in minors, so that should improve.

Schoeneweis,Scott		W	L	Sv	IP	K	ERA	WHIP	OBA	vL	vR	BF/G	H%	S%	xERA	G	L	F	Ctl	Dom	Cmd	hr/f	hr/9	RAR	BPV	R$
LH Reliever	04 CHW	6	9	0	112	69	5.61	1.59	290	244	303	25.3	31%	67%	4.95	44	19	36	3.9	5.5	1.4	12%	1.4	-16.4	16	$1
Age 35	05 TOR	3	4	1	57	43	3.32	1.39	251	188	306	3.1	31%	75%	3.76	59	17	24	3.9	6.8	1.7	5%	0.3	7.4	52	$5
Type GB	06 2TM	4	2	4	51	29	4.92	1.41	250	236	257	3.1	28%	65%	4.36	58	16	26	4.2	5.1	1.2	9%	0.7	-2.5	13	$4
Health A	07 NYM	0	2	2	59	41	5.03	1.53	271	204	316	3.7	30%	70%	4.41	51	19	30	4.3	6.3	1.5	14%	1.2	-4.4	27	$1
PT/Exp C	08 NYM	2	6	1	57	34	3.33	1.38	256	178	333	3.3	28%	80%	4.42	50	19	31	3.7	5.4	1.5	12%	1.1	6.6	26	$4
Consist A	1st Half	0	2	0	33	13	3.03	1.22	220			3.6	22%	81%	4.68	53	17	30	3.9	3.6	0.9	13%	1.1	5.0	-8	$2
LIMA Plan C+	2nd Half	2	4	1	24	21	3.75	1.58	300			3.1	36%	80%	4.07	45	23	32	3.4	7.9	2.3	12%	1.1	1.5	73	$2
+/- Score -57	09 Proj	2	4	0	44	29	4.14	1.47	268			3.5	30%	73%	4.40	51	19	30	3.9	6.0	1.5	10%	0.8	-0.3	31	$2

Why he shouldn't be on your list:
- Rising xERA trend
- Cmd stuck below 2.0
- GB/FB continuing to inch in wrong directions
- Second half Dom "rebound" was in only 24 IP

JOSHUA RANDALL

Seanez,Rudy

Seanez,Rudy			W	L	Sv	IP	K	ERA	WHIP	OBA	vL	vR	BF/G	H%	S%	xERA	G	L	F	Ctl	Dom	Cmd	hr/f	hr/9	RAR	BPV	R$
RH Reliever	04	2TM *	5	3	3	80	79	2.81	1.17	218	256	202	5.2	28%	79%	3.53	48	16	37	3.5	8.9	2.5	9%	0.8	15.2	91	$12
Age 40	05	SD	7	1	0	60	84	2.70	1.18	224	231	212	4.3	34%	79%	2.87	37	23	39	3.3	12.6	3.8	8%	0.6	11.5	153	$11
Type Pwr	06	2TM	3	3	0	53	54	4.92	1.70	280	266	273	5.0	34%	74%	4.87	31	24	45	5.4	9.2	1.7	12%	1.4	-2.6	27	$2
Health B	07	LA	6	3	1	76	73	3.79	1.38	267	269	264	4.5	32%	77%	4.10	36	20	44	3.2	8.6	2.7	10%	1.2	6.0	83	$8
PT/Exp D	08	PHI	5	4	0	43	30	3.53	1.45	237	247	232	4.5	28%	75%	4.68	47	24	29	5.2	6.2	1.2	5%	0.4	3.9	-3	$4
Consist B	1st Half		3	3	0	26	18	2.45	1.36	208			4.8	26%	80%	4.36	54	22	24	5.6	6.3	1.1	0%	0.0	5.8	-6	$3
LIMA Plan C+	2nd Half		2	1	0	18	12	5.11	1.59	277			4.2	31%	69%	5.04	39	25	36	4.6	6.1	1.3	10%	1.0	-1.8	3	$1
+/- Score -48	09	Proj	3	4	0	44	32	4.34	1.54	260			4.6	30%	74%	4.96	40	23	37	5.0	6.6	1.3	10%	1.0	-3.3	3	$2

Only a favorable H% and S% kept his ERA in check, but a glance at his 2H shows how things can go south. With advancing age and eroding BPIs, his xERA levels could become reality very quickly.

Seay,Bobby

Seay,Bobby			W	L	Sv	IP	K	ERA	WHIP	OBA	vL	vR	BF/G	H%	S%	xERA	G	L	F	Ctl	Dom	Cmd	hr/f	hr/9	RAR	BPV	R$
LH Reliever	04	TAM *	2	1	1	58	47	2.20	1.13	240			4.7	28%	85%	3.24				2.2	7.3	3.3		0.8	16.1	96	$8
Age 30	05	COL *	1	0	0	38	36	4.97	1.82	314			4.7	38%	75%	4.35	47	21	32	4.7	8.5	1.8	13%	1.2	-3.4	51	($1)
Type Pwr FB	06	DET *	1	2	0	39	24	6.23	1.51	281			4.5	31%	59%	4.89	37	28	35	3.7	5.5	1.5	11%	1.2	-8.0	15	$0
Health A	07	DET	3	0	1	46	38	2.33	1.14	225	209	250	3.2	29%	79%	4.16	38	18	44	2.9	7.4	2.5	2%	0.2	12.4	70	$7
PT/Exp D	08	DET	1	2	0	56	58	4.48	1.49	271	303	252	4.1	35%	70%	4.12	38	21	40	4.0	9.3	2.3	6%	0.6	-0.9	75	$3
Consist A	1st Half		1	1	0	24	19	3.42	1.43	264			3.6	32%	76%	4.32	44	21	35	3.8	7.2	1.9	4%	0.4	2.7	50	$2
LIMA Plan B	2nd Half		0	1	0	33	39	5.25	1.53	276			4.7	38%	66%	3.99	33	21	45	4.1	10.8	2.6	8%	0.8	-3.6	93	$1
+/- Score 17	09	Proj	1	1	0	44	39	4.34	1.45	264			4.0	32%	71%	4.38	38	21	41	3.9	8.1	2.1	8%	0.8	0.3	55	$2

While his BPIs show some life, 2007 gave false hope that he was making major gains. xERA was the truer indicator and reflects how similar '07 and '08 really were. Doesn't leave much optimism for 2009, however.

Sheets,Ben

Sheets,Ben			W	L	Sv	IP	K	ERA	WHIP	OBA	vL	vR	BF/G	H%	S%	xERA	G	L	F	Ctl	Dom	Cmd	hr/f	hr/9	RAR	BPV	R$
RH Starter	04	MIL	12	14	0	237	264	2.70	0.98	231	232	220	27.2	30%	78%	2.85	43	17	40	1.2	10.0	8.3	10%	0.9	45.8	169	$35
Age 30	05	MIL	10	9	0	156	141	3.34	1.07	244	234	241	28.3	29%	74%	3.51	37	21	42	1.4	8.1	5.6	10%	1.1	17.4	122	$20
Type FB	06	MIL	6	7	0	106	116	3.82	1.09	260	248	266	25.0	34%	66%	3.01	40	19	40	0.9	9.8	10.5	8%	0.8	8.7	170	$13
Health F	07	MIL	12	5	0	141	106	3.82	1.24	257	200	300	24.5	29%	73%	4.28	37	19	45	2.4	6.8	2.9	9%	1.1	10.5	72	$15
PT/Exp A	08	MIL	13	9	0	198	158	3.09	1.15	245	256	226	26.0	29%	76%	3.90	41	18	41	2.1	7.2	3.4	7%	0.8	29.0	90	$23
Consist B	1st Half		9	2	0	111	91	2.83	1.07	234			27.7	27%	79%	3.60	46	14	40	1.9	7.4	4.0	9%	1.0	19.8	106	$16
LIMA Plan C+	2nd Half		4	7	0	87	67	3.41	1.25	257			24.2	31%	73%	4.29	34	23	42	2.5	6.9	2.8	4%	0.5	9.2	70	$8
+/- Score -8	09	Proj	11	9	0	174	147	3.41	1.17	252			25.4	30%	74%	3.82	38	19	42	2.0	7.6	3.9	9%	1.0	11.1	100	$19

Extra! Sheets Healthy For Almost Entire Season! Reeled off 20 PQS-DOMinating starts, zero PQS-DISasters (in 29 starts) until elbow tear in Sept. IP spike adds to risk. Again.

Shell,Steven

Shell,Steven			W	L	Sv	IP	K	ERA	WHIP	OBA	vL	vR	BF/G	H%	S%	xERA	G	L	F	Ctl	Dom	Cmd	hr/f	hr/9	RAR	BPV	R$
RH Reliever	04		0	0	0	0	0	0.00	0.00																		
Age 26	05	aa	10	8	0	159	106	4.75	1.50	292			26.1	33%	70%	4.90				3.1	6.0	2.0		0.9	-8.7	47	$7
Type xFB	06	a/a	6	11	0	140	78	6.03	1.55	319			23.2	35%	61%	5.49				2.1	5.0	2.4		1.0	-26.2	42	$0
Health A	07	aa	7	3	0	83	57	5.47	1.63	328			10.5	35%	73%	6.91				2.3	6.2	2.7		2.0	-10.3	22	$2
PT/Exp D	08	WAS *	5	4	3	108	86	2.60	1.12	223	253	150	7.2	26%	80%	4.14	38	17	45	2.8	7.1	2.6	7%	0.8	22.3	70	$14
Consist F	1st Half		3	2	1	64	49	2.84	1.18	251			10.1	30%	77%	3.89	42	21	37	2.1	6.8	3.2	6%	0.6	11.3	85	$7
LIMA Plan B	2nd Half		2	2	2	44	37	2.25	1.02	179			5.0	20%	85%	4.11	38	16	46	3.7	7.6	2.1	9%	1.0	11.0	53	$7
+/- Score -36	09	Proj	3	3	0	59	44	4.00	1.37	267			9.0	30%	75%	4.58	38	16	46	3.1	6.8	2.2	10%	1.2	-1.8	55	$4

2-2, 2.16 ERA in 50 IP at WAS. The good news: At 25, showed growth in Dom and OBA, death against RH.
The bad news: xERA, H%, S%, hr/f, FB all say that ERA was a mirage. He's due for a fall.

Sherrill,George

Sherrill,George			W	L	Sv	IP	K	ERA	WHIP	OBA	vL	vR	BF/G	H%	S%	xERA	G	L	F	Ctl	Dom	Cmd	hr/f	hr/9	RAR	BPV	R$
LH Reliever	04	SEA *	6	3	13	74	70	3.00	1.23	257			5.4	32%	79%	3.78				2.2	8.5	3.8		0.9	13.0	108	$14
Age 32	05	SEA *	5	6	7	43	54	3.98	1.14	219	116	273	3.4	31%	67%	3.08	42	16	42	3.1	11.3	3.6	9%	0.8	2.1	139	$9
Type Pwr xFB	06	SEA	2	4	1	40	42	4.28	1.43	210	143	297	2.4	30%	67%	4.88	30	19	51	6.1	9.5	1.6	0%	0.0	1.4	14	$4
Health B	07	SEA	2	0	3	46	56	2.36	0.98	178	156	212	2.4	25%	80%	3.47	25	21	55	3.3	11.0	3.3	7%	0.8	12.1	111	$9
PT/Exp C	08	BAL	3	5	31	53	58	4.73	1.50	238	190	254	4.1	31%	70%	4.68	34	13	53	5.6	9.8	1.8	8%	1.0	-2.5	38	$13
Consist C	1st Half		2	3	26	37	37	3.68	1.25	201			3.9	24%	76%	4.69	29	9	61	4.9	9.1	1.9	9%	1.2	3.0	38	$13
LIMA Plan C+	2nd Half		1	2	5	17	21	7.05	2.05	310			4.6	44%	64%	4.59	44	20	36	7.0	11.4	1.6	6%	0.5	-5.5	37	$1
+/- Score -11	09	Proj	3	4	20	58	65	3.88	1.40	238			4.1	31%	75%	4.17	34	18	48	4.7	10.1	2.2	8%	0.9	1.8	68	$12

Does he have closer-worthy skills? BPV says "no," but that's premature. Doubled RHB faced as closer, but held his own. Real problem was Ctl, and assuming a return to health, he's not too old to recover that skill.

Shields,James

Shields,James			W	L	Sv	IP	K	ERA	WHIP	OBA	vL	vR	BF/G	H%	S%	xERA	G	L	F	Ctl	Dom	Cmd	hr/f	hr/9	RAR	BPV	R$
RH Starter	04	aa	0	3	0	18	13	8.50	1.94	339			21.9	36%	60%	8.30				4.5	6.5	1.4		2.5	-9.2	-18	($2)
Age 27	05	a/a	8	5	0	115	94	3.13	1.23	253			26.5	31%	74%	3.19				2.5	7.4	2.9		0.4	16.7	98	$13
Type	06	TAM *	9	10	0	185	159	4.37	1.38	289	266	309	25.7	34%	71%	3.75	43	23	34	2.1	7.7	3.6	11%	1.0	4.3	102	$15
Health A	07	TAM	12	8	0	215	184	3.85	1.11	250	243	250	27.9	29%	70%	3.53	43	16	40	1.5	7.7	5.1	11%	1.2	17.3	119	$26
PT/Exp A	08	TAM	14	8	0	215	160	3.56	1.15	255	255	253	26.5	29%	73%	3.73	46	16	37	1.7	6.7	4.0	10%	1.0	20.9	100	$24
Consist A	1st Half		6	5	0	109	88	3.71	1.14	254			26.1	30%	71%	3.64	45	16	39	1.6	7.2	4.4	10%	1.0	8.7	109	$12
LIMA Plan C+	2nd Half		8	3	0	106	72	3.41	1.16	257			27.0	29%	75%	3.83	47	16	36	1.7	6.1	3.6	10%	1.0	12.3	90	$13
+/- Score 24	09	Proj	16	7	0	218	172	3.68	1.19	260			27.1	30%	72%	3.72	45	17	38	1.8	7.1	4.0	10%	1.0	18.8	103	$25

This is what you call a nice "tight" skill set. Pinpoint control, just enough dominance that he doesn't need to blow batters away with every pitch, and keeps the ball down. Triple-digit BPVs are the result. A keeper.

Shields,Scot

Shields,Scot			W	L	Sv	IP	K	ERA	WHIP	OBA	vL	vR	BF/G	H%	S%	xERA	G	L	F	Ctl	Dom	Cmd	hr/f	hr/9	RAR	BPV	R$
RH Reliever	04	ANA	8	2	4	105	109	3.34	1.30	247	235	242	7.4	33%	75%	3.23	56	14	30	3.4	9.3	2.7	7%	0.5	14.2	110	$14
Age 33	05	ANA	10	11	7	91	98	2.76	1.13	204	202	203	4.7	28%	77%	3.03	54	17	28	3.7	9.7	2.6	8%	0.5	18.1	108	$18
Type Pwr GB	06	LAA	7	7	2	87	84	2.89	1.08	222	207	227	4.7	28%	77%	3.15	52	15	33	2.5	8.7	3.5	10%	0.8	17.9	119	$15
Health A	07	LAA	4	5	2	77	77	3.86	1.23	222	214	226	4.5	28%	70%	3.67	45	19	36	3.9	9.0	2.3	10%	0.8	6.2	80	$9
PT/Exp C	08	LAA	6	4	4	63	64	2.70	1.34	239	209	262	4.2	30%	84%	3.49	54	16	31	4.1	9.1	2.2	11%	0.9	12.9	84	$10
Consist A	1st Half		3	2	2	32	32	2.53	1.13	217			4.2	28%	79%	2.90	61	13	27	3.1	9.0	2.9	9%	0.6	7.2	117	$6
LIMA Plan B	2nd Half		3	2	2	31	32	2.88	1.57	260			4.3	32%	87%	4.09	48	18	34	5.2	9.2	1.8	13%	1.2	5.7	52	$4
+/- Score -18	09	Proj	6	5	5	68	68	3.47	1.29	234			4.5	30%	75%	3.51	51	17	33	3.9	9.1	2.3	10%	0.8	7.6	88	$10

Had been the 9th ining heir apparent to K-Rod for several years, but declining control is taking him out of the picture. Still has valuable skills, still LIMA-caliber, but also still an end-gamer.

Shouse,Brian

Shouse,Brian			W	L	Sv	IP	K	ERA	WHIP	OBA	vL	vR	BF/G	H%	S%	xERA	G	L	F	Ctl	Dom	Cmd	hr/f	hr/9	RAR	BPV	R$
LH Reliever	04	TEX	2	0	0	45	34	2.59	1.31	239	188	277	3.6	28%	84%	3.56	58	20	22	3.8	6.8	1.8	14%	0.8	10.2	56	$5
Age 40	05	TEX	3	2	0	53	35	5.25	1.37	269	209	337	3.6	29%	64%	3.82	54	21	25	3.1	5.9	1.9	17%	1.2	-5.8	57	$2
Type xGB	06	2TM	1	3	2	38	23	4.02	1.52	271	238	309	2.6	30%	76%	4.61	51	20	29	4.3	5.4	1.3	11%	0.9	2.4	12	$2
Health A	07	MIL	1	1	1	48	32	3.02	1.26	255	214	295	2.7	31%	73%	3.64	55	21	24	2.6	6.0	2.3	0%	0.0	8.3	71	$4
PT/Exp D	08	MIL	5	1	2	51	33	2.81	1.17	241	180	301	3.0	27%	80%	3.21	62	19	19	2.5	5.8	2.4	16%	0.9	9.3	78	$8
Consist B	1st Half		3	0	2	29	19	1.88	1.01	206			3.0	22%	92%	3.12	63	14	23	2.5	6.0	2.4	21%	1.3	8.5	81	$6
LIMA Plan C+	2nd Half		2	1	0	23	14	3.98	1.37	282			3.0	33%	70%	3.30	61	24	16	2.4	5.6	2.3	8%	0.4	0.8	74	$2
+/- Score -15	09	Proj	2	2	0	44	27	3.72	1.33	264			2.9	30%	73%	3.69	58	20	22	2.9	5.6	1.9	10%	0.6	3.5	58	$3

Faced higher mix of lefty batters, the most in 3 years. This helped cement 2007 skills, offset abnormal hr/f over-correction. Don't bet again on ERA under 3.00, as H% and S% will correct. And 40 is 40.

Silva,Carlos

Silva,Carlos			W	L	Sv	IP	K	ERA	WHIP	OBA	vL	vR	BF/G	H%	S%	xERA	G	L	F	Ctl	Dom	Cmd	hr/f	hr/9	RAR	BPV	R$
RH Starter	04	MIN	14	8	0	203	76	4.21	1.43	308	328	289	26.8	32%	73%	4.56	51	17	32	1.6	3.4	2.2	10%	1.0	5.5	48	$10
Age 30	05	MIN	9	8	0	188	71	3.44	1.17	286	302	277	28.5	29%	76%	4.04	49	20	31	0.4	3.4	7.9	12%	1.2	21.5	77	$16
Type Con	06	MIN	11	15	0	180	70	5.95	1.54	326	329	320	22.3	32%	66%	4.82	44	22	34	1.6	3.5	2.2	16%	1.9	-30.9	41	$2
Health A	07	MIN	13	14	0	202	89	4.19	1.31	287	294	280	25.9	30%	70%	4.44	48	19	34	1.6	4.0	2.5	8%	0.9	7.9	54	$15
PT/Exp A	08	SEA	4	15	0	153	69	6.46	1.60	330	348	312	24.7	35%	60%	4.81	44	23	33	1.9	4.1	2.2	10%	1.2	-39.9	44	($4)
Consist A	1st Half		4	9	0	100	39	5.69	1.46	316			25.7	33%	62%	4.75	46	18	35	1.4	3.5	2.4	10%	1.2	-16.5	49	$1
LIMA Plan D	2nd Half		0	6	0	54	30	7.89	1.85	354			23.2	39%	57%	4.91	40	31	29	2.7	5.0	1.9	12%	1.2	-23.4	36	($5)
+/- Score 58	09	Proj	7	15	0	174	79	5.02	1.51	316			24.1	33%	69%	4.65	45	23	32	1.8	4.1	2.3	11%	1.2	-4.7	47	$4

The oddest part of this season is that SEA paid money for it. On purpose. Contact pitchers are at the mercy of the team surrounding them. The hard truth: Skills-wise, 2008 was not any different than 2007 or 2006.

MICHAEL ROY

Slaten,Doug

		W	L	Sv	IP	K	ERA	WHIP	OBA	vL	vR	BF/G	H%	S%	xERA	G	L	F	Ctl	Dom	Cmd	hr/f	hr/9	RAR	BPV	R$
LH Reliever	04	0	0	0	0	0	0.00	0.00																		
Age 29	05 aa	2	2	1	61	59	5.73	1.75	311			4.9	40%	65%	5.24				4.3	8.6	**2.0**		0.3	-10.7	77	($0)
Type FB	06 a/a	4	4	10	63	63	2.06	1.23	231			4.5	31%	83%	2.63				3.5	9.0	**2.6**		0.2	19.1	112	$13
Health A	07 ARI	3	2	0	36	28	2.73	1.52	286	268	284	2.6	33%	86%	4.50	44	17	39	3.5	6.9	**2.0**	9%	1.0	7.6	53	$4
PT/Exp D	08 ARI	0	3	0	32	20	4.74	1.46	266	232	282	3.1	29%	70%	5.10	39	19	43	3.9	5.6	**1.4**	9%	1.1	-1.9	12	$0
Consist C	1st Half	0	2	0	24	15	4.07	1.32	243			3.3	26%	72%	4.74	42	19	39	3.7	5.6	**1.5**	10%	1.1	0.6	20	$1
LIMA Plan C+	2nd Half	0	1	0	8	5	6.75	1.87	328			2.7	36%	64%	6.20	31	17	52	4.5	5.6	**1.3**	7%	1.1	-2.4	-11	($1)
+/- Score -18	09 Proj	1	2	0	29	19	4.34	1.48	275			3.8	30%	74%	5.03	39	18	44	3.7	5.9	1.6	10%	1.2	-2.5	22	$1

Despite surface stat appearances, his skill set never made the leap to the majors. Knee strain cut into 2H stats, but 2008 was looking pretty tepid anyway. Next.

Slowey,Kevin

		W	L	Sv	IP	K	ERA	WHIP	OBA	vL	vR	BF/G	H%	S%	xERA	G	L	F	Ctl	Dom	Cmd	hr/f	hr/9	RAR	BPV	R$
RH Starter	04	0	0	0	0	0	0.00	0.00																		
Age 25	05	0	0	0	0	0	0.00	0.00																		
Type Con FB	06 aa	4	3	0	59	44	4.42	1.29	268			27.6	30%	69%	4.28				2.3	6.7	**2.9**		1.2	0.8	67	$5
Health A	07 MIN *	14	6	0	200	134	3.42	1.26	281	267	309	25.3	32%	76%	4.60	29	21	50	1.4	6.0	**4.2**	6%	0.9	26.7	77	$22
PT/Exp C	08 MIN	12	11	0	160	123	3.99	1.15	263	277	246	24.2	30%	70%	3.96	36	19	45	1.3	6.9	**5.1**	10%	1.2	7.1	102	$18
Consist A	1st Half	5	6	0	73	54	3.47	1.03	244			23.9	27%	72%	3.94	35	17	48	1.1	6.7	**6.0**	10%	1.2	7.9	103	$10
LIMA Plan C+	2nd Half	7	5	0	88	69	4.42	1.26	278			24.4	32%	68%	3.96	37	21	42	1.5	7.1	**4.6**	10%	1.2	-0.8	101	$8
+/- Score 29	09 Proj	16	9	0	209	152	3.54	1.19	266			25.2	30%	75%	4.03	38	19	42	1.5	6.6	4.3	9%	1.1	10.2	94	$24

With a 102 BPV, you'd think he's arrived, but elevated xERAs warn caution. The tipping point will be his G/F trend; it's headed in the right direction. A few more GBs and he's golden. UP: 18 wins, 3.00 ERA

Smith,Greg

		W	L	Sv	IP	K	ERA	WHIP	OBA	vL	vR	BF/G	H%	S%	xERA	G	L	F	Ctl	Dom	Cmd	hr/f	hr/9	RAR	BPV	R$
LH Starter	04	0	0	0	0	0	0.00	0.00																		
Age 25	05	0	0	0	0	0	0.00	0.00																		
Type xFB	06 aa	5	4	0	60	33	5.55	1.77	324			25.6	36%	69%	6.05				3.8	5.0	**1.3**		0.9	-7.6	21	$0
Health A	07 aa	9	5	0	122	82	4.64	1.50	304			24.5	34%	71%	5.28				2.4	6.1	**2.5**		1.1	-2.7	51	$7
PT/Exp C	08 OAK *	8	16	0	196	113	4.01	1.34	236	232	247	25.5	25%	72%	5.32	34	20	46	4.2	5.2	**1.2**	7%	1.0	8.1	-8	$12
Consist A	1st Half	5	6	0	99	70	3.44	1.23	227			25.7	26%	74%	4.65	37	20	44	3.6	6.3	**1.8**	6%	0.7	11.1	31	$10
LIMA Plan D	2nd Half	3	10	0	98	43	4.59	1.45	246			25.2	25%	71%	6.05	32	21	47	4.8	3.9	**0.8**	9%	1.2	-3.0	-48	$3
+/- Score -45	09 Proj	11	13	0	189	115	4.54	1.47	276			25.1	30%	72%	5.25	34	20	46	3.6	5.5	1.5	9%	1.2	-19.2	14	$10

Rookie hurled 5 PQS DOMinant starts in first 7, but collapsed in 2H. IP spike may be to blame. H%, hr/f made this look better than it was. Still owns '07 Cmd; look for that before investing.

Smith,Joe

		W	L	Sv	IP	K	ERA	WHIP	OBA	vL	vR	BF/G	H%	S%	xERA	G	L	F	Ctl	Dom	Cmd	hr/f	hr/9	RAR	BPV	R$
RH Reliever	04	0	0	0	0	0	0.00	0.00																		
Age 25	05	0	0	0	0	0	0.00	0.00																		
Type Pwr xGB	06	0	0	0	0	0	0.00	0.00																		
Health A	07 NYM *	3	2	2	53	50	3.38	1.50	268	298	266	3.8	34%	78%	3.31	62	17	21	4.2	8.4	**2.0**	9%	0.5	6.9	78	$5
PT/Exp D	08 NYM	6	3	0	63	52	3.55	1.30	222	320	192	3.3	27%	73%	3.29	63	20	18	4.4	7.4	**1.7**	13%	0.6	5.6	55	$7
Consist A	1st Half	0	1	0	31	27	3.45	1.15	214			3.4	26%	73%	2.59	68	18	14	3.5	7.8	**2.3**	25%	0.9	3.2	93	$3
LIMA Plan B	2nd Half	6	2	0	32	25	3.66	1.44	230			3.1	28%	73%	3.99	57	21	21	5.3	7.0	**1.3**	5%	0.3	2.4	18	$4
+/- Score 10	09 Proj	5	3	3	63	53	3.46	1.31	241			3.4	30%	74%	3.19	62	19	19	3.7	7.6	2.0	12%	0.6	8.9	76	$7

Sidearmer has become death to RHB. Combination of solid Dom and extreme GB should help LIMA status, but trouble with Ctl and LH holding him back. He's only 25, so worth watching.

Smoltz,John

		W	L	Sv	IP	K	ERA	WHIP	OBA	vL	vR	BF/G	H%	S%	xERA	G	L	F	Ctl	Dom	Cmd	hr/f	hr/9	RAR	BPV	R$
RH Starter	04 ATL	0	1	44	81	85	2.77	1.08	247	255	236	4.5	32%	79%	2.89	48	18	34	1.4	9.4	**6.5**	11%	0.9	14.9	157	$22
Age 42	05 ATL	14	7	0	229	169	3.06	1.15	245	252	233	28.3	29%	76%	3.59	48	22	30	2.1	6.6	**3.2**	9%	0.7	33.4	89	$26
Type Pwr	06 ATL	16	9	0	232	211	3.49	1.19	253	278	226	27.2	31%	74%	3.39	46	20	33	2.1	8.2	**3.8**	10%	0.9	28.5	114	$27
Health F	07 ATL	14	8	0	206	197	3.11	1.18	253	262	237	26.4	32%	76%	3.36	45	20	35	2.1	8.6	**4.2**	9%	0.8	33.5	122	$26
PT/Exp A	08 ATL	3	2	0	28	36	2.57	1.18	240	226	234	19.1	35%	81%	2.80	49	14	38	2.6	11.6	**4.5**	8%	0.6	5.9	165	$5
Consist A	1st Half	3	2	0	28	36	2.57	1.18	240			19.1	35%	81%	2.80	49	14	38	2.6	11.6	**4.5**	8%	0.6	5.9	165	$5
LIMA Plan A+	2nd Half	0	0	0	0	0	0.00	0.00																		
+/- Score 1	09 Proj	6	4	0	87	84	3.52	1.23	248			22.6	31%	74%	3.44	47	18	34	2.7	8.7	3.2	10%	0.8	9.7	109	$10

Labrum shoulder surgery cut short season in June. Reports say he won't be ready for start of 2009 and may decide to retire. If healthy, his skills have not deteriorated - yet. But at 41 after major surgery, he's a big risk.

Snell,Ian

		W	L	Sv	IP	K	ERA	WHIP	OBA	vL	vR	BF/G	H%	S%	xERA	G	L	F	Ctl	Dom	Cmd	hr/f	hr/9	RAR	BPV	R$
RH Starter	04 aa	11	7	0	151	120	3.75	1.34	280			24.8	33%	75%	4.47				2.2	7.2	**3.2**		1.0	10.9	80	$13
Age 27	05 PIT *	12	5	0	154	122	4.32	1.21	245	304	239	19.3	28%	67%	4.13	37	21	42	2.6	7.1	**2.7**	9%	1.1	-1.5	72	$15
Type Pwr	06 PIT	14	11	0	186	169	4.74	1.46	274	305	251	25.5	32%	72%	4.04	43	21	36	3.6	8.2	**2.3**	15%	1.4	-5.8	71	$13
Health A	07 PIT	9	12	0	208	177	3.76	1.33	263	284	245	27.6	31%	75%	3.94	46	17	37	2.9	7.7	**2.6**	9%	1.0	17.0	82	$17
PT/Exp A	08 PIT	7	12	0	164	135	5.42	1.77	303	314	295	24.8	36%	70%	5.02	38	25	37	4.9	7.4	**1.5**	9%	1.0	-23.4	17	($1)
Consist B	1st Half	3	7	0	86	64	5.99	1.93	324			26.0	38%	68%	5.36	41	24	35	5.1	6.7	**1.3**	7%	0.7	-18.1	1	($4)
LIMA Plan D+	2nd Half	4	5	0	79	71	4.81	1.59	277			23.6	33%	73%	4.67	34	26	40	4.6	8.1	**1.8**	12%	1.3	-5.2	34	$2
+/- Score 13	09 Proj	10	12	0	189	160	4.20	1.46	272			24.3	32%	74%	4.32	40	22	38	3.7	7.6	2.1	10%	1.0	0.5	56	$11

In Quest of Good Things:
- 36% hit rate should regress
- 25% LD rate should regress
- Has a history of good things
- Little pressure in Pittsburgh
- Will come cheap on Draft Day
- Has a history of good things

Sonnanstine,Andy

		W	L	Sv	IP	K	ERA	WHIP	OBA	vL	vR	BF/G	H%	S%	xERA	G	L	F	Ctl	Dom	Cmd	hr/f	hr/9	RAR	BPV	R$
RH Starter	04	0	0	0	0	0	0.00	0.00																		
Age 26	05	0	0	0	0	0	0.00	0.00																		
Type Con FB	06 aa	15	8	0	185	127	4.11	1.27	274			27.7	31%	70%	4.08				1.9	6.2	**3.2**		1.0	9.4	77	$18
Health A	07 TAM *	12	14	0	202	155	5.09	1.31	283	318	266	25.8	32%	64%	4.13	39	18	43	1.8	6.9	**3.9**	10%	1.2	-14.5	93	$14
PT/Exp B	08 TAM	13	9	0	193	124	4.38	1.29	280	265	289	25.4	31%	68%	4.30	42	17	41	1.7	5.8	**3.4**	8%	1.0	-0.7	78	$15
Consist A	1st Half	9	3	0	102	67	4.60	1.39	298			25.8	34%	67%	4.22	44	19	37	1.7	5.9	**3.5**	6%	0.7	-3.2	83	$8
LIMA Plan C+	2nd Half	4	6	0	92	57	4.13	1.18	258			25.0	28%	69%	4.38	40	14	46	1.8	5.6	**3.2**	10%	1.3	2.5	71	$8
+/- Score 22	09 Proj	14	10	0	204	140	4.07	1.28	277			25.9	31%	72%	4.23	41	17	42	1.8	6.2	3.5	10%	1.2	5.0	83	$19

If not for his drop in Dom this year, I'd say it would be a near guarantee that he'd break through the 4.00 ERA barrier in '09. Now I'm not so sure. Needs a few points of S%, a few more GB... he's right on the cusp.

Soriano,Rafael

		W	L	Sv	IP	K	ERA	WHIP	OBA	vL	vR	BF/G	H%	S%	xERA	G	L	F	Ctl	Dom	Cmd	hr/f	hr/9	RAR	BPV	R$
RH Reliever	04 SEA *	1	3	0	15	17	4.80	1.47	274			6.0	36%	70%	4.91				3.6	10.2	**2.8**		1.2	-0.7	85	$1
Age 29	05 SEA	0	0	0	7	9	2.54	0.99	231	571	100	4.0	35%	71%	3.04	32	16	53	1.3	11.4	**9.0**	0%	0.0	1.6	181	$1
Type Pwr xFB	06 SEA	1	2	2	60	65	2.25	1.08	206	244	179	4.5	27%	85%	3.84	27	19	54	3.2	9.8	**3.1**	7%	0.9	17.1	96	$10
Health F	07 ATL	3	3	9	72	70	3.00	0.86	188	164	197	3.8	21%	76%	3.41	33	16	51	1.9	8.8	**4.7**	13%	1.5	12.7	118	$14
PT/Exp D	08 ATL	0	1	3	14	16	2.57	1.14	151	222	103	4.1	20%	80%	4.48	23	16	61	5.8	10.3	**1.8**	5%	0.6	2.9	30	$3
Consist B	1st Half	0	0	3	9	11	2.00	1.22	136			4.1	22%	82%	4.64	25	15	60	7.0	11.0	**1.6**	0%	0.0	2.5	12	$2
LIMA Plan A	2nd Half	0	1	0	5	5	3.60	1.00	175			3.9	18%	75%	4.22	18	18	64	3.6	9.0	**2.5**	13%	1.8	0.4	61	$1
+/- Score -75	09 Proj	2	2	10	54	54	3.53	1.14	222			4.3	27%	75%	4.04	28	17	55	3.0	9.1	3.0	10%	1.3	2.0	88	$9

Now looks like 2007 was health "outlier" as only DL-free season in last 5 years. Elbow surgery in August ended 2008, bringing DL days to over 450 in 5 years. IF healthy, has closer-worthy skills, but what a big IF.

Soria,Joakim

		W	L	Sv	IP	K	ERA	WHIP	OBA	vL	vR	BF/G	H%	S%	xERA	G	L	F	Ctl	Dom	Cmd	hr/f	hr/9	RAR	BPV	R$
RH Reliever	04	0	0	0	0	0	0.00	0.00																		
Age 25	05 MEX	5	0	0	66	55	4.91	1.74	301			10.3	35%	75%	5.93				4.8	7.5	**1.6**		1.2	-4.9	36	$2
Type Pwr FB	06 MEX	0	0	15	37	28	4.38	1.43	277			4.1	33%	70%	4.31				3.2	6.8	**2.2**		0.7	0.6	64	$6
Health A	07 KC	2	3	17	69	75	2.48	0.94	191	167	200	4.3	26%	74%	3.14	39	20	40	2.5	9.8	**3.9**	4%	0.4	17.3	126	$17
PT/Exp B	08 KC	2	3	42	67	66	1.60	0.86	170	167	171	4.0	22%	87%	3.22	45	14	41	2.5	8.8	**3.5**	7%	0.7	22.8	113	$26
Consist B	1st Half	0	1	22	36	39	1.25	0.75	151			3.9	20%	88%	2.92	48	7	45	2.3	9.8	**4.3**	5%	0.5	13.8	140	$14
LIMA Plan C+	2nd Half	2	2	20	31	27	2.01	0.99	192			4.2	23%	86%	3.57	41	22	37	2.9	7.8	**2.7**	10%	0.9	9.0	82	$12
+/- Score -51	09 Proj	2	3	40	73	70	2.73	1.09	224			4.5	28%	79%	3.48	42	18	40	2.5	8.7	3.5	9%	0.9	8.5	109	$23

Both lucky and good in first full year as closer. ERA will spike when H% and S% regress, but fine Cmd will limit the damage. GB% trend also gives hope that HR won't be a future issue. Invest in this age-24 ace.

MICHAEL ROY

Sowers,Jeremy

		Yr	Tm	W	L	Sv	IP	K	ERA	WHIP	OBA	vL	vR	BF/G	H%	S%	xERA	G	L	F	Ctl	Dom	Cmd	hr/f	hr/9	RAR	BPV	R$
LH	Starter	04		0	0	0	0	0	0.00	0.00																		
Age	26	05	a/a	6	1	0	88	65	2.25	1.11	262			25.4	31%	84%	3.31				1.0	6.6	**6.5**		0.7	22.3	158	$13
Type	Con	06	CLE *	16	5	0	185	83	2.62	1.23	253	225	259	26.5	27%	80%	4.39	48	21	30	2.4	4.0	**1.7**	6%	0.5	44.2	33	$24
Health	A	07	CLE *	5	11	0	164	79	5.56	1.57	315	206	338	26.2	34%	65%	5.33	40	16	44	2.5	4.3	**1.8**	6%	0.9	-21.3	29	$0
PT/Exp	C	08	CLE *	8	12	0	181	102	4.68	1.47	290	258	303	24.8	31%	71%	4.67	42	24	34	2.8	5.0	**1.8**	11%	1.1	-7.4	34	$7
Consist	B	1st Half		4	7	0	95	55	4.57	1.59	311			25.2	34%	74%	4.78	41	26	34	2.9	5.2	**1.8**	12%	1.2	-2.6	35	$2
LIMA Plan	C	2nd Half		4	5	0	86	47	4.80	1.33	266			24.5	28%	66%	4.56	43	23	34	2.8	4.9	**1.7**	10%	1.0	-4.8	33	$4
+/- Score	-4	09	Proj	**5**	**6**	**0**	**104**	**56**	**4.41**	**1.40**	**285**			**25.0**	**30%**	**71%**	**4.66**	**42**	**21**	**36**	**2.5**	**4.8**	**1.9**	**10%**	**1.1**	**-3.0**	**40**	**$5**

4-9, 5.58 ERA in 121 IP at CLE. One could say he did better than '07, but that's damning with faint praise. Still getting lit up at ML level. Watch Dom; unless it approaches 5.6 tipping point, he'll remain cannon fodder.

Speier,Justin

		Yr	Tm	W	L	Sv	IP	K	ERA	WHIP	OBA	vL	vR	BF/G	H%	S%	xERA	G	L	F	Ctl	Dom	Cmd	hr/f	hr/9	RAR	BPV	R$
RH	Reliever	04	TOR	3	8	7	69	52	3.91	1.25	239	258	220	4.6	27%	72%	4.63	34	17	49	3.3	6.8	**2.1**	8%	1.0	4.4	46	$8
Age	35	05	TOR	3	2	0	66	56	2.58	0.95	205	167	219	3.9	23%	83%	3.79	35	16	49	2.0	7.6	**3.7**	11%	1.4	14.6	95	$10
Type	Pwr xFB	06	TOR	2	0	0	51	55	2.99	1.33	246	183	264	3.7	32%	81%	4.13	30	20	50	3.7	9.7	**2.6**	7%	0.9	9.9	83	$6
Health	D	07	LAA	2	3	0	50	47	2.88	0.96	203	222	186	3.8	24%	76%	3.64	37	12	50	2.2	8.5	**3.9**	9%	1.1	10.0	109	$8
PT/Exp	D	08	LAA	2	8	0	68	56	5.03	1.41	265	288	240	4.8	28%	72%	4.66	35	15	50	3.6	7.4	**2.1**	15%	2.0	-5.7	50	$3
Consist	B	1st Half		0	4	0	34	25	5.34	1.39	252			4.4	26%	69%	4.75	40	14	46	4.0	6.7	**1.7**	17%	2.1	-4.1	30	$1
LIMA Plan	B+	2nd Half		2	4	0	34	31	4.72	1.43	277			5.1	31%	74%	4.58	31	15	54	3.1	8.1	**2.6**	13%	1.8	-1.6	70	$2
+/- Score	8	09	Proj	**2**	**5**	**5**	**58**	**52**	**4.50**	**1.34**	**262**			**4.4**	**30%**	**72%**	**4.36**	**34**	**15**	**50**	**3.1**	**8.1**	**2.6**	**12%**	**1.6**	**0.4**	**74**	**$6**

Not as bad as it seemed, thanks to H% and S% regressing to mean and aberrantly bad hr/f. But xFB means HR issues aren't going away. He'll rebound, but forget '06-'07. He's no sub-3.00 ERA pitcher.

Speier,Ryan

		Yr	Tm	W	L	Sv	IP	K	ERA	WHIP	OBA	vL	vR	BF/G	H%	S%	xERA	G	L	F	Ctl	Dom	Cmd	hr/f	hr/9	RAR	BPV	R$
RH	Reliever	04	aa	3	1	37	62	53	3.38	1.23	210			4.2	25%	75%	3.06				4.3	7.7	**1.8**		0.8	7.4	72	$18
Age	29	05	COL *	4	3	6	75	46	4.89	1.74	323			5.3	37%	70%	5.02	46	20	34	3.5	5.5	**1.6**	2%	0.2	-6.0	27	$2
Type	GB	06	COL	0	0	0	0	0	0.00	0.00																		
Health	F	07	COL *	4	5	33	67	42	6.61	1.91	325			4.6	37%	65%	5.41	42	28	30	4.9	5.6	**1.1**	8%	0.8	-18.0	-13	$8
PT/Exp	F	08	COL *	3	1	0	64	41	3.80	1.34	259	272	273	5.1	30%	72%	4.13	53	18	29	3.2	5.8	**1.8**	7%	0.6	3.7	47	$4
Consist	C	1st Half		1	1	0	29	20	4.03	1.55	300			5.0	35%	74%	4.52	45	20	34	3.1	6.2	**2.0**	6%	0.6	0.8	51	$1
LIMA Plan	C+	2nd Half		2	0	0	35	21	3.60	1.17	221			5.1	25%	69%	3.61	63	15	22	3.3	5.4	**1.6**	8%	0.5	2.9	48	$3
+/- Score	-24	09	Proj	**2**	**1**	**0**	**44**	**28**	**4.55**	**1.47**	**277**			**4.8**	**31%**	**70%**	**4.34**	**51**	**20**	**29**	**3.5**	**5.8**	**1.6**	**10%**	**0.8**	**0.0**	**38**	**$2**

2-1, 4.06 ERA in 51 IP at COL. Big sidearmer is effective when sinker is working and Ctl is on, but as with most finesse types, is hittable otherwise. Profiles as a decent middle man, but not as a fanalytic option.

Springer,Russ

		Yr	Tm	W	L	Sv	IP	K	ERA	WHIP	OBA	vL	vR	BF/G	H%	S%	xERA	G	L	F	Ctl	Dom	Cmd	hr/f	hr/9	RAR	BPV	R$
RH	Reliever	04	HOU *	1	3	6	45	36	3.80	1.62	291			5.2	35%	78%	5.04				4.2	7.2	**1.7**		0.8	2.6	52	$3
Age	40	05	HOU	4	4	0	59	54	4.73	1.19	228	209	231	3.9	26%	64%	3.92	40	16	44	3.2	8.2	**2.6**	13%	1.4	-3.5	80	$5
Type	Pwr xFB	06	HOU	1	1	0	59	46	3.50	1.05	216	253	187	3.3	23%	75%	4.43	27	15	58	2.4	7.0	**2.9**	10%	1.5	7.2	65	$6
Health	B	07	STL	8	1	0	66	66	2.18	0.91	181	235	158	3.3	24%	77%	3.65	30	20	51	2.6	9.0	**3.5**	4%	0.4	18.3	100	$14
PT/Exp	D	08	STL	2	1	0	50	45	2.33	1.13	216	277	176	2.9	27%	83%	4.21	30	20	49	3.2	8.1	**2.5**	6%	0.7	12.1	66	$6
Consist	B	1st Half		1	0	0	25	21	2.16	1.12	194			3.2	24%	81%	4.44	33	19	48	4.0	7.6	**1.9**	3%	0.4	6.5	40	$3
LIMA Plan	C+	2nd Half		1	1	0	25	24	2.49	1.15	236			2.7	29%	85%	4.00	28	21	51	2.5	8.5	**3.4**	9%	1.1	5.6	93	$3
+/- Score	-78	09	Proj	**2**	**1**	**0**	**44**	**37**	**4.14**	**1.31**	**246**			**3.3**	**28%**	**73%**	**4.59**	**31**	**19**	**51**	**3.5**	**7.7**	**2.2**	**9%**	**1.2**	**-1.3**	**51**	**$3**

Returned to earth as forecast, but luck stayed in stratosphere. Don't get me wrong, most kids half his age would kill for this Dom, OBA. But when S% and hr/f regress, he may wish he'd have retired relatively on top.

Stokes,Brian

		Yr	Tm	W	L	Sv	IP	K	ERA	WHIP	OBA	vL	vR	BF/G	H%	S%	xERA	G	L	F	Ctl	Dom	Cmd	hr/f	hr/9	RAR	BPV	R$
RH	Reliever	04		0	0	0	0	0	0.00	0.00																		
Age	29	05	aa	4	5	0	85	50	4.86	1.54	297			25.3	33%	69%	5.02				3.2	5.2	**1.7**		0.9	-5.9	36	$2
Type		06	TAM *	8	7	0	157	99	5.51	1.66	308			21.2	35%	66%	5.37	40	15	45	3.6	5.6	**1.5**	5%	0.7	-18.4	21	$2
Health	B	07	TAM	2	7	0	62	35	7.08	1.85	339	346	341	5.0	36%	63%	5.17	48	17	35	3.6	5.1	**1.4**	14%	1.6	-19.8	20	($4)
PT/Exp	C	08	NYM *	11	8	1	164	89	6.22	1.78	323	316	250	16.3	36%	64%	5.55	39	24	38	3.9	4.9	**1.3**	6%	0.8	-39.3	-0	($4)
Consist	A	1st Half		7	7	0	97	47	7.16	1.85	344			27.3	38%	59%					3.3	4.3	**1.3**		0.6	-34.7	21	($5)
LIMA Plan	F	2nd Half		4	1	1	66	43	4.84	1.67	290			10.2	32%	73%	5.34	39	24	38	4.7	5.8	**1.2**	9%	1.0	-4.7	-7	$1
+/- Score	-8	09	Proj	**1**	**5**	**0**	**53**	**29**	**5.31**	**1.66**	**302**			**7.1**	**32%**	**70%**	**5.24**	**44**	**19**	**37**	**3.9**	**5.0**	**1.3**	**10%**	**1.2**	**-5.8**	**5**	**($1)**

1-0, 3.51 ERA in 33 IP at NYM. So after years of lousy skills and a so-so 1H in minors, he puts up a plus-3.0 Cmd in the majors. Of course. Just as expected. And now seems firmly in NYM's 'pen plans. Color me skeptical.

Street,Huston

		Yr	Tm	W	L	Sv	IP	K	ERA	WHIP	OBA	vL	vR	BF/G	H%	S%	xERA	G	L	F	Ctl	Dom	Cmd	hr/f	hr/9	RAR	BPV	R$
RH	Reliever	04	a/a	1	0	4	15	13	2.40	1.33	262			5.3	32%	84%	3.78				3.0	7.8	**2.6**		0.6	3.6	86	$3
Age	25	05	OAK	5	1	23	78	72	1.73	1.01	194	224	172	4.6	25%	84%	3.54	45	17	38	3.0	8.3	**2.8**	4%	0.3	25.5	91	$21
Type	Pwr FB	06	OAK	4	4	37	70	67	3.33	1.10	244	274	211	4.1	31%	70%	3.51	37	21	42	1.7	8.6	**5.2**	5%	0.5	10.6	125	$22
Health	C	07	OAK	5	2	16	50	63	2.88	0.94	199	224	162	4.0	28%	74%	2.81	40	15	45	2.2	11.3	**5.3**	10%	0.9	10.0	164	$16
PT/Exp	B	08	OAK	7	5	18	71	70	3.80	1.23	231	200	250	4.6	29%	70%	3.85	36	23	41	3.4	8.9	**2.6**	8%	0.8	4.8	81	$15
Consist	B	1st Half		1	2	15	35	38	4.08	1.05	213			4.2	25%	68%	3.29	39	17	44	2.5	9.7	**3.8**	15%	1.5	1.2	123	$9
LIMA Plan	B	2nd Half		6	3	3	36	32	3.53	1.40	247			5.0	32%	72%	4.46	33	29	38	4.3	8.1	**1.9**	0%	0.0	3.6	40	$6
+/- Score	16	09	Proj	**7**	**4**	**35**	**73**	**75**	**3.35**	**1.17**	**233**			**4.4**	**30%**	**74%**	**3.57**	**38**	**21**	**41**	**2.9**	**9.3**	**3.3**	**9%**	**0.9**	**7.6**	**106**	**$23**

His usual self early, but pulled groin cut into Dom, and bad hr/f luck cut into OAK's faith. Was again pitching well by Sept, but by then save opps were gone. Owns those 100+ BPVs, but now may need a change of venue.

Stults,Eric

		Yr	Tm	W	L	Sv	IP	K	ERA	WHIP	OBA	vL	vR	BF/G	H%	S%	xERA	G	L	F	Ctl	Dom	Cmd	hr/f	hr/9	RAR	BPV	R$
LH	Starter	04		0	0	0	0	0	0.00	0.00																		
Age	29	05	a/a	7	10	0	146	94	4.80	1.52	313			24.0	35%	71%	5.52				2.1	5.8	**2.7**		1.2	-9.0	49	$4
Type		06	LA *	11	11	0	170	110	4.50	1.49	274			23.5	31%	70%	5.05	40	19	41	3.9	5.8	**1.5**	6%	0.7	-0.3	18	$9
Health	A	07	LA *	6	11	0	128	89	9.14	2.28	390			20.1	44%	60%	5.81	39	21	39	4.3	6.3	**1.5**	10%	1.5	-74.3	15	($18)
PT/Exp	B	08	LA *	9	10	0	156	104	4.91	1.65	313	314	233	26.4	34%	74%	5.01	38	22	41	3.3	6.0	**1.8**	11%	1.4	-12.2	35	$2
Consist	B	1st Half		7	7	0	103	60	4.50	1.62	306			27.4	33%	75%	5.45	37	17	46	3.4	5.3	**1.5**	7%	1.1	-2.9	17	$3
LIMA Plan	C+	2nd Half		2	3	0	53	44	5.69	1.70	326			24.7	36%	73%	4.36	39	26	35	3.0	7.4	**2.4**	20%	2.1	-9.3	68	($1)
+/- Score	-4	09	Proj	**3**	**4**	**0**	**54**	**41**	**4.83**	**1.48**	**283**			**21.6**	**32%**	**71%**	**4.51**	**39**	**22**	**39**	**3.3**	**6.8**	**2.1**	**12%**	**1.3**	**-1.2**	**50**	**$2**

2-3, 3.49 ERA in 39 IP at LA. Best ML showing yet, though xERA shows it really wasn't all that. Which pretty much sums up his career so far. At 29, it might be a good time to, oh, actually flash a few skills about now.

Suppan,Jeff

		Yr	Tm	W	L	Sv	IP	K	ERA	WHIP	OBA	vL	vR	BF/G	H%	S%	xERA	G	L	F	Ctl	Dom	Cmd	hr/f	hr/9	RAR	BPV	R$
RH	Starter	04	STL	16	9	0	188	110	4.16	1.37	266	272	260	26.0	28%	73%	4.44	48	18	34	3.1	5.3	**1.7**	12%	1.2	2.2	37	$14
Age	34	05	STL	16	10	0	194	114	3.57	1.39	273	271	279	26.1	30%	78%	4.41	46	21	32	2.9	5.3	**1.8**	12%	1.1	16.2	41	$16
Type	Con	06	STL	12	7	0	190	104	4.12	1.45	279	302	257	26.0	30%	74%	4.59	47	23	31	3.3	4.9	**1.5**	11%	1.0	8.6	25	$11
Health	A	07	MIL	12	12	0	207	114	4.62	1.50	294	334	271	26.9	32%	70%	4.77	45	20	35	3.0	5.0	**1.7**	7%	0.8	-4.8	33	$8
PT/Exp	A	08	MIL	10	10	0	178	90	4.96	1.54	292	288	308	25.6	30%	72%	4.87	44	23	32	3.4	4.6	**1.3**	15%	1.5	-15.2	13	$4
Consist	A	1st Half		4	6	0	93	53	4.05	1.54	283			26.0	31%	76%	4.62	50	23	28	3.9	5.1	**1.3**	10%	0.9	2.5	15	$3
LIMA Plan	C	2nd Half		6	4	0	84	37	5.97	1.54	302			25.1	29%	68%	5.12	39	24	37	2.9	3.9	**1.4**	19%	2.2	-17.7	11	$0
+/- Score	-14	09	Proj	**9**	**13**	**0**	**189**	**99**	**4.87**	**1.50**	**290**			**26.0**	**31%**	**70%**	**4.80**	**45**	**22**	**33**	**3.2**	**4.7**	**1.5**	**11%**	**1.1**	**-10.6**	**23**	**$5**

Prior BPIs best labeled as "pedestrian." Now they're a big orange hand, flashing "Don't draft! Don't draft!" over and over. For those who think he's good enough in the end-game, PLEASE join my league.

Tallet,Brian

		Yr	Tm	W	L	Sv	IP	K	ERA	WHIP	OBA	vL	vR	BF/G	H%	S%	xERA	G	L	F	Ctl	Dom	Cmd	hr/f	hr/9	RAR	BPV	R$
LH	Reliever	04	a/a	1	1	1	32	23	6.45	1.86	314			8.1	38%	62%	5.33				5.2	6.6	**1.3**		0.0	-8.3	59	($1)
Age	31	05	aaa	6	5	0	97	49	4.48	1.40	288			19.1	30%	73%	5.07				2.4	4.6	**1.9**		1.4	-2.1	23	$5
Type	Pwr	06	TOR *	4	2	3	79	53	5.36	1.65	282	220	246	5.7	31%	70%	5.34	41	18	41	4.9	6.1	**1.2**	10%	1.2	-7.8	-4	$2
Health	A	07	TOR	2	4	0	62	54	3.47	1.24	218	247	194	5.4	28%	70%	4.25	40	19	40	4.0	7.8	**1.9**	1%	0.1	8.0	50	$6
PT/Exp	D	08	TOR	1	2	0	56	47	2.88	1.31	247	257	230	4.7	30%	80%	4.10	43	22	36	3.5	7.5	**2.1**	7%	0.6	10.2	61	$5
Consist	B	1st Half		0	1	0	32	29	3.09	1.47	262			4.7	33%	80%	4.33	41	22	38	4.2	8.2	**1.9**	6%	0.6	4.9	52	$2
LIMA Plan	C+	2nd Half		1	0	0	24	18	2.59	1.11	226			4.7	26%	80%	3.79	45	21	34	2.6	6.7	**2.6**	8%	0.7	5.3	73	$3
+/- Score	-28	09	Proj	**2**	**2**	**0**	**58**	**46**	**3.88**	**1.29**	**248**			**5.3**	**29%**	**72%**	**4.16**	**42**	**20**	**38**	**3.3**	**7.1**	**2.2**	**9%**	**0.9**	**1.9**	**60**	**$5**

Continues to hoodwink the ERA gods... last year it was hr/f, this year S%. And next year? We can't predict that stuff, we only project skills. And while his are improving, xERA still shouts than an ERA spike is coming.

ROD TRUESDELL

Taschner,Jack

		Yr	Tm		W	L	Sv	IP	K	ERA	WHIP	OBA	vL	vR	BF/G	H%	S%	xERA	G	L	F	Ctl	Dom	Cmd	hr/f	hr/9	RAR	BPV	R$
LH	Reliever	04	a/a		7	8	0	111	76	7.02	1.74	314			16.2	35%	61%	6.38				4.1	6.1	1.5		1.4	-36.7	18	($3)
Age	31	05	SF	*	5	0	10	71	68	1.70	1.15	188			4.3	25%	86%	4.35	35	13	52	4.4	8.6	1.9	2%	0.3	22.4	49	$15
Type	Pwr FB	06	SF	*	6	8	14	68	69	5.50	1.65	314			4.5	39%	69%	4.39	27	29	44	3.2	9.1	2.8	10%	1.2	-8.5	82	$8
Health	A	07	SF		3	1	0	50	51	5.40	1.46	238	316	176	3.5	31%	62%	4.67	33	18	49	5.2	9.2	1.8	6%	0.7	-6.0	35	$2
PT/Exp	D	08	SF		3	2	0	48	39	4.88	1.69	296	279	308	3.3	35%	72%	5.03	39	19	43	4.5	7.3	1.6	8%	0.9	-3.6	27	$1
Consist	A	1st Half			2	1	0	28	23	2.54	1.24	216			2.9	26%	82%	4.55	38	15	46	4.1	7.3	1.8	5%	0.6	6.0	36	$4
LIMA Plan	C+	2nd Half			1	1	0	20	16	8.22	2.33	386			3.8	45%	65%	5.75	39	22	39	5.0	7.3	1.5	10%	1.4	-9.6	13	($3)
+/- Score	-2	09	Proj		3	2	0	44	37	4.76	1.59	277			3.7	32%	73%	4.87	36	20	44	4.6	7.7	1.7	10%	1.2	-2.8	29	$2

Last year's book called him (a)nother FB pitcher with good Dom but Ctl issues." Well, he's still a FB pitcher with Ctl issues, and now with less-good Dom. xERA trend says all you need to know about his rosterability.

Tavarez,Julian

		Yr	Tm		W	L	Sv	IP	K	ERA	WHIP	OBA	vL	vR	BF/G	H%	S%	xERA	G	L	F	Ctl	Dom	Cmd	hr/f	hr/9	RAR	BPV	R$
RH	Reliever	04	STL		7	4	4	64	48	2.39	1.19	240	253	231	3.4	30%	79%	3.69	50	21	29	2.7	6.7	2.5	2%	0.1	14.8	77	$11
Age	35	05	STL		2	3	4	65	47	3.45	1.33	270	294	271	3.7	31%	77%	3.80	51	21	28	2.6	6.5	2.5	10%	0.8	6.4	74	$6
Type	Pwr GB	06	BOS		5	4	1	98	56	4.49	1.57	284	248	327	7.6	31%	73%	4.43	57	17	26	4.0	5.1	1.3	12%	0.9	0.8	19	$4
Health	A	07	BOS		7	11	0	135	77	5.14	1.50	284	260	300	17.5	31%	66%	4.47	54	16	30	3.4	5.1	1.5	10%	0.9	-10.6	32	$5
PT/Exp	C	08	2TM		1	5	0	55	51	5.10	1.85	321	374	270	5.0	40%	73%	3.88	53	27	21	4.6	8.4	1.8	14%	0.8	-5.4	57	($1)
Consist	A	1st Half			0	2	0	20	16	7.20	2.25	355			6.5	43%	64%	4.69	58	25	17	6.3	7.2	1.1	0%	0.0	-7.1	-5	($3)
LIMA Plan	D+	2nd Half			1	3	0	35	35	3.89	1.61	300			4.4	37%	80%	3.44	49	28	23	3.6	9.1	2.5	21%	1.3	1.8	92	$1
+/- Score	33	09	Proj		3	4	0	68	54	4.24	1.49	276			6.0	33%	73%	3.81	53	22	25	3.7	7.1	1.9	12%	0.8	4.8	60	$4

Move to ATL was just what the doctor ordered, as he flashed skills of old in 2nd half. Keeps making noise about wanting to start, but recent-year skills far better as RP. Still has profile to help in setup role on right team.

Tejeda,Robinson

		Yr	Tm		W	L	Sv	IP	K	ERA	WHIP	OBA	vL	vR	BF/G	H%	S%	xERA	G	L	F	Ctl	Dom	Cmd	hr/f	hr/9	RAR	BPV	R$
RH	Reliever	04	aa		8	14	0	150	117	5.52	1.46	273			24.3	30%	66%	5.22				3.6	7.0	2.0		1.6	-21.7	35	$5
Age	27	05	PHI	*	6	3	0	113	96	3.34	1.36	220	210	226	15.6	28%	75%	4.80	36	21	43	5.1	7.6	1.5	4%	0.4	12.7	14	$10
Type	Pwr xFB	06	TEX	*	11	7	0	153	108	4.52	1.56	271	331	250	23.7	30%	74%	5.27	37	18	45	4.6	6.3	1.4	10%	1.2	0.6	6	$9
Health	A	07	TEX	*	6	12	0	114	84	7.49	1.96	313	317	264	23.1	35%	62%	6.25	35	14	51	6.1	6.7	1.1	9%	1.3	-41.8	-31	($7)
PT/Exp	D	08	2AL	*	3	3	1	78	74	3.49	1.12	191	225	115	8.1	24%	70%	4.18	33	20	47	4.1	8.5	2.1	7%	0.7	8.3	53	$10
Consist	D	1st Half			1	1	1	42	36	3.53	1.17	210			10.7	25%	71%	4.49	24	28	48	3.8	7.7	2.0	6%	0.7	4.2	39	$5
LIMA Plan	C+	2nd Half			2	2	0	37	38	3.44	1.07	169			6.3	22%	69%	3.92	35	18	47	4.4	9.3	2.1	7%	0.7	4.1	62	$5
+/- Score	-43	09	Proj		3	4	0	64	56	4.68	1.45	257			9.9	30%	71%	4.70	35	17	48	4.3	7.9	1.9	10%	1.3	-2.2	41	$4

2-2, 3.97 ERA in 45 IP at 2AL. Solid for two of three months at KC, but H% made season look better than it was. Still has that power arm, but shaky Ctl (which spiked again in Sept) & extreme FB% make for a volatile mix.

Thompson,Brad

		Yr	Tm		W	L	Sv	IP	K	ERA	WHIP	OBA	vL	vR	BF/G	H%	S%	xERA	G	L	F	Ctl	Dom	Cmd	hr/f	hr/9	RAR	BPV	R$
RH	Reliever	04	a/a		9	2	0	87	59	3.31	1.13	253			22.0	28%	75%	3.56				1.6	6.1	3.9		1.0	11.1	93	$12
Age	27	05	STL	*	6	1	1	68	39	3.04	1.19	235	224	228	5.7	26%	77%	3.77	58	17	25	2.9	5.1	1.8	11%	0.8	10.2	50	$8
Type	Con GB	06	STL	*	3	2	0	98	61	3.11	1.28	265	284	256	7.3	30%	77%	3.67	55	21	24	2.4	5.6	2.3	9%	0.6	16.7	69	$8
Health	B	07	STL		8	6	0	129	53	4.73	1.52	301	343	267	13.1	30%	74%	4.91	49	17	34	2.8	3.7	1.3	15%	1.6	-4.9	19	$5
PT/Exp	C	08	STL	*	7	4	0	77	35	5.94	1.57	315	279	303	11.9	33%	63%	4.62	51	20	29	2.5	4.1	1.6	12%	1.1	-15.9	34	$1
Consist	B	1st Half			2	3	0	35	17	6.39	1.83	344			16.6	36%	67%	4.88	56	15	29	3.2	4.3	1.4	14%	1.4	-9.1	25	($2)
LIMA Plan	C+	2nd Half			5	1	0	42	18	5.57	1.36	288			9.5	30%	58%	4.38	48	23	29	1.9	3.9	2.0	9%	0.9	-6.7	44	$2
+/- Score	31	09	Proj		4	4	0	64	31	4.54	1.46	295			10.7	31%	71%	4.46	51	19	29	2.6	4.4	1.7	11%	1.0	-0.9	39	$3

6-3, 5.15 ERA in 65 IP at STL. Being punished at ML level due to lack of a strikeout pitch. GB profile still strong, but subject to whims of fortune with this K rate. Elbow pain may have played a role; hope for return of 5.6 Dom.

Thornton,Matt

		Yr	Tm		W	L	Sv	IP	K	ERA	WHIP	OBA	vL	vR	BF/G	H%	S%	xERA	G	L	F	Ctl	Dom	Cmd	hr/f	hr/9	RAR	BPV	R$
LH	Reliever	04	SEA	*	8	7	0	115	93	5.63	1.93	286	300	225	16.0	35%	69%	5.97	40	20	40	7.2	7.3	1.0	4%	0.5	-17.0	-45	($1)
Age	32	05	SEA		0	4	0	57	57	5.21	1.68	251	262	235	4.8	28%	76%	4.84	43	15	42	6.6	9.0	1.4	20%	2.1	-5.9	4	($0)
Type	Pwr	06	CHW		5	3	2	54	49	3.33	1.24	232	211	240	3.6	28%	76%	3.61	49	19	32	3.5	8.2	2.3	10%	0.8	8.2	80	$8
Health	A	07	CHW		4	4	2	56	55	4.80	1.51	271	283	260	3.7	35%	68%	3.98	47	19	34	4.2	8.8	2.1	7%	0.6	-2.0	71	$5
PT/Exp	C	08	CHW		5	3	1	67	77	2.67	1.00	202	170	218	3.6	28%	76%	2.57	53	20	27	2.5	10.3	4.1	11%	0.7	13.9	148	$12
Consist	B	1st Half			4	1	1	32	40	2.27	0.82	160			3.5	23%	75%	2.16	53	22	25	2.6	11.4	4.4	12%	0.6	8.1	167	$8
LIMA Plan	B+	2nd Half			1	2	0	36	37	3.03	1.15	236			3.6	31%	76%	2.96	53	18	29	2.5	9.4	3.7	11%	0.8	5.8	131	$4
+/- Score	12	09	Proj		5	4	0	73	75	3.60	1.24	233			3.8	30%	73%	3.31	50	19	31	3.5	9.3	2.7	10%	0.7	9.9	102	$9

Unexplained surprises are why we love this game. In 74 appearances, he was scored upon only 17 times, and allowed more than 1 run only twice. Those two multi-run outings... are when he was on my roster.

Timlin,Mike

		Yr	Tm		W	L	Sv	IP	K	ERA	WHIP	OBA	vL	vR	BF/G	H%	S%	xERA	G	L	F	Ctl	Dom	Cmd	hr/f	hr/9	RAR	BPV	R$
RH	Reliever	04	BOS		5	4	1	76	56	4.14	1.24	259	269	247	4.2	30%	69%	3.63	50	21	29	2.2	6.6	2.9	12%	0.9	2.7	86	$7
Age	43	05	BOS		7	3	13	80	59	2.25	1.32	276	296	257	4.2	33%	83%	3.84	45	27	29	2.2	6.6	3.0	3%	0.2	21.0	81	$15
Type	Con	06	BOS		6	6	9	64	30	4.36	1.47	302	306	303	4.1	32%	72%	5.01	40	21	39	2.3	4.2	1.9	8%	1.0	1.6	33	$7
Health	D	07	BOS	*	2	1	1	64	34	3.72	1.18	243	173	274	4.5	26%	72%	4.75	39	16	45	2.4	4.8	2.0	8%	1.0	6.1	37	$6
PT/Exp	D	08	BOS		4	4	1	49	32	5.66	1.62	301	337	269	4.8	32%	69%	4.88	44	18	38	3.7	5.8	1.6	14%	1.6	-8.0	28	$1
Consist	A	1st Half			3	3	1	22	12	7.05	1.84	322			4.3	35%	62%	5.45	48	17	35	4.6	5.0	1.1	11%	1.2	-7.2	-8	$0
LIMA Plan	C	2nd Half			1	1	0	28	20	4.57	1.45	285			5.2	30%	76%	4.45	40	20	40	2.9	6.5	2.2	17%	2.0	-0.7	56	$1
+/- Score	-19	09	Proj		2	4	0	44	24	4.76	1.49	285			4.6	30%	71%	4.99	42	19	39	3.3	5.0	1.5	10%	1.2	-3.1	20	$1

And the decline accelerates. H% in '07 predictably regressed, and skills were no better. Bottom line: there are SO many better ways to spend your last buck. Like dollar beverage night. Or 1/4 of a ballpark hot dog.

Tomko,Brett

		Yr	Tm		W	L	Sv	IP	K	ERA	WHIP	OBA	vL	vR	BF/G	H%	S%	xERA	G	L	F	Ctl	Dom	Cmd	hr/f	hr/9	RAR	BPV	R$
RH	Reliever	04	SF		11	7	0	194	108	4.04	1.34	264	294	233	25.8	29%	72%	4.69	42	21	37	3.0	5.0	1.7	8%	0.9	5.4	30	$12
Age	36	05	SF		8	15	1	190	114	4.50	1.38	277	282	264	24.8	30%	69%	4.64	40	22	38	2.7	5.4	2.0	8%	0.9	-5.9	42	$9
Type		06	LA		8	7	0	112	76	4.74	1.36	280	300	258	10.9	31%	69%	4.56	37	18	45	2.3	6.1	2.6	10%	1.4	-3.4	62	$8
Health	C	07	2NL		4	12	0	131	105	5.55	1.50	287	276	291	14.5	33%	65%	4.40	41	20	39	3.3	7.2	2.2	11%	1.2	-18.2	60	$2
PT/Exp	B	08	2TM		2	7	0	70	49	6.30	1.44	296	283	298	13.9	33%	58%	4.25	44	19	37	2.3	6.3	2.7	13%	1.4	-17.2	73	$0
Consist	A	1st Half			2	7	0	64	43	6.78	1.51	311			15.7	34%	56%	4.22	45	21	34	2.1	6.1	2.9	15%	1.6	-19.5	75	($1)
LIMA Plan	B	2nd Half			0	0	0	6	6	1.43	0.79	101			5.8	15%	80%	4.48	27	0	73	4.3	8.6	2.0	0%	0.0	2.2	43	$1
+/- Score	78	09	Proj		2	3	0	40	27	4.56	1.37	279			11.3	31%	69%	4.36	41	20	39	2.5	6.2	2.5	10%	1.1	0.1	62	$2

The most manic player box ever. BPIs truly getting better every year. But things presumably out of his control (S%, H%, hr/f) are all skidding, well, out of control. The results are what teams see; he may not get another shot.

Torres,Salomon

		Yr	Tm		W	L	Sv	IP	K	ERA	WHIP	OBA	vL	vR	BF/G	H%	S%	xERA	G	L	F	Ctl	Dom	Cmd	hr/f	hr/9	RAR	BPV	R$
RH	Reliever	04	PIT		7	7	3	92	62	2.64	1.18	251	254	257	4.5	29%	80%	3.43	59	15	26	2.2	6.1	2.8	8%	0.6	18.4	88	$11
Age	37	05	PIT		5	5	3	94	55	2.77	1.19	222	272	189	5.0	25%	79%	4.33	51	16	34	3.4	5.3	1.5	7%	0.7	17.1	30	$11
Type	GB	06	PIT		3	6	12	93	72	3.29	1.46	272	281	269	4.3	33%	78%	3.87	55	19	26	3.7	7.0	1.9	8%	0.6	13.8	59	$10
Health	B	07	PIT		2	4	12	53	45	5.46	1.40	277	275	278	4.1	33%	63%	3.82	48	19	34	2.9	7.7	2.6	13%	1.2	-6.8	86	$6
PT/Exp	B	08	MIL		7	5	28	80	51	3.49	1.35	250	258	250	4.8	28%	75%	3.96	56	20	24	3.7	5.7	1.5	10%	0.7	7.7	37	$17
Consist	A	1st Half			4	1	13	45	30	2.62	1.28	236			4.9	27%	81%	3.79	55	23	23	3.6	6.0	1.7	10%	0.6	9.1	43	$10
LIMA Plan	D	2nd Half			3	4	15	35	21	4.59	1.44	266			4.7	30%	69%	4.17	58	17	25	3.8	5.4	1.4	10%	0.8	-1.4	29	$7
+/- Score	-26	09	Proj																										

Before he decided to retire, this note contained reasons why he was primed to drop off in 2009. The media focused on his 28 saves and wondered why. We congratulate him for going out when it could get no better.

Troncoso,Ramon

		Yr	Tm		W	L	Sv	IP	K	ERA	WHIP	OBA	vL	vR	BF/G	H%	S%	xERA	G	L	F	Ctl	Dom	Cmd	hr/f	hr/9	RAR	BPV	R$
RH	Reliever	04			0	0	0	0	0	0.00	0.00																		
Age	26	05			0	0	0	0	0	0.00	0.00																		
Type	xGB	06			0	0	0	0	0	0.00	0.00																		
Health	A	07	aa		7	3	7	52	32	3.83	1.54	294			6.6	34%	75%	4.72				3.3	5.6	1.7		0.5	4.1	49	$7
PT/Exp	F	08	LA	*	5	1	0	68	52	5.16	1.74	317	254	278	5.9	38%	69%	3.71	61	22	18	3.9	6.9	1.8	8%	0.4	-7.5	57	$1
Consist	C	1st Half			4	0	0	41	25	5.92	2.09	349			6.3	40%	69%	4.39	63	22	15	5.2	5.5	1.1	5%	0.2	-8.4	1	($2)
LIMA Plan	B+	2nd Half			1	1	0	27	27	4.00	1.22	262			5.3	34%	68%	2.53	60	21	19	2.0	9.0	4.5	14%	0.7	0.9	146	$2
+/- Score	45	09	Proj		5	2	0	54	41	4.00	1.48	283			5.9	33%	74%	3.40	60	21	18	3.3	6.8	2.1	13%	0.7	6.3	71	$4

1-1, 4.26 ERA in 38 IP at LA. Extreme groundballer skipped Triple-A, but was sent down after poor April. Called up in 2H with less fanfare, and showed true skills. 2H Dom not his norm, but that GB rate is. A LIMA sleeper.

ROD TRUESDELL

Valverde,Jose

	Yr	Tm	W	L	Sv	IP	K	ERA	WHIP	OBA	vL	vR	BF/G	H%	S%	xERA	G	L	F	Ctl	Dom	Cmd	hr/f	hr/9	RAR	BPV	R$
RH Reliever	04	ARI	1	2	8	29	38	4.32	1.37	218	152	258	4.3	27%	79%	3.49	36	25	39	5.2	11.7	**2.2**	27%	2.2	-0.2	83	$5
Age 29	05	ARI	3	4	15	66	75	2.45	1.07	215	168	241	4.3	29%	80%	3.28	38	19	43	2.7	10.2	**3.8**	7%	0.7	14.6	126	$15
Type Pwr FB	06	ARI	2	3	18	49	69	5.87	1.47	265	323	192	4.9	39%	61%	3.28	35	24	41	4.0	12.6	**3.1**	12%	1.1	-8.3	132	$8
Health B	07	ARI	1	4	47	64	78	2.66	1.12	202	202	189	4.0	27%	82%	3.42	36	17	47	3.6	10.9	**3.0**	10%	1.0	14.0	112	$24
PT/Exp A	08	HOU	6	3	44	72	83	3.38	1.18	234	190	252	4.0	30%	77%	3.28	39	20	41	2.9	10.4	**3.6**	13%	1.3	8.0	126	$25
Consist A	1st Half		4	2	22	40	50	4.24	1.39	265			4.3	34%	77%	3.21	43	20	38	3.3	11.2	**3.3**	20%	1.8	0.1	131	$12
LIMA Plan C+	2nd Half		2	1	22	32	33	2.27	0.91	190			3.6	25%	78%	3.36	34	20	46	2.3	9.4	**4.1**	6%	0.6	7.8	119	$13
+/- Score 32	**09**	**Proj**	**4**	**4**	**45**	**73**	**83**	**2.73**	**1.09**	**224**			**4.0**	**30%**	**80%**	**3.23**	**37**	**20**	**43**	**2.5**	**10.3**	**4.2**	**10%**	**1.0**	**9.9**	**133**	**$26**

HOU wisely stayed with him when bad H% and hr/f luck hit, and he rewarded them in kind. Always will be a bit susceptible to the long ball, but they have to put the bat on his stuff first. He's now established as a top closer.

Vargas,Claudio

	Yr	Tm	W	L	Sv	IP	K	ERA	WHIP	OBA	vL	vR	BF/G	H%	S%	xERA	G	L	F	Ctl	Dom	Cmd	hr/f	hr/9	RAR	BPV	R$
RH Starter	04	MON	5	5	0	118	89	5.26	1.56	265	301	239	11.8	28%	73%	5.19	33	22	45	4.9	6.8	**1.4**	16%	2.0	-14.5	1	$2
Age 30	05	2NL *	11	11	0	160	124	5.10	1.44	276	268	288	23.3	31%	69%	4.54	35	23	41	3.3	6.9	**2.1**	14%	1.6	-16.8	49	$7
Type FB	06	ARI	12	10	0	167	123	4.84	1.42	282	275	272	23.4	31%	70%	4.46	40	18	42	2.8	6.6	**2.4**	12%	1.5	-7.4	61	$10
Health B	07	MIL	11	6	1	134	107	5.09	1.54	288	320	255	20.7	32%	71%	4.77	34	22	44	3.6	7.2	**2.0**	12%	1.5	-11.1	43	$7
PT/Exp B	08	NYM *	8	4	0	80	46	6.15	1.73	325	323	178	19.6	35%	66%	4.91	49	17	34	3.3	5.2	**1.6**	11%	1.3	-18.5	30	($0)
Consist A	1st Half		4	3	0	48	27	5.44	1.39	287			15.9	31%	62%	4.38	49	17	34	2.3	5.1	**2.2**	10%	1.0	-6.9	55	$2
LIMA Plan C	2nd Half		4	1	0	32	19	7.21	2.23	375			27.5	40%	70%					4.8	5.3	**1.1**		1.6	-11.6	-13	($2)
+/- Score 13	**09**	**Proj**	**4**	**2**	**0**	**40**	**23**	**5.01**	**1.57**	**292**			**19.7**	**31%**	**71%**	**5.19**	**39**	**20**	**41**	**3.6**	**5.2**	**1.4**	**11%**	**1.4**	**-4.1**	**13**	**$2**

3-2, 4.62 ERA in 37 IP at NYM. Another step back. Pitched poorly with NYM, even worse in minors, then went down with a sore elbow in Aug. 30-year-old journeyman with marginal skills AND a bad arm? Sign me up!

Vazquez,Javier

	Yr	Tm	W	L	Sv	IP	K	ERA	WHIP	OBA	vL	vR	BF/G	H%	S%	xERA	G	L	F	Ctl	Dom	Cmd	hr/f	hr/9	RAR	BPV	R$
RH Starter	04	NYY	14	10	0	198	150	4.91	1.29	259	253	256	26.0	28%	66%	4.29	39	18	43	2.7	6.8	**2.5**	13%	1.5	-11.6	66	$15
Age 32	05	ARI	11	15	0	215	192	4.43	1.25	269	244	285	27.2	31%	70%	3.46	43	23	34	1.9	8.0	**4.2**	16%	1.5	-5.0	114	$17
Type Pwr FB	06	CHW	11	12	0	202	184	4.85	1.30	265	256	261	25.8	32%	64%	3.86	40	20	41	2.5	8.2	**3.3**	10%	1.0	-7.3	98	$17
Health A	07	CHW	15	8	0	217	213	3.74	1.14	244	230	253	27.5	30%	72%	3.52	40	17	43	2.1	8.8	**4.3**	11%	1.2	20.5	121	$28
PT/Exp A	08	CHW	12	16	0	208	200	4.67	1.32	267	259	266	26.8	33%	67%	3.84	38	20	42	2.6	8.6	**3.3**	10%	1.1	-8.2	101	$17
Consist A	1st Half		7	6	0	106	104	4.49	1.39	279			27.0	34%	70%	3.97	35	23	43	2.7	8.8	**3.3**	10%	1.1	-1.8	98	$9
LIMA Plan B	2nd Half		5	10	0	102	96	4.85	1.25	254			26.6	31%	63%	3.71	42	17	40	2.6	8.5	**3.3**	10%	1.1	-6.4	104	$8
+/- Score 38	**09**	**Proj**	**15**	**10**	**0**	**203**	**191**	**4.03**	**1.21**	**249**			**26.2**	**30%**	**70%**	**3.70**	**40**	**19**	**41**	**2.4**	**8.5**	**3.5**	**10%**	**1.1**	**18.0**	**104**	**$23**

Anatomy of "underperforming":
Situation OOPS - Rel. to ML
Bases empty .714 - 6% better
Runners on .818 - 12% worse
Hence S% issues, multi-run HR. Same 4 of last 5 years, so it's the 800 lb. gorilla in the room.

Veras,Jose

	Yr	Tm	W	L	Sv	IP	K	ERA	WHIP	OBA	vL	vR	BF/G	H%	S%	xERA	G	L	F	Ctl	Dom	Cmd	hr/f	hr/9	RAR	BPV	R$
RH Reliever	04	a/a	7	6	0	94	60	6.70	1.82	327			13.5	36%	63%	6.43				4.0	5.7	**1.4**		1.1	-27.3	22	($3)
Age 28	05	aaa	3	5	24	61	62	4.26	1.63	286			4.9	37%	74%	4.81				4.6	9.1	**2.0**		0.6	0.3	77	$10
Type Pwr FB	06	aaa	5	3	21	59	55	3.07	1.31	256			5.0	32%	78%	3.60				3.1	8.4	**2.7**		0.6	10.6	93	$15
Health A	07	NYY	0	0	2	9	7	5.81	1.40	186			4.5	24%	54%	5.42	41	19	41	6.8	6.8	**1.0**	0%	0.0	-1.5	-42	$1
PT/Exp F	08	NYY *	5	3	9	71	80	3.33	1.34	236	217	254	4.1	31%	79%	3.72	41	18	41	4.2	10.2	**2.4**	11%	1.0	8.9	88	$12
Consist D	1st Half		2	0	9	38	40	2.62	1.14	220			4.2	28%	82%	3.64	36	19	44	3.1	9.4	**3.0**	9%	1.0	8.2	100	$9
LIMA Plan B	2nd Half		3	3	0	32	40	4.17	1.57	253			4.0	34%	77%	3.83	45	17	38	5.6	11.1	**2.0**	13%	1.1	0.7	73	$3
+/- Score 7	**09**	**Proj**	**5**	**4**	**0**	**68**	**70**	**3.97**	**1.38**	**247**			**4.7**	**31%**	**74%**	**3.95**	**41**	**18**	**40**	**4.1**	**9.3**	**2.3**	**11%**	**1.1**	**4.0**	**75**	**$7**

5-3, 3.59 ERA in 58 IP at NYY.
PRO: Showed he still has power stuff, moved up the NYY pecking order as the season progressed
CON: Poor Ctl almost cancels out flashy Dom
A work in progress, with upside.

Verlander,Justin

	Yr	Tm	W	L	Sv	IP	K	ERA	WHIP	OBA	vL	vR	BF/G	H%	S%	xERA	G	L	F	Ctl	Dom	Cmd	hr/f	hr/9	RAR	BPV	R$
RH Starter	04		0	0	0	0	0	0.00	0.00																		
Age 26	05	DET *	2	2	0	43	35	2.08	0.88	181			18.2	22%	78%	1.40				2.3	7.3	**3.2**		0.4	12.2	117	$8
Type Pwr FB	06	DET	17	9	0	186	124	3.63	1.33	263	279	253	26.3	29%	76%	4.33	42	23	35	2.9	6.0	**2.1**	10%	1.0	21.3	49	$21
Health A	07	DET	18	6	0	202	183	3.66	1.23	241	232	234	26.2	29%	73%	3.85	41	19	40	3.0	8.2	**2.7**	9%	0.9	21.1	85	$26
PT/Exp A	08	DET	11	17	0	201	163	4.84	1.40	256	254	254	26.3	30%	66%	4.56	40	18	42	3.9	7.3	**1.9**	7%	0.8	-12.1	44	$12
Consist B	1st Half		4	9	0	108	78	4.42	1.32	243			27.0	28%	68%	4.66	42	15	44	3.8	6.5	**1.7**	7%	0.8	-0.9	35	$7
LIMA Plan C	2nd Half		7	8	0	93	85	5.32	1.49	270			25.7	33%	64%	4.43	38	21	41	4.1	8.2	**2.0**	7%	0.8	-11.2	54	$5
+/- Score 9	**09**	**Proj**	**14**	**13**	**0**	**203**	**168**	**3.95**	**1.31**	**248**			**25.2**	**29%**	**72%**	**4.21**	**40**	**19**	**40**	**3.4**	**7.4**	**2.2**	**9%**	**0.9**	**5.4**	**61**	**$20**

Dodged the workload-spike burnout in '07; maybe this was it. In-season "dead arm" talk adds credence. Ctl issues not the norm either. Clearly young enough to rebound... a chance to buy low? Yes, but not risk-free.

Villanueva,Carlos

	Yr	Tm	W	L	Sv	IP	K	ERA	WHIP	OBA	vL	vR	BF/G	H%	S%	xERA	G	L	F	Ctl	Dom	Cmd	hr/f	hr/9	RAR	BPV	R$
RH Reliever	04		0	0	0	0	0	0.00	0.00																		
Age 25	05	aa	1	3	0	21	13	8.14	1.57	280			23.6	29%	48%	5.66				4.3	5.6	**1.3**		1.7	-9.9	8	($1)
Type Pwr	06	MIL *	13	8	0	181	146	4.22	1.22	246	226	204	23.5	28%	69%	4.01	43	16	41	2.7	7.2	**2.7**	11%	1.1	6.0	77	$18
Health A	07	MIL	8	5	1	114	99	3.94	1.35	239	250	227	8.3	28%	75%	4.56	36	17	47	4.2	7.8	**1.9**	11%	1.3	6.9	42	$11
PT/Exp C	08	MIL	4	7	1	108	93	4.07	1.31	268	227	300	9.7	31%	75%	3.68	47	19	35	2.5	7.7	**3.1**	16%	1.5	2.6	96	$8
Consist B	1st Half		3	5	0	68	50	5.40	1.46	293			14.3	32%	69%	4.19	46	18	37	2.6	6.6	**2.5**	17%	1.8	-9.5	71	$1
LIMA Plan B+	2nd Half		1	2	1	40	43	1.80	1.05	221			6.1	29%	89%	2.84	49	20	31	2.2	9.7	**4.3**	13%	0.9	12.2	140	$6
+/- Score 41	**09**	**Proj**	**4**	**4**	**8**	**73**	**66**	**3.58**	**1.25**	**246**			**8.9**	**29%**	**76%**	**3.81**	**43**	**18**	**39**	**3.0**	**8.1**	**2.8**	**11%**	**1.1**	**4.7**	**87**	**$10**

Excelled after moving to pen: 2H BPIs are representative of his season-total relief skills. Has he found his new niche? With the incumbent MIL closer looking tenuous at best...
UP: 30 Saves

Villarreal,Oscar

	Yr	Tm	W	L	Sv	IP	K	ERA	WHIP	OBA	vL	vR	BF/G	H%	S%	xERA	G	L	F	Ctl	Dom	Cmd	hr/f	hr/9	RAR	BPV	R$
RH Reliever	04	ARI *	0	4	0	29	28	9.93	2.03	365	250	400	6.2	43%	51%	4.68	29	35	35	3.7	8.7	**2.3**	17%	1.9	-20.3	63	($5)
Age 27	05	ARI *	2	3	0	31	12	5.52	1.35	262	207	278	5.8	27%	59%	5.36	33	29	38	3.2	3.5	**1.1**	7%	0.9	-4.9	-12	$1
Type	06	ATL	9	1	0	92	55	3.62	1.30	264	264	259	6.7	28%	78%	4.27	47	19	34	2.6	5.4	**2.0**	13%	1.3	9.9	50	$10
Health A	07	ATL	2	2	1	76	58	4.25	1.40	258	315	220	6.5	31%	70%	4.29	44	23	33	3.8	6.8	**1.8**	8%	0.7	1.7	44	$4
PT/Exp C	08	HOU *	2	4	1	61	38	5.46	1.59	283	258	306	6.4	28%	74%	5.19	41	17	43	4.3	5.6	**1.3**	19%	2.4	-8.9	4	($0)
Consist A	1st Half		1	3	0	37	21	4.90	1.53	284			4.8	26%	82%	5.07	40	17	43	3.7	5.1	**1.4**	23%	2.9	-2.9	12	$0
LIMA Plan C	2nd Half		1	1	1	24	17	6.30	1.69	283			12.4	31%	65%	4.53	67	0	33	5.2	6.3	**1.2**	15%	1.5	-6.1	18	($0)
+/- Score 1	**09**	**Proj**	**2**	**2**	**0**	**40**	**25**	**4.78**	**1.52**	**274**			**7.0**	**29%**	**72%**	**4.94**	**42**	**21**	**37**	**4.1**	**5.7**	**1.4**	**13%**	**1.4**	**-2.9**	**12**	**$1**

1-3, 5.02 ERA in 38 IP at HOU. Astros released him 3 months into a two-year deal. He's never had an xERA under 4, so the release was probably the better move. Signed with COL, so now you KNOW you don't want him.

Villone,Ron

	Yr	Tm	W	L	Sv	IP	K	ERA	WHIP	OBA	vL	vR	BF/G	H%	S%	xERA	G	L	F	Ctl	Dom	Cmd	hr/f	hr/9	RAR	BPV	R$
LH Reliever	04	SEA	8	6	0	117	86	4.08	1.42	236	203	247	9.1	27%	73%	5.04	38	19	43	4.9	6.6	**1.3**	8%	0.9	5.1	2	$8
Age 39	05	2TM	5	5	1	64	70	4.08	1.44	240	222	258	3.5	32%	72%	3.87	43	22	35	4.9	9.8	**2.0**	7%	0.6	1.8	66	$6
Type Pwr FB	06	NYY	3	3	0	80	72	5.06	1.57	249	179	289	5.1	30%	69%	5.24	31	21	48	5.7	8.1	**1.4**	8%	1.0	-4.9	-0	$3
Health A	07	NYY	0	0	0	42	25	4.26	1.28	232			4.8	25%	69%	4.99	37	19	43	3.8	5.3	**1.4**	9%	1.1	1.3	8	$2
PT/Exp D	08	STL	1	2	1	50	50	4.68	1.64	242	176	300	3.1	31%	72%	4.96	38	22	40	6.7	9.0	**1.4**	7%	0.7	-2.5	-2	$1
Consist A	1st Half		1	2	0	31	30	5.57	1.79	270			4.3	35%	68%	5.18	36	26	38	6.7	8.8	**1.3**	6%	0.6	-4.9	-9	($1)
LIMA Plan C	2nd Half		0	0	1	19	20	3.26	1.40	193			2.1	24%	80%	4.62	40	15	45	6.5	9.3	**1.4**	9%	0.9	2.4	10	$2
+/- Score -60	**09**	**Proj**	**1**	**2**	**0**	**44**	**38**	**4.97**	**1.54**	**241**			**3.5**	**29%**	**69%**	**5.03**	**37**	**20**	**43**	**5.8**	**7.9**	**1.4**	**9%**	**1.0**	**-3.7**	**0**	**$1**

He's not only a lefty with a pulse, he throws hard. So he has GMs willing to pay for this year after year. His BEST ERA in the last DECADE was 4.08. And he makes half a mil per. Dads, put the ball in Junior's left hand.

Vizcaino,Luis

	Yr	Tm	W	L	Sv	IP	K	ERA	WHIP	OBA	vL	vR	BF/G	H%	S%	xERA	G	L	F	Ctl	Dom	Cmd	hr/f	hr/9	RAR	BPV	R$
RH Reliever	04	MIL	4	4	1	72	63	3.75	1.18	231	163	290	4.0	26%	75%	4.14	35	17	48	3.0	7.9	**2.6**	12%	1.5	4.5	74	$8
Age 34	05	CHW	6	5	0	70	43	3.73	1.47	273	330	242	4.7	30%	78%	4.82	43	21	36	3.7	5.5	**1.5**	10%	1.0	5.6	20	$5
Type Pwr xFB	06	ARI	4	6	0	65	72	3.59	1.23	217	163	256	3.9	28%	75%	3.42	45	19	36	4.0	10.0	**2.5**	14%	1.1	7.2	94	$8
Health C	07	NYY	8	2	0	75	62	4.30	1.45	237	265	213	4.3	29%	71%	5.02	36	19	45	5.1	7.4	**1.4**	6%	0.7	1.9	8	$7
PT/Exp C	08	COL	1	2	0	46	49	5.28	1.46	270	372	170	4.7	32%	70%	4.17	33	18	50	3.7	9.6	**2.6**	16%	2.0	-5.7	83	$1
Consist C	1st Half		0	0	0	10	7	9.28	2.27	354			4.6	35%	67%	7.22	21	18	62	6.5	6.5	**1.0**	18%	3.7	-6.0	-60	($2)
LIMA Plan B	2nd Half		1	2	0	36	42	4.21	1.24	244			4.7	31%	72%	3.46	37	18	45	3.0	10.4	**3.5**	14%	1.5	0.2	122	$3
+/- Score 30	**09**	**Proj**	**4**	**4**	**0**	**64**	**61**	**4.11**	**1.31**	**238**			**4.3**	**29%**	**72%**	**4.27**	**34**	**18**	**48**	**3.8**	**8.6**	**2.3**	**10%**	**1.1**	**0.6**	**64**	**$6**

Troubles abound. Missed most of 1st half with shoulder trouble, then had hr/f trouble with COL, and legal trouble in Oct (DUI arrest). Skills were great in 2H, though; if he stays out of trouble, fairly safe end-game LIMA pick.

ROD TRUESDELL

Volquez,Edinson

Volquez,Edinson		Yr	W	L	Sv	IP	K	ERA	WHIP	OBA	vL	vR	BF/G	H%	S%	xERA	G	L	F	Ctl	Dom	Cmd	hr/f	hr/9	RAR	BPV	R$
RH	Starter	04	0	0	0	0	0	0.00	0.00																		
Age	25	05 TEX *	1	9	0	72	53	6.88	1.68	316			20.7	36%	60%	6.13				3.4	6.6	2.0		1.4	-22.2	31	($3)
Type	Pwr	06 TEX *	7	12	0	153	127	5.40	1.68	273			24.3	32%	70%	5.23				5.6	7.5	1.3		1.2	-16.0	36	$3
Health	A	07 TEX *	16	3	0	143	133	3.72	1.25	233	222	299	23.9	28%	73%	3.99	38	22	40	3.6	8.3	2.3	10%	1.0	13.9	69	$20
PT/Exp	B	08 CIN	17	6	0	196	206	3.21	1.33	232	248	214	25.2	31%	77%	3.66	46	20	34	4.3	9.5	2.2	8%	0.6	25.5	79	$23
Consist	B	1st Half	10	3	0	99	110	2.08	1.21	205			24.1	29%	84%	3.28	51	19	30	4.4	10.0	2.3	5%	0.4	26.8	91	$16
LIMA Plan	D+	2nd Half	7	3	0	97	96	4.37	1.45	258			26.4	32%	72%	4.04	42	20	38	4.2	8.9	2.1	10%	0.9	-1.2	68	$7
+/- Score	15	09 Proj	14	11	0	203	203	4.08	1.38	245			24.3	31%	72%	3.87	44	20	36	4.2	9.0	2.1	10%	0.9	11.7	71	$17

Season totals are misleading: xERA, S% show some 1H luck. 2H skills much like '07 - that's your baseline. Overall growth real -- so is its uneven nature. At 25, don't expect linear gains; a short-term step back is likely.

Volstad,Chris

Volstad,Chris		Yr	W	L	Sv	IP	K	ERA	WHIP	OBA	vL	vR	BF/G	H%	S%	xERA	G	L	F	Ctl	Dom	Cmd	hr/f	hr/9	RAR	BPV	R$
RH	Starter	04	0	0	0	0	0	0.00	0.00																		
Age	22	05	0	0	0	0	0	0.00	0.00																		
Type	GB	06	0	0	0	0	0	0.00	0.00																		
Health	A	07 aa	4	2	0	42	23	3.63	1.33	279			25.6	30%	75%	4.26				2.1	4.9	2.3		0.9	4.4	51	$4
PT/Exp	D	08 FLA *	10	8	0	175	102	3.39	1.36	258	243	236	25.0	30%	73%	4.33	53	18	29	3.4	5.2	1.5	2%	0.2	19.1	33	$13
Consist	A	1st Half	4	3	0	85	47	3.81	1.38	269			26.1	31%	69%					3.1	5.0	1.6		0.0	4.8	65	$5
LIMA Plan	C	2nd Half	6	5	0	90	55	2.99	1.35	248			24.1	29%	77%	4.32	53	18	29	3.8	5.5	1.4	4%	0.3	14.3	28	$8
+/- Score	-25	09 Proj	10	7	0	140	79	4.06	1.39	267			25.1	30%	72%	4.32	53	18	29	3.3	5.1	1.5	8%	0.7	0.4	34	$9

6-5, 2.88 ERA in 84 IP at FLA. Why he's not there yet:
- Subpar Cmd
- Miniscule hr/f
- He's only 22

Has a future, but don't pay for an ERA less than 4.00 in '09.

Wade,Cory

Wade,Cory		Yr	W	L	Sv	IP	K	ERA	WHIP	OBA	vL	vR	BF/G	H%	S%	xERA	G	L	F	Ctl	Dom	Cmd	hr/f	hr/9	RAR	BPV	R$
RH	Reliever	04	0	0	0	0	0	0.00	0.00																		
Age	25	05	0	0	0	0	0	0.00	0.00																		
Type		06	0	0	0	0	0	0.00	0.00																		
Health	A	07 aa	0	1	0	33	25	1.93	1.28	240			9.9	28%	88%	3.41				3.5	6.7	1.9		0.6	10.3	68	$3
PT/Exp	F	08 LA *	2	1	1	86	62	2.83	0.98	219	211	194	5.5	24%	77%	3.66	41	21	38	1.7	6.5	3.8	11%	1.1	15.2	90	$10
Consist	A	1st Half	0	1	1	45	30	3.36	1.10	255			5.9	28%	74%	3.84	39	25	36	1.2	5.9	4.9	10%	1.1	5.1	90	$4
LIMA Plan	B+	2nd Half	2	0	0	40	32	2.23	0.84	174			5.1	19%	83%	3.47	43	18	39	2.2	7.1	3.2	12%	1.1	10.1	89	$7
+/- Score	2	09 Proj	1	1	0	69	52	3.42	1.09	237			6.7	27%	73%	3.77	41	21	38	2.0	6.8	3.5	10%	1.1	4.8	89	$6

2-1, 2.27 ERA in 71 IP at LA. Another pitcher likely to be overvalued. Hit rate is certain to regress, meaning an ERA spike. Cmd is solid, so won't fall far. But as we often advise, use xERA as your benchmark.

Waechter,Doug

Waechter,Doug		Yr	W	L	Sv	IP	K	ERA	WHIP	OBA	vL	vR	BF/G	H%	S%	xERA	G	L	F	Ctl	Dom	Cmd	hr/f	hr/9	RAR	BPV	R$
RH	Reliever	04 TAM *	5	9	0	99	54	6.63	1.62	279	279	216	20.5	25%	69%	6.14	29	15	56	4.8	4.9	1.0	18%	3.0	-26.9	-34	($2)
Age	28	05 TAM *	5	14	0	171	102	5.95	1.48	302	310	283	23.5	32%	64%	4.73	38	21	41	2.3	5.4	2.3	14%	1.7	-33.2	50	$1
Type	Con FB	06 TAM *	2	16	0	132	63	9.20	2.01	373	284	331	23.3	40%	52%	6.15	33	23	44	3.0	4.3	1.4	6%	1.0	-75.6	7	($17)
Health	B	07 TAM	0	0	0	0	0	0.00	0.00																		
PT/Exp	D	08 FLA *	5	2	0	74	49	4.07	1.49	293	303	216	6.5	32%	77%	4.91	32	23	44	2.9	6.0	2.1	10%	1.3	1.8	42	$4
Consist	C	1st Half	1	2	0	55	38	3.48	1.37	269			9.1	30%	79%	4.73	36	19	45	3.0	6.3	2.1	8%	1.1	5.4	45	$3
LIMA Plan	C	2nd Half	4	0	0	19	11	5.81	1.83	356			3.7	38%	73%	5.41	26	31	43	2.4	5.3	2.2	13%	1.9	-3.5	35	$1
+/- Score	-13	09 Proj	2	5	0	44	25	5.17	1.59	310			7.8	32%	72%	5.26	31	24	44	2.9	5.2	1.8	12%	1.7	-5.0	24	$0

4-2, 3.69 ERA in 64 IP at FLA, a performance that will get him overvalued. Ancient Shandler Proverb #78: It's far easier and more dangerous to overvalue a player when he has no value to begin with. Fair warning.

Wagner,Billy

Wagner,Billy		Yr	W	L	Sv	IP	K	ERA	WHIP	OBA	vL	vR	BF/G	H%	S%	xERA	G	L	F	Ctl	Dom	Cmd	hr/f	hr/9	RAR	BPV	R$
LH	Reliever	04 PHI	4	0	21	48	59	2.43	0.77	186	103	197	3.9	25%	75%	2.41	45	14	41	1.1	11.0	9.8	11%	0.9	10.9	191	$16
Age	37	05 PHI	4	3	38	77	87	1.52	0.84	171	128	173	3.9	23%	88%	2.72	46	19	35	2.3	10.1	4.4	10%	0.7	26.0	143	$28
Type	Pwr FB	06 NYM	3	2	40	72	94	2.25	1.11	225	161	234	4.2	32%	85%	2.48	53	16	31	2.6	11.7	4.5	13%	0.9	19.9	171	$25
Health	C	07 NYM	2	2	34	68	80	2.64	1.13	222	241	209	4.2	30%	80%	3.34	37	18	45	2.9	10.5	3.6	8%	0.8	15.1	126	$20
PT/Exp	A	08 NYM	0	1	27	47	52	2.30	0.89	194	220	174	4.0	26%	79%	2.99	38	20	42	1.9	10.0	5.2	8%	0.8	11.4	144	$16
Consist	B	1st Half	0	1	18	33	38	1.91	0.94	198			4.0	27%	86%	2.97	40	18	42	2.2	10.4	4.8	9%	0.8	9.6	146	$11
LIMA Plan	C	2nd Half	0	0	9	14	14	3.21	0.79	186			4.0	24%	60%	3.02	33	25	42	1.3	9.0	7.0	7%	0.6	1.8	139	$5
+/- Score	-19	09 Proj	0	0	0	15	12	3.72	1.31	255			4.4	29%	76%	4.16	40	20	41	3.1	7.4	2.4	11%	1.2	0.3	68	$1

Likely to miss all of 2009 season after TJ surgery. Still showing elite skills, so even at 38 he should get another shot in... what are we calling it? Twenty-ten? Two thousand ten? Oh-Ten? The Great Depression?

Wainwright,Adam

Wainwright,Adam		Yr	W	L	Sv	IP	K	ERA	WHIP	OBA	vL	vR	BF/G	H%	S%	xERA	G	L	F	Ctl	Dom	Cmd	hr/f	hr/9	RAR	BPV	R$
RH	Starter	04 aaa	4	4	0	63	56	5.55	1.55	288			23.5	33%	68%	5.60				3.7	8.0	2.2		1.6	-9.4	44	$2
Age	27	05 aaa	9	10	0	176	123	4.86	1.48	301			27.7	35%	68%	4.91				2.4	6.3	2.6		0.8	-12.0	63	$7
Type		06 STL	2	1	3	75	72	3.12	1.15	232	301	182	5.0	29%	75%	3.38	48	17	35	2.6	8.6	3.3	8%	0.7	12.7	110	$10
Health	C	07 STL	14	12	0	202	136	3.70	1.40	271	249	283	27.2	31%	74%	4.34	48	18	34	3.1	6.1	1.9	6%	0.6	18.1	51	$16
PT/Exp	B	08 STL	11	3	0	132	91	3.20	1.18	247	264	234	27.1	28%	76%	3.94	46	19	35	2.3	6.2	2.7	9%	0.8	17.4	73	$15
Consist	B	1st Half	6	3	0	92	62	3.14	1.09	236			28.3	26%	76%	3.75	48	18	35	2.0	6.1	3.1	10%	1.0	12.8	82	$11
LIMA Plan	C	2nd Half	5	0	0	40	29	3.35	1.39	270			24.8	32%	76%	4.39	42	22	36	3.1	6.5	2.1	4%	0.4	4.6	52	$5
+/- Score	-8	09 Proj	14	8	0	203	151	3.50	1.28	261			25.8	31%	74%	3.98	46	19	35	2.6	6.7	2.6	8%	0.8	9.0	75	$19

Only a sprained finger kept him from a big season. Stats not quite as good as skills, but he keeps besting xERA as a starter. A breakout is not far off; a few more K's a bit more health. UP: 18 wins, 3.00 ERA

Wakefield,Tim

Wakefield,Tim		Yr	W	L	Sv	IP	K	ERA	WHIP	OBA	vL	vR	BF/G	H%	S%	xERA	G	L	F	Ctl	Dom	Cmd	hr/f	hr/9	RAR	BPV	R$
RH	Starter	04 BOS	12	10	0	188	116	4.88	1.38	271	230	298	25.3	29%	68%	4.58	47	14	40	3.0	5.6	1.8	12%	1.4	-10.4	43	$10
Age	42	05 BOS	16	12	0	225	151	4.16	1.24	249	202	278	28.3	27%	72%	4.35	41	17	42	2.7	6.0	2.2	12%	1.4	5.9	55	$21
Type	xFB	06 BOS	7	11	0	140	90	4.63	1.33	255	221	265	25.9	28%	68%	4.78	39	16	44	3.3	5.8	1.8	10%	1.2	-1.2	33	$10
Health	C	07 BOS	17	12	0	189	110	4.76	1.35	264	247	276	26.0	29%	67%	4.88	39	19	42	3.0	5.2	1.7	8%	1.0	-6.0	29	$15
PT/Exp	A	08 BOS	10	11	0	181	117	4.13	1.18	232	244	218	24.8	25%	69%	4.72	36	16	49	3.0	5.8	2.0	9%	1.2	4.9	38	$16
Consist	A	1st Half	5	5	0	102	69	3.88	1.25	230			26.6	25%	74%	4.81	36	18	46	3.7	6.1	1.6	10%	1.2	5.9	23	$9
LIMA Plan	D	2nd Half	5	6	0	79	48	4.44	1.09	234			22.6	25%	63%	4.61	35	13	52	2.1	5.5	2.7	9%	1.3	-0.9	56	$8
+/- Score	-63	09 Proj	10	10	0	145	90	4.47	1.28	254			25.4	27%	69%	4.79	38	16	46	2.9	5.6	1.9	9%	1.2	-6.5	38	$12

Season to season, amazingly consistent mediocrity. But that has value, especially on a team where notching 5 or more runs per gane is not a problem. IP always at risk, but always add up. Never bet against a knuckler.

Walker,Jamie

Walker,Jamie		Yr	W	L	Sv	IP	K	ERA	WHIP	OBA	vL	vR	BF/G	H%	S%	xERA	G	L	F	Ctl	Dom	Cmd	hr/f	hr/9	RAR	BPV	R$
LH	Reliever	04 DET	3	4	1	64	53	3.22	1.26	276	200	313	3.8	32%	79%	4.02	36	20	44	1.7	7.4	4.4	9%	1.1	9.6	102	$7
Age	37	05 DET	4	3	0	48	30	3.73	1.29	265	245	271	3.1	29%	74%	4.46	41	19	40	2.4	5.6	2.3	8%	0.9	3.8	55	$5
Type	Con xFB	06 DET	0	1	0	48	37	2.81	1.15	258	238	262	3.5	28%	85%	4.13	31	20	49	1.5	6.9	4.6	11%	1.5	10.3	93	$5
Health	B	07 BAL	3	2	7	61	41	3.23	1.21	248	216	268	3.1	28%	76%	4.56	34	21	46	2.5	6.0	2.4	7%	0.9	9.6	52	$9
PT/Exp	D	08 BAL	1	3	0	38	24	6.87	1.68	331	304	352	3.0	33%	67%	5.17	36	16	49	2.6	5.7	2.2	18%	2.8	-11.8	46	($2)
Consist	B	1st Half	1	0	0	22	18	4.98	1.61	314			2.7	34%	79%	4.76	34	15	51	2.9	7.5	2.6	17%	2.5	-1.7	68	$1
LIMA Plan	D	2nd Half	0	3	0	16	6	9.39	1.78	352			3.5	32%	52%	5.74	38	16	46	2.2	3.3	1.5	20%	3.3	-10.1	16	($2)
+/- Score	31	09 Proj	1	3	0	48	28	4.50	1.52	300			3.2	31%	77%	5.18	35	18	47	2.8	5.3	1.9	12%	1.7	-4.5	32	$1

Collapsed when elbow started hurting. Dom shows he wasn't right even after DL return. Even healthy, FB% means HR, and other skills not strong enough to offset it. Too risky for limited reward.

Walker,Tyler

Walker,Tyler		Yr	W	L	Sv	IP	K	ERA	WHIP	OBA	vL	vR	BF/G	H%	S%	xERA	G	L	F	Ctl	Dom	Cmd	hr/f	hr/9	RAR	BPV	R$
RH	Reliever	04 SF *	6	2	1	78	60	3.79	1.44	282	287	288	5.6	33%	77%	4.33	42	20	38	3.0	6.9	2.3	10%	1.0	4.6	63	$6
Age	33	05 SF	6	4	23	61	54	4.26	1.55	283	284	278	4.1	33%	77%	4.44	42	18	41	4.0	7.9	2.0	12%	1.3	-0.1	55	$12
Type	Pwr	06 2TM	1	4	10	25	19	7.17	1.55	276	333	226	4.3	33%	50%	4.91	35	28	37	4.3	6.8	1.6	3%	0.4	-8.2	19	$3
Health	F	07 SF *	3	2	7	37	26	4.46	1.63	299	182	308	4.8	33%	77%	5.28	35	18	48	3.8	6.3	1.6	10%	1.4	-0.1	23	$4
PT/Exp	D	08 SF	5	8	0	53	49	4.56	1.28	238	319	186	3.4	28%	67%	3.60	48	21	31	3.5	8.3	2.3	15%	1.2	-1.9	79	$5
Consist	C	1st Half	3	3	0	33	28	4.32	1.20	242			3.7	28%	67%	3.63	45	22	33	2.7	7.6	2.8	13%	1.1	-0.2	87	$3
LIMA Plan	B	2nd Half	2	5	0	20	21	4.95	1.40	232			3.1	28%	68%	3.54	52	20	28	4.9	9.4	1.9	21%	1.3	-1.7	66	$2
+/- Score	11	09 Proj	4	5	5	44	38	3.93	1.36	264			3.8	32%	74%	3.87	44	22	34	3.1	7.9	2.5	11%	1.0	2.5	80	$6

Dom returned in second year post-TJ surgery, but a mid-season groin injury, poor S% and hr/f did in ERA. A smart team will see skills rebound & take a shot, but odds for saves or fanalytic value are slim.

ROD TRUESDELL

Wang,Chien-Ming

Wang,Chien-Ming		Yr	W	L	Sv	IP	K	ERA	WHIP	OBA	vL	vR	BF/G	H%	S%	xERA	G	L	F	Ctl	Dom	Cmd	hr/f	hr/9	RAR	BPV	R$
RH	Starter	04 a/a	11	6	0	149	102	4.23	1.34	282			26.5	33%	68%	4.12				2.1	6.1	2.9		0.6	2.0	78	$11
Age	29	05 NYY	* 10	6	0	150	65	4.21	1.30	271	258	254	26.4	29%	69%	3.81	64	14	22	2.3	3.9	1.7	11%	0.8	3.0	50	$10
Type	Con xGB	06 NYY	19	6	1	218	76	3.63	1.31	275	275	279	27.1	29%	72%	3.93	63	17	20	2.1	3.1	1.5	8%	0.5	24.9	39	$21
Health	F	07 NYY	19	7	0	199	104	3.70	1.29	261	286	242	28.0	29%	71%	3.89	58	18	23	2.7	4.7	1.8	6%	0.4	19.7	49	$21
PT/Exp	A	08 NYY	8	2	0	95	54	4.07	1.32	251	261	238	26.8	29%	68%	4.00	55	22	23	3.3	5.1	1.5	6%	0.4	3.2	36	$8
Consist	A	1st Half	8	2	0	95	54	4.07	1.32	251			26.8	29%	68%	4.00	55	22	23	3.3	5.1	1.5	6%	0.4	3.2	36	$8
LIMA Plan	C	2nd Half	0	0	0	0	0	0.00	0.00																		
+/- Score	-8	09 Proj	16	9	0	189	101	3.92	1.34	265			26.7	29%	71%	3.94	58	18	23	2.9	4.8	1.7	8%	0.6	11.2	46	$17

Most infamous foot tendon injury since Achilles' (at least in NY) should be healed by 2009. Only skills concern is slowly eroding Ctl: it was 3.2 in 2H of '07, 3.3 here. Probably too early to raise red flag yet, but bears watching.

Washburn,Jarrod

Washburn,Jarrod		Yr	W	L	Sv	IP	K	ERA	WHIP	OBA	vL	vR	BF/G	H%	S%	xERA	G	L	F	Ctl	Dom	Cmd	hr/f	hr/9	RAR	BPV	R$
LH	Starter	04 ANA	11	8	0	149	86	4.65	1.33	274	225	283	25.4	29%	68%	4.69	38	20	41	2.4	5.2	2.2	10%	1.2	-4.0	45	$10
Age	34	05 ANA	8	8	0	177	94	3.20	1.33	269	266	276	25.9	29%	80%	4.79	39	21	40	2.6	4.8	1.8	8%	1.0	25.6	33	$14
Type	Con FB	06 SEA	8	14	0	187	103	4.67	1.35	273	317	257	25.8	29%	68%	4.84	40	18	42	2.6	5.0	1.9	10%	1.2	-2.6	36	$11
Health	A	07 SEA	10	15	0	194	114	4.32	1.38	269	213	288	26.1	29%	71%	5.04	37	18	45	3.1	5.3	1.7	8%	1.1	4.4	26	$12
PT/Exp	A	08 SEA	5	14	1	154	87	4.68	1.46	286	252	299	24.0	31%	70%	5.01	36	23	41	2.9	5.1	1.7	9%	1.1	-6.4	27	$5
Consist	A	1st Half	3	7	1	84	52	5.23	1.54	302			23.5	33%	68%	4.85	38	23	38	2.9	5.6	1.9	9%	1.1	-9.2	38	$2
LIMA Plan	C	2nd Half	2	7	0	69	35	4.02	1.35	266			24.7	28%	74%	5.20	33	22	45	3.0	4.5	1.5	9%	1.2	2.8	12	$4
+/- Score	-34	09 Proj	7	14	0	174	97	4.50	1.41	279			25.1	30%	71%	5.01	37	21	43	2.9	5.0	1.7	9%	1.2	-12.6	27	$8

Strained ab muscle cut season mercifully short. In truth, skills no different than past, but he fell into the SEA undertow. Subject of trade rumors, so watch carefully. With FB style, things could really turn sour in wrong home park.

Waters,Chris

Waters,Chris		Yr	W	L	Sv	IP	K	ERA	WHIP	OBA	vL	vR	BF/G	H%	S%	xERA	G	L	F	Ctl	Dom	Cmd	hr/f	hr/9	RAR	BPV	R$
LH	Starter	04	0	0	0	0	0	0.00	0.00																		
Age	28	05	0	0	0	0	0	0.00	0.00																		
Type	Pwr	06 aa	8	14	0	155	90	7.81	2.03	331			28.4	34%	64%	7.87				5.7	5.2	0.9		2.0	-62.9	-21	($12)
Health	A	07 a/a	8	9	0	158	91	6.61	1.96	318			27.5	34%	67%	6.87				5.8	5.2	0.9		1.3	-41.8	2	($8)
PT/Exp	D	08 BAL	* 11	11	0	187	103	6.05	1.68	301	303	263	24.5	32%	65%	5.20	48	17	36	4.2	5.0	1.2	11%	1.2	-39.1	2	($1)
Consist	C	1st Half	5	5	0	87	41	7.18	1.88	333			23.2	35%	63%					4.3	4.2	1.0		1.3	-30.4	-6	($5)
LIMA Plan	F	2nd Half	6	6	0	100	62	5.06	1.50	270			25.9	29%	68%	4.81	48	17	36	4.1	5.6	1.4	11%	1.1	-8.7	16	$4
+/- Score	-4	09 Proj	2	3	0	45	26	5.80	1.71	291			26.1	31%	69%	5.35	48	17	36	5.0	5.2	1.0	13%	1.4	-5.2	-16	($1)

3-5, 5.01 ERA in 65 IP in BAL. After one-hit debut, there was no place to go but down. Luckily, with a complete absence of any discernable skill, the trip was quick. For the MLB minimum, I'm pretty sure I could do this too.

Weathers,David

Weathers,David		Yr	W	L	Sv	IP	K	ERA	WHIP	OBA	vL	vR	BF/G	H%	S%	xERA	G	L	F	Ctl	Dom	Cmd	hr/f	hr/9	RAR	BPV	R$
RH	Reliever	04 2NL	7	7	0	82	61	4.17	1.46	269	241	294	5.5	30%	76%	4.28	49	18	33	3.8	6.7	1.7	14%	1.3	1.0	44	$6
Age	39	05 CIN	7	4	15	77	61	3.96	1.30	246	265	226	4.5	29%	71%	3.77	50	21	28	3.4	7.1	2.1	11%	0.8	2.7	65	$12
Type		06 CIN	4	4	12	73	50	3.57	1.30	228	219	230	4.6	24%	80%	4.55	45	17	38	4.2	6.1	1.5	14%	1.5	8.3	20	$11
Health	A	07 CIN	2	6	33	78	48	3.59	1.21	234	254	218	4.6	27%	70%	4.76	36	21	43	3.1	5.6	1.8	4%	0.5	8.0	29	$17
PT/Exp	B	08 CIN	4	6	0	69	46	3.25	1.53	280	245	296	4.3	32%	81%	4.66	44	24	32	3.9	6.0	1.5	8%	0.8	8.7	24	$4
Consist	A	1st Half	2	3	0	32	21	3.66	1.53	279			4.1	30%	82%	4.60	43	27	30	3.9	5.9	1.5	16%	1.4	2.4	21	$2
LIMA Plan	C	2nd Half	2	3	0	37	25	2.90	1.53	280			4.5	33%	80%	4.71	45	22	33	3.9	6.0	1.6	2%	0.2	6.3	27	$2
+/- Score	-64	09 Proj	3	4	3	58	38	4.50	1.50	275			4.6	30%	73%	4.77	43	22	36	3.9	5.9	1.5	10%	1.1	-3.0	22	$3

Third straight season using S% or H% or hr/f to dodge the fates of xERA. But nobody can escape the baseball gods' wrath forever. At 39, it's payback time.

Weaver,Jered

Weaver,Jered		Yr	W	L	Sv	IP	K	ERA	WHIP	OBA	vL	vR	BF/G	H%	S%	xERA	G	L	F	Ctl	Dom	Cmd	hr/f	hr/9	RAR	BPV	R$
RH	Starter	04	0	0	0	0	0	0.00	0.00																		
Age	26	05 aa	3	3	0	43	39	4.19	1.49	275			23.7	33%	75%	4.73				3.8	8.2	2.2		1.0	0.6	63	$3
Type	Pwr xFB	06 LAA	* 17	3	0	200	184	2.43	1.02	222	250	174	25.4	27%	82%	3.83	30	18	52	1.9	8.3	4.4	8%	1.0	52.5	106	$36
Health	A	07 LAA	13	7	0	161	115	3.91	1.39	282	291	269	24.8	32%	74%	4.68	36	17	47	2.5	6.4	2.6	7%	1.0	11.8	61	$15
PT/Exp	B	08 LAA	11	10	0	177	152	4.33	1.28	258	243	266	24.8	31%	69%	4.24	33	22	46	2.8	7.7	2.8	8%	1.0	0.4	76	$16
Consist	B	1st Half	7	8	0	103	77	4.29	1.27	257			25.3	29%	69%	4.37	36	19	44	2.6	6.7	2.6	9%	1.1	0.7	65	$9
LIMA Plan	C+	2nd Half	4	2	0	74	75	4.38	1.31	259			24.1	33%	69%	4.06	27	25	48	2.9	9.1	3.1	8%	1.0	-0.3	91	$7
+/- Score	17	09 Proj	14	8	0	194	172	3.80	1.29	261			24.8	31%	74%	4.21	33	20	47	2.7	8.0	3.0	9%	1.1	5.1	82	$21

Can't see it in results, but this was a growth season. Big 2H Dom, around nagging aches, mitigated FB%. 57/17 PQS split also a step up. Just hitting stride at 26. Durability still TBD, but there's more skills upside here.

Webb,Brandon

Webb,Brandon		Yr	W	L	Sv	IP	K	ERA	WHIP	OBA	vL	vR	BF/G	H%	S%	xERA	G	L	F	Ctl	Dom	Cmd	hr/f	hr/9	RAR	BPV	R$
RH	Starter	04 ARI	7	16	0	208	164	3.59	1.50	249	268	223	26.3	30%	78%	3.66	64	17	19	5.1	7.1	1.4	15%	0.7	17.2	31	$10
Age	30	05 ARI	14	12	0	229	172	3.54	1.26	262	298	228	29.0	31%	74%	2.85	65	19	16	2.3	6.8	2.9	18%	0.8	20.0	102	$21
Type	xGB	06 ARI	16	8	0	235	178	3.10	1.13	246	261	231	28.9	29%	74%	2.66	66	17	16	1.9	6.8	3.6	13%	0.6	40.2	115	$29
Health	A	07 ARI	18	10	0	236	194	3.01	1.19	239	272	199	28.6	29%	75%	3.00	62	18	20	2.7	7.4	2.7	9%	0.5	41.3	99	$29
PT/Exp	A	08 ARI	22	7	0	227	183	3.30	1.20	244	265	219	27.4	30%	73%	2.96	64	15	20	2.6	7.3	2.8	10%	0.5	27.3	103	$28
Consist	A	1st Half	12	4	0	112	94	3.21	1.13	235			26.6	29%	72%	2.69	66	16	18	2.3	7.6	3.2	10%	0.5	14.6	117	$16
LIMA Plan	C+	2nd Half	10	3	0	115	89	3.37	1.26	252			28.2	30%	74%	3.22	63	15	22	2.8	7.0	2.5	9%	0.5	12.7	90	$13
+/- Score	23	09 Proj	19	8	0	228	181	3.16	1.21	245			27.6	30%	75%	2.98	64	17	20	2.7	7.2	2.7	11%	0.6	38.3	99	$27

Pay for the consistency, the health, and the 220+ IP every year. Pay for the K's, the bullet-proof GB%, the low-3 ERAs, and the wins. Pay for the 100 BPV, and peak age. As close to a lock as you can get at SP.

Wellemeyer,Todd

Wellemeyer,Todd		Yr	W	L	Sv	IP	K	ERA	WHIP	OBA	vL	vR	BF/G	H%	S%	xERA	G	L	F	Ctl	Dom	Cmd	hr/f	hr/9	RAR	BPV	R$
RH	Starter	04 CHC	* 3	2	0	46	50	5.48	1.85	286	302	275	6.6	38%	70%	5.24	25	30	45	6.5	9.8	1.5	7%	0.8	-6.9	4	$0
Age	30	05 CHC	* 5	3	1	85	72	4.55	1.56	264	234	284	11.2	31%	73%	4.63	47	15	38	5.0	7.6	1.5	9%	1.0	-3.2	28	$4
Type	Pwr	06 2TM	1	4	1	78	54	4.15	1.51	236	208	265	7.5	27%	73%	5.10	49	14	37	5.8	6.2	1.1	7%	0.7	3.6	-17	$3
Health	B	07 2TM	3	3	0	79	60	4.54	1.48	256	311	200	10.9	29%	73%	4.85	40	18	41	4.5	6.8	1.5	11%	1.2	-0.8	18	$4
PT/Exp	B	08 STL	13	9	0	192	134	3.71	1.25	248	256	237	25.0	27%	75%	4.34	39	21	40	2.9	6.3	2.2	11%	1.2	13.3	52	$17
Consist	A	1st Half	7	2	0	88	68	3.47	1.19	236			24.2	27%	76%	4.12	40	19	41	2.9	6.9	2.4	10%	1.1	8.8	66	$10
LIMA Plan	D	2nd Half	6	7	0	103	66	3.92	1.31	257			25.7	28%	74%	4.53	39	23	39	3.0	5.7	1.9	11%	1.2	4.5	40	$8
+/- Score	-24	09 Proj	6	6	0	124	91	4.50	1.48	268			24.8	30%	72%	4.76	41	19	40	4.1	6.6	1.6	10%	1.1	-6.4	28	$5

Two reasons to avoid in 2009:
- ERA well below xERA
- More in-season elbow pain accompanied by 110 IP spike

A nice Ctl step up, however:
Small DN: 5.00+ ERA
Big DN: TJ surgery.

Wells,Kip

Wells,Kip		Yr	W	L	Sv	IP	K	ERA	WHIP	OBA	vL	vR	BF/G	H%	S%	xERA	G	L	F	Ctl	Dom	Cmd	hr/f	hr/9	RAR	BPV	R$
RH	Reliever	04 PIT	5	7	0	138	116	4.56	1.53	271	300	244	25.6	32%	72%	4.27	46	22	32	4.3	7.6	1.8	11%	0.9	-5.1	44	$5
Age	32	05 PIT	8	18	0	182	132	5.09	1.57	266	288	249	24.7	30%	69%	4.75	47	20	33	4.9	6.5	1.3	12%	1.1	-19.0	10	$3
Type	Pwr GB	06 2TM	2	5	0	44	20	6.53	1.86	329	353	323	23.4	36%	63%	5.41	51	20	29	4.3	4.1	1.0	6%	0.6	-10.9	-13	($2)
Health	F	07 STL	7	17	0	163	122	5.70	1.62	288	287	287	21.7	33%	66%	4.56	48	19	33	4.3	6.7	1.6	11%	1.1	-25.5	31	$1
PT/Exp	C	08 2TM	1	3	0	38	31	6.21	1.83	268	266	286	7.2	32%	66%	5.11	53	17	29	7.2	7.4	1.0	12%	1.0	-8.8	-29	($2)
Consist	B	1st Half	1	1	0	20	16	2.28	1.52	224			8.8	26%	89%	4.45	58	13	28	6.4	7.3	1.1	13%	0.9	4.9	-5	$2
LIMA Plan	F	2nd Half	0	2	0	18	15	10.50	2.17	312			6.1	37%	49%	5.84	48	21	30	8.0	7.5	0.9	11%	1.0	-13.8	-55	($3)
+/- Score	1	09 Proj	1	4	0	41	31	5.49	1.76	280			6.6	33%	69%	4.98	50	19	31	5.9	6.8	1.1	10%	0.9	-3.1	-9	($1)

Pitched out of bullpen a lot, and suffered more problems with blood clots. These seemingly unrelated items each contributed to his most beneficial season in years: didn't pitch as much, so RAR less negative than usual.

Westbrook,Jake

Westbrook,Jake		Yr	W	L	Sv	IP	K	ERA	WHIP	OBA	vL	vR	BF/G	H%	S%	xERA	G	L	F	Ctl	Dom	Cmd	hr/f	hr/9	RAR	BPV	R$
RH	Starter	04 CLE	14	9	0	215	116	3.39	1.25	255	255	247	27.2	28%	75%	3.67	63	14	23	2.6	4.9	1.9	12%	0.8	27.7	59	$20
Age	31	05 CLE	15	15	0	210	119	4.50	1.30	269	275	255	26.1	30%	66%	3.43	62	19	19	2.4	5.1	2.1	15%	0.8	-3.2	67	$15
Type	Con xGB	06 CLE	15	10	0	211	109	4.18	1.43	293	290	300	28.7	32%	71%	3.83	61	17	22	2.3	4.6	2.0	9%	0.6	9.9	59	$15
Health	F	07 CLE	6	9	0	152	93	4.32	1.41	271	288	263	26.3	30%	70%	4.13	54	20	27	3.3	5.5	1.7	10%	0.8	3.4	43	$9
PT/Exp	B	08 CLE	1	2	0	35	19	3.11	1.15	252	238	273	28.3	26%	80%	3.70	55	17	28	1.8	4.9	2.7	16%	1.3	5.3	73	$3
Consist	A	1st Half	1	2	0	35	19	3.11	1.15	252			28.3	26%	80%	3.70	55	17	28	1.8	4.9	2.7	16%	1.3	5.3	73	$3
LIMA Plan	C+	2nd Half	0	0	0	0	0	0.00	0.00																		
+/- Score	-2	09 Proj	2	4	0	58	30	4.66	1.47	284			23.1	31%	70%	4.16	58	18	24	3.1	4.7	1.5	12%	0.9	1.9	36	$2

First strained ribcage, then tore elbow ligament, requiring TJS. Preseason noise was a of new pitch to improve Dom, but that didn't show in this small sample. Due back mid-season; avoid until 2nd year post-surgery.

ROD TRUESDELL

Wheeler,Dan				W	L	Sv	IP	K	ERA	WHIP	OBA	vL	vR	BF/G	H%	S%	xERA	G	L	F	Ctl	Dom	Cmd	hr/f	hr/9	RAR	BPV	R$
RH	Reliever	04	2NL	3	1	0	65	55	4.29	1.48	293	380	226	6.2	34%	76%	4.22	38	22	40	2.8	7.6	**2.8**	12%	1.4	-0.2	79	$3
Age	31	05	HOU	2	3	3	73	69	2.22	0.98	205	206	204	4.0	25%	83%	3.53	38	18	44	2.3	8.5	**3.6**	8%	0.9	18.3	106	$12
Type	Pwr xFB	06	HOU	3	5	9	71	68	2.53	1.15	224	273	183	3.9	29%	81%	3.85	37	20	44	3.0	8.6	**2.8**	6%	0.6	17.2	87	$13
Health	A	07	2TM	1	9	11	75	82	5.30	1.30	260	260	253	4.5	33%	62%	3.64	37	18	45	2.8	9.9	**3.6**	12%	1.3	-7.7	118	$8
PT/Exp	C	08	TAM	5	6	13	66	53	3.12	1.00	191	215	163	3.7	20%	77%	4.31	28	17	54	3.0	7.2	**2.4**	10%	1.4	10.0	55	$14
Consist	A	1st Half		2	3	2	38	25	1.88	0.91	169			3.9	18%	87%	4.62	33	11	56	3.1	5.9	**1.9**	7%	0.9	11.7	34	$7
LIMA Plan	B	2nd Half		3	3	11	28	28	4.82	1.11	218			3.5	24%	64%	3.90	22	27	51	2.9	9.0	**3.1**	16%	1.9	-1.6	84	$7
+/- Score	-33	09	Proj	**6**	**3**	**15**	**73**	**72**	**3.60**	**1.16**	**230**			**4.0**	**28%**	**74%**	**3.87**	**32**	**20**	**49**	**2.9**	**8.9**	**3.1**	**11%**	**1.2**	**4.9**	**94**	**$15**

Just one fly in the ointment: a big FB spike, with nasty gopheritis. 2H Cmd back to prior levels: no worries there. FB should regress some as well. Know the HR risk, but on a team with an uncertain 9th inning... UP: 30 Saves

Willis,Dontrelle				W	L	Sv	IP	K	ERA	WHIP	OBA	vL	vR	BF/G	H%	S%	xERA	G	L	F	Ctl	Dom	Cmd	hr/f	hr/9	RAR	BPV	R$
LH	Starter	04	FLA	10	11	0	197	139	4.02	1.38	274	203	287	26.4	31%	73%	4.26	45	19	36	2.8	6.4	**2.3**	9%	0.9	5.9	62	$12
Age	27	05	FLA	22	10	0	236	170	2.63	1.14	242	222	247	28.2	29%	77%	3.73	45	24	32	2.1	6.5	**3.1**	5%	0.4	47.0	83	$33
Type	Pwr	06	FLA	12	12	0	223	160	3.87	1.42	271	231	281	28.5	31%	75%	4.25	48	20	33	3.3	6.5	**1.9**	9%	0.8	16.9	51	$15
Health	B	07	FLA	10	15	0	205	146	5.17	1.60	294	123	320	26.5	33%	70%	4.52	46	21	32	3.8	6.4	**1.7**	13%	1.3	-18.9	37	$4
PT/Exp	A	08	DET	* 3	3	0	52	36	7.27	2.06	276	125	242	18.5	31%	65%	7.08	43	12	46	8.8	6.2	**0.7**	9%	1.2	-18.7	-106	($4)
Consist	C	1st Half		1	2	0	27	15	7.66	1.96	249			16.7	26%	61%	7.91	41	6	53	9.3	4.8	**0.5**	9%	1.3	-11.2	-145	($3)
LIMA Plan	C	2nd Half		2	1	0	25	21	6.84	2.16	305			20.8	36%	69%	6.25	44	17	39	8.3	7.8	**0.9**	10%	1.1	-7.6	-62	($2)
+/- Score	-26	09	Proj	**4**	**4**	**0**	**62**	**42**	**5.37**	**1.63**	**283**			**21.7**	**31%**	**69%**	**4.99**	**45**	**19**	**36**	**4.6**	**6.1**	**1.3**	**11%**	**1.2**	**-4.4**	**8**	**$1**

0-2, 9.38 ERA in 24 IP at DET. Ctl was a jaw-dropping 13.1 in short stint with Tigers, but that's only the worst of an entire array of awfulness. He'll keep getting chances since DET's stuck with him. Thankfully, you're not.

Wilson,Brian				W	L	Sv	IP	K	ERA	WHIP	OBA	vL	vR	BF/G	H%	S%	xERA	G	L	F	Ctl	Dom	Cmd	hr/f	hr/9	RAR	BPV	R$
RH	Reliever	04		0	0	0	0	0	0.00	0.00																		
Age	27	05	a/a	1	1	8	27	35	2.00	1.00	155			4.4	25%	78%	1.02				4.3	11.7	**2.7**		0.0	7.7	150	$7
Type	Pwr GB	06	SF	* 3	6	8	58	50	4.50	1.60	252			4.8	31%	72%	4.63	45	26	29	5.9	7.8	**1.3**	8%	0.6	-0.1	3	$5
Health	A	07	SF	* 2	4	17	58	47	2.66	1.38	220	304	145	4.5	28%	80%	4.17	56	15	29	5.2	7.3	**1.4**	2%	0.2	12.6	24	$11
PT/Exp	C	08	SF	3	2	41	62	67	4.62	1.44	261	202	320	4.3	34%	70%	3.43	52	19	30	4.0	9.7	**2.4**	14%	1.0	-2.7	95	$18
Consist	B	1st Half		0	1	22	32	37	4.26	1.42	245			4.2	34%	70%	3.56	49	14	36	4.5	10.5	**2.3**	7%	0.6	0.0	94	$9
LIMA Plan	C+	2nd Half		3	1	19	31	30	5.00	1.47	277			4.5	33%	70%	3.27	54	22	24	3.5	8.8	**2.5**	24%	1.5	-2.8	95	$9
+/- Score	41	09	Proj	**2**	**2**	**35**	**44**	**44**	**3.52**	**1.33**	**246**			**4.3**	**31%**	**76%**	**3.37**	**52**	**19**	**29**	**3.7**	**9.1**	**2.4**	**12%**	**0.8**	**5.2**	**93**	**$16**

Were it not for a bad hr/f and H%, this would've looked even better. As it is, only shaky Ctl is keeping BPV from elite level. 2H gives hope, two prior years show dark side. Not risk- free, but saves look secure.

Wilson,C.J.				W	L	Sv	IP	K	ERA	WHIP	OBA	vL	vR	BF/G	H%	S%	xERA	G	L	F	Ctl	Dom	Cmd	hr/f	hr/9	RAR	BPV	R$
LH	Reliever	04	TEX	0	0	0	0	0	0.00	0.00											0.0	0.0						
Age	28	05	TEX	* 1	11	1	92	65	6.49	1.72	327	290	339	11.9	36%	64%	3.72	60	20	20	3.2	6.4	**2.0**	23%	1.4	-24.1	66	($3)
Type	Pwr GB	06	TEX	2	4	1	44	43	4.08	1.29	239	155	292	4.2	28%	74%	3.43	49	21	30	3.7	8.8	**2.4**	20%	1.4	2.6	86	$5
Health	D	07	TEX	2	1	12	68	63	3.03	1.22	206	112	275	4.3	26%	76%	3.60	49	24	27	4.3	8.3	**1.9**	8%	0.5	12.4	59	$12
PT/Exp	C	08	TEX	2	2	24	46	41	6.03	1.64	273	265	269	4.2	31%	66%	4.47	49	16	35	5.2	8.0	**1.5**	17%	1.6	-9.6	29	$8
Consist	B	1st Half		0	2	18	35	28	4.59	1.42	249			4.1	29%	70%	4.29	49	16	35	4.3	7.1	**1.6**	11%	1.0	-1.1	39	$7
LIMA Plan	C+	2nd Half		2	0	6	11	13	10.64	2.36	340			4.5	40%	59%	5.04	50	16	34	8.2	10.6	**1.3**	34%	3.3	-8.5	-1	$1
+/- Score	34	09	Proj	**1**	**4**	**10**	**58**	**50**	**4.34**	**1.41**	**252**			**4.7**	**30%**	**71%**	**3.97**	**50**	**19**	**31**	**4.2**	**7.8**	**1.9**	**11%**	**0.9**	**3.2**	**55**	**$6**

Elbow pain prior to bone spur surgery likely explains awful 2H. But skills hardly closer-worthy before that, and maturity also raised issues. Will have to re-win closer's job; without it, just a lefty setup guy with iffy Cmd.

Wolfe,Brian				W	L	Sv	IP	K	ERA	WHIP	OBA	vL	vR	BF/G	H%	S%	xERA	G	L	F	Ctl	Dom	Cmd	hr/f	hr/9	RAR	BPV	R$
RH	Reliever	04		0	0	0	0	0	0.00	0.00																		
Age	28	05	a/a	4	3	0	38	23	6.10	2.03	358			7.8	41%	68%	6.95				4.2	5.5	**1.3**		0.5	-8.4	30	($1)
Type	Con GB	06	aa	1	3	0	42	26	9.26	2.22	385			9.0	42%	58%	9.00				4.0	5.6	**1.4**		1.7	-24.6	-9	($7)
Health	B	07	TOR	3	1	0	45	22	2.98	0.99	220			4.7	23%	75%	3.82	56	12	32	1.8	4.4	**2.4**	11%	1.0	8.5	64	$6
PT/Exp	D	08	TOR	* 2	5	1	58	37	4.02	1.46	291	273	205	6.9	33%	74%	4.46	48	16	36	2.7	5.7	**2.1**	7%	0.8	2.3	55	$3
Consist	F	1st Half		0	2	1	21	13	2.57	1.21	255			4.1	28%	83%	4.10	48	17	35	2.2	5.5	**2.5**	8%	0.9	4.6	66	$2
LIMA Plan	B+	2nd Half		2	3	0	37	24	4.84	1.61	310			10.5	35%	70%	4.69	50	13	38	3.0	5.8	**1.9**	7%	0.8	-2.3	51	$1
+/- Score	-1	09	Proj	**3**	**4**	**0**	**54**	**34**	**4.04**	**1.42**	**291**			**6.3**	**32%**	**74%**	**4.15**	**53**	**13**	**34**	**2.4**	**5.7**	**2.4**	**10%**	**1.0**	**1.8**	**70**	**$4**

0-2, 2.45 ERA in 22 IP at TOR. Strained triceps in April, rode Syracuse Shuttle much of rest of season. Skills are just ok, and "non-prospect" reputation works against him. Decent ML bullpen filler, but not a fanalytic option.

Wolf,Randy				W	L	Sv	IP	K	ERA	WHIP	OBA	vL	vR	BF/G	H%	S%	xERA	G	L	F	Ctl	Dom	Cmd	hr/f	hr/9	RAR	BPV	R$
LH	Starter	04	PHI	5	8	0	136	89	4.30	1.33	274	254	276	25.2	30%	72%	4.59	35	21	43	2.4	5.9	**2.5**	10%	1.3	-0.6	55	$7
Age	32	05	PHI	6	4	0	80	61	4.39	1.41	278	238	293	26.7	31%	75%	4.47	35	23	42	2.9	6.9	**2.3**	13%	1.6	-1.4	58	$5
Type	Pwr FB	06	PHI	4	0	0	56	44	5.60	1.71	284	86	323	21.7	30%	73%	5.29	37	19	44	5.3	7.0	**1.3**	17%	2.1	-7.7	-1	$1
Health	F	07	LA	9	6	0	103	94	4.73	1.45	275	250	278	24.9	34%	68%	4.16	41	19	40	3.4	8.2	**2.4**	8%	0.9	-3.9	75	$8
PT/Exp	B	08	2NL	12	12	0	190	162	4.30	1.38	262	283	258	24.8	31%	71%	4.21	39	23	39	3.4	7.7	**2.3**	10%	1.0	-0.8	64	$13
Consist	B	1st Half		5	7	0	98	89	4.13	1.38	262			24.8	32%	73%	3.99	40	24	36	3.4	8.2	**2.4**	11%	1.0	1.7	74	$7
LIMA Plan	C	2nd Half		7	5	0	92	73	4.49	1.38	263			24.8	31%	69%	4.44	37	21	41	3.3	7.1	**2.1**	9%	1.0	-2.4	54	$6
+/- Score	5	09	Proj	**11**	**10**	**0**	**174**	**145**	**4.66**	**1.43**	**271**			**24.4**	**32%**	**70%**	**4.36**	**38**	**21**	**41**	**3.4**	**7.5**	**2.2**	**11%**	**1.2**	**-0.4**	**59**	**$10**

Dazzling Sept (2.23 ERA) driven by Ctl (1.9) he'll be unable to sustain. The big picture is the more accurate one: serviceable SP with a checkered injury past, and now a 90 IP spike. Still owns upside, but also owns big risk.

Wood,Kerry				W	L	Sv	IP	K	ERA	WHIP	OBA	vL	vR	BF/G	H%	S%	xERA	G	L	F	Ctl	Dom	Cmd	hr/f	hr/9	RAR	BPV	R$
RH	Reliever	04	CHC	8	9	0	140	144	3.73	1.27	243	262	227	26.7	31%	74%	3.47	46	19	35	3.3	9.3	**2.8**	12%	1.0	9.3	102	$14
Age	31	05	CHC	3	4	0	66	77	4.23	1.18	218	220	211	11.9	26%	73%	3.40	34	24	42	3.5	10.5	**3.0**	21%	1.9	0.1	105	$7
Type	Pwr FB	06	CHC	1	2	0	19	13	4.22	1.41	260	206	293	20.8	25%	82%	5.00	39	10	51	3.8	6.1	**1.6**	16%	2.3	0.6	26	$1
Health	F	07	CHC	1	1	0	24	24	3.33	1.28	208	148	233	4.6	29%	71%	4.48	34	18	48	4.8	8.9	**1.8**	0%	0.0	3.3	42	$2
PT/Exp	C	08	CHC	5	4	34	66	84	3.26	1.09	224	209	227	4.1	33%	70%	2.93	39	20	41	2.4	11.4	**4.7**	5%	0.4	8.3	157	$22
Consist	C	1st Half		4	1	20	41	51	2.43	0.86	185			3.9	28%	71%	2.83	35	19	46	2.0	11.3	**5.7**	2%	0.2	9.2	162	$15
LIMA Plan	C+	2nd Half		1	3	14	26	33	4.57	1.45	279			4.3	40%	69%	3.08	45	21	34	3.2	11.6	**3.7**	9%	0.7	-0.9	146	$6
+/- Score	9	09	Proj	**4**	**5**	**38**	**68**	**77**	**3.44**	**1.21**	**235**			**6.5**	**31%**	**76%**	**3.44**	**39**	**18**	**43**	**3.0**	**10.2**	**3.3**	**11%**	**1.1**	**7.6**	**118**	**$21**

Upside and injury risk, thy name is Wood. This year's injury was "only" a blister, and only cost him three weeks. Around that he was simply dominating. Closing has been career tonic for brittle arms before. But see first sentence.

Wright,Jamey				W	L	Sv	IP	K	ERA	WHIP	OBA	vL	vR	BF/G	H%	S%	xERA	G	L	F	Ctl	Dom	Cmd	hr/f	hr/9	RAR	BPV	R$
RH	Reliever	04	COL	* 10	9	0	182	96	5.28	1.69	307	253	281	26.3	32%	72%	4.88	50	22	28	4.0	4.7	**1.2**	15%	1.3	-22.9	5	($0)
Age	34	05	COL	8	16	0	171	101	5.47	1.65	294	314	279	23.0	32%	68%	4.65	53	20	27	4.3	5.3	**1.2**	14%	1.2	-25.9	11	($1)
Type	xGB	06	SF	6	10	0	156	79	5.19	1.48	275	261	300	20.2	29%	66%	4.30	58	18	23	3.7	4.6	**1.2**	13%	0.9	-13.6	18	$3
Health	C	07	TEX	* 6	6	0	97	48	4.29	1.59	286	268	253	18.2	31%	75%	4.80	55	17	28	4.1	4.5	**1.1**	10%	0.9	2.6	2	$4
PT/Exp	C	08	TEX	8	7	0	84	60	5.12	1.52	281	286	280	5.0	33%	65%	3.61	62	20	19	3.7	6.4	**1.7**	10%	0.5	-8.1	54	$5
Consist	B	1st Half		4	3	0	45	31	3.60	1.20	221			4.5	27%	68%	3.37	62	19	18	3.6	6.2	**1.7**	4%	0.2	4.1	55	$5
LIMA Plan	C+	2nd Half		4	4	0	39	29	6.87	1.88	340			5.6	39%	63%	3.87	61	20	19	3.9	6.6	**1.7**	16%	0.9	-12.2	54	($1)
+/- Score	16	09	Proj	**5**	**6**	**0**	**73**	**48**	**4.59**	**1.52**	**279**			**5.4**	**32%**	**70%**	**3.95**	**59**	**19**	**22**	**3.8**	**6.0**	**1.5**	**12%**	**0.7**	**4.3**	**40**	**$4**

Better results since he moved to pen. 2H ERA was mostly bad luck-driven, although pitching in 75 games contributed. Five of those 75 gms: (4/23) 1 IP, 5 ER (6/1) 0 IP 4 ER, (7/2) 1 IP, 6 ER, (8/28) .1 IP, 4 ER, (9/19) 1, 5 ER

Wright,Wesley				W	L	Sv	IP	K	ERA	WHIP	OBA	vL	vR	BF/G	H%	S%	xERA	G	L	F	Ctl	Dom	Cmd	hr/f	hr/9	RAR	BPV	R$
LH	Reliever	04		0	0	0	0	0	0.00	0.00																		
Age	24	05		0	0	0	0	0	0.00	0.00																		
Type	Pwr	06	aa	1	1	1	21	25	5.14	1.33	202			6.0	26%	64%	3.57				5.6	10.7	**1.9**		1.3	-1.6	81	$2
Health	A	07	a/a	7	4	2	78	75	4.50	1.68	272			8.2	33%	75%	5.18				5.7	8.7	**1.5**		1.0	-0.4	54	$5
PT/Exp	D	08	HOU	4	3	1	56	57	5.01	1.42	223	207	220	3.4	27%	68%	4.27	40	21	39	5.5	9.2	**1.7**	14%	1.3	-5.1	35	$4
Consist	C	1st Half		3	2	0	27	27	5.27	1.58	230			3.1	28%	69%	4.55	48	16	36	6.6	8.9	**1.4**	15%	1.3	-3.4	8	$2
LIMA Plan	B	2nd Half		1	1	1	28	30	4.75	1.27	215			3.7	26%	66%	3.98	32	26	42	4.4	9.5	**2.1**	13%	1.3	-1.7	61	$2
+/- Score	19	09	Proj	**3**	**2**	**0**	**44**	**44**	**4.55**	**1.38**	**241**			**4.3**	**30%**	**69%**	**4.06**	**38**	**22**	**40**	**4.3**	**9.1**	**2.1**	**11%**	**1.0**	**1.5**	**63**	**$3**

Rule 5 pick lasted the season, so now he'll likely get needed time in minors. Brought prior flashy Dom and poor Ctl to majors. If he can build on 2H improvement in the latter, he'll come fast. Tuck this name away.

ROD TRUESDELL

Wuertz,Mike

		Yr	Tm	W	L	Sv	IP	K	ERA	WHIP	OBA	vL	vR	BF/G	H%	S%	xERA	G	L	F	Ctl	Dom	Cmd	hr/f	hr/9	RAR	BPV	R$
RH	Reliever	04	CHC *	2	1	20	73	82	3.20	1.17	207	212	221	4.4	27%	77%	3.99	29	16	55	3.9	10.1	**2.6**	8%	1.0	9.6	82	$14
Age	30	05	CHC	6	2	0	75	89	3.83	1.33	221	260	197	4.3	30%	72%	3.67	43	17	40	4.8	10.7	**2.2**	8%	0.7	3.9	83	$8
Type	Pwr	06	CHC *	9	1	10	81	98	2.61	1.22	241	184	245	4.7	33%	83%	2.76	54	16	30	2.9	10.8	**3.7**	13%	0.9	18.9	148	$17
Health	A	07	CHC	2	3	0	72	79	3.49	1.37	239	238	233	4.2	31%	78%	3.82	44	15	41	4.4	9.8	**2.3**	10%	1.0	8.4	81	$6
PT/Exp	D	08	CHC *	1	2	4	65	55	3.74	1.48	247	230	288	4.6	29%	78%	4.28	46	25	29	5.0	7.6	**1.5**	13%	1.0	4.3	26	$4
Consist	B	1st Half		1	1	0	36	23	2.77	1.37	258			4.4	29%	83%	4.44	44	24	32	3.5	5.8	**1.6**	8%	0.8	6.6	31	$3
LIMA Plan	B+	2nd Half		0	1	4	29	32	4.91	1.60	232			4.9	29%	72%	3.67	52	30	17	6.8	9.8	**1.5**	30%	1.2	-2.3	25	$2
+/- Score	-0	09	Proj	**2**	**2**	**0**	**64**	**64**	**3.83**	**1.35**	**238**			**4.5**	**30%**	**75%**	**3.79**	**47**	**17**	**36**	**4.3**	**9.1**	**2.1**	**11%**	**1.0**	**4.3**	**74**	**$5**

2006 was an outlying peak year amidst four comparable 80ish BPV seasons. '08 was different from top to bottom - Ctl, Dom, OBA vs RH. LD rate shows that he was hit HARD. That'll regress. The rest might not, much.

Yabuta,Yasuhiko

		Yr	Tm	W	L	Sv	IP	K	ERA	WHIP	OBA	vL	vR	BF/G	H%	S%	xERA	G	L	F	Ctl	Dom	Cmd	hr/f	hr/9	RAR	BPV	R$
RH	Reliever	04	JPN	3	4	2	77	67	3.48	1.41	235			5.1	29%	77%	3.78				4.9	7.9	**1.6**		0.8	8.2	66	$6
Age	35	05	JPN	7	4	2	56	51	3.79	1.09	222			4.4	24%	76%	3.80				2.6	8.2	**3.2**		1.9	3.5	71	$9
Type		06	JPN	4	2	1	55	46	3.25	1.43	229			5.1	27%	80%	3.73				5.3	7.5	**1.4**		0.8	8.6	59	$6
Health	A	07	JPN	4	6	4	53	43	4.01	1.53	315			4.1	36%	79%	5.81				2.1	7.3	**3.4**		1.4	3.0	66	$5
PT/Exp	D	08	KC *	5	6	3	78	50	6.53	1.80	323	185	345	7.2	36%	64%	5.07	50	15	35	4.1	5.7	**1.4**	10%	1.1	-21.0	19	($1)
Consist	C	1st Half		1	4	0	35	22	6.03	1.89	317			6.1	34%	71%	5.36	50	17	33	5.2	5.5	**1.1**	15%	1.6	-7.3	-14	($2)
LIMA Plan	C+	2nd Half		4	2	3	42	28	6.95	1.74	328			8.6	37%	58%	5.31	50	0	50	3.2	5.9	**1.8**	4%	0.7	-13.6	47	$0
+/- Score	8	09	Proj	**3**	**3**	**0**	**44**	**30**	**4.91**	**1.57**	**287**			**5.5**	**32%**	**71%**	**4.64**	**50**	**15**	**36**	**3.9**	**6.1**	**1.6**	**12%**	**1.2**	**-1.2**	**33**	**$2**

1-3, 4.78 ERA in 37 IP at KC. Didn't pan out, and inconsistent skill history says we shouldn't be that surprised. GB% is solid, but if JPN Dom won't translate to U.S., he's in trouble. More data needed, so pass for now.

Yabu,Keiichi

		Yr	Tm	W	L	Sv	IP	K	ERA	WHIP	OBA	vL	vR	BF/G	H%	S%	xERA	G	L	F	Ctl	Dom	Cmd	hr/f	hr/9	RAR	BPV	R$
RH	Reliever	04	JPN	6	9	0	116	79	3.76	1.38	262			26.3	29%	76%	4.32				3.5	6.1	**1.8**		1.0	8.4	46	$8
Age	40	05	OAK	4	0	1	58	44	4.50	1.55	281	291	283	6.5	33%	73%	4.47	42	26	31	4.0	6.8	**1.7**	10%	0.9	-0.9	34	$3
Type	Pwr	06	MEX	1	1	5	12	8	3.75	1.50	307			4.8	35%	76%	4.96				2.3	6.0	**2.7**		0.8	1.1	63	$3
Health	B	07		0	0	0	0	0	0.00	0.00																		
PT/Exp	D	08	SF	3	6	0	68	48	3.57	1.40	247	355	181	4.9	29%	74%	4.40	47	23	30	4.2	6.4	**1.5**	5%	0.4	5.8	25	$4
Consist	B	1st Half		3	4	0	41	27	3.27	1.31	241			5.3	28%	75%	4.01	51	25	24	3.7	5.9	**1.6**	7%	0.4	5.1	35	$4
LIMA Plan	C	2nd Half		0	2	0	27	21	4.04	1.54	257			4.4	32%	73%	4.97	40	21	39	5.1	7.1	**1.4**	3%	0.3	0.7	9	$0
+/- Score	-70	09	Proj	**3**	**3**	**0**	**64**	**44**	**4.25**	**1.54**	**263**			**6.2**	**30%**	**74%**	**4.82**	**44**	**24**	**32**	**4.8**	**6.2**	**1.3**	**9%**	**0.9**	**-3.8**	**4**	**$2**

If you cherry-pick skills from his history, you can assemble a good pitcher, but he's shown no inclination to do that himself. So instead you get moments of brilliance (1.10 ERA in May) mixed with lots of mediocrity.

Yates,Tyler

		Yr	Tm	W	L	Sv	IP	K	ERA	WHIP	OBA	vL	vR	BF/G	H%	S%	xERA	G	L	F	Ctl	Dom	Cmd	hr/f	hr/9	RAR	BPV	R$
RH	Reliever	04	NYM *	8	6	4	85	69	5.48	1.70	285	330	296	7.7	34%	68%	4.28	55	21	25	5.2	7.3	**1.4**	12%	0.8	-12.8	24	$3
Age	31	05	NYM	0	0	0	0	0	0.00	0.00																		
Type	Pwr	06	ATL	2	5	1	50	46	3.96	1.46	230	217	235	3.9	27%	76%	4.52	41	22	37	5.6	8.3	**1.5**	12%	1.1	3.3	18	$4
Health	C	07	ATL	2	3	2	66	69	5.18	1.44	256	310	213	3.8	33%	64%	3.84	46	17	37	4.2	9.4	**2.2**	9%	1.4	-6.2	80	$3
PT/Exp	C	08	PIT	6	3	1	73	63	4.67	1.54	258	303	224	4.5	31%	70%	4.33	48	22	30	5.0	7.7	**1.5**	9%	0.7	-3.6	29	$4
Consist	B	1st Half		3	1	0	40	25	3.80	1.56	225			4.8	26%	75%	5.50	49	18	33	6.7	5.6	**0.8**	5%	0.4	2.4	-53	$2
LIMA Plan	B	2nd Half		3	2	1	33	38	5.73	1.52	295			4.3	39%	63%	3.14	46	27	27	3.0	10.4	**3.5**	16%	1.1	-5.9	130	$2
+/- Score	-10	09	Proj	**4**	**4**	**5**	**63**	**60**	**4.57**	**1.49**	**256**			**4.3**	**32%**	**70%**	**4.06**	**47**	**21**	**32**	**4.7**	**8.6**	**1.8**	**10%**	**0.9**	**2.2**	**52**	**$5**

If we take away 1H, then 2H continues Cmd growth trend that started in 2006. But with no documented injuries to explain away that 1H, we can't just push it aside. Treat him as end-game fodder with some LIMA upside.

Young,Chris

		Yr	Tm	W	L	Sv	IP	K	ERA	WHIP	OBA	vL	vR	BF/G	H%	S%	xERA	G	L	F	Ctl	Dom	Cmd	hr/f	hr/9	RAR	BPV	R$
RH	Starter	04	a/a	9	6	0	118	89	5.05	1.57	299			23.1	34%	70%	5.48				3.3	6.8	**2.1**		1.2	-10.3	43	$5
Age	29	05	TEX	12	7	0	164	137	4.28	1.26	259	281	220	22.1	30%	69%	4.32	33	18	49	2.5	7.5	**3.0**	8%	1.0	2.0	79	$16
Type	Pwr xFB	06	SD	11	5	0	179	164	3.47	1.13	210	175	234	23.4	24%	77%	4.38	25	18	56	3.5	8.2	**2.4**	10%	1.4	22.5	58	$22
Health	D	07	SD	9	8	0	173	167	3.12	1.10	195	231	155	23.2	25%	72%	4.26	29	16	54	3.7	8.7	**2.3**	4%	0.5	27.8	62	$22
PT/Exp	A	08	SD	7	6	0	102	93	3.96	1.29	226	259	189	23.9	27%	73%	4.73	22	25	53	4.2	8.2	**1.9**	9%	1.1	3.9	33	$9
Consist	A	1st Half		4	4	0	54	51	4.50	1.48	247			23.8	29%	74%	4.91	24	27	49	5.0	8.5	**1.7**	11%	1.5	-1.5	20	$3
LIMA Plan	C+	2nd Half		3	2	0	48	42	3.35	1.08	200			24.1	24%	72%	4.54	19	23	58	3.4	7.8	**2.3**	7%	0.9	5.5	47	$6
+/- Score	-34	09	Proj	**10**	**8**	**0**	**160**	**146**	**4.01**	**1.27**	**239**			**23.9**	**28%**	**73%**	**4.53**	**25**	**21**	**54**	**3.5**	**8.2**	**2.4**	**9%**	**1.2**	**-3.8**	**57**	**$15**

Don't read too much into this season because 1) Elbow stiffness in April, 2) Hit in face by line drive in May, 3) Strained forearm in August. xFB hurler survives because it's Petco, but be wary of those xERAs.

Zambrano,Carlos

		Yr	Tm	W	L	Sv	IP	K	ERA	WHIP	OBA	vL	vR	BF/G	H%	S%	xERA	G	L	F	Ctl	Dom	Cmd	hr/f	hr/9	RAR	BPV	R$
RH	Starter	04	CHC	16	8	0	209	188	2.75	1.22	228	232	218	27.9	28%	79%	3.58	51	18	31	3.5	8.1	**2.3**	8%	0.6	38.9	80	$26
Age	27	05	CHC	14	6	0	223	202	3.27	1.15	213	212	212	27.5	26%	74%	3.43	50	20	30	3.5	8.1	**2.3**	12%	0.8	26.9	81	$26
Type	Pwr	06	CHC	16	7	0	214	210	3.41	1.29	212	247	174	27.3	27%	76%	3.92	47	17	36	4.8	8.8	**1.8**	10%	0.8	28.5	53	$24
Health	A	07	CHC	18	13	0	216	177	3.95	1.33	235	268	200	27.0	27%	73%	4.22	47	17	37	4.2	7.4	**1.8**	10%	1.0	12.6	44	$21
PT/Exp	A	08	CHC	14	6	0	189	130	3.91	1.29	244	235	247	26.5	28%	72%	4.27	47	18	35	3.4	6.2	**1.8**	9%	0.9	8.4	44	$16
Consist	A	1st Half		8	3	0	106	68	3.13	1.33	259			28.2	30%	78%	4.30	49	18	34	3.0	5.8	**1.9**	6%	0.6	14.9	48	$10
LIMA Plan	D	2nd Half		6	3	0	82	62	4.91	1.25	224			24.5	25%	63%	4.24	45	18	37	3.9	6.8	**1.7**	13%	1.2	-6.6	39	$6
+/- Score	-17	09	Proj	**11**	**10**	**0**	**188**	**137**	**4.08**	**1.35**	**243**			**26.7**	**28%**	**72%**	**4.36**	**47**	**18**	**35**	**4.0**	**6.6**	**1.7**	**10%**	**0.9**	**-0.5**	**36**	**$13**

Dom continued falling as two shoulder injuries took a bite out of IP. "Rotator cuff tendinitis" are not words you want associated with a pitcher with his workload history. Warning flag remains... DN: 4.50 ERA, or worse

Ziegler,Brad

		Yr	Tm	W	L	Sv	IP	K	ERA	WHIP	OBA	vL	vR	BF/G	H%	S%	xERA	G	L	F	Ctl	Dom	Cmd	hr/f	hr/9	RAR	BPV	R$
RH	Reliever	04		0	0	0	0	0	0.00	0.00																		
Age	29	05	aa	2	1	0	21	18	7.71	1.67	329			24.1	40%	52%	5.84				2.6	7.7	**3.0**		0.9	-8.8	73	($0)
Type	Con xGB	06	a/a	9	7	0	162	74	4.78	1.71	336			27.8	35%	75%	6.46				2.6	4.1	**1.6**		1.3	-5.3	8	$2
Health	A	07	aa	12	3	2	78	44	3.47	1.40	288			6.8	34%	73%	3.79				2.4	5.1	**2.1**		0.0	9.6	73	$11
PT/Exp	D	08	OAK *	5	0	19	85	43	0.88	1.14	222	280	198	5.1	25%	93%	3.55	65	16	19	3.0	4.5	**1.5**	4%	0.2	36.2	43	$19
Consist	C	1st Half		3	0	8	37	17	0.32	1.02	225			4.6	26%	96%	2.69	70	19	11	1.8	4.1	**2.3**	0%	0.0	18.4	73	$10
LIMA Plan	C	2nd Half		2	0	11	48	26	1.32	1.24	220			5.7	25%	91%	3.89	63	16	21	4.0	4.9	**1.2**	6%	0.4	17.8	22	$10
+/- Score	-99	09	Proj	**5**	**3**	**13**	**73**	**38**	**3.35**	**1.32**	**266**			**6.5**	**30%**	**75%**	**3.76**	**62**	**16**	**22**	**2.7**	**4.7**	**1.7**	**8%**	**0.5**	**6.0**	**51**	**$11**

11 Sv, 1.06 ERA in 59 IP at OAK. As striking as these stats are, the skills were incredibly soft. Best that can be said is extreme GB rate offset some ills. ERA regression is a given, and a closer job is far from a lock.

Zito,Barry

		Yr	Tm	W	L	Sv	IP	K	ERA	WHIP	OBA	vL	vR	BF/G	H%	S%	xERA	G	L	F	Ctl	Dom	Cmd	hr/f	hr/9	RAR	BPV	R$
LH	Starter	04	OAK	11	11	0	213	163	4.48	1.39	264	263	248	27.0	30%	71%	4.62	37	19	44	3.4	6.9	**2.0**	10%	1.2	-1.2	47	$13
Age	31	05	OAK	14	13	0	228	171	3.87	1.20	223	215	223	26.9	25%	71%	4.19	42	21	37	3.5	6.7	**1.9**	11%	1.0	14.2	46	$23
Type	Pwr FB	06	OAK	16	10	0	221	151	3.83	1.40	253	260	257	28.1	28%	76%	5.00	38	17	45	4.0	6.1	**1.5**	9%	1.1	19.9	18	$20
Health	A	07	SF	11	13	0	197	131	4.53	1.35	247	242	244	24.7	27%	69%	4.76	39	20	41	3.8	6.0	**1.6**	10%	1.1	-2.5	22	$12
PT/Exp	A	08	SF	10	17	0	180	120	5.15	1.60	268	213	285	25.4	30%	68%	5.44	36	23	40	5.1	6.0	**1.2**	7%	0.8	-19.5	-15	$3
Consist	A	1st Half		3	12	0	86	50	5.99	1.84	303			24.0	33%	68%	5.92	39	24	37	5.6	5.3	**0.9**	8%	0.9	-18.1	-39	($4)
LIMA Plan	C	2nd Half		7	5	0	94	70	4.39	1.38	233			27.0	27%	68%	5.01	34	22	44	4.7	6.7	**1.4**	6%	0.7	-1.4	6	$6
+/- Score	-39	09	Proj	**8**	**10**	**0**	**134**	**92**	**4.63**	**1.50**	**263**			**25.8**	**29%**	**72%**	**5.09**	**37**	**21**	**41**	**4.4**	**6.2**	**1.4**	**10%**	**1.1**	**-12.3**	**7**	**$6**

xERA says this has been the same crappy pitcher for five years, with '08 a wee bit worse. It's time for SF to cut losses and salvage whatever remaining skill is left. He held LHers to .213 BA in 150 AB. Hello bullpen.

Zumaya,Joel

		Yr	Tm	W	L	Sv	IP	K	ERA	WHIP	OBA	vL	vR	BF/G	H%	S%	xERA	G	L	F	Ctl	Dom	Cmd	hr/f	hr/9	RAR	BPV	R$
RH	Reliever	04	aa	2	2	0	20	25	7.20	1.65	271			22.9	31%	65%	7.07				5.4	11.3	**2.1**		3.2	-7.0	17	$0
Age	24	05	a/a	9	5	0	151	181	3.46	1.25	212			24.2	30%	73%	2.88				4.4	10.8	**2.4**		0.6	15.7	110	$18
Type	Pwr FB	06	DET	6	3	1	83	97	1.95	1.18	193	183	188	5.5	27%	87%	3.74	34	21	45	4.5	10.5	**2.3**	7%	0.6	26.7	78	$15
Health	F	07	DET	2	3	1	34	27	4.27	1.19	195	271	135	4.9	23%	65%	4.67	36	16	48	4.5	7.2	**1.6**	7%	0.8	1.0	22	$4
PT/Exp	D	08	DET	0	2	1	23	22	3.48	1.97	268	161	317	5.4	32%	86%	5.97	40	20	40	8.5	8.5	**1.0**	11%	1.2	2.5	-58	$0
Consist	C	1st Half		0	0	1	5	3	3.40	2.45	349			5.7	40%	85%	7.36	37	37	26	8.5	5.1	**0.6**	0%	0.0	0.6	-123	($0)
LIMA Plan	B	2nd Half		0	2	0	18	19	3.50	1.83	240			5.3	29%	87%	5.57	41	14	45	8.5	9.5	**1.1**	14%	1.5	1.9	-39	$0
+/- Score	-84	09	Proj	**3**	**5**	**23**	**73**	**78**	**3.58**	**1.37**	**226**			**5.9**	**29%**	**77%**	**4.10**	**38**	**21**	**41**	**4.9**	**9.6**	**2.0**	**10%**	**1.0**	**2.9**	**56**	**$14**

Two years and three injuries since that magical '06 season, and Ctl, Cmd are a mess. Still in mix for saves, but he'll have to prove skills and health first. Reputation outstrips actual value at this point. Bid carefully.

BRANDON KRUSE

Batter Consistency Charts

by Dylan Hedges

The definition of consistency is the achievement of a level of performance that does not vary greatly in quality over time. Few things are as valuable to head-to-head points league success as filling your roster with players who can produce a solid weekly baseline of stats, week in and week out. In traditional leagues, while consistency is not as important — all we really care about are the end-of-season aggregate numbers — populating your fantasy team with consistent players can make roster management easier.

Consistent batters have good plate discipline, walk rate and on base percentage. These are foundation skills. Those who add power to the mix are obviously more valuable, however, the ability to hit home runs consistently is rare.

We can *track* consistency — and we do so in the accompanying charts — but *predicting* it is difficult. Many fantasy leaguers will try to predict a batter's hot or cold streaks, but that is typically a fool's errand. The best we can do is find players who demonstrate seasonal consistency over time; in-season, we want to manage players and consistency tactically.

For this process, we use the Base Performance Value (BPV) gauge. This primarily measures batting eye, batting average and power. BPV levels of 50 or above in a given week are defined as "DOMinating" weeks. Levels less than zero are defined as "DISaster" weeks. By comparing the DOM and DIS levels in individual weeks, we can analyze batters similarly to how we evaluate starting pitchers.

There are three elements to the process:

First, you want players who provide some **base level production**. This is no different than any other skills evaluation process. You want batters on your team that are projected to be highly productive. *Consistent* production in this context is almost secondary.

The second element is **risk mitigation**. Batters who perform poorly in individual weeks can have a much greater negative impact on a team's overall performance than the positive impact of batters doing well. The Quality-Consistency Score (QC) described earlier in the book reflects this by giving negative outcomes double the weight. We use this formula in the charts: (DOM − (2xDIS)) x 2

Third is the application of the DOM/DIS rates for use in **comparison of players** to uncover hidden value. The minimum level benchmark is a DOM/DIS split of 50/20. While this equates to a QC score of only 20, it keeps the available talent pool open while focusing on the best skills.

An example: Garrett Atkins and Stephen Drew put up comparable aggregate statistics in 2008. Atkins had 32 more RBIs but Drew had more runs, SBs and a higher batting average. In a 15-team, 5x5 mixed league, Atkins was valued at $16, Drew at $15 (the values in this book are higher due to a different definition of the player pool.) However, in terms of quality and consistency, these players' values are further apart. Atkins' DOM/DIS split was 41/19 for a QC score of 6. Drew's was 63/15 for a QC score of 66!

The following charts include:

- Up to three years of data for all batters who had at least five weeks of stats in 2008
- Base Performance Value for the year (BPV)
- Total number of weeks he accumulated stats (#Wks)
- Domination and Disaster percentages (DOM, DIS)
- Quality-Consistency Score (QC)
- The final chart lists all batters who achieved a single season QC score of 100 during the past three years

Some other observations...

Garrett Atkins, mentioned above, not only had a QC of only 6 but it is the most recent data point in a disturbing trend: 106, 68, 6.

Despite his marginal draft list status, **Casey Blake's** QC trend is at least a little bit encouraging: -44, -6, 24.

There are some players that we immediately label as "streaky." **Pat Burrell** is one of them. While his QC scores don't light up the stadium — 36, 24, 48 — they are at least all positive, if not a little bit "hippy."

We've been trying to put a positive spin on **Robinson Cano's** season. However, when it comes to consistency, QC puts a negative stamp on 2008. His trend: 128, 32, -50.

Here's a surprise... Despite his age and loss of power, **Brian Giles'** consistency is on a 3-year climb: 20, 64, 96.

A 20-97-.264 season would merit a mid-teens bid in most Rotisserie leagues, but when it comes to consistency, **Jose Guillen** likely gave his H2H owners fits all year. His DOM/DIS split of 48/41 equates to a QC of –68.

Traditional stats make **Raul Ibanez** look like a consistent producer. His QC scores show that talent waning: 82, 32, 8.

Health aside, **Chipper Jones** needs to be near the top of most H2H draft lists on his consistency alone: 104, 128, 122.

Carlos Pena had his breakout year in 2007 and a slight drop-off in 2008. QC says his consistency was actually better this past year (60 in 2007, 82 in 2008).

The highest QC score possible is 200. **Albert Pujols** has managed levels of 160 in 2006 and 170 in 2008.

BATTER CONSISTENCY CHART

Name	Year	BPV	#Wks	DOM	DIS	QC
Abercrombie,Reggie	06	14	27	22%	63%	-208
	07	5	11	9%	55%	-202
	08	87	14	43%	57%	-142
Abreu,Bobby	06	67	27	56%	7%	84
	07	55	27	48%	22%	8
	08	61	27	59%	15%	58
Abreu,Tony	07	36	13	46%	23%	0
Adams,Russ	06	13	21	29%	43%	-114
	07	32	8	38%	63%	-176
Alou,Moises	06	80	21	62%	5%	104
	07	76	17	53%	18%	34
	08	39	5	40%	20%	0
Ambres,Chip	08	-13	9	22%	56%	-180
Amezaga,Alfredo	06	19	27	22%	41%	-120
	07	25	27	33%	33%	-66
	08	24	26	35%	54%	-146
Anderson,Brian	06	23	27	37%	41%	-90
	08	43	27	30%	44%	-116
Anderson,Garret	06	42	26	50%	15%	40
	07	61	19	63%	26%	22
	08	42	27	33%	22%	-22
Anderson,Josh	07	51	5	40%	60%	-160
	08	43	9	33%	33%	-66
Anderson,Marlon	06	62	26	54%	31%	-16
	07	56	19	42%	42%	-84
	08	0	21	29%	62%	-190
Andino,Robert	06	-24	7	0%	86%	-344
	08	15	19	21%	74%	-254
Ankiel,Rick	07	68	9	56%	22%	24
	08	63	24	50%	21%	16
Antonelli,Matthew	08	0	5	0%	40%	-160
Ardoin,Danny	06	-14	14	21%	57%	-186
	08	4	13	31%	62%	-186
Arias,Joaquin	08	41	7	43%	43%	-86
Atkins,Garrett	06	87	27	67%	7%	106
	07	63	27	56%	11%	68
	08	47	27	41%	19%	6
Aubrey,Michael	08	14	5	20%	80%	-280
Aurilia,Rich	06	64	25	60%	12%	72
	07	26	24	29%	46%	-126
	08	40	27	37%	30%	-46
Ausmus,Brad	06	6	27	19%	48%	-154
	07	15	27	30%	48%	-132
	08	8	27	30%	59%	-176
Aviles,Mike	08	56	19	63%	21%	42
Aybar,Erick	06	2	14	21%	71%	-242
	07	0	21	19%	67%	-230
	08	28	22	36%	32%	-56
Aybar,Willy	06	45	16	25%	25%	-50
	08	39	21	48%	19%	20
Bailey,Jeff	08	56	11	36%	55%	-148
Baker,Jeff	06	147	5	60%	40%	-40
	07	13	24	29%	63%	-194
	08	60	26	38%	46%	-108
Baker,John	08	60	13	69%	15%	78
Bako,Paul	06	-16	22	9%	73%	-274
	07	-8	26	23%	65%	-214
	08	15	26	23%	54%	-170
Baldelli,Rocco	06	65	17	59%	12%	70
	07	19	7	29%	43%	-114
	08	61	8	50%	38%	-52
Balentien,Wladimir	08	19	16	38%	44%	-100
Bankston,Wes	08	4	5	20%	40%	-120
Barajas,Rod	06	32	26	31%	35%	-78
	07	41	22	41%	50%	-118
	08	34	24	50%	33%	-32
Barden,Brian	07	-25	9	11%	89%	-334
	08	-25	5	0%	80%	-320
Bard,Josh	06	78	26	50%	35%	-40
	07	48	25	40%	28%	-32
	08	4	16	25%	50%	-150
Barfield,Josh	06	38	27	37%	26%	-30
	07	10	27	15%	44%	-146
Barmes,Clint	06	10	27	22%	41%	-120
	07	12	10	20%	60%	-200
	08	50	23	48%	17%	28
Barrett,Michael	06	68	21	71%	19%	66
	07	23	23	30%	39%	-96
	08	5	8	13%	38%	-126
Bartlett,Jason	06	38	17	47%	24%	-2
	07	27	26	31%	50%	-138
	08	26	24	38%	29%	-40
Barton,Brian Deon	08	39	21	33%	48%	-126
Barton,Daric	08	21	27	33%	41%	-98
Bautista,Jose	06	39	22	32%	32%	-64
	07	44	25	36%	12%	24
	08	36	27	30%	48%	-132
Bay,Jason	06	75	27	70%	11%	96
	07	40	27	44%	37%	-60
	08	73	27	59%	7%	90
Belliard,Ronnie	06	35	27	41%	26%	-22
	07	45	27	41%	30%	-38
	08	63	20	50%	25%	0
Beltran,Carlos	06	91	27	74%	11%	104
	07	70	26	54%	12%	60
	08	70	27	63%	11%	82
Beltre,Adrian	06	49	27	48%	26%	-8
	07	56	27	44%	26%	-16
	08	49	25	44%	16%	24
Bennett,Gary	06	10	25	24%	60%	-192
	07	17	26	19%	54%	-178
	08	4	7	29%	71%	-226
Berkman,Lance	06	98	27	78%	0%	156
	07	68	27	59%	19%	42
	08	93	27	63%	11%	82
Bernadina,Rogearvin	08	-9	7	29%	57%	-170
Berroa,Angel	06	8	27	19%	48%	-154
	08	13	17	29%	47%	-130
Betancourt,Yuniesky	06	31	27	30%	26%	-44
	07	38	26	38%	31%	-48
	08	32	27	33%	30%	-54
Betemit,Wilson	06	55	27	59%	30%	-2
	07	58	27	59%	30%	-2
	08	45	22	45%	32%	-38
Bixler,Brian	08	-30	14	7%	86%	-330
Blake,Casey	06	57	22	50%	36%	-44
	07	47	27	41%	22%	-6
	08	55	27	56%	22%	24
Blalock,Hank	06	34	26	42%	27%	-24
	07	76	11	73%	18%	74
	08	64	14	50%	21%	16
Blanco,Gregor	08	17	26	35%	38%	-82
Blanco,Henry	06	36	27	33%	44%	-110
	07	-18	13	8%	69%	-260
	08	29	25	32%	44%	-112
Bloomquist,Willie	06	8	27	19%	44%	-138
	07	13	27	22%	63%	-208
	08	12	18	11%	67%	-246
Blum,Geoff	06	24	27	30%	48%	-132
	07	30	27	33%	37%	-82
	08	33	26	35%	35%	-70
Bocock,Brian	08	-37	6	0%	83%	-332
Boggs,Brandon	08	42	23	35%	39%	-86
Bonifacio,Emilio	07	15	5	0%	60%	-240
	08	15	14	29%	43%	-114
Boone,Aaron	06	26	25	24%	36%	-96
	07	47	13	46%	38%	-60
	08	30	23	30%	57%	-168
Botts,Jason	06	37	8	38%	63%	-176
	07	23	10	30%	30%	-60
	08	63	5	40%	60%	-160
Bourn,Michael	06	-51	6	17%	83%	-298
	07	29	22	27%	55%	-166
	08	3	27	19%	44%	-138
Bowen,Rob	06	36	25	36%	56%	-152
	07	42	25	40%	52%	-128
	08	6	22	36%	64%	-184
Bowker,John	08	33	24	38%	46%	-108
Bradley,Milton	06	51	19	42%	21%	0
	07	78	19	47%	32%	-34
	08	95	27	67%	15%	74
Branyan,Russell	06	68	26	54%	23%	16
	07	51	24	46%	38%	-60
	08	93	13	54%	31%	-16
Braun,Ryan	07	96	20	75%	0%	150
	08	73	27	70%	15%	80
Broussard,Ben	06	55	27	52%	26%	0
	07	35	25	44%	44%	-88
	08	-15	5	20%	60%	-200
Brown,Emil	06	57	27	59%	19%	42
	07	18	27	33%	41%	-98
	08	25	26	27%	38%	-98
Brown,Matt	08	-45	7	14%	86%	-316
Bruce,Jay	08	47	19	53%	37%	-42
Bruntlett,Eric	06	29	23	35%	57%	-158
	07	11	17	35%	59%	-166
	08	8	27	30%	59%	-176

BATTER CONSISTENCY CHART

Name	Year	BPV	#Wks	DOM	DIS	QC
Buck,John	06	32	26	31%	42%	-106
	07	43	26	38%	31%	-48
	08	28	27	41%	37%	-66
Buck,Travis	07	64	19	58%	16%	52
	08	40	10	50%	50%	-100
Budde,Ryan	07	-17	5	0%	60%	-240
	08	-99	5	0%	100%	-400
Burke,Chris	06	40	25	40%	44%	-96
	07	23	24	38%	42%	-92
	08	3	26	23%	73%	-246
Burke,Jamie	07	40	25	44%	44%	-88
	08	18	25	24%	60%	-192
Burrell,Pat	06	69	27	56%	19%	36
	07	73	27	56%	22%	24
	08	72	26	62%	19%	48
Burriss,Emmanuel	08	26	22	23%	59%	-190
Buscher,Brian	07	15	10	30%	50%	-140
	08	35	18	33%	22%	-22
Butler,Billy	07	52	18	50%	22%	12
	08	37	23	43%	39%	-70
Bynum,Freddie	06	45	19	47%	37%	-54
	07	52	20	35%	55%	-150
	08	-21	10	10%	70%	-260
Byrd,Marlon	06	19	15	27%	33%	-78
	07	50	19	42%	16%	20
	08	59	24	50%	17%	32
Byrnes,Eric	06	50	27	44%	26%	-16
	07	51	26	50%	27%	-8
	08	24	11	36%	36%	-72
Cabrera,Asdrubal	07	45	9	33%	11%	22
	08	33	23	30%	39%	-96
Cabrera,Jolbert	08	34	14	43%	43%	-86
Cabrera,Melky	06	43	22	41%	18%	10
	07	34	27	33%	44%	-110
	08	17	24	25%	38%	-102
Cabrera,Miguel	06	91	27	74%	19%	72
	07	86	27	74%	15%	88
	08	71	27	63%	15%	66
Cabrera,Orlando	06	46	26	42%	19%	8
	07	41	26	54%	15%	48
	08	35	27	37%	26%	-30
Cairo,Miguel	06	12	22	27%	50%	-146
	07	16	22	23%	59%	-190
	08	21	26	19%	50%	-162
Callaspo,Alberto	06	9	7	29%	57%	-170
	07	4	15	27%	53%	-158
	08	46	20	30%	35%	-80
Cameron,Mike	06	58	24	50%	25%	0
	07	46	27	41%	37%	-66
	08	62	23	43%	22%	-2
Cancel,Robinson	08	19	16	25%	69%	-226
Cano,Robinson	06	69	22	64%	0%	128
	07	59	26	46%	15%	32
	08	35	27	41%	33%	-50
Cantu,Jorge	06	31	22	41%	32%	-46
	07	30	19	37%	47%	-114
	08	55	27	56%	26%	8
Carlin,Luke	08	-13	17	12%	71%	-260
Carroll,Brett	07	-25	7	14%	86%	-316
	08	-48	8	0%	88%	-352
Carroll,Jamey	06	45	26	38%	19%	0
	07	13	27	30%	59%	-176
	08	23	26	38%	42%	-92
Carter,Chris	08	19	5	40%	40%	-80
Casanova,Raul	07	56	12	58%	25%	16
	08	29	9	22%	33%	-88
Casey,Sean	06	36	21	38%	19%	0
	07	46	27	48%	22%	8
	08	46	24	42%	46%	-100
Cash,Kevin	07	-33	6	0%	83%	-332
	08	24	27	26%	63%	-200
Casilla,Alexi	07	-7	13	8%	62%	-232
	08	32	19	32%	26%	-40
Castillo,Jose	06	26	27	33%	48%	-126
	07	18	27	30%	44%	-116
	08	28	25	36%	36%	-72
Castillo,Luis	06	37	27	41%	26%	-22
	07	40	26	54%	19%	32
	08	26	20	30%	35%	-80
Castillo,Wilkin	08	9	5	40%	60%	-160
Casto,Kory	07	-37	6	0%	100%	-400
	08	15	17	35%	41%	-94

BATTER CONSISTENCY CHART

Name	Year	BPV	#Wks	DOM	DIS	QC
Castro,Juan	06	16	27	26%	48%	-140
	07	-12	15	20%	53%	-172
	08	-5	15	0%	60%	-240
Castro,Ramon	06	35	17	35%	35%	-70
	07	74	23	43%	48%	-106
	08	44	20	40%	40%	-80
Catalanotto,Frank	06	66	26	62%	12%	76
	07	48	24	50%	38%	-52
	08	44	23	48%	39%	-60
Cedeno,Ronny	06	10	27	22%	37%	-104
	07	20	14	36%	57%	-156
	08	26	27	26%	44%	-124
Cervenak,Mike	08	-48	6	17%	67%	-234
Chavez,Endy	06	46	27	44%	30%	-32
	07	31	15	47%	40%	-66
	08	22	27	26%	56%	-172
Chavez,Eric	06	48	27	52%	22%	16
	07	47	17	41%	24%	-14
	08	35	6	17%	33%	-98
Chavez,Raul	06	-34	11	18%	82%	-292
	08	10	19	32%	42%	-104
Choo,Shin-Soo	06	58	12	67%	33%	2
	08	87	18	61%	17%	54
Christian,Justin	08	24	9	11%	44%	-154
Church,Ryan	06	78	18	67%	28%	22
	07	60	26	58%	4%	100
	08	48	18	61%	28%	10
Cintron,Alex	06	26	27	33%	48%	-126
	07	10	22	32%	55%	-156
	08	25	19	21%	42%	-126
Clark,Tony	06	19	20	30%	60%	-180
	07	58	27	52%	37%	-44
	08	20	26	23%	42%	-122
Clement,Jeff	08	24	15	33%	47%	-122
Cora,Alex	06	8	27	22%	48%	-148
	07	23	26	46%	46%	-92
	08	37	23	30%	35%	-80
Coste,Chris	06	62	20	45%	35%	-50
	07	30	15	33%	33%	-66
	08	40	27	44%	30%	-32
Counsell,Craig	06	21	22	23%	18%	-26
	07	16	26	19%	54%	-178
	08	23	27	30%	59%	-176
Crabbe,Callix	08	-16	6	0%	50%	-200
Crawford,Carl	06	50	26	46%	12%	44
	07	54	25	52%	24%	8
	08	30	21	33%	43%	-106
Crede,Joe	06	56	26	46%	23%	0
	07	6	10	20%	40%	-120
	08	48	19	47%	16%	30
Crisp,Coco	06	30	18	44%	28%	-24
	07	34	27	48%	26%	-8
	08	40	28	54%	32%	-20
Crosby,Bobby	06	16	20	15%	50%	-170
	07	16	17	18%	41%	-128
	08	24	27	33%	33%	-66
Cruz,Jose	06	39	18	50%	22%	12
	07	29	18	22%	33%	-88
	08	-26	10	0%	80%	-320
Cruz,Luis	08	19	5	0%	40%	-160
Cruz,Nelson	06	21	11	27%	55%	-166
	07	30	21	43%	38%	-66
	08	102	6	83%	0%	166
Cuddyer,Michael	06	67	27	74%	11%	104
	07	48	26	54%	23%	16
	08	29	15	40%	47%	-108
Cust,Jack	07	86	22	55%	27%	2
	08	76	28	54%	18%	36
D' Antona,James	08	-30	8	13%	63%	-226
Damon,Johnny	06	59	27	56%	22%	24
	07	41	27	33%	19%	-10
	08	57	25	44%	16%	24
Davis,Chris	08	82	15	67%	13%	82
Davis,Rajai	06	-11	7	14%	86%	-316
	07	36	18	33%	50%	-134
	08	14	25	28%	60%	-184
DeJesus,David	06	52	22	45%	18%	18
	07	32	26	38%	19%	0
	08	52	25	52%	20%	24
Delgado,Carlos	06	73	26	65%	23%	38
	07	48	26	54%	23%	16
	08	67	27	59%	15%	58

BATTER CONSISTENCY CHART

Name	Year	BPV	#Wks	DOM	DIS	QC
Dellucci,David	06	67	26	58%	31%	-8
	07	31	14	36%	36%	-72
	08	34	26	38%	50%	-124
Denker,Travis	08	69	8	25%	38%	-102
Denorfia,Chris	06	32	14	43%	50%	-114
	08	36	10	40%	30%	-40
DeRosa,Mark	06	54	25	44%	32%	-40
	07	47	27	44%	30%	-32
	08	63	26	50%	27%	-8
DeWitt,Blake	08	33	23	30%	48%	-132
Diaz,Matt	06	51	26	35%	35%	-70
	07	62	27	56%	22%	24
	08	0	10	10%	60%	-220
Dickerson,Chris	08	112	6	83%	17%	98
DiFelice,Mike	06	-42	8	13%	88%	-326
	07	20	6	0%	50%	-200
Dillon,Joe	07	71	10	70%	20%	60
	08	11	18	39%	56%	-146
Dobbs,Greg	06	76	10	30%	50%	-140
	07	49	27	41%	22%	-6
	08	58	26	58%	23%	24
Doumit,Ryan	06	31	15	40%	47%	-108
	07	57	19	47%	42%	-74
	08	64	25	48%	24%	0
Drew,J.D.	06	69	26	65%	15%	70
	07	52	26	46%	27%	-16
	08	78	23	52%	17%	36
Drew,Stephen	06	65	13	31%	23%	-30
	07	28	27	22%	22%	-44
	08	62	27	63%	15%	66
Dukes,Elijah	07	29	12	33%	42%	-102
	08	66	16	56%	31%	-12
Duncan,Chris	06	80	18	72%	11%	100
	07	65	24	46%	29%	-24
	08	30	16	31%	31%	-62
Duncan,Shelley	07	70	11	45%	45%	-90
	08	3	8	13%	50%	-174
Dunn,Adam	06	66	27	70%	19%	64
	07	86	26	62%	15%	64
	08	76	27	74%	11%	104
Duran,German	08	16	18	22%	56%	-180
Durham,Ray	06	71	26	69%	19%	62
	07	20	26	31%	31%	-62
	08	59	27	48%	19%	20
Dye,Jermaine	06	92	26	77%	0%	154
	07	58	26	58%	23%	24
	08	71	28	64%	25%	28
Easley,Damion	06	34	27	37%	52%	-134
	07	50	19	47%	47%	-94
	08	25	26	38%	58%	-156
Eckstein,David	06	27	22	18%	27%	-72
	07	46	24	42%	33%	-48
	08	34	24	29%	25%	-42
Edmonds,Jim	06	57	22	59%	23%	26
	07	35	23	43%	39%	-70
	08	60	26	58%	35%	-24
Ellis,Mark	06	31	24	42%	33%	-48
	07	46	27	44%	19%	12
	08	30	23	39%	22%	-10
Ellsbury,Jacoby	07	69	9	56%	33%	-20
	08	33	28	29%	25%	-42
Encarnacion,Edwin	06	57	24	46%	21%	8
	07	45	26	50%	31%	-24
	08	54	27	56%	26%	8
Ensberg,Morgan	06	59	24	38%	33%	-56
	07	37	26	42%	42%	-84
	08	-16	9	11%	78%	-290
Erstad,Darin	06	16	11	9%	73%	-274
	07	20	19	37%	42%	-94
	08	25	26	38%	38%	-76
Escobar,Yunel	07	59	19	58%	16%	52
	08	45	25	36%	24%	-24
Estrada,Johnny	06	43	27	33%	37%	-82
	07	31	26	38%	38%	-76
	08	-37	6	0%	67%	-268
Ethier,Andre	06	55	23	61%	26%	18
	07	54	27	44%	19%	12
	08	71	27	48%	7%	68
Evans,Nick	08	41	16	44%	50%	-112
Everett,Adam	06	19	27	22%	26%	-60
	07	12	13	23%	31%	-78
	08	16	16	25%	50%	-150

BATTER CONSISTENCY CHART

Name	Year	BPV	#Wks	DOM	DIS	QC
Fahey,Brandon	06	8	23	22%	57%	-184
	07	-25	14	14%	86%	-316
	08	20	16	25%	44%	-126
Fasano,Sal	06	23	24	46%	46%	-92
	07	19	8	38%	63%	-176
	08	34	11	45%	36%	-54
Feliz,Pedro	06	35	27	41%	26%	-22
	07	34	27	37%	30%	-46
	08	34	23	39%	22%	-10
Fielder,Prince	06	57	27	59%	15%	58
	07	96	26	81%	0%	162
	08	67	27	59%	19%	42
Fields,Josh	07	61	18	50%	39%	-56
	08	-23	7	0%	86%	-344
Figgins,Chone	06	30	26	35%	35%	-70
	07	53	22	64%	32%	0
	08	21	23	22%	26%	-60
Flores,Jesus	07	25	27	30%	63%	-192
	08	35	20	40%	45%	-100
Floyd,Cliff	06	34	23	39%	30%	-42
	07	45	26	38%	23%	-16
	08	53	22	50%	36%	-44
Fontenot,Mike	07	37	19	26%	47%	-136
	08	78	26	62%	27%	16
Fowler,Dexter	08	-48	5	0%	100%	-400
Francisco,Ben	07	69	11	36%	55%	-148
	08	48	23	48%	26%	-8
Francoeur,Jeff	06	36	27	41%	26%	-22
	07	48	27	41%	19%	6
	08	22	27	30%	37%	-88
Frandsen,Kevin	06	4	14	21%	64%	-214
	07	35	25	28%	48%	-136
Freel,Ryan	06	40	25	32%	36%	-80
	07	18	14	14%	36%	-116
	08	30	10	40%	30%	-40
Fukudome,Kosuke	08	37	26	50%	35%	-40
Furcal,Rafael	06	51	26	50%	15%	40
	07	29	24	33%	13%	14
	08	99	7	57%	14%	58
Garciaparra,Nomar	06	75	23	65%	22%	42
	07	33	24	29%	29%	-58
	08	63	14	50%	43%	-72
Gardner,Brett	08	4	12	25%	58%	-182
Garko,Ryan	06	54	10	50%	10%	60
	07	57	27	48%	19%	20
	08	37	27	48%	37%	-52
Gathright,Joey	06	7	26	15%	35%	-110
	07	26	17	41%	35%	-58
	08	0	23	17%	52%	-174
German,Esteban	06	62	27	56%	26%	8
	07	33	27	44%	37%	-60
	08	21	27	37%	48%	-118
Gerut,Jody	08	59	20	55%	25%	10
Getz,Christopher	08	-4	5	0%	80%	-320
Giambi,Jason	06	85	27	59%	19%	42
	07	45	18	44%	33%	-44
	08	64	27	63%	19%	50
Giles,Brian	06	56	27	48%	19%	20
	07	49	22	50%	9%	64
	08	76	27	56%	4%	96
Glaus,Troy	06	67	26	58%	8%	84
	07	60	23	57%	30%	-6
	08	65	27	67%	22%	46
Gload,Ross	06	50	24	42%	46%	-100
	07	45	22	45%	32%	-38
	08	24	25	24%	44%	-128
Golson,Gregory	08	-99	5	0%	100%	-400
Gomes,Jonny	06	47	21	43%	38%	-66
	07	60	24	50%	21%	16
	08	25	23	35%	52%	-138
Gomez,Carlos	07	4	12	25%	75%	-250
	08	21	27	37%	30%	-46
Gomez,Chris	06	53	18	44%	33%	-44
	07	31	25	36%	40%	-88
	08	20	25	36%	48%	-120
Gonzalez,Adrian	06	63	27	52%	7%	76
	07	65	27	63%	22%	38
	08	67	27	52%	15%	44
Gonzalez,Alberto	07	-55	6	0%	100%	-400
	08	32	17	24%	71%	-236
Gonzalez,Alex	06	31	24	42%	38%	-68
	07	51	23	43%	30%	-34

BATTER CONSISTENCY CHART

Name	Year	BPV	#Wks	DOM	DIS	QC
Gonzalez,Andy	07	-6	21	14%	71%	-256
	08	22	6	33%	67%	-202
Gonzalez,Carlos	08	26	17	35%	29%	-46
Gonzalez,Edgar	08	32	20	35%	50%	-130
Gonzalez,Luis	06	60	27	48%	19%	20
	07	51	26	50%	27%	-8
	08	49	27	37%	26%	-30
Gordon,Alex	07	40	27	44%	37%	-60
	08	51	24	50%	25%	0
Gotay,Ruben	07	46	23	48%	39%	-60
	08	25	25	44%	44%	-88
Granderson,Curtis	06	47	27	48%	22%	8
	07	75	27	74%	11%	104
	08	61	24	58%	13%	64
Greene,Khalil	06	40	25	32%	48%	-128
	07	50	27	56%	26%	8
	08	13	18	22%	39%	-112
Griffey Jr.,Ken	06	50	21	48%	19%	20
	07	65	25	60%	12%	72
	08	48	27	44%	19%	12
Gross,Gabe	06	65	26	38%	42%	-92
	07	47	24	54%	42%	-60
	08	41	27	41%	37%	-66
Grudzielanek,Mark	06	38	24	38%	17%	8
	07	45	24	50%	21%	16
	08	40	18	50%	33%	-32
Guerrero,Vladimir	06	77	26	73%	8%	114
	07	88	26	77%	8%	122
	08	69	26	65%	8%	98
Guillen,Carlos	06	76	27	63%	7%	98
	07	64	27	67%	19%	58
	08	56	22	59%	14%	62
Guillen,Jose	06	27	15	27%	40%	-106
	07	50	27	59%	22%	30
	08	42	27	48%	41%	-68
Gutierrez,Franklin	06	23	11	55%	36%	-34
	07	55	21	48%	33%	-36
	08	31	27	48%	33%	-36
Guzman,Cristian	07	55	11	36%	45%	-108
	08	47	26	31%	19%	-14
Gwynn,Tony	06	3	9	22%	56%	-180
	07	12	18	17%	44%	-142
	08	-15	9	11%	56%	-202
Hafner,Travis	06	114	22	73%	5%	126
	07	57	27	52%	19%	28
	08	16	13	23%	38%	-106
Hairston,Jerry	06	-8	27	22%	67%	-224
	07	1	21	24%	57%	-180
	08	67	20	45%	25%	-10
Hairston,Scott	06	97	5	80%	20%	80
	07	49	23	39%	22%	-10
	08	55	22	45%	36%	-54
Hall,Bill	06	81	27	63%	19%	50
	07	48	24	50%	21%	16
	08	36	26	38%	38%	-76
Hall,Toby	06	32	26	42%	42%	-84
	07	-13	19	11%	68%	-250
	08	11	26	27%	46%	-130
Hamilton,Josh	07	77	17	65%	24%	34
	08	72	27	67%	19%	58
Hammock,Robby	07	6	15	27%	53%	-158
	08	-15	11	18%	64%	-220
Hanigan,Ryan	08	35	8	25%	25%	-50
Hannahan,Jack	07	55	8	38%	38%	-76
	08	26	26	46%	35%	-48
Hardy,J.J.	06	28	7	43%	29%	-30
	07	49	27	52%	19%	28
	08	56	27	44%	22%	0
Harris,Brendan	06	23	10	20%	40%	-120
	07	48	26	50%	15%	40
	08	37	27	37%	33%	-58
Harris,Willie	06	-22	14	14%	86%	-316
	07	37	23	35%	39%	-86
	08	41	26	35%	35%	-70
Hart,Corey	06	51	24	42%	33%	-48
	07	69	27	56%	7%	84
	08	48	27	52%	22%	16
Hatteberg,Scott	06	69	26	54%	23%	16
	07	75	23	65%	13%	78
	08	-1	9	11%	67%	-246
Hawpe,Brad	06	71	27	59%	26%	14
	07	80	27	78%	11%	112
	08	68	26	54%	19%	32

BATTER CONSISTENCY CHART

Name	Year	BPV	#Wks	DOM	DIS	QC
Haynes,Nathan	07	3	17	24%	71%	-236
	08	-18	6	17%	67%	-234
Headley,Chase	08	46	16	38%	13%	24
Helms,Wes	06	84	27	56%	26%	8
	07	28	27	26%	41%	-112
	08	19	26	27%	54%	-162
Helton,Todd	06	73	26	58%	23%	24
	07	85	27	67%	4%	118
	08	48	16	56%	31%	-12
Hermida,Jeremy	06	29	21	29%	48%	-134
	07	69	21	71%	14%	86
	08	37	26	38%	31%	-48
Hernandez,Anderson	06	-26	9	22%	67%	-224
	08	53	7	29%	14%	2
Hernandez,Luis	07	18	9	22%	33%	-88
	08	-1	9	11%	78%	-290
Hernandez,Ramon	06	54	26	46%	23%	0
	07	33	22	45%	41%	-74
	08	35	27	33%	26%	-38
Herrera,Jonathan	08	-2	7	14%	71%	-256
Hill,Aaron	06	36	27	44%	30%	-32
	07	54	26	54%	15%	48
	08	30	9	22%	33%	-88
Hinske,Eric	06	63	27	48%	22%	8
	07	39	27	41%	48%	-110
	08	53	27	52%	37%	-44
Hoffpauir,Micah	08	92	11	36%	55%	-148
Holliday,Matt	06	83	27	70%	4%	124
	07	95	27	78%	4%	140
	08	82	24	67%	17%	66
Hollimon,Michael	08	77	5	40%	60%	-160
Holm,Stephen	08	49	19	47%	42%	-74
Hoover,Paul	08	-16	8	13%	63%	-226
Hopper,Norris	06	73	5	60%	0%	120
	07	40	25	40%	40%	-80
	08	-16	6	17%	67%	-234
Horwitz,Brian	08	26	6	33%	67%	-202
Howard,Ryan	06	111	27	85%	0%	170
	07	102	26	69%	4%	122
	08	78	27	56%	7%	84
Huber,Justin	07	-66	5	20%	80%	-280
	08	33	12	50%	50%	-100
Hudson,Orlando	06	52	27	44%	19%	12
	07	53	23	65%	17%	62
	08	56	19	42%	16%	20
Huff,Aubrey	06	54	25	52%	28%	-8
	07	48	26	50%	23%	8
	08	78	27	67%	15%	74
Hulett,Timothy	08	7	9	22%	67%	-224
Hundley,Nicholas	08	19	14	29%	36%	-86
Hunter,Torii	06	53	25	48%	12%	48
	07	63	27	56%	11%	68
	08	55	27	56%	19%	36
Hu,Chin-lung	07	46	6	17%	67%	-234
	08	-16	15	20%	67%	-228
Iannetta,Chris	06	39	5	40%	40%	-80
	07	23	24	21%	50%	-158
	08	72	27	48%	15%	36
Ibanez,Raul	06	65	27	63%	11%	82
	07	59	25	48%	16%	32
	08	61	27	48%	22%	8
Iguchi,Tadahito	06	42	26	54%	19%	32
	07	40	27	37%	19%	-2
	08	10	18	11%	44%	-154
Infante,Omar	06	36	25	16%	44%	-144
	07	21	24	25%	46%	-134
	08	45	20	45%	15%	30
Inge,Brandon	06	48	27	56%	11%	68
	07	30	27	37%	33%	-58
	08	26	26	35%	31%	-54
Inglett,Joe	06	29	16	38%	31%	-48
	08	40	25	44%	20%	8
Ishikawa,Travis	06	67	5	60%	40%	-40
	08	50	8	38%	25%	-24
Iwamura,Akinori	07	41	23	52%	17%	36
	08	33	27	30%	19%	-16
Izturis,Cesar	06	19	11	36%	55%	-148
	07	23	27	26%	48%	-140
	08	22	25	16%	40%	-128
Izturis,Maicer	06	51	22	41%	41%	-82
	07	44	21	38%	29%	-40
	08	34	19	37%	32%	-54

Name	Year	BPV	#Wks	DOM	DIS	QC
Jackson,Conor	06	50	27	59%	19%	42
	07	63	27	52%	15%	44
	08	57	26	46%	12%	44
Jacobs,Mike	06	56	26	58%	23%	24
	07	50	23	48%	26%	-8
	08	63	27	44%	19%	12
Janish,Paul	08	-10	11	36%	45%	-108
Jenkins,Geoff	06	46	27	41%	26%	-22
	07	54	27	48%	30%	-24
	08	33	24	38%	38%	-76
Jeter,Derek	06	67	27	59%	11%	74
	07	56	27	63%	11%	82
	08	41	26	42%	27%	-24
Johjima,Kenji	06	43	27	37%	26%	-30
	07	41	26	38%	35%	-64
	08	15	27	37%	56%	-150
Johnson,Dan	06	33	21	29%	43%	-114
	07	46	23	30%	35%	-80
	08	30	5	40%	60%	-160
Johnson,Kelly	07	54	27	44%	30%	-32
	08	52	27	52%	7%	76
Johnson,Nick	06	83	25	72%	4%	128
	08	62	7	43%	14%	30
Johnson,Reed	06	60	26	62%	12%	76
	07	11	16	25%	50%	-150
	08	44	26	38%	38%	-76
Johnson,Rob	08	-34	5	20%	80%	-280
Jones,Adam	06	8	10	20%	60%	-200
	07	32	10	50%	50%	-100
	08	31	23	22%	22%	-44
Jones,Andruw	06	69	27	52%	15%	44
	07	37	26	38%	19%	0
	08	-6	15	13%	67%	-242
Jones,Brandon	08	39	10	50%	30%	-20
Jones,Chipper	06	92	23	70%	9%	104
	07	102	25	80%	8%	128
	08	104	26	69%	4%	122
Jones,Jacque	06	58	27	52%	7%	76
	07	40	27	48%	37%	-52
	08	-23	10	10%	90%	-340
Joyce,Matthew	08	64	18	50%	28%	-12
Kaaihue,Kila	08	54	5	40%	60%	-160
Kapler,Gabe	06	31	17	35%	41%	-94
	08	61	24	58%	21%	32
Kazmar,Sean	08	-11	7	14%	86%	-316
Kearns,Austin	06	56	26	54%	23%	16
	07	43	27	44%	22%	0
	08	12	16	25%	44%	-126
Kemp,Matt	06	47	13	31%	62%	-186
	07	66	20	65%	25%	30
	08	54	27	48%	19%	20
Kendall,Jason	06	33	27	26%	11%	8
	07	15	27	33%	41%	-98
	08	28	27	30%	33%	-72
Kendrick,Howie	06	38	14	36%	43%	-100
	07	50	16	50%	13%	48
	08	43	19	37%	26%	-30
Kennedy,Adam	06	33	27	30%	26%	-44
	07	5	19	21%	63%	-210
	08	29	27	30%	37%	-88
Kent,Jeff	06	61	22	59%	18%	46
	07	71	26	69%	15%	78
	08	39	23	48%	35%	-44
Keppinger,Jeff	06	37	6	33%	50%	-134
	07	87	16	50%	31%	-24
	08	36	21	29%	24%	-38
Kinsler,Ian	06	52	22	68%	18%	64
	07	49	23	35%	17%	2
	08	72	21	57%	5%	94
Konerko,Paul	06	76	26	65%	4%	114
	07	63	27	63%	15%	66
	08	47	24	42%	17%	16
Koshansky,Joe	07	-19	6	0%	83%	-332
	08	94	8	50%	38%	-52
Kotchman,Casey	06	-20	6	17%	67%	-234
	07	70	26	58%	19%	40
	08	44	26	31%	31%	-62
Kotsay,Mark	06	38	27	48%	26%	-8
	07	17	12	25%	50%	-150
	08	41	23	43%	26%	-18
Kouzmanoff,Kevin	06	30	5	40%	40%	-80
	07	49	27	44%	26%	-16
	08	39	27	41%	22%	-6

Name	Year	BPV	#Wks	DOM	DIS	QC
Kubel,Jason	06	24	21	33%	48%	-126
	07	53	27	52%	15%	44
	08	53	27	59%	11%	74
LaHair,Bryan	08	20	11	18%	45%	-144
Laird,Gerald	06	57	27	52%	30%	-16
	07	18	26	35%	38%	-82
	08	38	22	45%	23%	-2
Lamb,Mike	06	57	27	37%	33%	-58
	07	53	27	37%	44%	-102
	08	13	24	33%	58%	-166
Langerhans,Ryan	06	33	27	41%	37%	-66
	07	9	24	29%	54%	-158
	08	42	18	33%	56%	-158
Larish,Jeffrey	08	33	12	42%	33%	-48
LaRoche,Adam	06	81	26	69%	8%	106
	07	57	27	52%	22%	16
	08	65	26	46%	19%	16
LaRoche,Andy	07	22	9	22%	33%	-88
	08	-7	17	35%	53%	-142
LaRue,Jason	06	16	24	38%	46%	-108
	07	3	25	16%	60%	-208
	08	21	25	28%	52%	-152
Lee,Carlos	06	73	26	62%	12%	76
	07	73	27	63%	7%	98
	08	81	19	68%	5%	116
Lee,Derrek	06	58	12	33%	25%	-34
	07	74	27	74%	11%	104
	08	58	27	59%	22%	30
Lewis,Fred	06	89	5	60%	40%	-40
	07	40	15	47%	47%	-94
	08	49	24	46%	17%	24
Lillibridge,Brent	08	17	13	31%	62%	-186
Lind,Adam	06	103	6	50%	17%	32
	07	30	18	44%	33%	-44
	08	41	18	39%	33%	-54
LoDuca,Paul	06	49	27	52%	19%	28
	07	31	24	38%	50%	-124
	08	25	18	17%	50%	-166
Loney,James	06	69	13	38%	31%	-48
	07	73	17	53%	18%	34
	08	46	27	33%	15%	6
Longoria,Evan	08	75	22	50%	9%	64
Lopez,Felipe	06	34	27	33%	37%	-82
	07	21	27	22%	37%	-104
	08	37	27	41%	37%	-66
Lopez,Jose	06	32	27	30%	22%	-28
	07	16	27	19%	48%	-154
	08	46	27	48%	19%	20
Loretta,Mark	06	33	27	33%	26%	-38
	07	41	27	37%	41%	-90
	08	42	27	37%	22%	-14
Lowell,Mike	06	59	27	56%	4%	96
	07	69	27	52%	11%	60
	08	53	23	52%	26%	0
Lowrie,Jed	08	47	17	47%	29%	-22
Ludwick,Ryan	07	58	22	55%	32%	-18
	08	94	27	74%	15%	88
Lugo,Julio	06	41	24	46%	29%	-24
	07	24	27	26%	41%	-112
	08	25	16	19%	31%	-86
Luis,Maza	08	-1	10	20%	60%	-200
Macias,Drew	08	51	5	40%	60%	-160
Mackowiak,Rob	06	40	27	33%	37%	-82
	07	32	25	28%	44%	-120
	08	-22	10	20%	70%	-240
Macri,Matthew	08	48	7	43%	43%	-86
Maier,Mitch	08	6	9	11%	56%	-202
Markakis,Nick	06	49	26	46%	23%	0
	07	62	26	69%	8%	106
	08	73	27	63%	7%	98
Marte,Andy	06	42	11	45%	36%	-54
	07	6	8	13%	63%	-226
	08	8	24	17%	46%	-150
Martinez,Victor	06	63	26	58%	12%	68
	07	70	25	64%	8%	96
	08	35	16	31%	13%	10
Martin,Russell	06	49	22	59%	14%	62
	07	59	27	56%	11%	68
	08	47	27	52%	19%	28
Mather,Joe	08	53	12	50%	33%	-32
Mathis,Jeff	06	0	10	20%	80%	-280
	07	25	13	38%	38%	-76
	08	10	26	23%	58%	-186

BATTER CONSISTENCY CHART

Name	Year	BPV	#Wks	DOM	DIS	QC
Matsui,Hideki	06	71	10	50%	30%	-20
	07	65	24	67%	13%	82
	08	49	18	39%	11%	34
Matsui,Kaz	06	27	15	40%	33%	-52
	07	39	21	29%	14%	2
	08	50	20	45%	25%	-10
MatthewsJr.,Gary	06	64	25	56%	16%	48
	07	40	26	35%	31%	-54
	08	24	27	33%	41%	-98
Mauer,Joe	06	86	27	78%	11%	112
	07	57	21	52%	24%	8
	08	75	27	63%	4%	110
Maybin,Cameron	07	4	8	25%	75%	-250
Maza,Luis	08	-1	10	20%	60%	-200
McAnulty,Paul	06	78	7	29%	57%	-170
	07	1	7	14%	57%	-200
	08	26	15	33%	53%	-146
McCann,Brian	06	84	26	69%	19%	62
	07	49	26	46%	15%	32
	08	77	27	59%	7%	90
McDonald,John	06	3	25	16%	72%	-256
	07	15	26	38%	50%	-124
	08	-2	23	9%	70%	-262
McLouth,Nate	06	27	19	37%	32%	-54
	07	54	27	52%	37%	-44
	08	65	27	56%	22%	24
McPherson,Dallas	06	56	10	40%	50%	-120
Melhuse,Adam	06	27	25	36%	56%	-152
	07	3	17	24%	59%	-188
	08	-20	9	22%	78%	-268
Mench,Kevin	06	37	26	23%	38%	-106
	07	47	26	42%	31%	-40
	08	35	19	42%	47%	-104
Metcalf,Travis	07	48	16	38%	50%	-124
	08	71	8	63%	38%	-26
Michaels,Jason	06	35	25	48%	32%	-32
	07	33	27	41%	30%	-38
	08	23	27	37%	48%	-118
Mientkiewicz,Doug	06	46	17	47%	18%	22
	07	52	14	43%	21%	2
	08	54	27	48%	37%	-52
Miles,Aaron	06	28	27	22%	41%	-120
	07	26	27	41%	41%	-82
	08	40	27	41%	19%	6
Millar,Kevin	06	51	26	50%	27%	-8
	07	47	27	44%	15%	28
	08	36	27	41%	33%	-50
Milledge,Lastings	06	24	14	29%	50%	-142
	07	45	15	40%	40%	-80
	08	34	24	38%	33%	-56
Miller,Corky	07	43	8	50%	50%	-100
	08	-52	19	5%	95%	-370
Moeller,Chad	06	-8	14	7%	64%	-242
	07	-23	16	13%	88%	-326
	08	18	19	26%	68%	-220
Molina,Bengie	06	45	26	50%	19%	24
	07	35	26	35%	31%	-54
	08	46	27	41%	30%	-38
Molina,Jose	06	25	26	35%	46%	-114
	07	19	26	38%	38%	-76
	08	9	27	19%	59%	-198
Molina,Yadier	06	14	27	22%	56%	-180
	07	33	22	27%	36%	-90
	08	46	26	27%	27%	-54
Monroe,Craig	06	54	27	48%	22%	8
	07	26	27	30%	44%	-116
	08	37	18	50%	44%	-76
Montanez,Luis	08	45	10	60%	20%	40
Montero,Miguel	07	28	27	41%	44%	-94
	08	52	24	42%	38%	-68
Montz,Luke	08	4	5	20%	60%	-200
Morales,Kendry	06	25	13	38%	46%	-108
	07	58	18	39%	56%	-146
	08	24	7	14%	71%	-256
Mora,Melvin	06	33	27	33%	26%	-38
	07	42	24	42%	25%	-16
	08	55	26	50%	15%	40
Morgan,Nyjer	07	40	6	50%	17%	32
	08	36	14	29%	36%	-86
Morneau,Justin	06	77	27	67%	11%	90
	07	60	27	56%	19%	36
	08	71	27	63%	11%	82
Morton,Colt	08	-69	5	0%	80%	-320

BATTER CONSISTENCY CHART

Name	Year	BPV	#Wks	DOM	DIS	QC
Moss,Brandon	07	56	7	43%	43%	-86
	08	48	18	33%	33%	-66
Murphy,Daniel	08	64	10	40%	30%	-40
Murphy,David	06	42	6	33%	33%	-66
	07	86	11	64%	9%	92
	08	52	19	63%	21%	42
Murphy,Donnie	07	49	13	31%	54%	-154
	08	7	14	21%	64%	-214
Murton,Matt	06	50	27	52%	30%	-16
	07	50	22	41%	41%	-82
	08	-18	9	33%	56%	-158
Myrow,Brian	07	-9	6	17%	83%	-298
	08	-9	7	29%	57%	-170
Nady,Xavier	06	46	25	48%	28%	-16
	07	53	27	52%	30%	-16
	08	65	26	62%	8%	92
Napoli,Mike	06	57	22	50%	32%	-28
	07	52	21	48%	29%	-20
	08	90	22	68%	23%	44
Navarro,Dioner	06	23	19	32%	32%	-64
	07	21	27	37%	52%	-134
	08	45	24	38%	17%	8
Newhan,David	06	21	9	22%	33%	-88
	07	-2	18	17%	56%	-190
	08	34	16	31%	50%	-138
Nieves,Wil	06	-99	5	0%	100%	-400
	07	-16	14	14%	79%	-288
	08	21	23	35%	57%	-158
Nix,Jayson	08	-33	6	0%	83%	-332
Norton,Greg	06	69	24	58%	29%	0
	07	28	21	43%	24%	-10
	08	55	25	56%	36%	-32
Ochoa,Ivan	08	-2	13	23%	54%	-170
Ojeda,Augie	07	32	17	35%	47%	-118
	08	19	27	30%	63%	-192
Olivo,Miguel	06	38	26	42%	35%	-56
	07	30	26	31%	35%	-78
	08	46	25	52%	36%	-40
Ordonez,Magglio	06	55	27	52%	4%	88
	07	103	27	85%	11%	126
	08	65	25	40%	4%	64
Orr,Pete	06	9	26	23%	58%	-186
	07	-22	20	15%	60%	-210
	08	3	15	40%	53%	-132
Ortiz,David	06	102	27	81%	4%	146
	07	112	27	78%	11%	112
	08	72	21	57%	19%	38
Ortmeier,Dan	07	56	15	53%	27%	-2
	08	22	9	33%	56%	-158
Overbay,Lyle	06	69	27	63%	19%	50
	07	37	22	36%	23%	-20
	08	47	27	52%	22%	16
Ozuna,Pablo	06	49	27	48%	30%	-24
	07	2	9	33%	56%	-158
	08	15	24	33%	54%	-150
Pagan,Angel	06	28	17	35%	47%	-118
	07	45	14	43%	36%	-58
	08	38	7	29%	29%	-58
Patterson,Corey	06	39	26	38%	23%	-16
	07	29	23	39%	35%	-62
	08	11	27	15%	52%	-178
Patterson,Eric	08	-8	12	17%	58%	-198
Paulino,Ronny	06	36	24	25%	13%	-2
	07	32	27	30%	37%	-88
	08	8	13	23%	62%	-202
Payton,Jay	06	39	27	30%	15%	0
	07	26	25	32%	40%	-96
	08	16	26	23%	42%	-122
Pearce,Steve	07	40	6	50%	33%	-32
	08	38	12	33%	33%	-66
Pedroia,Dustin	06	11	7	29%	43%	-114
	07	64	27	63%	19%	50
	08	72	28	57%	11%	70
Pena,Brayan	06	28	8	13%	50%	-174
	07	-10	9	22%	78%	-268
	08	31	5	40%	40%	-80
Pena,Carlos	06	49	6	33%	33%	-66
	07	108	27	74%	22%	60
	08	71	24	67%	13%	82
Pena,Tony	06	13	13	15%	54%	-186
	07	18	27	30%	37%	-88
	08	-28	26	12%	73%	-268

BATTER CONSISTENCY CHART

Name	Year	BPV	#Wks	DOM	DIS	QC
Pena,WilyMo	06	64	18	56%	22%	24
	07	47	27	37%	41%	-90
	08	-6	13	15%	62%	-218
Pence,Hunter	07	72	21	62%	0%	124
	08	50	27	52%	19%	28
Pennington,Cliff	08	15	8	25%	38%	-102
Peralta,Jhonny	06	32	27	30%	30%	-60
	07	46	26	46%	15%	32
	08	56	27	56%	19%	36
Perez,Fernando	08	45	5	40%	40%	-80
Petit,Gregorio	08	65	7	29%	57%	-170
Phelps,Josh	07	66	26	38%	54%	-140
	08	6	6	33%	50%	-134
Phillips,Andy	06	27	25	32%	44%	-112
	07	29	12	17%	25%	-66
	08	26	17	35%	59%	-166
Phillips,Brandon	06	39	26	50%	27%	-8
	07	50	26	46%	12%	44
	08	41	24	42%	17%	16
Pierre,Juan	06	37	27	41%	26%	-22
	07	31	27	22%	19%	-32
	08	25	25	20%	44%	-136
Pierzynski,A.J.	06	41	27	48%	26%	-8
	07	33	26	38%	31%	-48
	08	36	27	44%	41%	-76
Pie,Felix	07	14	18	22%	67%	-224
	08	13	10	30%	40%	-100
Podsednik,Scott	06	26	26	35%	35%	-70
	07	24	16	25%	44%	-126
	08	21	24	21%	46%	-142
Polanco,Placido	06	29	23	26%	39%	-104
	07	69	27	44%	4%	72
	08	48	26	50%	23%	8
Posada,Jorge	06	63	27	67%	11%	90
	07	88	26	81%	4%	146
	08	48	11	45%	27%	-18
Prado,Martin	06	33	7	43%	29%	-30
	07	24	9	44%	44%	-88
	08	61	20	50%	35%	-40
Pujols,Albert	06	120	25	80%	0%	160
	07	101	27	74%	11%	104
	08	130	26	85%	0%	170
Punto,Nick	06	33	27	37%	37%	-74
	07	2	27	15%	44%	-146
	08	35	22	32%	23%	-28
Quentin,Carlos	06	65	12	58%	17%	48
	07	22	19	21%	42%	-126
	08	82	23	83%	9%	130
Quinlan,Robb	06	53	26	46%	35%	-48
	07	23	26	42%	46%	-100
	08	8	24	21%	54%	-174
Quintanilla,Omar	06	-10	6	17%	50%	-166
	07	5	8	25%	63%	-202
	08	25	21	29%	52%	-150
Quintero,Humberto	06	51	6	33%	67%	-202
	07	-5	12	17%	42%	-134
	08	1	16	19%	56%	-186
Quiroz,Guillermo	07	83	5	20%	40%	-120
	08	-3	25	16%	64%	-224
Rabelo,Mike	07	22	26	35%	58%	-162
	08	-2	11	18%	64%	-220
Raburn,Ryan	07	69	14	64%	29%	12
	08	28	26	31%	35%	-78
Ramirez,Alexei	08	48	27	41%	26%	-22
Ramirez,Aramis	06	74	27	67%	7%	106
	07	76	26	58%	8%	84
	08	75	27	59%	15%	58
Ramirez,Hanley	06	57	27	52%	15%	44
	07	81	27	78%	4%	140
	08	80	26	65%	12%	82
Ramirez,Manny	06	105	24	75%	17%	82
	07	69	24	63%	13%	74
	08	99	27	70%	11%	96
Ramirez,Max	08	26	8	25%	63%	-202
Ransom,Cody	07	41	5	20%	80%	-280
	08	111	8	50%	38%	-52
Redmond,Mike	06	43	26	42%	35%	-56
	07	32	21	19%	43%	-134
	08	21	22	36%	50%	-128
Reed,Jeremy	06	15	14	29%	43%	-114
	08	27	19	32%	47%	-124
Renteria,Edgar	06	50	26	54%	8%	76
	07	61	23	57%	9%	78
	08	31	27	41%	33%	-50

BATTER CONSISTENCY CHART

Name	Year	BPV	#Wks	DOM	DIS	QC
Repko,Jason	06	29	17	35%	53%	-142
	08	-4	6	17%	67%	-234
Reyes,Argenis	08	-16	14	7%	79%	-302
Reyes,Jose	06	55	26	50%	15%	40
	07	49	27	52%	11%	60
	08	58	27	59%	22%	30
Reynolds,Mark	07	68	21	52%	33%	-28
	08	61	27	56%	22%	24
Riggans,Shawn	06	-16	5	40%	60%	-160
	08	34	23	35%	48%	-122
Rios,Alex	06	66	24	58%	17%	48
	07	63	27	59%	7%	90
	08	53	27	44%	22%	0
Rivas,Luis	08	6	25	16%	60%	-208
Rivera,Juan	06	67	24	58%	17%	48
	08	39	25	32%	44%	-112
Rivera,Mike	06	47	14	36%	21%	-12
	08	55	17	47%	53%	-118
Roberts,Brian	06	45	24	42%	25%	-16
	07	56	26	54%	15%	48
	08	60	27	63%	15%	66
Roberts,Dave	06	38	25	40%	32%	-48
	07	27	23	43%	35%	-54
	08	11	13	23%	46%	-138
Rodriguez,Alex	06	71	26	58%	12%	68
	07	105	27	74%	4%	132
	08	86	25	68%	8%	104
Rodriguez,Ivan	06	42	27	44%	15%	28
	07	36	26	42%	31%	-40
	08	32	27	41%	37%	-66
Rodriguez,Luis	06	19	24	29%	67%	-210
	07	11	23	13%	57%	-202
	08	36	14	36%	43%	-100
Rodriguez,Sean	08	13	15	27%	67%	-214
Rohlinger,Ryan	08	-39	8	0%	100%	-400
Rolen,Scott	06	72	27	67%	11%	90
	07	38	22	32%	36%	-80
	08	49	22	55%	27%	2
Rollins,Jimmy	06	55	27	56%	19%	36
	07	64	27	63%	7%	98
	08	55	24	54%	21%	24
Romero,Alexander	08	11	22	23%	59%	-190
Rosales,Adam	08	-13	8	13%	88%	-326
Ross,Cody	06	36	24	38%	58%	-156
	07	114	17	82%	6%	140
	08	58	27	52%	19%	28
Ross,Dave	06	86	25	68%	20%	56
	07	30	25	40%	36%	-64
	08	35	20	35%	50%	-130
Rowand,Aaron	06	36	20	30%	30%	-60
	07	69	27	63%	7%	98
	08	41	27	52%	33%	-28
Ruggiano,Justin	08	16	15	40%	53%	-132
Ruiz,Carlos	06	35	11	36%	55%	-148
	07	43	27	48%	26%	-8
	08	19	26	27%	54%	-162
Ruiz,Randy	08	26	8	25%	50%	-150
Ryan,Brendan	07	43	17	35%	29%	-46
	08	8	21	24%	57%	-180
Ryan,Dusty	08	69	5	20%	20%	-40
Salazar,Jeff	06	54	5	40%	20%	0
	07	38	11	27%	45%	-126
	08	22	22	36%	50%	-128
Salazar,Oscar	08	67	8	50%	25%	0
Saltalamacchia,J	07	39	23	39%	30%	-42
	08	38	19	53%	32%	-22
Sammons,Clint	08	-28	10	10%	90%	-340
Sanchez,Freddy	06	63	27	63%	7%	98
	07	48	25	44%	16%	24
	08	24	27	33%	37%	-82
Sandoval,Pablo	08	59	8	63%	13%	74
Santiago,Ramon	06	-14	21	19%	71%	-246
	07	29	8	25%	50%	-150
	08	64	21	48%	29%	-20
Santos,Omir	08	-66	5	0%	100%	-400
Sardinha,Dane	08	-29	10	20%	80%	-280
Schierholtz,Nate	07	30	10	40%	60%	-160
	08	64	5	60%	20%	40
Schneider,Brian	06	18	26	35%	42%	-98
	07	27	26	27%	31%	-70
	08	30	26	23%	27%	-62
Schumaker,Skip	06	-4	9	11%	78%	-290
	07	54	18	44%	39%	-68
	08	43	27	33%	19%	-10

BATTER CONSISTENCY CHART

Name	Year	BPV	#Wks	DOM	DIS	QC
Scott,Luke	06	100	13	69%	31%	14
	07	69	27	59%	33%	-14
	08	55	27	52%	26%	0
Scutaro,Marco	06	40	26	50%	31%	-24
	07	31	26	38%	31%	-48
	08	32	27	37%	30%	-46
Sexson,Richie	06	65	27	56%	11%	68
	07	33	24	38%	42%	-92
	08	32	20	30%	30%	-60
Shealy,Ryan	06	49	11	36%	27%	-36
	07	8	12	33%	50%	-134
	08	82	5	80%	20%	80
Sheffield,Gary	06	51	9	44%	33%	-44
	07	60	25	56%	32%	-16
	08	35	24	42%	21%	0
Shelton,Chris	06	52	22	41%	32%	-46
	08	24	9	33%	56%	-158
Shoppach,Kelly	06	38	20	35%	55%	-150
	07	66	26	50%	46%	-84
	08	83	27	52%	33%	-28
Sizemore,Grady	06	75	27	70%	7%	112
	07	59	27	59%	15%	58
	08	67	27	63%	15%	66
Smith,Jason	06	34	15	33%	67%	-202
	07	24	20	35%	50%	-130
	08	10	9	33%	67%	-202
Smith,Seth	08	51	17	35%	41%	-94
Snider,Travis	08	64	6	50%	17%	32
Snyder,Chris	06	44	26	38%	46%	-108
	07	47	26	46%	38%	-60
	08	59	24	50%	29%	-16
Soriano,Alfonso	06	76	27	63%	19%	50
	07	76	25	60%	12%	72
	08	71	21	57%	19%	38
Soto,Geovany	07	123	7	71%	29%	26
	08	70	26	58%	15%	56
Span,Denard	08	51	17	47%	24%	-2
Spilborghs,Ryan	06	40	17	35%	47%	-118
	07	60	20	55%	25%	10
	08	66	20	60%	30%	0
Stairs,Matt	06	42	25	52%	24%	8
	07	80	26	46%	23%	0
	08	39	27	41%	22%	-6
Stavinoha,Nick	08	-24	8	13%	75%	-274
Stewart,Chris	07	11	9	22%	44%	-132
Stewart,Ian	07	39	8	38%	50%	-124
	08	61	17	41%	41%	-82
Stewart,Shannon	06	31	10	30%	30%	-60
	07	39	27	33%	26%	-38
	08	20	10	20%	40%	-120
Sullivan,Cory	06	36	27	30%	41%	-104
	07	30	17	29%	53%	-154
	08	-9	5	20%	80%	-280
Suzuki,Ichiro	06	43	27	44%	26%	-16
	07	50	27	44%	11%	44
	08	38	27	37%	19%	-2
Suzuki,Kurt	07	41	17	53%	29%	-10
	08	31	28	29%	18%	-14
Sweeney,Mark	06	32	27	41%	41%	-82
	07	37	25	36%	44%	-104
	08	-30	23	17%	70%	-246
Sweeney,Mike	06	50	13	62%	31%	0
	07	36	18	39%	39%	-78
	08	49	11	18%	18%	-36
Sweeney,Ryan	06	-23	6	17%	83%	-298
	08	35	26	31%	31%	-62
Swisher,Nick	06	63	27	56%	22%	24
	07	60	27	52%	15%	44
	08	40	27	30%	22%	-28
Taguchi,So	06	28	26	31%	35%	-78
	07	34	27	26%	30%	-68
	08	9	26	27%	65%	-206
Tatis,Fernando	06	72	12	50%	50%	-100
	08	62	19	53%	16%	42
Taveras,Willy	06	18	27	19%	37%	-110
	07	32	22	36%	14%	16
	08	7	26	27%	46%	-130
Teagarden,Taylor	08	184	6	67%	17%	66
Teahen,Mark	06	65	20	60%	20%	40
	07	42	25	44%	20%	8
	08	35	27	41%	37%	-66
Teixeira,Mark	06	71	27	70%	4%	124
	07	85	22	68%	5%	116
	08	87	27	70%	7%	112

BATTER CONSISTENCY CHART

Name	Year	BPV	#Wks	DOM	DIS	QC
Tejada,Miguel	06	64	27	56%	7%	84
	07	48	24	42%	13%	32
	08	37	27	37%	26%	-30
Thames,Marcus	06	73	26	58%	19%	40
	07	58	24	54%	25%	8
	08	64	27	59%	30%	-2
Theriot,Ryan	06	78	15	47%	33%	-38
	07	32	26	27%	23%	-38
	08	42	27	44%	19%	12
Thigpen,Curtis	07	7	16	25%	56%	-174
	08	22	6	17%	67%	-234
Thomas,Clete	08	46	11	55%	27%	2
Thomas,Frank	06	73	26	62%	8%	92
	07	63	26	62%	12%	76
	08	30	14	36%	29%	-44
Thome,Jim	06	98	27	67%	7%	106
	07	91	24	83%	8%	134
	08	70	27	67%	7%	106
Tolbert,Matt	08	32	12	42%	33%	-48
Torrealba,Yorvit	06	40	15	40%	13%	28
	07	30	27	37%	33%	-58
	08	32	22	36%	36%	-72
Towles,J.R.	07	138	5	60%	20%	40
	08	-10	18	11%	72%	-266
Tracy,Chad	06	50	27	56%	15%	52
	07	56	18	56%	17%	44
	08	37	19	47%	32%	-34
Treanor,Matt	06	13	26	23%	46%	-138
	07	36	26	38%	38%	-76
	08	8	21	29%	57%	-170
Tuiasosopo,Matt	08	-10	5	40%	40%	-80
Tulowitzki,Troy	06	3	5	40%	60%	-160
	07	57	27	56%	11%	68
	08	40	19	37%	26%	-30
Uggla,Dan	06	50	27	59%	15%	58
	07	61	27	59%	30%	-2
	08	77	26	62%	23%	32
Upton,B.J.	06	3	10	10%	30%	-100
	07	75	22	68%	18%	64
	08	48	27	48%	22%	8
Upton,Justin	07	23	10	20%	60%	-200
	08	60	21	57%	14%	58
Uribe,Juan	06	35	26	42%	19%	8
	07	27	27	30%	41%	-104
	08	31	24	38%	38%	-76
Utley,Chase	06	69	27	63%	7%	98
	07	86	23	70%	0%	140
	08	73	26	58%	12%	68
Valbuena,Luis	08	30	5	40%	60%	-160
Valentin,Javier	06	38	27	37%	52%	-134
	07	42	26	46%	38%	-60
	08	42	26	35%	58%	-162
VanEvery,Jonathan	08	10	6	17%	50%	-166
Varitek,Jason	06	36	23	43%	22%	-2
	07	45	27	52%	22%	16
	08	26	28	46%	46%	-112
Vazquez,Ramon	06	0	14	21%	50%	-158
	07	26	21	29%	43%	-114
	08	50	27	44%	44%	-88
Velandia,Jorge	08	0	8	13%	88%	-326
Velez,Eugenio	08	27	21	38%	52%	-132
Venable,William	08	33	6	50%	33%	-32
Victorino,Shane	06	36	27	41%	44%	-94
	07	42	25	36%	28%	-40
	08	50	24	42%	38%	-68
Vidro,Jose	06	42	24	46%	25%	-8
	07	50	27	48%	19%	20
	08	15	19	26%	47%	-136
Vizquel,Omar	06	42	27	41%	41%	-82
	07	19	27	30%	41%	-104
	08	5	22	36%	50%	-128
Votto,Joey	07	76	5	60%	20%	40
	08	67	27	48%	11%	52
Ward,Daryle	06	78	26	54%	42%	-60
	07	93	22	59%	32%	-10
	08	41	21	48%	43%	-76
Weeks,Rickie	06	35	17	35%	12%	22
	07	49	25	40%	48%	-112
	08	36	24	42%	25%	-16
Wells,Vernon	06	72	27	63%	11%	82
	07	36	25	32%	28%	-48
	08	60	20	50%	5%	80
Werth,Jayson	07	59	22	41%	32%	-46
	08	64	26	62%	19%	48

BATTER CONSISTENCY CHART

Name	Year	BPV	#Wks	DOM	DIS	QC
Wigginton,Ty	06	58	23	48%	26%	-8
	07	51	27	44%	15%	28
	08	67	23	43%	13%	34
Wilkerson,Brad	06	45	19	53%	26%	2
	07	58	24	33%	21%	-18
	08	17	26	31%	42%	-106
Willingham,Josh	06	59	26	46%	23%	0
	07	56	25	56%	16%	48
	08	57	20	45%	30%	-30
Willits,Reggie	06	20	12	25%	67%	-218
	07	33	26	42%	31%	-40
	08	-3	23	17%	74%	-262
Wilson,Jack	06	27	27	44%	30%	-32
	07	52	26	46%	27%	-16
	08	24	18	28%	44%	-120
Wilson,Robert	08	-37	5	20%	80%	-280
Winn,Randy	06	37	26	35%	31%	-54
	07	51	27	56%	15%	52
	08	51	27	48%	19%	20
Wise,Dewayne	06	-19	9	11%	78%	-290
	08	41	17	35%	53%	-142
Wood,Brandon	07	-8	9	22%	78%	-268
	08	6	12	8%	50%	-184
Wright,David	06	73	27	59%	15%	58
	07	85	27	81%	7%	134
	08	79	27	59%	7%	90
Youkilis,Kevin	06	53	26	58%	8%	84
	07	59	26	54%	15%	48
	08	86	28	64%	18%	56
Young,Chris	06	29	8	38%	50%	-124
	07	49	26	38%	23%	-16
	08	50	27	52%	11%	60
Young,Delmon	06	52	6	33%	17%	-2
	07	37	27	37%	19%	-2
	08	36	27	41%	22%	-6
Young,Delwyn	06	-99	5	0%	100%	-400
	07	94	7	43%	43%	-86
	08	27	21	43%	43%	-86
Young,Dmitri	06	28	14	36%	43%	-100
	07	68	26	69%	19%	62
	08	47	10	40%	30%	-40
Young,Michael	06	55	27	48%	11%	52
	07	45	26	50%	19%	24
	08	39	27	41%	22%	-6
Zaun,Gregg	06	59	26	54%	31%	-16
	07	47	21	48%	29%	-20
	08	33	24	38%	38%	-76
Zimmerman,Ryan	06	57	27	59%	15%	58
	07	51	27	48%	11%	52
	08	47	19	53%	32%	-22
Zobrist,Ben	06	4	10	20%	60%	-200
	07	-29	9	11%	78%	-290
	08	62	17	47%	24%	-2

The QC-100 Elite List

Name	Year	BPV	#Wks	DOM	DIS	QC
Howard,Ryan	06	111	27	85%	0%	170
Pujols,Albert	08	130	26	85%	0%	170
Cruz,Nelson	08	102	6	83%	0%	166
Fielder,Prince	07	96	26	81%	0%	162
Pujols,Albert	06	120	25	80%	0%	160
Berkman,Lance	06	98	27	78%	0%	156
Dye,Jermaine	06	92	26	77%	0%	154
Braun,Ryan	07	96	20	75%	0%	150
Ortiz,David	06	102	27	81%	4%	146
Posada,Jorge	07	88	26	81%	4%	146
Ramirez,Hanley	07	81	27	78%	4%	140
Ross,Cody	07	114	17	82%	6%	140
Utley,Chase	07	86	23	70%	0%	140
Holliday,Matt	07	95	27	78%	4%	140
Wright,David	07	85	27	81%	7%	134
Thome,Jim	07	91	24	83%	8%	134
Rodriguez,Alex	07	105	27	74%	4%	132
Quentin,Carlos	08	82	23	83%	9%	130
Cano,Robinson	06	69	22	64%	0%	128
Johnson,Nick	06	83	25	72%	4%	128
Jones,Chipper	07	102	25	80%	8%	128
Hafner,Travis	06	114	22	73%	5%	126
Ordonez,Magglio	07	103	27	85%	11%	126
Holliday,Matt	06	83	27	70%	4%	124
Teixeira,Mark	06	71	27	70%	4%	124
Pence,Hunter	07	72	21	62%	0%	124
Howard,Ryan	07	102	26	69%	4%	122
Guerrero,Vladimir	07	88	26	77%	8%	122
Jones,Chipper	08	104	26	69%	4%	122
Hopper,Norris	06	73	5	60%	0%	120
Helton,Todd	07	85	27	67%	4%	118
Teixeira,Mark	07	85	22	68%	5%	116
Lee,Carlos	08	81	19	68%	5%	116
Konerko,Paul	06	76	26	65%	4%	114
Guerrero,Vladimir	06	77	26	73%	8%	114
Mauer,Joe	06	86	27	78%	11%	112
Hawpe,Brad	07	80	27	78%	11%	112
Ortiz,David	07	112	27	78%	11%	112
Sizemore,Grady	06	75	27	70%	7%	112
Teixeira,Mark	08	87	27	70%	7%	112
Mauer,Joe	08	75	27	63%	4%	110
Ramirez,Aramis	06	74	27	67%	7%	106
Thome,Jim	06	98	27	67%	7%	106
Atkins,Garrett	06	87	27	67%	7%	106
LaRoche,Adam	06	81	26	69%	8%	106
Markakis,Nick	07	62	26	69%	8%	106
Thome,Jim	08	70	27	67%	7%	106
Jones,Chipper	06	92	23	70%	9%	104
Cuddyer,Michael	06	67	27	74%	11%	104
Beltran,Carlos	06	91	27	74%	11%	104
Alou,Moises	06	80	21	62%	5%	104
Granderson,Curtis	07	75	27	74%	11%	104
Pujols,Albert	07	101	27	74%	11%	104
Lee,Derrek	07	74	27	74%	11%	104
Rodriguez,Alex	08	86	25	68%	8%	104
Dunn,Adam	08	76	27	74%	11%	104
Duncan,Chris	06	80	18	72%	11%	100
Church,Ryan	07	60	26	58%	4%	100

Starting Pitcher Consistency Charts

We've always approached performance measures on an aggregate basis. Each individual event that our statistics chronicle gets dumped into a huge pool of data. We then use our formulas to try to sort and slice and manipulate the data into more usable information.

Pure Quality Starts (PQS) take a different approach (see Glossary for complete definition). It says that the smallest unit of measure should not be the "event" but instead be the "game." Within that game, we can accumulate all the strikeouts, hits and walks, and evaluate that outing as a whole. After all, when a pitcher takes the mound, he is either "on" or "off" his game; he is either dominant or struggling, or somewhere in between.

PQS captures the array of events and slaps an evaluative label on that outing, on a scale of 0 to 5. It doesn't matter if a few extra balls got through the infield, or the pitcher was given the hook in the fourth or sixth inning, or the bullpen was able to strand their inherited baserunners. When we look at performance in the aggregate, those events do matter, and will affect a pitcher's BPIs and ERA. But with PQS, the minutia is less relevant than the overall performance.

In the end, a dominating performance is a dominating performance, whether Jake Peavy is hurling a 1-hit shutout or giving up 3 runs while striking out 7 in 6 IP. And a disaster is still a disaster, whether Daniel Cabrera gets a first inning hook after giving up 5 runs, or "takes one for the team" getting shelled for 9 runs in 5 IP.

With Gene McCaffrey's Domination and Disaster percentages, we can sort out the PQS scores even more.

Domination Percentage (DOM%) measures the portion of a pitcher's starts that scored a 4 or 5 on the PQS scale.

Disaster Percentage (DIS%) measures the portion of a pitcher's starts that scored a 0 or 1 on the PQS scale.

DOM/DIS percentages open up a new perspective, providing us with two separate scales of performance. In tandem, they measure consistency.

This is important because a pitcher might possess incredible skill but be unable to sustain it on a start-by-start basis. For instance, a pitcher who posts PQS scores of 5,0,5,0,5 might have an ERA that is identical to one who posts scores of 3,3,3,3,3 — less skill, but more consistent. ERAs, WHIPs, and even BPIs don't capture that subtle difference. DOM/DIS does capture that difference, and in doing so, helps us identify pitchers who might be better or worse than their stats — and sabermetrics — indicate.

The final step is to convert a pitcher's DOM/DIS split back to an equivalent ERA. By creating a grid of individual DOM and DIS levels, we can determine the average ERA at each cross point. The result is an ERA based purely on PQS, and so we can call it the PQS ERA, or qERA.

The following charts include:
- Up to six years of data for all pitchers who had at least five starts in 2008
- Total number of starts in that year (#)
- Average pitch counts for all starts (PC)
- Domination and Disaster percentages (DOM, DIS) for first half, second half and total season
- Quality-Consistency Score (QC)
- PQS Earned Run Average (qERA)

Some observations...

The ability to maintain positive QC scores for extended periods is rarer than we would think. That's why you have to take notice of a pitcher like **Bronson Arroyo**, who is a marginal pick in most leagues but has posted positive QC scores in four of the last five years.

Health will always be an issue, but **A.J. Burnett** has had no less than a 53% DOM and no more than a 19% DIS since 2004. Note that he has not posted even one DIS outing in the second half of the past two years.

In 2005, **Doug Davis** averaged 106 pitches per start, a workload level that few pitchers manage successfully. His QC score that year was 40. In the three subsequent years, his scores have been 4, -12 and –32.

A scan of **Livan Hernandez's** workload and QC scores provides a similar view of the possible impact of workload:

Year	PC	QC
2003	108	92
2004	112	90
2005	114	-8
2006	103	16
2007	102	-66
2008	90	-70

If "slow and steady wins the race," then you have to like **Felix Hernandez's** QC trend — 44, 58, 64 — and note that he's never posted a full-season DIS% of more than 13%.

On the flipside is the slow decline of future Hall-of-Famer **Greg Maddux**, whose six-year QC trend — 50, 68, 56, 34, 16, 18 — chronicles his fall from the Elite.

The epitome of consistency? His name is **Johan Santana**. Despite ERAs over the past five years that have fluctuated between 2.53 and 3.33, his QC scores have been unwavering: 140, 146, 140, 140, 146. Since 2005, he has posted no DIS starts in the first half of a season, and no more than one DIS in any second half.

Negative consistency might belong to **Jarrod Washburn**, whose last four QC scores have been –22, -20, -18 and -38.

And for anyone who still does not believe that a long-term investment in **Carlos Zambrano** is a bad idea, his QC scores present yet another argument: 124, 68, 92, 58, 26. His PC trend presents a compelling argument for workload management.

STARTING PITCHER CONSISTENCY CHART

				First Half		Second Half		Full Season			
Pitcher	Yr	#	PC	DOM	DIS	DOM	DIS	DOM	DIS	QC	qERA
Arroyo,Bronson	04	29	95	57%	14%	60%	13%	59%	14%	62	3.97
	05	32	101	53%	18%	27%	27%	41%	22%	-6	4.56
	06	34	110	79%	11%	47%	13%	65%	12%	82	3.61
	07	34	101	50%	11%	44%	13%	47%	12%	46	4.28
	08	34	101	40%	30%	64%	0%	50%	18%	28	4.37
Backe,Brandon	04	9	83			22%	33%	22%	33%	-88	5.21
	05	25	91	44%	17%	43%	43%	44%	24%	-8	4.56
	06	8	84	50%	50%	0%	17%	13%	25%	-74	5.08
	07	5	91			20%	20%	20%	20%	-40	4.75
	08	31	90	35%	20%	45%	45%	39%	29%	-38	4.82
Badenhop,Burke	08	8	84	25%	38%			25%	38%	-102	5.27
Baek,Cha Seung	04	5	101			20%	40%	20%	40%	-120	5.50
	06	6	96			67%	17%	67%	17%	66	3.73
	07	12	96	45%	27%	0%	0%	42%	25%	-16	4.74
	08	21	87	25%	25%	38%	46%	33%	38%	-86	5.19
Bailey,Homer	07	9	90	17%	33%	33%	0%	22%	22%	-44	4.75
	08	8	85	25%	50%	0%	50%	13%	50%	-174	7.08
Baker,Scott	05	9	90	100%	0%	50%	13%	56%	11%	68	3.97
	06	16	90	22%	56%	0%	43%	13%	50%	-174	7.08
	07	23	90	22%	22%	43%	7%	35%	13%	18	4.41
	08	28	96	43%	14%	57%	14%	50%	14%	44	4.23
Balester,Collin	08	15	90	0%	33%	42%	17%	33%	20%	-14	4.71
Banks,Josh	08	14	84	29%	14%	0%	71%	14%	43%	-144	5.70
Bannister,Brian	06	6	100	40%	20%	100%	0%	50%	17%	32	4.37
	07	27	96	38%	15%	36%	29%	37%	22%	-14	4.64
	08	32	98	42%	21%	31%	46%	38%	31%	-48	5.00
Batista,Miguel	03	29	93	60%	13%	50%	21%	55%	17%	42	4.10
	04	31	101	42%	16%	17%	42%	32%	26%	-40	4.90
	06	33	99	33%	22%	27%	13%	30%	18%	-12	4.60
	07	32	101	35%	12%	60%	7%	47%	9%	58	3.98
	08	20	86	13%	53%	0%	60%	10%	55%	-200	7.77
Beckett,Josh	03	22	97	60%	20%	83%	8%	73%	14%	90	3.51
	04	26	94	54%	23%	62%	15%	58%	19%	40	4.10
	05	29	97	81%	19%	69%	8%	76%	14%	96	3.41
	06	33	98	56%	17%	47%	13%	52%	15%	44	4.37
	07	30	103	63%	13%	86%	0%	73%	7%	118	3.25
	08	27	100	65%	12%	80%	10%	70%	11%	96	3.51
Bedard,Erik	04	26	100	33%	27%	45%	45%	38%	35%	-64	5.13
	05	24	103	67%	11%	40%	20%	50%	17%	32	4.37
	06	33	100	47%	32%	71%	7%	58%	21%	32	4.23
	07	28	105	74%	11%	78%	0%	75%	7%	122	3.13
	08	15	91	40%	27%			40%	27%	-28	4.74
Belisle,Matt	05	5	73	40%	40%			40%	40%	-80	5.21
	07	30	93	35%	18%	31%	31%	33%	23%	-26	4.71
	08	6	86	0%	50%			0%	50%	-200	7.46
Benoit,Joaquin	03	18	90	40%	40%	13%	75%	28%	56%	-168	7.14
	04	15	89	42%	33%	0%	100%	33%	47%	-122	5.83
	05	9	95			22%	33%	22%	33%	-88	5.21
Bergmann,Jason	06	6	87			33%	33%	33%	33%	-66	5.08
	07	21	90	55%	27%	30%	50%	43%	38%	-66	5.07
	08	22	94	62%	15%	33%	33%	50%	23%	8	4.50
Billingsley,Chad	06	16	95	0%	60%	36%	18%	25%	31%	-74	5.13
	07	20	95	25%	50%	50%	13%	45%	20%	10	4.53
	08	32	101	58%	5%	54%	8%	56%	6%	88	3.68
Blackburn,Nick	08	33	87	47%	21%	29%	50%	39%	33%	-54	5.00
Blanton,Joe	05	33	93	35%	29%	56%	6%	45%	18%	18	4.40
	06	31	101	28%	22%	23%	8%	26%	16%	-12	4.62
	07	34	102	63%	0%	40%	13%	53%	6%	82	3.85
	08	33	98	30%	15%	38%	23%	33%	18%	-6	4.60
Boggs,Mitchell	08	6	89	20%	20%	0%	100%	17%	33%	-98	5.29
Bonderman,J	03	28	86	39%	17%	10%	60%	29%	32%	-70	5.13
	04	32	90	41%	18%	53%	20%	47%	19%	18	4.40
	05	29	98	56%	6%	55%	27%	55%	14%	54	3.97
	06	34	97	61%	11%	38%	25%	50%	18%	28	4.37
	07	28	97	81%	0%	33%	33%	61%	14%	66	3.71
	08	12	98	33%	25%			33%	25%	-34	4.90
Bonine,Eddie	08	5	80	20%	40%			20%	40%	-120	5.50
Bonser,Boof	06	18	87	43%	43%	45%	9%	44%	22%	0	4.56
	07	30	92	39%	11%	25%	42%	33%	23%	-26	4.71
	08	12	89	42%	25%			42%	25%	-16	4.74
Braden,Dallas	07	14	85	25%	75%	10%	60%	14%	64%	-228	8.46
	08	10	89			40%	20%	40%	20%	0	4.56
Buchholz,Clay	08	15	91	22%	33%	17%	50%	20%	40%	-120	5.50
Buchholz,Taylor	06	19	87	53%	27%	0%	50%	42%	32%	-44	4.92
	07	8	79	29%	29%	0%	100%	25%	38%	-102	5.27
Buehrle,Mark	03	35	100	43%	19%	57%	0%	49%	11%	54	4.28
	04	35	106	58%	11%	44%	6%	51%	9%	66	3.85
	05	33	105	56%	0%	40%	7%	48%	3%	84	3.68
	06	32	97	28%	11%	21%	43%	25%	25%	-50	4.93
	07	30	103	41%	6%	31%	15%	37%	10%	34	4.41
	08	34	100	47%	11%	60%	20%	53%	15%	46	4.37
Burnett,A.J.	04	19	94	50%	38%	55%	0%	53%	16%	42	4.37
	05	32	103	65%	6%	60%	13%	63%	9%	90	3.50
	06	21	103	33%	33%	67%	13%	57%	19%	38	4.10
	07	25	106	60%	27%	70%	0%	64%	16%	64	3.83
	08	34	107	50%	20%	71%	0%	59%	12%	70	3.97
Burres,Brian	07	17	93	20%	40%	43%	43%	29%	41%	-106	5.40
	08	22	91	18%	35%	20%	60%	18%	41%	-128	5.60

STARTING PITCHER CONSISTENCY CHART

				First Half		Second Half		Full Season			
Pitcher	Yr	#	PC	DOM	DIS	DOM	DIS	DOM	DIS	QC	qERA
Bush,David	04	16	92	50%	0%	50%	21%	50%	19%	24	4.37
	05	24	88	30%	50%	43%	36%	38%	42%	-92	5.25
	06	32	93	63%	11%	46%	23%	56%	16%	48	4.10
	07	31	95	59%	6%	36%	21%	48%	13%	44	4.28
	08	29	92	35%	24%	42%	8%	38%	17%	8	4.52
Byrd,Paul	04	19	88	50%	25%	33%	13%	37%	16%	10	4.52
	05	31	94	35%	6%	43%	21%	39%	13%	26	4.41
	06	31	92	53%	18%	7%	43%	32%	29%	-52	4.90
	07	31	91	38%	6%	7%	27%	23%	16%	-18	4.63
	08	30	84	39%	44%	33%	8%	37%	30%	-46	5.00
Cabrera,Daniel	04	27	92	25%	8%	7%	47%	15%	30%	-90	5.29
	05	29	99	47%	24%	33%	25%	41%	24%	-14	4.56
	06	26	103	33%	20%	45%	36%	38%	27%	-32	4.82
	07	34	105	58%	11%	40%	20%	50%	15%	40	4.37
	08	30	101	30%	20%	10%	50%	23%	30%	-74	5.21
Cain,Matt	05	7	102			57%	0%	57%	0%	114	3.38
	06	31	106	38%	38%	67%	7%	52%	23%	12	4.50
	07	32	105	53%	12%	60%	27%	56%	19%	36	4.10
	08	34	106	60%	10%	50%	7%	56%	9%	76	3.68
Campillo,Jorge	08	25	86	45%	36%	36%	36%	40%	36%	-64	5.07
Capuano,Chris	03	5	84	50%	50%	33%	67%	40%	60%	-160	7.05
	04	17	87	50%	30%	43%	29%	47%	29%	-22	4.67
	05	35	104	37%	5%	38%	19%	37%	11%	30	4.41
	06	34	99	79%	5%	33%	20%	59%	12%	70	3.97
	07	25	91	47%	47%	30%	20%	40%	36%	-64	5.07
Carmona,Fausto	06	7	87	33%	33%	25%	25%	29%	29%	-58	4.93
	07	32	98	53%	12%	47%	0%	50%	6%	76	3.85
	08	22	92	10%	40%	25%	25%	18%	32%	-92	5.29
Carpenter,Chris	04	28	96	53%	6%	45%	27%	50%	14%	44	4.23
	05	33	103	89%	6%	60%	7%	76%	6%	128	3.13
	06	32	102	65%	0%	67%	7%	66%	3%	120	3.14
Chacon,Shawn	03	22	98	47%	18%	40%	40%	45%	23%	-2	4.53
	05	24	102	30%	30%	43%	7%	38%	17%	8	4.52
	06	20	86	18%	55%	0%	22%	10%	40%	-140	5.70
	08	15	94	27%	27%			27%	27%	-54	4.93
Chamberlain,Joba	08	12	94	50%	38%	75%	25%	58%	33%	-16	4.55
Chico,Matt	07	31	91	17%	44%	23%	38%	19%	42%	-130	5.60
	08	8	91	25%	50%			25%	50%	-150	6.56
Colon,Bartolo	03	34	104	63%	16%	40%	20%	53%	18%	34	4.37
	04	34	100	28%	33%	69%	19%	47%	26%	-10	4.67
	05	33	98	67%	6%	67%	0%	67%	3%	122	3.14
	06	10	85	14%	14%	33%	33%	20%	20%	-40	4.75
	07	18	88	36%	29%	25%	50%	33%	33%	-66	5.08
	08	7	83	50%	17%	0%	0%	43%	14%	30	4.32
Contreras,Jose	03	9	98	100%	0%	71%	29%	78%	22%	68	3.65
	04	31	97	43%	36%	47%	24%	45%	29%	-26	4.67
	05	32	99	47%	18%	53%	0%	50%	9%	64	3.85
	06	30	101	50%	6%	36%	21%	43%	13%	34	4.32
	07	30	97	35%	12%	46%	31%	40%	20%	0	4.56
	08	20	95	37%	26%	0%	100%	35%	30%	-50	5.00
Cook,Aaron	03	16	89	6%	38%			6%	38%	-140	5.63
	04	16	92	9%	18%	20%	20%	13%	19%	-50	4.66
	05	13	91			8%	31%	8%	31%	-108	5.45
	06	32	97	39%	6%	21%	21%	31%	13%	10	4.49
	07	25	96	32%	11%	67%	0%	40%	8%	48	4.11
	08	32	96	25%	0%	25%	17%	25%	6%	26	4.48
Correia,Kevin	03	7	82			29%	29%	29%	29%	-58	4.93
	05	11	82	0%	50%	44%	44%	36%	45%	-108	5.75
	07	8	88			63%	13%	63%	13%	74	3.71
	08	19	90	40%	40%	33%	22%	37%	32%	-54	5.00
Cruz,Juan	03	6	96			50%	17%	50%	17%	32	4.37
	06	15	84	56%	22%	33%	33%	47%	27%	-14	4.67
Cueto,Johnny	08	31	98	47%	21%	42%	25%	45%	23%	-2	4.53
Danks,John	07	26	93	25%	25%	20%	40%	23%	31%	-78	5.21
	08	33	95	58%	16%	50%	29%	55%	21%	26	4.23
Davies,Kyle	05	14	98	18%	27%	67%	0%	29%	21%	-26	4.73
	06	14	89	25%	38%	17%	67%	21%	50%	-158	6.74
	07	28	88	31%	50%	17%	50%	25%	50%	-150	6.56
	08	21	94	11%	33%	33%	33%	24%	33%	-84	5.21
Davis,Doug	03	20	94	8%	50%	50%	38%	25%	45%	-130	5.98
	04	34	100	47%	16%	60%	13%	53%	15%	46	4.37
	05	35	106	58%	26%	63%	13%	60%	20%	40	3.95
	06	34	103	21%	16%	47%	13%	32%	15%	4	4.60
	07	33	102	44%	22%	40%	27%	42%	24%	-12	4.56
	08	26	95	58%	17%	36%	43%	46%	31%	-32	4.82
de la Rosa,Jorge	04	5	82			0%	40%	0%	40%	-160	5.90
	06	13	84	0%	100%	10%	30%	8%	46%	-168	6.53
	07	23	91	33%	28%	0%	60%	26%	35%	-88	5.27
	08	23	92	27%	45%	58%	17%	43%	30%	-34	4.92
Dempster,Ryan	03	19	95	24%	29%	0%	0%	21%	26%	-62	4.98
	05	6	99	67%	17%			67%	17%	66	3.73
	08	33	101	55%	5%	77%	0%	64%	3%	116	3.29
Dickey,R.A.	03	13	96	0%	100%	50%	25%	46%	31%	-32	4.82
	04	15	95	31%	31%	0%	100%	27%	40%	-106	5.40
	08	14	97	14%	29%	14%	43%	14%	36%	-116	5.54
Duchscherer,J	08	22	93	63%	6%	17%	17%	50%	9%	64	3.85

STARTING PITCHER CONSISTENCY CHART

				First Half		Second Half		Full Season			
Pitcher	Yr	#	PC	DOM	DIS	DOM	DIS	DOM	DIS	QC	qERA
Duckworth,B	03	18	85	31%	38%	20%	40%	28%	39%	-100	5.27
	04	6	60	0%	80%	0%	100%	0%	83%	-332	12.14
	06	8	97	0%	40%	33%	33%	13%	38%	-126	5.54
	08	7	93			43%	29%	43%	29%	-30	4.74
Duke,Zach	05	14	91	100%	0%	42%	33%	50%	29%	-16	4.61
	06	34	96	32%	21%	33%	13%	32%	18%	-8	4.60
	07	19	88	6%	41%	0%	50%	5%	42%	-158	5.80
	08	31	94	21%	26%	50%	8%	32%	19%	-12	4.60
Dumatrait,Phil	07	6	67			0%	83%	0%	83%	-332	12.14
	08	11	92	27%	36%			27%	36%	-90	5.27
Eaton,Adam	03	31	98	50%	22%	46%	15%	48%	19%	20	4.40
	04	33	99	56%	6%	47%	13%	52%	9%	68	3.85
	05	22	100	50%	14%	38%	13%	45%	14%	34	4.28
	06	13	87			31%	31%	31%	31%	-62	5.08
	07	30	92	33%	22%	8%	50%	23%	33%	-86	5.21
	08	19	92	21%	26%			21%	26%	-62	4.98
Escobar,Kelvim	03	26	102	42%	25%	57%	7%	50%	15%	40	4.37
	04	33	104	41%	6%	63%	6%	52%	6%	80	3.85
	05	7	91	57%	14%			57%	14%	58	3.97
	06	30	97	53%	12%	69%	15%	60%	13%	68	3.71
	07	30	101	69%	13%	50%	21%	60%	17%	52	3.83
Estes,Shawn	03	28	93	37%	32%	33%	44%	36%	36%	-72	5.13
	04	34	99	32%	26%	20%	40%	26%	32%	-76	5.13
	05	21	92	29%	18%	0%	50%	24%	24%	-48	4.75
	08	8	88	25%	0%	0%	75%	13%	38%	-126	5.54
Eveland,Dana	06	5	97	0%	40%			0%	40%	-160	5.90
	08	29	93	32%	21%	30%	40%	31%	28%	-50	4.90
Feierabend,Ryan	07	9	83	0%	50%	0%	67%	0%	56%	-224	8.24
	08	8	85			13%	38%	13%	38%	-126	5.54
Feldman,Scott	08	25	94	21%	21%	27%	18%	24%	20%	-32	4.75
Figueroa,Nelson	08	6	98	33%	33%			33%	33%	-66	5.08
Floyd,Gavin	06	11	91	9%	55%			9%	55%	-202	7.99
	07	10	96	0%	100%	67%	22%	60%	30%	0	4.39
	08	33	98	39%	17%	47%	7%	42%	12%	36	4.32
Fogg,Josh	03	26	82	31%	23%	31%	38%	31%	31%	-62	5.08
	04	32	87	12%	35%	27%	13%	19%	25%	-62	5.03
	05	28	93	47%	18%	9%	27%	32%	21%	-20	4.71
	06	31	89	18%	18%	29%	43%	23%	29%	-70	4.98
	07	29	91	33%	20%	21%	29%	28%	24%	-40	4.73
	08	14	81	33%	50%	13%	63%	21%	57%	-186	7.36
Fossum,Casey	03	14	85	33%	25%	0%	50%	29%	29%	-58	4.93
	04	27	89	17%	58%	40%	33%	30%	44%	-116	5.29
	05	25	98	40%	20%	47%	27%	44%	24%	-8	4.56
	06	25	88	19%	31%	44%	33%	28%	32%	-72	5.13
	07	10	85	30%	50%			30%	50%	-140	6.37
Francis,Jeff	04	7	93			14%	29%	14%	29%	-88	5.08
	05	33	95	33%	17%	33%	40%	33%	27%	-42	4.90
	06	32	99	35%	18%	33%	13%	34%	16%	4	4.60
	07	34	103	56%	6%	50%	13%	53%	9%	70	3.85
	08	24	99	35%	24%	71%	14%	46%	21%	8	4.53
Franklin,Ryan	03	32	99	39%	17%	29%	14%	34%	16%	4	4.60
	04	32	100	24%	12%	53%	20%	38%	16%	12	4.52
	05	30	96	24%	12%	38%	23%	30%	17%	-8	4.60
Gabbard,Kason	07	15	90	0%	25%	18%	36%	13%	33%	-106	5.37
	08	12	85	8%	50%			8%	50%	-184	7.26
Galarraga,A	08	28	97	27%	7%	38%	15%	32%	11%	20	4.49
Gallagher,Sean	08	21	97	18%	18%	20%	60%	19%	38%	-114	5.45
Gallardo,Yovani	07	17	96	67%	0%	64%	14%	65%	12%	82	3.61
Garcia,Freddy	03	33	102	42%	11%	36%	36%	39%	21%	-6	4.64
	04	31	106	67%	6%	62%	8%	65%	6%	106	3.38
	05	33	103	50%	11%	27%	27%	39%	18%	6	4.52
	06	33	101	44%	17%	60%	0%	52%	9%	68	3.85
	07	11	95	36%	36%			36%	36%	-72	5.13
Garland,Jon	03	32	95	28%	33%	29%	21%	28%	28%	-56	4.93
	04	33	103	35%	18%	25%	6%	30%	12%	12	4.49
	05	32	104	47%	0%	33%	13%	41%	6%	58	4.11
	06	32	104	35%	18%	53%	7%	44%	13%	36	4.32
	07	32	103	29%	6%	40%	27%	34%	16%	4	4.60
	08	32	100	16%	16%	15%	31%	16%	22%	-56	4.77
Garza,Matt	06	9	89			22%	56%	22%	56%	-180	7.36
	07	15	95	100%	0%	29%	36%	33%	33%	-66	5.08
	08	30	98	41%	29%	31%	15%	37%	23%	-18	4.64
Gaudin,Chad	07	34	97	33%	28%	38%	44%	35%	35%	-70	5.13
	08	6	93	67%	17%			67%	17%	66	3.73
Geer,Joshua	08	5	94			0%	20%	0%	20%	-80	4.83
Germano,Justin	04	5	79	0%	33%	0%	100%	0%	60%	-240	9.02
	07	23	88	64%	18%	0%	33%	30%	26%	-44	4.90
	08	6	91	17%	33%			17%	33%	-98	5.29
Glavine,Tom	03	32	91	21%	32%	38%	23%	28%	28%	-56	4.93
	04	33	103	32%	0%	21%	29%	27%	12%	6	4.50
	05	33	99	28%	33%	47%	0%	36%	18%	0	4.52
	06	32	102	37%	11%	38%	15%	38%	13%	24	4.41
	07	34	98	32%	11%	27%	20%	29%	15%	-2	4.62
	08	13	84	25%	33%	0%	100%	23%	38%	-106	5.36
Gobble,Jimmy	03	9	92			44%	22%	44%	22%	0	4.56
	04	24	92	19%	31%	38%	38%	25%	33%	-82	5.13
	06	6	79	0%	67%	33%	33%	17%	50%	-166	6.90

STARTING PITCHER CONSISTENCY CHART

				First Half		Second Half		Full Season			
Pitcher	Yr	#	PC	DOM	DIS	DOM	DIS	DOM	DIS	QC	qERA
Gonzalez,Edgar	04	10	81	0%	100%	11%	56%	10%	60%	-220	8.46
	06	5	94	100%	0%	67%	0%	80%	0%	160	2.69
	07	12	79	25%	13%	0%	75%	17%	33%	-98	5.29
	08	6	81	0%	50%			0%	50%	-200	7.46
Gonzalez,Gio	08	7	89			29%	57%	29%	57%	-170	7.14
Gorzelanny,Tom	06	11	92	0%	50%	56%	22%	45%	27%	-18	4.67
	07	32	104	50%	6%	36%	14%	44%	9%	52	4.11
	08	21	91	6%	35%	25%	75%	10%	43%	-152	5.70
Greinke,Zack	04	24	95	56%	0%	53%	13%	54%	8%	76	3.85
	05	33	94	22%	33%	33%	33%	27%	33%	-78	5.13
	07	14	86	29%	29%	29%	43%	29%	36%	-86	5.27
	08	32	101	58%	16%	77%	8%	66%	13%	80	3.61
Guthrie,Jeremy	07	26	96	77%	0%	23%	38%	50%	19%	24	4.37
	08	30	102	50%	5%	50%	20%	50%	10%	60	4.23
Halladay,Roy	03	36	101	76%	5%	73%	7%	75%	6%	126	3.13
	04	21	98	47%	6%	25%	75%	43%	19%	10	4.44
	05	19	101	68%	5%			68%	5%	116	3.38
	06	32	95	56%	0%	57%	14%	56%	6%	88	3.68
	07	31	107	50%	13%	47%	7%	48%	10%	56	4.28
	08	33	107	68%	0%	86%	0%	76%	0%	152	2.84
Hamels,Cole	06	23	95	22%	33%	64%	14%	48%	22%	8	4.53
	07	28	100	61%	6%	70%	10%	64%	7%	100	3.50
	08	33	104	70%	5%	69%	8%	70%	6%	116	3.25
Hammel,Jason	06	9	89	0%	50%	14%	57%	11%	56%	-202	7.77
	07	14	89			21%	36%	21%	36%	-102	5.36
	08	5	89	40%	20%			40%	20%	0	4.56
Hampton,Mike	03	31	96	25%	31%	27%	13%	26%	23%	-40	4.73
	04	29	94	18%	29%	33%	33%	24%	31%	-76	5.21
	05	12	85	33%	22%	0%	100%	25%	42%	-118	5.40
	08	13	92			46%	23%	46%	23%	0	4.53
Harang,Aaron	03	15	82	17%	67%	33%	22%	27%	40%	-106	5.40
	04	28	97	50%	14%	36%	14%	43%	14%	30	4.32
	05	32	107	59%	6%	40%	0%	50%	3%	88	3.47
	06	34	106	63%	11%	47%	7%	56%	9%	76	3.68
	07	34	106	58%	5%	67%	7%	62%	6%	100	3.50
	08	29	103	53%	21%	60%	30%	55%	24%	14	4.23
Harden,Rich	03	13	97			38%	31%	38%	31%	-48	5.00
	04	31	102	44%	19%	67%	7%	55%	13%	58	3.97
	05	19	99	73%	9%	75%	0%	74%	5%	128	3.25
	06	9	89	33%	33%	33%	67%	33%	44%	-110	5.29
	08	25	98	79%	7%	64%	0%	72%	4%	128	2.99
Haren,Dan	03	14	83	33%	33%	27%	36%	29%	36%	-86	5.27
	04	5	89	0%	100%	25%	0%	20%	20%	-40	4.75
	05	34	99	53%	21%	47%	13%	50%	18%	28	4.37
	06	34	103	53%	5%	53%	7%	53%	6%	82	3.85
	07	34	107	68%	0%	80%	7%	74%	3%	136	2.99
	08	33	101	89%	5%	71%	14%	82%	9%	128	3.00
Harrison,Matt	08	15	91	0%	50%	23%	38%	20%	40%	-120	5.50
Heilman,Aaron	03	13	91	0%	50%	0%	33%	0%	38%	-152	5.72
	04	5	89			60%	20%	60%	20%	40	3.95
	05	7	90	57%	14%			57%	14%	58	3.97
Hendrickson,Mark	03	30	85	17%	28%	17%	50%	17%	37%	-114	5.45
	04	30	94	24%	29%	46%	31%	33%	30%	-54	5.08
	05	31	91	0%	25%	33%	27%	16%	26%	-72	5.03
	06	25	98	33%	13%	30%	40%	32%	24%	-32	4.71
	07	15	83	30%	30%	20%	40%	27%	33%	-78	5.13
	08	19	93	32%	37%			32%	37%	-84	5.19
Hernandez,Felix	05	12	102			83%	8%	83%	8%	134	3.00
	06	31	99	47%	18%	50%	7%	48%	13%	44	4.28
	07	30	100	36%	14%	50%	0%	43%	7%	58	4.11
	08	31	103	59%	12%	57%	14%	58%	13%	64	3.97
Hernandez,Livan	03	33	108	47%	11%	86%	7%	64%	9%	92	3.50
	04	35	112	58%	5%	56%	6%	57%	6%	90	3.68
	05	34	114	26%	16%	40%	20%	32%	18%	-8	4.60
	06	34	103	16%	11%	40%	7%	26%	9%	16	4.48
	07	33	102	22%	22%	20%	33%	21%	27%	-66	4.98
	08	31	90	35%	30%	18%	36%	29%	32%	-70	5.13
Hernandez,O	04	15	95	0%	0%	57%	21%	53%	20%	26	4.50
	05	22	100	36%	27%	45%	18%	41%	23%	-10	4.56
	06	29	98	41%	35%	67%	17%	52%	28%	-8	4.61
	07	24	100	54%	23%	64%	18%	58%	21%	32	4.23
Herrera,Yoslan	08	5	72	0%	100%	25%	75%	20%	80%	-280	10.46
Hill,Rich	06	16	101	0%	50%	67%	17%	50%	25%	0	4.61
	07	32	96	47%	12%	53%	13%	50%	13%	48	4.23
	08	5	71	20%	40%			20%	40%	-120	5.50
Hill,Shawn	06	6	96	0%	17%			0%	17%	-68	4.69
	07	16	90	63%	0%	50%	13%	56%	6%	88	3.68
	08	12	94	17%	33%			17%	33%	-98	5.29
Hirsh,Jason	06	9	86			33%	44%	33%	44%	-110	5.29
	07	19	93	35%	24%	0%	0%	32%	21%	-20	4.71
Hochevar,Luke	08	22	94	44%	31%	17%	17%	36%	27%	-36	4.82
Howell,J.P.	05	15	86	17%	50%	56%	33%	40%	40%	-80	5.21
	06	8	89			13%	50%	13%	50%	-174	7.08
	07	10	95	14%	29%	33%	33%	20%	30%	-80	5.21

STARTING PITCHER CONSISTENCY CHART

				First Half		Second Half		Full Season			
Pitcher	Yr	#	PC	DOM	DIS	DOM	DIS	DOM	DIS	QC	qERA
Hudson,Tim	03	34	103	70%	10%	71%	7%	71%	9%	106	3.25
	04	27	102	40%	13%	33%	8%	37%	11%	30	4.41
	05	29	100	29%	36%	40%	0%	34%	17%	0	4.60
	06	35	98	32%	21%	31%	19%	31%	20%	-18	4.71
	07	34	93	53%	21%	47%	7%	50%	15%	40	4.37
	08	22	91	45%	25%	50%	0%	45%	23%	-2	4.53
Hughes,Phil	07	13	95	50%	50%	36%	27%	38%	31%	-48	5.00
	08	8	79	17%	83%	50%	50%	25%	75%	-250	9.46
Hurley,Eric	08	5	88	25%	0%	0%	100%	20%	20%	-40	4.75
Jackson,Edwin	04	5	71	0%	33%	0%	100%	0%	60%	-240	9.02
	05	6	88			0%	33%	0%	33%	-132	5.53
	07	31	95	44%	38%	40%	20%	42%	29%	-32	4.74
	08	31	97	33%	17%	23%	38%	29%	26%	-46	4.93
Jackson,Zach	06	7	92	0%	33%	0%	0%	0%	29%	-116	5.18
	08	9	93			22%	11%	22%	11%	0	4.51
James,Chuck	06	18	99	33%	33%	53%	20%	50%	22%	12	4.50
	07	30	89	28%	22%	42%	33%	33%	27%	-42	4.90
	08	7	74	20%	40%	0%	100%	14%	57%	-200	7.77
Jennings,Jason	03	32	95	40%	30%	8%	33%	28%	31%	-68	5.13
	04	33	101	33%	22%	47%	13%	39%	18%	6	4.52
	05	20	99	28%	17%	100%	0%	35%	15%	10	4.52
	06	32	103	50%	0%	50%	21%	50%	9%	64	3.85
	07	18	87	50%	10%	13%	50%	33%	28%	-46	4.90
	08	6	87	0%	67%			0%	67%	-268	9.80
Jimenez,Ubaldo	07	15	90			40%	33%	40%	33%	-52	4.92
	08	34	99	40%	20%	71%	7%	53%	15%	46	4.37
Johnson,Josh	06	24	99	58%	0%	67%	17%	63%	8%	94	3.50
	08	14	101	0%	0%	54%	0%	50%	0%	100	3.47
Johnson,Randy	03	18	100	75%	25%	64%	0%	67%	6%	110	3.38
	04	35	104	89%	0%	94%	0%	91%	0%	182	2.39
	05	34	101	74%	11%	73%	13%	74%	12%	100	3.51
	06	33	99	58%	26%	57%	7%	58%	18%	44	4.10
	07	10	91	60%	20%			60%	20%	40	3.95
	08	30	97	47%	24%	62%	8%	53%	17%	38	4.37
Jurrjens,Jair	07	7	68			14%	43%	14%	43%	-144	5.70
	08	31	99	56%	11%	46%	15%	52%	13%	52	4.23
Karstens,Jeff	06	6	86			17%	17%	17%	17%	-34	4.65
	08	9	92			22%	22%	22%	22%	-44	4.75
Kazmir,Scott	04	7	83			29%	43%	29%	43%	-114	5.40
	05	32	103	50%	28%	71%	21%	59%	25%	18	4.39
	06	24	101	47%	16%	100%	0%	58%	13%	64	3.97
	07	34	106	47%	11%	80%	7%	62%	9%	88	3.50
	08	27	102	57%	14%	62%	23%	59%	19%	42	4.10
Kendrick,Kyle	07	20	88	20%	0%	33%	27%	30%	20%	-20	4.71
	08	30	87	26%	32%	9%	64%	20%	43%	-132	5.50
Kennedy,Ian	08	9	82	25%	50%	0%	100%	22%	56%	-180	7.36
Kershaw,Clayton	08	21	88	13%	38%	62%	31%	43%	33%	-46	4.92
Kuroda,Hiroki	08	31	88	41%	18%	71%	21%	55%	19%	34	4.10
Lackey,John	03	33	99	50%	15%	46%	23%	48%	18%	24	4.40
	04	32	100	41%	18%	20%	13%	31%	16%	-2	4.60
	05	33	106	39%	6%	73%	0%	55%	3%	98	3.38
	06	33	106	61%	11%	60%	27%	61%	18%	50	3.83
	07	33	103	61%	6%	60%	7%	61%	6%	98	3.50
	08	24	101	82%	0%	38%	8%	58%	4%	100	3.38
Laffey,Aaron	07	9	80			11%	22%	11%	22%	-66	4.79
	08	16	93	43%	7%	0%	100%	38%	19%	0	4.52
Lannan,John	07	6	94			0%	17%	0%	17%	-68	4.69
	08	31	95	28%	17%	31%	23%	29%	19%	-18	4.62
Ledezma,Wil	03	8	83	100%	0%	0%	83%	25%	63%	-202	7.72
	04	8	79			38%	25%	38%	25%	-24	4.82
	05	10	94	0%	50%			0%	50%	-200	7.46
	06	7	78			0%	29%	0%	29%	-116	5.18
	08	6	82	17%	83%			17%	83%	-298	10.80
Lee,Cliff	03	9	89	100%	0%	63%	25%	67%	22%	46	3.85
	04	33	96	56%	11%	33%	47%	45%	27%	-18	4.67
	05	32	97	56%	22%	79%	0%	66%	13%	80	3.61
	06	33	102	39%	11%	40%	27%	39%	18%	6	4.52
	07	16	97	23%	23%	33%	33%	25%	25%	-50	4.93
	08	31	106	72%	6%	62%	0%	68%	3%	124	3.14
Lester,Jon	06	15	101	33%	17%	0%	22%	13%	20%	-54	4.79
	07	11	97			36%	27%	36%	27%	-36	4.82
	08	33	100	50%	15%	69%	8%	58%	12%	68	3.97
Lieber,Jon	04	27	94	46%	15%	57%	7%	52%	11%	60	4.23
	05	35	89	32%	21%	75%	6%	51%	14%	46	4.23
	06	27	92	33%	25%	40%	27%	37%	26%	-30	4.82
	07	12	95	42%	17%			42%	17%	16	4.44
Lilly,Ted	03	31	94	28%	28%	69%	31%	45%	29%	-26	4.67
	04	32	103	39%	6%	36%	7%	38%	6%	52	4.29
	05	25	86	24%	35%	25%	50%	24%	40%	-112	5.50
	06	32	100	50%	22%	50%	14%	50%	19%	24	4.37
	07	34	95	78%	17%	50%	19%	65%	18%	58	3.73
	08	34	95	55%	30%	86%	7%	68%	21%	52	3.85
Lincecum,Tim	07	24	99	58%	33%	75%	8%	67%	21%	50	3.85
	08	33	109	74%	0%	86%	14%	79%	6%	134	3.13
Liriano,Francisco	06	16	89	80%	0%	50%	33%	69%	13%	86	3.61
	08	14	91	0%	67%	64%	18%	50%	29%	-16	4.61

STARTING PITCHER CONSISTENCY CHART

				First Half		Second Half		Full Season			
Pitcher	Yr	#	PC	DOM	DIS	DOM	DIS	DOM	DIS	QC	qERA
Litsch,Jesse	07	20	89	20%	60%	27%	20%	25%	30%	-70	5.13
	08	28	97	28%	17%	50%	10%	36%	14%	16	4.41
Liz,Radhames	08	17	91	25%	38%	11%	44%	18%	41%	-128	5.60
Lohse,Kyle	03	33	92	47%	21%	36%	14%	42%	18%	12	4.44
	04	34	98	22%	17%	13%	38%	18%	26%	-68	5.03
	05	30	95	33%	20%	20%	33%	27%	27%	-54	4.93
	06	19	89	25%	63%	45%	18%	37%	37%	-74	5.13
	07	32	94	39%	22%	36%	29%	38%	25%	-24	4.82
	08	33	96	50%	15%	54%	15%	52%	15%	44	4.37
Looper,Braden	07	30	93	19%	19%	57%	36%	37%	27%	-34	4.82
	08	33	98	32%	26%	50%	14%	39%	21%	-6	4.64
Lowe,Derek	03	33	95	21%	21%	21%	7%	21%	15%	-18	4.63
	04	33	93	18%	35%	25%	38%	21%	36%	-102	5.36
	05	35	95	42%	11%	56%	19%	49%	14%	42	4.28
	06	34	96	32%	26%	47%	20%	38%	24%	-20	4.64
	07	32	94	53%	16%	62%	31%	56%	22%	24	4.23
	08	34	92	65%	5%	64%	14%	65%	9%	94	3.38
Lowry,Noah	04	14	95	33%	33%	45%	9%	43%	14%	30	4.32
	05	33	107	50%	22%	67%	0%	58%	12%	68	3.97
	06	27	97	15%	23%	43%	36%	30%	30%	-60	5.08
	07	26	98	35%	12%	22%	33%	31%	19%	-14	4.60
Maddux,Greg	03	36	81	43%	14%	53%	7%	47%	11%	50	4.28
	04	33	89	44%	17%	60%	0%	52%	9%	68	3.85
	05	35	89	47%	11%	44%	6%	46%	9%	56	3.98
	06	34	82	50%	17%	44%	13%	47%	15%	34	4.40
	07	34	80	50%	17%	50%	25%	50%	21%	16	4.50
	08	33	78	35%	15%	46%	15%	39%	15%	18	4.52
Maholm,Paul	05	6	102			50%	17%	50%	17%	32	4.37
	06	30	97	28%	28%	42%	0%	33%	17%	-2	4.60
	07	29	91	39%	28%	36%	18%	38%	24%	-20	4.64
	08	31	98	56%	17%	46%	8%	52%	13%	52	4.23
Maine,John	05	8	79			0%	50%	0%	50%	-200	7.46
	06	15	100	0%	33%	42%	8%	33%	13%	14	4.49
	07	32	102	76%	18%	33%	33%	56%	25%	12	4.39
	08	25	102	63%	21%	17%	33%	52%	24%	8	4.50
Marcum,Shaun	06	14	88			21%	50%	21%	50%	-158	6.74
	07	25	91	45%	18%	43%	29%	44%	24%	-8	4.56
	08	25	93	67%	7%	30%	50%	52%	24%	8	4.50
Marquis,Jason	04	32	104	35%	12%	33%	13%	34%	13%	16	4.49
	05	32	100	33%	17%	21%	21%	28%	19%	-20	4.62
	06	33	93	28%	22%	27%	40%	27%	30%	-66	5.13
	07	33	91	44%	17%	40%	33%	42%	24%	-12	4.56
	08	28	94	29%	18%	18%	18%	25%	18%	-22	4.62
Marshall,Sean	06	24	86	35%	35%	0%	71%	25%	46%	-134	5.98
	07	19	84	67%	22%	30%	50%	47%	37%	-54	4.98
	08	7	87	67%	33%	50%	25%	57%	29%	-2	4.39
Martinez,Pedro	03	29	98	69%	13%	85%	15%	76%	14%	96	3.41
	04	33	106	72%	11%	73%	7%	73%	9%	110	3.25
	05	31	98	89%	0%	62%	8%	77%	3%	142	2.84
	06	23	92	88%	6%	29%	43%	70%	17%	72	3.63
	07	5	92			40%	0%	40%	0%	80	3.89
	08	20	94	11%	33%	36%	9%	25%	20%	-30	4.73
Masterson,Justin	08	9	96	56%	0%			56%	0%	112	3.38
Matsuzaka,D	07	32	109	72%	0%	50%	14%	63%	6%	102	3.50
	08	29	100	44%	13%	54%	15%	48%	14%	40	4.28
McCarthy,Brandor	05	10	95	40%	60%	60%	0%	50%	30%	-20	4.71
	07	22	84	23%	38%	22%	44%	23%	41%	-118	5.50
	08	5	75			40%	60%	40%	60%	-160	7.05
McClung,Seth	03	5	78	20%	40%			20%	40%	-120	5.50
	05	17	94	67%	0%	43%	43%	47%	35%	-46	4.98
	06	15	98	7%	47%			7%	47%	-174	6.53
	08	12	86	60%	30%	50%	50%	58%	33%	-16	4.55
McGowan,Dustin	05	7	89			14%	43%	14%	43%	-144	5.70
	07	27	100	42%	17%	67%	7%	56%	11%	68	3.97
	08	19	95	42%	21%			42%	21%	0	4.56
Meche,Gil	03	32	96	50%	6%	36%	36%	44%	19%	12	4.44
	04	23	101	30%	40%	46%	8%	39%	22%	-10	4.64
	05	26	98	33%	28%	0%	50%	23%	35%	-94	5.36
	06	32	103	56%	11%	43%	36%	50%	22%	12	4.50
	07	34	105	58%	11%	47%	13%	53%	12%	58	4.23
	08	34	105	45%	10%	86%	0%	62%	6%	100	3.50
Mendoza,Luis	08	11	79	17%	83%	20%	60%	18%	73%	-256	9.50
Miller,Andrew	07	13	94	17%	0%	0%	57%	8%	31%	-108	5.45
	08	20	91	30%	40%			30%	40%	-100	5.29
Millwood,Kevin	03	35	99	50%	15%	40%	20%	46%	17%	24	4.40
	04	25	94	67%	17%	57%	43%	64%	24%	32	3.95
	05	30	99	40%	13%	53%	0%	47%	7%	66	3.98
	06	34	97	56%	11%	63%	13%	59%	12%	70	3.97
	07	31	95	40%	20%	38%	25%	39%	23%	-14	4.64
	08	29	93	33%	17%	73%	27%	48%	21%	12	4.53
Miner,Zach	06	16	89	43%	14%	11%	44%	25%	31%	-74	5.13
	08	13	95			46%	23%	46%	23%	0	4.53
Misch,Pat	08	7	88	29%	43%			29%	43%	-114	5.40
Moehler,Brian	05	25	86	27%	33%	20%	50%	24%	40%	-112	5.50
	06	21	81	27%	47%	0%	67%	19%	52%	-170	6.90
	08	26	84	42%	17%	36%	21%	38%	19%	0	4.52

Pitcher	Yr	#	PC	First Half DOM	DIS	Second Half DOM	DIS	Full Season DOM	DIS	QC	qERA
Morales,Franklin	07	8	74			63%	38%	63%	38%	-26	4.53
	08	5	97	0%	40%			0%	40%	-160	5.90
Morris,Matt	03	27	93	37%	16%	63%	13%	44%	15%	28	4.44
	04	32	96	44%	6%	36%	29%	41%	16%	18	4.44
	05	31	93	69%	13%	27%	20%	48%	16%	32	4.40
	06	33	99	44%	17%	47%	20%	45%	18%	18	4.40
	07	32	95	24%	12%	27%	27%	25%	19%	-26	4.62
	08	5	92	0%	100%			0%	100%	-400	15.00
Morrow,Brandon	08	5	101			40%	40%	40%	40%	-80	5.21
Morton,Charlie	08	15	88	33%	17%	33%	44%	33%	33%	-66	5.08
Moseley,Dustin	07	8	82	50%	0%	0%	50%	13%	38%	-126	5.54
	08	10	81	17%	33%	25%	25%	20%	30%	-80	5.21
Moyer,Jamie	03	33	104	53%	11%	43%	14%	48%	12%	48	4.28
	04	33	102	39%	22%	13%	33%	27%	27%	-54	4.93
	05	32	102	33%	28%	43%	14%	38%	22%	-12	4.64
	06	33	99	39%	6%	27%	27%	33%	15%	6	4.60
	07	33	95	39%	22%	33%	13%	36%	18%	0	4.52
	08	33	96	32%	16%	29%	7%	30%	12%	12	4.49
Mulder,Mark	03	26	100	58%	5%	71%	14%	62%	8%	92	3.50
	04	33	100	67%	0%	20%	27%	45%	12%	42	4.28
	05	32	94	22%	22%	14%	29%	19%	25%	-62	5.03
	06	17	87	33%	27%	0%	100%	29%	35%	-62	5.27
Mussina,Mike	03	31	104	78%	11%	46%	0%	65%	6%	106	3.38
	04	27	96	28%	22%	78%	11%	44%	19%	12	4.44
	05	30	99	44%	11%	50%	33%	47%	20%	14	4.53
	06	32	95	79%	11%	69%	15%	75%	13%	98	3.41
	07	27	86	57%	29%	31%	31%	44%	30%	-32	4.92
	08	34	92	58%	16%	67%	0%	62%	9%	88	3.50
Myers,Brett	03	32	94	53%	16%	38%	46%	47%	28%	-18	4.67
	04	31	90	31%	38%	27%	27%	29%	32%	-70	5.13
	05	34	102	61%	11%	56%	13%	59%	12%	70	3.97
	06	31	104	56%	19%	73%	7%	65%	13%	78	3.61
	07	30	101	29%	29%	77%	15%	50%	23%	8	4.50
Nippert,Dustin	08	6	97			33%	33%	33%	33%	-66	5.08
Nolasco,Ricky	06	22	87	30%	40%	25%	33%	27%	36%	-90	5.27
	08	32	99	61%	33%	79%	0%	69%	19%	62	3.73
Ohlendorf,Ross	08	5	86			0%	60%	0%	60%	-240	9.02
Olsen,Scott	06	31	93	50%	19%	60%	13%	55%	16%	46	4.10
	07	33	93	26%	21%	21%	43%	24%	30%	-72	5.21
	08	33	94	42%	21%	36%	14%	39%	18%	6	4.52
Olson,Garrett	07	7	92	0%	100%	17%	50%	14%	57%	-200	7.77
	08	26	89	21%	36%	25%	42%	23%	38%	-106	5.36
Oswalt,Roy	03	21	92	64%	7%	57%	14%	62%	10%	84	3.71
	04	35	102	68%	5%	69%	19%	69%	11%	94	3.61
	05	35	103	68%	5%	63%	6%	66%	6%	108	3.38
	06	32	101	41%	6%	73%	0%	56%	3%	100	3.38
	07	32	103	60%	0%	50%	17%	56%	6%	88	3.68
	08	32	97	58%	16%	69%	0%	63%	9%	90	3.50
Owings,Micah	07	27	90	43%	29%	54%	31%	48%	30%	-24	4.82
	08	18	93	53%	24%	0%	100%	50%	28%	-12	4.61
Padilla,Vicente	03	32	99	56%	17%	64%	14%	59%	16%	54	4.10
	04	20	89	40%	10%	50%	30%	45%	20%	10	4.53
	05	27	95	8%	46%	57%	21%	33%	33%	-66	5.08
	06	33	100	56%	17%	33%	13%	45%	15%	30	4.40
	07	23	89	13%	40%	50%	25%	26%	35%	-88	5.27
	08	29	100	22%	17%	27%	9%	24%	14%	6	4.51
Park,Chan Ho	03	7	80	14%	57%			14%	57%	-200	7.77
	04	16	95	38%	38%	13%	38%	25%	38%	-102	5.27
	05	29	97	47%	24%	8%	42%	31%	31%	-62	5.08
	06	21	101	31%	6%	20%	40%	29%	14%	2	4.50
	08	5	87	60%	40%			60%	40%	-40	4.67
Parra,Manny	08	29	93	44%	39%	45%	18%	45%	31%	-34	4.82
Parrish,John	08	6	86	50%	0%	0%	100%	17%	67%	-234	8.85
Parr,James	08	5	89			20%	60%	20%	60%	-200	7.98
Pavano,Carl	03	32	94	63%	16%	62%	23%	63%	19%	50	3.83
	04	31	102	71%	6%	50%	7%	61%	6%	98	3.50
	05	17	91	29%	29%			29%	29%	-58	4.93
	08	7	81			0%	43%	0%	43%	-172	5.90
Peavy,Jake	03	32	101	32%	16%	69%	15%	47%	16%	30	4.40
	04	27	99	55%	9%	69%	0%	63%	4%	110	3.29
	05	30	105	71%	6%	69%	0%	70%	3%	128	2.99
	06	32	105	59%	12%	60%	13%	59%	13%	66	3.97
	07	34	106	72%	0%	81%	6%	76%	3%	140	2.84
	08	27	106	73%	20%	50%	17%	63%	19%	50	3.83
Pelfrey,Mike	07	13	94	13%	25%	40%	20%	23%	23%	-46	4.75
	08	32	104	33%	28%	36%	21%	34%	25%	-32	4.90
Penny,Brad	03	32	95	37%	16%	54%	15%	44%	16%	24	4.44
	04	24	95	67%	6%	33%	33%	58%	13%	64	3.97
	05	29	96	53%	13%	50%	29%	52%	21%	20	4.50
	06	33	98	61%	6%	20%	13%	42%	9%	48	4.11
	07	33	98	56%	11%	33%	13%	45%	12%	42	4.28
	08	17	98	40%	20%	0%	50%	35%	24%	-26	4.64

Pitcher	Yr	#	PC	First Half DOM	DIS	Second Half DOM	DIS	Full Season DOM	DIS	QC	qERA
Perez,Odalis	03	29	95	50%	11%	55%	36%	52%	21%	20	4.50
	04	31	91	69%	0%	27%	20%	48%	10%	56	4.28
	05	19	86	30%	20%	33%	33%	32%	26%	-40	4.90
	06	20	87	13%	75%	50%	33%	35%	50%	-130	6.25
	07	26	90	28%	22%	13%	50%	23%	31%	-78	5.21
	08	30	90	29%	29%	31%	31%	30%	30%	-60	5.08
Perez,Oliver	03	25	96	33%	42%	54%	31%	44%	36%	-56	5.07
	04	30	104	60%	7%	87%	7%	73%	7%	118	3.25
	05	20	94	40%	33%	20%	60%	35%	40%	-90	5.25
	06	22	96	40%	47%	43%	43%	41%	45%	-98	5.67
	07	29	104	73%	13%	57%	21%	66%	17%	64	3.73
	08	34	99	42%	26%	73%	13%	56%	21%	28	4.23
Perkins,Glen	08	26	91	46%	23%	15%	31%	31%	27%	-46	4.90
Petit,Yusmeiro	07	10	79	33%	0%	29%	57%	30%	40%	-100	5.29
	08	8	79	100%	0%	43%	43%	50%	38%	-52	4.87
Pettitte,Andy	03	33	102	53%	32%	71%	14%	61%	24%	26	3.95
	04	15	90	70%	20%	20%	0%	53%	13%	54	4.23
	05	33	97	76%	0%	88%	0%	82%	0%	164	2.69
	06	35	100	35%	20%	47%	13%	40%	17%	12	4.44
	07	34	99	39%	22%	50%	13%	44%	18%	16	4.44
	08	33	99	45%	20%	46%	23%	45%	21%	6	4.53
Pineiro,Joel	03	32	100	53%	0%	46%	15%	50%	6%	76	3.85
	04	21	107	56%	11%	67%	33%	57%	14%	58	3.97
	05	30	98	27%	27%	33%	27%	30%	27%	-48	4.90
	06	25	96	33%	33%	14%	43%	28%	36%	-88	5.27
	07	11	90			36%	36%	36%	36%	-72	5.13
	08	25	87	27%	20%	20%	30%	24%	24%	-48	4.75
Ponson,Sidney	03	31	92	72%	6%	31%	0%	55%	3%	98	3.38
	04	33	100	28%	28%	33%	0%	30%	15%	0	4.60
	05	23	90	28%	33%	0%	80%	22%	43%	-128	5.50
	06	16	82	23%	31%	33%	67%	25%	38%	-102	5.27
	07	7	90	14%	57%			14%	57%	-200	7.77
	08	24	90	42%	33%	17%	50%	29%	42%	-110	5.40
Prior,Mark	03	30	113	79%	5%	91%	0%	83%	3%	154	2.69
	04	21	98	43%	29%	57%	21%	52%	24%	8	4.50
	05	27	105	67%	17%	53%	7%	59%	11%	74	3.97
	06	9	93	25%	25%	0%	60%	11%	44%	-154	5.70
Purcey,David	08	12	93	0%	100%	60%	20%	50%	33%	-32	4.71
Rasner,Darrell	07	6	67	17%	67%			17%	67%	-234	8.85
	08	20	82	25%	17%	25%	38%	25%	25%	-50	4.93
Redding,Tim	03	32	91	42%	32%	46%	15%	44%	25%	-12	4.74
	04	17	90	7%	57%	33%	67%	12%	59%	-212	7.77
	05	7	71	17%	50%	0%	100%	14%	57%	-200	7.77
	07	15	93	0%	0%	31%	23%	27%	20%	-26	4.73
	08	33	95	35%	15%	23%	46%	30%	27%	-48	4.90
Redman,Mark	03	29	109	40%	13%	71%	7%	55%	10%	70	3.97
	04	32	97	29%	18%	33%	27%	31%	22%	-26	4.71
	05	30	91	44%	11%	17%	25%	33%	17%	-2	4.60
	06	29	95	14%	36%	20%	33%	17%	34%	-102	5.29
	07	8	78	0%	60%	0%	67%	0%	63%	-252	9.02
	08	9	83	11%	33%			11%	33%	-110	5.37
Reyes,Anthony	06	17	85	33%	17%	45%	36%	41%	29%	-34	4.74
	07	20	88	42%	17%	50%	25%	45%	20%	10	4.53
	08	6	87			17%	17%	17%	17%	-34	4.65
Reyes,Jo-jo	07	10	82	0%	100%	22%	33%	20%	40%	-120	5.50
	08	22	85	43%	36%	13%	75%	32%	50%	-136	6.37
Reynolds,Gregory	08	13	75	18%	45%	0%	100%	15%	54%	-186	6.90
Richard,Clayton	08	8	81			38%	63%	38%	63%	-176	7.25
Richmond,Scott	08	5	87			40%	0%	40%	0%	80	3.89
Robertson,Nate	03	8	95			50%	38%	50%	38%	-52	4.87
	04	32	93	47%	18%	47%	20%	47%	19%	18	4.40
	05	32	93	41%	18%	20%	7%	31%	13%	10	4.49
	06	32	97	39%	17%	36%	7%	38%	13%	24	4.41
	07	30	96	20%	27%	60%	13%	40%	20%	0	4.56
	08	28	90	26%	16%	33%	44%	29%	25%	-42	4.93
Rodriguez,Wandy	05	22	92	11%	22%	31%	23%	23%	23%	-46	4.75
	06	24	92	37%	26%	20%	40%	33%	29%	-50	4.90
	07	31	92	59%	0%	36%	29%	48%	13%	44	4.28
	08	25	91	46%	31%	42%	33%	44%	32%	-40	4.92
Rogers,Kenny	03	31	99	33%	17%	46%	8%	39%	13%	26	4.41
	04	35	100	42%	21%	19%	31%	31%	26%	-42	4.90
	05	30	100	29%	6%	31%	8%	30%	7%	32	4.48
	06	33	93	33%	28%	20%	20%	27%	24%	-42	4.73
	07	11	92	67%	33%	25%	13%	36%	18%	0	4.52
	08	30	95	26%	32%	18%	36%	23%	33%	-86	5.21
Rowland-Smith,R	08	12	99	0%	50%	40%	20%	33%	25%	-34	4.90
Rusch,Glendon	03	19	95	13%	38%	67%	33%	21%	37%	-106	5.36
	04	16	100	50%	10%	50%	17%	50%	13%	48	4.23
	05	19	99	30%	30%	33%	33%	32%	32%	-64	5.08
	06	9	84	33%	56%			33%	56%	-158	6.91
	08	9	87	50%	50%	0%	43%	11%	44%	-154	5.70

STARTING PITCHER CONSISTENCY CHART

				First Half		Second Half		Full Season			
Pitcher	Yr	#	PC	DOM	DIS	DOM	DIS	DOM	DIS	QC	qERA
Sabathia,C.C.	03	30	104	39%	6%	50%	0%	43%	3%	74	3.89
	04	30	104	47%	12%	46%	8%	47%	10%	54	4.28
	05	31	102	44%	25%	67%	7%	55%	16%	46	4.10
	06	28	105	64%	21%	71%	7%	68%	14%	80	3.61
	07	34	105	74%	5%	73%	0%	74%	3%	136	2.99
	08	35	109	70%	15%	80%	0%	74%	9%	112	3.25
Sampson,Chris	07	19	86	19%	25%	0%	67%	16%	32%	-96	5.29
	08	11	77	27%	36%			27%	36%	-90	5.27
Sanchez,Anibal	06	17	99	0%	50%	60%	13%	53%	18%	34	4.37
	07	6	95	0%	17%			0%	17%	-68	4.69
	08	10	88			40%	20%	40%	20%	0	4.56
Sanchez,Jonathan	08	29	98	53%	21%	30%	50%	45%	31%	-34	4.82
Santana,Ervin	05	23	98	38%	50%	60%	20%	52%	30%	-16	4.71
	06	33	97	50%	11%	27%	33%	39%	21%	-6	4.64
	07	26	97	56%	33%	38%	13%	50%	27%	-8	4.61
	08	32	107	79%	0%	69%	0%	75%	0%	150	2.84
Santana,Johan	03	18	95	100%	0%	64%	7%	72%	6%	120	3.25
	04	34	101	79%	16%	100%	0%	88%	9%	140	2.88
	05	33	101	78%	0%	80%	7%	79%	3%	146	2.84
	06	34	102	74%	0%	80%	7%	76%	3%	140	2.84
	07	33	101	89%	0%	60%	7%	76%	3%	140	2.84
	08	34	106	79%	0%	80%	7%	79%	3%	146	2.84
Saunders,Joe	06	13	89			54%	31%	54%	31%	-16	4.71
	07	18	99	20%	0%	23%	8%	22%	6%	20	4.49
	08	31	97	39%	11%	23%	23%	32%	16%	0	4.60
Scherzer,Max	08	7	94	33%	33%	50%	0%	43%	14%	30	4.32
Schilling,Curt	03	24	102	82%	9%	92%	8%	88%	8%	144	2.88
	04	32	107	78%	0%	64%	14%	72%	6%	120	3.25
	05	11	105	33%	0%	50%	0%	45%	0%	90	3.68
	06	31	105	79%	5%	58%	0%	71%	3%	130	2.99
	07	24	95	40%	20%	44%	0%	42%	13%	32	4.32
Schmidt,Jason	03	29	106	83%	6%	91%	9%	86%	7%	144	2.88
	04	32	113	65%	6%	73%	13%	69%	9%	102	3.38
	05	29	105	44%	25%	46%	23%	45%	24%	-6	4.53
	06	32	108	67%	0%	43%	14%	56%	6%	88	3.68
	07	6	79	17%	67%			17%	67%	-234	8.85
Sheets,Ben	03	34	99	52%	5%	46%	15%	50%	9%	64	3.85
	04	34	105	89%	6%	88%	0%	88%	3%	164	2.54
	05	22	104	62%	0%	89%	0%	73%	0%	146	2.99
	06	17	92	50%	25%	85%	8%	76%	12%	104	3.41
	07	24	94	67%	11%	50%	50%	63%	21%	42	3.95
	08	31	99	72%	0%	54%	15%	65%	6%	106	3.38
Shields,James	06	21	95	50%	0%	46%	15%	48%	10%	56	4.28
	07	31	102	61%	0%	77%	8%	68%	3%	124	3.14
	08	33	95	63%	11%	50%	7%	58%	9%	80	3.68
Silva,Carlos	04	33	88	17%	33%	7%	7%	12%	21%	-60	4.79
	05	27	85	38%	6%	64%	9%	48%	7%	68	3.98
	06	31	84	13%	33%	31%	38%	23%	35%	-94	5.36
	07	33	93	33%	17%	40%	20%	36%	18%	0	4.52
	08	28	88	35%	25%	0%	63%	25%	36%	-94	5.27
Slowey,Kevin	07	11	94	0%	29%	75%	0%	27%	18%	-18	4.62
	08	27	93	50%	21%	46%	15%	48%	19%	20	4.40
Smith,Gregory	08	32	97	39%	17%	29%	43%	34%	28%	-44	4.90
Smoltz,John	05	33	100	42%	11%	93%	0%	64%	6%	104	3.50
	06	35	101	74%	5%	75%	13%	74%	9%	112	3.25
	07	32	96	82%	12%	73%	7%	78%	9%	120	3.13
	08	5	87	80%	20%			80%	20%	80	3.55
Snell,Ian	05	5	80			0%	40%	0%	40%	-160	5.90
	06	32	95	39%	28%	50%	0%	44%	16%	24	4.44
	07	32	98	65%	0%	53%	13%	59%	6%	94	3.68
	08	31	97	39%	33%	38%	31%	39%	32%	-50	5.00
Sonnanstine,Andy	07	22	95	57%	0%	33%	27%	41%	18%	10	4.44
	08	32	91	32%	11%	54%	15%	41%	13%	30	4.32
Sowers,Jeremy	06	14	91	33%	33%	55%	18%	50%	21%	16	4.50
	07	13	82	8%	50%	100%	0%	15%	46%	-154	6.25
	08	22	92	11%	67%	23%	23%	18%	41%	-128	5.60
Stults,Eric	07	5	87			40%	60%	40%	60%	-160	7.05
	08	7	89	60%	20%	0%	100%	43%	43%	-86	5.21
Suppan,Jeff	03	31	101	44%	11%	31%	0%	39%	6%	54	4.29
	04	31	98	47%	12%	14%	21%	32%	16%	0	4.60
	05	32	95	17%	22%	50%	14%	31%	19%	-14	4.60
	06	32	96	6%	41%	40%	27%	22%	34%	-92	5.21
	07	34	98	32%	11%	27%	7%	29%	9%	22	4.48
	08	31	91	28%	28%	8%	31%	19%	29%	-78	5.03
Tejeda,Robinson	05	13	88	50%	33%	57%	14%	54%	23%	16	4.50
	06	14	90	0%	60%	33%	33%	21%	43%	-130	5.50
	07	19	94	12%	41%	0%	50%	11%	42%	-146	5.70
Thompson,Brad	07	17	82	20%	10%	14%	43%	18%	24%	-60	4.77
	08	6	74	33%	33%	33%	33%	33%	33%	-66	5.08
Tomko,Brett	03	33	99	21%	16%	21%	21%	21%	18%	-30	4.63
	04	31	101	25%	31%	47%	20%	35%	26%	-34	4.82
	05	30	100	35%	18%	46%	15%	40%	17%	12	4.44
	06	15	95	33%	33%			33%	33%	-66	5.08
	07	19	90	50%	38%	36%	18%	42%	26%	-20	4.74
	08	10	96	30%	30%			30%	30%	-60	5.08
Tucker,Ryan	08	6	93	17%	50%			17%	50%	-166	6.90

STARTING PITCHER CONSISTENCY CHART

				First Half		Second Half		Full Season			
Pitcher	Yr	#	PC	DOM	DIS	DOM	DIS	DOM	DIS	QC	qERA
Van Benschoten,J	04	5	84			40%	20%	40%	20%	0	4.56
	07	9	80	20%	60%	0%	75%	11%	67%	-246	9.15
	08	5	78	0%	100%	0%	50%	0%	80%	-320	12.14
Vazquez,Javier	03	34	109	70%	5%	79%	0%	74%	3%	136	2.99
	04	32	100	50%	0%	29%	36%	41%	16%	18	4.44
	05	33	101	67%	11%	53%	13%	61%	12%	74	3.71
	06	32	103	47%	6%	53%	20%	50%	13%	48	4.23
	07	32	108	82%	0%	67%	0%	75%	0%	150	2.84
	08	33	102	53%	16%	50%	29%	52%	21%	20	4.50
Verlander,Justin	06	30	99	47%	6%	38%	23%	43%	13%	34	4.32
	07	32	105	76%	6%	67%	13%	72%	9%	108	3.25
	08	33	107	50%	10%	46%	31%	48%	18%	24	4.40
Villanueva,Carlos	06	6	98	33%	33%	33%	0%	33%	17%	-2	4.60
	07	6	87	100%	0%	40%	0%	50%	0%	100	3.47
	08	9	96	11%	22%			11%	22%	-66	4.79
Volquez,Edinson	06	8	81			13%	63%	13%	63%	-226	8.46
	07	6	99			33%	17%	33%	17%	-2	4.60
	08	32	105	74%	11%	54%	8%	66%	9%	96	3.38
Volstad,Chris	08	14	92	100%	0%	31%	15%	36%	14%	16	4.41
Wainwright,Adam	07	32	99	18%	12%	60%	7%	38%	9%	40	4.29
	08	20	98	62%	0%	43%	14%	55%	5%	90	3.68
Wakefield,Tim	03	33	94	58%	11%	71%	14%	64%	12%	80	3.71
	04	30	98	31%	13%	21%	36%	27%	23%	-38	4.73
	05	33	103	44%	11%	47%	27%	45%	18%	18	4.40
	06	23	98	61%	6%	0%	60%	48%	17%	28	4.40
	07	31	93	35%	18%	36%	29%	35%	23%	-22	4.64
	08	30	93	42%	11%	45%	36%	43%	20%	6	4.56
Wang,Chien-Ming	05	17	90	33%	17%	40%	20%	35%	18%	-2	4.52
	06	33	92	26%	26%	21%	14%	24%	21%	-36	4.75
	07	30	95	40%	7%	53%	13%	47%	10%	54	4.28
	08	15	94	33%	13%			33%	13%	14	4.49
Washburn,Jarrod	03	32	101	37%	11%	38%	15%	38%	13%	24	4.41
	04	25	97	35%	18%	50%	25%	40%	20%	0	4.56
	05	29	93	33%	28%	27%	9%	31%	21%	-22	4.71
	06	31	99	50%	28%	31%	23%	42%	26%	-20	4.74
	07	32	102	35%	24%	47%	27%	41%	25%	-18	4.74
	08	26	100	39%	22%	25%	38%	35%	27%	-38	4.82
Waters,Chris	08	11	98			9%	45%	9%	45%	-162	6.53
Weaver,Jered	06	19	102	100%	0%	38%	15%	58%	11%	72	3.97
	07	28	98	50%	29%	50%	14%	50%	21%	16	4.50
	08	30	101	63%	16%	45%	18%	57%	17%	46	4.10
Webb,Brandon	03	28	100	79%	0%	57%	21%	68%	11%	92	3.61
	04	35	98	42%	5%	38%	25%	40%	14%	24	4.32
	05	33	102	61%	0%	67%	7%	64%	3%	116	3.29
	06	33	101	74%	0%	50%	7%	64%	3%	116	3.29
	07	34	101	53%	0%	80%	0%	65%	0%	130	3.14
	08	34	99	75%	10%	57%	14%	68%	12%	88	3.61
Wellemeyer,Todd	07	11	77	25%	38%	67%	33%	36%	36%	-72	5.13
	08	32	97	67%	11%	57%	0%	63%	6%	102	3.50
Westbrook,Jake	03	22	86	10%	50%	25%	33%	18%	41%	-128	5.60
	04	30	99	21%	7%	38%	6%	30%	7%	32	4.48
	05	34	94	42%	21%	33%	13%	38%	18%	4	4.52
	06	32	102	61%	17%	21%	14%	44%	16%	24	4.44
	07	25	99	44%	33%	31%	6%	36%	16%	8	4.52
	08	5	101	20%	0%			20%	0%	40	4.47
Willis,Dontrelle	03	27	99	69%	8%	50%	21%	59%	15%	58	4.10
	04	32	98	33%	33%	57%	7%	44%	22%	0	4.56
	05	34	105	78%	6%	56%	13%	68%	9%	100	3.38
	06	34	106	33%	17%	44%	19%	38%	18%	4	4.52
	07	35	100	47%	11%	19%	38%	34%	23%	-24	4.71
	08	7	71	0%	75%	0%	33%	0%	57%	-228	8.24
Wolf,Randy	03	33	99	74%	0%	43%	21%	61%	9%	86	3.50
	04	23	92	50%	21%	44%	22%	48%	22%	8	4.53
	05	13	100	38%	8%			38%	8%	44	4.29
	06	12	88			17%	33%	17%	33%	-98	5.29
	07	18	99	33%	11%			33%	11%	22	4.49
	08	33	96	60%	30%	38%	23%	52%	27%	-4	4.61
Wood,Kerry	03	32	110	68%	11%	77%	15%	72%	13%	92	3.51
	04	22	101	88%	13%	64%	14%	73%	14%	90	3.51
	05	10	88	38%	13%	50%	50%	40%	20%	0	4.56
Young,Chris	04	7	95			43%	43%	43%	43%	-86	5.21
	05	31	92	44%	28%	38%	38%	42%	32%	-44	4.92
	06	31	98	61%	11%	46%	31%	55%	19%	34	4.10
	07	30	96	65%	24%	62%	23%	63%	23%	34	3.95
	08	18	97	60%	20%	63%	13%	61%	17%	54	3.83
Zambrano,Carlos	03	32	106	47%	5%	77%	8%	59%	6%	94	3.68
	04	31	112	71%	12%	79%	0%	74%	6%	124	3.25
	05	33	108	61%	22%	67%	7%	64%	15%	68	3.83
	06	33	110	68%	11%	71%	14%	70%	12%	92	3.51
	07	34	109	68%	16%	47%	13%	59%	15%	58	4.10
	08	30	101	56%	6%	33%	33%	47%	17%	26	4.40
Zito,Barry	03	35	107	25%	10%	60%	20%	40%	14%	24	4.32
	04	34	108	44%	22%	50%	6%	47%	15%	34	4.40
	05	35	109	58%	5%	75%	19%	66%	11%	88	3.61
	06	34	108	47%	5%	33%	20%	41%	12%	34	4.32
	07	33	103	22%	22%	60%	27%	39%	24%	-18	4.64
	08	32	100	26%	42%	31%	23%	28%	34%	-80	5.13

Bullpen Indicator Charts

Closer Volatility Chart

CLOSERS DRAFTED refers to the number of saves sources purchased in both LABR and Tout Wars Leagues each year. These only include relievers drafted for at least $10, specifically for saves speculation. **AVG R$** refers to the average purchase price of these pitchers in the AL-only and NL-only leagues. **FAILED** is the number (and percentage) of closers drafted that did not return at least 50% of their value that year. The Failures include those that lost their value due to ineffectiveness, injury or managerial decision. **NEW SOURCES** are arms that were drafted for less than $10 (if they were drafted at all) but finished with at least double-digit saves.

Bullpen Indicators Chart

These charts offer insight for those looking to speculate on future closer candidates. The charts help focus on many of the statistical and situational factors that might go into a manager's decision to grant any individual pitcher a save opportunity. It's not all-encompassing, but it's a good start. The chart provides a four-year scan for nearly all pitchers who posted at least one save and/or three holds in 2008.

Saves Percentage: What it says is simple... "Who is getting it done?" Intuitively, this percentage should be a major factor in determining which closers might be in danger of losing their jobs. However, a Doug Dennis study showed little correlation between saves success rate alone and future opportunity. Better to prospect for pitchers who have *both* a high saves percentage (80% or better) *and* high skills, as measured by base performance value.

Base Performance Value: The components of BPV are evaluated in many ways. Big league managers tend to look for a pitcher who can strike out eight or nine batters per 9 IP, sometimes even if he's also walking that many. In using BPV, we set a benchmark of 75 as the minimum necessary for success. BPV's over 100 are much better, however.

Situational Performance is the last piece of the puzzle. The chart includes opposition batting averages for each pitcher versus right-handed and left-handed hitters, with runners on base, in his first 15 pitches, etc. which are all good indicators. We'll set a benchmark of a .250 BA; anything over and the risk level increases.

There are other variables that come into play as well. Left-handed relievers rarely move into a closer's role unless the team's bullpen has sufficient southpaw depth. Some managers do see the value of having a high-skills arm available for the middle innings, so those pitchers don't get promoted into a closer's role either.

The tools are here. Whether or not a manager will make a decision reflective of this information remains to be seen. But the data can help us increase our odds of uncovering those elusive saves and minimizing some of the risk.

NOTE: In the Bullpen Indicators Chart, BPV values for 2006 and 2007 use the previous version of the BPV formula. 2008 values use the new version.

2008 Closer Volatility Report

Closer value and volatility have hit a three-year plateau. While the cost of saves increased by a scant 11 cents over 2007 to $17.78, the range his been within 13 cents since 2006. The percentage of closers that failed also remained close to 33% for the third straight year.

While costs plateaued, risk aversion to closer investments increased. Thirty-two pitchers were drafted for saves speculation in 2008, a 13-year high. Nearly 40% of these pitchers cost $15 or less.

Five drafted closers managed to return 30% or more in profit: Kerry Wood ($22 return on $10 average draft price), B.J. Ryan ($16 on $10), Joakim Soria ($27 on $20), Jose Valverde ($25 on $19), and Brad Lidge ($25 on $19). Only eight closers total (28%) returned any type of profit. Eight returned $0 on their investments (which averaged $16). In all, 22 of 32 pitchers drafted for saves (69%) realized a loss on their purchase price. Saves remain extremely high risk investments.

The accompanying chart lists 10 closers who returned less than 50% of their draft value; these are classified as the "failures." However, the list does not include others who also lost their jobs but managed to return at least half their value. These pitchers were Takashi Saito, Huston Street, Matt Capps, Billy Wagner and Brandon Lyon. So, in some sense, the failure rate was even greater than indicated.

Of the 11 new sources that amassed at least 10 saves in 2008, only two might be considered strong front-line closer candidates for 2008 — Jonathan Broxton and Brian Fuentes — so volatility within the closer's role still remains.

Last year at this time, there were more settled bullpen situations and we concluded that this could push prices up in 2008. While the increase was only 11 pennies, it is a question we need to ask again for 2009.

Many incumbent closers are free agents this winter, including Kerry Wood, Francisco Rodriguez and Fuentes. With strong odds that these relievers will be closing out ninth innings on new clubs, there will be a potential ripple effect for all closer roles. Currently, there are only 6 of 14 firm bullpen situations in the AL; only 5 of 16 in the NL. The fallout from this high level of volatility could see fantasy leaguers investing in an even larger group of speculative closers come March, and a further decline in the average price for saves.

CLOSER VOLATILITY CHART

FAILURES	2002	2003	2004	2005	2006	2007	2008
	Alfonseca	Alfonseca	Biddle	Adams	Benitez	Benitez	Accardo
	Anderson,M	Anderson,M	Borowski	Affeldt	Dempster	Dotel	Isringhausen
	Foulke	Benitez	Guardado	Benitez	Foulke	Fuentes	Jones,T
	Fox	Dejean	Koch	Dotel	Gagne	Gagne	Soriano,R
	Gordon	Embree	Lopez,Aq	Foulke	Guardado	Gonzalez,M	Borowski
	Strickland	Escobar	MacDougal	Gagne	MacDougal	Gordon	Corpas
	Wickman	Hoffman	Mantei	Graves	Orvella	Ray	Cordero,C
	Zimmerman	Isringhausen	Nen	Kolb	Reitsma	Ryan	Gagne
		Jimenez	Rhodes	Mota	Turnbow	Torres	Putz
		Koch	Riske	Percival	Valverde	Wickman	Wilson,CJ
		Mesa	Wagner	Speier			
		Nen		Takatsu			
		Sasaki					
		Stewart					
		Urbina					
		Williams,M					
		Williamson					

NEW SOURCES	2002	2003	2004	2005	2006	2007	2008
	Acevedo	Beck	Affeldt	Brazoban	Burgos	Accardo	Broxton
	Baez	Biddle	Aquino	Bruney	Duchscherer	Capps	Franklin,R
	Cordero	Borowski	Chacon	Dempster	Julio,J	Corpas	Fuentes
	DeJean	Carter,L	Cordero	Farnsworth	Nelson,J	Embree	Gonzalez,M
	Gagne	Cordero,F	Frasor	Fuentes	Otsuka	Gregg	Lewis,J
	Irabu	Gordon	Herges	Hermanson	Papelbon	Hennessy	Morrow
	Julio	Hasegawa	Hermanson	Jones,T	Putz	Myers,B	Rauch
	Looper	Kolb,D	Hawkins	Lyon	Saito,T	Reyes,A	Rodney
	Marte	Lopez,Aq	Lidge	MacDougal	Timlin	Soria	Torres,S
	Nunez,V	MacDougal	Putz	Reitsma	Torres,S	Wheeler	Wheeler
	Osuna	Marte	Rodriguez,Fr	Rodney	Walker,T	Wilson,CJ	Ziegler
	Williamson	Politte	Takatsu	Street	Wheeler		
		Tavarez	Wickman	Turnbow			
		Worrell	Worrell	Walker,T			
			Yan	Weathers			

SUMMARY

NUMBER OF CLOSERS

YEAR	Drafted	Avg R$	Failed	Failure %	New Sources
1996	24	$30	3	13%	2
1997	26	$30	5	19%	8
1998	25	$32	11	44%	9
1999	23	$25	5	22%	7
2000	27	$25	10	37%	9
2001	25	$26	7	28%	7
2002	28	$22	8	29%	12
2003	29	$21.97	17	59%	14
2004	29	$19.78	11	38%	15
2005	28	$20.79	12	43%	15
2006	30	$17.80	10	33%	12
2007	28	$17.67	10	36%	11
2008	32	$17.78	10	31%	11

BULLPEN INDICATORS

Pitcher			Tm	BPIs			Results		Runners		Pitch Ct		Platoon	
				IP/g	bpv	S%	Sv%	Eff%	Emp	On	1-15	16-30	vLH	vRH
Aardsma,David	R	06	CHC	1.2	41	75%	0%	100%	189	247	219	197	190	225
		07	CHW	1.3	66	63%	0%	56%	262	338	274	356	283	310
		08	BOS	1.0	4	68%	0%	73%	202	298	223	316	253	245
Accardo,Jeremy	R	05	SF	1.0	48	67%	0%	45%	239	222	203	313	182	265
		06	TOR	1.1	72	62%	38%	62%	226	364	286	276	241	307
		07	TOR	1.1	85	83%	86%	80%	201	211	181	290	161	250
		08	TOR	0.8	13	56%	67%	55%	450	200	326	143	300	300
Acosta,Manny	R	07	ATL	1.1	87	84%	0%	83%	159	171	190	105	250	93
		08	ATL	1.2	7	79%	60%	59%	257	247	255	227	289	220
Adams,Mike	R	05	MIL	1.0	46	90%	50%	60%	231	240	278	167	200	258
		08	SD	1.2	130	82%	0%	71%	158	273	220	188	225	181
Affeldt,Jeremy	L	05	KC	1.0	55	68%	0%	86%	300	259	293	268	263	283
		06	COL	1.8	9	62%	33%	58%	165	315	260	180	213	240
		07	COL	0.8	58	74%	0%	65%	240	213	241	129	250	211
		08	CIN	1.1	116	79%	0%	75%	268	258	277	224	269	261
Albers,Matt	R	08	BAL	1.8	10	75%	0%	64%	226	233	203	227	159	292
Arredondo,Jose	R	08	LAA	1.2	86	87%	0%	74%	175	206	205	161	155	228
Ayala,Luis	R	05	WAS	1.0	64	83%	33%	78%	308	261	275	328	352	229
		07	WAS	1.0	52	80%	50%	75%	256	282	302	138	243	286
		08	NYM	0.9	52	61%	60%	65%	247	336	269	350	281	289
Balfour,Grant	R	08	TAM	1.1	128	86%	80%	89%	120	169	100	213	122	156
Bass,Brian	R	08	BAL	1.8	35	69%	50%	62%	368	233	287	237	279	309
Bautista,Denny	R	08	PIT	1.2	-40	70%	0%	74%	286	274	288	230	284	278
Beimel,Joe	L	06	LA	1.1	26	79%	100%	93%	258	267	286	185	232	279
		07	LA	0.8	42	67%	100%	91%	250	256	256	235	188	294
		08	LA	0.7	25	85%	0%	94%	268	260	265	250	278	250
Bell,Heath	R	07	SD	1.2	134	79%	33%	84%	162	214	182	206	216	157
		08	SD	1.1	83	71%	0%	69%	234	197	234	159	197	242
Bennett,Jeff	R	08	ATL	1.4	38	73%	75%	72%	229	239	249	228	273	212
Benoit,Joaquin	R	05	TEX	2.7	64	72%	0%	69%	143	133	172	106	119	156
		06	TEX	1.4	88	62%	0%	73%	240	210	231	178	191	245
		07	TEX	1.2	104	78%	46%	74%	250	192	218	216	172	268
		08	TEX	1.0	-36	72%	25%	77%	230	235	264	154	184	282
Betancourt,Raf	R	05	CLE	1.2	129	77%	33%	75%	215	238	233	200	264	204
		06	CLE	1.1	104	71%	50%	65%	214	278	248	236	221	254
		07	CLE	1.2	223	84%	50%	91%	190	173	191	157	239	148
		08	CLE	1.0	64	68%	50%	70%	275	270	303	200	243	295
Blevins,Jerry	L	08	OAK	1.0	86	74%	0%	60%	269	167	211	237	170	250
Borowski,Joe	R	05	TAM	1.1	32	64%	0%	70%	159	328	240	184	198	244
		06	FLA	1.0	63	75%	84%	80%	237	233	239	230	167	291
		07	CLE	1.0	77	67%	85%	79%	284	296	303	254	293	286
		08	CLE	0.9	-27	64%	60%	50%	395	265	333	357	333	333
Boyer,Blaine	R	08	ATL	0.9	89	58%	20%	63%	228	313	230	357	271	256
Bradford,Chad	R	05	BOS	0.8	64	72%	0%	83%	308	315	297	389	409	282
		06	NYM	0.9	108	73%	67%	84%	284	224	238	333	262	251
		07	BAL	0.8	36	75%	29%	68%	273	312	291	310	321	282
		08	TAM	0.9	34	85%	0%	83%	280	264	268	318	303	259
Bray,Bill	L	06	CIN	1.1	63	74%	67%	73%	302	267	259	283	329	254
		07	CIN	0.8	78	55%	100%	70%	269	290	313	111	158	342
		08	CIN	0.7	68	84%	0%	65%	305	235	275	207	253	276
Breslow,Craig	L	08	MIN	1.0	56	83%	50%	67%	214	200	196	229	190	224
Brocail,Doug	R	07	SD	1.1	42	78%	0%	94%	192	283	217	221	182	268
		08	HOU	1.0	92	71%	40%	79%	232	257	244	239	301	203
Broxton,Jonathan	R	06	LA	1.1	106	83%	43%	79%	253	172	234	192	244	196
		07	LA	1.0	137	77%	25%	79%	228	220	245	152	200	247
		08	LA	1.0	130	72%	64%	70%	173	255	199	238	260	177
Bruney,Brian	R	05	ARI	1.0	55	62%	75%	71%	227	364	277	339	280	314
		06	NYY	1.1	87	96%	0%	83%	195	182	184	200	115	229
		07	NYY	0.9	31	72%	0%	69%	256	232	262	204	303	209
		08	NYY	1.1	60	84%	50%	94%	105	212	192	71	119	179
Buchholz,Taylor	R	08	COL	1.1	85	81%	33%	78%	146	261	177	243	198	180
Burton,Jared	R	07	CIN	0.9	68	79%	0%	75%	195	176	179	222	130	219
		08	CIN	1.1	83	80%	0%	84%	250	257	284	190	242	262
Camp,Shawn	R	06	TAM	1.0	64	71%	67%	79%	316	310	300	365	370	284
		07	TAM	0.8	54	66%	0%	69%	382	362	397	212	370	368
		08	TOR	1.0	92	67%	0%	91%	228	301	279	167	356	204
Capps,Matt	R	06	PIT	1.0	95	72%	10%	70%	265	268	266	288	250	275
		07	PIT	1.0	99	80%	86%	79%	228	207	197	364	281	181
		08	PIT	1.1	106	72%	81%	74%	233	253	248	235	229	253
Carlson,Jesse	L	08	TOR	0.9	73	84%	100%	93%	202	185	188	220	200	189
Casilla,Santiago	R	07	OAK	1.1	73	68%	40%	81%	216	233	208	266	212	230
		08	OAK	1.0	60	77%	67%	85%	344	257	328	230	308	291
Chamberlain,Job	R	07	NYY	1.3	198	100%	100%	100%	179	74	158	125	132	156
		08	NYY	2.4	121	80%	0%	85%	192	224	165	282	197	212
Condrey,Clay	R	07	PHI	1.3	32	67%	100%	100%	290	309	322	206	299	302
		08	PHI	1.2	46	81%	100%	56%	293	314	340	191	317	292
Cordero,Chad	R	05	WAS	1.0	87	90%	87%	82%	194	204	242	74	192	205
		06	WAS	1.1	69	81%	88%	82%	236	183	239	113	219	212
		07	WAS	1.0	57	79%	80%	77%	247	276	275	224	221	295
		08	WAS	0.7	40	89%	0%	100%	375	273	286	400	250	429
Cordero,Francisc	R	05	TEX	1.0	98	76%	82%	82%	231	236	249	194	250	214
		06	MIL	1.0	90	74%	67%	75%	229	266	260	231	286	219
		07	MIL	1.0	156	74%	86%	80%	187	260	191	340	225	212
		08	CIN	1.0	61	78%	85%	80%	213	261	245	203	212	252

BULLPEN INDICATORS

Pitcher			Tm	BPIs			Results		Runners		Pitch Ct		Platoon	
				IP/g	bpv	S%	Sv%	Eff%	Emp	On	1-15	16-30	vLH	vRH
Corey,Bryan	R	08	SD	1.0	37	54%	0%	50%	269	325	311	255	274	309
Corpas,Manny	R	06	COL	0.9	91	76%	0%	67%	282	291	311	150	281	290
		07	COL	1.0	90	84%	86%	89%	211	245	213	300	234	214
		08	COL	1.0	59	70%	31%	67%	275	295	271	315	267	301
Cotts,Neal	L	05	CHW	0.9	90	82%	0%	89%	171	188	196	114	206	155
		06	CHW	0.8	21	75%	25%	76%	295	287	285	309	263	314
		08	CHC	0.7	117	77%	0%	69%	319	175	250	267	254	250
Crain,Jesse	R	05	MIN	1.1	15	79%	25%	75%	218	219	228	185	209	225
		06	MIN	1.1	91	74%	25%	65%	243	289	250	256	259	263
		07	MIN	0.9	47	68%	0%	78%	200	440	224	500	269	308
		08	MIN	0.9	55	76%	0%	76%	276	233	256	255	247	258
Cruz,Juan	R	07	ARI	1.2	120	80%	0%	91%	198	211	219	208	269	143
		08	ARI	0.9	74	83%	0%	86%	141	243	163	231	160	207
Delcarmen,Mann	R	06	BOS	1.1	91	66%	0%	80%	273	345	283	371	319	302
		07	BOS	1.0	93	85%	50%	92%	193	169	195	143	164	196
		08	BOS	1.0	92	72%	40%	81%	199	215	209	200	197	214
Devine,Joey	R	08	OAK	1.1	107	92%	50%	90%	138	164	139	200	200	112
Donnelly,Brendar	R	05	ANA	1.0	65	74%	0%	76%	258	228	260	194	213	274
		06	ANA	1.0	51	74%	0%	94%	234	246	256	194	290	204
		07	BOS	0.8	66	71%	0%	91%	235	234	225	300	212	250
		08	CLE	0.9	-73	61%	0%	100%	269	407	286	545	300	364
Dotel,Octavio	R	05	OAK	1.0	52	79%	64%	57%	143	212	175	273	269	107
		07	ATL	0.9	117	73%	73%	74%	322	164	278	133	265	225
		08	CHW	0.9	127	77%	20%	76%	242	188	235	167	250	201
Downs,Scott	L	06	TOR	1.3	54	72%	25%	72%	246	134	199	203	177	208
		07	TOR	0.7	97	84%	25%	85%	198	250	233	184	209	238
		08	TOR	1.1	82	86%	56%	81%	200	229	209	203	194	226
Estrada,Marco	R	08	WAS	1.2	55	61%	0%	75%	400	231	348	313	333	280
Feliciano,Pedro	L	06	NYM	0.9	87	86%	0%	77%	255	242	270	173	231	266
		07	NYM	0.8	87	75%	67%	88%	233	165	199	208	168	221
		08	NYM	0.6	60	78%	50%	81%	292	268	297	115	198	368
Foulke,Keith	R	05	BOS	1.1	32	65%	79%	70%	247	333	252	400	255	333
		06	BOS	1.1	98	70%	0%	94%	286	250	295	227	301	236
		08	OAK	1.0	26	79%	50%	69%	209	286	261	192	200	279
Francisco,Frank	R	07	TEX	1.0	42	71%	0%	96%	309	220	245	284	221	286
		08	TEX	1.1	117	77%	45%	65%	189	212	196	216	193	205
Franklin,Ryan	R	07	STL	1.2	92	74%	17%	77%	227	244	256	172	238	231
		08	STL	1.1	33	80%	68%	72%	269	284	283	278	258	287
Frasor,Jason	R	05	TOR	1.1	63	78%	33%	73%	248	246	250	244	236	257
		06	TOR	1.0	75	71%	0%	83%	207	293	248	235	211	262
		07	TOR	1.1	93	61%	50%	50%	217	222	213	224	245	200
		08	TOR	1.0	-10	72%	0%	63%	230	186	194	267	266	174
Fuentes,Brian	L	05	COL	1.0	101	79%	91%	83%	261	171	235	182	164	237
		06	COL	1.0	86	75%	83%	77%	240	173	216	184	183	218
		07	COL	1.0	82	76%	74%	72%	167	271	190	275	204	207
		08	COL	0.9	131	76%	88%	80%	188	235	180	300	184	210
Gagne,Eric	R	05	LA	0.9	203	82%	100%	100%	200	200	238	0	217	185
		06	LA	1.0	144	0%	100%	0%	0	0	0	0	0	0
		07	BOS	1.0	79	72%	80%	80%	243	247	247	229	224	265
		08	MIL	0.9	29	70%	59%	68%	337	175	246	359	244	281
Garcia,Jaime	L	08	STL	1.6	-2	67%	0%	80%	150	286	240	214	308	179
Geary,Geoff	R	05	PHI	1.5	58	73%	0%	71%	222	277	212	313	192	294
		06	PHI	1.1	81	79%	25%	85%	337	234	303	253	348	249
		07	PHI	1.2	35	72%	0%	71%	318	259	290	263	248	309
		08	HOU	1.2	29	79%	0%	74%	203	175	191	151	216	174
Gonzalez,Mike	L	05	PIT	1.0	91	80%	100%	86%	225	169	207	173	152	223
		06	PIT	1.0	102	83%	100%	88%	168	267	223	184	163	227
		07	ATL	0.9	51	87%	100%	100%	290	200	235	300	333	189
		08	ATL	0.9	115	71%	88%	74%	221	205	253	77	269	200
Gordon,Tom	R	05	NYY	1.0	70	81%	22%	78%	210	194	227	103	187	217
		06	PHI	1.0	86	80%	87%	80%	218	250	247	200	185	277
		07	PHI	0.9	69	70%	55%	77%	258	270	276	167	310	222
		08	PHI	0.9	16	69%	67%	81%	308	217	258	261	246	266
Grabow,John	L	05	PIT	0.8	48	66%	0%	80%	217	257	242	237	219	250
		06	PIT	1.0	70	73%	0%	79%	223	307	259	214	275	251
		07	PIT	0.8	63	71%	50%	80%	263	291	293	231	238	303
		08	PIT	1.0	28	83%	50%	79%	259	176	228	227	239	214
Green,Sean	R	06	SEA	1.3	33	69%	0%	75%	273	286	250	294	190	325
		07	SEA	1.1	57	75%	0%	78%	300	297	292	324	329	286
		08	SEA	1.1	56	66%	25%	73%	292	233	272	215	306	229
Gregg,Kevin	R	07	FLA	1.1	76	73%	89%	81%	194	220	166	276	162	247
		08	CHC	1.0	27	73%	76%	70%	182	228	206	200	179	224
Grilli,Jason	R	06	DET	1.2	27	71%	0%	79%	239	290	223	319	292	249
		07	DET	1.4	52	66%	0%	76%	245	280	305	226	237	275
		08	COL	1.3	41	78%	50%	67%	252	220	262	229	227	242
Guardado,Eddie	L	05	SEA	1.0	80	83%	88%	83%	234	244	240	239	231	242
		06	CIN	0.9	47	87%	72%	67%	303	288	308	250	234	327
		08	MIN	0.9	18	66%	80%	87%	257	233	277	108	213	268
Guerrier,Matt	R	06	MIN	1.8	31	81%	100%	100%	304	273	276	318	337	258
		07	MIN	1.2	92	83%	25%	71%	218	224	232	195	264	187
		08	MIN	1.0	30	71%	20%	68%	266	287	264	273	280	272
Hammel,Jason	R	08	TAM	2.0	9	73%	100%	64%	230	330	283	250	253	292
Hanrahan,Joel	R	08	WAS	1.2	72	74%	69%	72%	215	252	257	230	228	237
Hansen,Craig	R	06	BOS	1.0	49	61%	0%	71%	304	306	287	325	344	276
		08	PIT	1.0	-86	64%	43%	52%	202	250	250	111	230	225

BULLPEN INDICATORS

				BPIs			Results		Runners		Pitch Ct		Platoon	
Pitcher			Tm	IP/g	bpv	S%	Sv%	Eff%	Emp	On	1-15	16-30	vLH	vRH
Hawkins,LaTroy	R	05	SF	0.9	45	77%	40%	58%	203	370	236	345	228	297
		06	BAL	1.0	44	69%	0%	76%	313	287	314	278	323	285
		07	COL	0.9	53	76%	0%	67%	262	237	222	433	237	266
		08	HOU	1.1	62	67%	50%	89%	178	303	219	250	287	185
Heilman,Aaron	R	05	NYM	2.0	98	73%	83%	79%	198	216	207	213	185	225
		06	NYM	1.2	85	69%	0%	76%	205	267	228	239	231	231
		07	NYM	1.1	87	75%	17%	71%	197	261	211	237	234	218
		08	NYM	1.0	38	69%	38%	62%	216	309	262	240	308	225
Hensley,Clay	R	08	SD	1.2	-22	64%	0%	57%	231	259	263	231	315	179
Herges,Matt	R	05	ARI	1.0	-23	59%	0%	80%	317	288	346	154	256	333
		06	FLA	1.1	35	75%	0%	61%	318	323	296	386	300	340
		07	COL	1.4	61	73%	0%	73%	170	250	223	164	216	184
		08	COL	1.1	41	68%	0%	44%	273	328	306	313	282	318
Hinckley,Michael	L	08	WAS	1.0	78	100%	0%	100%	273	63	172	222	214	167
Hinshaw,Alex	L	08	SF	0.8	9	82%	0%	86%	227	197	245	125	197	227
Hoffman,Trevor	R	05	SD	1.0	131	74%	93%	83%	240	230	235	235	298	179
		06	SD	1.0	98	84%	90%	87%	257	122	212	133	194	214
		07	SD	0.9	70	73%	86%	79%	215	247	230	211	299	169
		08	SD	0.9	130	72%	88%	77%	211	268	217	333	299	170
Howell,J.P.	L	08	TAM	1.4	90	83%	60%	88%	207	178	215	116	188	197
Howry,Bob	R	05	CLE	0.9	84	74%	60%	87%	181	212	201	148	180	198
		06	CHC	0.9	110	76%	56%	77%	240	250	253	224	247	244
		07	CHC	1.0	95	75%	67%	77%	196	317	269	162	192	283
		08	CHC	1.0	102	68%	20%	72%	319	288	305	304	336	282
Isringhausen,Jas	R	05	STL	0.9	68	85%	91%	87%	200	205	208	175	168	229
		06	STL	1.0	31	83%	77%	67%	239	202	237	204	270	187
		07	STL	1.0	75	79%	94%	95%	185	170	183	180	196	167
		08	STL	1.0	38	66%	63%	56%	269	291	311	208	186	327
Jenks,Bobby	R	05	CHW	1.2	118	80%	75%	77%	224	227	221	268	105	298
		06	CHW	1.0	97	72%	91%	85%	241	266	254	261	227	268
		07	CHW	1.0	131	68%	87%	80%	149	269	202	176	237	169
		08	CHW	1.1	69	77%	88%	87%	244	209	244	156	219	240
Jimenez,Cesar	L	08	SEA	1.1	46	74%	0%	40%	191	339	301	240	327	208
Johnson,Jim	R	08	BAL	1.3	27	79%	100%	85%	236	200	198	250	227	212
Jones,Todd	R	05	FLA	1.1	131	79%	89%	81%	236	222	220	280	231	229
		06	DET	1.0	60	69%	86%	76%	236	340	249	409	264	284
		07	DET	1.0	31	69%	86%	80%	248	291	261	263	265	269
		08	DET	0.9	-28	71%	86%	85%	272	322	304	244	289	304
Kensing,Logan	R	08	FLA	1.2	21	75%	0%	67%	212	257	254	224	208	259
Kobayashi,Masa	R	08	CLE	1.0	70	72%	67%	60%	252	337	280	333	280	292
Kuo,Hong-Chih	L	08	LA	1.9	149	81%	33%	78%	204	181	214	188	167	207
League,Brandon	R	08	TOR	1.1	46	85%	100%	78%	246	211	235	219	250	210
Lewis,Jensen	R	07	CLE	1.1	107	83%	0%	86%	222	246	274	188	244	229
		08	CLE	1.3	39	77%	93%	77%	283	254	264	235	265	272
Lidge,Brad	R	05	HOU	1.0	154	83%	91%	85%	239	205	235	186	244	202
		06	HOU	1.0	100	64%	84%	78%	224	256	242	236	286	201
		07	HOU	1.0	116	79%	70%	74%	223	212	213	234	184	243
		08	PHI	1.0	109	84%	100%	100%	209	170	207	137	261	108
Lincoln,Mike	R	08	CIN	1.1	76	69%	0%	67%	253	248	243	284	225	270
Lindstrom,Matt	R	07	FLA	0.9	87	75%	0%	79%	230	289	247	280	263	255
		08	FLA	0.9	34	77%	83%	85%	276	270	288	152	327	218
Linebrink,Scott	R	05	SD	1.0	101	85%	17%	85%	227	186	208	200	197	221
		06	SD	1.0	81	75%	18%	78%	258	224	248	230	204	294
		07	MIL	1.0	54	79%	12%	68%	268	232	251	258	215	284
		08	CHW	0.9	111	74%	25%	81%	204	250	217	237	179	256
Logan,Boone	L	06	CHW	0.8	37	59%	50%	75%	194	378	302	176	357	244
		07	CHW	0.7	40	71%	0%	81%	301	295	248	465	221	357
		08	CHW	0.8	97	67%	0%	56%	264	371	315	379	291	351
Lopez,Aquilino	R	07	DET	1.7	7	64%	100%	100%	242	303	233	321	258	286
		08	DET	1.6	65	78%	0%	80%	279	291	279	298	306	273
Lopez,Javier	L	05	ARI	0.5	30	49%	50%	75%	231	417	354	333	278	421
		06	BOS	0.6	45	81%	100%	100%	222	237	204	1000	250	208
		07	BOS	0.7	50	77%	0%	83%	208	274	233	300	293	176
		08	BOS	0.8	31	84%	0%	92%	240	250	259	209	193	301
Lowe,Mark	R	08	SEA	1.1	30	70%	20%	25%	317	297	309	314	358	258
Lyon,Brandon	R	05	ARI	0.9	12	69%	93%	83%	382	311	356	320	317	364
		06	ARI	1.0	52	72%	0%	69%	290	226	294	143	244	270
		07	ARI	1.0	39	78%	40%	86%	294	210	278	146	233	267
		08	ARI	1.0	85	70%	84%	76%	294	318	301	314	283	323
Madrigal,Warner	R	08	TEX	1.2	16	67%	33%	50%	210	297	263	267	305	209
Madson,Ryan	R	05	PHI	1.1	81	70%	0%	76%	247	273	304	160	292	233
		06	PHI	2.7	41	68%	50%	63%	344	256	342	235	296	311
		07	PHI	1.5	64	79%	50%	77%	198	280	222	200	170	275
		08	PHI	1.1	92	77%	33%	85%	244	258	267	225	257	244
Marmol,Carlos	R	07	CHC	1.2	123	89%	50%	92%	183	154	150	208	209	146
		08	CHC	1.1	103	77%	78%	87%	126	151	128	162	187	94
Marshall,Sean	L	08	CHC	1.9	74	74%	50%	54%	269	150	242	95	219	217
Marte,Damaso	L	05	CHW	0.7	69	81%	50%	78%	222	291	269	222	267	244
		06	PIT	0.8	78	75%	0%	56%	257	230	238	206	225	258
		07	PIT	0.7	107	79%	0%	100%	202	197	211	160	94	271
		08	NYY	0.9	86	67%	71%	88%	197	224	220	146	235	197
Masset,Nick	R	08	CIN	1.5	39	78%	33%	71%	327	263	346	176	263	311
McClellan,Kyle	R	08	STL	1.1	67	72%	17%	73%	298	238	280	253	238	291
Mendoza,Luis	R	08	TEX	2.5	21	53%	50%	31%	222	351	326	318	294	282

BULLPEN INDICATORS

				BPIs			Results		Runners		Pitch Ct		Platoon	
Pitcher			Tm	IP/g	bpv	S%	Sv%	Eff%	Emp	On	1-15	16-30	vLH	vRH
Meredith,Cla	R	06	SD	1.1	153	91%	0%	88%	216	114	161	200	281	107
		07	SD	1.0	97	76%	0%	58%	267	327	295	262	286	303
		08	SD	1.0	74	73%	0%	55%	299	285	281	298	352	260
Messenger,Rand	R	06	FLA	1.0	44	66%	0%	58%	299	293	265	338	333	267
		07	SF	1.1	17	75%	20%	64%	314	343	357	292	342	320
		08	SEA	1.0	-1	80%	100%	100%	381	200	310	273	250	333
Miller,Jim	R	08	BAL	1.0	30	93%	50%	25%	308	278	333	200	333	250
Miller,Justin	R	07	FLA	1.0	108	72%	0%	88%	242	213	252	148	324	184
		08	FLA	1.0	51	71%	0%	79%	289	232	256	261	310	224
Miller,Trever	L	05	TAM	0.7	44	77%	0%	72%	239	308	282	257	267	289
		06	HOU	0.7	113	79%	33%	75%	271	176	234	161	221	228
		07	HOU	0.6	61	69%	33%	87%	205	290	242	333	209	289
		08	TAM	0.6	56	68%	67%	94%	313	173	248	250	209	299
Miner,Zach	R	07	DET	1.6	44	80%	0%	67%	326	222	318	210	219	312
		08	DET	2.6	14	70%	0%	64%	222	274	281	175	247	250
Morrow,Brandon	R	07	SEA	1.1	58	75%	0%	78%	222	265	277	187	278	221
		08	SEA	1.4	65	78%	83%	73%	125	174	131	185	200	99
Mota,Guillermo	R	05	FLA	1.2	68	67%	50%	82%	231	279	283	211	243	262
		06	NYM	1.1	32	75%	0%	81%	261	253	237	300	252	261
		07	NYM	1.1	65	59%	0%	62%	225	317	264	215	235	284
		08	MIL	1.0	43	74%	25%	65%	236	253	229	291	291	210
Motte,Jason	R	08	STL	0.9	185	88%	100%	100%	111	167	130	143	71	188
Moylan,Peter	R	07	ATL	1.1	76	87%	50%	78%	215	199	223	171	242	184
		08	ATL	0.8	144	100%	50%	71%	273	167	217	0	273	167
Nathan,Joe	R	05	MIN	1.0	143	75%	90%	85%	165	215	171	224	158	206
		06	MIN	1.1	188	82%	95%	96%	168	141	176	63	193	130
		07	MIN	1.1	129	84%	90%	87%	174	262	209	207	221	199
		08	MIN	1.0	133	91%	87%	83%	211	130	191	163	175	191
Nelson,Joe	R	08	FLA	0.9	93	88%	20%	75%	198	219	232	150	237	183
Neshek,Pat	R	06	MIN	1.2	219	87%	0%	78%	202	128	157	225	244	140
		07	MIN	1.0	99	75%	0%	81%	171	197	167	255	181	185
		08	MIN	0.9	114	64%	0%	67%	188	333	175	500	250	233
Nunez,Leo	R	08	FLA	1.1	29	76%	0%	73%	231	253	246	237	266	221
Ohlendorf,Ross	R	08	PIT	2.1	23	67%	0%	56%	288	310	318	227	349	247
Ohman,Will	L	05	CHC	0.6	58	84%	0%	75%	202	200	194	286	173	231
		06	CHC	0.8	82	70%	0%	91%	190	227	215	224	157	245
		07	CHC	0.6	54	69%	100%	79%	296	269	298	136	236	325
		08	ATL	0.7	66	70%	25%	88%	228	232	244	167	200	256
Okajima,Hideki	L	07	BOS	1.0	112	82%	71%	90%	230	168	219	155	236	182
		08	BOS	1.0	75	82%	11%	73%	182	269	213	241	188	242
Oliver,Darren	L	06	NYM	1.8	57	77%	0%	88%	215	259	259	161	208	244
		07	LAA	1.1	63	71%	0%	92%	222	263	219	221	289	209
		08	LAA	1.3	80	77%	0%	86%	252	263	247	229	231	275
Osoria,Franquelis	R	07	PIT	1.1	28	68%	0%	67%	278	300	307	241	353	263
		08	PIT	1.4	65	65%	0%	58%	355	319	304	367	373	312
Papelbon,Jon	R	05	BOS	2.0	64	87%	0%	78%	262	259	262	292	200	308
		06	BOS	1.2	169	92%	85%	83%	199	112	180	132	203	128
		07	BOS	1.0	189	82%	92%	87%	123	187	161	83	104	200
		08	BOS	1.0	178	77%	89%	84%	186	263	206	255	227	202
Pena,Tony	R	06	ARI	1.2	39	66%	100%	60%	253	356	309	289	382	179
		07	ARI	1.1	65	73%	40%	84%	209	205	211	205	245	176
		08	ARI	1.0	84	67%	38%	81%	264	277	279	230	280	260
Percival,Troy	R	05	DET	1.0	6	61%	73%	60%	206	207	211	200	176	244
		07	STL	1.2	106	84%	0%	100%	161	186	218	30	214	138
		08	TAM	0.9	-11	70%	88%	87%	165	218	190	167	188	179
Perez,Chris	R	08	STL	1.0	46	78%	64%	70%	267	169	202	258	245	207
Perez,Rafael	L	07	CLE	1.4	137	86%	50%	82%	185	191	147	254	145	213
		08	CLE	1.1	140	73%	29%	78%	202	276	230	236	216	244
Pinto,Renyel	L	06	FLA	1.1	66	84%	100%	100%	156	217	207	222	150	215
		07	FLA	1.0	71	76%	17%	68%	271	167	228	200	210	227
		08	FLA	1.0	14	72%	0%	73%	236	214	259	148	258	206
Putz,J.J.	R	05	SEA	0.9	46	78%	25%	78%	236	276	225	364	321	197
		06	SEA	1.1	226	76%	84%	85%	176	257	200	229	211	204
		07	SEA	1.1	194	89%	95%	94%	180	109	173	26	148	158
		08	SEA	1.0	61	77%	65%	62%	239	274	279	222	261	250
Qualls,Chad	R	05	HOU	1.0	72	75%	0%	88%	263	234	251	242	218	275
		06	HOU	1.1	46	71%	0%	77%	242	242	258	181	227	253
		07	HOU	1.0	96	82%	50%	76%	292	252	264	333	248	289
		08	ARI	1.0	131	75%	53%	69%	212	248	242	176	225	234
Ramirez,Edwar	R	07	NYY	1.0	84	59%	33%	62%	225	341	241	400	342	239
		08	NYY	1.0	84	72%	25%	73%	202	228	213	213	224	200
Ramirez,Ramon	R	06	COL	1.1	76	74%	0%	74%	241	218	265	141	274	194
		07	COL	0.8	51	44%	0%	71%	321	308	316	300	240	357
		08	KC	1.0	73	78%	20%	81%	218	225	226	222	294	157
Rauch,Jon	R	06	WAS	1.1	63	79%	40%	75%	215	252	257	180	254	216
		07	WAS	1.0	81	69%	40%	82%	200	278	230	232	208	249
		08	ARI	1.0	103	70%	75%	67%	233	296	252	267	268	242
Ray,Chris	R	05	BAL	1.0	74	85%	0%	56%	208	237	218	261	284	174
		06	BAL	1.1	41	84%	87%	80%	188	202	221	119	184	202
		07	BAL	1.0	90	67%	80%	68%	190	276	218	216	233	212
Reyes,Dennys	L	05	SD	1.4	39	74%	0%	100%	192	237	219	190	136	262
		06	MIN	0.8	105	96%	0%	95%	229	151	205	143	148	244
		07	MIN	0.6	38	78%	0%	91%	302	319	293	455	273	364
		08	MIN	0.6	95	84%	0%	87%	222	250	240	182	198	284

BULLPEN INDICATORS

				BPIs			Results		Runners		Pitch Ct		Platoon	
Pitcher			Tm	IP/g	bpv	S%	Sv%	Eff%	Emp	On	1-15	16-30	vLH	vRH
Rhodes,Arthur	L	05	CLE	0.9	117	81%	0%	83%	220	188	200	235	286	155
		06	PHI	0.8	79	67%	57%	77%	224	305	243	333	286	248
		08	FLA	0.6	73	82%	67%	94%	206	250	219	333	162	309
Rincon,Juan	R	05	MIN	1.0	111	79%	0%	74%	229	219	207	278	218	228
		06	MIN	1.0	97	77%	33%	91%	273	266	260	313	222	303
		07	MIN	0.9	50	70%	0%	77%	270	277	272	292	313	236
		08	CLE	1.2	27	66%	0%	67%	254	348	259	359	330	264
Riske,David	R	05	CLE	1.2	62	76%	100%	50%	201	220	212	187	213	204
		06	CHW	1.1	38	75%	0%	50%	236	247	254	233	280	224
		07	KC	1.1	56	86%	50%	72%	281	193	267	175	202	265
		08	MIL	0.9	-36	71%	29%	67%	275	298	303	250	344	250
Rivera,Mariano	R	05	NYY	1.1	142	85%	91%	86%	166	194	166	179	177	176
		06	NYY	1.2	132	83%	92%	83%	258	174	237	194	192	250
		07	NYY	1.1	168	72%	88%	80%	245	252	257	208	255	241
		08	NYY	1.1	186	84%	98%	88%	178	149	178	130	155	183
Rivera,Saul	R	06	WAS	1.1	46	78%	33%	87%	232	263	275	209	194	290
		07	WAS	1.1	48	71%	60%	76%	298	215	275	231	271	244
		08	WAS	1.1	54	72%	0%	65%	306	250	333	156	271	284
Rodney,Fernando	R	05	DET	1.1	73	82%	60%	61%	273	207	283	130	265	219
		06	DET	1.1	67	72%	64%	80%	185	208	176	214	202	192
		07	DET	1.1	92	69%	33%	65%	200	276	262	207	247	231
		08	DET	1.1	25	69%	68%	60%	222	237	261	186	260	197
Rodriguez,Francs	R	05	ANA	1.0	105	81%	90%	82%	190	173	184	154	213	153
		06	ANA	1.1	124	89%	92%	88%	201	191	202	176	215	179
		07	LAA	1.1	116	78%	87%	85%	205	204	230	138	187	217
		08	LAA	0.9	75	85%	90%	86%	252	183	235	160	228	208
Romero,J.C.	L	05	MIN	0.8	43	81%	0%	79%	248	223	244	214	198	268
		06	ANA	0.7	41	60%	0%	73%	225	363	300	333	202	382
		07	PHI	0.8	57	88%	50%	90%	250	158	209	176	208	198
		08	PHI	0.7	21	82%	20%	78%	228	174	209	138	101	287
Romo,Sergio	R	08	SF	1.2	109	76%	0%	89%	123	186	100	242	91	188
Ryan,B.J.	L	05	BAL	1.0	142	80%	88%	80%	229	181	193	246	211	206
		06	TOR	1.1	150	86%	90%	87%	190	142	196	85	120	182
		07	TOR	0.9	-8	50%	60%	43%	250	444	231	667	333	333
		08	TOR	1.0	59	79%	89%	81%	222	208	204	250	230	211
Saito,Takashi	R	06	LA	1.1	161	78%	92%	90%	159	206	170	164	227	129
		07	LA	1.0	192	88%	91%	89%	143	169	155	135	186	114
		08	LA	1.0	143	78%	82%	73%	188	288	226	255	250	213
Samardzija,Jeff	R	08	CHC	1.1	34	82%	25%	63%	212	235	188	310	170	268
Sampson,Chris	R	08	HOU	2.2	73	65%	0%	74%	203	256	179	295	303	183
Sanchez,Duaner	R	08	NYM	0.9	49	69%	0%	93%	213	270	246	216	200	268
Sarfate,Dennis	R	07	HOU	1.2	392	83%	0%	100%	105	300	211	125	182	167
		08	BAL	1.4	-3	71%	0%	58%	181	207	224	138	165	220
Schoeneweis,S	L	05	TOR	0.7	67	75%	25%	78%	238	252	246	240	188	306
		06	CIN	0.7	35	65%	67%	87%	200	310	233	364	236	257
		07	NYM	0.8	43	70%	67%	81%	319	221	243	373	204	316
		08	NYM	0.8	25	80%	20%	64%	227	299	238	342	172	336
Seay,Bobby	L	07	DET	0.8	74	79%	50%	93%	284	165	209	333	209	250
		08	DET	0.9	71	70%	0%	82%	271	283	315	186	302	250
Shell,Steven	R	08	WAS	1.3	50	86%	67%	79%	204	189	179	239	253	155
Sherrill,George	L	05	SEA	0.7	98	53%	0%	81%	188	200	204	182	156	273
		06	SEA	0.6	89	67%	100%	83%	194	232	217	158	143	297
		07	SEA	0.6	122	80%	43%	87%	222	143	174	208	156	212
		08	BAL	0.9	31	70%	84%	76%	233	242	259	176	194	257
Shields,Scot	R	05	ANA	1.2	99	77%	54%	75%	186	220	205	202	199	203
		06	ANA	1.2	101	77%	25%	75%	217	218	232	174	207	227
		07	LAA	1.1	88	70%	25%	77%	199	243	242	170	214	226
		08	LAA	1.0	81	84%	44%	82%	299	184	259	200	216	267
Shouse,Brian	L	05	TEX	0.8	41	64%	0%	78%	200	340	247	342	209	337
		06	MIL	0.6	31	76%	40%	75%	200	333	244	429	238	309
		07	MIL	0.7	68	73%	25%	85%	260	255	275	167	214	295
		08	MIL	0.7	78	80%	40%	85%	220	250	247	150	173	301
Slaten,Doug	L	07	ARI	0.6	47	86%	0%	77%	305	239	273	294	268	284
		08	ARI	0.7	12	70%	0%	57%	288	222	272	154	232	282
Smith,Joe	R	07	NYM	0.8	83	79%	0%	87%	203	327	274	257	298	266
		08	NYM	0.8	53	73%	0%	80%	195	262	212	293	340	196
Soriano,Rafael	R	06	SEA	1.1	97	85%	33%	78%	214	192	232	121	244	179
		07	ATL	1.0	132	76%	75%	84%	165	221	190	154	164	197
		08	ATL	1.0	23	80%	75%	60%	200	111	152	143	222	103
Soria,Joakim	R	07	KC	1.1	131	74%	81%	80%	173	211	168	246	167	200
		08	KC	1.1	112	87%	93%	88%	154	209	146	267	169	171
Speier,Justin	R	05	TOR	1.0	83	83%	0%	70%	191	211	210	137	167	219
		06	TOR	0.9	87	81%	0%	90%	235	235	254	143	183	264
		07	LAA	1.0	112	76%	0%	87%	220	179	193	257	222	186
		08	LAA	1.1	47	72%	0%	55%	263	262	280	224	293	238
Speier,Ryan	R	08	COL	1.2	49	70%	0%	71%	306	258	317	146	282	279
Stetter,Mitch	L	08	MIL	0.8	20	77%	0%	78%	149	194	193	130	167	170
Stokes,Brian	R	07	TAM	1.1	12	63%	0%	53%	354	333	341	344	346	341
		08	NYM	1.4	83	79%	33%	75%	263	286	295	269	333	220
Street,Huston	R	05	OAK	1.2	98	84%	85%	85%	192	197	194	195	224	172
		06	OAK	1.0	144	70%	77%	74%	205	276	238	242	274	211
		07	OAK	1.0	164	74%	76%	79%	179	213	184	222	224	162
		08	COL	1.1	76	71%	72%	72%	217	250	228	219	200	250

BULLPEN INDICATORS

				BPIs			Results		Runners		Pitch Ct		Platoon	
Pitcher			Tm	IP/g	bpv	S%	Sv%	Eff%	Emp	On	1-15	16-30	vLH	vRH
Tallet,Brian	L	08	TOR	1.1	60	80%	0%	71%	252	232	279	143	260	227
Tankersley,Taylor	L	06	FLA	0.8	71	84%	43%	84%	246	214	231	182	232	225
		07	FLA	0.7	68	75%	33%	88%	286	213	243	250	179	301
		08	FLA	0.7	9	58%	0%	57%	294	300	321	267	346	271
Taschner,Jack	L	05	SF	0.9	77	86%	0%	83%	238	128	193	182	265	128
		06	SF	0.8	31	59%	0%	60%	316	365	359	318	275	400
		07	SF	0.8	63	62%	0%	84%	236	235	250	214	316	176
		08	SF	0.7	24	72%	0%	74%	300	284	283	317	276	311
Tavarez,Julian	R	05	STL	0.9	66	77%	67%	88%	299	254	286	229	294	271
		06	BOS	1.7	30	73%	33%	57%	320	278	311	286	262	326
		08	ATL	1.1	54	73%	0%	58%	260	352	281	373	356	271
Thatcher,Joe	L	08	SD	1.0	1	61%	0%	42%	400	364	343	405	387	380
Thornton,Matt	L	05	SEA	1.0	21	76%	0%	50%	292	213	262	167	262	235
		06	CHW	0.9	73	76%	40%	81%	223	235	213	316	211	240
		07	CHW	0.8	71	68%	29%	72%	245	289	303	146	283	260
		08	CHW	0.9	145	76%	17%	76%	148	248	188	186	176	211
Timlin,Mike	R	05	BOS	1.0	95	83%	65%	81%	281	271	275	299	299	257
		06	BOS	0.9	35	72%	53%	72%	306	303	301	328	306	303
		07	BOS	1.1	49	74%	100%	92%	233	232	205	333	173	274
		08	BOS	1.0	29	69%	100%	56%	269	338	299	316	333	267
Torres,Salomon	R	05	PIT	1.2	44	79%	100%	76%	233	208	212	221	272	189
		06	PIT	1.0	64	78%	80%	80%	294	255	265	298	281	269
		07	PIT	0.9	74	63%	67%	66%	193	391	255	364	275	278
		08	MIL	1.1	36	75%	80%	77%	257	234	303	117	256	238
Turnbow,Derrick	R	05	MIL	1.0	87	88%	91%	91%	226	165	205	150	235	165
		06	MIL	0.9	65	60%	75%	65%	239	270	240	313	245	263
		07	MIL	0.9	98	64%	25%	83%	132	241	160	277	172	189
		08	MIL	0.8	-364	58%	100%	50%	400	417	474	125	500	353
Valverde,Jose	R	05	ARI	1.1	120	80%	88%	81%	222	200	236	172	168	241
		06	ARI	1.1	109	61%	82%	75%	245	268	270	246	323	192
		07	ARI	1.0	112	82%	87%	81%	197	194	203	173	202	189
		08	HOU	1.0	122	77%	86%	83%	231	200	228	190	174	253
Veras,Jose	R	07	NYY	1.0	48	54%	100%	100%	250	111	130	125	154	190
		08	NYY	1.0	69	78%	0%	75%	250	214	248	174	202	256
Villanueva,Carlos	R	07	MIL	1.9	57	75%	33%	78%	209	278	229	219	230	243
		08	MIL	2.3	95	75%	100%	70%	238	185	211	260	206	228
Wade,Cory	R	08	LA	1.3	84	81%	0%	85%	198	200	203	205	208	191
Wagner,Billy	L	05	PHI	1.0	131	88%	93%	88%	176	147	174	143	128	173
		06	NYM	1.0	138	85%	89%	86%	248	171	250	136	161	234
		07	NYM	1.0	119	80%	87%	84%	229	198	223	150	241	209
		08	NYM	1.0	142	79%	79%	77%	143	250	170	250	233	169
Walker,Jamie	L	05	DET	0.7	54	74%	0%	78%	250	264	268	185	245	271
		06	DET	0.9	94	85%	0%	92%	252	250	257	225	238	262
		07	BAL	0.8	53	76%	54%	79%	246	241	248	217	216	268
		08	BAL	0.6	47	67%	0%	59%	333	318	319	368	304	352
Walker,Tyler	R	05	SF	0.9	50	77%	82%	78%	231	343	292	241	287	276
		06	TAM	1.0	63	50%	71%	60%	350	224	253	364	333	226
		07	SF	1.0	55	88%	0%	90%	182	308	238	500	182	308
		08	SF	0.8	78	67%	0%	67%	239	239	238	242	329	189
Weathers,David	R	05	CIN	1.1	62	71%	79%	79%	229	258	244	222	265	226
		06	CIN	1.1	24	80%	63%	69%	234	216	230	239	219	230
		07	CIN	1.1	42	70%	85%	74%	222	248	247	188	254	218
		08	CIN	1.0	24	81%	0%	70%	331	215	288	232	235	296
Wheeler,Dan	R	05	HOU	1.0	101	83%	60%	81%	205	202	225	145	204	204
		06	HOU	1.0	92	81%	75%	82%	204	245	232	200	273	183
		07	TAM	1.1	103	62%	61%	65%	179	371	239	284	260	253
		08	TAM	0.9	53	77%	72%	80%	170	214	204	114	217	166
Wilson,Brian	R	06	SF	1.0	55	67%	50%	64%	404	177	280	294	348	235
		07	SF	1.0	90	77%	86%	84%	218	133	178	182	304	145
		08	SF	1.0	92	70%	87%	85%	234	271	240	288	194	308
Wilson,C.J.	L	05	TEX	2.0	41	58%	100%	46%	140	270	213	286	178	204
		06	TEX	1.0	60	74%	50%	67%	218	247	241	238	155	292
		07	TEX	1.0	84	76%	86%	91%	171	248	209	243	112	275
		08	TEX	0.9	26	66%	86%	82%	240	301	266	262	260	271
Wolfe,Brian	R	07	TOR	1.2	62	75%	0%	75%	231	214	228	190	348	130
		08	TOR	1.1	62	82%	0%	60%	234	233	238	214	273	205
Wright,Wesley	L	08	HOU	0.8	29	68%	100%	86%	198	242	194	308	207	230
Wuertz,Mike	R	05	CHC	1.0	89	72%	0%	83%	208	232	218	231	260	197
		06	CHC	1.0	78	85%	0%	82%	200	253	207	231	184	245
		07	CHC	1.0	84	78%	0%	77%	255	210	246	203	241	232
		08	CHC	1.0	23	77%	0%	50%	216	357	309	209	233	306
Yabu,Keiichi	R	08	SF	1.1	25	74%	0%	63%	220	268	238	227	356	183
Yates,Tyler	R	06	ATL	0.9	48	76%	17%	60%	196	268	240	188	217	235
		07	ATL	0.9	79	64%	67%	81%	222	283	257	220	310	213
		08	PIT	1.0	26	70%	20%	75%	259	267	277	235	308	234
Ziegler,Brad	R	08	OAK	1.3	36	93%	85%	92%	283	159	237	222	286	175
Zumaya,Joel	R	06	DET	1.3	92	87%	17%	82%	162	207	174	228	183	188
		07	DET	1.2	56	65%	20%	61%	141	241	200	156	271	135
		08	DET	1.1	-67	86%	20%	50%	275	255	276	241	161	317

Injuries

Off-Season Injury Report

by Rick Wilton

In 2008, 431 players landed on the disabled list. Of those, 241 were pitchers and 190 were hitters. These numbers were all-time records. Based on the total pool of players who compiled at least one at-bat or inning pitched in the majors, plus those who spent the entire season on the DL:

- One out of every 3.4 hitters spent at least some time on the disabled list in 2008. That's 29% of all batters.
- One out of every 2.7 pitchers spent at least some time on the disabled list in 2008. That's 37% of all pitchers.

Off-season updates...

Erik Bedard (LHP, SEA): The report on his fall surgery indicated he did not need either his labrum or rotator cuff repaired. He did have a cyst removed and minor labral debridement. The findings from the surgery don't equate to all of the difficulties he suffered through in 2008. We may learn more information about the shoulder down the road.

Jeremy Bonderman (RHP, DET) was recovering on schedule late in November from thoracic outlet syndrome. A rib was removed and the circulation in his right arm was normal with no signs of blood clots. He had begun a throwing program in mid-November and, barring a setback, should be close to ready by spring training.

Chris Carpenter (RHP, STL) had surgery in October to transpose the ulnar collateral nerve near his right elbow. The problem was a major cause of the discomfort in his right arm. Reportedly, this is common after pitchers have had Tommy John surgery (he had the surgery in July 2007). The Cardinals are hopeful he will be ready for spring training. The downside is he has had two surgeries in less than two years, a tough hurdle to overcome.

Eric Chavez (3B, OAK) needed surgery in August to repair major damage to the labrum in his right shoulder. The big question is how much flexibility and strength will he lose due to the surgery/injury. He is a candidate to start the 2009 season on the DL.

Carl Crawford (OF, TAM) underwent surgery in mid-August to repair damage to his right index finger. He was able to play in the post-season but was not 100%. Crawford will be 100% at the start of spring training.

Joe Crede (3B, CHW) has already had one surgery to repair a herniated disc in the lumbar region of his lower back. Late in 2008, he developed a new malady in his lower back. Reportedly, it is in a different location. With this second injury, it is unlikely that he will shake his back woes in 2009, or maybe even the rest of his career.

Chris Duncan (OF, STL) underwent what we believe is the first-of-its-kind surgery for a baseball player in August, having an artificial disc inserted in his cervical spine. If he can come back and play close to his prior productivity, surgeons may have a new option in helping players with disc problems in their neck.

Justin Duchscherer (RHP, OAK) underwent surgery just after the season ended to repair cartilage damage in his right hip. This is the second time in two years that he has needed surgery on the hip. You have to wonder if he will be able to avoid chronic hip issues in the future.

Mark Ellis (2B, OAK) underwent surgery on his right shoulder in the fall. He had cartilage and labral damage. This is the second labral surgery on his right shoulder in his career. The A's say he will be ready for the 2009 opener.

Rafael Furcal (SS, LA) underwent surgery in early July to repair a herniated disc in the lumbar (lower) region of his back. Question: Are these back issues becoming chronic?

Ryan Freel (OF, CIN) tried to come back from a right hamstring injury late in the year but was never able to get over the hump. His game is speed, and this could have an impact on that skill.

Yovani Gallardo (RHP, MIL) was able to return from a torn anterior cruciate ligament (ACL) in his right knee in September, much quicker than expected. He is now coming off both cartilage and ACL surgery the past year and he has to avoid developing more knee injuries.

Tom Glavine (LHP, ATL) had surgery in August to repair a torn flexor tendon in his pitching elbow, but there was no damage to the ulnar collateral ligament. Dr. James Andrews gave his opinion that Glavine should be able to recover and be ready close to spring training.

Tom Gorzelanny's (LHP, PIT) season ended in September due to ligament damage in his left middle finger. The Bucs expect him to be ready at the start of spring training.

Vlad Guerrero (OF, LAA) had the medial meniscus in his left knee repaired in October. The hope is he can play more in the field in 2009.

Travis Hafner (DH, CLE) underwent arthroscopic surgery this fall to clean out his shoulder joint. The Tribe believes he will be ready for spring training.

Eric Hurley (RHP, TEX) struggled with hamstring, biceps and shoulder issues in 2008. He needs to remain healthy in 2009 or his advancement will be restricted.

Phil Hughes (RHP, NYY) suffered a fractured rib in April and did return for a couple of outings late in September. By all accounts, he looked solid will be ready for the start of spring training.

Jason Isringhausen (RHP, STL) had surgery on the flexor tendon group in his pitching elbow this fall. He is a candidate to start the year on the DL. Remember, we have not heard anything regarding his chronic hip problem that almost ended his career two years ago.

Nick Johnson (1B, WAS) had surgery late in the year to have a tendon sheath repaired in his right wrist. There is a good chance he starts the year on the DL.

Kevin Kouzmanoff (3B, SD) underwent surgery on his right shoulder in mid-November. There were no reports of shoulder problems during the season so this surgery, though considered minor, is a surprise. He did have a slightly herniated disc in his lower back that cleared up before the end of the season.

Mike Lowell (3B, BOS) had surgery to repair damage to the labrum in his left hip during the post-season. Players with similar type surgery needed up to 4-6 months to recover, suggesting he could start the season on the DL.

Noah Lowry (LHP, SF) needed surgery in September to remove bone spurs from his pitching elbow. Though he was expected to resume throwing by the end of the year, his early 2009 status is up in the air.

Victor Martinez (C, CLE) had surgery to remove several loose bodies in his throwing elbow in June. He returned in late August and finally hit a couple of homers late in the season. He will be 100% at the start of spring training.

Gary Matthews Jr. (OF, LAA) will start the 2009 season on the disabled list after undergoing surgery in late October to repair damage to the patella tendon on his left knee. Look for Matthews to miss at least the first six weeks of the season, if not longer.

Dustin McGowan (RHP, TOR) underwent surgery in late July to have a frayed labrum repaired. His short-term future is in doubt entering spring training due to the nature of the surgery.

Pat Neshek (RHP, MIN) had Tommy John surgery in November and will miss the 2009 season.

Jorge Posada (C, NYY): The surgery done on in late July repaired damage to the rotator cuff and labrum in his throwing shoulder. The Yanks expect him back by the start of spring training.

Albert Pujols (1B, STL) underwent surgery at the end of the season to decompress and transpose the ulnar nerve in his right arm. The Cards believe he will be ready by spring training.

Carlos Quentin (OF, CHW) is spending the off-season rebuilding the strength in his surgically repaired right wrist. While he should be ready for spring training, his power numbers should suffer in 2009.

Mariano Rivera (RHP, NYY) had a calcium deposit removed from his pitching shoulder in the fall. The Yanks say he will be ready for the start of spring training.

Scott Rolen (3B, TOR) has developed more issues with his left shoulder. He has already had two surgeries to repair damage to the labrum. He will never hit 20 home runs again, and his career will continue in a downward spiral.

Johan Santana (LHP, NYM) had surgery on his left knee to clean up some cartilage damage. The Mets state he will be ready for the start of spring training.

Jason Schmidt (RHP, LA) had surgery in September to clean up scar tissue in his right shoulder. He still has not returned from major surgery on his right shoulder in June 2007 and is unlikely to return to his prior form.

John Smoltz (RHP, ATL) underwent surgery to repair damage to the labrum in his right shoulder in June. The Braves do not believe he will be back until May-June 2009.

BJ Upton (OF, TAM) was able to play with a torn labrum in his left shoulder for most of the season. He was expected to have surgery to repair it in the off-season and should be able to start 2009 on time.

Chase Utley (2B, PHI) has cartilage damage in his right hip that required surgery. He could miss up to a third of the 2009 season. *(Note that this late news is not reflected in Utley's projection.)*

Rickie Weeks (2B, MIL) had cartilage damage repaired via surgery on his left knee in the fall. The Brewers believe he will avoid starting the 2009 season on the disabled list.

Hidden Injuries:
2009 Speculations
by Ray Murphy

Rick Wilton's companion piece on injured players and their 2009 outlook represents the more straightforward injury-related analyses. In this day and age, thanks largely to Rick's exhaustive research, once a player's injury is identified, we have a good idea of his prognosis. But what about those injuries that are never publicly identified? We are left to speculate about how a hidden injury might have affected 2008, and whether it means we should expect a 2009 rebound.

Here is a collection of players who we think may have been impacted by under-reported injuries in 2008, and what that might mean for their 2009 outlook:

If you break **Jacoby Ellsbury's** (OF, BOS) season into thirds, June and July stick out as his worst months: a sub-600 OPS and only 9 SB for that stretch. The cause may have been a strained wrist suffered in early June, which did not DL him but may have affected him in the weeks that followed. If we look at Ellsbury's other two thirds of the season as his baseline, it improves his 2009 outlook considerably: .300 with 70 SB may be attainable in a fully healthy season.

Luke Scott (OF, BAL) tanked in the second half, but between the second half of 2007 and the first half of 2008 together, he established significantly better skills. Scott battled a few nagging injuries all year, and the dings may have gotten the better of him in the summer heat. Take a look at his 2008 first half (.280, 14 HR) and double it to reveal his healthy upside.

Anytime we see a catcher have a lost season at the plate, as **Kenji Johjima** (C, SEA) did this year, our first reaction is to suspect injury. Catchers are plagued by nicks and bruises, especially to the fingers and hands. Johjima didn't hit the DL, but did get numerous days off during the summer in favor of Jeff Clement. Finally in September, after weeks of lightened workload, Johjima's bat warmed up. He's not so old that we should have expected a sudden decline; instead we're inclined to give him a mulligan for 2008 on the basis of suspected injury issues.

Edgar Renteria's (SS, DET) career path is awfully odd: the two worst years of his career have been his only two in the American League. After the fact, his nightmarish 2005 in BOS was attributed to back trouble and weight issues, as well as a dislike of cold weather. The latter does not explain his poor summer this year in

Detroit, but we wonder if the other root causes of his bad year in BOS recurred in 2008. The similarities between 2008 and 2005 are striking. Note that 2006 became a nice rebound year for him.

Entering 2008, **Alex Rios'** (OF, TOR) pattern was to start out hot and fade in the second half. But this year he reversed that trend. There were a couple of minor health issues that were reported early in the season, none of which seemed consequential at the time. He had an April bout with the flu, which could have sapped his strength long after he returned to the lineup. Also, his first child was born in July in Puerto Rico; perhaps the stress of being on the road away from his pregnant wife and unborn child negatively impacted him in the first half. We're still waiting for Rios to put two good halves together, but 2009 may be the year.

Chris Young (OF, ARI) came on late, turning a disastrous year into a merely disappointing one. Was health a factor in this poor sophomore season? Perhaps. The best indicator might be his stolen base output: despite an on base average consistent with 2007, he stole only four bases in the first half. Like Rios, Young had an illness in April that could have had a lingering impact. Unlike Rios, he did not fully recover in the second half. But we know from 2007 that he owns better skills, so with better health, that 30-30 potential may emerge sooner than later.

Kosuke Fukudome's (OF, CHC) month-over-month batting average trend was startling in its consistency of direction: .305-.293-.264-.236-.193-.178. Playing time was stable until September, suggesting injury was not a factor. But perhaps fatigue got the better of him? The longer Major League schedule, with its rigorous travel and infrequent days off, may have sapped Fukudome of his endurance as the season wore on. If he comes back for 2009 better conditioned, he could join the ranks of Japanese players who took a significant step forward in their second season in the U.S.

Brett Myers' (RHP, PHI) season took several bizarre turns, but in the end his second half was back in line with prior skill levels. What happened along the way? The idea of a struggling veteran pitcher accepting an assignment to the low minors doesn't support injury as a root cause. Either a mechanical correction or perhaps an off-field issue would seem more consistent with that narrative. The lack of a clear explanation leaves us open to the risk of recurrence, but the late-season edition of Myers (10 straight PQS-Dom starts from 7/29 thru 9/14) looked like the vintage Myers, suggesting the issue was a temporary one.

Was **Jeff Francoeur's** (OF, ATL) awful 2008 just the continuation of his downward spiral, or did he hide an injury ? We get suspicious of injuries in cases where we see power hitters with BPIs that are stable, except for PX. In Francoeur's case, those BPIs were never a strong point in support of his production. Like Myers above, Francoeur's brief demotion in July suggests that the Braves thought the problem was not injury-related. One theory would be a

back problem that drained his power, or perhaps some ill-conceived weight training that left him overly muscle-bound and tight. Without question, Francoeur's main issue is with plate discipline. But that may not be the only factor limiting his production.

Deep in the dog days of August, when his team needed their ace to keep them in the pennant race, **Dan Haren** (RHP, ARI) came up small. This was the second straight year that he faded in the summer heat. This time, luck looked like a prime culprit, as Haren's hit rate reached a ridiculous 43% in August. But more than just bad luck, a previously dominant Haren getting tattooed might suggest another cause. Arizona likely would not have let him keep taking his turn if he were truly injured, but some sort of general fatigue or even a late-season dead arm period could explain this collapse. It may take an adjustment to Haren's routine, either in the off-season or between starts, for him to finish strong in 2009.

There were many oddities surrounding **Jon Rauch's** (RHP, ARI) trade from Washington to Arizona. At first, it seemed like the Nationals sold surprisingly low on an effective and cost-controlled closer. Then Rauch got to Arizona and was totally ineffective. Did Washington knowingly trade damaged goods? Did the Diamondbacks knowingly acquire an injured Rauch? The circumstantial evidence would seem to support this theory. Unfortunately, it does not tell us one way or the other whether to expect the effective Rauch to return in 2009, but it is something to monitor in the spring.

5-Year Injury Log

The following chart details the disabled list stints for all players during the past five years. For each injury, the number of days the player missed during the season is listed. A few DL stints are for fewer than 15 days; these are cases when a player was placed on the DL prior to Opening Day (only in-season time lost is listed).

There are a few abbreviations used in this table:

  Lt = left
  Rt = right
  fx = fractured
  R/C = rotator cuff
  surg = surgery
  TJS = Tommy John (ulnar collateral
      ligament reconstruction) surgery
  x 2 = two occurrences of the same injury
  x 3 = three occurrences of the same injury

**All data provided by
Baseball-Injury-Report.com**

BATTERS	Yr	Days	Injury
Abreu,Tony	08	184	Hip surgery 5/08
Alou,Moises	05	31	Right hamstring strain & calf
	06	49	Lumbar strain; sprained rt ankle
	07	75	Strained left quad
	08	161	Sports hernia; strained left calf muscle
Anderson,Garret	04	49	Arthritic upper back
	07	96	Hip flexor x 2; rt. elbow
Anderson,Marlon	08	47	Strained Lt hip x 2
Ankiel,Rick	04	150	Recovery from left elbow surgery
	06	182	Torn patella tendon
Atkins,Garrett	05	22	Strained right hamstring
Aurilia,Rich	05	18	Strained left hamstring
	06	15	Strained right groin
	07	25	Strained right hamstring; neck
Aybar,Erick	07	49	Strained left hamstring; bruised hand
	08	28	Dislocated right pinkie finger
Aybar,Willy	08	49	Strained Lt hamstring
Baker,Jeff	07	21	Concussion
Bako,Paul	05	128	Left knee surgery
	06	31	Partially torn right oblique
Baldelli,Rocco	04	18	Strained right quadriceps
	05	182	Recovery from right knee surgery
	06	65	Left hamstring strain
	07	167	Strained left hamstring; Rt groin
	08	133	Mitochondrial disorder
Barajas,Rod	07	29	Strained right groin
Bard,Josh	04	92	Strained left groin
	07	15	Strained left groin
	08	93	Sprained Rt. ankle; strained right triceps
Barfield,Josh	08	82	Strained middle finger - left hand
Barmes,Clint	05	119	Fractured left clavicle
Barrett,Michael	06	29	Intrascrotal hematoma
	07	21	Concussion
	08	135	Facial surgery; Strained Rt elbow
Bartlett,Jason	08	20	Sprained right knee
Barton,Brian	08	55	Strained Rt oblique; Bruised Rt hand
Barton,Daric	08	17	Strained neck
Bautista,José	04	33	Recovery from right shoulder surgery
	07	17	Puncture wound-left hand
Belliard,Ronnie	08	40	Strained Lt calf, Rt groin
Beltran,Carlos	07	16	Strained abdominal muscle
Bennett,Gary	08	134	Plantar Fasciitis Lt foot
Berkman,Lance	05	31	Right knee soreness
Betemit,Wilson	08	34	Strained Rt hamstring
Blake,Casey	06	48	Sprained right ankle; oblique
Blalock,Hank	07	107	Thoracic Outlet Syndrome
	08	108	Carpal tunnel Rt wrist; Inflam. Rt shoulder
Blanco,Henry	07	82	Herniated disc - neck
Bloomquist,Willie	04	19	Strained lower back
	08	51	Strained right hamstring
Blum,Geoff	05	18	Left chest contusion
Boone,Aaron	04	100	Torn left ACL
	07	98	Sprained MCL - left knee
Bourn,Michael	07	41	Sprained right ankle
Bowen,Rob	06	16	Left thumb sprain
Bradley,Milton	05	94	Ligament tear right finger; patella tendon
	06	79	Sprained right knee; Lt shoulder
	07	66	Calf; hamstring; wrist; oblique
Branyan,Russell	05	32	Fractured left middle finger
	08	42	Strained right oblique muscle
Buck,Travis	07	59	Strained left hamstring; Rt thumb
	08	20	Shin splints
Burke,Chris	06	15	Dislocated left shoulder
Burrell,Pat	04	30	Left wrist surgery
Buscher,Brian	07	16	Infection-right leg
Bynum,Freddie	06	57	Right shoulder inflammation
	07	44	Strained left hamstring
	08	39	Recovery from Rt. Knee surgery 3/2008
Byrd,Marlon	05	29	Broken right ring finger
	08	27	Inflammation Lt. knee
Byrnes,Eric	08	118	Strained Rt hamstring x 2
Cabrera,Orlando	05	15	Inflammation of the right elbow
Cairo,Miguel	05	17	Strained left hamstring
	06	32	Strained right hamstring
Callaspo,Jolbert	08	56	Unspecific medical condition
Cameron,Mike	05	83	Multiple facial fractures; Lt wrist
	06	20	Strained left oblique
Cano,Robinson	06	43	Strained left hamstring
Cantu,Jorge	06	43	Broken bone, left foot

BATTERS	Yr	Days	Injury
Carroll,Brett	08	100	Separated right shoulder
Casey,Sean	04	16	Strained right calf
	06	44	Fx vertebrae
	08	32	Strained neck; right hip flexor
Casilla,Alexi	08	23	Torn ligament right thumb
Castillo,Jose	05	69	Torn MCL - left knee; oblique
Castillo,Luis	08	53	Strained left hip flexor
Castro,Juan	04	21	Strained left ribcage
	05	22	Strained left knee
	07	84	Tendinitis right elbow x 2
Castro,Ramon	04	124	Right toe inflammation
	05	18	Strained right quadriceps
	06	62	Strained left oblique
	07	49	Arthritis - lower back
	08	56	Strained right hamstring x 2
Catalanotto,Frank	04	95	Groin injury x 3
	07	22	Acute strain - right biceps muscle
Chavez,Endy	07	82	Strained left hamstring
Chavez,Eric	04	37	Broken bone, right hand
	07	66	Lower back spasms
	08	155	Inflammation Rt shoulder; Back spasms
Choo,Shin-Soo	08	61	Recovery from surgery on Lt, elbow
Church,Ryan	05	35	Right rib cage sprain; fx toe
	08	70	Concussion x 2
Cintron,Alex	08	31	Strained left hamstring
Clark,Tony	06	39	Right shoulder strain
Cora,Alex	08	25	Sore Rt elbow
Costa,Shane	06	20	Strained left hamstring
	08	28	Recovery from surgery on his wrist
Coste,Chris	07	7	Strained hamstring
Cota,Humberto	04	66	Strained left oblique
	05	23	Strained oblique
	07	27	Strained left shoulder
Counsell,Craig	03	61	Dislocated right thumb
	06	38	Right rib fracture
Crawford,Carl	08	47	Dislocated right index finger
Crede,Joe	05	15	Stress fracture - right index finger
	07	118	Inflammation lower back
	08	34	Inflammation lower back
Crisp,Coco	05	15	Sprained right thumb
	06	49	Fractured left finger
Crosby,Bobby	05	77	Fractured rib; Lt ankle
	06	59	Lower back strain x 2
	07	68	Fractured left hand
	08	14	Strained left hamstring
Cuddyer,Michael	05	17	Bone bruise in right hand
	07	15	Torn ligament-left thumb
	08	96	Dislocated Rt finger; Fx Lt foot; Lt finger
Damon,Johnny	08	14	Sprained A/C joint right shoulder
De Aza,Alejandro	07	114	Sprained right ankle
	08	184	High ankle sprain Lt ankle
DeJesus,David	06	40	Strained left hamstring
Delgado,Carlos	04	37	Strained rib cage
	05	16	Sore left elbow
Dellucci,David	07	79	Severely strained left hamstring
Denorfia,Chris	07	183	Pending surgery - right elbow
	08	73	Lower back stiffness
DeRosa,Mark	06	15	Sprained left foot
Diaz,Matt	05	37	Strained oblique
	08	119	Strained ligament left knee
Doumit,Ryan	06	100	Strained left hamstring x 2
	07	46	High ankle sprain; Lt wrist sprain
	08	23	Fractured tip of Lt thumb
Drew,J.D.	05	91	Broken left wrist
	08	21	Herniated disc
Duffy,Chris	05	38	Strained left hamstring
	07	93	Sprained left ankle
	08	95	Lt. shoulder surgery
Dukes,Elijah	08	88	Rt. hamstring; Rt knee; Rt calf
Duncan,Chris	08	70	Pinched nerve -cervical spine
Durham,Ray	04	38	Strained left hamstring; knee
	06	15	Left hamstring strain
Easley,Damion	07	43	Sprained left ankle
Eckstein,David	06	27	Torn oblique muscle
	07	28	Lower back spasms
	08	20	Strained Rt hip flexor
Edmonds,Jim	07	33	Pinched nerve in lower back
	08	6	Strained Rt. Calf

BATTERS	Yr	Days	Injury
Ellis, Mark	04	183	Torn right labrum
	06	30	Broken right thumb
	08	9	Torn labrum - right shoulder
Encarnacion, Edwin	06	29	Sprained left ankle
Encarnacion, Juan	04	15	Left shoulder tendinitis
	07	43	Scar tissue left wrist; facial fx 9/07
	08	184	Left eye and orbital bone 8/07
Erstad, Darin	04	36	Strained right hamstring
	06	75	Right ankle irritation x 2
	07	59	Sprained left ankle x 2
Estrada, Johnny	05	16	Lumbar and cervical strain
	08	79	Sore Rt elbow; Neuritis Rt elbow
Everett, Adam	04	53	Broken bone in left wrist
	07	94	Fractured left fibula
	08	87	Strained Rt shoulder; tend. Rt shoulder
Feliz, Pedro	08	26	Inflammation lower back
Figgins, Chone	07	29	Fx- two fingers Rt hand
	08	37	Strained Rt hamstring x 2
Flores, Jesus	08	15	Sprained left ankle
Floyd, Cliff	04	31	Strained right quadriceps
	06	47	Left Achilles; Lt ankle
	08	32	Torn cartilage - Rt. Knee (surgery 4/11)
Frandsen, Kevin	06	15	Broken jaw
	08	181	Torn Lt Achilles tendon
Freel, Ryan	05	51	Left foot inflammation; Rt knee
	07	94	Torn cartilage Rt knee; neck bruise
	08	181	Strained right hamstring
Furcal, Rafael	07	12	Sprained left ankle
	08	141	Back surgery 7/08
Garciaparra, Nomar	04	67	Right Achilles tendinitis
	05	106	Torn left groin muscle
	06	34	Right knee sprain; ribcage
	07	21	Strained left calf
	08	97	Strained Lt knee; torn MCL Lt knee
Gathright, Joey	08	28	Bruised right shoulder
German, Esteban	04	27	Left oblique strain
Giambi, Jason	04	70	Benign tumor
	04	15	Sprained right ankle
	07	68	Torn Plantar fascia tendon - Lt foot
Gibbons, Jay	04	61	Left hip flexor strain; back
	06	61	Sprained right knee; Lt groin
	07	49	Torn labrum-left shoulder
	07	39	Bone bruise right knee
Giles, Marcus	04	60	Broken collarbone
	07	15	Sprained left knee
Glaus, Troy	04	109	Right shoulder surgery
	07	32	Left foot surgery; heel
Gload, Ross	05	83	Left shoulder inflammation
	07	47	Torn right quad muscle
Gomes, Jonny	06	41	Right shoulder surgery
Gomez, Carlos	07	64	Fractured hamate bone - left hand
Gomez, Chris	06	61	Broken hand
Gonzalez, Alex	06	15	Oblique strain
	08	184	Compression fx left lower leg/surgery 7/08
Gonzalez, Alberto	08	27	Strained left hamstring
Gonzalez, Luis	04	63	Right elbow surgery
Gordon, Alex	08	20	Torn right quadriceps
Gotay, Ruben	08	15	Strained left hamstring
Granderson, Curtis	04	24	Fractured 3rd metacarpal, Rt. Hand
Greene, Khalil	05	37	Fractured right finger; left toe
	06	16	Torn left middle finger ligament
	08	61	Fractured left hand
Griffey Jr., Ken	04	76	Torn right hamstring x 2
	06	28	Strained biceps tendon in right knee
Grudzielanek, Mark	04	70	Partial tear in right Achilles tendon
	07	23	Torn meniscus - left knee
	08	59	Torn deltoid ligament - right ankle
Guerrero, Vladimir	05	20	Partial dislocation of left shoulder
Guillen, Carlos	05	68	Sore right knee; Lt hamstring
Guillen, Jose	06	90	Left hamstring strain; Rt elbow
Gutierrez, Franklin	07	12	Strained left hamstring
Guzman, Christian	06	182	Right shoulder surgery
	07	122	Strained left hamstring; left thumb
Guzman, Freddy	05	182	Right elbow surgery
Gwynn, Tony, Jr.	08	19	Strained Lt. hamstring
Hafner, Travis	05	18	Post-concussion syndrome
	08	102	Strained right shoulder

FIVE-YEAR INJURY LOG

BATTERS	Yr	Days	Injury
Hairston Jr., Jerry	04	85	Fractured left ankle; finger
	05	15	Left elbow ligament injury
	07	73	Lower back soreness; neck
	08	50	Fractured Rt hamstring x 2; Fx Lt thumb
Hairston, Scott	05	31	Torn labrum
	06	39	Left biceps strain
	07	29	Strained left oblique muscle
	08	32	Torn ligament - left thumb
Hall, Bill	07	19	Sprained right ankle
Hall, Toby	07	46	Torn labrum - throwing shoulder
Hamilton, Josh	07	51	Sprained Rt wrist; stomach ailment
Hardy, J.J.	06	138	Right ankle surgery
Hawpe, Brad	05	52	Strained left hamstring
	08	16	Strained right hamstring
Helms, Wes	04	40	Torn meniscus, right knee
Helton, Todd	05	15	Left calf strain
	06	15	Stomach ailment
	08	71	Sore lower back
Hermida, Jeremy	06	40	Sore right hip flexor, groin strain
	07	43	Bruised right patellar
	08	9	Tight Lt hamstring
Hernandez, Ramon	04	35	Strained left knee
	05	58	Sprained Left wrist; surgery
	07	33	Groin contusion; oblique
Hill, Aaron	08	123	Post concussion syndrome symptoms
Holliday, Matt	05	40	Fractured right pinkie finger
	08	16	Strained left hamstring
Hopper, Norris	07	17	Bruised heel
	08	143	Tommy John surgery 7/08
House, J.R.	05	182	Right shoulder surgery
Howard, Ryan	07	15	Strained left quad muscle
Hudson, Orlando	04	23	Strained left hamstring
	08	51	Dislocated left wrist
Huff, Aubrey	06	23	Left knee sprain
Hunter, Torii	04	18	Strained right hamstring
	05	65	Fractured left ankle
	06	15	Stress fracture, left foot
Ibanez, Raul	04	37	Strained right hamstring
Iguchi, Tadahito	08	56	Separated right shoulder
Infante, Omar	08	54	Strained Lt hamstring; Fx Lt hand
Ingett, Joe	07	17	Strained left hamstring
Inge, Brandon	04	19	Broken finger
	08	17	Strained left oblique
Iwamura, Akinori	07	34	Strained right oblique
Izturis, Cesar	05	72	Lower back sprain; hamstring
	06	93	Post elbow surgery; hamstring
	08	15	Strained right hamstring
Izturis, Maicer	05	53	Sprained MCL, left knee
	06	46	Strained left hamstring
	07	63	Strained right hamstring x 2
	08	61	Strained back; torn thumb ligament
Jacobs, Mike	07	40	Fractured right thumb
Jenkins, Geoff	08	18	Right hip flexor strain
Johnson, Kelly	06	182	Right elbow surgery
Johnson, Nick	04	53	Strained lower back
	05	29	Right heel contusion
	07	183	Fx right femur + surgery x 2
	08	138	Torn tendon - right wrist
Johnson, Reed	07	85	Herniated disc lower back
	08	15	Lower back spasms
Jones, Adam	08	29	Fractured left foot
Jones, Andruw	08	82	Tendinitis -right patellar tendon
Jones, Chipper	04	19	Strained right hamstring
	05	42	Ligament strain, left foot
	06	44	Right ankle; oblique x 2
	07	20	Bone bruise right wrist/hand
	08	15	Strained left hamstring
Kearns, Austin	04	105	Rt thumb surgery; fx left forearm
	08	78	Stress fx Lt foot; surgery Rt elbow
Kemp, Matt	07	17	Separated right shoulder
Kendrick, Howie	07	78	Fx index finger lt hand x 2
	08	78	Strained Lt hamstring x 2
Kennedy, Adam	05	27	Recovery from right knee surgery
	07	50	Torn cartilage-right knee
Kent, Jeff	06	36	Abdominal strain; sprained lt wrist
	08	21	Surgery - right knee - cartilage

BATTERS	Yr	Days	Injury
Keppinger,Jeff	05	23	Left knee (tibia plate) fracture
	07	21	Fx right index finger
	08	39	Fractured left patellar (kneecap)
Kielty,Bobby	07	70	Strained left calf muscle
Kinsler,Ian	06	43	Dislocated left thumb
	07	29	Stress fracture left foot
	08	43	Sports hernia
Konerko,Paul	08	23	Strained left oblique
Kotchman,Casey	06	146	Mononucleosis
Kotsay,Mark	07	108	Lower back spasms; surgery
	08	36	Strained lower back
Kubel,Jason	05	182	Left knee surgery
Laird,Gerald	04	63	Torn ligament, left thumb
	08	35	Strained left hamstring
LaRoche,Adam	04	34	Separated left shoulder
	08	17	Right intercostal strain
LaRoche,Andy	08	34	Surgery Rt. Thumb
LaRue,Jason	04	15	Fractured right index finger
	06	15	Right knee surgery
	07	15	Contusion left shoulder
Lee,Carlos	08	51	Fractured left pink finger
Lee,Derrek	06	101	Inflammation, fx rt wrist
Lewis,Fred	07	20	Strained right oblique
Lo Duca,Paul	07	15	Strained right hamstring
	08	57	Bruised Rt hand; Fx Rt hand
Loewen,Adam	07	152	Stress fracture - right elbow
	08	151	Stress fracture - right elbow
Logan,Nook	07	34	Sprained left foot
Longoria,Evan	08	29	Fractured right hand
Lowell,Mike	08	42	Strained right oblique muscle; Rt thumb
Ludwick,Ryan	04	92	Right knee surgery
Lugo,Julio	06	31	Strained abdominal muscle
	08	80	Strained left quad
Marte,Andy	07	26	Strained left hamstring
Martinez,Victor	08	78	Surgery - right elbow
Matos,Luis	04	74	Fractured right shin
	05	39	Broken right index finger
	06	18	Right shoulder inflammation
Mather,Joel	08	28	Fractured left hand
Matsui,Hideki	06	123	Broken left wrist
	07	15	Strained left hamstring
	08	56	Inflammation left knee
Matsui,Kaz	04	46	Lower back strain
	05	52	Bruised left knee
	06	17	Sprained MCL, right knee
	07	36	Strained lower back
	08	54	Strained Rt hamst.; Fissure; Inflam Disc
Matthews Jr.,Gary	05	24	Strained left hamstring
	06	9	Ribcage strain
Mauer,Joe	04	136	Sprained left knee x 2
	07	34	Strained left quad muscle
McCann,Brian	06	16	Sprained right ankle
McDonald,John	06	15	Groin injury
	08	31	Sprained right ankle
McLouth,Nate	06	51	Left ankle sprain
McPherson,Dallas	05	87	Left hip surgery
	06	71	Lower back spasms
	07	183	Back surgery (1/07)
Mench,Kevin	04	19	Strained left oblique
Metcalf,Travis	07	15	Strained left hamstring
Michaels,Jason	06	18	Sprained right ankle
Mientkiewicz,Doug	04	16	Left wrist soreness
	05	49	Bruised lower back; hamstring
	06	68	Lower back strain
	07	91	Fractured right wrist
Miles,Aaron	05	33	Right intercostal strain
Milledge,Lastings	08	27	Strained right groin
Molina,Bengie	04	31	Fx rt index finger; calf
	05	25	Strained right quadriceps
Molina,Yadier	05	40	Hairline fracture, left pinkie finger
	07	29	Fractured left wrist
Monroe,Craig	04	17	Strained left hamstring
Montero,Miguel	08	24	Fractured index finger Rt. hand
Morales,Jose	07	22	Sprained left ankle
Mora,Melvin	04	15	Strained right hamstring
	07	23	Sprained left foot

BATTERS	Yr	Days	Injury
Morneau,Justin	05	15	Concussion
Moss,Brandon	08	21	Appendectomy
Munson,Eric	05	34	Bruised ribs
Murphy,David	08	54	Sprained posterior cruciate ligament - rt knee
Murphy,Donnie	05	15	Fractured finger - right hand
	07	15	Strained oblique
	08	32	Inflammation Rt elbow
Nady,Xavier	06	19	Appendectomy
Napoli,Mike	07	51	Strained right hamstring; ankle
	08	32	Inflammation right shoulder
Navarro,Dioner	06	41	Bruised right wrist
	08	17	Lacerations of two fingers on Rt. Hand
Newhan,David	06	133	Fractured right fibula
Niekro,Lance	04	6	Right ankle sprain
	06	31	Right groin strain; shoulder
Nixon,Trot	04	118	Strained lt quad; back
	05	27	Left oblique strain
	06	34	Strained right biceps
	08	93	Strained left groin/hernia surgery 7/08
Norton,Greg	04	37	Left knee inflammation
	07	46	Torn meniscus - Rt. Knee - surgery
Olivo,Miguel	04	15	Kidney stones
Ordonez,Magglio	04	117	Bone marrow edema; strain
	05	79	Hernia surgery
	08	18	Strained right oblique
Ortiz,David	08	54	Torn tendon sheath - left wrist
Overbay,Lyle	07	38	Fractured right hand
Owens,Jerry	06	15	Sprained right ankle
	08	20	Surgery to repair torn R/C Rt. shoulder
Ozuna,Pablo	07	126	Fractured right fibula, torn ligament
Pagan,Angel	06	75	Torn left hamstring
	07	54	Colitis
	08	140	Bruised labrum Lt shoulder
Payton,Jay	07	19	Strained right hamstring
Pena,Brayan	07	15	Concussion
	08	18	Lower back strain
Pena,Carlos	08	23	Fractured index finger left hand
Pena,Wily Mo	05	35	Strained left quadriceps muscle
	06	52	Left wrist surgery
	08	88	Lt shoulder surgery; Strained oblique
Pence,Hunter	07	29	Chip fracture-right wrist
Phillips,Andy	06	15	Strained left rib cage muscle
	07	26	Fractured right wrist
	08	6	Backs spasms
Phillips,Brandon	08	18	Fractured right index finger & surgery
Pierre,Juan	08	25	Sprained medial collateral ligament - lt knee
Podsednik,Scott	05	16	Strained left adductor muscle
	07	89	Strained lt rib cage muscle; adductor
	08	25	Fractured left pinky finger
Polanco,Placido	04	30	Strained left quadriceps
	05	15	Strained left hamstring
	06	37	Separated left shoulder
Posada,Jorge	08	108	Torn subscapularis muscle Rt shoulder
Prado,Martin	08	59	Sprained Lt thumb
Pujols,Albert	06	18	Strained right oblique
	08	15	Strained left calf
Punto,Nick	04	121	Fx right clavicle; oblique
	05	30	Pulled right hamstring
	08	40	Strained left hamstring x 2
Quentin,Carlos	07	45	Strained hamstring; torn labrum
Quinlan,Robb	04	49	Left oblique strain
	05	53	Bulging disc in neck
Quintanilla,Omar	06	19	Right shin contusion
	08	20	Concussion
Rabelo,Mike	08	12	Sprained Lt knee
Ramirez,Aramis	05	39	Strained left quadriceps
	07	15	Tendinitis - left patellar
Reed,Jeremy	06	91	Fractured right thumb
Renteria,Edgar	07	34	Sprained Rt ankle x 2
Richar,Danny	08	60	Stress fracture of Rib
Riggans,Shawn	07	119	Tendinitis - throwing elbow
	08	22	Surgery - right knee
Rios,Alex	06	30	Staph infection in lower left leg
Rivera,Juan	06	21	Rib cage tightness
	07	154	Fx left leg (1/07), surgery
Roberts,Brian	06	24	Strained groin

FIVE-YEAR INJURY LOG

BATTERS	Yr	Days	Injury
Roberts,Dave	04	23	Strained right hamstring
	05	14	Groin strain
	06	17	Right knee contusion
	07	29	Bone spurs and chip in left elbow
	08	105	Inflammation Lt. knee/surgery 4/08
Robles,Oscar	07	15	Torn tendon -- left wrist
Rodriguez,Alex	08	19	Grade 2 strain of Rt quad muscle
Rolen,Scott	05	111	Sprained Lt shoulder; tendinitis
	07	33	Sore left shoulder
	08	41	Fractured finger; Inflammation Rt shoulder
Rolins,Jimmy	08	19	Sprained Rt ankle
Ross,Cody	06	24	Bruised left pinky finger
	07	74	Strained left hamstring
Ross,Dave	06	18	Lower abdominal strain
	07	15	Concussion
	08	24	Back Spasms
Rowand,Aaron	06	56	Fx Lt ankle; Fx nose
Ryan,Brendan	08	24	Strained ribcage
Sanchez,Angel	07	183	Strained elbow
	08	28	Sprained finger left hand
Sanchez,Freddy	04	96	Recovery from right ankle surgery
	07	6	Sprained MCL right knee
Santiago,Ramon	08	33	Separated left shoulder
Schneider,Brian	06	15	Strained left hamstring
Sexson,Richie	04	156	Lt shoulder surgery; labrum
Shealy,Ryan	06	39	Right elbow strain
	07	60	Strained Lt hamstring x 2
Sheffield,Gary	06	129	Lt wrist contusion; surgery
	07	15	Sore right shoulder
	08	28	Strained left oblique
Snelling,Chris	04	182	Broken right wrist
	05	62	Sprained Lt knee; meniscus
	06	69	Post surgery; Lt shoulder strain
	07	143	Contusion - left knee
	08	46	Inflammation Lt knee
Snyder,Chris	08	19	Left testicular fracture
Soriano,Alfonso	07	22	Strained right quad muscle
	08	56	Fx metacarpal - Lt hand; Strained Rt calf
Spilborghs,Ryan	08	54	Strained left oblique
Stairs,Matt	04	15	Strained left oblique
Stewart,Shannon	04	58	Plantar fasciitis, right heel
	06	119	Torn plantaar fascia x 2
	08	64	High ankle sprain - right ankle
Sweeney,Mark	07	11	Bruised right foot
	08	23	Strained right hamstring
Sweeney,Mike	04	43	Herniated disc
	05	15	Sprained left wrist and elbow
	06	98	Bulging disc in upper back
	07	74	Cartilage damage right knee
	08	97	Inflammation - surgery on both knees 6/08
Sweeney,Ryan	08	29	Sprained t thumb; Bruised Lt foot
Swisher,Nick	05	23	Sprained right shoulder
Taveras,Willy	07	47	Strained right quad muscle
Teahen,Mark	05	21	Lower back strain
	07	15	Strained left forearm
Teixeira,Mark	04	16	Strained left oblique muscle
	07	34	Strained left quad muscle
Tejada,Miguel	07	35	Fractured radius left wrist
Terrero,Luis	05	22	Left groin strain
	07	39	Strained left groin
Thames,Marcus	07	21	Strained left hamstring
Thomas,Clete	08	15	Sprained right ankle
Thomas,Frank	04	89	Fracture, left foot
	05	130	Fracture, left foot; surgery
	06	15	Strained right quadriceps
	08	94	Strained right quad x 2
Thome,Jim	05	114	Back strain; Rt elbow surgery
	07	22	Strained right ribcage
Tolbert,Matt	08	109	Torn ligament Lt thumb
Torrealba,Yorvit	06	82	Right shoulder strain x 2
	08	31	Torn Meniscus - left knee/surgery 9/08
Tracy,Chad	07	57	Strained Rt knee; ribcage
	08	56	Recovery from microsurgery Rt. knee
Treanor,Matt	06	15	Left shoulder
	08	28	Strained left hip
Tulowitzki,Troy	08	67	Torn tendon rt. quad; Cut lt hand

FIVE-YEAR INJURY LOG

BATTERS	Yr	Days	Injury
Upton,B.J.	07	34	Strained left quad
Upton Justin	08	55	Strained left oblique muscle
Uribe,Juan	08	15	Strained left hamstring
Utley,Chase	07	31	Fractured right hand
Valentin,Jose	04	18	Pulled left hamstring
	05	88	Torn ligaments - right knee
	07	111	Strained Lt knee; Fx fibula
Varitek,Jason	06	33	Cartilage damage, left knee
Vazquez,Ramon	04	31	Strained right oblique
Victorino,Shane	07	22	Strained right calf
	08	16	Strained Rt calf
Vidro,Jose	04	39	Right knee surgery
	05	61	High left ankle sprain
	06	31	Left hamstring strain
Vizquel,Omar	08	40	Surgery Lt knee
Ward,Daryle	04	50	Right thumb ligament sprain
	07	40	Strained Rt calf; Lt hip
	08	41	Herniated disc - lumbar spine
Weeks,Rickie	06	69	Right wrist surgery
	07	19	Tendinitis right wrist
	08	15	Sprained left knee
Wells,Vernon	04	30	Strained right calf
	07	10	Left shoulder surgery (labrum & cyst)
	08	59	Fx Lt wrist; Strained Lt hamstring
Werth,Jayson	04	59	Strained oblique muscle
	05	65	Lt wrist fx; bursitis
	06	182	Left wrist surgery
	07	33	Sprained last wrist
	08	15	Strained right oblique
Wigginton,Ty	04	16	Ulcer
	06	33	Broken bone in left hand
	08	26	Fractured thumb left hand
Wilkerson,Brad	06	53	Right shoulder surgery
	07	24	Strained right hamstring
	08	15	Lower back spasms
Willingham,Josh	05	95	Stress fracture, left forearm
	06	15	Strained ligament - left hand
	08	57	Back spasms
Willits,Reggie	08	17	Concussion
Wise,DeWayne	08	15	Strained left adductor
Wilson,Jack	08	51	Strained Lt. calf
Wilson,Vance	04	41	Lt wrist surgery; hamstring
	07	183	Strained throwing elbow
	08	184	Tommy John surgery Rt. Elbow 6/2007
Woodward,Chris	04	27	Tightness in right hamstring
Youkilis,Kevin	04	16	Bruised right ankle
Young,Dmitri	04	54	Broken right leg
	06	80	Strained Rt quad x 2
	08	116	Diabetes; strained back; strained Lt hip
Zaun,Gregg	05	15	Concussion
	06	5	Muscle pull, right calf
	07	44	Fractured right thumb
	08	19	Strained right elbow
Zimmerman,Ryan	08	57	Torn labrum - left shoulder
Zobrist,Ben	07	43	Strained left oblique muscle

PITCHERS	Yr	Days	Injury
Aardsma,David	08	40	Strained right groin
Accrado,Jeremy	08	143	Tightness Rt forearm
Acosta,Manny	08	49	Strained Rt hamstring
Affeldt,Jeremy	04	55	Strained right rib cage
	05	67	Left groin strain x 2
Albaladejo,Jonathan	08	143	Sprained UCL Rt elbow
Albers,Matt	08	96	Torn labrum - pitching shoulder
Alvarez,Mario	08	25	Stiffness - right elbow
Aquino,Greg	05	68	Ulnar nerve irritation
	06	24	Sore right forearm
	07	34	Tightness in pitching forearm
	08	39	Strained left hamstring
Armas,Tony	04	56	Recovery from rotator cuff surgery
	05	35	Right groin strain
	06	27	Strained right forearm
	08	84	Strained ab muscle/hernia surgery 8/08
Ayala,Luis	06	182	Right elbow surgery
	07	80	Tommy John surgery 3/2006

PITCHERS	Yr	Days	Injury
Backe,Brandon	05	40	Left intercostal strain
	06	143	Right elbow sprain; elbow surgery
	07	153	Tommy John surgery 9/2006
Badenhop,Burke	08	100	Tendinitis right shoulder
Baek,Cha Seung	06	7	Right triceps tendinitis
	07	92	Inflammation right shoulder
Baez,Danys	06	40	Appendectomy
	07	27	Tendinitis pitching forearm
	08	184	Tommy John surgery 9/2007
Baker,Scott	08	32	Strained Rt groin
Bale,John	07	103	Strained left biceps and shoulder
	08	139	Tightness Lt shoulder & dead arm feeling
Bannister,Brian	06	120	Strained right hamstring
Bautista,Denny	05	144	Right shoulder tendinitis
	06	24	Sore right pectoral muscle
	08	33	Tendinitis Rt shoulder
Beckett,Josh	04	58	Finger injury x 2; lower back
	05	32	Strained left oblique; finger
	07	15	Avulsion of skin - right index finger
	08	32	Back spasms; Sore pitching elbow
Bedard,Erik	05	57	Strained left MCL
	07	22	Strained right oblique
	08	102	Torn labrum/surgery 10/08; Sore hip
Belisle,Matt	06	71	Lower back strain x 2
	08	44	Sore Rt knee; sore Rt forearm
Bell,Rob	05	56	Personal reasons
Benitez,Armando	04	20	Right elbow inflammation
	05	110	Torn right hamstring
	06	35	Left knee bursitis; Rt knee inflammation
Bennett,Jeff	08	22	Subluxation of right shoulder
Benoit,Joaquin	04	15	Sore right rotator cuff
	05	46	Sore right shoulder; Right elbow tendinitis
	08	34	Soreness - right shoulder
Benson,Kris	05	31	Strained right pectoral
	06	17	Right elbow tendinitis
	07	183	Torn rotator cuff
Bergmann,Jason	07	72	Tight left hamstring; sore elbow
Betancourt,Rafael	04	15	Right biceps tendinitis
	05	18	Right shoulder inflammation
	06	26	Right upper back strain
Bierd,Randor	08	80	Rotator cuff impingement Rt shoulder
Birkins,Kurt	08	17	Neuritis pitching elbow
Bonderman,Jeremy	07	15	Blister right middle finger
	08	115	Thoracic outlet syndrome
Bootcheck,Chris	06	19	Strained left hamstring
	08	45	Strained Lt oblique; Strained Rt forearm
Borowski,Joe	04	121	Slight tear, right rotator cuff
	05	46	Fractured right ulnar bone
	08	38	Strained triceps rt. arm
Bowie,Micah	06	53	Left latissimus dorsi strain
	07	154	Hernia; hip x 2
	08	64	Strained Lt forearm
Brackman,Andrew	08	184	Recovery from Tommy John surgery 8/07
Bradford,Chad	04	15	Lower back sprain
	05	100	Lower back surgery
Braun,Ryan	08	81	Recovery from surgery on his pitching elbow
Bray,Bill	07	110	Sprained left index finger
Brazoban,Yhency	06	172	Right elbow surgery
	07	157	Recovery from TJS; torn labrum
	08	74	Strained pitching shoulder
Britton,Chris	08	28	Strained ribcage muscle
Brocail,Doug	04	44	Left hamstring; Appendicitis
	06	113	Coronary angioplasy; hamstring
	07	16	Strained right gluteus muscle
Brown,Andrew	08	90	Soreness - right shoulder
Bruney,Brian	04	40	Inflamed right elbow
	08	97	Lisfranc injury Rt foot
Buchholz,Clay	08	18	Broken fingernail right hand
Burgos,Ambriorix	08	184	Tommy John surgery 8/07
Burnett,A.J.	04	59	Recovery from right elbow surgery
	06	73	Right elbow soreness x 2
	07	59	Sore pitching shoulder x 2
Burton,Jared	07	57	Lower back spasms; Lt hamstring
	08	45	Strained right lat muscle
Byrdak,Tim	06	102	Bone spurs in left elbow
	07	26	Strained flexor tendon - pitching arm
Byrd,Paul	04	75	Recovery from right elbow surgery

FIVE-YEAR INJURY LOG

PITCHERS	Yr	Days	Injury
Cabrera,Daniel	05	20	Lower back strain
	06	21	Tightness in right shoulder
	08	16	Sprained right elbow
Cabrera,Fernando	06	16	Bruised right heel
	08	88	Recovery from surgery on Rt. Elbow
Calero,Kiko	04	28	Right rotator cuff tendinitis
	05	27	Right elbow tendinitis
	07	17	Inflammation right shoulder
	08	66	Torn rotator cuff Rt shoulder 9/2007
Cameron,Kevin	08	82	Sprained right elbow
Capellan,Jose	06	15	Right shoulder strain
Capps,Matt	08	54	Bursitis - pitching shoulder
Capuano,Chris	04	93	Sore left elbow; Lt arm; Lt quad
	07	22	Strained left groin
	08	184	Tommy John surgery 5/08
Carlyle,Buddy	08	17	Strained neck muscle
Carmona,Fausto	08	63	Strained left hip
Carpenter,Chris	06	15	Right shoulder bursitis
	07	182	Bone chips right elbow
	08	184	TJS recovery; Compressed nerve Rt arm
Casilla,Santiago	08	33	Sore Rt elbow
Chacin,Gustavo	06	93	Left forearm strain and elbow sprain
	07	89	Strained pitching shoulder
Chacon,Shawn	05	33	Strained left hamstring
	06	25	Left leg hematoma
Chamberlain,Joba	08	26	Tendinitis - right rotator cuff
Cherry,Rocky	07	17	Strained right lat muscle
	08	54	Strained Rt. Shoulder
Chico,Matt	08	130	Surgery - left elbow
Choate,Randy	08	102	Fractured finger left hand
Chulk,Vinnie	07	35	Blood clot - right hand
	08	16	Tendinitis Rt shoulder
Clarke,Darren	07	46	Right shoulder inflamation
Corcoran,Tim	07	60	Strained pitching elbow
Colome,Jesus	04	20	Right shoulder tendinitis
	05	67	Right shoulder inflammation x 2
	07	56	Soft tissue infection
Colon,Bartolo	06	130	Inflammation & Rt R/C tear
	07	67	Sore pitching elbow; R/C
	08	82	Strained oblique
Contreras,Jose	03	78	Right shoulder strain
	06	16	Pinched nerve in right hip
	08	74	Ruptured Achilles; Strained Rt elbow
Cook,Aaron	04	57	Blood clots in both lungs
	05	117	Pulmonary embolism
	07	46	Strained right oblique
Cordero,Chad	08	166	Torn labrum/ biceps tendon - rt shoulder
Cormier,Lance	06	15	Strained left oblique
	07	84	Tired pitching arm; triceps
Corey,Brian	08	17	Strained left hamstring
Correia,Kevin	08	48	Strained left intercostals
Crain,Jesse	07	138	Torn R/C and Labrum
Cruz,Juan	06	29	Sore right shoulder
	07	18	Strained muscle - right shoulder
	08	27	Strained left oblique
Davies,Kyle	06	108	Strained right groin
Davis,Doug	08	23	Thyroid surgery
Day,Dewon	07	20	Strained lower back
De La Rosa,Jorge	06	45	Blisters on left hand
	07	41	Strained pitching elbow
Dempster,Ryan	04	119	Recovery from right elbow surgery
	07	27	Strained left oblique muscle
Devine,Joey	08	67	Inflammation - right elbow setback 7/08
Dinardo,Lenny	04	89	Blister left index finger; shoulder
	06	101	Neck strain
Dingman,Craig	06	182	Arterial bypass surgery
Dohmann,Scott	06	15	Viral infection
Donnelly,Brendan	04	73	Nasal fractures
	07	112	Strained pitching forearm
Dotel,Octavio	05	137	Right elbow surgery
	06	135	Recovery from right elbow surgery
	07	94	Strained left oblique; shoulder
Duchscherer,Justin	06	47	Right elbow tendinitis
	07	139	Strained right hip
	08	62	Strained Rt hip; Strained Rt biceps tendon
Duckworth,Brandon	06	63	Right elbow strain
	07	79	Torn left oblique

PITCHERS	Yr	Days	Injury
Dumatrait, Phil	08	95	Sore pitching shoulder/ surgery 8/08
Duke, Zach	05	23	Sprained left ankle
	07	75	Tightness in pitching elbow
Eaton, Adam	05	46	Strained right middle finger x 2
	06	113	Right finger surgery
	07	16	Strained pitching shoulder
Elarton, Scott	06	77	Right shoulder surgery
	07	75	Strained right foot; labrum surgery
	08	92	Personal reasons
Embree, Alan	06	15	Strained left groin
Escobar, Kelvim	05	89	Right elbow strain x 3
	06	15	Right elbow irritation
	07	15	Irritation right shoulder
	08	184	Torn labrum - Rt. Shoulder
Estes, Shawn	05	65	Stress fracture, left navicular bone
	06	179	Left elbow surgery
	07	183	Tommy John surgery 6/2006
	08	95	Fractured left thumb
Eyre, Scott	04	18	Lower back strain
	06	16	Strained right hamstring
	08	66	Bone spur Lt elbow; Strained Lt groin
Farnsworth, Kyle	04	15	Right knee contusion
Flores, Randy	05	15	Avulsed callus pad on left foot
	08	22	Tendinitis left ankle
Fogg, Josh	07	15	Strained left groin
	08	55	Strained Rt groin; Lower back spasms
Fossum, Casey	04	39	Left shoulder strain
	06	15	Groin strain
Francisco, Frank	05	181	Right elbow surgery
	06	77	Recovery from right elbow surgery
Francis, Jeff	08	38	Inflammation - pitching shoulder
Fuentes, Brian	04	69	Back strain
	07	41	Strained left LAT muscle
Fultz, Aaron	07	35	Strained rib cage muscle
Gabbard, Kason	08	110	Surgery bone spur - left elbow 7/08
Gagne, Eric	05	151	Right elbow sprain & surgery
	06	174	Back surgery & elbow surgery
	07	27	Strained right hip, back.elbow
	08	40	Tendinitis Rt. Shoulder
Gallagher, Sean	08	20	Fatigue - right shoulder
Gallardo, Yovani	08	165	Two knee surgeries
Garcia, Anderson	08	59	Inflammation Rt. Shoulder
Garcia, Freddy	07	127	Tendinitis right biceps; R/C; labrum
Garcia, Harvey	08	184	Tendinitis - Rt. Shoulder
Gardner, Lee	08	165	Inflammation pitching elbow
Garza, Matt	08	16	Inflamed radial nerve - Rt. Arm
Gaudin, Chad	08	14	Lt. hip surgery (labrum) 12/2007
Geary, Geoff	05	15	Right eye contusion
	08	18	Strained right groin
Giese, Dan	08	17	Inflammation - pitching shoulder
Glavine, Tom	08	125	Sore pitching forearm
Glover, Gary	08	34	Strained Lt calf; Rt shoulder
Gobble, Jimmy	08	42	Strained lower back
Gonzalez, Mike	05	54	Sprained MCL - left knee
	06	38	Left arm fatigue
	07	138	Torn UCL
	08	80	Tommy John surgery 6/2008
Gordon, Tom	06	21	Strained right shoulder
	07	74	Inflamed R/C Rt shoulder
	08	85	inflammation - right elbow
Gorzelanny, Tom	06	29	Left elbow soreness
	08	19	Irritated left middle finger
Grabow, John	07	23	Inflamed pitching elbow
Green, Sean	06	50	Back spasms; strained side
Greinke, Zack	06	79	Personal reasons
Guardado, Eddie	04	64	Left rotator tear
	06	43	Left elbow surgery
	07	128	Tommy John surgery 9/2006
	08	20	Sore pitching shoulder
Guerrier, Matt	06	53	Fractured right thumb
Guevara, Carlos	08	62	Strained Rt. Groin
Guthrie, Jeremy	08	21	Impingement - right rotator cuff
Guzman, Angel	07	121	Strained right elbow
	08	155	Tommy John surgery 9/2008
Halladay, Roy	04	81	Right shoulder fatigue x 2
	05	86	Fractured left tibia
	07	20	Appendectomy

PITCHERS	Yr	Days	Injury
Hamels, Cole	06	18	Left shoulder strain
	07	32	Strained pitching elbow
Hampson, Justin	08	64	Tendinitis Lt. shoulder
Hampton, Mike	08	118	Strained left pectoral muscle
Harang, Aaron	04	24	Sprained ligament, right elbow
	08	28	Strained pitching forearm
Harden, Rich	05	38	Strained left oblique
	06	146	Sprain Rt elbow; back strain
	07	151	Strained pitching shoulder x 2
	08	37	Strained Rt. subscapularis muscle
Hawkins, LaTroy	05	24	Right ulnar neuritis
	07	31	Inflammation in pitching elbow
Hendrickson, Mark	05	16	Left shoulder stiffness
	06	18	Left shoulder tightness
Henn, Sean	08	31	Inflammation Lt shoulder
Hensley, Clay	07	34	Strained groin; Labrum surgery
	08	68	Strained Rt. Shoulder
Herges, Matt	08	15	Lower back stiffness
Hernandez, Felix	07	26	Strained flexor muscle - right forearm
	08	16	Sprained left ankle
Hernandez, Orlando	04	103	Recovery from right shoulder surgery
	05	50	Strained right shoulder x 2
	07	30	Bursitis in pitching shoulder
	08	16	Sprained left ankle
Hill, Rich	08	30	Lower back soreness
Hill, Shawn	06	95	Right elbow soreness
	07	94	Strained left (non-throwing) shoulder
	08	117	Rt elbow (spurs) surgery 9/08; Forearm
Hirsh, Jason	07	84	Fractured right fibula; ankle
	08	74	Strained Rt. Shoulder
Hochevar, Luke	08	41	Ribcage contusion
Hoey, James	08	184	Biceps tendinitis/shoulder surgery 5/08
Hudson, Luke	05	66	Right shoulder strain
	07	182	Tendinitis right triceps x 2
	08	184	Ribcage contusion
Hudson, Tim	04	45	Left oblique strain
	05	32	Strained left oblique
	08	65	Torn ulnar collateral ligament - right elbow
Hughes, Philip	07	94	Strained left hamstring
	08	90	Fractured rib
Hurley, Eric	08	91	Strained Lt hamstring; sore Rt shoulder
Isringhausen, Jason	03	72	Sore right shoulder
	05	16	Strained right abdominal muscle
	08	73	Torn flexor tendon; Lacerated Rt hand
Jackson, Edwin	04	60	Strained right forearm
James, Chuck	06	32	Strained right hamstring
	07	15	Sore pitching shoulder
	08	10	Torn rotator cuff
Janssen, Casey	08	184	Torn labrum - Rt. Shoulder, surgery 3/08
Jenks, Bobby	08	18	Bursitis - left scapula area
Jennings, Jason	05	74	Fractured right finger
	07	91	Torn flexor tendon; elbow
	08	152	Irritated ulnar nerve - Rt elbow
Jimenez, Cesar	07	183	Stress Fx pitching elbow
Jiminez, Kelvin	08	17	Bruised right hand
Johnson, Jim	08	29	Impingement - right shoulder
Johnson, Josh	07	166	Tight pitching elbow; nueritis
	08	102	Tommy John surgery 8/2007
Johnson, Randy	03	98	Knee sprain; surgery
	07	134	Lower back pain x 3
	08	15	Recovery from back surgery
Johnson, Tyler	07	48	Tendinitis - left triceps
	08	184	R/C surgery 5/08
Jones, Todd	06	18	Pulled hamstring
	08	60	Inflammation right shoulder x 2
Julio, Jorge	07	17	Strained right calf
Jurrjens, Jair	07	16	Sore pitching shoulder
Karstens, Jeff	07	104	Fx right fibula; elbow
	08	50	Strained right groin
Kazmir, Scott	06	55	Lt shoulder sorenes x 2
	08	35	Strained Lt elbow
Kennedy, Ian	08	26	Strained right lat, bursitis, pitching shoulder
Kensing, Logan	05	130	Sore right elbow
	06	56	Right wrist flexor strain
	07	129	Tommy John surgery 8/2006
Kim, Byung-Hyun	04	26	Right shoulder strain
	06	27	Strained right hamstring
	07	27	Bruised Rt thumb

PITCHERS	Yr	Days	Injury
King,Ray	07	17	Tendinitis left shoulder
Kinney,Josh	07	184	Tommy John surgery 3/2007
	08	156	2 setbacks from 3/2007 TJS
Kuo,Hong-Chih	07	126	Irritation - left elbow x 2
Kuroda,Hiroki	08	19	Tendinitis - right shoulder
Lackey,John	08	44	Grade 2 strain, Rt. Triceps
Lawrence,Brian	06	182	Labrum - R/C surgery
	07	183	Labrum and R/C surgery 2/2006
League,Brandon	07	135	Strained lat; strained oblique
Lee,Cliff	07	32	Strained upper abdominal muscle
Leicester,Jon	07	66	Strained pitching shoulder
Lerew,Andrew	07	134	Ulnar nerve neuritis
	08	117	Tommy John surgery 7/2008
Lester,Jon	06	39	Lymphoma
	07	71	Recovery from lymphoma
Lidge,Brad	07	23	Stained left oblique
	08	6	Surgery (cartilage damage) Rt. Knee
Lieber,Jon	04	32	Groin strain
	06	38	Strained left groin
	07	110	Ruptured tendon Lt foot; oblique
	08	73	Strained Rt foot; Sprained Rt foot
Lilly,Ted	05	49	Left biceps tendinitis x 2
Linebrink,Scott	08	40	Inflamed subscapularis muscle
Liriano,Francisco	06	34	Sore left elbow and forearm
	07	183	Torn UCL - pitching elbow and surgery
Livingston,Bobby	07	40	Torn labrum - pitching shoulder
	08	109	Recovery from shoulder surgery
Loaiza,Esteban	06	40	Left shoulder and back strain
	07	143	Tightness in upper back; meniscus
	08	63	Inflamed Rt shoulder; Tight Rt shoulder
Loe,Kameron	06	45	Right elbow bone bruise
	07	14	Strained lower back
Looper,Braden	07	16	Strained pitching shoulder
Lopez,Rodrigo	07	106	Torn flexor tendon-pitching arm x 2
Loux,Shane	08	16	Oral surgery
Lowe,Mark	06	43	Right elbow tendinitis
	07	148	Sore right elbow; surgery
Lowry,Noah	06	31	Right oblique strain
	08	184	Lt forearm surgery
Lugo,Ruddy	06	23	Mid-back strain
Lyon,Brandon	04	182	Right elbow surgery
	05	92	Right elbow tendinitis
MacDougal,Mike	04	20	Stomach virus
	06	101	Right shoulder strain
	07	28	Inflamed pitching shoulder
Madson,Ryan	04	39	Sprained right finger
	07	81	Strained pitching shoulder; oblique
Mahay,Ron	05	16	Groin strain
	07	34	Strained ribcage muscle
	08	11	Plantar fasciitis - left foot
Maine,John	06	40	Inflammation in right middle finger
	08	46	Strained R/C, bone spur Rt shoulder
Marmol,Carlos	06	16	Right shoulder fatigue
Maroth,Mike	06	103	Bone chips, left elbow
	07	26	Tendinitis-pitching elbow
Marshall,Sean	06	40	Strained left oblique muscle
Marcum,Shaun	08	33	Strained pitching elbow
Marte,Damaso	05	17	Inflamed left trapezius
Martinez,Carlos	06	147	Right elbow strain; surgery
	07	183	Tommy John surgery 7/2006
Martinez,Pedro	06	60	Right hip inflammation; calf
	07	156	Rotator cuff surgery
	08	61	Strained Lt hamstring
Martin,Tom	07	23	Strained left groin
Mathis,Doug	08	84	Inflammation pitching shoulder
Mateo,Julio	04	50	Right elbow tendinitis
	06	56	Broken left hand; shoulder
Matsuzaka,Daisuke	08	24	Strained rotator cuff - right shoulder
Mathieson,Scott	06	29	Right elbow surgery
	07	183	Tommy John surgery 9/2006
	08	184	Setbacks from 2006 TJS
McCarthy,Brandon	07	53	Stress fx - Rt shoulder blade; blister
	08	146	inflammation Rt. Forearm/setback 4/08
McClung,Seth	04	126	Recovery from right elbow surgery
McGowan,Dustin	08	83	Frayed labrum, surgery 7/08
Meche,Gil	05	27	Right knee patellar tendinitis

FIVE-YEAR INJURY LOG

PITCHERS	Yr	Days	Injury
Mendoza,Luis	08	59	Inflammation Rt shoulder, Blister Rt hand
Mercker,Kent	08	119	Strained lower back
Mesa,Jose	07	16	Strained right groin
Messenger,Randy	07	28	fractured metatarsal-left hand
Miller,Andrew	07	20	Strained left hamstring
	08	49	Tendinitis in right patellar tendon
Miller,Justin	08	19	Inflammation - right elbow
Miller,Matt	05	79	Right forearm tightness
	06	138	Right elbow strain
	07	38	Strained right forearm
Miller,Trever	05	15	Right hamstring strain
	06	23	Left elbow sprain
Millwood,Kevin	04	37	Sprained ligament/tendon, Rt elbow
	05	21	Strained right groin
	07	50	Strained left hamstring x 2
	08	40	Strained right groin x 2
Miner,Zach	07	23	Tendinitis pitching shoulder
Mitre,Sergio	06	88	Right shoulder inflammation
	07	17	Torn callus on pitching hand
	08	184	Strained Rt. Forearm
Moehler,Brian	06	28	Sprained right ankle
Mosley,Dustin	08	22	Forearm stiffness pitching arm
Mota,Guillermo	05	26	Right elbow inflammation
Moylam,Peter	08	171	Soreness Rt. Elbow, TJS 5/08
Mulder,Mark	06	99	Lt shoulder soreness; surgery
	07	184	Recovery from shoulder surgery
	08	171	Recovery from shoulder surgery
Murray,A.J.	08	118	Strained rotator cuff - left shoulder
Mussina,Mike	04	42	Right elbow injury
	06	15	Groin strain
	07	22	Strained left hamstring
Myers,Brett	07	64	Soreness in pitching shoulder
Nelson,Joe	07	183	Shoulder surgery
Neshek,Pat	08	145	Partially torn UCL - Rt. Elbow
Nippert,Dustin	08	38	Blister - Rt foot
Nolasco,Ricky	07	119	Inflamed rt elbow x 2
Nunez,Leo	07	183	Hairline Fx - Rt wrist
	08	54	Strained right lat muscle
O'Connor,Mike	07	78	Elbow surgery 11/06
Ohka,Tomo	04	95	Fractured right forearm
	06	77	Partial right rotator cuff tear
Oliver,Darren	04	31	Tight left shoulder
Orvella,Chad	08	184	Surgery for impingement - Rt shoulder 5/08
Osoria,Franquelis	08	16	Bursitis - right ankle
Oswalt,Roy	06	15	Strained middle back
	08	16	Strained left abductor muscle
Otsuka,Akinori	07	74	Tightness pitching forearm
Owens,Henry	07	132	Inflamed pitching shoulder x 2
	08	184	Surgery to repair torn R/C Rt. Shoulder
Owings,Micah	07	15	Strained right hamstring
Padilla,Vicente	04	72	Right triceps tendinitis
	05	15	Right triceps tendinitis
	07	54	Strained right triceps
	08	30	Strained Lt hamstring; Strained neck
Park,Chan Ho	04	98	Strained lower back
	06	49	Abdominal pain; intestinal bleeding
Paronto,Chad	07	16	Strained right groin
Parra,Manny	07	21	Displaced chip fracture - left thumb
Parrish,John	05	27	Right elbow strain
	06	182	Recovery from left elbow surgery
Patterson,John	04	78	Right groin strain
	05	15	Lower back spasms
	06	146	Right forearm strain; surgery
	07	148	Strained right biceps
Patton,Troy	08	184	Torn labrum
Pauley,David	06	34	Strained right forearm
Paulino,Felipe	08	184	Pinched nerve in upper pitching arm
Pavano,Carl	05	97	Right shoulder tendinitis
	06	182	Back strain, bone chips in right elbow
	07	174	Torn ulnar collateral ligament
	08	145	Tommy John surgery 8/2007
Peavy,Jake	04	43	Strained tendon, right forearm
	08	28	Strained Rt elbow
Penny,Brad	04	44	Strained right biceps
	05	19	Nerve irritation - right arm
	08	95	Inflammation Rt shoulder

PITCHERS	Yr	Days	Injury
Penn,Hayden	06	58	Appendicitis
Percival,Troy	04	25	Right elbow inflammation
	05	113	Torn forearm muscle x 2
	06	182	Partial tear, right flexor pronator
	08	52	Strained Lt hamstring x 2; Sore Rt knee
Perez,Odalis	04	20	Inflamed left rotator cuff
	05	88	Lt shoulder soreness; oblique
	07	43	Strained left knee
	08	15	Tendinitis - left shoulder
Perez,Oliver	05	68	Fractured left big toe
	07	18	Lower back stiffness
Perkins,Glen	07	112	Strained teres major muscle
Pettitte,Andy	04	102	Strained elbow x 2; surgery
	08	6	Backs spasms
Pineiro,Joel	04	70	Right elbow strain
	05	11	Sore right shoulder
	07	15	Sprained right ankle
	08	36	Sore Rt shoulder; Sore Rt groin
Pinto,Renyel	07	42	Strained left shoulder
	08	15	Strained left hamstring
Prior,Mark	04	61	Inflamed right Achilles tendon
	05	38	Fractured right elbow; inflamed
	06	122	Rt shoulder tendinitis, strain x 2
	07	183	Right shoulder surgery
	08	184	Surgery repaired torn capsule Rt shoulder
Proctor,Scott	08	71	Tendinitis pitching elbow
Putz,J.J.	08	57	Costochondritis; Hyperextended Rt. elbow
Ramirez,Horacio	04	122	Left shoulder tendinitis
	06	105	Sprained finger; left hamstring strain
	07	51	Tendinitis pitching shoulder
Ramirez,Ramon (KC)	07	48	Inflammation right elbow x 2
Rapada,Clay	08	18	Biceps tendinitis Lt arm
Rasner,Darrell	06	83	Right shoulder tendinitis
	07	11	Fractured right index finger
Rauch,Jon	04	31	Left oblique strain
	05	103	Torn right labrum
Ray,Chris	07	72	Bone spur pitching elbow
	08	184	Tommy John surgery 8/2007
Redding,Tim	05	44	Strained right shoulder
Redman,Mark	06	13	Torn left knee cartilage
	07	16	Toe infection
Reyes,Al	07	15	Strained rotator cuff
	08	38	Tendinitis pitching shoulder
Reyes,Anthony	08	19	Strained pitching elbow
Reyes,Dennys	07	64	Inflamed elbow; shoulder
Rheinecker,John	07	65	Back spasms
	08	184	Thoracic outlet syndrome surgery 5/08
Riske,David	06	47	Lower back strain
	08	35	Hyperextended Rt elbow
Robertson,Connor	07	132	Fractured right thumb
Robertson,Nate	07	20	Tired pitching arm
Rodney,Fernando	04	183	Right elbow sprain
	05	66	Right shoulder inflammation
	07	56	Tendinitis Rt shoulder; biceps
	08	78	Tendinitis Rt. shoulder
Rodriguez,Francisco	05	17	Strained right forearm
Rodriguez,Wandy	08	38	Strained Lt. groin
Rogers,Kenny	07	123	Tendinitis Lt elbow; blood clot
Rosario,Francisco	07	107	Strained pitching shoulder
	08	184	Strained pitching shoulder
Rupe,Josh	06	87	Left elbow inflammation
	07	107	Sore pitching elbow
Ryan,BJ	07	169	Strained pitching elbow
	08	14	Tommy John surgery 5/2007
Saarloos,Kirk	04	66	Bone spur in right elbow
Sabathia,C.C.	05	13	Strained right oblique muscle
	06	30	Strained right oblique muscle
Sampson,Chris	07	29	Sprained ulnar collateral ligament
Saito,Takashi	08	31	Sprained pitching elbow
Sanchez,Anibal	08	123	Labrum surgery 6/2007 Rt. Shoulder
Sanchez,Duaner	06	64	Separated right shoulder
	07	184	Shoulder surg, Fx bone Rt. Shoulder
	08	16	Rehab of Rt shoulder surgery
Sanchez,Humberto	07	183	Tommy John surgery - 5/2007
	08	162	Recovery from TJS

FIVE-YEAR INJURY LOG

PITCHERS	Yr	Days	Injury
Sanchez,Jonathan	07	23	Strained rib cage muscle
	08	20	Strained left shoulder
Santos,Victor	06	25	Right rotator cuff strain
Sarfate,Dennis	08	20	Fractured clavicle
Schilling,Curt	05	90	Bruise Rt ankle; ankle pain
	07	48	Sore pitching shoulder
	08	191	Torn right biceps tendon
Schmidt,Jason	04	12	Right shoulder stiffness
	05	16	Strained right shoulder
	07	157	R/C surgery; bursitis
	08	184	Torn right biceps tendon
Schoeneweis,Scott	04	71	Inflamed Lt elbow; surgery
Seanez,Rudy	05	35	Right shoulder strain
	08	15	Strained pitching shoulder
Seay,Bobby	05	49	Strained left pectoral muscle
Seo,Jae	06	15	Left groin strain
Sheets,Ben	05	74	Torn back muscle; virus
	06	96	Rt shoulder strain; tendinitis
	07	45	Sprained index finger right hand
Shields,Scot	08	6	Strained Rt. Shoulder
Sherrill,George	04	17	Fatigue
	08	26	Inflammation left shoulder
Shouse,Brian	04	39	Inflamed left rotator cuff
	06	16	Strained right calf
Sisco,Andrew	08	185	Recovery from Tommy John surgery
Silva,Carlos	05	15	Torn meniscus in right knee
	08	15	Tendinitis right shoulder
Slaten,Doug	08	25	Strained right knee
Slowey,Kevin	08	25	Strained biceps muscle Rt arm
Smoltz,John	07	15	Inflamed pitching shoulder
	08	161	Torn labrum; Inflammed Trap; Rt biceps
Snell,Ian	08	15	Strained pitching elbow
Soriano,Rafael	04	147	Right elbow surgery
	05	154	Recovery from right elbow surgery
	06	15	Right shoulder fatigue
	08	154	Inflammation Rt elbow x 2
Soria,Joakim	07	15	Inflammation right shoulder
Sosa,Jorge	07	14	Strained left hamstring
Speier,Justin	04	28	Right elbow soreness
	06	32	Right forearm tightness
	07	74	Intestinal virus
Speier,Ryan	08	22	Bruised rotator cuff Rt shoulder
Springer,Russ	08	16	Irritated ulnar nerve Rt. Elbow
Stauffer,Tim	08	184	Torn Labrum/surgery 5/08
Street,Huston	06	20	Strained right groin
	07	71	Irritated pitching elbow
Suppan,Jeff	08	15	Irritation right elbow
Tallet,Brian	04	113	Recovery from left elbow surgery
	08	19	Fractured toe - right foot
Tankersley,Taylor	07	10	Shoulder tendinitis
Tata,Jordan	08	22	Fractured metacarpal bone right hand
Timlin,Mike	06	18	Strained right shoulder
	07	45	Tendinitis Rt shoulder; oblique
	08	35	Tendinitis Lt knee; Cut finger Rt hand
Thompson,Brad	08	57	Inflamed pitching elbow
Threets,Erick	08	44	Intercostal strain -right side
Tomko,Brett	04	16	Right elbow inflammation
	06	33	Strained left oblique
	08	49	Strained right elbow
Torres,Salomon	07	56	Inflamed Rt elbow x 2
Traber,Billy	04	183	Recovery from left elbow surgery
Trachsel,Steve	05	141	Herniated disc, lower back
	07	21	Strain gluteus muscle
Valdez,Merkin	07	183	Tommy John surgery 10/06
	08	138	Strained right shoulder
Valverde,Jose	04	112	Right shoulder tendinitis
	05	28	Right biceps tendinitis
VanBenschoten,John	05	185	Torn right labrum
	06	135	Recovery from right shoulder surgery
Vargas,Claudio	05	37	Right elbow sprain
	07	15	Lower back spasms
Vargas,Jason	07	9	Bone spur Rt elbow
	08	184	Left hip surgery (labrum) 3/08
Veras,Jose	07	136	Inflammation right arm

PITCHERS	Yr	Days	Injury
Villarreal, Oscar	04	147	Right flexor strain
	05	144	Right rotator cuff strain
Villone, Ron	07	14	Strained lower back
Vizcaino, Luis	08	64	Strained Rt. Shoulder
Wade, Cory	08	19	Inflammation right shoulder
Waechter, Doug	08	19	Strained rotator cuff - right shoulder
Wagner, Billy	04	75	Strained Lt R/C; groin
	08	58	Sprained left forearm
Wagner, Ryan	05	87	Right shoulder inflammation
	07	147	Torn labrum
	08	124	Labrum surgery 6/07
Wakefield, Tim	06	57	Stress fracture in rib cage
	08	18	Soreness - pitching shoulder
Wainwright, Adam	08	75	Sprained middle finger - right hand
Walker, Jaime	08	32	Inflammation pitching elbow
Walker, Tyler	05	18	Right shoulder inflammation
	06	111	Right elbow surgery
	07	183	Tommy John surgery 7/06
Wang, Chien-Ming	05	59	Right shoulder inflammation
	07	23	Strained right hamstring
	08	106	Lisfranc sprain, torn tendon - right foot
Washburn, Jarrod	04	43	Inflammation of chest ligament
	05	18	Left forearm strain
Weathers, David	08	15	Ulnar neuritis pitching elbow
Weaver, Jeff	07	29	Inflammation in pitching shoulder
Weaver, Jered	07	16	Tendinitis right biceps
Wellemeyer, Todd	04	55	Right shoulder strain
	07	81	Sore pitching elbow
Wells, Kip	04	22	Right elbow inflammation
	06	127	Sprained Rt foot; blood clot
	08	83	Blood clot Rt hand

FIVE-YEAR INJURY LOG

PITCHERS	Yr	Days	Injury
Westbrook, Jake	07	52	Strained left internal oblique muscle
	08	162	Tommy John surgery 06/08
Willis, Dontrelle	08	38	Hyperextended Rt. Knee
Wilson, C.J.	06	11	Right hamstring strain
	08	53	Bone spurs - left elbow, surgery 8/08
Wise, Matt	05	23	Strained left intercostal
	06	49	Right elbow surgery
	08	167	Bruise Rt forearm; weak Rt shoulder
Wolf, Randy	04	59	Lt elbow tendinitis x 2
	05	113	Left elbow surgery
	06	118	Recovery from left elbow surgery
	07	89	Soreness -pitching shoulder
Wolfe, Brian	08	48	Strained triceps Rt. Arm
Wood, Kerry	04	52	Tendinitis, lower right triceps
	05	108	Strained Rt shoulder; surgery
	06	162	Post surgical; R/C tear
	07	124	Shoulder stiffness
	08	22	Blister on pitching hand
Wright, Jamey	07	66	Inflamed right shoulder
Yabu, Keichi	08	16	Sprained middle finger - right hand
Yates, Tyler	05	182	Torn rotator cuff
Young, Chris	07	15	Strained left oblique
	08	89	Strained right forearm; nasal fractures
Zagurski, Mike	07	43	Pulled left hamstring
	08	184	Tommy John surgery 4/08
Zambrano, Victor	04	47	Right elbow inflammation
	06	148	Torn right elbow tendon
	07	60	Strained pitching forearm
Zambrano, Carlos	08	15	Strained right shoulder
Zumaya, Joel	07	107	Ruptured tendon right middle finger
	08	130	Recovery from surgery on Rt. Shoulder

IV.
PROSPECTS

Top Prospects for 2009

by Deric McKamey

Nick Adenhart (RHP, LAA) got out of the gate strong enough to earn a couple of spot starts for the Angels, but after getting bombed (9.00 ERA), he was never the same, going 9-13 with a 5.76 ERA, a 1.4 Cmd, 6.8 Dom, and a .306 oppBA in Triple-A. The high offensive environment didn't help, but his command was spotty and he didn't show much movement to his 88-93 MPH fastball and plus curveball.

Jake Arrieta (RHP, BAL) led the Carolina League (high Class-A) with a 2.87 ERA and showed solid base skills (2.4 Cmd, 9.6 Dom, and a .199 oppBA), earning the Pitcher of the Year award. A big-bodied starter with excellent arm strength, velocity (87-95 MPH), and two solid comps (slider and change-up), he repeated his drop-and-drive delivery more consistently and should arrive quickly.

Jimmy Barthmaier (RHP, PIT) resurrected his prospect status, establishing better fastball command and gaining trust in his secondary pitches, A strong-framed pitcher who throws hard (89-94 MPH), he went 5-6 with a 4.02 ERA, a 2.3 Cmd, 8.0 Dom, and a .237 oppBA between Triple and Double-A. His versatility allows him to be used in multiple ways, but he will be vying for a rotation spot.

Brian Bogusevic (OF, HOU) was drafted in the first round as a pitcher, but after three seasons of struggles on the mound, he made the transition to outfield, proceeding to hit .347/.432/.537 with a 0.80 Eye in 147 at-bats between Double and high Class-A. He has a classic LH swing with power and judges the strike zone well. It would not be surprising to see him make the Majors in 2009.

Michael Bowden (RHP, BOS) has been able to win and miss bats using pitch movement, command (4.1 Cmd), and deception, as opposed to overwhelming velocity (88-92 MPH). His curveball and circle-change are very advanced for his age and he went 9-7 with a 2.62 ERA, 8.1 Dom, and a .212 oppBA between Triple and Double-A. He should be the first starter recalled by Boston once the season starts.

Reid Brignac (SS, TAM) is about as enigmatic as prospects get, showing strong offense and marginal defense in the low minors, but reversing that trend at the upper levels. He hit .250/.299/.412 with a poor 0.27 Eye, but did show some power (26 doubles/9 HR). He moves well at shortstop with solid range, soft hands, and average arm strength. If his bat comes through in spring training, he could become the starter.

Trevor Cahill (RHP, OAK) elevated his prospect status immensely, proving to be an extreme groundball artist, but able to miss bats as well. He throws a very heavy, 86-93 MPH fastball and has two breaking pitches that he can go to. He went 11-5 with a 2.61 ERA, a 2.7 Cmd, 9.8 Dom, and a .179 oppBA between Triple and Double-A, and could have immediate impact when he makes his debut.

Carlos Carrasco (RHP, PHI) seems to get less respect the closer he gets to the Majors. However, he improved his overall game, showing better fastball command and trust in his comps (curveball and change-up). He can hit 94 MPH with his fastball and does a nice job of repeating his arm speed, but does tend to pitch with effort. Between Triple and Double-A, he went 9-9 with a 3.69 ERA, a 2.7 Cmd, 9.2 Dom, and a .253 oppBA.

Chris Coghlan (2B, FLA) makes the most out of his average tools and played well enough at Double-A that the Marlins could entertain moving incumbent 2B Dan Uggla to another position. The left-handed hitter can hit for average (.298) and will draw walks, giving him a solid .396 OBP. His power is limited to doubles (32), but he can handle the bat. Defensively, he makes the plays he gets to.

Daniel Cortes (RHP, KC) built on his strong '07 campaign by experiencing an increase in velocity, which helped him make the jump to Double-A. He went 10-4 with a 3.78 ERA, a 2.0 Cmd, 8.4 Dom, and a .241 oppBA. His tall frame allows him to generate good downhill plane to his pitches, which includes an 88-95 MPH fastball, curveball, and change-up. He will compete for a rotation spot by mid-season.

Aaron Cunningham (OF, OAK) has always been better than the sum of his parts, and though he is unlikely to be an All-Star, he keeps producing and providing value. Between Triple and Double-A, he hit .329/.400/.532 with 17 HR, 15 SB, and a 0.45 Eye, and hit .250 for the Athletics in September. His arm strength and average range can play at any outfield spot, but he likely begins 2009 in a platoon.

Wade Davis (RHP, TAM) may have the best pure arm strength of the Rays' pitching prospects, being able to maintain his 87-94 MPH fastball deep into games. He will cut his fastball to right-handed batters and he shows off an impressive curveball. His delivery needs to be repeated more often, which will help both his command (2.1 Cmd) and change-up. Between Triple and Double-A, he went 13-8 with a 3.47 ERA, 7.6 Dom, and a .243 oppBA.

Chris Dickerson (OF, CIN) hit much better for the Reds (.304 in 102 at-bats) than he ever did in the minors and provided the team with some much-needed spark. He is very athletic, possessing good speed and moderate power. At Triple-A, he hit .287/.384/.479 with 11 HR, 26 SB, and a 0.53 Eye. He can play all three outfield spots, but may be better suited for a fourth outfielder role.

Scott Elbert (LHP, LA) made a slow, but successful recovery from off-season shoulder surgery, regaining his fastball velocity (89-94 MPH) and movement to his curveball and change-up. Used in relief initially, he was recalled to make a spot-start for the Dodgers, only to be returned to the bullpen, where he may stay. In 41.1 innings at Double-A, he posted a 2.40 ERA, a 2.3 Cmd, 10.0 Dom, and a .157 oppBA.

Alcides Escobar (SS, MIL) is known for his plus defense that includes outstanding arm strength, range, and soft hands. The Venezuelan has also turned himself into an asset offensively, hitting .328/.363/.434 with eight HR and a 0.38 Eye at Double-A. Though he has a tendency to strike out, he should hit for average and will steal bases (34 SB) with his above average speed. J.J. Hardy could be traded to make room for him.

Dexter Fowler (OF, COL) has the makings of an all-around player and is beginning to put everything in place. He has plus speed and the swing mechanics to hit for both power and batting average. He judges the strike zone well (0.73 Eye), though his swing can get long. He hit .335/.431/.515 with nine HR and 20 SB in Double-A, and will be given a shot to win the everyday CF role with a good spring training.

Mat Gamel (3B, MIL) tore up the high minors (.325/.392/.531 with 35 doubles, 19 HR and 99 RBI) with a passive-aggressive approach that should make him a run producer in the Majors. He has a tendency to strike out, but will draw his share of walks. His indifferent defense presents problems on where to play him, as the positions he could possibly play are locked up by strong incumbents.

Gio Gonzalez (LHP, OAK) continued his streaky tendencies, being a world-beater one moment, but then struggling the next outing. His 12-6 curveball helps him register strikeouts, and he keeps hitters honest with his 85-92 MPH sinker. He tended to nibble too much at the Major League level (7.68 ERA), but was solid in Triple-A, going 8-7 with a 4.24 ERA, a 2.2 Cmd, 9.4 Dom, and a .233 oppBA.

Tommy Hanson (RHP, ATL) had as many dominating moments as any pitcher in the minors, and finished 11-5 with a 2.41 ERA, a 3.1 Cmd, 10.6 Dom, and a .175 oppBA between Double and high Class-A. A tall, projectable pitcher, he keeps the ball down with his 88-95 MPH sinker and can throw strikes with all three of his comps. He will be given the chance to earn the fifth rotation spot.

J.A. Happ (LHP, PHI) finds a way to miss bats (10.1 Dom and .234 oppBA) despite marginal velocity (84-91 MPH). He uses a three-pitch arsenal with excellent command (3.2 Cmd) and a deceptive delivery to fool hitters and induce ground balls. At Triple-A, he went 8-7 with a 3.60 ERA, and spun a 3.69 ERA in 8 appearances for the Phillies. He has the inside track for the fifth rotation spot.

Derek Holland (LHP, TEX) came out of nowhere, sporting a 90-96 MPH fastball that has plus movement. He posted one of the top seasons in the minors, going 13-1 with a 2.27 ERA, a 3.9 Cmd, 9.4 Dom, and a .209 oppBA at three levels. Improving both his slider and change-up was the key to success, as well as gaining better fastball command. He could be a factor by mid-season if his improvements are for real.

Eric Hurley (RHP, TEX) might have exhausted his rookie status, having taken the fifth rotation spot with a 5.47 ERA, but encountered some shoulder inflammation that ended his season. His 5.30 ERA was not impressive and he was hittable (.285 oppBA), but his command (2.5 Cmd) and dominance (8.7 Dom) were there. He can throw all three pitches for strikes and has the arm action and repeatable delivery to improve.

Will Inman (RHP, SD) takes his knocks for having an unconventional, high-effort delivery and being primarily a flyball pitcher, but all he does is win and miss bats. At Double-A, he went 9-8 with a 3.52 ERA, a 2.0 Cmd, 9.3 Dom, and a .234 oppBA. He battles at all times and has a very durable arm, which allows him to get the most out of his 86-91 MPH fastball, curveball, and slider.

Travis Ishikawa (1B, SF) resurrected his prospect status by improving his plate discipline, which in turn, allowed his power to play up and gave him a strong batting average. He hit .299/.377/.578 with 35 doubles and 24 HR between Triple and Double-A, and hit .274 over the last two months in the bigs. He has a very picturesque swing and complements his offense by being a very smooth defender.

Eddie Kunz (RHP, NYM) didn't provide the relief that the Mets needed down the stretch (13.50 ERA) when called-up, but was solid at the Triple and Double-A levels, saving 27 games with a 3.33 ERA, 7.8 Dom, and a .238 oppBA. He is tough on RH batters with his 89-94 MPH fastball and slider, and only allowed one HR, but his command was very inconsistent and may be relegated to setup work.

Matt LaPorta (OF/1B, CLE) was the big prize for dealing C.C. Sabathia at the July 31 trading deadline. The right-handed slugger provides pole-to-pole power with excellent bat speed and strike zone judgment. He only got 362 at-bats in Double-A due to playing for Team USA, but he hit .279/.386/.539 with 22 HR and a 0.66 Eye. His defense is a little stretched for the corner outfield, so he may be given a chance to win the 1B job.

Lou Marson (C, PHI) is one of the more athletic catchers in the minors and is rated a strong defender based on his arm strength, agility, and receiving skills. On offense, he is a good contact hitter who will draw walks, though his power is limited to doubles. At Double-A, he hit .314/.433/.416 with a 0.97 Eye, and could start 2009 in a shared role behind the plate.

Cameron Maybin (OF, FLA) was hoping to play a huge role for the Marlins in 2008, but struggled during spring training and spent most of the year in Double-A, where he hit .277/.375/.456 with 13 HR, 21 SB, and a 0.47 Eye. His tools are impressive, showing the ability to hit for power, run, and play solid defense in CF. As a precursor to 2009, he hit extremely well during his September call-up (.500 BA in 32 at-bats).

Andrew McCutchen (OF, PIT), based on talent and performance, probably deserved a chance to play in the Majors in 2008, but the Pirates were rewarded for their patience as he blossomed in Triple-A (.283/.372/.398 with nine HR and 34 SB). He is a high-energy player with plus speed, hitting ability, and solid defense in CF. He will get a chance to open as the Pirates' leadoff hitter.

James McDonald (RHP, LA) is a very athletic pitcher with solid average stuff and the performance to back it up. Between Triple and Double-A, he went 7-4 with a 3.26 ERA, a 2.6 Cmd, 9.0 Dom, and a .223 oppBA. His 88-93 MPH fastball, curveball, and change-up are all quality pitches. He does tend to pitch up in the zone, though that is less of an issue at Dodgers Stadium.

Kam Mickolio (RHP, BAL) presents an intimidating force with his 6'9" height and ability to touch 95 MPH with his fastball. He cuts his fastball and has a devastating slider that checks right-handed batters effectively. Between Triple and Double-A, he saved three games with a 3.70 ERA, a 3.0 Cmd, 9.7 Dom, and a .232 oppBA. He could thrive in a setup role immediately, and could close if his change-up develops.

Adam Miller (RHP, CLE) spent more time on the disabled list than on the mound, which is becoming more and more frequent. This time, finger tendon surgery limited him to six starts and 28.2 innings in Triple-A, where he posted a 1.88 ERA. The Indians are going to bring him to camp as a reliever, where he will unleash his 89-97 MPH fastball and nasty slider, in order to stabilize an erratic bullpen. He has the goods to close if left in that role.

Jason Motte (RHP, STL), in only his third year on the mound after being drafted as a catcher, possessed the most dominant set of base skills of any Triple-A reliever (4.2 Cmd, 14.9 Dom, and a .245 oppBA). Armed with an 88-98 MPH fastball and diving slider, he aggressively attacks hitters and actually pitched better in his brief stint for the Cardinals (0.82 ERA/13.1 Dom), making him a cinch to land a bullpen job in 2009.

Dan Murphy (2B/3B/OF, NYM) has always been able to hit, showing good bat speed and plate discipline. Between Double-A and short-season ball, he hit .315/.379/.496 with 13 HR, 14 SB, and a 0.81 Eye, and hit .313 for the Mets. Finding him a position has proven difficult, as he has played 2B, 3B, 1B, and LF, all at a below average level. He should open 2009 as the Mets' primary pinch-hitter/utilityman.

Jeff Niemann (RHP, TAM) once again battled an injury (shoulder), but rebounded strong and even made two spot starts for Tampa Bay. The tall, strong-framed pitcher went 9-5 with a 3.59 ERA, a 2.6 Cmd, 8.7 Dom, and a .207 oppBA at Triple-A, mowing down hitters with an 88-96 MPH fastball, two solid breaking pitches (knuckle-curve and slider), and the ability to change speeds.

Bud Norris (RHP, HOU) could impact the Astros' bullpen if the team will let him make the switch to relief. A strong-framed pitcher with excellent arm strength and velocity (90-95 MPH), he was mediocre as a starter in Double-A, going 3-8 with a 4.05 ERA, a 2.7 Cmd, 9.5 Dom, and a .286 oppBA. A newfound slider gave him a reliable second pitch, but he missed part of the season with an elbow strain.

David Price (LHP, TAM) enters 2009 as the top pitching prospect in baseball, featuring projectable size and incredible stuff. His 89-95 MPH fastball and hard slider are lethal pitches to any hitter, and to top it off, he knows how to pitch. Between Double and high Class-A, he went an astounding 12-1 with a 2.30 ERA, a 3.4 Cmd, 9.0 Dom, and a .228 oppBA, and should open 2009 in the Rays' rotation.

Max Ramirez (C/1B, TEX) made the most of a Taylor Teagarden injury to leap to the Majors, where he became an instant offensive success before cooling-down (.217 BA). He generates good bat speed through natural strength, and makes such good contact that he hit .347/.439/.628 with 19 HR at three levels. On defense, he is below average in most areas, but could make the Rangers' roster in a C/1B/DH role.

Colby Rasmus (OF, STL) was supposed to be manning CF for St. Louis during the year, but was inconsistent at the plate and suffered a minor knee injury in the second half. At Triple-A, he hit .251/.346/.396 with 11 HR, 15 SB, and a 0.68 Eye, proving that he wasn't quite ready. His offensive skills are diverse and he plays outstanding defense. The Cardinals hope he plays his way into their starting lineup.

Nolan Reimold (OF, BAL) is an underrated power hitter, possessing good bat speed and the ability to drive to all fields. He hit .284/.367/.501 with 25 HR and a 0.77 Eye at Double-A, showing improvement in all facets of his offense. His average speed gives him adequate range in the outfield and shows a very strong arm. He'll be in line for at least a platoon role to start 2009.

Jeff Samardzija (RHP, CHC) has elevated his game at every promotion, even though his numbers suggested otherwise. He had an ordinary 4.29 ERA between Triple and Double-A, including marginal base skills (1.4 Cmd, 6.7 Dom, and .248 oppBA), but thrived in the Cubs' bullpen (2.28 ERA), where he even closed with Kerry Wood out. The tall, athletic pitcher features an 88-95 MPH fastball and nasty slider.

Jordan Schafer (OF, ATL) missed a third of the season serving a 50-game suspension for PED usage. He started out slowly, creating naysayers, but rebounded strong. At Double-A, he hit .269/.378/.471 with ten HR, 12 SB, and a 0.56 Eye. He remains a solid talent, with moderate power, above average speed, and plus defense in CF, and will be in competition for a starting role during spring training.

James Simmons (RHP, OAK) pitched at Double-A all season, only a year removed from college, and was solid, going 9-6 with a 3.51 ERA, a 3.8 Cmd, 7.9 Dom, and a .282 oppBA. Extremely polished, being able to mix his pitches with outstanding command, he kept hitters off balance using his 86-93 MPH fastball, slider, curveball, and change-up. His upside isn't high, but he is durable and can pitch tons of innings.

Travis Snider (OF, TOR) made a light-speed ascension through the minors, culminating with at-bats in Toronto, where he hit .301. His short, muscular build, impressive bat speed, and ability to center the baseball gives him outstanding power and the ability to hit for aveage. At three levels, he hit .275/.358/.481 with 23 HR, and 91 RBI. He does tend to strike out and is only a fringe-average defender in the corner outfield.

Taylor Teagarden (C, TEX), based on his defense and power potential, has a chance to be an impact player in the Majors. Defensively, he has excellent receiving skills and a strong throwing arm. His contact ability is sporadic, but he will draw walks and has solid power to the pull field. He hit only .211/.319/.374 with nine HR between Triple and Double-A, but was impressive for Texas, hitting .319 with a .809 SLG.

Daryl Thompson (RHP, CIN) catapulted across three levels, going 8-4 with a 2.70 ERA, a 3.3 Cmd, 7.0 Dom, and a .231 oppBA, which earned him a shot at the Reds' fifth rotation spot. After three starts (6.91 ERA) he came down with some shoulder inflammation that grounded him the rest of the season. His 88-95 MPH fastball and solid complementary pitches puts him in line for a starting role.

Ryan Tucker (RHP, FLA) possesses one of the better fastballs in the Marlins' system, registering 90-96 MPH and showing explosive life. He pitched a fair number of innings in the Majors with sporadic results, but was incredible at Double-A, sporting a 1.58 ERA, a 2.0 Cmd, 7.3 Dom, and a .195 oppBA. He can fill multiple roles, but will need a strong spring training to earn a rotation spot.

Luis Valbuena (2B, SEA) has shifted over to 2B from his natural SS, where his diminishing range and stiff hands are less of an issue. His offense is the best part of his game, showing moderate power, batting average ability, excellent plate discipline (0.84 Eye), and above average speed. Between Triple and Double-A, he hit .303/.382/.431 with 11 HR and 18 SB, and may be given a shot at 2B or as the Mariners' utility infielder.

Matt Wieters (C, BAL) reigns as the top prospect in baseball. The switch-hitter torched Double and high Class-A, hitting .355/.454/.600 with 27 HR, 91 RBI, and a 1.08 Eye, and will be a force in the middle of the lineup at his peak. His receiving skills and arm strength are outstanding, but his height causes mobility problems. He should be the starter by the All-Star break.

Jordan Zimmermann (RHP, WAS) has quietly emerged as the Nationals' top pitching prospect, vaulting over more heralded hurlers. Movement is the name of his game, with his smooth arm action and repeatable delivery that makes his 88-93 MPH fastball, change-up, and slider play up. Between Double and high Class-A, he went 10-3 with a 2.89 ERA, a 2.9 Cmd, 9.0 Dom, and a .215 oppBA.

The Top Ranked Prospects for Impact in 2009

David Price (LHP, TAM)
Cameron Maybin (OF, FLA)
Andrew McCutchen (OF, PIT)
Travis Snider (OF, TOR)
Taylor Teagarden (C, TEX)
Colby Rasmus (OF, STL)
Matt Wieters (C, BAL)
Adam Miller (RHP, CLE)
Jason Motte (RHP, STL)
Jordan Zimmermann (RHP, WAS)

Jeff Samardzija (RHP, CHC)
Tommy Hanson (RHP, ATL)
Chris Dickerson (OF, CIN)
Ryan Tucker (RHP, FLA)
James McDonald (RHP, LAD)
Trevor Cahill (RHP, OAK)
Dan Murphy (2B/3B/OF, NYM)
Gio Gonzalez (LHP, OAK)
Jeff Niemann (RHP, TAM)
Dexter Fowler (OF, COL)

Jordan Schafer (OF, ATL)
Matt LaPorta (OF/1B, CLE)
Alcides Escobar (SS, MIL)
Aaron Cunningham (OF, OAK)
Travis Ishikawa (1B, SF)
Nolan Reimold (OF, BAL)
Eric Hurley (RHP, TEX)
Lou Marson (C, PHI)
JA Happ (LHP, PHI)
Nick Adenhart (RHP, LAA)

Scott Elbert (LHP, LAD)
Daryl Thompson (RHP, CIN)
Reid Brignac (SS, TAM)
Max Ramirez (C/1B, TEX)
Carlos Carrasco (RHP, PHI)
Eddie Kunz (RHP, NYM)
Mat Gamel (3B, MIL)
Kam Mickolio (RHP, BAL)
Chris Coghlan (2B, FLA)
Will Inman (RHP, SD)

Derek Holland (LHP, TEX)
James Simmons (RHP, OAK)
Daniel Cortes (RHP, KC)
Michael Bowden (RHP, BOS)
Brian Bogusevic (OF, HOU)
Wade Davis (RHP, TAM)
Jake Arrieta (RHP, BAL)
Luis Valbuena (2B, SEA)
Jimmy Barthmaier (RHP, PIT)
Bud Norris (RHP, HOU)

Top Japanese Prospects
by Tom Mulhall

Shinnosuke Abe (C, Yomiuri Giants) is a 28 year-old on Japan's most popular team. A solid defender, he has some power and a .360 career OBA. However, he plays for a team that does not post, and signed a new contract before the 2008 season making him the highest paid catcher in Japan. There is no indication he is interested in coming to MLB. *Possible ETA: 2010*

Norichika Aoki (OF, Yakult Swallows) could be the best position player on this list, and was just about the only Japanese hitter who hit well in the Olympics. However, he has just four years of service time towards free agency. Think "Ichiro-lite": high BA, plenty of speed and good defense. Aoki has expressed an interest in MLB "down the road" and his team will post (having previously posted Akinori Iwamura). Despite falling on hard times financially, it would still be surprising if the Swallows posted Aoki soon since he is their only marquee player. If you can afford to stash him on reserve for a few years, it may be worth the wait. *Possible ETA: 2010 but more likely 2011.*

Yu Darvish (RHP, Nippon Ham Fighters) is a hugely talented young pitcher who has posted two sub-2.00 ERA seasons in a row. He unanimously won the Sawamura Award in 2007, Japan's equivalent of the Cy Young. Half Iranian, some journalists wonder if he would feel comfortable playing in the U.S. With only three years of service time, he could be years away from MLB, but his owners may not be able to resist the huge posting fee they could be offered. *Possible ETA: 2010 at the earliest.*

Kyuji Fujikawa (RHP, Hanshin Tigers) is a very capable young closer whose team previously posted Kei Igawa. He has the talent to succeed in MLB, but it would be surprising if he is posted any time soon since he only has a few years' service time. His owner, however, has indicated he will never post Fujikawa. *Possible ETA: 2011 at the earliest with 2012 or later more likely.*

Hirokaza Ibata (SS, Chunichi Dragons) believes he is the best shortstop in Japan, which could mean he will want to test himself in the Majors at some point. He is a top defensive player (2008 Gold Glove winner) with good speed and a good eye. Several Dragons jumped to MLB last year and he could follow at some point. He's had issues with his front office which often portends a move, but it appears he will be staying put in 2009. *Possible ETA: 2010.*

Ryota Igarashi (RHP, Yakult Swallows) is a hard-throwing reliever who has hit 98 mph on the radar gun on several occasions. Usually a middle reliever, he had some success when required to close, including 37 saves with a 2.66 ERA in 2004. He will be a free agent in 2010 and has expressed a desire to test out MLB. He's a longshot to get some saves on the cheap if you can draft him now on reserve, but don't go overboard if you are bidding. *Probable ETA: 2010.*

Hirotoshi Ishii (LHP, Yakult Swallows) badly wants to join the Majors. His team agreed to post him after the 2006 season, but an injury derailed those plans and caused him to miss all of 2007 as well. Since time on the DL does not count towards free agency, he can only hope his team will agree to post him. *Probable ETA: 2010.*

Hitoki Iwase (LHP, Chunichi Dragons) is a closer coming off five straight successful years. A free agent after 2007, he chose to re-sign with his Japanese team for one year rather than testing the Majors. Now a free agent again, there would be no posting fee and he has expressed an interest in MLB. However, the latest rumors are that he is on the verge of signing another one-year extension with the Dragons. It appears he is just using MLB as leverage to get better contracts from his team. *Possible ETA: 2010.*

Kenshin Kawakami (RHP, Chunichi Dragons) has impressive credentials for someone with less hype than other Japanese pitchers: ROY in 1998; 2004 Central League MVP, Sawamura winner; and multiple All-Star selections. He is the highest paid starting pitcher in Japan and is now a free agent. Minor back problems did not affect his efficiency in 2008 when he finished with a 2.30 ERA. He could be a solid #3 SP in MLB, and has the highest combination of talent and immediate opportunity. *Probable ETA: 2009.*

Seung-yeop Lee (1B, Yomiuri Giants) is a Korean slugger who plays in the Japanese League and is constrained by their posting rules. He has two years remaining on a four-year contract, but can opt out and sign with a MLB team if the Giants win the championship. He'll be 34 when he could first make the move, so it's getting closer to the time to cross him off your list. *Possible ETA: 2010 at the earliest.*

Tomohiro Nioka (SS/3B, Nippon Ham Fighters) has decent power for a middle infielder. His eye is a little questionable and he may struggle at first. Nioka had huge PR problems in 2008, having been caught in a highly publicized affair with a popular TV newswoman. The image-conscience Giants traded him in the off-season, so he

may decide in favor of a change of scenery at some point. If he comes over, he might be worth a gamble, but only at the right price. *Possible ETA: 2010.*

Kazumi Saito (RHP, Softbank Hawks) statistically was Japan's best starting pitcher — even better than Matsuzaka. He had a huge year in 2006 when he led the Pacific League in ERA, wins, strikeouts and winning percentage. Unfortunately, he has a recurring shoulder problem similar to the one that plagued Mark Prior. He had surgery to repair a damaged rotator cuff in his pitching shoulder in 2008, causing him to miss most of the season. His team doesn't post so he'll have to wait until he attains free agency. Big risk due to his shoulder, but possible big reward. *Possible ETA: 2010.*

Yuki Saito (RHP, Waseda University) is a sensational young starting pitcher. Saito elected to attend college in 2007 rather than sign with a Japanese professional team and is therefore not bound by the posting system. According to a Mets scout, he could be "the next Pedro Martinez." He has the potential to be the best pitcher on this list, but is years away from MLB. *Possible ETA: MLB minors in 2010.*

Ken Takahashi (LHP, Hiroshima Carp) is reportedly drawing interest from the Mets, Cubs, Padres and Giants, who all appear to be in the market for a 40-year-old, inconsistent pitcher who has only won 10 games once in 14 years. He will be a free agent after the 2009 season and wants to try out MLB, where he'd probably be a long reliever and spot starter. *Probable ETA: 2010, if you are also in the market for a 40-year-old, inconsistent pitcher who has won 10 games once in 14 years.*

Junichi Tazawa (RHP, Nippon Oil) is a 22-year old who plays in a semi-professional "industrial" league. Since these leagues are independent of the professional leagues, the posting restrictions do not apply. Tazawa probably would have been the #1 selection in the professional draft this year, but he sent a letter to the owners of all 12 Japanese pro teams informing them that he intended to sign with a MLB team. (As a result, Japanese owners are attempting to extend their slipping control over players by banning any amateur player from returning to the Japanese league until three years after their MLB contract has expired.) Tazawa has a fastball in the low to mid-90's, complemented by a forkball and a slider. Several teams have been mentioned as being interested, including the Red Sox, Braves, Tigers, Pirates and Phillies. *Probable ETA: MLB minors in 2009.*

Koji Uehara (RHP, Yomiuri Giants) was once considered the best starting pitcher in Japan after Matsuzaka, but lately his stock has fallen. A control pitcher, he was used as a closer against his wishes in 2007 after coming off an injury. He was ineffective both in the rotation and out of the bullpen in 2008, even being demoted at one point, although he did finish strong after the Olympics. His team has really yanked him around, both with regard to his usage and his free agency, so there's little doubt he will leave after the 2008 season. Once almost a sure bet to succeed in MLB, he now must be considered a gamble. *Probable ETA: 2009.*

Major League Equivalents

In his 1985 *Baseball Abstract*, Bill James introduced the concept of major league equivalencies. His assertion was that, with the proper adjustments, a minor leaguer's statistics could be converted to an equivalent major league level performance with a great deal of accuracy.

Because of wide variations in the level of play among different minor leagues, it is difficult to get a true reading on a player's potential. For instance, a .300 batting average achieved in the high-offense Pacific Coast League is not nearly as much of an accomplishment as a similar level in the Eastern League. MLEs normalize these types of variances, for all statistical categories.

The actual MLEs are not projections. They represent how a player's previous performance might look at the major league level. However, the MLE stat line can be used in forecasting future performance in just the same way as a major league stat line would.

The model we use contains a few variations to James' version and updates all of the minor league and ballpark factors. In addition, we designed a module to convert pitching statistics, which is something James did not originally do.

Do MLEs really work?

Used correctly, MLEs are excellent indicators of potential. But, just like we cannot take traditional major league statistics at face value, the same goes for MLEs. The underlying measures of base skill — batting eye ratios, pitching command ratios, etc. — are far more accurate in evaluating future talent than raw home runs, batting averages or ERAs.

The charts we present here also provide the unique perspective of looking at two years' worth of data. These are only short-term trends, for sure. But even here we can find small indications of players improving their skills, or struggling, as they rise through more difficult levels of competition. Since players — especially those with any modicum of talent — are promoted rapidly through major league systems, a two-year scan is often all we get to spot any trends. Five-year trends do appear in the *Minor League Baseball Analyst*.

Here are some things to look for as you scan these charts:

Target players who...
- spent a full year in AA and then a full year in AAA
- had consistent playing time from one year to the next
- improved their base skills as they were promoted

Raise the warning flag for players who...
- were stuck at the same level both years, or regressed
- displayed marked changes in playing time from one year to the next
- showed large drops in BPIs from one year to the next

Players are listed on the charts if they spent at least part of 2007 or 2008 in Triple-A or Double-A and had at least 100 AB or 30 IP within those two levels. Each is listed with the organization with which they finished the season.

Only statistics accumulated in Triple-A and Double-A ball are included (players who split a season are indicated as a/a); Major League and Single-A stats are excluded.

Each player's actual AB and IP totals are used as the base for the conversion. However, it is more useful to compare performances using common levels, so rely on the ratios and sabermetric gauges. Complete explanations of these formulas appear in the Glossary.

Batters who had a BPV of at least 50, and pitchers who had a BPV of at least 90, and are less than 26 years of age (the "unofficial" break point between prospect and suspect) are indicated with an "a" after their age. This should provide a pool of the best rising prospects. Obvious prospects like Jay Bruce and Evan Longoria were tagged as "a" in 2007. However, there were also lesser players tagged in last year's book who ended up getting significant playing time in 2008. Among them were Willy Aybar, Jerry Blevins, Dallas Braden, Asdrubal Cabrera, Chris Davis, Joey Devine, Ben Francisco, Chase Headley, Jensen Lewis, Jed Lowrie, Kyle McClellan, Brandon Moss, Chris Perez and Ian Stewart.

Also keep an eye on players more than 26, but less than 30, with similarly high BPVs. These are your "Bull Durham" prospects, indicated with a "b" after their age. Keep these players on your end-game or reserve list radar as there could be hidden short-term value here. Among the players tagged as "b" is last year's book were Grant Balfour, Nelson Cruz, Scott Hairston, Edwar Ramirez and Ben Zobrist.

Major League Equivalent Statistics

BATTER	Yr	Age	Pos	Lev	Org	ab	r	h	d	t	hr	rbi	bb	k	sb	cs	ba	ob	slg	ops	bb%	ct%	eye	px	sx	rc/g	bpv
Abad,Andy	07	35	3	aaa	MIL	269	39	71	11	0	10	47	20	36	5	2	264	315	415	730	7%	87%	0.56	93	70	4.69	37
Abercrombie,Reg	07	27	8	aa	FLA	353	51	86	17	6	12	39	8	104	29	6	245	262	426	687	2%	71%	0.08	109	214	3.85	28
	08	28	8	aa	HOU	289	25	60	11	1	8	24	6	81	11	10	207	224	332	556	2%	72%	0.08	77	97	2.11	2
Abernathy,Brent	07	30	543	aaa	WAS	357	32	78	14	1	2	30	28	38	13	6	219	276	280	556	7%	89%	0.74	46	85	2.64	7
Abreu,Michel	08	30	3	aa	NYM	425	46	94	19	0	10	48	28	58	1	0	221	268	338	606	6%	86%	0.47	77	43	3.12	15
Abreu,Tony	07	23 a	4	aa	LA	234	41	75	20	3	2	15	12	29	4	0	321	354	457	811	5%	88%	0.41	100	133	6.36	56
Adams,Russ	07	27	4	aaa	TOR	431	50	100	21	2	10	44	32	52	3	3	231	285	355	640	7%	88%	0.63	81	68	3.47	23
	08	28	84	aaa	TOR	429	51	94	17	2	13	51	41	99	9	2	219	288	359	647	9%	77%	0.42	86	93	3.65	17
Affronti,Michael	08	25	4	aa	OAK	128	10	31	10	0	1	12	0	19	0	0	240	240	338	578	0%	85%	0.00	78	3	2.72	12
Aguila,Chris	07	29	8	aa	PIT	172	16	32	4	1	2	15	6	43	2	2	186	212	260	472	3%	75%	0.13	46	84	1.72	-16
	08	30	8	aa	NYM	420	54	95	15	1	21	53	39	100	9	4	227	292	416	708	8%	76%	0.39	111	80	4.16	29
Aldridge,Cory	07	28	8	aa	CHW	421	44	83	25	2	8	43	54	136	4	2	198	288	325	613	11%	68%	0.39	87	80	3.24	9
	08	29	0	aa	KC	167	17	36	5	1	7	30	19	36	2	3	216	296	381	677	10%	78%	0.52	96	60	3.66	22
Alexander,Manny	07	37	6	a/a	WAS	293	23	48	10	2	2	16	12	60	2	2	164	197	229	426	4%	80%	0.20	45	95	1.39	-23
Alfaro,Jason	07	30	6	aa	NYM	312	26	59	11	0	8	32	10	48	1	1	190	214	296	510	3%	85%	0.20	67	42	2.03	-5
Alfonzo,Eliezer	08	30	2	aa	SF	196	19	52	14	1	5	30	7	49	1	0	268	292	426	718	3%	75%	0.14	107	58	4.45	36
Allegra,Matthew	07	26	8	aa	MIN	373	41	70	23	1	9	41	22	92	2	2	187	231	324	556	6%	75%	0.24	94	69	2.42	6
Allen,Brandon	08	23 a	3	aa	CHW	153	27	41	6	1	15	29	18	37	3	1	268	345	614	959	11%	76%	0.49	192	91	7.67	78
Allen,Luke	07	29	8	aa	LA	106	9	17	3	0	1	5	8	19	2	2	156	217	205	422	7%	82%	0.44	36	63	1.35	-24
Alley,Joshua	08	25	80	aa	SD	287	30	67	12	2	3	24	44	40	6	3	233	335	318	653	13%	86%	1.09	59	80	3.94	24
Almonte,Erick	07	30	6	a/a	DET	297	30	66	13	1	3	34	42	67	5	3	224	319	306	626	12%	77%	0.62	59	65	3.53	11
	08	31	640	aaa	DET	395	36	78	20	1	7	36	40	68	3	2	198	272	306	577	9%	83%	0.59	74	53	2.84	8
Alomar Jr.,Sandy	07	41	2	aa	NYM	160	9	28	5	1	2	18	5	30	1	0	175	200	254	453	3%	81%	0.16	51	53	1.63	-17
Ambres,Chip	07	28	8	aa	NYM	427	56	87	17	0	13	49	49	106	5	0	204	286	338	624	10%	75%	0.46	84	73	3.43	12
	08	29	8	aa	SD	412	62	88	20	4	15	58	41	92	6	3	214	285	393	678	9%	78%	0.45	109	124	3.84	25
Anderson,Brian	07	26	1	aaa	CHW	200	26	49	7	1	9	28	18	43	3	2	243	305	421	725	8%	78%	0.41	104	78	4.43	32
Anderson,Bryan	07	21	2	aa	STL	389	44	107	14	1	5	45	28	59	0	1	275	325	356	681	7%	85%	0.48	54	39	4.24	24
	08	22	2	aa	STL	315	31	86	16	1	3	33	28	45	2	0	273	332	359	692	8%	86%	0.63	63	57	4.50	30
Anderson,Drew M	07	26	48	a/a	CIN	518	64	116	28	4	10	48	42	108	10	7	225	282	350	633	7%	79%	0.39	84	105	3.33	17
	08	27	4	a/a	CIN	238	25	52	13	1	4	20	18	34	4	0	217	272	328	600	7%	86%	0.52	77	85	3.15	15
Anderson,Drew T	07	26	48	a/a	MIL	420	54	101	31	4	4	37	23	100	14	8	240	280	356	636	5%	76%	0.23	85	129	3.32	20
	08	27	8	aaa	CIN	404	40	95	23	5	6	52	15	91	3	6	234	262	361	623	4%	77%	0.17	85	94	3.01	16
Anderson,Josh	07	25	8	aa	HOU	513	48	114	14	5	2	32	23	70	30	8	223	257	277	534	4%	86%	0.33	36	135	2.48	-4
	08	26	8	aaa	ATL	494	61	132	21	3	3	31	24	53	33	7	266	300	337	637	5%	89%	0.45	51	131	3.75	19
Anderson,Lars	08	21 a	3	aa	BOS	133	22	40	14	0	4	24	23	34	1	0	304	407	501	908	15%	75%	0.69	141	46	8.21	73
Andino,Robert	07	23	6	aa	FLA	598	70	146	22	10	11	42	35	121	17	15	245	287	368	655	6%	80%	0.29	75	143	3.44	18
	08	24	6	aa	FLA	181	22	45	12	2	5	21	15	29	7	6	249	308	419	727	8%	84%	0.53	111	116	4.18	40
Andrus,Elvis	08	20	6	aa	TEX	482	66	131	18	2	3	53	30	68	43	20	271	314	335	649	6%	86%	0.44	46	127	3.64	18
Andrus,Erold	07	23	8	aa	TAM	206	22	43	13	0	2	12	10	37	2	1	207	243	297	539	4%	82%	0.26	69	68	2.39	3
	08	24	8	aa	TAM	466	48	102	23	5	6	47	42	79	2	2	218	283	325	609	8%	83%	0.53	72	84	3.19	13
Ankiel,Rick	07	28	8	aa	STL	387	41	73	10	2	20	58	17	90	2	3	188	222	378	600	4%	77%	0.19	107	68	2.61	11
Antonelli,Matthew	07	22	4	aa	SD	187	31	50	9	1	6	22	27	34	9	3	267	360	422	782	13%	82%	0.79	97	108	5.71	45
	08	24	4	aa	SD	451	51	82	16	3	5	32	62	79	5	5	183	281	263	544	12%	83%	0.79	53	81	2.54	-1
Appert,Luke	07	27	8	aa	OAK	275	25	58	13	1	3	32	33	48	1	1	211	296	302	598	11%	82%	0.69	64	45	3.17	11
	08	28	4	aa	PHI	299	26	59	13	0	5	22	26	50	1	1	197	262	294	557	8%	83%	0.53	66	35	2.62	4
Ardoin,Danny	07	33	2	aa	STL	197	13	25	8	0	1	6	15	60	1	0	124	188	185	373	7%	70%	0.26	46	45	1.13	-35
Arencibia,JP	08	23	2	aa	TOR	262	26	68	13	0	13	35	5	46	0	0	260	273	458	731	2%	82%	0.11	121	17	4.36	38
Arhart,Josh	07	28	2	aa	TAM	167	12	26	7	0	2	11	12	36	0	0	153	210	225	435	7%	78%	0.33	53	26	1.54	-20
Arias,Joaquin	08	24	64	aa	TEX	432	44	110	13	7	6	36	14	43	17	6	256	280	358	637	3%	90%	0.34	62	145	3.47	17
Armstrong,Cole	08	25	2	a/a	CHW	356	33	82	25	0	8	40	13	53	0	1	230	257	364	622	4%	85%	0.25	96	30	3.14	21
Arnold,Derrick	08	25	46	a/a	ATL	202	10	39	7	1	1	11	8	45	5	2	191	223	247	470	4%	78%	0.19	40	78	1.80	-16
Asanovich,Robert	07	25	4	aa	TAM	401	36	83	16	1	4	28	32	64	6	6	206	265	280	545	7%	84%	0.50	52	65	2.45	0
	08	26	4	aa	TAM	282	29	55	9	1	3	23	45	44	0	5	193	305	263	568	14%	85%	1.03	48	36	2.74	5
Ashby,Chris	07	33	2	aa	FLA	152	11	22	4	0	3	14	15	39	0	1	143	222	221	443	9%	75%	0.40	49	28	1.59	-24
Ash,Jonathan	07	25	4	aa	HOU	280	25	69	13	2	3	25	19	16	2	3	248	295	334	629	6%	94%	1.22	60	62	3.40	32
	08	26	4	aa	HOU	275	22	52	8	1	0	7	27	17	1	4	187	259	224	483	9%	94%	1.53	30	46	1.91	5
Aubrey,Michael	07	25	30	aa	CLE	207	17	42	10	0	5	27	9	34	0	0	204	238	330	568	4%	83%	0.26	83	22	2.60	7
	08	26	30	a/a	CLE	388	36	94	25	1	7	44	21	52	0	0	242	281	368	649	5%	87%	0.41	88	32	3.61	25
Aviles,Mike	07	27	654	aa	KC	538	58	129	23	4	11	57	23	56	3	5	239	270	362	632	4%	90%	0.40	78	79	3.25	20
	08	28 b	4	aa	KC	214	32	62	20	5	7	32	9	21	3	0	290	319	526	845	4%	90%	0.43	153	150	6.22	68
Avlas,Phil	07	25	8	aa	ARI	228	22	41	3	1	1	12	22	38	3	1	179	251	213	463	9%	83%	0.58	21	78	1.86	-20
	08	26	8	aa	ARI	221	24	58	13	0	2	23	14	28	3	1	264	308	349	657	6%	87%	0.51	66	58	3.89	25
Badeaux,Brooks	07	31	84	aa	TAM	396	32	69	13	1	1	29	21	63	1	4	175	217	219	436	5%	84%	0.33	34	54	1.49	-21
Baez,Edgardo	08	23	8	aa	WAS	167	17	34	8	1	1	10	12	41	4	4	205	258	282	539	7%	76%	0.29	56	95	2.29	-3
Bailey,Jeff	07	29	3	aaa	BOS	404	54	89	23	1	12	50	49	96	7	6	221	306	373	679	11%	76%	0.52	99	76	3.91	25
	08	30	38	aaa	BOS	418	64	102	27	2	16	54	45	86	3	2	245	318	434	752	10%	79%	0.52	121	79	4.92	42
Baisley,Jeffrey	07	25	5	aa	OAK	404	48	90	20	2	9	37	23	72	3	1	223	265	346	611	5%	82%	0.32	81	83	3.13	14
	08	26	5	aa	OAK	299	33	72	21	1	6	32	23	34	0	1	242	295	374	669	7%	89%	0.66	93	43	3.86	32
Baker,John	07	27	2	aa	FLA	270	26	61	12	0	6	30	22	61	2	0	226	283	338	622	7%	77%	0.36	75	46	3.38	13
	08	28	2	aa	FLA	193	26	50	12	1	5	23	19	33	1	2	261	327	401	728	9%	83%	0.57	94	64	4.66	37
Baldiris,Aarom	07	25	5	aa	NYY	286	33	65	8	1	8	32	26	49	1	0	226	290	339	628	8%	83%	0.52	68	57	3.47	14
Balentien,Wladimi	07	23	8	aa	SEA	477	65	122	22	2	19	71	48	100	13	5	256	324	433	757	9%	79%	0.48	108	93	5.03	39
	08	24 a	8	aa	SEA	233	38	53	17	0	13	43	26	44	2	5	227	304	474	778	10%	81%	0.59	155	58	4.65	51
Ball,Jarred	07	24	8	aa	ARI	270	31	66	21	2	2	29	17	40	9	5	243	288	355	643	6%	85%	0.43	86	110	3.47	25
	08	25	8	aa	HOU	170	21	36	8	3	1	11	17	38	9	2	210	282	310	591	9%	77%	0.44	67	168	3.15	7
Bankston,Wes	07	24	30	aaa	TAM	390	44	88	22	1	15	56	24	85	2	0	226	271	403	673	6%	78%	0.28	112	63	3.75	27
	08	25	30	aa	OAK	375	41	86	16	1	13	54	15	54	0	2	230	261	387	647	4%	86%	0.28	96	42	3.34	22
Bannon,Jeff	07	28	8	aaa	CIN	313	27	65	11	1	4	33	18	58	3	0	208	250	285	536	5%	81%	0.30	53	70	2.45	-3
Barden,Brian	07	27	56	aa	STL	352	30	71	9	1	3	26	26	63	2	3	203	258	255	512	7%	82%	0.41	36	50	2.17	-10
	08	28	6	aa	STL	411	42	92	16	3	5	25	27	61	2	4	223	271	315	587	6%	85%	0.44	61	68	2.86	8
Barfield,Josh	08	26	4	a/a	CLE	303	25	66	16	1	4	20	13	60	8	5	217	250	313	563	4%	80%	0.22	69	83	2.53	5

BATTER	Yr	Age	Pos	Lev	Org	ab	r	h	d	t	hr	rbi	bb	k	sb	cs	ba	ob	slg	ops	bb%	ct%	eye	px	sx	rc/g	bpv
Barker,Kevin	07	32	3	aaa	TOR	470	52	103	19	1	15	58	56	113	3	0	218	301	360	661	11%	76%	0.49	88	57	3.87	19
	08	33	3	aaa	CIN	399	50	82	17	0	16	53	38	94	0	1	205	274	369	643	9%	76%	0.41	100	34	3.42	18
Barker,Sean	07	27	8	aa	COL	261	36	69	18	2	4	32	10	61	9	5	264	291	394	685	4%	76%	0.16	92	121	3.89	29
	08	28	8	aa	COL	362	35	69	20	3	1	30	14	78	8	4	190	220	267	487	4%	78%	0.18	60	118	1.87	-9
Barmes,Clint	07	29	6	aa	COL	428	45	98	15	4	8	29	15	50	6	6	230	256	340	597	3%	88%	0.30	69	98	2.83	11
Barnes,Larry	07	33	38	aa	LA	178	12	26	3	1	5	14	6	37	1	1	146	172	260	431	3%	79%	0.15	64	74	1.34	-22
Barnwell,Chris	07	29	6	aaa	MIL	456	58	105	21	2	7	32	29	70	10	4	230	276	328	605	6%	85%	0.41	67	102	3.14	13
	08	30	6	aa	FLA	330	35	71	15	1	4	30	30	50	11	3	214	279	305	584	8%	85%	0.60	64	95	3.03	10
Barton,Brian	07	25	8	a/a	CLE	476	54	126	20	1	8	55	42	111	18	10	265	325	359	684	8%	77%	0.38	64	84	4.12	22
Barton,Daric	07	22	3	aa	OAK	516	71	139	37	3	7	59	65	56	3	5	269	351	393	745	11%	89%	1.16	90	65	5.06	50
Basak,Chris	07	29	5	aaa	MIN	341	46	77	19	1	7	38	19	71	13	3	226	266	344	610	5%	79%	0.26	80	117	3.19	14
	08	30	456	aaa	NYY	319	28	65	15	1	5	22	15	66	9	7	205	240	307	547	4%	79%	0.22	70	84	2.28	2
Bass,Bryan	07	25	5	aa	BAL	339	39	63	14	0	8	27	26	103	12	5	186	244	300	544	7%	70%	0.25	75	93	2.41	-2
Bates,Aaron	08	25	30	aa	BOS	457	47	113	30	1	8	53	38	95	0	0	248	306	368	674	8%	79%	0.41	86	33	4.04	26
Batista,Tony	07	34	5	aaa	WAS	107	12	25	5	1	5	18	6	17	1	0	236	278	429	707	6%	84%	0.38	117	78	4.16	34
Batista,Wilson	07	27	4	aa	NYM	301	23	55	13	1	4	18	6	55	5	3	182	198	275	473	2%	82%	0.11	63	87	1.69	-11
Baxter,Michael J	08	24	80	aa	SD	324	34	75	15	3	6	40	32	38	2	2	233	303	351	653	9%	88%	0.86	76	76	3.72	26
Bear,Ryan	07	27	8	aa	FLA	357	35	71	14	0	7	37	27	85	3	1	200	256	297	553	7%	76%	0.32	65	54	2.59	-0
Beattie,Andrew	07	30	4	a/a	FLA	269	26	50	6	1	9	33	29	72	4	4	186	264	314	578	10%	73%	0.40	74	64	2.69	0
	08	31	4	aa	FLA	442	51	100	20	3	8	43	30	91	9	4	227	276	337	612	6%	80%	0.33	73	101	3.17	12
Bellhorn,Mark	07	33	40	aaa	CIN	326	31	70	20	0	11	45	50	91	0	0	215	319	375	694	13%	72%	0.54	105	13	4.30	26
	08	34	3	aa	LA	207	23	37	11	1	5	20	26	45	1	0	181	271	316	587	11%	78%	0.57	89	62	2.95	8
Bellorin,Edwin	07	26 a	2	aa	COL	221	29	62	15	0	7	33	13	23	1	0	281	320	448	768	5%	89%	0.54	112	46	5.27	51
	08	27	2	aa	COL	335	18	81	22	2	4	43	10	32	1	1	242	264	352	615	3%	91%	0.32	80	44	3.16	20
Bell,Bubba	07	25	8	aa	BOS	147	18	34	5	1	3	17	11	15	4	0	233	288	336	624	7%	90%	0.77	64	101	3.54	20
	08	26	8	aa	BOS	312	38	76	15	2	9	37	29	53	2	1	245	308	392	700	8%	83%	0.54	93	71	4.30	30
Bell,Michael	08	24	4	aa	MIL	444	40	93	25	2	8	40	21	69	1	4	210	245	327	571	4%	84%	0.30	80	54	2.56	9
Benjamin,Casey	07	27	6	aa	TEX	469	51	89	20	3	7	38	50	71	6	1	189	267	294	561	10%	85%	0.70	69	98	2.73	5
	08	28	6	aa	TEX	309	32	61	4	3	7	22	29	65	2	1	197	266	293	559	9%	79%	0.45	53	82	2.67	-4
Bennett,Paul	08	25	4	a/a	ATL	144	11	24	5	1	0	8	8	38	1	1	163	210	209	419	6%	73%	0.22	35	83	1.40	-27
Bergeron,Peter	07	30	8	aa	PIT	104	8	17	3	1	0	6	5	20	2	0	166	206	209	415	5%	81%	0.26	32	90	1.45	-26
Bergolla,William	07	25	4	aa	SF	356	49	95	20	1	5	29	24	41	10	3	267	313	368	681	6%	88%	0.58	73	97	4.19	30
	08	26	4	a/a	WAS	301	35	63	14	0	4	23	24	34	4	1	209	267	294	560	7%	89%	0.69	61	71	2.71	9
Berkery,Thomas	08	26	4	aa	TEX	256	25	49	12	3	3	18	23	54	1	5	190	257	291	548	8%	79%	0.42	68	85	2.35	-0
Bernadina,Rogear	07	23	8	a/a	WAS	413	56	96	16	2	5	33	40	81	35	16	232	300	317	617	9%	80%	0.49	57	129	3.24	11
	08	24	8	a/a	WAS	457	64	132	21	7	7	43	36	89	33	12	288	340	408	748	7%	81%	0.41	77	160	5.06	36
Bernier,Douglas	07	27	5	aa	COL	216	18	53	12	0	2	18	22	48	2	2	246	314	323	637	9%	78%	0.45	60	44	3.65	15
	08	28	6	aa	COL	337	36	68	8	3	6	26	40	60	1	2	201	285	295	580	11%	82%	0.66	56	67	2.91	3
Berroa,Angel	07	30	6	aa	KC	307	30	64	13	0	5	26	17	49	2	2	208	248	293	541	5%	84%	0.33	59	50	2.41	0
	08	31	6	aa	KC	189	25	44	11	0	7	20	6	25	3	2	234	257	400	658	3%	87%	0.24	107	74	3.40	27
Bigbie,Larry	07	30	8	a/a	ATL	312	36	71	18	2	3	28	27	68	4	0	226	288	326	614	8%	78%	0.40	72	93	3.37	13
Bixler,Brian	07	25	6	aa	PIT	475	62	116	22	7	4	41	42	115	23	5	244	305	342	647	8%	76%	0.36	65	161	3.84	16
	08	26	6	aa	PIT	321	36	80	8	4	6	29	22	98	19	8	249	296	348	645	6%	70%	0.22	58	146	3.58	11
Blalock,Jake	07	24	8	aa	KC	158	6	22	5	1	1	13	10	26	2	0	138	187	198	386	6%	83%	0.36	41	65	1.22	-30
	08	25	0	aa	PHI	153	9	29	5	0	2	11	9	31	0	0	190	237	258	495	6%	80%	0.30	46	16	2.05	-11
Blanco,Andres	08	24	6	aa	CHC	298	22	72	8	1	1	27	11	25	7	4	242	268	283	551	3%	92%	0.42	31	73	2.57	2
Blanco,Gregor	07	24	8	aaa	ATL	464	73	124	17	4	3	31	56	78	21	20	267	346	341	687	11%	83%	0.72	50	116	4.00	24
Blanco,Tony	07	26	80	aa	WAS	253	23	48	10	1	7	33	11	57	4	0	189	222	320	542	4%	78%	0.19	82	85	2.36	0
	08	27	50	aa	COL	390	40	104	29	0	16	59	20	54	4	3	267	303	460	763	5%	86%	0.37	127	45	4.88	49
Blanks,Kyle	08	22	3	aa	SD	492	65	141	19	4	16	92	43	82	4	5	287	344	439	783	8%	83%	0.52	92	77	5.49	44
Blasi,Nicholas	07	26	8	aa	OAK	341	43	88	11	1	3	32	21	85	8	4	258	301	319	619	6%	75%	0.25	43	88	3.38	9
	08	27	8	a/a	CHW	304	37	62	8	0	5	23	19	76	5	3	204	251	275	526	6%	75%	0.25	46	81	2.31	-8
Bocachica,Hiram	07	32	8	aa	SD	169	19	30	7	1	6	22	24	36	6	2	178	280	327	607	12%	79%	0.67	92	92	3.15	10
Bocock,Brian	08	24	6	aa	SF	123	12	19	3	0	0	3	12	34	6	3	151	225	175	401	9%	73%	0.35	21	93	1.34	-34
Boeve,Adam	07	27	8	aa	PIT	413	48	86	12	2	14	42	44	124	17	7	209	285	350	635	10%	70%	0.35	83	101	3.37	11
	08	28	3	aa	PIT	263	28	55	14	2	9	35	18	86	10	4	207	257	375	632	6%	67%	0.20	105	119	3.18	17
Boggs,Brandon	07	25	8	aa	TEX	354	55	85	19	3	16	45	56	89	9	4	239	343	445	788	14%	75%	0.63	125	107	5.50	44
Bogusevic,Brian	08	25 a	8	aa	HOU	124	15	38	9	1	2	14	12	20	6	1	310	368	441	810	9%	84%	0.58	92	106	6.46	53
Bohn,T.J.	07	28	8	a/a	ATL	230	27	44	10	0	2	16	27	67	9	3	193	278	257	535	10%	71%	0.40	49	86	2.52	-8
	08	29	8	aaa	PHI	316	23	55	16	1	4	20	18	85	3	2	175	221	265	486	6%	73%	0.22	64	64	1.88	-11
Bolivar,Luis	07	27	845	a/a	CIN	392	43	95	19	5	4	39	22	80	13	5	243	283	342	625	5%	80%	0.27	67	131	3.33	14
	08	28	564	a/a	CIN	370	41	81	16	2	8	34	20	80	15	5	219	259	338	597	5%	78%	0.25	77	117	2.97	10
Bonifacio,Emilio	07	22	46	aa	ARI	551	70	147	20	4	2	34	32	86	34	15	267	307	328	636	5%	84%	0.37	44	129	3.54	15
	08	23	4	a/a	WAS	398	47	109	18	4	1	26	25	58	17	12	273	315	345	660	6%	85%	0.42	52	119	3.71	21
Bonvechio,Brett	07	25 a	0	aa	SD	128	20	29	8	0	8	23	19	27	0	0	230	330	468	797	13%	79%	0.69	144	28	5.53	50
Boone,James	08	26	8	aa	PIT	329	29	63	11	1	8	33	31	97	2	3	191	261	300	561	9%	71%	0.32	68	52	2.59	-2
Borbon,Julio	08	23	8	aa	TEX	255	31	78	11	2	4	17	11	25	13	13	306	335	412	746	4%	90%	0.44	69	106	4.40	39
Borchard,Joe	08	30	8	aaa	ATL	117	12	25	4	1	3	9	9	29	3	2	213	272	331	603	7%	75%	0.33	73	94	2.99	8
Borowiak,Zach	07	26	45	a/a	BOS	271	32	52	7	0	2	25	19	49	3	0	193	245	239	484	7%	82%	0.39	34	75	2.03	-14
Boscan,Jean	07	28	2	a/a	CIN	107	5	18	1	0	1	8	22	25	1	0	171	311	203	514	17%	76%	0.86	20	21	2.49	-18
	08	29	2	aa	ATL	255	18	48	11	0	2	21	25	45	0	0	186	258	248	507	9%	82%	0.54	47	20	2.21	-8
Botts,Jason	07	27	80	aa	TEX	369	49	93	29	2	10	55	56	101	0	1	252	351	425	776	13%	73%	0.56	117	57	5.52	44
Boucher,Sebastier	07	26	8	a/a	BAL	395	57	83	13	1	3	29	50	80	16	12	209	299	269	568	11%	80%	0.63	43	98	2.72	0
	08	27	8	a/a	BAL	329	48	74	13	3	8	27	31	77	7	7	224	291	355	646	9%	77%	0.41	81	112	3.38	16
Bourgeois,Jason	07	26	84	a/a	CHW	500	67	139	25	4	10	48	41	66	33	10	277	332	399	731	8%	87%	0.62	80	130	4.92	38
	08	27	8	aaa	CHW	510	67	125	19	3	8	39	28	62	24	11	245	284	343	627	5%	88%	0.45	63	120	3.30	17
Bowers,Jason	07	30	4	aa	PIT	426	36	81	20	2	5	32	32	69	11	5	190	246	280	526	7%	84%	0.45	63	94	2.27	-2
	08	31	5	aa	PIT	368	35	75	20	1	4	31	20	62	10	3	203	245	298	543	5%	83%	0.33	69	96	2.47	3
Bowker,John	07	24	8	aa	SF	522	63	139	31	5	16	71	32	89	2	8	266	308	437	745	6%	83%	0.36	109	71	4.56	41
Bowman,Shawn	08	24	5	aa	NYM	113	10	25	6	0	2	8	2	30	3	1	217	230	321	551	2%	74%	0.07	73	75	2.42	4
Bozied,Tagg	07	28	3	aa	STL	449	45	83	18	1	15	54	35	96	2	0	185	245	331	576	7%	79%	0.37	90	54	2.71	6
	08	29	38	aa	FLA	425	62	101	22	2	18	58	38	79	5	2	237	299	425	724	8%	81%	0.48	116	87	4.46	36

BATTER	Yr	Age	Pos	Lev	Org	ab	r	h	d	t	hr	rbi	bb	k	sb	cs	ba	ob	slg	ops	bb%	ct%	eye	px	sx	rc/g	bpv
Brantley,Michael	07	20	8	aa	MIL	187	25	45	6	1	0	19	27	22	15	3	241	338	286	624	13%	88%	1.25	35	119	3.88	20
	08	21 a	83	aa	MIL	420	65	119	15	1	3	32	42	22	22	10	284	349	346	696	9%	95%	1.95	45	102	4.51	52
Branyan,Russell	08	33	5	aaa	MIL	153	16	42	12	0	9	24	17	47	3	1	272	345	517	862	10%	69%	0.36	155	41	6.55	62
Braun,Ryan	07	24 a	5	aaa	MIL	117	25	37	12	0	9	19	14	10	4	3	316	389	650	1039	11%	91%	1.40	210	80	9.20	120
Brazell,Craig	07	27	3	aa	KC	542	60	131	32	0	25	65	22	102	0	1	242	272	438	710	4%	81%	0.22	123	26	4.08	36
Breen,Patrick	07	25	80	aa	TAM	279	26	44	9	4	5	29	28	100	3	6	158	235	274	509	9%	64%	0.28	70	116	1.93	-13
Brewer,Jace	07	28	6	aa	KC	220	20	42	10	1	2	12	8	40	2	2	189	218	265	483	4%	82%	0.20	56	81	1.80	-10
Brignac,Reid	07	22	6	aa	TAM	527	77	124	27	4	15	69	48	82	13	6	235	299	387	686	8%	84%	0.59	96	115	4.02	30
	08	23	6	aaa	TAM	352	36	78	23	2	7	36	21	78	4	2	222	265	358	623	6%	78%	0.27	94	86	3.21	18
Brinkley,Dante	07	26	8	aa	FLA	311	35	63	15	1	8	24	23	118	11	7	201	257	330	588	7%	62%	0.20	84	100	2.71	6
	08	27	8	aa	FLA	216	30	40	11	1	4	18	26	70	3	3	183	271	292	563	11%	68%	0.37	74	89	2.64	-1
Brito,Javier	07	25 a	3	aa	ARI	440	57	129	27	2	10	58	64	78	1	0	294	383	428	810	13%	82%	0.82	91	52	6.44	52
	08	26	8	aa	ARI	246	33	55	13	0	12	39	38	48	1	0	222	325	424	749	13%	81%	0.79	124	38	4.96	41
Brito,Juan	07	28	2	aaa	WAS	196	11	41	12	0	3	21	12	46	0	0	208	255	315	570	6%	76%	0.27	78	12	2.73	7
Broadway,Larry	07	27	3	aaa	WAS	338	40	74	19	2	11	44	51	81	1	0	218	321	382	703	13%	76%	0.63	105	61	4.43	29
	08	28	3	aaa	WAS	429	43	92	24	2	6	42	43	101	3	8	214	286	323	609	9%	76%	0.43	77	56	3.00	11
Broussard,Ben	08	32	80	a/a	NYY	308	48	68	16	1	14	48	19	67	1	0	221	265	419	685	6%	78%	0.28	121	74	3.79	29
Brown,Andrew	08	24	3	aa	STL	247	27	51	12	0	9	29	22	65	1	0	206	271	358	629	8%	74%	0.34	95	42	3.33	15
Brown,Dee	07	30	8	aa	OAK	377	46	77	15	0	10	50	23	83	2	1	203	249	320	570	6%	78%	0.28	75	64	2.68	4
	08	31	08	aa	LAA	485	50	100	26	0	8	53	43	64	7	2	207	272	308	580	8%	87%	0.68	72	70	2.91	12
Brown,Dustin	07	25	2	a/a	BOS	281	36	67	19	1	7	38	25	67	0	0	237	298	382	680	8%	76%	0.37	99	48	4.04	27
	08	26	2	aaa	BOS	297	30	75	14	1	8	42	30	73	0	0	251	320	387	708	9%	75%	0.42	87	32	4.51	28
Brown,Jeremy	07	28	2	aa	OAK	339	32	71	17	1	10	41	32	70	0	0	211	279	355	634	9%	79%	0.46	93	30	3.43	18
Brown,Jordan	07	24 a	30	aa	CLE	483	73	145	35	1	9	65	57	53	10	2	299	373	430	803	11%	89%	1.09	94	84	6.30	60
	08	25	30	aaa	CLE	420	47	108	28	2	6	46	33	67	3	4	256	310	373	682	7%	84%	0.49	84	64	4.04	30
Brown,Matt	07	25	58	aa	LAA	391	57	90	25	1	15	49	36	107	5	9	230	295	417	712	8%	73%	0.34	120	70	3.94	33
	08	26 b	350	aa	LAA	400	59	109	29	3	16	52	25	73	3	2	271	314	476	790	6%	82%	0.34	132	87	5.34	52
Brown,Tim	07	25	3	aa	SD	351	48	83	13	0	11	43	34	64	0	0	235	303	371	674	9%	82%	0.53	84	33	4.01	24
Brown,Travis	08	28	5	a/a	BAL	116	8	15	1	1	0	8	8	25	0	2	129	185	152	336	6%	78%	0.32	13	76	0.83	-45
Brown,Willie Dee	07	25	8	aa	WAS	174	16	36	6	0	3	12	7	38	2	0	207	237	289	526	4%	78%	0.18	54	61	2.32	-5
Bruce,Jay	07	20 a	8	a/a	CIN	253	36	81	20	2	15	39	22	54	3	3	322	376	600	976	8%	79%	0.41	171	83	8.45	86
	08	22 a	8	aaa	CIN	184	28	63	8	3	9	30	10	37	7	1	340	375	565	940	5%	80%	0.28	130	148	8.49	73
Bruntlett,Eric	07	30	8	aa	HOU	227	20	43	6	3	1	14	19	40	8	4	188	250	251	501	8%	82%	0.47	40	130	2.11	-11
Buchanan,Brian	08	35	0	aa	KC	232	26	43	9	1	5	25	11	53	1	1	183	220	297	517	5%	77%	0.21	73	77	2.10	-5
Buck,Travis	08	25	8	aa	OAK	169	21	41	7	1	1	12	18	26	3	1	244	318	312	630	10%	85%	0.70	49	86	3.66	16
Budde,Ryan	07	28	2	aa	LAA	156	15	34	9	0	2	20	13	30	2	2	221	280	323	603	8%	81%	0.43	74	50	3.05	12
	08	29	2	aa	LAA	173	11	28	7	1	2	16	7	45	3	0	159	191	239	430	4%	74%	0.15	55	86	1.49	-21
Burgamy,Brian	07	26	8	aa	PHI	183	14	28	6	0	3	8	18	44	3	2	152	229	228	457	9%	76%	0.42	52	54	1.72	-20
Burgess,Brandon	08	26	5	aa	ARI	175	15	31	11	0	5	22	8	60	3	2	177	215	322	537	5%	66%	0.14	99	66	2.15	3
Burnham,Gary	07	33	3	aaa	PHI	493	45	122	31	0	10	65	53	71	0	1	246	320	369	688	10%	86%	0.75	86	18	4.26	33
Burrus,Josh	07	24	80	aa	ATL	239	25	45	10	0	5	27	27	77	7	3	187	268	286	554	10%	68%	0.35	66	73	2.62	-4
Buscher,Brian	07	26	50	a/a	MIN	379	47	98	23	1	11	48	33	42	3	2	259	319	408	727	8%	89%	0.79	99	58	4.67	43
	08	27	5	aaa	MIN	185	21	48	10	0	5	23	14	20	1	2	258	311	399	710	7%	89%	0.72	93	39	4.32	39
Butera,Andrew	07	24	2	aa	MIN	167	8	29	4	1	1	6	5	24	0	0	176	199	228	427	3%	86%	0.20	34	36	1.45	-23
	08	25	2	aa	MIN	302	30	55	15	1	5	30	26	51	0	1	184	249	286	535	8%	83%	0.52	71	47	2.37	1
Butler,Billy	07	21 a	83	aa	KC	203	34	54	10	1	10	40	38	27	1	0	266	382	473	855	16%	87%	1.41	124	61	6.95	68
	08	22 a	3	aa	KC	101	16	32	6	1	4	11	12	6	0	0	317	389	515	904	11%	94%	2.00	123	62	7.93	96
Butler,Brent	07	30	3	aaa	TAM	284	24	66	16	0	4	23	13	45	1	1	231	264	327	591	4%	84%	0.28	71	38	2.93	12
Butler,Jacob	08	26	380	aa	TOR	434	38	90	22	2	13	48	45	103	0	0	208	283	357	640	9%	76%	0.44	95	34	3.50	17
Buttler,Vic	07	27	8	aa	PIT	263	27	56	6	2	2	17	22	27	16	8	211	271	271	543	8%	90%	0.81	38	125	2.44	2
Bynum,Freddie	08	29	5	a/a	BAL	150	14	31	4	3	1	13	16	39	6	2	205	281	282	563	10%	74%	0.41	45	152	2.83	-5
Bynum,Seth	07	27	6	aa	WAS	212	16	37	3	1	4	25	14	44	3	2	176	227	263	490	6%	79%	0.32	50	66	1.93	-14
	08	28	64	aa	WAS	273	36	56	13	1	10	35	20	81	1	4	204	258	366	624	7%	70%	0.24	100	67	3.00	14
Byrd,Marlon	07	30	8	aa	TEX	176	18	42	10	1	4	19	8	36	2	1	239	271	370	640	4%	80%	0.22	87	89	3.38	20
Byrne,Bryan	08	24	3	aa	ARI	416	52	115	25	0	8	44	56	59	2	3	277	362	392	755	12%	86%	0.94	82	36	5.34	45
Cabrera,Asdrubal	07	22 a	6	a/a	CLE	406	78	122	27	2	6	53	45	43	23	8	300	370	424	794	10%	89%	1.05	88	124	6.00	57
	08	23	6	aaa	CLE	141	23	44	7	1	4	12	7	24	2	2	312	345	461	806	5%	83%	0.29	94	94	5.79	49
Cabrera,Jolbert	07	35	58	aa	COL	200	12	36	9	1	3	12	5	31	0	1	179	198	273	471	2%	84%	0.16	65	42	1.65	-11
	08	36	8	aaa	CIN	215	18	48	13	3	3	20	9	38	3	3	221	254	352	606	4%	82%	0.25	87	104	2.85	15
Cain,Lorenzo	08	22	8	a/a	MIL	167	16	38	8	3	3	15	18	38	5	2	228	303	365	668	10%	77%	0.47	86	139	3.88	21
Callaspo,Alberto	07	24 a	64	aa	ARI	226	38	69	14	2	5	24	23	15	1	2	307	370	450	820	9%	93%	1.55	96	78	6.30	73
Camarena,Jose	08	24	2	aa	ATL	213	13	45	8	0	2	19	9	41	1	1	212	243	275	517	4%	81%	0.21	46	35	2.21	-6
Campbell,Scott	08	24	4	aa	TOR	417	55	110	19	2	8	36	49	55	2	7	265	342	375	717	11%	87%	0.89	73	53	4.54	36
Campusano,Jose	07	24	8	aa	FLA	108	13	24	3	2	1	2	3	24	8	2	225	245	314	559	3%	78%	0.12	54	188	2.62	-1
Camp,Matt	08	24	68	aa	CHC	482	51	107	10	3	2	27	36	46	17	10	221	275	265	539	7%	90%	0.77	29	105	2.47	1
Cancel,Robinson	07	31	2	aa	NYM	236	13	39	11	1	4	18	8	54	2	1	163	192	258	450	3%	77%	0.15	65	60	1.53	-16
Canizares,Barbarc	07	28 b	3	aaa	ATL	163	21	50	12	1	3	29	10	27	0	0	309	351	449	799	6%	83%	0.38	99	52	6.02	52
	08	29	30	aaa	ATL	504	42	122	23	0	10	50	33	68	1	0	243	289	346	634	6%	86%	0.48	70	31	3.53	19
Cannizaro,Andy	07	29	46	a/a	NYY	198	26	46	10	0	2	18	18	38	0	1	232	295	309	604	8%	81%	0.47	59	45	3.20	11
	08	30	4	aaa	CLE	255	25	55	10	0	3	22	20	28	1	0	216	272	297	569	7%	89%	0.71	57	43	2.82	10
Cannon,Chip	07	26	3	aa	TOR	394	42	79	20	1	14	40	40	143	1	0	201	274	359	633	9%	64%	0.28	100	50	3.37	14
	08	27	3	aaa	TOR	251	22	51	12	0	5	25	34	86	1	0	202	297	304	601	12%	66%	0.40	71	33	3.24	4
Cantu,Jorge	07	26	3	aaa	CIN	185	21	48	13	1	3	20	11	32	0	0	257	298	385	683	6%	83%	0.34	91	51	4.10	30
Caraballo,Francisc	07	24	8	aa	HOU	390	37	88	23	1	11	47	21	96	4	2	226	266	373	640	5%	75%	0.22	97	65	3.36	20
Carlin,Luke	07	27	2	aa	SD	300	27	50	15	2	0	13	37	83	0	3	168	260	229	490	11%	72%	0.45	49	56	2.00	-15
Carp,Christopher	07	21	3	aa	NYM	359	46	80	15	0	8	40	32	62	2	1	223	286	331	618	8%	83%	0.52	71	56	3.32	14
	08	22	380	aa	NYM	478	57	129	27	1	14	61	67	74	1	2	270	360	418	778	12%	85%	0.91	97	35	5.64	48
Carroll,Brett	07	25 a	8	aa	FLA	417	56	110	29	5	17	67	26	84	0	7	264	307	481	788	6%	80%	0.30	136	78	4.92	50
Carson,Matt	07	26	8	aa	NYY	471	63	100	20	2	15	66	28	128	8	0	212	256	356	613	6%	73%	0.22	89	111	3.16	12
	08	27	8	a/a	NYY	417	59	102	14	6	14	53	24	86	9	4	244	286	406	691	6%	79%	0.28	94	147	4.00	26
Carter,Chris	08	26	80	aaa	BOS	470	51	122	25	1	17	63	31	75	0	0	260	306	423	729	6%	84%	0.42	103	29	4.65	38
Carter,William	07	25 a	38	a/a	BOS	548	65	158	42	2	14	72	44	68	1	0	288	340	449	789	7%	88%	0.64	111	49	5.74	54

Major League Equivalent Statistics

BATTER	Yr	Age	Pos	Lev	Org	ab	r	h	d	t	hr	rbi	bb	k	sb	cs	ba	ob	slg	ops	bb%	ct%	eye	px	sx	rc/g	bpv
Carte,Daniel	08	24	8	aa	COL	422	36	99	13	0	8	40	15	79	3	10	234	261	321	582	4%	81%	0.19	56	38	2.58	5
Casanova,Raul	07	35	2	aaa	TAM	141	12	35	8	0	5	18	11	34	0	0	249	302	402	704	7%	76%	0.31	100	12	4.33	31
	08	36	2	aa	NYM	157	13	35	9	0	3	17	8	28	0	0	222	258	330	588	5%	82%	0.27	78	22	2.90	12
Cash,Kevin	07	30	2	aaa	BOS	176	18	27	7	0	5	20	18	55	0	0	155	234	290	524	9%	69%	0.33	85	30	2.24	-7
Casilla,Alexi	07	23	46	aaa	MIN	320	52	84	13	1	3	20	31	51	24	12	263	328	338	665	9%	84%	0.61	53	120	3.88	22
Castillo,Alberto	07	38	2	aaa	BAL	203	21	48	5	0	3	21	29	36	0	0	235	330	301	632	12%	82%	0.81	44	21	3.72	13
Castillo,Javier	08	25	5	a/a	CHW	489	61	124	24	6	8	64	43	102	4	2	254	314	371	685	8%	79%	0.42	77	104	4.21	25
Castillo,Welington	08	21	2	aa	CHC	203	19	54	10	0	3	19	11	40	0	0	264	302	358	660	5%	80%	0.28	67	23	3.89	21
Castillo,Wilkin	07	23	2	aa	ARI	410	41	113	28	3	6	38	15	53	15	16	277	302	402	704	3%	87%	0.28	89	97	3.82	35
	08	24	25	a/a	CIN	428	32	91	16	1	5	36	19	49	4	4	213	247	289	536	4%	89%	0.39	53	55	2.33	1
Casto,Kory	07	26	58	aaa	WAS	408	50	91	18	2	9	50	48	98	4	4	223	304	342	646	10%	76%	0.48	77	74	3.62	16
	08	27	8	aaa	WAS	130	15	33	5	0	5	20	15	26	1	2	255	331	396	727	10%	80%	0.56	86	36	4.58	32
Castro,Bernie	07	28	4	aaa	WAS	428	53	102	17	5	1	27	31	63	29	8	239	290	306	596	7%	85%	0.48	48	150	3.20	9
	08	29	4	aaa	NYY	282	34	60	9	0	1	16	22	37	16	9	213	271	253	524	7%	87%	0.60	32	100	2.30	-4
Castro,Ofilio	07	24	5	aa	WAS	197	19	42	7	1	0	18	19	39	1	3	212	281	256	537	9%	80%	0.49	34	61	2.41	-5
	08	25	5	a/a	WAS	418	40	96	24	1	3	36	24	37	0	2	229	270	310	581	5%	91%	0.63	62	40	2.85	15
Cates Jr.,Gary	07	26	46	aa	CHC	343	21	72	9	1	2	20	13	43	11	7	211	239	256	496	4%	88%	0.31	33	77	1.96	-10
Cedeno,Ronny	07	25 a	6	aa	CHC	287	42	91	13	2	9	29	24	41	5	5	318	370	467	837	8%	86%	0.58	93	82	6.43	56
Cepicky,Matt	07	30	80	a/a	BAL	395	36	71	18	2	12	43	33	124	1	2	181	243	332	576	8%	69%	0.26	94	63	2.63	4
Cervenak,Mike	07	31	35	aaa	BAL	554	60	137	22	3	14	68	20	83	2	0	247	273	369	642	3%	85%	0.24	77	70	3.51	19
	08	32	053	aaa	PHI	456	48	113	24	1	9	48	9	67	3	3	248	263	360	623	2%	85%	0.14	77	63	3.17	17
Chang,Ray Bo-shu	07	24	6	aa	SD	267	21	60	14	0	3	29	14	58	1	2	224	263	310	573	5%	78%	0.25	64	35	2.72	6
Chaves,Brandon	07	28	6	aa	PIT	336	28	66	14	1	0	27	26	83	13	6	198	254	243	497	7%	75%	0.31	38	92	2.10	-12
	08	29	6	aa	CLE	247	19	39	2	2	2	12	23	49	9	3	157	229	198	428	9%	80%	0.48	23	104	1.55	-29
Chavez,Angel	07	26	546	aaa	NYY	430	55	114	23	1	10	58	23	76	5	3	266	304	393	696	5%	82%	0.31	85	74	4.22	30
	08	27	564	aa	LA	463	49	108	25	0	7	49	21	50	4	4	233	266	334	600	4%	89%	0.41	72	56	2.98	16
Chavez,Ozzie	07	24	64	aaa	MIL	306	31	73	12	2	4	28	35	48	4	9	239	317	330	647	10%	84%	0.73	61	67	3.43	19
	08	25	64	a/a	MIL	271	17	51	5	2	3	24	14	45	4	2	187	227	250	477	5%	84%	0.32	38	78	1.86	-16
Chavez,Raul	07	35	2	aaa	NYY	290	23	54	12	0	4	25	9	40	1	0	186	211	264	474	3%	86%	0.23	55	48	1.81	-11
Chen,Yung Chi	08	25	45	aa	SEA	249	28	52	9	0	2	19	17	30	7	2	208	258	268	526	6%	88%	0.57	45	86	2.40	-1
Chirinos,Robinson	07	23	6	aa	CHC	127	9	25	4	2	2	13	11	27	1	1	199	261	306	566	8%	79%	0.40	64	97	2.65	1
	08	24	5	aa	CHC	103	9	21	7	2	0	6	8	15	0	0	205	260	308	568	7%	86%	0.53	74	96	2.73	9
Choo,Shin-Soo	07	25	8	aaa	CLE	208	29	49	11	1	2	23	19	35	9	3	233	297	324	620	8%	83%	0.53	65	114	3.42	15
Choy Foo,Rodney	07	26	50	aa	CLE	367	36	76	14	2	9	36	56	80	11	4	206	311	326	637	13%	78%	0.70	75	86	3.65	13
Christianson,Ryan	07	26	2	aa	STL	114	12	18	3	0	3	10	8	32	0	1	160	214	282	497	6%	72%	0.24	74	49	1.87	-11
Christian,Justin	07	27	8	a/a	NYY	424	48	96	13	4	3	40	21	69	30	5	226	262	302	564	5%	84%	0.30	49	156	2.85	2
	08	28	8	aaa	NYY	268	38	68	14	1	5	35	15	35	18	4	253	292	371	663	5%	87%	0.42	80	127	3.94	26
Christy,Jeffrey	08	24	2	a/a	MIN	164	19	30	9	0	0	7	20	36	0	1	181	271	234	505	11%	78%	0.55	47	44	2.19	-9
Ciofrone,Peter	07	24	8	aa	SD	497	65	109	18	2	9	47	36	72	1	7	220	273	315	588	7%	86%	0.50	62	58	2.80	9
	08	25	58	aa	SD	437	64	110	17	3	13	52	37	69	2	0	252	310	394	703	8%	84%	0.53	87	84	4.41	30
Ciriaco,Juan	07	24	6	aa	SD	131	11	18	3	0	1	5	5	24	4	1	138	168	181	349	3%	82%	0.20	30	101	0.97	-38
Clark,Doug	07	32	8	aaa	ATL	451	60	105	20	3	12	56	48	92	16	5	233	307	367	674	10%	80%	0.52	84	114	4.04	23
Clark,Douglas	08	27	2	aa	KC	106	8	18	3	1	4	12	4	18	1	1	170	197	314	511	3%	83%	0.20	83	82	1.88	-5
Clark,Howie	08	35	84	aaa	MIN	338	36	76	14	4	4	34	17	31	2	1	224	261	327	588	5%	91%	0.56	66	99	2.90	13
Clement,Jeff	07	24	20	aa	SEA	455	62	107	31	2	16	66	52	85	0	0	236	315	420	734	10%	81%	0.61	120	47	4.72	40
	08	25 a	2	aa	SEA	172	31	49	15	0	10	33	28	27	0	0	284	385	552	937	14%	85%	1.06	170	29	8.16	86
Clevlen,Brent	07	24	8	aaa	DET	322	30	67	13	5	6	33	36	100	4	4	208	288	335	623	10%	69%	0.36	78	120	3.25	9
	08	25	8	aaa	DET	476	60	117	20	6	17	66	44	142	6	2	246	310	422	732	8%	70%	0.31	104	120	4.66	31
Closser,JD	07	28	20	a/a	OAK	334	39	60	15	1	9	37	42	70	2	3	180	271	307	578	11%	79%	0.60	82	58	2.78	6
	08	29	2	a/a	SD	207	14	34	6	0	4	17	20	42	0	1	166	240	247	487	9%	80%	0.48	53	21	1.95	-13
Coats,Buck	07	25	8	a/a	CIN	471	67	128	21	2	10	52	37	73	16	2	272	325	391	717	7%	85%	0.51	77	112	4.81	33
	08	26	8	aaa	TOR	447	56	113	21	5	6	37	29	92	12	6	253	299	364	664	6%	79%	0.32	73	122	3.78	21
Coghlan,Christoph	08	23	4	aa	FLA	483	68	127	28	4	6	61	58	59	27	12	264	342	375	718	11%	88%	0.98	78	123	4.69	40
Colamarino,Brant	07	27	3	aa	OAK	361	30	69	18	0	6	32	23	72	1	1	190	240	292	531	6%	80%	0.32	71	37	2.31	-1
Coles,Corey	07	26	8	aa	NYM	304	31	70	9	1	1	17	20	43	7	5	231	278	275	553	6%	86%	0.46	33	82	2.62	-0
Colina,Alvin	07	26	2	aa	COL	272	16	45	16	0	4	26	13	59	0	0	165	202	265	467	4%	78%	0.21	73	20	1.71	-10
	08	27	2	aaa	CIN	227	18	49	6	1	6	40	13	60	2	1	215	257	336	593	5%	74%	0.22	73	59	2.91	6
Colina,Javier	08	30	5	a/a	CHW	181	18	42	7	1	5	17	9	30	2	0	233	268	366	633	5%	83%	0.28	82	71	3.41	17
Collaro,Thomas	07	24	8	a/a	CHW	539	56	133	30	1	24	71	31	148	6	4	247	288	441	728	5%	72%	0.21	121	59	4.34	36
	08	26	08	a/a	COL	302	23	50	13	1	6	24	16	72	1	0	165	207	271	478	5%	76%	0.22	70	56	1.81	-12
Collier,Lou	07	34	8	aaa	PHI	168	17	43	7	1	2	17	7	34	2	1	257	288	343	631	4%	79%	0.21	59	76	3.46	14
Collins,Michael	07	23	3	aa	LAA	429	38	94	16	2	4	40	11	65	5	4	219	238	294	532	2%	85%	0.16	52	80	2.27	-2
	08	24	3	aa	LAA	250	36	59	16	1	4	30	12	32	7	7	234	271	353	624	5%	87%	0.39	85	107	3.00	21
Colonel,Christian	07	26	58	aa	COL	527	59	140	41	0	14	63	35	69	5	5	266	312	420	732	6%	87%	0.51	108	49	4.62	43
	08	27	853	aa	COL	429	48	109	28	1	8	43	22	48	5	6	255	292	382	673	5%	89%	0.46	89	63	3.77	31
Colvin,Tyler	07	22	8	aa	CHC	247	29	67	10	2	8	26	4	46	6	1	271	283	425	708	2%	81%	0.09	93	112	4.29	31
	08	23	8	aa	CHC	540	51	121	25	8	11	60	32	81	5	5	223	267	358	625	6%	85%	0.40	84	106	3.17	17
Concepcion,Albert	07	26	23	aa	LA	289	33	54	11	1	9	44	17	66	0	2	187	231	322	553	5%	77%	0.25	84	57	2.36	2
	08	27	3	aa	FLA	213	25	47	9	1	4	26	22	41	1	2	220	292	321	613	9%	81%	0.53	67	62	3.21	12
Concepcion,Ambio	08	27	8	aa	NYM	456	43	90	18	2	9	42	14	100	18	6	198	221	307	528	3%	78%	0.14	71	117	2.18	-2
Conrad,Brooks	07	28	4	aa	HOU	533	58	87	27	2	16	48	42	146	8	2	164	225	308	533	7%	73%	0.29	93	97	2.26	-1
	08	29	4	aa	OAK	465	58	84	23	3	18	62	31	105	3	1	182	233	356	588	6%	78%	0.29	107	93	2.70	11
Constanza,Jose	08	25	8	aa	CLE	338	37	82	10	4	0	28	24	40	20	7	242	293	295	588	7%	88%	0.60	37	137	3.10	8
Conway,Dan	07	28	2	a/a	NYY	118	9	17	3	0	2	9	7	39	0	1	140	188	206	394	6%	67%	0.18	42	41	1.18	-32
Cook,David	08	27	8	a/a	CHW	436	61	106	22	2	18	45	77	110	12	7	244	358	425	783	15%	75%	0.70	111	81	5.50	41
Coon,Bradley	07	25	8	aa	LAA	226	32	61	7	3	1	14	19	35	22	12	269	326	336	662	8%	85%	0.55	44	154	3.65	19
	08	26	8	aa	LAA	337	58	89	8	1	3	24	38	47	13	10	265	339	321	660	10%	86%	0.80	38	99	3.84	20
Cooper,Craig	08	24	8	aa	SD	408	38	98	20	2	6	46	35	81	4	3	240	301	341	642	8%	80%	0.44	69	66	3.60	17
Cooper,James	08	25	8	aa	NYY	168	12	36	5	1	0	15	19	28	3	3	211	292	251	544	10%	83%	0.68	30	66	2.54	-3
Cooper,Jason	07	27	80	aaa	CLE	339	50	78	25	5	8	43	45	74	8	3	229	319	401	719	12%	78%	0.60	114	139	4.54	35
	08	28	8	aaa	CLE	304	32	63	17	3	7	38	40	67	2	5	207	299	352	651	12%	78%	0.59	94	73	3.51	20
Copeland,Benjami	08	25	8	aa	SF	457	60	113	19	10	4	39	41	66	21	8	248	310	357	667	8%	86%	0.63	69	173	3.96	24

BATTER	Yr	Age	Pos	Lev	Org	ab	r	h	d	t	hr	rbi	bb	k	sb	cs	ba	ob	slg	ops	bb%	ct%	eye	px	sx	rc/g	bpv
Cordido,Julio	07	27	4	aa	SF	153	12	27	8	0	2	15	12	25	2	1	174	232	260	492	7%	83%	0.46	65	55	1.99	-6
	08	28	5	aa	SF	267	23	50	5	1	0	16	14	57	3	3	188	229	214	443	5%	79%	0.25	20	73	1.58	-24
Corley,William	08	25	80	aa	PIT	500	49	119	24	2	9	41	20	94	4	10	238	268	346	613	4%	81%	0.22	73	60	2.93	14
Cornejo,Eduardo	07	26	4	aa	OAK	224	19	53	10	0	2	23	14	27	3	2	237	283	305	588	6%	88%	0.54	52	50	2.99	11
	08	27	56	aa	COL	230	16	52	6	0	1	17	25	27	2	6	224	300	260	560	10%	88%	0.91	27	29	2.59	4
Coronado,Jose	07	21	6	aa	NYM	307	26	58	6	1	1	12	26	69	6	3	189	252	225	477	8%	78%	0.38	25	79	1.94	-19
	08	22	6	aa	NYM	507	47	119	22	0	1	33	48	66	8	3	235	301	284	585	9%	87%	0.73	41	63	3.10	10
Corona,Reegie	07	21	6	aa	NYY	140	20	32	6	0	0	6	19	29	7	2	225	317	270	587	12%	80%	0.66	40	93	3.26	5
	08	22	46	aa	NYY	457	70	121	26	2	3	37	47	73	24	4	265	334	351	686	9%	84%	0.65	65	124	4.54	28
Corporan,Carlos	07	24	2	aa	MIL	179	15	32	13	0	2	20	7	44	1	0	179	209	282	491	4%	75%	0.15	79	54	1.91	-5
	08	25	2	a/a	MIL	200	16	41	12	1	5	20	12	32	2	2	206	250	346	595	5%	84%	0.36	92	65	2.79	14
Corsaletti,Jeffrey	07	25	8	aa	BOS	462	73	109	22	2	5	46	65	76	16	8	236	330	323	653	12%	84%	0.85	61	105	3.89	21
	08	26	8	a/a	BOS	446	64	113	32	4	10	49	55	80	7	2	253	334	411	745	11%	82%	0.68	107	104	5.05	42
Cortes,Jorge	07	27	8	aa	CHC	355	45	84	17	2	2	29	42	55	5	2	235	316	309	625	11%	84%	0.76	55	87	3.58	16
Cortez,Fernando	07	26	45	aa	KC	304	30	71	13	1	3	18	19	40	9	1	235	280	309	589	6%	87%	0.48	54	93	3.13	10
	08	27	6	aaa	CHW	355	22	77	10	1	4	28	13	32	8	5	218	245	281	526	3%	91%	0.39	43	67	2.23	-2
Cosby,Rob	07	27	53	aa	TOR	437	36	103	28	1	12	50	17	76	0	1	235	264	386	650	4%	83%	0.23	101	28	3.46	25
	08	28	35	aa	HOU	369	23	63	16	1	7	32	9	40	1	0	171	190	278	469	2%	89%	0.23	71	47	1.67	-9
Cosme,Caonabo	07	29	36	aa	CIN	293	28	60	14	1	9	36	7	89	3	0	205	224	349	573	2%	70%	0.08	92	82	2.60	8
	08	30	4	a/a	DET	182	16	36	3	1	3	10	6	49	0	0	198	224	269	493	3%	73%	0.12	43	54	1.98	-14
Costanzo,Michael	07	24	5	aa	PHI	508	70	120	26	1	23	66	57	136	2	0	236	313	425	737	10%	73%	0.42	116	58	4.75	35
	08	25	530	aaa	BAL	483	44	107	24	1	9	50	41	136	2	2	222	283	333	616	8%	72%	0.30	75	46	3.26	11
Costa,Shane	07	26 a	8	aa	KC	233	35	64	18	2	4	11	21	19	6	2	274	333	413	747	8%	92%	1.10	99	110	5.11	54
	08	27	8	aa	KC	292	33	75	20	0	7	33	23	35	8	2	258	313	403	716	7%	88%	0.66	100	76	4.58	41
Coste,Chris	07	35	23	a/a	PHI	198	14	38	7	0	4	27	10	29	0	0	194	231	291	522	5%	85%	0.33	63	20	2.22	-2
Cota,Humberto	08	30	2	aa	COL	138	15	34	9	0	3	16	3	19	0	1	249	268	374	641	2%	87%	0.18	90	41	3.35	24
Cotto,Pedro	07	25	8	aa	DET	202	23	44	5	2	0	14	12	27	2	2	218	261	263	524	5%	87%	0.44	32	97	2.30	-5
	08	26	8	aa	DET	110	7	23	3	2	2	11	6	14	0	4	209	247	318	565	5%	87%	0.39	63	92	2.20	3
Cottrell,Patrick	08	27	5	aa	TAM	205	22	38	5	1	3	18	10	30	2	1	184	222	256	478	5%	85%	0.33	45	86	1.85	-14
Crabbe,Callix	07	25	48	aaa	MIL	457	74	122	22	7	8	33	62	64	15	16	267	355	398	753	12%	86%	0.97	83	131	4.84	43
	08	26	48	aaa	MIL	204	24	44	8	2	1	13	30	35	7	6	217	317	286	603	13%	83%	0.86	48	102	3.14	9
Craig,Allen	08	24	5	aa	STL	506	64	130	25	0	15	65	36	70	2	1	256	306	397	703	7%	86%	0.52	91	49	4.34	33
Craig,Matthew	07	26	53	aa	CHC	386	42	97	23	2	11	50	36	85	1	0	252	316	408	724	8%	78%	0.42	101	53	4.66	34
	08	27	3	aa	CHC	223	30	56	13	0	7	24	32	38	2	0	250	343	404	747	12%	83%	0.83	100	49	5.19	41
Creek,Greg	07	25	3	aa	ATL	232	23	48	13	0	1	14	21	58	2	5	206	271	272	542	8%	75%	0.36	54	49	2.32	-2
	08	26	35	aa	ATL	351	37	78	17	5	5	41	32	66	0	3	223	288	335	624	8%	81%	0.49	74	81	3.28	14
Crespo,Cesar	07	28	846	aaa	BAL	340	29	74	12	1	3	32	34	70	10	7	219	291	284	575	9%	79%	0.49	47	75	2.84	2
Crew,Ryan	07	24	8	aa	MIL	137	16	30	6	0	0	11	13	21	3	0	222	291	264	554	9%	85%	0.63	37	73	2.85	2
Crowe,Trevor	07	24	8	aa	CLE	518	74	119	25	2	4	43	55	66	24	10	230	305	309	614	10%	87%	0.84	58	113	3.36	17
	08	25	8	a/a	CLE	344	61	93	26	2	8	36	38	70	15	8	271	344	424	768	10%	80%	0.55	106	120	5.23	45
Crozier,Eric	07	29	3	aa	BOS	220	23	37	9	1	5	27	22	89	1	0	167	242	286	528	9%	59%	0.24	76	66	2.32	-8
Cruz,Enrique	07	26	5	aa	CIN	484	46	106	24	1	6	47	31	109	9	5	219	266	312	578	6%	78%	0.28	66	77	2.81	6
	08	27	54	aaa	ATL	230	10	41	12	0	2	17	8	54	0	2	180	208	256	464	3%	76%	0.15	58	19	1.64	-13
Cruz,Jose	07	23	4	aa	NYM	264	19	48	13	2	3	22	28	56	4	3	180	259	276	535	10%	79%	0.51	66	80	2.38	-3
Cruz,Lee	08	25	80	aa	CHW	197	22	49	11	1	10	24	10	38	0	3	248	286	472	758	5%	81%	0.27	136	47	4.40	44
Cruz,Luis	07	24	6	aa	SD	394	34	75	16	1	8	31	19	42	3	0	190	228	295	523	5%	89%	0.46	70	69	2.23	1
	08	25	6	aa	PIT	495	50	126	33	1	7	51	18	43	4	8	254	281	365	645	4%	91%	0.43	81	54	3.36	27
Cruz,Nelson	07	27 b	8	aa	TEX	162	22	45	7	1	12	32	15	34	1	2	277	338	548	886	8%	79%	0.44	156	56	6.56	66
	08	28 b	8	aa	TEX	383	64	105	14	2	27	69	38	77	17	9	273	339	533	872	9%	80%	0.49	147	104	6.29	62
Cumberland,Shau	07	23	8	aa	CIN	467	36	108	20	1	7	42	29	79	3	10	231	276	322	598	6%	83%	0.37	63	38	2.82	10
	08	24	8	a/a	CIN	436	57	108	18	4	8	31	36	84	14	7	247	305	359	664	8%	81%	0.43	72	120	3.83	21
Cunningham,Aaro	07	21 a	8	aa	ARI	118	21	32	8	3	5	17	10	22	1	3	271	328	517	845	8%	81%	0.45	148	169	5.60	61
	08	22	8	aa	OAK	423	67	121	21	4	12	51	38	80	12	6	286	345	440	785	8%	81%	0.48	96	119	5.55	45
Curreri,Frank	08	26	82	aa	ARI	335	27	76	19	0	5	33	40	48	3	1	227	310	325	636	11%	86%	0.84	71	41	3.66	22
Curtis,Colin	07	23	8	aa	NYY	240	32	57	11	1	3	15	17	48	1	1	238	288	329	617	7%	80%	0.35	64	73	3.30	12
	08	24	8	aa	NYY	495	64	119	19	2	10	67	50	84	6	3	240	309	344	654	9%	83%	0.60	67	79	3.81	20
Czarniecki,Jordan	07	27	8	aa	COL	427	53	100	26	0	10	42	41	67	13	4	234	301	363	664	9%	84%	0.61	89	84	3.87	27
	08	28	8	aa	LAA	393	41	87	19	3	6	27	33	60	8	10	222	283	331	614	8%	85%	0.56	74	87	3.01	15
D'Antona,James	07	25	532	aa	ARI	483	59	127	37	4	11	65	31	52	3	2	263	307	421	728	6%	89%	0.59	109	80	4.60	44
	08	26 b	5	aa	ARI	419	54	134	31	1	17	62	24	57	1	0	321	357	525	882	5%	87%	0.42	133	45	7.25	70
Daeges,Zachary	08	25 a	8	aa	BOS	394	49	110	36	2	4	49	56	59	2	2	280	369	409	779	12%	85%	0.94	99	58	5.76	53
Danielson,Sean P.	07	25	8	aa	STL	320	41	74	13	1	3	25	29	37	11	5	231	294	301	595	8%	89%	0.79	50	95	3.09	13
	08	26	8	a/a	BOS	346	34	79	13	3	1	17	25	83	19	5	229	280	290	570	7%	76%	0.30	44	130	2.94	0
Daniel,Mike	08	24	8	aa	WAS	485	47	102	11	1	10	43	44	105	14	12	210	276	295	571	8%	78%	0.42	52	74	2.63	-0
Davis,Ben	07	31	2	aa	LA	110	8	15	3	0	1	6	6	29	0	1	134	176	178	354	5%	74%	0.20	32	46	0.95	-38
	08	32	2	a/a	BAL	161	9	26	6	1	3	11	3	31	0	0	158	176	253	429	2%	81%	0.11	62	39	1.38	-19
Davis,Blake	07	24	6	aa	BAL	115	10	21	6	0	0	8	8	21	1	1	186	237	236	473	6%	82%	0.38	45	54	1.83	-12
	08	25	6	aa	BAL	457	48	114	19	5	4	44	22	70	7	8	250	285	338	623	5%	85%	0.32	59	100	3.20	14
Davis,Bradley	07	25	1	aa	FLA	152	10	38	15	1	3	17	16	37	0	1	250	322	419	741	10%	76%	0.44	123	42	4.76	43
	08	26	2	aa	FLA	249	24	42	13	1	5	22	28	53	0	2	170	254	287	541	10%	79%	0.53	79	46	2.38	-0
Davis,Christopher	07	22 a	5	aa	TEX	109	18	30	7	0	11	21	11	22	0	0	275	342	642	984	9%	80%	0.50	213	20	8.04	90
	08	23 a	3	aa	TEX	297	53	90	19	1	19	57	20	57	5	1	303	347	566	913	6%	81%	0.35	159	91	7.41	73
Davis,Leonard	08	25	8	a/a	WAS	221	23	53	12	2	8	31	9	46	2	1	239	268	417	685	4%	79%	0.19	111	88	3.79	29
Davis,Quentin	08	26	8	aa	ATL	199	14	32	5	0	4	17	8	41	8	5	161	191	241	432	4%	79%	0.18	50	83	1.35	-22
Davis,Rajai	07	27	8	aa	PIT	211	23	55	10	3	3	23	15	24	21	9	260	308	371	679	7%	89%	0.61	74	147	3.88	29
Dawkins,Gookie	07	28	46	a/a	PHI	421	34	84	15	1	4	27	21	86	9	5	200	238	271	509	5%	80%	0.25	50	77	2.09	-8
	08	29	56	a/a	KC	402	31	77	21	1	7	28	22	105	4	4	193	234	300	533	5%	74%	0.21	74	61	2.22	-1
De Jesus,Ivan	08	21	64	aa	LA	463	74	135	20	1	6	46	65	66	14	2	292	379	380	759	12%	86%	0.97	61	95	5.80	42
De Jesus,Michael	08	25	4	aa	CIN	178	24	40	8	0	2	11	24	24	2	1	227	317	301	618	12%	86%	0.96	54	57	3.49	17
De La Cruz,Christ	08	26	4	a/a	FLA	170	13	32	6	0	2	15	18	25	0	4	189	269	254	523	10%	85%	0.74	45	25	2.16	-3
de la Rosa,Tomas	07	30	54	aa	SF	459	40	90	20	2	6	44	21	71	13	6	196	231	284	516	4%	85%	0.30	61	95	2.12	-4
De Leon,Santo	08	25	5	aa	DET	169	19	39	10	1	5	19	6	21	1	1	233	258	386	644	3%	88%	0.28	99	76	3.32	24

BATTER	Yr	Age	Pos	Lev	Org	ab	r	h	d	t	hr	rbi	bb	k	sb	cs	ba	ob	slg	ops	bb%	ct%	eye	px	sx	rc/g	bpv
DeCaster,Yurende	07	28	38	aa	PIT	407	38	86	20	1	6	37	38	99	9	7	210	278	305	583	9%	76%	0.39	67	70	2.82	5
	08	29	5	a/a	WAS	366	39	72	18	1	9	45	26	101	4	5	197	250	322	572	7%	72%	0.26	82	71	2.56	5
Deeds,Doug	07	26	8	aaa	MIN	235	27	53	7	2	8	18	18	81	2	1	227	283	371	655	7%	65%	0.23	84	93	3.63	15
	08	27	83	aa	CHC	416	50	109	32	2	9	41	30	88	5	1	262	311	411	722	7%	79%	0.34	104	86	4.64	37
Delaney,Jason	07	25	38	aa	PIT	223	20	52	10	0	6	29	29	45	0	0	234	324	354	677	12%	80%	0.65	77	14	4.18	23
	08	26	3	aa	PIT	465	49	118	25	3	6	41	68	93	6	4	253	348	356	703	13%	80%	0.73	72	72	4.60	29
Dement,Dan	07	29	458	aa	WAS	407	43	76	20	2	6	43	28	115	2	0	186	238	286	524	6%	72%	0.24	68	74	2.28	-5
Denker,Travis	08	23	4	aa	SF	296	40	70	23	1	6	31	38	62	3	1	235	323	377	700	11%	79%	0.61	101	73	4.42	32
Denorfia,Chris	08	28	8	aa	OAK	189	23	44	11	1	1	13	8	26	4	4	233	264	312	576	4%	86%	0.30	61	94	2.59	9
Denove,Christoph	08	26	2	aa	CIN	164	8	33	10	0	0	10	14	24	1	2	201	264	264	528	8%	85%	0.58	56	27	2.30	1
Desmond,Ian	08	23	6	aa	WAS	323	32	69	13	0	9	34	24	64	10	10	212	266	334	600	7%	80%	0.37	77	69	2.73	10
Dewitt,Blake	07	22	5	aa	LA	178	17	45	12	1	5	17	6	22	0	1	253	277	416	693	3%	88%	0.27	108	51	3.91	34
	08	23	4	aa	LA	111	13	29	4	1	3	14	8	12	1	0	265	313	397	711	7%	89%	0.64	80	78	4.57	34
Diaz,Argenis	08	22	6	aa	BOS	139	16	38	9	1	1	19	8	24	0	1	276	316	378	694	5%	83%	0.34	76	66	4.24	30
Diaz,Einar	07	35	2	aa	PIT	118	9	20	6	0	1	8	5	10	3	1	166	199	249	449	4%	92%	0.49	60	76	1.60	-10
Diaz,Frank	07	24	8	aa	WAS	416	46	91	17	2	11	47	21	61	8	3	219	257	347	605	5%	85%	0.35	81	95	3.01	13
	08	25	8	aaa	WAS	117	14	29	6	1	0	8	5	17	3	2	249	278	313	591	4%	85%	0.28	50	108	2.94	9
Diaz,Robinzon	07	24	2	a/a	TOR	366	30	106	18	1	4	32	10	20	4	0	289	307	376	684	3%	95%	0.50	63	64	4.28	32
	08	25	2	a/a	PIT	145	6	33	7	1	1	13	4	9	1	3	227	246	305	551	3%	94%	0.44	56	48	2.30	8
Diaz,Victor	07	26	80	aa	TEX	271	30	74	13	2	12	50	16	74	3	0	272	313	462	775	6%	73%	0.22	114	80	5.30	42
	08	27	08	aa	SEA	485	52	112	33	0	18	80	48	158	6	4	231	300	414	714	9%	68%	0.30	119	54	4.30	32
Dickerson,Chris	07	25	8	a/a	CIN	468	57	108	13	4	12	46	48	147	25	8	231	304	355	659	9%	69%	0.33	73	131	3.84	14
	08	27	8	aaa	CIN	349	49	84	14	5	9	40	40	91	19	7	240	319	385	704	10%	74%	0.44	87	152	4.35	25
DiFelice,Mike	07	38	2	aa	NYM	248	22	44	6	0	4	22	12	71	0	1	178	215	243	458	5%	71%	0.17	42	39	1.68	-20
	08	39	2	aaa	TAM	217	14	36	10	0	2	17	10	52	0	0	165	202	235	437	4%	76%	0.20	54	24	1.52	-19
Dillon,Joe	07	32	5	aaa	MIL	319	55	85	24	2	16	58	41	34	5	1	265	350	505	855	11%	89%	1.20	151	91	6.55	75
	08	33	5	aaa	MIL	171	23	33	6	1	3	15	20	28	1	2	194	277	298	575	10%	83%	0.69	66	74	2.76	6
Dinkelman,Brian	08	25	4	aa	MIN	198	21	42	12	2	2	17	8	22	2	2	213	243	325	568	4%	89%	0.35	79	101	2.54	11
Dobson,Patrick	07	27	83	aa	SF	305	27	54	17	1	3	19	23	71	6	3	177	236	274	510	7%	77%	0.33	71	85	2.12	-5
Dominguez,Jeffrey	08	22	45	aa	SEA	351	28	63	13	0	2	26	25	64	15	5	179	234	234	468	7%	82%	0.39	42	89	1.85	-15
Donachie,Adam	07	24	2	aa	KC	271	28	49	12	0	7	29	26	65	0	0	183	255	301	555	9%	76%	0.40	77	29	2.59	1
	08	25	2	aa	KC	264	25	51	8	0	4	24	31	61	1	1	193	277	265	542	10%	77%	0.50	48	38	2.56	-6
Donald,Jason	08	24	6	aa	PHI	362	40	94	16	2	12	38	33	68	8	2	260	321	411	732	8%	81%	0.48	94	87	4.82	35
Donovan,Todd	08	30	8	aa	OAK	307	35	62	10	1	1	17	27	54	24	6	202	267	249	516	8%	82%	0.50	36	123	2.43	-8
Doolittle,Sean	08	22	3	aa	OAK	201	19	44	13	0	3	23	13	39	1	1	219	266	328	595	6%	81%	0.33	80	45	2.95	13
Dorn,Daniel	08	24	83	aa	CIN	336	47	81	18	1	17	44	31	68	1	0	240	304	454	758	8%	80%	0.45	130	57	4.89	43
Dorta,Melvin	07	26	6	a/a	WAS	356	35	72	15	3	1	24	21	45	10	11	203	247	270	517	6%	87%	0.46	49	108	2.00	-3
	08	27	45	aa	PIT	403	35	100	16	4	6	35	24	40	15	16	249	291	347	638	6%	90%	0.59	64	98	3.13	21
Dowdy,Brett	07	26	48	aa	SD	312	36	65	11	2	4	23	28	60	10	4	208	273	288	561	8%	81%	0.47	54	109	2.73	1
	08	27	64	aa	SD	479	66	112	20	3	9	40	30	83	10	6	234	280	346	626	6%	83%	0.37	72	108	3.30	15
Dragicevich,Jeffrey	07	25	4	aa	COL	117	9	24	6	0	4	14	8	33	0	1	208	259	354	613	6%	72%	0.24	95	23	2.98	13
	08	26	56	aa	COL	334	27	76	11	1	7	32	37	66	1	6	229	305	333	638	10%	80%	0.56	66	29	3.41	14
Duarte,Jose	08	24	8	aa	KC	528	58	123	20	2	8	39	43	77	24	9	232	290	321	611	8%	86%	0.56	59	103	3.26	13
Dubois,Jason	07	29	80	aaa	BAL	378	36	86	20	0	12	38	26	97	0	0	226	276	376	653	6%	74%	0.27	97	21	3.59	21
	08	30	83	a/a	CHC	330	45	71	13	0	20	47	25	84	3	2	214	269	433	702	7%	75%	0.30	127	57	3.88	30
Duenas,Tomas	07	26	2	aa	COL	218	14	38	7	0	4	23	7	49	1	0	176	201	267	468	3%	77%	0.14	59	37	1.73	-14
Duffy,Chris	08	28	8	aa	PIT	109	9	24	7	1	2	8	8	22	4	3	218	271	347	618	7%	80%	0.37	89	102	3.04	17
Duff,Timothy	07	26	2	aa	LAA	195	11	32	5	0	3	16	11	59	3	3	165	211	232	443	5%	70%	0.19	44	47	1.51	-23
	08	27	2	aa	LAA	235	13	41	7	0	2	16	12	60	3	1	172	212	226	438	5%	74%	0.20	39	49	1.56	-23
Duncan,Eric	07	23	30	aaa	NYY	411	44	98	25	1	11	59	45	71	2	2	238	313	381	694	10%	83%	0.63	96	49	4.22	31
	08	24	503	aaa	NYY	437	41	93	21	1	10	52	31	103	5	4	213	266	332	598	7%	76%	0.30	78	63	2.94	9
Duncan,Jeff	07	29	8	aaa	TOR	141	18	26	1	0	0	5	17	30	5	2	185	271	191	462	11%	79%	0.56	6	84	1.91	-25
Duncan,Shelley	07	28 b	8	aaa	NYY	336	49	87	16	1	22	67	37	82	2	2	260	334	512	846	10%	76%	0.46	147	53	6.12	56
	08	29	8	aaa	NYY	205	29	40	11	0	9	34	30	57	4	1	193	296	386	682	13%	72%	0.53	120	72	4.00	24
Dunlap,Cory	07	23	30	aa	LA	399	37	79	16	0	6	49	55	66	0	0	197	295	282	577	12%	83%	0.84	59	21	2.98	7
Duran,German	07	23 a	4	aa	TEX	480	67	132	30	4	19	69	28	65	9	2	275	315	475	790	6%	86%	0.43	125	109	5.44	52
Durrington,Trent	07	32	40	aaa	CLE	195	23	36	5	1	1	15	22	40	12	5	185	266	231	497	10%	79%	0.54	32	118	2.12	-15
Edwards,Mike	07	31	8	a/a	CIN	167	18	31	9	0	2	14	10	28	3	0	187	231	268	499	5%	84%	0.35	61	82	2.12	-5
Ehlers,Cody	07	25	30	aa	NYY	385	35	86	27	0	7	48	52	83	0	1	222	315	348	663	12%	78%	0.63	91	19	3.92	24
	08	26	3	aa	NYY	370	40	65	22	1	7	38	40	95	0	0	177	256	301	557	10%	74%	0.42	86	42	2.61	3
Einertson,Mitch	08	23	8	aa	HOU	382	38	86	22	1	9	46	19	67	4	4	225	262	359	620	5%	82%	0.28	90	66	3.08	18
Eldred,Brad	07	27	38	aa	PIT	311	26	50	8	1	10	32	13	90	7	2	160	195	288	483	4%	71%	0.15	76	89	1.74	-13
	08	28	3	aaa	CHW	427	48	88	18	1	31	77	22	141	3	3	206	245	468	713	5%	67%	0.16	150	52	3.69	34
Eldridge,Rashad	07	26	8	aa	MIN	361	49	86	17	3	5	31	23	63	5	5	237	282	337	618	6%	82%	0.36	68	102	3.16	14
	08	27	8	aa	TAM	435	53	104	16	5	4	42	49	80	18	11	239	316	321	637	10%	82%	0.61	54	123	3.54	14
Ellison,Jason	08	31	8	aa	TEX	477	43	86	16	3	2	30	41	69	9	10	180	245	235	480	8%	85%	0.59	40	85	1.82	-12
Ellis,Andrew	07	26	2	aa	LA	357	43	75	17	1	6	41	44	60	1	4	210	297	314	611	11%	83%	0.74	72	46	3.16	14
	08	28	2	aa	LA	274	32	70	14	2	3	42	38	41	0	2	256	346	348	695	12%	85%	0.92	65	50	4.45	30
Ellsbury,Jacoby	07	24	8	a/a	BOS	436	69	131	25	5	2	35	32	48	35	8	300	348	394	742	7%	89%	0.66	68	156	5.36	41
Ensberg,Morgan	08	33	5	aaa	CLE	159	19	24	8	0	4	18	26	48	1	1	150	267	278	545	14%	70%	0.53	84	47	2.52	-5
Erickson,Matt	07	32	46	aa	ARI	231	22	46	9	1	1	20	13	39	2	1	197	241	258	498	5%	83%	0.34	45	86	2.09	-9
Errecart,Christoph	08	24	3	aa	MIL	360	44	76	20	1	12	35	25	91	1	2	212	264	370	635	7%	75%	0.28	101	59	3.25	18
Escobar,Alcides	07	21	6	aa	MIL	226	24	62	5	3	1	25	11	31	3	3	274	306	339	646	4%	86%	0.33	40	108	3.62	15
	08	22	6	aa	MIL	547	77	160	23	3	7	61	26	67	28	10	292	324	384	708	5%	88%	0.39	62	121	4.55	31
Escobar,Alex	08	30	0	aaa	WAS	230	21	45	9	0	4	23	14	48	3	3	196	243	292	535	6%	79%	0.30	65	56	2.29	-2
Escobar,Yunel	07	25	6	aaa	ATL	180	18	57	10	2	2	26	13	25	6	3	317	363	428	790	7%	86%	0.52	76	103	5.87	47
Espinosa,David	07	26	80	aaa	DET	372	39	70	15	5	4	45	31	84	11	2	189	251	287	538	8%	77%	0.37	64	146	2.49	-3
Espino,Damaso	07	24	2	aa	KC	231	13	53	10	0	2	17	18	25	1	2	230	286	300	586	7%	89%	0.71	53	24	2.95	13
	08	25	2	aa	CLE	138	8	29	3	0	0	9	13	17	0	0	211	280	232	511	9%	88%	0.77	18	15	2.32	-7
Esposito,Brian	07	29	2	aa	STL	242	7	30	4	0	2	10	7	51	0	2	122	148	169	316	3%	79%	0.14	30	16	0.72	-44
	08	30	2	aa	COL	247	16	39	2	1	3	15	5	36	3	1	157	174	212	386	2%	85%	0.14	31	75	1.15	-32
Esquivel,Matt	07	25	8	aa	ATL	372	55	82	14	1	15	58	38	92	12	2	220	292	386	678	9%	75%	0.41	99	107	4.01	23

Major League Equivalent Statistics

BATTER	Yr	Age	Pos	Lev	Org	ab	r	h	d	t	hr	rbi	bb	k	sb	cs	ba	ob	slg	ops	bb%	ct%	eye	px	sx	rc/g	bpv
Eure,Jeffrey	07	27	5	aa	KC	163	10	25	5	2	2	12	8	53	2	1	153	194	234	428	5%	67%	0.16	52	100	1.43	-25
Evans,Nicholas	08	23 a	38	aa	NYM	296	44	83	17	5	11	45	22	54	2	1	280	330	483	813	7%	82%	0.41	123	124	5.84	52
Evans,Terry	07	26	8	aa	LAA	475	58	126	34	3	12	61	21	120	20	9	265	296	423	718	4%	75%	0.17	107	117	4.28	36
	08	27	8	aa	LAA	174	24	40	11	0	3	17	16	54	5	6	227	291	338	629	8%	69%	0.29	81	78	3.12	15
Everidge,Tommy	08	25	30	aa	OAK	531	65	120	28	0	15	84	39	103	0	0	227	280	365	645	7%	81%	0.38	91	33	3.55	21
Eylward,Mike	07	28	30	aa	LAA	479	52	110	23	0	8	58	33	73	1	4	229	278	327	606	6%	85%	0.45	69	35	3.06	14
	08	29	30	aa	PHI	230	15	39	9	0	3	19	12	45	0	1	168	210	254	464	5%	80%	0.27	60	28	1.68	-14
Eymann,Eric	08	25	56	aa	CIN	445	46	114	27	2	7	53	18	53	4	5	257	286	371	657	4%	88%	0.34	81	67	3.60	26
Fahey,Brandon	07	27	6	aaa	BAL	343	35	76	8	6	2	26	29	44	12	5	221	282	294	576	8%	87%	0.66	44	142	2.88	5
	08	28	6	aaa	BAL	222	20	46	6	0	1	18	16	42	1	5	207	261	247	508	7%	81%	0.38	31	40	2.03	-10
Faison,Vince	07	27	8	aa	OAK	348	26	63	15	5	3	34	17	77	8	3	180	217	283	500	5%	78%	0.21	66	139	1.98	-8
Falu,Irving	07	24	64	aa	KC	476	37	102	11	5	1	23	29	38	12	10	214	258	263	521	6%	92%	0.75	33	101	2.21	-0
	08	25	864	aa	KC	362	46	97	10	2	4	34	31	28	9	9	267	325	338	663	8%	92%	1.12	46	85	3.78	31
Fasano,James	07	24	30	aa	TEX	236	22	60	12	1	8	31	14	33	0	0	254	296	411	707	6%	86%	0.44	100	32	4.31	34
Fasano,Sal	07	36	2	aaa	TOR	145	14	32	4	0	6	11	5	31	1	0	223	247	379	625	3%	79%	0.14	89	39	3.16	14
Feiner,Korey	07	26	2	a/a	MIN	168	12	28	5	0	1	13	14	49	0	0	166	228	214	442	7%	71%	0.28	37	24	1.64	-24
Feliciano,Jesus	07	28	8	aa	NYM	235	23	54	8	0	2	18	14	25	3	2	228	273	293	565	6%	89%	0.58	46	60	2.75	6
	08	29	8	aa	NYM	509	52	122	16	3	2	40	30	56	9	14	240	282	292	575	6%	89%	0.54	38	76	2.63	6
Fernandez,Alexan	07	26	8	aa	PIT	215	17	38	10	0	2	17	9	29	1	0	178	210	247	457	4%	87%	0.30	52	49	1.69	-13
Fernando,Osvaldo	07	27	6	aa	HOU	105	7	20	3	0	0	3	1	13	4	2	191	197	224	421	1%	88%	0.07	29	16	1.38	-23
Ferris,Michael	07	25	30	aa	STL	227	22	42	9	0	4	19	25	57	2	2	184	264	272	536	10%	75%	0.43	59	48	2.42	-5
Fields,Josh	07	25 a	5	a/a	CHW	205	25	54	13	0	11	33	36	57	7	5	265	374	483	857	15%	72%	0.63	135	53	6.50	57
	08	26	5	aaa	CHW	276	34	60	13	2	9	29	31	90	7	2	218	297	381	678	10%	67%	0.34	101	106	3.98	21
Figueroa,Francisc	07	25	4	aa	BAL	350	48	86	16	1	1	15	35	44	12	12	244	313	304	617	9%	87%	0.80	47	90	3.16	17
Figueroa,Luis	07	34	6	aa	SF	443	39	86	15	2	2	31	16	40	4	7	194	223	251	474	4%	91%	0.40	41	76	1.71	-10
	08	35	645	aa	CHC	370	38	84	14	1	2	30	21	28	1	2	227	269	285	554	5%	92%	0.75	44	52	2.62	9
Finan,Ryan	08	27	3	aa	BAL	377	46	82	17	1	9	43	39	77	0	0	217	290	342	632	9%	80%	0.50	81	42	3.48	16
Fiorentino,Jeff	07	24	8	aa	BAL	436	54	106	15	2	12	52	36	76	7	5	244	302	373	674	8%	83%	0.48	79	80	3.90	23
	08	25	8	a/a	BAL	250	23	57	10	1	2	23	31	50	7	3	229	314	301	615	11%	80%	0.62	52	76	3.44	10
Flores,Joshua	07	22	8	aa	HOU	192	24	38	7	2	2	10	15	34	12	0	198	256	286	542	7%	82%	0.44	58	159	2.76	-1
Fontenot,Mike	07	27	6	aa	CHC	211	32	55	13	2	5	24	11	33	2	1	260	296	417	713	5%	85%	0.33	103	121	4.36	36
Ford,Joshua	07	25	2	aa	ARI	257	24	61	12	0	3	23	25	51	0	1	237	304	318	621	9%	80%	0.49	60	25	3.42	13
Ford,Lew	07	31	8	aaa	MIN	122	13	28	11	0	2	15	14	34	2	1	229	310	361	672	11%	72%	0.42	101	52	3.97	26
Ford,Shelby	08	24	4	aa	PIT	319	36	84	23	7	3	27	17	43	17	6	264	301	406	706	5%	87%	0.39	96	176	4.27	35
Fowler,Dexter	08	23 a	8	aa	COL	421	66	128	28	6	7	46	46	60	14	10	304	373	449	822	10%	86%	0.77	97	130	6.15	57
Fox,Adam	07	26	53	aa	TEX	352	37	82	14	3	6	32	18	58	4	4	233	270	343	613	5%	84%	0.31	71	86	3.08	13
	08	27	54	aa	TEX	384	36	72	12	2	7	33	27	73	6	0	187	240	285	525	6%	81%	0.37	61	93	2.34	-5
Fox,Jake	07	25	83	aa	CHC	458	59	109	25	1	20	59	16	90	6	2	238	264	426	690	3%	80%	0.18	117	87	3.83	31
	08	26	38	aa	CHC	505	65	120	33	1	23	74	33	89	5	2	237	284	443	726	6%	82%	0.37	130	71	4.33	40
Francia,Juan	07	26	4	a/a	NYY	227	29	54	5	1	0	19	14	28	10	10	239	284	268	551	6%	87%	0.50	22	106	2.34	-1
Francisco,Ben	07	26 a	8	aaa	CLE	377	51	109	27	1	10	44	33	60	19	9	289	346	444	789	8%	84%	0.55	106	97	5.53	51
Franco,Iker	07	26	2	aaa	ATL	177	14	36	8	0	2	23	17	31	0	2	203	274	279	554	9%	83%	0.56	56	24	2.55	2
Frazier,Jeffrey	07	25	8	aa	SEA	302	23	60	10	1	3	23	17	56	0	2	200	243	265	508	5%	82%	0.31	45	38	2.10	-9
	08	26	08	a/a	DET	458	41	114	17	1	5	42	24	47	1	1	249	286	321	608	5%	90%	0.51	51	42	3.24	14
Freeman,Choo	07	28	8	aa	LA	400	36	81	12	2	7	33	36	94	2	1	201	267	288	555	8%	77%	0.38	55	64	2.65	-3
Freese,David	08	25	5	aa	STL	464	62	117	24	2	18	68	29	91	4	2	251	295	427	723	6%	80%	0.32	110	78	4.43	35
Frey,Christopher	07	24	8	aa	COL	474	51	128	28	5	1	27	29	49	10	8	271	313	355	668	6%	90%	0.60	63	104	3.90	28
	08	25	8	aa	COL	421	34	103	21	4	2	28	15	38	8	5	246	272	326	598	3%	91%	0.39	58	96	3.00	14
Frostad,Emerson	07	25	3	aa	TEX	307	31	66	11	1	11	35	27	72	3	1	214	276	368	644	8%	77%	0.37	93	63	3.49	17
	08	26	253	aa	TEX	342	38	74	22	2	6	31	26	67	3	4	217	273	341	614	7%	80%	0.39	86	76	3.08	16
Frost,Jeremy	07	28	23	aa	CHW	238	22	46	4	1	6	16	12	71	2	1	192	232	289	521	5%	70%	0.18	56	73	2.22	-9
Fuld,Sam	07	26	8	aa	CHC	387	52	92	23	2	3	22	37	41	10	3	237	304	328	632	9%	89%	0.90	68	104	3.60	25
	08	27	8	aa	CHC	402	41	86	17	2	5	37	40	45	7	11	215	287	300	587	9%	89%	0.91	58	72	2.76	14
Fuller,Cody	07	25	8	aa	LAA	330	30	61	8	2	2	23	24	89	15	8	185	241	237	479	7%	73%	0.27	35	113	1.86	-18
	08	26	8	aa	LAA	166	13	29	5	1	3	8	6	25	3	6	172	198	260	459	3%	85%	0.22	55	87	1.37	-16
Fulse,Sheldon	07	26	8	aa	WAS	178	31	41	7	1	3	13	26	51	11	3	228	326	324	650	13%	71%	0.51	64	127	3.99	12
Furmaniak,J.J.	07	28	645	aa	OAK	424	47	90	14	1	10	34	33	106	14	7	213	270	317	587	7%	75%	0.31	65	91	2.86	4
Gaetti,Joe	07	26	8	aa	COL	421	48	93	22	4	15	45	33	121	4	5	220	277	398	675	7%	71%	0.27	109	88	3.61	24
	08	27	8	aa	MIN	289	41	67	15	2	13	40	23	87	2	0	232	289	430	719	7%	70%	0.26	120	91	4.36	32
Gaffney,Michael	07	26	4	aa	KC	218	15	44	9	0	2	13	14	30	2	0	202	249	268	517	6%	86%	0.45	49	46	2.30	-3
Gall,John	07	30	83	aa	FLA	413	48	85	20	2	8	38	26	59	7	4	205	253	320	572	6%	86%	0.45	76	91	2.67	9
	08	31	8	aa	FLA	359	35	86	23	0	9	54	23	53	6	4	239	285	374	659	6%	85%	0.43	93	58	3.61	27
Gamel,Mathew	08	23	5	a/a	MIL	529	76	148	31	4	16	76	46	101	5	9	280	337	443	780	8%	81%	0.46	105	80	5.24	46
Garciaparra,Micha	07	25	6	a/a	PHI	284	26	59	4	1	3	21	30	51	5	2	208	284	260	544	10%	82%	0.60	31	72	2.63	-6
	08	26	3	aa	MIL	103	9	29	4	1	2	15	3	22	2	1	283	302	392	694	3%	78%	0.13	69	90	4.21	25
Garcia,Emmanuel	08	23	4	aa	NYM	367	43	80	11	1	3	34	29	69	14	10	218	275	278	553	7%	81%	0.42	42	96	2.51	-2
Garcia,Isa	08	24	50	aa	STL	194	18	46	6	0	4	25	4	25	0	1	238	252	327	579	2%	87%	0.15	57	35	2.73	6
Garcia,Jesse	07	34	6	aa	HOU	270	20	45	9	0	5	19	6	53	1	4	166	183	254	437	2%	80%	0.11	58	51	1.34	-19
Garcia,Sergio	07	28	46	aa	LA	250	31	55	12	0	6	22	17	40	4	1	219	270	335	605	7%	84%	0.44	77	76	3.14	14
Gardenhire,Toby	08	26	536	aa	MIN	284	23	61	4	1	1	17	20	49	2	1	214	266	243	509	7%	83%	0.41	19	58	2.25	-12
Gardner,Brett	07	24	8	a/a	NYY	384	75	100	16	6	1	24	49	75	36	7	260	343	341	684	11%	80%	0.64	55	189	4.66	22
	08	25	8	aaa	NYY	341	57	88	10	7	3	27	57	72	31	9	259	366	353	719	14%	79%	0.79	57	185	5.04	26
Garrett,Shawn	07	29	30	aa	CHW	451	44	100	25	2	9	45	31	131	5	3	222	272	346	618	6%	71%	0.24	84	80	3.18	13
	08	30	83	aa	SEA	475	46	109	26	2	8	53	24	97	4	4	230	267	340	607	5%	80%	0.25	76	68	3.03	13
Garthwaite,Jay	07	27	80	aa	CIN	253	18	48	13	0	8	27	14	82	1	1	189	231	334	565	5%	68%	0.17	94	31	2.50	5
Gartrell,Maurice	08	25	80	aa	CHW	409	47	95	20	1	14	45	40	99	6	1	232	301	392	693	9%	76%	0.41	100	74	4.21	27
Gathright,Joey	07	26	8	aa	KC	223	33	62	9	3	0	18	33	23	18	8	277	370	339	710	13%	90%	1.44	45	136	4.81	40
Gautreau,Jake	07	28	4	aa	NYM	226	12	37	10	0	4	21	3	35	0	0	165	177	264	442	1%	85%	0.10	67	19	1.45	-15
Geiger,Kyle	07	25	2	aa	MIN	276	27	56	14	1	3	26	12	41	0	0	202	235	287	522	4%	85%	0.28	61	49	2.23	-2
Gentry,Craig	08	25	8	aa	TEX	360	36	82	15	0	3	25	19	58	12	10	227	266	293	559	5%	84%	0.33	50	78	2.48	3
Gerut,Jody	08	31	8	aa	SD	107	16	25	7	2	3	13	9	12	3	1	230	292	421	713	8%	89%	0.79	119	139	4.26	42

Major League Equivalent Statistics

BATTER	Yr	Age	Pos	Lev	Org	ab	r	h	d	t	hr	rbi	bb	k	sb	cs	ba	ob	slg	ops	bb%	ct%	eye	px	sx	rc/g	bpv
Getz,Christopher	07	24	4	aa	CHW	278	35	75	9	1	3	26	32	29	11	7	270	346	338	684	10%	89%	1.10	46	87	4.28	31
	08	25	46	aaa	CHW	404	51	107	21	1	10	43	35	49	10	4	265	323	398	721	8%	88%	0.71	87	83	4.68	39
Gibbons,Jay	08	32	8	a/a	MIL	120	9	27	8	0	3	11	6	19	0	0	227	263	375	639	5%	84%	0.32	100	15	3.37	23
Gillespie,Cole	08	24	8	aa	MIL	462	55	109	33	2	11	60	59	88	12	1	237	323	384	707	11%	81%	0.67	102	98	4.61	34
Gil,Jerry	08	26	8	a/a	CIN	185	12	26	10	0	4	18	4	50	4	0	142	159	259	418	2%	73%	0.08	81	85	1.30	-18
Gimenez,Chris	07	25	5	aa	CLE	113	17	22	6	0	5	10	8	29	1	0	193	244	370	614	6%	74%	0.26	110	76	3.02	15
	08	26	2	a/a	CLE	372	59	100	22	1	8	39	67	93	2	2	268	379	392	771	15%	75%	0.72	85	56	5.72	39
Gimenez,Hector	08	26	2	aaa	TAM	146	8	27	6	2	2	12	6	33	0	0	183	217	290	507	4%	78%	0.20	70	68	2.04	-6
Ginter,Keith	07	31	503	aaa	CLE	369	39	75	14	1	11	49	51	67	3	3	202	300	332	631	12%	82%	0.77	80	50	3.45	16
	08	32	54	aaa	BOS	444	35	89	20	0	4	38	39	88	3	1	201	266	274	539	8%	80%	0.44	54	50	2.53	-2
Godwin,Adam	08	26	8	aa	LA	417	43	91	14	2	2	27	39	59	24	6	219	286	275	561	9%	86%	0.67	41	114	2.89	3
Godwin,Tyrell	07	28	8	a/a	WAS	390	37	72	17	1	5	31	32	79	8	9	185	248	272	520	8%	80%	0.41	61	73	2.11	-5
Gold,Nate	07	27	3	aa	TEX	469	52	107	20	1	20	73	28	104	0	0	228	272	402	674	6%	78%	0.27	105	33	3.75	25
	08	28	03	aa	TEX	475	50	95	23	2	17	62	41	106	0	1	200	264	361	625	8%	78%	0.39	100	43	3.20	16
Goleski,Ryan	07	26	8	aa	CLE	471	40	100	16	2	6	58	42	101	7	9	212	277	294	571	8%	79%	0.42	55	64	2.67	2
	08	27	80	aa	CLE	338	40	71	15	2	9	30	34	97	2	2	210	282	346	628	9%	71%	0.35	86	73	3.33	12
Golson,Gregory	07	22	8	aa	PHI	153	16	33	5	1	3	13	2	40	4	0	216	226	320	546	1%	74%	0.05	65	118	2.48	-0
	08	23	8	aa	PHI	426	46	104	16	2	11	43	25	100	16	6	244	285	366	651	5%	77%	0.25	76	103	3.60	17
Gomes,Jonny	08	28	8	aaa	TAM	107	14	22	9	0	2	11	9	30	0	1	202	264	336	600	8%	72%	0.30	100	55	2.90	15
Gomez,Alexis	07	29	8	aa	COL	322	25	68	15	3	5	23	11	80	3	2	210	235	324	558	3%	75%	0.13	75	92	2.46	3
Gomez,Carlos	07	22	8	aa	NYM	140	20	36	7	1	2	11	13	19	14	5	257	320	364	685	8%	86%	0.68	73	137	4.15	29
Gonzalez,Adolfo	08	23	54	aa	LA	245	19	64	13	1	1	16	8	45	3	1	260	283	332	615	3%	82%	0.17	56	67	3.31	13
Gonzalez,Alberto	07	24	6	a/a	NYY	493	58	120	28	8	1	48	31	63	12	6	244	289	338	627	6%	87%	0.49	67	139	3.38	19
	08	25	6	aaa	WAS	221	20	48	9	0	4	24	12	32	3	2	217	258	310	568	5%	86%	0.38	64	55	2.67	6
Gonzalez,Andy	07	26	4	aaa	CHW	124	14	29	7	1	3	15	21	35	5	1	232	342	375	717	14%	71%	0.59	94	102	4.84	28
	08	27	4	aaa	CLE	289	31	61	12	0	6	30	34	73	2	2	210	293	309	602	11%	75%	0.47	66	44	3.16	7
Gonzalez,Carlos	07	22	8	aa	ARI	500	60	136	37	3	16	71	32	89	8	6	272	316	454	770	6%	82%	0.36	120	85	5.03	47
	08	23	8	aa	OAK	173	18	42	8	1	3	22	12	26	1	1	243	292	353	644	6%	85%	0.46	73	66	3.58	20
Gonzalez,Edgar	07	29	45	aa	STL	459	40	94	23	2	5	33	32	75	9	4	204	255	289	545	6%	84%	0.42	61	83	2.49	2
Gonzalez,Edwar	08	26	80	aa	NYY	396	52	106	27	0	13	60	18	76	8	5	268	300	437	737	4%	81%	0.24	112	73	4.53	40
Gonzalez,Juan	07	26	46	aa	LA	349	45	81	16	1	7	39	29	59	6	3	232	291	346	636	8%	83%	0.49	75	85	3.51	18
	08	27	46	aa	LA	360	33	77	18	0	11	43	43	75	2	1	215	299	358	657	11%	79%	0.58	93	35	3.76	21
Gonzalez,Wiki	07	33	2	aaa	CHW	235	21	53	6	0	10	33	13	19	1	1	226	265	379	644	5%	92%	0.67	89	30	3.39	25
Gorecki,Reid	08	28	8	a/a	ATL	253	41	63	7	0	7	33	25	47	13	5	249	317	363	680	9%	82%	0.54	69	97	4.07	22
Gorneault,Nick	07	28	8	aa	LAA	471	59	92	18	1	13	42	41	123	12	7	195	259	318	577	8%	74%	0.33	77	92	2.70	3
	08	29	8	aa	HOU	370	38	71	13	1	13	36	29	85	5	8	191	250	335	585	7%	77%	0.34	87	64	2.57	6
Gradoville,Tim	07	28	2	a/a	PHI	149	10	19	3	0	0	3	10	46	3	1	128	181	152	333	6%	69%	0.21	21	69	0.91	-44
	08	29	2	a/a	TEX	115	8	17	2	0	1	8	4	32	1	0	145	171	184	354	3%	72%	0.11	25	58	1.00	-39
Granadillo,Tony	08	24	4	a/a	BOS	351	40	74	21	1	4	34	43	64	1	1	211	297	309	606	11%	82%	0.68	73	53	3.25	14
Greenberg,Adam	07	27	8	aa	KC	467	54	101	25	7	5	32	56	102	17	8	216	300	333	633	11%	78%	0.54	78	144	3.48	15
	08	28	8	aa	LAA	262	36	59	7	2	2	12	24	51	13	7	223	289	285	574	8%	80%	0.48	41	123	2.80	1
Greene,Tyler	07	24	6	aa	STL	221	31	45	14	1	6	19	12	53	8	2	202	244	352	597	5%	76%	0.23	101	129	2.87	14
	08	25	6	aa	STL	485	58	100	18	3	10	36	24	109	15	7	205	244	318	561	5%	78%	0.23	71	122	2.53	2
Green,Andy	08	31	4	a/a	NYM	440	55	91	20	3	9	33	48	76	5	4	207	284	321	605	10%	83%	0.62	74	85	3.10	12
Green,Nick	07	29	648	aa	SEA	387	40	83	15	3	14	43	16	117	3	5	213	244	372	616	4%	70%	0.13	95	88	2.87	13
	08	30	64	aaa	NYY	391	31	72	12	1	9	38	19	107	3	2	185	222	291	513	5%	73%	0.17	66	58	2.08	-8
Griffin,John-Ford	07	28	80	aaa	TOR	484	55	109	26	3	23	67	47	129	3	0	226	294	432	725	9%	73%	0.36	125	76	4.45	34
	08	29	8	aa	LA	319	40	77	15	2	11	47	26	57	1	1	243	301	400	701	8%	82%	0.46	98	63	4.23	30
Griffin,Michael	07	24	8	aa	CIN	165	15	47	9	2	3	17	8	23	4	0	282	314	409	723	4%	86%	0.33	83	105	4.82	35
	08	25	584	a/a	CIN	452	34	105	28	3	4	30	15	73	9	9	233	258	333	590	3%	84%	0.20	74	85	2.71	12
Guarno,Rick	07	25	2	aa	COL	248	21	55	13	0	5	28	13	58	3	0	221	259	327	586	5%	77%	0.22	73	55	2.93	8
	08	26	2	aa	COL	197	19	43	8	1	5	17	2	28	1	2	219	227	341	568	1%	86%	0.07	77	72	2.43	6
Guerrero,Cristian	07	27	8	a/a	WAS	139	16	27	4	2	5	19	17	52	3	1	194	280	363	643	11%	63%	0.32	97	125	3.47	11
Gutierrez,Chris	08	25	64	a/a	TOR	282	35	61	15	3	2	29	36	63	0	4	218	305	313	619	11%	78%	0.57	68	75	3.25	12
Gutierrez,Franklin	07	25	8	aaa	CLE	129	25	41	7	0	3	14	7	18	6	3	318	353	442	795	5%	86%	0.39	84	100	5.74	48
Gutierrez,Jesse	07	29	30	a/a	CIN	308	25	66	16	1	7	28	15	56	0	1	216	252	335	587	5%	82%	0.26	80	35	2.81	10
Gutierrez,Tonys	07	24	3	aa	CIN	135	10	33	6	0	2	13	19	32	4	1	246	339	331	670	12%	77%	0.60	59	48	4.27	19
	08	25	3	aa	CIN	414	52	98	20	1	6	43	50	62	7	14	236	318	329	647	11%	85%	0.81	65	61	3.39	22
Guzman,Freddy	07	27	8	aa	TEX	535	68	117	18	6	3	25	45	83	42	14	220	280	296	576	8%	85%	0.55	50	158	2.91	5
	08	28	80	a/a	DET	518	74	115	14	12	4	43	38	49	51	12	222	275	316	591	7%	91%	0.77	55	213	3.13	12
Guzman,Garrett	07	25	8	aa	MIN	475	57	127	20	1	10	69	27	46	5	7	268	307	380	687	5%	90%	0.57	73	59	4.01	31
	08	26	8	a/a	WAS	385	42	78	17	3	7	49	33	38	7	7	203	265	313	578	8%	90%	0.86	72	92	2.69	14
Guzman,Javier	07	23	6	aa	PIT	171	16	49	13	0	2	20	4	18	6	0	284	300	391	691	2%	90%	0.22	83	78	4.42	33
	08	24	6	aa	ATL	387	39	85	13	3	3	28	15	43	7	5	221	251	293	543	4%	89%	0.36	49	100	2.40	1
Guzman,Jesus	08	24	54	aa	OAK	400	46	116	20	1	12	63	28	53	4	5	290	337	432	769	7%	87%	0.52	91	53	5.23	45
Guzman,Joel	07	23	50	aaa	TAM	414	44	100	17	2	16	64	23	108	9	2	241	281	406	687	5%	74%	0.21	99	96	3.98	26
	08	24	5	aaa	TAM	436	42	94	20	0	17	59	16	88	1	2	216	243	375	618	3%	80%	0.18	99	36	2.98	16
Gwynn,Tony	07	25	8	aaa	MIL	126	17	33	3	2	0	11	8	13	4	3	262	306	317	623	6%	90%	0.62	35	136	3.33	14
	08	26	8	aaa	MIL	375	33	82	7	2	2	18	21	47	14	6	218	260	263	523	5%	88%	0.45	29	99	2.31	-6
Haad,Yamid	07	30	2	aaa	CLE	113	11	28	4	0	2	11	7	22	2	0	247	292	327	619	6%	80%	0.32	53	53	3.47	11
	08	31	2	aaa	CLE	108	7	14	3	0	1	5	7	31	0	0	134	185	181	366	6%	72%	0.22	33	27	1.08	-37
Haerther,Cody	07	24	8	aa	STL	142	17	34	10	0	4	22	12	26	0	0	241	302	395	696	8%	81%	0.47	107	29	4.23	34
	08	25	8	aa	STL	332	28	71	18	0	3	23	25	53	2	5	212	268	292	560	7%	84%	0.48	61	39	2.55	5
Haines,Kyle	08	26	64	aa	SF	348	39	78	13	3	0	35	44	54	1	4	225	312	278	590	11%	84%	0.81	40	65	3.06	8
Hall,James	08	24	8	aa	TAM	189	22	39	12	1	4	15	16	53	1	1	208	271	340	612	8%	72%	0.31	90	74	3.12	13
Hall,Michael	08	23	8	aa	BOS	263	38	56	17	1	10	27	29	82	3	1	212	292	395	687	10%	69%	0.36	117	85	3.99	26
Hall,Noah	07	30	80	aa	NYY	271	27	54	13	1	6	35	23	60	1	3	199	262	320	582	8%	78%	0.39	79	53	2.74	7
	08	31	08	a/a	SEA	175	13	34	9	0	1	16	20	20	3	3	194	275	262	538	10%	89%	0.98	55	45	2.38	7
Halman,Gregory	08	21	8	aa	SEA	236	35	59	13	1	8	24	14	57	7	7	248	291	415	706	6%	76%	0.25	106	104	3.82	31
Hamilton,Mark	07	23	3	aa	STL	248	25	52	13	0	5	32	19	45	1	1	211	268	321	589	7%	82%	0.43	75	43	2.92	10
	08	24	3	aa	STL	245	20	49	10	0	6	22	26	53	0	0	200	276	310	586	10%	78%	0.49	71	16	2.97	6

BATTER	Yr	Age	Pos	Lev	Org	ab	r	h	d	t	hr	rbi	bb	k	sb	cs	ba	ob	slg	ops	bb%	ct%	eye	px	sx	rc/g	bpv
Hammock,Robby	07	30	2	aa	ARI	246	20	53	11	1	3	20	26	40	2	1	213	288	299	587	10%	84%	0.65	60	53	3.01	9
	08	31	2	aa	ARI	217	21	43	5	2	4	20	14	45	1	0	196	243	294	537	6%	79%	0.30	58	79	2.41	-5
Hammond,Joey	07	30	846	a/a	PHI	408	47	92	10	1	5	39	33	57	2	2	225	283	289	572	7%	86%	0.57	42	60	2.84	4
	08	31	3658	a/a	PHI	428	37	88	15	2	3	26	40	73	2	3	205	272	272	545	9%	83%	0.55	47	51	2.51	-1
Hanigan,Ryan	07	27	2	a/a	CIN	324	35	73	16	1	3	27	41	45	0	2	226	312	311	624	11%	86%	0.91	62	37	3.46	19
	08	28	2	aaa	CIN	272	26	71	11	0	4	25	18	36	1	0	262	309	343	652	6%	87%	0.51	57	38	3.87	21
Hankerd,Kevin	08	24	8	aa	ARI	436	29	100	16	3	5	43	18	55	2	7	229	259	312	572	4%	87%	0.32	55	52	2.57	6
Hannahan,Jack	07	28	405	aaa	DET	336	49	88	17	1	10	55	67	87	5	5	263	385	413	798	17%	74%	0.76	96	60	5.97	42
Hanson,Travis	07	27	5	aa	STL	254	11	42	3	1	3	10	6	53	1	1	164	184	212	396	2%	79%	0.12	28	44	1.21	-31
Harman,Bradley	08	23	46	aa	PHI	443	36	82	15	1	14	41	31	103	2	1	185	238	318	557	7%	77%	0.30	81	48	2.50	1
Harper,Brandon	07	31	2	aaa	WAS	276	23	41	11	0	2	22	20	51	2	0	150	207	209	416	7%	81%	0.39	45	61	1.43	-24
Harper,Brett	07	26	38	aa	NYM	476	50	110	20	0	17	64	24	114	2	0	232	270	378	648	5%	76%	0.21	91	47	3.52	19
	08	27	03	aa	SF	352	39	93	28	0	14	48	10	54	0	1	263	284	465	749	3%	85%	0.18	133	29	4.58	46
Harrison,Benjamin	08	27	80	aa	TEX	426	50	98	22	1	14	51	36	109	13	2	230	290	380	671	8%	74%	0.33	96	95	3.94	23
Harrison,Vince	07	28	5	aa	NYM	218	21	43	7	0	3	22	15	36	1	4	198	249	278	527	6%	83%	0.41	54	42	2.14	-4
Harris,Clay	08	26	3	aa	PHI	123	12	24	4	0	3	6	13	16	0	0	194	271	292	563	9%	87%	0.79	61	24	2.73	6
Hart,Bo	07	31	4	a/a	BAL	118	6	18	4	1	0	4	4	26	2	0	149	177	197	374	3%	78%	0.15	36	87	1.13	-32
Hart,Wilson Bregy	08	26	8	aa	HOU	319	36	67	19	1	6	27	28	52	7	9	209	273	327	601	8%	84%	0.54	82	77	2.76	14
Harvey,Kris	08	25	8	aa	FLA	209	19	26	8	1	5	14	17	65	2	0	124	191	239	430	8%	69%	0.27	72	89	1.47	-24
Harvey,Ryan	08	24	8	aa	CHC	111	6	20	6	0	2	11	5	31	1	1	182	216	285	501	4%	72%	0.15	73	37	1.92	-6
Hatch,Anthony	08	25	5	aa	TOR	255	19	51	10	0	5	21	13	36	0	1	199	238	295	533	5%	86%	0.36	64	25	2.29	0
Hattig,John	07	28	5	aaa	TOR	347	30	83	16	1	10	42	31	97	0	2	238	301	372	674	8%	72%	0.32	86	29	3.90	21
Hayes,Brett	07	24	2	aa	FLA	273	18	56	15	0	2	25	16	47	2	0	206	249	281	529	5%	83%	0.33	58	46	2.39	-1
	08	25	2	aa	FLA	297	32	65	10	1	9	28	12	60	2	6	220	249	346	595	4%	80%	0.19	77	63	2.64	9
Haynes,Nathan	07	28	8	aa	LAA	171	24	50	7	3	3	23	16	41	10	6	290	351	426	777	9%	76%	0.39	83	165	5.20	39
	08	29	8	aaa	TAM	277	20	54	6	2	2	17	8	57	9	3	196	217	248	466	3%	79%	0.14	34	109	1.79	-18
Headley,Chase	07	23 a	5	aa	SD	433	72	126	32	4	17	69	66	112	1	0	291	385	504	889	13%	74%	0.59	136	82	7.54	65
	08	24	8	aa	SD	259	40	66	19	1	10	33	25	61	0	0	256	321	448	770	9%	76%	0.41	126	53	5.21	45
Head,Stephen	08	25	38	aa	CLE	404	43	105	22	1	11	42	21	71	1	1	259	296	397	693	5%	82%	0.30	91	47	4.15	30
Heether,Adam	07	26	5	aa	MIL	432	47	107	23	4	7	49	42	89	2	6	248	315	369	684	9%	79%	0.48	81	67	3.98	26
	08	27	65	aaa	MIL	390	50	85	26	1	8	36	48	77	7	1	217	303	351	654	11%	80%	0.62	93	87	3.84	23
Heintz,Chris	07	33	2	aaa	MIN	167	16	41	7	0	1	14	9	37	0	0	243	281	302	583	5%	78%	0.25	46	30	2.99	5
	08	34	2	aaa	BAL	164	8	31	4	1	2	14	8	20	1	0	192	228	259	487	4%	88%	0.38	44	47	1.97	-10
Henry,Sean	08	23	8	aa	CIN	396	50	99	20	3	10	47	32	59	12	9	250	307	389	695	8%	85%	0.55	89	103	4.02	31
Hermansen,Chad	07	30	8	aa	NYM	392	33	69	13	1	6	34	22	133	6	2	177	221	264	486	5%	66%	0.17	56	89	1.91	-14
Hernandez,Anders	07	25	64	aa	NYM	554	67	143	25	3	4	33	25	72	12	10	259	291	334	625	4%	87%	0.35	55	96	3.30	16
	08	26	6	aa	NYM	479	45	81	18	5	4	28	30	84	8	8	169	218	249	467	6%	82%	0.36	54	113	1.86	-14
Hernandez,Diory	07	23	64	aa	ATL	433	43	121	23	1	6	50	24	63	18	22	280	318	379	697	5%	85%	0.39	70	76	3.70	30
	08	25	465	a/a	ATL	536	43	135	23	3	6	49	21	72	7	10	253	281	339	619	4%	87%	0.29	59	66	3.12	15
Hernandez,Jose	07	38	50	aa	PIT	322	24	50	11	1	7	33	20	94	1	1	157	205	261	466	6%	71%	0.21	66	47	1.70	-16
Hernandez,Luis	07	23	6	a/a	BAL	397	42	90	14	4	0	36	16	48	5	5	227	257	282	539	4%	88%	0.33	40	104	2.37	-1
	08	24	6	aaa	BAL	205	14	33	6	0	0	9	7	23	2	2	159	186	187	373	3%	89%	0.29	25	63	1.06	-31
Hernandez,Michel	07	29	2	aaa	TAM	170	19	41	4	0	4	16	15	14	0	1	241	301	327	627	8%	92%	1.02	52	33	3.44	22
	08	30	2	aa	PIT	252	21	54	12	1	2	13	12	35	0	2	213	248	287	535	5%	86%	0.34	55	46	2.32	0
Herrera,Javier	07	26	2	aa	WAS	167	14	31	4	0	3	18	19	24	1	2	183	266	253	520	10%	85%	0.77	44	37	2.26	-5
	08	27	2	a/a	WAS	210	28	43	9	1	2	16	28	48	4	4	206	299	283	582	12%	77%	0.58	55	83	2.91	3
Herrera,Javier A.	08	24	80	aa	OAK	255	33	58	12	1	6	27	17	53	6	5	227	274	350	624	6%	79%	0.31	80	94	3.12	15
Herrera,Jonathan	07	23	6	aa	COL	509	54	126	23	3	3	33	31	53	15	13	248	291	322	613	6%	90%	0.58	54	94	3.09	17
	08	24	64	aa	COL	226	28	62	6	0	2	22	14	20	11	3	273	315	325	640	6%	91%	0.67	36	91	3.81	20
Herr,Aaron	07	27	54	aaa	CIN	507	65	126	28	3	18	72	33	132	8	4	249	295	425	719	6%	74%	0.25	110	95	4.34	33
	08	28	5	aaa	CIN	308	27	56	7	2	9	29	11	88	1	0	181	209	304	513	3%	72%	0.12	71	72	2.05	-8
Hessman,Mike	07	30	5	aaa	DET	422	60	90	20	2	25	85	54	151	5	11	213	302	444	746	11%	64%	0.36	136	73	4.24	34
	08	31	5	aaa	DET	399	60	83	15	3	24	52	43	134	3	3	209	286	443	729	10%	66%	0.32	134	98	4.26	31
Hester,John	08	25	2	aa	ARI	306	30	73	24	2	9	39	13	67	3	2	240	271	421	692	4%	78%	0.20	121	78	3.85	34
Hill,Jamar	07	25	8	aa	NYM	170	17	41	7	0	5	17	5	40	3	3	244	267	365	632	3%	76%	0.14	78	59	3.17	16
Hill,Jason	07	31	23	aa	PHI	434	32	84	22	0	6	38	19	73	1	1	194	227	282	509	4%	83%	0.26	64	34	2.08	-4
Hill,Koyie	07	29	2	aa	CHC	149	15	36	12	0	2	16	7	25	1	1	242	277	354	631	5%	83%	0.29	88	49	3.35	23
	08	30	2	aa	CHC	364	37	77	19	1	12	42	26	70	2	2	210	263	366	629	7%	81%	0.37	99	53	3.21	18
Hodges,Wes	08	24	5	aa	CLE	504	60	130	27	2	15	83	46	99	3	1	257	319	410	729	8%	80%	0.47	98	64	4.74	35
Hoffmann,Jaime	08	24	8	aa	LA	478	49	113	17	2	8	54	43	61	22	11	237	300	329	630	8%	87%	0.70	60	96	3.43	18
Hoffpauir,Jarrett	07	24 a	4	aa	STL	393	39	106	22	0	9	45	44	34	4	5	271	344	392	735	10%	91%	1.30	83	37	4.87	50
	08	25	4	aa	STL	410	36	92	25	1	3	34	36	36	2	5	225	287	312	599	8%	91%	0.99	67	43	3.02	22
Hoffpauir,Micah	07	28	3	aa	CHC	310	39	76	19	0	12	51	17	35	2	1	246	285	428	713	5%	89%	0.48	117	52	4.23	40
	08	29 b	3	aa	CHC	290	42	84	28	1	18	68	11	41	2	0	291	318	586	904	4%	86%	0.28	187	66	6.86	80
Hollimon,Michael	07	25	46	a/a	DET	490	84	124	30	9	11	70	58	120	14	6	252	331	419	750	11%	76%	0.48	106	167	5.00	38
	08	26	4	aaa	DET	331	43	58	13	4	11	26	35	96	6	3	175	254	336	590	10%	71%	0.37	96	129	2.81	5
Hollins,Damon	08	34	8	aa	KC	363	39	64	14	2	11	40	37	78	2	2	176	253	314	566	9%	79%	0.48	84	66	2.62	3
Holm,Stephen	07	28	2	aa	SF	254	24	51	11	0	6	19	28	39	2	1	203	282	314	596	10%	85%	0.73	73	42	3.08	12
Holt,John	07	25	4	a/a	ATL	433	49	122	19	4	0	21	38	79	19	10	282	340	345	685	8%	82%	0.48	48	115	4.30	23
	08	26	4	a/a	ATL	472	51	111	15	6	2	40	42	80	23	13	235	298	303	601	8%	83%	0.53	45	130	3.07	7
Hooper,Kevin	07	31	4	aaa	DET	246	38	63	9	0	1	16	14	24	9	4	256	295	304	598	5%	90%	0.55	38	101	3.18	12
Hoover,Paul	08	32	2	aa	FLA	175	19	33	6	0	4	14	10	46	1	1	189	234	296	530	6%	74%	0.22	68	54	2.25	-4
Horwitz,Brian	07	25	8	aa	SF	400	39	111	24	2	2	25	27	27	3	1	278	323	361	684	6%	93%	0.97	64	65	4.31	39
	08	26	8	aa	SF	264	34	64	10	1	6	24	25	38	1	1	242	309	353	661	9%	85%	0.66	71	59	3.88	23
House,J.R.	07	28	203	aaa	BAL	419	48	115	29	1	10	62	41	58	1	5	274	339	424	763	9%	86%	0.71	103	36	5.12	48
	08	29	32	aa	HOU	454	41	106	18	0	12	40	34	45	1	3	235	288	357	645	7%	90%	0.76	78	25	3.53	25
Howard,Josh	07	24	8	aa	SD	205	25	37	3	0	0	11	29	58	8	4	181	284	195	478	13%	72%	0.51	12	82	2.05	-25
Howard,Kevin	07	26	4	aa	LA	243	25	56	9	1	5	20	17	25	6	2	229	281	337	617	7%	90%	0.69	68	85	3.31	18
	08	27	4	aa	SEA	247	25	54	13	0	8	33	28	32	1	5	219	298	368	666	10%	87%	0.87	96	29	3.59	30
Hubbard,Marshall	07	25	3	aa	SEA	488	57	106	26	3	12	60	52	138	1	1	218	293	354	647	10%	72%	0.38	89	64	3.63	17
	08	26	3	aa	SEA	309	40	74	20	2	8	40	44	60	2	5	238	333	396	729	13%	81%	0.74	105	64	4.59	37
Hubele,Ryan	07	27	2	a/a	BAL	258	30	48	10	1	5	21	13	54	3	1	185	225	293	518	5%	79%	0.24	70	89	2.15	-4

BATTER	Yr	Age	Pos	Lev	Org	ab	r	h	d	t	hr	rbi	bb	k	sb	cs	ba	ob	slg	ops	bb%	ct%	eye	px	sx	rc/g	bpv
Huber,Justin	07	25	83	aa	KC	286	30	65	12	1	13	52	16	44	1	0	227	268	406	674	5%	84%	0.36	107	49	3.73	27
	08	26	3	aa	SD	199	13	39	9	0	2	21	14	50	0	1	194	246	268	515	6%	75%	0.28	55	23	2.18	-7
Huckaby,Ken	07	37	2	aa	LA	237	8	41	4	0	1	17	6	63	0	0	174	193	198	391	2%	73%	0.09	18	11	1.22	-33
Hudson,Robert	08	25	46	aa	CHW	320	24	71	16	0	1	24	16	53	8	6	220	257	279	536	5%	83%	0.30	49	68	2.35	-0
Huffman,Chad	07	22	8	aa	SD	167	25	41	3	1	6	25	20	41	0	0	246	326	383	709	11%	75%	0.49	77	60	4.57	23
	08	23	8	aa	SD	437	57	106	25	1	7	49	56	77	1	1	242	328	350	678	11%	82%	0.73	76	50	4.20	27
Huffman,Royce	07	31	538	aa	SD	478	34	79	19	1	4	39	46	103	4	1	165	239	230	469	9%	78%	0.45	48	55	1.86	-16
	08	32	305	aaa	CHW	370	34	77	20	0	9	32	31	94	3	3	207	267	331	598	8%	75%	0.33	84	47	2.94	10
Hughes,John	08	25	3	aa	TAM	395	44	89	23	1	11	40	36	99	2	1	226	290	374	664	8%	75%	0.36	97	56	3.78	23
Hughes,Luke	07	23	48	aa	MIN	315	45	78	16	1	7	34	25	60	3	1	246	302	366	669	7%	81%	0.42	80	79	3.96	23
	08	24	5	a/a	MIN	391	57	105	19	3	13	49	27	92	5	1	268	315	435	749	6%	77%	0.29	103	103	4.97	38
Hulett,Timothy	07	25	4	aa	TEX	517	77	125	28	2	10	54	51	99	16	6	243	311	358	669	9%	81%	0.52	79	107	4.00	24
	08	26	64	aa	SEA	336	55	84	19	3	10	37	39	67	8	6	249	328	414	742	11%	80%	0.59	105	110	4.74	38
Hundley,Nicholas	07	24	2	aa	SD	373	47	79	18	1	17	61	36	75	0	2	211	281	402	683	9%	80%	0.48	116	40	3.80	28
	08	25	2	aa	SD	224	26	42	10	0	8	31	13	43	0	0	189	234	348	582	6%	81%	0.31	99	38	2.67	10
Hu,Chin-lung	07	24	6	aa	LA	517	73	147	35	3	12	50	26	45	13	9	285	320	432	751	5%	91%	0.58	100	99	4.84	48
	08	25	6	aa	LA	156	16	39	5	2	1	12	6	17	2	0	252	279	326	605	4%	89%	0.35	48	106	3.25	11
Inglett,Joe	07	29	48	aaa	CLE	392	35	82	14	5	3	45	33	60	5	13	209	270	293	562	8%	85%	0.54	54	101	2.39	3
Iorg,Eli	08	26	8	aa	HOU	459	38	100	17	3	8	41	16	90	15	10	217	243	322	565	3%	80%	0.18	67	100	2.44	3
Iribarren,Hernan	07	23	4	aa	MIL	479	61	132	21	10	4	44	39	102	16	17	275	330	385	714	7%	79%	0.38	70	153	4.19	28
	08	24	84	aaa	MIL	361	35	83	14	2	0	22	22	51	14	10	229	273	279	552	6%	86%	0.43	40	102	2.50	1
Ishikawa,Travis	07	24	3	aa	SF	173	13	31	3	1	2	13	13	41	1	0	181	240	242	481	7%	76%	0.32	36	65	1.97	-18
	08	25 a	3	aa	SF	405	58	105	32	2	18	79	40	74	8	6	260	327	480	808	9%	82%	0.54	142	88	5.50	56
Ivany,Devin	08	26	2	aa	WAS	206	24	43	7	1	6	18	11	43	3	4	210	250	335	585	5%	79%	0.25	77	84	2.62	7
Jackson,Austin	08	22	8	aa	NYY	520	73	143	31	3	9	67	53	107	18	6	276	342	400	742	9%	79%	0.49	86	110	5.11	37
Jacobs,Gregory	07	31	8	aa	PHI	462	43	92	26	1	13	47	24	76	1	4	200	239	345	585	5%	84%	0.31	96	43	2.62	12
	08	32	8	aa	LA	211	21	45	10	1	3	21	15	31	1	1	214	267	306	573	7%	86%	0.50	65	61	2.77	8
Janish,Paul	07	25	6	a/a	CIN	523	55	110	26	2	4	33	53	75	10	3	210	283	289	572	9%	86%	0.71	59	88	2.90	8
	08	26	6	aaa	CIN	318	34	69	18	1	6	32	20	62	2	0	216	262	331	593	6%	81%	0.32	80	69	2.98	11
Jaramillo,Jason	07	25	2	aaa	PHI	435	44	110	14	2	6	48	42	69	0	1	253	319	336	654	9%	84%	0.61	54	41	3.89	19
	08	26	2	aaa	PHI	421	39	97	17	0	7	31	33	78	1	1	229	286	323	609	7%	81%	0.42	64	33	3.23	11
Jaso,John	07	24 a	20	aa	TAM	380	50	104	21	2	10	58	49	45	2	2	273	356	413	769	12%	88%	1.09	92	59	5.50	51
	08	25	2	a/a	TAM	392	51	90	17	2	9	52	56	41	2	1	230	327	355	682	13%	89%	1.36	80	63	4.24	37
Jay,Jonathan	07	23	8	aa	STL	102	14	21	3	1	2	9	9	15	3	1	206	270	314	584	8%	85%	0.60	65	122	2.92	7
	08	24	8	aa	STL	430	51	116	18	3	9	44	34	44	8	10	269	323	385	708	7%	90%	0.78	74	80	4.24	36
Jenkins,Andrew	08	25	38	aa	FLA	347	29	75	13	1	6	41	16	62	2	3	217	251	309	560	4%	82%	0.26	61	52	2.54	3
Jennings,Jeffery	07	26	2	aa	SF	250	13	38	8	0	1	14	10	51	2	5	151	184	194	378	4%	80%	0.19	34	44	1.02	-32
Jennings,Robin	07	35	3	a/a	WAS	182	16	34	10	0	5	15	10	31	1	0	189	230	321	551	5%	83%	0.31	88	44	2.43	5
Jeroloman,Brian	08	23	2	a/a	TOR	301	29	70	16	0	6	30	47	58	0	0	231	335	342	677	14%	81%	0.81	76	17	4.25	25
Jimenez,D'Angelo	07	30 b	6	aaa	WAS	171	24	53	11	2	5	21	25	20	2	2	309	398	490	888	13%	88%	1.29	115	81	7.54	76
	08	31	46	aa	STL	303	25	54	9	1	3	24	28	31	4	1	180	249	250	499	8%	90%	0.92	47	70	2.15	-2
Jimenez,Jorge	08	24	5	aa	BOS	211	18	51	12	1	2	17	6	24	1	1	241	261	337	598	3%	89%	0.24	70	61	2.97	14
Jimenez,Luis	07	25	30	a/a	BAL	401	52	105	17	0	20	75	44	84	2	1	261	333	452	786	10%	79%	0.52	115	40	5.50	45
	08	26	30	a/a	WAS	337	34	75	10	0	10	40	35	60	2	1	224	297	344	641	9%	82%	0.58	73	39	3.60	16
Jimerson,Charlton	07	28	8	aa	SEA	387	42	79	17	2	17	56	25	160	24	9	205	253	387	639	6%	59%	0.16	109	125	3.14	16
	08	29	8	aa	SEA	210	16	37	6	1	8	22	3	80	9	7	176	186	324	510	1%	62%	0.03	86	115	1.60	-5
Johnson,Ben	07	26	8	aa	NYM	204	23	45	10	0	3	12	20	40	3	1	222	291	307	598	9%	80%	0.50	61	59	3.18	9
Johnson,Ben	07	26	30	aa	LAA	128	19	30	6	1	3	17	6	26	1	2	232	268	359	627	5%	80%	0.25	82	100	3.11	16
	08	27	2	aa	LAA	480	50	103	18	1	17	70	14	79	5	6	215	237	360	597	3%	83%	0.17	89	66	2.69	12
Johnson,Brent	07	25	80	aa	SEA	453	53	108	25	1	5	39	44	57	6	7	238	306	334	640	9%	87%	0.78	69	65	3.50	24
	08	26	8	aa	SEA	349	34	72	17	2	5	30	30	37	6	7	206	269	306	575	8%	89%	0.82	69	76	2.63	14
Johnson,Christoph	08	24	5	aa	HOU	431	38	108	21	1	10	48	18	69	4	0	249	280	370	650	4%	84%	0.27	80	65	3.67	21
Johnson,Dan	08	29	03	aaa	TAM	394	61	93	18	0	18	59	60	73	0	1	236	337	419	756	13%	81%	0.82	112	32	5.12	41
Johnson,Elliot	07	24	4	aaa	TAM	463	53	91	16	5	11	43	41	134	15	6	197	262	324	586	8%	71%	0.31	77	137	2.84	3
	08	25	46	aaa	TAM	387	39	86	22	4	7	39	26	91	12	3	223	272	352	624	6%	77%	0.29	86	126	3.32	16
Johnson,Gabe	08	29	2	aa	SEA	127	10	22	4	1	2	10	10	38	1	1	176	238	264	502	8%	70%	0.27	57	76	2.05	-12
Johnson,Jay	07	25	80	aa	BOS	411	37	98	28	3	4	50	34	68	4	3	238	297	347	643	8%	83%	0.50	80	75	3.59	22
Johnson,Mark	07	32	2	aa	ARI	242	21	50	7	0	2	18	32	24	0	1	208	299	263	563	12%	90%	1.30	39	23	2.80	11
	08	33	2	aa	STL	201	11	39	7	0	1	20	22	25	1	1	195	274	241	515	10%	88%	0.89	36	26	2.32	-2
Johnson,Michael	07	27	30	aa	HOU	341	37	61	12	2	13	41	43	117	0	1	180	272	343	615	11%	66%	0.37	97	50	3.15	7
Johnson,Rob	07	24	20	aa	SEA	422	47	97	23	0	5	32	33	60	6	8	230	286	317	603	7%	86%	0.55	65	58	3.00	15
	08	25	2	aa	SEA	417	42	107	25	0	7	38	29	56	6	7	257	306	365	671	7%	86%	0.52	78	51	3.81	28
Johnson,Russ	07	35	5	aa	PIT	360	26	62	14	1	5	29	27	44	3	3	171	228	255	483	7%	88%	0.60	57	52	1.87	-7
Johnston,Seth	08	26	5	aa	SD	460	54	93	20	0	12	53	32	87	3	2	202	254	325	579	6%	81%	0.37	79	59	2.76	7
Jones,Adam	07	22 a	8	aa	SEA	420	65	120	25	4	21	73	32	98	7	8	286	336	514	851	7%	77%	0.33	139	104	6.01	59
Jones,Brandon	07	24	8	a/a	ATL	535	75	149	32	5	17	89	54	109	15	8	279	345	452	797	9%	80%	0.50	110	113	5.65	48
	08	25	8	aaa	ATL	346	36	79	21	1	7	42	38	68	8	7	228	305	352	657	10%	80%	0.57	87	70	3.63	23
Jones,Daryl	08	21	8	aa	STL	124	15	31	5	1	4	11	17	23	5	1	253	343	407	751	12%	82%	0.75	94	101	5.27	38
Jones,Garrett	07	26	83	aaa	MIN	400	54	105	30	3	12	67	29	88	2	2	262	312	439	751	7%	78%	0.33	118	82	4.86	43
	08	27	38	aaa	MIN	527	62	119	27	2	16	69	36	96	7	2	225	275	376	651	6%	82%	0.38	96	87	3.57	22
Jones,Kennard	08	27	8	aa	BAL	140	14	30	5	1	1	13	12	19	5	2	212	273	276	549	8%	87%	0.62	44	99	2.62	1
Jones,Mitch	07	30	83	aa	LA	185	26	38	10	1	13	38	19	68	2	0	207	280	474	754	9%	63%	0.28	157	76	4.54	39
	08	31	8	aa	LA	200	26	42	11	1	11	31	14	53	3	0	208	262	438	699	7%	74%	0.27	138	85	3.90	32
Jorgensen,Ryan	07	28	2	aaa	CIN	249	24	51	14	0	2	21	17	49	1	0	205	255	284	539	6%	80%	0.34	61	49	2.49	0
	08	29	2	aaa	MIN	198	20	38	9	0	5	18	12	55	0	0	191	237	317	555	6%	72%	0.22	83	31	2.49	2
Joseph,Onil	07	26	8	aa	KC	347	30	74	11	3	2	23	15	67	8	12	213	246	275	521	4%	81%	0.23	42	96	1.98	-7
Joyce,Matthew	07	23	8	aa	DET	456	57	108	29	3	15	66	48	123	4	6	236	308	408	717	9%	73%	0.39	112	76	4.29	32
	08	24	8	aaa	DET	200	29	47	12	2	11	34	20	53	2	3	235	305	470	776	9%	73%	0.38	141	97	4.80	44
Jurich,Mark	07	27	38	aa	ATL	373	35	82	27	2	5	48	27	63	1	2	219	272	343	615	7%	83%	0.43	90	55	3.15	19
	08	28	8	a/a	ATL	246	20	45	14	1	3	20	15	59	0	1	183	231	278	509	6%	76%	0.26	69	48	2.08	-5
Justice,Justin	08	24	8	aa	DET	157	11	21	4	1	2	12	11	31	1	1	131	187	206	393	6%	81%	0.35	47	74	1.20	-30
Justis,Shane	08	26	54	aa	LA	338	35	74	14	1	2	27	31	43	8	9	220	285	284	569	8%	87%	0.73	48	75	2.63	8

BATTER	Yr	Age	Pos	Lev	Org	ab	r	h	d	t	hr	rbi	bb	k	sb	cs	ba	ob	slg	ops	bb%	ct%	eye	px	sx	rc/g	bpv
Kaaihue,Kala	07	23	3	aa	ATL	118	12	14	5	1	0	7	9	45	0	0	119	181	178	359	7%	62%	0.20	45	98	1.04	-38
	08	24	3	aa	ATL	376	51	91	21	1	11	49	72	101	0	5	242	363	388	752	16%	73%	0.71	95	31	5.11	34
Kaaihue,Kila	07	24	30	aa	KC	244	31	53	13	0	9	33	35	34	0	0	219	316	378	694	13%	86%	1.03	101	25	4.28	35
	08	25 a	30	aa	KC	401	76	113	15	0	29	84	88	58	3	2	282	412	536	948	18%	85%	1.51	145	44	8.60	84
Kata,Matt	08	31	84	aa	PIT	396	37	77	15	3	5	33	16	65	14	6	195	227	290	517	4%	84%	0.25	62	126	2.10	-4
Katin,Brendan	07	25	8	aa	MIL	450	59	102	22	0	20	77	35	155	3	2	226	282	407	689	7%	66%	0.23	112	55	3.93	26
	08	26	8	aaa	MIL	321	34	71	19	2	14	52	9	93	5	2	223	245	425	669	3%	71%	0.10	125	96	3.42	28
Kazmar,Sean	07	23	4	aa	SD	269	26	49	9	2	5	28	21	44	5	1	180	241	281	522	7%	84%	0.48	63	101	2.29	-4
	08	24	6	aa	SD	382	43	84	16	2	2	32	31	63	6	5	221	279	289	568	7%	84%	0.49	50	86	2.74	4
Kelly,Christopher	07	26	5	aa	CHW	459	30	91	16	0	5	37	15	99	0	0	198	224	263	487	3%	78%	0.15	46	21	1.93	-12
Kelly,Don	07	28	8	aa	PIT	150	14	29	4	1	0	7	12	17	4	3	194	255	232	488	8%	89%	0.74	29	91	1.94	-9
	08	29	465	aa	ARI	436	46	101	20	4	6	41	25	41	2	1	232	273	341	614	5%	91%	0.60	72	85	3.22	19
Kelly,Kenny	07	29	8	aaa	CHW	246	33	57	7	0	9	23	26	59	10	3	231	304	370	675	10%	76%	0.44	82	85	4.03	19
Kemp,Matt	07	23 a	8	aa	LA	161	26	47	15	2	4	16	9	23	8	2	289	326	476	802	5%	86%	0.38	128	149	5.71	57
Keppinger,Jeff	07	27 b	54	aaa	CIN	228	27	75	13	1	2	15	19	14	1	1	329	381	421	802	8%	94%	1.39	68	51	6.33	66
Keylor,Cory	07	28	8	a/a	BOS	414	40	82	22	3	6	37	30	118	5	3	199	253	312	565	7%	72%	0.25	77	101	2.63	3
Khoury,Ryan	08	25	54	aa	BOS	299	35	77	20	1	3	31	34	54	3	3	257	332	360	692	10%	82%	0.62	77	61	4.31	30
Kielty,Bobby	08	32	8	aaa	MIN	147	13	25	5	1	3	19	20	42	0	1	168	269	283	552	12%	71%	0.48	72	51	2.57	-5
Kiger,Mark	07	27	543	aa	NYM	424	56	94	22	2	7	36	57	107	11	7	221	314	333	647	12%	75%	0.53	76	90	3.67	16
	08	28	6	aa	SEA	376	35	65	10	1	2	28	54	95	2	6	173	276	218	494	12%	75%	0.56	32	44	2.04	-18
Kindel,Jeff	08	25	3	aa	COL	506	40	123	21	1	8	49	36	67	3	3	243	293	333	626	7%	87%	0.53	61	42	3.41	17
King,Brennan	07	27	5	aaa	PHI	465	45	116	16	1	10	49	32	67	1	0	250	299	350	649	6%	86%	0.48	64	43	3.75	19
	08	28	5	aaa	PHI	342	23	69	11	0	5	26	11	68	0	0	203	227	274	501	3%	80%	0.16	48	22	2.05	-9
King,Tom	08	24	5	aa	SD	175	12	29	6	0	2	8	15	27	0	0	165	232	230	462	8%	85%	0.57	46	22	1.79	-15
Kinkade,Mike	07	34	58	a/a	NYY	223	35	55	10	1	7	34	12	36	3	0	248	286	395	681	5%	84%	0.33	91	99	4.03	27
Kirkland,Kody	07	24	5	aa	DET	411	52	75	19	3	12	47	38	125	9	6	183	252	333	585	8%	70%	0.30	94	114	2.70	6
	08	25	5	a/a	DET	376	37	76	11	5	8	37	32	99	8	2	203	265	318	582	8%	74%	0.32	69	126	2.90	2
Klassen,Danny	07	32	65	aa	HOU	379	31	71	13	1	5	25	18	126	2	2	187	222	268	490	4%	67%	0.14	54	67	1.91	-13
	08	33	4	aa	HOU	105	6	17	3	1	1	9	10	22	0	2	162	236	227	463	9%	79%	0.46	41	58	1.66	-20
Klink,Simon	07	26	5	aa	SF	408	30	87	15	2	7	33	27	100	1	1	214	263	313	576	6%	75%	0.27	64	47	2.80	3
	08	27	35	aa	SF	349	28	68	17	1	2	29	27	97	2	0	195	252	264	516	7%	72%	0.28	52	60	2.29	-8
Klosterman,Ryan	07	25	54	aa	TOR	341	32	59	14	1	3	22	27	62	16	5	172	232	243	475	7%	82%	0.43	52	110	1.92	-13
	08	26	6	aa	TOR	318	35	60	11	2	5	29	33	68	8	6	188	265	278	542	9%	78%	0.48	58	97	2.40	-4
Knoedler,Justin	07	27	2	aa	SF	302	30	66	23	2	4	29	17	77	5	1	217	260	346	606	5%	74%	0.23	94	98	3.09	16
	08	28	2	aa	OAK	217	23	28	10	1	6	23	10	48	2	0	130	167	268	435	4%	78%	0.20	87	105	1.39	-17
Knott,Jon	07	29	8	aaa	BAL	288	37	64	13	1	12	30	43	82	4	2	221	322	395	717	13%	71%	0.52	106	68	4.52	28
	08	30	8	aaa	PHI	462	45	94	24	1	17	50	37	115	2	1	202	262	368	630	7%	75%	0.32	104	48	3.25	17
Koonce,Graham	07	32	30	a/a	ATL	253	22	43	11	1	10	40	27	85	0	1	171	251	335	586	10%	66%	0.32	101	37	2.76	5
Koshansky,Joe	07	25	3	aa	COL	498	59	127	26	2	16	74	51	111	3	3	255	324	412	736	9%	78%	0.46	100	56	4.79	35
	08	26	3	aa	COL	457	60	113	29	3	21	80	40	116	1	0	248	308	463	771	8%	75%	0.34	134	68	5.07	45
Kottaras,George	07	24	2	aaa	BOS	294	29	70	24	0	8	35	28	64	1	1	238	304	401	706	9%	78%	0.44	114	34	4.29	35
	08	25	20	aaa	BOS	395	50	85	19	0	16	52	50	97	0	0	214	302	383	685	11%	75%	0.51	105	26	4.08	25
Kratz,Erik	07	27	2	a/a	TOR	272	23	52	14	1	10	36	14	59	0	1	192	231	365	596	5%	78%	0.24	108	39	2.71	13
	08	28	2	a/a	TOR	247	26	49	13	1	13	33	16	59	3	0	200	248	420	668	6%	76%	0.27	133	72	3.49	27
Kreuzer,Joshua	08	26	3	aa	TOR	116	8	16	3	0	0	5	7	25	2	0	135	186	159	345	6%	78%	0.29	21	69	1.01	-40
Kroeger,Josh	07	25	8	aa	CHC	400	51	111	18	2	17	62	35	69	6	5	277	335	459	794	8%	83%	0.51	110	73	5.52	48
	08	26	8	aa	CHC	430	52	109	33	2	11	49	30	71	8	4	255	304	417	721	7%	84%	0.43	112	88	4.46	40
Labandeira,Josh	07	29	4	aa	FLA	292	22	64	14	1	2	24	20	61	1	4	219	269	288	557	6%	79%	0.33	52	41	2.53	1
	08	30	4	a/a	KC	173	13	28	3	0	2	10	15	40	0	2	164	229	209	438	8%	77%	0.37	29	31	1.53	-26
LaForest,Pete	07	30	25	aa	SD	296	35	47	4	0	20	48	37	115	2	0	157	250	367	618	11%	61%	0.32	113	43	3.05	5
Lahair,Bryan	07	25	3	aa	SEA	552	65	131	41	1	10	67	42	122	0	1	238	291	367	658	7%	78%	0.34	94	41	3.73	25
	08	26	3	aa	SEA	316	30	69	22	1	8	40	36	80	1	1	217	297	372	668	10%	75%	0.45	105	44	3.84	24
Lambin,Chase	07	28	64	aa	FLA	434	44	90	22	4	10	40	33	126	2	6	206	262	343	605	7%	71%	0.26	88	85	2.89	10
	08	29	84	aa	FLA	307	40	71	12	3	9	39	28	86	2	1	233	296	387	682	8%	72%	0.32	92	103	4.01	22
Lane,Jason	07	31	8	aa	HOU	185	22	38	9	0	6	24	13	31	1	1	204	258	344	602	7%	83%	0.42	90	57	2.97	14
	08	32	8	aaa	BOS	400	46	75	21	2	12	43	41	81	3	3	187	262	338	600	9%	80%	0.50	97	70	2.93	12
Langerhans,Ryan	08	29	8	aaa	WAS	213	30	53	13	2	2	24	29	57	9	3	248	338	351	689	12%	73%	0.51	75	121	4.45	24
Lansford,Joshua	08	24	5	aa	CHC	161	11	33	13	0	1	12	4	19	0	1	203	221	304	525	2%	88%	0.20	83	34	2.12	6
LaPorta,Matthew	08	24 a	8	aa	CLE	362	54	92	23	1	19	65	44	69	2	1	254	335	476	812	11%	81%	0.64	137	59	5.80	54
Larish,Jeffrey	07	25	3	aa	DET	454	66	109	22	2	25	93	80	107	5	2	241	354	460	815	15%	76%	0.74	131	69	5.99	49
	08	26	3	aaa	DET	384	39	82	17	2	16	51	40	95	0	1	213	288	392	680	10%	75%	0.43	108	41	3.87	24
Laroche,Andy	07	24 a	5	aa	LA	265	44	71	15	1	15	38	31	38	2	2	269	346	505	852	11%	86%	0.83	143	64	6.34	65
	08	25	5	aa	LA	145	30	36	4	0	4	22	31	18	2	1	246	379	350	729	18%	88%	1.72	63	65	5.17	42
Larson,Brandon	07	31	5	aa	WAS	189	18	28	6	0	4	11	8	47	1	1	148	181	244	426	4%	75%	0.16	61	72	1.37	-22
Leahy,Ryan	07	26	4	aa	LAA	173	10	30	3	0	0	5	10	24	0	3	171	218	191	409	6%	86%	0.43	18	30	1.27	-27
	08	27	64	aa	LAA	169	11	24	4	0	0	7	5	20	1	0	144	166	165	331	3%	88%	0.23	19	57	0.86	-40
LeCroy,Matthew	07	32	2	aaa	MIN	247	11	41	11	0	3	23	22	54	0	0	168	235	244	479	8%	78%	0.40	56	7	1.92	-13
Ledee,Ricky	07	34	8	aa	NYM	290	22	48	7	1	6	37	18	74	0	0	164	212	258	470	6%	74%	0.24	57	34	1.77	-17
Lee,Taber	07	27	46	aa	PIT	196	22	37	7	0	0	12	22	30	8	1	191	272	226	498	10%	85%	0.73	31	92	2.32	-9
Lefave,Andrew	08	24	38	aa	WAS	188	24	39	11	1	1	21	23	24	2	6	209	296	291	587	11%	87%	0.96	62	74	2.74	15
Leone,Justin	07	31	85	aa	SF	428	48	73	20	2	11	35	45	127	15	1	170	249	299	548	9%	70%	0.35	83	125	2.62	-2
	08	32	85	aa	SF	358	48	71	18	1	11	48	48	98	12	6	197	293	344	637	12%	73%	0.50	94	92	3.43	14
Leon,Carlos	07	28	6	a/a	PHI	222	20	37	7	0	0	9	14	35	0	5	165	213	195	408	6%	84%	0.39	27	48	1.20	-26
Leon,Maxwell	08	24	6	a/a	DET	296	31	76	6	3	0	23	37	60	13	8	256	340	295	635	11%	80%	0.62	26	110	3.69	8
Lerud,Steven	08	24	2	aa	PIT	146	15	31	7	0	3	16	12	37	1	0	215	273	322	596	7%	75%	0.32	73	46	3.08	8
Leslie,Myron	07	25	8	aa	OAK	386	41	92	24	1	4	36	49	68	1	1	238	323	333	656	11%	82%	0.72	72	44	3.93	23
	08	26	58	aa	OAK	367	33	72	15	0	6	30	36	74	2	4	196	267	288	555	9%	80%	0.49	63	37	2.56	1
Lewis,Fred	07	27	8	aa	SF	171	23	40	7	4	5	23	14	34	6	1	234	292	417	709	8%	80%	0.40	106	192	4.34	30
Lewis,Richard	07	27	45	aa	KC	342	31	62	11	1	3	27	16	67	2	2	182	218	248	466	4%	80%	0.23	45	70	1.74	-16
Liefer,Jeff	08	34	0	aaa	CHW	134	10	24	7	0	3	12	14	40	1	0	178	258	285	543	10%	70%	0.36	74	36	2.53	-3
Lillibridge,Brent	07	24	6	a/a	ATL	525	67	135	20	4	11	50	34	111	36	13	257	302	371	673	6%	79%	0.30	72	135	3.94	22
	08	25	6	aaa	ATL	355	37	67	15	5	3	31	26	82	19	8	188	244	281	525	7%	77%	0.32	62	158	2.25	-6

BATTER	Yr	Age	Pos	Lev	Org	ab	r	h	d	t	hr	rbi	bb	k	sb	cs	ba	ob	slg	ops	bb%	ct%	eye	px	sx	rc/g	bpv
Limonta,Johan	08	25	38	aa	SEA	360	39	89	27	3	8	45	30	80	2	2	248	306	402	708	8%	78%	0.38	106	76	4.33	34
Linden,Todd	08	28	8	a/a	CLE	402	51	96	23	1	13	50	55	130	4	2	239	330	398	728	12%	68%	0.42	103	61	4.75	31
Lindsey,John	07	31	30	aa	LA	454	46	92	20	1	18	71	21	114	0	0	202	237	370	607	4%	75%	0.18	103	34	2.90	13
	08	32	30	aa	LA	481	58	116	28	1	19	68	45	80	0	0	240	305	419	724	9%	83%	0.56	113	32	4.54	38
Lind,Adam	07	24	8	aaa	TOR	174	17	49	8	2	6	24	12	36	0	0	282	328	454	782	6%	79%	0.33	104	63	5.49	44
	08	25 a	8	aaa	TOR	189	21	56	16	2	6	43	16	36	1	1	298	353	492	845	8%	81%	0.44	130	74	6.50	62
Lisson,Mario	08	24	56	aa	KC	476	47	97	23	2	11	54	28	91	26	7	204	248	327	574	6%	81%	0.31	81	120	2.73	7
Lis,Erik	08	25	083	aa	MIN	405	39	96	32	2	9	41	21	84	1	1	237	275	389	664	5%	79%	0.25	106	58	3.67	28
Loadenthal,Carl	07	26	8	aa	ATL	476	57	121	14	4	0	24	49	80	32	18	253	323	299	621	9%	83%	0.61	33	120	3.37	10
	08	27	8	a/a	ATL	306	26	67	5	0	1	12	21	66	17	8	219	270	244	513	6%	78%	0.32	18	85	2.25	-13
Lobaton,Jose	08	24	2	aa	SD	294	29	65	17	0	7	37	32	69	1	1	220	297	347	644	10%	76%	0.47	86	35	3.61	18
Lombard,George	07	32	8	aaa	WAS	127	11	25	5	0	3	9	13	43	8	3	198	271	305	575	9%	66%	0.29	71	82	2.83	1
Loney,James	07	23	38	aa	LA	233	22	56	16	1	1	26	20	42	2	1	241	302	333	635	8%	82%	0.48	73	65	3.60	20
Longoria,Evan	07	22 a	5	a/a	TAM	485	91	142	28	0	25	90	70	96	4	0	292	382	507	889	13%	80%	0.73	132	68	7.55	67
Lopez,Gabe	07	28	4	aa	NYY	409	32	83	17	1	1	39	30	65	2	2	203	257	254	511	7%	84%	0.46	41	52	2.20	-6
	08	29	4	aa	SD	351	37	66	11	2	2	18	28	32	1	5	188	248	243	492	7%	91%	0.89	39	62	1.92	-4
Lopez,Jose	08	24	2	aa	HOU	130	9	24	2	0	2	7	4	23	0	0	181	205	241	446	3%	82%	0.17	37	24	1.59	-21
Lopez,Pedro	07	23	6	aaa	CIN	285	36	76	12	1	3	25	25	34	4	3	267	326	347	673	8%	88%	0.74	57	73	4.09	27
	08	24	64	aaa	TOR	339	34	73	12	1	2	24	28	63	4	1	215	275	272	547	8%	82%	0.45	41	73	2.64	-2
Lowrance,Marvin	08	24	8	aa	WAS	154	21	36	12	0	6	18	15	33	1	0	237	306	424	730	9%	78%	0.46	124	51	4.63	39
Lowrie,Jed	07	23 a	6	a/a	BOS	497	71	143	51	5	10	60	66	78	4	4	288	371	471	842	12%	84%	0.85	131	88	6.57	67
	08	24	6	aaa	BOS	198	28	49	14	1	4	26	25	36	1	0	247	332	388	719	11%	82%	0.68	99	69	4.75	37
Lubanski,Chris	07	23	8	aa	KC	409	45	98	20	3	12	48	38	75	3	8	240	304	391	695	9%	82%	0.51	95	67	3.92	29
	08	24	8	aa	KC	393	43	88	21	6	12	45	32	109	4	1	224	283	396	680	8%	72%	0.30	106	127	3.90	24
Lucas,Edward	07	25	5	aa	KC	125	14	29	5	1	2	14	7	21	2	1	230	272	331	604	5%	83%	0.34	67	93	3.08	11
	08	26	5	aa	KC	317	36	76	9	3	3	24	29	55	11	8	241	305	313	619	8%	83%	0.53	47	107	3.25	10
Lucena,Juan	07	24	45	aa	STL	303	28	66	11	1	2	26	14	16	1	1	218	251	279	530	4%	95%	0.82	44	57	2.35	7
Lucy,Donald	07	25	2	a/a	CHW	365	41	85	18	0	7	26	29	81	12	1	232	289	336	625	7%	78%	0.36	72	91	3.55	14
Ludwick,Ryan	07	29	8	aa	STL	106	17	24	5	0	5	23	6	21	1	1	226	268	403	671	5%	80%	0.28	110	70	3.60	26
Luna,Hector	07	28	6	aaa	TOR	390	44	92	23	1	7	35	24	56	3	4	236	280	351	631	6%	86%	0.43	80	62	3.31	20
	08	29	5	aaa	TOR	429	54	101	21	1	10	34	23	80	5	2	236	275	357	632	5%	81%	0.29	80	82	3.39	18
Lydon,Wayne	07	26	8	a/a	TOR	524	64	113	19	4	5	35	41	102	22	9	215	271	295	566	7%	80%	0.40	54	125	2.73	2
	08	27	8	aaa	TOR	499	59	111	17	3	1	35	46	89	35	9	222	287	272	560	8%	82%	0.52	38	130	2.89	-0
Machado,Alejandr	08	26	40	aaa	MIN	195	26	55	14	2	2	24	9	25	9	3	283	315	401	716	5%	87%	0.37	86	130	4.61	37
Machado,Andy	07	27	6	aaa	CIN	278	39	55	7	2	4	21	46	67	10	3	199	312	279	591	14%	76%	0.68	49	114	3.23	0
	08	28	5	aa	NYM	252	23	45	12	1	4	21	32	56	3	0	179	270	275	545	11%	78%	0.57	66	70	2.62	-2
Macias,Drew	07	25	8	aa	SD	441	48	98	17	5	9	52	62	78	7	10	222	317	340	658	12%	82%	0.79	74	89	3.66	20
	08	26	8	aa	SD	504	74	119	22	3	8	53	66	78	14	7	237	325	341	666	12%	85%	0.85	69	103	4.01	24
Macias,Jose	07	36	8	aaa	MIL	285	20	58	10	2	2	25	9	48	4	2	202	227	268	495	3%	83%	0.19	46	82	1.98	-10
Mackowiak,Rob	08	32	8	aaa	CIN	141	21	28	2	1	4	10	26	40	3	1	199	322	313	635	15%	72%	0.64	63	91	3.70	5
Macri,Matthew	07	25	54	a/a	MIN	331	45	86	24	0	12	37	18	69	4	4	261	299	445	744	5%	79%	0.26	121	62	4.56	42
	08	26	64	aaa	MIN	313	27	66	20	3	8	37	19	79	2	2	212	257	373	631	6%	75%	0.24	106	79	3.17	19
Maddox,Marc	08	25	4	aa	KC	453	55	115	29	0	3	24	39	64	12	12	253	313	336	649	8%	86%	0.62	67	71	3.54	24
Madera,Sandy	08	28	03	a/a	BOS	285	29	69	16	1	9	40	18	41	1	0	241	287	395	682	6%	86%	0.45	100	49	3.99	30
Mahar,Kevin	07	26	8	aa	TEX	482	50	106	20	3	7	37	18	115	5	1	220	249	316	565	4%	76%	0.16	64	96	2.67	3
Maier,Mitch	07	25	8	aa	KC	544	58	127	26	4	10	48	26	82	5	2	233	268	349	617	5%	85%	0.32	76	91	3.22	16
	08	26	8	aa	KC	345	45	96	23	1	6	32	24	38	9	3	277	324	405	730	6%	89%	0.63	90	90	4.83	42
Majewski,Dustin	07	26	8	aa	TOR	466	44	91	24	2	11	43	53	103	1	4	196	278	329	607	10%	78%	0.51	87	41	3.04	12
	08	27	8	aa	TEX	430	50	98	26	3	7	50	57	70	5	6	228	318	352	670	12%	84%	0.81	85	71	3.87	27
Majewski,Val	07	26	8	a/a	BAL	456	53	104	24	3	5	43	40	92	11	5	229	291	324	614	8%	80%	0.43	68	103	3.30	13
	08	27	8	aa	HOU	160	18	37	8	1	5	16	13	20	1	4	231	287	394	681	7%	88%	0.63	102	64	3.57	32
Maldonado,Carlos	07	29	2	aa	PIT	143	10	22	3	0	1	13	13	29	0	0	157	226	196	422	8%	80%	0.45	28	22	1.50	-27
	08	30	2	aa	PIT	125	7	25	8	0	2	12	9	23	0	1	200	251	303	554	6%	81%	0.37	76	19	2.48	5
Malec,Christopher	08	26	53	aa	NYY	405	57	104	24	2	5	45	58	59	0	2	257	350	359	709	13%	86%	0.99	74	48	4.67	36
Malo,Jonathan	08	25	45	aa	NYM	276	39	61	12	1	3	24	23	47	9	3	221	280	303	583	8%	83%	0.48	58	111	2.99	7
Mangini,Matthew	08	23	5	aa	SEA	237	18	42	4	0	2	20	10	55	0	1	177	211	219	430	4%	77%	0.18	28	36	1.47	-26
Manriquez,Salomc	07	25	20	aa	TEX	247	26	58	11	0	14	41	19	51	0	1	233	288	441	729	7%	79%	0.37	123	20	4.34	36
	08	26	2	aa	NYM	321	31	72	14	1	3	22	17	49	2	2	224	264	298	562	5%	85%	0.36	54	61	2.65	4
Manzella,Thomas	07	24	6	aa	HOU	228	28	57	10	2	1	12	15	36	8	2	250	297	325	622	6%	84%	0.42	54	118	3.50	14
	08	25	6	aa	HOU	452	32	95	21	4	3	35	24	60	3	9	210	249	291	540	5%	87%	0.39	58	66	2.22	2
Maples,Chris	07	28	80	aaa	DET	181	15	30	6	1	0	13	15	63	3	1	168	232	210	442	8%	65%	0.24	33	91	1.66	-26
Maroul,David	08	26	5	aa	SF	366	39	73	24	0	8	29	17	100	3	4	200	236	326	562	4%	73%	0.17	89	61	2.43	7
Marson,Louis	08	22	2	aa	PHI	322	41	89	16	0	4	34	50	53	2	4	276	374	363	737	13%	84%	0.94	63	36	5.12	37
Marte,Andy	07	24	5	aaa	CLE	352	41	86	17	1	13	52	19	57	0	0	244	283	409	692	5%	84%	0.33	102	39	4.04	30
Martinez-Esteve,E	07	24	8	aa	SF	134	8	28	2	1	1	8	10	28	1	1	206	258	255	513	7%	79%	0.33	30	60	2.22	-12
	08	25	80	aa	SF	396	35	103	13	0	5	35	44	34	2	1	261	335	330	665	10%	91%	1.30	48	34	4.14	33
Martinez,Fernandc	07	19	8	aa	NYM	236	31	66	12	1	3	20	20	37	2	6	278	333	380	713	8%	85%	0.54	70	68	4.31	32
Martinez,Gabriel	07	24	30	aa	TAM	386	35	90	13	1	12	67	26	92	0	1	234	282	369	651	6%	76%	0.28	82	31	3.58	17
	08	25	038	aa	TAM	511	54	118	24	0	16	72	39	95	0	0	232	286	373	659	7%	81%	0.41	91	24	3.73	23
Martinez,Jesus	08	20	8	aa	NYM	352	43	96	19	3	6	39	24	58	5	2	271	318	397	715	6%	83%	0.42	83	100	4.58	33
Martinez,Jose	07	22	6	aa	STL	250	30	66	11	0	8	38	12	19	0	0	264	298	404	702	5%	92%	0.63	88	30	4.30	37
	08	23	46	aa	STL	483	39	106	17	1	6	53	16	34	1	5	219	244	296	541	3%	93%	0.47	52	39	2.31	4
Martinez,Ramon	08	36	6	aa	NYM	187	17	42	6	0	2	13	15	16	1	1	223	282	282	563	8%	91%	0.93	42	40	2.76	10
Martin,Dustin	08	25	8	aa	MIN	510	55	128	30	6	8	58	37	114	18	12	250	302	376	678	7%	78%	0.33	85	123	3.80	25
Marti,Amaury	07	25	8	aa	STL	107	19	28	4	0	5	15	8	20	1	0	257	307	426	733	7%	81%	0.38	100	69	4.73	35
Massaro,Michael	08	24	8	aa	OAK	132	12	30	7	1	0	7	6	18	1	6	225	258	291	549	4%	87%	0.33	51	78	2.06	3
Mateo,Henry	07	31	48	aaa	DET	311	36	68	13	2	3	16	28	54	20	10	217	281	295	577	8%	82%	0.51	54	121	2.78	5
Mather,Joe	07	25	83	aa	STL	487	59	104	21	1	22	57	39	74	7	0	213	270	392	662	7%	85%	0.52	108	84	3.68	26
	08	26	8	aa	STL	211	33	51	11	1	11	30	23	30	6	2	240	315	458	772	10%	86%	0.76	131	95	5.08	49
Mathews,Aaron	07	25	8	aa	TOR	471	48	115	29	3	6	36	20	73	4	2	245	275	357	632	4%	84%	0.27	80	79	3.39	20
	08	26	8	aa	TOR	297	35	74	11	2	5	38	17	43	2	4	248	290	344	633	6%	85%	0.40	62	73	3.36	16
Mathis,Jeff	07	25	2	aa	LAA	250	33	54	12	1	4	22	14	43	3	1	217	259	319	578	5%	83%	0.33	71	93	2.81	8

BATTER	Yr	Age	Pos	Lev	Org	ab	r	h	d	t	hr	rbi	bb	k	sb	cs	ba	ob	slg	ops	bb%	ct%	eye	px	sx	rc/g	bpv
Matos,Luis	07	29	8	aa	NYM	392	33	70	19	1	2	22	16	66	6	7	180	212	251	463	4%	83%	0.24	55	79	1.59	-13
Matranga,Dave	07	31	6	aa	TEX	248	22	43	6	1	6	18	18	73	6	1	175	231	288	519	7%	71%	0.25	67	99	2.25	-9
	08	32	45	aa	KC	201	24	43	7	3	4	23	16	52	2	3	216	274	338	612	7%	74%	0.31	74	110	3.05	9
Matulia,Matt	08	24	645	aa	CHC	250	30	47	7	1	2	16	30	46	3	4	188	275	246	520	11%	82%	0.65	39	74	2.27	-8
Maxwell,Justin	08	25	8	aa	WAS	146	27	28	5	2	5	21	23	23	10	5	191	301	348	649	14%	84%	1.01	92	160	3.50	21
Mayberry,John	07	24	8	aa	TEX	245	29	53	10	0	13	31	16	53	6	1	218	267	412	679	6%	79%	0.31	115	74	3.77	26
	08	25	8	aa	TEX	519	48	118	33	5	15	53	25	84	8	4	228	263	398	661	5%	84%	0.30	110	98	3.50	27
Maybin,Cameron	08	22	8	aa	FLA	390	61	99	14	7	11	41	54	109	18	8	254	344	412	756	12%	72%	0.49	92	170	5.11	32
Mayorson,Manuel	07	25	45	aa	TOR	452	43	108	23	2	1	23	31	32	6	8	240	289	305	594	6%	93%	0.99	52	67	2.95	21
	08	26	6	aa	FLA	424	42	113	30	1	2	39	27	20	17	17	266	310	355	665	6%	95%	1.35	72	80	3.53	45
Maysonet,Edwin	07	26	64	aa	HOU	341	26	76	11	2	4	30	13	61	4	2	222	249	296	545	4%	82%	0.21	49	74	2.47	-2
	08	27	64	aa	HOU	406	40	87	18	1	5	23	30	58	3	4	215	270	299	569	7%	86%	0.53	60	57	2.71	7
May,Lucas	08	24	2	aa	LA	392	41	78	24	1	11	41	25	94	5	1	200	249	348	596	6%	76%	0.27	98	81	2.90	12
Maza,Luis	07	27	458	aa	LA	324	32	73	18	1	4	29	22	54	2	2	225	274	325	599	6%	83%	0.40	72	62	3.05	13
	08	28	48	aa	LA	238	36	71	9	3	2	20	23	28	1	2	299	361	381	742	9%	88%	0.81	54	87	5.20	38
Mc Fall,Brian	08	25	8	aa	KC	348	35	76	15	2	14	51	32	89	6	7	218	283	397	680	8%	75%	0.36	108	73	3.63	24
McAnulty,Paul	07	27	8	aa	SD	233	19	48	9	1	3	24	23	51	0	2	205	276	295	571	9%	78%	0.45	59	39	2.74	2
	08	28 b	8	aa	SD	181	26	49	11	1	9	39	27	39	0	0	269	363	487	851	13%	79%	0.69	134	44	6.67	59
McCarthy,Bill	07	28	8	a/a	KC	270	23	53	9	2	7	23	14	61	3	2	197	236	319	555	5%	77%	0.23	74	85	2.45	1
McClain,Scott	07	35	3	aa	SF	468	40	78	16	0	16	58	34	116	1	1	168	223	305	528	7%	75%	0.29	84	31	2.18	-4
	08	36	53	aa	SF	477	66	112	26	1	20	82	54	100	3	2	235	312	417	729	10%	79%	0.54	114	63	4.62	36
McCoy,Mike	07	27	68	aa	STL	306	25	57	8	1	2	18	43	52	10	7	185	284	233	518	12%	83%	0.82	34	73	2.30	-8
	08	28	4	a/a	COL	292	35	72	11	2	4	27	21	33	8	5	247	296	333	629	7%	89%	0.62	57	99	3.42	18
McCutchen,Andrew	07	21	8	aa	PIT	513	68	133	25	2	9	47	42	74	19	5	260	316	373	688	8%	86%	0.57	76	107	4.30	29
	08	22	8	aa	PIT	512	66	138	26	2	7	44	59	73	30	21	270	345	371	716	10%	86%	0.80	70	98	4.39	35
McDonald,Darnell	07	29	8	aaa	MIN	491	65	132	26	5	7	67	43	110	31	7	269	328	381	708	8%	78%	0.39	76	143	4.71	29
	08	30	8	aaa	MIN	369	38	78	20	3	8	41	25	83	14	3	212	262	343	605	6%	78%	0.30	86	121	3.11	12
McDougall,Marsha	07	29	5	aa	LA	515	48	106	26	1	15	62	22	94	2	2	205	237	346	583	4%	82%	0.23	91	49	2.68	11
	08	30	4	aa	SD	107	8	21	9	0	1	10	4	17	1	0	193	224	297	521	4%	84%	0.25	84	49	2.21	4
McEwing,Joe	07	35	45	aaa	BOS	477	41	112	23	1	6	41	23	104	5	9	234	268	326	595	5%	78%	0.22	66	51	2.80	9
McGehee,Casey	07	25	52	aa	CHC	436	45	100	26	2	9	48	33	75	1	3	229	283	355	639	7%	83%	0.44	86	51	3.42	21
	08	26	5	aa	CHC	497	49	123	26	0	9	66	28	74	0	4	248	288	357	646	5%	85%	0.38	76	23	3.51	22
McIntyre,Nick	07	27	65	aa	DET	278	28	49	7	1	2	15	11	77	4	0	175	207	225	433	4%	72%	0.15	35	103	1.57	-24
McPherson,Dallas	08	28	5	aa	FLA	448	69	97	18	2	30	71	59	169	11	6	216	307	464	771	12%	62%	0.35	142	94	4.81	37
Melian,Jackson	07	28	8	aa	DET	320	38	79	12	2	11	51	24	76	6	5	246	299	394	693	7%	76%	0.32	89	83	3.99	25
	08	29	8	a/a	HOU	175	13	29	6	0	4	13	4	31	2	2	166	186	277	463	2%	82%	0.14	70	59	1.54	-13
Melillo,Kevin	07	25	4	aa	OAK	382	48	82	23	4	7	41	41	90	6	7	214	290	351	641	10%	76%	0.45	92	104	3.35	18
	08	26	45	a/a	TOR	372	33	83	17	3	12	41	36	87	3	1	223	291	381	672	9%	77%	0.41	98	73	3.87	23
Melo,Juan	07	31	5	aa	WAS	188	8	28	5	0	2	14	9	34	1	4	149	188	209	397	5%	82%	0.27	40	27	1.11	-28
Mench,Kevin	08	31	8	a/a	TOR	184	18	42	10	2	3	22	10	26	0	0	226	267	356	623	5%	86%	0.39	86	62	3.26	19
Mendez,Carlos	07	33	30	aaa	ATL	263	23	62	16	0	5	28	6	38	0	2	236	254	349	603	2%	86%	0.17	81	32	2.91	15
Mendez,Victor	08	28	8	aa	NYM	105	7	19	2	0	2	7	11	23	1	1	184	259	251	510	9%	78%	0.46	41	34	2.19	-12
Mendoza,Carlos	07	28	5	aa	NYY	268	22	46	11	0	0	14	32	67	3	1	170	260	211	470	11%	75%	0.48	36	58	1.96	-19
Menechino,Frank	07	37	4	aa	SD	128	16	31	10	1	2	13	9	26	1	0	241	291	377	668	7%	80%	0.35	98	84	3.92	28
Mercado,Orlando	08	24	2	aa	ARI	194	19	41	6	0	2	19	33	23	0	2	212	328	273	600	15%	88%	1.42	42	22	3.24	17
Mercedes,Victor	07	28	64	aa	CHW	341	36	72	16	1	6	23	18	68	5	6	211	252	312	564	5%	80%	0.27	69	74	2.49	4
	08	29	4	aa	CHW	416	45	92	23	2	11	46	13	79	9	9	221	245	366	611	3%	81%	0.16	95	92	2.72	16
Merchan,Jesus	07	27	64	a/a	SEA	378	51	95	17	2	7	40	22	28	9	5	250	291	362	652	5%	93%	0.78	74	101	3.64	29
	08	28	6	aa	ARI	436	39	128	20	5	4	55	14	40	2	2	293	316	384	700	3%	91%	0.36	62	73	4.41	31
Merloni,Lou	07	36	5	aa	OAK	393	28	64	14	1	1	23	23	59	1	4	162	209	212	421	6%	85%	0.39	39	43	1.38	-22
Merrill,Ronnie	07	29	65	aa	ARI	377	40	73	13	3	10	38	30	84	10	4	193	253	320	574	7%	78%	0.36	77	114	2.69	3
	08	30	6	a/a	TAM	451	54	87	13	4	3	30	46	84	5	3	193	268	263	531	9%	81%	0.55	46	107	2.44	-6
Metcalf,Travis	07	25	5	aa	TEX	261	31	55	18	0	5	31	21	56	2	1	210	268	341	610	7%	79%	0.37	93	58	3.12	16
	08	26	5	aa	TEX	265	26	55	12	1	4	27	13	49	0	1	208	245	302	547	5%	82%	0.26	65	51	2.44	1
Meyer,Drew	07	26	6	aa	TEX	225	21	39	10	0	1	7	20	41	2	3	174	241	228	470	8%	82%	0.48	44	54	1.79	-14
	08	27	458	aa	TEX	284	30	58	8	4	2	17	25	39	7	2	203	268	276	543	8%	86%	0.65	46	126	2.59	-0
Miller,Corky	07	32	2	aaa	ATL	181	10	32	7	0	4	20	20	27	4	0	179	260	278	538	10%	85%	0.74	66	47	2.56	2
Miller,Jai	07	23	8	aa	FLA	406	46	96	24	2	12	49	50	115	10	6	236	320	394	714	11%	72%	0.43	102	86	4.41	30
	08	24	8	aa	FLA	434	54	102	20	4	15	45	45	120	16	7	235	307	400	707	9%	72%	0.37	100	121	4.25	27
Miller,Matthew	07	25	8	aa	COL	446	47	106	20	2	10	48	34	57	1	4	239	293	356	649	7%	87%	0.60	76	47	3.55	23
	08	26	8	aa	COL	531	67	154	30	0	8	72	39	44	4	3	290	339	389	729	7%	92%	0.91	72	52	4.92	45
Minaker,Christoph	07	24	6	aa	SEA	353	32	70	9	1	3	22	22	62	2	8	198	246	253	498	6%	82%	0.36	37	53	1.89	-12
Minicozzi,Mark	07	25	645	aa	SF	275	24	51	10	2	1	13	14	39	2	1	187	227	249	475	5%	86%	0.37	45	83	1.85	-12
Miranda,Juan	07	24	30	aa	NYY	196	28	48	15	1	7	44	21	49	0	1	247	320	436	756	10%	75%	0.42	125	58	4.92	43
	08	25	30	aaa	NYY	356	34	90	19	0	10	44	45	76	2	1	253	337	393	731	11%	79%	0.60	92	32	4.89	34
Mitchell,Lee	07	25	5	aa	FLA	451	56	103	23	2	15	56	59	154	2	1	227	316	389	705	11%	66%	0.38	102	62	4.40	25
	08	26	5	aa	FLA	324	28	63	19	2	5	40	52	84	3	3	196	306	310	616	14%	74%	0.62	80	62	3.33	11
Mitchell,Russell	08	24	53	aa	LA	485	50	111	20	2	13	58	35	80	6	5	228	281	356	636	7%	84%	0.44	80	70	3.37	18
Mohr,Dustan	07	31	8	aaa	TAM	201	22	40	13	0	8	21	15	84	1	1	197	254	381	634	7%	58%	0.18	118	44	3.18	18
Molina,Felix	07	24	4	aa	MIN	426	40	99	17	2	6	35	26	63	7	7	232	276	321	597	6%	85%	0.41	60	74	2.93	10
	08	25	46	a/a	MIN	302	23	62	15	2	2	27	15	48	4	8	205	243	286	529	5%	84%	0.31	59	73	2.05	-1
Molina,Gustavo	07	26	2	a/a	BAL	216	15	50	7	0	2	13	10	33	0	2	233	268	290	559	5%	85%	0.32	41	23	2.59	1
	08	27	2	aa	NYM	228	17	39	6	0	6	21	12	51	0	0	169	211	266	477	5%	78%	0.23	59	21	1.81	-15
Montanez,Luis	07	26	8	a/a	BAL	333	44	86	11	0	9	32	28	46	4	5	257	314	368	682	8%	86%	0.59	70	55	4.00	26
	08	27 b	8	aa	BAL	451	73	129	27	3	22	78	29	58	3	5	286	329	504	833	6%	87%	0.51	134	76	5.90	61
Montz,Luke	07	24	2	aa	WAS	146	18	29	4	1	4	15	7	45	0	0	195	230	312	543	4%	69%	0.15	69	78	2.37	-3
	08	25	2	a/a	WAS	388	38	86	19	1	11	55	33	73	1	2	223	284	363	647	8%	81%	0.45	90	41	3.52	20
Monzon,Erick	07	26	6	aa	SEA	230	15	41	9	1	5	23	21	53	3	3	180	248	286	533	8%	77%	0.39	68	57	2.29	-4
	08	27	6	aa	SEA	148	12	25	3	1	2	6	12	41	4	0	168	230	236	466	7%	72%	0.29	41	98	1.90	-21
Mooney,Michael	08	25	8	aa	SF	138	12	24	7	0	6	18	3	32	3	2	170	187	341	527	2%	77%	0.09	105	78	1.87	2
Moore,Adam	08	24	2	aa	SEA	428	47	118	31	1	11	56	34	70	0	1	276	329	426	755	7%	84%	0.48	104	33	5.12	44
Moore,Frank	07	29	8	aa	FLA	235	19	41	9	2	2	19	15	71	2	2	172	222	252	474	6%	70%	0.21	54	85	1.81	-16

Major League Equivalent Statistics

BATTER	Yr	Age	Pos	Lev	Org	ab	r	h	d	t	hr	rbi	bb	k	sb	cs	ba	ob	slg	ops	bb%	ct%	eye	px	sx	rc/g	bpv
Moore,Scott	07	24	5	aa	CHC	321	49	77	17	3	16	56	38	88	3	3	239	319	465	784	11%	73%	0.43	136	97	5.15	44
	08	25	5	aaa	BAL	287	33	61	17	1	6	36	18	56	3	0	214	261	341	602	6%	80%	0.32	87	82	3.07	14
Morales,Jose	07	25	2	aaa	MIN	376	41	114	24	1	2	37	28	45	1	4	303	351	388	740	7%	88%	0.62	67	40	5.04	41
	08	26	2	aaa	MIN	197	14	52	6	1	3	12	6	27	0	1	262	283	344	627	3%	86%	0.21	52	39	3.36	13
Morales,Kendry	07	24	30	aa	LAA	255	36	78	18	1	4	32	12	28	0	2	305	338	428	766	5%	89%	0.43	89	53	5.29	47
	08	25	3	aa	LAA	317	37	94	17	0	11	52	15	38	1	3	297	328	457	785	5%	88%	0.39	102	32	5.39	49
Moran,Javon	07	25	8	a/a	PHI	425	62	102	17	3	2	17	35	72	23	15	239	297	306	604	8%	83%	0.49	48	127	3.01	10
	08	26	8	a/a	PHI	363	39	77	17	1	2	17	24	52	17	2	213	262	279	540	6%	86%	0.46	50	116	2.65	1
Morgan,Matthew	07	26	24	aa	ARI	216	11	37	5	0	0	11	16	36	1	0	173	229	197	426	7%	84%	0.44	21	33	1.54	-25
	08	27	2	aa	ARI	152	13	33	8	1	1	7	8	24	1	0	219	259	302	561	5%	84%	0.33	62	67	2.69	5
Morgan,Nyjer	07	27	8	aa	PIT	164	22	39	3	1	0	7	10	28	18	7	238	282	268	550	6%	83%	0.36	22	142	2.64	-4
	08	28	8	aa	PIT	322	41	80	11	3	1	26	13	45	33	8	249	278	309	587	4%	86%	0.29	43	159	3.13	6
Morrissey,Adam	07	26	4	aa	LAA	486	67	104	22	1	7	39	71	136	10	7	213	314	304	618	13%	72%	0.53	63	78	3.38	8
	08	27	540	aa	LAA	393	32	93	19	0	10	37	25	89	3	2	236	282	360	641	6%	77%	0.28	82	39	3.50	18
Morris,Jed	08	29	2	aa	OAK	119	11	24	4	1	2	10	9	15	0	0	200	255	296	551	7%	88%	0.60	62	53	2.56	4
Morse,Mike	07	26	56	aa	SEA	291	38	74	22	0	5	31	21	49	4	3	254	303	374	677	7%	83%	0.42	90	65	3.97	30
Mortimer,Steve	07	26	38	aa	WAS	228	23	41	10	1	6	24	25	93	1	2	179	261	313	574	10%	59%	0.27	85	62	2.69	0
Morton,Colt	08	27	2	aa	SD	218	18	31	6	1	4	18	13	67	1	0	143	191	232	423	6%	69%	0.19	56	74	1.42	-25
Moses,Matt	07	23	5	a/a	MIN	436	40	100	30	0	5	55	18	87	11	3	229	260	333	592	4%	80%	0.21	79	82	2.96	13
	08	24	8	aa	MIN	387	34	78	19	2	2	28	27	61	6	5	203	255	276	531	7%	84%	0.45	55	81	2.32	-1
Moss,Brandon	07	24 a	8	aaa	BOS	493	59	136	46	1	13	70	54	133	3	5	276	347	452	800	10%	73%	0.41	125	47	5.68	52
	08	25	3	aaa	BOS	163	23	40	8	3	6	24	12	41	2	0	248	300	438	739	7%	75%	0.29	115	140	4.72	36
Moss,Steve	07	24	8	aa	MIL	443	47	91	19	4	10	48	61	114	10	6	206	302	333	635	12%	74%	0.53	80	100	3.49	12
Mottola,Chad	07	36	80	aaa	TOR	405	54	91	21	3	14	42	25	74	5	1	224	270	396	665	6%	82%	0.34	106	102	3.67	25
Muich,Joseph	08	26	2	aa	NYY	142	6	28	4	0	0	9	9	43	0	0	194	243	220	464	6%	69%	0.21	23	12	1.83	-22
Mulhern,Ryan	07	27	30	aaa	CLE	476	56	123	34	1	13	64	35	122	1	3	259	309	414	723	7%	74%	0.29	106	44	4.50	36
	08	28	03	a/a	PIT	316	34	62	14	0	9	32	27	89	0	1	197	260	325	584	8%	72%	0.30	82	33	2.82	5
Munson,Eric	07	30	2	aa	HOU	173	17	33	12	0	5	17	15	39	1	1	191	255	338	593	8%	78%	0.39	102	44	2.86	13
Murphy,Daniel	08	24 a	5	aa	NYM	361	48	98	24	1	11	56	33	40	12	6	271	333	432	765	8%	89%	0.84	106	86	5.15	51
Murphy,David	07	26	8	a/a	TEX	407	39	101	18	4	8	37	31	59	7	2	247	301	366	668	7%	86%	0.53	76	97	3.95	25
Murphy,Donnie	07	25	6	aa	OAK	175	25	50	17	1	2	18	13	38	3	2	288	338	429	767	7%	78%	0.35	108	89	5.29	48
	08	26	4	aa	OAK	141	18	31	8	1	8	20	6	36	1	0	220	250	453	703	4%	74%	0.16	142	87	3.82	35
Murphy,Steven	07	23	8	aa	TEX	488	57	123	31	3	10	54	23	88	4	4	252	286	388	674	5%	82%	0.27	92	80	3.80	28
	08	24	8	aa	TEX	508	62	115	31	7	15	64	27	100	12	5	227	266	404	670	5%	80%	0.27	112	140	3.60	27
Murphy,Tommy	07	28	8	aa	LAA	307	26	62	14	3	2	23	16	76	11	9	201	240	289	529	5%	75%	0.21	61	126	2.11	-4
	08	29	8	a/a	FLA	453	53	101	18	3	3	23	34	91	27	11	222	276	296	572	7%	80%	0.37	52	126	2.78	3
Murton,Matt	07	26 a	8	aa	CHC	151	23	41	14	1	5	21	14	17	1	0	274	334	483	817	8%	89%	0.81	140	73	5.97	65
	08	27	8	aa	OAK	321	32	73	19	2	1	20	29	32	5	4	227	291	306	596	8%	90%	0.89	61	77	3.07	19
Myers,Casey	07	28	0	aa	OAK	122	15	28	2	1	2	9	11	18	0	0	231	294	306	600	8%	85%	0.60	45	60	3.21	8
Myers,Corey	07	27	20	aa	LAA	174	13	34	5	0	2	22	17	29	2	2	196	266	267	533	9%	83%	0.57	47	46	2.36	-4
Myers,Michael	07	28	34	aa	CHW	278	22	40	7	1	2	24	25	67	5	6	143	214	203	417	8%	76%	0.37	40	75	1.33	-28
Myrow,Brian	07	31	3	aa	SD	347	39	78	19	2	8	47	36	101	1	0	226	299	365	665	9%	71%	0.36	91	66	3.88	20
	08	32	3	aa	SD	328	44	77	16	1	9	43	59	78	0	1	233	350	365	715	15%	76%	0.76	86	38	4.74	28
Nanita,Ricardo	07	26	8	aa	CHW	427	37	92	17	0	4	34	27	56	8	8	216	263	287	550	6%	87%	0.48	52	59	2.44	3
	08	27	8	aa	CHW	412	42	101	19	1	9	42	32	57	12	9	245	298	360	659	7%	86%	0.56	76	74	3.60	24
Natale,Jeff	07	25	34	aa	BOS	404	50	93	27	1	4	48	65	33	4	3	229	336	327	663	14%	92%	1.94	75	58	4.05	46
	08	26	3	a/a	BOS	111	12	26	4	1	3	11	13	11	2	1	232	312	356	668	10%	90%	1.18	75	80	3.95	32
Navarro,Oswaldo	07	23	64	aa	SEA	446	44	100	20	0	3	39	29	79	3	3	224	272	289	561	6%	82%	0.37	50	51	2.68	3
	08	24	6	aa	SEA	357	36	80	18	1	1	24	25	64	2	4	223	274	288	562	7%	82%	0.39	52	58	2.64	4
Negron,Miguel	07	25	8	aa	NYM	506	44	104	21	1	4	54	38	87	15	9	205	260	270	530	7%	83%	0.44	49	82	2.33	-3
	08	26	8	aa	CHW	479	61	124	15	3	6	48	54	59	21	16	259	335	342	677	10%	88%	0.92	53	98	3.97	27
Nelson,Brad	07	25	38	aaa	MIL	411	47	100	22	1	18	57	29	90	8	7	243	293	433	726	7%	78%	0.32	117	70	4.22	36
	08	26	3	aaa	MIL	475	56	111	30	1	13	56	55	66	9	9	234	314	384	698	10%	86%	0.84	101	66	4.07	36
Nelson,Christophe	08	23	6	aa	COL	283	26	59	16	1	2	29	25	47	4	1	208	271	291	562	8%	83%	0.52	63	76	2.75	6
Nelson,John	07	29	53	aa	CHC	263	25	42	7	0	11	30	18	91	0	1	158	211	313	524	6%	65%	0.19	90	31	2.08	-6
Nelson,Jon	07	28	8	aa	SEA	191	17	31	11	2	3	17	4	71	2	1	161	179	287	465	2%	63%	0.06	85	131	1.58	-10
	08	29	08	aa	SEA	375	34	80	19	2	7	31	11	98	2	2	214	235	331	566	3%	74%	0.11	79	71	2.53	6
Nelson,Justin	08	25	8	aa	COL	364	41	75	16	3	14	37	33	83	1	6	207	272	382	655	8%	77%	0.40	106	67	3.31	20
Nettles,Jeff	07	29	5	aa	KC	221	16	41	11	0	5	26	11	57	1	0	187	224	295	519	5%	74%	0.18	74	36	2.17	-4
	08	30	53	aa	BAL	510	54	101	19	0	19	57	32	82	0	1	198	246	345	591	6%	84%	0.39	89	31	2.81	11
Newhan,David	07	34	4	aa	NYM	173	16	38	8	1	4	18	12	33	4	4	218	269	340	609	6%	81%	0.36	78	95	2.94	12
	08	35	84	aa	HOU	198	25	45	10	1	6	23	9	29	5	3	228	259	378	637	4%	85%	0.29	96	101	3.23	21
Nicholson,David	07	25	48	aa	LA	182	22	31	5	1	2	16	18	40	2	3	172	247	240	487	9%	78%	0.45	44	87	1.91	-15
Nickeas,Mike	07	25	2	aa	NYM	212	20	39	9	0	1	11	14	32	2	3	184	235	238	473	6%	85%	0.45	43	58	1.78	-12
	08	26	2	aa	NYM	214	14	38	8	0	2	17	17	44	0	1	176	236	242	478	7%	80%	0.39	49	25	1.87	-14
Nicolas,Cesar	07	25	53	aa	ARI	310	40	63	15	0	7	39	36	71	2	7	203	286	322	608	10%	77%	0.51	80	46	2.93	11
	08	26	5	aa	ARI	296	29	67	20	0	6	33	44	53	1	2	227	327	351	678	13%	82%	0.83	89	29	4.12	29
Niekro,Lance	07	29	3	aa	SF	143	14	31	6	2	3	14	8	33	0	1	218	260	352	612	5%	77%	0.25	84	81	3.02	12
Nielsen,Eric	08	27	8	a/a	TOR	343	29	75	11	1	4	15	28	48	2	0	217	276	287	563	7%	86%	0.58	47	54	2.79	4
Nixon,Trot	08	35	8	aa	NYM	222	35	52	13	0	9	31	35	34	2	0	234	338	417	755	14%	85%	1.02	116	54	5.19	46
Nix,Jayson	07	25	4	aa	COL	439	59	111	29	2	9	43	23	68	18	8	252	290	387	677	5%	85%	0.35	93	114	3.83	29
	08	26	4	aa	COL	264	41	66	17	1	12	34	17	47	7	6	251	297	460	757	6%	82%	0.37	132	100	4.52	45
Nix,Laynce	07	27	8	a/a	MIL	358	49	81	18	1	20	63	26	107	4	0	226	279	447	726	7%	70%	0.24	132	80	4.33	35
	08	28	8	aaa	MIL	380	43	85	18	2	16	41	26	78	4	4	223	273	407	680	6%	80%	0.34	112	72	3.68	27
Nowak,Christophe	07	25	3	aa	TAM	368	44	97	18	3	6	45	45	67	14	3	263	343	374	717	11%	82%	0.66	74	112	4.90	32
	08	26	5	a/a	TAM	515	68	129	31	3	12	63	49	81	5	7	250	315	392	707	9%	84%	0.60	95	73	4.28	35
Nunez,Abraham	07	31	8	aaa	WAS	414	38	95	21	0	13	56	26	113	3	5	228	274	370	644	6%	73%	0.23	91	37	3.35	18
	08	33	54	a/a	NYM	323	28	51	4	0	3	20	39	53	6	1	158	249	195	444	11%	84%	0.74	24	69	1.75	-23
Ochoa,Ivan	07	25	6	aa	SF	179	17	46	10	2	2	16	8	26	7	2	255	285	361	646	4%	85%	0.29	73	119	3.63	21
	08	26	64	aa	SF	292	45	82	10	3	5	26	28	57	17	11	280	343	383	727	9%	80%	0.49	65	130	4.54	30
Oeltjen,Trent	07	25	8	aaa	MIN	244	32	56	9	4	2	23	9	45	14	7	230	257	324	581	4%	82%	0.20	60	177	2.66	5
	08	26	8	aa	ARI	442	60	127	25	9	5	48	20	59	12	8	287	318	419	737	4%	87%	0.34	86	161	4.68	38

Major League Equivalent Statistics

BATTER	Yr	Age	Pos	Lev	Org	ab	r	h	d	t	hr	rbi	bb	k	sb	cs	ba	ob	slg	ops	bb%	ct%	eye	px	sx	rc/g	bpv
Oliveros,Luis	07	24	2	aa	SEA	175	16	43	10	0	3	15	10	25	0	0	244	287	353	640	6%	86%	0.41	78	23	3.57	22
	08	25	2	aa	SEA	192	18	44	8	0	1	9	8	23	2	0	230	259	289	548	4%	88%	0.32	47	59	2.61	2
Olmedo,Ray	07	26	6	aaa	TOR	328	26	85	11	1	1	21	23	47	6	6	260	309	308	617	7%	86%	0.49	36	60	3.30	11
	08	27	6	aaa	WAS	353	29	73	13	2	3	24	14	38	8	12	207	238	275	513	4%	89%	0.38	48	83	1.89	-4
Ordaz,Luis	07	32	4	aa	PIT	351	23	70	15	1	1	22	11	63	6	4	199	224	257	481	3%	82%	0.18	45	68	1.83	-11
	08	33	4	aa	PIT	132	8	33	9	0	2	13	4	18	1	0	251	274	354	629	3%	87%	0.24	77	30	3.42	20
Orr,Pete	07	28	8	aaa	ATL	154	21	33	6	3	1	7	11	39	6	3	211	265	302	567	7%	75%	0.29	57	175	2.66	-0
	08	29	4	aaa	WAS	284	34	60	13	7	2	24	15	56	14	4	212	251	324	575	5%	80%	0.26	71	205	2.72	5
Ortiz,Wilberto	08	24	6	aa	LAA	254	22	61	11	0	2	20	13	33	3	1	239	276	305	580	5%	87%	0.39	50	54	2.94	8
Ortmeier,Dan	07	26	8	aa	SF	305	28	63	16	1	7	39	19	60	11	2	205	252	331	583	6%	80%	0.32	83	99	2.88	9
Osborn,Pat	07	27	5	aa	CLE	183	12	34	6	0	1	15	15	24	4	2	185	246	233	479	7%	87%	0.61	37	60	1.96	-11
Otness,John J.	07	26	2	aa	BOS	251	12	46	10	1	0	17	6	30	1	1	184	203	229	432	2%	88%	0.20	37	48	1.47	-20
	08	27	2	aa	BOS	251	25	56	14	1	1	24	19	28	0	3	222	277	294	571	7%	89%	0.68	56	47	2.71	11
Owens,Jeremy	07	31	8	aaa	TAM	341	36	77	14	5	6	27	16	132	13	2	224	260	346	605	5%	61%	0.12	75	166	3.14	8
Owens,Jerry	07	27	8	aaa	CHW	232	35	61	9	0	3	18	26	35	20	9	263	338	339	677	10%	85%	0.75	53	104	4.15	24
	08	28	8	aaa	CHW	351	31	81	9	0	1	17	31	54	23	13	231	292	264	557	8%	84%	0.56	27	85	2.64	-1
Pacheco,Jonel	08	26	8	aa	PIT	416	52	104	16	0	9	41	33	76	9	4	250	305	354	659	7%	82%	0.44	68	74	3.85	20
Padgett,Matt	07	30	83	a/a	PHI	454	29	83	22	1	9	36	22	98	1	0	183	222	294	516	5%	79%	0.23	75	37	2.13	-3
Padilla,Jorge	07	28	8	aa	KC	443	54	104	18	2	10	47	32	69	13	6	235	286	347	633	7%	84%	0.47	72	97	3.42	17
	08	29	8	a/a	WAS	388	45	94	12	1	3	28	30	50	10	11	242	296	304	600	7%	87%	0.60	43	77	2.95	10
Pagan,Angel	07	26	8	aa	CHC	116	13	23	3	2	3	7	7	20	4	1	203	248	330	578	6%	83%	0.36	75	147	2.78	5
Pagnozzi,Matt	07	25	2	aa	STL	182	11	33	8	0	2	10	7	40	1	0	183	212	256	467	4%	78%	0.17	53	41	1.77	-14
	08	26	2	aa	STL	221	18	42	9	0	2	15	13	38	2	1	191	237	259	496	6%	83%	0.34	51	53	2.04	-8
Palacios,Rodolfo	08	23	2	aa	MIN	116	10	21	4	0	1	7	2	23	0	0	177	191	237	428	2%	80%	0.08	43	41	1.43	-21
Pali,Matthew	07	27	803	aa	LAA	322	22	64	8	1	5	28	17	64	4	6	197	238	276	514	5%	80%	0.27	49	56	2.03	-9
Palmisano,Lou	07	25	2	aa	MIL	351	38	75	19	1	9	50	47	80	6	2	213	305	349	654	12%	77%	0.59	90	73	3.80	20
Paniagua,Salvado	08	25	2	aa	NYM	113	13	24	6	0	6	15	3	33	1	0	208	227	408	635	2%	71%	0.09	121	60	3.06	21
Panther,Nathan	08	27	8	aa	CLE	294	35	60	14	1	5	22	36	59	4	0	205	292	312	604	11%	80%	0.61	72	78	3.28	10
Parejo,Freddy	08	24	8	aa	MIL	334	30	78	10	2	2	25	7	49	10	5	235	250	293	544	2%	85%	0.14	40	103	2.42	-2
Parra,Gerardo	08	21	8	aa	ARI	265	30	71	13	6	4	28	20	28	14	10	267	319	408	727	7%	90%	0.73	88	164	4.27	40
Parrish,Dave	07	28	2	aa	PIT	250	15	38	10	0	3	18	12	56	1	1	150	189	227	417	5%	78%	0.21	54	39	1.34	-23
Pascucci,Val	07	29	3	aa	FLA	447	64	92	20	1	22	67	49	140	6	1	206	284	404	688	10%	69%	0.35	119	86	3.98	25
	08	30	83	a/a	NYM	478	54	102	20	0	19	63	68	128	3	2	214	312	374	686	12%	73%	0.53	98	39	4.13	22
Patchett,Gary	07	29	6	aa	LAA	221	23	40	2	0	0	12	11	59	1	1	180	220	187	406	5%	73%	0.19	6	59	1.35	-34
	08	30	46	aa	LAA	318	21	60	9	1	3	25	20	79	2	3	187	236	246	482	6%	75%	0.26	41	49	1.88	-16
Patterson,Eric	07	24	48	aa	CHC	516	75	135	26	5	12	52	42	76	19	10	261	317	401	718	7%	85%	0.55	89	125	4.46	35
	08	26	4	aa	OAK	312	38	83	21	3	7	35	15	57	14	2	265	299	413	712	5%	82%	0.26	99	135	4.53	35
Patterson,Ryan	07	24	8	aa	TOR	446	42	105	24	0	15	53	18	89	1	5	234	264	390	654	4%	80%	0.20	100	28	3.35	23
	08	25	8	aa	TOR	460	43	98	25	2	14	40	16	73	6	3	213	239	368	607	3%	84%	0.22	100	80	2.87	16
Paulino,Ronny	08	27 b	2	aa	PIT	111	13	29	12	1	3	14	10	30	0	2	259	320	454	774	8%	73%	0.33	138	72	4.91	50
Paul,Xavier	07	23	8	aa	LA	422	53	111	19	1	10	42	41	95	15	10	263	328	384	712	9%	77%	0.43	79	84	4.40	29
	08	24	8	aa	LA	443	65	123	25	3	8	53	35	82	14	8	277	330	398	728	7%	82%	0.43	82	109	4.69	35
Pavkovich,Adam	07	26	48	aa	LAA	281	35	63	21	1	2	26	23	58	3	7	224	284	323	607	8%	79%	0.41	78	71	2.90	15
	08	27	8	aa	LAA	450	59	106	22	3	16	63	29	99	6	3	235	282	401	683	6%	78%	0.30	103	99	3.89	27
Paz,Richard	08	31	04	aa	HOU	262	19	53	9	1	3	23	35	35	1	0	201	295	269	564	12%	87%	0.99	47	40	2.88	6
Pearce,Steve	07	24 a	3	aa	PIT	412	61	121	34	2	15	72	30	51	10	2	293	341	496	837	7%	88%	0.60	135	99	6.36	65
	08	25	83	aa	PIT	386	39	86	24	1	9	49	25	68	9	4	224	272	365	637	6%	82%	0.37	96	84	3.37	22
Pedroza,Sergio	08	25	8	aa	TAM	298	26	63	13	0	4	28	28	68	11	6	213	280	296	576	9%	77%	0.41	60	71	2.81	4
Peel,Aaron	07	25	8	aa	LAA	310	29	69	18	1	6	32	5	41	2	0	224	235	343	579	2%	87%	0.12	83	71	2.71	11
Pena,Brayan	07	26	23	aaa	ATL	345	38	98	19	1	5	43	17	35	5	8	284	317	387	705	5%	90%	0.48	73	62	4.16	34
	08	27 b	2	aa	KC	234	26	63	17	1	5	25	21	15	6	3	267	328	405	733	8%	93%	1.39	97	76	4.79	57
Pena,Ramiro	07	22	6	aa	NYY	203	23	50	7	1	0	10	21	33	7	3	246	317	291	608	9%	84%	0.64	35	94	3.38	9
	08	23	6	aa	NYY	443	53	111	19	5	2	42	37	84	8	6	250	308	327	636	8%	81%	0.45	54	110	3.54	14
Pennington,Clifton	07	23	6	aa	OAK	271	34	60	12	1	2	17	31	29	7	2	222	302	294	595	10%	89%	1.08	52	91	3.23	17
	08	24	64	aa	OAK	440	66	102	13	3	1	25	68	53	23	7	231	334	281	616	13%	88%	1.28	36	121	3.65	18
Peralta,Juan	07	24	4	aa	TOR	272	23	67	8	1	3	22	20	51	2	1	248	299	314	614	7%	81%	0.39	44	54	3.37	9
Perez,Fernando	07	24	8	aa	TAM	393	68	105	21	8	7	27	63	96	26	20	268	369	411	780	14%	76%	0.65	90	173	5.15	40
	08	25	8	aaa	TAM	511	67	125	14	8	4	28	45	139	34	13	245	306	327	633	8%	73%	0.32	50	176	3.55	9
Perez,Kenny	07	26	40	a/a	CHW	324	27	75	12	3	7	35	17	48	2	3	231	269	350	619	5%	85%	0.36	74	68	3.14	14
	08	27	5	aa	COL	133	15	37	11	1	1	13	10	12	1	0	277	328	392	720	7%	91%	0.81	88	71	4.80	45
Perez,Miguel	08	25	2	aa	PIT	171	11	42	4	0	2	18	8	29	1	1	247	279	302	581	4%	83%	0.26	36	31	2.92	3
Perez,Timo	07	32	80	aaa	DET	489	63	127	32	1	10	58	29	47	11	6	260	301	388	689	6%	90%	0.62	90	85	4.05	36
	08	34	80	aaa	DET	427	40	100	23	2	9	45	35	41	14	6	235	293	362	655	8%	90%	0.85	85	86	3.66	30
Perez,Tomas	07	34	6	a/a	CHW	476	45	92	18	0	6	41	23	90	3	1	193	231	266	496	5%	81%	0.26	51	63	2.04	-9
	08	35	54	aa	HOU	306	20	61	11	3	1	16	14	40	1	6	200	234	261	495	4%	87%	0.34	44	62	1.84	-9
Perez,Yohannis	07	25	6	aa	MIL	190	15	32	4	2	0	13	13	52	2	3	170	224	210	434	7%	73%	0.26	27	98	1.48	-27
Perry,Jason	07	27	8	a/a	DET	411	70	85	21	1	19	64	50	132	3	0	207	293	402	695	11%	68%	0.38	119	88	4.13	26
	08	28	8	a/a	ATL	365	53	78	17	1	17	48	36	105	4	0	215	285	403	688	9%	71%	0.35	114	87	4.02	25
Petersen,Joshua	08	25	8	aa	NYM	241	20	57	11	1	2	24	13	51	3	3	238	277	316	593	5%	79%	0.26	57	64	2.95	8
Peterson,Brian	07	29	2	aa	PIT	251	20	51	11	1	2	20	18	40	0	2	204	256	274	530	7%	84%	0.44	52	41	2.32	-2
	08	30	2	aa	BAL	177	13	34	7	0	2	15	11	26	0	1	189	238	258	495	6%	86%	0.44	49	29	2.00	-8
Peterson,Brock	07	24	30	aa	MIN	389	53	97	19	2	12	51	33	79	1	0	249	308	399	707	8%	80%	0.42	95	69	4.42	31
	08	25	3	a/a	MIN	461	55	101	29	2	12	59	35	108	1	1	219	273	364	638	7%	77%	0.32	98	63	3.40	20
Petit,Gregorio	07	23	6	aa	OAK	503	45	135	25	0	5	50	34	75	8	6	268	315	348	663	6%	85%	0.45	59	53	3.89	23
	08	24	6	aa	OAK	308	29	71	12	2	1	26	17	45	2	6	229	269	290	558	5%	85%	0.37	44	69	2.48	2
Pettit,Christopher	08	24	8	aa	LAA	222	22	48	12	1	5	21	12	34	4	2	216	258	342	600	5%	85%	0.36	83	82	2.94	14
Phelps,Josh	08	30	3	aa	STL	461	60	99	23	1	19	65	37	99	2	2	214	273	389	662	8%	79%	0.38	108	58	3.58	24
Phillips,Andy	07	31	4	aaa	NYY	249	31	64	9	1	9	30	25	44	2	1	257	325	408	733	9%	82%	0.57	91	59	4.82	34
	08	32	3	aaa	CIN	146	19	36	7	1	4	15	14	19	2	0	245	309	390	699	9%	87%	0.72	91	78	4.38	34
Phillips,Jason	08	32	2	aaa	ATL	120	10	26	5	0	3	11	5	14	0	1	213	245	319	563	4%	88%	0.36	71	34	2.52	7
Phillips,Kyle	08	25	3	aa	TOR	268	26	72	14	0	7	27	20	36	0	2	269	320	398	717	7%	86%	0.55	86	21	4.51	36

BATTER	Yr	Age	Pos	Lev	Org	ab	r	h	d	t	hr	rbi	bb	k	sb	cs	ba	ob	slg	ops	bb%	ct%	eye	px	sx	rc/g	bpv
Phillips,Paul	07	30	2	aa	KC	202	13	31	5	0	1	8	11	30	0	0	152	194	198	392	5%	85%	0.35	32	25	1.23	-29
	08	31	2	aaa	CHW	253	16	54	12	0	2	13	13	33	0	0	212	249	279	528	5%	87%	0.39	52	18	2.36	-0
Piedra,Jorge	07	28	8	aa	OAK	265	29	66	18	1	6	38	22	38	0	1	248	306	386	693	8%	86%	0.60	97	40	4.18	34
Pie,Felix	07	23 a	8	aa	CHC	229	43	77	9	4	8	37	16	34	8	7	336	380	515	895	7%	85%	0.47	104	148	7.11	65
	08	24	8	aa	CHC	335	42	84	19	3	8	41	17	43	8	9	252	287	395	682	5%	87%	0.39	93	106	3.62	30
Pilittere,Peter	07	26	2	aa	NYY	348	39	80	14	1	2	31	23	48	0	1	230	277	290	567	6%	86%	0.47	45	48	2.78	5
	08	27	2	aa	NYY	364	40	89	13	1	3	42	17	34	0	1	245	280	308	588	5%	91%	0.52	45	47	3.00	11
Pinckney,Andrew	07	25	5	aa	BOS	458	54	103	27	3	10	48	31	92	3	7	224	273	360	632	6%	80%	0.33	91	73	3.16	19
	08	27	5	aa	TOR	406	37	93	24	2	7	37	20	87	2	4	229	265	351	617	5%	79%	0.23	84	58	3.08	16
Pinckney,Brandon	07	25	6	aa	CLE	278	32	62	12	1	2	29	16	34	0	2	223	266	291	558	6%	88%	0.47	50	55	2.60	5
	08	26	46	aa	CLE	322	33	76	13	1	5	29	11	47	2	1	237	262	326	588	3%	85%	0.24	60	65	2.92	9
Plouffe,Trevor	07	21	6	aa	MIN	497	62	122	34	1	7	41	29	76	10	8	245	287	360	647	6%	85%	0.38	84	84	3.47	24
	08	22	654	a/a	MIN	477	55	112	31	5	7	50	24	78	4	3	235	271	365	636	5%	84%	0.31	90	103	3.35	21
Pope,Van	07	24	5	aa	ATL	421	41	85	21	3	5	37	30	71	9	6	203	256	302	558	7%	83%	0.42	69	98	2.53	4
	08	25	5	aa	ATL	350	37	79	18	1	3	39	28	47	7	6	225	282	307	589	7%	87%	0.59	61	77	2.90	12
Porter,Gregory	07	27	80	aa	LAA	472	51	116	21	2	8	59	25	106	12	6	246	284	350	634	5%	78%	0.23	69	93	3.42	15
	08	28	80	aaa	WAS	318	24	63	14	0	2	18	18	72	3	2	199	241	260	501	5%	77%	0.25	48	50	2.08	-9
Powell,Landon	07	26	2	aa	OAK	236	38	57	8	1	11	32	27	40	1	0	240	318	419	738	10%	83%	0.68	105	67	4.82	37
	08	27	2	aa	OAK	300	29	53	9	0	10	37	44	67	0	1	178	283	310	593	13%	78%	0.66	79	21	3.02	5
Prado,Martin	07	24	4	aaa	ATL	395	55	119	22	2	4	37	30	38	5	4	301	351	397	748	7%	90%	0.79	69	79	5.20	45
Prettyman,Ronald	07	26	5	aa	SEA	291	25	60	12	1	5	28	16	64	3	2	206	247	308	555	5%	78%	0.24	67	64	2.51	1
	08	27	5	aa	SEA	165	19	23	5	2	3	17	6	37	2	0	142	173	245	419	4%	78%	0.17	64	143	1.34	-23
Price,Jared	08	27	2	a/a	CHW	183	12	26	3	0	6	6	14	70	0	0	141	201	246	447	7%	62%	0.20	60	14	1.59	-24
Pride,Curtis	07	39	80	aa	LAA	215	17	32	9	1	2	17	18	84	6	3	147	211	225	435	8%	61%	0.21	55	94	1.52	-24
Pridie,Jason	07	24	8	a/a	TAM	525	80	149	30	10	13	59	33	85	23	11	284	326	453	779	6%	84%	0.39	106	170	5.22	46
	08	25	8	aaa	MIN	559	66	128	18	11	9	48	23	140	20	9	229	259	351	610	4%	75%	0.16	72	183	2.98	9
Prieto,Alex	07	31	6	aaa	BOS	182	18	39	11	1	3	17	15	32	2	3	213	274	326	600	8%	82%	0.47	80	70	2.92	13
Pritz,Bryan	07	25	8	a/a	BOS	372	41	98	23	2	6	40	33	53	4	1	263	324	381	704	8%	86%	0.63	82	75	4.53	34
	08	26	8	a/a	BOS	187	18	41	14	0	1	12	14	27	2	1	221	275	310	585	7%	85%	0.51	73	56	2.94	14
Psomas,Grant	07	25	3	aa	FLA	442	50	86	23	3	14	43	43	119	7	6	193	265	348	613	9%	73%	0.36	98	92	2.99	12
	08	26	3	aa	FLA	130	14	20	5	2	4	16	17	43	1	1	156	251	304	555	11%	67%	0.38	88	118	2.50	-4
Putnam,Danny	07	25	8	aa	OAK	223	17	44	15	1	2	24	16	40	3	5	198	252	299	551	7%	82%	0.41	77	65	2.34	6
	08	26	8	aa	OAK	326	40	71	15	1	10	45	34	72	2	2	217	291	361	653	9%	78%	0.47	91	59	3.62	19
Quentin,Carlos	07	25 a	8	aa	ARI	115	23	34	11	1	4	21	7	13	0	1	297	339	501	840	6%	88%	0.54	138	90	6.15	67
Quintanilla,Omar	07	26	64	aa	COL	348	41	96	26	3	3	32	23	57	2	1	277	322	391	713	6%	84%	0.41	85	79	4.62	36
Quintero,Humberto	07	28	2	aa	HOU	177	15	43	9	1	3	15	2	23	0	2	244	254	357	611	1%	87%	0.11	76	50	2.95	15
	08	29	2	aa	HOU	130	9	23	3	1	2	12	3	14	0	2	179	200	251	451	3%	89%	0.25	44	60	1.47	-17
Quiroz,Guillermo	07	26	2	aa	TEX	259	17	59	14	0	5	25	12	48	1	0	226	259	330	589	4%	82%	0.24	73	30	2.94	10
Raburn,John	07	29	84	aa	FLA	372	39	66	10	3	2	20	36	74	15	6	178	251	234	485	9%	80%	0.49	37	128	2.03	-15
	08	30	846	aa	TAM	353	29	64	5	3	0	23	22	45	10	5	180	227	214	442	6%	87%	0.47	22	117	1.60	-22
Raburn,Ryan	07	26 b	8	aaa	DET	315	53	83	18	3	15	57	46	67	11	4	265	358	480	838	13%	79%	0.68	131	120	6.34	56
Raglani,John	07	24	8	aa	LA	456	60	96	21	3	17	53	68	123	7	8	210	313	381	695	13%	73%	0.56	104	82	4.04	24
Ragsdale,Corey	08	26	4	aa	TEX	203	24	37	9	3	4	24	20	51	7	1	181	253	310	563	9%	75%	0.39	82	151	2.72	2
Rahl,Christopher	07	24	8	aa	ARI	423	49	98	24	4	7	41	13	73	13	6	232	254	355	609	3%	83%	0.17	84	131	2.97	15
	08	25	8	aa	ARI	421	38	83	23	2	5	20	22	97	14	12	196	236	294	530	5%	77%	0.23	70	103	2.07	-1
Raines Jr.,Tim	07	28	8	aa	HOU	367	39	84	11	2	9	38	14	69	17	4	229	258	344	602	4%	81%	0.21	70	124	3.05	9
	08	29	8	aa	ARI	502	70	130	25	11	14	57	20	91	21	8	259	287	435	722	4%	82%	0.22	106	192	4.28	34
Ramirez,Max	08	24 a	20	aa	TEX	280	41	84	16	2	16	43	30	55	2	2	301	369	539	908	10%	80%	0.55	142	70	7.49	70
Ramirez,Wilkin	07	22	8	aa	DET	121	14	25	3	1	2	13	8	35	6	2	207	256	298	553	6%	71%	0.23	55	132	2.58	-4
	08	23	8	a/a	DET	469	62	121	22	6	15	59	36	117	22	14	258	311	426	737	7%	75%	0.31	102	143	4.40	34
Ramirez,Yordany	07	23	8	aa	SD	127	16	35	3	0	4	16	5	21	5	6	275	302	390	691	4%	84%	0.24	68	73	3.57	24
	08	24	8	aa	HOU	432	36	83	18	2	9	37	8	51	13	11	191	205	302	507	2%	88%	0.15	72	102	1.79	-3
Ramos,Peeter	07	26	4	aa	PHI	282	30	71	7	0	6	27	23	36	4	5	252	309	345	654	8%	87%	0.66	57	46	3.62	21
Randel,Kevin	07	26	4	aa	FLA	125	10	18	6	0	2	5	21	44	3	1	146	268	237	505	14%	65%	0.48	65	51	2.26	-15
Ransom,Cody	07	32	563	aa	HOU	503	44	93	22	0	18	53	29	157	13	4	185	230	332	562	6%	69%	0.19	92	77	2.48	3
	08	33	56	aaa	NYY	423	53	86	19	2	18	54	37	121	7	4	203	266	382	648	8%	71%	0.30	108	88	3.35	18
Rapoport,James	08	23	8	aa	STL	183	19	38	4	2	1	14	6	28	9	1	209	233	268	501	3%	85%	0.21	37	145	2.20	-11
Rasmus,Colby	07	21	8	aa	STL	472	76	113	32	2	22	59	58	87	15	4	239	323	456	778	11%	82%	0.67	136	108	5.27	49
	08	22	8	aa	STL	331	44	72	13	0	8	28	38	55	12	4	218	298	329	627	10%	83%	0.69	72	87	3.48	16
Raynor,John	08	25	8	aa	FLA	452	84	123	26	5	11	40	53	114	38	12	272	348	421	769	10%	75%	0.47	96	164	5.40	40
Recker,Anthony	07	24	2	aa	OAK	201	12	35	10	0	3	16	13	54	0	1	175	226	269	495	6%	73%	0.25	68	23	1.95	-9
	08	25	2	aa	OAK	430	41	96	24	3	8	46	31	109	1	2	223	275	345	621	7%	75%	0.29	83	64	3.23	14
Reddick,William	08	22	8	aa	BOS	117	18	23	4	1	4	20	10	20	2	1	199	262	354	616	8%	83%	0.51	92	117	3.08	14
Redman,Prentice	07	28	80	aa	SEA	412	41	76	16	2	10	38	38	106	2	4	184	254	307	561	9%	74%	0.36	77	61	2.53	0
	08	29	8	aa	SEA	455	68	102	23	1	17	53	45	70	6	9	225	294	393	687	9%	85%	0.64	105	71	3.75	31
Redman,Tike	07	31	8	aaa	BAL	296	47	78	13	4	2	23	29	26	23	7	265	330	350	679	9%	91%	1.13	58	154	4.28	35
	08	32	80	aaa	BAL	463	55	105	14	3	3	26	35	47	9	12	226	280	285	565	7%	90%	0.74	41	89	2.57	7
Reed,Eric	07	27	8	aa	FLA	303	40	69	8	9	0	15	13	61	23	3	227	259	310	569	4%	80%	0.21	48	245	2.94	-0
	08	28	8	aa	NYM	135	14	23	3	0	0	6	8	22	5	3	173	220	193	413	6%	84%	0.36	18	90	1.37	-28
Reed,Jeremy	07	26	8	aa	SEA	563	70	132	30	3	10	47	37	78	10	9	235	282	349	631	6%	86%	0.47	78	91	3.28	20
	08	27 b	8	aa	SEA	149	19	42	9	1	5	15	13	13	5	1	284	340	447	787	8%	91%	0.95	106	91	5.72	57
Reese,Kevin	07	30	8	aaa	NYY	433	48	93	12	2	8	49	44	75	7	7	214	286	307	593	9%	83%	0.58	57	76	2.94	7
Reimold,Nolan	07	24 a	8	aa	BAL	186	24	50	14	0	10	28	15	39	2	3	271	324	501	825	7%	79%	0.37	145	46	5.58	58
	08	25	8	aa	BAL	507	73	128	26	2	22	70	53	71	6	3	252	322	441	764	9%	86%	0.75	116	77	5.09	47
Relaford,Desi	07	34	5	aa	TEX	316	27	55	11	1	4	31	24	63	4	0	175	233	253	485	7%	80%	0.38	52	82	2.00	-12
Repko,Jason	08	28	8	aa	LA	459	64	104	21	4	9	36	38	99	14	6	225	284	345	630	8%	78%	0.38	77	125	3.37	15
Requena,Alexande	07	27	8	aa	SF	117	9	20	5	1	0	8	10	28	9	5	170	235	227	462	8%	76%	0.36	44	127	1.66	-18
Restovich,Mike	07	29	80	aaa	WAS	356	35	81	17	2	16	49	27	108	3	2	227	282	418	700	7%	70%	0.25	115	67	4.01	28
Reyes,Argenis	07	25	4	aa	CLE	467	52	108	19	2	2	25	19	56	22	8	231	261	291	552	4%	88%	0.34	45	117	2.58	3
	08	26	4	aa	NYM	311	32	73	9	1	0	17	24	42	10	6	234	288	269	558	7%	86%	0.56	29	87	2.67	1
Reyes,Guillermo	08	27	64	aa	ARI	279	33	62	7	2	1	12	24	39	3	6	221	282	270	553	8%	86%	0.61	34	80	2.51	0
Reyes,Jose	07	25	2	aa	NYM	126	10	23	5	0	2	16	10	22	2	0	181	244	264	508	8%	82%	0.47	57	52	2.23	-7

BATTER	Yr	Age	Pos	Lev	Org	ab	r	h	d	t	hr	rbi	bb	k	sb	cs	ba	ob	slg	ops	bb%	ct%	eye	px	sx	rc/g	bpv
Reyes,Milver	07	25	2	aa	PIT	105	4	20	5	0	0	7	7	24	0	0	189	241	231	472	6%	77%	0.29	38	7	1.88	-16
	08	26	2	aa	PIT	150	8	24	4	0	1	6	6	28	0	0	159	189	202	392	4%	81%	0.20	31	23	1.22	-30
Reynolds,Kyle	07	24	5	aa	CHC	139	19	34	9	0	8	28	7	26	2	2	246	280	472	752	5%	81%	0.25	139	64	4.36	44
	08	25	53	aa	CHC	357	28	72	19	1	8	34	21	78	2	4	203	246	332	578	5%	78%	0.27	86	47	2.61	8
Reynolds,Mark	07	24 a	5	aa	ARI	134	22	37	9	2	6	17	16	27	3	1	276	354	496	851	11%	80%	0.59	135	126	6.54	60
Rhinehart,William	08	24	3	aa	WAS	219	18	43	13	0	5	23	21	40	0	0	197	266	322	588	9%	82%	0.52	86	17	2.93	11
Rhymes,William	07	25	4	aa	DET	155	19	37	6	0	1	19	6	20	5	1	239	266	294	560	4%	87%	0.29	42	91	2.76	3
	08	26	4	a/a	DET	541	62	141	18	7	2	47	36	59	13	7	261	306	328	635	6%	89%	0.61	45	120	3.59	18
Richardson,Antoai	08	25	8	aa	SF	365	53	77	5	5	4	25	45	73	27	7	211	298	281	579	11%	80%	0.61	39	164	3.13	-1
Richardson,Juan	07	29	50	aa	STL	430	42	88	15	1	11	51	31	120	0	2	205	258	322	580	7%	72%	0.26	73	36	2.77	4
	08	30	305	aa	KC	494	67	120	32	2	11	61	41	90	2	5	242	300	381	682	8%	82%	0.46	95	59	3.91	29
Richardson,Kevin	07	27	2	aa	TEX	320	30	56	7	0	11	32	17	84	0	2	174	216	296	512	5%	74%	0.21	71	33	2.01	-9
	08	28	2	aa	TEX	187	17	37	8	1	4	15	12	47	0	0	198	247	320	567	6%	75%	0.26	78	45	2.65	3
Richard,Chris	07	33	83	aaa	TAM	342	54	83	21	2	13	49	36	92	8	3	242	314	424	738	10%	73%	0.39	115	108	4.74	36
	08	34	3	aaa	TAM	467	58	105	25	3	19	62	39	126	3	0	224	284	408	692	8%	73%	0.31	114	86	4.04	28
Richar,Danny	07	24 a	4	a/a	CHW	398	53	113	22	6	14	54	34	67	6	5	283	339	470	809	8%	83%	0.51	115	115	5.73	52
	08	25	4	aaa	CIN	362	39	81	19	2	9	41	24	62	10	6	223	271	364	634	6%	83%	0.38	91	97	3.26	19
Richie,Anthony	07	26	2	aa	CHC	220	16	44	6	0	7	21	9	32	2	1	200	232	327	559	4%	85%	0.28	76	40	2.47	4
	08	27	2	aa	CHC	172	10	38	11	0	2	16	5	24	1	0	219	240	316	555	3%	86%	0.19	73	35	2.55	7
Rifkin,Aaron	07	29	3	aa	COL	453	40	94	28	0	10	50	26	115	2	1	208	251	339	590	5%	75%	0.22	90	42	2.85	11
Riggans,Shawn	07	27	2	aaa	TAM	121	10	30	9	1	4	14	4	31	0	3	251	274	432	706	3%	75%	0.12	118	62	3.65	35
Riggs,Eric	07	31	4	aa	FLA	297	32	55	16	3	6	30	21	57	2	2	186	240	323	563	7%	81%	0.37	89	97	2.50	6
Rivas,Luis	07	28	64	aaa	CLE	410	47	91	16	2	8	34	35	66	10	7	222	284	331	615	8%	84%	0.54	70	89	3.14	14
Rivera,Mike	07	31	2	aaa	MIL	349	29	62	13	0	15	48	20	72	4	5	178	222	346	568	5%	79%	0.27	100	43	2.31	6
Rivera,Rene	07	24	2	aa	SEA	323	24	59	14	0	4	31	20	83	1	2	182	230	262	492	6%	74%	0.24	57	36	1.94	-11
	08	25	23	aa	LA	252	19	53	10	0	8	23	17	46	0	1	209	259	339	598	6%	82%	0.37	83	18	2.92	11
Roberson,Chris	07	28	8	aaa	PHI	463	51	106	19	2	4	38	24	54	15	9	229	267	301	569	5%	88%	0.45	52	100	2.65	7
	08	29	8	aaa	BAL	437	38	95	10	1	4	41	28	60	15	17	218	265	276	540	6%	86%	0.46	38	74	2.19	-2
Roberson,Ryan	08	25	3	a/a	DET	465	59	112	18	1	19	67	26	106	6	5	241	281	404	686	5%	77%	0.25	98	71	3.83	26
Roberts,Brandon	07	23	8	aa	MIN	369	41	98	12	3	2	32	25	48	12	8	266	312	331	643	6%	87%	0.52	44	104	3.59	17
Roberts,Ryan	07	27	54	aaa	TOR	337	37	74	14	1	10	38	44	77	1	2	220	309	361	670	11%	77%	0.57	88	43	3.91	21
	08	28	45	aa	TEX	453	48	108	23	5	7	45	46	68	11	4	239	309	359	668	9%	85%	0.67	79	115	3.98	26
Robinson,Christop	07	23	2	aa	CHC	289	23	68	16	0	1	22	16	61	3	0	235	276	302	578	5%	79%	0.27	56	55	2.97	7
	08	24	2	aa	CHC	159	10	29	5	0	1	13	9	31	0	1	181	223	229	453	5%	80%	0.28	36	27	1.64	-19
Robinson,Shane	08	24	8	aa	STL	385	43	101	18	3	4	32	17	46	12	10	262	293	354	647	4%	88%	0.36	63	104	3.42	21
Robinson,Wade	07	27	4	aa	WAS	110	7	17	3	0	0	4	9	17	3	1	158	220	190	410	7%	84%	0.50	28	62	1.42	-26
Robles,Oscar	07	31	6	aa	SD	102	6	18	3	1	0	7	5	13	0	1	178	216	233	449	5%	87%	0.38	36	80	1.59	-18
	08	33	46	a/a	PHI	362	23	69	10	0	3	32	26	38	0	0	190	245	247	492	7%	90%	0.70	39	17	2.05	-6
Robnett,Richie	07	24	8	aa	OAK	523	64	118	35	1	14	60	30	124	3	3	225	268	378	646	5%	76%	0.24	103	65	3.40	23
	08	25	8	aa	OAK	293	29	57	18	0	3	20	27	66	2	0	196	264	286	550	9%	77%	0.41	69	55	2.62	2
Rodriguez,Guilder	07	24	6	aa	MIL	175	23	46	1	0	0	13	20	26	7	6	261	336	266	602	10%	85%	0.76	5	72	3.20	4
	08	25	4	aa	MIL	175	22	35	2	0	0	4	15	21	8	2	199	262	209	472	8%	88%	0.71	10	101	2.04	-16
Rodriguez,Guillern	07	29	2	aa	SF	103	9	17	5	0	1	10	7	9	1	0	167	219	233	452	6%	91%	0.72	50	55	1.70	-9
Rodriguez,John	07	30	0	aa	STL	157	21	27	8	1	4	16	14	37	1	0	172	241	301	542	8%	76%	0.38	83	85	2.43	-1
	08	31	8	a/a	NYM	211	23	44	7	1	7	22	19	52	0	1	209	274	346	620	8%	75%	0.36	82	49	3.20	11
Rodriguez,Joshua	08	24	64	aa	CLE	532	66	115	21	6	6	43	69	112	11	7	216	305	309	615	11%	79%	0.61	61	114	3.32	9
Rodriguez,Mike	07	27	8	aa	HOU	241	24	52	10	2	2	17	14	34	7	4	217	259	296	555	5%	86%	0.40	56	106	2.51	3
	08	28	8	aa	BAL	395	38	83	14	3	4	41	23	67	9	1	210	252	287	539	5%	83%	0.34	52	111	2.52	-2
Rodriguez,Sean	07	22	6	aa	LAA	508	76	120	29	1	15	66	48	119	14	9	236	302	386	688	9%	77%	0.40	98	93	3.96	27
	08	23 a	4	aa	LAA	248	57	69	18	1	17	43	25	39	3	1	277	342	557	899	9%	84%	0.63	170	102	6.98	75
Rogers,Eddie	07	29	654	aaa	BOS	405	34	89	16	0	5	28	16	65	7	5	220	251	294	545	4%	84%	0.25	53	65	2.43	0
	08	30	64	a/a	WAS	324	26	63	9	0	3	16	9	48	10	10	194	215	254	469	3%	85%	0.18	42	78	1.56	-15
Rogowski,Casey	07	26	38	aaa	CHW	453	54	103	25	0	15	48	55	102	15	5	227	311	379	690	11%	77%	0.54	99	78	4.19	27
	08	27	30	aa	OAK	415	47	89	18	2	9	44	36	90	11	4	215	277	332	609	8%	78%	0.40	76	98	3.18	11
Rogowski,Ryan	08	25	8	aa	LA	111	9	18	3	0	2	9	16	23	6	1	164	271	242	514	13%	79%	0.71	50	71	2.45	-10
Rohan,Jimmy	07	23	3	aa	LA	164	13	34	6	1	0	17	14	25	0	0	207	268	254	522	8%	85%	0.55	37	45	2.37	-5
Rohlinger,Ryan	08	25	5	aa	SF	159	23	41	11	1	5	16	10	18	1	1	260	305	432	737	6%	89%	0.57	114	78	4.63	45
Rojas,Carlos	07	24	64	aa	CHC	319	25	69	13	1	0	21	21	43	3	0	216	265	262	527	6%	86%	0.49	38	67	2.44	-3
	08	25	4	aa	BAL	441	61	97	12	1	2	32	41	66	1	3	220	287	263	550	9%	85%	0.63	32	59	2.63	-1
Romak,Jamie	08	23	3	aa	PIT	120	13	23	6	0	6	20	14	28	0	0	188	271	384	655	10%	77%	0.50	119	19	3.52	22
Romero,Alexandei	07	24	8	aa	ARI	533	66	148	29	5	5	52	30	45	10	10	278	317	378	695	5%	92%	0.67	71	98	4.13	35
	08	25	8	aa	ARI	173	23	51	8	2	3	15	9	17	3	3	293	330	413	743	5%	90%	0.55	78	100	4.83	41
Roneberg,Brett	07	29	83	aa	PIT	238	26	44	8	2	5	24	21	40	6	0	185	250	292	543	8%	83%	0.52	67	109	2.56	-0
Roof,Shawn	08	24	6	aa	DET	124	12	24	3	0	0	6	9	18	1	0	194	246	217	463	7%	86%	0.49	21	54	1.86	-17
Rosales,Adam	07	24	3	aa	CIN	255	41	62	16	3	11	25	29	59	3	5	242	321	462	783	10%	77%	0.50	135	107	4.97	46
	08	25	56	aaa	CIN	432	54	106	25	4	9	44	17	71	6	1	246	274	387	662	4%	84%	0.24	93	113	3.71	25
Rosales,Orlando	08	25	8	aa	HOU	106	10	19	3	0	1	4	4	14	0	2	181	210	235	445	3%	87%	0.28	38	53	1.43	-18
Rosario,Olmo	08	28	468	aa	SF	420	46	103	26	3	8	40	15	66	11	5	245	271	377	648	3%	84%	0.23	90	105	3.44	24
Rose,Mike	07	31	2	aaa	CLE	290	29	63	16	1	5	28	28	70	1	4	217	286	335	621	9%	76%	0.40	81	47	3.19	14
Rottino,Vinny	07	27	28	aaa	MIL	377	49	96	15	2	10	45	32	56	12	10	255	313	388	701	8%	85%	0.58	83	94	4.10	31
	08	29	2	aaa	MIL	431	40	85	24	2	5	37	22	65	6	4	198	237	298	535	5%	85%	0.34	71	83	2.28	2
Rouse,Mike	08	28	6	aaa	PHI	393	32	80	15	0	4	29	14	85	5	3	204	231	275	507	3%	78%	0.17	51	64	2.08	-8
Rowlett,Casey	07	25	48	aa	STL	246	28	49	10	2	2	15	15	34	5	0	201	247	278	525	6%	86%	0.45	53	115	2.40	-2
	08	26	84	aa	STL	216	25	44	7	2	4	21	16	35	6	8	205	259	305	564	7%	84%	0.46	62	109	2.35	3
Rozema,Mike	07	26	5	a/a	ATL	202	23	44	6	1	4	23	13	46	5	2	218	264	312	576	6%	77%	0.28	59	93	2.80	3
Ruan,Wilkin	07	29	8	aa	LA	369	32	71	9	2	2	25	8	45	7	2	191	207	240	447	2%	88%	0.17	33	109	1.62	-19
	08	30	8	aa	LA	211	20	55	6	3	0	12	6	20	3	3	262	282	314	596	3%	91%	0.30	36	96	2.95	8
Ruggiano,Justin	07	25 a	8	aaa	TAM	482	73	141	27	2	19	69	51	148	25	12	292	360	472	832	10%	69%	0.35	113	106	6.19	51
	08	26	8	aaa	TAM	257	38	67	15	2	8	40	17	71	16	4	261	306	430	736	6%	73%	0.23	107	140	4.74	36
Ruiz,Randy	07	30	38	a/a	SF	474	48	103	22	2	13	53	30	115	1	1	216	262	356	619	6%	76%	0.26	89	60	3.16	14
	08	31	03	aaa	MIN	416	42	102	26	2	11	48	15	119	1	2	245	272	394	666	4%	71%	0.13	99	55	3.65	25

Major League Equivalent Statistics BATTERS

BATTER	Yr	Age	Pos	Lev	Org	ab	r	h	d	t	hr	rbi	bb	k	sb	cs	ba	ob	slg	ops	bb%	ct%	eye	px	sx	rc/g	bpv
Rundgren,Rex	07	27	6	aa	FLA	250	17	41	3	1	2	16	12	49	1	3	164	202	205	408	5%	80%	0.25	26	54	1.27	-30
	08	28	6	aa	LA	108	8	16	1	0	1	5	3	14	1	0	150	171	183	354	2%	87%	0.19	20	63	0.99	-38
Rushford,Jim	07	34	83	aaa	PHI	413	21	92	21	0	2	36	23	30	2	0	222	262	285	548	5%	93%	0.75	51	33	2.60	10
Russo,Kevin	08	24	45	aa	NYY	267	42	76	15	2	2	31	20	42	8	3	284	334	378	712	7%	84%	0.48	68	115	4.69	33
Ryal,Rusty	07	25	45	aa	ARI	178	17	40	6	2	6	17	7	36	3	3	224	252	374	626	4%	80%	0.19	87	102	2.98	14
	08	26	45	aa	ARI	460	52	113	20	4	14	53	29	83	3	4	245	290	396	687	6%	82%	0.35	93	77	3.93	27
Ryan,Brendan	07	26	6	aa	STL	321	41	68	6	3	1	11	19	34	13	6	213	257	258	515	6%	89%	0.55	29	130	2.21	-6
Ryan,Dusty	08	24	2	a/a	DET	369	45	84	20	3	12	49	35	100	2	1	229	295	401	696	9%	73%	0.35	108	84	4.12	28
Ryan,Mike	07	30	8	aa	PIT	379	32	64	15	3	9	31	17	106	0	2	168	203	294	497	4%	72%	0.16	78	68	1.84	-9
	08	31	8	aa	FLA	109	11	27	5	2	6	20	5	27	1	0	250	283	491	774	4%	75%	0.19	140	106	4.88	45
Saccomanno,Mark	07	27	3	aa	HOU	470	44	99	17	3	16	59	22	116	1	2	210	246	360	606	5%	75%	0.19	89	64	2.91	11
	08	28	53	aa	HOU	528	55	121	25	1	18	55	23	82	3	4	228	260	383	644	4%	85%	0.28	97	51	3.31	22
Sadler,Donnie	07	32	6	aa	ARI	112	11	16	1	3	1	10	13	30	3	0	144	235	238	472	11%	73%	0.44	47	183	1.97	-24
Sadler,Ray	07	27	8	aa	HOU	491	50	94	17	2	17	64	36	122	9	8	191	246	340	586	7%	75%	0.29	89	79	2.62	6
	08	28	8	aa	HOU	452	48	94	21	4	18	51	20	92	4	4	208	242	387	630	4%	80%	0.22	109	87	3.02	19
Salas,Issmael	07	25	384	aa	CHC	344	35	70	16	0	6	41	20	34	2	2	204	247	306	553	5%	90%	0.57	70	52	2.50	8
Salazar,Jeff	07	27	8	aa	ARI	400	55	98	26	7	8	49	42	53	12	5	246	317	405	722	9%	87%	0.79	103	148	4.54	40
Salazar,Oscar	07	29	540	aa	BAL	532	47	105	26	1	14	61	17	84	2	2	197	222	330	551	3%	84%	0.20	86	53	2.34	5
	08	30	30	aaa	BAL	443	53	108	31	2	10	61	31	54	6	2	244	293	391	684	6%	88%	0.57	102	84	4.04	35
Salome,Angel	08	22 a	2	aa	MIL	367	53	117	27	1	11	66	28	47	2	2	319	367	488	855	7%	87%	0.60	114	56	6.86	65
Sammons,Clint	07	24	2	aa	ATL	296	23	64	10	0	4	30	22	67	1	1	215	269	286	555	7%	77%	0.32	48	33	2.64	-2
	08	25	2	aaa	ATL	278	19	56	15	0	1	18	17	54	6	2	203	249	267	516	6%	80%	0.31	53	64	2.26	-4
Sanchez,Alex	07	31	8	aaa	CHW	103	10	32	4	1	3	5	3	11	3	3	315	332	446	778	3%	89%	0.24	79	84	5.12	42
Sanchez,Angel	08	25	6	aa	KC	372	33	82	13	2	2	29	30	53	4	7	220	278	280	559	7%	86%	0.57	44	64	2.57	3
Sanchez,Gabriel	08	25 a	35	aa	FLA	478	55	127	37	1	13	72	57	66	13	8	265	344	429	773	11%	86%	0.87	112	70	5.28	52
Sanchez,Yunesky	08	24	6	aa	ARI	494	50	133	17	3	0	18	19	34	7	14	270	297	317	614	4%	93%	0.56	36	71	3.02	16
Sandoval,Danny	07	28	6	aaa	PHI	365	22	77	9	1	3	19	7	32	5	3	211	225	265	490	2%	91%	0.20	37	63	1.93	-10
	08	30	64	aaa	TOR	465	42	107	17	0	7	38	22	71	7	3	229	265	311	575	5%	85%	0.32	56	63	2.79	6
Sandoval,Freddy	07	25	5	aa	LAA	472	68	122	27	4	9	59	54	79	17	11	257	334	387	721	10%	83%	0.68	87	111	4.54	35
	08	26	534	aa	LAA	525	72	150	40	1	11	69	37	67	5	3	286	332	429	762	7%	87%	0.55	102	67	5.25	48
Sandoval,Pablo	08	22 a	2	aa	SF	175	26	55	13	0	6	33	7	17	0	1	314	341	491	832	4%	90%	0.41	119	41	6.20	62
Sansoe,Mike	07	25	8	aa	SD	301	32	61	9	2	1	14	26	66	9	6	202	265	252	517	8%	78%	0.39	36	104	2.23	-10
Santangelo,Louis	07	25	2	aa	HOU	206	24	43	8	2	4	13	18	51	2	0	208	271	318	590	8%	75%	0.36	69	100	3.02	5
	08	26	2	aa	HOU	388	26	74	8	0	8	31	21	81	1	1	191	232	279	511	5%	79%	0.26	53	29	2.12	-9
Santiago,Ramon	07	28	6	aaa	DET	365	34	85	16	4	3	26	14	58	7	9	232	260	318	579	4%	84%	0.24	59	101	2.56	7
Santos,Chad	07	26	3	aa	SF	103	16	20	6	0	3	10	11	29	0	1	194	274	329	603	10%	72%	0.39	92	56	2.99	10
Santos,Omir	07	26	2	a/a	NYY	205	14	41	8	0	3	16	9	46	1	1	198	231	277	508	4%	78%	0.20	55	38	2.08	-7
	08	27	2	aaa	BAL	297	23	65	10	0	1	27	15	51	1	2	218	256	261	517	5%	83%	0.30	34	37	2.24	-7
Santos,Sergio	07	24	6	a/a	TOR	479	54	106	33	2	17	53	35	93	3	0	221	274	407	681	7%	81%	0.38	121	74	3.84	31
	08	25	65	aaa	MIN	390	40	74	24	0	4	37	16	66	5	2	190	222	282	504	4%	83%	0.24	70	80	2.04	-3
Sardinha,Bronson	07	24	8	a/a	NYY	444	57	102	22	4	15	69	48	87	12	3	229	304	395	699	10%	80%	0.55	103	117	4.27	30
	08	26	8	a/a	CLE	402	47	99	16	3	7	48	40	74	4	4	246	314	348	663	9%	81%	0.54	67	78	3.88	20
Sardinha,Dane	07	28	2	aaa	DET	381	33	67	12	1	8	40	21	94	2	0	176	220	278	498	5%	75%	0.23	64	62	2.01	-10
	08	30	2	aaa	DET	183	14	28	7	0	4	13	6	56	1	0	155	182	263	445	3%	70%	0.11	70	50	1.51	-17
Sardinha,Duke	07	27	3	aa	COL	222	23	49	10	1	8	24	14	46	1	3	219	266	380	646	6%	79%	0.30	100	55	3.26	20
Saunders,Michael	08	22	8	aa	SEA	343	47	85	20	2	9	38	33	82	11	9	247	314	398	712	9%	76%	0.41	98	103	4.17	31
Scales,Bobby	07	30	843	aaa	BOS	432	53	113	28	5	8	46	41	93	12	3	261	325	409	734	9%	78%	0.44	98	132	4.89	36
	08	31	4	aa	CHC	387	61	94	16	1	10	38	38	84	4	5	244	312	369	681	9%	78%	0.46	80	74	3.98	23
Schafer,Jordan	08	22	8	aa	ATL	297	38	72	16	4	8	42	41	73	10	6	242	334	404	738	12%	75%	0.56	101	129	4.75	34
Schierholtz,Nate	07	24 a	8	aa	SF	411	54	122	28	6	12	55	14	49	8	5	297	320	479	799	3%	88%	0.27	117	124	5.48	53
	08	25 a	8	aa	SF	350	53	101	20	8	13	62	17	46	8	3	288	321	505	826	5%	87%	0.38	130	164	5.87	57
Schneider,John	07	28	2	a/a	TOR	193	16	26	7	0	4	15	21	57	0	0	135	220	239	459	10%	70%	0.36	67	24	1.73	-20
Schnurstein,Micah	08	24	3	aa	CHW	293	34	58	10	1	4	17	18	50	7	1	197	244	275	519	6%	83%	0.36	52	103	2.31	-6
Schuerholz,Jonath	07	27	4	a/a	ATL	152	17	26	6	0	3	15	12	33	6	1	172	233	263	496	7%	78%	0.37	62	96	2.12	-10
Schumaker,Skip	07	28	8	aa	STL	232	23	52	12	0	4	21	19	36	2	3	225	284	329	613	8%	84%	0.53	72	43	3.10	15
Scott Jr.,Lorenzo	08	27	[illegible]	aa	FLA	265	39	65	8	3	6	23	36	83	23	13	246	336	361	697	12%	69%	0.43	69	147	4.12	19
Scram,Deik	08	25	[illegible]	aa	DET	482	52	103	20	3	10	52	43	100	11	4	213	278	327	604	8%	79%	0.43	73	99	3.14	10
Seabol,Scott	07	32	5	aa	FLA	503	60	96	19	4	19	63	36	123	4	1	191	244	358	602	7%	76%	0.29	99	101	2.88	10
Self,Todd	07	29	3	aa	HOU	428	48	92	17	1	10	46	46	101	2	2	215	292	325	617	10%	76%	0.46	71	55	3.32	10
Sellers,Justin	08	23	64	aa	OAK	439	55	96	13	5	4	35	36	56	8	7	219	278	298	576	8%	87%	0.64	50	115	2.77	7
Sellers,Neil	08	27	5	aa	PHI	483	43	109	25	1	15	53	30	66	2	6	225	271	371	642	6%	86%	0.46	94	37	3.28	23
Sellers,Patrick	07	25	53	aa	HOU	358	37	83	19	1	5	32	14	58	0	2	231	261	334	595	4%	84%	0.25	72	45	2.91	12
Serrano,Ray	07	27	2	a/a	ATL	126	17	32	11	1	3	12	7	20	2	0	250	291	414	705	5%	84%	0.36	115	99	4.31	38
Shabala,Adam	07	30	8	aa	CHW	331	35	51	7	1	3	14	38	105	8	5	154	240	206	446	10%	68%	0.36	34	88	1.67	-27
Shealy,Ryan	07	28	0	aa	KC	122	10	23	6	0	4	17	10	29	0	0	190	254	334	588	8%	76%	0.36	91	14	2.85	8
	08	29	30	aa	KC	400	40	92	20	0	15	48	41	90	0	1	230	302	396	698	9%	78%	0.46	104	18	4.19	29
Sheldon,Ole	08	26	3	aa	HOU	373	42	86	12	1	9	39	40	57	2	1	229	305	343	647	10%	85%	0.70	70	54	3.73	19
Shelton,Chris	07	27	3	aaa	DET	498	66	119	27	1	11	57	73	133	4	2	238	336	364	700	13%	73%	0.55	84	61	4.51	25
	08	28	3	aa	TEX	256	26	70	18	2	8	35	21	48	0	0	272	327	447	774	8%	81%	0.44	115	46	5.36	47
Shorey,Mark	07	23	8	aa	STL	190	19	43	10	0	8	26	12	37	0	0	225	269	398	668	6%	80%	0.31	108	22	3.67	26
	08	24	8	aa	STL	388	37	99	24	1	8	50	22	89	1	0	255	295	381	676	5%	77%	0.25	88	48	4.01	26
Simokaitis,Joseph	07	25	6	aa	CHC	340	33	72	14	1	4	20	28	68	1	5	212	271	293	565	7%	80%	0.40	57	47	2.60	2
	08	26	6	aa	CHC	145	16	24	6	0	2	10	19	33	0	1	162	258	240	498	11%	77%	0.57	54	41	2.09	-12
Sing,Brandon	07	27	3	aa	BAL	214	12	31	8	0	2	10	10	53	3	1	146	183	207	390	4%	75%	0.18	45	58	1.20	-29
Sinisi,Vince	07	26	8	aa	SD	303	36	77	16	1	7	30	16	43	5	3	252	290	383	674	5%	86%	0.37	87	77	3.85	27
	08	27	83	aa	SD	279	17	63	9	1	3	27	13	45	0	1	228	262	297	558	4%	84%	0.29	47	31	2.62	1
Slayden,Jeremy	08	26	8	aa	PHI	483	50	117	28	1	14	55	36	87	1	6	242	294	389	683	7%	82%	0.41	96	33	3.81	29
Smith,Casey	07	29	46	aa	LAA	393	35	86	18	2	2	38	20	61	10	2	218	256	287	543	5%	84%	0.33	51	104	2.53	0
	08	30	4	aaa	PHI	300	15	41	5	0	3	15	11	65	3	1	138	169	181	349	4%	78%	0.17	29	53	0.95	-39
Smith,Coby	07	27	8	aa	LAA	243	32	51	9	1	2	16	26	34	19	7	208	284	273	557	10%	86%	0.76	47	123	2.72	4
	08	28	8	aa	LAA	329	32	66	12	1	2	18	26	49	11	5	201	260	259	519	7%	85%	0.54	44	90	2.28	-4

BATTER	Yr	Age	Pos	Lev	Org	ab	r	h	d	t	hr	rbi	bb	k	sb	cs	ba	ob	slg	ops	bb%	ct%	eye	px	sx	rc/g	bpv
Smith,Corey	08	26	530	aa	LAA	518	46	116	28	1	19	63	24	95	12	7	224	258	393	651	4%	82%	0.25	106	72	3.28	24
Smith,David	07	27	80	aa	TOR	458	60	103	29	1	19	50	37	99	3	5	224	283	416	699	8%	78%	0.38	122	57	3.88	33
	08	28	8	a/a	TOR	332	40	77	24	1	13	40	37	90	2	2	230	307	423	730	10%	73%	0.41	126	54	4.53	37
Smith,Jason	08	31	546	aa	KC	423	38	86	18	4	14	45	17	125	3	1	203	234	362	595	4%	71%	0.14	96	98	2.78	10
Smith,Ryan	07	28	2	aaa	CHW	103	3	12	1	0	1	3	3	31	0	0	117	141	153	294	3%	70%	0.09	22	7	0.65	-50
Smith,Sean	07	25	8	aa	CHW	269	22	50	4	0	1	12	15	64	11	6	187	231	211	442	5%	76%	0.24	17	82	1.57	-26
Smith,Seth	07	25	8	aa	COL	451	50	124	28	5	14	61	30	63	5	3	275	320	447	767	6%	86%	0.47	110	93	5.16	47
	08	26	8	aa	COL	248	37	66	13	1	7	35	30	34	7	0	267	347	415	763	11%	86%	0.90	95	97	5.59	46
Snider,Travis	08	21	80	a/a	TOR	426	65	113	26	0	19	74	47	115	2	1	266	339	457	796	10%	73%	0.41	121	50	5.70	47
Snyder,Brad	07	25	8	aaa	CLE	259	36	61	12	2	8	30	33	82	10	0	237	322	390	712	11%	68%	0.40	95	127	4.77	26
	08	26	8	aaa	CLE	411	45	87	25	3	10	52	24	127	6	3	213	256	360	616	5%	69%	0.19	98	106	3.08	15
Snyder,Brian	07	26	4	aa	OAK	370	48	77	27	1	6	36	56	90	1	1	209	313	338	651	13%	76%	0.62	93	53	3.78	21
	08	27	50	aa	SD	252	21	47	12	1	2	28	33	61	2	1	186	281	263	544	12%	76%	0.54	57	58	2.60	-4
Snyder,Earl	07	31	56	aaa	CHW	404	43	75	17	0	13	43	31	96	0	1	185	242	321	563	7%	76%	0.32	86	35	2.55	3
Solano,Donovan	08	21	6	aa	STL	106	9	25	4	0	1	9	4	17	2	1	233	262	301	563	4%	84%	0.25	49	60	2.67	3
Sollmann,Steven	07	26	3	aa	MIL	445	61	104	23	2	3	40	50	63	17	6	235	312	313	626	10%	86%	0.80	60	107	3.56	19
Sosa,Carlos	07	26	8	aa	SF	376	41	83	20	2	6	40	34	82	3	5	220	285	333	618	8%	78%	0.42	77	66	3.18	13
	08	27	8	aa	SF	411	45	90	22	1	7	43	37	95	2	2	219	284	331	615	8%	77%	0.39	77	55	3.24	13
Soto,Geovany	07	25 a	23	aa	CHC	385	61	122	29	2	23	87	42	84	0	0	316	383	577	960	10%	78%	0.50	162	45	8.64	82
Spann,Chad	07	24	5	a/a	BOS	347	30	76	19	0	6	37	27	94	1	4	219	275	326	601	7%	73%	0.29	75	30	2.96	10
	08	25	5	a/a	KC	256	21	49	7	0	3	25	13	56	1	1	191	232	251	483	5%	78%	0.24	41	44	1.91	-15
Spanos,Vasili	07	27	35	aa	OAK	392	37	86	21	2	7	38	12	64	3	2	220	243	335	578	3%	84%	0.19	79	74	2.69	9
Span,Denard	07	24	8	aaa	MIN	487	58	127	20	6	3	54	37	92	25	14	261	313	345	658	7%	81%	0.40	57	137	3.72	18
	08	25	8	aaa	MIN	156	26	46	10	1	2	12	20	33	12	9	295	376	406	782	11%	79%	0.60	79	119	5.28	43
Spearman,Jemel	07	27	84	aa	CHC	355	39	74	13	4	5	30	21	53	6	2	208	252	314	566	6%	85%	0.39	66	125	2.68	5
	08	28	8	a/a	WAS	141	12	28	5	1	2	14	11	24	6	0	198	255	287	542	7%	83%	0.44	59	108	2.68	-1
Spears,Nathaniel	07	22	4	aa	CHC	114	19	32	2	2	4	9	11	16	2	0	281	344	439	783	9%	86%	0.69	85	135	5.77	43
	08	23	4	aa	CHC	402	57	105	22	3	6	39	45	58	5	6	261	335	373	708	10%	86%	0.78	77	85	4.45	34
Spidale,Michael	07	26	8	aa	PHI	264	32	68	5	4	2	15	14	18	8	4	256	292	320	612	5%	93%	0.76	38	130	3.28	16
	08	27	8	a/a	PHI	359	40	81	12	2	6	28	17	37	16	1	226	260	323	583	4%	90%	0.45	62	125	3.02	10
Spilborghs,Ryan	07	28	8	aa	COL	124	17	30	6	1	3	11	12	19	2	2	245	312	381	692	9%	85%	0.64	86	88	4.03	30
Spring,Matthew	08	24	2	aa	TAM	246	23	53	14	1	7	25	18	58	1	1	215	268	363	630	7%	76%	0.30	96	54	3.27	17
Stansberry,Craig	07	26	465	aa	SD	466	68	103	25	2	12	61	58	100	8	10	220	306	357	663	11%	79%	0.58	90	82	3.64	22
	08	27	6	aa	SD	273	34	54	10	2	6	21	35	54	4	6	199	290	310	600	11%	80%	0.64	70	83	2.91	8
Statia,Hainley	08	23	6	aa	LAA	223	22	50	11	2	1	17	12	14	7	5	224	264	305	569	5%	94%	0.86	59	109	2.60	16
Stavinoha,Nick	07	25	8	aa	STL	499	37	103	14	0	9	36	23	72	5	1	206	241	287	528	4%	86%	0.32	52	58	2.34	-4
	08	26	8	aa	STL	427	50	117	18	2	11	54	15	42	2	1	274	298	403	701	3%	90%	0.35	82	64	4.29	32
Stavisky,Brian	08	28	80	aa	LAA	314	42	79	15	0	11	38	36	59	9	3	252	329	409	738	10%	81%	0.61	99	74	4.92	37
Stern,Adam	07	28	8	aaa	BAL	289	37	71	10	4	1	22	23	64	16	6	247	302	319	620	7%	78%	0.36	49	153	3.44	9
	08	29	8	aaa	BAL	122	11	21	4	1	1	6	4	20	4	2	173	196	238	434	3%	83%	0.17	43	127	1.46	-21
Stewart,Caleb	07	25	8	aa	NYM	433	47	87	12	1	11	51	27	93	3	7	202	248	308	556	6%	78%	0.29	64	57	2.38	-0
	08	26	8	aa	NYM	471	52	105	29	3	10	52	42	76	6	2	223	287	359	646	8%	84%	0.56	92	90	3.60	23
Stewart,Chris	07	26	2	aa	TEX	153	14	32	7	0	2	16	9	18	0	2	206	250	288	538	6%	88%	0.51	60	36	2.29	3
	08	27	2	aaa	NYY	272	27	65	16	0	2	19	22	37	2	1	240	297	318	615	8%	86%	0.60	61	48	3.37	17
Stewart,Ian	07	22 a	5	aa	COL	414	60	121	22	2	13	54	42	72	9	2	292	357	449	807	9%	83%	0.58	100	93	6.15	50
	08	24 a	5	aa	COL	257	46	64	13	4	14	40	24	45	5	3	248	311	488	799	8%	83%	0.52	140	144	5.24	51
Stinnett,Kelly	07	38	2	aa	STL	103	6	13	1	0	1	6	5	26	0	0	122	162	177	339	5%	75%	0.19	33	23	0.89	-42
Stocker,Mel	07	27	8	aa	MIL	267	40	52	7	7	0	17	20	54	24	6	196	252	270	522	7%	80%	0.37	44	238	2.41	-9
	08	28	8	aaa	MIL	145	16	30	5	0	0	4	9	19	12	1	206	252	243	495	6%	87%	0.46	32	119	2.37	-9
Stodolka,Michael	07	26	3	aa	KC	381	51	90	23	1	8	44	56	87	3	0	235	333	363	696	13%	77%	0.64	88	66	4.49	28
	08	27	38	aa	KC	227	25	56	11	0	4	16	22	39	0	1	246	311	341	652	9%	83%	0.56	67	31	3.79	21
Strait,William	07	24	8	aa	CIN	217	25	41	13	0	6	22	13	56	9	2	188	235	328	563	6%	74%	0.24	95	102	2.57	7
	08	25	8	aa	CIN	226	24	48	14	2	4	14	10	46	4	4	212	247	341	588	4%	80%	0.23	88	104	2.64	12
Strong,Jamal	07	29	8	a/a	NYY	292	38	57	5	2	0	16	40	52	11	2	194	291	222	513	12%	82%	0.77	20	115	2.47	-12
Stubbs,Robert	08	24	8	a/a	CIN	167	20	44	11	1	2	14	13	34	5	1	264	319	374	693	7%	79%	0.39	79	98	4.42	28
St. Pierre,Maxim	08	28	2	a/a	DET	306	23	55	10	0	5	33	14	39	0	1	181	217	265	482	4%	87%	0.36	55	29	1.84	-10
Suarez,Ignacio	07	26	64	aa	BOS	352	38	73	16	1	3	23	25	85	5	1	208	261	279	540	7%	76%	0.30	53	87	2.53	-3
	08	27	6	aa	BOS	442	41	90	23	0	4	36	30	78	11	5	204	254	279	533	6%	82%	0.38	58	77	2.36	-1
Suero,Ovandy	08	26	8	aa	KC	328	31	73	11	4	2	19	16	54	33	17	222	257	295	552	5%	83%	0.29	48	156	2.31	-0
Sullivan,Cory	07	28	8	aa	COL	206	19	42	7	2	1	14	12	43	2	2	202	246	264	510	6%	79%	0.28	44	91	2.11	-9
	08	29	8	aa	COL	381	43	95	25	2	4	29	19	50	8	8	248	284	357	640	5%	87%	0.38	79	87	3.32	23
Suomi,Richard	07	27	2	a/a	WAS	129	11	23	5	2	2	12	7	22	0	0	174	218	286	504	5%	83%	0.32	71	84	2.02	-6
	08	28	2	a/a	PHI	192	14	37	11	1	4	16	8	22	0	0	193	224	312	536	4%	89%	0.37	81	39	2.29	5
Sutil,Wladimir	08	24	6	aa	HOU	316	32	69	11	0	0	18	12	24	16	5	217	245	251	496	4%	92%	0.48	30	104	2.11	-6
Sutton,Nathanael	08	26	4	aa	LAA	453	45	106	11	4	6	34	21	62	15	10	234	268	311	578	4%	86%	0.34	48	108	2.71	4
Sutton,Stephen	07	24	54	aa	HOU	480	65	111	24	1	8	42	45	77	19	6	232	297	333	629	9%	84%	0.58	70	104	3.53	18
	08	25	4	aa	HOU	520	72	135	31	3	15	49	54	80	14	8	260	329	418	747	9%	85%	0.67	102	96	4.87	42
Suzuki,Kurt	07	24	2	aa	OAK	211	26	52	9	0	2	22	17	34	0	0	248	306	317	623	8%	84%	0.51	51	35	3.51	14
Swann,Pedro	07	37	8	a/a	PHI	308	23	57	14	1	5	23	17	75	2	5	184	227	281	507	5%	76%	0.22	66	56	1.94	-7
Sweeney,Ryan	07	23	8	aaa	CHW	397	47	107	17	1	12	45	47	62	7	5	270	347	405	752	11%	84%	0.76	85	64	5.13	40
Szymanski,Brandc	08	26	8	a/a	CIN	276	21	51	7	1	8	29	10	91	4	1	183	212	307	519	4%	67%	0.11	73	75	2.10	-7
Tabata,Jose	08	20	8	aa	PIT	383	50	101	15	1	5	44	30	55	16	2	264	317	350	666	7%	86%	0.54	59	108	4.20	23
Tatis,Fernando	07	33	5	aa	NYM	497	53	85	20	2	11	39	36	121	5	5	172	227	289	516	7%	76%	0.29	75	83	2.07	-6
	08	34	5	aa	NYM	120	13	22	4	0	9	22	12	22	0	0	184	258	432	690	9%	81%	0.53	141	11	3.69	30
Tatum,Craig	07	25	2	aa	CIN	173	17	34	9	1	2	18	13	43	0	1	198	255	291	546	7%	75%	0.31	66	62	2.45	-1
	08	26	2	a/a	CIN	332	24	69	16	1	7	45	20	63	1	1	207	251	320	571	6%	81%	0.31	76	41	2.68	6
Taylor,Reggie	08	32	8	aaa	ATL	153	12	30	4	2	2	8	8	28	3	3	194	233	278	511	5%	82%	0.27	52	108	2.03	-8
Teagarden,Taylor	07	24	0	aa	TEX	102	16	27	3	0	6	14	8	33	0	0	266	318	466	784	7%	68%	0.24	114	32	5.37	40
	08	25	2	aa	TEX	246	24	44	6	2	7	16	26	66	1	1	180	258	300	558	10%	73%	0.39	70	74	2.59	-3
Tejeda,Juan	07	26	30	aa	PHI	314	25	64	20	2	8	44	19	36	1	0	204	249	355	604	6%	89%	0.53	101	56	2.97	20
Terrero,Luis	08	28	80	aaa	BAL	497	54	108	24	4	10	65	33	108	10	11	218	266	342	608	6%	78%	0.30	80	103	2.85	12

Major League Equivalent Statistics

BATTER	Yr	Age	Pos	Lev	Org	ab	r	h	d	t	hr	rbi	bb	k	sb	cs	ba	ob	slg	ops	bb%	ct%	eye	px	sx	rc/g	bpv
Thibault,Kiel	08	25	2	aa	KC	100	6	14	6	0	0	8	4	20	4	0	144	176	202	377	4%	80%	0.19	51	90	1.21	-27
Thigpen,Curtis	07	24	2	aaa	TOR	179	17	48	10	0	3	17	14	20	1	0	268	321	374	696	7%	89%	0.70	75	37	4.45	34
	08	25	23	aaa	TOR	361	24	71	22	0	3	36	17	59	2	1	198	234	281	515	4%	84%	0.29	65	44	2.17	-1
Thomas,Charles	07	29	8	a/a	MIL	264	24	48	9	0	3	19	19	62	6	1	180	235	245	479	7%	76%	0.30	46	79	1.97	-15
Thomas,Clete	07	24	8	aa	DET	528	91	138	27	6	7	49	55	106	16	11	261	331	373	704	9%	80%	0.52	75	135	4.37	28
	08	25	8	aaa	DET	291	36	62	15	2	7	36	31	75	23	12	214	289	350	639	10%	74%	0.41	88	130	3.23	16
Thompson,Kevin	07	28	8	aaa	NYY	267	33	65	16	2	5	32	34	56	20	8	244	330	369	699	11%	79%	0.62	86	123	4.33	29
	08	29	8	aa	PIT	195	27	45	9	1	3	14	15	36	15	3	229	283	326	609	7%	82%	0.41	67	134	3.39	12
Thompson,Rich	07	28	8	aa	ARI	324	40	73	14	4	2	27	19	50	10	2	225	268	314	582	6%	85%	0.38	60	146	2.98	7
	08	29	8	a/a	PHI	362	29	74	14	3	3	29	27	70	17	2	204	259	290	549	7%	81%	0.38	57	131	2.71	-1
Thomson,Gregory	08	24	8	aa	ARI	164	18	31	7	1	1	11	13	31	3	3	187	249	258	506	8%	81%	0.43	51	95	2.06	-8
Thorman,Scott	08	27	3	aaa	ATL	387	37	82	18	1	15	44	15	77	6	1	212	240	378	618	4%	80%	0.19	103	77	3.04	17
Thurston,Joe	07	28	48	a/a	PHI	509	51	120	26	4	4	43	32	56	12	14	235	281	327	608	6%	89%	0.57	65	95	2.91	17
	08	29	48	aaa	BOS	507	61	131	27	3	7	46	25	72	14	10	258	293	361	654	5%	86%	0.35	72	98	3.55	23
Tiffee,Terry	07	28	5	aaa	BAL	475	41	116	23	1	9	50	22	54	0	1	245	279	356	635	4%	89%	0.42	75	30	3.44	21
	08	29	538	aa	LA	392	51	114	31	2	7	48	20	42	1	2	292	326	432	758	5%	89%	0.47	101	58	5.14	48
Timmons,Wes	07	28	5	aaa	ATL	355	39	80	16	0	4	44	20	29	7	5	225	268	301	569	5%	92%	0.70	56	72	2.69	12
	08	29	5	aaa	ATL	239	28	47	14	0	2	19	34	24	9	0	198	297	277	574	12%	90%	1.37	62	90	3.13	19
Timpner,Clay	07	24	8	aa	SF	392	40	103	10	3	5	30	29	59	7	12	262	312	337	649	7%	85%	0.48	47	76	3.41	16
	08	25	8	aa	SF	436	54	94	17	2	2	39	27	55	10	7	216	262	276	538	6%	87%	0.49	45	102	2.40	0
Tolbert,Christophe	07	25	4	aaa	MIN	417	63	118	23	6	6	51	34	58	11	3	283	336	408	744	7%	86%	0.58	83	141	5.14	40
Tolleson,Steven	08	25	64	aa	MIN	343	43	88	25	1	7	40	34	68	10	7	257	324	395	718	9%	80%	0.50	97	83	4.45	36
Tomlin,James	07	25	8	aa	LA	289	31	59	16	0	0	20	14	49	11	2	206	241	262	503	4%	83%	0.28	50	104	2.19	-6
	08	26	8	aa	LA	383	43	98	26	1	2	26	28	42	10	6	257	307	343	650	7%	89%	0.65	69	83	3.68	27
Torbert,Wallace	07	24	8	aa	HOU	300	23	65	13	1	1	25	24	71	3	8	215	273	276	548	7%	76%	0.34	47	52	2.36	-2
Toregas,Wyatt	07	25	2	aa	CLE	284	30	62	15	0	5	32	24	42	3	1	217	278	321	599	8%	85%	0.56	73	59	3.10	14
	08	26	2	a/a	CLE	317	32	72	15	0	12	52	28	51	2	1	228	291	391	683	8%	84%	0.55	102	39	3.97	29
Torrealba,Steve	07	30	2	aa	DET	298	28	50	7	0	7	32	18	79	1	0	166	214	257	470	6%	74%	0.23	55	48	1.79	-17
	08	31	0	aa	BAL	120	12	26	6	0	6	20	9	21	1	0	220	276	418	694	7%	82%	0.44	121	35	3.98	32
Torres,Andres	07	30	8	a/a	DET	473	58	110	16	16	7	40	38	116	17	9	232	289	381	670	7%	76%	0.33	84	235	3.70	19
	08	31	8	aa	CHC	409	60	95	21	6	8	33	36	95	19	4	233	294	370	664	8%	77%	0.37	88	168	3.89	21
Torres,Eider	07	25	46	aaa	BAL	393	37	102	15	0	4	40	24	52	21	11	260	302	328	630	6%	87%	0.46	50	82	3.40	16
	08	26	4	aaa	BAL	473	55	124	17	4	1	37	30	52	23	12	262	306	320	626	6%	89%	0.58	42	117	3.40	16
Toussaint,Andrew	08	26	8	aa	LAA	126	12	24	1	1	3	10	2	37	0	1	187	198	276	474	1%	70%	0.05	48	87	1.66	-17
Towles,J.R.	07	24	2	aa	HOU	259	43	73	11	2	10	42	21	37	9	9	281	336	449	785	8%	86%	0.57	101	108	5.04	47
	08	25	2	aa	HOU	168	20	42	7	1	6	20	10	25	3	4	251	292	406	698	5%	85%	0.38	94	81	3.84	30
Tracy,Andy	07	34	3	aa	NYM	472	51	80	15	1	13	51	52	130	1	2	169	251	285	536	10%	72%	0.40	72	50	2.38	-6
	08	35	3	aaa	PHI	430	52	100	27	0	19	63	47	100	3	0	233	308	427	735	10%	77%	0.47	123	54	4.71	38
Trumbo,Mark	08	23	3	aa	LAA	123	11	31	7	1	5	21	6	24	1	2	252	287	447	734	5%	80%	0.25	120	69	4.20	39
Trzesniak,Nick	07	27	2	aa	DET	123	15	30	5	0	3	14	11	22	0	1	248	311	354	665	8%	82%	0.52	70	36	3.86	22
	08	28	2	a/a	TEX	134	10	24	5	1	3	13	5	40	0	0	181	208	289	497	3%	70%	0.11	67	56	1.93	-10
Tucker,Jonathan	08	25	546	aa	BAL	418	60	99	22	3	6	39	40	56	7	8	236	303	342	645	9%	87%	0.72	73	94	3.51	23
Tucker,Michael	07	36	0	aaa	BOS	235	22	46	16	0	5	21	38	62	1	2	195	307	322	629	14%	74%	0.61	91	29	3.44	15
Tuiasosopo,Matt	07	21	5	aa	SEA	446	64	105	25	3	8	49	68	104	3	9	235	337	359	695	13%	77%	0.65	83	71	4.17	26
	08	22	5	aa	SEA	437	71	109	29	1	10	60	40	90	3	0	249	312	389	701	8%	79%	0.44	96	83	4.42	32
Tupman,Matt	07	28	2	aa	KC	299	15	65	13	0	1	22	26	34	2	2	217	279	269	548	8%	89%	0.76	44	27	2.60	5
	08	29	2	aa	KC	288	27	55	9	1	3	26	17	41	0	1	189	234	254	488	5%	86%	0.41	44	50	1.95	-11
Turner,Justin	08	24	4	aa	CIN	280	34	72	13	1	7	31	25	43	2	1	256	318	382	699	8%	85%	0.59	81	63	4.38	31
Tyner,Jason	08	31	8	aaa	CHW	307	29	60	9	0	1	14	28	27	9	1	194	261	233	494	8%	91%	1.04	31	83	2.21	-2
Upton,Justin	07	20 a	8	aa	ARI	259	42	80	17	4	13	46	34	40	8	8	308	388	551	939	11%	85%	0.84	147	128	7.60	80
Ust,Brant	07	29	4	aa	SEA	151	7	25	6	0	2	11	7	45	0	0	164	200	248	448	4%	70%	0.15	58	10	1.58	-18
Valaika,Christophe	08	23	6	aa	CIN	379	44	100	17	1	10	38	22	59	5	5	264	303	390	694	5%	84%	0.36	81	66	4.08	29
Valbuena,Luis	07	22	4	aa	SEA	444	47	95	21	2	9	38	43	76	9	7	214	283	331	614	9%	83%	0.57	77	82	3.14	14
	08	23	4	aa	SEA	452	69	122	19	1	9	49	50	60	15	9	270	343	376	719	10%	87%	0.83	70	89	4.66	36
Valdez,Wilson	07	29	6	aa	LA	361	51	85	13	1	3	18	28	39	9	5	235	289	299	589	7%	89%	0.72	46	94	3.00	12
Valencia,Daniel	08	24	5	aa	MIN	266	33	66	16	2	8	26	13	64	2	1	249	285	411	697	5%	76%	0.21	105	88	4.08	31
Valentin,Geraldo	07	25	48	aa	KC	437	37	106	17	2	2	41	20	42	4	11	243	276	303	579	4%	90%	0.47	45	54	2.62	9
	08	26	8	aa	KC	256	15	56	9	1	2	15	8	23	1	4	219	244	284	528	3%	91%	0.36	46	41	2.17	-1
Valido,Robert	07	22	6	aa	CHW	266	21	44	7	1	0	16	9	39	9	6	165	193	199	392	3%	85%	0.23	27	107	1.15	-29
	08	23	6	a/a	CHW	407	31	78	9	4	3	25	18	82	16	11	193	226	255	481	4%	80%	0.22	39	120	1.76	-15
Vallejo,Jose	08	22	4	aa	TEX	259	27	69	14	2	2	24	12	35	12	1	266	299	359	658	4%	86%	0.34	67	123	4.03	23
Van Every,Jonatha	07	28	8	a/a	CLE	309	34	76	17	3	9	44	34	108	4	8	245	320	405	725	10%	65%	0.31	101	101	4.28	30
	08	29	8	aaa	BOS	380	62	82	14	2	18	52	40	148	4	1	215	289	401	690	9%	61%	0.27	109	105	4.04	22
Varner,Noochie	07	27	80	aa	HOU	352	24	80	17	2	4	37	22	56	3	1	227	272	321	594	6%	84%	0.39	65	60	3.03	10
Vazquez,Ramon	07	31	6	aa	TEX	132	16	22	7	1	1	8	14	31	2	1	170	249	276	525	10%	76%	0.45	73	119	2.33	-5
Velandia,Jorge	07	33	6	aaa	TAM	433	38	93	21	4	5	27	24	102	5	5	214	256	310	566	5%	76%	0.24	66	91	2.58	3
	08	34	64	aaa	CLE	300	27	56	4	1	3	16	28	75	2	0	187	257	232	489	9%	75%	0.37	28	62	2.09	-19
Velazquez,Gilbert	07	28	56	a/a	MIN	228	25	45	9	3	2	23	17	52	3	0	198	253	282	535	7%	77%	0.32	56	124	2.48	-4
	08	29	6	aaa	BOS	350	40	75	17	3	7	34	16	68	3	3	214	248	337	585	4%	81%	0.23	80	93	2.72	9
Velez,Eugenio	07	25	84	aa	SF	394	45	97	14	6	1	19	21	62	41	18	247	284	322	606	5%	84%	0.33	50	176	2.99	10
	08	26	8	aa	SF	171	20	46	10	3	4	12	14	30	11	9	269	324	425	749	7%	82%	0.45	100	148	4.27	40
Venable,William	07	25	8	aa	SD	515	56	123	15	2	7	58	33	83	18	2	238	284	314	598	6%	84%	0.40	49	109	3.26	8
	08	26	8	aa	SD	442	56	106	21	3	10	47	35	100	6	3	240	296	370	666	7%	77%	0.35	83	94	3.83	21
Vento,Mike	07	29	80	aaa	TOR	295	29	66	18	0	6	32	19	63	0	0	222	269	349	618	6%	79%	0.31	88	27	3.23	16
Von Schell,Tyler	07	28	3	aa	SF	243	22	42	8	0	9	28	14	66	0	0	171	215	313	528	5%	73%	0.21	85	27	2.17	-4
Votto,Joey	07	24	38	aaa	CIN	496	66	138	20	1	22	82	62	98	15	11	278	358	456	814	11%	80%	0.63	106	70	5.85	49
Wagner,Mark	08	24	2	aa	BOS	342	35	67	19	0	7	37	29	65	0	0	196	259	312	570	8%	81%	0.45	80	29	2.74	7
Wald,Jake	07	27	6	aa	SF	361	32	69	17	3	4	27	22	89	8	3	190	236	289	526	6%	75%	0.25	68	109	2.27	-4
	08	28	6	aa	SF	365	45	76	20	3	4	31	33	102	6	1	207	273	306	579	8%	72%	0.33	70	116	2.94	4
Walker,Brian	08	23	2	aa	LAA	148	10	25	6	0	3	12	5	32	0	2	166	192	265	457	3%	79%	0.15	66	35	1.48	-15
Walker,Christophe	07	27	8	aa	CHC	267	16	46	5	0	2	17	8	57	8	6	174	199	221	420	3%	79%	0.15	31	72	1.31	-26
	08	28	8	aa	LAA	319	33	66	10	4	1	20	12	55	11	10	207	236	268	504	4%	83%	0.23	41	132	1.89	-10

BATTER	Yr	Age		Pos	Lev	Org	ab	r	h	d	t	hr	rbi	bb	k	sb	cs	ba	ob	slg	ops	bb%	ct%	eye	px	sx	rc/g	bpv
Walker,Neil	07	22		5	aa	PIT	495	71	128	33	2	10	56	45	72	8	6	259	320	394	714	8%	85%	0.63	94	85	4.46	37
	08	23		5	aa	PIT	505	59	113	25	5	13	69	24	89	9	7	223	258	367	625	4%	82%	0.26	91	113	3.06	17
Wallace,David	07	28		2	a/a	CLE	179	17	23	3	0	5	13	18	62	0	1	126	207	228	436	9%	65%	0.29	58	37	1.50	-28
	08	29		2	aaa	WAS	125	12	24	5	0	2	9	14	32	0	1	190	272	275	547	10%	75%	0.44	59	34	2.52	-3
Washington,Rico	07	29		53	aa	STL	262	23	51	11	1	7	26	15	37	2	0	195	238	318	556	5%	86%	0.40	78	57	2.53	5
	08	30		385	aa	STL	252	37	47	11	0	8	27	35	44	0	2	186	284	320	605	12%	83%	0.80	86	43	3.08	13
Wathan,Derek	07	31		5	aa	KC	189	13	30	6	1	1	12	9	30	1	1	159	198	219	416	5%	84%	0.30	41	65	1.35	-24
	08	32		63	aaa	DET	283	20	47	4	3	2	20	8	52	6	4	165	187	216	403	3%	82%	0.15	31	110	1.21	-29
Wathan,Dusty	07	34		32	a/a	PHI	248	17	50	10	1	0	15	12	41	2	1	200	237	248	485	5%	83%	0.29	40	58	1.96	-11
Watkins,Tommy	07	27		685	aaa	MIN	349	49	87	21	0	7	46	34	68	11	7	250	317	367	685	9%	80%	0.50	82	83	4.08	28
	08	28		8	aaa	MIN	233	24	40	7	2	1	13	18	31	4	4	174	232	230	462	7%	87%	0.57	39	97	1.67	-14
Watson,Brandon	07	26		8	aaa	WAS	399	42	113	10	5	2	26	18	48	16	9	282	314	345	659	4%	88%	0.38	40	122	3.81	18
	08	27		8	aaa	PHI	518	61	134	18	1	5	32	20	52	9	9	259	286	328	615	4%	90%	0.38	48	75	3.15	14
Watson,Matt	08	30		08	aa	TOR	252	29	60	15	0	4	24	35	53	1	0	236	329	347	676	12%	79%	0.66	80	38	4.23	25
Webb,Trey	07	26		486	aa	SF	322	32	64	12	3	2	18	5	71	7	3	198	209	268	478	1%	78%	0.06	48	129	1.80	-13
Weber,Jon	07	30		8	aaa	TAM	136	17	31	5	2	3	18	18	25	0	0	228	319	348	667	12%	81%	0.72	73	82	4.03	20
	08	31		8	aaa	TAM	389	41	78	18	3	9	36	28	98	8	6	201	255	332	587	7%	75%	0.29	84	98	2.72	7
Webster,Anthony	07	24		80	aa	TEX	411	53	102	23	3	7	31	17	47	24	11	247	277	365	643	4%	88%	0.36	80	133	3.33	23
	08	26		8	aa	PIT	292	34	59	10	4	4	28	18	19	8	7	203	249	303	551	6%	93%	0.93	63	130	2.36	12
Wells,Casper	08	24	a	8	aa	DET	270	46	68	16	5	13	40	24	51	6	4	250	311	486	797	8%	81%	0.46	141	157	5.16	51
Wesson,Barry	07	30		8	aa	HOU	222	12	34	5	1	2	10	16	66	6	1	155	212	211	423	7%	70%	0.25	37	77	1.50	-28
West,Jeremy	07	26		30	aa	CHW	190	16	45	3	0	0	15	13	29	1	1	237	284	251	535	6%	85%	0.44	13	40	2.52	-7
West,Kevin	07	28		803	aa	TEX	371	32	80	16	0	11	37	24	89	0	1	215	263	345	607	6%	76%	0.27	83	22	3.05	11
Whitesell,Josh	07	25		30	aa	WAS	387	60	88	19	1	15	58	66	103	5	2	228	340	400	740	15%	73%	0.64	106	71	4.97	33
	08	26	b	3	aa	ARI	475	67	137	32	0	22	86	60	121	1	2	289	368	496	864	11%	75%	0.50	132	30	6.89	61
Whiteside,Eli	07	28		2	a/a	BAL	202	18	42	6	3	5	29	7	44	1	3	207	233	340	573	3%	78%	0.16	78	98	2.39	4
	08	29		2	a/a	SF	175	11	31	5	0	2	16	9	28	2	0	176	215	236	452	5%	84%	0.31	42	48	1.70	-18
Whitney,Matthew	08	25		30	aa	CLE	463	49	110	27	1	9	50	52	88	0	0	238	315	357	672	10%	81%	0.59	82	31	4.07	25
Wieters,Matthew	08	22	a	2	aa	BAL	208	36	71	13	1	11	45	34	24	1	0	341	434	572	1006	14%	88%	1.42	141	57	10.37	100
Williams,Glenn	07	30		3	aaa	MIN	405	38	83	17	2	7	50	24	107	1	2	204	249	309	558	6%	74%	0.23	69	58	2.55	1
Williams,Marland	07	26		8	aa	CIN	322	28	55	5	3	9	30	24	139	13	2	170	229	284	512	7%	57%	0.18	63	137	2.21	-14
Wilson,Craig	08	32		3	aa	SEA	391	39	75	13	0	14	46	31	113	2	2	191	252	335	586	7%	71%	0.28	86	41	2.78	5
Wilson,Josh	08	28		64	a/a	BOS	405	32	90	23	1	5	32	22	63	10	5	222	262	318	579	5%	84%	0.34	70	77	2.76	10
Wilson,Michael	07	24		8	aa	SEA	208	25	33	6	1	8	23	14	85	3	0	160	214	306	520	6%	59%	0.17	85	107	2.15	-8
	08	25		8	aa	SEA	407	58	93	23	1	20	65	49	109	7	0	229	311	434	746	11%	73%	0.45	126	86	4.88	37
Wilson,Neil	08	25		2	aa	COL	158	12	36	7	0	5	10	6	16	0	1	225	252	358	611	4%	90%	0.37	85	21	2.96	17
Wilson,Robert	07	24		2	aa	LAA	313	33	78	20	1	8	42	26	42	5	3	249	306	392	697	8%	87%	0.61	97	68	4.20	35
	08	26		2	aa	LAA	260	26	71	18	0	3	36	24	40	0	0	271	332	372	704	8%	84%	0.58	78	23	4.59	34
Wimberly,Corey	07	24		4	aa	COL	365	50	91	14	1	3	26	16	41	29	10	250	280	316	597	4%	89%	0.38	48	131	3.09	10
	08	25		46	aa	COL	388	45	98	14	1	0	18	28	31	40	19	252	302	294	597	7%	92%	0.89	35	118	3.01	16
Winfree,David	07	22		350	aa	MIN	460	47	110	24	3	9	42	20	91	0	0	239	271	363	634	4%	80%	0.22	82	56	3.40	18
	08	23		8	aa	MIN	453	48	100	25	2	15	72	32	78	2	3	221	273	381	653	7%	83%	0.42	102	58	3.47	24
Wise,Dewayne	07	30		8	aaa	CIN	207	27	44	9	4	6	16	6	55	6	2	211	235	382	617	3%	73%	0.12	102	184	2.94	15
	08	31		8	aaa	CHW	191	29	48	11	2	8	17	17	33	11	7	254	315	449	764	8%	83%	0.52	121	130	4.62	45
Witter,Adam	08	26		2	aa	SF	400	47	82	16	2	15	64	53	94	0	6	204	297	367	664	12%	77%	0.56	98	42	3.59	20
Woodward,Chris	08	32		64	aaa	MIL	297	20	60	13	1	2	26	18	40	2	1	200	246	266	512	6%	87%	0.45	49	51	2.20	-4
Wood,Brandon	07	23		56	aa	LAA	437	66	111	25	1	20	70	40	109	9	1	254	317	453	770	8%	75%	0.37	124	94	5.23	43
	08	24	a	6	aa	LAA	395	69	105	20	1	25	70	37	90	5	6	265	329	506	835	9%	77%	0.41	142	74	5.76	55
Wood,Jason	08	39		35	aa	FLA	346	37	71	11	0	3	30	20	61	2	0	204	248	258	506	6%	82%	0.33	40	61	2.19	-9
Wooten,Shawn	07	35		2	aa	NYM	146	6	22	3	0	0	8	7	21	0	0	149	188	168	355	5%	85%	0.33	17	18	1.01	-37
	08	36		2	aa	SD	164	10	23	4	0	2	11	14	39	0	0	140	206	197	403	8%	76%	0.35	39	21	1.33	-30
Worth,Danny	08	23		6	a/a	DET	297	35	67	16	3	4	26	25	47	6	0	224	286	337	622	8%	84%	0.54	76	119	3.47	17
Yan,Ruddy	07	26		8	a/a	BAL	420	48	93	12	2	3	19	31	38	13	10	222	276	280	556	7%	91%	0.83	41	97	2.54	7
Yarbrough,Brando	08	24		20	aa	STL	306	30	63	12	5	2	28	34	78	2	1	205	285	295	580	10%	75%	0.44	58	116	2.95	1
Yepez,Marcos	07	26		64	a/a	WAS	224	29	56	7	1	1	17	17	49	4	2	250	303	301	605	7%	78%	0.35	37	89	3.28	5
	08	27		4	aa	WAS	167	16	34	7	2	1	22	17	33	6	5	204	276	286	562	9%	80%	0.51	57	113	2.56	2
Young Jr.,Eric	08	23		4	aa	COL	403	52	103	21	3	2	24	42	53	32	20	255	326	336	661	9%	87%	0.79	59	125	3.66	25
Young,Delwyn	07	25		8	aa	LA	490	81	134	44	3	14	74	30	100	3	4	274	315	457	773	6%	80%	0.30	127	87	5.10	50
Young,Ernie	07	38		0	aaa	CHW	374	36	69	10	0	13	34	32	99	0	0	185	249	313	561	8%	74%	0.32	76	24	2.60	-1
Young,Matt	08	26		8	aa	ATL	491	56	119	13	7	2	38	52	55	23	13	242	314	309	623	9%	89%	0.93	42	137	3.40	17
Zeringue,Jonathar	08	26		8	aa	OAK	478	55	99	19	2	15	64	38	94	3	5	206	264	348	612	7%	80%	0.40	87	64	3.01	13
Zobrist,Ben	07	26	b	6	aaa	TAM	222	39	57	13	2	7	20	41	38	8	3	258	373	424	797	16%	83%	1.07	105	113	5.98	51

					Actual				Major League Equivalents																
PITCHER	Yr	Age	Lev	Org	w	l	g	sv	ip	h	er	hr	bb	k	era	whip	bf/g	oob	ctl	dom	cmd	hr/9	h%	s%	bpv
Aardsma,David	07	26	aaa	CHW	3	2	28	15	35	32	23	10	12	40	5.96	1.27	5.2	240	3.1	10.2	3.3	2.6	27%	62%	59
Abraham,Paul	07	28	aa	SD	1	3	47	8	52	53	20	2	25	38	3.53	1.50	4.9	258	4.4	6.6	1.5	0.4	32%	76%	62
	08	29	aa	SD	1	1	30	0	41	61	29	6	30	26	6.28	2.21	7.1	337	6.6	5.6	0.9	1.4	38%	74%	-2
Abreu,Winston	07	30	aaa	WAS	3	0	37	5	52	31	10	2	23	62	1.73	1.04	5.6	170	4.0	10.7	2.7	0.4	25%	85%	130
Aceves,Alfredo	08	26	a/a	NYY	4	5	17	0	93	100	42	13	21	62	4.07	1.30	23.1	269	2.0	6.0	2.9	1.2	30%	73%	62
Acosta,Manny	07	26	aaa	ATL	9	3	40	12	59	56	19	0	38	47	2.82	1.58	6.7	244	5.8	7.1	1.2	0.0	32%	80%	74
Adenhart,Nicholas	07	21	aa	LAA	10	8	26	0	153	184	78	8	66	98	4.59	1.63	26.8	292	3.9	5.8	1.5	0.5	35%	71%	48
	08	22	aa	LAA	9	13	26	0	145	197	111	15	74	95	6.88	1.87	26.7	317	4.6	5.9	1.3	0.9	37%	63%	26
Adkins,James	08	23	aa	LA	1	3	8	0	38	46	22	5	28	23	5.21	1.95	23.1	293	6.6	5.4	0.8	1.2	33%	75%	11
Adkins,Jon	07	30	aa	NYM	2	4	48	5	65	111	46	11	23	27	6.32	2.06	6.8	370	3.2	3.7	1.2	1.6	39%	72%	-20
	08	31	aaa	CIN	1	4	57	30	62	75	31	6	14	32	4.43	1.43	4.7	292	2.0	4.7	2.4	0.9	32%	71%	47
Aguilar,Omar	08	24	aa	MIL	0	3	28	4	38	29	13	5	23	37	3.17	1.36	5.8	206	5.4	8.7	1.6	1.2	25%	82%	64
Aguilar,Salvador	07	26	aa	NYM	7	9	28	0	119	203	99	4	44	50	7.47	2.08	21.3	369	3.4	3.7	1.1	0.3	41%	61%	17
	08	27	aa	NYM	10	3	24	0	111	131	53	9	43	58	4.28	1.56	20.8	288	3.4	4.7	1.4	0.7	32%	73%	32
Akin,Brian	07	26	aa	LA	2	4	44	2	82	98	52	4	56	87	5.72	1.87	8.9	290	6.1	9.6	1.6	0.5	39%	68%	73
	08	27	aa	LA	3	7	32	1	53	90	56	7	63	35	9.55	2.88	9.6	366	10.7	5.9	0.6	1.2	42%	66%	-6
Alaniz,Adrian	08	25	aa	WAS	0	5	13	0	66	67	31	8	29	37	4.16	1.47	22.3	259	4.0	5.0	1.3	1.1	28%	75%	26
Albaladejo,Jonathan	07	25	a/a	WAS	7	3	36	2	60	52	25	5	23	46	3.70	1.23	6.9	227	3.4	6.8	2.0	0.8	27%	72%	70
Albers,Matt	07	25	aa	HOU	2	3	9	0	53	60	27	7	23	34	4.65	1.57	26.4	279	3.9	5.8	1.5	1.3	31%	74%	27
Alexander,Mark	07	27	aa	LA	5	1	48	5	79	91	69	15	62	73	7.85	1.93	8.0	282	7.1	8.3	1.2	1.7	34%	61%	22
Alfonzo,Edgar	08	24	aa	NYM	2	2	28	0	38	49	22	7	14	27	5.13	1.68	6.2	308	3.4	6.4	1.9	1.7	35%	75%	20
Alvarado,Giancarlo	08	31	aa	LAA	7	5	26	0	130	200	106	20	90	79	7.31	2.23	25.8	345	6.2	5.5	0.9	1.4	38%	68%	-4
Alvarez,Abe	07	25	aaa	BOS	5	8	25	0	100	123	72	10	48	59	6.48	1.71	18.5	296	4.3	5.3	1.2	0.9	34%	61%	26
Alvarez,Mario	08	25	aa	LA	1	5	10	0	40	59	38	5	24	17	8.48	2.07	20.1	334	5.4	3.8	0.7	1.2	36%	58%	-9
Alvarez,Oscar	07	27	aa	BAL	11	7	25	0	135	180	112	22	65	48	7.47	1.81	25.6	313	4.3	3.2	0.7	1.4	32%	59%	-16
Ambriz,Hector	08	24	aa	ARI	5	13	27	0	152	194	114	29	49	100	6.72	1.60	25.5	304	2.9	5.9	2.0	1.7	33%	61%	20
Anderson,Brett	08	21 a	aa	OAK	2	1	6	0	31	28	9	3	8	34	2.49	1.14	21.0	234	2.2	9.8	4.4	0.8	32%	82%	134
Anderson,Brian	07	24	aa	SF	1	5	47	29	50	65	27	4	21	37	4.92	1.72	4.9	308	3.8	6.7	1.8	0.8	37%	72%	48
Anderson,Craig	07	27	a/a	BAL	12	4	28	0	166	223	104	24	41	75	5.66	1.59	26.8	315	2.2	4.0	1.8	1.3	34%	67%	15
	08	28	a/a	BAL	7	10	29	0	128	231	128	34	28	63	8.96	2.02	21.8	382	1.9	4.4	2.3	2.4	40%	58%	-20
Anderson,Jason	07	28	a/a	PHI	4	3	37	1	64	94	47	11	18	37	6.60	1.74	8.1	334	2.5	5.2	2.1	1.5	37%	64%	20
	08	29	a/a	PHI	3	3	47	2	64	111	48	7	32	34	6.68	2.23	7.0	372	4.5	4.7	1.1	1.0	41%	70%	0
Andrade,Steve	07	30	aaa	TAM	3	2	38	0	59	70	45	5	37	40	6.86	1.82	7.4	290	5.7	6.1	1.1	0.8	34%	61%	31
	08	31	a/a	TAM	5	4	41	5	60	64	28	6	45	48	4.11	1.81	6.9	266	6.7	7.2	1.1	0.9	32%	79%	39
Antonini,Michael	08	23	aa	NYM	1	3	8	0	45	49	23	10	16	27	4.52	1.46	24.7	273	3.3	5.4	1.6	2.1	28%	78%	6
Aquino,Greg	07	30	aaa	MIL	3	2	35	7	38	33	14	2	22	37	3.37	1.44	4.8	228	5.2	8.8	1.7	0.5	30%	77%	82
Ardoin,Kevin	07	25	aa	DET	3	5	34	0	47	70	32	9	29	14	6.17	2.10	6.9	338	5.5	2.8	0.5	1.7	34%	74%	-37
Arias,Alberto	08	25	aa	HOU	4	4	38	1	69	79	31	3	21	46	3.98	1.45	7.9	281	2.7	5.9	2.2	0.4	34%	72%	68
Arias,Marlon	08	24	aa	LA	7	3	15	0	68	94	44	9	31	42	5.85	1.83	21.5	321	4.0	5.5	1.4	1.3	36%	70%	15
Armas Jr.,Tony	08	30	aa	NYM	5	7	17	0	102	136	49	13	27	53	4.28	1.59	27.1	313	2.4	4.7	2.0	1.1	34%	76%	28
Arredondo,Jose	07	24	aa	LAA	0	1	25	10	28	22	10	2	14	24	3.31	1.29	4.7	209	4.6	7.8	1.7	0.7	26%	76%	75
Asadoorian,Eric	07	27	aa	CIN	1	1	37	0	52	55	31	7	34	34	5.40	1.71	6.5	267	5.8	5.9	1.0	1.2	30%	71%	21
	08	28	aa	LA	4	4	17	1	42	70	45	4	24	16	9.60	2.22	12.8	362	5.1	3.4	0.7	0.8	39%	54%	-7
Asahina,Jonathan	07	27	aa	COL	3	5	10	0	49	80	44	13	29	11	7.99	2.22	25.3	359	5.3	2.1	0.4	2.3	35%	68%	-66
Ascanio,Jose	07	22 a	aa	ATL	2	2	44	10	78	77	28	1	19	61	3.23	1.23	7.4	253	2.2	7.0	3.2	0.1	32%	72%	111
	08	23	aa	CHC	2	1	40	11	54	61	36	11	24	49	5.99	1.56	6.1	278	3.9	8.1	2.0	1.9	32%	66%	34
Aselton,Kyle	08	26	aa	MIN	8	6	38	1	110	141	68	8	68	64	5.54	1.90	14.0	305	5.5	5.2	0.9	0.6	35%	70%	26
Asencio,Miguel	07	27	aa	HOU	2	6	38	3	84	151	81	17	40	32	8.65	2.27	11.5	380	4.3	3.4	0.8	1.8	39%	63%	-38
	08	28	a/a	BOS	2	4	41	1	71	93	59	4	40	35	7.44	1.87	8.3	309	5.1	4.4	0.9	0.4	35%	57%	25
Asher,David	07	25	aa	SEA	0	0	23	2	19	27	16	1	9	12	7.48	1.94	4.0	330	4.5	5.9	1.3	0.5	39%	59%	36
Astacio,Ezequiel	07	28	aa	TEX	3	5	31	2	52	69	51	13	30	40	8.74	1.90	8.1	311	5.2	6.9	1.3	2.3	34%	56%	-7
Atchison,Scott	07	32	aa	SF	3	2	38	4	53	59	16	1	9	37	2.79	1.28	5.9	275	1.6	6.3	4.0	0.2	34%	77%	116
Atencio,Greg	07	26	aa	KC	4	7	36	0	113	167	94	15	52	68	7.50	1.93	15.2	335	4.1	5.4	1.3	1.2	38%	61%	12
	08	27	aa	KC	4	4	36	4	79	98	51	5	43	62	5.76	1.78	10.3	297	4.9	7.1	1.4	0.5	37%	66%	52
Atkins,Mitch	08	23	aa	CHC	17	7	28	0	164	176	85	28	52	110	4.64	1.39	25.3	269	2.8	6.0	2.1	1.5	30%	72%	36
Austen,David	08	27	aa	LAA	3	4	20	0	70	128	66	11	16	28	8.52	2.05	17.4	385	2.0	3.6	1.8	1.4	41%	58%	-4
Avery,James	07	23	aa	CIN	11	10	27	0	146	193	108	21	62	80	6.66	1.74	25.2	311	3.8	4.9	1.3	1.3	34%	63%	11
	08	24	aa	CIN	7	8	24	0	130	177	86	19	46	77	5.97	1.71	25.1	317	3.2	5.3	1.7	1.3	35%	67%	19
Avery,Matt	07	24	aa	CHC	2	2	31	0	49	61	31	11	20	29	5.61	1.65	7.2	299	3.7	5.2	1.4	1.9	32%	72%	-1
	08	25	aa	CHC	4	2	32	1	66	81	41	12	39	40	5.59	1.81	9.8	296	5.3	5.4	1.0	1.7	32%	73%	-0
Ayala,Manny	08	24	aa	SD	7	4	21	0	90	93	57	12	43	56	5.66	1.51	19.0	261	4.3	5.6	1.3	1.2	29%	64%	27
Babula,Shaun	07	30	aaa	CHW	3	3	37	0	61	82	49	10	36	36	7.20	1.93	8.0	315	5.2	5.3	1.0	1.5	35%	64%	1
	08	31	a/a	CHW	2	0	25	0	38	61	36	4	19	21	8.38	2.09	7.7	354	4.5	4.9	1.1	1.0	39%	59%	5
Backe,Brandon	07	29	aa	HOU	4	2	6	0	30	48	24	8	17	19	7.20	2.18	25.5	354	5.2	5.6	1.1	2.4	38%	72%	-31
Bacsik,Mike	07	30	aaa	WAS	1	3	9	0	36	51	22	7	7	21	5.49	1.59	18.0	325	1.6	5.2	3.2	1.6	35%	70%	39
	08	31	aaa	WAS	7	5	36	1	77	110	49	13	22	48	5.71	1.72	9.9	329	2.6	5.6	2.1	1.6	36%	70%	21
Baek,Cha Seung	07	27	aa	SEA	1	1	6	0	31	45	16	1	13	13	4.55	1.87	24.7	330	3.8	3.9	1.0	0.3	37%	74%	23
Baerlocher,Ryan	07	30	a/a	ATL	4	5	17	0	98	163	69	10	28	43	6.31	1.94	28.0	362	2.5	4.0	1.6	0.9	40%	67%	12
Bailey,Andrew	08	24	aa	OAK	5	9	37	0	110	111	58	13	52	89	4.73	1.47	13.1	256	4.2	7.3	1.7	1.0	31%	70%	53
Bailey,Cory	07	37	aa	CHC	5	3	44	5	91	136	42	9	19	43	4.18	1.70	9.6	339	1.9	4.3	2.3	0.9	37%	77%	33
Bailey,Homer	07	21	aaa	CIN	6	3	12	0	67	53	27	5	30	55	3.66	1.23	23.2	212	4.0	7.4	1.8	0.6	26%	71%	77
	08	22	aaa	CIN	4	7	19	0	111	130	69	12	45	88	5.55	1.57	26.2	285	3.6	7.1	2.0	1.0	34%	65%	52
Baker,Brad	07	27	a/a	MIN	2	7	29	0	94	142	87	18	37	56	8.29	1.90	15.6	341	3.5	5.3	1.5	1.7	37%	57%	-0
Baker,Chris	07	30	aa	TEX	4	6	18	0	74	164	97	26	36	25	11.78	2.70	23.1	431	4.3	3.0	0.7	3.1	43%	59%	-93
Baker,Scott	07	26 b	aaa	MIN	3	2	7	1	42	44	23	4	5	32	4.84	1.17	24.7	265	1.1	6.8	6.2	0.9	32%	59%	147
Baldwin,Andrew	07	25 a	aa	SEA	5	12	27	0	166	227	96	14	21	98	5.19	1.50	27.2	319	1.1	5.3	4.6	0.7	37%	65%	98
	08	26	aa	SEA	10	5	30	0	147	216	97	14	47	70	5.91	1.78	23.1	334	2.9	4.3	1.5	0.9	37%	67%	19
Balester,Collin	07	21	a/a	WAS	4	10	27	0	150	165	74	11	46	103	4.45	1.40	24.0	273	2.7	6.2	2.3	0.7	32%	68%	64
	08	22	aaa	WAS	9	3	15	0	78	82	36	11	21	57	4.17	1.32	22.1	264	2.4	6.5	2.7	1.3	30%	73%	59
Balfour,Grant	07	30 b	a/a	MIL	1	1	32	7	43	35	13	2	20	51	2.80	1.27	5.6	219	4.1	10.6	2.6	0.5	32%	79%	114
Ballard,Michael	08	25	aa	TEX	11	6	25	0	134	197	85	8	41	77	5.72	1.77	25.2	334	2.8	5.2	1.9	0.6	38%	67%	42
Banks,Josh	07	25	aaa	TOR	12	10	27	0	169	227	112	28	25	85	5.97	1.49	27.6	315	1.3	4.5	3.4	1.5	34%	63%	45
	08	26	a/a	SD	1	3	12	0	47	69	37	3	14	26	7.02	1.77	18.4	334	2.8	5.0	1.8	0.6	38%	58%	37

Major League Equivalent Statistics

					Actual				Major League Equivalents																
PITCHER	Yr	Age	Lev	Org	w	l	g	sv	ip	h	er	hr	bb	k	era	whip	bf/g	oob	ctl	dom	cmd	hr/9	h%	s%	bpv
Bard,Daniel	08	23 a	aa	BOS	4	1	31	7	49	35	13	3	27	53	2.45	1.26	6.6	196	4.9	9.8	2.0	0.6	27%	82%	99
Barnes,John	07	31	a/a	BOS	2	3	7	0	36	28	14	1	38	20	3.60	1.82	24.4	209	9.4	4.9	0.5	0.3	25%	79%	46
Barnette,Anthony	08	25	aa	ARI	11	7	27	0	153	179	91	23	44	112	5.32	1.46	24.8	286	2.6	6.6	2.5	1.4	33%	66%	50
Barone,Daniel	07	24	aa	FLA	8	3	23	0	136	151	73	14	35	79	4.80	1.36	25.3	275	2.3	5.2	2.3	0.9	31%	66%	52
	08	25	aa	FLA	4	6	16	0	81	114	57	11	23	48	6.28	1.70	23.4	326	2.6	5.3	2.0	1.2	36%	64%	28
Barratt,Jonathan	07	23	aa	TAM	4	10	20	0	90	107	66	10	60	42	6.59	1.85	21.5	289	6.0	4.2	0.7	1.0	31%	64%	7
Barrett,Ricky	07	27	aaa	MIN	2	1	22	1	30	39	21	4	16	27	6.14	1.84	6.5	308	4.9	8.1	1.6	1.2	38%	68%	40
	08	28	aaa	MIN	4	5	50	2	70	65	31	4	41	63	3.92	1.52	6.2	242	5.3	8.1	1.5	0.5	31%	74%	71
Barry,Kevin	07	29	aaa	ATL	5	7	24	0	112	154	76	16	47	65	6.08	1.79	22.0	320	3.8	5.2	1.4	1.3	35%	68%	11
Barthmaier,James	07	24	aa	HOU	2	9	24	0	90	135	76	13	45	60	7.63	2.00	18.5	339	4.5	6.0	1.3	1.3	39%	62%	11
	08	25	aa	PIT	5	5	26	0	125	136	74	8	51	88	5.30	1.49	21.2	271	3.6	6.4	1.7	0.6	33%	63%	57
Barzilla,Phil	07	29	aa	HOU	9	7	31	1	135	236	103	9	59	51	6.83	2.18	22.2	375	3.9	3.4	0.9	0.6	41%	67%	1
	08	30	aa	SD	3	3	41	0	64	85	45	8	37	44	6.37	1.91	7.6	313	5.2	6.2	1.2	1.1	36%	67%	21
Basner,Ryan	07	26	a/a	ATL	4	5	36	1	91	123	54	14	34	61	5.38	1.73	11.8	317	3.4	6.0	1.8	1.4	36%	72%	22
	08	27	a/a	ATL	4	2	39	0	68	113	75	15	36	36	9.86	2.17	8.9	361	4.7	4.7	1.0	2.0	38%	55%	-27
Bass,Adam	07	26	aa	ARI	3	1	19	0	50	57	17	5	18	27	3.10	1.52	11.7	282	3.3	4.9	1.5	0.8	32%	82%	34
	08	27	aa	SD	2	2	50	1	63	112	75	10	46	40	10.64	2.50	6.8	378	6.5	5.7	0.9	1.4	43%	56%	-9
Bass,Brian	07	26	aaa	MIN	7	3	37	1	103	121	59	10	27	64	5.11	1.44	12.1	287	2.4	5.6	2.4	0.9	33%	65%	54
Bastardo,Antonio	08	23	aa	PHI	1	5	14	0	67	62	31	15	37	50	4.15	1.48	21.0	240	5.0	6.8	1.4	2.1	25%	81%	14
Bateman,Joe	07	27	aa	SF	4	1	29	0	56	71	25	6	25	33	4.06	1.72	9.0	303	4.1	5.3	1.3	1.0	34%	79%	25
	08	28	a/a	MIL	3	1	49	8	77	79	24	5	26	59	2.75	1.36	6.7	259	3.0	6.8	2.3	0.5	32%	81%	75
Bauer,Rick	07	31	a/a	LA	2	6	41	2	68	115	53	15	55	45	6.95	2.50	9.0	367	7.3	5.9	0.8	2.0	40%	76%	-25
	08	32	aaa	TOR	0	0	34	18	34	35	12	1	20	34	3.05	1.60	4.5	258	5.3	9.0	1.7	0.3	35%	80%	85
Baugh,Kenneth	07	29	aa	FLA	7	9	21	0	96	188	128	18	78	43	11.93	2.75	26.0	400	7.3	4.0	0.6	1.6	43%	56%	-38
	08	30	aa	FLA	3	1	15	0	36	65	36	8	27	17	8.95	2.54	13.2	382	6.6	4.1	0.6	2.0	40%	67%	-43
Bautista,Denny	07	27	aa	COL	3	2	51	0	64	80	35	1	37	46	4.90	1.82	6.0	298	5.2	6.5	1.2	0.2	37%	71%	56
Bayliss,Jonah	08	28	a/a	TOR	3	5	54	5	72	111	54	12	31	38	6.75	1.96	6.5	344	3.8	4.8	1.3	1.5	37%	67%	-3
Bazardo,Yorman	07	23	aaa	DET	10	6	23	0	136	159	74	9	43	60	4.89	1.48	26.1	286	2.8	4.0	1.4	0.6	32%	66%	33
	08	24	aaa	DET	4	13	25	0	130	202	117	20	43	66	8.10	1.88	25.0	347	3.0	4.6	1.5	1.4	38%	57%	4
Beam,T.J.	07	27	aaa	NYY	4	3	29	3	47	63	26	7	11	36	5.03	1.56	7.3	315	2.0	6.9	3.4	1.4	37%	71%	63
	08	28	aa	PIT	2	1	30	5	43	53	24	3	18	27	4.95	1.62	6.5	294	3.6	5.7	1.6	0.5	35%	69%	47
Bean,Colter	07	31	aaa	NYY	2	0	28	0	59	87	56	4	36	42	8.47	2.07	10.5	335	5.4	6.5	1.2	0.7	40%	57%	31
	08	32	a/a	TAM	3	5	45	11	60	71	34	6	31	54	5.17	1.70	6.2	289	4.7	8.1	1.7	0.8	36%	70%	57
Beckstead,Jentry	07	27	aa	COL	3	1	45	1	71	113	66	13	39	37	8.38	2.13	8.0	353	4.9	4.7	1.0	1.7	38%	62%	-17
Begg,Chris	07	28	aa	SF	14	5	27	0	166	283	110	24	33	57	5.96	1.90	29.6	368	1.8	3.1	1.7	1.3	39%	70%	-2
Belisario,Ronald	08	26	aa	PIT	4	4	38	9	57	81	41	6	28	27	6.49	1.91	7.2	328	4.4	4.3	1.0	0.9	36%	66%	9
Belisle,Matt	08	28	a/a	CIN	6	1	27	4	47	67	28	1	13	22	5.41	1.70	8.0	328	2.5	4.2	1.7	0.2	37%	66%	44
Bell,Rob	07	31	aaa	BAL	4	3	10	0	66	83	34	8	20	46	4.68	1.56	29.7	301	2.7	6.2	2.3	1.1	35%	72%	49
	08	32	aaa	CHW	1	5	12	0	37	65	45	7	11	22	11.01	2.05	15.3	377	2.6	5.3	2.1	1.8	41%	45%	1
Beltran,Francis	07	28	aaa	BAL	2	9	47	8	59	95	46	3	17	39	7.05	1.89	6.0	354	2.6	5.9	2.3	0.5	42%	60%	54
	08	29	aaa	DET	3	5	37	3	44	54	30	5	12	31	6.16	1.49	5.2	295	2.4	6.3	2.6	1.1	34%	59%	55
Bennett,Jeff	07	27	a/a	ATL	3	5	42	1	95	123	53	7	48	38	5.01	1.80	10.7	307	4.6	3.6	0.8	0.7	34%	72%	12
Benson,Kris	08	34	aaa	PHI	1	4	11	0	60	105	51	11	16	27	7.57	2.01	27.0	375	2.4	4.0	1.7	1.6	40%	64%	-8
Bergesen,Bradley	08	23	aa	BAL	15	6	24	0	148	170	67	13	27	61	4.07	1.33	26.2	282	1.6	3.7	2.3	0.8	31%	71%	44
Berg,Christopher	07	23	aa	CHC	7	7	27	0	140	189	98	5	73	56	6.30	1.87	24.8	316	4.7	3.6	0.8	0.3	35%	64%	20
Berg,Justin	08	24	aa	CHC	4	9	32	0	118	139	80	14	62	48	6.09	1.70	17.1	287	4.7	3.6	0.8	1.0	30%	65%	4
Berken,Jason	08	25	aa	BAL	12	4	26	0	145	171	75	12	39	104	4.63	1.44	24.4	287	2.4	6.4	2.7	0.7	34%	68%	70
Bierd,Randor	07	24 a	aa	DET	3	2	27	1	45	39	24	1	10	44	4.72	1.09	6.7	229	2.1	8.7	4.2	0.2	31%	53%	144
Birkins,Kurt	07	27	aaa	BAL	8	4	20	0	105	133	54	8	41	81	4.59	1.65	24.0	302	3.5	6.9	2.0	0.7	37%	73%	56
	08	28	aaa	TAM	2	3	36	0	40	69	42	4	30	23	9.39	2.46	6.0	370	6.7	5.2	0.8	1.0	42%	60%	-0
Bisenius,Joe	07	25	aaa	PHI	3	4	35	0	46	62	35	6	32	35	6.92	2.04	6.5	314	6.3	6.8	1.1	1.2	37%	67%	20
	08	26	a/a	PHI	3	5	43	0	63	71	43	8	47	41	6.17	1.86	7.0	278	6.6	5.9	0.9	1.1	32%	68%	20
Bittner,Tim	07	27	aa	CHW	2	4	48	0	66	136	55	13	39	22	7.55	2.64	7.7	414	5.2	3.1	0.6	1.8	43%	74%	-51
	08	28	a/a	WAS	2	6	45	5	72	78	45	6	53	47	5.57	1.81	7.6	269	6.6	5.8	0.9	0.7	31%	69%	33
Blackburn,Nick	07	26	a/a	MIN	10	4	25	0	148	164	54	9	22	58	3.26	1.26	24.8	275	1.3	3.5	2.6	0.6	30%	75%	59
Blackley,Travis	07	25	aa	SF	10	8	28	0	162	186	105	22	71	98	5.84	1.58	26.1	282	3.9	5.4	1.4	1.2	31%	65%	23
	08	26	aaa	PHI	5	10	28	0	123	158	96	20	63	73	7.02	1.79	20.7	305	4.6	5.4	1.2	1.5	33%	62%	6
Blazek,Christopher	08	25	aa	HOU	4	4	47	2	69	75	38	8	27	68	4.93	1.48	6.5	270	3.6	8.9	2.5	1.1	34%	69%	74
Blevins,Jerry	07	24 a	aa	OAK	4	5	41	4	54	51	17	3	13	57	2.81	1.17	5.4	243	2.1	9.5	4.5	0.5	33%	77%	142
	08	25 a	aa	OAK	2	2	28	10	32	37	11	3	6	28	3.12	1.32	4.9	281	1.6	7.8	5.0	0.9	35%	80%	123
Bloom,Kyle	08	26	aa	PIT	5	8	28	0	109	132	71	10	61	70	5.86	1.77	18.3	293	5.0	5.8	1.1	0.8	34%	67%	30
Boggs,Mitch	07	24	aa	STL	11	7	26	0	152	190	75	15	61	100	4.45	1.65	26.7	299	3.6	5.9	1.6	0.9	35%	75%	38
	08	25	aa	STL	9	3	21	0	125	121	55	11	44	66	3.94	1.32	25.3	249	3.2	4.7	1.5	0.8	28%	71%	42
Bogusevic,Brian	08	25	aa	HOU	2	6	17	0	88	104	58	16	32	28	5.91	1.54	23.1	288	3.2	2.8	0.9	1.6	29%	65%	-16
Bohorquez,Carlos	07	26	aa	CIN	3	2	22	0	30	36	19	1	21	18	5.65	1.88	6.6	288	6.3	5.4	0.9	0.3	34%	68%	38
Bongiovanni,Vincent	08	26	aa	ARI	3	3	42	3	61	86	43	9	40	40	6.38	2.05	7.2	324	5.9	5.8	1.0	1.3	37%	70%	7
Bonilla,Henry	07	29	aa	LAA	12	8	29	0	165	316	179	32	68	57	9.75	2.33	29.9	396	3.7	3.1	0.8	1.7	41%	58%	-40
	08	30	aa	LAA	5	2	51	3	71	116	69	16	46	39	8.68	2.27	7.2	358	5.8	4.9	0.8	2.0	38%	64%	-29
Bonine,Eddie	07	26	a/a	DET	15	5	26	0	162	221	102	17	29	60	5.67	1.54	27.8	318	1.6	3.3	2.1	0.9	34%	63%	28
	08	27	a/a	DET	12	5	18	0	110	143	67	11	22	54	5.45	1.49	27.0	307	1.8	4.4	2.5	0.9	34%	64%	44
Booker,Chris	07	31	aaa	WAS	2	5	55	30	58	48	27	4	44	63	4.14	1.59	4.8	220	6.9	9.8	1.4	0.7	30%	75%	79
Borkowski,Dave	08	32	aa	HOU	2	2	27	2	40	49	13	4	8	19	2.90	1.43	6.5	296	1.8	4.2	2.3	0.8	33%	83%	45
Borrell,Danny	07	29	aa	OAK	3	3	19	0	64	61	30	11	33	50	4.21	1.46	14.8	247	4.6	7.0	1.5	1.6	28%	77%	32
	08	30	aa	OAK	4	2	8	0	37	59	28	5	19	16	6.77	2.08	23.2	351	4.5	3.8	0.8	1.3	37%	69%	-13
Bostick II,Adam	07	25	aa	NYM	6	7	21	0	97	125	75	21	46	75	6.93	1.77	21.7	307	4.3	7.0	1.6	2.0	34%	64%	11
	08	26	aa	NYM	2	2	11	0	44	60	39	7	21	23	7.92	1.84	19.1	317	4.3	4.8	1.1	1.4	35%	57%	3
Bouknight,Kip	07	29	aa	PIT	12	7	27	0	156	220	105	20	54	64	6.05	1.75	27.0	325	3.1	3.7	1.2	1.2	35%	67%	2
	08	30	aa	PHI	3	8	16	0	79	151	88	20	44	25	10.03	2.46	26.6	395	5.0	2.8	0.6	2.3	40%	61%	-64
Bowden,Michael	07	21	aa	BOS	8	6	19	0	96	121	57	9	33	69	5.33	1.60	22.9	301	3.1	6.5	2.1	0.8	36%	67%	52
	08	22 a	a/a	BOS	9	7	26	0	144	129	52	10	29	111	3.25	1.10	22.3	235	1.8	6.9	3.8	0.6	29%	72%	111
Bowers,Cedrick	08	31	aa	COL	6	1	35	1	65	79	43	7	56	44	5.93	2.07	9.3	293	7.7	6.1	0.8	1.0	34%	72%	20
Boyer,Blaine	07	26	aaa	ATL	4	3	21	2	73	93	46	1	55	51	5.71	2.02	17.2	303	6.7	6.3	0.9	0.1	37%	69%	48

Major League Equivalent Statistics

					Actual				Major League Equivalents																
PITCHER	Yr	Age	Lev	Org	w	l	g	sv	ip	h	er	hr	bb	k	era	whip	bf/g	oob	ctl	dom	cmd	hr/9	h%	s%	bpv
Braden,Dallas	07	24 a	aa	OAK	3	3	13	0	76	67	31	6	21	70	3.61	1.16	23.9	233	2.5	8.3	3.3	0.7	30%	71%	106
	08	25	aa	OAK	3	1	11	0	53	58	17	7	11	41	2.82	1.30	20.4	271	1.9	7.0	3.7	1.1	32%	84%	87
Brandt,Douglas	08	24	aa	LAA	2	4	42	0	60	84	52	10	34	46	7.73	1.96	7.0	323	5.1	6.8	1.3	1.5	37%	62%	13
Braun,Ryan	07	27	aa	KC	2	2	23	9	33	27	6	1	14	27	1.64	1.24	6.0	216	3.9	7.2	1.8	0.3	28%	88%	84
Bray,Stephen	08	28	a/a	MIL	2	8	46	1	75	99	56	17	32	57	6.76	1.75	7.6	311	3.9	6.8	1.8	2.1	34%	66%	8
Bray,Steve	07	27	aaa	MIL	5	2	42	1	77	71	19	5	29	64	2.16	1.30	7.7	240	3.4	7.5	2.2	0.6	30%	86%	80
Brazelton,Dewon	07	27	aa	PIT	5	9	19	0	105	154	71	10	30	46	6.08	1.75	25.9	334	2.6	3.9	1.5	0.8	37%	65%	19
Breslow,Craig	07	27	aaa	BOS	2	3	49	1	68	89	44	7	27	59	5.84	1.72	6.4	310	3.6	7.8	2.2	1.0	38%	66%	56
Bresnehan,Patrick	08	23	aa	PIT	0	1	38	6	50	53	31	1	52	33	5.56	2.08	6.6	264	9.3	5.9	0.6	0.2	32%	71%	46
Bright,Adam	07	23	aa	COL	1	3	52	0	46	55	28	4	27	35	5.45	1.77	4.1	289	5.2	6.8	1.3	0.8	35%	69%	41
	08	24	aa	COL	3	8	47	0	49	65	28	4	13	30	5.22	1.59	4.7	313	2.3	5.6	2.4	0.8	36%	67%	53
Brito,Eude	07	29	aaa	PHI	1	6	20	0	58	95	56	13	38	25	8.68	2.29	15.1	358	6.0	3.8	0.6	2.0	37%	64%	-42
	08	30	a/a	NYM	4	3	51	1	81	116	65	9	38	46	7.21	1.90	7.7	329	4.2	5.1	1.2	1.0	37%	61%	16
Britton,Chris	07	25 a	aaa	NYY	4	2	37	8	57	60	21	4	15	49	3.31	1.31	6.5	265	2.4	7.7	3.3	0.6	33%	76%	98
Broadway,Lance	07	24	aaa	CHW	8	9	27	0	155	189	110	25	83	96	6.39	1.75	26.8	295	4.8	5.6	1.2	1.5	32%	66%	10
	08	25	aaa	CHW	11	7	24	0	145	199	99	33	45	89	6.14	1.69	27.8	320	2.8	5.5	2.0	2.1	34%	69%	3
Brooks,Frank	07	29	aa	SD	3	1	25	1	31	27	9	3	13	20	2.70	1.29	5.2	227	3.9	5.9	1.5	0.8	26%	82%	54
Broshuis,Garrett	07	26	aa	SF	3	17	26	0	153	208	88	13	39	57	5.16	1.61	26.7	317	2.3	3.3	1.5	0.8	34%	68%	19
	08	27	aa	SF	13	9	28	0	157	239	95	18	40	73	5.47	1.78	26.3	343	2.3	4.2	1.8	1.1	37%	70%	18
Brower,Jim	07	35	a/a	NYY	5	2	44	22	55	71	22	3	18	37	3.64	1.62	5.7	307	2.9	6.0	2.1	0.5	36%	78%	57
	08	36	a/a	HOU	2	2	36	8	47	67	20	3	23	34	3.83	1.91	6.3	327	4.5	6.5	1.5	0.6	39%	81%	41
Browning,Barret	08	24	aa	LAA	1	1	27	1	31	36	26	2	14	28	7.43	1.62	5.2	284	4.2	8.1	1.9	0.6	36%	51%	70
Brownlie,Robert	07	27	aa	CLE	1	2	9	0	48	55	24	6	16	30	4.52	1.48	23.5	282	3.0	5.5	1.8	1.1	32%	72%	38
	08	28	a/a	WAS	9	7	30	0	150	201	96	29	54	72	5.78	1.70	23.1	315	3.2	4.3	1.3	1.8	33%	70%	-7
Brown,Andrew	07	27	aa	OAK	2	3	37	4	40	43	18	5	16	37	4.12	1.46	4.8	266	3.6	8.2	2.3	1.0	33%	74%	68
Brown,Brooks	07	22	aa	ARI	4	4	12	0	66	88	41	4	42	41	5.61	1.98	27.0	314	5.8	5.6	1.0	0.5	37%	70%	31
	08	23	aa	ARI	6	15	26	0	144	186	90	10	69	97	5.60	1.77	26.0	306	4.3	6.1	1.4	0.6	36%	68%	40
Brown,Eric	08	25	aa	NYM	6	9	30	0	123	169	85	16	29	66	6.24	1.62	18.6	321	2.2	4.8	2.2	1.2	35%	62%	32
Brummett,Tyson	08	24	aa	PHI	2	9	14	0	80	119	74	12	46	38	8.28	2.06	28.5	337	5.2	4.3	0.8	1.3	36%	60%	-9
Buchholz,Clay	07	23 a	a/a	BOS	8	5	24	0	125	103	44	10	36	146	3.17	1.11	21.0	220	2.6	10.5	4.1	0.7	31%	74%	138
	08	24 a	a/a	BOS	5	2	11	0	58	52	20	3	19	50	3.03	1.20	21.8	233	2.9	7.8	2.7	0.5	30%	75%	98
Buckner,Billy	07	24	aa	KC	10	10	31	0	124	156	71	16	33	81	5.12	1.52	17.8	301	2.4	5.9	2.5	1.1	34%	68%	48
	08	25	aa	ARI	5	10	21	0	116	179	92	13	48	55	7.15	1.95	26.9	345	3.7	4.3	1.1	1.0	38%	63%	5
Bueno,Francisley	07	27	a/a	ATL	5	6	25	0	132	198	74	14	33	74	5.08	1.75	24.7	339	2.3	5.0	2.2	1.0	38%	72%	34
	08	28	aaa	ATL	2	6	19	0	84	120	62	8	31	48	6.65	1.79	20.8	328	3.3	5.2	1.6	0.9	37%	62%	27
Bukvich,Ryan	07	29	aaa	CHW	1	3	23	9	28	32	13	3	11	25	4.24	1.53	5.4	280	3.5	8.2	2.3	1.1	35%	75%	65
	08	30	aaa	BAL	8	4	34	1	85	103	57	6	57	47	5.99	1.88	12.0	294	6.0	4.9	0.8	0.6	34%	67%	26
Bulger,Jason	07	29	aa	LAA	5	2	49	10	52	75	35	5	31	55	6.03	2.04	5.3	330	5.4	9.5	1.8	0.9	43%	70%	57
	08	30 b	aa	LAA	4	0	37	16	43	37	5	0	29	49	1.12	1.55	5.2	229	6.1	10.2	1.7	0.0	34%	92%	105
Bullington,Bryan	07	27	aa	PIT	11	9	26	0	150	201	98	12	70	62	5.85	1.80	27.3	314	4.2	3.7	0.9	0.7	34%	67%	12
	08	28	a/a	CLE	5	9	25	1	128	215	113	20	47	81	7.94	2.05	25.4	365	3.3	5.7	1.7	1.4	41%	62%	10
Bumatay,Mike	07	28	a/a	OAK	4	2	55	3	52	74	44	6	38	46	7.56	2.14	4.8	326	6.6	8.0	1.2	1.0	40%	64%	33
Bump,Nate	08	32	aa	SF	4	3	17	0	58	65	25	2	26	20	3.83	1.56	15.3	276	4.0	3.2	0.8	0.4	30%	75%	24
Bumstead,Michael	07	30	aa	TEX	1	2	20	1	31	81	69	11	30	15	19.91	3.59	10.1	474	8.7	4.5	0.5	3.3	49%	43%	-102
Burch,Jason	08	26	aa	TOR	3	3	31	0	45	73	29	6	18	32	5.76	2.02	7.2	358	3.5	6.3	1.8	1.1	41%	73%	25
Burke,Greg	08	26 b	aa	SD	2	7	59	23	84	95	26	7	20	69	2.83	1.37	6.1	280	2.1	7.4	3.5	0.7	34%	82%	95
Burnett,Sean	07	25	aa	PIT	4	5	15	0	70	106	47	4	42	23	5.99	2.11	23.5	340	5.4	3.0	0.6	0.6	37%	71%	-1
Burnside,Adrian	07	31	aa	SD	0	0	35	0	45	74	39	4	29	19	7.68	2.28	6.7	360	5.7	3.8	0.7	0.9	39%	65%	-6
Burns,Mike	07	29	aaa	BOS	4	9	35	3	112	166	87	19	34	62	6.98	1.79	15.1	337	2.7	5.0	1.8	1.5	37%	62%	11
	08	30	aa	CHC	8	12	37	2	133	236	110	29	34	60	7.44	2.03	17.8	378	2.3	4.1	1.8	1.9	40%	66%	-17
Burton,TJ	07	24	aa	CLE	2	2	29	0	37	57	21	2	23	26	5.11	2.16	6.5	344	5.6	6.2	1.1	0.5	41%	76%	31
	08	25	aa	CLE	2	2	29	0	30	53	18	1	17	18	5.33	2.33	5.4	378	5.0	5.4	1.1	0.3	44%	76%	24
Buschmann,Matthew	08	25	aa	SD	10	6	27	0	148	157	57	13	61	96	3.46	1.47	24.1	266	3.7	5.8	1.6	0.8	31%	78%	47
Butcher,Brok	08	25	aa	LAA	5	5	17	0	96	146	81	15	34	47	7.60	1.88	27.1	343	3.2	4.4	1.4	1.4	37%	60%	0
Buzachero,Edward	07	26	a/a	CLE	6	8	52	3	77	113	62	9	23	41	7.26	1.77	7.0	335	2.7	4.8	1.8	1.0	37%	58%	23
	08	27	a/a	CLE	3	4	45	11	71	94	37	9	29	44	4.66	1.73	7.3	312	3.6	5.6	1.5	1.2	35%	76%	24
Cahill,Trevor	08	21	aa	OAK	6	1	7	0	37	24	9	2	16	29	2.08	1.08	21.1	181	3.9	7.2	1.8	0.5	23%	83%	86
Calero,Kiko	08	34	aa	TEX	2	3	26	1	30	41	29	6	25	23	8.79	2.19	5.9	319	7.4	6.9	0.9	1.8	36%	61%	-1
Cali,Carmen	07	29	aaa	MIN	5	1	31	1	47	57	20	1	17	21	3.90	1.57	6.8	293	3.3	4.1	1.2	0.2	33%	74%	41
	08	30	aaa	MIN	5	1	50	2	65	95	43	5	29	36	5.92	1.89	6.3	332	3.9	5.0	1.3	0.8	38%	68%	23
Camacho,Eddie	07	25	aa	NYM	2	1	37	3	58	76	30	7	18	41	4.65	1.61	7.1	308	2.8	6.3	2.3	1.0	36%	73%	48
	08	26	aa	NYM	5	3	51	0	79	89	37	9	34	40	4.18	1.55	6.9	277	3.9	4.5	1.2	1.0	30%	76%	20
Cameron,Ryan	07	30	a/a	PHI	0	1	45	1	68	123	66	13	58	49	8.77	2.65	8.4	382	7.6	6.5	0.8	1.7	43%	68%	-14
Campbell,Brett	07	26	aa	WAS	3	5	48	9	58	68	41	6	38	45	6.36	1.81	5.7	285	5.8	7.0	1.2	0.9	34%	64%	39
Campillo,Jorge	07	29	aa	SEA	9	6	24	0	149	225	79	15	55	67	4.75	1.88	29.8	341	3.3	4.0	1.2	0.9	37%	76%	10
Campusano,Edward	08	26	aa	CHC	3	3	34	1	49	63	45	13	33	33	8.20	1.96	7.1	306	6.1	6.0	1.0	2.3	32%	62%	-18
Capellan,Jose	07	27	aaa	DET	3	3	26	4	37	42	24	4	15	22	5.75	1.56	6.4	281	3.8	5.4	1.4	1.0	32%	63%	32
	08	28	aa	KC	4	1	9	0	53	66	37	6	23	22	6.33	1.68	27.1	299	3.9	3.8	1.0	1.0	32%	62%	8
Caridad,Esmailin	08	25	aa	CHC	7	3	14	0	82	78	35	17	22	41	3.80	1.22	24.3	245	2.4	4.5	1.8	1.8	24%	78%	16
Carignan,Gary	08	22	aa	OAK	3	3	46	24	52	38	14	4	34	57	2.41	1.38	4.9	200	5.9	9.8	1.7	0.7	27%	85%	89
Carlson,Jesse	07	27	aa	TOR	8	2	58	6	70	102	54	6	21	60	6.94	1.75	5.6	333	2.7	7.7	2.9	0.7	41%	59%	73
Carlyle,Buddy	07	30 b	aaa	ATL	5	2	9	0	48	52	20	7	11	44	3.69	1.30	22.6	268	2.1	8.2	4.0	1.2	33%	76%	97
Carpenter,Andrew	08	23	a/a	PHI	6	9	17	0	100	135	72	17	33	63	6.47	1.68	27.1	316	3.0	5.7	1.9	1.5	35%	64%	20
Carrasco,Carlos	07	21	aa	PHI	6	4	14	0	70	70	43	10	44	44	5.50	1.63	22.8	256	5.6	5.7	1.0	1.3	28%	69%	19
	08	22	a/a	PHI	9	9	26	0	151	154	70	16	55	138	4.14	1.39	25.0	259	3.3	8.2	2.5	1.0	32%	72%	76
Carrasco,D.J.	07	30	aa	ARI	5	14	34	0	137	309	184	29	86	64	12.10	2.88	23.4	435	5.6	4.2	0.7	1.9	46%	57%	-48
Carrasco,Hector	08	39	aa	CHC	5	6	42	1	67	80	39	12	29	43	5.20	1.63	7.3	290	3.9	5.8	1.5	1.6	32%	72%	16
Carr,Adam	08	25	aa	WAS	3	4	30	11	33	43	27	6	21	22	7.42	1.93	5.4	308	5.7	5.9	1.0	1.7	34%	64%	-1
Carvajal,Marcos	07	23	aa	NYM	5	10	28	0	119	138	82	13	63	77	6.24	1.69	19.6	284	4.8	5.8	1.2	1.0	33%	63%	28
	08	24	aa	FLA	1	2	24	0	53	78	49	8	46	33	8.39	2.34	11.6	334	7.9	5.6	0.7	1.4	37%	65%	-6
Casadiego,Gerardo	07	27	aa	COL	4	3	41	9	50	70	33	13	26	43	5.98	1.92	5.9	324	4.7	7.6	1.6	2.3	37%	75%	2
	08	28	aa	BAL	5	6	55	1	70	92	37	5	35	40	4.79	1.80	6.0	309	4.5	5.1	1.1	0.6	35%	73%	29
Casilla,Santiago	07	27	aa	OAK	2	1	22	3	24	22	14	1	16	21	5.42	1.56	4.9	236	5.9	7.8	1.3	0.5	30%	63%	69

Major League Equivalent Statistics

					Actual				Major League Equivalents																
PITCHER	Yr	Age	Lev	Org	w	l	g	sv	ip	h	er	hr	bb	k	era	whip	bf/g	oob	ctl	dom	cmd	hr/9	h%	s%	bpv
Cassel,Jack	07	27	aa	SD	7	14	27	0	156	277	98	17	53	85	5.62	2.11	29.1	378	3.1	4.9	1.6	1.0	42%	74%	13
	08	28	aa	HOU	9	5	19	0	107	149	56	13	35	50	4.73	1.72	26.1	322	2.9	4.2	1.4	1.1	35%	74%	14
Cassel,Justin	08	24	aa	CHW	10	4	28	0	165	218	81	11	63	88	4.42	1.70	27.2	311	3.4	4.8	1.4	0.6	35%	74%	34
Cassidy,Scott	07	32	aa	SD	4	4	40	10	40	74	41	6	18	37	9.26	2.29	5.2	388	4.0	8.2	2.1	1.3	47%	59%	30
Castellanos,Hugo	07	27	aa	STL	4	3	46	0	67	81	34	8	43	32	4.52	1.85	7.0	291	5.8	4.3	0.7	1.1	32%	78%	5
	08	28	aa	STL	2	1	28	0	67	105	56	5	41	35	7.54	2.18	12.2	349	5.5	4.7	0.9	0.7	39%	64%	11
Castellanos,Jonathan	07	26	aa	ARI	5	6	13	0	68	109	43	7	22	29	5.62	1.92	25.4	354	2.9	3.8	1.3	0.9	39%	71%	7
Castillo,Jesus	08	24	aa	LA	7	4	23	0	114	142	48	8	36	66	3.82	1.56	22.2	299	2.8	5.2	1.8	0.7	34%	76%	45
Castillo,Osbek	07	27	aa	ARI	1	3	29	1	67	74	62	9	60	45	8.31	1.98	11.4	273	8.0	6.1	0.8	1.2	31%	57%	16
Castorri,Christian	08	25	aa	PIT	1	3	23	2	51	85	49	7	23	18	8.71	2.12	11.2	364	4.1	3.2	0.8	1.3	38%	58%	-21
Castro,Angel	08	26	aa	DET	2	2	26	2	43	38	20	3	20	26	4.17	1.34	7.1	230	4.2	5.4	1.3	0.7	26%	69%	48
Castro,Fabio	07	23	a/a	PHI	7	5	32	2	75	75	38	9	40	61	4.56	1.53	10.4	255	4.8	7.3	1.5	1.1	30%	73%	48
	08	24	a/a	PHI	8	4	30	0	120	138	74	19	52	89	5.55	1.58	18.0	282	3.9	6.7	1.7	1.4	32%	68%	32
Cate,Troy	07	27	aa	STL	2	5	33	0	71	111	70	16	33	46	8.88	2.04	10.7	349	4.2	5.8	1.4	2.0	38%	58%	-12
	08	28	a/a	MIL	5	3	27	1	72	87	45	9	26	31	5.60	1.58	12.0	293	3.3	3.9	1.2	1.1	31%	66%	10
Cavazos,Andy	07	27	aa	STL	2	5	44	0	47	51	22	6	29	37	4.16	1.68	4.9	268	5.5	7.0	1.3	1.1	32%	78%	37
	08	28	aa	CHC	2	1	26	1	33	39	30	5	28	20	8.17	2.00	6.3	285	7.5	5.4	0.7	1.3	31%	59%	6
Cecil,Brett	08	22	a/a	TOR	8	5	24	0	108	109	45	6	41	98	3.75	1.39	19.4	257	3.4	8.2	2.4	0.5	33%	73%	88
Ceda,Jose	08	22 a	aa	CHC	2	1	22	9	30	29	9	2	14	36	2.69	1.43	5.9	248	4.2	10.8	2.6	0.6	36%	83%	106
Cedeno,Juan	07	24	aa	KC	3	2	35	0	69	108	64	11	28	39	8.35	1.98	9.7	349	3.7	5.1	1.4	1.4	39%	58%	3
	08	25	aa	DET	3	2	28	1	54	69	34	2	27	21	5.73	1.77	9.1	304	4.4	3.4	0.8	0.4	34%	65%	20
Cedeno,Xavier	08	22	aa	COL	7	7	19	0	102	138	53	11	33	44	4.67	1.67	24.7	316	2.9	3.9	1.3	1.0	34%	74%	14
Chamberlain,Joba	07	22 a	a/a	NYY	5	2	11	0	48	45	20	5	17	70	3.74	1.29	18.4	243	3.2	13.1	4.1	0.9	38%	74%	143
Chavez,Jesse	07	24	aa	PIT	3	3	46	2	80	113	44	4	19	51	4.97	1.64	7.9	325	2.1	5.8	2.7	0.5	38%	69%	67
	08	25	aa	PIT	2	6	51	14	68	74	40	9	24	53	5.28	1.45	5.8	272	3.2	7.0	2.2	1.2	32%	65%	53
Chenard,Kenneth	07	29	aa	TEX	3	8	34	2	68	123	85	17	59	58	11.26	2.66	11.2	381	7.7	7.6	1.0	2.3	44%	59%	-23
Cherry,Rocky	07	28	aa	CHC	2	0	43	7	51	73	41	8	24	38	7.28	1.89	5.7	327	4.2	6.6	1.6	1.3	38%	62%	23
	08	29	a/a	BAL	0	1	30	0	39	50	17	4	13	29	3.93	1.62	5.9	305	3.1	6.6	2.1	0.8	36%	78%	53
Chiavacci,Ron	07	30	aaa	DET	12	6	26	0	151	194	82	18	48	98	4.90	1.60	26.3	306	2.8	5.8	2.1	1.1	35%	71%	40
	08	31	a/a	HOU	6	12	25	0	131	204	109	29	52	85	7.47	1.96	25.6	348	3.6	5.8	1.6	2.0	38%	65%	-5
Chick,Travis	07	23	aa	SEA	6	7	20	0	91	107	65	13	43	64	6.42	1.65	20.8	287	4.3	6.3	1.5	1.3	33%	62%	27
	08	24	aa	SEA	7	5	32	0	129	132	62	11	62	94	4.33	1.50	17.8	259	4.3	6.6	1.5	0.7	31%	72%	52
Childers,Jason	07	33	aaa	CHW	3	2	46	0	53	67	34	9	23	32	5.72	1.71	5.3	303	3.9	5.5	1.4	1.6	33%	70%	8
	08	34	aaa	CHW	4	2	50	17	59	42	11	3	15	51	1.61	0.96	4.6	196	2.2	7.8	3.5	0.5	25%	86%	121
Childers,Matt	07	29	aaa	PHI	7	4	19	0	102	173	81	15	29	58	7.10	1.98	26.3	367	2.6	5.1	2.0	1.3	41%	65%	14
	08	30	aaa	PHI	3	5	53	20	66	95	40	11	21	53	5.38	1.74	5.8	328	2.8	7.2	2.5	1.5	38%	73%	41
Choate,Randy	07	32	aa	ARI	3	1	54	3	62	92	32	5	19	45	4.60	1.78	5.4	336	2.7	6.5	2.4	0.7	40%	74%	57
	08	33	aaa	MIL	0	4	26	2	39	47	25	4	21	27	5.83	1.75	7.0	294	4.9	6.1	1.3	1.0	34%	67%	30
Christensen,Daniel	07	24	aa	KC	3	15	27	0	140	211	126	24	58	83	8.11	1.91	25.1	340	3.7	5.3	1.4	1.6	37%	58%	2
	08	25	aa	DET	7	10	27	0	158	204	89	19	60	77	5.06	1.67	26.9	307	3.4	4.4	1.3	1.1	33%	71%	15
Claggett,Anthony	08	24	aa	NYY	4	2	29	9	58	67	20	1	34	44	3.09	1.74	9.3	284	5.2	6.8	1.3	0.2	36%	81%	61
Clarke,Darren	08	28	aa	COL	2	2	29	1	30	45	24	7	25	17	7.23	2.33	5.4	337	7.6	5.2	0.7	2.2	36%	73%	-32
Clark,Zachary	08	25	a/a	BAL	5	4	14	0	78	96	44	8	19	29	5.09	1.47	24.5	296	2.2	3.4	1.6	1.0	31%	66%	20
Clippard,Tyler	07	23	a/a	NYY	6	5	20	0	96	126	65	15	50	70	6.09	1.83	22.8	310	4.7	6.6	1.4	1.4	36%	69%	20
	08	24	aaa	WAS	6	13	27	0	143	140	81	13	63	105	5.10	1.42	23.0	251	4.0	6.6	1.7	0.8	30%	64%	55
Coffey,Todd	08	28	aaa	CIN	3	3	34	2	39	60	25	5	16	35	5.69	1.95	5.6	345	3.7	8.1	2.2	1.2	42%	73%	44
Coke,Phillip	08	26	a/a	NYY	11	6	37	0	135	166	62	10	51	104	4.14	1.60	16.5	295	3.4	6.9	2.0	0.7	36%	75%	60
Collazo,Willie	07	28	aa	NYM	6	5	53	4	98	123	37	6	22	50	3.42	1.47	8.1	300	2.0	4.6	2.3	0.6	34%	77%	54
	08	29	aa	NYM	4	9	37	2	135	188	89	23	43	49	5.91	1.70	16.9	322	2.8	3.2	1.1	1.5	33%	68%	-11
Colon,Bartolo	08	35	aaa	BOS	3	1	9	0	31	28	11	2	6	17	3.04	1.11	14.0	238	1.8	4.9	2.7	0.6	27%	74%	76
Colon,Roman	08	29	aa	KC	7	5	33	2	112	199	101	23	41	47	8.14	2.14	17.2	378	3.3	3.7	1.1	1.8	40%	64%	-29
Connolly,Jonathan	07	24	a/a	DET	8	8	25	1	135	179	93	24	35	70	6.19	1.59	24.3	313	2.3	4.7	2.0	1.6	33%	64%	15
	08	25	a/a	DET	0	8	12	0	67	104	55	8	22	24	7.35	1.89	26.8	348	3.0	3.2	1.1	1.1	37%	61%	-7
Connolly,Michael	07	25	aa	KC	4	7	29	1	110	167	88	14	37	57	7.18	1.85	18.1	341	3.0	4.6	1.5	1.2	37%	61%	12
Cooper,Mike	07	24	aa	STL	1	2	21	0	28	41	28	6	20	17	8.95	2.17	6.8	335	6.3	5.6	0.9	2.0	36%	60%	-19
Corcoran,Roy	07	27	aa	FLA	4	4	53	15	61	84	34	1	41	40	4.98	2.05	5.7	321	6.0	5.9	1.0	0.2	39%	74%	41
Corcoran,Tim	07	29	a/a	TAM	3	2	24	3	32	35	17	2	20	24	4.77	1.70	6.2	273	5.5	6.6	1.2	0.7	33%	72%	45
	08	30	aa	FLA	4	2	16	0	55	97	46	6	24	34	7.45	2.20	17.7	376	4.0	5.5	1.4	0.9	43%	65%	14
Corey,Bryan	07	34	aaa	BOS	6	8	58	3	68	73	40	7	22	54	5.28	1.39	5.1	267	2.9	7.1	2.4	1.0	32%	63%	67
Corey,Mark	07	33	aa	PIT	1	1	23	0	32	48	21	1	29	16	5.92	2.41	7.5	339	8.2	4.5	0.5	0.3	39%	74%	16
Cormier,Lance	07	27	a/a	ATL	5	3	12	0	60	86	36	7	18	28	5.34	1.74	23.3	330	2.8	4.2	1.5	1.0	36%	71%	15
Cortes,Daniel	08	22	aa	KC	10	4	23	0	116	121	63	14	54	96	4.88	1.51	22.4	263	4.2	7.4	1.8	1.1	32%	70%	52
Cory,Forrest	08	25	aa	ARI	3	2	37	1	68	103	58	9	28	30	7.65	1.93	8.9	342	3.8	4.0	1.1	1.3	37%	60%	-4
Cotts,Neal	07	28	aa	CHC	2	2	24	0	50	60	41	6	37	33	7.36	1.95	10.2	292	6.7	6.0	0.9	1.1	33%	62%	19
Cowart,Adam	08	25	aa	SF	8	7	32	0	138	220	81	8	32	56	5.28	1.83	20.5	353	2.1	3.6	1.7	0.5	39%	70%	27
Cox,Benjamin	07	26	aa	SF	0	8	17	0	54	75	37	5	32	28	6.13	1.98	15.6	321	5.4	4.6	0.9	0.8	36%	69%	14
Cox,James	08	24	a/a	NYY	5	4	33	1	42	41	28	4	21	17	5.94	1.47	5.6	251	4.4	3.7	0.8	0.9	27%	59%	19
Cramer,Bob	07	28	aa	OAK	5	1	12	0	52	61	16	4	12	36	2.71	1.41	18.8	288	2.1	6.2	3.0	0.6	34%	83%	78
Crawford,Tristan	07	25	a/a	MIN	8	6	30	0	84	129	69	16	35	51	7.43	1.95	13.7	345	3.7	5.5	1.5	1.7	38%	64%	-1
	08	26	aa	WAS	2	3	12	0	35	56	24	2	14	21	6.21	2.00	14.4	355	3.5	5.4	1.5	0.6	41%	68%	30
Crist,Kyle	08	25	aa	KC	4	1	42	6	74	88	46	13	37	44	5.54	1.68	8.1	289	4.5	5.4	1.2	1.6	31%	71%	6
Cromer,Jason	07	27	aa	KC	3	8	36	1	85	138	71	6	32	44	7.53	2.00	11.6	357	3.4	4.6	1.4	0.6	40%	60%	21
	08	28	aa	TAM	5	3	29	0	75	123	46	6	29	39	5.49	2.02	12.8	359	3.5	4.7	1.3	0.7	40%	73%	18
Crowell,Jim	07	33	aaa	TOR	1	4	28	0	56	93	62	4	29	19	9.98	2.18	10.2	362	4.7	3.1	0.6	0.7	39%	51%	-6
Cruceta,Francisco	07	26	aa	TEX	3	0	25	1	65	52	33	3	46	52	4.60	1.50	11.5	214	6.3	7.2	1.1	0.5	27%	68%	65
	08	27 b	aaa	DET	2	3	32	3	42	46	25	0	24	51	5.39	1.67	6.1	273	5.2	10.9	2.1	0.0	41%	64%	111
Cueto,Johnny	07	22 a	a/a	CIN	8	4	14	0	83	83	31	10	12	88	3.41	1.15	24.1	255	1.3	9.6	7.1	1.0	33%	74%	180
Cullen,Ryan	07	28	aa	NYM	2	5	48	0	80	116	41	13	19	45	4.61	1.69	7.7	331	2.2	5.0	2.3	1.5	36%	77%	23
Cummings,Jeremy	07	31	aaa	TOR	6	8	29	0	120	160	78	18	40	77	5.83	1.67	19.0	313	3.0	5.7	1.9	1.3	35%	67%	27
	08	32	aaa	TAM	8	3	16	1	87	89	34	12	24	64	3.48	1.30	23.0	260	2.5	6.6	2.6	1.2	30%	78%	62
Currin,Pat	08	24	aa	OAK	4	3	28	1	46	68	39	6	14	28	7.60	1.78	7.7	337	2.7	5.4	2.0	1.2	38%	57%	25
Cyr,Eric	07	29	aa	LA	9	9	28	0	145	224	95	21	51	74	5.89	1.89	25.0	345	3.2	4.6	1.4	1.3	38%	71%	4
	08	30	aa	LA	3	2	17	1	45	85	52	15	35	33	10.40	2.67	14.8	394	6.9	6.6	1.0	2.9	43%	65%	-52

Major League Equivalent Statistics

					Actual				Major League Equivalents																
PITCHER	Yr	Age	Lev	Org	w	l	g	sv	ip	h	er	hr	bb	k	era	whip	bf/g	oob	ctl	dom	cmd	hr/9	h%	s%	bpv
Daigle,Casey	07	26	aa	ARI	9	5	41	0	107	208	116	26	36	73	9.76	2.28	13.6	399	3.0	6.1	2.1	2.2	44%	59%	-12
	08	28	aaa	MIN	1	5	44	1	69	74	38	9	37	50	4.94	1.60	7.1	268	4.8	6.6	1.4	1.2	31%	72%	32
Daley,Matt	07	25	aa	COL	2	6	43	0	95	112	57	18	24	68	5.36	1.44	9.6	288	2.3	6.4	2.8	1.7	32%	67%	43
	08	26	aa	COL	4	6	63	1	66	77	34	7	36	49	4.70	1.70	4.9	285	4.9	6.6	1.4	0.9	34%	74%	38
Daniels,Adam	07	25	aa	STL	5	7	15	0	72	103	60	6	36	34	7.48	1.92	23.3	329	4.4	4.3	1.0	0.7	37%	59%	14
	08	26	aa	STL	1	4	17	0	55	89	45	6	38	28	7.31	2.29	16.9	354	6.2	4.5	0.7	0.9	39%	68%	-1
Darensbourg,Vic	07	37	aaa	DET	6	2	50	0	52	54	14	0	18	34	2.36	1.37	4.5	261	3.1	5.9	1.9	0.0	32%	81%	78
Davidson,Daniel	07	27	aa	LAA	2	4	7	0	43	46	15	5	9	18	3.11	1.28	25.9	267	1.9	3.8	2.0	1.0	29%	80%	37
	08	28	aa	LAA	1	0	24	0	53	58	24	5	18	33	4.08	1.43	9.6	271	3.1	5.6	1.8	0.8	31%	73%	49
Davidson,Dave	07	23	aa	PIT	4	1	45	2	67	60	37	3	33	52	4.98	1.38	6.4	234	4.4	7.0	1.6	0.4	29%	62%	71
	08	24	aa	PIT	4	2	35	0	64	71	32	3	38	41	4.43	1.69	8.5	273	5.3	5.7	1.1	0.4	32%	73%	44
Davies,Kyle	08	25	aa	KC	6	2	11	0	57	61	19	4	23	30	2.97	1.48	22.9	268	3.7	4.7	1.3	0.7	30%	82%	35
Davis,Allen	07	32	aa	PHI	3	2	31	1	47	84	35	6	21	28	6.76	2.23	7.8	378	4.1	5.4	1.3	1.1	43%	70%	6
Davis,Jason	08	28	aa	PIT	6	9	21	0	116	164	89	5	59	46	6.88	1.92	26.7	326	4.6	3.5	0.8	0.4	36%	61%	16
Davis,Kane	07	32	aaa	PHI	3	3	41	4	53	57	24	3	28	48	4.11	1.61	5.9	269	4.8	8.2	1.7	0.5	35%	74%	70
	08	33	aaa	TOR	6	7	16	0	86	122	57	5	33	48	5.93	1.80	25.4	327	3.4	5.1	1.5	0.5	38%	65%	35
Davis,Wade	07	22	aa	TAM	7	3	14	0	80	84	34	3	31	71	3.83	1.44	24.9	264	3.5	8.0	2.3	0.3	34%	72%	88
	08	23	a/a	TAM	13	8	28	0	160	159	71	13	65	117	3.99	1.40	24.7	254	3.7	6.6	1.8	0.7	30%	73%	60
Day,Dewon	07	27	a/a	CHW	2	5	34	2	39	51	32	1	39	49	7.41	2.29	6.0	307	9.0	11.2	1.2	0.3	45%	65%	79
	08	28	a/a	CHW	1	9	35	0	71	113	74	9	41	45	9.38	2.17	10.3	352	5.2	5.7	1.1	1.2	40%	55%	6
Day,Zach	07	29	aa	KC	1	1	11	0	36	52	27	3	35	8	6.63	2.39	17.5	330	8.6	1.9	0.2	0.7	34%	71%	-15
De Jong,Jordan	07	28	a/a	TOR	6	5	38	2	66	75	35	6	32	58	4.80	1.62	7.9	280	4.3	7.9	1.8	0.8	35%	71%	60
	08	29	aaa	TOR	6	2	53	5	71	92	47	12	45	54	5.98	1.93	6.5	308	5.7	6.8	1.2	1.5	35%	72%	13
De La Cruz,Eulogio	07	24	a/a	DET	7	5	33	0	104	114	54	6	38	71	4.67	1.46	13.8	273	3.3	6.1	1.9	0.5	33%	67%	61
	08	25	aa	FLA	13	8	25	0	147	163	86	14	66	103	5.28	1.56	26.4	275	4.1	6.3	1.5	0.8	32%	66%	45
De La Cruz,Jose	07	24	aa	SEA	1	2	42	5	61	74	38	4	36	40	5.58	1.79	6.9	292	5.3	5.9	1.1	0.6	34%	68%	37
De La Cruz,Julio	07	27	aa	PHI	1	4	48	6	64	85	48	6	37	44	6.77	1.90	6.4	312	5.2	6.1	1.2	0.8	37%	63%	30
De La Vara,Gilbert	08	24	aa	KC	3	0	21	2	32	28	14	0	16	17	3.82	1.37	6.6	232	4.4	4.8	1.1	0.0	28%	69%	60
De Los Santos,Richa	07	23	a/a	TAM	6	5	46	0	87	102	43	7	19	38	4.45	1.39	8.2	286	2.0	3.9	2.0	0.7	31%	68%	42
	08	24	aa	TAM	5	5	14	1	79	87	36	4	25	32	4.08	1.43	24.5	275	2.9	3.7	1.3	0.5	30%	71%	35
De Los Santos,Valeri	08	36	aa	COL	4	5	23	0	78	115	65	16	29	48	7.46	1.85	16.2	336	3.4	5.5	1.6	1.9	36%	62%	-2
Deago,Roger	07	30	aa	SD	6	8	34	0	132	220	124	21	74	75	8.47	2.23	20.0	363	5.1	5.1	1.0	1.5	40%	62%	-10
	08	31	aa	TAM	2	5	59	4	82	102	36	5	44	45	4.00	1.78	6.5	299	4.8	4.9	1.0	0.5	34%	78%	31
Deaton,Kevin	07	26	aa	OAK	0	4	6	0	34	55	36	7	14	17	9.40	2.02	28.1	357	3.6	4.4	1.2	1.8	38%	54%	-20
Debarr,Nick	07	24	aa	TAM	3	4	53	4	83	94	41	6	36	44	4.45	1.56	7.0	279	3.9	4.7	1.2	0.7	31%	72%	33
	08	25	aaa	TAM	7	5	50	1	78	87	47	11	38	46	5.48	1.61	7.1	276	4.4	5.3	1.2	1.3	30%	68%	18
Deduno,Samuel	07	24	aa	COL	5	8	21	0	124	154	106	18	69	104	7.72	1.80	27.9	298	5.0	7.5	1.5	1.3	36%	57%	33
DeHoyos,Gabe	07	27	aa	KC	6	1	38	4	69	81	29	5	29	39	3.76	1.58	8.2	285	3.8	5.1	1.3	0.6	33%	77%	38
	08	28	aa	SD	6	4	60	4	83	96	34	3	41	75	3.65	1.65	6.3	284	4.5	8.1	1.8	0.3	37%	77%	77
DeJean,Mike	07	37	aa	COL	0	3	20	0	30	62	42	15	11	18	12.62	2.42	8.1	414	3.2	5.3	1.7	4.6	41%	53%	-97
Delaney,Robert	08	24 a	aa	MIN	2	1	24	5	34	23	5	2	7	29	1.39	0.90	5.4	189	1.9	7.8	4.0	0.6	24%	89%	131
Delcarmen,Manny	07	26 a	aaa	BOS	3	2	20	0	29	34	15	1	15	32	4.69	1.70	6.7	288	4.7	9.8	2.1	0.3	40%	71%	91
Delgado,Jesus	07	23	aa	FLA	5	7	31	1	93	111	60	6	48	67	5.77	1.71	13.9	290	4.7	6.5	1.4	0.6	35%	65%	47
	08	24	aa	FLA	5	2	48	1	68	74	44	4	39	50	5.85	1.66	6.5	271	5.2	6.7	1.3	0.6	33%	63%	51
Denham,Dan	08	26	aa	LAA	9	10	25	0	146	198	96	18	63	77	5.89	1.79	27.5	317	3.9	4.8	1.2	1.1	35%	68%	13
DePaula,Jorge	07	29	aa	COL	9	6	20	0	104	204	125	26	59	39	10.81	2.52	28.3	401	5.1	3.4	0.7	2.3	41%	58%	-59
Depaula,Julio	07	25	aaa	MIN	12	5	49	2	83	83	39	10	31	51	4.22	1.37	7.3	255	3.4	5.5	1.6	1.1	28%	72%	39
	08	26	aaa	MIN	3	5	51	2	77	97	58	11	42	52	6.72	1.81	7.1	301	5.0	6.1	1.2	1.3	34%	64%	19
Desalvo,Matt	07	27	aaa	NYY	9	5	20	0	113	115	46	5	61	81	3.69	1.55	25.3	258	4.9	6.4	1.3	0.4	31%	76%	57
	08	28	aaa	ATL	2	11	34	0	92	120	65	8	60	73	6.30	1.96	13.2	309	5.9	7.2	1.2	0.7	38%	67%	40
Devaney,Michael	07	25	aa	NYM	6	9	22	0	104	130	72	12	47	55	6.25	1.70	21.8	300	4.0	4.8	1.2	1.1	33%	64%	17
Devine,Joey	07	24 a	a/a	ATL	5	4	50	20	57	49	15	2	21	65	2.44	1.23	4.7	229	3.3	10.3	3.2	0.3	33%	80%	127
Dew,Joshua	08	24	aa	STL	1	2	38	2	50	63	28	3	22	45	5.01	1.69	6.1	301	3.9	8.0	2.1	0.6	38%	70%	70
Deza,Fredy	07	25	aa	BAL	7	8	36	0	124	157	77	25	43	84	5.58	1.61	15.6	302	3.1	6.1	1.9	1.8	33%	70%	17
Dials,Zach	08	23	aa	TOR	2	3	36	15	36	51	24	4	14	29	5.90	1.79	4.7	323	3.6	7.2	2.0	1.0	39%	68%	45
Diamond,Thomas	08	26	aa	TEX	3	3	12	0	53	67	47	3	39	36	7.89	1.98	21.7	300	6.6	6.1	0.9	0.6	36%	58%	34
Diaz,Amalio	07	21	aa	LAA	0	2	6	0	37	50	24	3	7	13	5.82	1.54	27.6	316	1.7	3.2	1.9	0.7	34%	61%	28
	08	22	aa	LAA	3	4	10	0	57	70	34	5	27	33	5.36	1.70	26.4	296	4.3	5.2	1.2	0.8	34%	68%	29
Diaz,Felix	07	27	a/a	BOS	9	8	30	0	129	192	120	26	52	77	8.33	1.89	20.7	337	3.6	5.3	1.5	1.8	37%	57%	-5
Diaz,Joselo	08	28	aa	TEX	3	6	35	6	70	78	65	15	69	45	8.33	2.08	10.0	274	8.8	5.7	0.7	1.9	29%	62%	-9
Dickey,R.A.	07	33	aaa	MIL	13	6	31	0	169	196	94	22	67	103	4.99	1.56	24.4	284	3.6	5.5	1.5	1.2	32%	70%	28
	08	34	aa	SEA	2	5	7	0	49	75	25	2	9	23	4.52	1.72	32.6	344	1.7	4.2	2.4	0.4	39%	73%	50
Difelice,Mark	07	31	a/a	MIL	10	3	36	0	124	123	44	11	18	101	3.22	1.14	14.0	254	1.3	7.3	5.7	0.8	31%	74%	143
	08	32	aaa	MIL	5	1	13	0	64	57	26	5	8	56	3.69	1.02	19.4	233	1.2	7.9	6.7	0.7	29%	65%	173
Dillard,Tim	07	24	aaa	MIL	8	4	34	0	133	196	91	15	39	56	6.16	1.77	18.3	335	2.6	3.8	1.4	1.0	36%	65%	10
	08	25	aaa	MIL	6	1	37	2	63	62	15	5	27	50	2.16	1.41	7.4	251	3.9	7.1	1.8	0.7	31%	88%	64
DiNardo,Lenny	08	29	aa	OAK	6	5	15	0	71	152	73	8	19	32	9.28	2.40	25.2	423	2.4	4.0	1.7	1.0	46%	60%	-1
Dittler,Jake	07	25	a/a	CLE	9	2	27	0	92	121	58	5	33	43	5.64	1.67	15.7	309	3.2	4.2	1.3	0.5	35%	65%	30
Dixon,Kevin	08	25	aa	CLE	9	11	27	1	157	196	102	20	53	96	5.85	1.58	26.2	299	3.0	5.5	1.8	1.1	34%	64%	32
Dobies,Andrew	07	24	aa	BOS	4	3	34	0	75	109	58	11	29	57	6.93	1.85	10.5	333	3.5	6.8	1.9	1.3	39%	63%	32
Dohmann,Scott	07	30	aaa	TAM	4	1	37	5	48	49	16	3	15	38	3.08	1.35	5.6	260	2.9	7.1	2.5	0.6	32%	79%	80
	08	31	aaa	TAM	0	2	33	20	41	43	20	2	13	38	4.37	1.38	5.4	265	2.9	8.3	2.8	0.5	34%	67%	97
Done,Juan	07	27	aa	SEA	4	11	32	1	107	149	76	10	55	42	6.37	1.91	16.2	323	4.6	3.5	0.8	0.9	35%	66%	1
Doolittle,Michael	08	26	aa	FLA	5	3	36	8	44	47	20	3	23	50	4.09	1.59	5.5	266	4.8	10.3	2.2	0.7	37%	75%	88
Dorman,Rich	08	30	aa	SEA	9	6	25	0	127	176	73	14	56	69	5.16	1.82	24.1	321	3.9	4.9	1.2	1.0	36%	73%	16
Douglass,Chance	07	24	aa	HOU	6	9	27	0	145	176	88	18	61	82	5.43	1.63	24.5	294	3.8	5.1	1.4	1.1	33%	68%	23
	08	25	aa	HOU	6	11	28	0	148	181	85	24	54	68	5.18	1.58	23.8	295	3.3	4.2	1.3	1.5	31%	71%	4
Dowdy,Justin	08	25	aa	OAK	1	3	41	1	61	81	51	4	46	41	7.54	2.08	7.4	313	6.7	6.0	0.9	0.7	37%	62%	27
Downs,Brodie	08	29	aa	SEA	5	2	36	2	94	144	64	8	59	41	6.12	2.15	13.3	344	5.6	3.9	0.7	0.8	38%	71%	2
Doyne,Michael	07	26 b	aaa	BAL	0	1	42	29	44	29	15	0	18	42	3.16	1.05	4.2	183	3.6	8.5	2.4	0.0	26%	67%	119
Driskill,Travis	07	36	aa	HOU	4	3	44	9	65	80	38	9	19	45	5.20	1.52	6.6	296	2.6	6.2	2.4	1.3	34%	68%	44
DuBose,Eric	07	31	a/a	CLE	5	8	22	0	100	158	91	13	52	[illegible]	8.20	2.10	22.8	351	4.7	5.8	1.2	1.2	40%	60%	10
Duckworth,Brandon	08	33	aa	KC	5	11	27	1	134	182	107	29	56	77	7.18	1.78	23.4	318	3.8	5.2	1.4	2.0	34%	63%	-8

					Actual				Major League Equivalents																
PITCHER	Yr	Age	Lev	Org	w	l	g	sv	ip	h	er	hr	bb	k	era	whip	bf/g	oob	ctl	dom	cmd	hr/9	h%	s%	bpv
Duensing,Brian	07	25	a/a	MIN	15	6	28	0	167	198	76	18	41	98	4.11	1.43	26.0	289	2.2	5.3	2.4	0.9	33%	73%	51
	08	26	aaa	MIN	5	11	25	0	138	170	78	16	35	62	5.07	1.48	24.3	296	2.3	4.1	1.8	1.1	32%	67%	26
Dumatrait,Phil	07	26	aaa	CIN	10	6	22	0	125	139	66	13	53	63	4.75	1.53	25.3	276	3.8	4.5	1.2	1.0	30%	71%	23
Durbin,J.D.	07	26	aaa	PHI	2	4	10	0	59	79	38	12	22	38	5.85	1.71	27.4	313	3.4	5.7	1.7	1.8	34%	70%	7
	08	27	a/a	PHI	5	14	34	0	130	192	110	21	66	68	7.62	1.98	18.7	336	4.5	4.7	1.0	1.5	36%	62%	-6
Edell,Ryan	08	25	aa	CLE	7	8	26	0	144	189	86	18	24	79	5.34	1.48	24.4	310	1.5	4.9	3.2	1.1	34%	65%	57
Edwards,Bill	07	27	aa	LAA	4	4	54	4	68	94	52	8	43	36	6.84	2.01	6.2	322	5.6	4.7	0.8	1.1	36%	66%	5
	08	28	aa	LAA	0	2	19	0	39	54	29	5	34	23	6.67	2.26	10.6	323	7.8	5.4	0.7	1.1	36%	71%	4
Egbert,John	07	24 a	aa	CHW	12	8	28	0	161	178	81	5	49	140	4.53	1.41	24.9	274	2.8	7.8	2.8	0.3	35%	66%	97
	08	25	a/a	CHW	4	12	25	0	133	174	95	22	46	103	6.40	1.65	24.4	309	3.1	6.9	2.2	1.5	36%	63%	37
Ekstrom,Michael	07	24	aa	SD	7	10	27	0	143	218	95	6	52	81	5.95	1.88	25.5	343	3.2	5.1	1.6	0.4	40%	66%	38
	08	25	aa	SD	11	8	41	1	108	166	67	14	38	77	5.56	1.88	12.7	344	3.1	6.5	2.0	1.2	40%	72%	32
Elarton,Scott	07	32	a/a	CLE	4	4	19	0	71	98	56	17	28	31	7.04	1.77	17.5	320	3.5	3.9	1.1	2.1	32%	64%	-26
Elbert,Scott	08	23 a	aa	LA	4	1	25	0	41	25	12	2	20	41	2.71	1.08	6.6	171	4.3	8.9	2.1	0.5	23%	76%	104
Elliott,Matthew	07	23	aa	ARI	1	6	46	5	63	72	39	8	34	59	5.60	1.69	6.3	282	4.9	8.5	1.7	1.2	35%	68%	51
Ellis,Jonathan	07	25	aa	SD	3	4	55	2	51	57	34	8	35	33	5.93	1.79	4.4	276	6.1	5.9	1.0	1.5	30%	70%	11
	08	26	aa	SD	10	7	60	1	77	97	36	5	38	53	4.16	1.74	6.0	300	4.4	6.2	1.4	0.5	36%	76%	45
Embry,Byron	07	31	aa	SEA	0	6	25	4	36	51	32	5	38	31	7.92	2.44	7.7	324	9.4	7.8	0.8	1.2	39%	68%	20
Englebrook,Evan	08	26	aa	HOU	2	2	34	4	55	66	29	3	26	24	4.69	1.67	7.4	289	4.3	4.0	0.9	0.6	32%	71%	23
Ennis,John	07	28	aaa	PHI	4	4	37	1	88	111	44	9	35	67	4.52	1.65	10.9	301	3.6	6.9	1.9	1.0	36%	74%	48
	08	29	aaa	PHI	4	3	40	0	55	71	30	8	19	47	4.93	1.64	6.3	306	3.2	7.8	2.5	1.2	37%	73%	55
Espineli,Eugene	07	25	aa	SF	8	10	29	0	140	179	71	9	40	81	4.56	1.56	21.7	304	2.6	5.2	2.0	0.6	35%	70%	51
	08	26	aa	SF	1	1	38	1	61	75	26	2	13	36	3.90	1.43	7.0	296	1.9	5.3	2.8	0.3	35%	72%	77
Esposito,Mike	07	26	aa	COL	5	6	28	1	109	197	110	24	47	40	9.09	2.23	20.1	381	3.9	3.3	0.8	2.0	39%	61%	-43
Estes,Shawn	08	36	aa	SD	5	2	8	0	44	58	24	4	12	21	4.79	1.57	24.8	309	2.4	4.3	1.8	0.7	34%	70%	36
Estrada,Jesse	08	25	aa	CHC	7	3	39	1	75	99	51	12	24	50	6.05	1.64	8.8	311	2.9	6.0	2.1	1.4	35%	65%	31
Estrada,Marco	08	25	a/a	WAS	9	6	25	0	139	152	53	7	53	95	3.40	1.47	24.4	272	3.4	6.1	1.8	0.5	33%	77%	61
Estrada,Paul	07	25	aa	HOU	1	8	53	8	70	91	53	8	47	52	6.85	1.97	6.5	308	6.0	6.7	1.1	1.0	36%	65%	27
Evans,Cody	08	25	aa	ARI	5	8	33	0	74	100	52	13	31	35	6.34	1.77	10.5	316	3.8	4.3	1.1	1.6	33%	67%	-8
Evans,Dustin	08	24	aa	ATL	1	5	8	0	31	64	46	2	19	17	13.40	2.67	21.7	414	5.5	4.9	0.9	0.6	47%	45%	3
Fairchild,Thomas	08	25	aa	HOU	2	8	22	1	61	86	65	11	31	36	9.61	1.91	13.4	326	4.5	5.3	1.2	1.6	36%	49%	0
Falkenborg,Brian	07	30	aa	STL	3	4	51	23	52	80	28	3	21	38	4.83	1.94	5.0	344	3.7	6.6	1.8	0.5	42%	74%	50
	08	31	aa	LA	1	1	32	13	35	51	23	4	11	26	5.88	1.80	5.2	335	2.9	6.7	2.3	1.1	39%	68%	43
Faris,Stephen	08	24	aa	SD	8	5	26	0	138	165	68	8	41	83	4.46	1.50	23.4	291	2.7	5.4	2.0	0.5	34%	70%	55
Farley,Christopher	08	26	aa	OAK	2	2	36	1	62	71	36	6	33	47	5.14	1.68	7.9	281	4.8	6.8	1.4	0.8	34%	70%	45
Feierabend,Ryan	07	22	aa	SEA	6	4	19	0	108	147	56	9	35	63	4.66	1.68	26.2	318	2.9	5.2	1.8	0.7	36%	73%	38
	08	23	aa	SEA	7	1	13	0	75	72	20	5	15	42	2.35	1.17	23.6	248	1.9	5.0	2.7	0.6	28%	83%	74
Feldkamp,Derek	07	24	aa	TAM	2	7	22	0	77	118	71	19	29	44	8.23	1.91	16.9	344	3.4	5.1	1.5	2.2	36%	60%	-18
Feldman,Scott	07	25	aa	TEX	1	1	21	2	30	35	20	1	13	20	6.00	1.58	6.4	284	3.8	6.0	1.6	0.3	34%	59%	58
Felix,Francisco	08	25	aa	LA	0	1	15	1	31	39	24	6	12	24	7.10	1.65	9.4	301	3.5	7.1	2.0	1.6	35%	59%	31
Feliz,Neftali	08	20 a	aa	TEX	4	3	10	0	45	35	16	1	21	42	3.23	1.25	18.8	211	4.2	8.4	2.0	0.2	29%	72%	99
Fernandez,Jason	08	24	aa	OAK	1	4	9	0	40	56	28	3	19	27	6.23	1.85	21.3	322	4.2	6.1	1.5	0.7	38%	65%	37
Field,Nate	07	32	aa	FLA	6	6	44	11	46	48	25	7	21	35	4.82	1.51	4.6	264	4.1	6.8	1.6	1.4	30%	72%	36
	08	33	aa	NYM	1	3	50	13	50	55	35	11	33	41	6.35	1.76	4.7	275	5.9	7.3	1.2	1.9	31%	68%	13
Fien,Casey	08	25	a/a	DET	5	3	52	13	60	60	23	7	15	50	3.39	1.25	4.8	254	2.3	7.5	3.3	1.1	31%	77%	86
Figueroa,Nelson	08	34	aa	NYM	4	7	20	0	113	159	76	18	38	71	6.08	1.74	26.4	325	3.0	5.7	1.9	1.4	36%	67%	22
Fillinger,Chad	07	25	aa	SEA	1	2	20	1	33	41	23	3	15	28	6.30	1.69	7.6	298	4.0	7.5	1.9	0.9	37%	62%	54
Fisher,Charles	07	25	aa	CIN	5	9	21	0	113	162	74	16	47	72	5.92	1.85	25.7	329	3.7	5.7	1.5	1.2	37%	70%	19
	08	26	a/a	CIN	6	5	50	8	68	83	30	4	32	52	3.97	1.70	6.3	296	4.3	6.9	1.6	0.6	36%	77%	54
Fiske,Justin	08	24	aa	STL	4	0	26	0	69	71	26	4	28	60	3.42	1.43	11.6	259	3.7	7.8	2.1	0.5	33%	77%	78
Fister,Douglas	07	24	aa	SEA	7	8	24	0	131	180	80	15	35	74	5.52	1.64	24.9	320	2.4	5.1	2.1	1.1	36%	68%	34
	08	25	aa	SEA	6	14	31	0	134	179	96	13	48	88	6.43	1.70	20.0	314	3.2	5.9	1.8	0.8	36%	61%	41
Flanagan,Jeremy	07	26	aa	TAM	5	3	40	1	76	114	61	10	41	30	7.21	2.04	9.4	339	4.9	3.6	0.7	1.2	36%	65%	-12
Flannery,Mike	07	28	aa	OAK	0	2	30	1	35	53	39	4	33	22	9.96	2.43	6.2	339	8.4	5.8	0.7	1.0	39%	57%	7
Flores,Ron	07	28	aa	OAK	1	2	40	1	36	54	16	5	20	18	4.05	2.04	4.5	338	5.0	4.4	0.9	1.2	37%	84%	-5
	08	29	aa	STL	7	4	59	4	63	103	43	7	40	38	6.09	2.26	5.5	358	5.7	5.3	0.9	1.0	41%	74%	7
Floyd,Gavin	07	25	aaa	CHW	7	3	17	0	106	113	51	13	36	85	4.32	1.40	27.0	267	3.1	7.2	2.4	1.1	32%	72%	61
Floyd,Jesse	07	27	aa	MIN	7	9	27	0	130	179	99	20	61	70	6.84	1.85	23.0	321	4.2	4.9	1.2	1.4	35%	64%	4
Foley,Travis	07	25	aa	OAK	5	4	46	4	54	63	36	3	23	46	5.96	1.60	5.3	286	3.9	7.6	2.0	0.5	36%	61%	69
Foli,Daniel	07	27	a/a	WAS	0	2	24	1	45	69	40	4	34	35	8.00	2.30	9.8	344	6.9	7.0	1.0	0.9	41%	64%	23
Foppert,Jesse	08	28	aa	SF	2	1	24	1	41	66	55	11	54	19	12.04	2.92	10.0	356	11.8	4.2	0.4	2.5	36%	60%	-57
Forystek,Brian	07	29	aa	MIN	1	1	16	1	40	56	31	3	28	26	7.03	2.09	12.5	325	6.2	5.8	0.9	0.6	38%	65%	27
Fossum,Casey	08	31	aaa	DET	3	0	11	0	46	27	13	4	20	38	2.61	1.01	16.5	166	3.9	7.4	1.9	0.9	19%	79%	80
Fowler,Eric	07	25	aa	TOR	4	4	9	0	40	77	41	9	19	17	9.21	2.39	23.7	396	4.3	3.8	0.9	2.1	41%	63%	-46
French,Lucas	08	23	aa	DET	9	11	27	0	170	220	87	16	58	76	4.58	1.63	28.7	307	3.1	4.0	1.3	0.9	33%	73%	19
Fritz,Benjamin	07	27	aa	OAK	11	11	28	0	149	226	130	10	75	65	7.85	2.02	26.3	342	4.5	3.9	0.9	0.6	38%	59%	10
	08	28	aa	DET	3	5	18	0	84	153	80	16	33	33	8.51	2.21	24.0	384	3.5	3.6	1.0	1.7	40%	62%	-29
Fruto,Emiliano	07	23	a/a	ARI	3	10	24	0	98	96	63	7	66	72	5.78	1.65	18.7	251	6.1	6.6	1.1	0.6	30%	64%	48
	08	24	aa	ARI	6	6	49	2	89	109	72	25	62	86	7.24	1.93	8.8	296	6.3	8.7	1.4	2.6	34%	68%	1
Fukumori,Kazuo	08	32	aa	TEX	1	6	38	2	64	102	52	9	20	29	7.28	1.91	8.1	354	2.8	4.1	1.4	1.3	38%	63%	-1
Fulchino,Jeff	07	28	aa	FLA	6	2	16	0	88	146	80	16	48	42	8.13	2.20	28.2	362	4.9	4.2	0.9	1.6	39%	64%	-22
	08	29	aa	KC	3	4	27	6	64	109	56	3	35	42	7.89	2.24	12.3	367	4.9	5.8	1.2	0.4	43%	62%	31
Fussell,Christopher	07	31	aa	LA	4	1	24	2	38	54	36	7	27	25	8.64	2.14	8.0	328	6.4	5.8	0.9	1.7	36%	60%	-7
Gabbard,Kason	07	25	aaa	BOS	7	2	14	0	75	81	37	11	26	54	4.48	1.43	23.3	270	3.2	6.5	2.1	1.3	31%	73%	44
Gabino,Armando	08	25	aa	MIN	6	5	49	3	81	104	37	7	36	45	4.07	1.73	7.7	306	3.9	5.0	1.3	0.7	35%	78%	28
Gagnier,Lauren	08	24	a/a	DET	5	5	11	0	50	70	51	6	28	36	9.16	1.96	22.2	324	5.0	6.5	1.3	1.1	38%	51%	24
Galarraga,Armando	07	26	aa	TEX	11	8	27	0	152	191	101	21	64	104	5.98	1.68	25.9	301	3.8	6.1	1.6	1.2	34%	66%	28
Gallagher,Sean	07	22	aa	CHC	10	3	19	0	101	101	44	5	38	76	3.91	1.37	22.9	255	3.4	6.8	2.0	0.4	31%	71%	73
Gallardo,Yovani	07	22 a	aaa	MIL	8	3	13	0	77	56	29	5	27	110	3.39	1.08	23.8	200	3.2	12.8	4.0	0.5	32%	69%	161
Gallo,Mike	07	31	aa	COL	2	6	56	6	60	111	67	13	41	27	10.07	2.55	5.9	389	6.2	4.1	0.7	1.9	41%	61%	-42
Gamble,Jerome	08	29	aa	ATL	3	10	31	0	98	127	81	12	46	56	7.45	1.76	14.8	307	4.2	5.2	1.2	1.1	34%	57%	18
Garcia,Anderson	07	27	a/a	PHI	1	7	51	11	77	101	54	11	24	47	6.36	1.63	6.9	310	2.9	5.5	1.9	1.3	35%	62%	27
Garcia,Dumas	08	25	aa	CHC	2	2	33	2	47	46	22	4	29	32	4.24	1.58	6.4	248	5.5	6.2	1.1	0.8	29%	75%	41

					Actual				Major League Equivalents																
PITCHER	Yr	Age	Lev	Org	w	l	g	sv	ip	h	er	hr	bb	k	era	whip	bf/g	oob	ctl	dom	cmd	hr/9	h%	s%	bpv
Garcia,Edgar	08	21	aa	PHI	1	7	11	0	58	75	57	11	28	29	8.84	1.78	24.8	307	4.3	4.5	1.0	1.7	32%	50%	-9
Garcia,Harvey	07	24	aa	FLA	6	3	60	1	72	92	53	12	41	62	6.56	1.84	5.7	304	5.1	7.7	1.5	1.5	36%	67%	26
Garcia,Jaime	07	21	aa	STL	5	9	18	0	103	103	48	14	43	85	4.19	1.42	24.8	255	3.8	7.4	2.0	1.2	30%	74%	53
	08	22	aa	STL	7	6	19	0	106	108	46	5	38	86	3.91	1.38	24.0	259	3.2	7.3	2.3	0.4	33%	71%	82
Garcia,Jose	07	26	aa	STL	2	2	18	0	36	61	30	9	13	17	7.47	2.04	9.9	367	3.2	4.1	1.3	2.3	38%	68%	-35
Garcia,Rosman	07	29	aa	BAL	3	5	33	1	86	153	85	9	45	40	8.90	2.30	13.6	378	4.7	4.2	0.9	0.9	42%	60%	-4
Gardner,Michael	07	26	aa	NYY	3	5	44	2	81	105	45	1	38	47	4.97	1.76	8.6	306	4.2	5.2	1.2	0.1	36%	69%	47
	08	27	aa	NYY	3	5	33	5	53	80	55	11	53	35	9.41	2.50	8.7	339	9.0	5.9	0.7	1.8	37%	63%	-19
Gardner,Richard	07	26	a/a	CIN	6	6	19	0	99	135	64	15	31	60	5.83	1.67	23.9	318	2.8	5.4	2.0	1.3	35%	67%	25
	08	27	aaa	MIL	6	5	30	1	120	156	76	18	66	74	5.72	1.85	19.1	308	4.9	5.5	1.1	1.3	34%	71%	11
Garrison,Stevenson	08	22	aa	SD	7	7	24	0	129	134	60	12	37	92	4.18	1.32	22.8	262	2.6	6.4	2.5	0.8	31%	70%	68
Garr,Brennan	08	25	aa	TEX	2	1	32	7	44	51	22	2	26	44	4.52	1.75	6.4	282	5.4	8.9	1.7	0.4	38%	73%	74
Garza,Matt	07	24	aaa	MIN	4	6	16	0	92	116	54	6	35	77	5.28	1.64	26.2	302	3.4	7.5	2.2	0.6	38%	67%	68
Gassner,Dave	07	29	aaa	MIN	6	12	26	0	149	214	128	23	52	63	7.73	1.78	26.9	330	3.1	3.8	1.2	1.4	35%	57%	-3
	08	30	aa	BOS	8	5	16	0	82	165	85	15	20	20	9.37	2.26	26.5	408	2.2	2.2	1.0	1.6	42%	59%	-40
Geer,Joshua	07	24	aa	SD	17	6	27	0	177	202	79	11	31	89	4.01	1.31	27.8	281	1.6	4.5	2.9	0.5	32%	69%	71
	08	25	aa	SD	8	9	28	0	166	226	102	22	50	82	5.54	1.66	27.2	317	2.7	4.4	1.6	1.2	34%	68%	16
George,Chris	07	28	aa	FLA	7	11	26	0	139	219	124	26	88	70	8.01	2.20	27.4	350	5.7	4.5	0.8	1.7	37%	65%	-22
	08	29	a/a	TOR	1	6	49	1	67	118	67	7	43	41	8.98	2.40	7.3	376	5.7	5.5	1.0	1.0	43%	61%	3
George,Jonathan	08	24	aa	COL	0	2	25	0	40	55	32	11	7	15	7.07	1.54	7.2	318	1.6	3.4	2.1	2.4	31%	59%	-16
Germano,Justin	07	25 a	aa	SD	4	0	5	0	32	29	8	0	3	15	2.19	1.01	25.1	236	0.9	4.3	4.6	0.0	28%	76%	130
	08	26	aa	SD	2	9	17	0	98	148	76	13	29	50	6.97	1.81	27.2	341	2.6	4.6	1.7	1.2	37%	62%	15
German,Franklyn	07	28	aa	TEX	2	2	47	7	59	63	36	7	55	51	5.50	2.00	6.2	266	8.4	7.8	0.9	1.1	32%	74%	35
	08	29	a/a	CHW	2	2	29	0	34	42	22	7	28	24	5.92	2.08	5.9	299	7.5	6.3	0.8	1.9	33%	76%	-5
Gervacio,Samuel	08	24	aa	HOU	3	5	50	5	73	81	34	8	28	80	4.19	1.49	6.5	276	3.4	9.8	2.9	1.0	37%	74%	88
Giese,Dan	07	30	aa	SF	3	1	47	2	73	106	39	3	14	46	4.75	1.64	7.1	331	1.8	5.6	3.2	0.4	39%	70%	79
	08	31	aaa	NYY	4	2	13	0	59	54	18	2	15	41	2.73	1.16	18.5	238	2.2	6.2	2.8	0.3	29%	76%	93
Ginter,Matt	07	30	a/a	MIL	2	6	32	2	69	126	52	7	13	32	6.83	2.01	10.6	384	1.7	4.2	2.4	1.0	42%	66%	25
	08	31	aaa	CLE	6	6	18	0	100	147	74	13	38	52	6.70	1.84	26.5	334	3.4	4.7	1.4	1.2	37%	64%	9
Giron,Roberto	07	32	aa	KC	2	5	39	6	85	80	51	16	34	69	5.36	1.34	9.3	244	3.6	7.3	2.0	1.7	27%	65%	40
	08	33	aa	KC	3	3	20	1	43	56	42	16	20	29	8.86	1.78	10.1	310	4.2	6.0	1.4	3.4	30%	57%	-44
Gissell,Chris	08	31	aa	OAK	7	3	25	1	81	120	46	13	24	40	5.07	1.78	15.2	336	2.7	4.4	1.6	1.4	36%	75%	6
Glant,Dustin	07	26	aa	ARI	5	3	47	5	79	124	59	10	30	45	6.68	1.95	8.2	350	3.4	5.2	1.5	1.2	39%	66%	12
	08	27	aa	ARI	3	3	40	0	74	153	98	11	52	43	11.85	2.76	10.5	414	6.3	5.2	0.8	1.3	46%	55%	-18
Glen,William	08	31	aa	FLA	9	5	25	0	96	101	44	9	59	57	4.15	1.67	17.6	266	5.5	5.3	1.0	0.8	30%	76%	30
Gogal,Jeff	08	26	aa	FLA	6	2	47	1	58	70	25	7	29	49	3.92	1.70	5.7	292	4.5	7.5	1.7	1.1	35%	80%	45
Gomez,Mariano	07	25	aa	CLE	3	3	48	2	66	69	41	7	28	43	5.59	1.46	6.0	263	3.8	5.9	1.6	0.9	30%	62%	43
	08	26	aaa	MIN	5	2	54	1	65	78	24	3	23	36	3.28	1.55	5.4	292	3.1	5.0	1.6	0.4	34%	79%	47
Gonzalez III,Jino	08	26	aa	TAM	2	4	37	2	87	114	70	8	64	52	7.24	2.04	11.7	309	6.6	5.4	0.8	0.8	35%	64%	18
Gonzalez,Alfredo	08	29	aa	TEX	5	2	36	2	75	129	60	13	25	39	7.19	2.06	10.4	371	3.0	4.7	1.5	1.6	40%	67%	-7
Gonzalez,Enrique	07	25	aa	ARI	8	10	27	0	153	241	124	16	68	94	7.31	2.02	28.0	350	4.0	5.5	1.4	0.9	40%	63%	20
	08	26	aa	SD	7	5	35	0	99	132	62	10	57	61	5.64	1.91	13.7	314	5.2	5.5	1.1	0.9	36%	71%	20
Gonzalez,Gio	07	22 a	aa	CHW	9	7	27	0	150	142	74	15	61	165	4.44	1.35	23.7	245	3.7	9.9	2.7	0.9	33%	69%	95
	08	23	aa	OAK	8	7	23	0	123	116	63	11	56	106	4.60	1.40	23.1	245	4.1	7.7	1.9	0.8	30%	68%	67
Gonzalez,Luis	07	25	aa	LA	3	4	33	3	42	31	24	2	54	41	5.19	2.01	6.3	199	11.5	8.8	0.8	0.5	27%	73%	70
Gonzalez,Marco	08	24	aa	STL	7	0	47	2	57	54	26	4	21	29	4.14	1.31	5.1	243	3.3	4.5	1.4	0.7	27%	69%	42
Gonzalez,Miguel	07	23	aa	LAA	8	4	30	1	130	154	64	14	44	67	4.42	1.52	19.3	288	3.1	4.6	1.5	1.0	32%	73%	27
Goocher,Clint	07	25	aa	ARI	5	4	52	6	76	91	41	10	26	52	4.86	1.53	6.5	291	3.0	6.2	2.0	1.2	33%	71%	41
Goodson,Matthew	08	26	aa	BOS	4	4	14	0	59	89	51	10	34	30	7.70	2.08	21.1	339	5.3	4.6	0.9	1.6	36%	64%	-14
Gordon,Brian	07	29	aa	HOU	6	2	39	1	61	88	35	7	27	32	5.11	1.88	7.5	330	3.9	4.8	1.2	1.0	37%	74%	13
	08	30	aa	TEX	6	5	34	3	95	151	60	23	27	42	5.68	1.88	13.4	353	2.6	4.0	1.5	2.2	36%	76%	-24
Gorzelanny,Tom	08	26 b	aa	PIT	3	1	7	0	35	37	11	1	5	24	2.96	1.18	20.5	265	1.2	6.3	5.3	0.3	32%	74%	142
Gosling,Mike	07	27	aaa	CIN	5	3	13	0	78	88	36	9	25	53	4.13	1.46	26.3	280	2.9	6.1	2.1	1.1	32%	75%	47
	08	28	aaa	TOR	5	6	58	7	68	101	41	4	26	49	5.39	1.86	5.6	337	3.4	6.5	1.9	0.6	40%	70%	50
Gothreaux,Jared	07	28	aa	HOU	5	8	36	1	133	213	105	28	47	52	7.08	1.95	18.0	354	3.2	3.5	1.1	1.9	36%	67%	-27
	08	29	aa	TOR	1	6	37	1	79	156	85	14	39	30	9.67	2.47	11.5	404	4.4	3.5	0.8	1.6	43%	61%	-35
Graves,Danny	08	35	a/a	MIN	6	6	32	1	94	154	82	11	36	29	7.86	2.02	14.5	360	3.4	2.8	0.8	1.1	38%	60%	-15
Gray,Jeffrey	07	26	aa	OAK	4	4	54	15	67	82	33	2	26	44	4.47	1.61	5.6	296	3.4	5.9	1.7	0.3	36%	71%	59
	08	27	aa	OAK	2	7	54	4	67	105	40	9	23	37	5.39	1.90	6.0	348	3.1	5.0	1.6	1.2	39%	74%	13
Green,Matthew	07	26	aa	ARI	12	6	28	0	148	197	91	21	61	102	5.54	1.74	24.6	313	3.7	6.2	1.7	1.3	36%	70%	26
	08	27	aa	ARI	3	2	17	0	53	91	51	15	21	32	8.56	2.10	15.7	369	3.5	5.4	1.6	2.5	39%	63%	-29
Green,Nick	07	23	aa	LAA	10	8	28	0	178	197	95	20	34	88	4.79	1.30	26.8	275	1.7	4.5	2.6	1.0	30%	64%	52
	08	24	aa	LAA	8	8	28	0	159	222	119	33	45	92	6.73	1.68	26.1	324	2.6	5.2	2.0	1.8	35%	63%	9
Green,Steve	07	30	aaa	BAL	2	4	52	3	67	98	56	9	42	55	7.52	2.08	6.5	333	5.6	7.3	1.3	1.2	40%	64%	24
	08	31	aaa	PHI	5	1	35	0	66	73	33	6	34	53	4.55	1.63	8.6	276	4.7	7.2	1.5	0.8	34%	73%	53
Gregerson,Luke	08	24	aa	STL	7	6	57	10	75	71	32	5	25	64	3.78	1.28	5.5	243	3.0	7.6	2.5	0.6	31%	71%	86
Gronkiewicz,Lee	07	29 b	a/a	TOR	6	3	47	13	74	98	30	11	12	58	3.70	1.48	6.9	310	1.5	7.1	4.8	1.3	36%	80%	96
Grube,Jarrett	07	26	aa	COL	7	3	52	0	67	78	29	6	23	49	3.87	1.50	5.7	284	3.1	6.5	2.1	0.7	34%	76%	59
	08	27	aa	COL	4	3	49	0	67	89	41	14	34	34	5.54	1.83	6.5	311	4.6	4.5	1.0	1.8	32%	75%	-15
Gryboski,Kevin	08	35	aa	SF	2	6	52	10	53	91	58	12	29	23	9.75	2.26	5.3	368	5.0	3.9	0.8	2.0	38%	58%	-39
Guevara,Carlos	07	26 a	aa	CIN	1	2	51	16	62	66	22	6	26	67	3.23	1.47	5.3	266	3.7	9.7	2.6	0.8	36%	81%	90
Gulin,Lindsay	07	31	a/a	MIL	12	6	24	0	129	163	78	24	63	88	5.40	1.74	25.1	301	4.4	6.1	1.4	1.7	33%	73%	11
	08	32	aaa	MIL	7	7	26	0	137	126	61	17	76	104	4.01	1.47	23.2	240	5.0	6.8	1.4	1.1	28%	76%	43
Gunderson,Kevin	08	24	aa	ATL	2	2	36	3	43	54	28	2	15	18	5.92	1.58	5.4	299	3.1	3.8	1.2	0.4	33%	60%	30
Gutierrez,Juan	07	24	aa	HOU	5	10	26	0	156	184	91	21	66	86	5.22	1.61	27.2	288	3.8	5.0	1.3	1.2	32%	70%	18
	08	25	aa	ARI	5	11	25	0	116	200	114	16	49	69	8.86	2.14	23.5	371	3.8	5.4	1.4	1.2	42%	58%	7
Gwyn,Marc	07	30	aa	LAA	2	1	47	15	57	105	39	8	23	35	6.11	2.25	6.3	388	3.6	5.4	1.5	1.3	44%	74%	4
	08	31	aa	FLA	1	0	36	5	44	70	33	6	26	24	6.72	2.18	6.2	353	5.3	4.9	0.9	1.2	39%	70%	-2
Haberer,Eric	07	25	aa	STL	13	8	28	0	152	199	91	13	77	57	5.39	1.81	25.7	309	4.5	3.4	0.7	0.8	33%	70%	5
Hacker,Eric	08	26	aa	NYY	7	4	17	0	91	112	43	4	33	63	4.28	1.60	24.2	297	3.3	6.2	1.9	0.4	36%	72%	60
Hackman,Luther	07	33	a/a	TEX	1	3	45	18	46	47	24	6	28	30	4.77	1.61	4.6	257	5.4	5.8	1.1	1.1	29%	73%	28
Haeger,Charlie	07	24	aaa	CHW	5	16	24	0	147	168	92	24	71	112	5.63	1.62	27.9	281	4.3	6.8	1.6	1.5	32%	68%	29
	08	25	aaa	CHW	10	13	28	0	178	200	116	18	80	103	5.87	1.57	28.6	278	4.0	5.2	1.3	0.9	31%	63%	30

Major League Equivalent Statistics

PITCHER	Yr	Age	Lev	Org	Actual				Major League Equivalents																
					w	l	g	sv	ip	h	er	hr	bb	k	era	whip	bf/g	oob	ctl	dom	cmd	hr/9	h%	s%	bpv
Haehnel,David	07	25	aa	BAL	2	1	40	0	69	88	61	10	50	45	7.97	2.00	8.5	303	6.5	5.9	0.9	1.3	34%	60%	9
Haigwood,Daniel	07	24	aa	BOS	3	5	17	0	69	80	56	12	51	60	7.26	1.90	19.6	285	6.6	7.8	1.2	1.6	34%	63%	22
	08	25	aa	BOS	2	3	38	1	67	66	32	6	43	57	4.24	1.63	8.0	253	5.8	7.7	1.3	0.8	31%	76%	53
Halama,John	08	37	aaa	CLE	8	6	16	0	107	156	78	17	21	35	6.54	1.65	30.6	332	1.8	3.0	1.7	1.4	34%	62%	-1
Hale,Beau	07	29	aa	BAL	6	5	15	0	71	130	61	10	34	30	7.74	2.30	24.8	385	4.3	3.8	0.9	1.3	41%	67%	-18
Hall,Bo	07	27	aa	MIL	5	2	34	1	54	58	31	8	46	42	5.20	1.91	7.7	268	7.6	7.0	0.9	1.4	31%	76%	21
	08	28	a/a	HOU	5	3	32	2	54	79	41	16	21	30	6.86	1.85	8.1	333	3.5	5.0	1.4	2.7	34%	70%	-35
Hall,Josh	07	27	a/a	WAS	3	4	31	1	67	79	44	3	38	36	5.97	1.74	10.1	287	5.1	4.8	1.0	0.4	33%	64%	33
	08	28	aa	COL	4	8	15	0	75	133	77	16	37	28	9.24	2.26	25.9	377	4.5	3.4	0.8	1.9	39%	60%	-40
Hamilton,Clayton	08	26	aa	TEX	1	3	20	1	35	43	26	6	14	12	6.80	1.61	7.9	294	3.5	3.1	0.9	1.5	30%	59%	-11
Hamman,Corey	07	27	a/a	DET	1	9	35	1	83	149	69	18	34	36	7.46	2.21	12.2	381	3.7	3.9	1.0	2.0	40%	69%	-36
	08	28	aa	PIT	9	9	28	0	133	209	94	15	54	52	6.34	1.97	23.3	349	3.6	3.5	1.0	1.0	37%	68%	-4
Hammel,Jason	07	25	aaa	TAM	4	5	13	0	76	75	40	4	30	65	4.78	1.38	25.2	252	3.6	7.7	2.2	0.5	32%	64%	82
Hammes,Zachary	07	23	aa	LA	5	8	26	0	94	127	66	12	31	65	6.30	1.67	16.6	316	3.0	6.2	2.1	1.2	36%	63%	38
	08	24	aa	LA	2	5	38	4	59	71	41	3	37	39	6.25	1.82	7.4	290	5.6	5.9	1.1	0.5	35%	64%	40
Hammond,Steve	07	25	aa	MIL	7	9	29	1	142	211	103	24	51	89	6.55	1.85	23.3	337	3.2	5.6	1.7	1.5	37%	67%	12
	08	26	a/a	SF	12	11	28	0	155	199	99	18	57	101	5.74	1.65	25.3	305	3.3	5.8	1.8	1.0	35%	66%	35
Hand,Donovan	08	22	aa	MIL	3	4	16	0	81	110	51	11	26	37	5.66	1.68	23.3	317	2.9	4.1	1.4	1.2	34%	68%	9
Hankins,Derek	08	25	aa	PIT	2	11	24	0	119	174	83	17	29	68	6.30	1.71	23.0	334	2.2	5.1	2.3	1.3	37%	64%	30
Hanrahan,Joel	07	26	aaa	WAS	5	4	15	0	75	77	39	11	37	58	4.72	1.52	22.2	259	4.5	7.0	1.6	1.3	30%	73%	38
Hansack,Devern	07	30	aaa	BOS	10	7	25	0	139	167	84	20	46	102	5.40	1.53	24.8	291	3.0	6.6	2.2	1.3	34%	67%	44
	08	31	aaa	BOS	6	10	25	0	139	159	88	19	46	98	5.68	1.47	24.4	281	2.9	6.4	2.2	1.2	32%	63%	45
Hansen,Craig	07	24	aaa	BOS	3	1	40	3	51	70	30	2	34	41	5.28	2.04	6.3	319	6.0	7.2	1.2	0.4	40%	73%	49
Hanson,Thomas	08	22 a	aa	ATL	8	4	18	0	98	78	38	9	41	99	3.49	1.21	22.5	214	3.8	9.1	2.4	0.8	28%	74%	93
Happ,J.A.	07	25	aaa	PHI	4	6	24	0	118	138	84	15	65	100	6.40	1.72	22.8	286	5.0	7.6	1.5	1.1	35%	63%	42
	08	26	aaa	PHI	8	7	24	0	135	138	71	19	52	127	4.71	1.41	24.3	260	3.4	8.4	2.5	1.3	32%	70%	67
Harang,Daryl	08	26	aa	TOR	4	6	59	2	65	90	48	8	44	41	6.61	2.07	5.5	321	6.1	5.6	0.9	1.1	36%	68%	11
Hardy,Rowdy	08	26	aa	KC	6	11	28	0	155	254	122	17	34	69	7.09	1.86	26.5	360	2.0	4.0	2.0	1.0	39%	61%	20
Harikkala,Tim	07	36	aa	COL	3	1	8	0	32	55	25	4	13	9	6.91	2.12	20.3	370	3.6	2.4	0.7	1.0	39%	67%	-21
Harrell,Lucas	08	23	aa	CHW	3	3	11	0	54	70	30	4	21	29	4.96	1.67	22.6	307	3.4	4.8	1.4	0.7	35%	70%	32
Harrison,Matt	07	22	aa	ATL	5	7	20	0	116	138	56	7	35	67	4.34	1.49	25.6	289	2.7	5.2	1.9	0.5	33%	70%	52
	08	23	aa	TEX	6	3	15	0	84	101	37	6	28	46	3.98	1.53	24.9	292	3.0	4.9	1.6	0.7	33%	75%	40
Harris,Jeff	07	33	aaa	CLE	6	9	27	0	138	174	92	25	39	71	5.97	1.54	22.8	301	2.5	4.6	1.8	1.6	32%	65%	12
	08	34	aaa	CLE	3	5	18	1	79	121	62	18	20	47	7.08	1.79	20.7	344	2.3	5.3	2.3	2.0	37%	64%	6
Hart,Kevin	07	25	aa	CHC	12	6	27	0	158	192	93	25	54	105	5.28	1.55	26.2	293	3.1	6.0	1.9	1.4	33%	69%	30
	08	26	aa	CHC	4	2	27	5	60	49	23	3	24	50	3.49	1.22	9.2	218	3.7	7.5	2.1	0.5	28%	71%	85
Harville,Chad	07	31	aa	ARI	6	4	46	24	52	60	32	7	25	32	5.50	1.63	5.1	283	4.3	5.6	1.3	1.2	32%	68%	23
Hawksworth,Blake	07	25	aa	STL	4	13	25	0	129	174	91	24	41	74	6.31	1.66	23.7	315	2.9	5.2	1.8	1.7	34%	65%	10
	08	26	aa	STL	5	7	18	0	88	133	72	12	39	64	7.37	1.95	23.9	341	4.0	6.5	1.6	1.2	40%	63%	23
Hayes,Chris	08	26	aa	KC	5	2	40	12	65	64	17	4	14	31	2.30	1.21	6.7	253	2.0	4.2	2.1	0.6	28%	84%	56
Hayhurst,Dirk	07	27	aa	SD	4	1	34	2	62	82	38	10	10	43	5.51	1.48	8.0	311	1.5	6.2	4.1	1.5	35%	66%	71
	08	28	aa	SD	2	3	46	2	84	110	46	7	34	70	4.91	1.71	8.4	309	3.6	7.5	2.1	0.8	38%	72%	58
Heath,Deunte	08	23	aa	ATL	4	5	13	0	66	88	48	5	33	39	6.60	1.82	24.1	312	4.5	5.3	1.2	0.7	36%	63%	28
Hedrick,Justin	07	25	aa	SF	4	6	41	1	71	69	22	4	40	56	2.81	1.53	7.7	249	5.1	7.1	1.4	0.6	31%	83%	60
	08	26	aa	SF	2	3	43	9	65	55	15	5	24	55	2.06	1.22	6.3	225	3.3	7.6	2.3	0.6	28%	86%	84
Hellickson,Jeremy	08	22	aa	TAM	4	4	13	0	75	93	38	16	15	68	4.55	1.44	25.2	298	1.8	8.1	4.5	1.9	35%	76%	82
Henderson,Brian	07	25	aa	TAM	6	3	59	1	66	79	29	7	28	36	3.93	1.61	5.1	290	3.8	4.9	1.3	0.9	32%	78%	26
	08	26	a/a	TAM	1	3	44	1	50	77	32	7	26	23	5.79	2.04	5.6	344	4.6	4.0	0.9	1.2	37%	73%	-7
Henderson,Jim	07	25	aa	CHC	7	3	50	10	71	81	26	12	34	44	3.34	1.62	6.4	281	4.3	5.5	1.3	1.5	31%	86%	15
Hendrickson,Ben	07	27	aa	KC	11	5	27	0	135	180	89	11	61	50	5.90	1.79	23.6	314	4.1	3.4	0.8	0.8	34%	67%	7
	08	28	aaa	TAM	10	9	29	0	149	183	100	14	66	67	6.04	1.67	23.6	296	4.0	4.0	1.0	0.8	32%	63%	16
Hennessey,Brad	08	29	aa	SF	7	10	21	0	132	229	113	28	46	46	7.66	2.08	31.5	372	3.2	3.2	1.0	1.9	38%	66%	-36
Henn,Sean	07	26	aaa	NYY	1	2	15	0	31	32	13	1	9	23	3.88	1.33	8.8	260	2.7	6.7	2.5	0.3	32%	69%	87
Hensley,Clay	07	28	aa	SD	1	7	13	0	71	145	79	14	44	35	9.98	2.66	30.5	412	5.5	4.5	0.8	1.7	44%	63%	-36
	08	29	aa	SD	1	1	16	0	48	67	31	8	21	22	5.75	1.83	14.3	322	4.0	4.1	1.0	1.5	34%	72%	-9
Herges,Matt	07	38	aa	COL	2	1	32	1	35	34	8	4	12	25	2.11	1.31	4.6	250	3.0	6.3	2.1	0.9	29%	89%	60
Hernandez,Buddy	07	29	aaa	ATL	9	3	47	3	74	97	37	9	20	57	4.43	1.58	7.1	309	2.5	6.9	2.8	1.0	37%	74%	62
Hernandez,Chris	07	27	aa	PIT	6	4	52	7	69	88	37	7	29	45	4.86	1.69	6.1	303	3.8	5.8	1.6	0.9	35%	73%	34
	08	28	aa	PIT	4	1	27	4	39	70	31	4	8	27	7.19	1.98	7.1	380	1.7	6.3	3.6	0.9	44%	63%	67
Hernandez,David	08	23	aa	BAL	10	4	27	0	141	133	54	12	71	141	3.42	1.45	22.8	244	4.5	9.0	2.0	0.8	32%	78%	78
Hernandez,Fernando	07	23	aa	CHW	1	3	60	9	85	92	41	6	26	73	4.36	1.38	6.1	270	2.7	7.7	2.8	0.7	34%	69%	87
	08	24	aa	CHW	6	5	41	0	58	77	43	3	32	40	6.70	1.87	6.8	312	4.9	6.2	1.3	0.5	37%	62%	42
Hernandez,Gabriel	07	21	aa	FLA	9	11	28	0	153	162	85	14	58	103	4.99	1.44	23.8	266	3.4	6.1	1.8	0.8	31%	66%	51
	08	22	aa	SEA	6	9	23	0	120	169	91	20	46	84	6.83	1.79	24.6	325	3.5	6.3	1.8	1.5	37%	64%	21
Hernandez,Moises	07	24	a/a	ATL	2	3	11	0	54	74	47	9	33	19	7.80	1.97	24.1	319	5.5	3.2	0.6	1.5	33%	61%	-23
Hernandez,Runelvys	07	29	a/a	PIT	1	7	17	0	82	138	60	18	35	35	6.54	2.11	24.3	365	3.9	3.9	1.0	2.0	38%	73%	-34
	08	30	aa	HOU	8	8	24	0	124	180	100	26	57	57	7.25	1.91	25.0	332	4.1	4.1	1.0	1.9	34%	65%	-22
Hernandez,Yoel	07	27	aaa	PHI	1	3	22	5	29	41	17	0	16	13	5.19	1.95	6.5	325	4.9	4.1	0.8	0.0	37%	70%	32
Herrera,Daniel	07	23 a	aa	TEX	5	2	34	0	52	51	29	4	20	55	5.01	1.36	6.6	251	3.5	9.5	2.8	0.7	34%	63%	99
	08	24 a	a/a	CIN	7	4	58	6	72	67	26	5	17	52	3.24	1.16	5.1	241	2.1	6.5	3.1	0.6	29%	73%	91
Herrera,Yoslan	07	26	aa	PIT	6	9	25	0	128	199	93	13	43	51	6.54	1.88	24.6	347	3.0	3.6	1.2	0.9	38%	65%	6
	08	27	aa	PIT	7	9	22	0	121	169	69	13	45	52	5.10	1.76	25.8	323	3.3	3.9	1.2	1.0	35%	72%	9
Herrmann,Frank	08	24	a/a	CLE	11	8	25	0	144	187	84	12	45	86	5.21	1.61	26.1	307	2.8	5.4	1.9	0.8	35%	68%	43
Herron,Tyler	08	22	aa	STL	5	5	15	0	81	109	51	8	27	50	5.66	1.68	24.9	315	3.0	5.5	1.9	0.9	36%	66%	38
Hertzler,Barry	07	27	a/a	BOS	4	3	40	1	70	117	68	4	30	22	8.70	2.09	8.8	363	3.9	2.8	0.7	0.6	39%	55%	-3
Hietpas,Joe	08	29	aa	NYM	3	5	43	0	65	109	72	17	40	31	9.95	2.29	7.9	365	5.5	4.3	0.8	2.4	38%	59%	-48
Hill,Joshua	07	25	aa	MIN	3	2	16	0	53	67	33	2	29	35	5.52	1.82	15.8	302	5.0	5.9	1.2	0.4	36%	68%	45
	08	26	aa	PIT	4	11	22	0	111	153	78	14	53	49	6.30	1.86	24.1	321	4.3	3.9	0.9	1.2	34%	67%	-2
Hinckley,Michael	07	25	aa	WAS	9	10	25	0	117	172	94	16	61	56	7.20	1.99	23.0	334	4.7	4.3	0.9	1.2	36%	64%	-3
	08	26	a/a	WAS	5	5	43	1	90	126	53	6	58	55	5.32	2.03	10.4	323	5.8	5.5	1.0	0.6	38%	73%	27
Hines,Carlos	07	27	aa	SF	1	1	29	2	40	61	28	2	27	17	6.22	2.19	7.1	344	5.9	3.9	0.7	0.5	38%	70%	7
Hinshaw,Alex	07	25 a	aa	SF	3	1	17	0	41	26	12	2	20	41	2.54	1.13	9.8	180	4.4	8.9	2.0	0.5	24%	79%	102

					Actual				Major League Equivalents																
PITCHER	Yr	Age	Lev	Org	w	l	g	sv	ip	h	er	hr	bb	k	era	whip	bf/g	oob	ctl	dom	cmd	hr/9	h%	s%	bpv
Hinton,Robert	07	23	aa	MIL	2	3	39	2	53	60	45	5	30	39	7.70	1.69	6.3	279	5.1	6.6	1.3	0.9	33%	52%	40
	08	24	aa	MIL	3	4	30	3	53	57	37	8	32	49	6.23	1.66	8.1	268	5.3	8.4	1.6	1.4	32%	64%	42
Hirsh,Jason	08	27	aa	COL	4	4	18	0	99	145	83	20	54	38	7.52	2.01	27.1	334	4.9	3.5	0.7	1.8	34%	65%	-29
Hochevar,Luke	07	24	aa	KC	4	9	27	0	152	198	107	25	48	116	6.36	1.62	25.6	308	2.9	6.9	2.4	1.5	36%	63%	40
Hodges,Trey	07	29	aaa	ATL	6	6	30	1	122	163	91	13	74	63	6.73	1.94	19.8	313	5.4	4.6	0.9	1.0	35%	65%	9
	08	30	aa	TEX	8	8	26	0	104	179	107	23	71	45	9.25	2.40	21.3	370	6.2	3.9	0.6	2.0	38%	63%	-42
Hoelscher,Nate	07	28	aa	KC	5	3	35	3	80	122	69	12	25	32	7.73	1.84	10.9	343	2.8	3.5	1.2	1.4	36%	58%	-7
Hoey,James	07	25 a	a/a	BAL	3	0	40	16	45	34	5	1	14	58	1.03	1.07	4.5	205	2.9	11.6	4.0	0.2	32%	91%	162
Holdzkom,Lincoln	07	26	a/a	BOS	5	1	42	1	63	67	28	5	47	44	4.05	1.82	7.1	267	6.7	6.2	0.9	0.7	32%	79%	36
	08	27	aaa	BOS	6	5	36	0	50	68	39	1	34	24	7.02	2.03	6.9	317	6.1	4.3	0.7	0.2	36%	62%	27
Holliman,Mark	07	24	aa	CHC	10	11	27	0	161	193	84	20	62	86	4.70	1.58	26.9	291	3.5	4.8	1.4	1.1	32%	73%	21
	08	25	aa	CHC	4	5	31	0	108	148	70	18	72	71	5.82	2.03	17.3	319	6.0	5.9	1.0	1.5	36%	74%	3
Honel,Kristopher	07	25	aa	CHW	2	2	17	0	60	73	57	9	59	37	8.50	2.19	18.1	292	8.8	5.5	0.6	1.4	32%	61%	0
Hoorelbeke,Casey	07	27	aa	LA	4	4	63	2	94	153	81	11	37	36	7.73	2.03	7.4	358	3.6	3.4	1.0	1.0	38%	61%	-7
Horne,Alan	07	25	aa	NYY	12	4	27	0	153	196	80	15	66	131	4.70	1.71	26.3	305	3.9	7.7	2.0	0.9	38%	74%	56
	08	26	aaa	NYY	2	3	8	0	32	41	26	2	23	20	7.39	2.02	19.8	307	6.5	5.6	0.9	0.6	36%	61%	28
Hottovy,Thomas	07	26	aa	BOS	4	10	24	0	120	191	106	21	56	51	7.92	2.06	24.9	352	4.2	3.8	0.9	1.6	37%	62%	-20
Houlton,D.J.	07	28	aa	LA	6	4	23	0	106	148	63	16	49	65	5.31	1.85	22.0	323	4.1	5.5	1.3	1.4	36%	74%	10
Houser Jr.,James	07	23	aa	TAM	5	4	20	0	103	100	51	11	40	80	4.45	1.36	22.1	249	3.5	7.0	2.0	1.0	30%	69%	60
	08	24	aa	TAM	3	3	20	0	94	79	35	9	40	65	3.35	1.27	19.7	224	3.8	6.2	1.6	0.9	26%	77%	55
Housman,Jeff	07	26	aa	MIL	3	2	32	0	40	64	34	3	36	22	7.74	2.49	6.8	355	8.0	4.9	0.6	0.8	40%	68%	3
Houston,Ryan	07	28	aaa	TOR	2	2	50	5	60	69	42	9	32	49	6.27	1.68	5.5	281	4.8	7.4	1.5	1.3	33%	64%	36
	08	29	aa	HOU	1	3	39	1	45	76	52	12	31	23	10.38	2.37	6.1	366	6.1	4.6	0.8	2.4	38%	58%	-46
Howard,Adam	08	25	aa	ARI	7	8	28	0	117	184	97	22	54	63	7.43	2.04	20.7	350	4.2	4.8	1.2	1.7	38%	66%	-13
Howard,Ben	07	29	aa	CHC	6	10	55	2	82	123	61	20	31	46	6.72	1.88	7.1	338	3.4	5.0	1.5	2.2	36%	69%	-18
	08	30	a/a	MIL	2	7	35	1	65	98	48	6	32	32	6.57	1.98	9.1	339	4.4	4.4	1.0	0.8	38%	66%	10
Howell,J.P.	07	24	aaa	TAM	7	8	21	0	128	133	65	20	37	128	4.57	1.33	25.9	262	2.6	9.0	3.5	1.4	33%	70%	87
Hrynio,Michael	07	25	aa	SEA	3	1	21	2	35	35	18	0	21	25	4.58	1.58	7.6	253	5.4	6.3	1.2	0.0	32%	68%	67
	08	26	aa	CIN	3	1	39	0	53	66	41	11	33	35	6.98	1.87	6.5	298	5.7	6.0	1.1	1.9	32%	66%	-3
Huber,Jon	07	26	aa	SEA	1	4	24	5	33	55	38	6	10	22	10.28	1.97	6.8	363	2.8	5.9	2.1	1.6	41%	46%	15
	08	27	aa	SEA	4	3	52	6	70	125	67	8	25	42	8.66	2.15	6.8	380	3.2	5.3	1.6	1.1	43%	58%	13
Hudspeth,Casey	08	24	aa	HOU	4	5	10	0	55	63	36	4	27	29	5.86	1.65	25.1	282	4.5	4.8	1.1	0.7	32%	63%	29
Huff,David	08	24 a	a/a	CLE	11	5	27	0	146	137	55	15	32	123	3.37	1.16	22.1	243	2.0	7.6	3.9	1.0	30%	74%	104
Hughes,Dustin	07	25	aa	KC	6	2	25	1	108	126	51	6	49	61	4.26	1.62	19.6	285	4.1	5.1	1.3	0.5	33%	73%	41
	08	26	aa	KC	8	4	32	3	108	152	71	14	47	61	5.94	1.84	16.1	325	3.9	5.1	1.3	1.1	36%	69%	13
Hughes,Philip	07	21 a	a/a	NYY	4	1	7	0	35	24	10	0	10	35	2.68	0.97	19.6	188	2.7	8.9	3.3	0.0	27%	69%	140
Hughes,Travis	07	29	aaa	BOS	7	6	57	24	75	81	31	3	34	56	3.69	1.54	5.9	271	4.1	6.8	1.7	0.4	33%	75%	64
Hughes,William	08	23	aa	PIT	2	2	6	0	31	42	22	4	16	15	6.29	1.90	24.9	318	4.8	4.2	0.9	1.2	34%	68%	-1
Hull,Eric	07	28	aa	LA	4	3	49	11	65	80	28	4	31	59	3.83	1.70	6.1	295	4.3	8.1	1.9	0.5	38%	78%	69
	08	29	aaa	BOS	2	3	40	0	54	83	34	2	23	51	5.71	1.94	6.6	343	3.7	8.5	2.3	0.4	44%	69%	74
Humber,Philip	07	25	aa	NYM	11	9	25	0	139	152	81	22	45	99	5.25	1.42	24.1	272	2.9	6.4	2.2	1.4	31%	66%	42
	08	26	aaa	MIN	10	8	31	0	136	165	82	21	51	86	5.41	1.58	19.8	293	3.3	5.7	1.7	1.4	33%	69%	24
Hunter,Christopher	07	27	aa	LAA	3	4	22	1	38	77	56	10	28	17	13.34	2.75	9.8	410	6.5	3.9	0.6	2.5	42%	51%	-64
Hunter,Tommy	08	22	aa	TEX	8	4	16	0	105	118	44	12	25	48	3.77	1.36	28.1	278	2.1	4.1	1.9	1.0	30%	76%	34
Hurley,Eric	07	22	aa	TEX	11	9	28	0	162	161	93	33	55	115	5.17	1.33	24.6	254	3.1	6.4	2.1	1.8	27%	67%	31
	08	23	aa	TEX	3	5	14	0	82	102	52	16	30	61	5.66	1.61	26.5	299	3.3	6.7	2.0	1.8	33%	70%	24
Hyatt,Jared	08	24	aa	TEX	5	3	11	0	60	59	25	3	18	42	3.78	1.28	22.9	251	2.7	6.3	2.3	0.5	30%	70%	77
Hynick,Brandon	08	24	aa	COL	10	7	27	0	172	207	98	30	29	81	5.12	1.37	27.4	292	1.5	4.2	2.8	1.6	30%	67%	34
Igawa,Kei	07	28	aaa	NYY	5	4	11	0	68	86	39	13	17	55	5.12	1.52	27.5	302	2.3	7.3	3.2	1.7	35%	71%	54
	08	29	aaa	NYY	14	6	26	0	156	182	85	21	51	89	4.88	1.49	26.5	286	2.9	5.1	1.8	1.2	32%	70%	30
Ingram,Jesse	07	25	aa	TEX	3	1	56	26	62	57	42	14	31	54	6.13	1.42	4.8	238	4.5	7.8	1.7	2.1	26%	62%	28
Inman,William	07	21	aa	SD	4	8	15	0	80	76	49	13	34	76	5.45	1.38	23.0	245	3.8	8.5	2.2	1.5	29%	64%	58
	08	22	aa	SD	9	8	28	0	135	129	58	9	72	120	3.86	1.49	21.3	246	4.8	8.0	1.7	0.6	31%	74%	71
Iriki,Yusaku	07	35	a/a	TOR	3	6	19	0	88	127	66	12	42	47	6.70	1.92	22.4	330	4.3	4.8	1.1	1.2	36%	66%	4
Isenberg,Kurt	07	26	aa	TOR	4	11	23	0	123	209	104	11	44	69	7.63	2.06	26.7	367	3.2	5.1	1.6	0.8	42%	61%	20
Jackson,Kyle	07	24	aa	BOS	4	9	42	1	70	84	61	9	51	67	7.83	1.92	8.1	291	6.5	8.6	1.3	1.2	36%	59%	40
	08	26	aa	BOS	5	3	28	0	80	111	79	10	48	42	8.85	1.98	14.0	322	5.4	4.7	0.9	1.1	35%	54%	4
Jackson,Steven	07	26	a/a	NYY	4	9	28	1	90	144	78	16	43	52	7.79	2.08	16.1	354	4.3	5.2	1.2	1.6	39%	64%	-6
	08	27	a/a	NYY	4	3	49	6	79	96	54	6	37	68	6.19	1.67	7.4	292	4.2	7.8	1.9	0.6	37%	61%	63
Jackson,Zach	07	24	aaa	MIL	11	10	29	0	169	216	107	15	68	112	5.69	1.68	26.8	304	3.6	6.0	1.6	0.8	36%	66%	41
	08	25	aaa	CLE	4	6	30	0	84	128	84	16	25	48	8.98	1.83	13.3	343	2.7	5.1	1.9	1.7	37%	51%	4
Jacobsen,Landon	07	28	a/a	PHI	8	12	29	0	163	247	122	16	80	60	6.76	2.01	27.7	342	4.4	3.3	0.8	0.9	37%	66%	-5
Jakubauskas,Chris	07	29	aa	SEA	0	4	16	0	51	74	41	4	28	28	7.28	1.99	15.6	331	4.9	4.9	1.0	0.7	38%	62%	20
	08	30	aa	SEA	8	1	18	0	88	113	28	8	28	49	2.86	1.60	22.1	306	2.9	5.0	1.7	0.8	35%	85%	36
James,Brad	07	23	aa	HOU	1	5	9	0	47	62	33	2	21	18	6.32	1.75	24.4	311	3.9	3.5	0.9	0.4	34%	62%	21
	08	24	aa	HOU	6	6	18	0	93	119	49	9	35	36	4.79	1.65	23.6	305	3.4	3.5	1.0	0.9	33%	72%	9
James,Chuck	08	27	aaa	ATL	5	5	16	0	86	90	35	5	40	63	3.66	1.51	23.8	263	4.2	6.6	1.6	0.5	32%	76%	59
James,Craig	07	25	aa	SEA	5	4	44	10	58	84	49	5	28	39	7.65	1.94	6.4	331	4.4	6.0	1.4	0.8	39%	59%	29
	08	26	aa	SEA	1	4	28	3	39	63	33	3	24	31	7.69	2.25	7.2	357	5.6	7.1	1.3	0.8	43%	64%	29
James,Justin	07	26	a/a	TOR	3	5	43	2	88	111	53	10	30	45	5.45	1.60	9.3	302	3.1	4.6	1.5	1.0	33%	67%	23
James,Michael	07	26	aa	BOS	2	3	55	22	57	75	34	9	43	44	5.44	2.05	5.2	309	6.7	7.0	1.0	1.4	36%	77%	14
	08	27	aa	BOS	5	4	46	2	76	92	47	7	34	46	5.56	1.65	7.6	292	4.0	5.5	1.4	0.9	33%	66%	33
Jamison,Neil	07	24	aa	SD	3	5	53	12	58	78	35	8	28	37	5.38	1.83	5.2	315	4.4	5.7	1.3	1.3	35%	73%	15
	08	25	aa	SD	1	2	29	2	35	39	12	1	11	20	3.13	1.42	5.3	275	2.8	5.1	1.8	0.3	32%	77%	59
Jepsen,Kevin	08	24	aa	LAA	3	4	40	13	54	46	14	3	32	46	2.27	1.44	5.9	226	5.2	7.6	1.4	0.5	29%	86%	70
Jimenez,Cesar	08	24 a	aa	SEA	1	3	29	3	38	42	18	3	8	41	4.15	1.33	5.6	276	2.0	9.6	4.9	0.7	37%	70%	139
Jimenez,Kelvin	07	27	aa	STL	2	3	30	1	39	59	16	2	13	26	3.69	1.82	6.2	339	2.9	6.0	2.1	0.5	40%	80%	51
	08	28	aa	STL	1	6	46	12	52	71	22	4	13	20	3.75	1.62	5.1	318	2.3	3.4	1.5	0.6	35%	78%	25
Jimenez,Ubaldo	07	24	aa	COL	8	5	19	0	103	138	95	12	64	77	8.29	1.96	26.5	315	5.6	6.7	1.2	1.1	37%	57%	25
Johnson,Alan	08	25	aa	COL	4	14	28	0	175	264	127	22	54	71	6.51	1.82	29.7	341	2.8	3.7	1.3	1.1	36%	65%	2
Johnson,Blake	08	23	aa	KC	10	9	26	0	143	204	102	23	39	74	6.42	1.70	25.4	328	2.5	4.6	1.9	1.4	36%	64%	14
Johnson,David	07	25	aa	MIL	1	1	26	4	41	46	31	7	21	38	6.80	1.62	7.2	275	4.6	8.3	1.8	1.5	33%	59%	44
	08	26	aa	MIL	5	3	40	3	62	68	29	6	31	57	4.16	1.59	7.0	272	4.5	8.2	1.8	0.8	34%	75%	63

PITCHER	Yr	Age	Lev	Org	w	l	g	sv	ip	h	er	hr	bb	k	era	whip	bf/g	oob	ctl	dom	cmd	hr/9	h%	s%	bpv
					Actual				Major League Equivalents																
Johnson,Grant	07	24	aa	CHC	1	1	28	3	48	44	31	6	22	34	5.71	1.38	7.4	239	4.1	6.4	1.5	1.2	27%	60%	43
	08	25	aa	CHC	2	5	21	0	60	83	47	8	29	24	7.00	1.87	13.7	322	4.3	3.6	0.8	1.2	34%	63%	-5
Johnson,Jason	08	35	aa	LA	11	5	20	0	113	165	64	19	35	73	5.06	1.77	26.5	333	2.8	5.8	2.1	1.5	37%	75%	22
Johnson,Jeremy	07	25	a/a	DET	5	3	41	2	73	83	39	5	27	40	4.80	1.51	7.9	280	3.4	4.9	1.5	0.6	32%	68%	40
	08	26	aaa	DET	5	3	23	1	81	118	56	10	29	50	6.17	1.80	16.7	331	3.2	5.6	1.7	1.1	38%	67%	25
Johnson,Jim	07	24	aaa	BAL	6	12	26	0	148	202	94	20	50	95	5.72	1.70	26.3	319	3.0	5.8	1.9	1.2	36%	68%	29
Johnson,Jonathan	07	33	aaa	ATL	1	4	10	0	44	71	44	8	23	21	9.00	2.12	22.3	353	4.7	4.3	0.9	1.7	37%	58%	-23
Johnson,Kristofer	08	24	aa	BOS	8	9	27	0	136	173	69	5	57	89	4.57	1.69	23.2	304	3.7	5.9	1.6	0.3	36%	72%	53
Jones,David	07	24	aa	BOS	2	1	23	2	42	41	19	3	16	36	3.97	1.37	7.9	251	3.5	7.7	2.2	0.7	32%	72%	77
	08	25 a	a/a	BOS	7	3	48	12	73	91	26	3	19	63	3.17	1.49	6.7	298	2.3	7.8	3.4	0.4	38%	79%	102
Jones,Geoffrey	07	28	aa	CHC	4	4	50	9	59	83	24	0	26	47	3.61	1.84	5.6	323	4.0	7.2	1.8	0.0	41%	78%	71
Jones,Greg	07	31	aa	LAA	4	2	36	3	53	113	54	11	20	23	9.18	2.50	8.0	421	3.4	3.9	1.2	1.9	44%	65%	-39
	08	32	aa	LA	3	3	28	0	42	59	29	9	39	30	6.30	2.32	7.9	324	8.3	6.4	0.8	2.0	36%	77%	-16
Jones,Jason	07	25	aa	NYY	8	11	28	0	131	171	80	16	36	62	5.49	1.57	21.1	308	2.5	4.2	1.7	1.1	33%	66%	23
	08	26	a/a	NYY	13	8	27	0	160	192	81	15	56	81	4.56	1.55	26.5	291	3.1	4.5	1.4	0.8	32%	71%	30
Jones,Justin	08	24	aa	WAS	2	5	12	0	55	72	37	3	25	35	6.02	1.76	21.5	308	4.1	5.7	1.4	0.5	36%	64%	42
Jones,Mike	08	25	aa	MIL	1	6	18	0	57	66	48	12	50	26	7.52	2.02	15.7	282	7.9	4.1	0.5	1.9	28%	66%	-23
Juarez,William	07	26	aa	LA	10	8	29	0	142	221	113	23	71	87	7.14	2.06	24.4	347	4.5	5.5	1.2	1.5	39%	67%	1
Jukich,Benjamin	08	26	a/a	CIN	11	5	27	0	161	211	87	11	61	105	4.88	1.68	27.5	309	3.4	5.8	1.7	0.6	36%	71%	47
Julianel,Ben	07	28	aa	FLA	2	2	36	0	53	84	48	8	36	38	8.04	2.26	7.6	350	6.1	6.4	1.0	1.3	40%	64%	7
	08	29	aa	MIN	3	2	56	26	68	93	28	4	41	48	3.70	1.98	6.0	319	5.5	6.3	1.2	0.5	38%	82%	38
Julio,Jorge	08	30	aaa	ATL	1	2	38	13	39	42	12	1	25	35	2.78	1.71	4.8	267	5.8	8.1	1.4	0.3	35%	83%	72
Junge,Eric	07	31	aaa	NYY	3	1	8	0	29	34	24	4	17	14	7.53	1.75	17.0	288	5.1	4.4	0.9	1.4	31%	57%	1
Jung,Sung Ki	08	29	aa	ATL	2	2	49	6	63	93	48	0	32	38	6.85	1.99	6.3	336	4.6	5.5	1.2	0.0	40%	62%	46
Jurrjens,Jair	07	22	aa	DET	7	5	19	0	112	136	55	8	32	81	4.41	1.50	26.1	293	2.6	6.5	2.5	0.6	35%	71%	69
Kaiser,Marc	07	25	aa	COL	6	8	27	0	131	227	132	20	88	39	9.08	2.40	25.8	372	6.0	2.7	0.4	1.4	38%	62%	-35
Karnuth,Jason	07	31	aaa	DET	2	2	30	6	37	45	19	6	7	22	4.61	1.42	5.4	295	1.8	5.3	3.0	1.5	32%	73%	44
Karstens,Jeff	07	25	a/a	NYY	4	0	7	0	36	37	11	3	13	26	2.63	1.37	22.1	260	3.2	6.4	2.0	0.8	31%	84%	61
	08	26	aaa	NYY	6	4	12	0	68	80	38	10	15	45	5.03	1.41	24.6	288	2.0	5.9	2.9	1.4	32%	67%	53
Keefer,Ryan	08	27	aa	BAL	2	4	39	1	65	83	52	14	45	42	7.15	1.96	8.2	304	6.2	5.8	0.9	2.0	33%	67%	-11
Keisler,Randy	07	32	aa	STL	8	11	25	0	156	231	111	21	58	77	6.38	1.85	29.8	336	3.3	4.4	1.3	1.2	37%	67%	5
	08	33	a/a	BAL	6	9	22	0	114	170	69	10	54	70	5.44	1.97	25.3	338	4.3	5.5	1.3	0.8	39%	73%	24
Kelley,Shawn	08	24 a	aa	SEA	3	1	29	9	42	36	12	2	18	38	2.47	1.27	6.1	225	3.8	8.1	2.1	0.4	29%	82%	90
Kelly,Steven	07	28	a/a	CIN	1	9	27	0	78	154	87	13	41	33	10.02	2.50	15.7	403	4.7	3.8	0.8	1.5	43%	59%	-30
Kendrick,Kyle	07	23	aa	PHI	4	7	12	0	81	96	35	4	19	42	3.89	1.41	29.3	288	2.1	4.6	2.2	0.5	33%	72%	59
Kennard,Jeff	07	26	aa	LAA	3	4	47	6	72	91	39	5	36	43	4.89	1.76	7.2	302	4.5	5.3	1.2	0.6	35%	72%	35
	08	27	aa	LAA	4	4	47	0	63	111	64	13	39	32	9.11	2.37	7.1	376	5.5	4.5	0.8	1.9	40%	63%	-33
Kennedy,Ian	07	23 a	a/a	NYY	6	2	15	0	83	63	30	5	30	76	3.25	1.12	22.4	206	3.2	8.2	2.5	0.5	27%	72%	100
	08	24 a	aaa	NYY	5	3	13	0	69	61	23	5	18	60	3.00	1.14	21.6	232	2.3	7.8	3.3	0.7	29%	76%	106
Keppel,Bob	07	25	aa	COL	8	10	26	0	138	219	128	20	67	51	8.33	2.07	26.5	352	4.3	3.3	0.8	1.3	37%	59%	-18
	08	26	aa	FLA	9	11	28	0	159	267	140	31	69	68	7.93	2.11	28.6	365	3.9	3.8	1.0	1.8	38%	64%	-27
Kershaw,Clayton	08	21 a	aa	LA	2	3	13	0	61	41	14	0	18	57	2.10	0.97	18.3	187	2.7	8.4	3.1	0.0	26%	76%	134
Kershner,Jason	07	31	aaa	CIN	5	4	39	1	63	76	41	10	22	32	5.87	1.55	7.2	291	3.2	4.6	1.5	1.4	31%	65%	12
	08	32	aa	SEA	6	4	34	1	47	75	35	5	21	26	6.74	2.05	6.9	354	4.0	5.0	1.2	0.9	40%	67%	14
Kester,Tim	07	36	aaa	BAL	9	9	28	0	127	184	101	14	32	57	7.16	1.70	21.0	332	2.2	4.0	1.8	1.0	36%	57%	22
Ketchner,Ryan	07	25	aa	SD	1	11	19	0	99	139	82	20	43	67	7.47	1.84	24.8	324	3.9	6.0	1.5	1.8	36%	62%	4
	08	26	aa	SEA	7	6	25	0	115	184	78	13	43	55	6.11	1.97	22.5	353	3.3	4.3	1.3	1.0	39%	69%	7
Key,Chris	07	30	aa	PHI	5	2	58	18	74	115	35	7	16	18	4.20	1.76	6.0	346	1.9	2.2	1.1	0.8	36%	77%	-2
Kilby,Brad	07	25	aa	OAK	3	3	47	0	65	76	26	6	22	56	3.63	1.50	6.1	285	3.1	7.7	2.5	0.9	35%	78%	72
	08	26	aa	OAK	7	2	51	2	70	60	31	9	26	50	4.00	1.22	5.7	227	3.3	6.5	2.0	1.1	26%	71%	56
Kim,Sun-Woo	07	30	aaa	SF	8	8	25	0	118	213	109	16	49	53	8.27	2.21	24.3	382	3.7	4.0	1.1	1.2	41%	62%	-11
King,Ray	08	35	a/a	HOU	2	1	36	5	36	34	12	2	16	22	3.04	1.38	4.3	246	3.9	5.4	1.4	0.6	29%	79%	51
Kinney,Matt	07	31	aa	SF	12	10	27	0	156	266	119	36	50	85	6.83	2.02	28.6	368	2.9	4.9	1.7	2.1	39%	70%	-16
Kinsey,Chris	07	25	aa	ARI	4	7	28	0	121	167	81	14	63	70	6.02	1.90	20.9	321	4.7	5.2	1.1	1.0	36%	69%	15
Knight,Brandon	08	33	aa	NYM	5	1	12	1	43	36	15	6	14	41	3.19	1.17	14.7	225	2.9	8.5	2.9	1.2	27%	79%	85
Knotts,Gary	07	31	a/a	PHI	2	4	6	0	39	48	21	6	21	18	4.89	1.76	30.5	294	4.9	4.2	0.9	1.4	31%	76%	-3
	08	32	aaa	BAL	2	7	39	0	102	139	73	15	52	81	6.40	1.86	12.5	318	4.5	7.1	1.6	1.3	37%	67%	28
Knox,Brad	07	25	aa	OAK	10	7	27	0	163	214	108	18	52	61	5.94	1.63	27.5	310	2.9	3.4	1.2	1.0	33%	64%	8
	08	26	aa	OAK	7	5	29	0	146	207	105	20	46	70	6.44	1.73	23.4	327	2.8	4.3	1.5	1.2	35%	64%	11
Koehler,Kurt	07	23	aa	FLA	1	1	21	5	25	33	21	0	11	9	7.42	1.77	5.6	311	4.1	3.1	0.8	0.0	35%	53%	28
Kohn,Shawn	07	28	aa	OAK	1	6	50	1	86	117	71	20	41	66	7.43	1.83	8.2	317	4.3	6.9	1.6	2.1	35%	63%	3
Kolb,Dan	07	27	a/a	WAS	2	2	31	2	55	63	45	8	46	32	7.32	1.98	8.7	282	7.5	5.3	0.7	1.3	31%	64%	5
Kometani,Paul	07	25	aa	TEX	3	4	39	8	78	102	51	4	31	57	5.83	1.70	9.2	310	3.5	6.6	1.9	0.5	38%	64%	57
	08	26	aa	TEX	4	5	47	2	60	80	47	12	28	39	7.00	1.80	6.0	313	4.2	5.8	1.4	1.8	34%	64%	1
Komine,Shane	07	27	aa	OAK	5	12	23	0	133	187	100	25	51	74	6.77	1.79	27.2	325	3.4	5.0	1.5	1.7	35%	65%	-1
Kontos,George	08	23	aa	NYY	6	11	27	0	151	169	89	20	63	123	5.28	1.53	24.9	277	3.7	7.3	2.0	1.2	33%	67%	50
Koplove,Mike	07	31	aaa	CLE	4	2	51	14	54	59	19	3	23	38	3.16	1.52	4.7	272	3.9	6.3	1.6	0.5	33%	80%	57
	08	32	aa	LA	2	1	41	9	54	55	28	6	21	36	4.69	1.41	5.7	259	3.5	5.9	1.7	1.0	30%	68%	45
Korecky,Robert	07	28	aaa	MIN	5	6	66	35	85	108	55	6	42	54	5.81	1.76	6.0	302	4.4	5.7	1.3	0.7	35%	66%	35
	08	29	aaa	MIN	6	5	53	26	74	81	31	3	24	53	3.74	1.42	6.1	273	2.9	6.4	2.2	0.4	33%	73%	73
Koronka,John	07	27	a/a	CLE	9	7	23	0	132	198	84	13	63	64	5.72	1.98	28.1	339	4.3	4.4	1.0	0.9	38%	71%	9
	08	28	aa	COL	5	3	13	0	67	120	50	8	40	20	6.70	2.38	27.4	379	5.4	2.7	0.5	1.0	40%	72%	-24
Kown,Andrew	07	25	aa	DET	6	8	27	1	120	163	80	12	39	70	6.00	1.68	20.5	318	2.9	5.3	1.8	0.9	36%	64%	35
	08	26	a/a	WAS	8	9	22	0	113	167	83	17	41	42	6.64	1.84	24.4	336	3.3	3.4	1.0	1.3	35%	65%	-10
Kozlowski,Ben	07	27	aaa	NYY	5	7	42	1	81	88	37	11	34	64	4.09	1.51	8.5	272	3.7	7.1	1.9	1.2	32%	76%	48
Kroenke,Zachary	08	24	a/a	NYY	7	0	41	1	53	43	24	5	30	44	4.01	1.38	5.6	218	5.1	7.4	1.5	0.9	26%	73%	60
Kunz,Edward	08	23	aa	NYM	1	5	50	27	54	54	23	1	26	41	3.83	1.48	4.8	255	4.3	6.8	1.6	0.2	32%	72%	73
Laffey,Aaron	07	22	a/a	CLE	13	4	22	0	131	135	51	7	31	90	3.50	1.27	24.9	261	2.1	6.2	2.9	0.5	31%	72%	86
	08	23	aaa	CLE	6	2	11	0	61	86	40	2	19	42	5.88	1.72	25.8	325	2.8	6.2	2.2	0.3	39%	63%	65
Lahey,Timothy	07	26	a/a	MIN	8	4	52	14	81	102	45	9	40	46	5.02	1.75	7.3	301	4.4	5.1	1.1	1.1	34%	73%	18
	08	27	aaa	MIN	5	5	48	8	63	79	45	7	24	42	6.48	1.64	6.0	301	3.4	6.0	1.8	1.0	35%	60%	36
Lambert,Chris	07	25	a/a	DET	1	6	34	0	90	123	80	18	41	65	8.04	1.82	12.6	318	4.1	6.5	1.6	1.8	36%	57%	11
	08	26	aaa	DET	12	8	26	0	149	165	71	7	46	108	4.27	1.42	24.9	274	2.8	6.5	2.3	0.4	34%	69%	75

PITCHER	Yr	Age	Lev	Org	w	l	g	sv	ip	h	er	hr	bb	k	era	whip	bf/g	oob	ctl	dom	cmd	hr/9	h%	s%	bpv
					Actual				Major League Equivalents																
Lamura,BJ	07	27	aa	LA	2	7	36	0	68	78	48	9	63	52	6.39	2.08	9.4	282	8.4	6.9	0.8	1.2	33%	70%	21
	08	28	aa	LA	4	4	21	1	87	141	77	19	41	55	7.97	2.09	20.8	357	4.2	5.7	1.3	2.0	39%	64%	-14
Lannan,John	07	23	a/a	WAS	6	3	13	0	74	70	24	3	27	33	2.92	1.31	24.1	245	3.3	4.0	1.2	0.4	28%	78%	45
Lara,Juan	07	27	a/a	CLE	4	3	54	2	59	69	33	3	31	42	5.08	1.69	5.0	285	4.7	6.4	1.4	0.5	35%	69%	50
Large,Terry	08	25	aa	BOS	0	2	22	1	33	47	30	3	26	29	8.13	2.18	7.7	325	6.9	7.8	1.1	0.9	40%	61%	33
Larrison,Preston	07	27	aaa	DET	2	2	45	1	58	66	34	2	30	31	5.26	1.65	5.9	280	4.6	4.8	1.0	0.3	32%	66%	40
	08	28	aaa	CLE	3	4	48	1	60	76	33	5	24	34	4.89	1.66	5.7	302	3.6	5.1	1.4	0.8	34%	71%	31
Laughter,Andrew	08	24	aa	TEX	2	3	30	9	45	45	28	3	21	30	5.57	1.47	6.6	257	4.1	6.0	1.5	0.6	30%	61%	52
Lavigne,Tim	07	29	a/a	HOU	1	4	35	7	58	89	45	9	21	33	6.98	1.89	8.0	344	3.2	5.1	1.6	1.3	38%	64%	10
	08	30	aa	NYM	2	6	43	9	44	76	40	11	43	22	8.18	2.69	5.7	371	8.8	4.4	0.5	2.3	39%	73%	-52
Lawrence,Brian	07	31	aa	NYM	8	5	16	0	104	158	75	11	16	49	6.50	1.67	29.9	341	1.4	4.3	3.0	0.9	38%	60%	48
	08	32	aaa	ATL	6	6	16	0	86	136	67	4	20	45	7.05	1.81	25.4	351	2.1	4.7	2.2	0.4	40%	58%	47
Lawson,Donald	08	23	aa	BOS	1	1	6	0	31	33	18	1	18	15	5.09	1.63	23.5	267	5.1	4.2	0.8	0.3	30%	67%	35
Leach,Brent	08	26	aa	LA	2	2	40	12	59	53	23	2	38	40	3.55	1.54	6.6	236	5.8	6.0	1.0	0.3	29%	76%	56
League,Brandon	08	26	aaa	TOR	2	3	20	2	34	43	20	3	11	27	5.33	1.60	7.7	304	2.9	7.1	2.4	0.8	37%	67%	63
Leblanc,Wade	07	23	aa	SD	7	3	12	0	57	56	27	9	21	47	4.22	1.34	20.3	250	3.2	7.3	2.3	1.5	29%	74%	53
	08	24	aaa	SD	11	9	26	0	138	156	95	20	44	113	6.17	1.45	23.2	279	2.9	7.4	2.6	1.3	33%	58%	58
Lecure,Samuel	07	23	aa	CIN	7	5	21	0	110	141	65	15	47	86	5.31	1.72	24.3	305	3.9	7.1	1.8	1.3	36%	71%	37
	08	24	aa	CIN	9	7	27	0	155	172	72	15	60	106	4.15	1.49	25.4	275	3.5	6.2	1.8	0.9	32%	74%	49
Lee,Cliff	07	29	a/a	CLE	2	3	9	0	46	48	23	1	33	43	4.53	1.75	23.9	261	6.4	8.3	1.3	0.2	35%	72%	73
Lee,Derek	07	33	aa	TEX	1	3	8	0	30	54	25	4	14	14	7.36	2.26	19.6	380	4.2	4.1	1.0	1.1	41%	67%	-8
	08	34	aa	TEX	1	6	8	0	44	74	34	6	13	16	6.96	1.97	27.0	365	2.6	3.3	1.2	1.2	39%	65%	-8
Lehr,Justin	07	30	aa	SEA	7	1	27	1	119	211	89	11	61	39	6.69	2.29	23.0	378	4.6	2.9	0.6	0.9	40%	70%	-16
	08	31	aaa	CIN	6	2	16	1	64	62	19	6	12	34	2.66	1.15	16.3	249	1.6	4.8	3.0	0.9	28%	81%	69
Leicester,Jon	07	29	aaa	BAL	3	3	13	0	65	63	25	8	25	44	3.42	1.36	21.4	251	3.4	6.1	1.8	1.0	29%	79%	47
	08	30	aaa	BAL	3	8	39	1	106	155	80	18	42	76	6.81	1.86	13.0	334	3.5	6.4	1.8	1.5	38%	65%	20
Lerew,Anthony	08	26	aaa	ATL	1	4	9	0	37	49	21	5	20	19	5.16	1.88	19.7	314	4.9	4.6	0.9	1.2	34%	75%	2
Lester,Jon	07	24	a/a	BOS	5	5	15	0	77	85	41	4	36	47	4.78	1.57	23.1	274	4.2	5.5	1.3	0.5	32%	68%	47
Lewis Jr.,Rommie	07	25	aa	BAL	5	5	47	1	69	101	54	12	31	50	7.10	1.92	7.1	334	4.1	6.6	1.6	1.6	38%	65%	14
	08	26	aa	BAL	1	6	38	0	66	107	36	6	29	48	4.86	2.06	8.6	357	3.9	6.5	1.7	0.8	42%	77%	34
Lewis,Colby	07	28	aa	OAK	8	3	15	0	95	100	30	11	28	66	2.84	1.34	27.0	265	2.6	6.3	2.4	1.1	31%	84%	59
Lewis,Jensen	07	23 a	a/a	CLE	3	0	34	2	52	37	12	3	17	55	2.08	1.04	6.1	196	2.9	9.5	3.2	0.5	27%	82%	125
Lewis,Scott	07	24	aa	CLE	7	9	27	0	134	163	71	14	37	105	4.73	1.49	21.9	294	2.5	7.0	2.8	0.9	35%	69%	70
	08	25 a	a/a	CLE	8	4	17	0	97	101	36	5	15	69	3.32	1.19	23.5	263	1.4	6.4	4.7	0.5	32%	72%	125
Lincecum,Timothy	07	23 a	aa	SF	4	0	5	0	31	14	1	0	11	38	0.30	0.83	23.3	138	3.3	11.0	3.3	0.0	23%	96%	163
Link,Jon	08	25	aa	CHW	5	4	56	35	56	61	27	4	29	56	4.38	1.61	4.5	271	4.7	9.0	1.9	0.7	36%	73%	74
Liriano,Francisco	08	25 a	aaa	MIN	10	2	19	0	118	114	50	8	32	93	3.81	1.24	25.8	249	2.4	7.1	2.9	0.6	31%	70%	91
Liriano,Pedro	07	27	aa	LAA	4	12	28	0	130	226	117	24	53	50	8.11	2.15	23.5	373	3.7	3.4	0.9	1.7	39%	64%	-30
Litsch,Jesse	07	23	a/a	TOR	8	2	12	0	76	73	24	6	17	48	2.84	1.18	26.0	247	2.0	5.7	2.8	0.7	29%	79%	78
Littleton,Wes	07	25	aa	TEX	0	1	23	2	32	41	26	7	9	16	7.17	1.56	6.2	305	2.5	4.5	1.8	1.9	32%	56%	3
	08	26	aa	TEX	7	1	44	6	58	70	33	3	28	44	5.16	1.68	6.1	292	4.3	6.7	1.6	0.5	36%	68%	54
Livingston,Bobby	07	25	aaa	CIN	3	4	17	0	104	147	58	9	18	53	4.98	1.59	27.6	327	1.6	4.6	2.9	0.8	37%	69%	56
	08	26	aaa	CIN	4	4	9	0	56	74	39	8	18	30	6.30	1.64	28.4	312	2.8	4.8	1.7	1.3	34%	63%	18
Liz,Radhames	07	24	aa	BAL	11	4	25	0	137	121	61	15	71	133	4.01	1.40	23.7	232	4.6	8.7	1.9	1.0	30%	74%	72
	08	25	aaa	BAL	3	7	15	0	87	88	41	7	30	73	4.28	1.36	24.8	257	3.1	7.6	2.4	0.7	32%	69%	78
Lockwood,Luke	07	26	aa	CIN	1	7	14	0	70	120	61	11	25	38	7.83	2.07	24.9	369	3.3	4.9	1.5	1.5	40%	63%	-2
Loe,Kameron	08	27	aa	TEX	3	5	26	1	58	93	49	10	23	22	7.67	1.99	11.0	354	3.6	3.5	1.0	1.5	37%	63%	-19
Lofgren,Charles	07	22	a/a	CLE	12	8	27	0	151	174	89	14	69	124	5.28	1.61	25.3	283	4.1	7.4	1.8	0.9	35%	68%	55
	08	23	aa	CLE	2	6	28	0	85	109	72	10	54	64	7.61	1.91	14.7	305	5.7	6.8	1.2	1.1	36%	59%	28
Lopez,Aquilino	07	32	aaa	DET	3	5	48	26	53	58	19	6	12	48	3.21	1.31	4.7	272	2.0	8.0	4.1	1.1	33%	80%	103
Lopez,Javier	07	25	aa	SD	2	2	30	0	35	41	22	3	20	23	5.65	1.73	5.5	285	5.1	5.8	1.1	0.8	33%	67%	33
Lopez,Wilton	08	25	aa	SD	0	2	28	0	39	51	27	2	12	19	6.14	1.62	6.3	309	2.8	4.4	1.5	0.5	35%	60%	36
Loux,Shane	08	29	aa	LAA	12	6	22	0	138	233	97	19	52	50	6.35	2.07	31.3	367	3.4	3.3	1.0	1.2	39%	71%	-15
Lowery,Devon	08	26	aa	KC	2	1	40	7	72	73	21	4	39	48	2.64	1.56	8.1	258	4.9	6.0	1.2	0.6	31%	85%	48
Lo,Ching	07	22	aa	COL	8	8	26	0	139	197	119	26	66	77	7.69	1.89	25.7	326	4.3	5.0	1.2	1.7	35%	61%	-6
	08	23	aa	COL	8	8	19	0	97	115	66	18	22	41	6.11	1.41	22.2	289	2.0	3.8	1.9	1.6	30%	59%	11
Lugo,Ruddy	07	27	a/a	OAK	5	1	28	10	34	22	6	0	21	22	1.51	1.24	5.1	179	5.4	5.7	1.1	0.0	23%	86%	76
	08	28	aa	NYM	7	12	24	0	134	193	116	23	63	73	7.80	1.90	26.9	330	4.2	4.9	1.2	1.5	36%	60%	-2
Lujan,John	08	24	aa	CHW	3	2	50	4	76	81	41	9	43	43	4.86	1.63	6.9	268	5.1	5.1	1.0	1.1	29%	72%	19
Lumsden,Tyler	07	24	aa	KC	9	6	25	0	119	172	102	12	61	62	7.72	1.95	23.2	330	4.6	4.7	1.0	0.9	37%	59%	12
	08	25	aa	KC	3	13	28	1	107	180	122	18	68	35	10.27	2.31	20.0	365	5.7	2.9	0.5	1.5	38%	55%	-34
Lundberg,Spike	07	30	aa	LA	7	7	33	0	120	281	154	34	51	49	11.55	2.77	20.7	445	3.9	3.7	1.0	2.6	46%	60%	-69
Lutz,Derrik	08	23	aa	CIN	2	2	52	3	50	72	33	2	28	37	5.93	2.00	4.7	330	5.0	6.6	1.3	0.4	40%	68%	45
Lynn,Kevin	08	30	a/a	TAM	1	2	18	0	41	59	37	13	20	20	8.01	1.90	11.0	328	4.3	4.3	1.0	2.9	32%	64%	-52
Macdonald,Michael	07	26	a/a	TOR	9	9	28	0	163	235	106	15	46	76	5.87	1.72	27.0	330	2.6	4.2	1.6	0.8	36%	66%	24
	08	27	a/a	TOR	1	7	39	5	104	149	63	17	29	51	5.48	1.71	12.3	329	2.5	4.4	1.8	1.4	35%	71%	10
MacDougal,Mike	08	32	aaa	CHW	0	4	38	4	49	59	28	3	33	55	5.21	1.87	6.2	291	6.0	10.1	1.7	0.6	40%	71%	75
Machi,Jean	07	25	aa	TOR	2	4	48	2	81	82	41	11	25	46	4.55	1.32	7.2	257	2.8	5.1	1.8	1.2	28%	68%	37
	08	26	aa	TOR	2	6	21	1	69	92	47	4	46	38	6.07	1.99	16.2	313	5.9	4.9	0.8	0.6	36%	68%	22
Mackintosh,Jason	07	27	aa	SEA	2	2	30	1	53	92	42	11	20	33	7.13	2.11	8.9	371	3.5	5.6	1.6	1.8	41%	69%	-6
	08	28	aa	PHI	5	4	43	2	60	65	25	6	20	26	3.74	1.41	6.1	270	3.0	3.8	1.3	0.9	29%	76%	23
Maclane,Evan	07	25	aa	ARI	7	7	32	0	115	234	132	28	39	45	10.28	2.37	19.0	410	3.0	3.5	1.1	2.2	42%	58%	-49
	08	26	aa	ARI	7	8	30	0	152	242	121	30	34	67	7.17	1.82	24.0	353	2.0	3.9	1.9	1.8	37%	63%	-5
Madrigal,Warner	08	25	aa	TEX	1	0	31	14	36	36	15	3	16	35	3.68	1.43	5.1	254	3.9	8.8	2.2	0.8	33%	76%	80
Madsen,Michael	07	25	aa	OAK	10	3	21	0	123	126	67	12	57	88	4.92	1.49	25.9	260	4.2	6.5	1.6	0.8	31%	67%	49
Maeda,Yukinaga	08	38	aa	TEX	5	3	36	1	55	74	38	9	13	43	6.15	1.58	6.9	315	2.1	6.9	3.3	1.5	36%	64%	56
Magee,Brandon	08	25	aa	TOR	7	13	28	0	163	229	111	19	74	50	6.13	1.86	27.8	325	4.1	2.8	0.7	1.0	34%	68%	-10
Magrane,Jim	07	29	a/a	WAS	7	10	30	0	148	228	98	13	50	64	5.93	1.88	23.7	345	3.0	3.9	1.3	0.8	38%	68%	12
Mahon,Reid	08	25	aa	ARI	0	2	52	24	65	88	40	11	27	41	5.54	1.76	5.9	316	3.7	5.6	1.5	1.5	35%	72%	11
Majewski,Gary	07	28	aaa	CIN	1	1	38	4	38	41	23	3	17	25	5.46	1.52	4.5	269	4.0	5.8	1.5	0.7	31%	63%	45
Maldonado,Ivan	07	27	aa	NYM	2	1	39	9	42	54	25	5	19	32	5.40	1.74	5.0	306	4.1	6.9	1.7	1.0	36%	70%	40
	08	28	aa	NYM	4	5	47	3	66	103	44	8	48	45	5.96	2.27	7.3	347	6.5	6.1	0.9	1.0	40%	75%	11

PITCHER	Yr	Age	Lev	Org	Actual				Major League Equivalents																
					w	l	g	sv	ip	h	er	hr	bb	k	era	whip	bf/g	oob	ctl	dom	cmd	hr/9	h%	s%	bpv
Mallett,Justin	07	26	a/a	CIN	4	6	45	1	96	106	64	9	51	76	6.01	1.63	9.7	275	4.7	7.1	1.5	0.9	33%	63%	48
	08	27	a/a	CIN	6	3	30	0	108	128	71	16	44	60	5.93	1.59	16.3	288	3.7	5.0	1.4	1.3	31%	65%	17
Maloney,Matthew	07	24	a/a	CIN	13	10	28	0	170	168	88	24	55	151	4.65	1.31	25.7	253	2.9	8.0	2.7	1.3	30%	68%	72
	08	25	aaa	CIN	11	5	25	0	140	164	89	23	40	115	5.72	1.46	24.5	286	2.6	7.4	2.9	1.5	33%	64%	58
Malone,Corwin	07	27	a/a	CHW	2	7	43	1	77	138	79	8	53	61	9.27	2.48	9.7	380	6.2	7.1	1.2	0.9	45%	61%	18
Manning,Charlie	07	29	a/a	NYY	4	2	41	3	61	65	40	4	33	48	5.89	1.60	6.7	266	4.9	7.1	1.5	0.5	33%	61%	60
Manon,Julio	07	34	a/a	OAK	2	1	20	1	21	13	9	3	11	25	3.79	1.16	4.3	178	4.7	10.7	2.3	1.4	23%	74%	89
	08	35	aa	BAL	2	7	56	32	63	48	36	6	31	60	5.19	1.25	4.7	207	4.4	8.5	1.9	0.8	26%	58%	80
Manship,Jeffrey	08	24	aa	MIN	3	6	14	0	76	104	45	8	26	49	5.36	1.70	25.2	319	3.0	5.8	1.9	1.0	37%	69%	37
Manuel,Robert	08	25 a	a/a	CIN	5	3	48	3	79	58	15	2	16	76	1.68	0.93	6.3	201	1.8	8.7	4.8	0.2	28%	82%	161
Marceaux,Jacob	08	25	aa	FLA	4	1	45	2	59	58	35	4	47	39	5.30	1.78	6.2	252	7.2	5.9	0.8	0.6	30%	70%	38
Marek,Stephen	08	25	aa	ATL	3	8	44	4	60	63	31	3	29	53	4.65	1.53	6.1	265	4.3	7.9	1.8	0.5	34%	69%	73
Markray,Thad	07	28	aa	KC	8	7	37	2	87	139	70	13	30	44	7.22	1.94	11.4	353	3.1	4.5	1.5	1.3	38%	63%	4
Marmol,Carlos	07	25	aa	CHC	4	1	8	0	41	37	24	5	13	38	5.31	1.21	21.1	235	2.8	8.3	3.0	1.2	29%	57%	87
Marquez,Jeffrey	07	23	aa	NYY	15	9	27	0	155	213	94	15	51	77	5.44	1.70	26.5	320	2.9	4.4	1.5	0.9	35%	68%	23
	08	24	a/a	NYY	7	8	17	0	96	130	65	15	34	37	6.09	1.71	26.1	317	3.2	3.5	1.1	1.4	33%	67%	-8
Marshall,Jay	08	26	aa	OAK	4	6	57	3	70	92	33	4	27	32	4.28	1.70	5.7	311	3.4	4.2	1.2	0.6	35%	75%	26
Marshall,Sean	08	26	aa	CHC	1	1	7	0	31	33	15	2	7	18	4.31	1.29	18.8	268	2.0	5.3	2.6	0.7	31%	67%	69
Marte,Jose	08	25	aa	ARI	4	2	36	7	49	66	34	9	27	29	6.31	1.88	6.5	314	4.9	5.3	1.1	1.6	34%	69%	-2
Marte,Luis	08	22	aa	DET	4	4	10	0	57	62	35	8	24	28	5.53	1.51	25.2	271	3.8	4.4	1.2	1.3	29%	65%	14
Martinez,Anastacio	07	29	a/a	DET	6	9	29	0	96	132	78	8	69	57	7.26	2.09	16.6	319	6.5	5.3	0.8	0.8	37%	64%	17
	08	30	a/a	DET	2	7	35	1	99	154	80	16	54	52	7.31	2.09	14.2	347	4.9	4.7	1.0	1.4	38%	66%	-9
Martinez,Carlos	07	25	aa	FLA	2	1	23	0	23	30	11	2	7	17	4.31	1.58	4.5	307	2.6	6.6	2.6	0.9	37%	74%	61
	08	26	aa	FLA	4	4	45	3	53	62	33	9	24	42	5.66	1.63	5.4	286	4.1	7.1	1.7	1.6	33%	69%	30
Martinez,Edgar	07	26	aaa	BOS	2	6	42	1	68	84	54	13	30	50	7.09	1.68	7.4	297	4.0	6.6	1.6	1.7	33%	60%	17
	08	27	aaa	BOS	8	3	33	2	113	115	66	16	60	72	5.25	1.55	15.3	259	4.8	5.7	1.2	1.3	29%	69%	23
Martinez,Jonathan	07	25	a/a	MIN	3	6	35	2	56	68	40	3	40	39	6.41	1.93	7.8	294	6.4	6.2	1.0	0.5	35%	65%	39
Martinez,Joseph	08	26	aa	SF	10	10	27	0	148	170	58	7	41	86	3.51	1.43	23.8	282	2.5	5.2	2.1	0.4	33%	75%	61
Martinez,Roman	08	24	aa	SEA	2	2	37	0	43	57	27	5	19	27	5.71	1.76	5.4	311	4.0	5.6	1.4	1.1	35%	69%	23
Martin,J.D.	07	25	aa	CLE	2	3	9	0	42	51	25	4	17	20	5.40	1.60	21.1	291	3.6	4.3	1.2	0.9	32%	67%	20
	08	26	a/a	CLE	12	3	35	0	89	99	33	8	23	67	3.29	1.37	10.9	275	2.3	6.7	2.9	0.8	33%	79%	75
Martis,Shairon	08	22	a/a	WAS	5	6	21	0	116	116	47	6	40	87	3.62	1.35	23.6	255	3.1	6.8	2.2	0.4	31%	73%	77
Mason,Christopher	07	23	aa	TAM	15	4	28	0	161	172	57	8	46	116	3.17	1.36	24.6	268	2.6	6.5	2.5	0.5	33%	77%	79
	08	24	aaa	TAM	3	10	33	0	108	161	87	20	40	78	7.24	1.86	15.7	338	3.3	6.5	2.0	1.7	38%	63%	17
Masset,Nick	07	25	aaa	CHW	0	4	11	0	45	63	32	9	10	29	6.45	1.61	18.6	322	2.0	5.7	2.8	1.8	35%	63%	30
Masterson,Justin	07	22	aa	BOS	4	3	10	0	58	66	40	5	21	43	6.21	1.50	25.6	280	3.3	6.6	2.0	0.7	34%	57%	59
	08	24	a/a	BOS	2	3	12	0	47	50	26	1	17	38	4.96	1.42	17.1	266	3.2	7.2	2.2	0.2	34%	62%	86
Mastny,Tom	08	28 b	aaa	CLE	2	2	28	0	35	33	9	1	14	36	2.43	1.32	5.3	241	3.5	9.3	2.6	0.3	33%	81%	110
Mata,Frank	07	24	aa	MIN	0	4	32	3	48	76	34	4	24	22	6.35	2.07	7.5	352	4.4	4.2	0.9	0.8	39%	69%	6
	08	25	aa	MIN	1	1	23	1	30	42	29	7	19	17	8.84	2.04	6.5	325	5.7	5.1	0.9	2.2	34%	59%	-27
Mateo,Juan	07	25	aa	CHC	2	3	8	0	40	61	24	11	12	23	5.45	1.82	23.7	343	2.6	5.1	2.0	2.4	36%	78%	-13
	08	26	aa	PIT	8	1	38	5	76	90	43	9	24	49	5.12	1.50	8.9	288	2.9	5.7	2.0	1.1	33%	67%	42
Mateo,Julio	07	30	aa	PHI	4	1	35	15	50	63	14	9	4	26	2.56	1.34	6.1	300	0.8	4.6	6.0	1.5	32%	90%	104
	08	31	aa	SF	3	4	25	4	61	112	58	11	13	28	8.48	2.04	12.1	385	1.9	4.1	2.2	1.6	41%	59%	2
Mathes,JR	07	26	aa	CHC	10	8	27	0	151	263	131	28	42	65	7.80	2.02	27.7	374	2.5	3.9	1.5	1.7	39%	63%	-14
	08	27	aa	CHC	9	5	27	0	140	198	86	20	37	54	5.53	1.67	23.8	326	2.4	3.5	1.5	1.3	34%	69%	4
Mathis,Douglas	07	24	aa	TEX	11	10	25	0	144	201	96	12	48	82	5.98	1.73	26.8	323	3.0	5.1	1.7	0.7	37%	65%	35
	08	25	aa	TEX	5	1	10	0	53	62	26	9	14	28	4.32	1.44	23.2	286	2.4	4.7	1.9	1.5	30%	75%	22
Matos,Osiris	07	23	aa	SF	5	0	35	4	56	59	22	3	22	36	3.48	1.44	7.0	264	3.5	5.8	1.7	0.5	31%	76%	57
	08	24 a	aa	SF	1	0	32	9	46	37	6	0	14	40	1.23	1.10	5.8	215	2.7	7.8	2.9	0.0	29%	88%	120
Mattheus,Ryan	07	24	aa	COL	9	11	26	0	158	228	138	18	57	88	7.86	1.80	28.7	330	3.2	5.0	1.6	1.0	37%	55%	22
	08	25	aa	COL	2	5	58	17	57	58	24	5	25	46	3.81	1.45	4.3	257	4.0	7.2	1.8	0.8	31%	76%	60
Mattox Jr,David	07	27	aa	KC	0	4	8	0	38	53	45	7	24	19	10.53	2.02	23.5	323	5.7	4.5	0.8	1.7	34%	47%	-17
Matumoto,Jo	07	37	aa	TOR	3	4	45	1	86	100	49	6	52	56	5.16	1.76	9.0	285	5.4	5.9	1.1	0.6	34%	70%	38
	08	38	a/a	TOR	2	1	42	0	64	100	36	10	36	39	5.00	2.12	7.7	349	5.0	5.4	1.1	1.4	39%	80%	-1
Mays,Joe	07	32	aa	LA	1	2	8	0	45	71	35	5	12	22	7.04	1.83	26.8	349	2.3	4.4	1.9	0.9	39%	61%	23
Mazone,Brian	07	31	aaa	PHI	3	2	6	0	36	37	12	5	8	16	2.88	1.25	25.2	258	2.1	4.0	1.9	1.3	27%	84%	28
	08	32	aaa	PHI	9	12	28	0	164	218	102	28	40	93	5.60	1.57	26.3	312	2.2	5.1	2.3	1.6	34%	68%	25
Mazzaro,Vince	08	22 a	aa	OAK	15	6	28	0	171	174	54	5	40	112	2.84	1.25	25.5	258	2.1	5.9	2.8	0.3	31%	77%	90
McBeth,Marcus	07	27	a/a	CIN	2	1	38	17	41	54	16	6	11	26	3.52	1.59	4.9	310	2.5	5.7	2.3	1.3	35%	83%	37
	08	28	aaa	BOS	2	1	28	2	31	32	26	8	17	25	7.44	1.59	5.0	261	5.0	7.2	1.5	2.2	28%	56%	12
McBride,Macay	07	25	aaa	DET	2	2	12	0	31	41	13	4	12	26	3.77	1.71	12.0	312	3.5	7.5	2.2	1.2	38%	82%	49
McCall,Derell	08	27	aa	FLA	1	4	8	0	35	53	30	4	18	19	7.72	2.03	21.7	341	4.6	4.9	1.1	0.9	38%	61%	11
McClaskey,Tim	07	32	aa	PHI	4	4	13	0	57	74	35	12	14	23	5.57	1.55	19.6	308	2.2	3.6	1.6	1.9	31%	69%	-6
McClellan,Kyle	07	23 a	aa	STL	2	0	24	0	30	27	9	2	6	25	2.77	1.09	5.0	233	1.8	7.5	4.1	0.6	29%	77%	121
McClung,Seth	07	27	aaa	MIL	3	5	45	5	77	63	21	6	53	81	2.40	1.50	7.6	218	6.1	9.5	1.5	0.7	29%	87%	79
McCrory,Robert	07	25	aa	BAL	1	2	22	13	23	29	13	0	17	17	5.22	1.98	5.1	301	6.5	6.7	1.0	0.0	38%	71%	57
	08	26	aaa	BAL	2	3	35	5	45	47	24	1	24	30	4.74	1.58	5.8	265	4.7	6.0	1.3	0.2	32%	68%	58
McCulloch,Kyle	08	24	aa	CHW	8	11	28	0	156	235	113	13	65	74	6.53	1.92	27.0	340	3.7	4.2	1.1	0.8	38%	65%	13
McCurdy,Nick	07	28	a/a	BAL	3	6	45	3	76	95	40	11	25	50	4.76	1.59	7.6	301	3.0	5.9	2.0	1.4	34%	74%	30
McCutchen,Daniel	07	25	aa	NYY	3	2	7	0	41	41	18	3	14	27	3.90	1.36	25.0	256	3.2	5.9	1.9	0.7	30%	72%	57
	08	26	a/a	PIT	11	12	28	0	171	210	92	30	39	113	4.85	1.45	26.7	296	2.0	6.0	2.9	1.6	33%	72%	45
McDonald,James	07	23 a	aa	LA	7	2	10	0	52	46	10	6	16	56	1.72	1.19	21.4	232	2.8	9.7	3.5	1.0	30%	93%	109
	08	24	aa	LA	7	4	27	0	141	131	59	16	55	124	3.75	1.32	22.1	241	3.5	7.9	2.3	1.1	30%	75%	70
McGee,Jacob	08	22	aa	TAM	6	4	15	0	77	72	39	6	36	56	4.55	1.40	22.2	242	4.2	6.5	1.6	0.7	29%	68%	57
McGinley,Blake	07	29	aa	FLA	6	9	43	1	81	119	65	15	41	45	7.26	1.98	9.2	334	4.6	5.0	1.1	1.6	36%	65%	-8
McKae,Dave	07	26	aa	SF	6	4	17	0	104	120	64	10	19	50	5.58	1.34	26.0	283	1.6	4.4	2.7	0.9	31%	58%	55
	08	27	aa	SF	8	9	28	0	124	186	92	11	40	55	6.67	1.83	21.0	340	2.9	4.0	1.4	0.8	37%	63%	15
McKeller,Ryan	08	25	aa	HOU	4	6	45	1	70	103	52	11	38	55	6.70	2.01	7.7	335	4.9	7.0	1.5	1.4	39%	68%	18
McLeary,Marty	07	33	aa	PIT	5	8	24	0	122	171	89	15	61	68	6.59	1.90	24.5	323	4.5	5.0	1.1	1.1	36%	66%	10
McLemore,Mark	07	27	aa	HOU	0	1	21	0	52	45	22	2	40	38	3.78	1.64	11.3	228	7.0	6.6	1.0	0.4	28%	76%	57
McNab,Timothy	07	27	aa	NYM	8	6	46	2	91	124	43	5	27	37	4.28	1.65	9.1	318	2.6	3.6	1.4	0.5	35%	74%	28
	08	28	aa	NYM	3	3	50	0	73	105	66	14	31	27	8.17	1.87	7.0	330	3.9	3.4	0.9	1.7	34%	57%	-23

Major League Equivalent Statistics

PITCHER	Yr	Age	Lev	Org	Actual w	l	g	sv	Major League Equivalents ip	h	er	hr	bb	k	era	whip	bf/g	oob	ctl	dom	cmd	hr/9	h%	s%	bpv
McNiven,Brooks	07	26	aa	SF	7	6	30	0	116	160	63	11	32	30	4.90	1.65	17.7	320	2.5	2.4	0.9	0.9	33%	71%	-2
	08	27	aa	SF	2	4	26	0	75	98	51	6	25	21	6.06	1.63	13.2	308	3.0	2.5	0.8	0.7	32%	62%	4
Meacham,Cory	07	23	aa	STL	11	8	28	0	144	168	88	15	53	68	5.47	1.53	22.9	285	3.3	4.2	1.3	1.0	31%	65%	22
Meaux,Ryan	07	29	aa	OAK	0	4	36	0	42	78	43	5	15	27	9.06	2.19	6.0	386	3.2	5.8	1.8	1.1	44%	57%	19
Medders,Brandon	07	28	aa	ARI	5	3	35	5	48	77	39	5	29	27	7.23	2.21	7.0	355	5.4	5.1	0.9	0.9	40%	67%	8
	08	29	aa	ARI	1	2	26	0	38	66	53	6	30	23	12.37	2.52	8.0	373	7.1	5.5	0.8	1.5	42%	49%	-15
Medlen,Kris	08	23 a	aa	ATL	7	8	36	1	120	139	56	8	28	102	4.17	1.39	14.4	284	2.1	7.6	3.7	0.6	36%	70%	102
Medlock,Calvin	07	25	a/a	TAM	6	3	51	2	79	74	39	6	30	72	4.46	1.32	6.6	243	3.4	8.2	2.4	0.7	31%	66%	85
	08	26	aaa	TAM	3	3	41	0	63	76	37	7	32	35	5.34	1.72	7.1	292	4.6	5.0	1.1	1.0	32%	70%	19
Meek,Evan	07	24	aa	TAM	2	1	44	1	67	88	41	2	37	58	5.51	1.87	7.3	311	4.9	7.8	1.6	0.3	40%	68%	64
	08	25	aa	PIT	1	1	32	4	57	57	22	2	19	39	3.50	1.32	7.6	254	3.0	6.1	2.0	0.4	31%	73%	73
Megrew,Michael	07	24	aa	LA	6	6	21	0	93	111	66	8	47	77	6.38	1.71	20.5	291	4.6	7.4	1.6	0.8	36%	62%	51
Melancon,Mark	08	24 a	a/a	NYY	7	1	31	3	69	52	21	5	17	58	2.73	1.00	8.7	205	2.2	7.5	3.4	0.7	26%	75%	111
Melendez,German	07	27	aa	HOU	6	5	44	4	79	92	53	18	40	48	6.02	1.66	8.2	284	4.5	5.5	1.2	2.1	30%	69%	-5
Meloan,Jonathan	07	23 a	aa	LA	7	2	49	20	66	41	18	6	28	78	2.38	1.04	5.4	176	3.8	10.5	2.8	0.8	24%	82%	116
	08	24	a/a	CLE	5	11	33	0	119	160	87	9	75	96	6.54	1.97	17.7	315	5.7	7.3	1.3	0.7	39%	66%	41
Mendez,Adalberto	07	26	aa	CHC	3	4	40	1	59	68	44	14	38	38	6.76	1.78	7.0	282	5.7	5.7	1.0	2.2	29%	67%	-12
Mendoza,Luis	07	24	aa	TEX	15	4	26	0	148	177	87	14	49	78	5.26	1.53	25.4	291	3.0	4.7	1.6	0.9	32%	66%	32
	08	25	aa	TEX	2	3	9	0	36	51	25	1	11	16	6.30	1.69	18.5	324	2.6	4.0	1.5	0.3	37%	60%	39
Meque,Jacobo	08	25 a	aa	LA	2	1	25	5	33	32	17	1	14	32	4.55	1.41	5.7	251	3.9	8.6	2.2	0.3	34%	66%	93
Messenger,Randy	08	27	aa	SEA	9	4	41	4	63	87	37	7	28	34	5.32	1.81	7.3	320	3.9	4.8	1.2	1.0	36%	72%	15
Meyer,Dan	07	26	aa	OAK	8	2	22	0	119	141	62	17	61	79	4.69	1.70	25.0	289	4.6	6.0	1.3	1.3	33%	76%	21
	08	27	aa	OAK	10	5	22	0	122	145	77	11	55	77	5.68	1.64	25.3	288	4.1	5.7	1.4	0.8	33%	65%	37
Michalak,Chris	07	37	aaa	WAS	5	8	20	0	100	121	48	12	28	37	4.36	1.49	22.1	293	2.6	3.3	1.3	1.0	31%	73%	13
	08	38	aa	OAK	1	4	35	0	51	74	36	12	31	20	6.44	2.05	7.2	332	5.4	3.5	0.6	2.1	33%	73%	-40
Mickolio,Kameron	07	23	aa	SEA	6	4	32	3	53	49	20	3	24	48	3.31	1.38	7.1	242	4.0	8.0	2.0	0.5	31%	76%	81
	08	24	a/a	BAL	3	1	45	3	58	61	30	2	31	53	4.63	1.58	5.8	264	4.8	8.3	1.7	0.3	35%	69%	78
Middleton,Kyle	07	27	aa	HOU	3	2	44	23	51	63	28	6	22	31	4.89	1.65	5.3	296	3.8	5.4	1.4	1.1	33%	72%	26
	08	28	aa	HOU	1	2	17	4	39	51	29	6	10	17	6.62	1.57	10.3	310	2.3	3.9	1.7	1.4	32%	59%	8
Mijares,Jose	07	23	a/a	MIN	5	4	51	9	69	58	39	11	57	66	5.07	1.66	6.2	223	7.4	8.6	1.2	1.4	27%	73%	43
Mikrut,Jonathan	08	26	aa	STL	4	3	44	0	65	76	37	13	20	35	5.06	1.47	6.5	284	2.8	4.8	1.8	1.8	29%	72%	9
Mildren,Paul	07	23	aa	KC	6	8	24	0	119	161	106	19	61	65	8.03	1.86	23.7	316	4.6	4.9	1.1	1.4	34%	57%	2
	08	24	aa	KC	2	6	23	1	46	69	42	7	31	31	8.24	2.17	10.2	341	6.0	6.1	1.0	1.4	39%	63%	2
Miller,Adam	07	23 a	aaa	CLE	5	4	19	0	65	73	40	4	20	65	5.53	1.43	14.9	278	2.8	9.0	3.3	0.5	37%	60%	106
Miller,Andrew	07	22 a	a/a	DET	2	0	6	0	36	34	12	2	10	29	2.98	1.22	25.0	243	2.5	7.2	2.9	0.5	30%	76%	96
Miller,Derek	07	26	aa	MIL	6	2	11	0	68	74	33	13	19	53	4.41	1.37	26.5	273	2.5	7.0	2.8	1.8	31%	75%	49
	08	27	aa	MIL	6	2	16	0	73	106	48	7	44	33	5.94	2.04	22.7	331	5.4	4.1	0.8	0.8	36%	71%	4
Miller,Greg	07	23	aa	LA	2	3	34	1	76	73	58	3	89	85	6.85	2.13	11.3	247	10.5	10.0	1.0	0.4	35%	65%	75
	08	24	aa	LA	2	3	48	0	53	64	54	3	65	47	9.07	2.42	5.9	292	11.0	7.9	0.7	0.5	37%	60%	43
Miller,Jason	07	25	aaa	MIN	1	5	31	0	75	106	48	13	27	30	5.81	1.78	11.4	326	3.3	3.6	1.1	1.6	34%	71%	-13
	08	26	aa	MIN	1	3	36	0	85	129	71	13	40	57	7.55	1.99	11.6	342	4.3	6.1	1.4	1.3	39%	63%	13
Miller,Jim	07	25	a/a	BAL	3	5	52	7	66	63	34	4	43	66	4.59	1.61	5.8	247	5.9	8.9	1.5	0.6	33%	71%	74
	08	26	a/a	BAL	3	6	56	10	80	78	38	7	29	76	4.25	1.33	6.1	250	3.3	8.5	2.6	0.8	32%	69%	89
Miller,Joshua	07	29	aa	HOU	6	6	35	3	137	205	83	23	31	54	5.41	1.72	18.2	338	2.0	3.6	1.7	1.5	35%	72%	1
	08	30	aa	HOU	8	9	28	1	148	261	121	40	24	47	7.38	1.93	25.6	377	1.5	2.9	2.0	2.4	37%	67%	-35
Miller,Matt	07	36	aaa	CLE	0	1	38	1	37	29	15	4	22	31	3.57	1.39	4.2	214	5.4	7.6	1.4	1.0	26%	78%	57
	08	37	aa	PIT	4	7	33	8	43	60	41	4	27	33	8.60	2.02	6.5	323	5.7	6.9	1.2	0.7	39%	55%	36
Mills,Adam	08	24 a	aa	BOS	0	5	11	0	63	79	35	2	8	31	5.01	1.39	24.7	301	1.2	4.4	3.8	0.3	35%	61%	92
Mills,Alan	07	41	aa	DET	1	1	29	23	29	31	14	1	13	16	4.38	1.50	4.4	265	4.0	5.0	1.2	0.4	31%	69%	47
Mills,Bradley	08	24	aa	TOR	3	2	6	0	32	28	5	2	12	26	1.44	1.25	22.4	228	3.5	7.3	2.1	0.6	29%	92%	80
Miner,Zach	07	26	a/a	DET	1	4	13	0	53	59	41	5	24	29	6.94	1.56	18.3	275	4.1	4.8	1.2	0.9	31%	54%	27
Minix,Travis	08	31	a/a	PHI	3	7	24	0	63	79	43	7	27	37	6.17	1.67	12.1	299	3.8	5.3	1.4	0.9	34%	63%	27
Misch,Pat	07	26	aa	SF	2	5	34	1	66	70	30	5	22	55	4.06	1.39	8.4	266	3.0	7.5	2.5	0.6	33%	71%	80
	08	27	aa	SF	6	5	20	0	87	142	80	18	33	39	8.23	2.01	21.4	359	3.4	4.0	1.2	1.9	38%	61%	-23
Mitchell,Andy	07	29	aaa	BAL	8	8	39	0	116	167	79	9	45	56	6.14	1.83	14.1	330	3.5	4.3	1.2	0.7	37%	65%	20
	08	30	aaa	BAL	12	8	32	0	138	171	87	16	61	56	5.65	1.68	19.9	298	4.0	3.6	0.9	1.0	32%	67%	6
Mobley,Chris	07	24	aa	FLA	7	2	39	11	41	58	24	3	14	25	5.29	1.74	4.9	325	3.0	5.4	1.8	0.7	37%	69%	40
	08	25	aa	FLA	5	3	58	28	62	79	40	4	22	59	5.80	1.63	4.9	303	3.2	8.6	2.7	0.6	39%	63%	83
Mock,Garrett	07	24	aa	WAS	1	5	11	0	51	78	40	5	29	32	7.05	2.10	23.3	343	5.2	5.7	1.1	0.9	39%	66%	16
	08	25 a	aaa	WAS	6	3	19	0	104	108	38	8	24	79	3.32	1.27	23.0	262	2.1	6.8	3.3	0.7	32%	76%	91
Molldrem,Craig	07	26	aa	FLA	5	4	53	0	70	90	48	8	46	43	6.20	1.93	6.4	305	5.9	5.5	0.9	1.0	34%	68%	15
Morales,Alexis	07	25	a/a	WAS	4	3	28	2	38	32	24	2	44	42	5.62	2.01	6.7	224	10.5	9.9	0.9	0.5	31%	71%	75
Morales,Franklin	07	22	aa	COL	5	4	20	0	112	118	60	12	58	83	4.81	1.57	25.2	265	4.7	6.7	1.4	1.0	31%	71%	43
	08	23	aa	COL	10	5	21	0	110	119	75	15	74	71	6.13	1.75	24.5	270	6.0	5.8	1.0	1.2	30%	66%	19
Morales,Ricardo	07	24	aa	NYM	3	2	13	0	44	53	31	7	11	22	6.31	1.45	14.8	290	2.3	4.6	2.0	1.5	31%	58%	21
Moreno,Edwin	08	28	aa	SD	5	8	60	26	71	73	43	10	40	45	5.39	1.58	5.3	259	5.1	5.7	1.1	1.3	29%	68%	23
Moreno,Victor	07	28	aaa	BAL	2	5	39	3	64	91	55	5	35	42	7.71	1.98	8.0	328	5.0	5.9	1.2	0.8	38%	59%	27
Morillo,Juan	07	24	aa	COL	6	5	53	0	67	64	27	3	32	61	3.60	1.43	5.5	246	4.3	8.2	1.9	0.4	32%	74%	83
	08	25	aa	COL	1	0	52	0	59	61	41	3	54	45	6.24	1.94	5.5	261	8.2	6.8	0.8	0.5	32%	66%	47
Morlan,Eduardo	08	23	aa	TAM	4	2	30	1	47	49	22	5	15	39	4.21	1.36	6.7	263	2.9	7.5	2.6	1.0	32%	71%	73
Morrow,Brandon	08	24	aa	SEA	1	2	12	0	30	23	16	2	18	29	4.71	1.36	10.8	208	5.3	8.8	1.6	0.6	27%	65%	82
Mortensen,Clayton	08	23	aa	STL	8	10	26	0	139	162	86	16	61	87	5.53	1.60	24.2	285	3.9	5.6	1.4	1.1	32%	67%	30
Morton,Charlie	07	24	aa	ATL	4	6	41	0	79	96	49	3	40	55	5.62	1.72	9.0	293	4.6	6.3	1.4	0.4	36%	65%	52
	08	25 a	aaa	ATL	5	2	13	0	79	58	22	0	27	63	2.51	1.08	24.3	201	3.1	7.2	2.3	0.0	27%	74%	107
Moscoso,Guillermo	08	25 a	aa	DET	3	1	6	0	34	27	14	4	7	42	3.60	1.02	22.4	215	1.9	11.0	5.7	1.1	30%	69%	164
Mosebach,Robert	08	24	aa	LAA	9	12	29	0	177	251	115	6	72	72	5.83	1.82	28.9	326	3.6	3.7	1.0	0.3	36%	66%	23
Moseley,Dustin	08	27	aa	LAA	7	10	20	0	116	195	124	26	38	63	9.61	2.01	28.6	365	2.9	4.9	1.7	2.0	39%	53%	-16
Moss,Damian	08	32	aaa	ATL	5	9	41	0	96	126	54	8	66	71	5.03	2.00	11.5	310	6.2	6.7	1.1	0.8	37%	75%	32
Motte,Jason	07	25	aa	STL	3	3	45	8	49	44	13	3	23	50	2.45	1.38	4.7	237	4.3	9.1	2.1	0.6	32%	84%	88
	08	26 b	aa	STL	4	3	63	9	66	79	30	6	28	82	4.06	1.61	4.8	291	3.8	11.1	3.0	0.8	41%	76%	102
Muecke,Joshua	07	26	aa	HOU	9	5	32	0	131	168	76	23	50	59	5.19	1.66	18.8	305	3.4	4.1	1.2	1.6	32%	73%	-5
	08	27	aa	HOU	8	13	29	0	165	205	106	26	69	79	5.76	1.66	26.1	298	3.8	4.3	1.1	1.4	32%	68%	2
Muegge,Danny	08	28	aa	LA	0	5	23	1	65	102	48	5	23	27	6.66	1.92	13.7	350	3.2	3.7	1.2	0.7	38%	64%	11

					Actual				Major League Equivalents																
PITCHER	Yr	Age	Lev	Org	w	l	g	sv	ip	h	er	hr	bb	k	era	whip	bf/g	oob	ctl	dom	cmd	hr/9	h%	s%	bpv
Mujica,Edward	07	23 a	aaa	CLE	2	1	34	14	37	40	25	4	9	40	6.05	1.32	4.6	269	2.2	9.7	4.4	1.0	36%	53%	124
Mullins,Ryan	07	24	a/a	MIN	4	6	18	0	101	136	73	8	30	64	6.50	1.64	25.6	316	2.7	5.7	2.1	0.7	37%	59%	50
	08	25	aa	MIN	9	9	30	0	148	200	87	19	63	77	5.31	1.78	23.2	316	3.8	4.7	1.2	1.2	35%	72%	11
Mulvey,Kevin	07	22	aa	NYM	12	10	27	0	157	164	65	4	42	98	3.72	1.31	24.6	263	2.4	5.6	2.3	0.2	32%	70%	78
	08	23	aaa	MIN	7	9	27	0	148	171	72	16	49	99	4.38	1.49	24.2	284	3.0	6.0	2.0	1.0	33%	73%	48
Muniz,Carlos	07	27 b	aa	NYM	2	4	47	23	64	61	22	2	20	50	3.07	1.26	5.7	246	2.7	7.0	2.5	0.3	31%	75%	91
	08	28	aa	NYM	2	4	33	9	36	41	23	6	17	22	5.69	1.60	5.0	279	4.2	5.6	1.3	1.5	30%	67%	16
Munoz,Arnie	07	25	aaa	WAS	3	1	54	0	52	54	19	5	18	39	3.31	1.37	4.2	260	3.1	6.7	2.1	0.9	31%	79%	61
Munoz,Luis	07	26	aa	PIT	14	6	28	0	153	193	82	14	39	79	4.83	1.52	24.3	302	2.3	4.7	2.0	0.8	34%	69%	40
	08	27	aa	SEA	5	9	27	0	129	198	110	22	67	61	7.69	2.05	23.8	344	4.6	4.2	0.9	1.5	37%	64%	-15
Munter,Scott	07	28	aa	SF	1	6	48	1	58	84	39	4	29	10	5.97	1.95	5.9	332	4.5	1.5	0.3	0.6	34%	68%	-12
	08	29	a/a	SF	3	1	46	0	57	91	28	6	18	21	4.44	1.89	6.0	352	2.8	3.3	1.2	0.9	38%	78%	2
Mura,Kyle	08	24	aa	STL	3	5	11	0	62	79	21	5	9	20	2.99	1.43	24.5	304	1.3	3.0	2.2	0.7	32%	81%	36
Murphy,Bill	07	26	aa	ARI	3	3	54	1	100	125	60	15	49	78	5.37	1.75	8.6	300	4.4	7.0	1.6	1.3	35%	72%	30
	08	27	aaa	TOR	8	10	32	2	142	197	119	20	97	120	7.54	2.07	22.1	322	6.1	7.6	1.2	1.3	39%	64%	24
Murray,Arlington	07	26	aa	TEX	3	3	41	5	52	56	26	3	28	40	4.41	1.60	5.8	267	4.8	6.8	1.4	0.6	33%	72%	55
Murray,A.J.	08	27	aa	OAK	2	2	9	0	45	62	24	3	15	27	4.83	1.71	23.2	321	3.0	5.4	1.8	0.7	37%	72%	40
Musser,Neal	07	27 b	aa	KC	4	1	32	8	55	45	5	1	13	34	0.79	1.05	6.8	217	2.2	5.6	2.6	0.2	26%	94%	93
	08	28	aa	KC	3	5	37	6	56	69	44	13	46	45	7.03	2.05	7.5	296	7.4	7.2	1.0	2.0	33%	70%	-1
Nall,Brandon	07	26	aa	NYM	2	0	34	0	43	62	29	0	18	29	6.03	1.86	6.1	331	3.7	6.0	1.6	0.0	40%	64%	59
Nall,T.J.	07	27	a/a	BOS	3	12	18	0	88	158	82	21	42	46	8.41	2.27	25.4	380	4.3	4.7	1.1	2.2	40%	66%	-35
Nannini,Micke	07	27	aa	CHC	1	2	28	1	53	73	41	11	31	35	6.96	1.98	9.3	322	5.3	5.9	1.1	1.8	35%	68%	-6
Narron,Sam	07	26	aa	MIL	7	9	27	0	151	236	102	15	32	75	6.09	1.77	26.3	348	1.9	4.5	2.3	0.9	39%	65%	34
	08	27	a/a	MIL	15	5	28	0	172	226	100	25	59	62	5.23	1.66	28.1	311	3.1	3.2	1.1	1.3	32%	71%	-5
Narveson,Chris	07	26	aa	STL	3	2	9	0	45	50	37	7	22	28	7.30	1.60	22.7	275	4.4	5.6	1.3	1.3	30%	54%	20
	08	27	aaa	MIL	6	13	28	0	136	156	91	24	58	110	6.00	1.57	21.8	282	3.8	7.3	1.9	1.6	33%	65%	35
Neal,Blaine	07	29	aaa	TOR	5	7	47	11	56	74	36	11	31	39	5.82	1.86	5.7	310	4.9	6.3	1.3	1.8	34%	73%	4
	08	31	aaa	DET	1	0	38	26	37	37	7	3	13	31	1.62	1.35	4.2	253	3.2	7.4	2.3	0.8	31%	93%	73
Nelson,Brad	07	26	a/a	ATL	6	2	32	0	87	97	47	6	28	47	4.90	1.44	11.9	276	2.9	4.8	1.6	0.7	31%	65%	43
	08	27	a/a	ATL	3	3	43	2	82	129	62	6	29	44	6.83	1.92	9.2	350	3.2	4.8	1.5	0.6	40%	63%	28
Nelson,Bubba	07	26	a/a	PHI	5	8	36	1	112	117	66	17	49	65	5.26	1.48	13.7	263	3.9	5.2	1.3	1.3	28%	67%	21
Ness,Joe	07	24	aa	CLE	4	3	26	0	71	94	62	7	46	53	7.83	1.97	13.4	311	5.9	6.8	1.1	0.9	37%	59%	30
Nestor,Scott	07	23	aa	FLA	2	4	58	1	75	75	44	5	43	77	5.32	1.58	5.8	256	5.2	9.2	1.8	0.6	34%	65%	78
	08	24	aa	FLA	1	1	55	0	61	63	62	9	54	56	9.13	1.91	5.4	261	7.9	8.2	1.0	1.4	32%	51%	32
Newman,Josh	07	25	aa	COL	3	2	55	0	62	99	42	4	33	40	6.13	2.13	5.7	353	4.8	5.7	1.2	0.6	41%	70%	24
	08	26	aa	KC	1	2	27	1	44	53	26	1	25	30	5.41	1.78	7.7	292	5.2	6.2	1.2	0.2	36%	67%	52
Newsom,Randy	07	25	aa	CLE	4	1	47	18	49	67	23	3	19	18	4.29	1.75	4.9	318	3.5	3.3	1.0	0.6	35%	76%	13
	08	26	a/a	CLE	5	2	56	30	54	70	26	2	41	27	4.24	2.05	4.8	307	6.8	4.5	0.7	0.4	35%	79%	23
Nicoll,Christopher	08	25 a	aa	KC	4	1	19	3	43	54	20	2	8	46	4.17	1.44	9.9	299	1.8	9.5	5.4	0.4	40%	70%	153
Niemann,Jeff	07	25	aaa	TAM	12	6	25	0	131	175	79	16	50	108	5.43	1.72	24.3	314	3.4	7.4	2.2	1.1	38%	70%	49
	08	26	aaa	TAM	9	5	24	0	133	114	62	16	49	110	4.17	1.23	23.0	227	3.3	7.4	2.2	1.1	27%	69%	68
Niese,Jonathon	08	22	aa	NYM	11	8	29	0	164	171	67	9	56	124	3.68	1.38	24.3	263	3.1	6.8	2.2	0.5	32%	73%	75
Nieve,Fernando	08	26	aa	HOU	2	5	36	6	72	106	54	15	29	47	6.74	1.87	9.6	334	3.6	5.9	1.6	1.9	37%	67%	2
Nippert,Dustin	07	26	aa	ARI	0	3	10	0	36	31	28	5	26	36	6.90	1.60	16.3	228	6.6	8.9	1.3	1.1	29%	57%	57
	08	27	aa	TEX	6	2	12	0	63	87	39	11	18	31	5.50	1.66	24.1	320	2.6	4.4	1.7	1.5	34%	71%	7
Nix,Michael	07	24	aa	ATL	4	6	44	0	69	71	24	2	33	59	3.15	1.49	6.9	259	4.2	7.7	1.8	0.3	33%	78%	79
	08	25	a/a	ATL	5	4	47	1	64	79	49	4	46	48	6.95	1.95	6.6	297	6.5	6.7	1.0	0.6	36%	63%	39
Norris,Bud	08	24	aa	HOU	3	8	19	0	80	97	38	8	30	70	4.29	1.59	19.0	293	3.4	7.9	2.3	0.9	36%	75%	65
Norrito,Giuseppe	07	25	aa	LA	8	5	24	0	117	166	71	20	29	45	5.46	1.66	22.4	326	2.2	3.5	1.6	1.5	34%	71%	-3
Nottingham,Shawn	07	23	aa	CLE	9	12	27	0	149	180	97	11	60	87	5.86	1.61	25.0	293	3.6	5.3	1.5	0.7	34%	62%	39
	08	24	aa	CLE	0	2	19	0	33	48	34	6	18	28	9.28	2.00	8.5	335	4.8	7.7	1.6	1.7	39%	53%	17
Novoa,Roberto	08	29	a/a	SF	3	2	42	2	60	104	51	7	34	34	7.67	2.29	7.5	371	5.1	5.0	1.0	1.1	41%	66%	-1
Novoa,Yunior	08	24	aa	WAS	2	1	32	0	51	40	15	2	23	40	2.59	1.23	6.6	211	4.1	7.0	1.7	0.4	27%	79%	80
Nunez,Leo	07	24	aa	KC	2	2	11	0	43	32	12	4	11	27	2.41	0.97	15.3	200	2.2	5.5	2.5	0.9	22%	81%	75
Nunez,Vladimir	07	33	aaa	CHW	4	10	29	1	111	144	97	23	52	66	7.84	1.76	17.9	308	4.2	5.3	1.3	1.9	33%	57%	-4
	08	34	aaa	ATL	3	1	37	3	57	65	28	1	29	50	4.48	1.66	7.1	281	4.6	7.9	1.7	0.2	37%	71%	77
O'Connor,Mike	07	27	aa	WAS	3	7	15	0	71	116	78	25	23	32	9.91	1.95	23.1	358	2.9	4.1	1.4	3.2	35%	53%	-58
	08	28	aaa	WAS	5	3	16	0	99	96	28	10	17	55	2.54	1.14	25.2	248	1.6	5.0	3.2	0.9	28%	82%	76
O'Day,Darren	07	25	aa	LAA	3	4	29	10	29	34	17	3	15	18	5.21	1.66	4.6	284	4.6	5.6	1.2	1.0	32%	70%	28
	08	26	aa	LAA	2	2	21	7	33	37	16	3	8	23	4.24	1.35	6.7	276	2.1	6.4	3.0	0.9	32%	70%	74
O'Malley,Ryan	07	27	aa	CHC	5	9	29	0	122	240	142	37	48	51	10.47	2.36	22.2	402	3.5	3.7	1.1	2.8	41%	58%	-63
	08	29	aa	CHW	4	3	20	0	64	151	65	5	21	32	9.13	2.69	18.0	447	3.0	4.5	1.5	0.7	50%	64%	3
Obermueller,Wes	07	31	aa	FLA	4	1	11	0	63	107	53	9	40	29	7.54	2.33	30.1	368	5.7	4.1	0.7	1.2	40%	68%	-16
Ohka,Tomo	07	32	aa	SEA	0	5	7	0	41	86	55	9	15	12	12.14	2.47	31.6	418	3.4	2.6	0.8	2.1	42%	50%	-59
	08	33	aaa	CHW	5	11	28	0	135	182	86	34	38	95	5.75	1.63	22.0	316	2.5	6.3	2.5	2.2	34%	72%	15
Ohlendorf,Ross	07	25	aaa	NYY	3	4	22	0	68	106	51	9	25	41	6.67	1.93	15.0	348	3.3	5.4	1.6	1.2	39%	66%	15
	08	26	a/a	PIT	5	4	12	0	69	94	38	8	14	49	4.93	1.58	25.9	319	1.9	6.3	3.4	1.0	37%	70%	69
Ojeda,Alvis	07	24	aa	LA	4	7	26	0	106	160	82	14	60	57	6.96	2.07	20.4	340	5.1	4.8	1.0	1.2	38%	67%	1
Olenberger,Kasey	07	30	aa	LAA	10	7	29	0	180	319	177	52	63	74	8.87	2.12	31.3	377	3.1	3.7	1.2	2.6	38%	62%	-52
	08	31	aa	LAA	4	6	36	0	116	191	106	26	74	49	8.20	2.29	16.8	361	5.8	3.8	0.7	2.0	37%	67%	-40
Olson,Garrett	07	24	aaa	BAL	9	7	22	0	128	117	63	17	40	105	4.43	1.23	24.1	238	2.8	7.4	2.6	1.2	28%	67%	71
	08	25 a	aaa	BAL	1	2	7	0	36	40	14	1	15	34	3.49	1.52	22.9	275	3.7	8.5	2.3	0.2	37%	76%	91
Omogrosso,Brian	08	24	aa	CHW	2	3	17	1	39	41	23	3	27	22	5.34	1.75	10.7	265	6.3	5.0	0.8	0.7	30%	69%	27
Ool,Kevin	07	27	aa	STL	4	2	21	0	56	101	41	5	18	27	6.63	2.13	13.5	381	2.9	4.3	1.5	0.7	42%	68%	13
Orenduff,Justin	07	24	aa	LA	8	5	27	0	109	132	62	19	47	95	5.13	1.64	18.4	292	3.9	7.8	2.0	1.6	35%	73%	39
	08	25	aa	LA	3	7	31	1	110	173	100	30	73	77	8.18	2.24	18.3	350	6.0	6.3	1.1	2.5	38%	68%	-29
Ortega,Anthony	08	23	aa	LAA	14	7	28	0	174	198	82	13	56	88	4.26	1.46	27.2	280	2.9	4.6	1.6	0.7	31%	71%	39
Orvella,Chad	07	27	aaa	TAM	3	3	42	20	52	49	26	8	22	45	4.55	1.38	5.3	246	3.8	7.7	2.0	1.5	29%	72%	51
Oseguera,Paul	08	25	aa	SF	3	2	19	0	57	66	39	7	31	36	6.15	1.70	13.9	285	4.8	5.7	1.2	1.2	32%	65%	22
Osoria,Franquelis	07	26	aa	PIT	2	5	39	11	54	67	22	3	22	24	3.63	1.63	6.3	296	3.6	4.0	1.1	0.6	33%	78%	26
Ostlund,Ian	07	29	a/a	DET	2	1	29	1	38	52	22	7	8	30	5.27	1.57	5.9	317	1.9	7.0	3.6	1.7	36%	71%	60
	08	30 b	aaa	DET	3	0	44	0	69	78	25	7	18	62	3.29	1.38	6.8	279	2.3	8.0	3.5	0.9	35%	79%	96
Ottavino,Adam	08	23	aa	STL	3	7	24	0	115	143	72	14	48	82	5.63	1.66	22.0	298	3.8	6.4	1.7	1.1	35%	67%	37

					Actual				Major League Equivalents																
PITCHER	Yr	Age	Lev	Org	w	l	g	sv	ip	h	er	hr	bb	k	era	whip	bf/g	oob	ctl	dom	cmd	hr/9	h%	s%	bpv
Outman,Joshua	07	23	aa	PHI	2	3	7	0	42	44	26	6	24	28	5.52	1.62	27.2	265	5.1	6.0	1.2	1.3	30%	68%	23
	08	24	aa	OAK	7	4	42	1	98	101	38	4	42	70	3.48	1.46	10.2	261	3.9	6.4	1.7	0.4	32%	76%	65
Overbey,Seth	07	23	aa	TOR	2	4	30	2	50	65	31	4	15	26	5.54	1.60	7.6	307	2.8	4.7	1.7	0.7	35%	65%	35
	08	24	aa	TOR	4	3	53	1	74	96	41	7	40	42	4.99	1.83	6.6	307	4.9	5.1	1.0	0.9	35%	74%	19
Overholt,Patrick	07	23	aa	PHI	6	9	15	0	79	122	73	14	51	39	8.30	2.19	26.9	346	5.8	4.4	0.8	1.6	37%	63%	-20
	08	25	aa	PHI	3	8	49	10	78	86	58	12	49	59	6.67	1.74	7.4	275	5.7	6.8	1.2	1.3	32%	63%	26
Oxspring,Chris	07	30	aaa	MIL	7	5	18	0	96	118	53	12	51	86	5.00	1.76	25.0	296	4.8	8.1	1.7	1.1	36%	74%	46
Oyervidez,Jose	07	26	aa	SD	0	1	7	0	30	46	28	2	13	16	8.33	1.96	20.9	342	4.0	4.9	1.2	0.7	39%	55%	21
	08	27	aa	HOU	1	3	43	3	76	115	63	7	45	41	7.48	2.10	8.9	341	5.3	4.8	0.9	0.8	38%	63%	11
Palazzolo,Steve	08	27	aa	SF	5	6	29	1	50	54	37	1	45	32	6.59	1.97	8.5	269	8.0	5.8	0.7	0.2	33%	64%	45
Palmer,Jonathan	07	29	aa	SF	11	8	30	0	155	231	116	24	65	69	6.75	1.91	25.0	338	3.8	4.0	1.1	1.4	36%	66%	-8
Palmer,Matt	08	30	aa	SF	6	10	26	0	142	215	111	15	95	91	7.01	2.18	27.8	341	6.0	5.8	1.0	0.9	39%	67%	14
Parisi,Mike	07	24	aa	STL	8	13	28	0	165	223	106	21	65	93	5.80	1.75	27.5	317	3.6	5.1	1.4	1.1	35%	68%	18
	08	25	aa	STL	8	2	15	0	84	96	43	7	33	45	4.64	1.53	24.9	280	3.6	4.8	1.4	0.7	32%	70%	35
Parker,Zack	07	26	aa	COL	2	1	16	0	33	49	38	6	29	15	10.34	2.37	10.9	339	7.8	4.0	0.5	1.6	36%	56%	-25
	08	27	aa	TEX	3	1	27	0	74	90	39	2	47	42	4.68	1.85	13.1	295	5.7	5.0	0.9	0.3	34%	73%	36
Park,Chan Ho	07	34	aa	HOU	6	14	24	0	135	219	126	36	47	86	8.38	1.97	27.5	357	3.1	5.7	1.8	2.4	38%	61%	-17
Parnell,Robert	07	23	aa	NYM	5	5	17	0	88	113	56	9	38	62	5.68	1.72	24.1	306	3.9	6.3	1.6	0.9	36%	67%	38
	08	24	aa	NYM	12	8	29	0	148	178	94	15	67	93	5.70	1.66	23.4	292	4.1	5.7	1.4	0.9	33%	66%	33
Paronto,Chad	08	33	aa	HOU	0	2	35	3	52	75	21	2	15	42	3.65	1.74	6.9	331	2.6	7.2	2.7	0.4	41%	79%	77
Parque,Jim	07	32	aa	SEA	1	3	11	0	45	96	53	7	24	19	10.59	2.67	22.9	423	4.7	3.7	0.8	1.4	45%	59%	-33
Parra,Manuel	07	25 a	a/a	MIL	10	4	17	0	106	102	38	3	36	93	3.23	1.30	26.4	248	3.1	7.9	2.6	0.3	32%	74%	99
Parrish,John	08	31	aaa	TOR	10	1	17	0	91	107	43	8	48	75	4.29	1.70	24.7	286	4.7	7.4	1.6	0.8	35%	76%	52
Parr,James	07	22	aa	ATL	4	5	18	0	98	130	63	9	26	64	5.79	1.59	24.6	312	2.4	5.9	2.5	0.8	36%	63%	55
	08	23	a/a	ATL	13	7	28	0	150	154	70	13	51	109	4.19	1.36	23.0	260	3.1	6.5	2.1	0.8	31%	70%	64
Patterson,Scott	07	28 b	a/a	NYY	4	2	44	2	77	65	14	1	19	65	1.65	1.08	7.0	223	2.2	7.6	3.5	0.1	29%	84%	125
	08	29	aaa	NYY	2	1	42	5	47	60	29	10	14	41	5.46	1.59	5.1	305	2.7	7.8	2.9	1.9	35%	71%	44
Patton,Troy	07	22	aa	HOU	10	8	24	0	151	159	70	17	44	80	4.17	1.34	26.8	265	2.6	4.8	1.8	1.0	29%	72%	38
Pauley,David	07	24	aaa	BOS	6	6	27	0	153	198	100	21	52	94	5.87	1.63	25.8	307	3.1	5.5	1.8	1.2	34%	66%	28
	08	25	aaa	BOS	14	4	25	0	147	173	74	10	41	87	4.51	1.46	25.7	287	2.5	5.3	2.1	0.6	33%	69%	55
Paulino,Felipe	07	24	aa	HOU	4	5	22	0	112	121	56	7	51	90	4.47	1.53	22.6	269	4.1	7.2	1.8	0.6	33%	70%	65
Paulk,Robert	07	27	aa	NYM	2	5	36	2	82	133	52	11	32	42	5.68	2.02	11.2	358	3.5	4.6	1.3	1.3	39%	74%	0
Payano,Nelson	08	26	aa	SEA	4	3	41	0	67	84	39	3	48	51	5.22	1.97	8.0	301	6.4	6.9	1.1	0.4	37%	72%	45
Peguero,Jailen	07	27	aa	ARI	6	2	53	4	66	63	21	7	30	52	2.81	1.41	5.4	246	4.1	7.1	1.7	0.9	30%	84%	57
	08	28	aa	ARI	6	4	51	5	70	101	52	7	48	50	6.65	2.13	6.9	331	6.2	6.4	1.0	0.9	39%	69%	21
Peguero,Tony	07	27	a/a	TAM	3	5	29	0	93	148	96	26	64	41	9.23	2.28	16.7	352	6.2	4.0	0.6	2.5	36%	63%	-52
Pelfrey,Mike	07	24	aa	NYM	3	6	14	0	74	86	39	6	26	47	4.76	1.50	23.4	284	3.1	5.7	1.8	0.8	33%	69%	48
Pelland,Tyler	07	24	a/a	CIN	6	5	54	2	89	94	47	9	40	84	4.74	1.50	7.3	265	4.0	8.5	2.1	0.9	34%	70%	70
	08	25	aaa	CIN	1	2	36	1	44	45	24	5	28	44	4.95	1.67	5.6	261	5.8	8.9	1.5	1.0	33%	72%	58
Pena,Luismar	07	25 a	aa	MIL	0	4	35	12	46	44	20	1	16	36	3.90	1.30	5.6	247	3.1	7.0	2.3	0.2	31%	68%	90
	08	26	aaa	MIL	2	3	52	15	49	59	41	4	46	44	7.59	2.14	4.8	290	8.5	8.0	0.9	0.7	36%	63%	42
Penn,Hayden	08	24	aaa	BAL	6	7	21	0	99	124	63	16	33	57	5.72	1.58	21.3	300	3.0	5.2	1.7	1.5	33%	67%	19
Perdomo,Luis	08	24	aa	STL	4	2	24	2	33	34	17	3	13	31	4.58	1.40	6.0	258	3.4	8.5	2.5	0.9	33%	68%	81
Pereira,Nick	07	25	aa	SF	9	9	26	0	143	157	71	17	71	95	4.47	1.59	24.8	273	4.5	5.9	1.3	1.0	31%	74%	33
	08	26	aa	SF	7	8	19	0	101	155	93	14	54	64	8.30	2.07	26.5	345	4.8	5.7	1.2	1.2	39%	59%	8
Perez,Beltran	07	26	a/a	WAS	7	7	24	0	124	172	80	19	39	56	5.81	1.70	23.9	322	2.8	4.1	1.4	1.4	34%	68%	4
	08	27	aa	WAS	3	5	36	2	59	91	48	10	32	43	7.36	2.08	8.2	345	4.9	6.5	1.3	1.6	39%	66%	5
Perez,Christopher	07	22 a	aa	STL	2	1	54	36	54	25	20	5	39	68	3.32	1.18	4.1	136	6.5	11.3	1.7	0.8	19%	75%	107
Perez,Juan	07	29	aa	PIT	3	2	40	2	55	79	47	7	33	40	7.61	2.03	6.8	328	5.4	6.5	1.2	1.1	38%	62%	21
Perez,Marcelo	07	27	aa	NYM	1	5	47	0	70	109	57	7	37	52	7.39	2.09	7.5	348	4.7	6.7	1.4	0.9	41%	64%	29
	08	28	aa	DET	1	1	30	2	39	63	35	10	28	20	8.02	2.31	6.8	354	6.4	4.6	0.7	2.2	37%	69%	-40
Perez,Oneli	07	24 a	aa	CHW	6	2	59	16	77	80	26	8	22	75	3.08	1.33	5.5	262	2.6	8.8	3.4	1.0	33%	81%	97
	08	25	a/a	NYY	2	3	38	2	60	87	56	14	34	61	8.34	2.01	7.8	332	5.0	9.1	1.8	2.0	40%	61%	20
Perez,Rafael	07	26	aaa	CLE	3	3	8	0	46	61	23	3	11	28	4.53	1.55	25.8	310	2.2	5.4	2.5	0.6	36%	71%	60
Periard,Alexandre	08	21	aa	MIL	2	4	8	0	38	46	27	3	16	18	6.39	1.63	21.6	293	3.8	4.3	1.1	0.7	33%	59%	24
Perkins,Glen	08	26	aaa	MIN	2	1	7	0	33	31	13	2	19	22	3.57	1.53	21.0	245	5.2	5.9	1.1	0.5	29%	77%	49
Perrault,Josh	08	26	a/a	WAS	4	2	49	1	70	90	41	10	21	49	5.27	1.58	6.5	305	2.7	6.2	2.3	1.3	35%	69%	41
Peterson,John	07	26	aa	OAK	3	6	13	0	75	101	51	7	34	30	6.13	1.81	27.3	316	4.1	3.6	0.9	0.8	34%	66%	7
Peterson,Matt	07	26	aa	PIT	4	2	54	29	68	68	20	4	33	44	2.65	1.49	5.5	254	4.4	5.8	1.3	0.6	30%	84%	49
Petit,Yusmeiro	07	23	aa	ARI	8	4	17	0	93	97	53	14	38	53	5.12	1.45	23.9	263	3.7	5.1	1.4	1.4	28%	68%	22
	08	24 a	aa	ARI	3	3	11	0	60	78	43	9	8	58	6.49	1.44	23.8	309	1.2	8.7	7.1	1.4	38%	56%	152
Petrick,William	07	23	aa	CHC	2	2	27	2	42	46	20	8	10	33	4.18	1.34	6.7	274	2.2	7.0	3.2	1.8	31%	77%	57
Pettyjohn,Adam	07	30	a/a	MIL	16	6	28	0	161	234	115	35	45	99	6.42	1.73	26.8	332	2.5	5.5	2.2	2.0	36%	67%	9
	08	31	aaa	CIN	15	6	28	0	174	227	115	26	46	79	5.93	1.57	27.9	309	2.4	4.1	1.7	1.4	33%	64%	13
Phillips,Heath	07	26	aaa	CHW	13	7	28	0	173	243	115	34	61	95	5.98	1.76	28.9	325	3.1	4.9	1.6	1.8	35%	70%	-1
	08	27	aaa	TAM	4	5	44	0	77	103	48	7	34	51	5.65	1.78	8.2	314	4.0	6.0	1.5	0.8	37%	68%	35
Pichardo,Kelvin	08	23	aa	SF	2	4	46	7	61	57	21	4	33	52	3.09	1.47	5.8	242	4.9	7.6	1.6	0.6	31%	80%	68
Pignatiello,Carmen	07	25	aa	CHC	2	0	50	4	55	54	21	7	21	38	3.44	1.37	4.7	252	3.4	6.2	1.8	1.1	29%	79%	46
	08	26	aa	CHC	0	1	45	3	39	66	45	8	22	26	10.29	2.23	4.5	364	5.0	6.0	1.2	1.8	40%	54%	-12
Pimentel,Julio	08	23	aa	KC	7	13	28	0	157	227	121	19	51	101	6.93	1.77	26.3	331	2.9	5.8	2.0	1.1	38%	61%	32
Pinango,Miguel	07	25	aa	LA	10	7	23	0	126	168	71	22	40	77	5.03	1.65	25.1	314	2.9	5.5	1.9	1.6	34%	74%	18
	08	26	aa	LA	5	9	27	0	136	202	98	24	42	76	6.47	1.80	23.8	337	2.8	5.0	1.8	1.6	37%	67%	7
Pino,Johan	07	24	aa	MIN	2	4	9	0	47	66	33	6	9	31	6.30	1.60	23.6	324	1.8	5.9	3.3	1.2	37%	61%	61
	08	25	aa	MIN	7	7	26	0	109	136	67	17	40	59	5.56	1.61	19.0	299	3.3	4.9	1.5	1.4	32%	68%	14
Pinto,Julio	08	24	aa	TOR	4	3	20	0	45	72	38	5	16	24	7.61	1.97	11.0	354	3.3	4.8	1.5	1.0	39%	60%	13
Plexico,Gerald	07	28	aa	WAS	2	5	43	1	66	88	42	13	40	26	5.74	1.93	7.5	313	5.4	3.5	0.6	1.8	32%	75%	-27
Plummer,Jarod	07	24 a	aa	KC	5	6	46	11	82	84	41	15	19	78	4.53	1.24	7.4	259	2.0	8.5	4.2	1.7	31%	70%	91
	08	25	aa	KC	4	1	29	3	58	71	37	14	16	54	5.72	1.49	8.8	294	2.5	8.4	3.4	2.1	34%	68%	55
Pollok,Dwayne	07	27	a/a	LA	2	3	46	2	82	133	53	8	21	25	5.84	1.88	8.6	357	2.3	2.8	1.2	0.9	38%	69%	-0
	08	28	aa	LA	10	5	40	4	105	160	75	14	24	47	6.40	1.75	12.3	343	2.1	4.1	2.0	1.2	37%	65%	15
Pope,Justin	07	28	a/a	NYY	4	3	42	6	62	72	46	14	21	34	6.67	1.50	6.5	286	3.0	4.9	1.6	2.0	29%	59%	2
	08	29	aa	PHI	1	1	36	10	40	36	14	8	19	16	3.09	1.37	4.8	236	4.2	3.6	0.9	1.7	23%	87%	-3
Poreda,Aaron	08	22	aa	CHW	3	4	15	0	87	98	39	7	23	64	4.03	1.39	25.0	278	2.4	6.6	2.8	0.7	33%	72%	76

					Actual				Major League Equivalents																
PITCHER	Yr	Age	Lev	Org	w	l	g	sv	ip	h	er	hr	bb	k	era	whip	bf/g	oob	ctl	dom	cmd	hr/9	h%	s%	bpv
Powers,Daniel	07	25	aa	MIN	2	5	34	1	59	96	46	4	27	32	6.93	2.06	8.7	356	4.1	4.8	1.2	0.7	40%	65%	17
Price,David	08	23	a/a	TAM	8	1	13	0	75	71	24	7	25	62	2.88	1.28	24.2	245	3.0	7.4	2.5	0.8	30%	81%	78
Prinz,Bret	07	30	a/a	PIT	1	2	37	7	44	55	16	4	28	31	3.32	1.88	5.7	300	5.6	6.4	1.1	0.8	36%	84%	34
Prochaska,Mike	07	27	a/a	TAM	8	8	26	0	138	164	83	23	57	70	5.40	1.61	24.0	290	3.7	4.5	1.2	1.5	31%	70%	5
	08	28	a/a	TAM	7	10	27	0	136	236	124	22	52	48	8.17	2.12	25.4	373	3.4	3.2	0.9	1.5	39%	62%	-26
Puffer,Brandon	07	32	aa	TEX	3	3	51	1	64	85	35	9	25	35	4.95	1.70	5.8	311	3.5	4.9	1.4	1.3	34%	74%	12
	08	33	aa	TEX	8	0	46	1	76	111	49	7	20	39	5.85	1.72	7.7	333	2.4	4.6	2.0	0.8	37%	66%	32
Pullin,Aaron	07	27	aa	LAA	5	5	51	0	61	77	43	7	33	31	6.27	1.81	5.7	302	4.9	4.6	0.9	1.0	33%	66%	12
Purcey,David	07	25	aa	TOR	3	5	11	0	62	86	51	6	18	42	7.42	1.67	25.9	321	2.6	6.1	2.4	0.8	38%	53%	53
	08	26	aaa	TOR	8	6	19	0	117	121	48	11	38	96	3.73	1.36	26.3	261	2.9	7.4	2.5	0.9	32%	75%	74
Rainville,Jay	08	23	aa	MIN	9	9	24	0	123	160	92	22	45	68	6.73	1.67	23.5	308	3.3	5.0	1.5	1.6	33%	62%	7
Rainwater,Josh	08	24	aa	DET	10	7	24	0	132	152	68	7	61	67	4.64	1.61	24.9	282	4.1	4.6	1.1	0.5	32%	70%	34
Rakers,Aaron	07	31	aa	SD	4	5	61	0	79	163	86	26	30	36	9.76	2.44	6.9	414	3.4	4.1	1.2	2.9	42%	64%	-66
Ramirez,Edwar	07	27 b	a/a	NYY	4	0	34	7	56	36	8	1	27	77	1.25	1.11	6.7	178	4.3	12.3	2.9	0.2	30%	89%	148
Ramirez,Elizardo	07	25	aaa	CIN	4	3	12	0	65	84	35	5	20	38	4.85	1.60	24.5	307	2.8	5.3	1.9	0.7	35%	70%	44
	08	26	aa	TEX	10	7	27	0	160	237	100	29	36	66	5.63	1.70	27.4	336	2.0	3.7	1.8	1.6	35%	71%	-0
Ramirez,Erasmo	07	31	aa	FLA	5	1	41	3	43	61	18	4	7	16	3.69	1.59	4.7	328	1.5	3.4	2.3	0.7	35%	78%	36
	08	32	aaa	MIL	3	5	42	1	54	66	24	7	12	42	4.02	1.44	5.6	295	1.9	6.9	3.6	1.2	35%	76%	77
Ramirez,Ismael	07	27	a/a	TOR	2	5	20	0	72	141	66	12	24	33	8.17	2.29	18.8	401	3.0	4.2	1.4	1.5	43%	65%	-17
Ramirez,Luis	07	25	aa	OAK	4	6	14	0	70	96	53	7	26	41	6.84	1.73	23.3	318	3.3	5.3	1.6	0.9	36%	59%	32
Ramirez,Ramon	07	25	a/a	CIN	6	1	21	1	46	45	21	4	19	41	4.12	1.40	9.5	252	3.7	8.0	2.2	0.8	32%	72%	73
	07	26	aa	COL	4	0	25	0	27	25	11	3	18	27	3.80	1.61	4.9	241	6.1	8.9	1.5	1.1	31%	80%	57
Ramirez,Ramon	08	27	a/a	CIN	6	8	30	1	145	147	77	19	63	113	4.76	1.45	21.1	257	3.9	7.0	1.8	1.2	30%	70%	48
Ramos,Cesar	07	23	aa	SD	13	9	27	0	163	178	76	16	46	77	4.21	1.38	26.0	272	2.6	4.2	1.7	0.9	30%	71%	33
	08	24	aa	SD	9	11	28	0	149	209	101	17	60	86	6.10	1.81	25.2	325	3.6	5.2	1.4	1.0	36%	67%	20
Ramos,Mario	07	30	aa	OAK	2	3	17	1	54	107	53	7	27	27	8.86	2.46	17.2	403	4.4	4.5	1.0	1.1	44%	63%	-11
Randolph,Stephen	07	33	aa	HOU	10	2	31	4	52	31	15	7	26	56	2.65	1.09	6.7	168	4.5	9.7	2.2	1.2	21%	83%	89
	08	34	a/a	PHI	3	1	46	6	62	47	21	4	47	73	3.06	1.51	6.0	205	6.8	10.6	1.6	0.6	29%	81%	91
Rapada,Clay	07	27	a/a	DET	7	2	57	17	57	80	37	6	30	41	5.77	1.92	4.9	324	4.7	6.5	1.4	0.9	38%	70%	32
	08	28 b	aaa	DET	0	1	28	2	35	38	12	2	15	38	2.98	1.50	5.5	270	3.8	9.8	2.6	0.5	37%	81%	97
Rasner,Darrell	08	28 b	aaa	NYY	4	0	5	0	31	22	4	0	6	22	1.22	0.92	23.8	196	1.8	6.3	3.5	0.0	25%	85%	126
Ray,Ken	07	33	a/a	MIL	3	4	37	3	63	83	39	10	38	50	5.56	1.92	8.2	312	5.4	7.1	1.3	1.4	36%	74%	20
Ray,Robert	08	25	aa	TOR	8	6	16	0	96	127	41	7	29	57	3.84	1.63	27.3	312	2.8	5.3	1.9	0.7	36%	77%	45
Ray,Ronald	08	24	aa	SF	6	4	46	1	72	98	34	3	25	38	4.20	1.71	7.3	317	3.1	4.7	1.5	0.4	36%	75%	40
Redding,Tim	07	30	aaa	WAS	9	5	17	0	89	141	73	10	27	48	7.32	1.88	25.2	351	2.8	4.9	1.8	1.0	39%	60%	21
Redman,Mark	07	34	a/a	COL	3	6	17	0	98	160	74	12	43	45	6.84	2.07	28.8	359	4.0	4.1	1.0	1.1	39%	67%	-4
	08	35	aa	COL	8	4	18	0	85	124	66	6	24	37	6.98	1.73	22.0	332	2.5	4.0	1.6	0.6	37%	58%	27
Redmond,Todd	08	23	aa	ATL	13	5	28	0	166	189	77	18	34	113	4.19	1.34	25.3	280	1.8	6.1	3.3	0.9	32%	71%	77
Regilio,Nick	08	30	aa	HOU	4	4	50	9	60	87	30	10	41	35	4.50	2.14	6.1	332	6.2	5.3	0.8	1.5	37%	83%	-7
Register,Steven	07	24	aa	COL	1	3	61	37	58	81	38	4	17	41	5.88	1.69	4.4	324	2.6	6.3	2.4	0.7	39%	64%	60
	08	25	aa	COL	5	3	56	16	59	70	28	4	19	40	4.24	1.51	4.7	289	2.9	6.0	2.1	0.7	34%	72%	57
Reichert,Dan	08	32	a/a	PIT	4	8	18	0	97	133	67	9	46	47	6.18	1.84	25.7	320	4.2	4.3	1.0	0.8	35%	66%	14
Reid,Ryan	08	23	aa	TAM	5	4	31	4	46	47	29	1	32	45	5.64	1.72	6.9	261	6.2	8.7	1.4	0.2	35%	64%	78
Reineke,Chad	07	25	aa	HOU	5	5	32	0	100	124	69	9	58	72	6.20	1.82	14.8	299	5.2	6.5	1.2	0.8	35%	65%	36
	08	27	aa	SD	5	10	23	0	129	161	79	21	47	84	5.52	1.61	25.4	299	3.3	5.9	1.8	1.4	33%	69%	25
Reinhard,Gregory	07	24	aa	CHC	1	1	20	0	28	35	19	6	17	21	6.05	1.83	6.7	297	5.4	6.7	1.2	2.0	33%	72%	1
	08	25	aa	CHC	5	4	45	4	85	90	48	10	46	67	5.05	1.59	8.5	266	4.8	7.0	1.5	1.1	32%	70%	43
Resop,Chris	07	25	aa	LAA	1	3	27	0	45	61	31	4	17	31	6.09	1.73	7.8	317	3.4	6.3	1.9	0.8	37%	64%	43
Reyes,Anthony	07	26	aa	STL	1	1	6	0	36	33	16	4	12	25	3.87	1.26	25.2	240	3.0	6.3	2.1	1.1	27%	73%	55
	08	27	a/a	CLE	4	3	13	0	65	80	33	9	29	44	4.60	1.67	23.0	296	4.0	6.1	1.5	1.2	34%	76%	28
Reyes,Jo-Jo	07	23	a/a	ATL	12	1	19	0	109	103	42	8	49	94	3.46	1.39	24.8	244	4.0	7.8	1.9	0.7	31%	76%	73
	08	24	aaa	ATL	1	1	8	0	39	35	12	2	16	33	2.77	1.31	20.6	235	3.7	7.6	2.1	0.5	30%	80%	83
Reynolds,Gregory	07	22 a	aa	COL	4	1	8	0	50	39	11	3	9	31	1.97	0.96	24.3	210	1.6	5.6	3.4	0.5	25%	82%	103
	08	23	aa	COL	1	3	13	0	63	95	35	4	21	31	5.00	1.83	23.1	340	2.9	4.4	1.5	0.6	38%	72%	28
Reynoso,Paulino	07	27	aaa	CHW	3	0	21	0	22	34	15	1	22	15	6.03	2.54	5.7	344	9.0	6.2	0.7	0.4	41%	75%	25
Rheinecker,John	07	28	aa	TEX	4	2	9	0	58	88	38	6	15	21	5.82	1.77	30.2	341	2.3	3.2	1.4	1.0	36%	68%	6
Rhoades,Chad	08	26	aa	BOS	5	3	41	2	61	90	48	7	31	50	7.04	1.98	7.3	335	4.6	7.4	1.6	1.0	41%	64%	37
Richardson,Dustin	08	25	aa	BOS	7	10	22	0	106	131	96	18	53	92	8.12	1.72	22.4	296	4.5	7.8	1.8	1.5	35%	53%	34
Richard,Clayton	08	25 a	a/a	CHW	12	6	20	0	127	125	49	7	22	73	3.50	1.16	25.9	252	1.6	5.2	3.3	0.5	29%	70%	89
Richmond,Scott	08	29	a/a	TOR	6	11	24	0	137	188	104	30	55	84	6.80	1.77	26.8	319	3.6	5.5	1.5	2.0	34%	66%	-3
Ridgway,Jeff	07	27	aaa	TAM	2	3	54	4	64	69	32	11	34	56	4.43	1.61	5.4	270	4.7	7.9	1.7	1.5	32%	77%	39
	08	28	aaa	ATL	4	0	44	4	52	82	42	3	28	47	7.23	2.10	6.0	349	4.8	8.0	1.7	0.6	44%	64%	52
Righter,Matthew	07	26	aa	DET	3	4	19	0	54	89	46	13	20	27	7.65	2.00	14.0	359	3.3	4.5	1.4	2.1	38%	65%	-24
	08	27	a/a	DET	1	1	18	0	35	48	29	5	25	7	7.37	2.10	9.8	320	6.5	1.8	0.3	1.2	32%	65%	-28
Riley,Matt	07	28	aa	LA	5	5	45	4	69	90	58	11	61	58	7.49	2.19	7.8	308	8.0	7.6	1.0	1.5	37%	67%	15
	08	29	aa	LA	2	1	25	1	40	55	20	7	32	38	4.48	2.16	8.2	318	7.2	8.4	1.2	1.5	39%	83%	22
Ring,Royce	07	27	a/a	ATL	5	2	42	2	44	51	21	2	21	45	4.31	1.64	4.8	284	4.3	9.2	2.1	0.5	38%	73%	84
Rivera,Mumba	07	27	aa	SEA	4	7	42	6	56	70	44	16	46	56	7.01	2.07	6.7	300	7.4	8.9	1.2	2.6	35%	72%	-3
	08	28	aa	SEA	5	3	41	11	51	64	33	5	29	39	5.73	1.82	5.9	300	5.1	6.9	1.3	0.8	36%	68%	39
Rleal,Sendy	07	27	aa	BAL	5	3	29	1	45	47	24	7	22	26	4.82	1.53	6.9	263	4.3	5.1	1.2	1.4	28%	73%	15
Roach,Jason	07	31	aa	PIT	4	3	33	1	63	102	49	5	32	28	7.06	2.13	9.6	357	4.5	4.0	0.9	0.7	39%	65%	6
Robbins,Jake	07	31	aaa	CHW	0	0	20	0	24	40	20	0	18	10	7.44	2.39	6.4	361	6.7	3.9	0.6	0.0	41%	65%	18
Robertson,Connor	07	26	aa	OAK	4	1	31	2	39	56	26	3	23	30	6.09	2.03	6.2	330	5.3	6.8	1.3	0.8	40%	70%	33
	08	27	aa	ARI	7	4	47	1	71	99	63	11	36	53	7.92	1.90	7.3	322	4.6	6.7	1.5	1.4	37%	58%	21
Robertson,David	08	24 a	a/a	NYY	4	0	30	3	53	34	13	1	24	65	2.20	1.09	7.1	180	4.1	11.0	2.7	0.2	28%	79%	137
Rodriguez,Derek	08	25	a/a	CHW	5	2	49	2	79	68	41	11	36	74	4.67	1.32	6.8	229	4.1	8.4	2.1	1.2	28%	67%	67
Rodriguez,Fernando	07	23	aa	LAA	8	4	21	0	117	159	79	15	45	48	6.10	1.74	26.0	317	3.5	3.6	1.0	1.2	34%	66%	-0
	08	24	aa	LAA	7	11	33	0	136	183	106	11	64	70	7.03	1.82	19.5	315	4.2	4.6	1.1	0.7	35%	60%	22
Rodriguez,Francisco	08	26	aa	LAA	5	5	50	2	75	96	42	10	36	54	5.06	1.75	7.0	303	4.3	6.5	1.5	1.2	35%	73%	29
Rodriguez,Henry	08	22	aa	OAK	2	7	14	0	41	54	36	1	39	37	7.90	2.27	15.2	311	8.6	8.1	0.9	0.2	40%	62%	55
Rodriguez,Jesus	08	23	aa	LA	5	5	13	0	67	80	44	15	32	38	5.95	1.68	23.7	291	4.3	5.1	1.2	2.1	30%	70%	-10
Rodriguez,Jose	07	26	aa	HOU	4	4	52	4	72	97	53	12	37	43	6.67	1.85	6.6	315	4.6	5.4	1.2	1.5	35%	66%	3

					Actual				Major League Equivalents																
PITCHER	Yr	Age	Lev	Org	w	l	g	sv	ip	h	er	hr	bb	k	era	whip	bf/g	oob	ctl	dom	cmd	hr/9	h%	s%	bpv
Rodriguez,Rafael	07	23	aa	LAA	0	6	46	0	71	95	43	7	32	35	5.48	1.78	7.3	314	4.0	4.4	1.1	0.9	35%	70%	14
	08	24	aa	LAA	4	4	51	11	67	79	26	5	18	46	3.52	1.44	5.7	287	2.4	6.1	2.5	0.7	34%	77%	67
Rodriguez,Ricardo	07	29	aa	PIT	2	6	16	0	61	140	76	9	21	21	11.18	2.64	21.3	439	3.1	3.1	1.0	1.4	46%	56%	-35
Roehl,Scott	08	27	aa	CLE	1	2	40	7	49	53	22	2	24	39	3.97	1.57	5.5	270	4.4	7.1	1.6	0.4	34%	74%	65
Roenicke,Joshua	08	26	a/a	CIN	6	2	57	13	61	69	26	6	29	56	3.77	1.60	4.8	279	4.3	8.2	1.9	0.8	35%	78%	65
Roe,Chaz	08	22	aa	COL	5	4	16	0	105	108	56	16	31	60	4.80	1.32	27.9	260	2.7	5.1	1.9	1.4	28%	67%	33
Rogers,Brian	07	25	aa	PIT	2	1	48	2	65	63	30	1	34	49	4.15	1.50	6.0	250	4.8	6.7	1.4	0.2	32%	70%	70
	08	26	a/a	NYM	2	2	37	1	53	67	26	4	22	41	4.32	1.67	6.6	300	3.8	7.0	1.9	0.8	36%	75%	54
Rohrbaugh,Robert	07	24	aa	SEA	13	8	28	0	170	194	71	16	51	97	3.76	1.44	26.5	281	2.7	5.1	1.9	0.9	32%	76%	44
	08	25	aa	SEA	7	5	19	1	96	126	66	8	31	65	6.22	1.63	23.0	311	2.9	6.1	2.1	0.8	36%	61%	50
Rojas,Chris	07	31	aa	PHI	7	4	19	0	78	114	63	20	71	32	7.24	2.38	21.8	334	8.2	3.7	0.5	2.3	33%	74%	-49
Rojas,Jose	08	26	aa	OAK	2	2	31	1	41	44	29	4	29	34	6.33	1.78	6.2	270	6.3	7.5	1.2	1.0	33%	65%	42
Roman,Orlando	08	30	aa	TOR	1	1	21	2	32	59	40	8	25	19	11.25	2.63	8.4	386	7.1	5.3	0.7	2.3	41%	58%	-42
Romero,Davis	08	26	aaa	TOR	5	9	25	0	106	130	60	14	32	72	5.05	1.53	18.9	296	2.7	6.1	2.2	1.2	34%	69%	44
Romero,Felix	07	27	aa	BAL	2	7	46	0	80	105	53	11	49	70	5.95	1.92	8.4	309	5.5	7.8	1.4	1.2	38%	71%	33
	08	28	a/a	BAL	8	3	45	1	85	95	44	11	28	78	4.60	1.45	8.3	277	3.0	8.3	2.8	1.1	34%	71%	74
Romero,Ricky	07	23	aa	TOR	3	6	18	0	88	113	59	11	52	68	6.03	1.87	23.5	305	5.3	6.9	1.3	1.1	36%	69%	29
	08	24	a/a	TOR	8	8	28	0	164	210	103	15	79	96	5.65	1.76	27.4	305	4.3	5.3	1.2	0.8	35%	68%	26
Romo,Sergio	08	26 a	aa	SF	1	3	27	11	33	32	17	1	10	28	4.55	1.28	5.1	251	2.7	7.6	2.8	0.3	32%	62%	100
Roney,Matt	07	28	a/a	TOR	4	3	29	4	45	71	34	2	18	37	6.87	1.98	7.6	351	3.7	7.4	2.0	0.5	43%	63%	59
Roquet,Rocky	07	25	aa	CHC	4	0	28	7	39	39	21	5	20	33	4.83	1.50	6.2	254	4.6	7.6	1.7	1.2	30%	71%	49
	08	26	aa	CHC	4	2	39	3	48	49	24	3	30	41	4.56	1.64	5.6	258	5.6	7.7	1.4	0.6	33%	72%	60
Rosales,Leonel	07	26	aa	SD	1	1	24	14	24	30	13	3	11	21	4.70	1.71	4.7	297	4.3	7.8	1.8	1.3	36%	76%	42
	08	27	aa	ARI	2	2	29	9	36	55	28	7	17	21	6.91	2.00	6.1	345	4.2	5.2	1.2	1.8	37%	69%	-11
Rosa,Carlos	07	23	aa	KC	6	6	21	1	97	121	60	8	43	60	5.55	1.69	21.3	299	4.0	5.6	1.4	0.8	34%	67%	35
	08	24 a	aa	KC	8	5	19	0	95	100	39	5	20	72	3.68	1.26	20.9	265	1.9	6.8	3.6	0.5	33%	71%	104
Rosen,Mark	07	23	aa	ARI	4	4	50	7	66	97	30	8	23	67	4.07	1.81	6.3	334	3.1	9.1	3.0	1.1	43%	81%	71
Rouwenhorst,Jonathc	07	28	aa	LAA	10	10	33	0	158	288	138	23	56	56	7.83	2.18	24.4	384	3.2	3.2	1.0	1.3	40%	64%	-20
	08	29	aaa	ATL	9	10	41	1	112	176	88	11	48	62	7.05	2.00	13.5	349	3.9	5.0	1.3	0.9	39%	64%	15
Rowe,Steven	07	27	aa	TEX	6	4	39	0	82	134	89	19	34	37	9.79	2.04	10.4	358	3.7	4.0	1.1	2.1	37%	53%	-33
	08	28	aa	TEX	4	5	27	0	78	136	58	16	41	33	6.62	2.27	15.0	374	4.7	3.8	0.8	1.9	39%	74%	-36
Rowland-Smith,Ryan	07	25	aa	SEA	3	4	25	1	41	41	21	2	24	43	4.60	1.58	7.4	254	5.3	9.3	1.8	0.5	35%	70%	83
Rundles,Rich	07	26	a/a	CLE	5	4	40	2	61	70	20	1	30	40	2.95	1.64	7.0	282	4.4	5.8	1.3	0.2	34%	81%	56
	08	27	aaa	CLE	5	4	55	4	52	51	24	4	27	50	4.17	1.49	4.2	249	4.7	8.7	1.8	0.7	32%	73%	74
Rupe,Josh	07	25	aa	TEX	2	2	7	0	37	51	28	6	16	15	6.76	1.80	25.0	321	3.8	3.7	1.0	1.4	34%	64%	-7
Rusch,Glendon	08	34	aa	COL	1	2	7	0	41	62	27	5	14	18	5.94	1.87	28.0	342	3.1	3.9	1.3	1.0	37%	69%	6
Rusch,Matt	07	24	aa	DET	6	1	40	3	53	54	29	5	20	46	5.00	1.39	5.7	258	3.4	7.7	2.3	0.9	32%	65%	71
	08	25	a/a	DET	4	1	48	1	73	97	47	13	21	52	5.83	1.61	6.9	312	2.6	6.4	2.5	1.6	35%	67%	37
Russell,Adam	07	24	aa	CHW	9	11	38	1	138	204	107	13	65	81	6.99	1.95	17.7	336	4.3	5.3	1.2	0.8	38%	63%	21
	08	25	aaa	CHW	3	2	25	0	37	33	16	4	20	25	3.92	1.44	6.5	235	4.9	6.0	1.2	1.0	27%	76%	40
Russell,James	08	23	aa	CHC	4	8	18	0	86	122	68	20	25	53	7.11	1.71	22.1	327	2.6	5.5	2.1	2.1	35%	62%	5
Russ,James	07	27	aa	FLA	1	6	21	1	89	99	51	9	37	48	5.11	1.52	18.8	275	3.7	4.8	1.3	0.9	31%	67%	28
Ryan,Patrick	08	25	aa	MIL	5	5	39	6	64	76	22	3	32	31	3.12	1.68	7.6	288	4.5	4.3	0.9	0.5	32%	82%	29
Ryu,Jae Kuk	07	24	aaa	TAM	5	4	14	0	71	81	44	6	23	59	5.57	1.46	22.3	281	2.9	7.5	2.6	0.8	35%	61%	75
Saarloos,Kirk	07	28	aaa	CIN	0	2	18	0	41	60	26	4	10	22	5.66	1.70	10.5	335	2.1	4.9	2.3	0.9	37%	67%	38
	08	29	aa	OAK	9	4	22	0	140	212	92	21	43	51	5.91	1.82	30.2	341	2.7	3.3	1.2	1.4	36%	70%	-10
Sack,Darren	07	25	aa	SF	2	5	9	0	39	70	49	8	24	19	11.22	2.41	23.2	379	5.6	4.3	0.8	1.8	40%	53%	-32
Sadler,Billy	07	26	aa	SF	3	2	49	7	54	51	40	7	46	57	6.68	1.78	5.2	242	7.6	9.5	1.2	1.1	31%	63%	56
	08	27	aa	SF	1	0	22	1	33	27	6	0	25	29	1.64	1.57	6.7	216	6.9	7.9	1.1	0.0	29%	88%	84
Sadlowski,Kyle	08	24	aa	STL	2	1	15	0	37	47	24	3	20	9	5.86	1.81	11.7	304	4.8	2.1	0.4	0.8	31%	67%	-7
Sadowski,Ryan	07	25	aa	SF	4	3	35	1	68	66	28	3	28	41	3.76	1.39	8.4	250	3.8	5.4	1.4	0.4	30%	72%	55
	08	26	aa	SF	9	4	40	0	91	143	68	8	48	60	6.69	2.09	11.4	349	4.8	5.9	1.2	0.8	41%	67%	23
Saenz,Chris	07	26	aa	LAA	1	7	19	0	46	83	62	3	37	17	12.14	2.60	13.4	381	7.2	3.4	0.5	0.7	41%	50%	-11
Salas,Juan	08	30 b	aaa	TAM	4	5	28	1	44	40	16	2	12	42	3.36	1.17	6.5	235	2.5	8.5	3.5	0.4	31%	71%	119
Salas,Marino	07	27	a/a	MIL	0	1	51	17	61	68	27	11	26	44	3.92	1.53	5.3	275	3.8	6.5	1.7	1.6	31%	81%	26
	08	28	aa	PIT	4	4	40	4	57	55	33	7	36	37	5.14	1.61	6.5	250	5.7	5.9	1.0	1.1	28%	70%	28
Salas,Noel	08	23 a	aa	STL	7	3	60	25	74	72	33	11	15	83	4.01	1.18	5.1	250	1.9	10.1	5.4	1.4	33%	72%	138
Salmon,Brad	07	28	aaa	CIN	2	2	37	4	43	52	25	4	19	32	5.29	1.64	5.3	291	4.0	6.8	1.7	0.9	35%	68%	47
	08	29	aa	KC	8	7	47	3	101	155	84	15	66	63	7.46	2.19	11.0	344	5.9	5.6	1.0	1.3	39%	67%	-0
Samardzija,Jeff	07	23	aa	CHC	3	3	6	0	34	38	16	10	9	17	4.22	1.38	24.4	276	2.4	4.5	1.9	2.6	26%	84%	-13
	08	24	aa	CHC	7	6	22	0	113	116	63	12	60	70	5.00	1.56	23.0	261	4.8	5.6	1.2	1.0	29%	69%	31
Sanches,Brian	07	29 b	aaa	PHI	2	3	36	16	47	71	35	7	9	40	6.72	1.70	6.0	342	1.7	7.7	4.6	1.3	41%	61%	90
	08	30	aaa	WAS	2	1	32	13	33	29	11	2	10	34	3.01	1.17	4.2	230	2.7	9.3	3.4	0.6	31%	76%	118
Sanchez,Jose	07	23	aa	NYM	4	9	27	0	145	189	88	14	58	82	5.44	1.70	24.8	308	3.6	5.1	1.4	0.9	35%	68%	27
	08	24	aa	NYM	13	7	29	0	152	189	80	12	45	97	4.73	1.54	23.4	299	2.7	5.7	2.1	0.7	35%	69%	54
Sanchez,Romulo	07	23	aa	PIT	6	3	40	1	57	51	23	8	18	43	3.57	1.19	5.9	232	2.8	6.7	2.4	1.3	26%	76%	61
	08	24	aa	PIT	5	1	33	4	54	61	27	5	20	26	4.54	1.50	7.3	278	3.3	4.3	1.3	0.9	30%	71%	26
Sandoval,Juan	07	27	aa	SEA	2	6	40	3	67	108	57	11	29	27	7.71	2.04	8.3	355	3.9	3.6	0.9	1.5	37%	63%	-21
	08	28	aa	MIL	2	6	45	20	48	54	24	6	33	27	4.52	1.81	5.0	279	6.1	5.1	0.8	1.1	31%	78%	14
Santana,Ervin	07	25	aa	LAA	2	1	5	0	32	48	24	4	11	26	6.79	1.84	30.5	341	3.0	7.2	2.4	1.2	41%	63%	46
Santiago,Jose	07	33	aa	NYM	7	8	32	0	119	204	101	16	45	38	7.64	2.08	18.6	369	3.4	2.9	0.9	1.2	39%	63%	-21
	08	34	aa	NYM	5	2	43	1	87	153	72	20	18	33	7.42	1.96	9.9	376	1.8	3.4	1.9	2.1	39%	66%	-22
Santiago,Tomas	08	27	aa	COL	4	8	32	0	106	141	67	14	54	61	5.66	1.84	15.8	314	4.6	5.2	1.1	1.2	35%	71%	12
Santos,Arthur	07	26	aa	KC	1	2	19	2	33	72	33	7	20	13	9.04	2.78	10.0	427	5.4	3.4	0.6	1.8	45%	69%	-51
Santos,Jarrett	07	26	aa	FLA	3	1	22	0	43	63	21	5	24	21	4.32	2.03	9.7	334	5.0	4.4	0.9	1.0	37%	81%	4
	08	27	aa	FLA	5	2	33	0	65	95	42	6	20	25	5.84	1.78	9.3	334	2.8	3.4	1.2	0.8	36%	67%	9
Santos,Reid	07	25	aa	CLE	8	3	39	2	96	102	39	11	34	69	3.65	1.42	10.7	267	3.2	6.5	2.0	1.0	31%	78%	52
	08	26	a/a	CLE	4	3	45	2	77	112	61	10	26	55	7.13	1.79	8.1	333	3.0	6.4	2.1	1.2	39%	60%	37
Santos,Victor	08	32	aa	SF	5	8	29	0	139	224	147	34	81	77	9.51	2.19	24.5	355	5.2	5.0	1.0	2.2	38%	58%	-32
Sarfate,Dennis	07	26	aaa	MIL	2	7	45	4	61	74	41	7	52	60	6.06	2.06	6.8	293	7.6	8.8	1.2	1.1	37%	71%	42
Sauerbeck,Scott	07	36	a/a	TOR	2	1	41	1	42	67	27	1	23	38	5.71	2.14	5.2	352	5.0	8.1	1.6	0.2	45%	71%	60
Saunders,Joe	07	26	aa	LAA	4	7	14	0	86	120	71	13	23	62	7.45	1.66	28.1	322	2.4	6.5	2.7	1.3	37%	55%	46
Savickas,Russell	07	24	aa	TOR	3	3	8	0	33	63	39	9	24	10	10.59	2.64	23.0	395	6.6	2.8	0.4	2.6	39%	62%	-75

					Actual				Major League Equivalents																
PITCHER	Yr	Age	Lev	Org	w	l	g	sv	ip	h	er	hr	bb	k	era	whip	bf/g	oob	ctl	dom	cmd	hr/9	h%	s%	bpv
Sawatski,Jay	07	25	a/a	MIN	4	3	42	0	70	100	49	6	28	43	6.35	1.83	7.9	328	3.6	5.5	1.5	0.8	38%	65%	30
	08	26	aa	MIN	1	4	22	0	38	66	45	7	25	28	10.59	2.38	9.2	371	6.0	6.6	1.1	1.6	42%	55%	-5
Scalamandre,Rich	07	27	a/a	ATL	3	6	38	3	55	86	48	9	29	22	7.89	2.09	7.3	349	4.7	3.6	0.8	1.5	37%	63%	-23
Schappert,Paul	07	26	aa	CHC	3	7	27	0	82	134	91	28	36	24	10.00	2.07	15.2	360	3.9	2.7	0.7	3.0	34%	55%	-78
Scherer,Matthew	07	25	aa	STL	4	3	55	1	70	81	34	6	24	58	4.33	1.50	5.6	284	3.1	7.5	2.4	0.8	35%	72%	69
	08	26	aa	STL	2	3	45	1	59	67	30	6	18	29	4.57	1.43	5.7	279	2.7	4.4	1.6	0.8	31%	69%	34
Scherzer,Max	07	23	aa	ARI	4	4	14	0	73	77	42	4	41	65	5.20	1.62	23.7	266	5.1	8.0	1.6	0.5	34%	67%	68
	08	24 a	aa	ARI	1	1	13	0	53	43	22	3	23	67	3.75	1.25	17.0	218	3.9	11.3	2.9	0.5	33%	70%	123
Schlact,Michael	07	22	aa	TEX	3	3	6	0	33	43	25	8	8	20	6.78	1.54	24.7	307	2.2	5.4	2.5	2.2	32%	60%	14
	08	23	aa	TEX	7	11	26	0	149	188	98	13	63	61	5.91	1.68	26.4	301	3.8	3.7	1.0	0.8	33%	64%	14
Schlichting,Travis	08	24	aa	LA	6	4	33	0	59	66	29	4	19	43	4.39	1.43	7.8	276	2.8	6.5	2.3	0.6	33%	69%	68
Schmoll,Steve	07	28	aa	NYM	2	3	54	4	76	113	45	6	20	34	5.27	1.76	6.6	337	2.4	4.0	1.7	0.7	37%	70%	25
	08	29	aa	WAS	3	5	46	7	70	101	30	4	20	35	3.85	1.73	7.1	331	2.6	4.5	1.8	0.5	38%	78%	38
Schreiber,Zach	07	25	a/a	ATL	4	6	58	6	78	63	27	5	37	62	3.16	1.28	5.7	217	4.3	7.1	1.7	0.6	27%	77%	71
	08	26	aaa	ATL	2	2	34	6	39	34	16	6	27	24	3.80	1.56	5.1	230	6.2	5.6	0.9	1.4	24%	81%	19
Schroder,Chris	07	29 b	aaa	WAS	2	2	26	1	33	30	9	0	19	35	2.40	1.47	5.6	235	5.1	9.4	1.9	0.0	34%	82%	103
	08	30	aaa	WAS	5	4	43	8	45	58	24	3	21	41	4.88	1.75	4.9	305	4.2	8.3	2.0	0.7	39%	72%	65
Schultz,Mike	07	28	aa	ARI	4	5	54	4	77	118	52	6	42	37	6.06	2.08	7.1	344	4.9	4.3	0.9	0.7	38%	70%	9
Searles,Jonathan	07	27	aa	SD	4	3	37	0	68	71	34	6	43	38	4.56	1.67	8.4	264	5.6	5.1	0.9	0.8	30%	73%	29
Seddon,Chris	07	24	aa	FLA	6	10	26	0	139	157	86	13	52	87	5.53	1.50	23.6	278	3.3	5.6	1.7	0.9	32%	63%	43
	08	25	aa	FLA	10	9	28	0	152	200	104	25	76	109	6.17	1.81	25.7	311	4.5	6.5	1.4	1.5	35%	68%	17
Segovia,Zach	07	24	a/a	PHI	6	12	23	0	135	195	105	15	53	43	7.01	1.83	27.9	331	3.5	2.8	0.8	1.0	35%	61%	-8
	08	25	aa	WAS	4	2	12	0	42	67	39	6	20	19	8.29	2.05	17.5	351	4.3	4.0	0.9	1.2	38%	59%	-7
Sencion,Carlos	08	24	aa	ATL	6	4	25	0	76	85	47	6	44	53	5.61	1.69	14.0	276	5.2	6.3	1.2	0.7	33%	66%	41
Seo,Jae	07	30	aaa	TAM	9	4	17	0	97	132	61	11	17	50	5.66	1.53	25.5	318	1.5	4.7	3.0	1.0	35%	64%	52
Serfass,Joseph	07	26	aa	NYM	3	3	32	0	46	69	40	9	10	23	7.85	1.72	6.7	339	2.0	4.6	2.3	1.8	36%	56%	9
Serrano,Alex	07	27	aa	LAA	3	5	47	4	69	125	56	10	11	34	7.33	1.98	7.2	383	1.5	4.4	3.0	1.3	42%	64%	27
Serrano,Jimmy	07	31	aa	FLA	5	3	24	0	71	100	51	9	26	37	6.40	1.77	13.9	325	3.3	4.6	1.4	1.2	36%	65%	12
Shackelford,Brian	07	31	aaa	TAM	0	5	52	1	44	58	32	4	19	17	6.44	1.74	4.0	310	3.9	3.5	0.9	0.9	33%	62%	7
Shafer,David	07	26	aa	OAK	1	1	51	8	58	71	48	11	34	34	7.40	1.82	5.4	295	5.3	5.3	1.0	1.7	32%	61%	-3
	08	27	aa	OAK	2	2	34	1	56	51	24	8	39	33	3.87	1.60	7.5	236	6.3	5.3	0.8	1.3	25%	80%	19
Shappi,Austin	07	25	aa	ARI	1	7	40	2	76	94	41	8	18	48	4.86	1.47	8.3	297	2.1	5.6	2.7	1.0	34%	68%	55
	08	26	aa	ARI	2	6	38	1	84	140	61	17	21	53	6.53	1.91	10.7	363	2.3	5.7	2.5	1.8	40%	69%	16
Sharpe,Steven	07	26	aa	OAK	3	1	26	8	28	37	13	3	7	10	4.06	1.56	4.8	310	2.2	3.4	1.5	1.1	33%	77%	12
	08	27	aa	OAK	1	0	19	1	31	55	34	2	16	11	9.79	2.29	8.5	380	4.5	3.1	0.7	0.7	41%	54%	-9
Sharpless,Josh	07	27	aa	PIT	1	5	43	3	64	80	44	11	44	50	6.13	1.94	7.2	301	6.1	7.1	1.2	1.6	35%	71%	13
	08	28	aa	SF	1	1	24	0	33	33	19	4	35	21	5.24	2.04	6.8	252	9.5	5.6	0.6	1.0	28%	75%	21
Shearn,Tom	07	30	aaa	CIN	7	10	26	0	143	202	98	13	59	84	6.15	1.82	26.1	326	3.7	5.3	1.4	0.8	37%	66%	26
	08	31	aaa	MIN	7	4	16	0	86	116	57	13	23	45	5.94	1.61	24.4	315	2.4	4.7	1.9	1.3	34%	65%	21
Shell,Steven	07	25	aa	LAA	7	3	36	0	83	115	51	19	21	57	5.47	1.63	10.5	321	2.3	6.2	2.7	2.0	35%	73%	23
	08	26 a	aaa	WAS	3	2	22	1	58	54	19	4	13	45	2.97	1.15	10.7	240	2.0	6.9	3.4	0.6	29%	76%	101
Shibilo,Andy	08	32	aaa	ATL	1	1	32	1	41	64	37	3	31	32	8.09	2.31	6.7	349	6.7	7.1	1.1	0.7	42%	63%	29
Shiell,Jason	07	31	aa	KC	2	4	29	3	85	157	74	17	39	28	7.86	2.30	15.3	387	4.1	3.0	0.7	1.8	40%	68%	-44
	08	32	a/a	MIL	3	6	39	0	53	80	41	10	36	40	6.97	2.18	6.9	340	6.0	6.7	1.1	1.7	39%	71%	-0
Shipman,Andy	07	26	aa	OAK	4	7	28	0	117	182	102	13	50	69	7.85	1.98	20.5	347	3.8	5.3	1.4	1.0	39%	59%	16
	08	27	aa	OAK	2	2	37	1	54	90	37	6	17	30	6.12	1.98	7.2	362	2.9	5.1	1.8	1.0	41%	69%	21
Shoemaker,Scott	07	26	aa	TEX	6	3	29	0	96	129	76	22	40	43	7.10	1.76	15.5	314	3.8	4.0	1.1	2.0	32%	63%	-23
	08	27	aa	SEA	3	3	32	0	90	153	83	20	42	44	8.31	2.17	14.3	368	4.2	4.4	1.0	2.0	39%	64%	-32
Shortslef,Josh	07	26	aa	PIT	5	13	27	0	149	216	98	13	64	64	5.90	1.88	26.5	331	3.9	3.9	1.0	0.8	36%	68%	9
Shortslef,Joshua	08	27	aa	PIT	5	2	29	3	62	78	34	3	29	37	5.00	1.72	9.9	301	4.2	5.4	1.3	0.5	35%	70%	40
Shuey,Paul	07	37	a/a	BAL	0	0	22	1	24	39	16	2	10	19	5.83	2.04	5.4	357	3.8	7.1	1.9	0.8	43%	71%	41
Sierra,Eduardo	07	25	a/a	CHW	2	7	47	2	62	76	45	4	42	51	6.55	1.90	6.4	294	6.1	7.4	1.2	0.6	37%	64%	48
	08	26	aa	LA	5	2	43	8	57	54	40	6	44	39	6.33	1.71	6.2	244	6.9	6.2	0.9	0.9	28%	63%	35
Silva,Jesus	07	25	aa	FLA	1	5	10	0	43	71	40	8	12	17	8.37	1.91	20.8	360	2.4	3.6	1.5	1.8	37%	57%	-17
Simmons,James	07	21	aa	OAK	0	0	13	0	29	41	16	2	8	20	4.93	1.68	10.3	325	2.5	6.2	2.5	0.6	38%	70%	61
	08	22 a	aa	OAK	9	6	25	0	136	159	55	10	28	103	3.64	1.38	23.4	286	1.9	6.8	3.7	0.7	35%	75%	96
Simon,Alfredo	07	26	aa	TEX	5	10	22	0	119	207	126	28	53	54	9.56	2.18	27.6	373	4.0	4.1	1.0	2.1	39%	57%	-36
Sinkbeil,Brett	08	24	aa	FLA	5	9	26	0	143	198	95	12	55	58	5.97	1.77	25.8	321	3.4	3.7	1.1	0.8	35%	66%	12
Sisco,Andy	07	25	aaa	CHW	3	6	23	0	78	92	52	15	47	68	5.98	1.78	16.0	287	5.4	7.8	1.4	1.7	34%	70%	23
Slocum,Brian	08	28	aaa	CLE	3	7	30	1	85	103	63	15	47	68	6.68	1.77	13.3	293	5.0	7.2	1.4	1.6	34%	64%	23
Slowey,Kevin	07	23 a	aaa	MIN	10	5	20	0	133	138	41	5	21	87	2.77	1.19	27.4	262	1.4	5.9	4.1	0.3	32%	77%	115
Smith,Brett	07	24	aa	NYY	7	4	17	0	91	80	45	11	55	64	4.48	1.48	23.6	231	5.4	6.3	1.2	1.0	26%	72%	40
Smith,Chris	07	26	a/a	BOS	6	9	32	1	109	181	74	13	48	63	6.15	2.10	17.1	363	3.9	5.2	1.3	1.1	41%	72%	8
	08	27	aaa	BOS	1	5	37	15	59	66	27	6	12	42	4.17	1.32	6.8	278	1.8	6.4	3.6	1.0	32%	71%	85
Smith,Dan	07	24	a/a	ATL	7	7	23	0	109	115	61	8	64	66	5.02	1.65	21.6	266	5.3	5.4	1.0	0.7	31%	69%	36
	08	25	aa	ATL	1	7	14	0	61	101	54	6	38	37	8.02	2.27	22.7	362	5.6	5.4	1.0	0.8	41%	63%	11
Smith,Gregory	07	24	aa	ARI	9	5	22	0	122	151	63	14	33	82	4.64	1.50	24.5	297	2.4	6.1	2.5	1.1	34%	71%	53
Smith,Jordan	08	23	aa	CIN	2	6	11	0	55	80	38	7	17	37	6.22	1.76	23.4	333	2.8	6.1	2.2	1.1	38%	66%	36
Smith,Mike	07	30	aa	STL	11	13	31	0	159	287	149	23	69	78	8.40	2.23	26.5	382	3.9	4.4	1.1	1.3	42%	62%	-10
Smith,Sean	07	24	aaa	CLE	9	7	24	0	133	148	76	16	59	82	5.14	1.56	24.8	276	4.0	5.5	1.4	1.1	31%	69%	30
	08	25	a/a	COL	6	8	22	0	114	127	78	18	54	72	6.17	1.58	23.4	276	4.2	5.7	1.3	1.4	30%	63%	21
Snyder,Benjamin	08	23	aa	SF	1	6	13	0	61	93	54	9	24	36	7.88	1.90	22.7	342	3.5	5.3	1.5	1.4	38%	59%	9
Snyder,Kyle	08	31	aaa	BOS	1	4	14	1	37	42	29	5	13	25	7.13	1.47	11.7	279	3.1	6.0	2.0	1.3	31%	51%	38
Soler,Alay	07	28	aa	PIT	1	1	14	1	39	66	37	4	23	17	8.62	2.29	14.5	368	5.3	3.8	0.7	0.8	40%	61%	-5
Songster,Judd	07	28	aa	COL	5	5	42	2	67	104	53	11	37	41	7.12	2.10	8.0	346	5.0	5.5	1.1	1.5	38%	68%	-2
Sonnanstine,Andrew	07	25 a	aaa	TAM	6	4	11	0	71	73	29	10	14	58	3.68	1.23	26.8	260	1.8	7.4	4.1	1.3	31%	75%	96
Sosa,Jorge	07	30	aa	NYM	4	0	5	0	32	46	7	1	6	18	2.01	1.61	29.0	329	1.6	4.9	3.1	0.4	38%	89%	71
	08	31	aa	SEA	2	2	27	4	36	44	21	6	25	27	5.28	1.89	6.4	292	6.2	6.8	1.1	1.5	34%	75%	16
Sosa,Oswaldo	07	22	aa	MIN	1	4	9	0	48	51	28	4	23	28	5.25	1.54	23.8	267	4.3	5.3	1.2	0.8	30%	66%	36
	08	23	aa	MIN	2	5	13	0	62	81	48	4	45	38	7.03	2.05	23.7	310	6.6	5.5	0.8	0.6	36%	64%	25
Sowers,Jeremy	07	24	aaa	CLE	4	5	15	0	96	128	53	6	24	55	4.96	1.58	28.9	313	2.2	5.1	2.3	0.6	36%	68%	55
	08	25	aaa	CLE	4	3	10	0	60	68	19	5	18	38	2.87	1.43	26.2	278	2.7	5.6	2.1	0.8	32%	83%	54
Speier,Ryan	07	28	aa	COL	1	4	50	33	49	71	41	5	29	29	7.56	2.04	4.9	332	5.3	5.3	1.0	0.9	38%	62%	14

					Actual				Major League Equivalents																
PITCHER	Yr	Age	Lev	Org	w	l	g	sv	ip	h	er	hr	bb	k	era	whip	bf/g	oob	ctl	dom	cmd	hr/9	h%	s%	bpv
Speigner,Levale	07	27	aaa	WAS	3	4	17	0	49	77	36	1	22	27	6.57	2.02	14.2	349	4.1	4.9	1.2	0.2	40%	65%	34
	08	28	a/a	WAS	4	0	35	0	59	55	15	4	14	29	2.33	1.17	6.9	243	2.1	4.4	2.0	0.5	27%	82%	60
Spoone,Chorye	08	23	aa	BAL	3	3	9	0	41	47	27	5	27	27	5.87	1.81	21.6	283	5.9	5.9	1.0	1.1	32%	69%	21
Stammen,Craig	08	25	a/a	WAS	4	5	15	0	81	92	45	3	26	53	5.03	1.45	23.6	279	2.9	5.9	2.1	0.3	34%	63%	68
Stanford,Jason	07	31	aaa	CLE	5	1	18	0	87	107	53	9	39	49	5.50	1.67	22.2	295	4.0	5.0	1.2	0.9	33%	67%	25
	08	32	a/a	CHC	6	6	18	0	79	114	59	10	39	41	6.70	1.94	21.4	331	4.4	4.6	1.0	1.1	36%	66%	4
Stark,Denny	08	34	aa	SEA	6	3	23	1	63	89	35	5	29	34	5.04	1.89	13.2	327	4.2	4.9	1.2	0.7	37%	73%	23
Starling,Wardell	07	25	aa	PIT	3	8	32	1	84	116	78	5	33	41	8.33	1.76	12.3	320	3.5	4.4	1.3	0.6	36%	49%	27
Startup,Will	07	23	a/a	SD	3	2	57	1	68	57	24	5	29	57	3.17	1.26	5.0	223	3.8	7.5	2.0	0.7	28%	77%	77
Stauffer,Tim	07	25	aa	SD	8	5	25	0	130	186	83	14	41	76	5.76	1.74	24.3	328	2.8	5.2	1.8	1.0	37%	68%	29
Stertzbach,Von	07	26	aa	LAA	1	2	21	0	25	39	26	5	16	17	9.48	2.20	6.1	348	5.8	6.2	1.1	1.6	39%	57%	-4
Stetter,Mitch	07	27 b	a/a	MIL	1	0	26	1	15	10	10	1	6	17	5.92	1.02	2.3	184	3.3	10.1	3.1	0.7	26%	38%	124
Stevens,Jeffrey	07	24 a	aa	CLE	3	1	34	2	48	48	22	4	17	56	4.14	1.36	6.1	256	3.2	10.5	3.3	0.8	36%	71%	113
	08	25 a	a/a	CLE	5	4	36	6	58	47	28	6	31	68	4.40	1.34	6.9	218	4.7	10.6	2.2	1.0	30%	69%	93
Stidfole,Sean	07	24	aa	TOR	1	0	30	0	52	54	19	4	31	32	3.21	1.63	7.9	261	5.4	5.5	1.0	0.7	30%	82%	36
	08	25	a/a	TOR	2	4	50	4	69	73	37	6	39	45	4.83	1.63	6.3	266	5.1	5.8	1.1	0.8	31%	71%	36
Stiller,Erik	08	24	aa	CLE	6	5	35	0	56	58	35	6	23	47	5.56	1.44	7.0	261	3.7	7.5	2.0	1.0	32%	62%	59
Stockman,Phil	07	28	a/a	ATL	2	0	21	3	31	21	6	1	16	23	1.67	1.19	6.1	186	4.7	6.8	1.5	0.3	23%	87%	79
	08	29	aaa	ATL	1	1	19	2	30	18	9	3	19	21	2.58	1.25	6.6	173	5.8	6.4	1.1	1.0	19%	84%	53
Stokes,Brian	08	29	aa	NYM	10	8	23	0	130	185	100	9	63	63	6.91	1.90	27.3	328	4.3	4.4	1.0	0.6	37%	62%	17
Stoner,Tobi	08	24	aa	NYM	4	6	15	0	79	92	45	7	29	49	5.17	1.53	23.4	285	3.3	5.6	1.7	0.8	33%	66%	43
Stone,Ricky	07	33	aaa	CIN	5	6	59	16	62	62	18	5	12	31	2.59	1.18	4.3	255	1.7	4.5	2.7	0.8	28%	82%	65
Strickland,Scott	08	32	aaa	NYY	4	0	52	12	66	62	35	9	29	57	4.73	1.39	5.5	243	4.0	7.8	1.9	1.3	29%	69%	55
Stults,Eric	07	28	aa	LA	5	7	21	0	89	181	105	16	43	59	10.59	2.52	23.1	410	4.4	6.0	1.4	1.6	46%	57%	-10
	08	29	aa	LA	7	7	20	0	117	163	70	19	44	74	5.38	1.76	27.4	322	3.4	5.7	1.7	1.4	36%	73%	17
Sturtze,Tanyon	08	38	aa	LA	2	2	39	5	51	73	33	7	21	30	5.80	1.84	6.2	328	3.7	5.2	1.4	1.2	37%	70%	13
Stutes,Kyle	07	26	aa	SD	0	1	27	2	31	47	27	6	17	19	7.69	2.03	5.7	339	4.8	5.5	1.1	1.6	37%	63%	-4
Sues,Jeffrey	08	25	aa	PIT	3	1	24	1	43	46	24	3	22	41	5.12	1.58	8.1	266	4.7	8.7	1.9	0.7	35%	67%	72
Swarzak,Anthony	07	22	aa	MIN	5	4	15	0	86	88	37	6	24	62	3.87	1.30	24.2	259	2.5	6.5	2.6	0.6	31%	71%	77
	08	23	a/a	MIN	8	8	27	0	146	187	85	16	52	84	5.23	1.63	24.7	305	3.2	5.2	1.6	1.0	34%	69%	29
Swindle,Robert	08	25 a	a/a	PHI	3	1	38	1	53	48	12	1	8	54	1.97	1.07	5.6	238	1.4	9.2	6.4	0.2	33%	81%	192
Switzer,Jon	07	28	aaa	TAM	0	0	23	1	33	34	4	0	10	19	1.17	1.34	6.1	263	2.6	5.1	1.9	0.0	32%	90%	73
	08	29	aaa	BOS	5	1	52	3	75	109	52	14	21	51	6.18	1.72	6.7	331	2.5	6.1	2.4	1.7	37%	68%	25
Tabor,Lee	08	24	aa	CIN	1	1	37	1	42	64	31	4	23	28	6.60	2.05	5.7	342	4.8	6.0	1.2	0.9	40%	68%	22
Tadano,Kazuhito	07	27	aa	OAK	8	7	29	0	129	195	101	27	42	95	7.05	1.84	21.2	341	2.9	6.6	2.2	1.8	38%	65%	18
Talbot,Mitch	07	24	aaa	TAM	13	9	29	0	161	205	110	16	64	109	6.15	1.67	25.5	304	3.6	6.1	1.7	0.9	35%	63%	40
	08	25 a	aaa	TAM	13	9	28	0	161	184	80	9	35	122	4.47	1.36	24.6	281	2.0	6.8	3.5	0.5	35%	66%	98
Tankersley,Dennis	07	29	aaa	DET	10	7	24	0	138	213	96	15	55	64	6.23	1.94	28.0	345	3.6	4.2	1.2	1.0	38%	68%	6
	08	30	aaa	WAS	4	4	30	0	100	145	68	14	43	49	6.12	1.88	16.0	331	3.8	4.4	1.1	1.3	36%	69%	1
Tankersley,Taylor	08	26	aa	FLA	2	1	29	0	31	40	8	2	20	23	2.24	1.92	5.2	305	5.8	6.8	1.2	0.6	37%	90%	40
Tata,Jordan	07	26	aaa	DET	4	5	14	0	82	81	37	9	29	42	4.06	1.34	25.0	253	3.2	4.6	1.4	1.0	28%	72%	32
Taubenheim,Ty	07	25	a/a	TOR	6	8	24	0	120	154	91	18	46	84	6.80	1.67	22.9	305	3.5	6.3	1.8	1.3	35%	60%	31
	08	26	aa	PIT	4	9	19	0	98	131	84	14	43	50	7.76	1.78	24.2	314	4.0	4.5	1.1	1.3	34%	56%	4
Tejeda,Robinson	08	27 b	aa	TEX	1	1	10	1	33	25	10	2	11	29	2.82	1.11	13.3	208	3.1	7.8	2.5	0.6	26%	77%	94
Tejera,Michael	07	31	aa	PIT	8	5	27	0	127	187	96	20	60	41	6.78	1.95	22.9	335	4.3	2.9	0.7	1.4	35%	67%	-23
	08	32	aaa	BOS	3	6	34	2	77	94	59	14	35	38	6.87	1.66	10.4	294	4.0	4.4	1.1	1.6	31%	61%	-2
Thatcher,Joe	07	26 a	a/a	SD	4	1	46	1	46	46	8	0	11	53	1.64	1.23	4.2	256	2.1	10.4	5.1	0.0	38%	85%	172
	08	27	aa	SD	5	2	37	3	39	49	16	2	13	32	3.61	1.61	4.8	303	3.1	7.3	2.4	0.6	37%	78%	71
Thayer,Dale	07	27	a/a	TAM	9	0	55	21	69	59	26	6	27	50	3.33	1.24	5.2	226	3.5	6.4	1.9	0.7	27%	75%	66
	08	28	aaa	TAM	3	1	52	9	68	85	25	2	25	63	3.34	1.62	5.9	300	3.3	8.3	2.5	0.3	39%	79%	88
Thomas,Brad	07	30	aa	SEA	8	6	34	2	116	207	97	11	59	68	7.55	2.29	17.8	379	4.5	5.2	1.2	0.8	43%	66%	10
Thomas,Justin	07	24	aa	SEA	4	9	24	0	119	170	88	11	66	87	6.62	1.98	24.3	328	5.0	6.6	1.3	0.9	39%	66%	31
	08	25	aa	SEA	9	8	32	1	135	152	76	14	71	108	5.05	1.64	19.3	277	4.7	7.2	1.5	0.9	34%	70%	48
Thompson,Aaron	08	22	aa	FLA	2	5	16	0	81	124	59	9	42	49	6.54	2.04	25.2	343	4.7	5.4	1.2	1.0	39%	68%	13
Thompson,Daryl	08	23 a	a/a	CIN	8	2	17	0	107	93	31	7	23	78	2.61	1.08	25.2	229	1.9	6.6	3.4	0.6	28%	78%	102
Thompson,Lavon	07	25	aa	HOU	4	3	38	3	54	66	30	17	10	41	4.99	1.40	6.1	293	1.7	6.7	4.1	2.8	30%	77%	39
	08	26	aa	HOU	1	3	19	0	36	48	28	7	9	29	6.86	1.59	8.6	314	2.3	7.1	3.1	1.7	36%	59%	49
Thompson,Mike	07	27	aa	SD	4	11	23	0	132	223	126	23	48	54	8.61	2.05	28.6	366	3.3	3.7	1.1	1.6	39%	58%	-20
	08	28	aa	PIT	3	3	22	0	59	101	42	6	27	19	6.42	2.16	13.6	370	4.0	2.9	0.7	0.9	39%	70%	-14
Thompson,Richard	07	23 a	aa	LAA	5	3	37	1	74	62	22	8	21	67	2.63	1.11	8.1	223	2.5	8.1	3.2	1.0	27%	82%	97
Thompson,Sean	07	25	aa	COL	9	8	27	0	133	161	79	16	61	68	5.33	1.67	22.6	293	4.1	4.6	1.1	1.1	32%	69%	16
Thomson,John	07	34	a/a	KC	2	7	10	0	47	76	49	9	19	29	9.32	2.00	23.2	354	3.6	5.5	1.5	1.7	39%	53%	-2
Thorpe,Tracy	07	27	aa	TOR	5	4	46	10	56	61	41	7	34	41	6.63	1.70	5.6	271	5.5	6.5	1.2	1.1	31%	61%	32
	08	28	a/a	SEA	5	4	39	5	73	86	54	14	44	61	6.64	1.77	8.8	287	5.4	7.5	1.4	1.7	33%	65%	21
Thorp,Paul	07	27	aa	NYY	0	1	15	1	30	39	14	5	25	15	4.34	2.13	10.1	306	7.6	4.5	0.6	1.4	33%	84%	-10
Threets,Erick	07	26	aa	SF	3	1	40	1	54	58	28	4	38	31	4.61	1.76	6.3	267	6.3	5.1	0.8	0.7	30%	74%	27
	08	27	aa	SF	4	5	37	0	66	71	37	6	41	34	5.01	1.70	8.3	270	5.6	4.6	0.8	0.8	30%	71%	23
Thurman,Corey	07	29	aa	MIL	5	8	30	0	95	118	74	26	39	65	6.99	1.64	14.5	298	3.7	6.1	1.7	2.5	31%	63%	-7
Tillman,Christopher	08	20 a	aa	BAL	11	4	28	0	135	126	56	11	60	141	3.74	1.37	20.7	242	4.0	9.4	2.3	0.8	32%	74%	89
Till,Brock	07	27	a/a	CIN	4	1	42	1	47	71	29	1	18	23	5.49	1.90	5.4	341	3.5	4.3	1.2	0.2	39%	69%	32
Todd,Jesse	08	22	aa	STL	5	6	21	0	125	106	47	14	32	86	3.38	1.10	24.0	225	2.3	6.2	2.7	1.0	26%	73%	73
Tomey,Anthony	07	26	a/a	DET	4	0	37	2	51	52	21	2	32	39	3.71	1.65	6.3	259	5.7	6.8	1.2	0.4	32%	77%	58
	08	27	aa	LA	5	5	39	0	64	78	47	12	43	54	6.61	1.90	7.9	295	6.1	7.6	1.2	1.7	34%	68%	17
Torra,Matthew	08	24	aa	ARI	10	10	27	0	157	235	91	24	33	81	5.19	1.70	26.9	338	1.9	4.6	2.5	1.4	37%	73%	25
Torres,Carlos	07	25	aa	CHW	2	2	36	1	56	74	34	5	25	49	5.41	1.77	7.3	311	4.1	7.9	2.0	0.8	39%	70%	56
	08	26	a/a	CHW	9	5	29	0	121	138	64	8	44	95	4.78	1.51	18.5	281	3.3	7.1	2.1	0.6	34%	68%	68
Torres,Joseph	08	26	aa	CHW	3	1	59	0	50	40	23	3	38	45	4.13	1.56	3.8	216	6.8	8.1	1.2	0.6	28%	74%	67
Totten,Heath	07	29	a/a	PHI	3	10	20	0	89	154	71	7	27	30	7.15	2.03	22.0	372	2.7	3.0	1.1	0.7	40%	63%	-0
	08	30	a/a	LA	8	7	29	0	101	184	68	9	23	42	6.01	2.04	17.3	384	2.0	3.8	1.9	0.8	42%	70%	17
Towers,Josh	08	32	aa	COL	6	7	31	0	116	201	107	15	31	58	8.30	2.00	18.4	372	2.4	4.5	1.9	1.2	41%	58%	12
Traber,Billy	07	28	aaa	WAS	2	3	14	0	40	49	17	2	8	22	3.86	1.42	12.4	297	1.7	5.0	3.0	0.5	34%	73%	73
	08	29	aaa	NYY	2	1	40	4	47	59	25	4	14	31	4.82	1.56	5.3	301	2.7	5.9	2.2	0.8	35%	70%	51

					Actual				Major League Equivalents																
PITCHER	Yr	Age	Lev	Org	w	l	g	sv	ip	h	er	hr	bb	k	era	whip	bf/g	oob	ctl	dom	cmd	hr/9	h%	s%	bpv
Trahern,Dallas	07	22	a/a	DET	13	6	27	0	169	207	90	13	52	85	4.82	1.53	27.9	295	2.8	4.5	1.6	0.7	33%	69%	36
	08	23	aa	FLA	5	11	21	0	111	157	88	21	47	65	7.14	1.84	25.1	326	3.8	5.3	1.4	1.7	35%	63%	-1
Trinidad,Polin	08	24	aa	HOU	6	5	18	0	107	118	45	13	21	62	3.81	1.29	25.0	273	1.7	5.2	3.0	1.1	30%	74%	61
Trolia,Aaron	07	26	aa	SEA	3	2	21	1	43	68	44	6	22	30	9.14	2.09	10.2	351	4.6	6.4	1.4	1.2	41%	55%	16
Troncoso,Ramon	07	25	aa	LA	7	3	35	7	52	61	22	3	19	32	3.83	1.54	6.6	287	3.3	5.6	1.7	0.5	34%	75%	51
	08	26	aa	LA	4	0	22	0	30	52	21	1	18	14	6.29	2.32	7.2	372	5.3	4.3	0.8	0.3	42%	71%	13
Tucker,Ryan	08	22	aa	FLA	5	3	25	0	91	71	18	2	38	68	1.78	1.20	15.0	211	3.8	6.7	1.8	0.2	27%	85%	85
Tyler,Scott	07	25	aa	FLA	0	2	28	1	30	32	39	2	51	27	11.59	2.76	6.1	268	15.2	8.0	0.5	0.7	34%	55%	41
Ungs,Nick	07	28	aa	FLA	5	5	29	1	112	170	90	21	59	48	7.23	2.04	19.2	342	4.7	3.9	0.8	1.7	36%	67%	-24
	08	29	a/a	MIL	6	4	15	0	79	104	51	13	24	38	5.82	1.62	24.0	310	2.8	4.3	1.5	1.5	33%	67%	6
Urdaneta,Lino	07	28	aa	NYM	2	1	26	9	35	51	28	5	12	10	7.13	1.79	6.3	331	3.1	2.6	0.8	1.2	34%	60%	-16
Urquidez,Jason	08	26	aa	ARI	3	1	18	0	32	38	23	5	16	29	6.43	1.68	8.2	287	4.5	8.0	1.8	1.3	35%	63%	45
Vaclavik,Justin	07	23	aa	PIT	2	6	24	0	34	59	40	3	23	22	10.61	2.39	7.5	371	6.0	5.9	1.0	0.8	43%	53%	12
Valdez,Edward	07	28	a/a	WAS	2	5	46	3	84	132	59	9	46	47	6.27	2.12	9.2	350	4.9	5.0	1.0	1.0	39%	71%	7
	08	29	aa	COL	5	4	50	2	74	109	54	6	29	49	6.54	1.86	7.1	335	3.5	5.9	1.7	0.8	39%	64%	36
Valdez,Luis	08	24	aa	ATL	4	3	55	28	65	57	24	3	38	64	3.35	1.46	5.2	230	5.2	8.8	1.7	0.4	31%	77%	84
Valdez,Miguel	08	24	aa	ARI	3	5	12	0	64	77	39	3	24	51	5.50	1.58	24.0	292	3.3	7.2	2.2	0.4	36%	63%	72
Valdez,Raul	07	30	aa	NYM	0	1	20	1	29	52	19	4	12	17	5.77	2.20	7.4	380	3.7	5.3	1.4	1.2	43%	76%	4
Van Allen,Cory	08	24	aa	WAS	3	3	10	0	47	69	28	3	10	29	5.32	1.69	21.7	334	2.0	5.6	2.8	0.6	39%	68%	63
Van Benschoten,Johr	07	27	aa	PIT	10	7	19	0	109	135	46	10	60	55	3.78	1.79	27.0	298	5.0	4.5	0.9	0.8	33%	81%	18
	08	28	aa	PIT	7	4	22	0	80	101	55	4	40	42	6.18	1.76	17.1	302	4.5	4.7	1.0	0.4	35%	63%	32
Van Buren,Jermaine	07	27	a/a	OAK	1	3	47	3	64	72	36	10	34	44	5.01	1.67	6.3	279	4.8	6.1	1.3	1.5	31%	74%	19
Van Hekken,Andy	08	29	aa	HOU	6	3	11	0	67	115	33	8	12	36	4.46	1.88	29.4	369	1.6	4.8	3.0	1.1	41%	79%	41
Vanden Hurk,Rick	07	22 a	aa	FLA	4	2	11	0	65	54	28	8	25	69	3.87	1.21	24.5	221	3.5	9.5	2.8	1.1	29%	72%	93
	08	23	aa	FLA	5	4	14	0	73	71	40	11	32	68	4.96	1.41	22.6	250	3.9	8.4	2.1	1.4	30%	69%	58
Vaquedano,Jose	07	26	aa	BOS	2	1	22	0	38	49	24	6	21	17	5.69	1.84	8.3	307	4.9	4.1	0.8	1.4	33%	71%	-5
	08	27	a/a	BOS	8	1	43	1	62	80	32	6	34	30	4.67	1.85	6.9	308	5.0	4.4	0.9	0.8	34%	76%	14
Vargas,Claudio	08	30	aa	NYM	5	2	8	0	43	76	36	7	19	26	7.46	2.19	27.5	376	3.9	5.4	1.4	1.5	42%	67%	-3
Vargas,Jason	07	25	aa	NYM	9	7	24	0	125	166	86	15	45	88	6.21	1.69	24.0	313	3.3	6.4	2.0	1.1	36%	64%	40
Vasquez,Carlos	07	25	a/a	CHW	4	3	52	4	76	73	33	3	39	49	3.90	1.47	6.4	248	4.6	5.8	1.3	0.4	30%	73%	56
Vasquez,Esmerling	07	24	aa	ARI	10	6	29	0	165	151	72	14	62	129	3.93	1.29	23.9	238	3.4	7.0	2.1	0.8	29%	71%	70
	08	25	aa	ARI	3	6	24	0	83	99	85	15	77	48	9.25	2.12	17.4	290	8.3	5.3	0.6	1.6	31%	56%	-6
Vasquez,Jorge	07	29	aa	TEX	2	3	34	0	52	63	40	11	53	44	6.90	2.22	7.9	291	9.2	7.6	0.8	1.8	34%	72%	5
Vasquez,Virgil	07	25	aaa	DET	12	5	25	0	155	167	79	20	33	109	4.57	1.29	26.1	269	1.9	6.3	3.3	1.2	31%	67%	73
	08	26	aaa	DET	12	12	27	0	159	210	105	30	37	98	5.95	1.56	26.4	312	2.1	5.5	2.6	1.7	34%	65%	31
Vaughan,Beau	07	26	aa	BOS	1	3	42	6	59	69	31	2	36	48	4.73	1.77	6.6	286	5.4	7.3	1.3	0.4	36%	72%	59
	08	27	a/a	BOS	3	2	46	17	58	63	22	3	28	51	3.39	1.57	5.7	272	4.3	8.0	1.9	0.5	35%	79%	71
Vazquez,Camilo	07	24	aa	CIN	4	8	21	0	112	158	81	11	43	71	6.54	1.79	25.1	325	3.5	5.7	1.6	0.9	37%	63%	31
	08	25	a/a	CIN	3	4	10	0	40	65	34	15	20	27	7.56	2.13	20.2	358	4.5	6.0	1.3	3.3	37%	73%	-52
Veal II,Donald	07	23	aa	CHC	8	10	28	0	130	152	93	14	77	107	6.42	1.76	21.7	285	5.3	7.4	1.4	1.0	35%	63%	41
	08	24	aa	CHC	5	10	29	0	145	174	87	22	84	100	5.42	1.78	23.5	291	5.2	6.2	1.2	1.4	33%	72%	18
Vega,Marwin	08	22	aa	SEA	3	3	46	2	68	74	40	3	45	45	5.28	1.74	6.9	271	5.9	5.9	1.0	0.4	33%	68%	46
Venafro,Mike	07	34	a/a	STL	1	2	51	2	50	74	33	2	21	23	5.99	1.91	4.7	337	3.8	4.0	1.1	0.4	38%	67%	22
Ventura,Ronnie	07	24	aa	HOU	4	9	20	0	87	113	69	8	31	47	7.18	1.64	19.9	307	3.2	4.8	1.5	0.9	34%	55%	28
Vermilyea,Jamie	07	26	aaa	TOR	2	2	25	1	43	47	25	5	21	27	5.27	1.59	7.8	274	4.4	5.6	1.3	1.1	31%	68%	29
	08	27	aa	TOR	3	3	20	0	39	69	44	9	26	19	10.05	2.44	10.5	377	6.1	4.4	0.7	2.1	40%	60%	-42
Villafuerte,Brandon	08	33	aa	FLA	7	3	62	7	64	89	34	6	31	44	4.79	1.87	5.0	323	4.3	6.2	1.4	0.8	38%	75%	33
Villa,Kelvin	07	22	aa	ATL	8	12	28	0	143	197	109	16	69	103	6.85	1.86	24.4	320	4.3	6.5	1.5	1.0	38%	63%	31
Viola,Pedro	08	25	aa	CIN	4	7	52	2	82	109	52	8	39	66	5.72	1.80	7.5	312	4.3	7.2	1.7	0.9	38%	68%	46
Volquez,Edinson	07	24	aa	TEX	14	2	19	0	109	88	42	12	42	104	3.47	1.20	23.6	217	3.5	8.5	2.5	1.0	27%	74%	86
Volstad,Chris	07	21	aa	FLA	4	2	7	0	42	46	17	4	10	23	3.63	1.33	25.6	272	2.1	4.9	2.3	0.9	30%	75%	53
	08	22	aa	FLA	4	4	15	0	91	96	39	0	31	50	3.86	1.40	26.2	265	3.1	4.9	1.6	0.0	32%	69%	65
Waddell,Jason	08	27	aa	SF	0	3	44	2	64	66	36	7	43	49	5.08	1.71	6.7	262	6.1	6.9	1.1	1.0	31%	72%	37
Wade,Cory	07	24	aa	LA	0	1	14	0	33	29	7	2	13	25	1.93	1.28	9.9	234	3.5	6.7	1.9	0.6	28%	88%	69
Waldrop,Steven	07	22	aa	MIN	3	6	11	0	59	83	41	7	20	27	6.25	1.75	25.0	325	3.1	4.1	1.4	1.1	35%	65%	11
Walker,Kevin	07	31	aa	COL	4	6	15	0	79	138	75	9	24	30	8.56	2.04	26.2	373	2.7	3.4	1.3	1.1	40%	57%	-5
Walker,Sean	08	26	aa	HOU	1	6	26	0	87	147	80	6	34	39	8.28	2.08	16.7	366	3.6	4.0	1.1	0.6	41%	58%	12
Walker,Tyler	07	31	aa	SF	1	2	20	7	23	33	16	6	12	17	6.45	1.94	5.6	329	4.6	6.7	1.4	2.3	36%	73%	-10
Walrond,Les	07	31	aa	CHC	11	5	27	0	137	277	131	23	70	55	8.62	2.53	27.7	409	4.6	3.6	0.8	1.5	43%	67%	-34
	08	32	a/a	PHI	6	9	28	0	122	158	63	7	52	91	4.67	1.72	20.2	307	3.9	6.7	1.7	0.5	37%	72%	56
Walters,Phillip	07	23	aa	STL	3	4	8	0	49	46	15	4	14	33	2.75	1.22	25.4	243	2.6	6.0	2.4	0.7	28%	80%	70
	08	24	aa	STL	10	6	29	0	158	175	88	20	66	129	4.99	1.53	24.2	275	3.8	7.3	2.0	1.1	33%	69%	52
Warden,Jim Ed	07	28	a/a	CLE	5	5	56	6	74	119	49	7	34	53	5.99	2.06	6.6	354	4.1	6.4	1.5	0.9	42%	71%	29
	08	29	a/a	WAS	4	7	57	9	77	93	37	1	38	40	4.27	1.69	6.2	292	4.4	4.7	1.1	0.1	34%	73%	43
Ward,Zachary	08	25	aa	MIN	5	6	46	1	93	113	48	4	55	63	4.69	1.80	9.5	293	5.3	6.1	1.1	0.4	35%	73%	45
Wasdin,John	07	35	aa	PIT	1	1	7	0	35	58	35	12	4	29	9.05	1.74	23.4	360	0.9	7.4	8.2	3.0	40%	52%	109
	08	36	aa	STL	9	6	41	3	110	129	54	16	21	71	4.42	1.37	11.5	287	1.7	5.8	3.3	1.3	32%	72%	62
Wassermann,Ehren	07	27	aaa	CHW	2	4	38	5	42	42	14	0	20	28	3.08	1.47	4.9	255	4.2	6.0	1.4	0.0	32%	77%	70
	08	28 b	aaa	CHW	3	0	32	7	39	36	7	1	14	35	1.70	1.27	5.1	239	3.2	8.1	2.6	0.2	32%	87%	102
Waters,Chris	07	27	a/a	BAL	8	9	28	0	158	208	116	23	101	91	6.61	1.96	27.5	311	5.8	5.2	0.9	1.3	34%	67%	4
	08	28	a/a	BAL	8	6	24	0	122	156	89	16	58	70	6.60	1.76	23.8	305	4.3	5.1	1.2	1.2	34%	63%	14
Watkins,Steve	07	29	aa	SD	2	5	34	0	78	133	72	19	60	37	8.30	2.48	12.4	369	6.9	4.2	0.6	2.2	38%	69%	-45
Watson,Sean	08	23	aa	CIN	1	2	31	3	35	31	21	1	29	38	5.30	1.71	5.2	232	7.4	9.7	1.3	0.3	33%	67%	86
Watson,Tanner	08	26	aa	CHC	1	3	17	0	57	98	46	8	25	25	7.25	2.15	17.0	369	4.0	4.0	1.0	1.3	40%	67%	-12
Wayne,Brett	07	27	aa	TAM	2	0	29	0	47	77	36	8	41	26	6.92	2.51	8.8	360	7.8	4.9	0.6	1.6	39%	75%	-23
Weatherby III,Charles	07	29	a/a	PHI	2	2	17	0	45	69	42	8	24	19	8.47	2.07	13.2	346	4.7	3.7	0.8	1.6	36%	60%	-24
Weathers,Casey	08	23 a	aa	COL	2	1	44	2	44	38	18	1	26	45	3.58	1.45	4.4	229	5.3	9.1	1.7	0.2	32%	74%	94
Weaver,Jeff	08	32	aaa	CLE	4	6	22	0	84	129	82	20	34	49	8.78	1.94	18.6	345	3.6	5.3	1.5	2.1	37%	57%	-16
Webber,Nick	07	23	aa	STL	1	3	33	0	50	70	28	4	22	25	4.99	1.83	7.2	324	3.9	4.5	1.2	0.7	36%	73%	20
	08	24	aa	STL	4	1	25	0	42	49	28	4	29	8	6.06	1.87	8.1	286	6.3	1.6	0.3	0.9	29%	68%	-14
Webb,John	07	28	aa	CHC	4	6	31	1	80	143	73	8	49	35	8.16	2.39	13.7	379	5.5	4.0	0.7	0.8	41%	65%	-7
Webb,Ryan	08	23	aa	OAK	9	8	25	0	130	175	78	11	39	80	5.40	1.65	23.7	316	2.7	5.5	2.1	0.8	36%	67%	45
Weiser,Keith	08	24	aa	COL	1	2	5	0	35	43	17	2	5	10	4.33	1.38	30.1	297	1.4	2.7	2.0	0.5	32%	68%	37

					Actual				Major League Equivalents																
PITCHER	Yr	Age	Lev	Org	w	l	g	sv	ip	h	er	hr	bb	k	era	whip	bf/g	oob	ctl	dom	cmd	hr/9	h%	s%	bpv
Welch,David	08	25	aa	MIL	11	4	26	0	147	177	79	27	57	77	4.82	1.59	25.5	291	3.5	4.7	1.4	1.6	31%	75%	5
Wells,Jared	07	26	aa	SD	4	7	47	8	92	134	71	11	56	68	6.94	2.06	9.8	333	5.4	6.7	1.2	1.1	39%	66%	22
	08	27	aa	SEA	1	5	52	20	60	79	54	8	41	44	8.08	2.00	5.7	311	6.2	6.5	1.1	1.2	36%	59%	18
Wells,Randy	07	25	aa	CHC	5	6	40	2	95	129	67	16	47	77	6.30	1.84	11.3	317	4.4	7.2	1.6	1.5	37%	68%	25
	08	26	aa	CHC	10	4	27	0	118	161	68	18	39	76	5.16	1.69	20.2	318	3.0	5.8	1.9	1.4	36%	73%	25
Whelan,Kevin	07	24	aa	NYY	4	2	31	4	54	43	27	3	47	55	4.46	1.68	8.0	215	7.9	9.2	1.2	0.5	29%	73%	76
Whisler,Wesley	07	24	aa	CHW	6	13	28	0	156	252	127	16	47	63	7.34	1.91	27.0	355	2.7	3.6	1.3	0.9	38%	61%	6
	08	26	aaa	CHW	12	10	27	0	156	209	87	17	46	62	5.01	1.64	26.3	315	2.7	3.6	1.3	1.0	34%	71%	12
White,Bill	07	29	aa	TEX	2	0	44	2	50	74	39	6	35	45	6.96	2.17	5.8	335	6.3	8.0	1.3	1.1	41%	68%	29
	08	30	aa	TEX	4	1	50	6	53	67	32	5	39	40	5.42	1.98	5.2	301	6.6	6.7	1.0	0.9	36%	73%	30
White,Cody	08	24	aa	LA	4	6	16	0	85	116	67	11	41	43	7.09	1.85	25.4	319	4.4	4.5	1.0	1.2	35%	62%	4
White,Matt	07	30	aa	LA	2	4	40	0	51	81	36	10	24	27	6.28	2.06	6.4	353	4.3	4.8	1.1	1.8	38%	73%	-16
White,Sean	08	27	aa	SEA	6	11	22	0	125	233	102	14	53	39	7.37	2.28	29.6	389	3.8	2.8	0.7	1.0	41%	68%	-22
White,Steven	07	26	aaa	NYY	6	4	16	1	91	103	45	4	34	45	4.48	1.50	25.2	279	3.4	4.4	1.3	0.4	32%	69%	41
	08	27	a/a	NYY	4	5	28	0	91	140	97	20	66	43	9.54	2.26	16.8	345	6.5	4.2	0.7	1.9	36%	59%	-33
Wideman,Aaron	08	23	aa	TOR	3	8	13	0	63	98	54	12	31	20	7.65	2.04	24.1	347	4.4	2.9	0.7	1.8	35%	65%	-36
Wigdahl,Jeffrey	07	25	aa	HOU	2	2	22	0	37	56	30	7	24	31	7.28	2.16	8.6	339	5.9	7.4	1.3	1.6	40%	68%	10
Wilhite,Matt	07	26	aa	LAA	3	4	49	3	74	120	61	10	23	30	7.39	1.92	7.3	356	2.8	3.6	1.3	1.3	38%	62%	-5
	08	27	aa	LAA	7	0	47	0	63	102	48	11	19	42	6.88	1.93	6.5	358	2.8	6.0	2.2	1.5	40%	66%	19
Wilkerson,Wes	07	31	a/a	ATL	3	4	44	1	63	98	56	8	32	32	7.91	2.06	7.1	346	4.6	4.6	1.0	1.1	38%	61%	1
Williams,Dave	07	29	aa	NYM	3	4	10	0	61	81	39	14	16	26	5.71	1.60	27.6	313	2.4	3.9	1.6	2.0	32%	70%	-11
Williams,Jerome	07	26	a/a	MIN	0	4	23	1	52	94	66	11	28	29	11.43	2.34	11.9	381	4.9	4.9	1.0	1.8	41%	50%	-25
Williams,Randy	07	32	aa	TEX	3	2	50	1	64	100	58	16	24	37	8.08	1.92	6.2	348	3.3	5.2	1.6	2.3	37%	62%	-19
Wilson,Brian	07	26	aa	SF	1	2	31	11	34	30	11	0	27	29	2.93	1.66	5.0	232	7.0	7.6	1.1	0.0	31%	80%	77
Windsor,Jason	07	25	aa	OAK	5	3	10	0	56	84	46	3	27	32	7.30	1.98	27.5	340	4.3	5.0	1.2	0.5	39%	61%	26
Wing,Ryan	07	26	aa	CHW	6	6	35	0	114	121	63	13	54	75	5.00	1.54	14.5	267	4.3	5.9	1.4	1.1	30%	69%	34
	08	27	aa	OAK	2	1	47	0	54	54	17	2	26	35	2.87	1.49	5.1	255	4.4	5.8	1.3	0.4	31%	81%	55
Winkelsas,Joe	07	34	a/a	ATL	2	2	19	0	36	42	17	0	17	22	4.17	1.64	8.6	287	4.2	5.4	1.3	0.0	35%	72%	57
Wise,Brendan	08	23	aa	DET	2	1	30	3	43	47	18	4	13	18	3.75	1.39	6.2	271	2.7	3.8	1.4	0.8	29%	75%	27
Wlodarczyk,Michael	08	26	aa	TAM	0	4	10	0	30	69	38	3	22	12	11.30	3.03	17.9	439	6.6	3.5	0.5	1.0	47%	61%	-31
Woerman,Joseph	07	25	aa	SEA	7	7	27	0	144	140	74	8	75	105	4.60	1.49	23.5	250	4.7	6.6	1.4	0.5	30%	68%	58
	08	26	aa	SEA	3	11	26	0	117	163	108	12	92	59	8.29	2.18	23.0	323	7.1	4.6	0.6	0.9	36%	61%	3
Wolfe,Brian	08	28	aaa	TOR	2	3	17	1	36	49	20	3	12	23	4.97	1.69	9.8	319	2.9	5.7	2.0	0.9	37%	71%	43
Wolf,Ross	07	25	aa	FLA	4	3	46	2	47	63	22	5	19	20	4.22	1.74	4.8	315	3.6	3.8	1.1	1.0	34%	78%	7
	08	26	aa	FLA	5	2	38	1	39	58	22	4	18	16	5.13	1.94	5.0	337	4.1	3.7	0.9	1.0	36%	75%	-2
Woodard,Steve	08	33	aaa	FLA	1	2	16	0	53	89	49	11	16	37	8.36	1.99	10.4	365	2.8	6.2	2.2	1.8	41%	59%	12
Woods,Jake	07	26	aa	SEA	5	7	25	1	114	194	118	21	51	62	9.33	2.14	23.1	368	4.0	4.9	1.2	1.6	40%	56%	-13
	08	27	aa	SEA	6	1	32	1	64	84	39	8	34	41	5.42	1.84	9.5	311	4.7	5.7	1.2	1.2	35%	73%	17
Woody,Abraham	07	25	aa	ARI	8	6	48	5	72	108	49	9	26	40	6.18	1.87	7.2	340	3.3	5.0	1.5	1.2	38%	68%	13
	08	26	aa	ARI	2	7	45	3	70	98	49	4	40	41	6.27	1.96	7.6	323	5.1	5.2	1.0	0.5	37%	67%	26
Wood,Blake	08	23	aa	KC	5	7	18	0	86	116	67	8	33	65	7.00	1.73	22.3	316	3.4	6.8	2.0	0.9	38%	58%	48
Wood,Mike	07	27	aa	TEX	9	3	16	0	97	118	54	11	25	51	5.02	1.48	26.7	294	2.3	4.8	2.0	1.0	33%	67%	37
Wood,Travis	08	22	aa	CIN	4	9	17	0	80	101	73	11	47	50	8.21	1.85	22.4	302	5.3	5.6	1.1	1.2	34%	55%	14
Wordekemper,Eric	08	25	aa	NYY	3	2	33	6	50	80	34	9	31	35	6.19	2.22	7.8	354	5.6	6.3	1.1	1.6	40%	75%	-2
Worrell,Mark	07	25	aa	STL	3	2	49	4	67	67	27	6	25	55	3.68	1.38	5.9	256	3.4	7.4	2.2	0.8	31%	76%	69
	08	26	a	STL	3	3	53	5	58	54	17	2	31	61	2.58	1.47	4.8	243	4.8	9.5	2.0	0.3	34%	83%	94
Wright,Brae	08	25	aa	MIL	6	10	27	0	170	188	79	9	63	104	4.17	1.48	27.7	275	3.3	5.5	1.6	0.5	32%	71%	52
Wright,Chase	07	25	a/a	NYY	13	5	25	1	145	168	88	20	70	66	5.44	1.64	26.5	284	4.4	4.1	0.9	1.2	30%	69%	6
	08	26	a/a	NYY	10	3	22	0	131	140	58	8	47	57	3.97	1.43	25.9	268	3.2	3.9	1.2	0.6	30%	72%	33
Wright,Matt	07	26	aa	KC	10	5	28	0	137	182	86	23	42	77	5.62	1.64	22.3	313	2.8	5.1	1.8	1.5	34%	69%	15
	08	27	aa	KC	4	10	27	0	148	229	133	37	68	69	8.11	2.00	27.0	346	4.1	4.2	1.0	2.2	36%	63%	-35
Wright,Steven	08	24	aa	CLE	4	3	14	0	75	98	47	17	19	49	5.68	1.56	24.0	309	2.3	5.9	2.6	2.0	33%	69%	23
Wright,Wesley	07	23	aa	LA	7	4	44	2	78	82	39	9	49	75	4.50	1.68	8.2	265	5.7	8.7	1.5	1.0	33%	75%	55
Yabuta,Yasuhiko	08	35	aa	KC	4	3	20	0	40	64	36	4	19	25	8.19	2.05	10.0	352	4.2	5.5	1.3	0.8	40%	58%	22
Yan,Esteban	08	33	aaa	BAL	1	2	37	0	47	61	38	3	15	46	7.24	1.61	5.8	307	2.8	8.7	3.1	0.6	40%	52%	93
Yates,Kyle	07	25	aa	TOR	9	9	27	0	151	223	99	28	46	80	5.90	1.78	26.3	336	2.8	4.8	1.7	1.7	36%	71%	2
Youman,Shane	07	28	aa	PIT	4	6	15	0	82	129	63	4	42	42	6.87	2.08	27.4	350	4.6	4.6	1.0	0.4	40%	65%	22
Young,Christopher	07	26	aa	FLA	0	3	42	1	45	86	38	8	18	15	7.55	2.31	5.6	395	3.7	2.9	0.8	1.6	41%	69%	-38
Yourkin,Matt	07	26	aa	FLA	1	1	52	0	57	76	36	3	29	38	5.63	1.84	5.2	313	4.5	6.0	1.3	0.5	37%	68%	40
	08	27	aa	FLA	2	5	35	0	47	80	45	6	33	32	8.52	2.38	7.1	366	6.2	6.0	1.0	1.2	42%	64%	4
Zambrano,Victor	07	32	a/a	PIT	5	2	14	0	74	99	62	7	34	50	7.56	1.80	25.0	314	4.2	6.0	1.4	0.8	37%	56%	34
	08	33	a/a	NYY	2	7	17	0	56	107	76	13	41	37	12.14	2.64	18.3	395	6.6	5.9	0.9	2.1	44%	54%	-34
Zarate,Mauro	07	25	aa	FLA	2	1	42	1	59	51	16	4	23	48	2.40	1.24	5.9	226	3.5	7.2	2.1	0.6	28%	83%	77
	08	26	aa	SD	3	0	46	0	71	86	29	8	20	49	3.66	1.48	6.8	292	2.5	6.2	2.4	1.0	34%	78%	55
Zell,Danny	07	26	a aa	DET	2	5	47	2	48	63	29	7	9	41	5.42	1.50	4.5	311	1.7	7.8	4.7	1.3	38%	66%	100
	08	27	aa	DET	4	2	47	1	49	72	33	6	15	29	6.11	1.78	4.9	336	2.7	5.3	1.9	1.1	38%	66%	28
Ziegler,Brad	07	28	aa	OAK	12	3	50	2	78	89	30	0	20	44	3.47	1.40	6.8	281	2.4	5.1	2.1	0.0	34%	73%	74
Zimmermann,Jordan	08	22	aa	WAS	7	2	20	0	106	93	38	7	36	86	3.22	1.21	22.0	231	3.1	7.3	2.4	0.6	29%	75%	85
Zinicola,Zechry	07	23	aa	WAS	0	4	42	6	57	59	41	3	36	38	6.45	1.66	6.2	261	5.7	6.0	1.1	0.5	31%	59%	47
	08	24	aa	WAS	6	5	39	6	53	70	37	5	28	29	6.27	1.85	6.5	311	4.7	4.9	1.0	0.8	35%	66%	19
Zink,Charlie	07	28	a/a	BOS	11	6	24	0	140	199	109	18	86	57	7.03	2.03	28.9	327	5.5	3.7	0.7	1.1	35%	66%	-9
	08	29	aaa	BOS	14	6	28	0	174	185	78	15	54	83	4.03	1.37	26.7	266	2.8	4.3	1.5	0.8	29%	72%	36
Zuercher,Zachary	07	23	aa	STL	3	0	37	1	43	42	15	3	22	24	3.22	1.48	5.1	251	4.5	5.1	1.1	0.6	29%	80%	39
	08	24	aa	STL	1	1	29	0	30	41	20	6	17	19	5.98	1.92	5.0	318	5.0	5.7	1.1	1.9	35%	73%	-8
Zumwalt,Alec	07	27	a/a	MIL	0	5	34	1	52	78	49	11	31	40	8.43	2.09	7.7	338	5.4	6.8	1.3	1.9	38%	61%	-2

VI.
RATINGS,
RANKINGS,
CHEAT
SHEETS

Ratings, Rankings, Cheat Sheets

Here is what you will find in this section:

Skills Rankings

We start by looking at some important component skills. For batters, we've ranked the top players in terms of pure power, speed, and batting average skill, breaking each down in a number of different ways to provide more insight. For pitchers, we rank some of the key base skills, differentiating between starters and relievers, and provide a few interesting cuts that might uncover some late round sleepers.

These are clearly not exhaustive lists of sorts and filters. If there is another cut you'd like to see, drop me a note and I'll consider it for next year's book. Also note that the database at BaseballHQ.com allows you to construct your own custom sorts and filters. Finally, remember that these are just tools. Some players will appear on multiple lists — even mutually exclusive lists — so you have to assess what makes most sense and make decisions for your specific application.

POWER

Top PX, 400+ AB: Top power skills from among projected full-time players.

Top PX, -300 AB: Top power skills from among projected part-time players. Possible end-game options are here.

Position Scarcity: A quick scan to see which positions have deeper power options than others.

Top PX, Ct% over 85%: Top power skills from among the top contact hitters. Best pure power options here.

Top PX, Ct% under 75%: Top power skills from among the worst contact hitters. These are free-swingers who might be prone to streakiness or lower batting averages.

Top PX, FB% over 40%: Top power skills from among the most extreme fly ball hitters. Most likely to convert their power into home runs.

Top PX, FB% under 35%: Top power skills from among those with lesser fly ball tendencies. There may be more downside to their home run potential.

SPEED

Top SX, 400+ AB: Top speed skills from among projected full-time players.

Top SX, -300 AB: Top speed skills from among projected part-time players. Possible end-game options here.

Position Scarcity: A quick scan to see which positions have deeper speed options than others.

Top SX, OB% over .350: Top speed skills from among those who get on base most often. Best opportunities for stolen bases here.

Top SX, OB% under .310: Top speed skills from among those who have trouble getting on base. These names may bear watching if they can improve their on base ability.

Top SX, SBO% over 20%: Top speed skills from among those who get the green light most often. Most likely to convert their speed into stolen bases.

Top SX, SBO% under 15%: Top speed skills from among those who are currently not getting the green light. There may be sleeper SB's here if given more opportunities to run.

BATTING AVERAGE

Top Ct%, 400+ AB: Top contact skills from among projected full-time players. Contact does not always convert to higher BAs, but is still strongly correlated.

Top Ct%, -300 AB: Top contact skills from among projected part-time players. Possible end-gamers here.

Low Ct%, 400+ AB: The poorest contact skills from among projected full-time players. Potential BA killers.

Top Ct%, bb% over 10%: Top contact skills from among the most patient hitters. Best batting average upside here.

Top Ct%, bb% under 6%: Top contact skills from among the least patient hitters. These are free-swingers who might be prone to streakiness or lower batting averages.

Top Ct%, GB% over 50%: Top contact skills from among the most extreme ground ball hitters. A ground ball has a higher chance of becoming a hit than a non-HR fly ball so there may be some batting average upside here.

Top Ct%, GB% under 40%: Top contact skills from among those with lesser ground ball tendencies. These players are making contact but hitting more fly balls, which tend to convert to hits at a lower rate than GB.

PITCHING SKILLS

Top Command: Leaders in projected K/BB rates.

Top Control: Leaders in fewest projected walks allowed.

Top Dominance: Leaders in projected strikeout rate.

Top Ground Ball Rate: GB pitchers tend to have lower ERA's (and higher WHIP) than fly ball pitchers.

Top Fly Ball Rate: FB pitchers tend to have higher ERA's (and lower WHIP) than ground ball pitchers.

High GB, Low Dom: GB pitchers tend to have lower K rates, but these are the most extreme examples.

High GB, High Dom: The best at dominating hitters and keeping the ball down. These are the pitchers who keep runners off the bases and batted balls in the park, a skills combination that is the most valuable a pitcher can own.

Lowest xERA: Leaders in projected skills-based ERA.

Top BPV: Two lists of top skilled pitchers here. For starters, those projected to be rotation regulars (180+ IP) and fringe starters with skill (-150 IP). For relievers, those projected to be frontline closers (10+ saves) and high-skilled bullpen fillers (9- saves).

+/- Scores

These lists rank those players with the highest and lowest +/- scores. The scores measure potential 2009 performance as compared to 2008. As such, the highest "+" scores represent both players who have the potential to break out as well as those who we expect to rebound from poor seasons. Note that, typically productive players who had awful 2008 seasons, even due to injury, might be ranked high just because 2009 has to be better than 2008. The flipside is similar. The lowest "-" scores represent players who are likely to collapse as well as those who are due for a correction. For instance, a pitcher like Brad Ziegler sits high on this list because the odds of him maintaining a sub-2.00 ERA are slim. A more detailed description of how these scores work appears in the Glossary.

Risk Management

Lists include players who've accumulated the most days on the disabled list over the past five years (Grade "F" in Health) and whose performance was the most consistent over the past three years. Also listed are the most reliable batters and pitchers overall, with a focus on positional and skills reliability. As a reminder, reliability in this context is not tied to skill level; it is a gauge of which players manage to accumulate playing time and post consistent output from year to year, whether that output is good or bad.

Portfolio3 Plan

Players are sorted and ranked based on how they fit into the three draft tiers of the Portfolio3 Plan. A full description of how this plan works appears in the Gaming section.

Position Scarcity Chart

There has been much discussion about position scarcity, its importance and how to leverage it in your draft. This chart provides a visual representation of the depth of talent for the top 45 players at each position and shows you why, in a snake draft league, it might make sense to draft a Dan Uggla before you draft a Nick Markakis.

Rotisserie Auction Draft

This list is presented with both AL and NL players, mostly because we don't know who is going to end up on what team yet. The values are representative of standard 75%-plus depth leagues. However, remember that these values are for player-to-player comparative purposes only, and allow us to provide rankings. You should not use these as actual in-draft bid values (see the Consumer Advisory earlier in the book for a full explanation).

The free projections update in March will provide better estimates of playing time, and as such, better information for drafting purposes. The custom draft guides on Baseball HQ are available to those who wish to produce accurate valuations for their particular league configuration. But in the interim, you can still use this information to plan out the core of your draft. For those who subscribe to Baseball HQ, full projections begin appearing online in December.

Rotisserie Snake Draft

This ranking takes the previous auction list, re-sets it into rounds and adjusts the rankings based on position scarcity. Given the growing popularity of 15-team mixed leagues, like the National Fantasy Baseball Championship, we've set this list up for that type of format.

In the first eight rounds, your target players should be those that are shaded (though your first round pick may depend upon your seed). These are the position scarcity picks. Also pay attention to the bolded players; these are categorical scarcity picks (primarily steals and saves).

If you reach a point where there are still undrafted players from earlier rounds, you can judiciously target those. To build the best foundation, you should come out of the first 10 rounds with all your middle infielders, all your corner infielders, one outfielder, at least one catcher and two pitchers (at least one closer).

The reason we target scarce positions first is that there will be plenty of solid outfielders and starting pitchers later on. The Position Scarcity Chart shows you why. The 25th best catcher on the list is Carlos Ruiz; the 25th best starting pitcher is A.J. Burnett. Which one would you rather have on your team?

Simulation League Draft

Using Runs Above Replacement creates a more real-world ranking of player value, which serves simulation gamers well. Batters and pitchers are integrated, and value break-points are delineated.

The Missing Piece of Information

The auction and snake draft rankings do not represent average draft positions (ADP) or average auction values (AAV). They represent where each player's true value may lie. It is the variance between this true value and the ADP/AAV market values — or better, the value that your league-mates place on each player — where you will find your potential for profit or loss.

How to leverage this? For instance, if we project Carlos Lee as a first round pick but you know the other owners see him as a third-rounder, you can probably wait to pick him up in round 2. If you are in an auction league in Boston with owners who still see David Ortiz as a $30+ player, a $26 projection could mean that you will take a loss on his purchase price should you decide to chase the bidding.

The Universal Disclaimer

This section is intended solely as a preliminary look based on current factors. Do not treat this guide as the Draft Day gospel. Use the ratings and rankings as a rough guide to get a general sense of where a player falls. For Draft Day, you will need to make your own adjustments based upon about 8,319 different criteria that can impact the world between now and then.

Daily updates appear online at BaseballHQ.com. And don't forget the free projections update in March at
http://www.baseballhq.com/books/freeupdate/index.shtml

BATTER SKILLS RANKINGS - POWER

TOP PX, 400+ AB

NAME	POS	PX
Howard,Ryan	3	212
Dunn,Adam	79	194
Cust,Jack	70	184
Pena,Carlos	3	182
Davis,Chris	35	176
Braun,Ryan	7	176
Rodriguez,Alex	5	174
Thome,Jim	0	173
Ortiz,David	0	172
Jacobs,Mike	3	171
Fielder,Prince	3	169
Cabrera,Miguel	3	169
Ludwick,Ryan	97	164
Reynolds,Mark	5	164
Soriano,Alfonso	7	162
Longoria,Evan	5	161
Pujols,Albert	3	160
Burrell,Pat	7	160
LaRoche,Adam	3	159
Teixeira,Mark	3	156
Dye,Jermaine	9	156
Wright,David	5	155
Bay,Jason	7	155
Upton,Justin	9	155
Ramirez,Manny	70	154
Cameron,Mike	8	153
Berkman,Lance	3	150
Bruce,Jay	98	149
Delgado,Carlos	3	149
Uggla,Dan	4	149
Hamilton,Josh	89	148
Gordon,Alex	5	148
Ramirez,Hanley	6	147
Ramirez,Aramis	5	146
Hawpe,Brad	9	146
Quentin,Carlos	7	145
Holliday,Matt	7	145
Scott,Luke	70	144

TOP PX, -300 AB

NAME	POS	PX
Branyan,Russell	5	199
Thames,Marcus	7	177
Joyce,Matthew	79	154
Ward,Daryle	3	142
Hoffpauir,Micah	7	142
Edmonds,Jim	8	138
Betemit,Wilson	35	137
Johnson,Nick	3	136
Hinske,Eric	970	136
Ruggiano,Justin	7	135
Castro,Ramon	2	134
Ross,Dave	2	132
Monroe,Craig	0	132
Boggs,Brandon	7	131
Anderson,Brian	8	130
Gomes,Jonny	09	130
Tatis,Fernando	79	130
Wilkerson,Brad	97	129
Norton,Greg	7	129
Murphy,Donnie	5	128
Baker,Jeff	43	127
Rodriguez,Sean	4	125
Cunningham,Aaron	7	124
Ishikawa,Travis	3	124
Mather,Joe	7	123

POSITIONAL SCARCITY

NAME	POS	PX
Thome,Jim	DH	173
Ortiz,David	2	172
Bradley,Milton	3	139
Hafner,Travis	4	139
Huff,Aubrey	5	133
Monroe,Craig	6	132
Shoppach,Kelly	CA	181
Napoli,Mike	2	179
Snyder,Chris	3	141
Iannetta,Chris	4	140
Castro,Ramon	5	134
Ross,Dave	6	132
Soto,Geovany	7	130
Posada,Jorge	8	126
Howard,Ryan	1B	212
Pena,Carlos	2	182
Davis,Chris	3	176
Jacobs,Mike	4	171
Fielder,Prince	5	169
Cabrera,Miguel	6	169
Pujols,Albert	7	160
LaRoche,Adam	8	159
Teixeira,Mark	9	156
Berkman,Lance	10	150
Uggla,Dan	2B	149
Utley,Chase	2	139
Baker,Jeff	3	127
Kinsler,Ian	4	126
Rodriguez,Sean	5	125
Fontenot,Mike	6	124
Weeks,Rickie	7	124
Johnson,Kelly	8	115
Branyan,Russell	3B	199
Rodriguez,Alex	2	174
Reynolds,Mark	3	164
Longoria,Evan	4	161
Wright,David	5	155
Gordon,Alex	6	148
Ramirez,Aramis	7	146
Hall,Bill	8	140
Wood,Brandon	9	136
Wigginton,Ty	10	132
Ramirez,Hanley	SS	147
Hardy,J.J.	2	123
Drew,Stephen	3	121
Peralta,Jhonny	4	119
Lowrie,Jed	5	118
Tulowitzki,Troy	6	112
Zobrist,Ben	7	111
Greene,Khalil	8	107
Dunn,Adam	OF	194
Cust,Jack	2	184
Thames,Marcus	3	177
Braun,Ryan	4	176
Ludwick,Ryan	5	164
Soriano,Alfonso	6	162
Burrell,Pat	7	160
Ross,Cody	8	156
Dye,Jermaine	9	156
Bay,Jason	10	155
Upton,Justin	11	155
Ramirez,Manny	12	154
Joyce,Matthew	13	154
Cameron,Mike	14	153
Hairston,Scott	15	151
Bruce,Jay	16	149

TOP PX, Ct% over 85%

NAME	Ct%	PX
Pujols,Albert	90	160
Ramirez,Aramis	86	146
Lee,Carlos	89	133
Huff,Aubrey	85	133
Morneau,Justin	85	132
Jones,Chipper	85	128
Kinsler,Ian	86	126
Guerrero,Vladimir	88	125
McCann,Brian	87	124
Gerut,Jody	87	123
Hardy,J.J.	85	123
Montanez,Luis	85	118
Wells,Vernon	87	115
Murphy,David	85	114
Sandoval,Pablo	90	113
Ordonez,Magglio	87	112
Schierholtz,Nate	87	109
Smith,Seth	85	108
Mora,Melvin	85	108
Lowell,Mike	86	108
Jackson,Conor	88	107
Martinez,Victor	87	106
Hill,Aaron	86	105
Atkins,Garrett	85	105
Pedroia,Dustin	92	105
Ramirez,Alexei	88	104
Rollins,Jimmy	89	104
Helton,Todd	86	102
Reyes,Jose	88	101
Furcal,Rafael	87	101
Mench,Kevin	86	101
Garciaparra,Nomar	92	101
Crede,Joe	87	100
Murphy,Daniel	87	99
Alou,Moises	90	99
Matsui,Hideki	85	99
Butler,Billy	88	98
Cano,Robinson	88	98

TOP PX, Ct% under 75%

NAME	Ct%	PX
Howard,Ryan	67	212
Branyan,Russell	63	199
Dunn,Adam	68	194
Cust,Jack	62	184
Pena,Carlos	69	182
Shoppach,Kelly	64	181
Napoli,Mike	70	179
Thames,Marcus	72	177
Thome,Jim	70	173
Ludwick,Ryan	73	164
Reynolds,Mark	65	164
Burrell,Pat	74	160
Upton,Justin	73	155
Joyce,Matthew	73	154
Cameron,Mike	70	153
Uggla,Dan	73	149
Hawpe,Brad	74	146
Snyder,Chris	74	141
Hall,Bill	70	140
Werth,Jayson	71	138
Betemit,Wilson	70	137
Swisher,Nick	73	137
Hinske,Eric	74	136
Ruggiano,Justin	70	135
Castro,Ramon	74	134

TOP PX, FB% over 40%

NAME	FB%	PX
Branyan,Russell	53	199
Dunn,Adam	47	194
Pena,Carlos	48	182
Shoppach,Kelly	42	181
Napoli,Mike	48	179
Thames,Marcus	51	177
Davis,Chris	40	176
Braun,Ryan	44	176
Rodriguez,Alex	40	174
Thome,Jim	41	173
Ortiz,David	45	172
Jacobs,Mike	45	171
Fielder,Prince	41	169
Ludwick,Ryan	47	164
Reynolds,Mark	45	164
Soriano,Alfonso	48	162
Longoria,Evan	41	161
Burrell,Pat	47	160
LaRoche,Adam	42	159
Ross,Cody	42	156
Dye,Jermaine	44	156
Bay,Jason	45	155
Upton,Justin	44	155
Ramirez,Manny	40	154
Joyce,Matthew	47	154
Cameron,Mike	45	153
Hairston,Scott	49	151
Uggla,Dan	47	149
Gordon,Alex	46	148
Ramirez,Hanley	40	147
Ramirez,Aramis	47	146
Quentin,Carlos	42	145
Scott,Luke	42	144
Cruz,Nelson	42	144
Young,Chris	45	143
Sizemore,Grady	45	143
Ward,Daryle	45	142
Granderson,Curtis	41	141

TOP PX, FB% under 35%

NAME	FB%	PX
Hamilton,Josh	33	148
Holliday,Matt	34	145
Betemit,Wilson	34	137
Markakis,Nick	34	136
Ruggiano,Justin	33	135
Ethier,Andre	33	135
Tatis,Fernando	34	130
Votto,Joey	32	126
Church,Ryan	32	124
Ishikawa,Travis	28	124
Kemp,Matt	34	122
Pena,Wily Mo	32	122
Lind,Adam	33	119
Upton,B.J.	32	116
Abreu,Bobby	31	116
Clark,Tony	30	115
Snider,Travis	29	114
Evans,Nick	34	114
Sandoval,Pablo	29	113
Overbay,Lyle	32	110
Schierholtz,Nate	29	109
Phillips,Brandon	34	109
Fukudome,Kosuke	31	108
Milledge,Lastings	33	106
Harris,Brendan	32	105

BATTER SKILLS RANKINGS - SPEED

TOP SX, 400+ AB

NAME	POS	SX
Bourn,Michael	8	168
Reyes,Jose	6	168
Crawford,Carl	7	163
Rollins,Jimmy	6	162
Weeks,Rickie	4	156
Victorino,Shane	8	155
Granderson,Curtis	8	153
Velez,Eugenio	4	153
Lewis,Fred	7	150
Furcal,Rafael	6	143
Ellsbury,Jacoby	879	140
Figgins,Chone	5	139
Kemp,Matt	89	139
Rios,Alex	98	135
Span,Denard	9	133
Gomez,Carlos	8	132
Aybar,Erick	6	132
Roberts,Brian	4	131
Suzuki,Ichiro	98	131
Sizemore,Grady	8	131
Anderson,Josh	8	130
Hart,Corey	9	128
McLouth,Nate	8	127
Kinsler,Ian	4	126
Damon,Johnny	780	126
Ramirez,Hanley	6	125
Werth,Jayson	987	125
Bartlett,Jason	6	125
Braun,Ryan	7	124
Phillips,Brandon	4	121
Punto,Nick	64	120
Patterson,Corey	8	119
Young,Chris	8	119
Beltran,Carlos	8	117
Holliday,Matt	7	116
Byrnes,Eric	7	116
Jones,Adam	8	115
Cameron,Mike	8	114

TOP SX, -300 AB

NAME	POS	SX
Davis,Rajai	8	170
Gardner,Brett	8	158
Roberts,Dave	7	152
Bernadina,Rogearvi	8	143
Wise,Dewayne	78	141
Morgan,Nyjer	7	135
Pierre,Juan	7	135
Arias,Joaquin	4	133
Lillibridge,Brent	6	131
Bynum,Freddie	6	131
Patterson,Eric	4	127
Harris,Willie	7	126
Cairo,Miguel	3	126
Bixler,Brian	6	125
German,Esteban	74	124
Cunningham,Aaron	7	123
Podsednik,Scott	8	121
Ruggiano,Justin	7	119
Pagan,Angel	7	118
Gathright,Joey	8	117
Pie,Felix	8	115
Schierholtz,Nate	9	114
Freel,Ryan	8	114
Burke,Chris	7	112
Willits,Reggie	79	112

POSITIONAL SCARCITY

NAME	POS	SX
Bradley,Milton	DH	76
Gomes,Jonny	2	72
Huff,Aubrey	3	69
Sheffield,Gary	4	67
Baldelli,Rocco	5	66
Floyd,Cliff	6	64
Olivo,Miguel	CA	88
Inge,Brandon	2	86
Rodriguez,Ivan	3	85
Martin,Russell	4	84
Napoli,Mike	5	83
Towles,J.R.	6	80
Mauer,Joe	7	76
Ruiz,Carlos	8	64
Cairo,Miguel	1B	126
Gload,Ross	2	82
Barton,Daric	3	80
Blalock,Hank	4	77
Berkman,Lance	5	76
Loney,James	6	75
Davis,Chris	7	69
Catalanotto,Frank	8	68
Lee,Derrek	9	68
Salazar,Oscar	10	67
Weeks,Rickie	2B	156
Velez,Eugenio	2	153
Bonifacio,Emilio	3	135
Matsui,Kaz	4	134
Arias,Joaquin	5	133
Roberts,Brian	6	131
Patterson,Eric	7	127
Kinsler,Ian	8	126
Figgins,Chone	3B	139
Tolbert,Matt	2	119
Duran,German	3	101
Reynolds,Mark	4	100
Guillen,Carlos	5	99
Rodriguez,Alex	6	95
Wright,David	7	92
Stewart,Ian	8	91
Dobbs,Greg	9	91
Quinlan,Robb	10	89
Reyes,Jose	SS	168
Rollins,Jimmy	2	162
Furcal,Rafael	3	143
Aybar,Erick	4	132
Lillibridge,Brent	5	131
Bynum,Freddie	6	131
Ramirez,Hanley	7	125
Bartlett,Jason	8	125
Davis,Rajai	OF	170
Bourn,Michael	2	168
Crawford,Carl	3	163
Gardner,Brett	4	158
Victorino,Shane	5	155
Granderson,Curtis	6	153
Roberts,Dave	7	152
Lewis,Fred	8	150
Maybin,Cameron	9	148
Taveras,Willy	10	146
Bernadina,Rogearvi	11	143
Wise,Dewayne	12	141
Ellsbury,Jacoby	13	140
Kemp,Matt	14	139
Morgan,Nyjer	15	135
Pierre,Juan	16	135

TOP SX, OB% over .350

NAME	OB%	SX
Reyes,Jose	350	168
Granderson,Curtis	351	153
Roberts,Dave	355	152
Maybin,Cameron	357	148
Furcal,Rafael	380	143
Figgins,Chone	358	139
Roberts,Brian	374	131
Suzuki,Ichiro	364	131
Sizemore,Grady	366	131
Kinsler,Ian	367	126
Damon,Johnny	365	126
Ramirez,Hanley	381	125
Werth,Jayson	366	125
Beltran,Carlos	371	117
Holliday,Matt	385	116
Utley,Chase	366	114
Willits,Reggie	360	112
Johnson,Kelly	351	111
Choo,Shin-Soo	351	110
Upton,B.J.	377	110
Theriot,Ryan	358	109
DeJesus,David	360	109
Castillo,Luis	366	109
Pedroia,Dustin	385	106
Blanco,Gregor	359	106
Dukes,Elijah	353	103
Abreu,Bobby	383	103
Fukudome,Kosuke	372	102
Bay,Jason	363	101
Guillen,Carlos	375	99
Drew,J.D.	396	95
Rodriguez,Alex	381	95
Hamilton,Josh	367	94
Jeter,Derek	350	93
Wright,David	397	92
Ethier,Andre	367	89
Polanco,Placido	350	88
Jackson,Conor	365	88

TOP SX, OB% under .310

NAME	OB%	SX
Davis,Rajai	301	170
Velez,Eugenio	303	153
Wise,Dewayne	296	141
Morgan,Nyjer	305	135
Bonifacio,Emilio	292	135
Arias,Joaquin	296	133
Gomez,Carlos	288	132
Aybar,Erick	304	132
Lillibridge,Brent	277	131
Bynum,Freddie	267	131
Anderson,Josh	298	130
Cairo,Miguel	301	126
Bixler,Brian	277	125
Patterson,Corey	284	119
Burke,Chris	306	112
Barmes,Clint	294	112
Hu,Chin-Lung	291	108
Ozuna,Pablo	302	104
Ortmeier,Dan	268	103
Aviles,Mike	308	102
Romero,Alex	297	102
Duran,German	287	101
McDonald,John	276	100
Ochoa,Ivan	285	100
Newhan,David	286	98

TOP SX, SBO% over 20%

NAME	SBO	SX
Davis,Rajai	58%	170
Bourn,Michael	38%	168
Reyes,Jose	42%	168
Crawford,Carl	33%	163
Rollins,Jimmy	28%	162
Gardner,Brett	35%	158
Weeks,Rickie	22%	156
Victorino,Shane	30%	155
Velez,Eugenio	45%	153
Roberts,Dave	23%	152
Lewis,Fred	21%	150
Maybin,Cameron	22%	148
Taveras,Willy	43%	146
Furcal,Rafael	24%	143
Bernadina,Rogear	38%	143
Wise,Dewayne	27%	141
Ellsbury,Jacoby	31%	140
Figgins,Chone	33%	139
Kemp,Matt	27%	139
Morgan,Nyjer	44%	135
Pierre,Juan	39%	135
Bonifacio,Emilio	30%	135
Rios,Alex	20%	135
Span,Denard	26%	133
Arias,Joaquin	27%	133
Gomez,Carlos	32%	132
Aybar,Erick	26%	132
Dickerson,Chris	26%	131
Lillibridge,Brent	33%	131
Roberts,Brian	25%	131
Bynum,Freddie	30%	131
Sizemore,Grady	21%	131
Anderson,Josh	34%	130
Hart,Corey	27%	128
Patterson,Eric	27%	127
Harris,Willie	21%	126
Crisp,Coco	23%	126
Ramirez,Hanley	25%	125

TOP SX, SBO% under 15%

NAME	SBO	SX
Werth,Jayson	14%	125
Beltran,Carlos	12%	117
Holliday,Matt	11%	116
Izturis,Maicer	14%	115
Jones,Adam	14%	115
Schierholtz,Nate	12%	114
Iwamura,Akinori	8%	114
Utley,Chase	9%	114
Inglett,Joe	14%	113
Guzman,Cristian	7%	112
Johnson,Kelly	10%	111
Chavez,Endy	11%	110
Amezaga,Alfredo	14%	110
Carroll,Jamey	10%	109
Kennedy,Adam	12%	109
DeJesus,David	10%	109
Hu,Chin-Lung	11%	108
Pedroia,Dustin	13%	106
Winn,Randy	12%	104
Cuddyer,Michael	7%	104
Langerhans,Ryan	8%	102
Aviles,Mike	10%	102
Fukudome,Kosuke	8%	102
Duran,German	8%	101
Bay,Jason	6%	101

BATTER SKILLS RANKINGS - BATTING AVERAGE

TOP Ct%, 400+ AB

NAME	Ct%	BA
Callaspo,Alberto	94	292
Polanco,Placido	94	313
Pedroia,Dustin	92	331
Betancourt,Yuniesk	92	281
Johjima,Kenji	91	277
Kotchman,Casey	91	294
Kendall,Jason	91	248
Molina,Yadier	91	281
Molina,Bengie	91	285
Wilson,Jack	90	279
Burriss,Emmanuel	90	268
Suzuki,Ichiro	90	319
Pujols,Albert	90	343
Cabrera,Orlando	90	278
Theriot,Ryan	90	289
Sandoval,Pablo	90	294
Giles,Brian	90	290
Sanchez,Freddy	89	285
Rollins,Jimmy	89	291
Mauer,Joe	89	320
Lee,Carlos	89	309
Aviles,Mike	89	277
Tejada,Miguel	89	285
Ramirez,Alexei	88	289
Lopez,Jose	88	282
Reyes,Jose	88	291
Cano,Robinson	88	300
Jackson,Conor	88	293
Butler,Billy	88	287
Guzman,Cristian	88	302
Guerrero,Vladimir	88	317
Wells,Vernon	87	294
Morales,Kendry	87	283
Furcal,Rafael	87	309
Aybar,Erick	87	272
Rivera,Juan	87	266
Victorino,Shane	87	286
Ellsbury,Jacoby	87	294

LOW Ct%, 400+ AB

NAME	Ct%	BA
Cust,Jack	62	236
Reynolds,Mark	65	255
Howard,Ryan	67	271
Dunn,Adam	68	247
Pena,Carlos	69	258
Jones,Andruw	69	231
Hall,Bill	70	247
Thome,Jim	70	270
Cameron,Mike	70	250
Werth,Jayson	71	275
Headley,Chase	72	274
Uggla,Dan	73	252
Upton,Justin	73	269
Ludwick,Ryan	73	270
Swisher,Nick	73	248
Hawpe,Brad	74	276
Flores,Jesus	74	238
Burrell,Pat	74	253
Upton,B.J.	74	281
Hermida,Jeremy	74	259
Weeks,Rickie	74	256
Bay,Jason	75	278
Church,Ryan	75	276
Giambi,Jason	75	243
Balentien,Wladimir	75	230
Hafner,Travis	75	271
Iannetta,Chris	75	265
Wood,Brandon	75	250
LaRoche,Adam	76	275
Greene,Khalil	76	251
Young,Chris	76	247
Longoria,Evan	76	278
Ankiel,Rick	76	257
Gordon,Alex	76	270
Jacobs,Mike	76	271
Bruce,Jay	77	275
Davis,Chris	77	285
Lewis,Fred	77	265
Cruz,Nelson	77	271
Shealy,Ryan	77	242
Choo,Shin-Soo	77	274
Peralta,Jhonny	77	276
Soriano,Alfonso	77	284
Willingham,Josh	77	262
Glaus,Troy	77	265
Teahen,Mark	77	269
Stewart,Ian	77	267
Rodriguez,Alex	77	293
Soto,Geovany	77	278
Iwamura,Akinori	77	264
Kemp,Matt	78	283
Granderson,Curtis	78	278
Blake,Casey	78	270
Fielder,Prince	78	278
Scott,Luke	78	265
Sizemore,Grady	78	275
Clement,Jeff	78	247
Jones,Adam	78	272
Drew,J.D.	78	271
Delgado,Carlos	78	269
Gonzalez,Adrian	79	283
Gomez,Carlos	79	245
Rowand,Aaron	79	268
Ramirez,Manny	79	306
Kearns,Austin	79	262
Bourn,Michael	79	249

TOP Ct%, bb% over 10%

NAME	bb%	Ct%
Pujols,Albert	15	90
Theriot,Ryan	10	90
Giles,Brian	13	90
Mauer,Joe	13	89
Ojeda,Augie	10	89
Jackson,Conor	10	88
Mientkiewicz,Doug	11	88
Gonzalez,Luis	11	88
Ruiz,Carlos	11	88
Pennington,Cliff	12	88
Furcal,Rafael	10	87
Martinez,Victor	10	87
Scutaro,Marco	10	87
Castillo,Luis	12	86
Helton,Todd	16	86
Damon,Johnny	10	86
Ramirez,Aramis	10	86
Morneau,Justin	10	85
Roberts,Dave	12	85
Matsui,Hideki	11	85
Martin,Russell	13	85
Bard,Josh	10	85
Schneider,Brian	11	85
Jones,Chipper	16	85
Hudson,Orlando	10	85
Roberts,Brian	12	84
LaRoche,Andy	12	84
Barton,Daric	13	84
Counsell,Craig	14	84
Rolen,Scott	10	84
Quentin,Carlos	10	84
Sheffield,Gary	12	84
Guillen,Carlos	11	83
Ethier,Andre	10	83
Carroll,Jamey	10	83
Spilborghs,Ryan	10	83
Zaun,Gregg	13	83
Durham,Ray	11	83

TOP Ct%, GB% over 50%

NAME	GB%	Ct%
Keppinger,Jeff	50	95
Pierre,Juan	54	94
Rodriguez,Luis	50	92
Frandsen,Kevin	52	92
Kotchman,Casey	54	91
Ozuna,Pablo	59	91
Burriss,Emmanuel	65	90
Chavez,Endy	57	90
Vidro,Jose	50	90
Suzuki,Ichiro	56	90
Miles,Aaron	54	90
Theriot,Ryan	54	90
Mauer,Joe	51	89
Tejada,Miguel	50	89
Schumaker,Skip	58	88
Hernandez,Luis	55	88
Hu,Chin-Lung	61	88
Ruiz,Carlos	52	88
Guzman,Cristian	55	88
Aybar,Erick	53	87
Ellsbury,Jacoby	52	87
Murton,Matt	54	87
Reed,Jeremy	51	87
Ryan,Brendan	54	87
Escobar,Yunel	57	87
Hanigan,Ryan	51	87
Anderson,Josh	55	86
Casilla,Alexi	54	86
Reyes,Argenis	62	86
Castillo,Luis	67	86
Winn,Randy	51	86
Rivas,Luis	50	86
Nieves,Wil	53	86
Roberts,Dave	51	85
Gathright,Joey	70	85
Martin,Russell	50	85
Bard,Josh	50	85
Schneider,Brian	50	85

TOP Ct%, -300 AB

NAME	Ct%	BA
Keppinger,Jeff	95	289
Pierre,Juan	94	291
Lo Duca,Paul	93	276
Rodriguez,Luis	92	247
Eckstein,David	91	272
Redmond,Mike	91	280
Ozuna,Pablo	91	277
Chavez,Endy	90	277
Vidro,Jose	90	277
Arias,Joaquin	90	269
Miles,Aaron	90	284
Loretta,Mark	90	287
Alou,Moises	90	294
Vizquel,Omar	90	241
Cora,Alex	90	254
Kotsay,Mark	90	269
Gload,Ross	89	283
Stewart,Shannon	89	250
Ojeda,Augie	89	238
Romero,Alex	89	260
Hernandez,Luis	88	238
Casey,Sean	88	280
Catalanotto,Frank	88	273
Mientkiewicz,Doug	88	274
Hu,Chin-Lung	88	247

TOP Ct%, bb% under 6%

NAME	bb%	Ct%
Pierre,Juan	5	94
Polanco,Placido	5	94
Frandsen,Kevin	4	92
Betancourt,Yuniesk	3	92
Johjima,Kenji	5	91
Redmond,Mike	4	91
Molina,Bengie	4	91
Ozuna,Pablo	3	91
Wilson,Jack	5	90
Arias,Joaquin	4	90
Sandoval,Pablo	4	90
Sanchez,Freddy	4	89
Gload,Ross	5	89
Aviles,Mike	4	89
Romero,Alex	5	89
Tejada,Miguel	5	89
Lopez,Jose	4	88
Hernandez,Luis	5	88
Cano,Robinson	5	88
Guzman,Cristian	5	88
Morales,Kendry	5	87
Hall,Toby	4	87
Aybar,Erick	4	87
Rivera,Juan	5	87
Schierholtz,Nate	4	87

TOP Ct%, GB% under 40%

NAME	GB%	Ct%
Garciaparra,Noma	39	92
Molina,Bengie	37	91
Loretta,Mark	38	90
Lee,Carlos	36	89
Jackson,Conor	39	88
Sweeney,Mike	38	88
Pennington,Cliff	36	88
Hall,Toby	34	87
McCann,Brian	37	87
Crede,Joe	32	87
Burke,Jamie	38	87
Kent,Jeff	38	87
Lowell,Mike	34	86
Salazar,Oscar	39	86
Helton,Todd	37	86
Kinsler,Ian	33	86
Hairston,Jerry	34	86
Ramirez,Aramis	34	86
Atkins,Garrett	36	85
Ellis,Mark	35	84
Infante,Omar	34	84
Barton,Daric	35	84
Duran,German	37	84
Rolen,Scott	36	84
Buscher,Brian	35	84

PITCHER SKILLS RANKINGS - Starting Pitchers

Top Command (k/bb)

NAME	Cmd
Slowey,Kevin	4.3
Sabathia,C.C.	4.2
Halladay,Roy	4.1
Haren,Dan	4.1
Hamels,Cole	4.0
Beckett,Josh	4.0
Shields,James	4.0
Santana,Ervin	4.0
Sheets,Ben	3.9
Maddux,Greg	3.7
Santana,Johan	3.6
Nolasco,Ricky	3.5
Sonnanstine,Andy	3.5
Vazquez,Javier	3.5
Baker,Scott	3.4
Chamberlain,Joba	3.4
Greinke,Zack	3.4
Oswalt,Roy	3.3
Cueto,Johnny	3.3
Smoltz,John	3.2
Duchscherer,Justin	3.2
Liriano,Francisco	3.1
Petit,Yusmeiro	3.1
Lackey,John	3.1
Peavy,Jake	3.1
Myers,Brett	3.0
Weaver,Jered	3.0
Johnson,Randy	3.0
Gallardo,Yovani	2.9
Lincecum,Tim	2.8
Bush,David	2.8

Top Control (bb/9)

NAME	Ctl
Maddux,Greg	1.3
Slowey,Kevin	1.5
Halladay,Roy	1.6
Byrd,Paul	1.8
Sonnanstine,Andy	1.8
Shields,James	1.8
Silva,Carlos	1.8
Blackburn,Nick	1.9
Richard,Clayton	2.0
Sheets,Ben	2.0
Lieber,Jon	2.0
Hamels,Cole	2.0
Sabathia,C.C.	2.0
Haren,Dan	2.0
Buehrle,Mark	2.0
Oswalt,Roy	2.1
Baker,Scott	2.1
Lewis,Scott	2.1
Bush,David	2.1
Duchscherer,Justin	2.1
Beckett,Josh	2.1
Nolasco,Ricky	2.1
Santana,Ervin	2.1
Reynolds,Greg	2.2
Lowe,Derek	2.2
Cook,Aaron	2.2
Duke,Zach	2.2
Petit,Yusmeiro	2.2
Mussina,Mike	2.3
Litsch,Jesse	2.3
Looper,Braden	2.3

Top Dominance (k/9)

NAME	Dom
Chamberlain,Joba	10.7
Lincecum,Tim	10.1
Scherzer,Max	10.1
Harden,Rich	9.9
Kazmir,Scott	9.9
Morrow,Brandon	9.8
Sanchez,Jonathan	9.2
Burnett,A.J.	9.1
Volquez,Edinson	9.0
Peavy,Jake	9.0
Gallardo,Yovani	8.9
Cueto,Johnny	8.8
Liriano,Francisco	8.8
Gonzalez,Gio	8.7
Smoltz,John	8.7
Perez,Oliver	8.7
Myers,Brett	8.7
Buchholz,Clay	8.6
Billingsley,Chad	8.6
Matsuzaka,Daisuke	8.5
Beckett,Josh	8.5
Santana,Ervin	8.5
Vazquez,Javier	8.5
Bedard,Erik	8.5
Happ,J.A.	8.5
Santana,Johan	8.4
Kershaw,Clayton	8.3
Sabathia,C.C.	8.3
Rodriguez,Wandy	8.3
Johnson,Randy	8.3
Young,Chris	8.2

Top Ground Ball Rate

NAME	GB
Webb,Brandon	64
Lowe,Derek	63
Carmona,Fausto	63
Gabbard,Kason	61
Hudson,Tim	61
Estes,Shawn	59
Westbrook,Jake	58
Wang,Chien-Ming	58
Cook,Aaron	57
Hernandez,Felix	56
Halladay,Roy	55
Laffey,Aaron	54
Maholm,Paul	54
Carpenter,Chris	54
Boggs,Mitch	54
Volstad,Chris	53
Lannan,John	53
Ponson,Sidney	53
Jimenez,Ubaldo	52
Jackson,Zach	52
Hampton,Mike	52
Miller,Andrew	52
Kuroda,Hiroki	52
Hochevar,Luke	51
Burnett,A.J.	51
Oswalt,Roy	51
Mendoza,Luis	50
Maddux,Greg	50
Morton,Charlie	50
Parra,Manny	50
Pettitte,Andy	50.1

Top Fly Ball Rate

NAME	FB
Hurley,Eric	57
Young,Chris	54
Hirsh,Jason	53
Lewis,Scott	51
James,Chuck	51
Petit,Yusmeiro	51
Kennedy,Ian	48
Morrow,Brandon	48
Perez,Oliver	48
Hill,Rich	48
Weaver,Jered	47
Liz,Radhames	47
Wakefield,Tim	46
McCarthy,Brandon	46
Purcey,David	46
Smith,Greg	46
Lilly,Ted	45
Baker,Scott	45
Cain,Matt	45
Rowland-Smith,Rya	44
Karstens,Jeff	44
Kazmir,Scott	44
Braden,Dallas	44
Gallagher,Sean	44
Matsuzaka,Daisuke	43
Banks,Josh	43
Santana,Ervin	43
Harang,Aaron	43
Washburn,Jarrod	43
Harden,Rich	43
Happ,J.A.	42.6

High GB, Low Dom

NAME	GB	Dom
Hudson,Tim	61	4.9
Estes,Shawn	59	4.1
Westbrook,J	58	4.7
Wang,Chien-M	58	4.8
Cook,Aaron	57	3.8
Laffey,Aaron	54	5.3
Carpenter,C	54	5.5
Boggs,Mitch	54	4.9
Volstad,Chris	53	5.1
Ponson,S	53	4.1
Jackson,Zach	52	5.4
Hampton,Mike	52	4.5
Mendoza,Luis	50	4.7
Maddux,Greg	50	4.8
Richard,C	50	5.5
Hill,Shawn	50	5.4
Pelfrey,Mike	49	5.2
Germano,J	49	4.6
Duke,Zach	49	4.6
Moseley,D	48	5.4
Litsch,Jesse	48	5.1
Miner,Zach	48	5.0
Pineiro,Joel	48	5.2
Marquis,J	48	5.0
Waters,Chris	48	5.2
Looper,B	48	5.0
Buehrle,Mark	47	5.5
Pavano,Carl	47	4.8
Penny,Brad	47	5.0
Saunders,Joe	46	5.0
Moehler,Brian	46	4.9

High GB, High Dom

NAME	GB	Dom
Webb,B	64	7.2
Lowe,Derek	63	6.1
Carmona,F	63	5.6
Gabbard,K	61	6.1
Hernandez,F	56	8.1
Halladay,Roy	55	6.7
Maholm,Paul	54	6.0
Lannan,John	53	5.9
Jimenez,U	52	7.5
Miller,Andrew	52	8.0
Kuroda,Hiroki	52	5.8
Hochevar,L	51	5.7
Burnett,A.J.	51	9.1
Oswalt,Roy	51	6.9
Morton,Charlie	50	6.4
Parra,Manny	50	8.1
Pettitte,Andy	50	6.9
Jurrjens,Jair	50	6.6
Price,David	50	7.5
Chamberlain,J	50	10.7
Eveland,D	49	6.4
Liriano,F	49	8.8
Dempster,R	49	8.0
Kershaw,C	48	8.3
Bonderman,J	48	7.1
Myers,Brett	48	8.7
Reyes,Jo-Jo	47	6.9
Zambrano,C	47	6.6
Smoltz,John	47	8.7
Buchholz,Clay	47	8.6
Davis,Doug	46	6.9

Lowest xERA

NAME	xERA
Chamberlain,Joba	2.94
Webb,Brandon	2.98
Lowe,Derek	3.19
Halladay,Roy	3.25
Liriano,Francisco	3.27
Hernandez,Felix	3.29
Burnett,A.J.	3.30
Lincecum,Tim	3.30
Sabathia,C.C.	3.31
Scherzer,Max	3.39
Beckett,Josh	3.40
Myers,Brett	3.41
Smoltz,John	3.44
Haren,Dan	3.46
Oswalt,Roy	3.50
Peavy,Jake	3.54
Hamels,Cole	3.55
Parra,Manny	3.55
Santana,Johan	3.58
Kershaw,Clayton	3.59
Harden,Rich	3.65
Buchholz,Clay	3.68
Santana,Ervin	3.69
Cueto,Johnny	3.69
Vazquez,Javier	3.70
Shields,James	3.72
Carpenter,Chris	3.74
Hudson,Tim	3.75
Pettitte,Andy	3.77
Gallardo,Yovani	3.77
Lackey,John	3.77

Top BPV, 180+ IP

NAME	BPV
Chamberlain,Joba	134
Sabathia,C.C.	120
Beckett,Josh	118
Haren,Dan	116
Santana,Ervin	111
Liriano,Francisco	110
Hamels,Cole	109
Lincecum,Tim	109
Halladay,Roy	109
Burnett,A.J.	106
Santana,Johan	106
Myers,Brett	104
Vazquez,Javier	104
Cueto,Johnny	104
Shields,James	103
Peavy,Jake	102
Webb,Brandon	99
Hernandez,Felix	99
Greinke,Zack	97
Oswalt,Roy	97
Slowey,Kevin	94
Nolasco,Ricky	93
Lowe,Derek	91
Lackey,John	91
Rodriguez,Wandy	88
Kazmir,Scott	86
Parra,Manny	86
Baker,Scott	85
Sonnanstine,Andy	83
Weaver,Jered	82
Pettitte,Andy	81

Top BPV, -150 IP

NAME	BPV
Smoltz,John	109
Scherzer,Max	94
Johnson,Randy	92
Harden,Rich	87
Duchscherer,Justin	85
Buchholz,Clay	83
Bonser,Boof	77
Petit,Yusmeiro	77
Richard,Clayton	73
Marshall,Sean	70
Lieber,Jon	67
Price,David	66
Martinez,Pedro	65
Lewis,Scott	65
Happ,J.A.	65
Capuano,Chris	64
Bonderman,Jeremy	64
Gonzalez,Gio	64
Carpenter,Chris	62
McGowan,Dustin	61
Braden,Dallas	60
Perez,Odalis	59
Owings,Micah	58
Marcum,Shaun	58
Hughes,Phil	57
Kennedy,Ian	57
Colon,Bartolo	56
Hill,Shawn	55
Reynolds,Greg	55
Bailey,Homer	54
Aceves,Alfredo	53

PITCHER SKILLS RANKINGS - Relief Pitchers

Top Command (k/bb)

NAME	Cmd
Papelbon,Jonathan	6.7
Capps,Matt	4.8
Rivera,Mariano	4.5
Valverde,Jose	4.2
Howry,Bob	4.1
Perez,Rafael	3.8
Blevins,Jerry	3.7
Nathan,Joe	3.7
Linebrink,Scott	3.6
Qualls,Chad	3.6
Betancourt,Rafael	3.6
Soria,Joakim	3.5
Wade,Cory	3.5
Romo,Sergio	3.4
Dotel,Octavio	3.4
Hoffman,Trevor	3.4
Mujica,Edward	3.4
Wood,Kerry	3.3
Broxton,Jonathan	3.3
Street,Huston	3.3
Meredith,Cla	3.2
Fuentes,Brian	3.2
Pena,Tony	3.2
Rauch,Jon	3.2
Kuo,Hong-Chih	3.2
Wheeler,Dan	3.1
Soriano,Rafael	3.0
Neshek,Pat	3.0
Devine,Joey	2.9
Ryan,B.J.	2.9
Bell,Heath	2.8

Top Control (bb/9)

NAME	Ctl
Capps,Matt	1.4
Papelbon,Jonathan	1.5
Rivera,Mariano	1.9
Howry,Bob	1.9
Wade,Cory	2.0
Sampson,Chris	2.0
Meredith,Cla	2.1
Hoffman,Trevor	2.1
Pena,Tony	2.1
Mujica,Edward	2.2
Kobayashi,Masa	2.2
Linebrink,Scott	2.2
Qualls,Chad	2.3
Bradford,Chad	2.3
Blevins,Jerry	2.3
Betancourt,Rafael	2.3
Corpas,Manny	2.4
Wolfe,Brian	2.4
Ayala,Luis	2.4
Oliver,Darren	2.4
Romo,Sergio	2.4
Lyon,Brandon	2.4
Giese,Dan	2.5
Perez,Rafael	2.5
Corey,Bryan	2.5
Valverde,Jose	2.5
Soria,Joakim	2.5
Tomko,Brett	2.5
Buchholz,Taylor	2.5
Rauch,Jon	2.6
Gonzalez,Edgar	2.6

Top Dominance (k/9)

NAME	Dom
Dotel,Octavio	12.0
Lidge,Brad	11.5
Balfour,Grant	11.5
Cruz,Juan	11.0
Broxton,Jonathan	11.0
Robertson,David	11.0
Fuentes,Brian	10.9
Perez,Chris	10.7
Bray,Bill	10.6
Ramirez,Edwar	10.6
Gonzalez,Mike	10.6
Putz,J.J.	10.4
Valverde,Jose	10.3
Marmol,Carlos	10.3
Wood,Kerry	10.2
Rodriguez,Francisco	10.2
Francisco,Frank	10.2
Sherrill,George	10.1
Kuo,Hong-Chih	10.0
Marte,Damaso	9.9
Cordero,Francisco	9.9
Papelbon,Jonathan	9.9
Ryan,B.J.	9.8
Eyre,Scott	9.7
Cabrera,Fernando	9.7
Nathan,Joe	9.7
Devine,Joey	9.7
Rodney,Fernando	9.6
Zumaya,Joel	9.6
Nelson,Joe	9.6
Hinshaw,Alex	9.5

Top Ground Ball Rate

NAME	GB
Meredith,Cla	70
Corcoran,Roy	70
Bradford,Chad	65
Moylan,Peter	64
League,Brandon	64
Johnson,Jim	62
Ziegler,Brad	62
Downs,Scott	62
Reyes,Dennys	62
Smith,Joe	62
Green,Sean	62
Bennett,Jeff	61
Troncoso,Ramon	60
Romero,J.C.	60
Wright,Jamey	59
Qualls,Chad	58
Bass,Brian	58
Lopez,Javier	58
Shouse,Brian	58
Perez,Rafael	57
Camp,Shawn	56
Masterson,Justin	56
Rivera,Mariano	55
Jenks,Bobby	55
O'Day,Darren	55
Rupe,Josh	55
Badenhop,Burke	54
Loe,Kameron	54
Torres,Salomon	54
Acosta,Manny	54
Cormier,Lance	54.1

Top Fly Ball Rate

NAME	FB
Percival,Troy	61
Soriano,Rafael	55
Marmol,Carlos	54
Giese,Dan	53
Romo,Sergio	53
Foulke,Keith	53
Guardado,Eddie	51
Hinshaw,Alex	51
Springer,Russ	51
Speier,Justin	50
Betancourt,Rafael	50
Beam,T.J.	50
Brown,Andrew	49
Benoit,Joaquin	49
Wheeler,Dan	49
Rauch,Jon	48
Mujica,Edward	48
Cruz,Juan	48
Sherrill,George	48
Lopez,Aquilino	48
Kensing,Logan	48
Tejeda,Robinson	48
Vizcaino,Luis	48
Borowski,Joe	47
Neshek,Pat	47
Hoffman,Trevor	47
Madrigal,Warner	47
Cabrera,Fernando	47
Walker,Jamie	47
Gobble,Jimmy	47
Farnsworth,Kyle	47.0

High GB, Low Dom

NAME	GB	Dom
Bradford,Chad	65	3.6
Johnson,Jim	62	5.5
Ziegler,Brad	62	4.7
Bass,Brian	58	4.8
Rupe,Josh	55	5.5
Loe,Kameron	54	4.6
Cormier,Lance	54	5.3
Sampson,C	53	4.3
Hensley,Clay	53	5.0
Condrey,Clay	52	4.3
Ramirez,H	52	3.4
Thompson,B	51	4.4
Osoria,F	51	4.8
Davis,Jason	50	4.4
Feldman,S	49	5.0
Belisle,Matt	48	5.2
Beimel,Joe	48	5.2
Dickey,R.A.	46	4.6

High GB, High Dom

NAME	GB	Dom
Meredith,Cla	70	6.6
Corcoran,Roy	70	5.9
Moylan,Peter	64	6.8
League,B	64	6.3
Downs,Scott	62	7.4
Reyes,D	62	7.1
Smith,Joe	62	7.6
Green,Sean	62	6.3
Bennett,Jeff	61	5.7
Troncoso,R	60	6.8
Romero,J.C.	60	7.2
Wright,Jamey	59	6.0
Qualls,Chad	58	8.4
Lopez,Javier	58	5.8
Shouse,Brian	58	5.6
Perez,Rafael	57	9.5
Camp,Shawn	56	7.2
Masterson,J	56	7.1
Rivera,M	55	8.3
Jenks,Bobby	55	6.4
O'Day,Darren	55	6.0
Badenhop,B	54	6.5
Torres,S	54	6.0
Acosta,Manny	54	6.6
Carrasco,D.J.	54	6.4
Tavarez,J	53	7.1
Wolfe,Brian	53	5.7
Affeldt,Jeremy	53	8.1
Hansen,Craig	53	7.1
Feliciano,P	53	8.4
Lincoln,Mike	53	7.2

Lowest xERA

NAME	xERA
Meredith,Cla	2.67
Perez,Rafael	2.77
Papelbon,Jonathan	2.85
Qualls,Chad	2.91
Broxton,Jonathan	2.92
Rivera,Mariano	2.97
Lidge,Brad	3.09
Dotel,Octavio	3.18
Smith,Joe	3.19
Nathan,Joe	3.19
Valverde,Jose	3.23
Downs,Scott	3.27
Thornton,Matt	3.31
League,Brandon	3.31
Bell,Heath	3.32
Howell,J.P.	3.34
Rodney,Fernando	3.36
Wilson,Brian	3.37
Putz,J.J.	3.39
Fuentes,Brian	3.39
Robertson,David	3.40
Troncoso,Ramon	3.40
Kuo,Hong-Chih	3.40
Wood,Kerry	3.44
Reyes,Dennys	3.45
Gonzalez,Mike	3.45
Bray,Bill	3.46
Moylan,Peter	3.48
Soria,Joakim	3.48
Devine,Joey	3.49
Balfour,Grant	3.50

Top BPV, 10+ Saves

NAME	BPV
Papelbon,Jonathan	159
Perez,Rafael	138
Valverde,Jose	133
Rivera,Mariano	133
Broxton,Jonathan	133
Qualls,Chad	126
Nathan,Joe	124
Wood,Kerry	118
Lidge,Brad	116
Fuentes,Brian	116
Soria,Joakim	109
Putz,J.J.	109
Street,Huston	106
Gonzalez,Mike	104
Bell,Heath	104
Saito,Takashi	104
Devine,Joey	103
Ryan,B.J.	101
Rodney,Fernando	94
Wheeler,Dan	94
Wilson,Brian	93
Capps,Matt	93
Cordero,Francisco	90
Soriano,Rafael	88
Francisco,Frank	88
Rauch,Jon	86
Hoffman,Trevor	85
Adams,Mike	84
Rodriguez,Francisco	83
Marmol,Carlos	83
Corpas,Manny	78

Top BPV, 9- Saves

NAME	BPV
Dotel,Octavio	137
Blevins,Jerry	115
Kuo,Hong-Chih	114
Meredith,Cla	112
Robertson,David	110
Bray,Bill	104
Thornton,Matt	102
Ramirez,Edwar	102
Howry,Bob	101
Linebrink,Scott	100
Logan,Boone	99
Balfour,Grant	96
Howell,J.P.	96
Betancourt,Rafael	94
Romo,Sergio	93
Neshek,Pat	93
Cruz,Juan	93
Eyre,Scott	90
Pena,Tony	89
Wade,Cory	89
Shields,Scot	88
Villanueva,Carlos	87
Delcarmen,Manny	87
Marte,Damaso	84
Mujica,Edward	82
Downs,Scott	82
Accardo,Jeremy	81
Camp,Shawn	81
Affeldt,Jeremy	80
Madson,Ryan	80
Walker,Tyler	80

+/- SCORES

BREAKOUTS and REBOUNDS

BATTERS	Pos	+
Ishikawa, Travis	3	57
Murton, Matt	7	56
Hernandez, Anderson	4	54
Gomes, Jonny	09	52
Sweeney, Ryan	98	52
Schierholtz, Nate	9	45
Mench, Kevin	7	43
LaRue, Jason	2	42
Riggans, Shawn	2	42
Hernandez, Luis	6	41
Howard, Ryan	3	40
Hafner, Travis	0	40
Wise, Dewayne	78	39
Castillo, Jose	5	38
Peralta, Jhonny	6	38
Bruntlett, Eric	765	38
Patterson, Corey	8	37
Johjima, Kenji	2	36
Reyes, Argenis	4	36
Weeks, Rickie	4	35
Pena, Wily Mo	7	33
Francoeur, Jeff	9	33
Murphy, Donnie	5	33
Konerko, Paul	3	32
Longoria, Evan	5	30
Cuddyer, Michael	9	29
Berroa, Angel	6	29
Jacobs, Mike	3	29
Teagarden, Taylor	2	29
Pena, Tony	6	28
Moss, Brandon	79	28
Dillon, Joe	4	28
Edmonds, Jim	8	27
Snider, Travis	7	27
Rivera, Juan	7	27
LaRoche, Andy	5	26
Hoffpauir, Micah	7	26
Gonzalez, Alberto	6	26
Antonelli, Matt	4	26
Murphy, Daniel	7	26
Ellis, Mark	4	25
Ruiz, Carlos	2	25
Mather, Joe	7	25
German, Esteban	74	25
Tejada, Miguel	6	25
Balentien, Wladimir	98	25
Anderson, Brian	8	25
Crosby, Bobby	6	24
Burrell, Pat	7	24
Inge, Brandon	25	24
Davis, Rajai	8	24
McCann, Brian	2	23
Metcalf, Travis	5	22
Kearns, Austin	9	22
Bako, Paul	2	22
Willingham, Josh	7	22
Montanez, Luis	7	22
Keppinger, Jeff	6	22
Smith, Seth	9	21
Encarnacion, Edwin	5	21
Ross, Cody	89	21
Cantu, Jorge	53	21
Joyce, Matthew	79	21
Swisher, Nick	83	21
Span, Denard	9	21
Quintero, Humberto	2	20
Hundley, Nicholas	2	20
Stewart, Ian	5	19
Larish, Jeff	5	19
Milledge, Lastings	8	19

PITCHERS	+
Moseley, Dustin	133
Jackson, Zach	112
Mendoza, Luis	100
Boyer, Blaine	96
Logan, Boone	87
Fogg, Josh	85
Tomko, Brett	78
Gobble, Jimmy	78
Misch, Pat	74
Mujica, Edward	72
Petit, Yusmeiro	71
Bonser, Boof	68
Owings, Micah	68
Hughes, Phil	65
Perez, Rafael	63
Silva, Carlos	58
Osoria, Franquelis	55
Accardo, Jeremy	54
Germano, Justin	53
Buchholz, Clay	52
Badenhop, Burke	52
Meredith, Cla	51
Majewski, Gary	49
Cueto, Johnny	49
Proctor, Scott	47
Beckett, Josh	47
Troncoso, Ramon	45
Howry, Bob	43
Myers, Brett	42
Wilson, Brian	41
Ayala, Luis	41
Villanueva, Carlos	41
Harang, Aaron	39
League, Brandon	39
Vazquez, Javier	38
Ohlendorf, Ross	38
Dotel, Octavio	37
Bailey, Homer	36
Belisle, Matt	36
Parra, Manny	35
Affeldt, Jeremy	35
Robertson, Nate	34
Reynolds, Greg	34
Sanchez, Anibal	34
Wilson, C.J.	34
Tavarez, Julian	33
Chico, Matt	32
Pineiro, Joel	32
Scherzer, Max	32
Valverde, Jose	32
Farnsworth, Kyle	32
Thompson, Brad	31
Burnett, A.J.	31
Walker, Jamie	31
Martinez, Pedro	31
Vizcaino, Luis	30
Haren, Dan	30
Sanchez, Jonathan	30
Balester, Collin	29
Slowey, Kevin	29
Miller, Andrew	29
Corpas, Manny	28
Rauch, Jon	28
Hernandez, Felix	27
McClellan, Kyle	27
Lackey, John	27
Heilman, Aaron	26
Santana, Ervin	26
Lyon, Brandon	26
Chamberlain, Joba	25

COLLAPSES and CORRECTIONS

BATTERS	Pos	-
Alou, Moises	7	-94
Blanco, Henry	2	-85
Kapler, Gabe	8	-77
Jones, Chipper	5	-75
Cash, Kevin	2	-58
Rivera, Mike	2	-55
Guzman, Cristian	6	-55
Erstad, Darin	78	-53
Clark, Tony	3	-50
Johnson, Reed	87	-50
Freel, Ryan	8	-49
Valentin, Javier	2	-49
Baldelli, Rocco	0	-49
Dobbs, Greg	5	-47
Young, Dmitri	3	-47
Vazquez, Ramon	56	-46
Floyd, Cliff	0	-46
Gonzalez, Edgar	4	-45
Gotay, Ruben	5	-45
Burke, Jamie	2	-45
Young, Delwyn	8	-44
Bradley, Milton	09	-44
Matsui, Hideki	07	-43
Ausmus, Brad	2	-43
Aurilia, Rich	35	-42
Casey, Sean	3	-41
Miles, Aaron	46	-40
Bloomquist, Willie	8	-40
Gomez, Chris	5	-40
Ludwick, Ryan	97	-39
Lugo, Julio	6	-38
Ankiel, Rick	8	-38
Stairs, Matt	0	-37
Grudzielanek, Mark	4	-37
Durham, Ray	4	-36
Theriot, Ryan	6	-35
Hairston, Jerry	67	-35
Ramirez, Manny	70	-35
Treanor, Matt	2	-34
Bartlett, Jason	6	-34
Figgins, Chone	5	-33
Ordonez, Magglio	9	-33
Rowand, Aaron	8	-33
Suzuki, Kurt	2	-32
Damon, Johnny	780	-32
Kent, Jeff	4	-31
Chavez, Raul	2	-31
Molina, Yadier	2	-31
Wells, Vernon	8	-31
Saltalamacchia, Jarro	2	-31
Easley, Damion	4	-30
Church, Ryan	9	-29
Carroll, Jamey	45	-27
Punto, Nick	64	-27
Loretta, Mark	4	-27
Cintron, Alex	6	-27
Cabrera, Orlando	6	-26
Buscher, Brian	5	-26
Schneider, Brian	2	-25
Raburn, Ryan	79	-25
Vizquel, Omar	6	-25
Salazar, Jeff	7	-25
Lee, Carlos	7	-25
Hudson, Orlando	4	-25
Giles, Brian	9	-25
Sweeney, Mike	0	-23
Norton, Greg	7	-23
Chavez, Eric	5	-23
Soriano, Alfonso	7	-23
Ibanez, Raul	7	-23

PITCHERS	-
Ziegler, Brad	-137
Devine, Joey	-117
Carpenter, Chris	-110
Beimel, Joe	-103
Balfour, Grant	-92
Bruney, Brian	-91
Zumaya, Joel	-84
Bradford, Chad	-79
Guardado, Eddie	-79
Cordero, Chad	-78
Nathan, Joe	-78
Springer, Russ	-78
Geary, Geoff	-77
Lopez, Javier	-77
Rhodes, Arthur	-76
Soriano, Rafael	-75
Percival, Troy	-74
Breslow, Craig	-72
Johnson, Jim	-71
Yabu, Keiichi	-70
Sadler, Billy	-68
Brown, Andrew	-67
Romero, J.C.	-67
Moylan, Peter	-66
Weathers, David	-64
Wakefield, Tim	-63
Albers, Matt	-60
Villone, Ron	-60
McCarthy, Brandon	-59
Grabow, John	-58
Schoeneweis, Scott	-57
Downs, Scott	-56
Moyer, Jamie	-54
Durbin, Chad	-53
Colome, Jesus	-53
Nunez, Leo	-52
Soria, Joakim	-51
Dolsi, Freddy	-51
Rivera, Mariano	-49
Ledezma, Wil	-48
Seanez, Rudy	-48
Rogers, Kenny	-47
Carlson, Jesse	-47
Arredondo, Jose	-46
Matsuzaka, Daisuke	-46
Giese, Dan	-46
Smith, Greg	-45
Frasor, Jason	-45
Beam, T.J.	-44
Duchscherer, Justin	-44
Corcoran, Roy	-44
Foulke, Keith	-44
Burnett, Sean	-43
Davies, Kyle	-43
Tejeda, Robinson	-43
Ramirez, Horacio	-41
Grilli, Jason	-41
Hampson, Justin	-41
Lidge, Brad	-41
Benoit, Joaquin	-40
Cabrera, Fernando	-39
Ryan, B.J.	-39
Zito, Barry	-39
Julio, Jorge	-39
Acosta, Manny	-39
Harden, Rich	-38
Bautista, Denny	-38
Riske, David	-38
Oliver, Darren	-38
Parrish, John	-38

RISK MANAGEMENT

GRADE "F" in HEALTH

Batters	Pitchers
Alou,Moises	Accardo,Jeremy
Baldelli,Rocco	Adams,Mike
Barrett,Michael	Ayala,Luis
Blalock,Hank	Backe,Brandon
Boone,Aaron	Baez,Danys
Bradley,Milton	Balfour,Grant
Byrnes,Eric	Bedard,Erik
Castro,Ramon	Bennett,Jeff
Chavez,Eric	Bonderman,Jeremy
Crede,Joe	Brocail,Doug
Crosby,Bobby	Capuano,Chris
Diaz,Matt	Carpenter,Chris
Doumit,Ryan	Chico,Matt
Erstad,Darin	Colon,Bartolo
Everett,Adam	Cordero,Chad
Frandsen,Kevin	Dotel,Octavio
Freel,Ryan	Duchscherer,Justin
Furcal,Rafael	Dumatrait,Phil
Garciaparra,Nomar	Escobar,Kelvim
Gerut,Jody	Estes,Shawn
Gonzalez,Alex	Foulke,Keith
Guzman,Cristian	Francisco,Frank
Hill,Aaron	Gagne,Eric
Izturis,Maicer	Gallardo,Yovani
Johnson,Nick	Glavine,Tom
Kendrick,Howie	Gonzalez,Mike
Kotsay,Mark	Gordon,Tom
Matsui,Hideki	Guardado,Eddie
Matsui,Kaz	Hampton,Mike
Mientkiewicz,Doug	Harden,Rich
Pagan,Angel	Hensley,Clay
Pena,Wily Mo	Hill,Shawn
Posada,Jorge	Hirsh,Jason
Rivera,Juan	Hughes,Phil
Roberts,Dave	Johnson,Josh
Sheffield,Gary	Johnson,Randy
Stewart,Shannon	Karstens,Jeff
Sweeney,Mike	Lieber,Jon
Thomas,Frank	Lincoln,Mike
Young,Dmitri	Liriano,Francisco
	Lowry,Noah
	Martinez,Pedro
	McCarthy,Brandon
	Moylan,Peter
	Nelson,Joe
	Neshek,Pat
	Pavano,Carl
	Percival,Troy
	Ramirez,Horacio
	Ray,Chris
	Rhodes,Arthur
	Rodney,Fernando
	Rogers,Kenny
	Rusch,Glendon
	Ryan,B.J.
	Sanchez,Anibal
	Sanchez,Duaner
	Sheets,Ben
	Smoltz,John
	Soriano,Rafael
	Speier,Ryan
	Walker,Tyler
	Wang,Chien-Ming
	Wells,Kip
	Westbrook,Jake
	Wolf,Randy
	Wood,Kerry
	Zumaya,Joel

Highest Reliability Grades - Health / Experience / Consistency (Min. Grade = BBB)

CA	POS	Rel
Kendall,Jason	2	AAB
Martin,Russell	2	AAB
Pierzynski,A.J.	2	ABA
Inge,Brandon	25	ABB
Johjima,Kenji	2	ABB
Molina,Bengie	2	ABB
Rodriguez,Ivan	2	ABB

1B/DH	POS	Rel
Gonzalez,Adrian	3	AAA
Teixeira,Mark	3	AAA
Cabrera,Miguel	3	AAB
Morneau,Justin	3	AAB
Youkilis,Kevin	35	AAB
Garko,Ryan	3	ABB
Loney,James	3	ABB
Millar,Kevin	3	ABB
Votto,Joey	3	ABB
Konerko,Paul	3	BAB
Jacobs,Mike	3	BBA
Belliard,Ronnie	354	BBB

2B	POS	Rel
DeRosa,Mark	4975	AAA
Iwamura,Akinori	4	AAA
Pedroia,Dustin	4	AAA
Cano,Robinson	4	AAB
Phillips,Brandon	4	AAB
Roberts,Brian	4	AAB
Uggla,Dan	4	AAB
Utley,Chase	4	AAB
Loretta,Mark	4	BBA
Kent,Jeff	4	BBB

3B	POS	Rel
Beltre,Adrian	5	AAA
Ramirez,Aramis	5	AAA
Huff,Aubrey	053	AAB
Wright,David	5	AAB
Bautista,Jose	5	ABA
Encarnacion,Edwin	5	ABA
Uribe,Juan	54	ABA
Feliz,Pedro	5	BAA
Mora,Melvin	5	BAA
Zimmerman,Ryan	5	BAA
Blake,Casey	53	BAB
Guillen,Carlos	53	BAB
Lowell,Mike	5	BAB
Wigginton,Ty	57	BBB

SS	POS	Rel
Betancourt,Yuniesky	6	AAA
Cabrera,Orlando	6	AAA
Young,Michael	6	AAA
Jeter,Derek	6	AAB
Peralta,Jhonny	6	AAB
Ramirez,Hanley	6	AAB
Reyes,Jose	6	AAB
Rollins,Jimmy	6	AAB
Bartlett,Jason	6	ABA
Harris,Brendan	645	ABA
Scutaro,Marco	645	ABA
Theriot,Ryan	6	ABB
Tejada,Miguel	6	BAB

OF	POS	Rel
Burrell,Pat	7	AAA
Ibanez,Raul	7	AAA
Rios,Alex	98	AAA
Sizemore,Grady	8	AAA
Winn,Randy	9	AAA
Young,Chris	8	AAA
Abreu,Bobby	9	AAB
Beltran,Carlos	8	AAB
Damon,Johnny	780	AAB
Dunn,Adam	79	AAB
Guerrero,Vladimir	90	AAB
Markakis,Nick	9	AAB
Suzuki,Ichiro	98	AAB
Swisher,Nick	83	AAB
Jackson,Conor	73	ABA
Victorino,Shane	8	ABA
Ethier,Andre	97	ABB
Kemp,Matt	89	ABB
Nady,Xavier	97	ABB
Scott,Luke	70	ABB
Young,Delmon	7	ABB
Hunter,Torii	8	BAA
Lee,Carlos	7	BAA
Pierre,Juan	7	BAA
Cameron,Mike	8	BAB
Crawford,Carl	7	BAB
Giles,Brian	9	BAB
Hawpe,Brad	9	BAB
Holliday,Matt	7	BAB
Crisp,Coco	8	BBA
Gonzalez,Luis	79	BBA
Fukudome,Kosuke	9	BBB
Payton,Jay	78	BBB

RP		Rel
Jenks,Bobby		AAA
Papelbon,Jonathan		AAA
Rodriguez,Francisco		AAA
Cordero,Francisco		AAB
Hendrickson,Mark		AAB
Hoffman,Trevor		AAB
Nathan,Joe		AAB
Rivera,Mariano		AAB
Gregg,Kevin		ABA
Owings,Micah		ABA
Weathers,David		ABA
Gaudin,Chad		ABB
Soria,Joakim		ABB
Lidge,Brad		BAA
Valverde,Jose		BAA
Capps,Matt		BBA
Rauch,Jon		BBA
Saito,Takashi		BBA
Vargas,Claudio		BBA
Fuentes,Brian		BBB

SP	Rel
Arroyo,Bronson	AAA
Buehrle,Mark	AAA
Bush,David	AAA
Byrd,Paul	AAA
Cain,Matt	AAA
Dempster,Ryan	AAA
Garland,Jon	AAA
Guthrie,Jeremy	AAA
Haren,Dan	AAA
Hernandez,Livan	AAA
Lohse,Kyle	AAA
Lowe,Derek	AAA
Maddux,Greg	AAA
Maholm,Paul	AAA
Marquis,Jason	AAA
Meche,Gil	AAA
Moyer,Jamie	AAA
Robertson,Nate	AAA
Sabathia,C.C.	AAA
Santana,Johan	AAA
Shields,James	AAA
Silva,Carlos	AAA
Suppan,Jeff	AAA
Vazquez,Javier	AAA
Washburn,Jarrod	AAA
Webb,Brandon	AAA
Zambrano,Carlos	AAA
Zito,Barry	AAA
Batista,Miguel	AAB
Blanton,Joe	AAB
Looper,Braden	AAB
Matsuzaka,Daisuke	AAB
Olsen,Scott	AAB
Santana,Ervin	AAB
Snell,Ian	AAB
Verlander,Justin	AAB
Bonser,Boof	ABA
Floyd,Gavin	ABA
Garza,Matt	ABA
Greinke,Zack	ABA
Jackson,Edwin	ABA
Redding,Tim	ABA
Saunders,Joe	ABA
Sonnanstine,Andy	ABA
Billingsley,Chad	ABB
Jimenez,Ubaldo	ABB
Moehler,Brian	ABB
Volquez,Edinson	ABB
Weaver,Jered	ABB
Cabrera,Daniel	BAA
Davis,Doug	BAA
Francis,Jeff	BAA
Hamels,Cole	BAA
Harang,Aaron	BAA
Hernandez,Felix	BAA
Lackey,John	BAA
Lilly,Ted	BAA
Oswalt,Roy	BAA
Peavy,Jake	BAA
Perez,Oliver	BAB
Pettitte,Andy	BAB
Baker,Scott	BBA
Wellemeyer,Todd	BBA
Gorzelanny,Tom	BBB
Myers,Brett	BBB
Rodriguez,Wandy	BBB

RISK MANAGEMENT

GRADE "A" in CONSISTENCY

Batters (min 400 AB)	Pitchers (min 120 IP)
Bartlett,Jason	Arroyo,Bronson
Beltre,Adrian	Bannister,Brian
Betancourt,Yuniesky	Beckett,Josh
Burrell,Pat	Buehrle,Mark
Cabrera,Orlando	Burnett,A.J.
DeRosa,Mark	Bush,David
Ellsbury,Jacoby	Byrd,Paul
Encarnacion,Edwin	Cabrera,Daniel
Flores,Jesus	Cain,Matt
Glaus,Troy	Chamberlain,Joba
Gonzalez,Adrian	Cook,Aaron
Grudzielanek,Mark	Davis,Doug
Hamilton,Josh	Dempster,Ryan
Hudson,Orlando	Duke,Zach
Hunter,Torii	Francis,Jeff
Ibanez,Raul	Garland,Jon
Iwamura,Akinori	Garza,Matt
Jackson,Conor	Greinke,Zack
Jacobs,Mike	Guthrie,Jeremy
Lee,Carlos	Hamels,Cole
Morales,Kendry	Harang,Aaron
Mora,Melvin	Harden,Rich
Pedroia,Dustin	Haren,Dan
Pierzynski,A.J.	Hernandez,Felix
Ramirez,Aramis	Hernandez,Livan
Reynolds,Mark	Jackson,Edwin
Rios,Alex	Kazmir,Scott
Sizemore,Grady	Lackey,John
Soriano,Alfonso	Lilly,Ted
Stewart,Ian	Lincecum,Tim
Suzuki,Kurt	Lohse,Kyle
Teixeira,Mark	Lowe,Derek
Upton,Justin	Maddux,Greg
Uribe,Juan	Maholm,Paul
Victorino,Shane	Maine,John
Werth,Jayson	Marquis,Jason
Willingham,Josh	Martinez,Pedro
Winn,Randy	Meche,Gil
Wood,Brandon	Millwood,Kevin
Young,Chris	Moyer,Jamie
Young,Michael	Oswalt,Roy
Zimmerman,Ryan	Peavy,Jake
	Penny,Brad
	Pineiro,Joel
	Redding,Tim
	Robertson,Nate
	Sabathia,C.C.
	Santana,Johan
	Saunders,Joe
	Shields,James
	Silva,Carlos
	Slowey,Kevin
	Sonnanstine,Andy
	Suppan,Jeff
	Vazquez,Javier
	Wakefield,Tim
	Wang,Chien-Ming
	Washburn,Jarrod
	Webb,Brandon
	Young,Chris
	Zambrano,Carlos
	Zito,Barry

TOP COMBINATION OF SKILLS AND RELIABILITY
Maximum of one "C" in Reliability Grade

BATTING POWER

PX over 120	PX	Rel
Howard,Ryan	212	AAC
Dunn,Adam	194	AAB
Rodriguez,Alex	174	AAC
Jacobs,Mike	171	BBA
Cabrera,Miguel	169	AAB
Reynolds,Mark	164	ACA
Soriano,Alfonso	162	CAA
Pujols,Albert	160	AAC
Burrell,Pat	160	AAC
LaRoche,Adam	159	AAC
Teixeira,Mark	156	AAA
Wright,David	155	AAB
Cameron,Mike	153	BAB
Uggla,Dan	149	AAB
Gordon,Alex	148	ABC
Ramirez,Hanley	147	AAB
Ramirez,Aramis	146	AAA
Hawpe,Brad	146	BAB
Holliday,Matt	145	BAB
Scott,Luke	144	ABB
Young,Chris	143	AAA
Sizemore,Grady	143	AAA
Pence,Hunter	142	ABC
Granderson,Curtis	141	AAC
Youkilis,Kevin	140	AAB
Utley,Chase	139	AAB
Willingham,Josh	138	CBA
Swisher,Nick	137	AAB
Hart,Corey	137	ABC
Wood,Brandon	136	ACA
Markakis,Nick	136	AAB
Gonzalez,Adrian	135	AAA
Ethier,Andre	135	ABB
Beltran,Carlos	134	AAB
Lee,Carlos	133	BAA
Huff,Aubrey	133	AAB
Konerko,Paul	133	BAB
Wigginton,Ty	132	BBB
Morneau,Justin	132	AAB
Glaus,Troy	131	CAA
Hunter,Torii	128	BAA
Blake,Casey	126	BAB
Votto,Joey	126	ABB
Nady,Xavier	125	ABB
Guerrero,Vladimir	125	AAB
Encarnacion,Edwin	124	ABA
Stewart,Ian	124	ACA
Hardy,J.J.	123	CBB
Olivo,Miguel	123	ACB
Kemp,Matt	122	ABB
Lee,Derrek	122	CBB
Beltre,Adrian	122	AAA
Drew,Stephen	121	AAC
Rios,Alex	121	AAA
Sexson,Richie	120	BBC

RUNNER SPEED

SX over 100	SX	Rel
Reyes,Jose	168	AAB
Crawford,Carl	163	BAB
Rollins,Jimmy	162	AAB
Victorino,Shane	155	ABA
Granderson,Curtis	153	AAC
Taveras,Willy	146	ABC
Ellsbury,Jacoby	140	ACA
Kemp,Matt	139	ABB
Pierre,Juan	135	BAA
Rios,Alex	135	AAA
Roberts,Brian	131	AAB
Suzuki,Ichiro	131	AAB
Sizemore,Grady	131	AAA
Anderson,Josh	130	ACB
Hart,Corey	128	ABC
Crisp,Coco	126	BBA
Damon,Johnny	126	AAB
Ramirez,Hanley	125	AAB
Bartlett,Jason	125	ABA
Phillips,Brandon	121	AAB
Patterson,Corey	119	ACB
Young,Chris	119	AAA
Beltran,Carlos	117	AAB
Holliday,Matt	116	BAB
Cameron,Mike	114	BAB
Iwamura,Akinori	114	AAA
Utley,Chase	114	AAB
Soriano,Alfonso	112	CAA
Milledge,Lastings	111	ACB
Amezaga,Alfredo	110	ACA
Theriot,Ryan	109	ABB
DeJesus,David	109	AAC
Castillo,Luis	109	CBA
Pedroia,Dustin	106	AAA
Blanco,Gregor	106	ACA
Winn,Randy	104	AAA
Young,Delmon	103	ABB
Abreu,Bobby	103	AAB
Fukudome,Kosuke	102	BBB
Reynolds,Mark	100	ACA
Ellis,Mark	100	CBB
Murphy,David	100	BCB
Teahen,Mark	100	ABC

OVERALL PITCHING SKILL

BPV over 75	BPV	Rel
Papelbon,Jonathan	159	AAA
Valverde,Jose	133	BAA
Rivera,Mariano	133	AAB
Broxton,Jonathan	133	ACA
Qualls,Chad	126	ACA
Nathan,Joe	124	AAB
Sabathia,C.C.	120	AAA
Beckett,Josh	118	CAA
Lidge,Brad	116	BAA
Haren,Dan	116	AAA
Fuentes,Brian	116	BBB
Meredith,Cla	112	ACA
Santana,Ervin	111	AAB
Soria,Joakim	109	ABB
Hamels,Cole	109	BAA
Lincecum,Tim	109	ACA
Halladay,Roy	109	CAB
Putz,J.J.	109	CBB
Street,Huston	106	CBB
Santana,Johan	106	AAA
Myers,Brett	104	BBB
Bell,Heath	104	ACB
Vazquez,Javier	104	AAA
Cueto,Johnny	104	ACA
Saito,Takashi	104	BBA
Shields,James	103	AAA
Peavy,Jake	102	BAA
Thornton,Matt	102	ACB
Howry,Bob	101	ACA
Linebrink,Scott	100	BCB
Webb,Brandon	99	AAA
Hernandez,Felix	99	BAA
Greinke,Zack	97	ABA
Oswalt,Roy	97	BAA
Howell,J.P.	96	ACA
Slowey,Kevin	94	ACA
Wheeler,Dan	94	ACA
Wilson,Brian	93	ACB
Capps,Matt	93	BBA
Lowe,Derek	91	AAA
Lackey,John	91	BAA
Cordero,Francisco	90	AAB
Pena,Tony	89	ACA
Shields,Scot	88	ACA
Rodriguez,Wandy	88	BBB
Villanueva,Carlos	87	ACB
Rauch,Jon	86	BBA
Kazmir,Scott	86	CAA
Parra,Manny	86	ACB
Baker,Scott	85	BBA
Hoffman,Trevor	85	AAB
Marte,Damaso	84	ACA
Rodriguez,Francisco	83	AAA
Sonnanstine,Andy	83	ABA
Downs,Scott	82	ACA
Weaver,Jered	82	ABB
Pettitte,Andy	81	BAB
Maddux,Greg	80	AAA

POSITION SCARCITY CHART

30	$30+ players	29	$20-29 players	15	$15-19 players	10	$10-14 players

FIRST BASE
NAME

Pujols, Albert
Cabrera, Miguel
Howard, Ryan
Teixeira, Mark
Berkman, Lance
Fielder, Prince
Votto, Joey
Davis, Chris
Morneau, Justin
Lee, Derrek
Gonzalez, Adrian
Delgado, Carlos
Youkilis, Kevin
Pena, Carlos
Konerko, Paul
Jacobs, Mike
LaRoche, Adam
Loney, James
Kotchman, Casey
Sandoval, Pablo
Garko, Ryan
Blalock, Hank
Giambi, Jason
Overbay, Lyle
Tracy, Chad
Helton, Todd
Shealy, Ryan
Millar, Kevin
Belliard, Ronnie
Barton, Daric
Johnson, Nick
Ishikawa, Travis
Gload, Ross
Young, Dmitri
Betemit, Wilson
Aurilia, Rich
Catalanotto, Frank
Sexson, Richie
Mientkiewicz, Doug
Bowker, John
Boone, Aaron
Salazar, Oscar
Cairo, Miguel
Casey, Sean
Ward, Daryle

SECOND BASE
NAME

Pedroia, Dustin
Utley, Chase
Kinsler, Ian
Roberts, Brian
Phillips, Brandon
Ramirez, Alexei
Polanco, Placido
Weeks, Rickie
Cano, Robinson
Uggla, Dan
Lopez, Jose
Johnson, Kelly
DeRosa, Mark
Ellis, Mark
Velez, Eugenio
Iwamura, Akinori
Sanchez, Freddy
Cabrera, Asdrubal
Matsui, Kaz
Lopez, Felipe
Kendrick, Howie
Hill, Aaron
Hudson, Orlando
Kent, Jeff
Barmes, Clint
Fontenot, Mike
Callaspo, Alberto
Casilla, Alexi
Antonelli, Matt
Grudzielanek, Mark
Kennedy, Adam
Castillo, Luis
Bonifacio, Emilio
Inglett, Joe
Baker, Jeff
Frandsen, Kevin
Durham, Ray
Patterson, Eric
Loretta, Mark
Miles, Aaron
Arias, Joaquin
Carroll, Jamey
Easley, Damion
Cedeno, Ronny
Rodriguez, Sean

THIRD BASE
NAME

Wright, David
Rodriguez, Alex
Ramirez, Aramis
Longoria, Evan
Beltre, Adrian
Atkins, Garrett
Jones, Chipper
Reynolds, Mark
Wigginton, Ty
Gordon, Alex
Glaus, Troy
Zimmerman, Ryan
Figgins, Chone
Mora, Melvin
Guillen, Carlos
Kouzmanoff, Kevin
Cantu, Jorge
Blake, Casey
Lowell, Mike
Encarnacion, Edwin
Stewart, Ian
Wood, Brandon
Rolen, Scott
Hall, Bill
LaRoche, Andy
DeWitt, Blake
Crede, Joe
Tolbert, Matt
Fields, Josh
Uribe, Juan
Prado, Martin
Dobbs, Greg
Feliz, Pedro
Buscher, Brian
Aybar, Willy
Chavez, Eric
Blum, Geoff
Bautista, Jose
Lamb, Mike
Vazquez, Ramon
Branyan, Russell
Marte, Andy
Quinlan, Robb
Hannahan, Jack
Duran, German

SHORTSTOP
NAME

Reyes, Jose
Ramirez, Hanley
Rollins, Jimmy
Furcal, Rafael
Tulowitzki, Troy
Hardy, J.J.
Drew, Stephen
Young, Michael
Peralta, Jhonny
Jeter, Derek
Theriot, Ryan
Cabrera, Orlando
Tejada, Miguel
Renteria, Edgar
Bartlett, Jason
Aviles, Mike
Guzman, Cristian
Escobar, Yunel
Betancourt, Yuniesk
Burriss, Emmanuel
Aybar, Erick
Greene, Khalil
Lowrie, Jed
Izturis, Maicer
Garciaparra, Nomar
Lugo, Julio
Wilson, Jack
Punto, Nick
Gonzalez, Alex
Hairston, Jerry
Scutaro, Marco
Zobrist, Ben
Izturis, Cesar
Santiago, Ramon
Harris, Brendan
Keppinger, Jeff
Crosby, Bobby
Lillibridge, Brent
Hu, Chin-Lung
Eckstein, David
Ochoa, Ivan
Everett, Adam
Vizquel, Omar
Berroa, Angel
Cintron, Alex

CATCHERS
NAME

Mauer, Joe
McCann, Brian
Doumit, Ryan
Martinez, Victor
Martin, Russell
Soto, Geovany
Molina, Bengie
Posada, Jorge
Napoli, Mike
Iannetta, Chris
Hernandez, Ram
Shoppach, Kelly
Snyder, Chris
Pierzynski, A.J.
Johjima, Kenji
Clement, Jeff
Suzuki, Kurt
Molina, Yadier
Towles, J.R.
Rodriguez, Ivan
Saltalamacchia, J
Navarro, Dioner
Laird, Gerald
Barajas, Rod
Ruiz, Carlos
Schneider, Brian
Baker, John
Buck, John
Varitek, Jason
Bard, Josh
Flores, Jesus
Torrealba, Yorvit
Olivo, Miguel
Barrett, Michael
Valentin, Javier
Castro, Ramon
Montero, Miguel
Teagarden, Taylor
Inge, Brandon
Ramirez, Max
Coste, Chris
Kendall, Jason
Hundley, Nicholas
Zaun, Gregg
Hanigan, Ryan

OUTFIELDERS
NAME

Holliday, Matt
Lee, Carlos
Braun, Ryan
Hamilton, Josh
Sizemore, Grady
McLouth, Nate
Soriano, Alfonso
Kemp, Matt
Beltran, Carlos
Crawford, Carl
Victorino, Shane
Markakis, Nick
Bay, Jason
Upton, B.J.
Hart, Corey
Rios, Alex
Suzuki, Ichiro
Abreu, Bobby
Ramirez, Manny
Hunter, Torii
Granderson, Curtis
Guerrero, Vladimir
Ethier, Andre
Pence, Hunter
Werth, Jayson
Damon, Johnny
Dye, Jermaine
Ellsbury, Jacoby
Wells, Vernon
Ludwick, Ryan
Milledge, Lastings
Dunn, Adam
Bruce, Jay
Cruz, Nelson
Quentin, Carlos
Ordonez, Magglio
Nady, Xavier
Jackson, Conor
Hawpe, Brad
DeJesus, David
Byrnes, Eric
Young, Chris
Span, Denard
Young, Delmon
Choo, Shin-Soo

STARTERS
NAME

Chamberlain, Joba
Sabathia, C.C.
Halladay, Roy
Santana, Johan
Santana, Ervin
Webb, Brandon
Liriano, Francisco
Hamels, Cole
Peavy, Jake
Oswalt, Roy
Shields, James
Lincecum, Tim
Slowey, Kevin
Haren, Dan
Vazquez, Javier
Greinke, Zack
Lackey, John
Beckett, Josh
Billingsley, Chad
Hernandez, Felix
Kazmir, Scott
Baker, Scott
Lee, Cliff
Meche, Gil
Burnett, A.J.
Weaver, Jered
Harden, Rich
Myers, Brett
Verlander, Justin
Gallardo, Yovani
Matsuzaka, D
Sheets, Ben
Wainwright, Adam
Lilly, Ted
Cueto, Johnny
Lowe, Derek
Danks, John
Sonnanstine, Andy
Dempster, Ryan
Buehrle, Mark
Duchscherer, J
Garza, Matt
Nolasco, Ricky
Volquez, Edinson
Pettitte, Andy

RELIEVERS
NAME

Papelbon, Jonathan
Valverde, Jose
Nathan, Joe
Lidge, Brad
Soria, Joakim
Rivera, Mariano
Street, Huston
Fuentes, Brian
Capps, Matt
Rodriguez, F
Wood, Kerry
Cordero, Francisco
Qualls, Chad
Jenks, Bobby
Ryan, B.J.
Putz, J.J.
Devine, Joey
Perez, Chris
Gonzalez, Mike
Francisco, Frank
Broxton, Jonathan
Wilson, Brian
Saito, Takashi
Wheeler, Dan
Hoffman, Trevor
Hanrahan, Joel
Zumaya, Joel
Buchholz, Taylor
Arredondo, Jose
Marmol, Carlos
Rauch, Jon
Rodney, Fernando
Sherrill, George
Gregg, Kevin
Bell, Heath
Perez, Rafael
Corpas, Manny
Lindstrom, Matt
Ziegler, Brad
Escobar, Kelvim
Shields, Scot
Lewis, Jensen
Balfour, Grant
Howell, J.P.
Villanueva, Carlos

PORTFOLIO3 PLAN

TIER 1

High Skill, Low Risk — Filters: BBB 80 100 100

BATTERS	Age	Bats	Pos	REL	Ct%	PX	SX	R$
Reyes,Jose	25	B	6	AAB	88	101	168	$36
Wright,David	26	R	5	AAB	81	155	92	$34
Ramirez,Hanley	25	R	6	AAB	82	147	125	$34
Holliday,Matt	29	R	7	BAB	81	145	116	$33
Lee,Carlos	32	R	7	BAA	89	133	61	$32
Pedroia,Dustin	25	R	4	AAA	92	105	106	$31
Rollins,Jimmy	30	B	6	AAB	89	104	162	$30
Utley,Chase	30	L	4	AAB	82	139	114	$30
Teixeira,Mark	29	B	3	AAA	81	156	51	$29
Beltran,Carlos	32	B	8	AAB	83	134	117	$27
Crawford,Carl	27	L	7	BAB	85	85	163	$26
Victorino,Shane	28	B	8	ABA	87	93	155	$26
Markakis,Nick	25	L	9	AAB	82	136	76	$26
Rios,Alex	28	R	98	AAB	83	121	135	$26
Roberts,Brian	31	B	4	AAB	84	93	131	$26
Suzuki,Ichiro	35	L	98	AAB	90	48	131	$25
Abreu,Bobby	35	L	9	AAB	80	116	103	$25
Hunter,Torii	33	R	8	BAA	81	128	92	$25
Guerrero,Vladimir	33	R	90	AAB	88	125	62	$25
Ethier,Andre	27	L	97	ABB	83	135	89	$25
Ramirez,Aramis	30	R	5	AAA	86	146	54	$25
Votto,Joey	25	L	3	AAB	81	126	67	$25
Morneau,Justin	28	L	3	AAB	85	132	54	$24
Damon,Johnny	35	L	780	AAB	86	94	126	$24
Huff,Aubrey	32	L	053	AAB	85	133	69	$23
Phillips,Brandon	27	R	4	AAB	84	109	121	$23
Youkilis,Kevin	30	R	35	AAB	80	140	64	$22
Nady,Xavier	30	R	97	ABB	80	125	63	$21
Beltre,Adrian	30	R	5	AAA	83	122	85	$21
Jackson,Conor	27	R	73	ABA	88	107	88	$21
Konerko,Paul	33	R	3	BAB	82	133	36	$20
Young,Delmon	23	R	7	ABB	82	86	103	$19
Ibanez,Raul	36	L	7	AAA	82	117	56	$19
Wigginton,Ty	31	R	57	BBB	81	132	52	$19
Winn,Randy	34	B	9	AAA	86	81	104	$18
Zimmerman,Ryan	24	R	5	BAA	83	109	61	$18
Theriot,Ryan	29	R	6	ABB	90	44	109	$18
Mora,Melvin	37	R	5	BAA	85	108	52	$17
DeRosa,Mark	34	R	4975	AAA	80	104	81	$17
Guillen,Carlos	33	B	53	BAB	83	109	99	$17
Garko,Ryan	28	R	3	ABB	82	109	41	$17
Bartlett,Jason	29	R	6	ABA	85	69	125	$16
Lowell,Mike	35	R	5	BAB	86	108	48	$15
Encarnacion,Edwin	26	R	5	ABA	81	124	59	$15
Pierre,Juan	31	L	7	BAA	94	36	135	$12
Crisp,Coco	29	B	8	BBA	84	78	126	$12
Millar,Kevin	37	R	3	ABB	82	103	32	$9
Belliard,Ronnie	34	R	354	BBB	83	105	44	$9
Uribe,Juan	30	R	54	ABA	80	105	52	$8
Harris,Brendan	28	R	645	ABA	80	105	72	$6

TIER 2

High Skill, Mod Risk — Filters: BBC 80 100 100 <$20

BATTERS	Age	Bats	Pos	REL	Ct%	PX	SX	R$
*Pujols,Albert	29	R	3	AAC	90	160	57	$37
*Hart,Corey	27	R	9	ABC	81	137	128	$26
*Pence,Hunter	26	R	9	ABC	80	142	99	$25
*Ellsbury,Jacoby	25	L	879	ACA	87	69	140	$23
*Lee,Derrek	33	R	3	CBB	80	122	68	$23
*Milledge,Lastings	24	R	8	ACB	80	106	111	$23
*Atkins,Garrett	29	R	53	AAC	85	105	62	$21
*DeJesus,David	29	L	789	AAC	86	92	109	$20
*Hardy,J.J.	26	R	6	CBB	85	123	59	$20
Drew,Stephen	26	L	6	AAC	83	121	80	$19
Taveras,Willy	27	R	8	ABC	84	35	146	$17
Kouzmanoff,Kevin	27	R	5	ABC	80	118	50	$17
Cantu,Jorge	27	R	53	ACB	82	114	60	$17
Murphy,David	27	L	97	BCB	85	114	100	$16
Guillen,Jose	33	R	970	BBC	82	102	67	$15
Francisco,Ben	27	R	79	ACB	82	113	78	$15
Ellis,Mark	31	R	4	CBB	84	99	100	$15
Overbay,Lyle	32	L	3	BAC	80	110	48	$13
Griffey Jr.,Ken	39	L	98	BBC	81	109	42	$13
Anderson,Josh	26	L	8	ACB	86	60	130	$13
Patterson,Corey	29	L	8	ACB	83	88	119	$12
Castillo,Luis	33	B	4	CBA	86	34	109	$9
Amezaga,Alfredo	31	B	8	ACA	86	54	110	$4

* Tier 2 players should be less than $20 If you are going to spend more
than $20 here, be aware of the added risk.

TIER 1

High Skill, Low Risk — Filters: BBB 75

PITCHERS	Age	Thrw	REL	BPV	R$
Santana,Johan	30	L	AAA	106	$28
Webb,Brandon	30	R	AAA	99	$27
Hamels,Cole	25	L	BAA	109	$26
Peavy,Jake	27	R	BAA	102	$26
Oswalt,Roy	31	R	BAA	97	$25
Shields,James	27	R	AAA	103	$25
Vazquez,Javier	32	R	AAA	104	$23
Greinke,Zack	25	R	ABA	97	$23
Lackey,John	30	R	BAA	91	$23
Billingsley,Chad	24	R	ABB	75	$22
Hernandez,Felix	23	R	BAA	99	$22
Baker,Scott	27	R	BBA	85	$22
Capps,Matt	25	R	BBA	93	$22
Rodriguez,Francisco	27	R	AAA	83	$22
Meche,Gil	30	R	AAA	76	$21
Weaver,Jered	26	R	ABB	82	$21
Myers,Brett	28	R	BBB	104	$20
Cordero,Francisco	34	R	AAB	90	$20
Lowe,Derek	35	R	AAA	91	$19
Sonnanstine,Andy	26	R	ABA	83	$19
Pettitte,Andy	36	L	BAB	81	$17
Rodriguez,Wandy	30	L	BBB	88	$17
Saito,Takashi	39	R	BBA	104	$15
Hoffman,Trevor	41	R	AAB	85	$15
Maddux,Greg	43	R	AAA	80	$13
Rauch,Jon	30	R	BBA	86	$12

TIER 2

High Skill, Mod Risk — Filters: BBC 50 <$20

PITCHERS	Age	Thrw	REL	BPV	R$
Qualls,Chad	30	R	ACA	126	$19
Wainwright,Adam	27	R	CBB	75	$19
Lilly,Ted	33	L	BAA	73	$19
Cueto,Johnny	23	R	ACA	104	$19
Jenks,Bobby	28	R	AAA	73	$19
Danks,John	24	L	ABC	78	$19
Putz,J.J.	32	R	CBB	109	$19
Dempster,Ryan	32	R	AAA	67	$18
Buehrle,Mark	30	L	AAA	69	$18
Garza,Matt	25	R	ABA	62	$18
Volquez,Edinson	25	R	ABB	71	$17
Cain,Matt	24	R	AAA	53	$17
Broxton,Jonathan	24	R	ACA	133	$16
Wilson,Brian	27	R	ACB	93	$16
Mussina,Mike	40	R	BAC	69	$15
Maine,John	28	R	CBA	57	$15
Parra,Manny	26	L	ACB	86	$15
Wheeler,Dan	31	R	ACA	94	$15
Kuroda,Hiroki	34	R	AAC	72	$15
Harang,Aaron	31	R	BAA	74	$15
Jurrjens,Jair	23	R	ACB	66	$15
Arroyo,Bronson	32	R	AAA	66	$14
Bush,David	29	R	AAA	72	$14
Buchholz,Taylor	27	R	ACA	72	$14
Maholm,Paul	26	L	AAA	63	$14
Looper,Braden	34	R	AAB	54	$14
Millwood,Kevin	34	R	CAA	74	$13
Gregg,Kevin	30	R	ABA	53	$12
Bell,Heath	31	R	ACB	104	$12
Corpas,Manny	26	R	ACA	78	$11
Lohse,Kyle	30	R	AAA	55	$11
Snell,Ian	27	R	AAB	56	$11
Shields,Scot	33	R	ACA	88	$10
Howell,J.P.	26	L	ACA	96	$10
Villanueva,Carlos	25	R	ACB	87	$10
Downs,Scott	33	L	ACA	82	$10
Sanchez,Jonathan	26	L	BCA	69	$10
Howry,Bob	35	R	ACA	101	$10
Thornton,Matt	32	L	ACB	102	$9
Francis,Jeff	28	L	BAA	53	$9
Linebrink,Scott	32	R	BCB	100	$9
Okajima,Hideki	33	L	ACB	71	$8
Heilman,Aaron	30	R	ACA	70	$8
Meredith,Cla	25	R	ACA	112	$7
Pena,Tony	27	R	ACA	89	$7
Pineiro,Joel	30	R	CBA	56	$7
Gaudin,Chad	26	R	ABB	64	$6
Grabow,John	30	L	ACA	50	$6
Rivera,Saul	31	R	ACA	61	$6
Aceves,Alfredo	26	R	ACB	53	$5
Peralta,Joel	33	R	ACA	65	$5
Duke,Zach	26	L	CAA	50	$5
Owings,Micah	26	R	ABA	58	$5

PORTFOLIO3 PLAN

TIER 3

High Skill, High Risk

BATTERS	Age	Bats	Pos	REL	Ct%	PX	SX	R$
			Filters:	n/a	80	100	100	<$10
Burriss,Emmanuel	24	B	64	AFF	90	27	107	$12
Aybar,Erick	25	B	6	CDC	87	60	132	$12
Lowrie,Jed	25	B	65	AFC	80	118	80	$12
Izturis,Maicer	28	B	64	FCB	90	77	115	$11
Garciaparra,Nomar	35	R	6	FCC	92	101	55	$11
Barmes,Clint	30	R	46	CCC	82	95	112	$11
Fontenot,Mike	28	L	4	ADD	81	124	76	$11
Davis,Rajai	28	R	8	ADB	84	60	170	$10
Roberts,Dave	36	L	7	FCB	85	57	152	$10
Lugo,Julio	33	R	6	DBB	83	74	110	$10
Buck,Travis	25	L	9	CFD	80	103	98	$10
Punto,Nick	31	B	64	CBF	83	61	120	$9
Kennedy,Adam	33	L	4	CCD	87	60	109	$9
Gonzalez,Alex	32	R	6	FDC	81	102	60	$9
Hairston,Jerry	32	R	67	DFF	86	81	105	$9
Crede,Joe	31	R	5	FCF	87	100	41	$9
Pearce,Steven	26	R	9	ADF	83	104	86	$9
Tolbert,Matt	27	B	5	DFB	83	72	119	$9
Pie,Felix	24	L	8	ADB	82	96	115	$9
Harris,Willie	30	L	7	ADC	80	88	126	$9
Bonifacio,Emilio	24	B	4	ADA	81	48	135	$9
Tatis,Fernando	34	R	79	AFC	80	130	53	$9
Schierholtz,Nate	25	L	9	ADA	87	109	114	$8
Zobrist,Ben	28	B	6	CDC	81	111	96	$8
Evans,Nick	23	R	7	AFF	81	114	79	$8
Dobbs,Greg	30	L	5	ADB	83	110	91	$8
Inglett,Joe	30	L	47	ADF	86	58	113	$8
Gathright,Joey	28	L	8	ACD	85	24	117	$8
Willits,Reggie	27	B	79	ADB	83	50	112	$8
Hoffpauir,Micah	29	L	7	AFD	83	142	71	$8
Freel,Ryan	33	R	8	FDC	83	68	114	$8
Mather,Joe	26	R	7	AFC	82	123	70	$7
Kapler,Gabe	33	R	8	AFD	84	102	80	$7
Barajas,Rod	33	R	2	BDB	82	102	38	$7
Patterson,Eric	26	L	4	ADB	82	84	127	$7
Santiago,Ramon	29	B	64	BFF	83	61	110	$6
Young,Dmitri	35	B	3	FDC	81	101	49	$6
Arias,Joaquin	24	R	4	ADA	90	61	133	$6
Carroll,Jamey	35	R	45	ACC	83	51	109	$5
Podsednik,Scott	33	L	8	DDA	82	69	121	$5
Montanez,Luis	27	R	7	ADB	85	118	68	$5
Chavez,Endy	31	L	97	CDB	90	52	110	$5
Bloomquist,Willie	31	R	8	CFA	83	23	102	$5
Valentin,Javier	33	B	2	AFA	83	122	10	$5
Hu,Chin-Lung	25	R	64	ADD	88	58	108	$5
Cunningham,Aaron	23	R	7	AFB	80	124	123	$5
Gardner,Brett	25	L	8	AFA	80	48	158	$5
Morgan,Nyjer	28	L	7	AFA	84	43	135	$5
Smith,Seth	26	L	9	ADA	85	108	72	$5
German,Esteban	31	R	74	ADD	82	68	124	$4
Cairo,Miguel	35	R	3	BFA	86	60	126	$4
Duran,German	24	R	5	AFF	84	97	101	$4
Anderson,Marlon	35	L	7	BFF	82	100	61	$3
Pennington,Cliff	24	B	4	AFA	88	40	100	$3
Pagan,Angel	27	B	7	FFB	81	82	118	$3
Ochoa,Ivan	26	B	6	AFA	81	56	100	$3
Rivera,Mike	32	R	2	AFF	82	102	39	$3
Mench,Kevin	31	R	7	ADB	86	101	75	$3
Ozuna,Pablo	34	R	4	DFD	91	44	104	$3
Romero,Alex	25	L	9	AFA	89	71	102	$2
McDonald,John	34	R	6	BDB	86	51	100	$2
Bernadina,Rogearvin	24	L	8	AFC	80	68	143	$2
Burke,Chris	29	R	7	ADB	80	80	112	$2
Young,Delwyn	26	B	8	BDD	81	102	36	$2
Dillon,Joe	33	R	4	AFF	82	100	59	$1

PITCHERS	Age	Thrw	REL	BPV	R$
		Filters:	n/a	75	<$10
Scherzer,Max	24	R	ADC	94	$14
Johnson,Randy	45	L	FAB	92	$13
Buchholz,Clay	24	R	ADD	83	$13
Marmol,Carlos	26	R	ACC	83	$12
Rodney,Fernando	32	R	FCA	94	$12
Perez,Rafael	27	L	ADB	138	$11
Petit,Yusmeiro	24	R	ADB	77	$11
Escobar,Kelvim	33	R	FBA	75	$11
Balfour,Grant	31	R	FFA	96	$10
Smoltz,John	42	R	FAA	109	$10
Soriano,Rafael	29	R	FDB	88	$9
Cruz,Juan	30	R	CCB	93	$9
Kuo,Hong-Chih	27	L	CDD	114	$9
Accardo,Jeremy	27	R	FCC	81	$8
Ramirez,Edwar	28	R	AFA	102	$8
Betancourt,Rafael	34	R	BCC	94	$8
Smith,Joe	25	R	ADA	76	$7
Blevins,Jerry	25	L	AFB	115	$7
Madson,Ryan	28	R	CCB	80	$7
Delcarmen,Manny	27	R	ADA	87	$7
Adams,Mike	30	R	FFC	84	$7
Veras,Jose	28	R	AFD	75	$7
Carlson,Jesse	28	L	ADC	78	$7
Dotel,Octavio	35	R	FDF	137	$7
Romo,Sergio	26	R	AFF	93	$6
Crain,Jesse	27	R	DDB	77	$6
Wade,Cory	25	R	AFA	89	$6
Nelson,Joe	34	R	FDB	77	$6
Robertson,David	24	R	AFF	110	$6
Walker,Tyler	33	R	FDC	80	$6
Neshek,Pat	28	R	FDB	93	$6
Cordero,Chad	27	R	FBA	75	$6
Bray,Bill	25	L	CDA	104	$5
Eyre,Scott	36	L	DDD	90	$5
Affeldt,Jeremy	29	L	BCC	80	$4
Farnsworth,Kyle	33	R	ACC	79	$4
Mujica,Edward	25	R	ADA	82	$4
Logan,Boone	24	L	ADB	99	$4
Camp,Shawn	33	R	ADA	81	$3

ROTISSERIE AUCTION DRAFT — Top 560 players ranked for 75% depth leagues

NAME	POS	5x5	NAME	POS	5x5	NAME	POS	5x5	NAME	POS	5x5
Pujols,Albert	3	$37	Lee,Derrek	3	$23	Cano,Robinson	4	$19	Drew,J.D.	9	$16
Reyes,Jose	6	$36	Gonzalez,Adrian	3	$23	Reynolds,Mark	5	$19	Bourn,Michael	8	$16
Wright,David	5	$34	Wells,Vernon	8	$23	Ryan,B.J.	P	$19	Morales,Kendry	9	$16
Rodriguez,Alex	5	$34	Ludwick,Ryan	97	$23	Jeter,Derek	6	$19	Johnson,Josh	P	$16
Ramirez,Hanley	6	$34	Soria,Joakim	P	$23	Ibanez,Raul	7	$19	Gerut,Jody	8	$15
Holliday,Matt	7	$33	Lackey,John	P	$23	Danks,John	P	$19	Mussina,Mike	P	$15
Lee,Carlos	7	$32	Rivera,Mariano	P	$23	Fukudome,Kosuke	9	$19	Perez,Oliver	P	$15
Braun,Ryan	7	$31	Huff,Aubrey	053	$23	Wigginton,Ty	57	$19	Maine,John	P	$15
Pedroia,Dustin	4	$31	Milledge,Lastings	8	$23	LaRoche,Adam	3	$19	Aviles,Mike	64	$15
Rollins,Jimmy	6	$30	Phillips,Brandon	4	$23	Cameron,Mike	8	$19	Litsch,Jesse	P	$15
Cabrera,Miguel	3	$30	Beckett,Josh	P	$23	Uggla,Dan	4	$19	Lowell,Mike	5	$15
Utley,Chase	4	$30	Dunn,Adam	79	$23	Gordon,Alex	5	$19	Bradley,Milton	09	$15
Howard,Ryan	3	$30	Street,Huston	P	$23	Putz,J.J.	P	$19	Parra,Manny	P	$15
Kinsler,Ian	4	$30	Bruce,Jay	98	$22	Sonnanstine,Andy	P	$19	Cust,Jack	70	$15
Furcal,Rafael	6	$29	Billingsley,Chad	P	$22	Lopez,Jose	4	$19	Saito,Takashi	P	$15
Chamberlain,Joba	P	$29	Delgado,Carlos	3	$22	Glaus,Troy	5	$19	Hafner,Travis	0	$15
Sabathia,C.C.	P	$29	Youkilis,Kevin	35	$22	Dempster,Ryan	P	$18	Lester,Jon	P	$15
Teixeira,Mark	3	$29	Hernandez,Felix	P	$22	Ankiel,Rick	8	$18	Encarnacion,Edwin	5	$15
Hamilton,Josh	89	$29	Kazmir,Scott	P	$22	Loney,James	3	$18	Blalock,Hank	35	$15
Halladay,Roy	P	$29	Fuentes,Brian	P	$22	Winn,Randy	9	$18	Wheeler,Dan	P	$15
Sizemore,Grady	8	$29	Baker,Scott	P	$22	Johnson,Kelly	4	$18	Kuroda,Hiroki	P	$15
McLouth,Nate	8	$28	Capps,Matt	P	$22	Zimmerman,Ryan	5	$18	Harang,Aaron	P	$15
Soriano,Alfonso	7	$28	Lee,Cliff	P	$22	Devine,Joey	P	$18	Giles,Brian	9	$15
Papelbon,Jonathan	P	$28	Cruz,Nelson	9	$22	Theriot,Ryan	6	$18	Church,Ryan	9	$15
Santana,Johan	P	$28	Rodriguez,Francisco	P	$22	Burrell,Pat	7	$18	Jurrjens,Jair	P	$15
Santana,Ervin	P	$27	Quentin,Carlos	7	$21	Perez,Chris	P	$18	Morrow,Brandon	P	$15
Webb,Brandon	P	$27	Ramirez,Alexei	4	$21	Buehrle,Mark	P	$18	Guillen,Jose	970	$15
Kemp,Matt	89	$27	Ordonez,Magglio	9	$21	Figgins,Chone	5	$18	Hoffman,Trevor	P	$15
Beltran,Carlos	8	$27	Meche,Gil	P	$21	Duchscherer,Justin	P	$18	Molina,Bengie	2	$15
Berkman,Lance	3	$27	Nady,Xavier	97	$21	Doumit,Ryan	2	$18	Hanrahan,Joel	P	$15
Crawford,Carl	7	$26	Wood,Kerry	P	$21	Garza,Matt	P	$18	Hermida,Jeremy	9	$15
Victorino,Shane	8	$26	Burnett,A.J.	P	$21	Willingham,Josh	7	$17	Young,Chris	P	$15
Liriano,Francisco	P	$26	Beltre,Adrian	5	$21	Martinez,Victor	2	$17	Swisher,Nick	83	$15
Fielder,Prince	3	$26	Atkins,Garrett	53	$21	Butler,Billy	03	$17	Byrd,Marlon	897	$15
Ortiz,David	0	$26	Jackson,Conor	73	$21	Nolasco,Ricky	P	$17	Francisco,Ben	79	$15
Markakis,Nick	9	$26	Weaver,Jered	P	$21	Taveras,Willy	8	$17	Ellis,Mark	4	$15
Valverde,Jose	P	$26	Hawpe,Brad	9	$21	Mora,Melvin	5	$17	Saunders,Joe	P	$14
Bay,Jason	7	$26	Harden,Rich	P	$21	DeRosa,Mark	4975	$17	Posada,Jorge	2	$14
Upton,B.J.	8	$26	Polanco,Placido	4	$20	Volquez,Edinson	P	$17	Zumaya,Joel	P	$14
Hamels,Cole	P	$26	DeJesus,David	789	$20	Upton,Justin	9	$17	Arroyo,Bronson	P	$14
Peavy,Jake	P	$26	Myers,Brett	P	$20	Pettitte,Andy	P	$17	Dukes,Elijah	9	$14
Hart,Corey	9	$26	Tulowitzki,Troy	6	$20	Guillen,Carlos	53	$17	Napoli,Mike	2	$14
Rios,Alex	98	$26	Pena,Carlos	3	$20	Kotchman,Casey	3	$17	Cuddyer,Michael	9	$14
Roberts,Brian	4	$26	Byrnes,Eric	7	$20	Kouzmanoff,Kevin	5	$17	Rowand,Aaron	8	$14
Suzuki,Ichiro	98	$25	Young,Chris	8	$20	Gonzalez,Mike	P	$17	Scherzer,Max	P	$14
Abreu,Bobby	9	$25	Span,Denard	9	$20	Sandoval,Pablo	3	$17	Bush,David	P	$14
Oswalt,Roy	P	$25	Cordero,Francisco	P	$20	Cain,Matt	P	$17	Kubel,Jason	09	$14
Ramirez,Manny	70	$25	Thome,Jim	0	$20	Cantu,Jorge	53	$17	Guzman,Cristian	6	$14
Shields,James	P	$25	Mauer,Joe	2	$20	Rodriguez,Wandy	P	$17	Buchholz,Taylor	P	$14
Hunter,Torii	8	$25	McCann,Brian	2	$20	Wang,Chien-Ming	P	$17	Giambi,Jason	30	$14
Granderson,Curtis	8	$25	Verlander,Justin	P	$20	Jones,Adam	8	$17	Stewart,Ian	5	$14
Guerrero,Vladimir	90	$25	Gallardo,Yovani	P	$20	Francisco,Frank	P	$17	Iannetta,Chris	2	$14
Ethier,Andre	97	$25	Konerko,Paul	3	$20	Lewis,Fred	7	$17	Carmona,Fausto	P	$14
Ramirez,Aramis	5	$25	Matsuzaka,Daisuke	P	$20	Lind,Adam	7	$17	Velez,Eugenio	4	$14
Pence,Hunter	9	$25	Hardy,J.J.	6	$20	Garko,Ryan	3	$17	Iwamura,Akinori	4	$14
Votto,Joey	3	$25	Sheets,Ben	P	$19	Bedard,Erik	P	$16	Anderson,Garret	70	$14
Lincecum,Tim	P	$25	Drew,Stephen	6	$19	Martin,Russell	2	$16	Wood,Brandon	56	$14
Werth,Jayson	987	$25	Qualls,Chad	P	$19	Cabrera,Orlando	6	$16	Escobar,Yunel	6	$14
Davis,Chris	35	$25	Wainwright,Adam	P	$19	Kershaw,Clayton	P	$16	Maholm,Paul	P	$14
Slowey,Kevin	P	$24	Weeks,Rickie	4	$19	Scott,Luke	70	$16	Ross,Cody	89	$14
Nathan,Joe	P	$24	Jones,Chipper	5	$19	Broxton,Jonathan	P	$16	Floyd,Gavin	P	$14
Lidge,Brad	P	$24	Lilly,Ted	P	$19	Tejada,Miguel	6	$16	Sanchez,Freddy	4	$14
Morneau,Justin	3	$24	Cueto,Johnny	P	$19	Renteria,Edgar	6	$16	Looper,Braden	P	$14
Damon,Johnny	780	$24	Jacobs,Mike	3	$19	Blake,Casey	53	$16	Cabrera,Asdrubal	46	$14
Dye,Jermaine	9	$24	Jenks,Bobby	P	$19	Bartlett,Jason	6	$16	Hairston,Scott	87	$14
Haren,Dan	P	$24	Young,Delmon	7	$19	Murphy,David	97	$16	Matsui,Kaz	4	$13
Vazquez,Javier	P	$23	Choo,Shin-Soo	97	$19	Soto,Geovany	2	$16	Guthrie,Jeremy	P	$13
Ellsbury,Jacoby	879	$23	Young,Michael	6	$19	Headley,Chase	7	$16	Zambrano,Carlos	P	$13
Greinke,Zack	P	$23	Lowe,Derek	P	$19	Wilson,Brian	P	$16	Johnson,Randy	P	$13
Longoria,Evan	5	$23	Peralta,Jhonny	6	$19	Matsui,Hideki	07	$16	Lopez,Felipe	4	$13

ROTISSERIE AUCTION DRAFT — Top 560 players ranked for 75% depth leagues

NAME	POS	5x5	NAME	POS	5x5	NAME	POS	5x5	NAME	POS	5x5
Buchholz,Clay	P	$13	DeWitt,Blake	54	$11	Fields,Josh	5	$9	Eveland,Dana	P	$7
Maddux,Greg	P	$13	Garland,Jon	P	$11	Scutaro,Marco	645	$9	Patterson,Eric	4	$7
Overbay,Lyle	3	$13	Bonderman,Jeremy	P	$11	Floyd,Cliff	0	$9	Veras,Jose	P	$7
Griffey Jr.,Ken	98	$13	Thames,Marcus	7	$11	Bonifacio,Emilio	4	$9	Carlson,Jesse	P	$7
Arredondo,Jose	P	$13	Balentien,Wladimir	98	$11	Cruz,Juan	P	$9	Cabrera,Melky	8	$7
Kendrick,Howie	4	$13	Callaspo,Alberto	4	$10	Matthews Jr.,Gary	978	$9	Campillo,Jorge	P	$7
Kearns,Austin	9	$13	Shields,Scot	P	$10	Kuo,Hong-Chih	P	$9	League,Brandon	P	$7
Teahen,Mark	97	$13	Torres,Salomon	P	$10	Laffey,Aaron	P	$9	Pena,Tony	P	$7
Anderson,Josh	8	$13	Martinez,Pedro	P	$10	Brown,Emil	79	$9	Schneider,Brian	2	$7
Rolen,Scott	5	$13	Lewis,Jensen	P	$10	Tatis,Fernando	79	$9	Baker,John	2	$7
Jones,Brandon	7	$13	Snider,Travis	7	$10	Okajima,Hideki	P	$8	Gload,Ross	3	$7
Price,David	P	$13	Casilla,Alexi	4	$10	Schierholtz,Nate	9	$8	Wise,Dewayne	78	$7
Millwood,Kevin	P	$13	Schumaker,Skip	879	$10	Gross,Gabe	9	$8	Sanchez,Anibal	P	$7
Rowland-Smith,Rya	P	$13	Wolf,Randy	P	$10	Uribe,Juan	54	$8	Dotel,Octavio	P	$7
Pelfrey,Mike	P	$13	Gonzalez,Gio	P	$10	Prado,Martin	5	$8	Carpenter,Chris	P	$7
Marmol,Carlos	P	$12	Byrd,Paul	P	$10	Zobrist,Ben	6	$8	Harrison,Matt	P	$7
Betancourt,Yuniesk	6	$12	Pierzynski,A.J.	2	$10	Infante,Omar	756	$8	Rasner,Darrell	P	$7
Dickerson,Chris	7	$12	Davis,Rajai	8	$10	Evans,Nick	7	$8	Buscher,Brian	5	$7
Hill,Aaron	4	$12	Gutierrez,Franklin	9	$10	Reed,Jeremy	8	$8	Baldelli,Rocco	0	$7
Hudson,Orlando	4	$12	Balfour,Grant	P	$10	Accardo,Jeremy	P	$8	Aybar,Willy	50	$7
Hernandez,Ramon	2	$12	Marshall,Sean	P	$10	Washburn,Jarrod	P	$8	Pineiro,Joel	P	$7
Lewis,Scott	P	$12	Moyer,Jamie	P	$10	Moss,Brandon	79	$8	Santiago,Ramon	64	$6
Rauch,Jon	P	$12	Roberts,Dave	7	$10	Jones,Andruw	8	$8	Miner,Zach	P	$6
Rodney,Fernando	P	$12	Lugo,Julio	6	$10	Johnson,Nick	3	$8	Marte,Damaso	P	$6
Sherrill,George	P	$12	Shealy,Ryan	3	$10	Bonser,Boof	P	$8	Romo,Sergio	P	$6
Rivera,Juan	7	$12	Howell,J.P.	P	$10	Saltalamacchia,Jarr	2	$8	Crain,Jesse	P	$6
Murphy,Daniel	7	$12	Villanueva,Carlos	P	$10	Dobbs,Greg	5	$8	Oliver,Darren	P	$6
Tracy,Chad	3	$12	Smoltz,John	P	$10	Feliz,Pedro	5	$8	Wade,Cory	P	$6
Sheffield,Gary	0	$12	Jimenez,Ubaldo	P	$10	Navarro,Dioner	2	$8	Wilson,C.J.	P	$6
Gomez,Carlos	8	$12	Wilson,Jack	6	$10	Ramirez,Edwar	P	$8	Pena,Wily Mo	7	$6
Gregg,Kevin	P	$12	Johjima,Kenji	2	$10	Inglett,Joe	47	$8	Nelson,Joe	P	$6
Helton,Todd	3	$12	Buck,Travis	9	$10	Gathright,Joey	8	$8	Baek,Cha Seung	P	$6
Hall,Bill	5	$12	Blackburn,Nick	P	$10	Garcia,Freddy	P	$8	Robertson,David	P	$6
Pierre,Juan	7	$12	Clement,Jeff	20	$10	Edmonds,Jim	8	$8	Gaudin,Chad	P	$6
Burriss,Emmanuel	64	$12	Downs,Scott	P	$10	Baker,Jeff	43	$8	Buck,John	2	$6
Aybar,Erick	6	$12	Sanchez,Jonathan	P	$10	Lyon,Brandon	P	$8	Masterson,Justin	P	$6
Kent,Jeff	4	$12	Smith,Greg	P	$10	Olsen,Scott	P	$8	Reyes,Jo-Jo	P	$6
Francoeur,Jeff	9	$12	Hughes,Phil	P	$10	Ishikawa,Travis	3	$8	Grabow,John	P	$6
Greene,Khalil	6	$12	Suzuki,Kurt	2	$10	McGowan,Dustin	P	$8	Varitek,Jason	2	$6
Patterson,Corey	8	$12	Howry,Bob	P	$10	Perez,Odalis	P	$8	Bard,Josh	2	$6
Wakefield,Tim	P	$12	Ray,Chris	P	$9	Blanco,Gregor	78	$8	Young,Dmitri	3	$6
Crisp,Coco	8	$12	Punto,Nick	64	$9	Gorzelanny,Tom	P	$8	Loretta,Mark	4	$6
Blanton,Joe	P	$12	Antonelli,Matt	4	$9	Willits,Reggie	79	$8	Hurley,Eric	P	$6
Shoppach,Kelly	2	$12	Hochevar,Luke	P	$9	Betancourt,Rafael	P	$8	Penny,Brad	P	$6
Snyder,Chris	2	$12	Volstad,Chris	P	$9	Hoffpauir,Micah	7	$8	Marquis,Jason	P	$6
Lowrie,Jed	65	$12	Grudzielanek,Mark	4	$9	McClellan,Kyle	P	$8	Walker,Tyler	P	$6
Bell,Heath	P	$12	Kennedy,Adam	4	$9	Frandsen,Kevin	4	$8	Harris,Brendan	645	$6
Padilla,Vicente	P	$12	Soriano,Rafael	P	$9	Heilman,Aaron	P	$8	Karstens,Jeff	P	$6
Lannan,John	P	$11	Millar,Kevin	3	$9	Freel,Ryan	8	$8	Flores,Jesus	2	$6
Izturis,Maicer	64	$11	Gonzalez,Alex	6	$9	Durham,Ray	4	$7	McCarthy,Brandor	P	$6
Happ,J.A.	P	$11	Galarraga,Armando	P	$9	Smith,Joe	P	$7	Neshek,Pat	P	$6
Maybin,Cameron	8	$11	Hairston,Jerry	67	$9	Mather,Joe	7	$7	Lowry,Noah	P	$6
Perez,Rafael	P	$11	Crede,Joe	5	$9	Kapler,Gabe	8	$7	Cordero,Chad	P	$6
Petit,Yusmeiro	P	$11	Pearce,Steven	9	$9	Meredith,Cla	P	$7	Torrealba,Yorvit	2	$6
Cook,Aaron	P	$11	Thornton,Matt	P	$9	Laird,Gerald	2	$7	Ayala,Luis	P	$6
Corpas,Manny	P	$11	Castillo,Luis	4	$9	Izturis,Cesar	6	$7	Miles,Aaron	46	$6
Lohse,Kyle	P	$11	Tolbert,Matt	5	$9	Blevins,Jerry	P	$7	Boggs,Brandon	7	$6
Garciaparra,Nomar	6	$11	Davies,Kyle	P	$9	Hinske,Eric	970	$7	Chavez,Eric	5	$6
Lindstrom,Matt	P	$11	Pie,Felix	8	$9	Madson,Ryan	P	$7	Albers,Matt	P	$6
Hill,Rich	P	$11	Johnson,Reed	87	$9	Joyce,Matthew	79	$7	Anderson,Brian	8	$6
Kennedy,Ian	P	$11	Molina,Yadier	2	$9	Alou,Moises	7	$7	Betemit,Wilson	35	$6
Snell,Ian	P	$11	de la Rosa,Jorge	P	$9	Pavano,Carl	P	$7	Kotsay,Mark	8	$6
Sweeney,Ryan	98	$11	Towles,J.R.	2	$9	Davis,Doug	P	$7	Diaz,Matt	7	$6
Purcey,David	P	$11	Rodriguez,Ivan	2	$9	Barajas,Rod	2	$7	Arias,Joaquin	4	$6
Richard,Clayton	P	$11	Belliard,Ronnie	354	$9	Spilborghs,Ryan	79	$7	Thomas,Frank	0	$6
Ziegler,Brad	P	$11	Harris,Willie	7	$9	Delcarmen,Manny	P	$7	Speier,Justin	P	$6
Barmes,Clint	46	$11	Francis,Jeff	P	$9	Ruiz,Carlos	2	$7	Nunez,Leo	P	$6
LaRoche,Andy	5	$11	Barton,Daric	3	$9	Ramirez,Ramon	P	$7	Zito,Barry	P	$6
Fontenot,Mike	4	$11	Linebrink,Scott	P	$9	Liz,Radhames	P	$7	Reyes,Anthony	P	$6
Escobar,Kelvim	P	$11	Braden,Dallas	P	$9	Adams,Mike	P	$7	Olivo,Miguel	20	$6

ROTISSERIE SNAKE DRAFT — 15 TEAM MIXED LEAGUE

#	NAME	POS
1	Reyes, Jose	6
	Ramirez, Hanley	6
	Wright, David	5
	Rodriguez, Alex	5
	Pujols, Albert	3
	Pedroia, Dustin	4
	Rollins, Jimmy	6
	Utley, Chase	4
	Kinsler, Ian	4
	Furcal, Rafael	6
	Holliday, Matt	7
	Lee, Carlos	7
	Papelbon, Jonathan	P
	Braun, Ryan	7
	Roberts, Brian	4
2	Cabrera, Miguel	3
	Howard, Ryan	3
	Chamberlain, Joba	P
	Sabathia, C.C.	P
	Teixeira, Mark	3
	Hamilton, Josh	89
	Halladay, Roy	P
	Valverde, Jose	P
	Sizemore, Grady	8
	McLouth, Nate	8
	Soriano, Alfonso	7
	Ramirez, Aramis	5
	Santana, Johan	P
	Davis, Chris	35
	Nathan, Joe	P
3	Lidge, Brad	P
	Santana, Ervin	P
	Webb, Brandon	P
	Kemp, Matt	89
	Beltran, Carlos	8
	Berkman, Lance	3
	Crawford, Carl	7
	Victorino, Shane	8
	Longoria, Evan	5
	Liriano, Francisco	P
	Fielder, Prince	3
	Ortiz, David	0
	Markakis, Nick	9
	Bay, Jason	7
	Upton, B.J.	8
4	Hamels, Cole	P
	Peavy, Jake	P
	Hart, Corey	9
	Rios, Alex	98
	Suzuki, Ichiro	98
	Abreu, Bobby	9
	Oswalt, Roy	P
	Ramirez, Manny	70
	Shields, James	P
	Hunter, Torii	8
	Granderson, Curtis	8
	Guerrero, Vladimir	90
	Ethier, Andre	97
	Pence, Hunter	9
	Votto, Joey	3

#	NAME	POS
5	Lincecum, Tim	P
	Werth, Jayson	987
	Slowey, Kevin	P
	Morneau, Justin	3
	Damon, Johnny	780
	Dye, Jermaine	9
	Haren, Dan	P
	Vazquez, Javier	P
	Ellsbury, Jacoby	879
	Greinke, Zack	P
	Lee, Derrek	3
	Gonzalez, Adrian	3
	Wells, Vernon	8
	Ludwick, Ryan	97
	Soria, Joakim	P
6	Lackey, John	P
	Rivera, Mariano	P
	Huff, Aubrey	053
	Milledge, Lastings	8
	Phillips, Brandon	4
	Beckett, Josh	P
	Dunn, Adam	79
	Street, Huston	P
	Bruce, Jay	98
	Billingsley, Chad	P
	Delgado, Carlos	3
	Youkilis, Kevin	35
	Hernandez, Felix	P
	Kazmir, Scott	P
	Fuentes, Brian	P
7	Baker, Scott	P
	Capps, Matt	P
	Lee, Cliff	P
	Cruz, Nelson	9
	Rodriguez, Francisco	P
	Quentin, Carlos	7
	Ramirez, Alexei	4
	Ordonez, Magglio	9
	Meche, Gil	P
	Nady, Xavier	97
	Wood, Kerry	P
	Burnett, A.J.	P
	Beltre, Adrian	5
	Atkins, Garrett	53
	Jackson, Conor	73
8	Weaver, Jered	P
	Hawpe, Brad	9
	Harden, Rich	P
	Polanco, Placido	4
	DeJesus, David	789
	Myers, Brett	P
	Tulowitzki, Troy	6
	Pena, Carlos	3
	Byrnes, Eric	7
	Young, Chris	8
	Span, Denard	9
	Cordero, Francisco	P
	Thome, Jim	0
	Mauer, Joe	2
	McCann, Brian	2

#	NAME	POS
9	Verlander, Justin	P
	Gallardo, Yovani	P
	Konerko, Paul	3
	Matsuzaka, Daisuke	P
	Hardy, J.J.	6
	Sheets, Ben	P
	Drew, Stephen	6
	Qualls, Chad	P
	Wainwright, Adam	P
	Weeks, Rickie	4
	Jones, Chipper	5
	Lilly, Ted	P
	Cueto, Johnny	P
	Jacobs, Mike	3
	Jenks, Bobby	P
10	Young, Delmon	7
	Choo, Shin-Soo	97
	Young, Michael	6
	Lowe, Derek	P
	Peralta, Jhonny	6
	Cano, Robinson	4
	Reynolds, Mark	5
	Ryan, B.J.	P
	Jeter, Derek	6
	Ibanez, Raul	7
	Danks, John	P
	Fukudome, Kosuke	9
	Wigginton, Ty	57
	LaRoche, Adam	3
	Cameron, Mike	8
11	Uggla, Dan	4
	Gordon, Alex	5
	Putz, J.J.	P
	Sonnanstine, Andy	P
	Lopez, Jose	4
	Glaus, Troy	5
	Dempster, Ryan	P
	Ankiel, Rick	8
	Loney, James	3
	Winn, Randy	9
	Johnson, Kelly	4
	Zimmerman, Ryan	5
	Devine, Joey	P
	Theriot, Ryan	6
	Burrell, Pat	7
12	Perez, Chris	P
	Buehrle, Mark	P
	Figgins, Chone	5
	Duchscherer, Justin	P
	Doumit, Ryan	2
	Garza, Matt	P
	Willingham, Josh	7
	Martinez, Victor	2
	Butler, Billy	03
	Nolasco, Ricky	P
	Taveras, Willy	8
	Mora, Melvin	5
	DeRosa, Mark	4975
	Volquez, Edinson	P
	Upton, Justin	9

#	NAME	POS
13	Pettitte, Andy	P
	Guillen, Carlos	53
	Kotchman, Casey	3
	Kouzmanoff, Kevin	5
	Gonzalez, Mike	P
	Sandoval, Pablo	3
	Cain, Matt	P
	Cantu, Jorge	53
	Rodriguez, Wandy	P
	Wang, Chien-Ming	P
	Jones, Adam	8
	Francisco, Frank	P
	Lewis, Fred	7
	Lind, Adam	7
	Garko, Ryan	3
14	Bedard, Erik	P
	Martin, Russell	2
	Cabrera, Orlando	6
	Kershaw, Clayton	P
	Scott, Luke	70
	Broxton, Jonathan	P
	Tejada, Miguel	6
	Renteria, Edgar	6
	Blake, Casey	53
	Bartlett, Jason	6
	Murphy, David	97
	Soto, Geovany	2
	Headley, Chase	7
	Wilson, Brian	P
	Matsui, Hideki	07
15	Drew, J.D.	9
	Bourn, Michael	8
	Morales, Kendry	9
	Johnson, Josh	P
	Gerut, Jody	8
	Mussina, Mike	P
	Perez, Oliver	P
	Maine, John	P
	Aviles, Mike	64
	Litsch, Jesse	P
	Lowell, Mike	5
	Bradley, Milton	09
	Parra, Manny	P
	Cust, Jack	70
	Saito, Takashi	P
16	Hafner, Travis	0
	Lester, Jon	P
	Encarnacion, Edwin	5
	Blalock, Hank	35
	Wheeler, Dan	P
	Kuroda, Hiroki	P
	Harang, Aaron	P
	Giles, Brian	9
	Church, Ryan	9
	Jurrjens, Jair	P
	Morrow, Brandon	P
	Guillen, Jose	970
	Hoffman, Trevor	P
	Molina, Bengie	2
	Hanrahan, Joel	P

ROTISSERIE SNAKE DRAFT — 15 TEAM MIXED LEAGUE

#	NAME	POS	#	NAME	POS	#	NAME	POS	#	NAME	POS
17	Hermida,Jeremy	9	21	Hernandez,Ramon	2	25	Snider,Travis	7	29	Fields,Josh	5
	Young,Chris	P		Lewis,Scott	P		Casilla,Alexi	4		Scutaro,Marco	645
	Swisher,Nick	83		Rauch,Jon	P		Schumaker,Skip	879		Floyd,Cliff	0
	Byrd,Marlon	897		Rodney,Fernando	P		Wolf,Randy	P		Bonifacio,Emilio	4
	Francisco,Ben	79		Sherrill,George	P		Gonzalez,Gio	P		Cruz,Juan	P
	Ellis,Mark	4		Rivera,Juan	7		Byrd,Paul	P		Matthews Jr.,Gary	978
	Saunders,Joe	P		Murphy,Daniel	7		Pierzynski,A.J.	2		Kuo,Hong-Chih	P
	Posada,Jorge	2		Tracy,Chad	3		Davis,Rajai	8		Laffey,Aaron	P
	Zumaya,Joel	P		Sheffield,Gary	0		Gutierrez,Franklin	9		Brown,Emil	79
	Arroyo,Bronson	P		Gomez,Carlos	8		Balfour,Grant	P		Tatis,Fernando	79
	Dukes,Elijah	9		Gregg,Kevin	P		Marshall,Sean	P		Okajima,Hideki	P
	Napoli,Mike	2		Helton,Todd	3		Moyer,Jamie	P		Schierholtz,Nate	9
	Cuddyer,Michael	9		Hall,Bill	5		Roberts,Dave	7		Gross,Gabe	9
	Rowand,Aaron	8		Pierre,Juan	7		Lugo,Julio	6		Uribe,Juan	54
	Scherzer,Max	P		Burriss,Emmanuel	64		Shealy,Ryan	3		Prado,Martin	5
18	Bush,David	P	22	Aybar,Erick	6	26	Howell,J.P.	P	30	Zobrist,Ben	6
	Kubel,Jason	09		Kent,Jeff	4		Villanueva,Carlos	P		Infante,Omar	756
	Guzman,Cristian	6		Francoeur,Jeff	9		Smoltz,John	P		Evans,Nick	7
	Buchholz,Taylor	P		Greene,Khalil	6		Jimenez,Ubaldo	P		Reed,Jeremy	8
	Giambi,Jason	30		Patterson,Corey	8		Wilson,Jack	6		Accardo,Jeremy	P
	Stewart,Ian	5		Wakefield,Tim	P		Johjima,Kenji	2		Washburn,Jarrod	P
	Iannetta,Chris	2		Crisp,Coco	8		Buck,Travis	9		Moss,Brandon	79
	Carmona,Fausto	P		Blanton,Joe	P		Blackburn,Nick	P		Jones,Andruw	8
	Velez,Eugenio	4		Shoppach,Kelly	2		Clement,Jeff	20		Johnson,Nick	3
	Iwamura,Akinori	4		Snyder,Chris	2		Downs,Scott	P		Bonser,Boof	P
	Anderson,Garret	70		Lowrie,Jed	65		Sanchez,Jonathan	P		Saltalamacchia,Jarro	2
	Wood,Brandon	56		Bell,Heath	P		Smith,Greg	P		Dobbs,Greg	5
	Escobar,Yunel	6		Padilla,Vicente	P		Hughes,Phil	P		Feliz,Pedro	5
	Maholm,Paul	P		Lannan,John	P		Suzuki,Kurt	2		Navarro,Dioner	2
	Ross,Cody	89		Izturis,Maicer	64		Howry,Bob	P		Ramirez,Edwar	P
19	Floyd,Gavin	P	23	Happ,J.A.	P	27	Ray,Chris	P			
	Sanchez,Freddy	4		Maybin,Cameron	8		Punto,Nick	64			
	Looper,Braden	P		Perez,Rafael	P		Antonelli,Matt	4			
	Cabrera,Asdrubal	46		Petit,Yusmeiro	P		Hochevar,Luke	P			
	Hairston,Scott	87		Cook,Aaron	P		Volstad,Chris	P			
	Matsui,Kaz	4		Corpas,Manny	P		Grudzielanek,Mark	4			
	Guthrie,Jeremy	P		Lohse,Kyle	P		Kennedy,Adam	4			
	Zambrano,Carlos	P		Garciaparra,Nomar	6		Soriano,Rafael	P			
	Johnson,Randy	P		Lindstrom,Matt	P		Millar,Kevin	3			
	Lopez,Felipe	4		Hill,Rich	P		Gonzalez,Alex	6			
	Buchholz,Clay	P		Kennedy,Ian	P		Galarraga,Armando	P			
	Maddux,Greg	P		Snell,Ian	P		Hairston,Jerry	67			
	Overbay,Lyle	3		Sweeney,Ryan	98		Crede,Joe	5			
	Griffey Jr.,Ken	98		Purcey,David	P		Pearce,Steven	9			
	Arredondo,Jose	P		Richard,Clayton	P		Thornton,Matt	P			
20	Kendrick,Howie	4	24	Ziegler,Brad	P	28	Castillo,Luis	4			
	Kearns,Austin	9		Barmes,Clint	46		Tolbert,Matt	5			
	Teahen,Mark	97		LaRoche,Andy	5		Davies,Kyle	P			
	Anderson,Josh	8		Fontenot,Mike	4		Pie,Felix	8			
	Rolen,Scott	5		Escobar,Kelvim	P		Johnson,Reed	87			
	Jones,Brandon	7		DeWitt,Blake	54		Molina,Yadier	2			
	Price,David	P		Garland,Jon	P		de la Rosa,Jorge	P			
	Millwood,Kevin	P		Bonderman,Jeremy	P		Towles,J.R.	2			
	Rowland-Smith,Ryan	P		Thames,Marcus	7		Rodriguez,Ivan	2			
	Pelfrey,Mike	P		Balentien,Wladimir	98		Belliard,Ronnie	354			
	Marmol,Carlos	P		Callaspo,Alberto	4		Harris,Willie	7			
	Betancourt,Yuniesky	6		Shields,Scot	P		Francis,Jeff	P			
	Dickerson,Chris	7		Torres,Salomon	P		Barton,Daric	3			
	Hill,Aaron	4		Martinez,Pedro	P		Linebrink,Scott	P			
	Hudson,Orlando	4		Lewis,Jensen	P		Braden,Dallas	P			

SIMULATION LEAGUE DRAFT TOP 500

NAME	POS	RAR
Pujols,Albert	3	44.4
Ramirez,Hanley	6	42.3
Rodriguez,Alex	5	39.3
Webb,Brandon	P	38.3
Chamberlain,Joba	P	36.4
Cabrera,Miguel	3	36.1
Wright,David	5	34.8
Ramirez,Manny	70	34.5
Pedroia,Dustin	4	33.0
Howard,Ryan	3	32.8
Dunn,Adam	79	32.0
Ortiz,David	0	31.6
Halladay,Roy	P	31.6
Mauer,Joe	2	31.4
Teixeira,Mark	3	30.9
Utley,Chase	4	30.1
Hamilton,Josh	89	29.5
Cust,Jack	70	29.3
Liriano,Francisco	P	28.9
Sabathia,C.C.	P	28.8
Beltran,Carlos	8	28.7
Hernandez,Felix	P	28.4
Furcal,Rafael	6	28.0
Lowe,Derek	P	27.4
Holliday,Matt	7	27.1
Kinsler,Ian	4	27.1
Pena,Carlos	3	26.9
McCann,Brian	2	26.2
Sizemore,Grady	8	25.4
Burnett,A.J.	P	25.4
Lincecum,Tim	P	25.3
Napoli,Mike	2	25.1
Reyes,Jose	6	24.3
McLouth,Nate	8	24.1
Thome,Jim	0	24.1
Braun,Ryan	7	23.8
Berkman,Lance	3	23.8
Jones,Chipper	5	23.7
Haren,Dan	P	23.7
Posada,Jorge	2	23.6
Bay,Jason	7	23.5
Beckett,Josh	P	23.1
Ethier,Andre	97	23.0
Youkilis,Kevin	35	22.8
Markakis,Nick	9	22.8
Iannetta,Chris	2	22.7
Oswalt,Roy	P	22.5
Rollins,Jimmy	6	22.2
Granderson,Curtis	8	22.2
Hawpe,Brad	9	22.2
Martinez,Victor	2	21.6
Myers,Brett	P	21.2
Lee,Carlos	7	21.1
Roberts,Brian	4	20.9
Soto,Geovany	2	20.8
Santana,Johan	P	20.5
Hamels,Cole	P	20.4
Burrell,Pat	7	20.4
Longoria,Evan	5	19.8
Peavy,Jake	P	19.4
Quentin,Carlos	7	19.2
Ramirez,Aramis	5	19.0
Werth,Jayson	987	18.9
Shields,James	P	18.8
Davis,Chris	35	18.6
Guerrero,Vladimir	90	18.5

NAME	POS	RAR
Drew,Stephen	6	18.5
Drew,J.D.	9	18.5
Santana,Ervin	P	18.4
Upton,Justin	9	18.4
Vazquez,Javier	P	18.0
Doumit,Ryan	2	17.8
Fielder,Prince	3	17.6
Scherzer,Max	P	17.4
Parra,Manny	P	17.4
Morneau,Justin	3	17.2
Snyder,Chris	2	16.5
Upton,B.J.	8	16.5
Lackey,John	P	16.3
Kershaw,Clayton	P	16.2
Meredith,Cla	P	16.1
Ludwick,Ryan	97	16.1
Tulowitzki,Troy	6	16.0
Guillen,Carlos	53	16.0
Cueto,Johnny	P	16.0
Shoppach,Kelly	2	15.9
Lowrie,Jed	65	15.8
Pettitte,Andy	P	15.7
Peralta,Jhonny	6	15.4
Hairston,Scott	87	15.1
Hardy,J.J.	6	15.1
Greinke,Zack	P	15.1
Gordon,Alex	5	14.9
Cameron,Mike	8	14.7
Gerut,Jody	8	14.6
Abreu,Bobby	9	14.4
Papelbon,Jonathan	P	14.1
Johnson,Kelly	4	14.1
Scott,Luke	70	14.0
Martin,Russell	2	13.9
Uggla,Dan	4	13.8
Dempster,Ryan	P	13.7
Ramirez,Alexei	4	13.6
Soriano,Alfonso	7	13.5
Kazmir,Scott	P	13.5
Billingsley,Chad	P	13.3
Buchholz,Clay	P	13.2
Konerko,Paul	3	13.1
Giles,Brian	9	13.1
Rivera,Mariano	P	13.0
Harden,Rich	P	13.0
Qualls,Chad	P	12.9
Broxton,Jonathan	P	12.9
Carmona,Fausto	P	12.7
Pence,Hunter	9	12.7
Bradley,Milton	09	12.6
Kuroda,Hiroki	P	12.6
Gallardo,Yovani	P	12.6
Ross,Cody	89	12.3
Weeks,Rickie	4	12.2
Dye,Jermaine	9	12.0
Perez,Rafael	P	11.8
Maholm,Paul	P	11.8
Downs,Scott	P	11.8
Rodriguez,Wandy	P	11.7
Volquez,Edinson	P	11.7
Bruce,Jay	98	11.6
Fontenot,Mike	4	11.5
League,Brandon	P	11.4
Fukudome,Kosuke	9	11.4
Wells,Vernon	8	11.3
Swisher,Nick	83	11.3

NAME	POS	RAR
Kemp,Matt	89	11.3
Wang,Chien-Ming	P	11.2
Lidge,Brad	P	11.2
Sheets,Ben	P	11.1
Ibanez,Raul	7	11.1
Jurrjens,Jair	P	11.0
Nathan,Joe	P	11.0
Maddux,Greg	P	10.8
Meche,Gil	P	10.8
Hunter,Torii	8	10.7
DeRosa,Mark	4975	10.5
Damon,Johnny	780	10.5
Glaus,Troy	5	10.4
Jeter,Derek	6	10.4
Ordonez,Magglio	9	10.3
Slowey,Kevin	P	10.2
Duchscherer,Justin	P	10.2
Hafner,Travis	0	10.1
DeJesus,David	789	10.0
Thornton,Matt	P	9.9
Valverde,Jose	P	9.9
Cano,Robinson	4	9.8
Smoltz,John	P	9.7
Howell,J.P.	P	9.7
Polanco,Placido	4	9.6
Bedard,Erik	P	9.5
Richard,Clayton	P	9.4
Jackson,Conor	73	9.3
Putz,J.J.	P	9.3
Votto,Joey	3	9.3
Bell,Heath	P	9.2
Wainwright,Adam	P	9.0
Johnson,Randy	P	9.0
Smith,Joe	P	8.9
Renteria,Edgar	6	8.7
Edmonds,Jim	8	8.6
Kuo,Hong-Chih	P	8.5
Huff,Aubrey	053	8.5
Soria,Joakim	P	8.5
Johnson,Josh	P	8.4
Johnson,Nick	3	8.4
Saltalamacchia,Jarr	2	8.4
Nolasco,Ricky	P	8.3
Victorino,Shane	8	8.2
Young,Chris	8	8.1
Danks,John	P	8.1
Fuentes,Brian	P	8.0
Gonzalez,Mike	P	7.9
Dukes,Elijah	9	7.8
Milledge,Lastings	8	7.8
Devine,Joey	P	7.8
Giambi,Jason	30	7.7
Young,Michael	6	7.7
Escobar,Yunel	6	7.7
Street,Huston	P	7.6
Wood,Kerry	P	7.6
Rodney,Fernando	P	7.6
Shields,Scot	P	7.6
Willingham,Josh	7	7.5
Sanchez,Jonathan	P	7.5
Helton,Todd	3	7.4
Lee,Cliff	P	7.4
Blalock,Hank	35	7.3
Buehrle,Mark	P	7.2
Millwood,Kevin	P	7.1
Garciaparra,Nomar	6	7.1

NAME	POS	RAR
Cabrera,Asdrubal	46	7.1
Reyes,Dennys	P	7.0
Baker,Scott	P	6.9
Zobrist,Ben	6	6.8
Hill,Aaron	4	6.8
Masterson,Justin	P	6.8
Dotel,Octavio	P	6.7
Reynolds,Mark	5	6.7
Balfour,Grant	P	6.6
Izturis,Maicer	64	6.6
Ankiel,Rick	8	6.5
Ryan,B.J.	P	6.4
Hudson,Orlando	4	6.4
Blevins,Jerry	P	6.3
Rodriguez,Francis	P	6.3
Cook,Aaron	P	6.3
Troncoso,Ramon	P	6.3
Cordero,Francisco	P	6.2
Robertson,David	P	6.2
Bonderman,Jerem	P	6.1
Jenks,Bobby	P	6.1
Lee,Derrek	3	6.1
Carpenter,Chris	P	6.0
Ramirez,Edwar	P	6.0
Mussina,Mike	P	6.0
Hochevar,Luke	P	6.0
Ziegler,Brad	P	6.0
Joyce,Matthew	79	5.9
Green,Sean	P	5.8
Beltre,Adrian	5	5.8
Church,Ryan	9	5.8
Moylan,Peter	P	5.8
Delcarmen,Manny	P	5.7
Lowell,Mike	5	5.7
Laffey,Aaron	P	5.5
Price,David	P	5.5
Gonzalez,Gio	P	5.5
Cruz,Nelson	9	5.4
Francisco,Frank	P	5.4
Cruz,Juan	P	5.4
Verlander,Justin	P	5.4
Madson,Ryan	P	5.3
Saito,Takashi	P	5.3
Wilson,Brian	P	5.2
McClellan,Kyle	P	5.2
Miller,Andrew	P	5.2
Headley,Chase	7	5.1
Weaver,Jered	P	5.1
Linebrink,Scott	P	5.1
Affeldt,Jeremy	P	5.1
Choo,Shin-Soo	97	5.0
McGowan,Dustin	P	5.0
Rolen,Scott	5	5.0
Perez,Chris	P	5.0
Bradford,Chad	P	5.0
Sonnanstine,Andy	P	5.0
Arredondo,Jose	P	5.0
Wheeler,Dan	P	4.9
Guzman,Cristian	6	4.9
LaRoche,Adam	3	4.8
Wade,Cory	P	4.8
Tavarez,Julian	P	4.8
Bray,Bill	P	4.7
Villanueva,Carlos	P	4.7
Bonser,Boof	P	4.7
Matsuzaka,Daisuk	P	4.7

SIMULATION LEAGUE DRAFT — TOP 500

NAME	POS	RAR	NAME	POS	RAR	NAME	POS	RAR	NAME	POS	RAR
Litsch,Jesse	P	4.6	Padilla,Vicente	P	2.8	Happ,J.A.	P	1.4	Osoria,Franquelis	P	0.1
Hernandez,Ramon	2	4.6	Ramirez,Ramon	P	2.8	Byrd,Marlon	897	1.4	Tomko,Brett	P	0.1
Callaspo,Alberto	4	4.6	Crain,Jesse	P	2.8	Ayala,Luis	P	1.4	Rodriguez,Ivan	2	0.1
Accardo,Jeremy	P	4.6	Jacobs,Mike	3	2.8	Rhodes,Arthur	P	1.4	Mujica,Edward	P	0.1
Camp,Shawn	P	4.5	O'Day,Darren	P	2.8	Gaudin,Chad	P	1.4	Rodriguez,Sean	4	0.1
Bush,David	P	4.5	Betancourt,Rafael	P	2.8	Montanez,Luis	7	1.3	Peralta,Joel	P	0.0
Ross,Dave	2	4.4	Blake,Casey	53	2.8	Carlyle,Buddy	P	1.3	Speier,Ryan	P	0.0
Castro,Ramon	2	4.4	Maine,John	P	2.7	Gabbard,Kason	P	1.3	Pie,Felix	8	0.0
Wuertz,Mike	P	4.3	Matsui,Kaz	4	2.7	Romo,Sergio	P	1.2	Flores,Randy	P	-0.1
Logan,Boone	P	4.3	Bailey,Homer	P	2.7	Eveland,Dana	P	1.2	Duncan,Chris	73	-0.1
Rivera,Saul	P	4.3	Theriot,Ryan	6	2.6	Spilborghs,Ryan	79	1.2	Bruney,Brian	P	-0.1
Nelson,Joe	P	4.3	Garza,Matt	P	2.6	Hoffman,Trevor	P	1.2	Majewski,Gary	P	-0.1
Wright,Jamey	P	4.3	Torres,Salomon	P	2.6	Boyer,Blaine	P	1.2	Encarnacion,Edwi	5	-0.2
Marte,Damaso	P	4.2	Kapler,Gabe	8	2.5	Buchholz,Taylor	P	1.1	Gordon,Tom	P	-0.2
Maybin,Cameron	8	4.2	Schneider,Brian	2	2.5	Overbay,Lyle	3	1.1	Hermida,Jeremy	9	-0.2
Molina,Bengie	2	4.2	Walker,Tyler	P	2.5	Hairston,Jerry	67	1.1	Corey,Bryan	P	-0.3
Hart,Corey	9	4.2	Martinez,Pedro	P	2.5	de la Rosa,Jorge	P	1.1	Lowe,Mark	P	-0.3
Delgado,Carlos	3	4.2	Navarro,Dioner	2	2.5	Molina,Yadier	2	1.0	Sanchez,Anibal	P	-0.3
Corpas,Manny	P	4.1	Hill,Shawn	P	2.4	Ruiz,Carlos	2	1.0	Schoeneweis,Scot	P	-0.3
Pena,Tony	P	4.1	Lopez,Jose	4	2.3	Keppinger,Jeff	6	1.0	Suzuki,Kurt	2	-0.3
Lincoln,Mike	P	4.1	Montero,Miguel	2	2.3	Sanchez,Duaner	P	0.9	Hoffpauir,Micah	7	-0.3
Branyan,Russell	5	4.0	Gonzalez,Adrian	3	2.2	Murphy,David	97	0.9	Holm,Stephen	2	-0.4
Ellis,Mark	4	4.0	Ohman,Will	P	2.2	Ohlendorf,Ross	P	0.9	Bierd,Randor	P	-0.4
Heilman,Aaron	P	4.0	Hawkins,LaTroy	P	2.2	Grabow,John	P	0.9	Moseley,Dustin	P	-0.4
Lannan,John	P	4.0	Yates,Tyler	P	2.2	Cunningham,Aaron	7	0.8	Wolf,Randy	P	-0.4
Jimenez,Ubaldo	P	4.0	Zaun,Gregg	2	2.2	Chavez,Eric	5	0.8	Matsui,Hideki	07	-0.4
Veras,Jose	P	4.0	Lewis,Jensen	P	2.2	Cordero,Chad	P	0.8	Cabrera,Fernando	P	-0.4
Bennett,Jeff	P	4.0	Arroyo,Bronson	P	2.2	Casilla,Santiago	P	0.7	Reyes,Jo-Jo	P	-0.4
Harris,Brendan	645	3.9	Julio,Jorge	P	2.1	Cormier,Lance	P	0.7	Cotts,Neal	P	-0.4
Johnson,Jim	P	3.9	Wigginton,Ty	57	2.0	Aviles,Mike	64	0.7	Rincon,Juan	P	-0.5
Lilly,Ted	P	3.9	Guerrier,Matt	P	2.0	Isringhausen,Jason	P	0.7	Inge,Brandon	25	-0.5
Valentin,Javier	2	3.9	Soriano,Rafael	P	2.0	Ray,Chris	P	0.7	Zambrano,Carlos	P	-0.5
Rios,Alex	98	3.8	Looper,Braden	P	2.0	Hughes,Phil	P	0.7	Aceves,Alfredo	P	-0.5
Feliciano,Pedro	P	3.8	Miller,Justin	P	2.0	Pineiro,Joel	P	0.7	Young,Delwyn	8	-0.5
Kobayashi,Masa	P	3.7	Park,Chan Ho	P	1.9	Romero,J.C.	P	0.6	Dillon,Joe	4	-0.5
Kent,Jeff	4	3.7	Tallet,Brian	P	1.9	Pelfrey,Mike	P	0.6	Fossum,Casey	P	-0.6
Byrdak,Tim	P	3.7	Smith,Seth	9	1.9	Hendrickson,Mark	P	0.6	Thomas,Frank	0	-0.6
Marmol,Carlos	P	3.6	Westbrook,Jake	P	1.9	Sampson,Chris	P	0.6	Owings,Micah	P	-0.6
Boggs,Brandon	7	3.6	Gross,Gabe	9	1.9	Kubel,Jason	09	0.6	Guthrie,Jeremy	P	-0.6
Phillips,Brandon	4	3.6	Perez,Odalis	P	1.9	Vizcaino,Luis	P	0.6	Tatis,Fernando	79	-0.6
Iwamura,Akinori	4	3.6	Lester,Jon	P	1.9	Lieber,Jon	P	0.5	Germano,Justin	P	-0.6
Shouse,Brian	P	3.5	Bartlett,Jason	6	1.9	Breslow,Craig	P	0.5	Boggs,Mitch	P	-0.7
Lind,Adam	7	3.5	Aardsma,David	P	1.8	Alou,Moises	7	0.5	Colon,Bartolo	P	-0.7
Norton,Greg	7	3.4	Miller,Trever	P	1.8	Brocail,Doug	P	0.5	Wood,Brandon	56	-0.7
Durham,Ray	4	3.4	Wolfe,Brian	P	1.8	Gagne,Eric	P	0.5	Chulk,Vinnie	P	-0.7
Bass,Brian	P	3.3	Sherrill,George	P	1.8	Mota,Guillermo	P	0.5	Nunez,Leo	P	-0.8
Varitek,Jason	2	3.3	Baker,Jeff	43	1.8	Atkins,Garrett	53	0.5	Lopez,Aquilino	P	-0.8
Corcoran,Roy	P	3.2	Morrow,Brandon	P	1.8	Snell,Ian	P	0.5	Samardzija,Jeff	P	-0.8
Wilson,C.J.	P	3.2	Barrett,Michael	2	1.7	Jimenez,Cesar	P	0.5	Condrey,Clay	P	-0.8
Marshall,Sean	P	3.2	Lopez,Javier	P	1.6	Scutaro,Marco	645	0.5	Francis,Jeff	P	-0.9
Bard,Josh	2	3.2	Adams,Mike	P	1.6	Teagarden,Taylor	2	0.5	Burke,Jamie	2	-0.9
Eyre,Scott	P	3.2	Griffey Jr.,Ken	98	1.6	Gregg,Kevin	P	0.4	Baez,Danys	P	-0.9
Mora,Melvin	5	3.2	Ramirez,Max	2	1.6	Volstad,Chris	P	0.4	Loe,Kameron	P	-0.9
Hanrahan,Joel	P	3.2	Baker,John	2	1.6	Speier,Justin	P	0.4	Contreras,Jose	P	-0.9
Carrasco,D.J.	P	3.2	Carlson,Jesse	P	1.6	Capuano,Chris	P	0.4	Cabrera,Orlando	6	-0.9
Oliver,Darren	P	3.1	Hudson,Tim	P	1.6	Loretta,Mark	4	0.4	Thompson,Brad	P	-0.9
Escobar,Kelvim	P	3.1	Rauch,Jon	P	1.6	Ruggiano,Justin	7	0.4	Schumaker,Skip	879	-1.0
Thames,Marcus	7	3.1	Burton,Jared	P	1.5	Lo Duca,Paul	2	0.4	Riggans,Shawn	2	-1.0
Harang,Aaron	P	3.0	Farnsworth,Kyle	P	1.5	Crawford,Carl	7	0.3	Ramirez,Horacio	P	-1.0
Kendrick,Howie	4	3.0	Badenhop,Burke	P	1.5	Wagner,Billy	P	0.3	Petit,Yusmeiro	P	-1.0
Capps,Matt	P	3.0	Frasor,Jason	P	1.5	Grilli,Jason	P	0.3	Proctor,Scott	P	-1.0
Howry,Bob	P	2.9	Johjima,Kenji	2	1.5	Seay,Bobby	P	0.3	Kennedy,Ian	P	-1.0
Nady,Xavier	97	2.9	Wright,Wesley	P	1.5	Tejada,Miguel	6	0.2	Dolsi,Freddy	P	-1.0
Zumaya,Joel	P	2.9	Lindstrom,Matt	P	1.5	Marcum,Shaun	P	0.2	Borowski,Joe	P	-1.1
Neshek,Pat	P	2.9	Clement,Jeff	20	1.5	Schierholtz,Nate	9	0.2	Hansen,Craig	P	-1.1
Okajima,Hideki	P	2.9	Lyon,Brandon	P	1.5	Acosta,Manny	P	0.1	Murphy,Daniel	7	-1.1

VII.
SABERMETRIC
TOOLS

One Glossary
Abbreviations and Beginner Concepts

Avg: Batting average (see also BA)

BA: Batting average (see also Avg)

BABIP: Batting average on balls-in-play (see Hit rate)

Base Performance Indicator (BPI): A statistical formula that measures an isolated aspect of a player's situation-independent raw skill or a gauge that helps capture the effects that random chance has on skill. Although there are many such formulas, there are only a few that we are referring to when the term is used in this book. For batters, the skills BPIs are linear weighted power index (PX), speed score index (SX), walk rate (bb%), contact rate (ct%), batting eye (Eye), ground ball/line drive/fly ball ratios (G/L/F), home run to fly ball rate (hr/f) and expected batting average (xBA). Random chance is measured with hit rate on balls in play (H%). For pitchers, our BPIs are control (bb/9), dominance (k/9), command (k/bb), opposition on base avg (OOB), ground/line/fly ratios (G/L/F) and expected ERA (xERA). Random chance is measured with hit rate (H%), strand rate (S%) and home run to fly ball ratio (hr/f).

Batting Average (BA, or Avg): A grand old nugget that has long outgrown its usefulness. We revere .300 hitting superstars and scoff at .250 hitters, yet the difference between the two is 1 hit every 20 ABs. This 1 hit every five games is not nearly the wide variance that exists in our perceptions of what it means to be a .300 or .250 hitter. BA is a poor evaluator of baseball performance in that it neglects the offensive value of the base on balls and assumes that all hits are created equal.

bb%: Walk rate (hitters)

bb/9: Opposition walks per 9 IP

BF/G: Batters faced per game

BIP: Balls-in-play

BPI: Base performance indicator

BPV: Base performance value

Ceiling: The highest professional level at which a player maintains acceptable BPIs. Also, the peak performance level that a player will likely reach, given his BPIs.

Cmd: Command ratio

Ct%: Contact rate

Ctl: Control rate

DIS%: PQS disaster rate

Dom: Dominance rate

DOM%: PQS domination rate

Eye: Batting eye

Fanalytics: The serious, scientific approach to fantasy baseball analysis. A contraction of "fantasy" and "analytics," fanalytic gaming might be considered a mode of play that requires a more strategic and quantitative approach to player analysis and game decisions.

FB%: Fly ball per cent

G/L/F: Ground balls, line drives, and fly balls as percentages of total balls in play (hits *and* outs)

GB%: Ground ball per cent

Gopheritis (also, Acute Gopheritis and Chronic Gopheritis): The dreaded malady in which a pitcher is unable to keep the ball in the ballpark. Pitchers with gopheritis have a fly ball rate of at least 40%. More severe cases have a FB% over 45%.

H%: Hit rate (batters) or Hits allowed per balls in play (pitchers)

hr/9: Opposition home runs per 9 IP

hr/f: Home runs hit (batters), or allowed (pitchers), per fly ball

IP/G: Innings pitched per game appearance

k/9: Dominance rate (opposition strikeouts per 9 IP)

LD%: Line drive per cent

Leading Indicator: A statistical formula that can be used to project potential future performance.

LW: Linear weights

LWPwr: Linear weighted power

Major League Equivalency (*Bill James*): A formula that converts a player's minor or foreign league statistics into a comparable performance in the major leagues. These are not projections, but conversions of current performance. Contains adjustments for the level of play in individual leagues and teams. Works best with Triple-A stats, not quite as well with Double-A stats, and hardly at all with the lower levels. Foreign conversions are still a work in process. James' original formula only addressed batting. Our research has devised conversion formulas for pitchers, however, their best use comes when looking at BPI's, not traditional stats.

Mendoza Line: Named for Mario Mendoza, it represents the benchmark for batting futility. Usually refers to a .200 batting average, but can also be used for low levels of other statistical categories. Note that Mendoza's lifetime batting average was actually a much more robust .215.

MLE: Major league equivalency

Noise: Irrelevant or meaningless pieces of information that can distort the results of an analysis. In news, this is opinion or rumor that can invalidate valuable information. In forecasting, these are unimportant elements of statistical data that can artificially inflate or depress a set of numbers.

OB: On base average (batters)

OBA: Opposition batting average (pitchers)

OOB: Opposition on base average (pitchers)

Opposition Strikeouts per Game: See Dominance rate.

Opposition Walks per Game: See Control rate.

OPS: On base plus slugging average

PQS: Pure Quality Starts

Pw: Linear weighted power

PX: Linear weighted power index

R$: Rotisserie value

RAR: Runs above replacement

RC: Runs created

RC/G: Runs created per game

REff%: Relief efficiency percentage

Rotisserie Value (R$): The dollar value placed on a player's performance in a Rotisserie league, and designed to measure the impact that player has on the standings. These values are highly variable depending upon a variety of factors:
- the salary cap limit
- the number of teams in the league
- each team's roster size
- the impact of any protected players
- each team's positional demands at the time of bidding
- the statistical category demands at the time of bidding
- external factors, e.g. media inflation or deflation of value

In other words, **a $30 player is only a $30 player if someone in your draft pays $30 for him.**

There are a variety of methods to calculate value, most involving a delineation of a least valuable performance level (given league size and structure), and then assigning a certain dollar amount for incremental improvement from that base. The method we use is a variation of the Standings Gain Points method described in the book, *How to Value Players for Rotisserie Baseball,* by Art McGee. (2nd edition available now)

People play Rotisserie in many variations. The most popular game is the 5x5 format. Mixed league participation is soaring; here, player pool penetration falls short of the standard 75%.

Since we currently have no idea who is going to close games for the Angels, or whether Travis Snider is going to break camp with Toronto, all the projected values are slightly inflated. They are roughly based on a 12-team AL and 13-team NL league. We've attempted to take some contingencies into account, but the values will not total to anywhere near $3120, so don't bother adding them up and save your irate e-mails.

A $25 player in this book might actually be worth $21. Or $28. This level of precision is irrelevant in a process that is going to be driven by market forces anyway. *So, don't obsess over it.*

How do other writers publish perfect Rotisserie values over the winter? Do they make arbitrary decisions as to where free agents are going to sign and who is going to land jobs in the spring? I'm not about to make those massive leaps of faith. Bottom line... Some things you can predict, to other things you have to react. As roles become more defined over the winter, our online updates will provide better approximations of playing time, and projected Roto values that add up to $3120.

S%: Strand rate

Save: There are six events that need to occur in order for a pitcher to post a single save...
1. The starting pitcher and middle relievers must pitch well.
2. The offense must score enough runs.
3. It must be a reasonably close game.
4. The manager must choose to put the pitcher in for a save opportunity.
5. The pitcher must pitch well and hold the lead.
6. The manager must let him finish the game.

Of these six events, only one is within the control of the relief pitcher. As such, projecting saves for a reliever has little to do with skill and a lot to do with opportunity. However, pitchers with excellent skills sets may create opportunity for themselves.

SBO: Stolen base opportunity per cent

Situation Independent: Describing a statistical gauge that measures performance apart from the context of team, ballpark, or other outside variables. Home runs, as they are unaffected by the performance of a batter's team, are often considered a situation independent stat (they are, however, affected by park dimensions). Strikeouts and Walks are better examples.

Conversely, RBI's are situation dependent because individual performance varies greatly by the performance of other batters on the team (you can't drive in runs if there is nobody on base). Similarly, pitching wins are as much a measure of the success of a pitcher as they are a measure of the success of the offense and defense performing behind that pitcher, and are therefore a poor measure of pitching performance alone.

Situation independent gauges are important for us to be able to separate a player's contribution to his team and isolate his performance so that we may judge it on its own merits.

Slg: Slugging average

Soft Stats (also, Soft Skills): Batting eyes less than 0.50. Command ratios less than 2.0. Strikeout rates less than 5.0. Etc.

Soft-tosser: A pitcher with a strikeout rate of 5.5 or less.

Spd: Speed score

Strikeouts per Game: See Opposition strikeouts per game.

Surface Stats: Traditional statistical gauges that the mainstream uses to measure performance. Stats like batting average, wins, and ERA only touch the surface of a player's skill. Component skills analysis digs beneath the surface to reveal true skill.

Sv%: Saves conversion rate

SX: Speed Score Index

Vulture: A pitcher, typically a middle reliever, who accumulates an unusually high number of wins by preying on other pitchers' misfortunes. More accurately, this is a pitcher typically brought into a game after a starting pitcher has put his team behind, and then pitches well enough and long enough to allow his offense to take the lead, thereby "vulturing" a win from the starter.

Walks per Game: See Opposition walks per game.

Wasted talent: A player with a high level skill that is negated by a deficiency in another skill. For instance, base path speed can be negated by poor on base ability. Pitchers with strong arms can be wasted because home plate is an elusive concept to them.

WHIP: Walks plus Hits divided by Innings Pitched

Wins: There are five events that need to occur in order for a pitcher to post a single win...
1. He must pitch well, allowing few runs.
2. The offense must score enough runs.
3. The defense must successfully field all batted balls.
4. The bullpen must hold the lead.
5. The manager must leave the pitcher in for 5 innings, and not remove him if the team is still behind.

Of these five events, only one is within the control of the pitcher. As such, projecting wins can be an exercise in futility.

xBA: Expected batting average

xERA: Expected ERA

The Other Glossary
Sabermetrics, Fanalytics and Advanced Concepts

Balls-in-play (BIP)

Batting: (AB – K) *Pitching: ((IP x 2.82)) + H – K*

The total number of batted balls that are hit fair, both hits and outs. An analysis of how these balls are hit – on the ground, in the air, hits, outs, etc. – can provide analytical insight, from player skill levels to the impact of luck on statistical output.

Base Performance Value (BPV): A single value that describes a player's overall raw skill level. This is more useful than traditional statistical gauges to track player performance trends and project future statistical output. The BPV formula combines and weights several BPIs.

Batting BPV: (Batting Eye x 20) + ((Batting Average - .300) / .003) + (Linear Weighted Power Index x 0.43)

This formula combines the individual raw skills of batting eye, the ability to hit safely, and the ability to hit with power. **BENCHMARKS:** The best hitters will have a BPV of 50 or greater. (Note: Batting BPV appears in this edition in the Batter Consistency Charts only.)

Pitching BPV1: (Dominance Rate x 6) + (Command Ratio x 21) - (Expected Opp. HR Rate x 30) - ((Opp. Batting Average - .275) x 200)

Pitching BPV2: ((Dominance Rate - 5.0) x 17) + (4.0 - Walk Rate) x 28)) + (Ground ball rate - 40%)

The new formula combines the individual raw skills of power, control and the ability to keep the ball down in the zone, all characteristics that are unaffected by most external factors. In tandem with a pitcher's strand rate, it provides a more complete picture of the elements that contribute to ERA, and therefore serves as an accurate tool to project likely changes in ERA. **BENCHMARKS:** A BPV of 50 is the minimum level required for long-term success. The elite of the bullpen aces will have BPV's in excess of 100 and it is rare for these stoppers to enjoy long term success with consistent levels under 75.

Note: BPV2 is used in the player boxes for years when G/L/F data is available. Other years use the BPV1 formula.

Batters faced per game (*Craig Wright*)

((IP x 2.82) + H + BB) / G

A measure of pitcher usage and one of the leading indicators for potential pitcher burnout. (See Usage Warning Flags in the Forecaster's Toolbox.)

Batting average on balls in play (*Voros McCracken*)

Batting BABIP: (H—HR) / (AB – HR – K)

Pitching BABIP: (H—HR) / ((IP x 2.82) + H - K - HR)

Also called Hit rate (H%). The percent of balls hit into the field of play that fall for hits. See Forecaster's Toolbox for a complete discussion. **BENCHMARK:** The league average H% is 30%, which is also the level that individual pitching performances will regress to on a year to year basis. Any +/- variance of 3% or more can affect a pitcher's ERA. Batters tend to regress to their own historical three-year mean level.

Batting eye (Eye)

(Walks / Strikeouts)

A measure of a player's strike zone judgment. **BENCHMARKS:** The best hitters have eye ratios more than 1.00 (indicating more walks than strikeouts) and are the most likely to be among a league's .300 hitters. Ratios less than 0.50 represent batters who likely also have lower BA's. (See Forecaster's Toolbox for more.)

Command ratio (Cmd)

(Strikeouts / Walks)

A measure of a pitcher's ability to get the ball over the plate. There is no more fundamental a skill than this, and so it is used as a leading indicator to project future rises and falls in other gauges, such as ERA. **BENCHMARKS:** Baseball's best pitchers will have ratios in excess of 3.0. Pitchers with ratios less than 1.0 — indicating that they walk more batters than they strike out — have virtually no potential for long term success. If you make no other changes in your approach to drafting a pitching staff, limiting your focus to only pitchers with a command ratio of 2.0 or better will substantially improve your odds of success. (See the Forecaster's Toolbox for more command ratio research.)

Contact rate (ct%)

((AB - K) / AB)

Measures a batter's ability to get wood on the ball and hit it into the field of play. **BENCHMARKS:** Those batters with the best contact skill will have levels of 90% or better. The hackers of society will have levels of 75% or less.

Control rate (bb/9), or Opposition walks per game

BB Allowed x 9 / IP

Measures how many walks a pitcher allows per game equivalent. **BENCHMARK:** The best pitchers will have bb/9 levels of 3.0 or less.

Dominance rate (k/9), or Opposition Strikeouts per Game

(K Allowed x 9 / IP)

Measures how many strikeouts a pitcher allows per game equivalent. **BENCHMARK:** The best pitchers will have k/9 levels of 5.6 or higher.

ERA variance: The variance between a pitcher's ERA and his xERA, which is a measure of over or underachievement. A positive variance indicates the potential for a pitcher's ERA to rise. A negative variance indicates the potential for ERA improvement. (See Expected ERA) **BENCHMARK:** Discount variances that are less than 0.50. Any variance more than 1.00 (one run per game) is regarded as a indicator of future change.

Expected batting average (*John Burnson*)

*xCT% * [xH1% + xH2%]*

where

$xH1\% = GB\% * [0.0004\ PX + 0.062\ ln(SX)]$
$\qquad + LD\% * [0.93 - 0.086\ ln(SX)]$
$\qquad + FB\% * 0.12$

and

$xH2\% = FB\% * [0.0013\ PX - 0.0002\ SX - 0.057]$
$\qquad + GB\% * [0.0006\ PX]$

A hitter's batting average as calculated by multiplying the percentage of balls put in play (contact rate) by the chance that a ball in play falls for a hit. The likelihood that a ball in play falls for a hit is a product of the speed of the ball and distance it is hit (PX), the speed of the batter (SX), and distribution of ground balls, fly balls, and line drives. We further split it out by non-homerun hit rate (xH1%) and homerun hit rate (xH2%). **BENCHMARKS:** In general, xBA should approximate batting average fairly closely. Those hitters who have large variances between the two gauges are candidates for further analysis.

Expected earned run average (Gill and Reeve)

$(.575 \times H \text{ [per 9 IP]}) + (.94 \times HR \text{ [per 9 IP]}) + (.28 \times BB \text{ [per 9 IP]}) - (.01 \times K \text{ [per 9 IP]}) - \text{Normalizing Factor}$

"xERA represents the expected ERA of the pitcher based on a normal distribution of his statistics. It is not influenced by situation-dependent factors." xERA erases the inequity between starters' and relievers' ERA's, eliminating the effect that a pitcher's success or failure has on another pitcher's ERA.

Similar to other gauges, the accuracy of this formula changes with the level of competition from one season to the next. The normalizing factor allows us to better approximate a pitcher's actual ERA. This value is usually somewhere around 2.77 and varies by league and year.

BENCHMARKS: xERA should approximate a pitcher's ERA fairly closely. Those pitchers who have large variances between the two gauges are candidates for further analysis.

Projected xERA or projected ERA? Projected xERA is more accurate for looking ahead on a purely skills basis. Projected ERA includes situation-*dependent* events — bullpen support, park factors, etc. — which are reflected better by ERA. The optimal approach is to use *both* gauges as a range of the expectation for the coming year.

Expected earned run average2 (John Burnson)

$(xER \times 9)/IP$, where xER is defined as

$xER\% \times \{ FB/10 + (1-xS\%) \times [(0.3 \times BIP) + BB] \}$

where

$xER\% = 0.96 - (0.0284 \times (GB/FB))$

and

$xS\% = (64.5 + (K/9 \times 1.2) - (BB/9 \times (BB/9 + 1))) / 20$
$+ ((0.0012 \times (GB\%^2)) - (0.001 \times GB\%) - 2.4)$

Note: xERA2 is used in the player boxes for years when G/L/F data is available. Other years use the Gill and Reeve formula.

Expected home run rate (xHR/9): *See Home runs to fly ball rate*

Ground ball, fly ball, line drive percentages (G/F/L): The percentage of all Balls-in-Play that are hit on the ground, in the air and as line drives. For batters, increased fly ball tendency may foretell a rise in power skills; increased line drive tendency may foretell an improvement in batting average. For a pitcher, the ability to keep the ball on the ground can contribute to his statistical output exceeding his demonstrated skill level .

*BIP Type	Total%	Out%
Ground ball	45%	72%
Line drive	20%	28%
Fly ball	35%	85%
TOTAL	*100%*	*69%*

* Data only includes fieldable balls and is net of home runs.

Hit rate (H%): *See Batting average on balls in play*

Home runs to fly ball rate

HR / FB

Also, expected home run rate = $(FB \times 0.10) \times 9 / IP$

The percent of fly balls that are hit for HRs. **BENCHMARK:** The league average level is 10%, which is also the level that individual pitching performances will regress to on a year to year basis. Batters tend to regress to their own historical three-year mean level.

Linear weights (Pete Palmer)

$((\text{Singles} \times .46) + (\text{Doubles} \times .8) + (\text{Triples} \times 1.02) + (\text{Home runs} \times 1.4) + (\text{Walks} \times .33) + (\text{Stolen Bases} \times .3) - (\text{Caught Stealing} \times .6) - ((\text{At bats} - \text{Hits}) \times \text{Normalizing Factor})$

(Also referred to as Batting Runs.) Formula whose premise is that all events in baseball are linear, that is, the output (runs) is directly proportional to the input (offensive events). Each of these offensive events is then weighted according to its relative value in producing runs. Positive events — hits, walks, stolen bases — have positive values. Negative events — outs, caught stealing — have negative values.

The normalizing factor, representing the value of an out, is an offset to the level of offense in a given year. It changes every season, growing larger in high offense years and smaller in low offense years. The value is about .26 and varies by league.

LW is no longer included in the player forecast boxes, but the LW concept is used with the linear weighted power gauge.

Linear weighted power (LWPwr)

$((\text{Doubles} \times .8) + (\text{Triples} \times .8) + (HR \times 1.4)) / (\text{At bats} - K) \times 100$

A variation of the linear weights formula that considers only events that are measures of a batter's pure power. **BENCHMARKS:** Baseball's top sluggers typically top the 17 mark. Weak hitters will have a LWPwr level of less than 10.

Linear weighted power index (PX)

(Batter's LWPwr / League LWPwr) x 100

LWPwr is presented in this book in its normalized form to get a better read on a batter's accomplishment in each year. For instance, a 30-HR season today is not nearly as much of an accomplishment as 30 HRs hit in a lower offense year like 1995. **BENCHMARKS:** A level of 100 equals league average power skills. Any player with a value more than 100 has above average power skills, and those more than 175 are the Slugging Elite.

On base average (OB)

$(H + BB) / (AB + BB)$

Addressing one of the two deficiencies in BA, OB gives value to those events that get batters on base, but are not hits. An OB of .350 can be read as "this batter gets on base 35% of the time." When a run is scored, there is no distinction made as to how that runner reached base. So, two thirds of the time — about how often a batter comes to the plate with the bases empty — a walk really is as good as a hit.

Note that the "official" version of this formula includes hit batsmen. We do not include it here because our focus is on purely skills-based gauges; research has shown that HBP is not a measure of batting skill but a measure of pitching deficiency. **BENCHMARKS:** We all know what a .300 hitter is, but what represents "good" for OB? That comparable level would likely be .400, with .275 representing the comparable level of futility.

On base plus slugging average (OPS): A simple sum of the two gauges, it is considered one of the better evaluators of overall performance. OPS combines the two basic elements of offensive production — the ability to get on base (OB) and the ability to advance baserunners (Slg). **BENCHMARKS:** The game's top batters will have OPS levels more than .900. The worst batters will have levels less than .600.

Opposition batting average (OBA)

(Hits Allowed / ((IP x 2.82) + Hits Allowed))

A close approximation of the batting average achieved by opposing batters against a particular pitcher.

BENCHMARKS: The converse of the benchmark for batters, the best pitchers will have levels less than .250; the worst pitchers levels more than .300.

Opposition home runs per game (hr/9)

(HR Allowed x 9 / IP)

Measures how many home runs a pitcher allows per game equivalent. **BENCHMARK**: The best pitchers will have hr/9 levels of less than 1.0.

Opposition on base average (OOB)

(Hits Allowed + BB) / ((IP x 2.82) + H + BB)

A close approximation of the on base average achieved by opposing batters against a particular pitcher. **BENCHMARK**: The best pitchers will have levels less than .300; the worst pitchers levels more than .375.

Plus/Minus score: A gauge that measures the probability that a player's future performance will exceed or fall short of the immediate past year's numbers. Positive scores indicate both rebounds and potential breakouts. Negative scores indicate both corrections and potential breakdowns. The further the score is from zero, the higher the likelihood of a performance swing. Two types of variables are tracked for batters and pitchers:

Batting: Multi-year trends in bb%, ct%, PX and SX. Outlying levels for h%, hr/f, xBA and LH/RH variance.

Pitching: Multi-year trends in BPV. Outlying levels for h%, s%, hr/f, xERA and LH/RH variance.

Power/contact rating

(BB + K) / IP

Measures the level by which a pitcher allows balls to be put into play and helps tie a pitcher's success to his team's level of defensive ability. In general, extreme power pitchers can be successful even with poor defensive teams. Power pitchers tend to have greater longevity in the game. Contact pitchers with poor defenses behind them are high risks to have poor W-L records and ERA. **BENCHMARKS**: A level of 1.13 or greater describes the pure throwers. A level of .93 or less describes the high contact pitcher. Tip... if you have to draft a pitcher from a poor defensive team, going with power over contact will usually net you more wins in the long run.

PQS disaster rate *(Gene McCaffrey)*: The percentage of a starting pitcher's outings that rate as a PQS-0 or PQS-1. See the Pitching Consistency Chart section for more information on DIS%.

PQS domination rate *(Gene McCaffrey)*: The percentage of a starting pitcher's outings that rate as a PQS-4 or PQS-5. See the Pitching Consistency Chart for more information on DOM%.

Pure Quality Starts: PQS is a method of evaluating individual starting pitcher performances. The old Quality Start method — minimum 6 IP, maximum 3 earned runs — is simplistic and does not measure any real skill. Bill James' "game score" methodology is better, but is not feasible for quick calculation.

In PQS, we give a starting pitcher credit for exhibiting certain skills in each of his starts. Then by tracking his "PQS Score" over time, we can follow his progress. A starter earns one point for each of the following criteria...

1. The pitcher must go a minimum of 6 innings. This measures stamina. If he goes less than 5 innings, he automatically gets a total PQS score of zero, no matter what other stats he produces.

2. He must allow no more than an equal number of hits to the number of innings pitched. This measures hit prevention.

3. His number of strikeouts must be no fewer than two less than his innings pitched. This measures dominance.

4. He must strike out at least twice as many batters as he walks. This measures command.

5. He must allow no more than one home run. This measures his ability to keep the ball in the park.

A perfect PQS score would be 5. Any pitcher who averages 3 or more over the course of the season is probably performing admirably. The nice thing about PQS is it allows you to approach each start as more than an all-or-nothing event.

Note the absence of earned runs. No matter how many runs a pitcher allows, if he scores high on the PQS scale, he has hurled a good game in terms of his base skills. The number of runs allowed — a function of not only the pitcher's ability but that of his bullpen and defense — will tend to even out over time.

Reliever efficiency per cent (REff%)

(Wins + Saves + Holds) / (Wins + Losses + SaveOpps + Holds)

This is a measure of how often a reliever contributes positively to the outcome of a game. A record of consistent, positive impact on game outcomes breeds managerial confidence, and that confidence could pave the way to save opportunities. For those pitchers suddenly thrust into a closer's role, this formula helps gauge their potential to succeed based on past successes in similar roles. **BENCHMARK**: Minimum of 80%.

Runs above replacement (RAR): An estimate of the number of runs a player contributes above a "replacement level" player. "Replacement" is defined as the level of performance at which another player can easily be found at little or no cost to a team. What constitutes replacement level is a topic that is hotly debated. There are a variety of formulas and rules of thumb used to determine this level for each position (replacement level for a shortstop will be very different from replacement level for an outfielder). Our estimates appear below.

One of the major values of RAR for fantasy applications is that it can be used to assemble an integrated ranking of batters and pitchers for drafting purposes.

Batters create runs; pitchers save runs. But are batters and pitchers who have comparable RAR levels truly equal in value? Pitchers might be considered to have higher value. Saving an additional run is more important than producing an additional run. A pitcher who throws a shutout is guaranteed to win that game, whereas no matter how many runs a batter produces, his team can still lose given poor pitching support.

To calculate RAR for batters:

Start with a batter's runs created per game (RC/G).

Subtract his position's replacement level RC/G.

Multiply by number of games played: (AB - H + CS) / 25.5.

Replacement levels used in this book, for 2008:

POS	AL	NL
C	4.19	4.21
1B	5.27	5.73
2B	4.89	4.77
3B	4.88	5.37
SS	4.33	4.63
LF	4.85	5.42
CF	5.35	4.74
RF	5.36	5.19
DH	4.93	

To calculate RAR for pitchers:

Start with the replacement level league ERA.

Subtract the pitcher's ERA. (To calculate *projected* RAR, use the pitcher's xERA.)

Multiply by number of games played, calculated as plate appearances (IP x 4.34) divided by 38.

Multiply the resulting RAR level by 1.08 to account for the variance between earned runs and total runs.

RAR can also be used to calculate rough projected team won-loss records. *(Roger Miller)* Total the RAR levels for all the players on a team, divide by 10 and add to 53 wins.

Runs created *(Bill James)*

(H + BB - CS) x (Total bases + (.55 x SB)) / (AB + BB)

A formula that converts all offensive events into a total of runs scored. As calculated for individual teams, the result approximates a club's actual run total with great accuracy.

Runs created per game *(Bill James)*

Runs Created / ((AB - H + CS) / 25.5)

RC expressed on a per-game basis might be considered the hypothetical ERA compiled against a particular batter. Another way to look at it... a batter with a RC/G of 7.00 would be expected to score 7 runs per game if he were cloned nine times and faced an average pitcher in every at bat. However, cloning batters is not a practice we recommend.

BENCHMARKS: Few players surpass the level of a 10.00 RC/G in any given season, but any level more than 7.50 can still be considered very good. At the bottom are levels less than 3.00.

Runs created per game2 *(Neil Bonner)*

(SS x 37.96) + (ct% x 10.38) + (bb% x 14.81) – 13.04

where SS, or "swing speed" is defined as

((1B x 0.5) + (2B x 0.8) + (3B x 1.1) + (HR x 1.2)) / (AB - K)

This is the version that is currently used in this book.

Saves conversion rate (Sv%)

Saves / Save Opportunities

The percentage of save opportunities that are successfully converted. **BENCHMARK:** We look for a minimum 80% for long-term success.

Slugging average (Slg)

(Singles + (2 x Doubles) + (3 x Triples) + (4 x HR)) / AB

A measure of the total number of bases accumulated (or the minimum number of runners' bases advanced) per at bat. It is a misnomer; it is not a true measure of a batter's slugging ability because it includes singles. Slg also assumes that each type of hit has proportionately increasing value (i.e. a double is twice as valuable as a single, etc.) which is not true. For instance, with the bases loaded, a HR always scores four runs, a triple always scores three, but a double could score two or three and a single could score one, or two, or even three.

BENCHMARKS: The top batters will have levels more than .500. The bottom batters will have levels less than .300.

Speed score *(Bill James):* A measure of the various elements that comprise a runner's speed skills. Although this formula (a variation of James' original version) may be used as a leading indicator for stolen base output, SB attempts are controlled by managerial strategy which makes Spd somewhat less valuable.

The speed scores in this book are calculated as the mean value of the following four elements...

1. Stolen base efficiency = *(((SB + 3)/(SB + CS + 7)) - .4) x 20*
2. Stolen base freq. = *Square root of ((SB + CS)/(Singles + BB)) / .07*
3. Triples rating = *(3B / (AB - HR - K))* and the result assigned a value based on the following chart:

< 0.001	0
0.001	1
0.0023	2
0.0039	3
0.0058	4
0.008	5
0.0105	6
0.013	7
0.0158	8
0.0189	9
.0223+	10

4. Runs scored as a percentage of times on base = *(((R - HR)/(H + BB - HR)) - .1) / .04*

Speed score index (SX)

(Batter's Spd / League Spd) x 100

Normalized speed scores are presented in this book to get a better read on a runner's accomplishment in context. A level of 100 equals league average speed skill. Values more than 100 indicate above average skill, more than 200 represent the Fleet of Feet Elite.

Stolen base opportunity per cent (SBO)

(SB + CS) / (BB + Singles)

A rough approximation of how often a base-runner attempts a stolen base. Provides a comparative measure for players on a given team and, as a team measure, the propensity of a manager to give a "green light" to his runners.

Strand rate (S%)

(H + BB - ER) / (H + BB - HR)

Measures the percentage of allowed runners a pitcher strands (earned runs only), which incorporates both individual pitcher skill and bullpen effectiveness. **BENCHMARKS:** The most adept at stranding runners will have S% levels more than 75%. Once a pitcher's S% starts dropping down less than 65%, he's going to have problems with his ERA. Those pitchers with strand rates more than 80% will have artificially low ERAs, which will be prone to relapse. (See the Forecaster's Toolbox for more research.)

Walks plus hits divided by innings pitched (WHIP): Decreed as a base Rotisserie category. **BENCHMARKS:** Usually, a WHIP of less than 1.20 is considered top level and more than 1.50 is indicative of poor performance. Levels less than 1.00 — allowing fewer runners than IP — represent extraordinary performance and are rarely maintained over time.

Walk rate (bb%)

(BB / (AB + BB))

A measure of a batter's plate patience. **BENCHMARKS:** The best batters will have levels more than 10%. Those with poor plate patience will have levels of 5% or less.

2009 CHEATER'S BOOKMARK

BATTING STATISTICS | BENCHMARKS

Abbrv	Term	Formula / Descr.	BAD UNDER	'08 LG AVG AL	'08 LG AVG NL	BEST OVER
Avg	Batting Average	h/ab	250	268	260	300
xBA	Expected Batting Average	See glossary		255	268	
OB	On Base Average	(h+bb)/(ab+bb)	300	336	331	375
Slg	Slugging Average	total bases/ab	350	420	413	500
OPS	On Base plus Slugging	OB+Slg	650	756	744	875
bb%	Walk Rate	bb/(ab+bb)	5%	9%	9%	10%
ct%	Contact Rate	(ab-k) / ab	75%	81%	80%	85%
Eye	Batting Eye	bb/k	0.50	0.51	0.48	1.00
PX	Power Index	Normalized power skills	80	100	100	120
SX	Speed Index	Normalized speed skills	80	100	100	120
SBO	Stolen Base Opportunity %	(sb+cs)/(singles+bb)		8%	8%	
G/F	Groundball/Flyball Ratio	gb / fb		1.2	1.2	
G	Ground Ball Per Cent	gb / balls in play		43%	43%	
L	Line Drive Per Cent	ld / balls in play		20%	21%	
F	Fly Ball Per Cent	fb / balls in play		37%	36%	
RC/G	Runs Created per Game	See glossary	3.00	4.81	4.67	7.50
RAR	Runs Above Replacement	See glossary	-0.0			+25.0

PITCHING STATISTICS | BENCHMARKS

Abbrv	Term	Formula / Descr.	BAD OVER	'08 LG AVG AL	'08 LG AVG NL	BEST UNDER
ERA	Earned Run Average	er*9/ip	5.00	4.35	4.29	4.00
xERA	Expected ERA	See glossary		4.48	4.35	
WHIP	Baserunners per Inning	(h+bb)/ip	1.50	1.39	1.39	1.25
BF/G	Batters Faced per Game	((ip*2.82)+h+bb)/g	28.0			
PC	Pitch Counts per Start		120	94	95	
OBA	Opposition Batting Avg	Opp. h/ab	290	265	263	250
OOB	Opposition On Base Avg	Opp. (h+bb)/(ab+bb)	350	333	333	300
BABIP	BatAvg on balls in play	(h-hr)/((ip*2.82)+h-k-hr)		304	304	
Ctl	Control Rate	bb*9/ip		3.3	3.4	3.0
hr/9	Homerun Rate	hr*9/ip		1.0	1.0	1.0
hr/f	Homerun per Fly ball	hr/fb		9%	10%	10%
S%	Strand Rate	(h+bb-er)/(h+bb-hr)		71%	71%	
DIS%	PQS Disaster Rate	% GS that are PQS 0/1		24%	24%	20%

Abbrv	Term	Formula / Descr.	BAD UNDER	'08 LG AVG AL	'08 LG AVG NL	BEST OVER
RAR	Runs Above Replacement	See glossary	-0.0			+25.0
Dom	Dominance Rate	k*9/ip		6.6	7.0	6.5
Cmd	Command Ratio	k/bb		2.0	2.0	2.2
G/F	Groundball/Flyball Ratio	gb / fb		1.18	1.25	
BPV	Base Performance Value	See glossary	50	48	53	75
DOM%	PQS Dominance Rate	% GS that are PQS 4/5		40%	43%	50%
Sv%	Saves Conversion Rate	(saves / save opps)		67%	62%	80%
REff%	Relief Effectiveness Rate	See glossary		66%	64%	80%

NOTES

First Pitch
Forums & Conferences

"The general wealth and depth of knowledge of not only the panelists, but attendees as well, was amazing. I'm a first-time attendee and am extremely impressed with the content and quality of the information."
— B.DeMent, Glen Ellyn IL

Get a head start on the 2009 season with a unique opportunity to go one-on-one with some of the top writers and analysts in the fantasy baseball industry. First Pitch Forums bring the experts to some of the top cities in the USA for lively and informative symposium sessions.

This year's theme: "55 Brainstorms for 2009"

These 3-hour sessions combine player analysis with fantasy drafting, interactive activities and fun! You've never experienced anything so informational and entertaining! We've selected the top issues, topics, players and strategies that could make or break your fantasy season. PLUS... 55 brainstorms from the game's leading experts. Among the topics covered:

- ◘ First-rounders who won't return first round value
- ◘ Bullpens that will have new closers by June
- ◘ Minor league end-gamers who will become full-timers after Opening Day
- ◘ Players who will open the season on the disabled list
- ◘ Player pool observations that need to shape your draft strategy
- ◘ Hitters who will post their first $30 season
- ◘ Pitchers you don't want at the price they will probably cost
- ◘ and much more!

Ron Shandler and *Baseball Injury Report's* Rick Wilton chair the sessions, bringing a dynamic energy to every event. They are joined by guest experts from Baseball HQ and some of the leading sports media sources.

What you get for your registration...

- ◘ Three hours of baseball talk with some of the industry's top analysts
- ◘ The chance to have *your* questions answered, one-on-one with the experts
- ◘ The opportunity to network with fellow fantasy leaguers from your area
- ◘ Freebies and discounts from leading industry vendors

Program description, forum sites and directions at
http:// www.baseballhq.com /seminars/

2009 SITES

February 21	**SF BAY AREA** (Milpitas, CA)
February 22	**LOS ANGELES** (Arcadia, CA)
February 28	**CLEVELAND downtown**
March 1	**CHICAGO** (Oak Brook, IL)
March 13	**DC/BALTIMORE** (Columbia, MD)
March 14	**NEW YORK** (Saddle Brook, NJ)
March 15	**BOSTON** (Natick, MA)

REGISTRATION: $29 per person in advance
$39 per person at the door

And... November 6-8, 2009 in **PHOENIX, AZ**

Deric McKamey's 2009
MINOR LEAGUE BASEBALL ANALYST

Available January 2009

Deric McKamey's **Minor League Baseball Analyst** is the first book to fully integrate sabermetrics and scouting. A long-term Bill James disciple and graduate of Major League Baseball's scout school, Deric provides his unique brand of analysis for over 1000 minor leaguers. For baseball analysts and those who play in fantasy leagues with farm systems, the *Analyst* is the perfect complement to the *Baseball Forecaster* and is designed exactly for your needs:

- ▪ *Stats and Sabermetrics...* Over three dozen categories for 1000 minor leaguers, including batter skills ratings, pitch repertoires and more
- ▪ *Performance Trends...* spanning each player's last five minor league stops, complete with leading indicators
- ▪ *Scouting reports...* for all players, including expected major league debuts, potential major league roles and more
- ▪ *Major League Equivalents...* Five year scans for every player
- ▪ *Mega-Lists...* The Top 100 of 2009, retrospective looks at the Top 100's of 2004-2008, organizational Top 15's, top prospects by position, power and speed prospects, and more
- ▪ *Strategy essays...* on drafting and managing your fantasy team's farm system
- ▪ *Player Potential Ratings...* Deric's exclusive system that evaluates each player's upside potential and chances of achieving that potential.

BOOKS

Art McGee's
HOW TO VALUE PLAYERS FOR ROTISSERIE® BASEBALL

Learn how to calculate the best player values for your draft or auction! Art McGee applies concepts from economics, finance, and statistics to develop a pricing method that far surpasses any other published. His method is highly sophisticated, yet McGee explains it in terms that any fantasy baseball owner can understand and apply.

In the 2nd Edition...

- ▪ Discover the power of Standings Gain Points (SGP)
- ▪ Learn how to adjust values for position scarcity, injury risk and future potential
- ▪ Set up your own pricing spreadsheet, as simple or sophisticated as you want
- ▪ Make better decisions on trades, free agents, and long-term contracts
- ▪ Apply these methods even if your league uses non-standard categories or has a non-standard number of teams
- ▪ PLUS... 10 additional essays to expand your knowledge base.

NOTES

NOTES

NOTES